THE
CREATIVE
IMPULSE

FIFTH EDITION

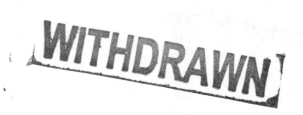

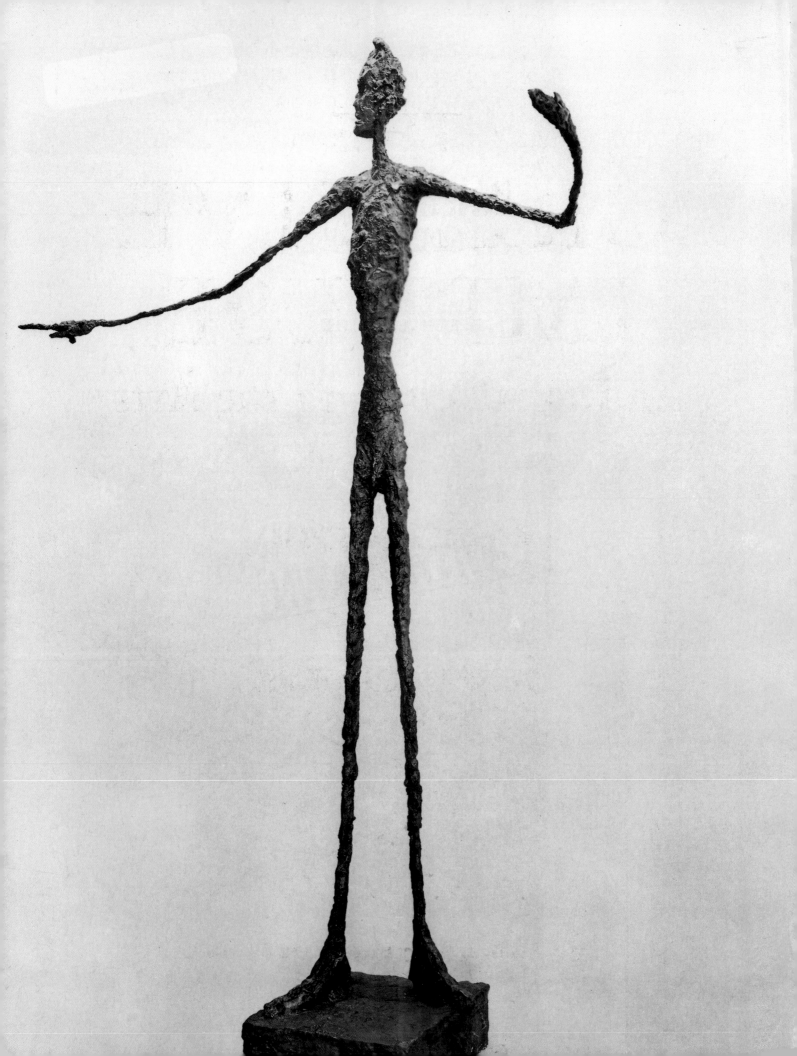

THE
CREATIVE
IMPULSE

An Introduction to the Arts

FIFTH EDITION

DENNIS J. SPORRE

ELON COLLEGE

Prentice Hall Inc., Upper Saddle River, NJ 07458

Copyright © 2000, 1996, 1993, 1990, 1987 by Prentice-Hall, Inc.
A Division of Pearson Education
Upper Saddle River, NJ 07458

10 9 8 7 6 5 4

ISBN 0–13–040035–1

This book was designed and produced by
Calmann & King Ltd, London
www.calmann-king.com

Publisher: Bud Therien
Editorial Director: Charlyce Jones Owen
Marketing Manager: Sheryl Adams
Manufacturing Manager: Nick Sklitsis
Assistant Editor: Marion Gottlieb

For Calmann & King Ltd.
Designer: Andrew Shoolbred
Picture Researcher: Maureen Cowdroy
Editor: Nell Graville

Printed in China

Cover picture: Page showing Thamyris, from Giovanni
Boccaccio's *De Claris Mulieribus* (*Concerning Famous
Women*), 1402. Ink and tempera on vellum. Bibliothèque
Nationale, Paris

Frontispiece: Alberto Giacometti, *Man Pointing*, 1947.
Bronze, 70½ x 40¾ x 16⅜ ins (179 x 103.4 x 41.5 cm),
at base 12 x 13¼ ins (30.5 x 33.7 cm). Museum of Modern
Art, New York. Gift of Mrs John D. Rockefeller 3rd. Photo
© Museum of Modern Art, New York. © ADAGP, Paris
and DACS, London 1999

Prentice Hall International (UK) Limited, *London*
Prentice-Hall of Australia Pty. Limited, *Sydney*
Prentice-Hall Canada Inc., *Toronto*
Prentice-Hall Hispanoamericana, S.A., *Mexico*
Prentice-Hall of India Private Limited, *New Delhi*
Prentice-Hall of Japan, Inc., *Tokyo*
Pearson Education Pte. Ltd., *Singapore*
Editora Prentice-Hall do Brasil, Ltda, *Rio de Janeiro*

Contents

Picture Credits and Literary Acknowledgments *10*
Preface *11*

Introduction: What are the Arts and How do We Evaluate and Describe them? *12*

THE HUMANITIES AND THE ARTS *14*

WHAT IS ART *14*
Nonrestrictiveness *15* Human Enterprise *15*
Medium of Expression *15* Communication *16*

THE FUNCTIONS OF ART *16*
Entertainment *16* Political and Social Commentary *16*
Therapy *17* Artifact *17*

EVALUATING WORKS OF ART *17*
Types of Criticism *17* Formal Criticism *17* Contextual
Criticism *18* **Making Judgments** *18* Craftsmanship *18*
Communication *18*

Getting Started *19*

TWO-DIMENSIONAL ART *20*
Media *20* **Composition** *20* Elements *20* *Techniques:
Linear Perspective 22* Principles *22*

SCULPTURE *22*
Techniques: Lost-Wax Casting 23 **Dimensionality** *23*
Texture *23*

ARCHITECTURE *23*
Structure *24*

MUSIC *25*
Genres *25* *Techniques: Musical Notation 25* **Melody
and Form** *26*

THEATRE *26*
Genres *26* Plot, Character, Thought, and Visual
Elements *26*

LITERATURE *27*
Genres *27* Point of View, Character, and Plot *27*
Theme and Language *27*

FILM *27*

DANCE *28*
Line, Form, and Repetition *28*

FEATURES *28*
Pronunciation *28* Profiles *29* Technology *29*
Masterwork *29* Focal Point *29* Our Dynamic World *29*
Maps and Timelines *29* Chapter Opener *29* Chapter
Review *29*

1 The Ancient World *30*

THE HUMAN JOURNEY *32*
Technology: Our Earliest Tools 33

OUR EARLIEST ART *34*
Venus Figures *34* The Cave of Lascaux *35*

MESOPOTAMIA *36*
Sumer *36* *Technology: The Invention of the Wheel 37*
Religion *38* Writing *38* *Masterwork: The Tell Asmar
Statues 39* Art *40* Music *40* Hammurabi and
Babylonia *40* The Assyrians *41*

ANCIENT EGYPT *42*
Religion *42* *Our Dynamic World: Ancient China 43*
Pyramid Architecture *43* Sculpture *46* Music *46*
*FOCAL POINT: AKHENATON AND MONOTHEISM: THE TELL EL
AMARNA PERIOD 47* *Profile: Akhenaton and Nefertiti 48*

2 Archaic Greece and the Aegean *50*

THE MINOANS *52*

THE MYCENAEANS *54*

BETWEEN MYTH AND HISTORY *55*

THE ARCHAIC GREEK WORLD *55*
The Polis *56* *Technology: The Olive Press 56*
The Hellenes *57* The Persian War *58* Religion *58*
Philosophy *59* Vase Painting *59* Protogeometric Style *59*
Geometric Style *60* Archaic Style *61* *Masterwork:
The Dipylon Vase 61* *Our Dynamic World: Native
America 63* Red- and Black-Figure Pottery *63*
Sculpture *65* Archaic Style *65* **Architecture–The Doric
Order** *67* **Music** *68* *Profile: Sappho 69* **Literature** *69*
Sappho *69* Hesiod *69* *Masterwork: Sappho–"God's
Wildering Daughter" 70* **Dance** *71*
FOCAL POINT: THE ILIAD AND ODYSSEY OF HOMER 72

3 Greek Classicism and Hellenism *74*

THE CLASSICAL WORLD *76*
The Persian War *76* The Age of Pericles *77* The
Peloponnesian War *78* Philosophy *79* Intellectualism *79*
Sophistry: The Distrust of Reason *79* Socrates, Plato,
and Aristotle *80* **Literature: The Platonic Dialogues** *82*
History and Science *83* **Classical Style in Vase Painting
and Sculpture** *83* Vase Painting *84* Sculpture *85*
Masterwork: Myron—Discus Thrower 86 Late Classical
Style *89* *Masterwork: The Parthenon 90* **Architecture** *92*
Our Dynamic World: The Nok Style of Africa 94
Theatre *95* Aeschylus *95* *Profile: Aeschylus 95*
Sophocles *96* Euripides *96* Aristotle's Theory of
Tragedy *96* *Masterwork: Sophocles—Oedipus the King 97*

Contents

Costume 97   Aristophanes 97   Theatre Design 98
Music 99   Dance 99

THE HELLENISTIC AGE 100
Alexander and the Spread of Hellenistic Culture 100
Technology: Hero's Steam Turbine 102   **Theatre and
Literature 102   Philosophy and Religion 102   Hellenistic
Style 103**   Sculpture 103   Architecture 105
*FOCAL POINT: FROM IDEALISM TO REALISM—PROMETHEUS
AND HECUBA 107*

4 The Roman Period *110*

THE ROMAN REPUBLIC 112
**Military Expansion 113   The Roman Civil War 113
The Visual Arts and Architecture 114   Wall Painting 114**
Sculpture 116   Architecture 117   Theatre 117   Comedy 117
Blood Sport 118   Philosophy and Religion 118

THE ROMAN EMPIRE 119
**Augustus 119   Pax Romana 121   Roman Law 122
Philosophy 122**   Seneca 122   Marcus Aurelius and
Epictetus 122   Plotinus: Beauty and Symbol 123
**Religion 124   Two-Dimensional Art 124   Sculpture 125
Architecture 125**   *Our Dynamic World: Chinese Painting 127
Masterwork: The Pantheon 130   Technology: Cement 133*
**Music 133   Literature 134   *Profile: Vergil 134*
Dance 136**
FOCAL POINT: AUGUSTUS—CLASSICAL VISIONS 137

5 Judaism and Early Christianity *140*

THE PEOPLE OF ISRAEL 142
**The Patriarchs 142   Abraham 142   Moses 142   The
Selection of Israel 143   The Ten Commandments 144
Conquest and the Judges 144   The United Monarchy 146
The Divided Kingdom and Exile 146   The Post-Exilic
Period and Beyond 146**   *Profile: Solomon 147*   **The
Hebrew Bible 147   The Torah 148   The Prophets 148
The Writings 149   Jewish Art and Architecture 149**
Visual Art 149   *Masterwork: The Temple of Jerusalem 150*
Music and Dance 152

CHRISTIANITY 152
Jesus Christ and His Teachings 152   *Our Dynamic World:
Shinto Sculpture in Japan 152*   **The Apostolic Mission 154
The Early Christian Church 155**   The Popes 156   Early
Christian Thought 157

**CHRISTIANITY AND THE LATE ROMAN
EMPIRE 158**
Diocletian 159   Constantine 160

LATE ROMAN AND EARLY CHRISTIAN ART 160
The Visual Arts and Architecture 160   Visual Art 160
Architecture 164   **Literature 168   Music 168**
Technology: Matches 169
*FOCAL POINT: ST PAUL AND THE WESTERNIZATION OF
CHRISTIANITY 170*

6 Byzantium and the Rise of
Islam *174*

BYZANTIUM 176
Justinian 178   The Isaurian Emperors and Iconoclasm 178

**From Rise to Fall (867–1453) 179   Byzantine
Intellectualism 180   The Arts of Byzantium 181   Two-
Dimensional Art 181   Hieratic Style 182   Sculpture 186
Literature 186   *Masterwork: The Harbaville Triptych 188
Our Dynamic World: Chinese Theatre 189   Theatre,
Music, and Dance 190   Architecture 192   Byzantine Art
and Culture 192**

THE RISE OF ISLAM 193
The Religion of Islam 193   The Spread of Islam 194
Profile: Muhammad 195   **Islamic Style in the Arts 196
Visual Art 196   Literature 196   Architecture 197**
*FOCAL POINT: IN PRAISE OF THE EMPEROR—THE MARK OF
JUSTINIAN 200   Profile: Anthemius of Tralles 200
Technology: Spanning Space with Triangles and Pots 203*

7 The Early Middle Ages: The
Monastic and Feudal Romanesque
Period *206*

THE MIDDLE AGES 208

THE MEDIEVAL CHURCH 209
**Devils and Division 209   The Roman Papacy 209
Monasticism 209**   *Profile: Pope Gregory I, the Great 210*

CHARLEMAGNE'S EMPIRE 211

FEUDALISM 212
Feudal Lords 212   Serfs and Women 213

THE VISUAL ARTS 213
Manuscript Illumination and Sculpture 213   *Technology:
The Viking Ships 215*   **Romanesque Style in Architecture
and Sculpture 217**   *Masterwork: The Bronze Doors of
Hildesheim Cathedral 218   Our Dynamic World:
Igbo-Ukwu 222*

MUSIC 223
**Sacred Music 223   Gregorian Chant 223   Polyphony:
Organum 223   Secular Music 223**

LITERATURE 224
Profile: Hildegard of Bingen 225

THEATRE 226

DANCE 226
FOCAL POINT: THE CAROLINGIAN RENAISSANCE 227
Manuscript Illumination and Wall Painting 228
Sculpture 231   Architecture 231

8 The High Middle Ages:
The Gothic Age *234*

**THE SOCIAL ORDER OF THE HIGH MIDDLE
AGES 236**
The Rise of Cities 236   *Technology: A Better Horse
Collar 236*   **The Middle Class 237   Feudal Monarchs and
Monarchies 237   Chivalry 238**

THE CHRISTIAN CHURCH 239
**Reform in the Christian Church 239   St Bernard of
Clairvaux and Mysticism 241   The Crusades 241**

PHILOSOPHY AND THEOLOGY 242
The Rise of Universities 242   Abelard and Realism 242

Profile: St Francis of Assisi 243   St Thomas Aquinas and Aristotelianism 244

LITERATURE 244
    Courtly Romances 244   Dante and the *Divine Comedy 245*

GOTHIC STYLE 246
    Architecture 246   *Masterwork: Suger and the Abbey Church of Saint-Denis 250*   **Sculpture 251**   **Painting 252**

MUSIC 254
    Our Dynamic World: Japanese Sculpture 255

THEATRE 255
FOCAL POINT: CHARTRES CATHEDRAL 258

9 The Late Middle Ages 264

THE END OF THE MIDDLE AGES 266
    Secularism and Transition 266   **The Hundred Years' War 266**   **The Secular Monarchies 266**   **The Plague 267**   *Profile: Joan of Arc 268*   **Economics and Industrialization 269**   *Technology: Keeping Time 270*   **Religion and the Great Schism 270**

LITERATURE 271
    Petrach and Boccaccio 271   **Petrach 271**   **Boccaccio 272**   **Froissart's Chronicles 272**   **Christine de Pisan 272**

ART AND ARCHITECTURE 273
    Late Gothic Architecture 273   *Profile: Geoffery Chaucer 274*   **Late Gothic Sculpture 277**   **Painting 278**   **Italy 278**   *Profile: Giotto—The Lamentation 281*

MUSIC 281
    Ars Nova 281   **Guillaume de Machaut 283**   **Francesco Landini 283**

THEATRE 283
    Our Dynamic World: Noh Theatre of Japan 284

DANCE 284
FOCAL POINT: WOMEN MYSTICS OF THE LATE MIDDLE AGES 285

10 The Early Renaissance 288

THE RENAISSANCE 290

THE RENAISSANCE VIEWPOINT 290
    Antiquity Revisited and Measured 290   **Humanism 291**   *Profile: Niccolò Machiavelli 292*   **Capitalism 294**   **Discovery 294**   **The Papal States 294**   **Italian City-States 295**

THE BEGINNINGS OF RENAISSANCE ARCHITECTURE 295
    Technology: Flywheels and Connecting Rods 296   **Alberti 296**   **Brunelleschi 297**

SCULPTURE 300
    Donatello 300   **Ghiberti 301**

PAINTING 303
    Masaccio 303   *Masterwork: Masaccio—The Tribute Money 304*   **The Heritage of Masaccio 305**   **Fra Angelico 306**   **Paolo Uccello 306**   **Lyrical Poetry in Painting 308**   **Botticelli 308**   *Our Dynamic World: Chinese Painting 309*   **Beyond Florence 310**

MUSIC 310

THEATRE 311

DANCE 312
FOCAL POINT: FLORENCE IN THE QUATTROCENTO 313
Cosimo de' Medici 314   Piero de' Medici 315
Lorenzo de' Medici 316

11 The High Renaissance and Mannerism 318

THE HIGH RENAISSANCE 320

SOUTHERN EUROPE IN THE SIXTEENTH CENTURY 320
    The Expanding World 320   **The Ottoman Turks 322**   **The Papal States 322**   *Technology: Leonardo: Turning the Screw 324*   **Spain's Golden Century 325**

THE VISUAL ARTS 326
    The High Renaissance 326   **Leonardo da Vinci 326**   *Our Dynamic World: Painting in India 327*   **Michelangelo 329**   *Profile: Michelangelo 330*   *Masterwork: Michelangelo—David 332*   **Raphael 334**   **Titian and Tintoretto: The High Renaissance in Venice 334**   **Mannerism 336**

ARCHITECTURE 338

THE PERFORMING ARTS 340
    Music 340   **Sacred Music 340**   **Secular Music 341**   **Instrumental Music 341**   **Theatre 341**   **Commedia dell'arte 342**

LITERATURE 344
    Baldassare Castiglione 344   **Ludovico Ariosto 345**
FOCAL POINT: PAPAL SPLENDOR—THE VATICAN 346

12 Renaissance and Reformation in Northern Europe 352

THE REFORMATION 354
    The Background 354   **Erasmus and Christian Humanism 354**   **Martin Luther 357**   **Ulrich Zwingli and Zurich 358**   **John Calvin and the New Jerusalem 359**

SCIENCE AND THE INTELLECT 360
    The Scientific Revival 360   *Technology: Naval Artillery 361*   **Michel de Montaigne 362**

THE VISUAL ARTS AND ARCHITECTURE 362
    Flanders 362   **Van Eyck and van der Weyden 362**   **The Netherlands 364**   **Hieronymus Bosch 364**   **Pieter Bruegel the Elder 365**   **Germany 366**   **Albrecht Dürer 366**   **Matthias Grünewald 368**   **Albrecht Altdorfer 369**   **France 370**   *Our Dynamic World: Ming Dynasty Porcelain 371*

MUSIC 372
    The Renaissance Style in Flanders 372   **Lutheranism and *Lieder* 373**   **Parisian Chanson 374**

DANCE 374
FOCAL POINT: THE GREAT AGE OF THE TUDORS 375
Visual Art and Architecture 376   Literature and Drama 377
Profile: William Shakespeare 378   *Profile: Shakespeare—Hamlet 379*   Music 381

Contents

13 The Baroque Age 384

SCIENTIFIC REVOLUTION AND SYSTEMATIC
RATIONALISM 386
Francis Bacon 386   Galileo Galilei 386   Johannes
Kepler 386   René Descartes 387   Isaac Newton 387

PHILOSOPHY 388
Thomas Hobbes 388   Technology: Standardized
Measurement 389   John Locke 389

THE COUNTER-REFORMATION 390
The Council of Trent 390   The Wars of Religion 391

ABSOLUTISM 392

THE VISUAL ARTS AND ARCHITECTURE 393
Baroque Style 393   Counter-Reformation Baroque 393
Caravaggio 393   El Greco 394   Sculpture 395
Architecture 397   Aristocratic Baroque 398
Rubens 398   Poussin 398   Sculpture 400
Architecture 400   Our Dynamic World: The Taj Mahal 404
Bourgeois Baroque 405   Rembrandt 405   Masterwork:
Rembrandt—The Night Watch 406   Van Ruisdael 407
Vermeer 408

LITERATURE 408
Poetry and Satire 408   The Rise of the Novel 409

MUSIC 409
Baroque Style 409   Instrumental Music 410   Concerto 410
Sonata 410   Masterwork: Bach—Fugue in G Minor 411
Vocal Music 411   Cantata 411   Opera 412
Profile: Johann Sebastian Bach 413

FRENCH NEOCLASSICAL THEATRE 414

DANCE 415
FOCAL POINT: ENGLISH BAROQUE—SEVENTEENTH-CENTURY
LONDON 417   Profile: Sir Christopher Wren 418
English Baroque Architecture 418   English Baroque
Music 419   English Baroque Theatre 419   Masterwork:
Wren—St Paul's Cathedral 420

14 The Enlightenment 424

THE ENLIGHTENMENT 426
Technology: James Watt and the Steam Engine 427
Technology 427   Philosophy 428   The Philosophes 429
Profile: Voltaire 430   Profile: Maria Theresa 431
Economics and Politics 431   Aesthetics and Classicism 433

THE VISUAL ARTS AND ARCHITECTURE 433
Rococo Style 433   Humanitarianism and Hogarth 437
Landscape and Portraiture 439   Genre 439
Neoclassicism 440   Masterwork: David—The Oath of the
Horatii 443

LITERATURE 445
Rococo 445   Pamphlets and Essays 445   Genre 446
The Pre-Romantics 446

MUSIC 447
Pre-Classical 447   Expressive Style 447   Classical Style 448
The Classical Sonata and Sonata Form 448   The Classical
Symphony 448   Other Classical Forms 449   Haydn 449
Mozart 450   Beethoven 451

THEATRE 452

Britain 452   America 452   France 452
Our Dynamic World: Japanese Kabuki Theatre 453

DANCE 454
FOCAL POINT: THE ENLIGHTENED DESPOT—FREDERICK THE
GREAT 457

15 The Romantic Age 462

THE AGE OF INDUSTRY 464
Technology 464   Social Changes 464   Marxism 465
Science 465   Philosophy 466   Idealism 466   Hegel's
Aesthetic Theory 467   Positivism and Materialism 468
Technology: Exact Tolerance 468   Internationalism 469
Patronage 470

ROMANTICISM IN THE VISUAL ARTS AND
ARCHITECTURE 470
Masterwork: Géricault—The Raft of the "Medusa" 472
Profile: Rosa Bonheur 475

ROMANTICISM IN LITERATURE 478
Wordsworth 478   Our Dynamic World: Japanese
Painting 479   Jane Austen 479   Masterwork: Austen—
Pride and Prejudice 480   Other Nineteenth-Century
Romantics 480

ROMANTICISM IN MUSIC 481
Lieder 481   Piano Works 482   Program Music 483
Symphonies 484   Trends 484   Choral Music 484
Profile: Joannnes Brahms 485   Opera 486

ROMANTICISM IN THEATRE 487
Popularism and Historical Accuracy 487   Melodrama 488

ROMANTICISM IN DANCE 489
FOCAL POINT: THE VICTORIANS 491

16 The Beginnings of Modernism 496

THE WORLD IN TURMOIL 498
European Migration 498   Business and Industry 499
Workers and Socialism 499   The German Reich 500
A Scientific Explosion 502   Physics 502   Technology:
Coca-Cola 502   Biology 503

PHILOSOPHY AND PSYCHOLOGY 503
Friedrich Nietzsche 503   Sigmund Freud 503

THE VISUAL ARTS AND ARCHITECTURE 504
Realism 504   Impressionism 509   Masterwork: Renoir—
Le Moulin de la Galette 510   Post-Impressionism 511
Our Dynamic World: Japanese Painting 513
Experimentation and Art Nouveau 515   Profile: Louis
Sullivan 517   Cubism 517   Mechanism and Futurism 519
Expressionism 521   Fauvism 521

LITERATURE 522
Realism 522   Naturalism 523   Symbolism 523

MUSIC 524
Impressionism 524   Profile: Igor Stravinsky 524
Naturalism in Opera 525   Nontraditional Transitions 527
Stravinsky 527   Schoenberg 527   Jazz 528

THEATRE 528
Realism and Naturalism 528   Symbolism 529

FILM: ART AND MECHANIZATION 529

DANCE *531*
Ethnic Foundations *531*   Diaghilev and the *Ballets
russes 531*   Duncan and the Modern Dance Movement *533*
FOCAL POINT: AMERICA'S GILDED AGE 534   The Breakers *535*
Whitehall *536*   Biltmore House *536*

17 Modernism *538*

THE MODERN WORLD IN CONFLICT *540*
Toward World War I *540*   The Great War *541*
Revolution and Civil War in Russia *543*   The Aftermath *543*

BETWEEN THE WARS *545*
The Great Depression *545*   Hitler's Conquests *545*
Technology: Computers 547

WORLD WAR II *547*
Europe and Africa *547*   The Pacific *548*

SCIENCE AND WAR *548*

PHILOSOPHY *549*   Pragmatism *549*   Existentialism *549*

LITERATURE *550*
Fiction *550*   Profile: *Langston Hughes 551*   Poetry *552*

THE VISUAL ARTS AND ARCHITECTURE *552*
Abstraction *552*   Dada *553*   Fantasy and Surrealism *555*
American Painting *556*   The Harlem Renaissance *557*
Profile: Georgia O'Keeffe 558   Central American
Painting *559*   African and Primitive Influences *559*
Our Dynamic World: African Masks 560   Architectural
Modernism *562*   *Masterwork: Wright—Kaufmann
House 563*

MUSIC *565*
Modern Traditionalism *565*   Departures *565*
Hindemith *565*   Bartók *566*   Berg and Webern *566*
Ives and Copland *566*

THEATRE *567*
Expressionism *567*   Epic Theatre *567*   Absurdism *567*
Masterwork: Martha Graham—Appalachian Spring 568

MODERN DANCE *569*
Native American Dance *569*

PHOTOGRAPHY *570*

FILM *570*
European Film *570*   *Masterwork: Dorothea Lange—
Migrant Mother 571*   The Rise of the Studio *571*   New
Genres *572*   Social Commentary *572*
FOCAL POINT: THE BAUHAUS—INTEGRATION OF THE ARTS 573

18 Postmodernism: The Pluralistic Age *576*

A PLURALISTIC WORLD ORDER *578*
Decolonization *578*   The Cold War *580*   A Unified
Europe *580*   Science and Liberty *580*   Another
Millennium *580*   *Technology: Robots 581*
Postmodernism *581*

THE VISUAL ARTS AND ARCHITECTURE *583*
Abstract Expressionism *583*   Pop Art *584*   *Masterwork:
Helen Frankenthaler—Buddha 585*   Op Art *587*
Hard Edge *587*   Photorealism and Conceptualism *588*
Neo-Expressionism *588*   Primary Structures *590*
Abstraction *591*   *Profile: Pablo Picasso 593*   Found
Sculpture and Junk Culture *594*   Minimalism *594*
Ephemeral and Environmental Art *595*   Installations *596*
Light Art *597*   Postmodernism *597*   Neo-Abstraction *598*
Video Art *598*   "New" Realism *599*   Architectural
Modernism *600*   Architectural Postmodernism *603*

PLURALISM IN LITERATURE *606*

MUSIC *607*
Serialism *608*   Aleatory Music *608*   Improvisation and
Musique Actuelle 608   Electronic Music *608*
Pluralism *609*

THEATRE *610*
Realism *610*   Absurdism *610*   Performance Art and
Postmodernism *611*   Alternative Social Theatre *611*

FILM *612*
International Film and the Demise of the Studio *612*
New Directors *613*

DANCE *613*
Modern *613*   Jazz Dance *614*   Ballet *614*   Postmodern *614*
FOCAL POINT: AN OUTPOURING OF ETHNICITY 615
Native American Poetry *615*   Native American Ceramics
and Painting *615*   Native American Music *616*
Native American Ritual/Theatre *616*   African American
Music—Jazz *616*   African American Theatre *617*   African
American Writers *618*   African American Film-Makers *618*
Hispanic Theatre *619*   Yiddish and Hebrew Theatre *619*
Asian American Theatre *619*

Glossary *621*
Notes *626*
Further Reading *627*
Index *631*

Picture Credits and Literary Acknowledgments

Picture Credits

The author, the publishers, and Calmann & King Ltd wish to thank the museums, galleries, collectors, and other owners who have kindly allowed their works to be reproduced in this book. In general, museums have supplied their own photographs; other sources are listed below: AKG, London: 1.7, 5.12, 5.15, 7.3, 8.5, 9.3, 9.17, 10.13, 10.14, 10.15, 10.19, 10.21, 10.24, 10.27, 10.28, 10.29, 10.30, 11.2, 11.6, 11.13, 11.20, 11.21, 11.34, 12.2, 12.3, 12.11, 12.12, 12.14, 12.15, 12.16, 12.17, 12.18, 12.24, 12.25, 13.2, 13.3, 13.4, 14.4, 15.20, 17.23, 17.24, 17.25; Ansel Adams Publishing Rights Trust/Corbis: 17.31; Ancient Art & Architecture Collection, London: 4.28 (photo: C.M. Dixon), 5.2, 8.17, 13.25; Wayne Andrews, Chicago: 14.23; © Araldo de Luca, Rome: 11.17; Arcaid: 16.40; The Architectural Association, London: 17.28, 18.35, 18.40; Archivi Alinari, Florence: 10.3, 11.30; James Austin, Cambridge: 10.4; Bildarchiv Foto Marburg, Germany: 3.33, 5.23, 5.26, 14.39, 14.40; Bildarchiv Preussischer Kulturbesitz, Berlin: 1.20, 14.36; Bilderberg/Wolfgang Volz, Hamburg: 0.3, 18.26; Bridgeman Art Library: 7.9, 9.16, 11.3, 11.7, 11.11, 12.1, 12.26, 14.7, 14.20, 14.31, 15.4, 16.6; British Library, London: 9.6; British Museum, London: 16.18; CNMHS/SPADEM, Paris: 7.16, 7.25; The Carnegie Museum of Art (Museum purchase: gift of Kaufmann's, the Women's Committee and the Fellows of the Museum of Art 85.62): 18.15; Cement & Concrete Association, Slough: 18.41; Trudy Lee Cohen © 1986, Philadelphia: 16.34; © Donald Cooper/Photostage, U.K.: 18.46; Corbis/Bettmann: 12.20; Courtauld Institute of Art, London: 13.11; James Davis Travel Photography: 18.45; Deutsches Archäologisches Institut, Athens: 2.9; Deutsches Archäologisches Institut, Rome: 4.32; Jean Dieuzaide, Toulouse: 7.11; John Donat, London: 17.24; Dumbarton Oaks (Byzantine Photograph Collection), Trustees of Harvard University, Washington D.C.: 6.16; Esto Photographics, Inc., Mamaroneck, New York: 18.36; ET Archive: 9.7; Mary Evans Picture Library: 7.21, 9.23, 11.28, 12.4, 12.5, 13.5; Fisk University (Vechten Gallery of Fine Arts) Nashville, Tennessee: 17.17; Fotografica Foglia, Naples: 4.10; Werner Forman Archive, London: 5.27, 9.20; Fotomas Index: 15.3; Alison Frantz, Princeton, New Jersey: 3.21, 3.24, 6.19; Sonia Halliday, Weston Turville, U.K.: 3.1 6.30, 6.34, 8.26, 8.28; Robert Harding Pictures Library, London: 11.35, 13.22, 13.23; Clive Hicks, London: 7.13, 8.10, 8.24, 8.25; Colorphoto Hans Hinz, Allschwil, Switzerland: 1.1, 1.5; Hirmer Fotoarchiv, Munich: 1.16, 1.19, 2.17, 2.20, 3.6, 3.17, 3.20, 3.29, 6.3, 6.4, 6.5, 6.10, 6.36, 8.8; Hirshhorn Museum and Sculpture Garden, Smithsonian Institution, Gift of Joseph H. Hirshhorn, 1972 (photo Lee Stalsworth): 18.8; Holly Solomon Gallery, New York: 18.22; Angelo Hornak, London: 16.39; Hulton Getty Picture Collection: 6.14, 12.23, 14.35, 17.29, 17.30; Dewitt Jones/Corbis: 17.30; A.F. Kersting: 1.15, 3.16, 3.31, 7.17, 8.1, 8.12, 8.13, 9.8, 9.9, 9.11, 9.14, 11.25, 13.1, 13.35, 13.38, 14.10, 15.11; Lauros-Giraudon/Bridgeman, London: 8.27, 8.29, 8.30, 13.14; Library of Congress, Washington, D.C.: 17.32; Ralph Liebermann, North Adams, MA: 16.24, 17.25, 18.38; Louisiana Office of Tourism/Al Godoy: 18.44; © Paul Maeyaert, Mont de L'Enclus (Orroir), Belgium: 4.26, 7.21; Mansell Collection: 3.4, 3.7, 3.8, 3.18, 4.15, 4.16, 4.20, 4.22, 4.25, 9.18, 10.6, 10.9, 10.10, 10.11, 10.25, 11.9, 11.26, 11.31, 13.10; Jean Mazenod, L'Art de L'Ancienne Rome, Editions Mazenod, Paris: 4.12; Menil Collection: 18.12; Lucia Moholy, Zürich: 17.34; © Gérard Monico, Saint-Denis, France: 8.7; Peter Moore, New York: 18.31; Ann Münchow, Aachen: 7.28; Musée d'Art et d'Histoire, Auxerre: 7.24; Musei Capitolini, Rome/Barbara Malter: 4.29; National Film Archive, London: 16.36, 17.33; Courtesy of the Oriental Institute, University of Chicago: 1.8, 1.10, 1.11; Österreichische Akademie der Wissenschaften-Mosaikenkommission, Vienna: 6.6; Pentogram Design/Theo Crosby: 12.27; Photoresources, Canterbury: 2.3; Josephine Powell, Rome: 6.2; Prestel Verlag Munich: 18.25; Quattrone Mario Fotostudio, Florence: 10.18; Range/Bettmann: 17.6; Réunion des Musées Nationaux, Paris: 2.10 (© Photo RMN-Hervé Lewandowski), 2.11, 6.12, 6.13, 7.26, 13.7, 13.16, 13.21, 14.15; Eric Robertson, New York: 17.20; Scala, Florence: 2.1, 5.1, 5.6, 6.1, 6.9, 6.31, 7.1, 9.1, 9.19, 10.1, 10.16, 10.20, 11.12, 11.15, 11.19, 11.33, 11.38, 11.39, 11.43, 13.6, 13.12, 13.13, 13.19, 13.20; Peter Sanders Collection: 6.20; Bob Schalkwijk, Mexico City: 17.19; Schomburg Center for Research in Black Culture (Art & Artifacts Division); The New York Public Library; Astor Lenox and Tilden Foundations: 17.18; Science Photo Library/Hank Morgan: 18.2; Edwin Smith, Saffron Walden: 14.37, 14.38; By courtesy of the Trustees of Sir John Soane's Museum, London: 14.12; SOA Photo Agency/Jahns: 18.43; Spectrum Colour Library: 8.9; Sperone Westwater: 18.14; © Steffans/SOA Photo Agency, London: 7.29; Stifts-bibliothek, St Gallen: 10.26; Studio Fotografico Quattrone, Florence: 11.16, 11.23, 13.9; Telegraph Colour Library/T. Yamada: 12.27; V&A Picture Library: 16.38; Vatican Museums: 11.36; Roger-Viollet: 9.13; Weidenfeld & Nicolson, London: 14.21; Wim Swaan: 9.10.

Literary Acknowledgments

Every effort has been made to trace or contact copyright holders and to obtain their permission for use of copyright material. The publishers will gladly receive any information enabling them to rectify any error or omission in subsequent editions. The author, the publishers, and Calmann & King Ltd wish to thank the following for permission to use copyright material:

Ch. 3 W.W. Norton & Company Inc. for extracts from *Agamemnon* and *Prometheus Bound* by Aeschylus, from *Three Greek Plays*, trs. Edith Hamilton, © 1937 W.W. Norton, Inc., renewed © 1965 Doris Fielding Reid

University of Chicago Press for an extract from *Hecuba* by Euripides, from *Complete Greek Tragedies*, ed. David Grene and Richmond Lattimore (1982)

Ch. 15 Bantam Doubleday Dell for "Der Erlkonig" by Johann Wolfgang von Goethe, trs. Philip L. Miller, from *The Ring of Words: An Anthology of Song Texts* (1963)

Ch. 17 Alfred A. Knopf Inc. for "The Negro Speaks of Rivers" by Langston Huges, from *Collected Poems*, © 1994 The Estate of Langston Hughes

Ch. 18 The author for "Recuerdo" from *Shadow Country* (American Indian Studies Center, University of California), © 1982 The Regents of the University of California

Preface

This is the fifth edition of a work used by more than one hundred programs in the United States, with separate editions in Great Britain and Australia. This edition maintains the book's overall focus and intent—that is, to present an overview of the arts in the Western tradition in the contexts of the philosophy, religion, aesthetic theory, economics, and politics surrounding them. The text remains an historical introduction to the humanities from which the reader will gain a basic familiarity with major styles and their implications as well as a sense of the historical development of individual arts disciplines.

In this edition, I have given close attention to making the text clear and relevant to today's student. I also have added material to broaden the scope of coverage and to include the most up-to-date artistic movements and achievements—for example, young contemporary realist painters, ethnic and social alternative theatre, and performance art.

I've included introductory and concluding essays for each chapter to highlight important themes and to stimulate critical thinking about material and its contemporary relevance. Where possible, I have linked topics among chapters—for example, the story of Phocion excerpted from Plutarch's *Lives* (Chapter 4) with Poussin's painting of the same subject (Chapter 13), and Christopher Marlowe's and Goethe's treatments of the Faust story. I also have given women a greater emphasis. In addition, a complete history of dance is traced throughout the text.

An emphasis fundamental to this text remains, and that is an emphasis on formal analysis of works of art to supplement discussion *about* them. This is critical if students are to carry an interest in the arts beyond the confines of the classroom and into the rest of their lives: that, I would hope, is the ultimate purpose of humanities courses. When encountering an artwork for the first time—whether in a museum, a theatre, a concert hall, or on the street—we usually do not have access to biographical or contextual materials. We have only the artwork and the ability to confront it, either with or without confidence. Thus, the analyses, which examine how artworks work in terms of line, form, color, melody, plot, and so on, teach students a means by which artworks can be approached,

responded to, and shared in an on-the-spot manner: the way we actually meet them in real life.

Throughout the text, a pronunciation prompt follows the first occurrence of important names and terms. The use of vowels and consonants to suggest those in the names and terms is straightforward and obvious, with the following exception: the letter Y suggests the vowel sound "eye."

Those familiar with the French and German languages (which account for a significant number of names and terms) know that no English vowels or consonants accurately suggest the nasal and gutteral sounds of those languages. I have tried to come as close as possible without indulging in the arcane. My guides, throughout, have been *Grolier's Encyclopedia* and *The American Heritage Dictionary*.

New to this edition is a corresponding compact disc with eighteen musical selections referenced in the text. It is available from Prentice Hall.

Finally, it should be clear that a book such as this depends upon a multitude of sources other than the general knowledge of its author. In the interest of readability and in recognition of the generalized purpose of this text, copious footnoting has been avoided. I hope the method chosen for presentation and documentation of the works of other authors meets the needs of both responsibility and practicality. The Further Reading section at the end of the book comprises the works used in the preparation of this text. I am indebted to these authors, to many colleagues around the country, and specifically to John Myers, Sherrill Martin, David Kechley, Pat Taylor, and Alan Pizer. For reviewing the manuscript, I would like to thank Madeline Archer, Duquesne University; David C. Bradley, Minot State University; Beverly Carter, Grove City College; Judith Chambers, Hillsborough Community College; Leslie Lambert, Santa Fe Community College; Michael Mallard, Union University; James E. Mattimore, Suffolk Community College; Rodney Oakes, L.A. Harbor College; Joyce Porter, Moraine Valley Community College; Sharon Rooks, Edison Community College; Lisa Odham Stokes, Seminole Community College; and Robert Turley, University of Toledo.

D.J.S.

What are the Arts and How do We Evaluate and Describe them?

OUTLINE

THE HUMANITIES AND THE ARTS

WHAT IS ART?
Nonrestrictiveness
Human Enterprise
Medium of Expression
Communication

THE FUNCTIONS OF ART
Entertainment
Political and Social Commentary
Therapy
Artifact

EVALUATING WORKS OF ART
Types of Criticism
Making Judgments

GETTING STARTED

Two-Dimensional Art
TECHNIQUES: Linear Perspective
Sculpture
TECHNIQUES: Lost-Wax Casting
Architecture
Music
TECHNIQUES: Musical Notation
Theatre
Literature
Film
Dance
Features

0.1 Antonio Canova, *Perseus Holding the Head of Medusa*, 1804–08. Marble, 7 ft 2⁵/₈ ins (2.20 m) high. The Metropolitan Museum of Art, New York (Fletcher Fund) 1967.

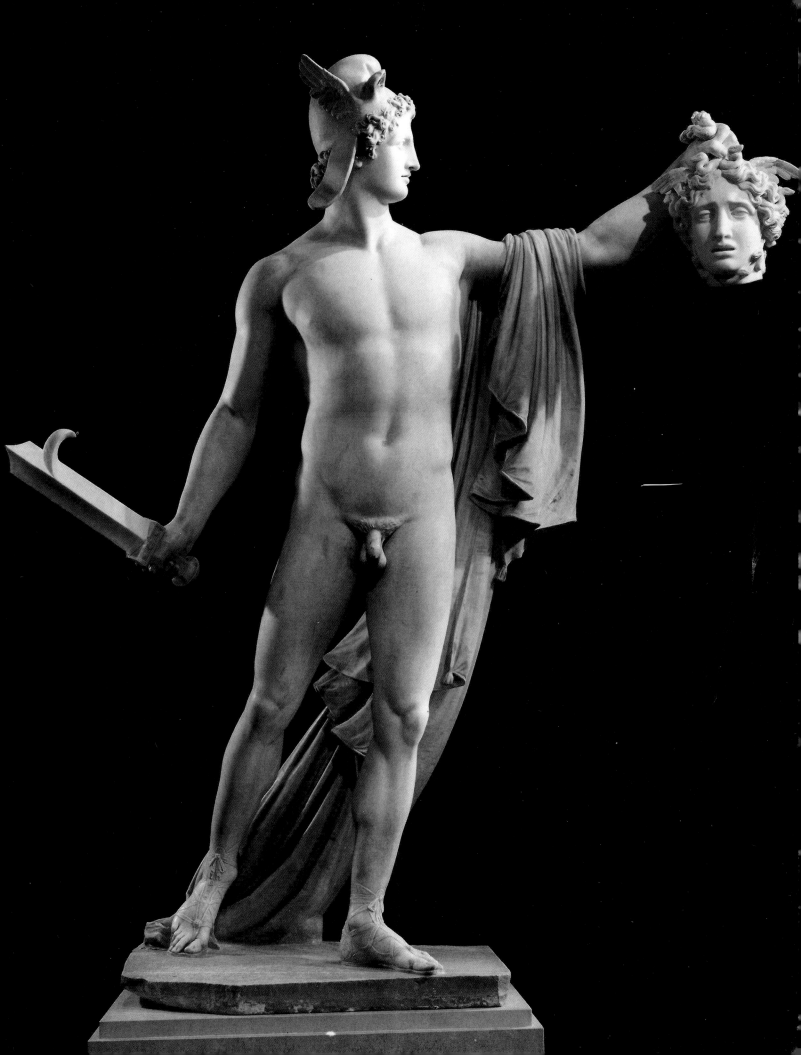

Humans are a creative species. Whether in science, politics, business, technology, or the arts, we depend on our creativity almost as much as anything else to meet the demands of daily life. That is why this book, which traces all aspects of human history, is called *The Creative Impulse*. It is a story about us: our perceptions of the world as we have come to see it, respond to it, and communicate our understandings to each other since the Ice Age, more than 35,000 years ago (Fig. **0.2**). At that time, we were already fully human. Although we have learned a great deal about our world and how it functions, and we have changed our patterns of existence, the fundamental characteristics that make us human—that is, our ability to intuit and to symbolize—have been with us from the beginning. Our art—the major remaining evidence of our earliest times—tells us this in inescapable terms.

Thus, as we begin our study, which will focus to a large extent on artistic creativity, we need some touchstones to help us to understand, evaluate, perceive, and respond to works of art. This chapter gives us that necessary foundation. As we proceed, you will note occasionally terms that appear in small capital letters. These terms are defined in the Glossary at the end of the book.

THE HUMANITIES AND THE ARTS

When we study human culture, we often use the terms "science" and "humanities." The humanities can broadly be defined as those aspects of culture that look into the human spirit. But despite our desire to categorize, there really is no clear boundary between the humanities and the sciences. The basic difference lies in the approach that distinguishes investigation of the natural universe, technology, and social science from the sweeping search of the arts for human reality and truth.

Within the educational system, the humanities have traditionally included the fine arts, literature, philosophy, and, sometimes, history. All these subjects concern the exploration of what it means to be human, what human beings think and feel, what motivates their actions and shapes their thoughts. Many of the "answers" lie in the millions of artworks all around the globe, from the earliest sculpted fertility figures to the video art of the end of the twentieth century. These ARTIFACTS and images are themselves expressions of the humanities, not merely illustrations of past or present ways of life.

Change in the arts differs from change in the sciences in one significant way. Whereas new technology usually displaces the old, and new scientific theory explodes the old, new art does not invalidate earlier human expression.

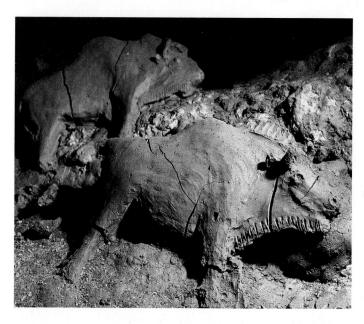

0.2 Bison, after 15,000 B.C. Modeled clay, 25 and 24 ins (63.5 and 61 cm) long. Tuc d'Audoubert, Ariège, France.

Obviously, not all artistic styles survive, but Picasso cannot do to Rembrandt what the theories of Einstein did to those of Newton.

Works of art also remain, in a curious way, always in the present. We react at the time we hear or see it to the sound of a symphony or to the color and composition of a painting. No doubt, an historical perspective on the composer or painter and a knowledge of the circumstances in which the art was created enhance our understanding and appreciation, but for most of us, today's reaction remains most important.

WHAT IS ART?

In a broad sense, the arts are *processes*, *products*, and *experiences* that communicate aspects of the human condition in a variety of means, many of which are nonverbal. *Processes* are the creative thoughts, materials, and techniques artists combine to create *products*—the artworks. *Experiences* are the human interactions and responses that occur when people encounter the vision of the artist in the artwork.

But what is art? Attempts to answer this question have been made by scholars, philosophers, and aestheticians for centuries without yielding many adequate answers. The late pop artist Andy Warhol (pronounced WOR-hohl) reportedly said that "Art is anything you can get away with." Perhaps we should be a little less cynical—and a little more specific. Instead of asking "What is art?", let us ask "What is a work of art?" *A work of art is one person's vision of human reality* (our hopes, desires, fears, and experiences), *expressed in a particular artistic medium, and shared with other people.* Now we can explore the terms of this definition.

Nonrestrictiveness

First, our definition is fairly nonrestrictive: an artwork is anything that attempts to communicate a vision of human reality through a means traditionally associated with the arts—drawing, painting, printmaking, sculpture, as well as works of music, dance, literature, film, architecture, and theatre. If the originator intends it as a work of art, it is one. Whether it is good or bad matters little. A child's drawing that expresses some feeling about mother, father, and home is as much an artwork as Michelangelo's (pronounced mih-kul-AN-juh-loh) Sistine Chapel frescoes. The music of REM and that of Mozart both qualify as artworks under our definition, even though the qualities we might give to these artworks probably would be different. (We will discuss value judgments later in this chapter.)

Human Enterprise

The second implication of our definition is that art is a human enterprise: whenever we experience a work of art, we come into contact with another human being. Artworks are intended to engage us and to animate a desire to respond. In the theatre, for example, we are exposed to a variety of visual and aural stimuli that attempts to make us feel, think, or react as the artists wish us to react.

Medium of Expression

Although we can readily accept the traditional media—painting, traditional sculpture, music using traditional instruments, theatre using a script and performed in an auditorium, and so on—sometimes, when a medium of expression does not conform to our expectations or experiences, we may reject the artwork. For example, Figure 0.3 shows a gigantic environmental installation, consisting of a 24½-mile-long nylon and steel fence, created (and financed) by the artist Christo (pronounced KRIS-toh). For Christo, this work—which existed for only a short time—

0.3 Christo, *Running Fence*, Sonoma and Marin Counties, California, 1972–6. Woven nylon fabric and steel cables, 18 ft (5.49 m) high, 24½ miles (39.2 km) long. Erected September 1976, two weeks.

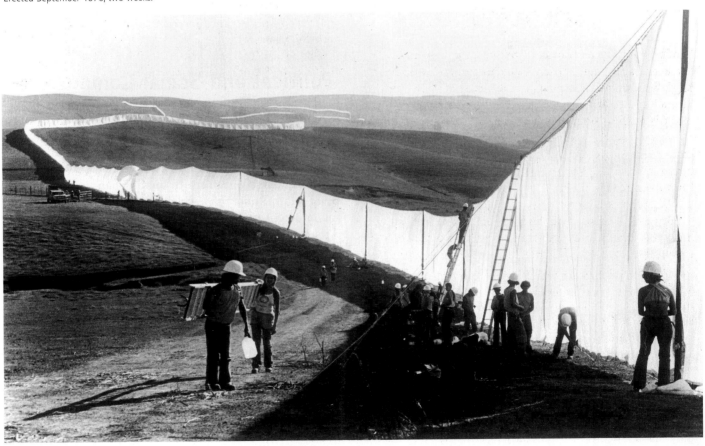

was an artwork. For other people, it most definitely was not. Even though the medium was unconventional, and the work transitory, our working definition would allow it because the intent of the work was artistic.

Communication

Artworks involve communication and sharing. When artworks and humans interact, a wide range of possibilities occurs. Interaction may be casual and fleeting, as in the first meeting of two people, when one or both are not at all interested in interaction. Similarly, the artist may not have much to say or may not say it very well. For example, a play may be written poorly or fail to engage the audience. Or audience members may be ignorant, self-absorbed, preconditioned, or distracted; their preconceptions may be rigid or may not be met by the production, or they may be so preoccupied by something that occurred outside the theatre that they find it impossible to perceive what the production offers. In such circumstances, the artistic experience fails. On the other hand, all conditions may be optimum, resulting in a profoundly exciting and meaningful experience. The play may treat a significant subject in a unique manner, the acting, directing, and design may be excellent, and the audience may be receptive. Or, the interaction may fall somewhere between these two extremes. In any case, a human interchange occurs, and that is fundamental to art.

In discussing art as communication, we need to note one important term, and that is SYMBOL. Symbols suggest something intangible or unobvious. Symbols differ from signs, which suggest facts or conditions. Signs are what they denote. Symbols carry deeper, wider, and richer meanings. Look at Figure 0.4. What do you see? You might identify this figure as a sign, which looks like a plus sign in arithmetic—it is what it seems to be. On the other hand, it might be a Greek cross, in which case it is a symbol because it suggests a wide variety of images, meanings, and implications. Artworks use symbols to convey meaning that goes well beyond the surface of the work, offering glimpses of human reality that cannot be sufficiently described in any other manner. Symbols make artworks into doorways, through which we pass in order to experience, in limited time and space, more of life.

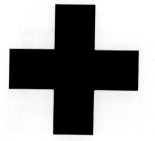

0.4 Greek cross?

THE FUNCTIONS OF ART

Art can function in many ways: as *entertainment*, as *political or social weapon*, as *therapy*, and as *artifact*. One function is no more important than the others. Nor are they mutually exclusive: a single artwork can pursue any or all of them. Nor are these the only functions of art. Rather, they serve as indicators of how art has functioned in the past, and can function in the present. Like the types and styles of art we will examine later in the book, these four functions are options for artists and depend on what artists wish to do with their artworks.

Entertainment

Plays, paintings, concerts, and so on can provide escape from everyday cares, treat us to a pleasant time, and engage us in social occasions; they entertain us. They also give us insights into our hopes and dreams, likes and dislikes, as well as other cultures; and we can find healing therapy in entertainment.

The function of any one artwork depends on us. An artwork in which one person finds only entertainment may function as a social and personal comment for someone else. A Mozart (pronounced MOHT-sahrt) symphony, for example, can relax us, but it may also comment on the life of the composer and/or the conditions of eighteenth-century Austria.

Political and Social Commentary

When art seeks to bring about political change or to modify the behavior of large groups of people, it has political or social functions. In ancient Rome, for example, the authorities used music and theatre to keep masses of people occupied in order to quell urban unrest. On the other hand, Roman playwrights used their plays to attack incompetent or corrupt officials. The Greek playwright Aristophanes used comedy in such plays as *The Birds* to attack the political ideas of the leaders of fourth-century B.C. Athenian society. In *Lysistrata* he attacked war by creating a story in which all the women of Athens go on a sex strike until Athens is rid of war and warmongers.

In late nineteenth-century Norway, Henrik Ibsen (IB-suhn) used his play *An Enemy of the People* (1882) as a platform for airing the issue of whether a government should ignore pollution in order to protect jobs or industry. In the United States at the turn of the twenty-first century, many artworks advance social and political causes and sensitize viewers, listeners, or readers to particular cultural situations.

Therapy

As therapy, art can help treat a variety of illnesses, both physical and mental. Role-playing, for example, frequently acts as a counseling tool in treating dysfunctional family situations. In this context, often called psychodrama, mentally ill patients act out their personal circumstances in order to find and cure the cause of their illness. The focus of this use of art as therapy is the individual. However, art in a much broader context acts as a healing agent for society's general illnesses as well. Artworks can illustrate society's failings and excesses in hopes of saving us from disaster. The laughter caused by comedy releases endorphins, chemicals produced by the brain, which strengthen the immune system.

Artifact

Art also functions as an artifact: a product that represents the ideas and technology of time and place. Artifacts, such as plays, paintings, poems, and buildings, connect us to our past. In this text, the function of art as artifact—as an example of a particular culture—takes on a central role.

When we examine art in the context of cultural artifact, one of the issues we face is the use of artworks in religious ritual. We could consider ritual as a separate function of art. Although we may not think of religious ritual as "art," in the broad context we have adopted for this text, ritual often meets our definition of human communication using an artistic medium. Music, for example, when part of a religious ceremony, meets the definition, and theatre—if seen as an occasion planned and intended for presentation—would include religious rituals as well as events that take place in playhouses. Often, it is difficult to discern when ritual stops and secular production starts—for example, ancient Greek tragedy seems clearly to have evolved from ritual. When ritual, planned and intended for presentation, uses traditionally artistic media like music, dance, and theatre, we can study it as "art" and artifact of its particular culture.

EVALUATING WORKS OF ART

One of the questions everyone seems to ask about an artwork is, "Is it any good?" Whether it is rock music, a film, a play, a painting, or a classical symphony, judgments about the quality of a work often vary from one extreme to the other, ranging from "I liked it" and "It was interesting," to specific reasons why the artwork is thought to be effective or ineffective.

Value judgments are intensely personal, but such a statement is not a satisfying one. Some opinions are more informed than others and represent more authoritative judgment. However, sometimes even knowledgeable people disagree. The best we can conclude is that value judgments simply may not be important or essential. Disagreements about quality, however, can enhance the experience of a work of art when they lead to thought about why the differences exist, resulting in a deeper understanding of the artwork. Nonetheless, evaluation—or criticism—can be exercised without involving any judgment. We can thoroughly dissect any work of art, describe what it consists of—recount and analyze, for example, plot, character, language, aural and visual elements, and thought—and how all of these factors affect an audience and its response. We can spend a significant amount of time doing this and never pass a value judgment at all.

Does this mean that all artworks are equal in value? Not at all. It means that in order to understand what criticism involves, we must separate descriptive analysis, which can be satisfying in and of itself, from the act of passing value judgments. Analysis necessarily leads to enhanced understanding. We may not like the work we have analyzed, but we have understood something that we did not understand before. One important value of criticism is the sharing process: our mutual agreement is less important than the enhanced perception that results from going through the process of understanding and sharing it with someone else.

Now that we have examined briefly what criticism is and why we might do it, what criteria or approaches can we use?

Types of Criticism

There are two basic types of criticism. Examination of a single artwork is called *formal criticism*. Examination of the same work in the context of the events surrounding it, and perhaps the circumstances of its creation, is called *contextual criticism*.

Formal Criticism

Here, we are interested primarily in the artwork itself. We can allow the work to stand by itself, applying no external conditions or information. We analyze the artwork just as we find it: if it is a painting, we look only within the frame; if it is a play, we analyze only what we see and hear. Formal criticism approaches the artwork as an entity within itself. As an example, we will do a brief analysis of Molière's (mohl-YAIR) comedy *Tartuffe* (tahr-TOOF; 1664):

Orgon, a rich bourgeois, has allowed a religious conman, Tartuffe, to gain complete hold over him. Tartuffe has moved into Orgon's house and tries to seduce Orgon's wife at the same time that he is planning to marry Orgon's daughter. Tartuffe is unmasked, and Orgon orders him out. Tartuffe seeks his revenge by claiming title to Orgon's house and blackmailing him with some secret papers. At the very last instant, Tartuffe's plans are foiled by the intervention of the king, and the play ends happily.

We have just described a story. Were we to go one step further and analyze the plot, we would look, among other things, for points at which *crises* occur and cause the characters to make important decisions; we would also want to know how those decisions moved the play from one point to the next. In addition, we would try to locate the extreme crisis—the *climax*. Meanwhile, we would discover auxiliary parts of the plot such as reversals: for example, when Tartuffe is discovered and the characters become aware of the true situation. Depending on how detailed our criticism were to become, we could work our way through each and every aspect of the plot. We might then devote some time to describing and analyzing the driving force—the character—of each person in the play and how the characters relate to each other. Has Molière created fully developed characters? Are they types, or do they seem to behave more or less like real individuals? In examining meaning, we would no doubt conclude that the play deals with religious hypocrisy, and that Molière had a particular point of view on that subject. In this approach, information about the playwright, previous performances, historic relationships, and so on is irrelevant.

Contextual Criticism

On the other hand, contextual criticism seeks meaning by examining related information "outside" the artwork, such as the artist's life, his or her culture, social, and political conditions and philosophies, public and critical reactions to the work, and so on. These can all be researched and applied to the work in order to enhance perception and understanding. This approach tends to view the artwork as an artifact generated from particular contextual needs, conditions, and/or attitudes. If we carry our criticism of *Tartuffe* in this direction, we would note that certain historical events help to clarify the play. For example, the object of Molière's attention probably was the Company of the Holy Sacrament, a secret, conspiratorial, and influential society in France at the time. Like many fanatical religious sects—including those of our own time—the society sought to enforce its own view of morality by spying on the lives of others and seeking out heresies,

in this case, in the Roman Catholic Church. Its followers were religious fanatics, and they had a considerable effect on the lives of the citizenry at large. If we were to follow this path of criticism, any and all such contextual matters that might illuminate or clarify what happens in the play would be pursued.

Making Judgments

Now that we have defined criticism and noted two approaches we might take in pursuing it, we can move on to the final step—making value judgments.

There are several approaches to the act of judgment. Two characteristics, however, apply to all artworks: they are *crafted*, and they *communicate* something to us about our experiences as humans. Making a judgment about the quality of an artwork should address each of these.

Craftsmanship

Is the work well made? To make this judgment, we first need some understanding of the medium in which the artist works. For example, if the artist proposes to give us a realistic vision of a tree, does the artist's handling of the paint yield a tree that looks like a tree? If craftsmanship depended only on the ability to portray objects realistically, judgment would be quite simple. However, we must remember that judgments about the craftsmanship of the artwork require some knowledge about the techniques of its medium. Although we may not yet be ready to make judgments about all of the aspects of craftsmanship in any art form, we can apply what we do know.

Communication

Evaluating what an artwork is trying to say offers more immediate opportunity for judgment and less need for expertise. Johann Wolfgang von Goethe (GUR-te), the nineteenth-century poet, novelist, and playwright, set out a basic, commonsense approach to communication. Because it provides an organized means for discovering an artwork's communication by progressing from analytical to judgmental functions, Goethe's approach is a helpful way in which to end our discussion on criticism. Goethe posed three questions: What is the artist trying to say? Does he or she succeed? Was the artwork worth the effort? These questions focus on the artist's communication by making us identify, first, what was being attempted and, second, the artist's success in that attempt. Whether or not the project was worth the effort asks us to decide if the communication was important. Was it worthwhile?

Getting Started

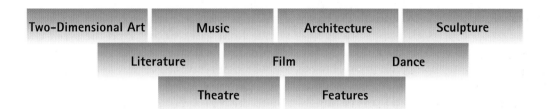

Two-Dimensional Art	Music	Architecture	Sculpture
Literature	Film	Dance
Theatre	Features

Getting Started takes us into the land of basic terminology and fundamental artistic concepts. In other words, we are about to sample some of the things that will help us to identify and communicate important characteristics appropriate to the works of two-dimensional art, sculpture, music, theatre, dance, literature, and film that are presented later in the text.

Although it may not seem so on first reading, the terms and concepts discussed here represent only a fraction of what we might study. The terms are technical, and, undoubtedly, you will want to return to this section as you encounter works of art in the chapters that follow, especially when you seek to describe and compare paintings, musical selections, and so on, using accurate terminology.

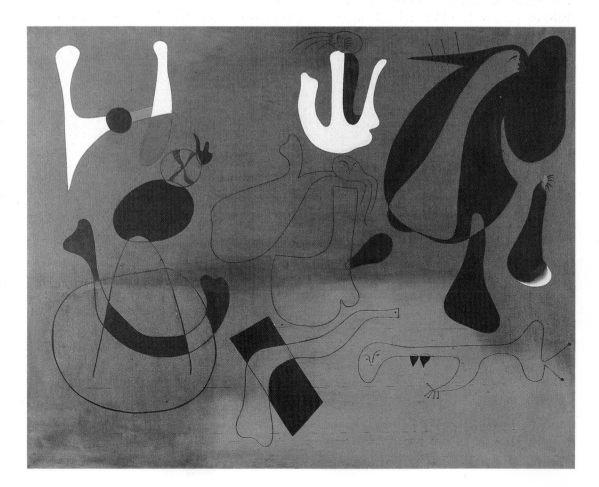

0.5 Joan Miró, *Composition*, 1933. Oil on canvas, 51³/₈ × 64 ins (130.5 × 165 cm). Wadsworth Atheneum, Hartford, Connecticut. © ADAGP, Paris and DACS, London 1999.

Two-Dimensional Art

Two-dimensional art consists of paintings, drawings, prints, and photographs, which differ from each other primarily in the technique of their execution. Probably, our initial response to all four is a response to subject matter—that is, we first notice what the painting, drawing, print, or photograph is about. Such recognition leads us into the work's meaning and begins to shape our response to it. Beyond the recognition of subject, however, lie the technical elements chosen by artists to make their vision appear the way they wish it to appear, and these include MEDIA and COMPOSITION.

Media

The media of the two-dimensional arts are paintings, drawings, prints, and photography. Paintings and drawings can be executed with oils, watercolors, tempera, acrylics, ink, and pencils, to name a few of the more obvious. Each physical medium has its own characteristics. As an example, let us look at *oils*.

Oils are one of the most popular of the painting media and have been since their development around the beginning of the fifteenth century. They offer artists a broad range of color possibilities; they do not dry quickly and can, therefore, be reworked; they present many options for textural manipulation; and they are durable. Look at the texture in the brushwork of Van Gogh's (van-GOH or van GAHK) *The Starry Night* (see Fig. **16.21**). This kind of manipulation is a characteristic of oil. Whatever the physical medium—that is, painting, drawing, print, or photograph—we can find identifiable characteristics that shape the final work of art. Had the artist chosen a different physical medium, the work—all other things being equal—would not look the same.

Composition

The second area we can isolate and respond to involves artists' use of the *elements* and *principles of composition*. These are the building blocks of two-dimensional works of art. Among others, these elements and principles include LINE, FORM, COLOR, REPETITION, and BALANCE.

Elements

The primary element of composition is line. In Joan Miró's (hoh-AHN mee-ROH) *Composition* (Fig. **0.5**) we see amorphous shapes. Some of these are like cartoon figures—identifiable because of their outline—but the other shapes also exemplify line, and they do so because they create boundaries between areas of color and between

0.6 Color wheel.

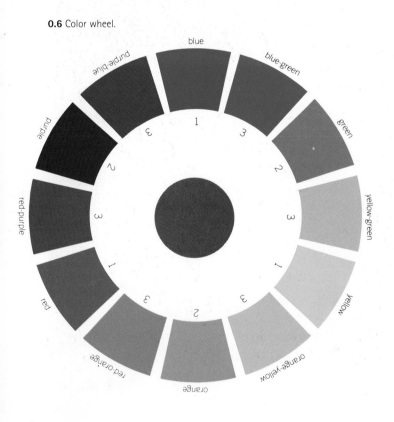

0.7 Value scale.

White		W	
High Light		HL	Yellow
Light	Yellow-green	L	Yellow-orange
Medium Light	Green	ML	Orange
Medium (grey)	Blue-green	M	Red-orange
High dark	Blue	MD	Red
Dark	Blue-violet	D	Red-violet
Low dark	Violet	LD	
Black		B	

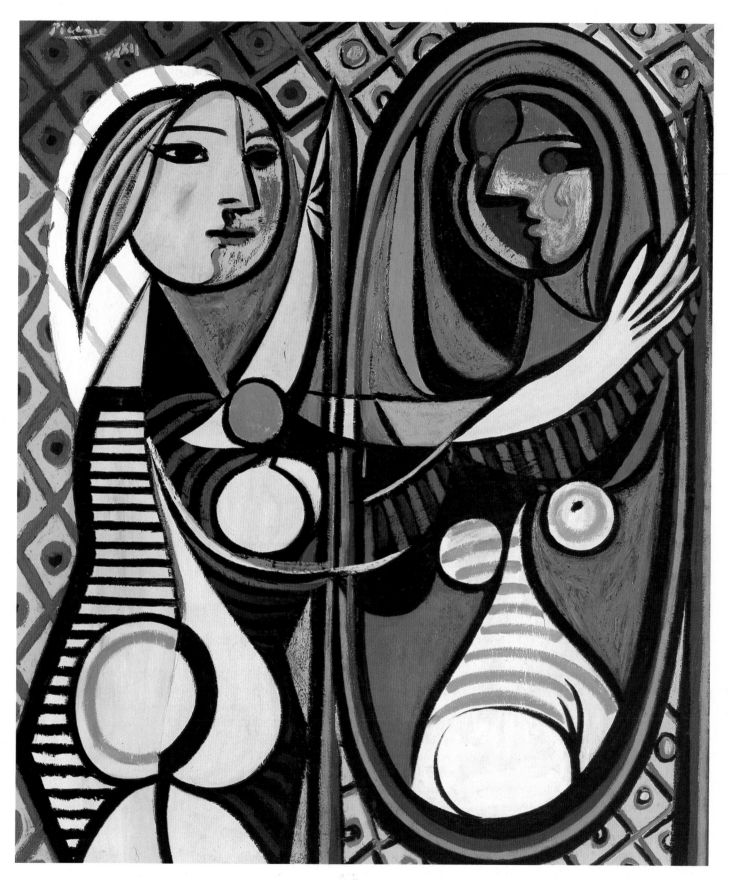

0.8 Pablo Picasso, *Girl Before a Mirror*, 1932. Oil on canvas, 64 × 51¼ ins (162.3 × 130.2 cm). Collection,
Museum of Modern Art, New York (Gift of Mrs. Simon Guggenheim). Photo: © 1998 The Museum of Modern Art, New York. © Succession Picasso/DACS 1999.

Linear Perspective

Throughout the text, we will witness how two-dimensional artists utilize "deep space"—that is, the illusion of depth in their works. One of the methods for creating deep space that appears rational or NATURALISTIC is the use of LINEAR PERSPECTIVE (Fig. **0.9**). Very simply, *linear perspective* is the creation of the illusion of distance in a two-dimensional artwork through the convention of line and foreshortening— that is, the illusion that parallel lines come together in the distance. Linear perspective is also called *scientific, mathematical one-point,* or *Renaissance perspective* and was developed in fifteenth-century Italy (see Chapter 10). It uses mathematical formulas to construct illusionistic images in which all elements are shaped by imaginary lines called *orthogonals* that converge in one or more *vanishing points* on a *horizon line.* Linear perspective is the system most people in the Euro-American cultures think of as perspective, because it is the visual code they are accustomed to seeing.

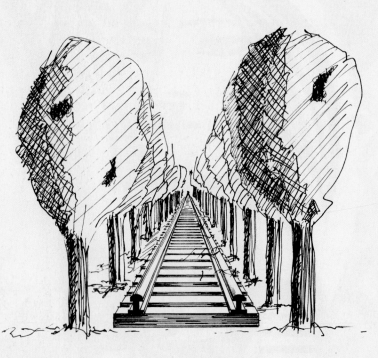

0.9 Linear perspective.

other shapes or forms. Essentially, line is either curved or straight, and it is used by artists to control our vision and to create unity, emotional value, and, ultimately, meaning.

Form and line are closely related. Form as a compositional element is the SHAPE of an object. It is the space described by line. A building is a form. So is a tree. We perceive them as buildings or trees, and we perceive their individual details, because of the line by which they are composed. *Color* is a somewhat complex compositional element. The word HUES is used to describe the basic colors of the spectrum (Fig. 0.6). The apparent whiteness or grayness of a color is its VALUE (Fig. 0.7). When we observe a work of art, we can, among other aspects of color, identify, respond to, and describe the breadth of the *palette*—how many different hues and values the artist has used—and the way the artist has used those hues and values.

Principles

The principles of composition include *repetition* (how the elements of the picture are repeated or alternated) and *balance* (how the picture stands on its axes). In Picasso's

(pee-KAH-soh) *Girl Before a Mirror* (Fig. 0.8), the artist has ordered the recurrence of elements in a regular manner. He has placed hard angles and soft curves side by side, and, in addition, has used two geometric forms, the oval and the diamond, over and over again to build up the forms of the work. He also has balanced the picture with nearly identical shapes on each side of the central axis. When identical shapes and colors appear on either side of the axis, it creates a condition called SYMMETRY. Balance achieved by using unequal shapes, as in Figures 0.5 and 0.8, indicates asymmetry, the balancing of unlike objects—also called psychological balance.

Sculpture

Sculpture is a medium of three dimensions. Thus, in addition to those qualities of composition just noted, we can approach sculpture by another element of composition

TECHNIQUES

Lost-Wax Casting

The LOST-WAX technique, sometimes known by the French term *cire-perdue*, is a method of casting sculpture in which the basic mold is created by using a wax model, which is then melted to leave the desired spaces in the mold. The technique probably began in Egypt. By 200 B.C., the technique was used in China and ancient Mesopotamia, and it was used soon after that by the Benin people of Africa. It spread to Greece sometime in the late sixth century B.C.

The drawings indicated in Figure **0.10** illustrate the steps Benin sculptors would have utilized. A heat-resistant "core" of clay—approximately the shape of the sculpture—was covered by a layer of wax approximately the thickness of the final work. The sculptor carved the details in the wax. Rods and a pouring cup made of wax were attached to the model, and then the model, rods, and cup were covered with thick layers of clay. When the clay was dry, the mold was heated to melt the wax. Molten metal could then be poured into the mold. When the molten metal had dried, the clay mold was broken and removed, which meant that the sculpture could not be duplicated.

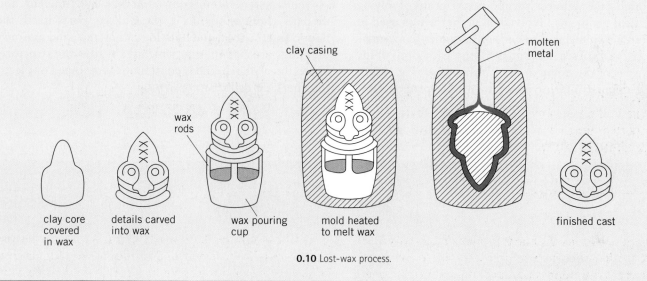

0.10 Lost-wax process.

called MASS: the size, shape, and volume of the forms. Sculpture appeals to us by how large or small it is and by the appearance of weight and density in its materials.

Dimensionality

As we have noted, sculpture defines actual space. Sculpture may be FULL-ROUND, RELIEF, or LINEAR. Full-round works are freestanding and fully three-dimensional. They are meant to be viewed from any angle. Relief sculpture projects from a background and cannot be seen from all sides. It maintains a two-dimensional quality, as compared to full-rounded sculpture. Linear sculpture emphasizes construction with thin, tubular items such as wire or neon tubing.

Texture

The surface treatment (called texture) of a work of sculpture is as important as its dimensionality. Michelangelo carved *David* (see Fig. **11.1**) from marble, but he made the stone seem alive and warm like living flesh by giving it a lustrous, polished texture.

Architecture

Architecture is often described as the art of sheltering, and it is the one art form that combines aesthetic considerations with intensely practical ones. Our formal responses to architecture often involve the purpose of the building: a church, an office building, a residence, and so on. The way architects merge interior function with exterior form provides much of our encounter with works of architecture.

Although a variety of fundamental technical elements exist in architecture, we will only discuss one: *structure.*

Structure

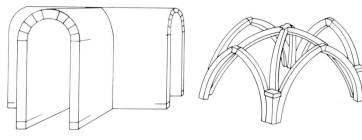

0.11 Groin vault.   **0.12** Ribbed vault.

Architecture contains many systems of structure. As we travel through the centuries in our examination of human creativity, we will see examples of POST-AND-LINTEL, CANTILEVER, ARCH, bearing wall, and skeleton frame structures. Laying horizontal pieces (LINTELS) across vertical supports (posts) gives us one of our oldest structural systems—that is, post-and-lintel (see Fig. **4.26**). When unimpeded interior space became an architectural necessity, the arch gave architects an additional means of solving the practical problems involved. Whether it was used in VAULTS (arches joined end to end) or in domes (concentric arches), as we shall see in the great Gothic cathedrals of the Middle Ages or the dome of the Pantheon (see Fig. **4.23**), the arch opened interior space to usable proportions.

When vaults cross at right angles, they create a GROIN VAULT (Fig. **0.11**). The protruding masonry that indicates a diagonal juncture of arches in a tunnel vault is a RIBBED VAULT (Fig. **0.12**). Cantilever, as exemplified in the Zarzuela (zahr-ZWAY-luh) Race Track (Fig. **0.13**), provided architects with dramatic means for expression, for here, unsupported, overhanging precipices define space.

The system of *bearing wall* has had ancient and modern applications. In it, the wall supports itself, the floors, and the roof, and both log cabins and solid masonry buildings are examples in which the wall is the structure. When the wall material is continuous (not joined or pieced together) it is called MONOLITHIC.

0.13 Eduardo Torroja, Grandstand, Zarzuela Race Track, Madrid, 1935.

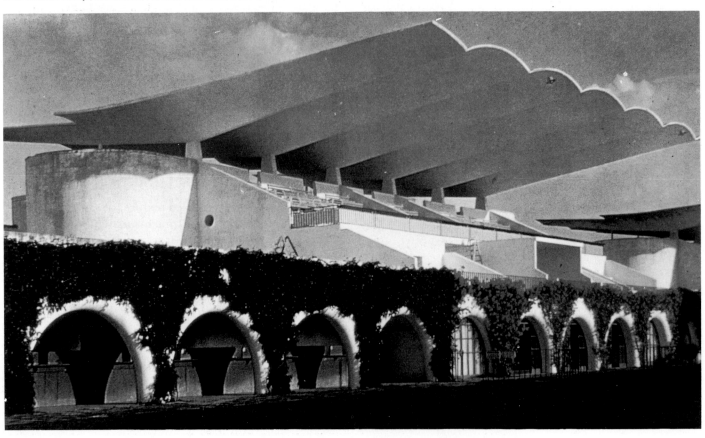

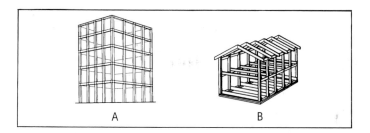

0.14 Skeleton frame structures: A. Steel-Cage Construction; B. Balloon Construction.

Finally, *skeleton frame* structure uses a framework to support the building. The walls are attached to the frame, thus forming an exterior skin. When skeleton framing makes use of wood, as in house construction, the technique is called *balloon construction*. When metal forms the frame, as in skyscrapers, the technique is known as steel-cage construction (Fig. **0.14**).

Music

Genres

Listening to music often begins with genre identification, simply because it helps us to know exactly what kind of composition we are hearing. Being aware that we are listening to a SYMPHONY—a large musical composition for orchestra, typically consisting of four separate sections called "movements"—provides us with clues that are different from a MASS—a choral setting of the Roman Catholic service, the Mass. A CONCERTO (kahn-CHAIR-toh), a composition for solo instrument with accompaniment, gives us different experiences from an OPERA or

---

TECHNIQUES

Musical Notation

Musical notation is a system of writing music so the composer can communicate clearly to the performer the pitches and rhythms (among other things) of the piece. A brief familiarity with this method of communication is important because later in the text we will illustrate characteristics of musical compositions with written notation.

The pitches of music are indicated with symbols, called *notes*, placed on a *staff*—five parallel lines on which each line and space represent a pitch (Fig. **0.15A**). The higher a note's placement on the staff, the higher the pitch. Seven of the twelve pitches of an octave in Western music are named after the first seven letters of the alphabet: A, B, C, D, E, F, G. The remaining five tones are indicated by the use of two signs, the *sharp* sign (♯) and the *flat* sign (♭) (Fig. **0.15B**). A *clef* (in French, "key") is placed at the beginning of the staff to show the pitch of each line and space (Figs. **0.15C** and **D**). Music is written in different *keys*—each associated with the presence of a central note, scale, and chord—which are indicated by a *key signature* (Figs. **0.15E** and **F**). *Rhythms* are indicated with notes indicating time values relative to each other (Fig. **0.15G**). The duration of silences in a musical piece is indicated by a symbol called a *rest* (Fig. **0.15H**).

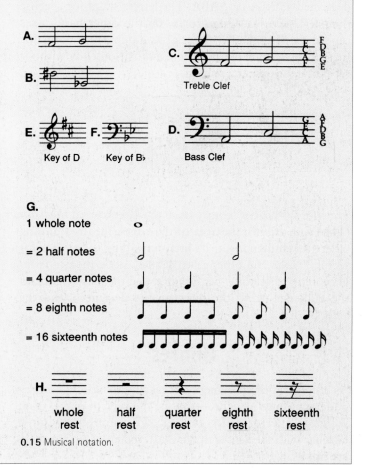

0.15 Musical notation.

ORATORIO, a large-scale choral work such as Handel's *Messiah* performed in concert form.

Melody and Form

Whatever the generic category, all music employs the same technical elements, of which MELODY and form are perhaps the two most obvious. We will introduce others at appropriate points in the text.

Melody is a succession of sounds with rhythmic and tonal organization. Any combination of musical tones constitutes a melody, but melody usually has particular qualities beyond being a mere succession of sounds. Musical ideas, for example, come to us in melodies called THEMES; shorter versions, brief melodic or rhythmic ideas, are called MOTIVES or MOTIFS (moh-TEEF).

Form, like the principles of composition in visual art, gives musical compositions shape and organization. Composers use form to arrange musical elements and relationships into successive events or sections. Basically, we can listen for two types of form: *closed* and *open*. Closed forms direct our attention back into the composition by restating at the end of a thematic section the element that formed the beginning. This pattern of development often is described as ABA or AABA. The letters stand for specific thematic sections. Open form, on the other hand, uses repetition of thematic material as a departure point for further development, and the composition ends without repeating the opening section.

Theatre

The word "theatre" comes from the Greek word *theatron* (THAY-uh-trahn): the area of the Greek theatre building where the audience sat. Its literal meaning is "a place for seeing." Like the other PERFORMING ARTS, theatre is an interpretive discipline, because between the playwright and the audience stand the director, the designers, and the actors.

Genres

As in music, our enjoyment of theatre can be enhanced by understanding the genre—that is, the type of play—from which the performance evolves. We are probably most familiar with the genres of TRAGEDY and *comedy*, but there are others.

We commonly describe a tragedy as a play with an unhappy ending, and typically, tragic heroes make free choices that cause suffering and defeat or sometimes triumph out of defeat. Often, the hero—the *protagonist*—undergoes a struggle that ends disastrously. In many respects, comedy is much more complex than tragedy and even harder to define. Comedy embraces a wide range of theatrical approaches, and when it is defined in its broadest terms, comedy may not even involve laughter. Although we can say, probably with some accuracy, that humor forms the root of all comedy, many comedies employ satire, and comedies often treat serious themes while remaining basically lighthearted in spirit.

These and the other genres of theatre guide our expectations as we witness a production. If we know the genre in advance, our responses move according to those expectations. If we do not know the genre, we have to work it out as the production unfolds.

Plot, Character, Thought, and Visual Elements

Technically, theatrical productions are shaped to a large degree by *plot*—that is, the structure of the play—the skeleton that gives it shape. The plot determines how a play works—how it moves from one moment to another, how conflicts are structured, and, ultimately, how the play comes to an end.

Plays also turn on *character*: the motivating psychological makeup of the people in the play. Although many plays focus on visual elements such as settings, lighting, and costumes, we find theatre engrossing because of the way plays reflect human behavior and conflict in human decisions and actions. Thus, when we attend a performance of a play, our primary attention focuses on how dialogue reveals character and how actors portray actions. Most plays hinge on the actions and decisions of one major character, called the *protagonist*, and when we follow his or her development and the consequences of his or her actions, we are led to an understanding of the play's meaning.

The meaning of the play—sometimes called its *thought*—like the meaning of any work of art, reveals what artists are trying to communicate to us about our universe.

The visual elements of a play comprise a number of factors including the relationship of the audience to the acting area—for example, the arena form in which the audience surrounds the stage area. Visual elements also include scenery, costumes, lighting, and actor movement.

Literature

Literature operates through a system of language in which the words themselves trigger our understanding.

Genres

Like many of the other arts, we approach literature first through the formal door of its genres. These are fiction, poetry, biography, and essay.

Fiction is a work created from the author's imagination rather than from fact. Normally, it takes one of two approaches to its subject matter: realistic—the appearance of observable, true-to-life details—or nonrealistic—fantasy. Other literary forms, such as narrative poetry, however, can also be fiction, and fictional elements can be introduced into forms such as biography and epic poetry. Traditionally, fiction is divided into novels and short stories.

Poetry, on the other hand, is a type of work designed to convey a vivid and imaginative sense of experience. It uses concentrated language, selected for its sound, suggestive power, and meaning, and employs specific technical devices such as meter, rhyme, and metaphor. Poetry can be divided into three major types: *narrative*, which tells a story, *dramatic*, which utilizes dramatic form or technique, and LYRIC, which consists of brief, subjective treatments employing strong imagination, melody, and feeling to create a single, unified, and intense impression of the personal emotion of the poet.

Over the centuries, *biography*, a written account of a person's life, has taken many forms, including literary narratives, simple catalogues of achievement, and psychological portraits. Biographies of saints and other religious figures are called hagiographies.

Traditionally, the *essay* is a short literary composition on a single subject, usually presenting the personal views of the author. Essays include many subforms and a variety of styles, but they uniformly present a personal point of view with a conscious attempt to achieve grace of expression. Characteristically, the best essays are marked by clarity, good humor, wit, urbanity, and tolerance.

Point of View, Character, and Plot

In writing fiction, authors usually employ one of four *points of view*: (1) first person; (2) epistolary (the use of letters written by the characters); (3) third person; or (4) stream of consciousness (wherein a flow of thoughts and feelings come from a specific character's psyche).

As in theatre, *character* also represents an important focus. The people in the work and their struggles with some important human problem give literature much of its appeal.

Plot in a work of literature may be a major or subordinate focus. Like theatrical plots, literary plots unfold the structure of the work and may come to a climax and resolution or leave the characters in a convenient place, allowing us to imagine their future lives continuing as their characters dictate.

Theme and Language

Most good stories have an overriding idea or *theme* by which the other elements are shaped. Although some critics argue that the quality of a theme is less important than what the author does with it, the best artworks are often those in which the author has taken a meaningful theme and developed it exceptionally.

In poetry, *language* that includes imagery—figures, which take words beyond their literal meaning, and METAPHORS, which give new implication to words—also provides an important focus.

Film

A product of modern technology, film brings us into a world that, apart from a lack of three-dimensionality, is often mistaken for reality. We are most familiar with the *narrative* film—that is, one that tells a story, such as the films directed by Alfred Hitchcock (Fig. 0.16). Two other types of film also exist—documentary film and absolute film. *Documentary* film is an attempt to record actuality, using either a sociological or a journalistic approach, and it is normally not reenacted by professional actors but shot as the event occurs. *Absolute* film is film that exists for its own sake, for its record of movement or form. It does not use narrative techniques—although documentary techniques can be used in some instances. Created neither in the camera nor on location, absolute film is built carefully, piece by piece, on the editing table or through special effects and multiple-printing techniques.

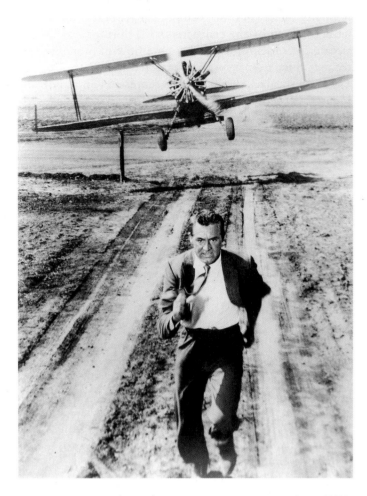

0.16 Alfred Hitchcock (director), *North by Northwest*, 1959. 136 minutes, MGM Studios, USA.

Dance

Dance deals with the human form in time and space. In general, it follows one of three traditions: ballet, modern dance, and folk dance. *Ballet* comprises what can be called classical or formal dance; it is rich in tradition and rests heavily on a set of prescribed movements and actions. In general, ballet is a highly theatrical dance presentation consisting of solo dancers, duets, and choruses, or *corps de ballet* (kohr duh ba-LAY). According to the *Dance Encyclopedia*, ballet's basic principle is "the reduction of human gesture to bare essentials, heightened and developed into meaningful patterns."

Modern dance is a label given to a broad variety of highly individualized dance works limited to the twentieth century, essentially American in derivation, and antiballetic in philosophy. The basic principle of modern dance probably could be stated as an emphasis on natural and spontaneous or uninhibited movement in strong contrast with the conventionalized and specified movement of the ballet. Although narrative elements often exist in modern dance, the form emphasizes them less than does traditional ballet. Modern dance also differs significantly from ballet in its use of the human body and interaction with the dance floor.

Folk dance, somewhat like folk music, comprises a body of group dances performed to traditional music. As in folk music, the creator (in this case, the *choreographer*) remains unknown. Folk dance began as a necessary or formative part of various cultures with characteristics identifiable with a given culture. Each folk dance has its prescribed movements, rhythms, music, and costumes. At its core, folk dancing establishes an individual sense of participation in a society, tribe, or mass movement, and strengthens individuals' sense of belonging through collective dancing. On the other hand, however, folk dance often takes on the characteristics of concert dance—as many tourists can relate.

Line, Form, and Repetition

The compositional elements of line, form, and repetition apply to the human body in dance in exactly the same manner as they apply to painting and sculpture. As in all artworks occupying space, dance can create meaning by using horizontal line to suggest placidity, vertical line to suggest grandeur, and diagonal line to suggest movement. Dancers' bodies become like sculptures in motion as they move from one pose to another, and, because dancers move through time, the element of repetition serves a vital part of how choreographers put dances together and how we respond to them. Patterns of shapes and movement occur, and through them, like themes and variations in music, we find structure and meaning in dance works.

Features

Pronunciation

Throughout the text, whenever a name or term (whose pronunciation may be problematical) appears for the first time, a pronunciation guide follows immediately in parentheses. The stressed syllable appears in capital letters. The vowel and consonant selections to guide you in pronouncing the word are straightforward. The only usage that may be questionable is the use of the letter Y to suggest a long I sound—for example, the first person pronoun "I" would appear "Y," and the word "aisle," would appear "YL."

Profiles

Profile boxes appear throughout the text in order to draw our attention to the biography of a prominent person in the chapter. Profile boxes give us a chance to get to know these people a little better, spending more time with them than regular treatment in the text might allow.

Technology

Throughout history, humans have made discoveries and then turned those discoveries into tools or other useful devices that enhance the quality of life. As the text suggests, being a human being isn't much different today from what it was thousands of years ago. On the other hand, the nature of our world, as the result of our technological advancement, is considerably different. Thus, in each chapter we have a feature box to highlight some important technology that developed during the time covered in that chapter.

Masterwork

In a text such as this, which discusses nearly a thousand works of art in painting, sculpture, architecture, theatre, literature, dance, music, and film, we need occasionally to rest, to draw away from the flow of the material, and focus on a single, significant work of art. That is the purpose of the Masterwork boxes in each chapter. The presence of one particular work of art singled out as a Masterwork does not necessarily mean it is any better than the other works which have not been so designated. The works selected are "masterworks" by whatever criteria we wish to define that term, but the selection is not intended as a hierarchical ranking system.

Focal Point

At the conclusion of each chapter a "Focal Point" section appears. Here we take the time to isolate a group of works, a special time, a combination of artists, or a locale that represents some important facet of the preceding chapter. In a way, the Focal Point section serves as a summary, because the material has a representative quality. Nonetheless, it is complete in itself, and we might even think that it belongs in the body of the chapter itself.

Our Dynamic World

The boxes in each chapter labeled "Our Dynamic World" are intended to give us a taste of what was happening in the arts in a non-Western culture at the same time as the topics in the chapter occurred in the West. Although these boxes are brief, and to some may appear tokenistic, they remind us that there is a world beyond the Western one, and they give us another chance to apply our skills of perception and analysis. The artworks in the box may be similar to or quite different from the style of their Western counterparts. How they are similar or different is a question we should attempt to answer—using only the evidence of the art itself and the descriptive terminology we studied earlier in this section. The works of art in the Dynamic World boxes do have a relationship to the art of the chapter, and we should take the time to understand that relationship.

Maps and Timelines

Maps and timelines appear, mostly, at the beginning of each chapter. They contain information to help locate and correlate the art, history, philosophy, geography, etc. covered in the chapter. They also can be used to relate one chapter to another in time and place.

Chapter Opener

The opening pages of each chapter prepare you for what lies ahead. Firstly, an outline of the chapter is given, followed by key terms and definitions that will help you to understand the material covered. A short essay connects ideas and issues in the chapter with today's problems and circumstances.

Chapter Review

At the end of each chapter a Chapter Review box helps you connect the information you have just studied. The **Critical Thought** section stimulates your critical thinking about material in the chapter, again tying it to today's themes and concerns. The **Summary** prompts your comprehension with statements concerning what you should be able to do, having studied the chapter. Each box ends with a directive for you to practice your use of terminology and understanding of concepts by comparing works of art.

CHAPTER ONE

The Ancient World

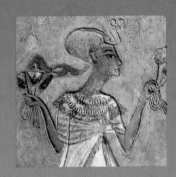

OUTLINE

THE HUMAN JOURNEY
  TECHNOLOGY: Our Earliest Tools

OUR EARLIEST ART
Venus Figures
The Cave of Lascaux

MESOPOTAMIA
Sumer
  TECHNOLOGY: The Invention of
    the Wheel
  MASTERWORK: The Tell Asmar
    Statues
Hammurabi and Babylonia
The Assyrians

ANCIENT EGYPT
Religion
  OUR DYNAMIC WORLD: Ancient
    China
Pyramid Architecture
Sculpture
Music

FOCAL POINT: AKHENATON AND
MONOTHEISM—THE TELL EL
AMARNA PERIOD
  PROFILE: Akhenaton and Nefertiti

VIEW

ART: THE CREATIVE IMPULSE

This chapter takes us from the beginnings of humankind through the great civilization of ancient Egypt. What it shows us, among other things, is the interrelationship of humankind in its desire to create art—something that began when our ancestors still lived in caves. More than that, however, we will see that these three cultures—Ice Age humans, Mesopotamians, and ancient Egyptians—made choices about the ways in which they represented the figures of humans and animals. As a result, we can identify their representations and differentiate them from each other and from the representations of other cultures and times we will study in subsequent chapters. In addition, we will see relationships in the manners in which these cultures viewed death and the afterlife. Finally, we will note how, as early as ancient Mesopotamia and Egypt, literacy meant power.

KEY TERMS

Some basic terms and concepts we will encounter in this chapter include the following:

Paleolithic, the first stage of human culture, in which humans discovered fire, clothing, basic techniques for hunting and gathering, and simple social organization.

Venus figures were widespread representations of the female form, probably with mystical significance.

Pantheon, a word meaning "all the gods."

Cuneiform was Sumerian writing involving two types of sign—one for syllables and one for words—consisting of wedge marks and combinations of wedge marks pressed into damp clay.

Pyramid, an Egyptian burial tomb of great size and scale containing hidden chambers.

Above Detail of Fig. **1.18**.

1.1 Black bull, detail, c. 16,000–14,000 B.C. Paint on limestone, 13 ft (3.96 m) long. Lascaux, France.

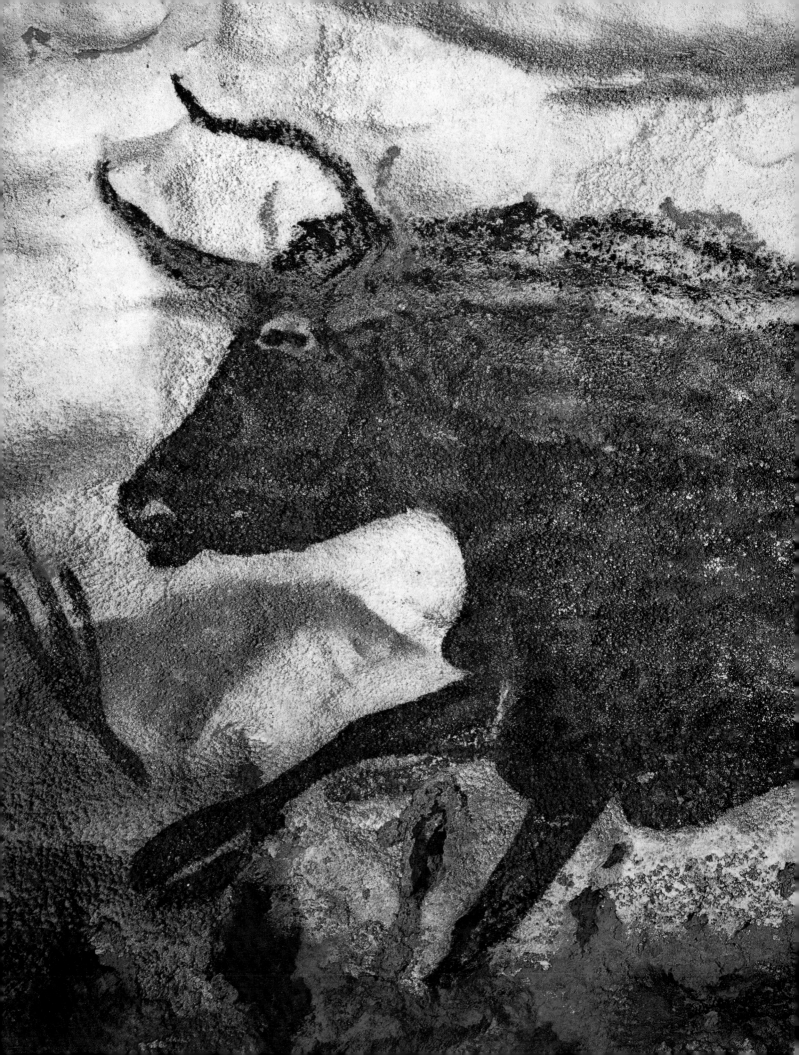

THE HUMAN JOURNEY

The human journey began long before the chronicles of history. Several million years may have passed as humankind journeyed from prehistory to city life, civilization, and history. As humans evolved culturally, they adapted to a changing environment with creative discoveries and ingenious applications of those discoveries in technology and social inventions. They migrated across the globe.

The first stage of human culture was the Paleolithic (pay-lee-oh-LITH-ik) or Old Stone Age, reaching back beyond one million years B.C. Here, humans were hunters and gatherers. But in the Paleolithic period, humans discovered fire, clothing, basic techniques for hunting and gathering food, and simple social organization. Toward the end of the period, our ancestors probably began to think in artistic and religious terms (Map **1.1**).

The second stage of human culture was the Neolithic period or New Stone Age. Between approximately 8000 B.C. and 3000 B.C., people began to settle down and to raise crops rather than to hunt and gather. This was the agricultural phase. Stone tools improved dramatically, and humans learned to make pottery and textiles. Social structure changed as well, as humans learned how to live together in small villages.

When villages evolved into cities, a third stage of cultural development occurred, called *civilization*. From that time on, humans have engaged in complex cultures evolving around urban centers and empire building. They learned how to work with metals, to build monumental

Map 1.1 Sites of prehistoric importance in Europe.

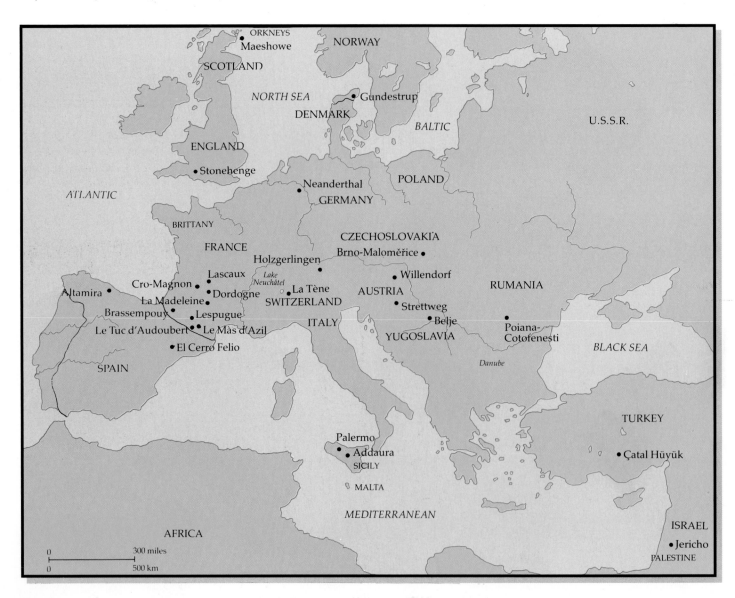

B.C.	GENERAL EVENTS	LITERATURE & PHILOSOPHY	VISUAL ART & ARCHITECTURE	PERFORMING ARTS
1,000,000				
	Stone weapons			
50,000				
	Homo neanderthalensis	Human symbols		
30,000				
	Homo sapiens		Woman from Willendorf (**1.4**)	
20,000				
			Horse from Gargas (**1.3**) Cave at Lascaux (**1.1, 1.5**)	
10,000				
	Last glaciers in Europe			
	Agricultural settlements Pottery			

Timeline 1.1 The prehistoric world.

architecture, to write, to organize centralized bureaucracies, and to stratify social classes.

Some 50,000 years ago, humankind began to grasp the notions of selfhood and individuality. They began to make symbols as part of a strategy for comprehending reality and for telling each other what they discovered. They learned to make art in order to express more fully what they believed was their unique essence. They became aware of death and buried their dead with care and reverence. They realized that they had a complex relationship with the world into which they were born in mystery, in which they lived in mystery, and from which they departed in mystery. Progress since that early time in technological and socioeconomic sophistication has been immense, but we are no more human now than they were then.

TECHNOLOGY: PUTTING DISCOVERY TO WORK

Our Earliest Tools

The technology that accompanied the transition of early humans into social organizations helped them to survive. Perhaps as early as one million years ago, our forebears began to use crudely split stones for cutting and scraping. In the millennia that followed, throughout Africa, Europe, and Asia, scrapers, spears, axes, and knives emerged, followed by bows and arrows with chipped flint heads. As early as 250,000 years ago, hand axes were made either from flint or from a fine-grained rock that would provide a sharp edge. Beginning with a suitable piece of stone, flakes were hammered off in a series around the edge, so that eventually both sides of the tool were covered with scars from which the flakes had been detached. At first, the flakes seem to have been discarded, but in time they were used unaltered as small tools, while, later still, they were often trimmed to provide knives and scrapers (Fig. **1.2**).

1.2 Hand-axe from Swanscombe, Kent, UK, c. 25,000 B.C. Flint, 6³/₈ ins (15.8 cm) high.

1.3 Horse's head, c. 17,000–13,000 B.C. Engraving on rock, about 8 ins (20 cm) high. Gargas, France.

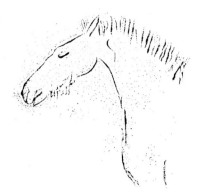

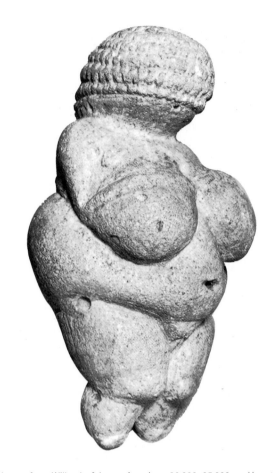

1.4 Woman from Willendorf, Lower Austria, c. 30,000–25,000 B.C. Limestone, 4¹⁄₂ ins (11 cm) high. Naturhistorisches Museum, Vienna.

If we have any tendency to think of our prehistoric predecessors as somehow less human than ourselves, we have only to consider the profundity of their art to set our thinking straight. However, because we are dealing with prehistory—that is, before recorded history—we can make only the broadest of conjectures, based on the slimmest of evidence. Studies of prehistoric societies and art leave us without a consensus on which to build, but even if we cannot accurately grasp all the whys or wherefores of the artifacts (see Introduction) that remain for us to study, we cannot escape the power of the human spirit that they express.

OUR EARLIEST ART

The first known drawings date from approximately 30,000 to 15,000 B.C. Figures were scratched on stones that have been found in deposits on cave floors, among tools and weapons that scholars have used to date them. Among these early works is a horse engraved on a cave wall at Gargas, France, dating from approximately 17,000 to 13,000 B.C. (Fig. **1.3**). The strong, curving outline captures the grace and strength of the horse, and in this smooth and sophisticated depiction, the artist uses realistic proportions and captures details like the hair under the muzzle. Although the use of line is economical, the essentials of the subject are nevertheless there. The caves at Gargas were also occupied by much later peoples, which raises some questions about the date of the drawings there, but they still provide us with a remarkable illustration of the perceptions and style of our prehistoric ancestors.

Venus Figures

Venus figures have been found in burial sites in a band stretching approximately 1,100 miles (1,770 kilometers) from western France to the central Russian plain. Many

scholars believe that these figures are the first works in a REPRESENTATIONAL style—that is, they are works that attempt to portray their subjects in a lifelike manner. The figures, which share certain stylistic features and are remarkably similar in overall design, may be fertility figures or they may have been no more than objects for exchange. Whatever their purpose, all the figures have the same tapering legs, wide hips, and sloping shoulders.

The Woman from Willendorf (VIH-lehn-dorf; Fig. **1.4**) is the best-known example of the Venus figures. Like the others, she is a human portrayal within a stylized framework. The emphasis on swollen thighs and breasts and prominent genitals suggest that the image is a fertility symbol. Carved from limestone, the figure was originally colored red, the color of blood, perhaps symbolizing life itself (corpses were painted red by many primitive peoples). She may be pregnant. She may very well be an Earth Mother, or goddess of fertility. She is generalized in her facelessness.

Although faceless, these Venus figures usually have hair, often wear bracelets, beads, aprons, or waistbands, and often show markings which may represent tattoos.

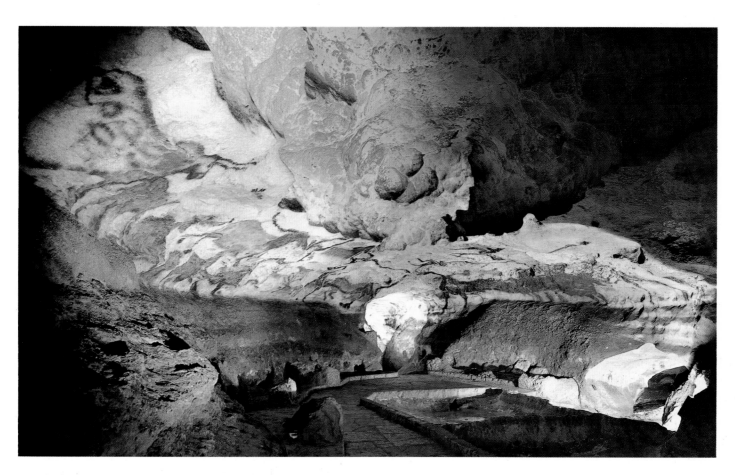

1.5 Main Hall, or Hall of the Bulls, Lascaux, France.

Although the culture would have been dominated by the male hunting ethos, the statues we have largely represent females and emphasize their sexuality. The mystery and apparent miracle of birth must have held great importance for these people. Thus, the Venus figurines, which seem to blend women's practical and symbolic roles, probably had a powerful, if unnameable, mystical significance.

The Cave of Lascaux

The Cave of Lascaux (lahs-KOH) in France lies slightly over a mile (about 2 kilometers) from the little town of Montignac, in the valley of the Vézère (vay-ZAIR) River. The cave itself was discovered in 1940 by a group of children who, while investigating a tree uprooted by a storm, scrambled down a fissure into a world undisturbed for thousands of years. The cave was sealed in 1963 to protect it from atmospheric damage, and visitors now see Lascaux II, an exact replica, which is sited in a quarry 600 feet (180 meters) away.

Perhaps a sanctuary for the performance of sacred rites and ceremonies, the Main Hall, or Hall of the Bulls (Fig. **1.5**), elicits a sense of power and grandeur. The thundering herd moves below a sky formed by the rolling contours of the stone ceiling of the cave, sweeping our eyes forward as we travel into the cave itself. At the entrance of the main hall, the 8-foot (2.4-meter) "unicorn" begins a larger-than-lifesize montage of bulls, horses, and deer, which are up to 12 feet (3.7 meters) tall. Their shapes intermingle with one another, and their colors radiate warmth and power. These magnificent creatures remind us that their creators were capable technicians who, with artistic skills at least equal to our own, were able to capture the essence beneath the visible surface of their world. The paintings in the Main Hall were created over a long period of time and by a succession of artists, yet their cumulative effect in this 30-by 100-foot (9 by 30 meters) domed gallery is that of a single work, carefully composed for maximum dramatic and communicative impact. We must remember, however, that we see the work, illuminated by electric floodlighting, very differently from the people by and for whom it was created, who could only ever see small areas at a time, lit by flickering stone lamps of oil or animal fat.

We cannot reconstruct what life was like during the latter half of the Old Stone Age, when the artistic achievements we have just examined occurred. There is some evidence that perhaps as early as 100,000 B.C. these people had some sort of religion. Some historians have suggested that they put up the skulls of cave bears as though to worship these rivals for the spaces in which they lived. By 50,000 B.C., Neanderthal people are known to have buried their dead with ceremony and care, behavior suggesting a belief in the hereafter, for ancient corpses were painted with red ochre, positioned with their knees raised, and provided with weapons. There is no proof for such conjecture, but the evidence does suggest that religion was among the earliest examples of human capacity to think in the abstract. As we have seen, there can be little doubt that art was another example.

In the New Stone Age—that is, the period from around 8000 B.C. to around 3000 B.C.—the final link was forged from our earliest, unknown ancestors to our earliest known ancestors, who emerged from the darkness of prehistory into the light of history and civilization. That link leads us from Europe to a place in the Middle East called Mesopotamia.

MESOPOTAMIA

In myth, the Tower of Babel (BAY-buhl) rose to connect heaven and earth. In much the same way, the arts of the Mesopotamians symbolized the people's relationship to their kings and, through them, to their gods. Bridging prehistory and history, the cities and empires of the Fertile Crescent, the land "between the rivers"—the Tigris and the Euphrates—were our PROTOTYPE civilizations. Here, for the first time, agriculture, metal technology, literacy, the specialization of labor, and a hierarchically organized urban community were combined. Kingdoms rose and fell as one power plundered its enemies and obliterated their cities, only in turn to be itself plundered and obliterated. Some time around 6000 B.C. the first recognizable civilization appeared in that part of the Near East that we call Mesopotamia (Maps **1.2** and **1.3**), and the earliest recognizable culture to emerge in this area was that of Sumer.

Sumer

The Sumerians (soo-MEER-ee-uhns) had a way of life similar to that of the other peoples in the region. They lived in villages and organized themselves around several important religious centers, which grew rapidly into cities.

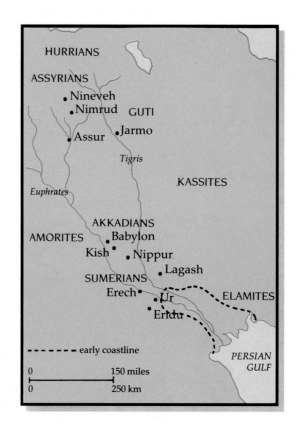

Map 1.2 Mesopotamia.

Map 1.3 Ancient Egypt and the Middle East.

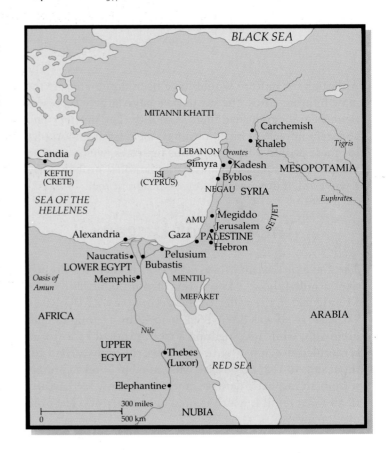

B.C.	GENERAL EVENTS	LITERATURE & PHILOSOPHY	VISUAL ART & ARCHITECTURE	PERFORMING ARTS
8000				
	Mesopotamian farming villages	Cuneiform writing		Religious and secular music
	Sumerian civilization			
3000				
	Invention of the wheel		Tell Asmar temple and statues (**1.8**)	
	Bronze casting		He-goat from Ur (**1.9**)	
	Old Kingdom of Egypt		Pyramid of Cheops (**1.14, 1.15**)	
	Sargon I		Rahotep and Nofret (**1.16**)	
2000				
	Hammurabi		Ceremonial vessel (**1.12**)	
	Middle Kingdom of Egypt			
	Shang Dynasty in China		Tell el Amarna (**1.18**)	
	Akhenaton and Nefertiti			
	Tutankhamun			
1000				
	New Kingdom of Egypt			
	Assyrian Empire			Funeral dances
900				
	Sargon II		Citadel at Dur Sharrukin (**1.10, 1.11**)	
700				
		Gilgamesh epic		
300				

Timeline **1.2** The Ancient Near East and Ancient Egypt.

The Invention of the Wheel

Insofar as Sumerians were capable of discerning scientific knowledge, they were also capable of applying that knowledge as technology. Sumerian mathematics employed a system of counting based on 60, and that system was used to measure time (we still have 60 minutes in 1 hour) and circles, divided into 360 degrees. The invention of number positioning—for example, 6 as a component of 6 or 60—made Sumerian mathematics unusually sophisticated. Mathematical calculation formed the basis for architectural endeavor, which, in turn, gave rise to higher levels of brick-making technology. Pottery was mass-produced and made the first known use of the potter's wheel. The wheel itself appeared as a transportation device in Sumer as early as 3000 B.C. By the same time, Sumerian technology had accomplished the casting of bronze and the invention of glass.

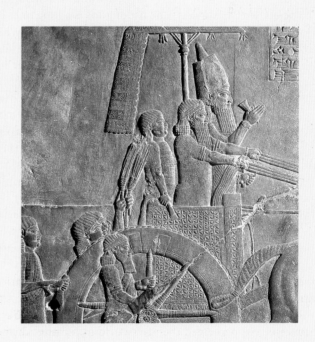

1.6 Ashurnasirpal II killing lions, from the Palace of Ashurnasirpal II, Nimrud (Calah), Iraq, c. 850 B.C. Limestone, 3 ft 3 ins × 8 ft 4 ins (99 × 254 cm). British Museum, London.

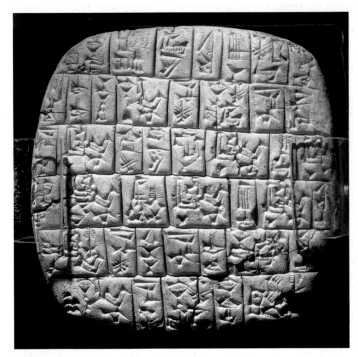

1.7 Clay tablet with cuneiform writing from Palace G, Elba, c. 2400 B.C. National Museum of Aleppo, Syria.

Religion

Religion and government shared a close relationship in Sumer. Religion permeated the social, political, and economic, as well as the spiritual and ethical life of society. A long EPIC poem, the *Gilgamesh* (GIL-guh-mesh) *Epic*, gives us an insight into this religion, around which Sumerian society was organized. The list of gods is a long one. By about 2250 B.C., the Sumerians worshipped a well-developed and generally accepted PANTHEON (PAN-thee-ahn) of gods. Temples were erected throughout Sumer for the sacrifices that were thought necessary to ensure good harvests. It appears that each individual city had its own god, and these local gods had their places in a larger HIERARCHY (HY-er-ahrk-ee). Like the Greeks later (see Chapter 2), the Sumerians gave human forms and attributes to their gods. The gods also had individual responsibilities. Ishtar was the goddess of love and procreation, for example. There was a god of the air, one of the water, one of the plow, and so on. Three male gods at the top of the hierarchy demanded sacrifice and obedience. To those who obeyed the gods came the promise of prosperity and longevity. Elaborate and intricate rituals focused on cycles involving marriage and rebirth: a drama of creation witnessed in the changing seasons.

Sumerian religion was concerned with life, and it seems to have perceived the afterworld as a rather dismal place. Nonetheless, there is evidence to suggest not only the practice of ritual suicide but also the belief that kings and queens would need a full complement of earthly possessions when they entered the next world.

Sumerian religion had important political ramifications as well. It ascribed ownership of all lands to the gods. The king was a king–priest, responsible to the gods alone. Below him, an elaborate class of priests enjoyed worldly power, privilege, and comfort, and to this class fell the responsibility for education and the writing of texts. And it is writing that undoubtedly represents the Sumerians' greatest contribution to the advancement of general civilization.

Writing

Various primitive peoples had used picture writing to convey messages. Sumerian writing, however, initiated the use of pictorial symbols that were qualitatively different: the Sumerians (and later the Egyptians) used pictures to indicate the syllabic sounds that occurred in different words rather than simply to represent the objects themselves. Sumerian language consisted of monosyllables used in combination, and so Sumerian writing came to consist of two types of sign, one for syllables and one for words. Writing materials were an unbaked clay tablet and a reed stylus, which, when pressed into the soft clay, produced a wedge-shaped mark. The wedges and combinations of wedges that made up Sumerian writing are called "cuneiform," from the Latin *cuneus* (KYOO-nee-uhs), meaning "wedge" (Fig. **1.7**).

Written language can cause many things to happen in a society, and it also reveals many things about that society. As well as opening up new possibilities for communication, it has a stabilizing effect on society, because it fixes the past by turning it into a documentable chronicle. In Sumer, records of irrigation patterns and practices, tax collections, and harvest and storage details were among the first things written down. Writing was also a tool of control and power. In the earliest times, the government and the priestly class of Sumer held a monopoly on literacy, and literacy served to strengthen their government.

But literacy also led to literature, and the oldest known story in the world comes to us from earliest Sumer. The *Gilgamesh* epic, an episodic tale of a hero's adventures, is from this era, although its most complete version dates from as late as the seventh century B.C. Gilgamesh probably was a real person, a ruler at Uruk (OO-ruk) who lived during the first half of the third millennium B.C., although there is no historical evidence actually to document that. One fascinating part of this epic describes a flood, which parallels that in the story of Noah's ark in the Bible. It is a hero's quest against nature, man, and the gods. Other epics too, and even love songs, have survived from the literature of ancient Sumer.

MASTERWORK

The Tell Asmar Statues

Undoubtedly the most striking features of these figures are their enormous, staring eyes, with their dramatic exaggeration. Representing Abu (AH-boo), the god of vegetation (the large figure), a goddess assumed to be his spouse, and a crowd of worshippers, the statues occupied places around the inner walls of an early temple, as though they were at prayer, awaiting the divine presence. The figures have great dignity, despite the stylization and somewhat crude execution. In addition to the staring eyes, our attention is drawn to the distinctive carving of the arms, which are separate from the body. The lines of each statue focus the eye of the viewer on the heart, adding to the emotion suggested by the posture. The composition is closed and self-contained, reflecting the characteristics of prayer.

Certain geometric and expressive qualities characterize these statues. In typical Sumerian style, each form is based on a cone or cylinder, and the arms and legs are stylized and pipelike, rather than being lifelike depictions of the subtle curves of human limbs.

The god Abu and the mother goddess may be distinguished from the rest by their size and by the large diameter of their eyes. The meaning in these statues clearly bears out what we know of Mesopotamian religious thought. The gods were believed to be present in their images. The statues of the worshippers were substitutes for the real worshippers, even though no attempt appears to have been made to make the statues look like any particular individual: every detail is simplified, focusing attention on the remarkable eyes, which are constructed from shell, lapis lazuli, and black limestone.

Large and expressive eyes appear to be a basic convention of Sumerian art—although it is a convention found in other ancient art as well. Its basis is unknown, but the idea of the eye as a source of power permeates ancient folk-wisdom. The eye could act as a hypnotizing, controlling force, for good or for evil—hence the term "evil eye," which is still used today. Symbolic references to the eye range from "windows of the soul" to the "all-seeing" vigilance of the gods.

The Sumerians used art, like language, to communicate through conventions. Just as cuneiform script condensed wider experiences and simplified pictures into signs, so Sumerian art took lifelikeness, as it was perceived by the artist, and reduced it to a few conventional forms, which, to those who understood the conventions, communicated larger truths about the world.

1.8 Statues of worshippers and deities from the Square Temple at Tell Asmar, Iraq, c. 2750 B.C. Gypsum, tallest figure 30 ins (76 cm) high. Iraq Museum, Baghdad, and Oriental Institute, University of Chicago.

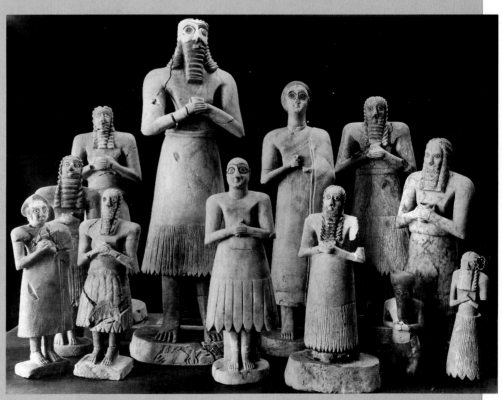

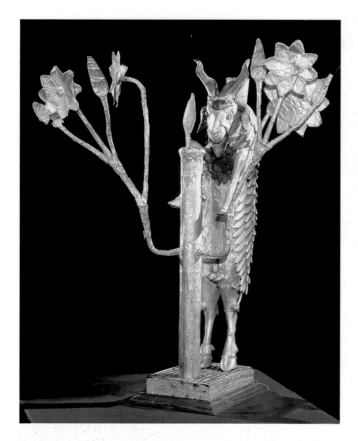

1.9 He-goat from Ur, c. 2600 B.C. Wood with gold and lapis lazuli overlay, 20 ins (50.8 cm) high. University Museum, University of Pennsylvania.

Art

Sumerian art progressed from stereotypical and anonymous portrayals to depictions of actual individuals, usually kings, who were portrayed in devotional acts rather than as warlords. The famous statues from Tell Asmar (as-MAR) and the Temple of Abu illustrate this well (see Fig. **1.8**).

But if crudity marks the depiction of the human figure in these votive statues, grace and delicacy are evident in works from the golden splendor of the Sumerian court. Inlaid in gold, the he-goat symbolizes the royal leadership of ancient Sumer and masculine fertility (Fig. **1.9**). Here, we glimpse an idea basic to Sumerian culture: the wisdom and perfection of divinity embodied in animal power. In this case, the goat is the earthly manifestation of the god Tammuz, and his superhuman character is crisply and elegantly conveyed.

Music

The early Sumerians made music as an essential and lively part of their culture, and they had many musical instruments. Music fulfilled a variety of functions in Sumerian life. It seems to have been most popular as secular enter-

tainment, but religious ceremonies also employed music. Solo performances, instrumental ensembles of single and mixed instruments, and solo and choral vocal music with instrumental accompaniment are all documented in surviving artifacts.

We can only speculate on what Sumerian music would have sounded like. Stringed instruments were predominant, while percussion and rhythm instruments seem to have been less popular, and the trumpet was mainly military in application. Thus, we may assume that Sumerian music favored lyrical, soft, restrained tones, rather than loud, brash ones.

Hammurabi and Babylonia

As Sumerian civilization coalesced, the region remained in flux until the next great ruler emerged in the early 1700s B.C. This ruler was Hammurabi (hah-moo-RAH-bee). His capital was Babylon, and Babylon became the hub of the world—at least for a while. The first Babylonian empire encompassed the lands from Sumer and the Persian Gulf to Assyria. It included the cities of Nineveh (NIHN-uh-vuh) and Nimrud (nim-ROOD) on the Tigris and Mari on the Euphrates, and extended up the Euphrates to presentday Aleppo (see Map **1.3**). This empire, of approximately 70,000 square miles (181,300 square kilometers), rested on an elaborate, centralized, administrative system. It maintained its order through a wideranging judicial code, which we have come to call the Code of Hammurabi. These laws consist of 282 articles, which address the legal questions of the time.

Foremost in importance among the articles was the precept of "an eye for an eye." Before Hammurabi's time, damages for bodily injury were assessed on a monetary basis—for example, a lost eye would be assessed at 60 shekels. Under Hammurabi, the monetary system was retained only for an injury inflicted by a free man on one of lower status. If, however, the parties were of equal status, exact retribution was called for: "An eye for an eye, a tooth for a tooth," and so forth. We do not know what retribution was exacted for injury inflicted on a person of higher degree, but the penalty in such a case was undoubtedly even more severe. Hammurabi's code was pragmatic and clearly based on a rigid class system. Only the rich were allowed to escape retributive mutilation by monetary payment. A sliding scale, based on ability to pay, determined compensation for medical expenses and legal fees.

The rights and place of women, likewise, were specifically spelled out. The purpose of a wife was to provide her husband with legitimate sons and heirs. The penalty for adultery (by a wife) was drowning for both wife and paramour. Men were allowed "secondary" or "temporary" wives as well as slave concubines. On the other hand, beyond the area of procreation, women were largely inde-

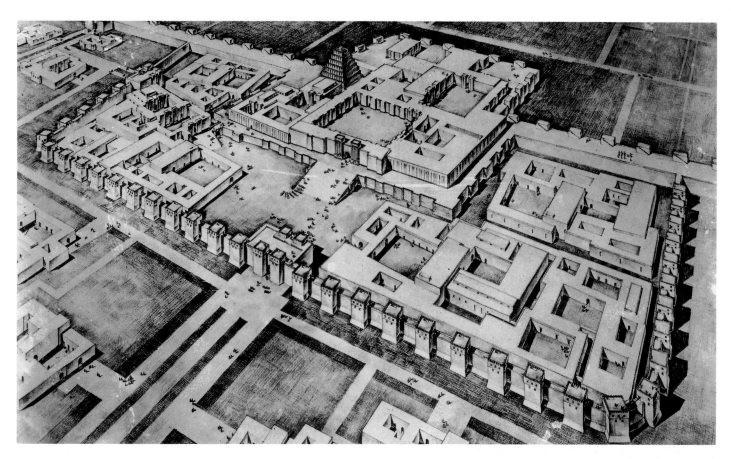

1.10 Reconstruction of Sargon II's citadel at Dur Sharrukin (Khorsabad), Iraq.

pendent. They could own property, run businesses, and lend and borrow money. A widow could remarry, which allowed greater population growth than was possible in cultures where the wife had to throw herself on her husband's funeral pyre.

In essence, the Code of Hammurabi dealt with wages, divorce, fees for medical services, family matters, commerce, and land and property, which included slaves. Hammurabi, like the rulers who preceded him, took his authority and also his law from the gods. Thus the concept of law as derived from extraordinary and supernatural powers continued unchallenged.

Hammurabi reigned for forty-two years. Some 125 years after his death, his dynasty ended.

The Assyrians

By the year 1000 B.C., a new power had arisen in Mesopotamia—the Assyrians. These were northern peoples from Ashur on the River Tigris. Their military power and skill enabled them to maintain supremacy over the region, including Syria, the Sinai peninsula, and as far as lower Egypt. For nearly 400 years they appear to have engaged in almost continuous warfare, ruthlessly destroying their enemies and leveling the conquered cities. Finally, they, too, felt the conqueror's sword, and all their cities were utterly destroyed.

Under Sargon II, who came to power in 722 B.C., the high priests of the country regained many of the privileges they had lost under previous kings, and the Assyrian Empire reached the peak of its power. Early in his reign, Sargon II founded the new city of Dur Sharrukin (door-shah-ROO-kihn; Khorsabad, Iraq). His vast royal CITADEL, which occupied some 250,000 square feet (23,225 square meters), was built as an image not only of his empire, but also of the cosmos itself. This citadel, a reconstruction of which appears in Figure 1.10, synthesizes the developments in Assyrian architecture and demonstrates the priorities of Assyrian civilization. In Sargon's new city, secular architecture clearly takes precedence over religious architecture, and the rulers of Assyria seem to have been far more concerned with building fortifications and imposing palaces than with erecting religious shrines. The citadel

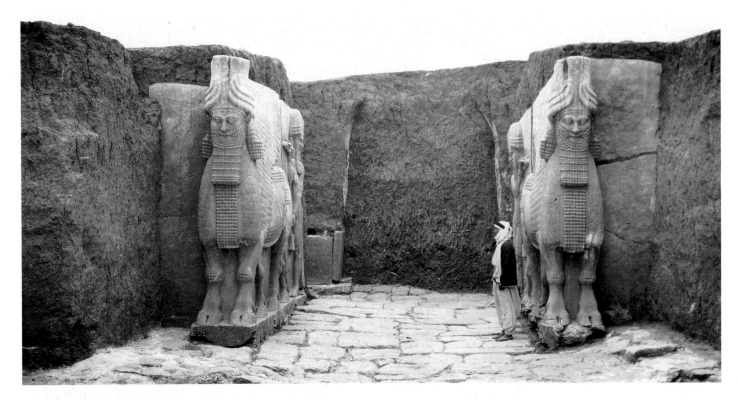

1.11 Gate of Sargon II's citadel at Dur Sharrukin (during excavation) with pair of winged and human-headed bulls. Limestone.

rises like the hierarchy of Assyrian gods, from the lowest levels of the city, through a transitional level, to the king's palace, which stands on its own elevated terrace. Two gates connect the walled citadel to the outside world. The first was undecorated; the second was adorned with, and guarded by, winged bulls (Fig. **1.11**).

ANCIENT EGYPT

Protected by deserts and confined to a narrow river valley (see Map **1.3**), Ancient Egypt experienced a relatively isolated cultural history, virtually unbroken for thousands of years. It was a civilization unique in its dependence upon the regular annual flooding of a single river, for each year, as the Nile overflowed its banks to deposit a rich and fertile silt on the surrounding fields, it bore witness to the rhythm of a beneficent natural order that would continue beyond the grave. Death—or, rather, everlasting life in the hereafter—was the focus of the life and the arts of the Egyptians. Created mostly in the service of the cult of a god, or to glorify the power and wealth of a pharaoh, art and architecture centered on the provision of an eternal dwelling place for the dead. Life was celebrated and recreated in images intended to provide an eternal substitute for the mortal body.

Religion

From the beginning of Egyptian civilization, the king was always identified with a god. At the time when Upper and Lower Egypt were united (c. 3000 B.C.), the king was considered to be the earthly manifestation of the god Horus, deity of the sky. The king was also considered to be the "Son of Ra," and thus represented a direct link between the royal line and the creator sun god.

Egyptian religion was a complex combination of local and national gods, and in a cumulative process new beliefs and gods were added over the thousands of years of Egyptian history. Two gods could be amalgamated and yet retain their separate entities. The same god could appear in various manifestations.

Religion played a central role in an Egyptian's personal and social life, as well as in civil organization. Death was believed to be a doorway to an afterlife, in which the departed could cultivate his or her own portion of the elysian fields with water apportioned by the gods. Life continued for the dead as long as the corpse, or some material image of it, continued to exist. Careful burial in dry sand, which preserved the corpse, was therefore essential, as was skillful mummification. The art of embalming had reached a proficient level as early as 3000 B.C. Great pains were taken to ensure a long existence for the corpse, and

Ancient China

One thousand years after Sumerian artists created the magnificent golden goat (see Fig. **1.9**), and the Hebrews were enslaved in Egypt (see p. 142), the ancient Chinese had mastered bronze casting. The ceremonial vessel shown here comes from the Shang Dynasty, c. 1400 B.C., and exhibits craftsmanship of magnificent quality. Each line has perfectly perpendicular sides and a flat bottom, meeting at a precise 90-degree angle, in contrast, for example, with incising, which forms a groove. The animal representation reveals a vision unlike that of Western culture but similar to that of Pacific northwest Native American design, in which the animal appears as if it had been skinned and laid out with the pelt divided on either side of the nose. A rigid bilateral balance results. Deftly placed ridges and gaps play against graceful curves, and, although the designs are delicate, the overall impression exhibits solidity and stability.

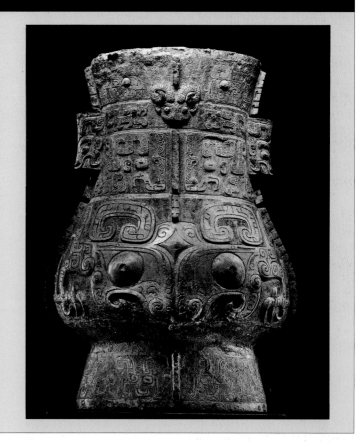

1.12 Shang Dynasty ritual wine vessel. Bronze, 16 × 11 ins (40.6 × 27.9 cm). The Nelson-Atkins Museum of Art, Kansas City, Missouri. (Purchase Nelson Trust).

mortuary buildings became the most important architectural features of the culture, reflecting their role as eternal homes. These tombs and burial places, rich in funereal imagery and narrative, have provided most of what we know of Egyptian history. Religious practice dictated that only good things be said of the departed, however. Thus the picture of a country populated by young, handsome, well-fed men and women, and ruled by beneficent pharaohs who inspired reverence, optimism, and productivity, even among the lowest slaves, may need careful adjustment.

The pharaoh (FAIR-oh) acted as a link between mortals and the eternal. Priests, or servants of the god, were delegates of the pharaoh. The common people relied on their ruler for their access to the afterlife: the offerings that would secure the pharaoh's existence in the afterlife were the people's only key to the eternal. It was, therefore, in every Egyptian's interest to be sure that the pharaoh's tomb could sustain and maintain him. Images and inscriptions in the tombs included the lowliest servants, ensuring that they, too, would participate forever in the pharaoh's immortality. Magic charms for the revivification of the deceased king, which were at one time spoken by priests,

came to be inscribed on the walls of the tomb so that, if necessary, the deceased could read them. Eventually the nobility began to usurp these magic formulas, and by the end of the twenty-first century B.C., they were copied regularly, and almost everyone could share the once unique privileges of the pharaoh.

The pharaoh joined the gods in the nether world after death. As befitting a ruler whose entourage also existed in the afterlife, he came to be associated with Osiris, king of the dead.

Pyramid Architecture

Pyramid building (c. 2700 B.C.) produced the most remarkable edifices of Egyptian civilization. Egypt's pyramids are the oldest existing buildings in the world. These ancient tombs are also among the world's largest structures. The largest stands taller than a forty-story building and covers an area greater than that of ten football fields. More than eighty pyramids still exist, and their once smooth limestone surfaces hide secret passageways and rooms. The pyramids of ancient Egypt served a vital purpose: to protect the pharaohs' bodies after death. Each pyramid originally held not only a pharaoh's preserved body but also all the goods he would need in his life after death.

Typical of Egyptian pyramids is a temple complex constructed a short distance from the pyramid and connected by a causeway. The most elaborate example of the temple complex is found at Giza, where the pyramids of Kings Khufu, Khafre, and Menkaura were built in close proximity to each other (Fig. **1.13**). Beginning in the 10th century A.D., the entire Giza complex served as a source of building materials for the construction of Cairo. The result was that all three pyramids were stripped of their original smooth outer facing of limestone.

The three pyramids at Giza have a carefully planned layout. Each is placed along the north–south meridian, with the faces of the pyramids pointing directly north, south, east, and west. The larger two are neatly placed along a southwest diagonal, with the third slightly offset

and smaller. It is assumed that this peculiar layout was a deliberate choice made by the architects, but the reasons for such a choice (if one existed) remain mysterious. Perhaps they were part of a plan, not of individual pyramids, but a group symbolizing Orion's belt: a group of stars that the pyramids match precisely. The intensity of the stars is reflected directly in the size of the pyramids.

The largest pyramid, that of Khufu, or Cheops (KEE-ahps; Fig. **1.14**), measures approximately 750 feet square (70 meters square) and rises at an angle of approximately 51 degrees to a height of 481 feet (147 meters). The burial chamber of the king lay hidden in the middle of the pyramid (Fig. **1.15**). Construction consisted of irregularly placed, rough-hewn stone blocks covered by a carefully dressed limestone facing, approximately 17 feet (5 meters) thick. The pyramid of Cheops' son Chephren (Khafre) originally measured 707 feet square (65 meters square), and rose, at an angle of 52 degrees, to a height of 471 feet (144 meters).

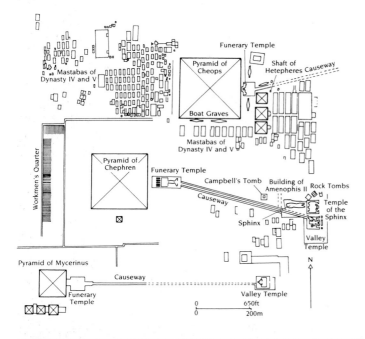

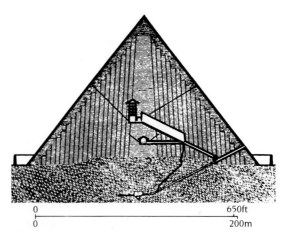

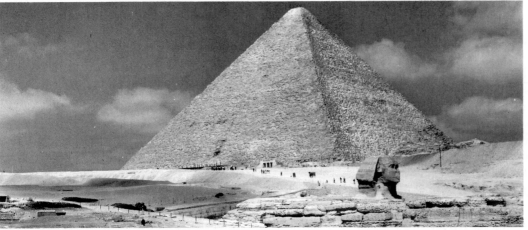

1.13 (*above left*) Plan of the Giza pyramid complex.

1.14 (*left*) Great Pyramid of Cheops, Giza, Egypt, Dynasty IV (2680–2565 B.C.).

1.15 (*above*) Longitudinal section, direction south–north, of the Great Pyramid of Cheops, Giza, Egypt, Dynasty IV (2680–2565 B.C.).

1.16 (*right*) Prince Rahotep and his wife Nofret from Maidum, c. 2580 B.C. Painted limestone, 3 ft 11½ ins (1.2 m) high. Egyptian Museum, Cairo.

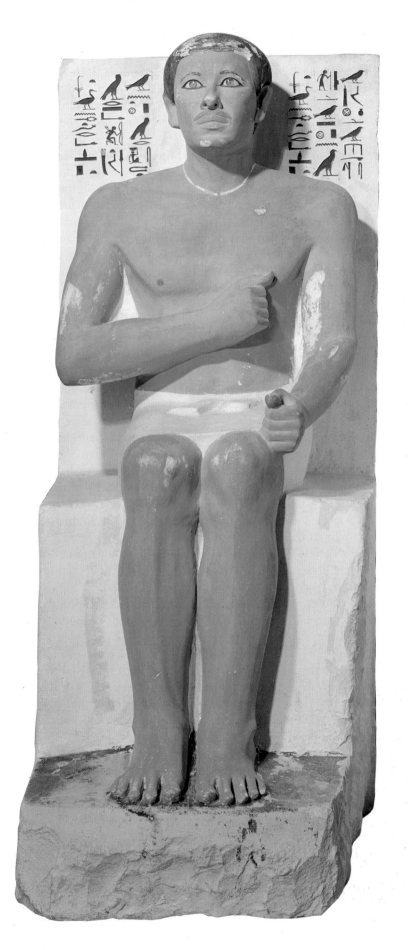
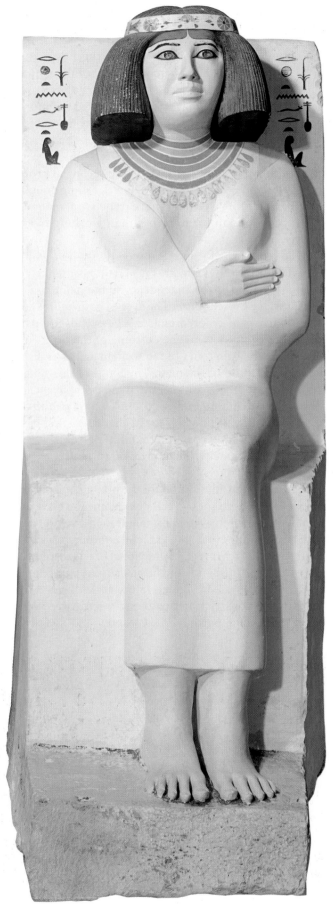

Sculpture

Sculpture was the major art form of the Egyptians. By 2700 B.C., sculptors had overcome many of the difficulties that plagued their predecessors. During those archaic times, religious tenets may have confounded sculptors, for many primitive peoples throughout history have regarded the lifelike portrayal of the human figure as dangerous. A close likeness of a person may have been thought capable of capturing the soul. There were also technical problems to be overcome. Early sculpture left detailing rough and simple. Sculptors seem to have relied on memory to portray the human form, rather than working from live models.

The sculpture of Prince Rahotep (RAH-hoh-tehp) and his wife Nofret (NOH-freht; Fig. **1.16**) has lifelike colors exemplifying the Egyptian tendency to use paint as a decorative surface for sculpture. The eyes of both figures consist of dull- and light-colored quartz. The eyelids are painted black. Both figures wear the costume of the time. As was customary, the skin tones of the woman are several shades lighter than those of the man. The kings of this time rose from peasant stock, an ancestry that is apparent in the sturdy, broad-shouldered, well-muscled physique of the prince. At the same time, his facial characteristics, particularly the eyes and expression, exhibit alertness, wisdom, strength, and capacity. The portrayal of Nofret expresses similar individuality.

The Egyptian admiration for the human body is clearly revealed in both statues. Precise modeling and attention to detail are evident in even the smallest items. Nofret's gown both covers and reveals the graceful contours of her body. Her facial features reveal an individual of less distinct character than her husband: she has a sensual and pampered face. She wears a wig shaped in the style of the day, but beneath the constricting headband we can see Nofret's much finer hair, parted in the center and swept back beneath the wig. The treatment of the hand held open against the body reveals not only the artist's skill and perceptiveness, but also the care and attention Nofret has bestowed on it. The hand is, indeed, delicate: small dimples decorate the fingers, and the nails exhibit extraordinary detail. The unpainted nails are correctly observed as being lighter than skin tone.

The artist's attention and precision, so carefully expressed in the upper body, deteriorate almost to the point of crudity in the lower body, as is typical of sculpture of this era. The legs of both figures are lumpy, ill-defined, and coarse. The feet are nearly unrecognizable as parts of the human anatomy, except in that they have five toes. Parts of the thrones on which the figures sit show even less attention to detail—they remain rough blocks of limestone, still bearing the marks of the quarry.

Music

The modern world is fairly well acquainted with Egyptian musical instruments: sculptures and paintings depict them, and fragments and even nearly complete instruments have been found. Harps, lyres, and numerous other stringed instruments, along with pipes, flutes, cymbals, and bells were all in the storechest of the Egyptian musician. As in Mesopotamia, the basic instrument in the Egyptian scheme was probably the harp. Harps varied tremendously in size, complexity, shape, and ornamentation (Fig. **1.17**). Harps are depicted with four, seven, and ten strings. Some are very plain, others ornate and brightly colored. How much of this variety is real and how much lies in the imagination of the painter, we do not know, but the frequent depiction of the harp does assure us of its popularity. Wall paintings also indicate that the larger harps, some of which appear to stand nearly six feet tall, were played essentially as modern harps are.

The tamboura (tuhm-BOO-ruh) of ancient Egypt had two basic shapes, one oval and the other with sides slightly incurved, like a modern violin or guitar. Illustrations show from two to four tuning pegs, and also indicate that the tamboura could be either with or without frets. Analysis of tambouras found with strings intact shows that the Egyptians used cat gut for stringing. Additional stringed instruments of innumerable shapes and sizes defy classification, but this variety certainly indicates that music held an important place among the arts of ancient Egypt.

Wind instruments were very varied in shape, size, and ornamentation. Small pipes made of reed with three, four, five, and more finger holes have been found in great quantity. Some of these appear to have been played by blowing directly across the opening at the end, and others seem to have required a reed, like the modern clarinet or oboe.

1.17 Egyptian harps.

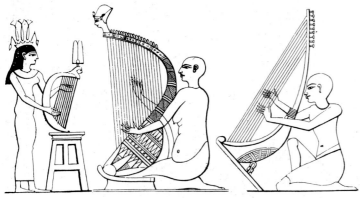

Focal Point

Akhenaton and Monotheism: The Tell el Amarna Period

The reign of Akhenaton (ahk-ehn-AH-tuhn; c. 1385–1358 B.C.) marked a break in the continuity of artistic style. The stiff poses of earlier art disappeared, to be replaced by a more natural form of representation (Fig. **1.18**). The pharaoh, moreover, was depicted in intimate scenes of domestic life, rather than in the ritual or military acts that were traditional. He is no longer seen associating with the traditional gods of Egypt. Rather, he and his queen are depicted worshipping the disc of the sun, whose rays end in hands that bless the royal pair or hold to their nostrils the *ankh*, the symbol of life.

The cause of this revolution is not certain, but some evidence suggests that the priesthood of Heliopolis, the ancient seat of the sun cult, were seeking to reestablish the primacy of their god.

In the fifth or sixth year of his reign, Akhenaton moved his court to the city of Tell el Amarna (uhm-AHR-nuh), newly constructed in the sandy desert on the east bank of the Nile. It was a new city for a new king intent on establishing a new order based on a new religion. Akhenaton failed, and Tell el Amarna, abandoned at his death, was never built over again because it lay away from cultivated land. It thus provides us with an unspoiled record of Akhenaton's social and cultural vision.

The town is dominated by the large estates of the wealthy. They chose the best sites and laid them out in the style of the Egyptian country house, with large gardens, numerous outbuildings, and a wall enclosing the entire

1.19 King Amenhotep IV, later Akhenaton, from a pillar statue in the temple of Aton near the temple of Amun at Karnak, 1364–1347 B.C. Sandstone, 13 ft (3.96 m) high. Egyptian Museum, Cairo.

1.18 *King Smenkhkare and Meritaten*, Tell el Amarna, Egypt, c. 1360 B.C. Painted limestone relief, about 5 ft (1.53 m) high. Staatliche Museen, Berlin.

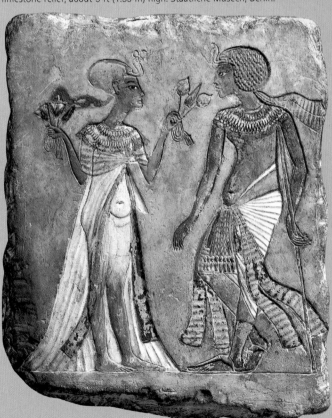

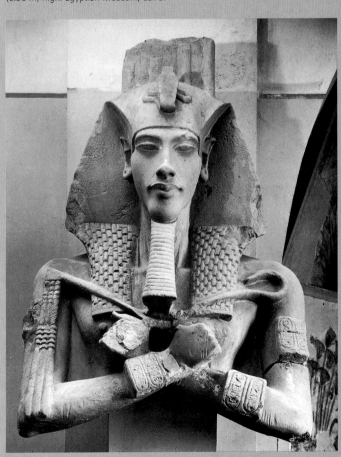

Akhenaton and Nefertiti

Amenhotep IV, as Akhenaton was called before changing his name to reflect his god, was himself unusual. He possessed a "strange genius" for religious experience and its expression. He is shown as having a misshapen body, an elongated head, and a drooping jaw. Yet the eyes are deep and penetrating. The effect is one of brooding intensity.

In a hymn of praise to Aton, the sun god, thought to have been written by the king, Akhenaton exhibits a spirit of deep joy and devotion to the deity. In his lyrical description of the way the earth and humankind react to the rising and setting of the sun, we glimpse a man of sensitive character. His vision is universal: Aton is not merely a god of Egypt, but of all people, and Akhenaton himself is the sole mediator between the two.

Nefertiti (c. 1372–1350 B.C.; Fig. **1.20**) was Akhenaton's Great Royal Wife. Scholars debate whether she was a princess from another land or an Egyptian. Those believing her to be of Egyptian origin are themselves divided. One group claims she was the daughter of Aye and Tiy, and the other claims her as the oldest daughter of Amenhotep III and another wife besides Tiye, possibly Sitamun. Whatever her parentage, Nefertiti was married to Akhenaton and while living in Memphis gave birth to six daughters. It is possible that she also had sons, although no record has been found of this. It was a practice in Egyptian art not to portray the male heirs as children. Possibly, she may have been the mother of Tutankhamun, the boy pharaoh who succeeded to the throne at the age of eleven and died nine years later. Nefertiti achieved a prominence unknown to other Egyptian queens. Her name is enclosed in a royal *cartouche* (a frame for a hieroglyphic inscription formed by a rope design surrounding an oval space), and there are, in fact, more statues and drawings of her than of Akhenaton. Some have even claimed that it was Nefertiti, not Akhenaton, who instigated the monotheistic religion of Aton. Around year 15 of Akhenaton's reign, Nefertiti mysteriously disappeared from view. Perhaps she died, but no indication of this can be found. Some scholars think that she was banished for some reason, and lived the rest of her years in the northern palace, raising Tutankhamun. Whatever may have happened, she was replaced by her oldest daughter, Meritaten, and disappeared from history.

Akhenaton's own words describe Nefertiti: "The Hereditary Princess, Great of Favor, Mistress of Happiness, Gay with the two feathers, at hearing whose voice one rejoices, Soothing the heart of the king at home, pleased at all that is said, the Great and Beloved Wife of the King, Lady of the Two Lands, Neferu-aton Nefertiti, living forever."

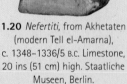

1.20 *Nefertiti*, from Akhetaten (modern Tell el-Amarna), c. 1348–1336/5 B.C. Limestone, 20 ins (51 cm) high. Staatliche Museen, Berlin.

establishment. Between these large estates lay the smaller dwellings of the less wealthy. The new city was complete, it seems, with a slum area outside the northern suburb. Near this area stood the grand North Palace.

In many ways, the architecture of Tell el Amarna reflects the common features of New Kingdom domestic architecture, although it is less sumptuous. Its lines and style seem relatively simple. Structures are open. At Amarna, numerous unroofed areas lead to the altar of the sun god, Aton, left open to provide access to his rays.

Sculpture at Tell el Amarna departs from tradition. It is more secular, with less apparent emphasis on statues and reliefs for tombs and temples. The Amarna sculptors seem to have sought to represent the uniqueness of human beings through their faces (see Fig. **1.20**). Amarna sculpture is highly lifelike, but it transcends the merely natural and enters the spiritual realm. The statue of Akhenaton shown in Figure **1.19** depicts the curious physical features of the king, and yet the stylization of the approach is also clear.

In the relief sculptures and wall paintings, the conventions of body proportions differ significantly from those of the other periods. In other periods, head and body proportions seem to be close to a ratio of 1:8. The total figure is thus nine head lengths from top to bottom. At Tell el Amarna, the total figure is seven to eight head lengths: in other words, the head is larger. Body proportions are also different. Arms are thinner and hands are larger. Abdominal and pelvic areas are emphasized in contrast to the focus on the shoulders and upper torso of earlier periods.

Many of the structural details of Amarna architecture are strikingly original. Plant motifs seem to have been favored, and palm-shaped columns are found in abundance. Also popular at Amarna were papyrus-bundle columns with CAPITALS of clustered, open flowers, some-times made of alabaster inlaid with blue paste. Most original are kiosk-like structures carved with convolvulus vines. The palace walls dazzled the eye with colored glazed tiles and painted stone reliefs. Indeed, the entire city must have shimmered in the sunlight of Akhenaton's single god.

Isolated from other periods by geographical and religious circumstance, the Tell el Amarna period encapsulates the artistic expressions of a single religious and philosophical concept. The religious reforms of Akhenaton were doomed to fail. Yet this Egyptian experiment in MONOTHE-ISM has left us with a vivid portrait of an integrated life-scheme.

CHAPTER REVIEW

Critical Thought

One of the critical challenges facing any culture is the manner in which it accommodates the viewpoints of those who dwell in it. By today's standards, the earliest "civilizations" were hardly more than counties on our political maps, but what distinguished them from other "civilizations" were what we might call their cultural ethos: that spirit of community that held them together as a people. Military conquest seems always to have been a major means of expanding that ethos beyond the immediate confines of the civilization, but once one people had conquered another, the question arose of how those who had been conquered were to be incorporated into the ethos of the ruling civilization. The question this raises, as we look back at the history of humankind's earliest civilization, is why do we find it so difficult to get along with people who are different from ourselves?

Summary

Having read this chapter, you should be able to:

- Discuss the contention, and support your ideas with illustrations drawn from the art of the period, that earliest humans were "fully human," as we are.
- Identify the characteristics of Stone Age, Mesopotamian, and Egyptian art by citing specific examples.
- Explain the linkages among politics, religion, and art in Mesopotamian and Egyptian societies.
- Analyze (describe) the works of art illustrated in this chapter using appropriate terms, such as line and form. For example, how does the statue of Queen Nofret employ line in comparison with the statues from Tell Asmar?

CHAPTER TWO

Archaic Greece and the Aegean

OUTLINE

THE MINOANS

THE MYCENAEANS

BETWEEN MYTH AND HISTORY

THE ARCHAIC GREEK WORLD
The Polis
The Hellenes
   TECHNOLOGY: The Olive Press
The Persian War
Religion
Philosophy
Vase Painting
   MASTERWORK: The Dipylon Vase
Sculpture
   OUR DYNAMIC WORLD: Native
      America
Architecture—The Doric Order
Music
Literature
   PROFILE: Sappho
   MASTERWORK: Sappho—"God's
      Wildering Daughter"
Dance

FOCAL POINT: THE *ILIAD* AND
ODYSSEY OF HOMER

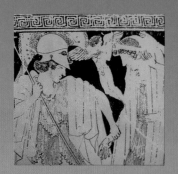

VIEW

RELIGION: TYING SOCIETY TOGETHER

In the previous chapter, as in the chapter to come (indeed in many of the chapters which follow), religion plays a central role in the cultures and arts we examine. It seems that in addition to creative impulses, we also find relationships among peoples in their search for communion with a power or powers higher than themselves. Greek culture was no exception and, in fact, much of its cultural ethos derived from its religion. Such an observation leads to one other, and that is the question, what does hold a society together? Can a society survive without some unifying characteristic with which most of its citizens can identify?

KEY TERMS

Some of the basic terms and concepts we will encounter in this chapter include the following:

Polis, the basic Greek city-state, consisting of a collection of self-governing people.

Acropolis, the "high city"—the elevated place in the center of the city occupied by the temples of the gods.

Geometric style was a style of vase painting that made use of bold, simple, linear designs.

Archaic style was a style of two-dimensional and three-dimensional art. In two-dimensional art, it utilized a sense of three-dimensional space, whereas in sculpture, it consisted of figures that exhibit a stiff, frontal pose.

Kouroi is a term describing a freestanding statue of a nude male youth.

Kore describes a sculpture of a fully-dressed female—that is, the female counterpart of the kouroi.

Doric order refers to a style of architecture employing columns capped by heavy lintels and a pedimented roof.

Above Detail of Fig. **2.11**.

2.1 Geometric amphora, c. 760 B.C. National Archeological Museum, Athens.

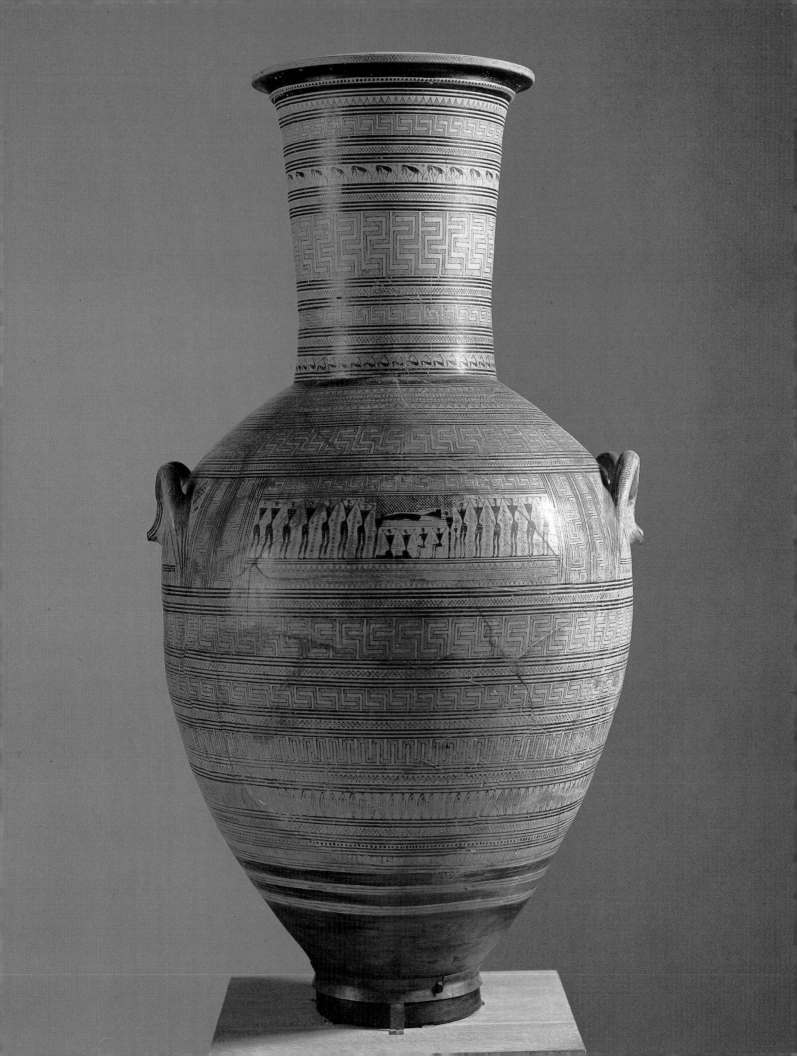

We leave the cradle of civilization in the Middle East and turn northeastward to the Aegean Sea and the area we know as Greece (Map **2.1**). Here the roots of Western civilization took hold. Undoubtedly, Egypt and Mesopotamia had an effect on the emerging culture of Greece—the Greeks of the classical period noted this, and the latest holders of Mesopotamian power, the Persians, conquered parts of the Grecian world, including Athens—but before there were "Greeks," there were others in the region.

THE MINOANS

Around 3000 B.C., while pyramids were rising in Egypt and sizable cities were being built in Mesopotamia, small towns on the island of Crete began to expand into large urban centers. The Minoan (mih-NOH-uhn) civilization, named after the legendary King Minos (MY-nuhs), emerged at this time, and by 1800 B.C. a great palace had arisen in the city of Knossos (NAHS-uhs) on Crete. Not much is known about the Minoans, but we can tell from

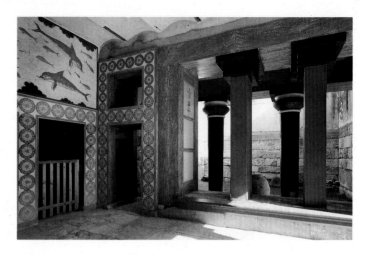

2.2 Queen's chamber, Palace of Minos at Knossos, Crete, c. 1500 B.C.

the ruins of their palaces and their wall paintings that they were rich and adventurous. They depended on their naval power for defense, and their palaces, which were not fortified, were elaborate complexes, with the private homes of

Timeline 2.1 Archaic Greece and the Aegean.

B.C.	GENERAL EVENTS	LITERATURE & PHILOSOPHY	VISUAL ART & ARCHITECTURE	PERFORMING ARTS
3000				
	Minoan civilization Mycenaean traders in the Aegean	Pictorial writing	Palace of Minos, Knossos (**2.2**)	
1500				
	Destruction of Troy		Lion Gate, Mycenae (**2.4**) *Boar Hunt* (**2.3**)	
1200				
	Greek "Middle Ages"		Protogeometric vases (**2.8**) Olmec art (**2.12**)	
800				
	Archaic period First Olympic games	Homer, *Iliad, Odyssey* Hesiod, *Works and Days*	Geometric vases (**2.1**) Dipylon Vase (**2.9**)	
700				
		Sappho of Lesbos	Doric order (**2.19**) Kouroi (**2.13, 2.14**)	
600				
	Persian Empire	Pythagoras	Perseus bowl (**2.10**) Korai (**2.15, 2.16**) "Basilica," Paestum (**2.20**)	Choric dance festivals First tragic competitions Development of modes
500				
	Persian War		Makron, skyphos (**2.11**) *Kritios Boy* (**2.17**) Red figure krater (**2.7**)	
400				

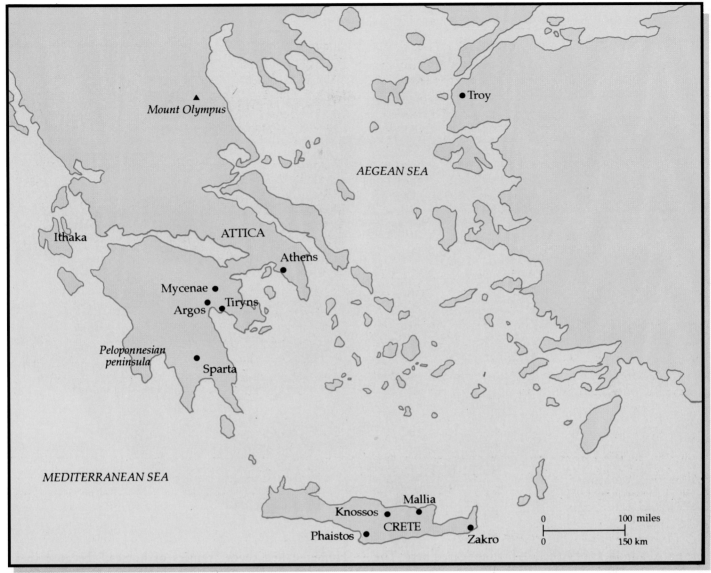

Map 2.1 The Aegean.

the aristocracy and religious leaders clustered around them. These palaces had running water and elaborate drainage systems, and, below ground, storage areas contained large earthenware pots of grains, oil, and wine. They also had systems for cooling during the summer and heating in winter. Through trading posts around the Aegean, Minoan Crete carried on a lively and rewarding commerce as far away as Egypt, exporting pottery, bronze, olive oil, and timber.

Many well-preserved archeological sites allow us to deduce a certain amount of information about the Minoan lifestyle and culture, even though their writing has yet to be fully deciphered. Wall paintings, executed in brilliant colors and displaying spontaneity and a deep love of nature, reveal accurately depicted portraits of royalty and scenes of nature. They reflect a flighty court life with high-born, bare-breasted ladies, bedecked in jewels, and strolling in lovely gardens. Sportive youths frolic and raise golden goblets of wine. Life was lavish in the labyrinthine

palaces of Knossos, with their complex rooms and passageways. There were bureaucrats in abundance, but few soldiers, and Minoan civilization clearly had trade, not militarism or politics, at its center.

The Minoans were a wealthy and secure people. If the so-called Palace of Minos (Fig. 2.2) is representative, they not only enjoyed comfort, but were also capable of sophisticated elegance in decor and design. The palace had so many rooms that it was remembered in Greek myth as the "labyrinth of the Minotaur (MIHN-oh-tohr)." The walls were built of masonry and decorated with murals and geometric motifs. Rectangular and circular COLUMNS, employed as supports, took the form of tapering wooden SHAFTS, perhaps reflecting their origin as unworked treetrunks, with heavy, geometric capitals. The total impression is one of openness and lightness, combined with luxury and attention to detail.

The religion had a variety of gods, goddesses, and myths. Early versions of Athena—who later emerged as

53

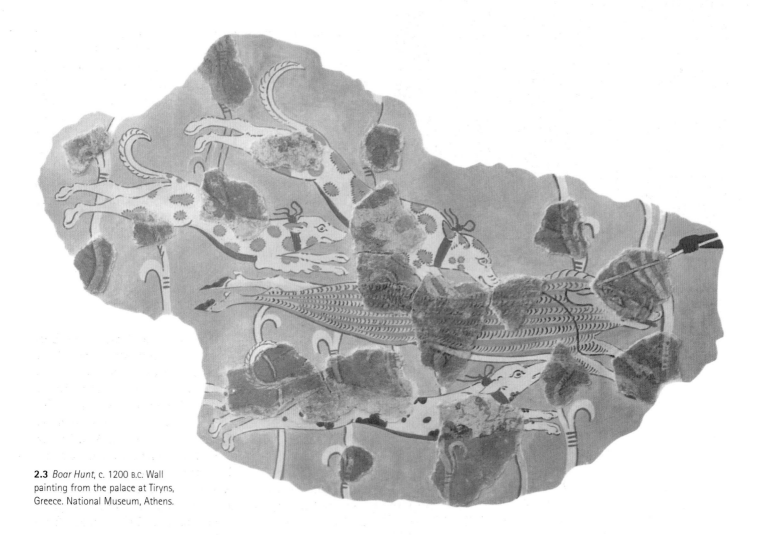

2.3 *Boar Hunt*, c. 1200 B.C. Wall painting from the palace at Tiryns, Greece. National Museum, Athens.

the patron goddess of Athens—first appeared here. The Minoans also had a cult of the sacred bull, which was celebrated by terrifying "bull dancing" or "bull leaping," a rite performed by naked young men and women on the backs and over the horns of the bulls. This was probably the origin of the Minotaur of Greek legend.

Minoan culture, however, experienced a short-lived glory. By 1500 B.C., the Minoans had been swept into darkness, perhaps by a series of earthquakes and volcanic eruptions or perhaps merely through conquest by their neighbors. However, their influence was felt on a later civilization that also emerged in the Aegean, that of the Mycenaeans (my-SEEN-ee-uhns).

THE MYCENAEANS

The Mycenaeans were early, barbaric, Indo-European conquerors who settled the rugged southeastern coastline of mainland Greece and who, by the fourteenth century B.C., had supplanted the Minoans as rulers of Crete.

Homer called them "tamers of horses," because they fought from chariots, and they left the lands they conquered in ruins. Unlike the Minoans, of whom the later Greeks were unaware, the Mycenaeans, through Homer, provided Greece with myths, legends, and heroes such as the mighty Achilles (uh-KIL-lees) in the *Iliad* (IHL-ee-uhd) and the wandering Odysseus (oh-DIHS-ee-uhs) in the *Odyssey* (AHD-ih-see). The Greeks also found in this people a source of ethics and moral order, and Homer's epics give a glimpse of a social organization in which the *oikos* (household domain) was the center of economic and social power.

Although conquest seems to have been their main occupation, the Mycenaeans did engage in some trade, their traders traveling throughout the Mediterranean between 1400 and 1200 B.C. Above all, however, they were warriors, and their rule was maintained by the strength of their military. It was their soldiers and armada of ships that reportedly conquered the legendary Troy and gave Homer the basis for his epic the *Iliad*.

A variety of local deities and household gods and goddesses, some of which appear also to have been prede-

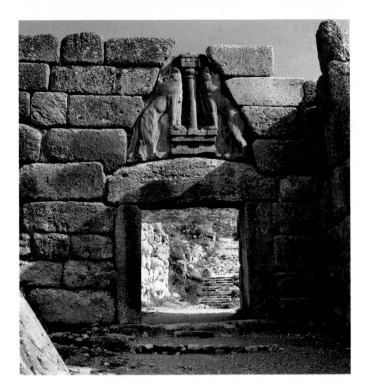

2.4 The Lion Gate, Mycenae, Greece, c. 1250 B.C.

alcove on top of the lintel, two lions, obviously intended as guardians, flank a tapering column similar to those found in Minoan palaces. The careful carving of the animals' musculature expresses strength, and it contrasts with the rough stone masonry, creating a slightly uncomfortable effect, which is reinforced by the cramped nature of the composition within the alcove. Yet, despite any crudity in the design, the execution is remarkably skillful, and the jointure of the stone is tight.

In spite of its great defenses and massively fortified palaces, the Mycenaean civilization collapsed shortly after 1200 B.C.

BETWEEN MYTH AND HISTORY

Between the time of the Mycenaean civilization, with its art and palaces, and that of the Greek city-states of the eighth century B.C., lies a historical vacuum of four centuries. Historians call this time the "Greek Middle Ages" or the "dark centuries," and it was during this period that wave upon wave of Indo-European peoples filtered into the area and spread throughout Asia Minor. The building of palaces ceased and what little artistic activity existed—for example, pottery—was crude. Although the Mycenaeans had writing, the skill seems to have vanished during this time, leaving only archeology to testify to the existence of these peoples. Life switched from fortified cities to isolated farming communities, and trade and commerce among communities isolated by the mountainous terrain was minimal if it had not ceased altogether.

Nonetheless, life was not static nor all dark. During this time, iron replaced bronze for tools and weapons, significant changes occurred in burial practices, the political hierarchy shifted from kings to powerful families, and new peoples drifted into the valleys, to neighboring islands, and to the shores of Asia Minor. Toward the end of the eighth century B.C., gatherings of Greeks listened rapturously to the epic poems of Homer and Hesiod, looking back on the heroes of Mycenae. And indeed, they did look backward, because it seemed that all glory lay in the past, with little to look forward to.

cessors of Greek deities, were worshipped in caves and at natural shrines. Religious practice included burying the dead with honor, and, like the Egyptians, the Mycenaeans mummified corpses and buried them with precious objects.

Most of what we know of the world of the ancient Mycenaeans comes from fragmentary remains of their art. The walls of their palaces bear decorative paintings, which also represent the activities of the time. The *Boar Hunt* (Fig. 2.3) shows a group of dogs, hunting as a pack and attacking their prey. That the hounds are domesticated is evident from their collars, which appear to be tied around the neck. The hand and what looks like the lance of the hunter at the extreme right of the fragment indicate that the dogs have chased the boar into the vicinity of the hunters. This painting is clearly a testament not only to a successful hunt, but also to the dog breeder, whose well-trained dogs carry out their owner's commands.

The central city of Mycenae boasted a great palace complex and great wealth. The palaces of the Mycenaeans were very different from those of the Minoans, for they were fortresses constructed of large, rough stone blocks placed at the center of a settlement on top of the highest hill. The individual boulders were so huge that the Greeks who viewed them centuries later called them "Cyclopean," believing that only cyclopses—mythological giants with one eye in the center of their foreheads—could have moved them.

The Lion Gate at the Palace of Mycenae (Fig. **2.4**) demonstrates the powerful effect of juxtaposing smoothly carved elements with the massive blocks of stone. In an

THE ARCHAIC GREEK WORLD

The time from approximately 800 to 480 B.C. is called the "archaic period" in order to contrast this phase of development in Greek civilization from a more vigorous cultural advancement called the "classical period" which occurred in the middle third of the fifth century B.C.

The Polis

The Greek city-states that developed at the beginning of the archaic period were already well established and functioning by the time recorded history began, but we do know, at least, that they did not all spring up simultaneously. Each city, or polis (POH-lis; plural poleis), consisted of a collection of self-governing people. The Greeks referred to cities by the collective name of their citizens—thus, for example, Athens was "the Athenians." Each polis was surrounded by a group of villages and a rural territory, and each was self-governing, functioning as an independent state. No central, unifying government drew these cities together, and each polis developed its own ethos—that is, a sense of self. Some, such as Athens, emerged as relatively peaceful, with a high esteem for the arts and philosophy. Others, such as Sparta, were militaristic and seemingly indifferent to high culture.

All the cities formed their social orders on distinct class structures: some people were free and others were slaves.

Among free males there existed a clear demarcation between those who were citizens and those who were not: only citizens could participate in political decision-making, own land, or serve in wars. But access to citizenship could alter according to the city's circumstances at a given time.

Physically, the polis was formed of two cities: a lower city, in which the people lived, and a high city, or *acropolis* (uh-KRAHP-oh-lis), an elevated place in the center of the city occupied by the temples of the gods. (This practice was little different from the ways in which towns developed in the Middle Ages, when the cathedral was built on the highest elevation in the center of a city to symbolize the centrality and elevation of the Christian church.) The citizens of the Greek polis owned the city, including the acropolis, and the pantheon of gods was more often a focus of civic pride than of reverence.

Originally, the typical polis had an organization similar to the tribal structure brought down from the north by the invaders, whose tribes were governed by an aristocracy or council of leading families. Typically, the leading landowners were part of such an aristocracy, and, occasionally, a polis might have a "king," like that of the ancient Minoans or Mycenaeans. Power in the polis actually belonged, however, to the landowners and tribal leaders, and the concept of a king gradually faded away, and

---

TECHNOLOGY: PUTTING DISCOVERY TO WORK

The Olive Press

Often, one of the interesting things about the record of history is not its claims, but the fact that particular individuals are recorded as having invented particular pieces of technology, and the Greeks had a great regard for technological innovation. The status of the technician in Greece was raised high—much more so than in neighboring Asiatic countries—and an interest in technology was respectable, with inventors being regarded as benefactors.

As Greek civilization spread through the Aegean and Mediterranean during the archaic age, trade became increasingly important. One of the few products that Greece, with its mountainous terrain and poor soil, could produce in sufficient abundance to export was olive oil, which, together with wine and pottery, became their principal export. Manufacturing oil in quantity required technological advances in the presses by which olive oil is produced. Initially, the oil

was extracted in a simple beam press illustrated in relief sculpture and vase paintings, but later, pulleys and screws worked the beam to press the oil (Fig. **2.5**).

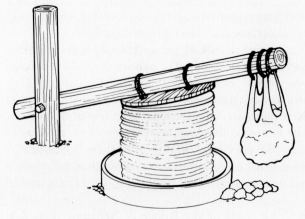

2.5 Reconstruction of an early beam press.

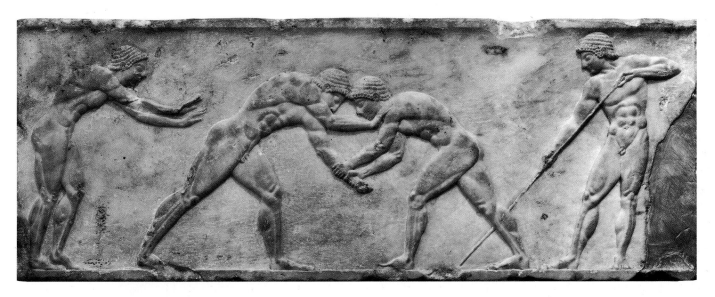

2.6 Wrestlers, from a statue base, c. 500 B.C. Marble, 12¼ ins (31.8 cm) high. National Archeological Museum, Athens.

was replaced by a group of elected magistrates. In the seventh and sixth centuries B.C., the aristocracy went into decline, giving rise to a new degree of freedom. The rise of trade and the increasing wealth of the merchant class siphoned power from the landowners.

As the polis developed, land, money, and military service became important qualifications for political power. Farmers, merchants, and craftsmen who could afford to buy weapons—each member of the army was self-armed—demanded inclusion in political decision-making. Often, *tyrants*—that is, spokesmen for the citizenry and quasi-rulers—arose from the ranks of the military. The word "tyrant" here does not have the negative connotations usually associated with it today.

By the end of the sixth century B.C., these unique Greek poleis were scattered throughout the Aegean and Mediterranean area. Although they did not match the cities of Egypt, Mesopotamia, or even Minoa or Mycenae in wealth and splendor, they contained thriving populations living in simple houses who, as a group, built impressive temples, theatres, and stadiums.

We look back on the Greek poleis and call them "democracies," seeing them as the forebears of our own "democratic" form of government. They were, of course, far from democratic in the modern sense of the word, for only native-born, free, adult males of a specific economic standing were citizens, and so had any voice in government. Nevertheless, the polis was a democracy in that the rule lay in the hands of the many and not in the hands of a few or, as in the monarchies of Ancient Egypt and Mesopotamia, in the hands of a god king.

The Hellenes

There was a unifying spirit among these independent poleis of Greek derivation—they saw themselves as "Hellenes (heh-LEENZ)." All the different peoples of the area—for example, the Ionians, Dorians, and Aculians—had a common language, which, although old, had only recently developed a written form. The earliest surviving Greek written characters are found on a jug dating from 725 B.C. These characters appear to be adapted from Phoenician script, one example of the many outside influences, especially Middle Eastern, that helped to shape Greek culture.

The Hellenes used a common calendar, which dated from the first Olympic games in 776 B.C. These games embodied much more than a mere sporting event—they represented life's struggles ("athletics" is a Greek word, meaning contest or struggle), and they symbolized the joy that can be found in toil and cost. The contests were undertaken for the honor of competing, and victory was regarded as a sufficient prize. But although the victors gained nothing more than a simple wreath of wild olive leaves, the citizens of a victorious athlete's polis often complemented the simple prize with more lucrative ones, such as free meals for life. Only men and boys could compete in the five-day festival of the Olympic games, held every four years, at Olympia. They competed in the nude—married women were forbidden even to attend the games—and the principal event was a foot race to honor Zeus (ZOOS), king of the gods (see the discussion on religion on page 58). Later, boxing, wrestling (Fig. **2.6**), other field sports, and chariot racing were added. The first day of the Olympic festival witnessed peripheral events, such as poetry readings and art exhibitions, and the third day was reserved for solemn religious sacrifices at the altar of Zeus.

The Persian War

Built by Cyrus the Great in the middle of the sixth century B.C., the Persian Empire stretched from the eastern Mediterranean to the River Indus and from the Caucasus Mountains to the Arabian Sea. The Persians had conquered Babylon, Mesopotamia, and Egypt. Unlike his barbarian father, Cyrus, Darius (duh-RY-uhs) I had a more enlightened vision of power. He built roads and canals, divided his empire into twenty sub-areas called satrapies, and built splendid palaces in his capital cities of Persepolis (purh-SEHP-oh-luhs) and Susa (SOOZ-uh). However, like any emperor, he could not tolerate rebellion, and when trouble arose in the Greek city–states of Ionia in 499 B.C., he moved to quash it. The result was what the Greeks called the great Persian War.

The revolt began in the trading city of Miletus (my-LEET-uhs), but the Ionians were no match for the Persians, and the revolt was soon crushed. The city of Athens responded to a plea for help, and that response prompted Darius to set his face to mainland Greece to punish the upstarts in 490 B.C. Darius drew his fleet ashore near the plain of Marathon, northeast of Athens, and 20,000 Persians and Medes outnumbered the Athenians two to one. The Athenian phalanx (a tight formation of infantry carrying overlapping shields and long spears) charged at the dead run, but the center broke and the Persians poured through. However, the vulnerable flanks of the Persian phalanx were turned by the aggressive Athenians, and, as a result, the Persians were forced to withdraw to their ships in disarray.

Darius died before he could take retributive action, and his son, Xerxes I (ZERK-sees), spent the next decade preparing for a new invasion of the Greek mainland, which set the stage for the great classical era of Athens, which we will trace in the next chapter.

Religion

The Greek mind was an earthy one, and Greek thought and religion centered on this life, rather than on the one to come. Ancient Greeks may often have looked for meaning in the order of the stars, but there, as on earth, the human mind was "the measure of all things."

At the core of Greek religion was a large family of superhuman gods. Their history in myth had been traced by the poet Homer in the *Iliad*. Greek religion had no holy

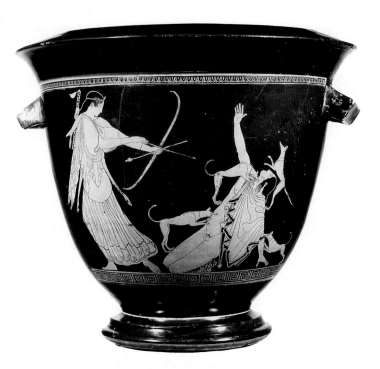

2.7 The Pan Painter, Attic Red Figure Krater showing Artemis Shooting Actaeon, c. 470 B.C. 16³⁄₄ ins (42.5 cm) high. Museum of Fine Arts, Boston.

books or scriptures. The stories of the gods were well known, however, through oral tradition and through writings such as Hesiod's *Theogony* (thee-AHG-oh-nee). These gods were called "Olympian" because they dwelt on the mythical (and also real) Mount Olympus. All were descended from a pair of older gods: Uranus (you-RAYN-uhs), representing the heavens, and Gaia (GAY-uh), representing the earth. But their genealogies were the subjects of so many varied myths that, although central to Greek religion, they are confusing, and, to some degree, confused. In addition to the central family of gods, the Greeks worshipped local deities who were thought to preside over certain human activities and to protect various specific geographical features such as streams and forests.

Unlike the Egyptians and Mesopotamians, the Greeks represented their gods in human terms, sometimes superior to humans, sometimes worse than us. This is a radical departure from, for example, the gods of Assyria and Babylonia, and the implication is clear: if the gods can be like humans, humans can also be godlike. Thus, an intimacy existed between the gods and their human companions, and life on earth for the Greeks was similar to that of the gods.

Homer had elaborated many of the often bizarre relationships of the gods in the Olympic pantheon, and some of the gods took shape from earlier religions of the Minoans and Mycenaeans, which may account for what often are confusing traits and characteristics.

In the Greek pantheon, Zeus, the sky god, functioned as the king of the gods on Mount Olympus. He hurled thunderbolts and presided over councils of gods. Endowed with a rapacious sexual appetite, Zeus sired both gods and mortals. Hera (HIH-ruh), Zeus' wife—and also his sister—functioned as the patron of women, who appealed to her for help. In legend, she also spent a good deal of time trying to keep an eye on her philandering husband. Zeus' two brothers, Poseidon (poh-SY-duhn) and Hades (HAY-deez), ruled the rest of the universe: Poseidon ruled the seas, waters, and earthquakes; while Hades ruled the underworld and land of the dead. Zeus had twin children, Apollo and Artemis (ART-uhm-ihs), who symbolized the sun and the moon, respectively. Apollo represented the intellect and reason, while Artemis was patroness of childbirth and wild creatures (Fig. 2.7).

Zeus' other children included Athena, goddess of wisdom and patron of the city of Athens. She sprang, fully developed, from the head of Zeus, and was worshipped as a virgin goddess. Ares was the god of war, who engaged in an incestuous and adulterous liaison with his half-sister Aphrodite, goddess of love and beauty, who was married to another of Zeus' sons, Hephaestus (hih-FEHS-tuhs), the god of craftsmen. According to legend, Hephaestus was both ugly and lame. Another son of Zeus, Hermes (HUHR-meez), served as the gods' messenger and patron of merchants and thieves. Zeus' sister Hestia (HEHS-tee-uh) protected the hearth in the Greek home.

Two other important deities headed large cults. Demeter (dih-MEE-tuhr), sister of Zeus, was goddess of the harvest, whose power made the earth fertile and crops grow. Initiates from all over Greece traveled to Eleusis, a small village in Attica, to worship her in quiet dignity and to join her cult with its promise of immortality. In contrast, Dionysus (dih-ohn-EE-suhs) was the god of wine and reveling, and his devotees participated wildly in search of rejuvenation and rebirth. His annual ceremonies in Athens gave birth to the festivals of drama we will study in the next chapter.

Philosophy

The age of great Greek philosophers was yet to come, but during the archaic period the groundwork was laid for rationalism and intellectual acuity that would blossom in the fifth century B.C. The word philosophy means "love of wisdom," and its practice developed into searches for the meaning and significance of the human condition. In the archaic period, philosophy first turned away from its roots in religion and began to apply reason to the discovery of the origins of the universe and the place of human beings in it.

In deference to the great philosopher of the Greek classical age yet to come, succeeding generations have called the philosophers of the archaic period the *pre-Socratics*, a term that does not refer to any specific philosophic system, of which there were several during the archaic period. Undoubtedly, the best-known and, arguably, the most important was the system of philosophy developed by Pythagoras (pih-THAG-uh-ruhs) and called *Pythagoreanism*. In his search for truth, Pythagoras concluded that mathematical relationships were universal—that is, that there were universal constants that applied throughout life. For example, his deduction of what we call the Pythagorean theorem postulates that the square of the hypotenuse of a right-angled triangle equals the sum of the squares of the other two sides. We see this as a mathematical given, but Pythagoras rationalized that this mathematical truth revealed the larger, universal truth about the cosmos: that the universe has a single reality existing apart from substance. He called this the "harmony of spheres." He further believed that all living things were related. Beyond his philosophical contributions, his mathematical inquiries deduced the numerical relationships among musical harmonies, his research in this area forming the basis of contemporary musical practice that divides a musical scale into an OCTAVE or eight tones.

Another important school of pre-Socratic philosophy was that of the *atomists*. Led by Leucippus (loo-SIH-puhs) and Democritus (de-MAHK-rit-uhs; c. 460 B.C.), this system believed that the universe is an ultimate and unchangeable reality based on atoms—that is, small "indivisible" and invisible particles. A second quality of the universe was "the void" or nothingness. Of course, we recognize both the term and the definition of "atom" as a part of the twentieth-century physical science of quantum mechanics.

Other pre-Socratic schools included the *materialists*, headed by Thales (THAY-leez) of Miletus (c. 585 B.C.), who believed that water was the primary element underlying the changing world of nature. A century later, another materialist, Empedocles (ehm-PEHD-oh-klees) of Acragas (c. 495 B.C.) postulated that the elements of nature consisted of fire, earth, air, and water. Combined (love) and separated (war and strife), they accounted for the progress of creatures and of civilizations.

Vase Painting

Protogeometric Style

Our earliest impressions of art during the "dark ages" between 1200 and 800 B.C. are given by the only artifacts that have survived: pots or vases. Whether the ornamentation on the objects qualifies as an art form is arguable;

2.8 Protogeometric
amphora, c. 950 B.C. 21³/₄ ins
(56 cm) high. Kerameikos
Museum, Athens.

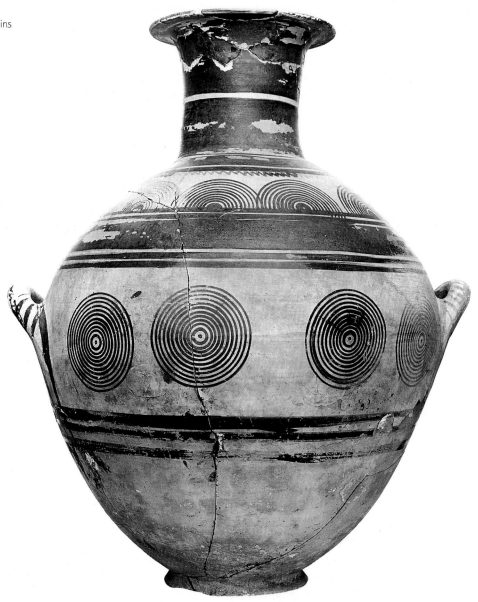

moreover, the term "vases" is somewhat misleading. Unlike modern fine-art ceramics, which are objects intended to convey beauty and comment on reality, these pots were designed to serve exclusively utilitarian purposes. They were cups, jugs, and vessels for storing and carrying water, wine, and oil. Vase painting was thus, at best, a minor art form among the Greeks.

Nevertheless these vessels do provide some insights into their time. The earliest examples, which date from around 1000 B.C., fall into a category known as "proto-geometric," a term that simply means "earliest forms of geometric." During this time, artists made use of bold, simple designs consisting mostly of circles and semicircles (Fig. **2.8**). The patterns are symmetrically balanced although the execution, while finely detailed, is somewhat haphazard. For example, the semicircles at the top of the

AMPHORA (AM-fuh-ruh) in Figure **2.8** are irregularly spaced: they overlap in one place, touch in another, and are separated by a gap in a third. Nonetheless, the overall composition here and elsewhere reveals a concern for rational order and for fine detail. The quality of the potter's technique is also quite high. The vases are wheel-thrown, and exhibit an exceptionally smooth surface. Decoration was applied by brush while the vase was turned on the wheel, or, in the case of the circular motifs, with a pair of compasses.

Geometric Style

Within the next two centuries, vase painting progressed to its full geometric phase. Figure **2.1** shows a geometric amphora in which the circular design of the protogeometric style has been replaced by linearity, using zigzags, diamonds, and the meander or maze pattern. The vessels themselves are more intricate in shape and larger in size. Some examples are nearly six feet (1.8 meters) high—so large, in fact, that they had to be constructed in sections.

Virtually every space on the vase is filled. The decoration is composed in horizontal bands called *registers*. When it appears, the human form is depicted in silhouette, with the head, legs, and feet in profile while the torso faces forward. In general, geometric vase design expresses absolute symmetry.

Archaic Style

Figure representation remained two-dimensional until the middle of the sixth century B.C. Depiction was restricted to full profile, or a full-frontal torso attached to legs in profile. The head, shown in profile, contained a full-frontal eye. Fabric was stiff and conventionalized. But by 500 B.C., artists were attempting to portray the body in a three-quarter position, between profile and full frontal. At the same time, a new feeling for three-dimensional space developed, and artists began to depict eyes more accurately. Fabric began to assume the drape and folds of real cloth. All these

MASTERWORK

The Dipylon Vase

The Dipylon (DIHP-ih-lahn) Vase (Fig. **2.9**), from slightly later in the eighth century B.C. than Figure **2.8**, was found in the Dipylon Cemetery in Athens. This pot and others like it served as grave monuments. Holes in the bottom allowed liquid offerings to filter down into the grave.

The vase in Figure **2.9** shows the body of the deceased lying on a funeral bier, surrounded by mourners. Also depicted on the vase is a funeral procession with warriors on foot and in chariots drawn by horses. Every human and animal figure in this complex design suggests a geometric shape and clearly represents a stylized approach, harmonizing with the other elements on the vase. Although recognizable and narrative in purpose, the figures appear as just another type of ornamentation within the larger context of the overall design. They follow the convention of portraying the torso frontally while the head and legs are in profile; turning the head to the rear would denote a figure in motion.

One of the amazing features of this vase is the amount and intricacy of detail that occupies every inch of its surface. Another important point is the organization of that detail into carefully balanced horizontal bands, each displaying a different geometric pattern. With only a few shapes, the artist has created a tremendously detailed painting with a subtle and sophisticated balance and focus. The dark, wide bands on the base and at the bottom of the bowl ground the design and help the viewer to focus on the story of the dead person. The patterns at the top and bottom of the vase are completely different, and yet they seem harmonious. Also notable is the balanced juxtaposition

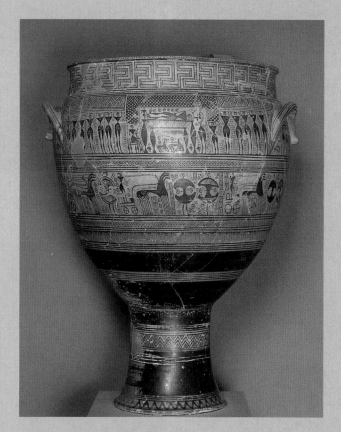

2.9 Dipylon Vase, Attic geometric amphora, eighth century B.C. 3 ft 6⅝ ins (1.08 m) high. Metropolitan Museum of Art, New York (Rogers Fund, 1914).

of straight lines and curves: the snake-like design and circles sit quite naturally alongside rectangles and triangles.

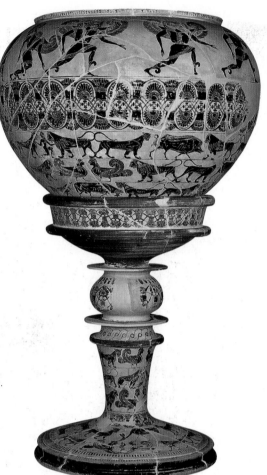

2.10 (*right*) Attic bowl showing Perseus and the Gorgons, early sixth century B.C. 36¹/₂ ins (93 cm) high. Louvre, Paris. © Photo RHM (Hervé Lewandowski).

2.11 (*below*) Skyphos by Hieron, painted by Makron, showing Paris abducting Helen, 500–480 B.C. 8¹/₂ ins (21.5 cm) high. Museum of Fine Arts, Boston (Francis Bartlett Donation).

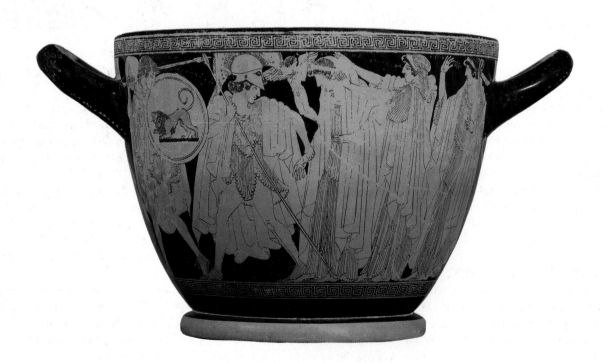

OUR DYNAMIC WORLD

Native America

We recognize the approach to human figures illustrated in the Greek sculptures of this chapter. Native American artists, however, developed a different set of conventions as Figure **2.12** illustrates. Among the many tribes of Native Americans, there is no specific word equivalent for the term "art." In Native American culture, art is anything that is technically well done. The "artist" is simply someone who is better at a job than someone else. Only a few tribes had a group of professionals who earned a living producing what we would call art.

The earliest identifiable art in Mexico comes from the Olmec people—called the "rubber people"—and can be dated to the

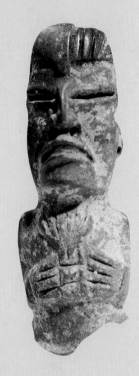

same period we are studying in this chapter, approximately 1000 B.C. These people carved a number of subjects—for example, the delicate, baby-faced figure shown in Figure **2.12**. This finely carved figurine has a noticeably turned-down mouth, a facial feature that is a common characteristic of Olmec sculpture of this period. Even though much of the body is missing, we can see that the carefully carved details on the green-gray stone effigy make a powerful statement.

2.12 Fragment of carved stone figurine; Olmec-style head with trace of red paint inlay. Xochipala, Guerrero, Mexico, 1250–750 B.C. 3 × 1 ins (7.6 × 2.5 cm). National Museum of the American Indian, Smithsonian Institution.

characteristics mark vase painting of the sixth century B.C., and they typify the various stages of the archaic style.

Individual vase painters' styles differed greatly from each other. We know some of these artists from their signatures. Others have been assigned names based on the subject or the location of their work. The Gorgon (GOHRG-uhn) Painter (Fig. **2.10**) was named after the Gorgons that decorate his work. In this example of the sixth-century style, the design is arranged in graduated registers, with an intricate and lovely geometric design as a focus on the middle band.

Red- and Black-Figure Pottery

Pottery of this period can be divided into two types—black-figure and red-figure. In black-figure vases, the design appears in black against the light red clay background. Details are incised, and white and dark colors are added. White tends to be used for women's flesh and for old men's beards. Red is used for hair, horses' manes, and for parts of garments (Fig. **2.10**).

Red-figure work, which first appears around 530 B.C., reverses the basic scheme, with the figures appearing in the natural red clay against a glazed black background (Fig. **2.11**). Contours and other internal lines appear in glaze and often stand out in slight relief. In early red-figure work, incision is occasionally used for the contours of the hair, with touches of white and red. Other techniques that appeared in the fifth and fourth centuries B.C. include the use of PALMETTES and other motifs impressed in the clay and covered with black glaze. The firing process for both types was the same.

Painters discovered that figures were more lifelike when they appeared in the natural red color of the terracotta, with the background filled in in black. At first, the change from black-figure to red-figure was tentative. Some vases appeared with red-figure work on one side and black-figure on the other.

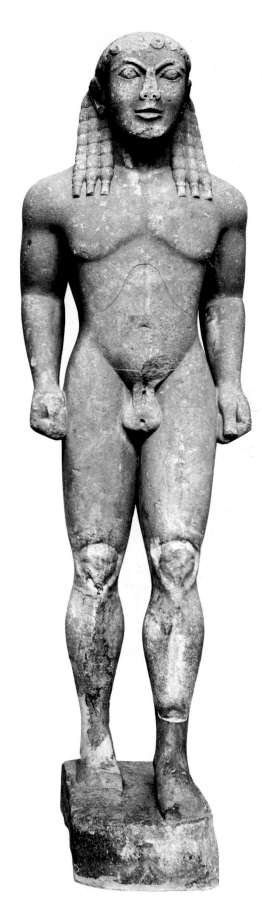

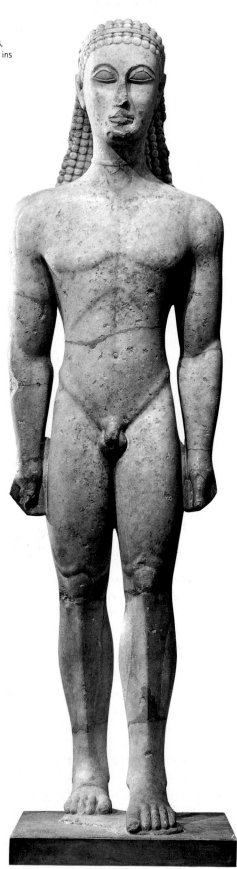

2.13 (*left*) Polymedes of Argos, Kouros, c. 600 B.C. Stone, 6 ft 5¹/₂ ins (1.97 cm) high. Archeological Museum, Delphi, Greece.

2.14 (*right*) Kouros, c. 615 B.C. Marble, 6 ft 4 ins (1.93 m) high. Metropolitan Museum of Art (Fletcher Fund, 1932).

Sculpture

Stone and metal are more durable than pottery, and sculpture often surpasses all other art forms in its survival of the centuries. However, Greek sculpture does not exist in great quantity, and it is unfortunately more than likely that some of the greatest examples have been lost to humanity forever.

Archaic Style

Most of the freestanding statues in the archaic style are of nude youths, and are known as kouroi (KOO-roy). The term means, simply, "male youth," and the singular form is kouros (KOO-rohs). More than a hundred examples have survived. All exhibit a stiff, fully frontal pose. The head is raised, eyes are fixed to the front, and arms hang straight down at the sides, with the fists clenched. The emphasis of these statues is on physicality and athleticism. The shoulders are broad, the pectoral muscles well developed, and the waist narrow. The legs show the musculature of a finely tuned athlete with solid buttocks and hardened calves. Nevertheless, these figures are clearly not lifelike. The sculptor seems overconscious of the block of stone from which the figures have been cut. Features are simplified, and the posture, despite the movement of one foot into the forward plane, is rigid. In spite of these limitations, however, these works represent a sculptural innovation. They are the first examples of truly freestanding sculpture. By freeing the statue of any support, the artist is able to represent the human form independently of any non-living matter. This accomplishment prepares the way for later, more successful representations of living beings.

Most of the kouroi were sculpted as funerary and temple art. Many of them were signed by the artist: "So-and-so made me." Whether the statues were intended to represent humans or gods—they are most definitely not portraits of individuals—is debatable. The fact that all are nudes is perhaps a celebration of the physical perfection of youth and of the marvelous nature of the human body. The kouroi may also represent, more directly, the naked athletes who took part in the games loved by the Greeks. The Greeks explained the practice of competing in the nude by telling the story of a runner who dropped his loin-cloth and, thus unimpeded, won the race. Other more symbolic explanations of the nudity of these statues have been offered, but no one view has prevailed.

Two significant characteristics are exemplified by the kouros from around 600 B.C. shown in Figure **2.13**. First is the fact that although there is an obvious attempt by the sculptor to depict the human figure in a fairly lifelike manner, the figure does not represent a particular person. Rather, it is a stereotype, or a symbol, and an idealization, perhaps of heroism. But it does not depict ideal human

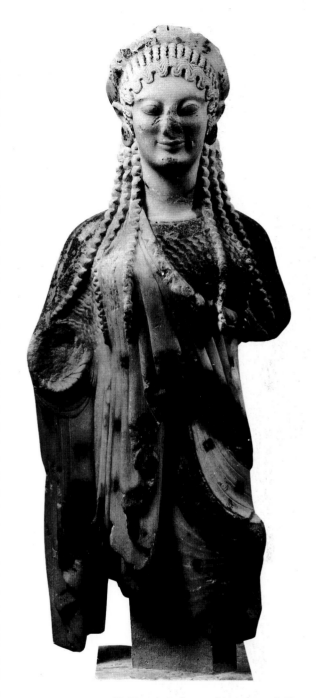

2.15 Kore, c. 510 B.C. Marble, 21¹/₂ ins (54.6 cm) high. Acropolis Museum, Athens.

form. The sculpture lacks refinement, and this is a characteristic that helps to differentiate the archaic from the classical style.

The second characteristic is the attempt to indicate movement. Even though the sculpture is firmly rooted, the left foot extends forward. This creates a greater sense of motion than if both feet were side by side in the same plane, yet the weight of the body remains equally divided between the two feet.

The striking similarity of form and style among the kouroi can be seen when we compare Figure **2.13** with the statue in Figure **2.14**. The same physical emphases, the same frontality and the same slight departure from the horizontal plane, with the left feet forward, occur. The stylized treatment of the hair is nearly identical, except that

one figure has the curls pushed back behind the ears, while the other wears his hair over the shoulders. In both statues the kneecaps are curiously overarticulated. Nevertheless, the kouroi differ in proportion and in facial details.

The kouros had a female counterpart in the *kore* (KOH-ray, plural korai, meaning "maidens"). These figures are always fully dressed, and in other ways, too, the kourai show far more variety than the kouroi. Some of these differences may stem from variations in regional dress, but clearly the sculptor's interest lies in the treatment of that dress, in the technical mastery required for an accurate depiction of cloth in stone.

Figure **2.15** shows a typical kore. In this delicate and refined portrayal, the sculptor seems to be reaching beyond the world of mortals, perhaps to depict an eastern goddess or queen. In contrast to the kouroi, the carving of this statue shows a lightness of touch and delicacy, not only in its anatomical features, but also in the precise folds of the

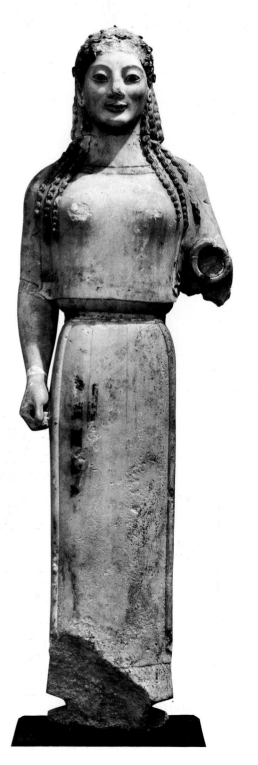

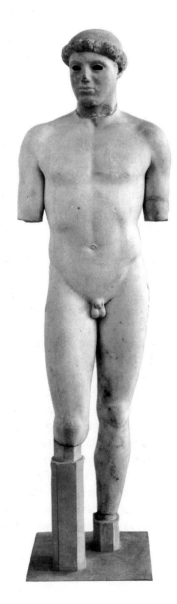

2.16 (*left*) Kore in Dorian peplos, c. 530 B.C. Marble, 4 ft (1.22 m) high. Acropolis Museum, Athens.

2.17 (*right*) *Kritios Boy*, c. 480 B.C. Marble, about 34 ins (86 cm) high. Acropolis Museum, Athens.

robes, finely detailed jewelry, and stylized hair. These elements combine to give the statue a greater degree of verisimilitude than the kouroi we have examined.

In comparison with Figure **2.15**, the kore shown in Figure **2.16** lacks detail, but it thereby achieves cleaner, more graceful, lines. Although anatomical details are disguised by the heavy fabric, the body, with the waist emphasized, is convincingly present beneath the robes. The kore's smile exhibits more personality than the blank stare of many archaic statues, and the extension of the left arm forward into space indicates a new interest in movement outside the main block of the statue.

By the early fifth century B.C. the stiffness of the archaic style had begun to modify. The human form began to be portrayed with subtlety and to display movement. The transition began with the *Kritios Boy* (KRIHT-ee-ohs; Fig. **2.17**), named for its presumed sculptor. Here is a statue in which the body truly stands at rest. The artist has discovered the principle of weight shift—that is, the way in which the body parts position themselves around the flexible axis of the spine. The *Kritios Boy* is the first known portrayal of this important principle, and in it we can discern the beginnings of the classical style.

Architecture—The Doric Order

The archaic period witnessed the building of temples in a new adaptation of the POST-AND-LINTEL structure. The style employed imposing vertical posts or columns capped by heavy lintels and a PEDIMENTED roof, and it was probably drawn from elements of Egyptian, Mycenaean, and pre-archaic Greek structures—for example, the FLUTED or vertically grooved column was used in Egypt nearly two thousand years before its appearance in Greece. The style of these temples was called Doric after one of the Hellenic peoples, the Dorians, and it seems to have been well established by 600 B.C. Although the style itself changed over time, the early version had a cumbersome appearance, with thick columns and blocky, oversized capitals. Many of its characteristics came from earlier wooden buildings. We can sense the qualities and details of the order by examining a reconstruction drawing of the west front of the Temple of Artemis at Corfu (Fig. **2.18**). In this example, tapering columns sit directly on the STYLOBATE (STYL-uh-bayt) or uppermost element of the foundation. The fluted SHAFT, the tubular main trunk of the column, tapers inward as it rises. The shaft leads to a flared ECHINUS (ehk-IHN-uhs), a round collar-like cushion between the shaft and a square ABACUS (AB-uh-kuhs): the slab at the top of the column on which the ARCHITRAVE (AR-kih-trayv), or bottom portion of the lintel, rests (Fig. **2.19**). In the ENTABLATURE we can see a FRIEZE or band of relief elements

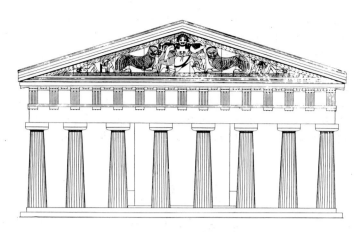

2.18 Reconstruction drawing of the west front of the Temple of Artemis, Corfu. [After Rodenwaldt.]

2.19 The Doric order.

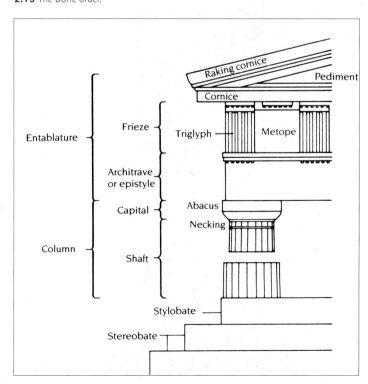

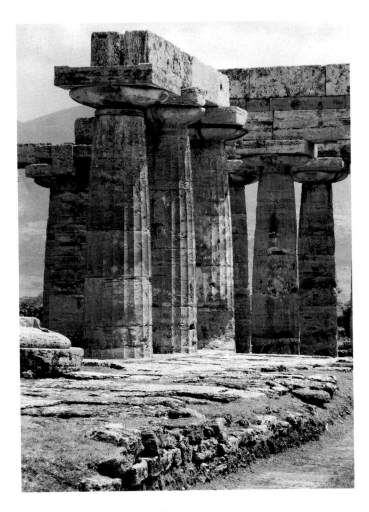

2.20 Corner of the "Basilica," Paestum, Italy, c. 550 B.C.

known as triglyphs and metopes (MEHT-uh-peez). Above the frieze rest two CORNICES. One is horizontal and the other rises at an angle creating a triangular space called a PEDIMENT, which was often filled with relief sculptures (see Figs. **3.9** and **3.10** in the next chapter).

The best-preserved temple from this period is the "Basilica" at Paestum (PEEHS-tuhm; Fig. **2.20**). It was dedicated to the goddess Hera. Here, the flaring of the columns is exaggerated and the capitals seem unduly large, as if the architect were afraid that the lintels of the architrave would collapse if not supported along their length. The PROPORTION, or relationship of the width of the columns to their height, gives the Basilica a squat appearance with none of the grace of its classical successors.

Music

Although we cannot play any Greek music, because we simply do not know how to interpret the surviving records,

we do know that music played a fundamental role in Greek life and education, and in Greek mythology, music had tremendous power to influence behavior. The gods themselves invented musical instruments, and the deities and heroes of Greek legend played them to remarkable effect. Apollo played the lyre (Fig. **2.21**), and Athena, the flute. Achilles, Homer's great hero of the *Iliad*, played proficiently.

Surviving records tell us that Greek music consisted of a series of MODES, the equivalent of our scales. Each mode—for example, the Dorian and Phrygian—had a name and a particular characteristic sound, not unlike the difference between our major and minor scales, and the Greeks attributed certain behavioral outcomes to each mode. Just as we say that minor scales sound sad or exotic, the Greeks held that the Dorian mode exhibited strong, even warlike, feelings, while the Phrygian elicited more sensual emotions.

2.21 Attributed to the Eucharides painter, amphora showing Apollo playing a lyre and Artemis holding an aulos before an altar, c. 490 B.C. 18½ ins (47 cm) high. Metropolitan Museum of Art, New York (Rogers Fund, 1907).

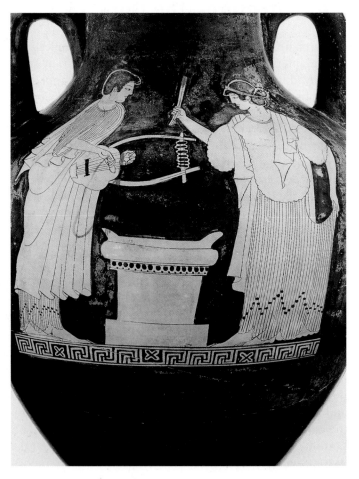

PROFILE

Sappho

One of the great Greek lyrists and few known female poets of the ancient world, Sappho was an aristocrat who married a prosperous merchant, and she had a daughter named Cleis. Her wealth afforded her the opportunity to live her life as she chose, and she chose to spend it studying the arts on the isle of Lesbos.

In the seventh century B.C., Lesbos was a cultural center. Sappho spent most her time on the island, though she also traveled widely throughout Greece. She was exiled for a time because of political activities in her family, and she spent this time in Sicily. By this time she was known as a poet, and the residents of Syracuse were so honored by her visit that they erected a statue to her. Sappho was much honored in ancient times. Coins of Lesbos were minted with her image during her own lifetime. Plato elevated her from the status of great lyric poet to one of the muses. Upon hearing one of her songs, Solon, himself an Athenian ruler, lawyer, and a poet, asked that he be taught the song "Because I want to learn it and die."

Although her work enjoyed great fame, it did not survive intact: only one of Sappho's poems is available in its entirety. All the rest exist solely as fragments. At one time, there were perhaps nine complete volumes of her poetry, but over the years neglect, natural disasters, and possibly some censorship took their toll. Late in the nineteenth century, however, manuscripts dating back to the eighth century A.D. were discovered in the Nile Valley, and some of these manuscripts contained pieces of her works. Many translations of these fragments have been made, and each offers a slightly different approach to her work. Translating Sappho's poetry is exceedingly challenging, in no small part because of the fragmented nature of the material. Sappho has remained an important literary and cultural figure, her works continue to be studied and translated, and speculation on her life remains popular.

We have a fairly good picture of what Greek musical instruments looked like from vase paintings. Figure **2.21** illustrates the aulos, a double-reed instrument, and the lyre, a stringed instrument. The Greeks were particularly fond of vocal music, and instruments were used principally to accompany vocal music. The lyrics of songs have survived, and these include songs to celebrate acts by the various gods, from whom some mortal had gained special favor.

Literature

Homer, whose work we examine in more detail at the end of this chapter, is probably the best-known of the ancient Greek poets, but he was by no means the only one. The growth of individualism in Greece produced a new literature: personal LYRIC poetry. Ancient lyrics, anonymous and often intended for use in rituals, had been concerned with experiences common to all. But by the end of the seventh century B.C., poets appeared along the Ionian coast who tell us their names, and sing of themselves, their travels, military adventures, political contests, homesickness, drinking parties, poverty, hates, and loves.

Sappho

The lyric poet Sappho (SAF-oh), who was born around 615 B.C., lived all her life on the island of Lesbos. She gathered around her a coterie of young women interested in poetry, and who may have been worshippers of the cult of Aphrodite. Many of Sappho's poems are written in honor of one or other of these young women.

Hesiod

Born at the end of the eighth century B.C., Hesiod (HEE-see-uhd) was the son of an emigrant farmer from Asia Minor. He depicts this hard life in his poem *Works and Days*. Hesiod's lesson is that men must work, and he sketches the work that occupies a peasant throughout the year, recounting how an industrious farmer toils and how work brings prosperity, in contrast to the ruin brought about by idleness. He captures the changing seasons and countryside with vivid word pictures. He also describes life at sea, and concludes with a catechism detailing how people should deal with each other. His style is similar to Homer's, but his subject matter is quite different, for rather than telling of heroes and gods, Hesiod dwells on the mundane and mortal.

MASTERWORK

Sappho—"God's Wildering Daughter"

Sappho was called a *lyrist* because, as was the custom of the time, she wrote her poems to be performed with the accompaniment of a lyre. Sappho composed her own music and refined the prevailing lyric meter to a point that it is now known as *sapphic meter.* She innovated lyric poetry both in technique and style, becoming part of a new wave of Greek lyrists that moved from writing poetry from the point of view of gods and muses to the point of view of the individual. She was one of the first poets to write from the first person, describing love and loss as they affected her personally.

Her style was sensual and melodic; primarily songs of love, yearning, and reflection. Frequently the object of her affections was female—usually one of the women sent to her for education in the arts. She nurtured these women, wrote poems of love and adoration to them, and when they eventually left the island to be married, she composed their wedding songs. Sappho's tone is emotional and frank, her language simple and sensuous. One of her longer fragments, "He seems to be a God, that Man," was much admired and imitated by later poets. In it, Sappho gazes at a young bride sitting and laughing next to her bridegroom and is overcome with emotion. In "God's Wildering Daughter," Sappho entreats Aphrodite, the immortal child of the god Zeus.

God's Wildering Daughter
Sappho

God's wildering daughter deathless Aphrodite,
A whittled perplexity your bright abstruse chair,
With heartbreak, lady, and breathlessness
Tame not my heart.

But come down to me, as you came before,
For if ever I cried, and you heard and came,
Come now, of all times, leaving
Your father's golden house

In that chariot pulled by sparrows reined and bitted,
Swift in their flying, a quick blur aquiver,
Beautiful, high. They drew you across steep air
Down to the black earth:

Fast they came, and you behind them. O
Hilarious heart, your face all laughter.
Asking, What troubles you this time, why again
Do you call me down?

Asking, In your wild heart, who now
Must you have? Who is she that persuasion
Fetch her, enlist her, and put her into bounden love?
Sappho, who does you wrong?

If she balks, I promise, soon she'll chase,
If she's turned from gifts, now she'll give them.
And if she does not love you, she will love,
Helpless, she will love.

Come, then, loose me from cruelties.
Give my tethered heart its full desire.
Fulfill, and, come, lock your shield with mine
Throughout the siege.

Hesiod's most famous work, however, is the *Theogony*, in which he traces the mythological history of the Greek gods. He describes the rise of the earth out of chaos, the overthrow of the Titans by Zeus, and the emergence of each god and goddess (see p. 59). Scholars attempting to understand Greek art and religion have found this work invaluable as a source of information.

Dance

The ancient Greeks believed that the Gods invented dancing. They believed that the Gods offered this gift to some select mortals only, who in turn taught dancing to the rest of humanity. The oldest Greek historical sources on dance come from Crete and the Minoan civilization, which cultivated music, song, and dance as part of their religious life and for their entertainment as well. The religious rituals of ancient Greece centered on dance. Beginning around 600 B.C., great festivals brought choruses of fifty dancers from each tribe together on special occasions for competitions. Most scholars agree that the Greek theatre developed directly from these dances. (The Greek tragic chorus had fifty members.)

Dance, music, and drama were inseparably entwined, and all played a fundamental part in early (and classical) Greek philosophy, religion, and life. The term "dance" had a broader definition for the Greeks than it does for us. In fact, it denoted almost any kind of rhythmic movement. Just as dance and music were inseparable, so were dance and poetry. A Greek could dance a poem, using rhythmic movements of his hands, arms, body, face, and head to interpret the verses recited or sung by himself or another person.

Focal Point

The *Iliad* and *Odyssey* of Homer

Homer's *Iliad* and *Odyssey* created the mythical history that later Greeks accepted as their historic heritage. They took the dark and unknown past and created in a literary, originally oral, form a cultural foundation for an entire people. They told of heroes and described the gods. They depicted places and events, and they did so in a form that represented a supreme artistic achievement: epic poetry. Both poems deal with minor episodes in the story of the battle of Troy, which ended, with the destruction of the city, in about 1230 B.C.

Divided into twenty-four books, the *Odyssey* tells the story of Odysseus, king of Ithaca, as he travels home from the Trojan War to recover his house and kingdom.

The poem opens on the island of Orgygia (ohr-Gihj-uh), where, ten years after the end of the Trojan War, Odysseus has been detained for seven years by the nymph Calypso. After setting the scene, the poem shifts to Ithaca, where Odysseus' wife, Penelope (pehn-EL-oh-pee), and son, Telemachus (tuh-LEHM-uh-kuhs), struggle to retain their authority during Odysseus' long absence. In Book V, Zeus orders Calypso to release Odysseus, and Odysseus sets sail on a raft, which is destroyed by Poseidon, god of the sea, washing ashore on the land of the Phaeacians (FAY-uh-shuns). Odysseus recounts for the Phaeacians his adventures since leaving Troy: the land of the Lotus-Eaters; struggling with lotus-induced lethargy; blinding Polyphemus (pahl-ee-FEEM-uhs) the Cyclops, a son of Poseidon; losing eleven of his twelve ships; reaching the island of Circe (SUHR-see) the enchantress, who turned some of his companions into swine; visiting the Land of Departed Spirits and learning from the Theban seer Tiresias (teer-EE-see-uhs) how to calm Poseidon's wrath; encountering the Sirens, Scylla (SIHL-uh) and Charybdis (kuh-RIB-dis), and the Cattle of the Sun, which his companions, despite warnings, kill for food; finally, surviving, alone, the following storm and reaching Calypso's idyllic island.

The Phaeacians return Odysseus to Ithaca, where the goddess Athena (uh-THEEN-uh) disguises him as a beggar and he reveals his true identity to his son. Together they plot to rid their home of the suitors hounding Penelope. Still in disguise, Odysseus passes the clever test Penelope has devised to choose one of the suitors. After passing the test, Odysseus kills the suitors with the help of Telemachus and two faithful servants and is accepted by Penelope as her long-lost husband and as the king of Ithaca.

Set in twenty-four books, like the *Odyssey*, and exploring the *heroic ideal* with all its contradictions, the *Iliad* begins with an explanation of the quarrel between King Agamemnon (ag-uh-MEM-nahn), commander of the Greek army, and Achilles, the Greeks' greatest warrior. When the action opens, the Greeks have been besieging Troy for nine years, trying to rescue Helen, wife of Agamemnon's brother Menelaus (mehn-uh-LAY-uhs), from Paris, one of the sons of the Trojan King Priam (PRY-uhm). As a result of his quarrel with Agamemnon, Achilles leaves the Greek forces, taking his followers with him. Without Achilles, the Greeks suffer many losses. Unable to bear it when the Trojans set fire to the Greek fleet, one of Achilles' close friends asks permission to rejoin the fight. Achilles agrees and lends him his armor. When his friend is killed by the Trojan hero Hector, Achilles exacts revenge by killing Hector. Hector's father, King Priam, asks Achilles for his son's body so that it can be properly buried. Achilles agrees, and his anger is assuaged. The work ends with Hector's funeral.

Homer develops events on the battlefield and behind the lines of both adversaries. From his descriptions, an elaborate evocation emerges of the splendor and tragedy of war and the inconsistencies of mortals and gods. The heroes are types, not real people, and their characters were established in legend long before they were described in this epic poem. Here is a brief extract from Book XX:

So these now, the Achaians, beside the curved ships
were arming around you, son of Peleus, insatiate of
battle, while on the other side at the break of the plain
the Trojans armed. But Zeus, from the many-folded
peak of Olympos, told Themis to summon all the gods
into assembly. She went everywhere, and told them to
make their way to Zeus' house. There was no river
who was not there, except only Ocean, there was not
any one of the nymphs who live in the lovely groves,
and the springs of rivers and grass of the meadows,
   who came not.   10
These all assembling into the house of Zeus cloud
   gathering

took places among the smooth-stone cloister walks
   which Hephaestus
had built for Zeus the father by his craftsmanship
   and contrivance.
So they were assembled within Zeus' house; and the
   shaker
of the earth did not fail to hear the goddess, but
   came up among them
from the sea, and sat in the midst of them, and asked
   Zeus of his counsel:
"Why, lord of the shining bolt, have you called the
   gods to assembly
once more? Are you deliberating Achaians and
Trojans? For the onset of battle is almost broken to
   flame between them."
In turn Zeus who gathers the clouds spoke to him in
   answer:
"You have seen, shaker of the earth, the counsel
   within me,   20
and why I gathered you. I think of these men though
   they are dying.

Even so, I shall stay here upon the fold of Olympos
sitting still, watching, to pleasure my heart.
      Meanwhile all you others
go down, wherever you may go among the Achaians
   and Trojans
and give help to either side, as your own pleasure
   directs you,
for if we leave Achilles alone to fight with the
   Trojans
they will not even for a little hold off swift-footed
   Peleion.
For even before now they would tremble whenever
   they saw him,
and now, when his heart is grieved and angered for
   his companion's
death, I fear against destiny he may storm their
   fortress."   30
So spoke the son of Kronos and woke the incessant
   battle.

CHAPTER REVIEW

Critical Thought

We have now arrived at the birthing place of Western culture. Here, in archaic Greece, politics, art, architecture, literature, music, and dance reveal themselves as PROTOTYPES. We begin to see things we recognize—not from history books or even museums, but on the streets of our own towns. That is what prototypes are: the original ideas or forms on which later ideas and forms are based. Some of our public buildings emulate the Greek original, and certainly our form of government grew from concepts basic to the polis.

Summary

After reading this chapter you should be able to:

- Identify and describe four pre-Socratic schools of philosophical thought.
- Characterize the Minoan, Mycenaean, and archaic Greek styles of architecture.
- Explain the differences among protogeometric, geometric, and archaic styles of pottery.
- Define the term polis and discuss its role as a fundamental concept in the Greek cultural ethos.
- Describe the characteristics of archaic Greek sculpture.
- Apply the elements and principles of composition to analyses and comparisons of archaic Greek, Egyptian, and Mesopotamian art and architecture.

CHAPTER THREE

Greek Classicism and Hellenism

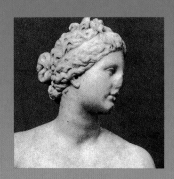

OUTLINE

THE CLASSICAL WORLD
The Persian War
The Age of Pericles
The Peloponnesian War
Philosophy
Literature: The Platonic Dialogues
History and Science
Classical Style in Vase Painting
  and Sculpture
  MASTERWORK: Myron—*Discus
    Thrower*
  OUR DYNAMIC WORLD: The Nok
    Style of Africa
Architecture
  MASTERWORK: The Parthenon
Theatre
  PROFILE: Aeschylus
  MASTERWORK: Sophocles—*Oedipus
    the King*
Music
Dance

THE HELLENISTIC AGE
Alexander and the Spread of
  Hellenistic Culture
Theatre and Literature
Philosophy and Religion
  TECHNOLOGY: Hero's Steam
    Turbine
Hellenistic Style

FOCAL POINT: FROM IDEALISM
TO REALISM—*PROMETHEUS* AND
HECUBA

VIEW

THE CLASSICAL IDEAL

The foundations of Western civilization rest firmly on the bedrock of classicism. The term classicism denotes the ideals and styles of ancient Greece and Rome as embodied primarily in their arts. Almost universally, these ideals and styles have been translated into notions of simplicity, harmony, restraint, proportion, and reason. We are related to the Greeks by these ideals, and, in fact, as we read subsequent chapters, we will see Greek classical ideas recur again and again. At times we will hear the classical/anti-classical struggle called the struggle between "form" and "feeling" or intellect versus emotion. That postulation means the struggle of artistic ideas in which appeal to rationality, simplicity, and restraint (form) comes up against ideals that appeal to emotion, complexity, and abandon (feeling). Classicism believes in the power of reason and searches for rational principles. Anti-classicism in its various styles promotes individualism and subjectivity.

Above Detail of Fig. **3.13**.

3.1 The Parthenon, Athens, 447–438 B.C.

KEY TERMS

Some of the basic terms and concepts we will encounter in this chapter include the following:

Oligarchy is government by the few, especially by a small faction of persons or families—as opposed to a **democracy**.

Aesthetics is a branch of philosophy dealing with the nature of beauty and art and their relation to human beings.

Classicism is a style of art relying on the fundamentals of simplicity, clarity of structure, and appeal to the intellect.

Ionic order, one of the Greek architectural decorative and elevational conventions and systems of proportion, characterized by columns with scroll-like capitals and circular bases.

Corinthian order, one of the Greek architectural decorative and elevational conventions and systems of proportion, characterized by columns employing an elaborate leaf motif in the capital.

Hellenistic style is an approach to art characterized by individuality, virtuosity, and emotion.

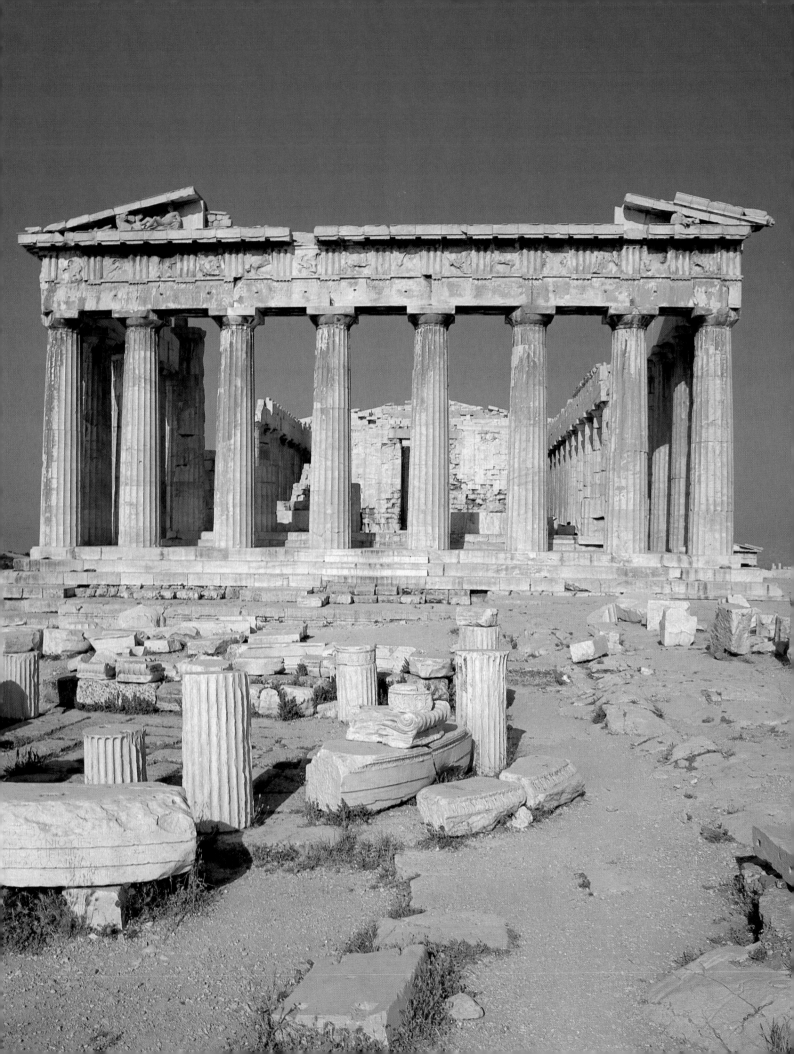

THE CLASSICAL WORLD
The Persian War

The Persians, defeated at Marathon in 490 B.C., spent the next ten years regrouping under Xerxes I and preparing for another invasion of the Greek mainland. That invasion took place in 480, when an army of perhaps as many as 60,000 men proved unstoppable, completely overrunning northern Greece. It must have been a frightening spectacle: Medes and Persians clad in leather breeches and fishtail iron jerkins, with short, powerful bows; Assyrians in bronze helmets and carrying long lances; Arabs in flowing robes; and Ethiopians in leopard and lion skins. A coalition army headed by the Spartans battled valiantly, at a narrow northern pass named Thermopylae—the Hot Gates—which has gone down in history largely because a traitor revealed to the Persians how to take the defenders from the rear. As the Persian army moved steadily south, its fleet sailed north against southern Attica. Athens was taken and destroyed, and ultimate victory for the Persians seemed a certainty.

The Greeks were, however, fighting on territory they knew well, they had brilliant leaders, and they were motivated by the desire to save their homeland. For years the Athenian Themistocles (thuh-MIS-tuh-kleez) had championed the Greek navy, and hundreds of new triremes (ships with three banks of oars; Fig. **3.2**) had been built. These long warships, manned by disciplined citizen–sailors, took to the sea against the Persian fleet. The critical battle came off the port of Athens, near the small island of Salamis, where the triremes (TRY-reemz) massed against the Persians, ramming them as Greek warriors swarmed aboard. The battle of Salamis was a Greek triumph, totally destroying the Persian fleet and leaving the Persian army unsupported.

The Persian army wintered in Thessaly, and in 479 B.C. it marched south again. Under Spartan command, the Greek army emerged victorious at the critical battle of Plataea. The beaten Persians withdrew, never again to set foot in Greece. The Persian War did not end for another thirty years, but after the battles of Salamis in 480 and Plataea in 479, the "war" consisted largely of annual raids by the Greeks on coastal lands of the Persian Empire.

Timeline 3.1 Greek Classicism and Hellenism.

B.C.	GENERAL EVENTS	LITERATURE & PHILOSOPHY	VISUAL ARTS & ARCHITECTURE	PERFORMING ARTS
500				
	Battle of Marathon Persian invasion Delian League	Herodotus	*Charioteer* (**3.6**) Myron, *Discus Thrower* (**3.8**)	Aeschylus Sophocles
450				
	Pericles Peloponnesian War	Protagoras Socrates Thucydides	Polyclitus, *Lance Bearer* (**3.7**) Parthenon (**3.1, 3.9, 3.10, 3.15, 3.16, 3.17**) Temple of Athena Nike (**3.21**) *Riace Warrior* (**3.12**) Propylaea (**3.20**)	Euripides Aristophanes
400				
	City-states defeated by Philip II Alexander the Great Invasion of Persia	Plato Aristotle Epicurus	Mausoleum, Halicarnassus (**3.11**) Praxiteles (**3.13, 3.14**) Lysippus, *Scraper* (**3.18**)	Theatre at Epidaurus Menander
300				
	Library at Alexandria Ptolemy I	Hippocrates Zeno the Stoic Theocritus	*Dying Gaul* (**3.31**)	
200				
			Nike of Samothrace (**3.29**) Temple of Olympian Zeus (**3.32**)	
100				
			Laocoön and his Two Sons (**3.30**)	

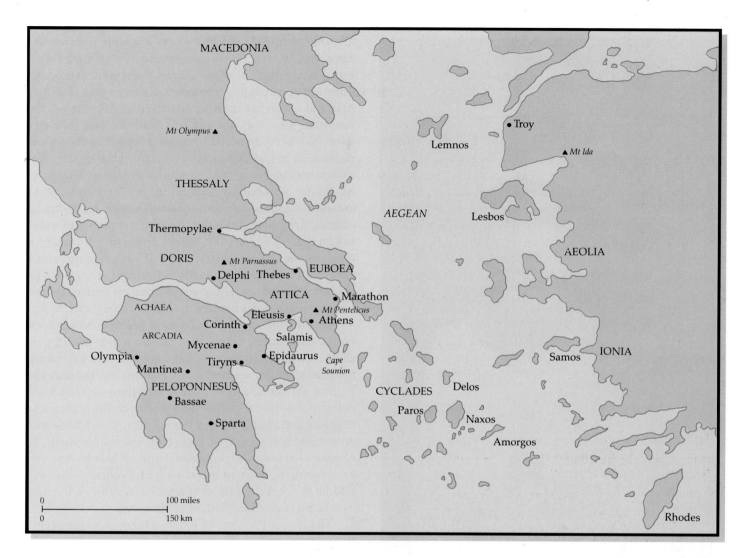

Map 3.1 Ancient Greece.

3.2 Reconstruction of a Greek trireme.

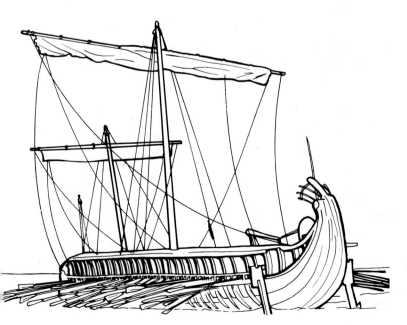

The Age of Pericles

Claiming to be the saviors of Greece, the Athenians set about liberating the rest of the country. Several city–states banded together with Athens to form the Delian (DEL-ee-uhn) League in 478 B.C. The league took its name from the Ionian island of Delos, where the group met and stored its money. Delos was the site of the shrine of Apollo, and such sanctuaries were always chosen as treasuries so that the god would guard them. The states made a contract, and the signatories agreed to follow a common foreign policy and to contribute ships and/or money, as Athens deemed necessary. Athens contributed the most money and commanded the fleet. What followed was a systematic liberation of the Greek cities around the Aegean and the conquest of some islands populated by non-Greeks. The Delian League became, in fact, a highly prosperous Athenian empire.

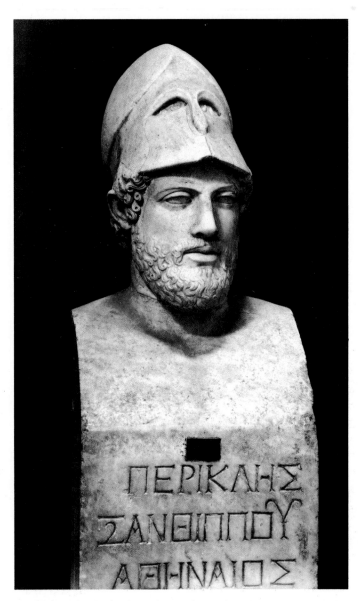

3.3 Kresilas, *Pericles*, Roman copy after original of c. 440 B.C. Marble, Vatican Museum, Rome.

230,000 people. About 40,000 of these were free male citizens; 40,000 were Athenian women; 50,000 were foreign born; and 100,000 were slaves. Athenian democracy, however, allowed only free male citizens to vote. The long-believed view that in the golden age of Athens, women, although honored as wives and mothers, had little freedom, has been disputed by some recent historians who claim that, although women were denied the right to vote, they otherwise associated with men as equals. The tyrant, or ruler, wielded considerable power. This power emanated principally from ownership of land. Private estates provided not only for the tyrant's individual welfare, but also for the horses and arms necessary to make him a leader in warfare. The Greek tyrants seem in general to have been especially benevolent. They were not necessarily aristocrats, and their claims to leadership were often based on their popularity among the citizens.

By the fifth century B.C., Athens was the richest of the Greek city–states. Greek law had been reformed by the great Athenian lawmaker Solon, and after 508 B.C., constitutional changes created a complex of institutions that became the foundations of an almost pure form of democracy. All political decisions were made, in principle at least, by a majority vote of the citizens. Conditions were now right for an age of high cultural achievement. By historical standards, the golden age of Athens was very brief—indeed, it lasted less than half a century—but that middle third of the fifth century B.C. was one of the most significant periods in Western civilization.

The tyrant Pericles (PER-i-kleez; Fig. **3.3**) dominated Athenian politics between 450 and 429 B.C. A descendant of the old aristocracy, he flourished under the new democracy. The Athenian historian Thucydides (thoo-SID-ih-deez) wrote that Pericles was enormously popular and known for his financial integrity. He clearly had a vision of Athenian greatness that he was able to bring to fruition.

The Peloponnesian War

Although they had joined forces to defeat the external threat of the Persians, the Greeks, with their independent city–states, never really coexisted peacefully, and toward the end of the fifth century B.C., that contentiousness led to a war of attrition between Athens and Sparta that effectively brought to a close the golden age of Athens. The Peloponnesian (pel-oh-pah-NEEZ-ee-uhn) War, which began in 431 B.C., constituted a clash between two completely opposite ways of life.

If Athens was a cultured society, democratic, and artistic, Sparta represented the old ways of warriors, courage, militarism, and OLIGARCHY (AH-lih-gar-kee). Sparta was ruled by a council of elders, and its males were required to

The destruction of Athens, the victory over the Persians, and the formation of the Delian League helped to transform the young democracy of Athens, with its thriving commerce, unique religion, and inquisitive philosophies, into a culture of immense artistic achievement. The ruined city had to be rebuilt, and the spirit of victory and heroics prevailed. The Delian treasury, moved to Athens by Pericles, was used to help finance the immense costs of reconstruction.

Athens had witnessed a succession of rulers, and an interesting form of democracy had gradually emerged. Historians estimate that when Pericles came to power, in 461 B.C., the population of Athens was approximately live in barracks, as soldiers, until they were thirty years old. In reality, every citizen had to be a soldier, because Sparta's agriculture depended on the labor of subject peoples, who far outnumbered the Spartans. In order to keep the population subdued, Sparta's men had to remain militarily expert. Spartans were, in consequence, the best soldiers in all of Greece.

In 404 B.C., the Spartans were victorious. Athens and the Athenians were humiliated, losing their navy and being forced to watch their empire collapse. Sparta made Athens tear down the defenses that guarded and connected Athens to its port, and also put Athens under the control of a council of conspirators called the Thirty Tyrants.

Although Sparta achieved political dominance, it did not assume any kind of cultural leadership nor much longlasting influence. Athens regained its freedom almost immediately, and although it was politically weakened and its role as a political power was diminished, its intellectual and aesthetic dominance continued to flourish.

Philosophy

Intellectualism

The classical Greeks laid great emphasis on human rationality and the intellect. However, such an emphasis did not preclude a profound respect for the irrational and the mysterious. The Greeks recognized oracles and omens. They made pilgrimages to the shrines of Apollo's oracle at Delphi (DEL-fy) and at Didyma (did-uh-MA) and there solicited advice which, if not always lucid, was respected. Numerous religious cults celebrated the cycle of the seasons and encouraged the fertility of the earth by performing mysterious and secret rites. Greek dance and drama developed from these rites, and belief in the supernatural and the darker forces of human irrationality lies close to the heart of the great classical tragedies.

Philosophy was an important discipline in Greek culture. A keen mind and a desire to answer life's critical questions were considered noble qualities. Under Pericles, philosophers such as Thales (THAY-leez), Anaximander (an-AK-suh-man-dur), and Heraclitus (hair-uh-KLY-tuhs) had great influence. They wrestled with questions such as "What is the basic element of which the universe is composed?" [Water.] "How do specific things emerge from the basic elements?" [By "separating out."] "What guides the process of change?" [The universe is in a constant flow. Nothing is; everything is becoming.]

Sophistry: The Distrust of Reason

Humankind: "The measure of all things"

The middle of the fifth century B.C. was the end of a cycle of constructive activity and the beginning of a period of criticism and skepticism. The attention was now turning toward humanity and ethics in a practical way. The rise of Sophistic philosophy demonstrated the contemporary concern of humankind, thinking in a relativistic way, challenging the existence of truth. All established beliefs and standards, whether religious, moral, or scientific, came under fire. Reason, it was argued, had led only to deception.

Skepticism emerged in an Athens torn by disputes and ruled by a form of democracy that depended on persuasion and practicality. Debating skills were thus an absolute necessity, and these conditions produced teachers of rhetoric. Those who championed this new utilitarian art of persuasion were called Sophists, or "wise ones." They were well versed in rhetoric, grammar, diction, and logical argument, as well as in behind-the-scenes intrigue. They set up schools and charged high fees for their services—a most unethical act, according to traditional Greek thinking.

The outstanding Sophist, Protagoras (pro-TAG-uh-ruhs), reduced the entire mental life of the individual to perceptions, as expressed in his contention "Man is the measure of all things." According to Protagoras, knowledge, truth, and reality possess only a subjective existence—that is, they are only opinions in each person's mind. There are no objective facts or real truths applying to all people. What seems true for one individual is true for that individual alone. Inasmuch as objectivity cannot be achieved, people must be content with subjective knowledge or mere opinion.

Protagoras based his conclusion that truth was relative on the observation that human knowledge of the *phenomenal* world (the world we sense) is imperfect because human senses are imperfect. Further, Protagoras maintained, even if human sense equipment were perfect, it would still be inadequate for accurately perceiving real objects. Therefore, humans can obtain only a partial knowledge based on partial experience, which is different for every human.

In his treatise *On the Gods*, Protagoras indicates that one "cannot feel sure that they [the gods] are, or that they are not, nor what they are like in figure, for there are many things that hinder sure knowledge, the obscurity of the subject and the shortness of human life." He then amplifies this religious doubt into a denial of any absolute truths at all. The individual person is "the measure of all things, of things that are that they are, and of things that are not that they are not." Truth is therefore relative and subjective. What appears true to any given person at any given moment is true, and what appears as real is real so far as any one person is concerned. But one such truth cannot be measured against another.

Socrates, Plato, and Aristotle

Socrates

Socrates (c. 470–399 B.C.), the father of ethics and initiator of the Socratic method, called himself the "gadfly" of Athens. He did not hesitate to condemn the Sophists for their lack of belief in a universal moral and intellectual order, but he also opposed many of the traditional values of Athens. He called on Athenians to examine their own lives and to think seriously about the real meaning of life. Sitting in the agora, or marketplace, he questioned everyone who passed by about subjects ranging from justice to art. He had no qualms about cornering a judge and asking him to explain justice, or in forcing an artist to define art, and was passionate in his defense of the right of individuals—including himself—to speak freely. He gathered around him young people, challenging them to examine their lives, and discussing with them how society should be organized and how life should be lived. For Socrates, the unexamined life was not worth living.

At the center of Socrates' thinking lay the *psyche*: the mind or soul. This, he believed, was immortal and much more important than the body, which perished. It was the responsibility of every individual to raise his or her psyche to its highest potential—that is, to fill it with knowledge acquired through rigorous debate and contemplation of abstract virtues and moral values. He believed that knowledge created virtuous behavior, and that those who did evil did so because they did not have knowledge—evil-doing was clear evidence of lack of knowledge.

As Plato reveals in his *dialogues*, Socrates' method was to question his students, and an inability to answer revealed the deficiency of their learning. His rigor was particularly upsetting to the elders of Athens who, in the years following the Peloponnesian War, believed Socrates to be a disruptive element in society, and many found evidence of blasphemy and even treason in his public arguments. In 399 B.C., Socrates was arrested for impiety and corrupting youth. He was tried by a jury, found guilty, and sentenced to death by drinking a cup of poisonous hemlock.

One of his mourners, a young man named Plato, was so moved by the apparent injustice of Socrates' death that he dedicated his life to immortalizing his teacher and explaining his philosophy.

Plato

Plato was born in Athens in 427 B.C., two years after the death of Pericles, and he grew up during the years of the Peloponnesian War, which brought an end to the Athenian Empire. His family belonged to the old Athenian aristocracy, but it escaped the financial ruin that befell many Athenian aristocrats, and managed to give him a good education. He emerged a thoroughly well-rounded individual, a good athlete, and with experience of painting, poetry, music, literature, and drama. He received military training and fought in the wars. Although well suited and well connected enough for a career in politics, Plato turned instead to philosophy and fell more and more under the influence of the teacher Socrates.

Plato's masterwork, *The Republic*, a series of dialogues involving Socrates, lays out Plato's concept of an ideal political state ruled one day by *philosopher kings*. His Theory of Forms, or Ideas, held that the material reality we humans perceive is only a shoddy copy of an unconditionally perfect reality that mere mortals can never know through sensory experience.

After Socrates' execution for "corrupting Athenian youth," Plato concentrated entirely on philosophy. Anti-Socratic feeling ran high in Athens, and for ten years Plato found it expedient to live outside the city, writing many of the early dialogues during this period. Much of his aesthetic theory can be found in these dialogues, which follow Socrates' customary question-and-answer format.

Plato invented AESTHETICS as a branch of philosophy, and Western thought has been profoundly influenced by his metaphysical approach to the philosophy of art. We find in Plato's dialogues a clear, though not very systematic, theory of art and beauty.

For Plato, art derived primarily from the skill of knowing and making, or *techne* (TEK-nay). Techne was the ability of an artist to be in command of a medium, to know what the end result would be, and to know how to execute the artwork to achieve that result. The fundamental principles of techne were measurement and proportion. Standards of taste—what is good and what is beautiful—could not be considered unless the work was correct in proportion and measure.

Plato's theory of beauty and the creation of beauty, or art, rests on his concept of imitation. According to Plato, the artist imitates the Ideal that exists beyond the universe. Indeed, the universe itself is only an imitation of ideas, or unchanging forms. This point is crucial to all Platonic thought, yet it is a difficult one. To simplify a complex notion, Ideas, or Forms, are reality. Everything on earth is an imitation of reality. Ideals are thus not thoughts conceived by an individual human mind (or a divine one). Forms are rather the objects of thought. They exist independently, no matter whether, or what, we think of them.

The arts are practiced to create imitations of Forms. Plato mistrusted the arts, and especially drama, however, because the individual artist may fail to understand the ultimate reality, and may instead present merely an "appearance of perceivable nature." Therefore, art must be judged by the statesman, who "envisages the human community according to the Ideas of justice, the good, courage, temperance, and the beautiful."[1] In the end, what is proper as art depends upon the "moral ends of the polis."

In addition to possessing technical ability and the ability to know and imitate Ideas, the artist must have a third quality, artistic inspiration. No one can ascend to the highest levels of artistry without divine inspiration and assistance. Plato calls artistry a form of "divine madness."

Aristotle

Born in 384 B.C., Aristotle (Fig. **3.4**) did not have Plato's advantages of birth. His family was middle-class, and his father was court physician to Amyntas of Macedon, grandfather of Alexander the Great. Aristotle was orphaned when he was quite young, and gained a home and his education through the generosity of a family friend. When he was eighteen years old he became a student at Plato's ACADEMY, where his affectations and self-

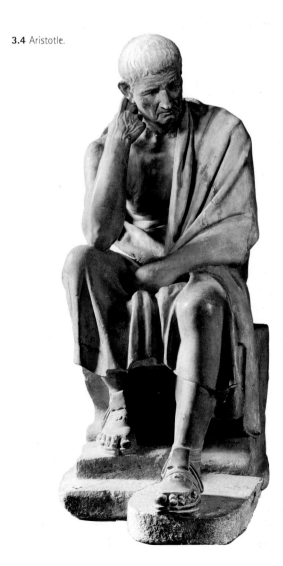

3.4 Aristotle.

absorption caused some trouble with the school's authorities. After Plato's death, Aristotle left the Academy and married. Around 343 B.C., he gained a favorable position as tutor to Alexander the Great. Aristotle sought to teach Alexander to revere all things Greek and despise anything barbarian—that is, non-Greek.

When Alexander acceded to the throne in 336 B.C., Aristotle returned to Athens to set up his own school, the Lyceum (ly-SEE-uhm). Over the next twelve years he produced a prolific outpouring of writings as well as research in physics, astronomy, biology, physiology, anatomy, natural history, psychology, politics, ethics, logic, rhetoric, art, theology, and metaphysics. Aristotle's "is probably the only human intellect that has ever compassed at first hand and assimilated the whole body of existing knowledge on all subjects, and brought it within a single focus."[2]

Aristotle's writings on nature make him the world's first real scientist, although many of his conclusions have been superseded. In contrast to Plato, Aristotle believed that the material world is real and not a creation of eternal Forms. He taught that individual things combine form and matter in ways that determine how they grow and change. He was also the founder of formal logic.

Aristotle's major work on the philosophy of art is the *Poetics*. There he maintains that all the arts imitate nature, and that imitative character is rooted in human psychology. For Aristotle, the end of artistic creation determines the appropriate means for its realization. In order to assess the excellence of a work, we must determine whether the work has a perfection of form and a soundness of method that make it a satisfactory whole. The elements of composition must display symmetry, harmony, and definition.

Aristotle's theory differs considerably from Plato's. Plato insists that artistic imitation, especially tragedy, fuels the passions and misleads the seeker of truth. Aristotle, by contrast, believes that the arts repair deficiencies in nature and that tragic drama in particular makes a moral contribution. Therefore the arts are valuable and justifiable. Aristotle rejects Plato's notion of the centrality of beauty and erotic love, as well as his metaphysical idealism. He sees beauty as a property of an artwork rather than its purpose, whereas for Plato the search for beauty is the proper end of art. He does agree with Plato "that art is a kind of *techne*, and that the most important human arts, such as music, painting, sculpture, and literature are imitative of human souls, bodies, and actions."[3]

The purpose of art, however, is not edification, nor the teaching of a moral lesson. The purpose of art is to give pleasure, and to the degree that it does that, it is good art. The pleasure Aristotle refers to comes when art excites our emotions and passions. These are then purged in response to the art and our souls lighten, delighted and healed. High art makes us think, of course, but the highest art must produce this CATHARSIS (kuh-THAR-sis), or purging effect.

Art can also provide entertainment for the lower classes, who, he maintains, are incapable of appreciating high art properly. It is better that they enjoy some kind of art than none at all, and they are entitled to this pleasure. Thus, Aristotle's aesthetics encompassed both the higher and the lower arts.

Literature: The Platonic Dialogues

Perhaps the greatest of Plato's dialogues is *The Republic*, in which Socrates seeks answers to the question "What is justice?" and describes the ideal society. The *Apology*, another of Plato's dialogues, gives his version of the speech Socrates gave in his own defense at his trial. Socrates was accused, and found guilty, of corrupting the youth of Athens and of believing in gods of his own devising rather than the gods of Athens.

Apology
Part I: Socrates' Defense Speech
(Section 2) The Old Accusers' Charges

And first, I have to reply to the older charges and to my first accusers, and then I will go on to the later ones. For of old I have had many accusers, who have accused me falsely to you during many years; and I am more afraid of them than of Anytus and his associates, who are dangerous, too, in their own way. But far more dangerous are the others, who began when you were children, and took possession of your minds with their falsehoods, telling of one Socrates, a wise man, who speculated about the heaven above, and searched into the earth beneath and made the worse appear the better cause. The disseminators of this tale are the accusers whom I dread; for their hearers are apt to fancy that such inquirers do not believe in the existence of the gods. And they are many, and their charges against me are of ancient date, and they were made by them in the days when you were more impressible than you are now—in childhood, or it may have been in youth—and the cause when heard went by default, for there was none to answer. And hardest of all, I do not know and cannot tell the names of my accusers; unless in the chance case of a comic poet. All who from envy and malice have persuaded you— some of them having first convinced themselves—all this class of men are most difficult to deal with; for I cannot have them up here, and cross-examine them, and therefore I must simply fight with shadows in my own defense, and argue when there is no one who answers. I will ask you then to assume with me, as I was saying, that my opponents are of two kinds; one recent, the other ancient: and I hope that you will see the propriety of my answering the latter first, for these accusations you heard long before the others, and much oftener.

Well, then, I must make my defense, and endeavor to clear away in a short time, a slander which has lasted a long time. May I succeed, if to succeed be for my good and yours, or

likely to avail me in my cause! The task is not an easy one: I quite understand the nature of it. And so leaving the event with God, in obedience to the law I will now make my defense.

I will begin at the beginning, and ask what is the accusation which has given rise to the slander of me, and in fact has encouraged Meletus to prefer this charge against me. Well, what do the slanderers say? They shall be my prosecutors, and I will sum up their words in an affidavit: "Socrates is an evildoer, and a curious person, who searches into things under the earth and in heaven, and he makes the worse appear the better cause; and he teaches the aforesaid doctrines to others." Such is the nature of the accusation: it is just what you have yourselves seen in the comedy of Aristophanes, who has introduced a man whom he calls Socrates, going about and saying that he walks in air, and talking a deal of nonsense concerning matters of which I do not pretend to know either much or little—not that I mean to speak disparagingly of any one who is a student of natural philosophy. I should be very sorry if Meletus could bring so grave a charge against me. But the simple truth is, O Athenians, that I have nothing to do with physical speculations. Very many of those here present are witnesses to the truth of this, and to them I appeal. Speak then, you who have heard me, and tell your neighbors whether any of you have ever known me hold forth in few words or in many upon such matters . . . You hear their answer. And from what they say of this part of the charge you will be able to judge of the truth of the rest.

As little foundation is there for the report that I am a teacher, and take money; this accusation has no more truth in it than the other. Although, if a man were really able to instruct mankind, to receive money for giving instruction would, in my opinion, be an honor to him. There is Gorgias of Leontium, and Prodicus of Ceos, and Hippias of Elis who go the round of the cities and are able to persuade the young men to leave their own citizens by whom they might be taught for nothing, and come to them whom they not only pay, but are thankful if they may be allowed to pay them. There is at this time a Parian philosopher residing in Athens, of whom I have heard; and I came to hear of him in this way:—I came across a man who has spent a world of money on the Sophists, Callias, the son of Hipponicus, and knowing that he had sons, I asked him: "Callias," I said, "if your two sons were foals or calves, there would be no difficulty in finding someone to put over them; we should hire a trainer of horses, or a farmer probably, who would improve and perfect them in their own proper virtue and excellence; but as they are human beings, whom are you thinking of placing over them? Is there any one who understands human and political virtue? You must have thought about the matter, for you have sons; is there any one?" "There is," he said. "Who is he?" said I; "and of what country? and what does he charge?" "Evenus the Parian," he replied, "he is the man, and his charge is five minae." Happy is Evenus, I said to myself, if he really has this wisdom, and teaches at such a moderate charge. Had I the same, I should have been very proud and conceited; but the truth is that I have no knowledge of the kind.

(Section 7) The Philosopher as Gadfly

And now, Athenians, I am not going to argue for my own sake, as you may think, but for yours, that you may not sin against the God by condemning me, who am his gift to you. For if you kill me you will not easily find a successor to me, who, if I may use such a ludicrous figure of speech, am a sort of gadfly, given to the state by God; and the state is a great and noble steed who is tardy in his motions owing to his very size, and requires to be stirred into life. I am that gadfly which God has attached to the state, and all day long and in all places am always fastening upon you, arousing and persuading and reproaching you. You will not easily find another like me, and therefore I would advise you to spare me. I dare say that you may feel out of temper (like the person who is suddenly awakened from sleep), and you think that you might easily strike me dead as Anytus advises, and then you sleep on for the remainder of your lives, unless God in his care of you sent you another gadfly. When I say that I am given to you by God, the proof of my mission is this:—if I had been like other men, I should not have neglected all my own concerns or patiently seen the neglect of them during all these years, and have been doing yours, coming to you individually like a father or elder brother, exhorting you to regard virtue; such conduct, I say, would be unlike human nature. If I had gained anything, or if my exhortations had been paid, there would have been some sense in my doing so; but now, as you will perceive, not even the impudence of my accusers dares to say that I have ever exacted or sought pay of any one; of that they have no witness. And I have a sufficient witness to the truth of what I say—my poverty.

History and Science

The Greek intellect probed the mysteries of this world as well as the more ethereal realms that were the domain of the philosophers. Before the fifth century B.C., accounts of the past were part of an oral tradition, more myth than fact, but at this time, history—the word derives from *historia*, meaning inquiry—became a written form, put together from careful research. The first to view history as a specialized discipline was Herodotus (huh-RAHD-uh-tuhs; c. 484–430 B.C.), and he wrote nine great volumes called *History of the Persian Wars*. The change from telling the narrative story in the form of epic or lyric poetry to relating it in a new descriptive form earned Herodotus the title "Father of History."

Although he was not an historian in our sense of the word—his writing tends to be filtered through the personalities of the people involved and he often invented inspiring speeches for kings and generals—he retained a neutrality and freedom from patriotic bias. He described the wars in colorful detail, seeking to show how human beings, in this case Greeks and Persians, settled their differences by resorting to arms, and he made full use of his tremendous powers of observation and recorded as much

information as he could unearth, including conflicting points of view. He also examined the reliability of his sources and presented them so that his readers could draw their own conclusions about their veracity. However, he did not shy away from drawing his own conclusions about the causes of events. He believed that the present had its causes in the past, and his analysis of the Persian War concluded that the Greeks defeated the Persians because the Greeks were morally right and the Persians were morally wrong. The moral fault in the Persians lay in their HUBRIS (HYOO-bris), or excessive pride and ambition. There was also a religious undertone to Herodotus' judgment, for he believed that the gods supported justice and truth and would ensure their victory.

Thucydides (thoo-SID-i-deez; d. c. 401 B.C.), who wrote a history of the Peloponnesian War, took history in a more subtle and thoughtful direction. He shared Herodotus' passion for the truth, and, although he had been an Athenian commander in the war, he dispassionately lists the foibles, follies, and errors made by the Athenians. Although it should be borne in mind that Thucydides was exiled from Athens for his failure as a naval commander early in the contest, his writing does not include self-justification. Rather, it is an unbiased compilation that strives to reveal human motives in ordinary events in order to draw a larger picture of history. His object was to instruct his readers so that they would be armed with knowledge when events of the past recurred—not in simplistic but in similar ways—in the future.

Greek intellects also turned to science and the natural world. Although they often erred in their observations, they also gave us many of our basic theories. Euclid's elements of geometry, for example, remained a standard text well into the twentieth century, and physicians still begin their careers by reciting the "oath" of the Greek physician Hippocrates (hip-AH-kruh-teez). Greek astronomers recognized that the earth was a sphere, and they even calculated its size and distance from the sun and moon through mathematics and trigonometry.

Classical Style in Vase Painting and Sculpture

Throughout history, people have sought rationality, intellectual challenge, and order from chaos. But the existence of emotion and intuitive feeling cannot be denied, and the struggle between intellect and emotion is one of the most significant problems in human existence. Although the two forces are not mutually exclusive—that is, the presence of the intellect does not necessarily mean the absence of emotion—the conflict between them has been a theme of Western art.

The fifth-century Athenians recognized this struggle. Indeed, Greek mythology tells a story that demonstrates the Periclean belief in the superiority of the intellect over the emotions. Marsyas (MAHR-see-uhs), a mortal, discovered an aulos (AW-lohs) discarded by the goddess Athena. (An aulos is a flute-like musical instrument which is associated with the wild revelries of the cult of Dionysus: see Fig. **2.21**.) With Athena's aulos in hand, Marsyas challenged the god Apollo to a musical contest. Apollo, patron of the rational arts, chose the lyre as his instrument, and he won the contest, symbolizing the dominance of intellect over emotion.

Vase Painting

Fifth-century Athenian vase painting reflects some characteristics of earlier work, including the principally geometric nature of design. What distinguishes the classical style in vase painting (our only visual evidence of Greek two-dimensional art of this period) from earlier styles such as the archaic, is a new sense of idealized reality in figure depiction, which reflects a technical advance as well as a change in attitude. Many of the problems of foreshortening (the contracting of lines to produce an illusion of projection in space) had been solved. As a result, figures have a new sense of depth. The illusion could be strengthened in some cases by the use of light and shadow. Records imply that mural painters of this period were extremely skilled in realistic representation, but we have no surviving examples to study. Vase painting does demonstrate, however, artists' concern for formal design—that is, logic and balance in the organization of space.

In the fifth century B.C., many of the most talented artists were engaged in sculpture, mural painting, and architecture. Nonetheless, vase painters such as the Achilles painter continued to express the idealism and dignity of the classical style. In Figure **3.5**, a quiet grandeur infuses the elegant and stately figures. The portrayal of the feet in the frontal position is significant, reflecting the new skill of foreshortening.

By the end of the fifth century B.C., vase painters had begun to break with the convention of putting all the figures along the base line: spatial depth was sometimes suggested by placing some figures higher than others. But it was not until the end of the next century that this convention was completely abandoned.

In general, we can identify four characteristics that define the classical style in vase painting. These are: (1) the figures are portrayed in simple line drawings; (2) the palette or color scheme is monochromatic—for example, red on black or black on red; (3) the palette depends on earthen tones—for example, red; and (4) the subject matter is heroic and idealized.

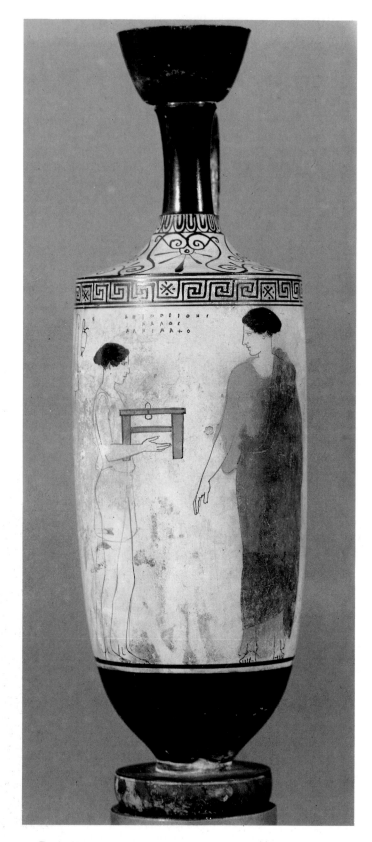

3.5 The Achilles painter, white ground lekythos from Gela(?), showing a woman and her maid, 440 B.C. 15 ins (38.4 cm) high. Museum of Fine Arts, Boston (Francis Bartlett Fund).

Sculpture

Styles do not start on a given date and end on another, even in Athens during the rule of Pericles. Although much of what we can surmise about Greek classical sculpture is actually based on inferior copies made at a later time, we know that the Greek classical style, especially in sculpture, was continually in a state of change. One artist's works differ from another's even though, in general, they reflect the basic characteristics of classicism. In classical sculpture, the tenets of Greek philosophy are reflected in the idealized, vigorous, youthful bodies that make a positive statement about the joys of earthly life.

From early in the fifth century B.C., we find an example of bronze sculpture representative of the new, developing classical style. The *Charioteer* from Delphi (Fig. **3.6**) records a victory in the games of 478 or 474 B.C. The figure is elegantly idealized, with subtle variation in the sleeves and drapery folds. The balance departs from absolute symmetry: the weight is slightly shifted to one leg, and the head turns gently away from the center line. The excellent preservation of this statue allows full appreciation of the relaxed control of the sculptor.

However, the age of Greek classical style properly began with the sculptors Myron (MY-ruhn) and Polyclitus (pah-luh-KLY-tuhs) in the middle of the fifth century B.C. Both contributed to the development of cast metal sculpture. (The example in Figure 3.7 is a marble copy of a bronze original, as is also Figure 3.8.) In his *Lance Bearer* (*Doryphorus*; Fig. **3.7**), Polyclitus is reputed to have achieved the ideal proportions for a male athlete: the *Lance Bearer* thus represents *the* male athlete, not *a* male athlete. The body's weight is thrown onto one leg in the *contrapposto* (cahn-truh-POHS-toh) stance. The resulting sense of relaxation, controlled motion, and subtle play of curves stand in contrast to the rigidity of the archaic style we witnessed in Chapter 2.

Polyclitus developed a set of rules for constructing the ideal human figure that he laid out in his treatise *The*

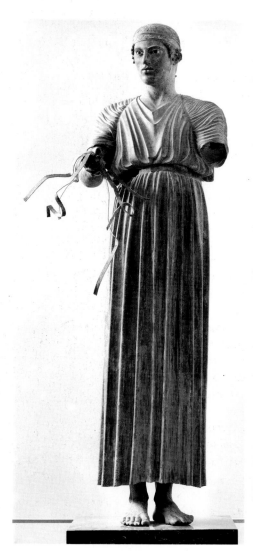

3.6 (*right*) *Charioteer*, from the Sanctuary of Apollo, Delphi, c. 478 or 474 B.C. Bronze, lifesize. Archeological Museum, Delphi, Greece.

3.7 (*far right*) Polyclitus, *Lance Bearer* (*Doryphorus*). Roman copy after a bronze original of c. 450–440 B.C. Marble, 6 ft 6 ins (1.98 m) high. Museo Archeologico Nazionale, Naples, Italy.

MASTERWORK

Myron—*Discus Thrower*

Myron's *Discus Thrower* (or *Discobolus;* Fig. **3.8**), exemplifies the classical concern for restraint in its subdued vitality and subtle suggestion of movement coupled with balance. But it also expresses the sculptor's interest in the flesh of the idealized human form. This example of the *Discus Thrower* is, unfortunately, a much later marble copy. Myron's original was in bronze, a medium that allowed more flexibility of pose than marble. A statue, as opposed to a relief sculpture, must stand on its own, and supporting the weight of the marble on a small area, such as one ankle, poses a significant structural problem. Metal has greater TENSILE STRENGTH (the ability to withstand twisting and bending), and thus this problem does not arise.

In *Discovery of the Mind: The Greek Origins of European Thought*, Bruno Snell writes: "If we want to describe the statues of the fifth century in the words of their age, we should say that they represent beautiful or perfect men, or, to use a phrase employed in the early lyrics for purposes of eulogy: 'god-like' men. Even for Plato the norm of judgment still rests with the gods, and not with men."[4] Even though Greek statuary may take the form of portraiture, the features are idealized. Human beings may be the measure of all things, but in art the individual is raised above human reality to the state of perfection found only in the gods.

Myron's representation of this young athlete contributes a sense of dynamism to Greek sculpture. Here Myron tackles a vexing problem for the sculptor: how to condense a series of movements into a single pose without making the sculpture appear static or frozen. His solution dramatically intersects two opposing arcs: one created by the downward sweep of the arms and shoulders, the other by the forward thrust of the thighs, torso, and head.

As is typical of Greek freestanding statues, the *Discus Thrower* is designed to be seen from one direction only. It is thus a sort of freestanding, three-dimensional "super-relief." The beginnings of classical style represented by celebration of the powerful nude male figure are an outgrowth of what is known as the "severe style." Myron was trained in this style, and the suggestions of moral idealism, dignity, and self-control in the statue are all qualities inherent in classicism. However, the *Discus Thrower* marks a step forward, in the increasing vitality of figure movement, a process we can trace from the frozen pose of the archaic kouros (see Fig. **2.13**), through the counterpoised balance of the *Kritios Boy* (see Fig. **2.17**), to Myron. Warm, full, and dynamic, Myron's human form achieves a new level of expressiveness and power. It is fully controlled and free of the unbridled emotion of later sculpture. For Myron, balanced composition remains the focus of the work, and form takes precedence over feeling.

3.8 Myron, *Discus Thrower* (*Discobolus*), c. 450 B.C. Roman marble copy after a bronze original, lifesize. Museo Nazionale Romano, Rome.

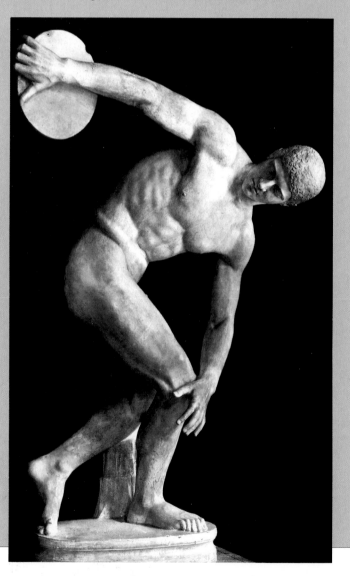

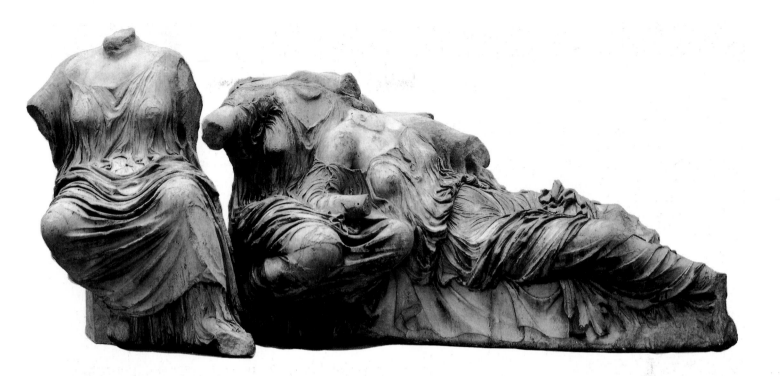

3.9 The *Fates*, from the east pediment of the Parthenon, c. 438–432 B.C. Marble, over lifesize. British Museum, London.

Canon (*kanon* is the Greek word for "rule" or "law"). The *Lance Bearer* supposedly illustrates his theory, but because neither the treatise nor the original statue has survived, we do not know what set of proportions Polyclitus thought to be ideal. Probably, it was based on the ratios between some basic unit and the length of some body part or parts. Myron's best-known work is the *Discus Thrower* (see the Masterwork box).

The east pediment of the Parthenon once contained marvelous sculptural elements (Figs **3.9** and **3.10**). The group of *Three Goddesses*, or *Fates*, is now on display in the British Museum in London. (This group of sculptures is known as the "Elgin Marbles" [EL-ghin] after Lord Elgin, who removed them from the Parthenon between 1801 and 1803 and took them to London. British possession of these treasures is a continuing controversy between Britain and Greece.) Originally, this group formed part of the architectural decoration high on the Parthenon. There, its diagonal curvilinearity would have offset the straight lines, and strong verticals and horizontals, of the temple. The scene depicted on this pediment was an illustration of the myth of the birth of Athena, patron goddess of Athens, from her father Zeus' head. Also from this east pediment is the figure of Dionysus (sometimes thought to be Heracles; pronounced HAIR-uh-kleez) shown in Figure **3.10**.

We can learn much from these battered but superb figures. What strikes us first is the brilliant arrangement of the figures within the geometric confines of the pediment. This triangular design encloses curving lines that flow rhythmically through the reclining figures, leading the eyes

3.10 *Dionysus* (*Heracles* (?)), from the east pediment of the Parthenon, c. 438–432 B.C. Marble, over lifesize. British Museum, London.

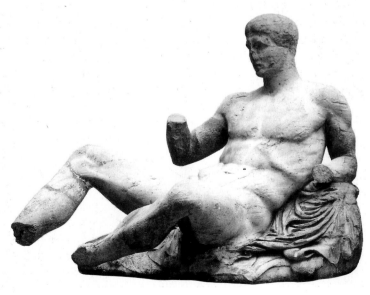

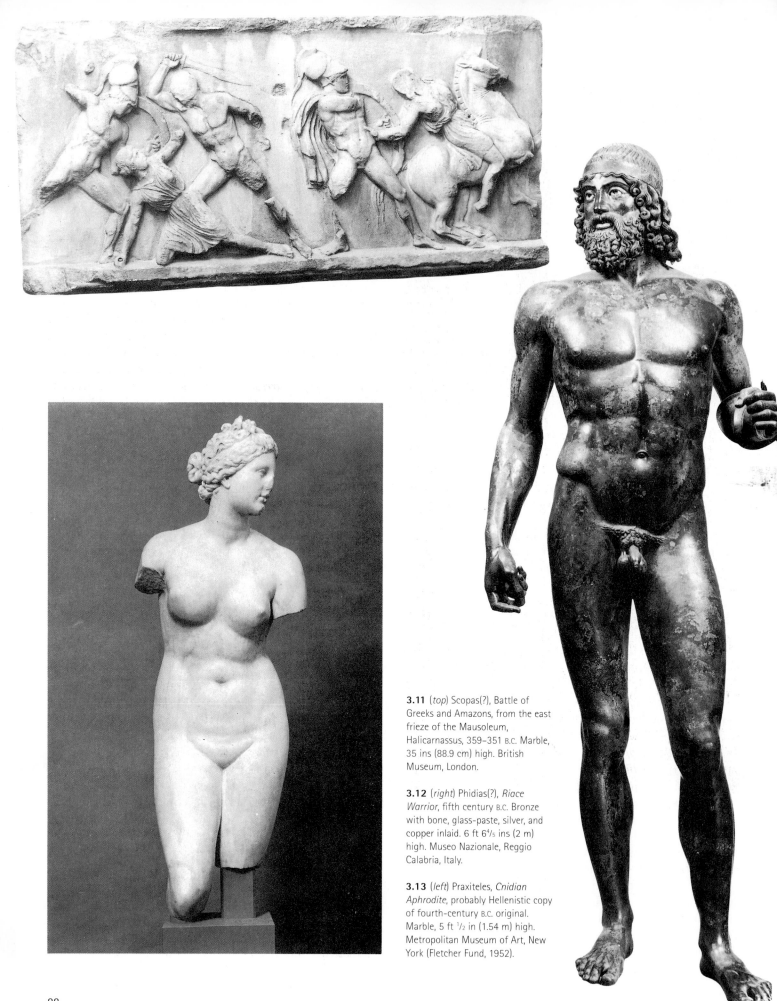

3.11 (*top*) Scopas(?), Battle of Greeks and Amazons, from the east frieze of the Mausoleum, Halicarnassus, 359–351 B.C. Marble, 35 ins (88.9 cm) high. British Museum, London.

3.12 (*right*) Phidias(?), *Riace Warrior*, fifth century B.C. Bronze with bone, glass-paste, silver, and copper inlaid. 6 ft 6⁴/₅ ins (2 m) high. Museo Nazionale, Reggio Calabria, Italy.

3.13 (*left*) Praxiteles, *Cnidian Aphrodite*, probably Hellenistic copy of fourth-century B.C. original. Marble, 5 ft ¹/₂ in (1.54 m) high. Metropolitan Museum of Art, New York (Fletcher Fund, 1952).

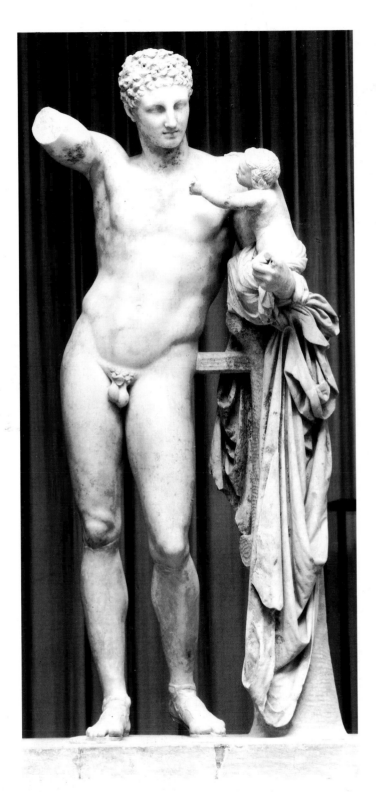

3.14 Followers of Praxiteles, *Hermes and the Infant Dionysus*, probably a Roman copy after an original of c. 300–250 B.C. Marble with remnants of red paint on the lips and hair, 7 ft 1 in. (2.16 m) high. Archeological Museum, Olympia. Discovered in the rubble of the ruined Temple of Hera at Olympia in 1875, this statue is now widely accepted as a very good Roman copy.

naturally from one part to the next. The treatment of the draperies of the female figures is highly sophisticated, for not only do the drape and flow of the stone fabric reinforce the simple lines of the whole, but they also reveal the perfected human female form beneath. These, and the Dionysus, are forms raised beyond the merely specific and human, to the level of symbols, as is appropriate to their intended position on a temple.

Even in their repose, these figures show grace and subtle movement. This formal restraint is made more evident when we compare these figures with those of a later style in Figure **3.11**. The composition here is more open, its movement less fluid, and the geometric groups of figures jerk the eye between sections of work, rather than leading.

Perhaps the most impressive sculptural finds of recent years are the two statues discovered in 1972 in the seabed off the coast of Riace, in southern Italy. Figure **3.12** shows one of these masterpieces, which are known as the *Riace* (ree-AH-chay) *Warriors*. The statue has been restored, but it shows the bone and glass eyes, silver teeth, and copper lips and nipples that would have adorned many ancient Greek bronzes. The simplicity with which the imposing musculature is portrayed, and the confident handling of the CONTRAPPOSTO, mark the work of a great sculptor of the mid-fifth century B.C. Some scholars even claim that the statues can be identified as part of a set of thirteen sculpted by Phidias (FID-ee-uhs), dedicated to the Athenian victory at Marathon in 490 B.C. They were probably shipwrecked around the first century B.C., on their way to Rome, having been plundered from Greece.

Late Classical Style

Sculpture of the fourth century B.C. changes toward greater emphasis on emotion. Praxiteles (prak-SIT-uh-leez) is famous for the individuality, delicacy, elegance, and grace in his treatment of subjects, such as the *Cnidian Aphrodite* (NY-dee-uhn af-roh-DY-tee; Fig. **3.13**). (Note that this is again a copy; the original has never been found.) His work looks inward in a way that differs from the formal detachment of earlier sculptors evident in the *Dionysus* (see Fig. **3.10**), for example. Originally, Aphrodite rested her weight on one foot: her body sways to the left in the famous Praxitelean S-curve. Strain on the ankle of the sculpture was minimized by the attachment of the arm to drapery and a vase.

The elegance of the work of Praxiteles and his followers can also be seen in the *Hermes and the Infant Dionysus* (Fig. **3.14**). Although this marble statue is probably a copy, it nonetheless exhibits fine subtlety of modeling and detailed individuality.

From the late fourth century, the sculpture of Lysippus (ly-SIP-uhs), a favorite of Alexander the Great, displays a dignified naturalness and a new concept of space.

MASTERWORK

The Parthenon

On the summit of the Acropolis at Athens (Figs. **3.1** and **3.15**) stands the Parthenon, the greatest temple built by the Greeks and the prototype for all classical buildings thereafter. When the Persians sacked Athens in 480 B.C., they destroyed the existing temple and its sculpture. And when Pericles rebuilt the Acropolis later in the fifth century B.C. Athens was at its zenith, and the Parthenon was its crowning glory. The Parthenon (Figs. **3.16** and **3.17**) exemplifies Greek classical architecture. Balance is achieved through geometric symmetry, and the clean, simple lines represent a perfect balance of forces holding the composition together. For the Greeks, deities were only slightly superior to mortals, and in the Greek temple, deity and humanity met in an earthly rendezvous. This human-centered philosophy is reflected by the scale of the temple.

In plan, the Parthenon has short sides slightly less than half the length of the long sides. Its interior, or *naos*, which is divided into two parts, housed a 40-foot (12-meter) high ivory and gold statue of Athena. The temple is peripteral—that is, it is surrounded by a single row of columns. The number of columns across the front and along the sides of the temple is determined by a specific convention. The internal harmony of the design rests in the regular repetition of virtually unvaried forms. All the columns appear alike and to be spaced equidistantly. But at the corners the spacing is adjusted to give a sense of grace and perfect balance, while preventing the monotony of unvaried repetition.

All the elements are carefully adjusted. A great deal has been written about the "refinements" of the Parthenon—those features that seem to be intentional departures from strict geometric regularity. According to some, the slight bulge of the horizontal elements compensates for the eye's tendency to see a downward sagging when all elements are straight and parallel. Each column swells toward the middle by about 7 inches (18 centimeters), to compensate for the tendency of parallel vertical lines to appear to curve inward. This swelling is known as ENTASIS. The columns also tilt inward slightly at the top, in order to appear perpendicular. The stylobate is raised toward the center so as not to appear to sag under the immense weight of the stone columns and roof. Even the white marble, which in other circumstances might appear stark, may have been chosen to reflect the intense Athenian sunlight.

3.15 Plan of the Acropolis, Athens.

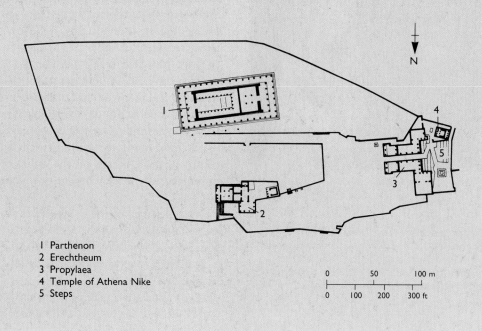

I Parthenon
2 Erechtheum
3 Propylaea
4 Temple of Athena Nike
5 Steps

| 0 | 50 | 100 m |

| 0 | 100 | 200 | 300 ft |

N

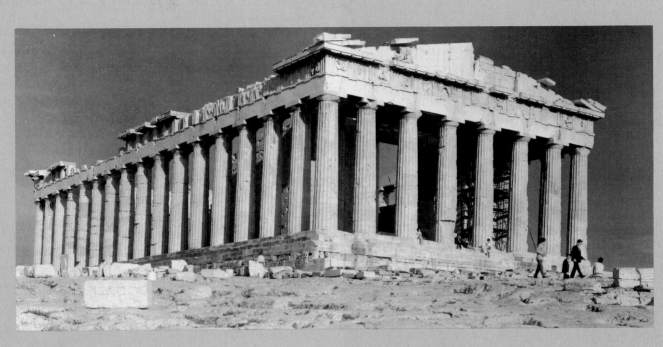

3.16 (*above*) Ictinos and Callicrates, the Parthenon, Acropolis, Athens, from the northwest, 447–438 B.C. Marble.
3.17 (*below*) The Parthenon, frieze on the west cella, c. 440 B.C.

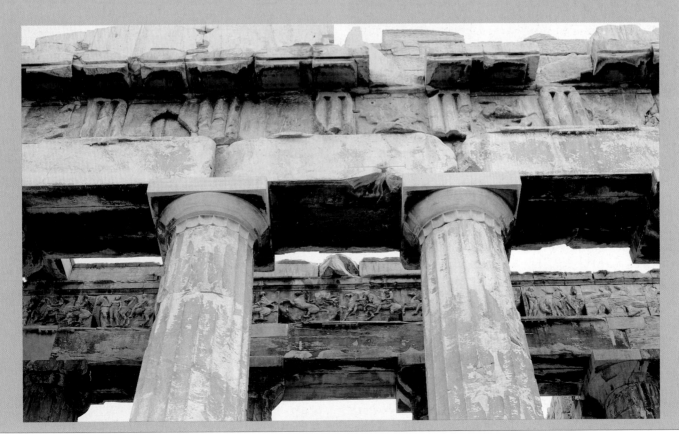

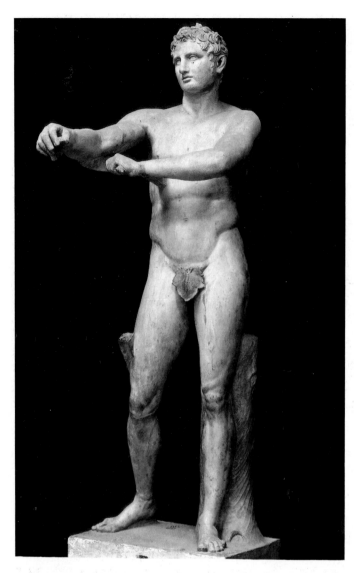

acteristics of a Greek temple is so complete that when we think of one Greek temple, we think of all Greek temples. Even so familiar a structure as a Gothic cathedral does not quite do this, because, despite the consistent form of the Gothic arch, it is used in such diverse ways that no one work can typify the many.

The classical Greek temple has a structure consisting of horizontal blocks of stone laid across vertical columns. This is called "post-and-lintel" structure. It is not unique to Greece, but the Greeks refined it to its highest aesthetic level. Structures of this type have some very basic problems. Stone has no great tensile strength, although it is high in COMPRESSIVE STRENGTH (the ability to withstand crushing). Downward thrust works against the tensile qualities of horizontal slabs (lintels) but for the compressive qualities of the vertical columns (posts). As a result, columns can be relatively delicate, whereas lintels must be massive.

This structural system allows for only limited open interior space. This was no great problem for the Greeks, because their temples were built to be seen and used from the outside. The Greek climate does not drive worshippers inside a building. Thus, exterior structure and aesthetics were the primary concern.

3.18 Lysippus, *Scraper (Apoxyomenos)*, Roman copy, probably after a bronze original of c. 330 B.C. Marble, 6 ft 9 ins (2.06 m) high. Vatican Museum, Rome.

His *Scraper* (Fig. **3.18**) illustrates an attempt to depict the figure in motion, in contrast to the poses we have seen previously. The subject of the *Scraper* is mundane—an athlete scraping dirt and oil from his body. The proportions of the figure are even more naturalistic than those of Polyclitus (see Fig. **3.7**), but the naturalism is still far from complete.

Architecture

Existing examples of Greek architecture offer a clear and consistent picture of the basic classical style, and nothing brings that picture so clearly to mind as the Greek temple. H. W. Janson makes an interesting point in *A Basic History of Art* when he suggests that the crystallization of the char-

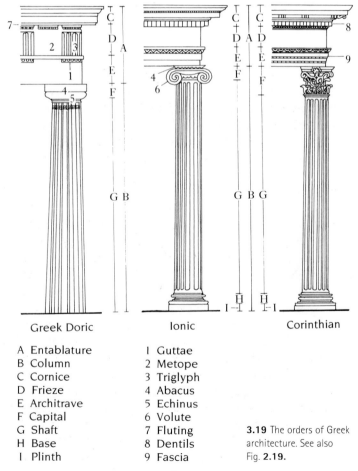

Greek Doric	Ionic	Corinthian

A Entablature	I Guttae
B Column	2 Metope
C Cornice	3 Triglyph
D Frieze	4 Abacus
E Architrave	5 Echinus
F Capital	6 Volute
G Shaft	7 Fluting
H Base	8 Dentils
I Plinth	9 Fascia

3.19 The orders of Greek architecture. See also Fig. **2.19**.

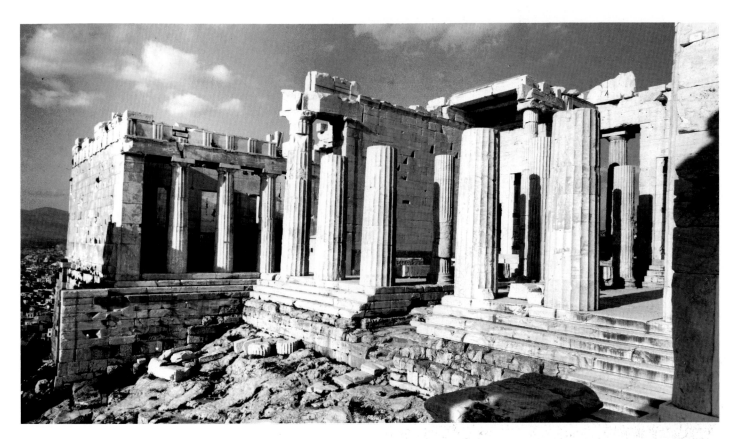

3.20 The Propylaea, Athens, from the west, c. 437–432 B.C.

Greek temples used three orders, Doric, IONIC, and CORINTHIAN. These are not just decorative and elevational conventions, but systems of proportion. The first, as we noted in the last chapter, is archaic in origin, although it was modified and used in classical style. The second is classical; the third, though of classical derivation, is of the later, Hellenistic style that we will examine further on in this chapter. As Figure **3.19** shows, simplicity was important to the Greek classical style, and the Doric and Ionic orders maintain clean lines even in their capitals. The Corinthian order has more ornate capitals. Taken in the context of an entire building, this detail may not seem significant. But columns, and particularly their capitals, are convenient ways of identifying the order of a Greek temple. Differences are also apparent in column bases and the configuration of the lintels, but the capitals tell the story at a glance. The earlier of the two classical orders, the Doric (see Fig. **2.19**), has a massive appearance compared with the Ionic. The Ionic column, with its round base, is raised above the baseline of the building. The flutings of the Ionic order, usually twenty-two per column, are deeper and more widely separated than those of the Doric, giving it a more delicate appearance. Ionic capitals consist of paired spiral shaped forms, known as VOLUTES (vuh-LOOTS). The Ionic architrave, or lintel, is divided into three horizontal bands, which diminish in size downward, creating a sense of lightness, unlike the massive Doric architrave.

The structure that serves as the entrance portal to the Parthenon is one of the most imposing monuments on the Acropolis. The Propylaea (Fig. **3.20**) was begun soon after the Parthenon was finished. It combines Doric and Ionic elements—two Doric temple-like FAÇADES (fuh-SAHD) are linked by an Ionic COLONNADE—in a design of some complexity which accommodates the awkward, sloping site. Work on the project was interrupted by the onset of the Peloponnesian War, and the building was never completed.

A final example of classical architecture takes us slightly beyond the classical period of the late fifth century B.C. Although no inscriptional information or other evidence provides a certain date for the Temple of Athena Nike (Fig. **3.21**), this small Ionic temple probably dates from the last quarter of the century. The pediments contained sculptures, but none of these has survived. What remain are sculptures from the frieze. The battle of Marathon of 490 B.C., the Athenians' greatest victory over the Persians, is the subject matter for the frieze on the south side of the temple. It is "the only known example in temple sculpture of a conflict from near-contemporary

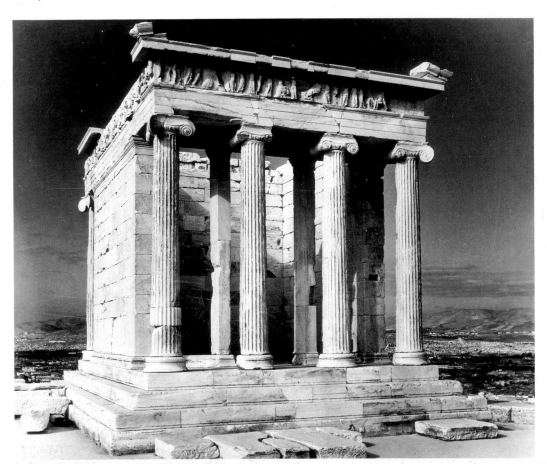

OUR DYNAMIC WORLD

The Nok Style of Africa

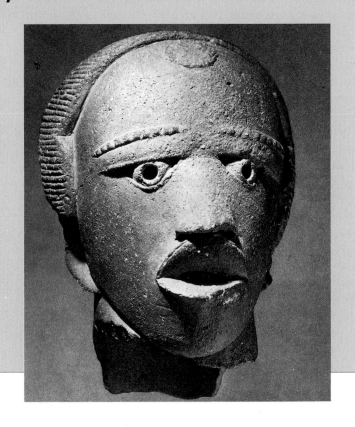

For thousands of years, African artists and craftsmen have created objects of sophisticated vision and masterful technique. While the Greeks produced classical sculpture, on the Jos plateau of northern Nigeria, the Noks, a nonliterate culture of farmers, entered the Iron Age and developed their own accomplished artistic style. Working in terracotta, these artists produced boldly designed sculptures (Fig. **3.22**). Although they are stylized—with flattened noses and segmented lower eyelids, for example—each work reveals individualized character. Curiously, the unusual combination of human individuality and artistic stylization makes the works powerfully appealing. Probably, these heads are portraits of ancestors of the ruling class, because the technique and medium of execution seem to have been chosen to ensure permanence and for magical rather than artistic reasons.

3.22 Head from Jemaa, c. 400 B.C. Terracotta, 10 ins (25 cm) high. National Museum, Lagos, Nigeria.

rather than legendary history".[5] The battle had apparently assumed a legendary status even by 420 B.C.

Theatre

In contrast to sculpture and painting, which used more-or-less lifelike images to portray the ideal, Greek classical theatre pursued the same ends through quite different means. The theatre of Periclean Athens was theatre of convention, in which neither scenery nor costumes employs representational details. The audience accepts descriptions in poetic dialogue, without demanding to see the objects described. Imagination is the key to this kind of theatre.

Theatre productions in ancient Greece were part of three annual religious festivals: the City Dionysia (dy-uh-NY-see-uh), the Rustic Dionysia, and the Lenaea (leh-NAY-uh). The first of these was a festival of tragic, and the last, of comic plays. The City Dionysia took place at the Theatre of Dionysus in Athens. Contests held at these festivals were begun in 534 B.C., before the classical era. Although we do not have most of the plays themselves, we do know the titles and the names of the authors who won the contests, from the earliest to the last. From inscriptions we know that three playwrights figured prominently and repeatedly as winners. They were Aeschylus (EHS-kih-luhs), Sophocles (SAHF-oh-kleez), and Euripides (yoo-RIP-i-deez). All the complete tragedies we have were written by these playwrights—seven by Aeschylus, seven by Sophocles, and eighteen by Euripides.

Playwrights entering the contests for tragedy or comedy were required to submit their plays to a panel of presiding officers, who selected three winners for production. The early classical plays had only one actor, plus a chorus. At the time of selection, the playwright was assigned the chief actor and the patron who paid all the expenses for the production. The author was also director, CHOREOGRAPHER, and musical composer, and often played the leading role as well.

Aeschylus

At the time the *Kritios Boy* (see Fig. **2.17**) was created, Aeschylus, the most famous poet of Ancient Greece, began to write for the theatre. He wrote magnificent tragedies of high poetry and on lofty moral themes. For example, in

Aeschylus (c. 525–456 B.C.)

Aeschylus was the first and perhaps the greatest classical Greek tragedian. Together with Sophocles and Euripides, he is one of only three ancient Greek playwrights whose works have survived, and although he wrote fewer plays and won fewer contests than Sophocles, his contributions to the development of theatre are enormous. His contributions to dramaturgy and production make him, if not the greatest writer, then certainly the most important person in Western theatre history. He was instrumental in establishing tragedy as a genre, and some have referred to him as "the creator of tragedy." According to Aristotle, Aeschylus was responsible for adding the second actor to tragic performance.

Born into an aristocratic family, he fought in the important battles of Marathon and Salamis (between the Greeks and the Persians), and his firsthand knowledge of battle infuses his works, which illumine the miseries—not the glories—of war. Apart from a few documented travels to as far as Sicily, little else is known of the life of this major figure in Western literature and theatre. It is known that he won his first contest in 484 B.C., and won at least thirteen first prizes at the major festivals. His victory total increased to twenty-eight after his death because he was granted the singular honor of being allowed to compete through posthumous revivals. He may have written as many as ninety tragedies and satyr plays, although only eighty titles are known and only seven tragedies have survived.

The characters in Aeschylus' tragedies are "types" in the classically idealized mold. He treats history loosely and seeks to describe a broad religious view underwritten by patriotic exultation. He always remains within the controlled formality of the classic viewpoint, with its focus on intellect (form) as opposed to emotion (feeling), and he writes in an exalted style, using vocabulary that is clearly linked to the epic and lyric traditions of Homer (see p. 72). He handles the problems of evil and divine justice grandly and powerfully, and although his style may seem foreign to us, his questions and insights do not.

Agamemnon, the first play in the *Oresteia* (or-es-TEE-uh) trilogy, Aeschylus' chorus warns that success and wealth are insufficient without goodness.

> Justice shines in sooty dwellings
> Loving the righteous way of life,
> But passes by with averted eyes
> The house whose lord has hands unclean,
> Be it built throughout of gold,
> Caring naught for the weight of praise
> Heaped upon wealth by the vain, but turning
> All alike to its proper end.[6]

Aeschylus poses questions that we still ask, such as: How responsible are we for our own actions? How subject are we to uncontrollable forces? His characters are larger than life, to be read as types rather than individuals, in accordance with the contemporary emphasis on the ideal. Yet in their strivings, as in their flaws, they are also undeniably human. Aeschylus' casts for his early plays consist of one actor and a chorus of fifty, conforming to the convention of the time. He is credited with the addition of a second actor, and, by the end of his long career, a third actor had been introduced and the chorus had been reduced to twelve.

Sophocles

Sophocles' career overlapped with that of Aeschylus. With *Oedipus* (EH-dih-puhs or EE-dih-puhs) *the King*, his personal career reached its peak at the zenith of the Greek classical style. Sophocles' plots and characterizations illustrate a trend toward increasing REALISM similar to that in classical sculpture. The move toward realism did not involve any illusion of reality onstage, however, and even Euripides' plays, the least idealistic of the Greek tragedies, are not realistic as we understand the word.

Sophocles was certainly a less formal poet than Aeschylus, however. His themes are more human, and his characters more subtle, although he explores the themes of human responsibility, dignity, and fate with the same intensity and high seriousness that we see in Aeschylus. His plots show increasing complexity, but within the formal restraints of the classical spirit.

Sophocles lived and wrote after the death of Pericles in 429 B.C., and he experienced the shame of Athenian defeat. Even so, his later plays did not shift toward emotionalism and interest in action. Classical Greek theatre consisted mostly of discussion and narration. The stories often dealt with bloodshed, but, though the play might lead up to the violence, and action was resumed when it was over, it is important to note that blood was never seen to be shed on stage.

Euripides

Euripides was younger than Sophocles, although both died in 406 B.C. They did, however, compete with each other, despite the fact that their works have quite different styles. Euripides' plays carry realism further than any other Greek tragedies and deal more with psychological probings and individual emotions than with great events. His language, though still basically poetic, has greater verisimilitude and much less formality than that of his predecessors. Euripides also experiments with, or ignores, many of the conventions of his theatre, relying less heavily on the chorus. He also explores the mechanical potential of scenery shifting and questions the religion of the day in his plays. They are more TRAGICOMEDIES than pure tragedies, and some critics have described many of them as MELODRAMAS.

Plays such as *The Bacchae* (BAHK-ee) reflect the changing Athenian spirit and dissatisfaction with contemporary events. Euripides was not particularly popular in his time, perhaps because of his less idealistic, less formal, and less conventional treatment of dramatic themes and characters. Was he perhaps too close to the reality of his age? His plays were received with enthusiasm in later years, however, and they are unquestionably the most popular of the Greek tragedies today.

Aristotle's Theory of Tragedy

We cannot leave the discussion of Greek classical theatre without noting Aristotle's analysis of tragedy. His ideas are still basic to dramatic theory and criticism, despite the fact that they have often been misunderstood and misapplied over the past 2,400 years. Drawing principally on Sophocles as a model, Aristotle laid out in the *Poetics* the six elements of tragedy. In order of importance they are: (1) *plot*, the basic structure of the play, which includes such things as decision-points for the characters and a climax, or high point of action; (2) *character*, the people of the play and their motivating psychological characteristics; (3) *thought*, what we would call the ideas explored by the play; (4) *diction*, the words of the play and their style, e.g. prose or poetry; (5) *music*, or what we would call the sounds of the production—for example, the manner in which the actors speak their lines, etc.; and (6) *spectacle*, all of the visual elements of the production, including scenery and costumes.

Plot, in tragedy, is far more than the simple storyline. For Aristotle, plot creates the basic structure of the play, just as form is the cornerstone of classical design. The parts of plot give shape to the play with a beginning (exposition), a middle (complication), and an end (dénouement), ensuring that the audience understands the progress of the drama. Additional points in the plot include *discoveries*, in which characters learn about themselves and others; *foreshadowing*, in which the playwright alerts the audience to

MASTERWORK

Sophocles—*Oedipus the King*

The story of Oedipus is one of the great legends of Western culture. When Sophocles used the legend in *Oedipus the King*, the story was familiar to all Athenians. In fact, it had also formed the basis for plays by Aeschylus and Euripides.

At the beginning of the play, Oedipus is the beloved ruler of the city of Thebes, whose citizens have been stricken by a plague. Consulting the Delphic oracle, Oedipus is told that the plague will cease only when the murderer of Queen Jocasta's (joh-CAS-tuh) first husband, King Laius (LAY-uhs), has been found and punished for his deed. Oedipus resolves to find Laius's killer. Only to discover that the old man he himself killed when he first approached Thebes as a youth, was none other than Laius. Finally, Oedipus learns the truth about himself and his past. Laius was Oedipus' father, and Jocasta, now Oedipus' wife and mother of his children, is, in fact, his mother. At the end, Jocasta hangs herself, and guilt-stricken Oedipus blinds himself with Jocasta's brooch pin.

The action moves from one moment of dramatic tension to another, rising to a climax. The protagonist, or central character, Oedipus, starts with no knowledge of his true identity. Slowly he discovers the truth about himself and the terrible deeds he has unknowingly committed: the murder of his father and marriage to his mother. However, his tragedy lies in the discovery of his guilt, rather than in the heinous acts themselves.

In *Oedipus*, Sophocles explores the reality of the dual nature we all share. He poses the eternal question, can we control our destinies or are we the pawns of fate? In exploring this question, he vividly portrays the circumstances in which one's strengths become one's weaknesses. Oedipus's HAMARTIA, or tragic flaw, is the excessive pride, or *hubris*, which drives him to pursue the truth, as a king—or a man—should, only to find the awful answer in himself.

Although the play is a tragedy, the message is one of uplift and positive resolution. (This type of structure is more fully described in the section below on Aristotle's theory of tragedy.) When Oedipus recognizes his own helplessness in the face of the full horror of his past, he performs an act of contrition: he blinds himself, and then exiles himself. As grotesque as this may seem, it nevertheless releases Oedipus onto a higher plane of understanding. The chorus chants, "I was blind," while seeing with normal eyes, and Oedipus moans, "I now have nothing beautiful left to see in this world." Yet, being blind, Oedipus is now able to "see" the nobler, truer reality of his self-knowledge.

future action; *reversals*, in which fortunes change; and *crises*, in which tension is created and characters grow.

For Aristotle, tragedy is a form of drama in which a protagonist goes through a significant struggle which ends in disaster. However, the protagonist is always a heroic character, who gains a moral victory even in physical defeat. Tragedy therefore asserts the dignity of humanity, as well as the existence of larger moral forces. In the end, tragedy is a positive experience, which evokes a catharsis, or purging, of pity and fear in the audience.

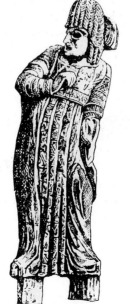

3.23 Greek statuette of a tragic actor, wearing a mask and a rich costume.

Costume

If the plays of the Greek classical tragedy treated lofty themes with theatrical, poetic language, the style of the productions displayed no less formality, idealism, and convention. The larger-than-life characters were portrayed by actors, always men, in larger-than-life, conventionalized costumes. Actors and chorus wore bright robes, whose colors conveyed specific information to the audience. The robes were padded to increase the actor's size; height was increased by thick-soled boots called *kothurnoi* (koh-THUHR-noy), and large masks whose fixed, conventionalized expressions were readily identified by the sophisticated and knowledgeable audience (Fig. **3.23**). Height was further increased by an *onkos* (AHN-kohs), a wiglike protrusion on top of the mask.

Aristophanes

Tragedies were not the only works produced in the theatre of the classical era in Athens. The Athenians were

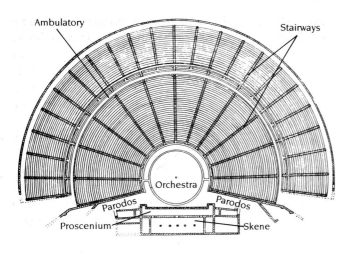

3.24 Plan of the theatre at Epidaurus, Greece, c. 350 B.C.

3.25 Polyclitus the Younger, theatre at Epidaurus, Greece, c. 350 B.C. Diameter 373 ft (114 m), orchestra 66 ft (20 m) across.

extremely fond of comedy, although no examples survive from the Periclean period. Aristophanes (eh-ris-TAH-fuh-neez; c. 450–c. 380 B.C.), of whose plays we have eleven, was the most gifted of the comic poets. His comedies of the post-classical period, such as *Lysistrata* (lis-is-TRAH-tuh), are highly satirical, topical, sophisticated, and often obscene. Productions of his comedies are still staged, in translation, but as the personal and political targets of his invective are unknown to us, these modern productions are mere shadows of what took the stage at the turn of the fourth century B.C.

Theatre Design

Scholars do not agree about the exact layout of the classical Greek theatre building and the precise nature of the acting area and scenery. But we can summarize some of the architectural and archeological speculation, bearing in mind that it is only speculation.

The form of the Greek theatre owes much to its origins in the choral dances associated with the worship of Dionysus. In 534 B.C., Thespis is reported to have introduced a single actor to these dances. In 472 Aeschylus added a second actor, and in 458 Sophocles added a third.

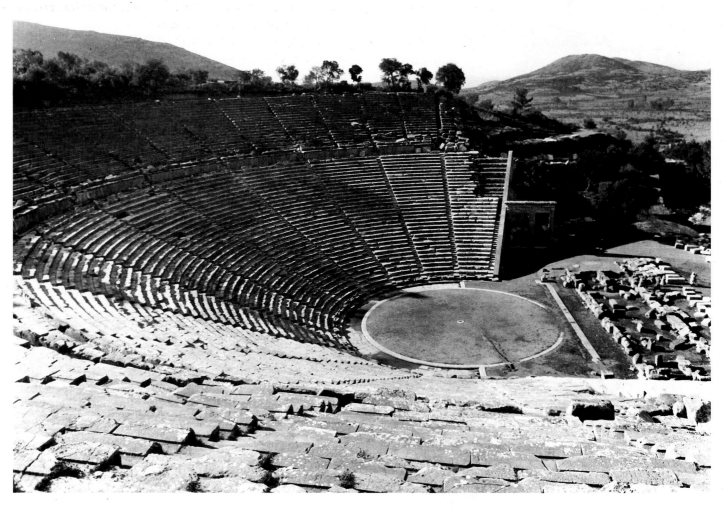

Throughout its history the Greek theatre was composed of a large circular *orchestra*—the acting and dancing area—with the vestige of an altar at its center, and a semicircular *theatron* (THAY-uh-trahn)—auditorium or viewing place—usually cut into or occupying the slope of a hill. Since the actors played more than one role, they needed somewhere to change costume, and so a *skene* (SKEEN-ay)—scene-building or retiring place—was added. The process by which the *skene* developed into a raised stage is somewhat obscure.

The earliest theatre still in existence is the Theatre of Dionysus on the south slope of the Acropolis. It dates from the fifth century B.C., and is where the plays of Aeschylus, Sophocles, Euripides, and Aristophanes were staged. Its current form dates from a period of reconstruction around 338–326 B.C. The theatre at Epidaurus (ehp-ih-DOHR-uhs; Figs **3.24** and **3.25**) is the best preserved. It was built by Polyclitus the Younger about 350 B.C. Its size demonstrates the monumental character the theatre had assumed by that time. The orchestra measures 66 feet (20 meters) in diameter, with an altar to Dionysus in the center. The auditorium, comprising slightly more than a semicircle, is divided by an AMBULATORY about two-thirds of the way up, and by radiating stairways. All the seats were of stone, and the first or lowest row consisted of seats for the dignitaries of Athens. These seats had backs and arm rests, some decorated with relief sculptures.

The design of theatres undoubtedly differed from place to place but time has removed most examples. The many theories about how Greek theatre productions worked, how scenery was used, and whether or not a raised stage was present, make fascinating reading, and the reader is encouraged to explore the area in detail elsewhere.

Music

Few examples of Ancient Greek music survive from any era—a handful of fragments with no clue as to how they were supposed to sound. The lyre and the aulos (see Fig. **2.21**) were the instruments basic to Greek music, and each had a significant role in pre-classical ritual. In the classical era the lyre and the aulos were used as solo instruments and as accompaniment.

The spirit of contest popular among the Greeks apparently extended to instrumental and vocal music. As with all the arts, music was regarded as essential to life, and almost everyone in Athens participated. Perhaps the word "dilettante," an amateur lover of the arts, would best describe the average Athenian. Professionalism and professional artists, however, were held in low esteem, and Aristotle urged that skill in music stop short of the professional. Practice should develop talent only to the point where one

could "delight in noble melodies and rhythms," as he says in the *Poetics*. He also discouraged excessive complexity. We should not infer too much from such an observation: complexity for the ancient Greeks would no doubt still be simplicity by our musical standards. It appears reasonably clear, for instance, that all Greek music of this era was MONOPHONIC—that is without harmony. "Complexity" might therefore mean technical difficulty, and perhaps melodic ornamentation.

Aristotle said that music should lead to noble thought, but some music in the Greek repertoire certainly led the other way. Rituals in praise of the god Dionysus were emotional and frenetic, and music played an important role in these.

If Plato's *Republic* can be taken as an accurate guide, Greek music seems to have relied on convention. Most of the performances in Periclean Athens appear to have been improvised, which may seem at odds with formal order. However, "improvisation" should not be interpreted here as spontaneous or unrehearsed. The Greeks had formulas or rules concerning acceptable musical forms for nearly every occasion. So the musician, though free to seek the momentary inspiration of the Muses—the mythological sisters who presided over the arts—was constrained by all the rules applicable to the occasion.

Pythagoras taught that an understanding of numbers was the key to an understanding of the entire spiritual and physical universe. Those views, expressed in music, as well as the other arts, led to a system of sounds and rhythms ordered by numbers. The intervals of the musical scale were determined by measuring vibrating strings. As a result, sounds in Greek music were calculated on relationships of 2 to 1 (one note having exactly double the vibrations per second as another—we call it an octave: middle C compared to C^1, for example); 5 to 1 (what we call a fifth—for example, the relationship between C and the G above), or perhaps, 4 to 1 (what we call a fourth—for example, the relationship between C and the F above).

Dance

Dance in the age of Pericles reflected both classical and anti-classical styles. The dances of the Dionysiac cult revels, which may have decreased in popularity but certainly continued under Periclean rule, disregarded form, order, restraint, and idealization. They were characterized by emotional frenzy, not intellect. However, the philosophies of the era, the relationship of dance to music and drama, and the treatment of dance by Plato and Aristotle, indicate that those aspects of dance which were associated with the theatre, at least, must have reflected classical values.

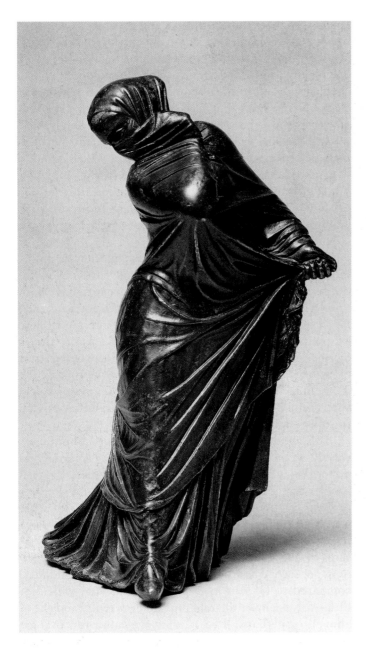

3.26 Statuette of a veiled dancer, c. 225–175 B.C. Bronze, 8¹/₈ ins (20.6 cm) high. Metropolitan Museum of Art, New York (Bequest of Walter C. Baker, 1972).

Dance is an evanescent art form, however. Today, even with labanotation (lab-uh-noh-TAY-shun)—a system of writing down dance movements—we cannot know what a dance piece looks like if we do not see the event. So the literary treatises, the musical fragments, and the archeological evidence from which so many have tried to reconstruct the dances of the Greeks can give us very little idea. In fact, the conventional nature of Greek art is our most

formidable obstacle. Some vase paintings and sculptures clearly depict dancers (Fig. **3.26**), but we do not know the conventions that apply to these poses, and so we are unable to reconstruct any actual dances.

THE HELLENISTIC AGE

Alexander and the Spread of Hellenistic Culture

Peace finally came to the Greek peninsula after the Macedonian conquest of the powerful King Philip II, who had seized the throne of Macedon in the middle of the fourth century. He assembled and trained a powerful army, conquered his neighbors, and became involved in the tangled alliances of the Greeks. In 338 B.C., at the battle of Chaeronea, Philip and his army routed the combined army of Athens and Thebes.

Two years later, Philip was assassinated by his own men, and his son, Alexander, ascended the throne as king and commander. A pupil of Aristotle, Alexander proved to be not only an able king and general, but also a man of sophisticated vision. Unlike his father, he was more interested in a world order than in mere conquest and pillage. His rule began with a twelve-year expedition in which he led an army, one quarter of which was Greek, into Asia. The brilliant 22-year-old carried Greek—that is, Athenian—culture further afield than ever before. According to legend, when he reached Asia, Alexander undid the Gordian knot tied by King Gordius of Phrygia. An oracle had foretold that whoever could untie the knot would be the next ruler of Asia. Alexander then defeated the Persian king, Darius III, at the battle of Issus. From there, Alexander led his forces against the city of Tyre in Syria, and pressed on to Egypt where, in the delta of the Nile, he founded Alexandria, one of the most influential and important cities in the Hellenistic world. A second defeat of Darius and the subsequent sacking of his capital, Persepolis, led to Alexander's installation as successor to the Persian throne. After pushing as far as the River Indus in India, Alexander's army balked, and so, after following the Indus south to the Indian Ocean, Alexander returned across the great desert and ended his odyssey in Babylon. According to legend, when Alexander the Great could find no more worlds to conquer, he sat down and wept. In any case, his destiny fulfilled, Alexander died of a sudden fever in Babylon at the age of thirty-three (Fig. **3.27**). He had married a Persian princess, declared himself a king and a god, and founded twenty-five Greek city–states. Along the way, his soldiers married native women and established

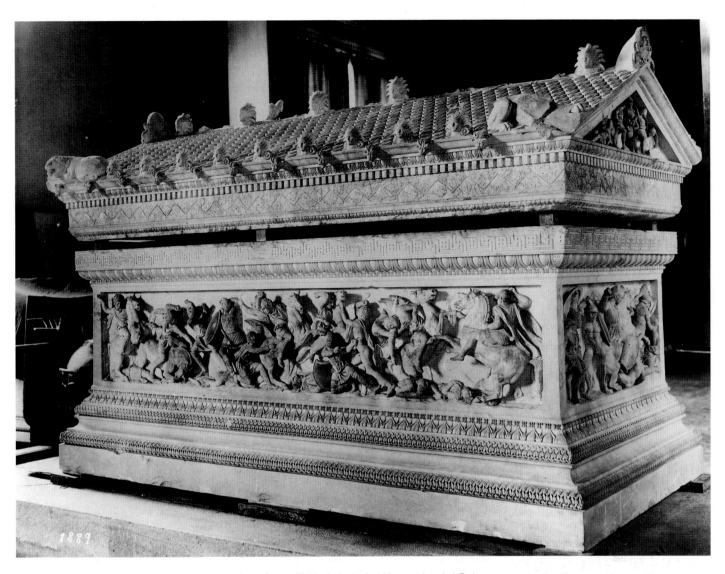

3.27 *Alexander Sarcophagus*, c. 310 B.C. Marble, 6 ft 4½ ins (1.94 m) high. Archeological Museum, Istanbul, Turkey.

Greek customs, trade, administration, and artistry throughout half of Asia.

Under the Alexandrine, or *Hellenistic*, Empire, which stretched from Egypt in the west to the Indus in the east, civilization and the arts flourished, and the influence of Hellenistic art continued for centuries after the fall of the empire to the Romans.

The success of Alexander's conquests depended to a great extent on his forceful personality. On his death, the empire began to crumble as regional fragmentation and struggles for power marked the post-Alexandrian Hellenistic world. Nevertheless, the creation of so vast an empire fostered an internationalism of culture that persisted into, and was strengthened under, the Roman Empire. Commerce flourished, and international communication carried Greek thought and artistic influence to all parts of

the known world. Intercultural relationships blossomed: Buddhist sculpture in India, for example, shows signs of Greek influence, and the European pantheon of gods began to reflect Eastern emotionalism. Athens, thus, remained an important center for ideas and cultural accomplishments, in spite of the weakness of its commercial and military power.

The source of Hellenistic culture was Alexandria, which was, at this time, the greatest city in the world and was endowed with phenomenal wealth. Legally it was a Greek city "by" not "in" Egypt. Brilliant writers and new literary forms emerged, and the Ptolemies (TAH-loh-meez) patronized science and scholarship. Royal funds paid for many splendid buildings, including an enormous library, which became the focal point of the Hellenistic intellectual world.

TECHNOLOGY: PUTTING DISCOVERY TO WORK

Hero's Steam Turbine

After the death of Alexander the Great, Ptolemy I became ruler of Egypt, proclaimed himself king, and gave himself the name Soter, or Savior. Despite a somewhat exaggerated view of his own importance, Ptolemy established what was essentially a research institute by founding the museum at Alexandria, the library of which was to become the most famous in the world. The museum attracted scholars from around the Hellenistic world to teach and to learn. One of these was Hero, whose tutor, Strato, had been a contemporary of Aristotle at the Lyceum in Athens. Hero compiled a textbook of engineering and invented a number of useful pieces of equipment, including a water clock. From his written account, it is clear that he gave a great deal of thought to maintaining an even flow of water into the mechanism so that it would keep accurate time. His steam turbine (Fig. **3.28**), which depended on the expansion of air and the vaporization of water when heated, could probably have been developed further to provide a useful source of power, but the machine appears to have been regarded merely as an entertaining toy.

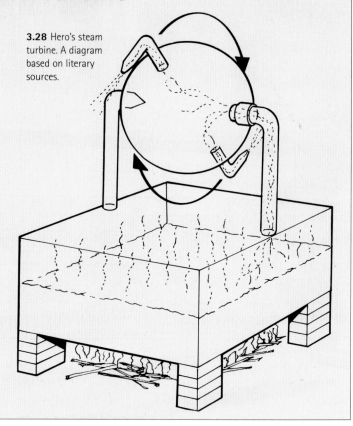

3.28 Hero's steam turbine. A diagram based on literary sources.

Theatre and Literature

The period from roughly the fourth century B.C. to the Roman infiltration, about 250 B.C., is called the Hellenistic period. This was a time of great expansion for the theatre in Greece. The general plan of the theatres did not change, but the *skene* frequently was two stories tall. After the chorus disappeared, in later Hellenistic times, a stage as high as twelve feet (3.6 meters) was not unusual.

In this period, comedy was the staple of the theatre. Only five, incomplete, plays by Menander (meh-NAN-duhr c. 343–c. 291 B.C.) survive. The action is bawdy; the situations are pleasant and domestic, and for the most part superficial and without satire. Religion no longer played a central role in the theatre, and, as we have noted, the chorus disappeared entirely.

Non-dramatic literature flourished, especially in Alexandria. The Ptolemies' support of the museum and library lured poets as well as scholars, and a variety of forms was pursued—for example, poetry, history, essays, and biography. A new form, the *pastoral*, which was devel-oped by the poet Theocritus (thee-AHK-ri-tuhs; c. 310–250 B.C.), focuses on rural scenes—for example, farmers and shepherds—and treats the subject with idealization and artificiality. Perhaps his works appealed because they played on the nostalgia of the readers, reminding them of the quiet country life that they had left for the hustle and bustle of the cities. Theocritus also wrote in a form called the *idyll*, which drew poetic pictures of common, everyday life and its affairs.

Philosophy and Religion

Four schools of thought vied for philosophical supremacy in the Hellenistic period. These were Cynicism, Skepticism, Stoicism, and Epicureanism (ehp-i-kyoo-REE-uhn-izm). Led by Diogenes (dy-AH-jen-eez; c. 412–c. 323 B.C.), the Cynics taught that humans are animals and that the good life lay simply in satisfying their animal needs. Since those needs can be troublesome, however, a wise person will have as few needs as possible but will disregard any social conventions that stand in the way of his own satisfaction.

In other words, if a person wanted nothing, then he could lack nothing. The Cynics had little use for society as an organizing principle, believing that it stood in the way of individual freedom and independence, and they therefore isolated themselves as much as possible from society. Needless to say, Cynicism had little appeal either to the masses or the aristocracy.

Followers of Pyrrho (PEER-oh) of Elis, the Skeptics, asserted that nothing was certain and that the senses were completely unreliable as sources of knowledge. Ultimately, the only certainty was that truth was unachievable. They questioned everything and admitted the truth of nothing. For the Skeptic, everything was relative. Universal doubt ruled their world. Less popular, even, than Cynicism, Skepticism did make inroads in later times, particularly during the Roman era.

Stoicism, founded by Zeno (ZEEN-oh), held that humans were the incarnation of reason or *logos* (LOH-gohs), which produces and directs the world and gave a spark to the individual soul in the form of rationality. The good life was defined as that which follows reason, wisdom, and virtue, but the only way to achieve these goals lay through renunciation and asceticism. The Stoic tended to leave everything to God and to accept whatever came his way. Once this state of mind was achieved, it was possible to disregard public opinion, misfortune, and even death—that is, one approached life with apathy. Stoicism maintained that happiness was the ultimate goal of the individual. It also stressed the importance of the senses in perceiving underlying moral law and the divine plan for the world. In the end, the Stoics perceived an ideal state, guided by *logos* and law, that included all humanity regardless of race, sex, nationality, or social standing. Stoicism proved a popular philosophy, especially among intellectuals and political leaders. Essentially Stoicism was an optimistic viewpoint that stood in strong contrast to the pessimism of the other philosophies of the time.

Epicurus (c. 342–270 B.C.) led Epicureans to a life of strict quietude. They concluded that human beings consisted of a temporary arrangement of atoms that dissolved at death. Because everything was temporary, the good life was simply an untroubled one. Wisdom dictated that one should avoid entanglements, maintain good health, tolerate pain, and accept death without fear. Epicurus founded a school in Athens, and his pupils, including women and slaves, gathered to discuss ideas. Epicureans believed that the senses could be relied upon to give an accurate picture of reality and that the mind functioned as a storehouse for those observations. Free will allowed humans to reach moral conclusions based on ethical constructs.

Hellenistic times were uncertain times, and human confidence in the ability to control anything waned. At such times, people tend to develop a belief that fate will do whatever fate will do and to adopt pietistic religious beliefs—that is, beliefs in which emotionalism takes the place of intellectualism or rationalism. In the Hellenistic world, a variety of mystery cults emerged from the East and from Egypt. The cult of Dionysus, god of revelry and wine, was particularly appealing in Greece proper. To unite Egyptians and Greeks, Ptolemy I, founder of the Alexandrian Museum, invented a new god, Serapis (suh-RAY-pis), who became popular throughout the Hellenistic world. Another powerful mystery cult that spread throughout the Mediterranean world and, later, became one of the most antagonistic forces met by the early Christians, was the cult of Isis. Originating in Egypt in the eighteenth century B.C., Isis was a nature goddess, who became the prototype for all goddesses. In Egyptian mythology she was the faithful wife and sister of Osiris and mother of Horus. After Osiris was slain by their brother, Set, and his body scattered in pieces, Isis gathered the pieces together; Osiris was then restored and became ruler of the dead. The legend symbolized the sun (Osiris) overwhelmed by night (Set), followed by the birth of the sun of a new day (Horus) from the eastern sky (Isis). Thus, it was a religion that emphasized resurrection after death: one of the characteristics that later put it into direct conflict with Christianity. Isis was universal mother and mistress of all magic, and her cult prevailed until the middle of the sixth century A.D. Probably, the appeal of the mystery cults lay in their mystery—that is, in secret initiation rites that gave the member a special status and, thus, satisfied a universal need to belong.

Hellenistic Style

Sculpture

In actuality a diversity of approaches, the Hellenistic style in sculpture continued to dominate the Mediterranean world until the first century B.C. As time progressed, it began to reflect an increasing interest in the differences between individual humans. Hellenistic sculptors turned away from idealization, often toward PATHOS, trivia, even banality, or flights of technical virtuosity. These characteristics appear in Figures 3.29, 3.30 and 3.31. The *Dying Gaul* (Fig. 3.31) is a powerful expression of emotion and pathos. This Roman copy of a statue from Pergamon places the figure on a stage, as if acting out a drama. The noble warrior, a Gallic casualty in the war between Pergamon and barbarian invaders, is slowly bleeding to death from a chest wound.

The *Nike of Samothrace* (NYK-ee; sam-oh-THRAYS), or *Winged Victory* (Fig. 3.29), displays a dramatic virtuosity of technique. As the symbol of the victory of one of

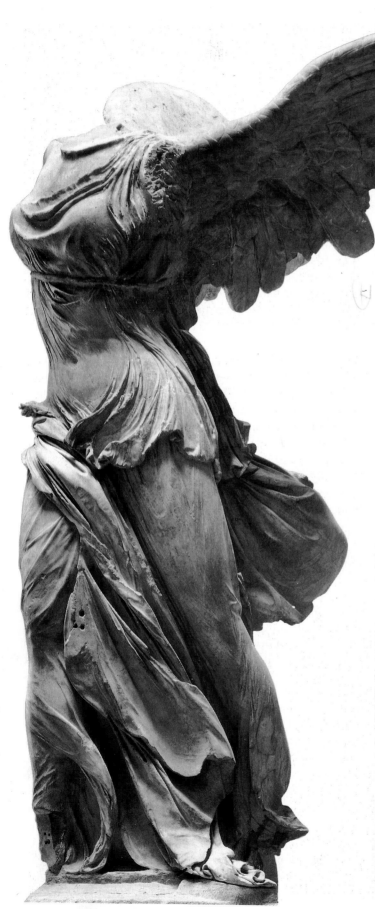

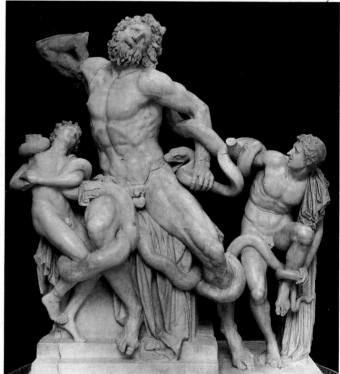

3.29 *Nike of Samothrace* (*Winged Victory*), c. 190 B.C. Marble, 8 ft (2.44 m) high. Louvre, Paris.

3.30 (*below*) Hagesandrus, Polydorus, and Athenodorus, *Laocoön and his Two Sons*, first century A.D. Marble, 8 ft (2.44 m) high. Vatican Museum, Rome.

Alexander's successors, she is strong, heavy, and yet amazingly agile and graceful. The unsupported wings and flying garments represent an achievement one does not expect to find in a carved work of marble. The sculptor has treated stone with an almost painterly technique, creating highlights and shadows that intensify the dramatic swirl of the draperies. As a result, we are able to sense the reality of the wind and sea into which she once faced.

The frequent Hellenistic theme of suffering receives violent treatment in the *Laocoön* (lay-AH-koh-ahn) group (Fig. **3.30**), attributed to three sculptors from the first century A.D., Hagesandrus (hag-uh-SAN-druhs), Polydorus (pah-lih-DOHR-uhs), and Athenodorus (ah-thehn-uh-DOHR-uhs). The Trojan priest Laocoön and his sons

3.31 *Dying Gaul*, Roman copy of a bronze original of c. 230–220 B.C. Marble, lifesize. Museo Capitolino, Rome.

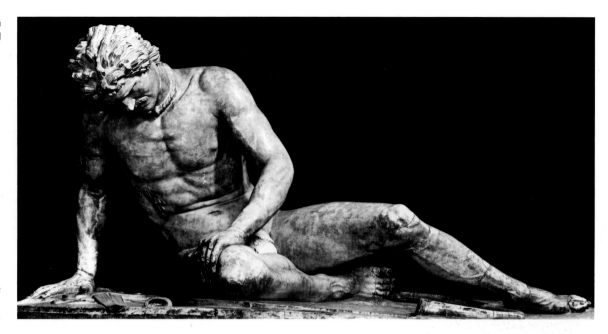

3.32 (*below*) The Temple of Olympian Zeus, Athens, 174 B.C.–A.D. 130.

are being strangled by sea serpents. According to Greek myth, this was Laocoön's punishment for defying Poseidon, god of the sea, by warning the Trojans of the Greek trick of the Trojan horse, in which soldiers were concealed. The expression of emotion is almost unrestrained. The figures writhe before our eyes, their straining muscles and bulging veins indicating mortal agony.

Architecture

The Temple of Olympian Zeus (Fig. **3.32**) illustrates the

Hellenistic modifications of classical style in architecture. The scale and complexity of the building are considerably different from the Parthenon. Order, balance, moderation, and harmony are still present, but these huge ruins reveal a change in proportions, with the use of slender and ornate Corinthian columns: temple architecture in this style was designed to produce an overpowering emotional experience. Begun by the architect Cossutius (koh-SOO-shuhs) for King Antiochus (an-TY-oh-kuhs) IV of Syria, this is the first major Corinthian temple. Its elaborate detail pushed

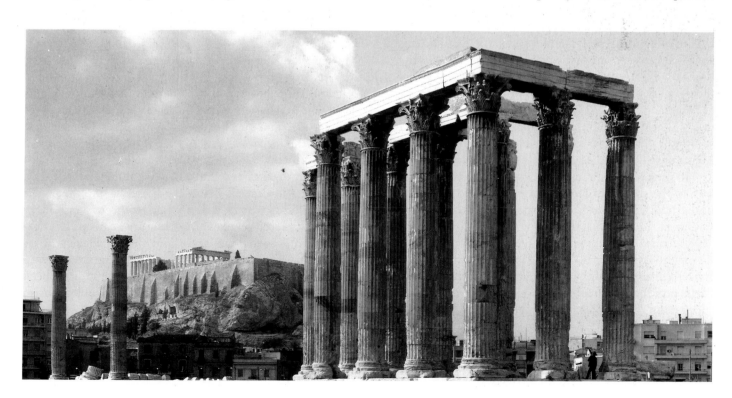

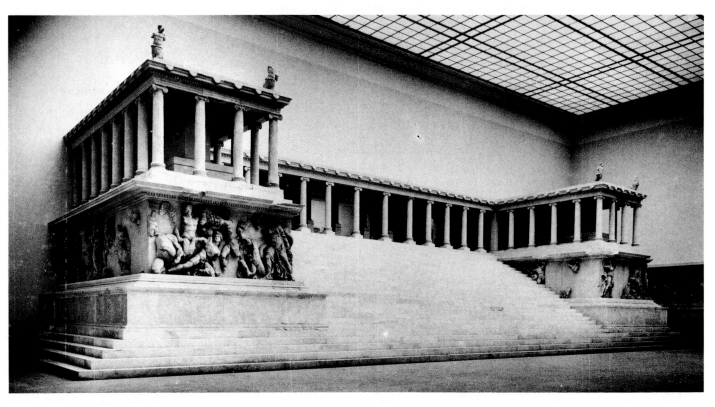

3.33 The west front of the Altar of Zeus, from the temple at Pergamon (restored), 197–159 B.C. Pergamonmuseum, Staatliche Museen, Berlin.

its completion date into the second century A.D. under the Roman emperor Hadrian. The ruins can only vaguely suggest the size and richness of the original building, which was surrounded by an immense walled precinct.

One center of Hellenistic power in Asia Minor was the city of Pergamon. Here, we find an example of Hellenistic style that ranks as one of the major accomplishments of the time. It was, in fact, considered to be one of the wonders of the then known world. The Altar of Zeus from the temple at Pergamon (Fig. 3.33) was excavated in pieces beginning in 1873 and reassembled in a painstaking process that took more than fifty years. The altar was built by King Eumenes (YOO-min-eez) II as a means to glorify the king and to impress the Greek world with Eumenes' contribution to the spread of Hellenism by his victories over the barbarians. The great frieze of the altar stands more than seven feet (2.1 meters) tall and runs for more than 450 feet (137 meters) around the entire perimeter of the building. The frieze represents a radical departure from the design concept of the classical Greek temple. For example, in the Parthenon the colonnade serves as a part of the structure, supporting the entablature, which, in turn, elevates the

frieze into a position of ethereal space and sustains the pediment and roof. In the Altar of Zeus, the frieze stands independently on a podium consisting of five steps. The colonnade retains no structural reason for being and becomes, rather, a unifying design device to give a boundary to the frieze.

The sculptures of the frieze narrate a typical battle between gods and giants, but the gods—now less potent in religious thought—symbolize qualities of good; the giants represent malevolent natural forces such as earthquakes and floods, and the portrayal symbolizes the struggle between the forces of light and the forces of darkness. An entire pantheon of gods is depicted, including Zeus, Helios the sun god, Hemera the winged goddess of the day, Artemis, and Heracles. Below the frieze we find the names of the sculptors who executed this magnificent work.

The technical details of the frieze are nearly as interesting as the power of its scale and the intricacies of its proportion. Throughout, great care was given to surface texture. Cloth, saddles, belt buckles, and flesh have been patiently finished to create textures of the real objects. Also of note is the depth of the relief.

Focal Point

From Idealism to Realism—*Prometheus* and *Hecuba*

In this chapter, we have been able to compare the various art forms of classical and Hellenistic Greece, to isolate some shared themes, and to draw some general conclusions about them. Here we'll focus on the process of change in Greek culture. In particular, we can see how much change occurred over a brief time in a single discipline, the theatre. To do this, we will use two plays that bracket the classical period in Athens: Aeschylus' *Prometheus* (proh-MEE-thee-uhs) *Bound* and Euripides' *Hecuba* (HEHK-yoo-buh).

According to legend, Prometheus frustrated the plans of Zeus by giving fire to a race of mortals whom Zeus sought to destroy. Here is classical Greek idealism at work: through reason, application, and vision, human beings can defy the gods and win. They are capable of nobility and infinite improvement. As punishment for his presumption, however, Zeus has Prometheus chained to a rock. In Prometheus' justification of what he did, he suggests that humankind, through technology and reason, can have dominion over nature.

Prometheus is a play unusual even for Aeschylus in its heavy dependence on dialogue and character, and in its lack of action. The hero is motionless, chained to a rock. Nothing happens. There is only conversation between a parade of different people, through which the playwright reveals character and situation.

In this extract, the scene is set for an exchange between Force, Violence, and Hephaestus, the fire god. Violence does not speak, however, as there are only two actors. Force presents the situation:

Far have we come to this far spot of earth,
This narrow Scythian land, a desert all untrodden.
God of the forge and fire, yours the task
The Father laid upon you.
To this high-piercing, headlong rock
In adamantine chains that none can break
Bind him—him here, who dared all things.
Your flaming flower he stole to give to men,
Fire, the master craftsman, through whose power
All things are wrought, and for such error now
He must repay the gods; be taught to yield
To Zeus' lordship and to cease
From his man-looking way.

Through speeches such as these, the characters are revealed—Force as a villain, and Hephaestus as a weak but kindly fool. After Force, Violence, and Hephaestus exit, Prometheus appears. He may have been revealed on a low wagon, called an *eccyclema* (ehk-i-KLAY-muh), which was rolled out from the central door of the *skene*. He speaks:

O air of heaven and swift winged winds,
O running river waters,
O never numbered laughter or sea waves,
Earth, mother of all, eye of the sun, all-seeing,
On you I call.
Behold what I, a god, endure for gods.
See in what tortures I must struggle
Through countless years of time.
This shame, these bonds, are put upon me
By the new ruler of the gods.
Sorrow enough in what is here and what is still to
    come.

And so the myth unfolds itself in high poetry as Prometheus discourses with the chorus, a group of kindly sea-nymphs, with Hermes, with Ocean, a humorous old busybody, and with Io, an ephemeral creature. When the dialogue has run its course, Prometheus declaims:

An end to words. Deeds now,
The world is shaken,
The deep and secret way of thunder
Is rent apart.
Fiery wreaths of lightning flash.
Whirlwinds toss the swirling dust.
The blasts of all the winds are battling in the air,
And sky and sea are one.
On me the tempest falls.
It does not make me tremble.
O holy Mother Earth, O air and sun,
Behold me. I am wronged.[7]

Prometheus is an idealistic exploration of human capacity, achievement, and power, written as the height of the golden age of Athens approached.

Euripides' play *Hecuba*, on the other hand, is a bitter tragedy of the interrelationships between those who rule and those who obey. It was written at a time when failure of leadership had dragged Athens downward through a long war of attrition with Sparta. Here again the playwright deals with myth, in this case, the story of the sack of Troy.

Two separate events are related, giving the plot an episodic character. Hecuba is the wife of Priam, king of Troy, whose city has at last fallen to the Greeks. She endures first the slaughter of her daughter Polyxena (pahl-ee-ZEEN-uh) by the Greeks, then she discovers the body of her son, Polydorus, who has been murdered by Polymestor (pahl-ee-MEHS-tohr). Each of these events takes her one step further from grief and nearer to despair. She seeks the help of the Greek king, Agamemnon, in her quest for revenge on Polymestor, but receives only pity and the question, "What woman on this earth was ever cursed like this?" Hecuba replies in language less poetic and more realistic than that of Prometheus:

There is none but goddess Suffering herself.

But let me tell you why I kneel
At your feet. And if my suffering seem just,
Then I must be content. But if otherwise,
Give me my revenge on that treacherous friend
Who flouted every god in heaven and in hell
To do this brutal murder.

At our table
He was our frequent guest; was counted first
Among our friends, respected and honoured by me,
Receiving every kindness that a man could meet—
And then, in cold deliberation killed
My son.

Murder may have its reasons, its motives,
But this—to refuse my son a grave, to throw him
To the sea, unburied! . . .

See me whole, observe
My wretchedness—

Once a queen, now
A slave; blessed with children, happy once,
Now old, childless, utterly alone,
Homeless, lost, unhappiest of women
On this earth . . .[8]

Step by step she moves inevitably toward her final acts of atrocity. The play focuses on how she is forced to yield, one at a time, her values, her self-respect, and "the faith which makes her human." Underlying the play is a stark condemnation of the logic of political necessity. When faced with power over which she has no control, she pleads the case of honor, decency, the gods, and moral law. All these appeals fail. As despair destroys her humanity, she passes beyond the reach of judgment. The chorus condemns the tragic waste of war and questions the necessity and logic of imperialism. Finally, Euripides attacks the gods themselves. Even if they exist, he implies, their justice is so far removed from humans that it has no relevance.

The transition from idealism, form, order, and restraint to greater realism and emotion represented by these two plays parallels the changes we have seen in painting, sculpture, and architecture. In all the arts, the idealization of classicism turned to the increasing realism of succeeding styles; restraint gave way to emotion, and form gave way to feeling.

CHAPTER REVIEW

Critical Thought

Given the complete defeat of Athens by Sparta and their different ways of life and philosophy, but the continuing influence of Athenian culture, it is possible to conclude that artistic culture is more important than power and conquest. One can certainly speculate on the kinds of social conditions that are necessary for a culture to flourish, provide adequately for its citizenry, and have a lasting positive impact on the future.

It may well be that Socrates has as much to say about life today as he had about life in Athens 2,400 years ago. Is an unexamined life not worth living? Would you like to be one of his students, pummeled constantly by questions designed to illumine your weaknesses, or would you rather sit in a classroom letting a professor lecture to you and provide you with the answers?

We often classify some people as "rational" and others as "emotional," putting classical principles into our personal relationships. Sometimes, men are described as more logical or more mathematically inclined than women, who are then described as more intuitive and artistic. Is that an accurate way of assessing individuals? Perhaps we're more comfortable dealing with classicism in a less personal manner—for example, finding examples of classicism in the buildings of our campus and community or in the music we listen to. Obviously these are not Greek classical buildings or songs, because they were made long after the Greek classical period, but you will easily recognize some basic characteristics of classicism in them.

Summary

After reading this chapter you should be able to:

- Explain the factors that coalesced to make Athens the cradle of Western civilization.
- Define and compare the several philosophical systems of the classical and Hellenistic eras.
- Identify works and artists, and characterize the visual art and architecture of the classical and post-classical periods.
- Compare Plato's and Aristotle's theories about art.
- Discuss Aristotle's theory of tragedy and its relationship to the major playwrights and production circumstances of the classical and post-classical periods.
- Describe the music and dance of the classical period.
- Apply the elements and principles of composition to analyze and compare individual works of art illustrated in this chapter.

CHAPTER FOUR

The Roman Period

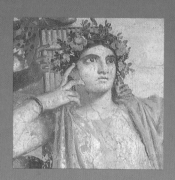

OUTLINE

THE ROMAN REPUBLIC
Military Expansion
The Roman Civil War
The Visual Arts and Architecture
Theatre
Philosophy and Religion

THE ROMAN EMPIRE
Augustus
Pax Romana
Roman Law
Philosophy
Religion
Two-Dimensional Art
Sculpture
  OUR DYNAMIC WORLD: Chinese
    Painting
Architecture
  MASTERWORK: The Pantheon
  TECHNOLOGY: Cement
Music
Literature
  PROFILE: Vergil
Dance

FOCAL POINT: AUGUSTUS—
CLASSICAL VISIONS

VIEW

DEMOCRACY AND LAW

Is it better to have a participatory government (democracy), than to have a monarchial or dictatorial government? For the second time in our study, we now watch as a relatively small and homogeneous citizenry cope with governing themselves. In ancient Rome, as life and population became more expansive, complicated, and diverse, the governmental form itself became problematical. Amazingly, the citizens of Rome willingly gave up their democracy in favor of a dictator. We wonder what might have transpired to bring about such an event and think of modern parallels such as Germany under Adolf Hitler and the Nazis. We also wonder, as we examine how democracy succeeded and failed in cultures such as those of ancient Greece and Rome, whether a country can become too large and too fragmented to sustain democracy. For example, could democracy ever work in a nation as large as modern China? Will the United States reach the point at which it is too diverse to continue as a representative democracy and still maintain any kind of social order? Interestingly, however, as Rome grew and its emperors became all-powerful, it witnessed nearly two hundred years of peace and stability—the *Pax Romana*—and entered a period in which the rule of law flourished. So, is it governmental form or something else that gives a society a high quality of life?

Above Detail of Fig. **4.10**.

4.1 *Gemma Augustea* (detail of the crowning of Augustus), early first century A.D. Onyx cameo, whole cameo 7¹/₂ × 9 ins (19 × 23 cm). Kunsthistorisches Museum, Vienna.

KEY TERMS

Some of the basic terms and concepts we will encounter in this chapter include the following:

S.P.Q.R.—*Senatus Populusque Romanus*—the Roman Senate and the People.

Pax Romana, "The Roman Peace," was a 200-year span of stability during the Roman Empire, beginning with the Emperor Augustus.

Trompe l'oeil, "trick of the eye" or "fool the eye." A two-dimensional artwork designed to make the viewer believe it is in three dimensions.

Engaged columns are columns, often decorative, that are part of, and project from, a wall surface.

Cella is the principal enclosed room of a Roman temple.

Sarcophagi are stone coffins, a notable type of Roman sculpture.

Masonry is stone or brickwork, a structural architectural feature at which the Romans excelled.

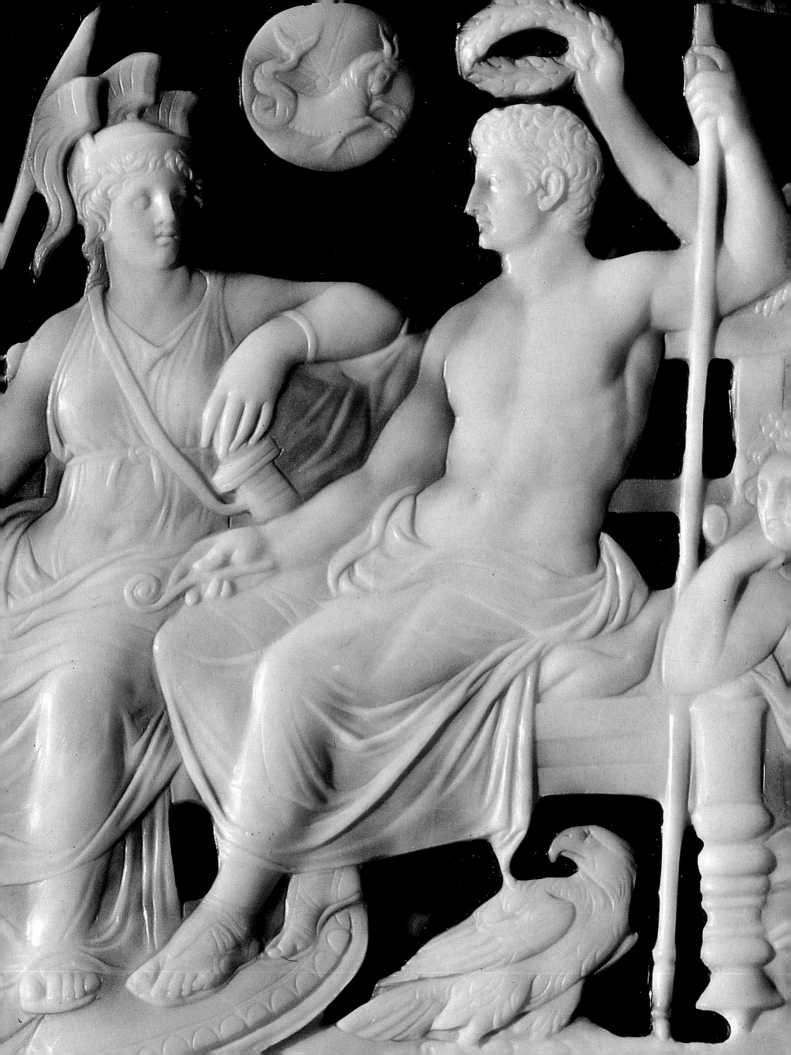

The civilization that would become the Roman one arose at the same time as that of Ancient Greece. By the sixth century B.C., Etruscan invaders who had come out of Asia by way of Greece dominated the Italian peninsula. The Etruscans brought to their new land a militaristic and practical society, an ANTHROPOMORPHIC conception of the deities, and arts roughly equivalent to those of archaic Greece, whose style had influenced them (Fig. **4.2**). Roman legend held that Rome was founded in 753 B.C. by Romulus (RAHM-yoo-luhs), an orphan, who, with his twin brother, Remus (REEM-uhs), had been suckled by a wolf as the boys' foster-mother. One Etruscan religious cult revered wolves, and this legend is taken as further evidence that Roman civilization had Etruscan roots.

Toward the end of the sixth century B.C., Rome, an important location as a convenient bridging point across the River Tiber, joined with other Latin cities in a revolt against Etruscan domination. In 509 B.C., according to Roman tradition, the last Etruscan king was expelled from Rome. This set the Romans on a 900-year course that would lead them to all corners of the then known world. Etruscan influence continued, however, and it was largely due to that influence and its inherited links with Greece

that the Romans carried forward the classical ideas that continue to permeate the Western approach to life today.

THE ROMAN REPUBLIC

Once free of Etruscan domination, the Romans developed a republican form of government that lasted until the first century B.C. This political stability provided important continuity for other Roman institutions. The motto "S.P.Q.R."—*Senatus Populusque Romanus* (the Roman Senate and People)—reflected the early Roman political and social order, and remained the watchword of Roman society until Imperial times. It meant that sovereignty rested in the people themselves, and not in any particular form of government. In many ways the Roman Republic functioned as a democracy. Decisions affecting society were made at a series of assemblies, which all citizens attended to express their will. The Senate, on the other hand, conducted the actual business of government, including the passage of legislation and the supervision of elected magistrates. Over the centuries, the greatest issues

Map 4.1 The Roman Republic, showing important battles and dates (B.C.) that areas came under dominion.

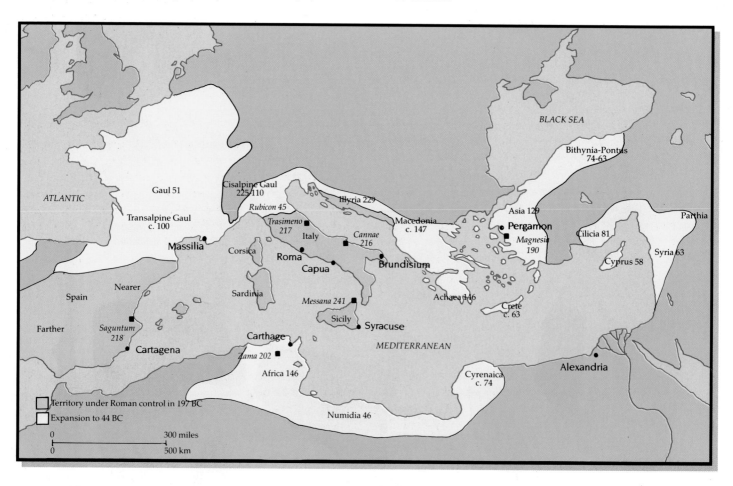

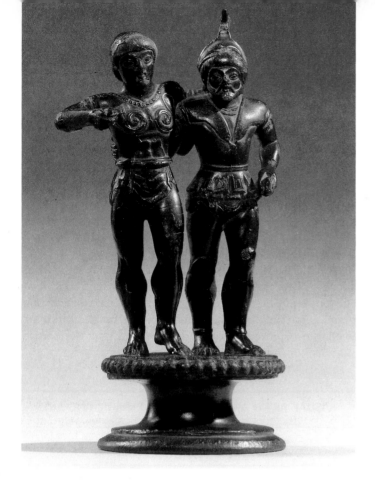

4.2 Etruscan warrior supporting a wounded comrade, early fifth century B.C. Bronze, 5¼ ins (13.4 cm) high (without base). Metropolitan Museum of Art, New York (Rogers Fund, 1947).

Military Expansion

Roman expansion was based on military conquest. Through conquest Rome assumed a position of political dominance in the Hellenistic world during the third and second centuries B.C. (Map **4.1**) The internationalization of culture, evident in Hellenic times, grew under the Romans. Later, Rome would extend its control throughout Europe and eventually as far as the British Isles.

By 272 B.C., the Romans had conquered western Greece. Then they took on Carthage, the other major power of the period, in the first of the Punic wars. Over the next hundred years, in three great stages, Rome and Carthage battled each other for control of the whole Mediterranean world. It was during the second Punic war, which began in 218 B.C., that the Carthaginian general Hannibal marched his legions over the Alps into Italy. The end of the second Punic war in 202 B.C. left Rome in a position of advantage and at a watershed.

Rome had the choice either to consolidate order and security in the west by ridding itself of the Carthaginian threat or to expand toward the east. The Romans chose to move eastward, hoping to gain new riches from the conquered territories. The outcome, though unforeseen, was to leave Rome overlord of the entire Hellenistic world. But with the third Punic war, which began in 149 B.C., Rome also accomplished its other objective: within three years Carthage was destroyed.

The Roman Civil War

The continuous state of war on the borders of the Roman provinces, as well as the practical requirements for effective government, led to an increase of power and authority in the hands of the Roman Senate and a decrease in the participation of ordinary citizens. Unlike Athens, Rome had very little commerce or industry, and the quality of life in Rome came to depend directly upon the wealth of conquered regions brought back to Rome as spoils.

The greatest danger to Rome did not lie in foreign wars, however, but in the threat of civil war. Conquests had made the Romans rich, and the *proconsuls* who governed the provinces took advantage of their positions, the availability of cheap land, slaves, and tribute money. Corruption was a temptation few could resist. They built vast estates and, in general, abused the poor, who became poorer. Rome itself became a Mecca for the rich and poor alike, and the widening gap between the two increased tension and bitterness among the masses. This was exacerbated by the violent excesses of generals who, having conquered the hinterlands, returned home with their armies intact. The result was a period of upheaval, which

affecting Roman society were played out as dramas between the people and the Senate.

The Senate itself was an hereditary institution composed of an assembly of the heads, or *patres*, of old families and, later, of wealthy members of the citizenry, or *plebs*. The Senate's 300 members therefore represented old and new money, power, and social interest. It was a self-renewing OLIGARCHY. The two most important officers who ruled the state were the *consuls*, who were elected by the representative assemblies for one-year terms, at the end of which they became members of the Senate.

In Rome, the rich ruled via the Senate and the general citizenry were little more than peasants. By the third century B.C., the division between aristocrat and peasant had widened appreciably, the former growing in riches and the latter sinking further and further into poverty. Yet as long as Rome remained reasonably small, the constitutional framework of the Republic held the social order together. It warded off revolution while permitting change and provided the body politic with reasonably well-trained leaders who knew how, above all else, to keep the Republic functioning and alive. It was, in fact, the internal stability of the Republic that made expansion possible, bringing about the next phase of Roman history.

lasted from approximately 133 to 31 B.C. and which brought the Roman Republic to a close.

During this time a succession of men attempted leadership. Marius (MAR-ee-uhs) was the first of these. Then came a power struggle in the late first century B.C. from which the dictator Sulla emerged, to be followed by Pompey (PAHM-pee).

In 59 B.C., Marius' nephew Julius Caesar (Caesar was the family name) was elected consul. During a five-year campaign against the Gauls, he kept a close watch on Roman politics. Corruption, intrigue, and murder were disfiguring public life and discrediting the Senate. Having returned to Italy in 49 B.C., he declared war on Pompey by crossing the River Rubicon, which marked the limit of his province. By 44 B.C., he had returned to Rome in triumph, to be voted dictator for life. His life was cut short only days

later, however, on 15 March 44 B.C., at the hands of assassins in the Senate.

One of Caesar's most lasting achievements was the invention of the Julian calendar, in which the year has 365 days, with an additional day every four years. The new calendar was used from 1 January 45 B.C.

The Visual Arts and Architecture

Wall Painting

Very little Roman painting has survived. Most of what survives appears to have been done in bright colors, in FRESCO—that is, painting on wet plaster that becomes a permanent part of the wall surface—and much of that art was an outright copy of Greek classical and Hellenistic

Timeline 4.1 The Roman period.

	GENERAL EVENTS	LITERATURE & PHILOSOPHY	VISUAL ART & ARCHITECTURE	PERFORMING ARTS
800 B.C.	Founding of Rome			
500 B.C.			Hermes (4.5)	
400 B.C.				Mime Hydraulos

300 B.C.	Roman Republic
	Roman conquest of
	    Western Greece
	First Punic war
	Second Punic war
				Development of Roman
				    comedy
				Plautus

200 B.C.	Third Punic war	Diogenes	Temple of Fortuna Virilis (4.7)	Terence First stone theatres in Rome
100 B.C.	Julius Caesar elected consul Julian calendarl Battle of Actium Augustus	Catullus Panaetius Posidonius Horace Vergil	Portrait of an Unknown Roman (4.6) Villa at Boscoreale (4.4) Lady Playing the Cithara (4.3) Ara Pacis (4.34)	 Pantomime
0	Expansion of Roman Empire Eruption of Mount Vesuvius Cult of Mithra	Seneca Plutarch	Vitruvius Colosseum (4.20, 4.21) Arch of Titus (4.25)	
A.D. 100	Destruction of Temple of Jerusalem	Livy Epictetus Juvenal Marcus Aurelius	Trajan's Column (4.15, 4.16) Pantheon (4.22, 4.23, 4.24) Forum of Augustus (4.32) Hercules and Telephos (4.10)	
A.D. 200		Plotinus	Sarcophagus (4.17)	

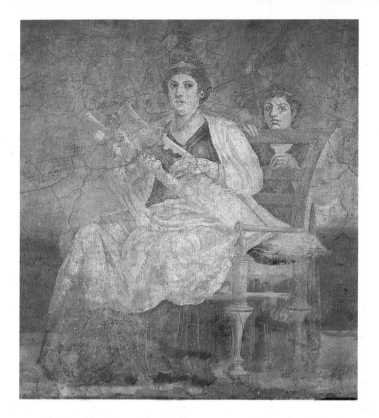

work. Many Greek artists and craftspeople were brought to Rome, and it was they who produced most early Roman art, so it is not surprising that Roman painting reflected classical and Hellenistic themes and styles, although certain uniquely Roman qualities were added. The illustrations that appear in this chapter may not be typical of Roman painting. They are, however, typical of what survives.

One of the characteristics common to Roman painting is an insistence on naturalistic figure depiction, such as we witnessed in Hellenistic style. In the painting of the *Lady Playing the Cithara* (Fig. **4.3**), naturalistic detail merges with an everyday subject matter. From this illustration we get a taste of Roman clothing, hair style, accessories, and furniture. The ornately turned legs of the chair and the gold embossing indicate careful and skilled craftsmanship as well as opulence. Notice how carefully and naturalistically the folds of the fabric are rendered, but notice, too, how careless the artist has been in the treatment of perspective. The legs and back of the chair have been

4.3 *Lady Playing the Cithara* c. 50 B.C. Wall painting, 6 ft 1½ ins (1.87 m) square. Metropolitan Museum of Art, New York (Rogers Fund, 1903).

4.4 Bedroom of a villa at Boscoreale, Italy, showing painted decorations, c. 50 B.C. Wall painting, average height 8 ft (2.44 m). Metropolitan Museum of Art, New York (Rogers Fund, 1903).

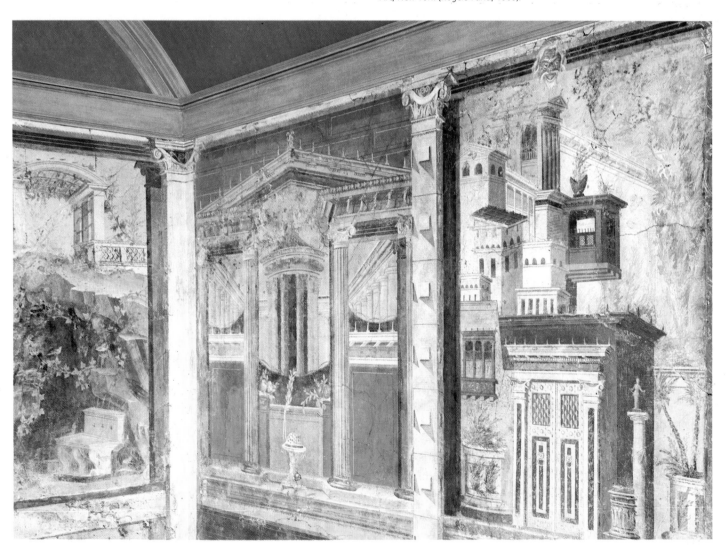

drawn without regard to the way lines and shapes actually recede into the distance. Nonetheless, this fresco is a formally composed picture, fitting its imposed boundary.

Roman wall painting may combine landscape representation with painted architectural detail (Fig. **4.4**). Often, the outdoor view appears as a panoramic vista seen through a TROMPE L'OEIL (trahmp-LOY) window. Rooms painted in this style reflect the tastes of late Republican aristocratic society. They took as their models the opulence and stylishness of the late Hellenistic princely courts, which were still influential around the Mediterranean.

Scenes from Greek mythology were very popular in Roman wall decoration, and it is possible that the treatment of subject matter in wall painting had some relationship to the painting of scenery in the theatres. The Roman architectural historian Vitruvius (vih-TROOV-ee-uhs; first century A.D.) indicates in his book *De Architectura* (day ar-kih-tek-TOOR-uh) that wall painters imitated theatrical scenery for tragedies, comedies, and satyr plays. Different styles prevailed in the different genres, and examples of each may be seen in surviving Roman wall paintings. Tragic scenery depicted columns, pediments, statues, and palace decor. Comic scenery portrayed private dwellings with balconies and windows. Satyric scenery illustrated trees, mountains, and rustic scenes. If the villa at Boscoreale (bahs-koh-ray-AHL-ay; Fig. **4.4**) does indeed reflect theatrical scenery, it seems clear that all three types are represented. The left panel seems satyric, the center panel tragic, and the right panel comic.

Mystery cults, especially that of Dionysus, were fashionable, and are represented in various manifestations in wall paintings, particularly in the so-called Villa of the Mysteries, which is located just outside the boundaries of the city of Pompeii.

Sculpture

Not all Roman art was an imitative reconstruction of Greek prototypes, although some Roman statues do fit this category. Figure **4.5** illustrates a Roman copy of a Greek statue of Hermes dating to c. 400 B.C. It would have represented to the Romans not only a mythological subject, but also the qualities of the earlier Hellenic era.

Some Roman sculpture, however, expresses a vigor that is uniquely Roman. Scholars do not always agree on what particular works of Roman sculpture mean or on why they were made. For example, the *Portrait of an Unknown Roman* (Fig. **4.6**) dates from a time when Hellenistic influence was becoming well established in Rome. It is tempting to attribute the highly lifelike representation of this work to the same artistic viewpoint that governed Hellenistic style and to conclude that it is a copy of a Hellenistic work. An important Etruscan–Roman religious practice undoubtedly had a stronger influence,

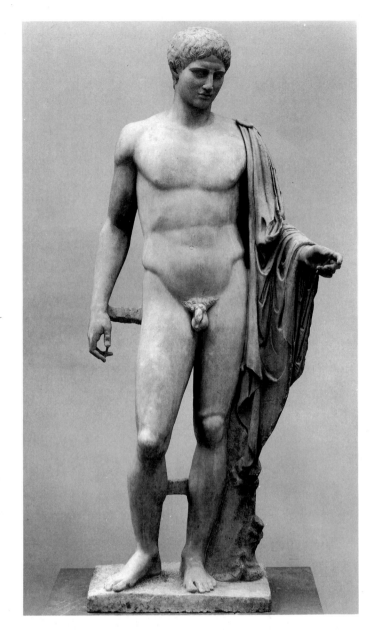

4.5 *Hermes*, Roman copy of a Greek work of c. 400 B.C. Marble, 5 ft 11 ins (1.8 m) high. Metropolitan Museum of Art, New York (Gift of the Hearst Foundation, 1956).

however. Portraits were an integral part of household and ancestor worship, and wax death masks were often made and kept by the family to remember a loved one. Wax is not a substance ideally suited for immortality, and it is possible that the bust in Figure **4.6** was made from a death mask. There may be more to this portrait, however, than mere accuracy. Some scholars point to an apparent emphasis on certain features which reinforces the ideas of ruggedness and character.

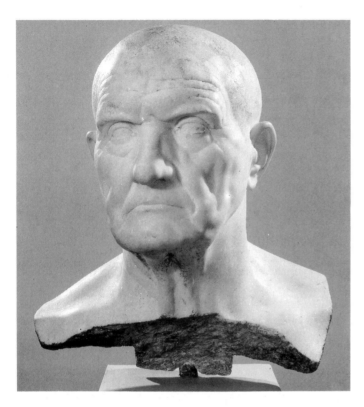

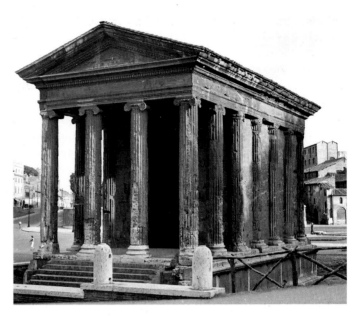

4.7 Temple of Fortuna Virilis, Rome, late second century B.C. Stone.

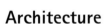

4.6 *Portrait of an Unknown Roman*, first century B.C. Marble, 14³/₈ ins (36.5 cm) high. Metropolitan Museum of Art, New York (Rogers Fund, 1903).

Architecture

Given the practicality of the Roman mind, it is not surprising to find that a distinctive Roman style is most evident in architecture. The clarity of form we found in the post-and-lintel structure of the classical Greek temple is also present in the Roman arch, but while in Greek architectural composition the part is subordinate to the whole, in Roman architecture each part often carries its own significance. The result is that we can usually surmise the appearance of a whole structure from one element.

Little survives of the architecture of the Republican period, but the use of Corinthian features and the graceful lines of what remains suggest a strong Hellenistic influence. There are notable differences, however. Hellenistic temples were built on an impressive scale (see Fig. **3.32**; Temple of the Olympian Zeus). Classical Greek temples were smaller, and Roman temples were smaller still, principally because Roman worship was mostly a private rather than a public matter.

Roman temple architecture employed ENGAGED COLUMNS—that is, columns partly embedded in the wall—and as a result, Roman temples lacked the open colonnades of their Greek counterparts, and this gave them a closed, slightly mysterious atmosphere. The Temple of Fortuna Virilis (Fig. **4.7**), which dates from the second century B.C. is the earliest well-preserved example of its kind. Greek influence may be seen in the delicate Ionic columns and entablature, but Etruscan elements are also present in the deep porch and in the engaged columns that are necessitated by the wide CELLA, or main enclosed space. (The one-room cella departs from the Etruscan convention of three rooms.) The Romans used the cella for displaying trophies from military campaigns, as well as to house the image of the deity.

Theatre

Comedy

The Romans loved entertainment. Roman comedy was wild, unrestrained, lewd, and highly realistic. Accounts of stage events suggest that very little was left to the audience's imagination. Actors wore various masks, and grotesquely padded costumes.

As Roman comedy developed in the third and second centuries B.C., it borrowed much from Hellenistic comedy, with its large theatres, high stages, and elaborate scene buildings (see Chapter 3). The Romans were receptive to comedy, and assimilated it quickly, and the importation of Greek comedy led to the rise of two of Rome's most important playwrights, Plautus (c. 254–184 B.C.) and Terence (c. 185–159 B.C.).

The twenty plays by Plautus (PLAW-tuhs) that survive provide a picture of a playwright who was principally a translator and adaptor. He copied Greek originals, changing the locations to Rome and inserting details of Roman domestic life. His characters were types, not individuals: the braggart soldier, the miser, the parasite, and the wily but mistreated slave. With their slapstick humor and "sight gags," Plautus' plays are full of farcical energy and appeal directly to the emotions, not to the intellect. They are not particularly well written, but they work well enough on stage.

Terence, who was better educated than Plautus and a more literary writer, enjoyed the support of a wealthy patron. In his six extant plays he appears to be a dramatist capable of drawing universal situations and characters. Like Plautus, he had a great influence on the theatre of later ages, but he was not particularly popular with Roman audiences, perhaps because he did not use banality and buffoonery.

Theatre fulfilled an important social function in keeping the minds of the masses off their problems. Yet it also served as a forum in which the general public could address grievances to the bureaucracy. When an official of the state had betrayed his trust, when a wrong had been suffered, or when an impropriety of state had become flagrant, the bite of Roman satire could be fierce, direct, and penetrating.

Blood Sport

Although we may not think of it in formal terms as theatre, blood sport had most of the trappings of theatre for the Romans and for other Mediterranean cultures that embraced it. A typical "performance" opened with the *pompa* or procession which featured the trainers, sponsors, and, of course, the gladiators. The acts included "lesser" animal fights, and, finally, the intermissions when public executions took place. These intermission–executions had nothing directly to do with blood sport. The gladiatorial fights were the featured performances and the majority of Gladiators, by the late Republic, were not slaves but volunteers who willingly forfeited their rights and property, and pledged not only to suffer intensely but to die fighting.

Although Gladiators may have been considered monsters outside the arena, they displayed, or "performed," what it meant to be Roman while they fought. The concept of *virtus* (honor above life), a specifically male trait to the Romans, was most often applied to the gladiator who fought well or continued to fight even after defeat. If a gladiator displayed these honorable traits but was clearly at the end of a losing bout, a display of *virtus* would enable him or her to raise one finger—the plea for clemency or mercy. Because Romans were more

interested in a good fight rather than bloodshed for its own sake, they could, and it seems usually did, grant *missio* or clemency for combatants so that the Gladiator could fight another day.

Interestingly, this need for Gladiators to display *virtus* in victory as well as in defeat (as in "baring one's neck") caused more conservative Romans to find it difficult to appreciate the Christian concept of martyrdom. Marcus Aurelius, when witnessing Christians making, in his mind, a show out of their deaths, complained that "Christians were shameless exhibitionists in their zeal for martyrdom." Marcus Aurelius expressed in Stoic fashion (see next section and p. 122) that Christians were essentially debasing the games.

The animal fights, however, provide evidence of the most elaborate theatrical performances. They included elaborate costumes and stage props, and a strong interest in illusions which would accompany the performing of debased Greek myths. For example, in one documented case, in Rome, the myth of Icarus was performed and involved the illusion of flight. The "fantasy" was abruptly shattered when the sorry individual came crashing back to earth—only to be met by a group of hungry lions.[1]

Philosophy and Religion

Rome assimilated much of its philosophical thought from the Greeks and the Hellenistic world. The earliest divinities of Rome were nature-spirits who dwelt in trees, in springs, and on hilltops. In addition to Jupiter, the sky-spirit, Saturnus, a spirit of agriculture, and Mars, a spirit of agriculture and of war, there were gods of the home—for example, Janus, god of the doorway, and Vesta, goddess of the hearth-fire. No shrine was regarded with greater veneration than that of Vesta, where the sacred fire was kept burning. The round base of the shrine can still be seen in the Roman Forum.

As Rome's influence spread outward and interreacted with other cultures, other divinities took their place in the Roman pantheon, in some cases displacing and in other cases merging with earlier Roman gods and goddess. In time, the gods of Rome were identified with the gods of Olympus and assumed their functions while retaining their Roman names. In 500 B.C., a great temple was dedicated to the triad Jupiter, Juno, and Minerva, the equivalents of the Greek gods Zeus, Hera, and Athena.

Roman culture was particularly receptive to Stoicism. For the Stoic, reason, or *logos*, governed the world, and the Great Intelligence was god. The main tenets of Stoicism were acceptance of fate and duty, and the kinship of all people. The latter idea gave to Roman law the goal of providing justice for everyone, and this was one of Rome's great contributions to subsequent Western culture. Essentially, however, Stoicism was deterministic. The Great Intelligence controlled all things, and a person could do nothing but submit to this greater will.

On its way to Rome, Stoicism passed into the hands of Diogenes of Babylon in the second century B.C., a period known as the Middle Stoa. Diogenes (dy-AH-jen-eez) brought Stoicism to Rome in 156–155 B.C., and he lectured on his philosophy, favorably impressing the Romans. In the early first century B.C., Stoicism finally lost much of its cynicism, became more cultured and universal, and more attuned to the Roman spirit. It adopted Aristotle's definition of virtue as a "golden mean," and espoused the belief that material goods might not only be a means to right living, but could also be pursued as an end in themselves. An emphasis on temperance, propriety in daily life, and the performance of daily duty made Stoicism even more attractive to the Roman way of thinking.

As a result, Rome became the home of Stoic philosophy. The worldliness and common sense of the Romans made it into a mellow, urbane, and tolerant set of beliefs, and freed it from intellectual and moral dogmatism.

THE ROMAN EMPIRE

Augustus

If anyone had hoped that the assassination of Julius Caesar would bring about the return of Republican rule, they must surely have been disappointed, for the political turbulence simply continued. Caesar's assassins and his old commanders battled for control, while orators like Cicero labored to save the old Republic. In the end, Julius Caesar's great nephew and adopted son Octavian—known to history as Augustus Caesar—outmaneuvered and outfought everyone.

The year after his uncle's death, Octavian and his allies of the Caesarian faction joined forces in an alliance called the Second Triumvirate. By means of intrigue and threat, they coerced the Senate into granting them—and their legions—the power to restore peace to the Roman state. In the battle of Philippi (fil-IP-y), in northern Greece in 42 B.C., Octavian and his allies defeated the conspirators who had assassinated Julius Caesar. However, peace was not at

Map 4.2 The Roman Empire A.D. 14–284.

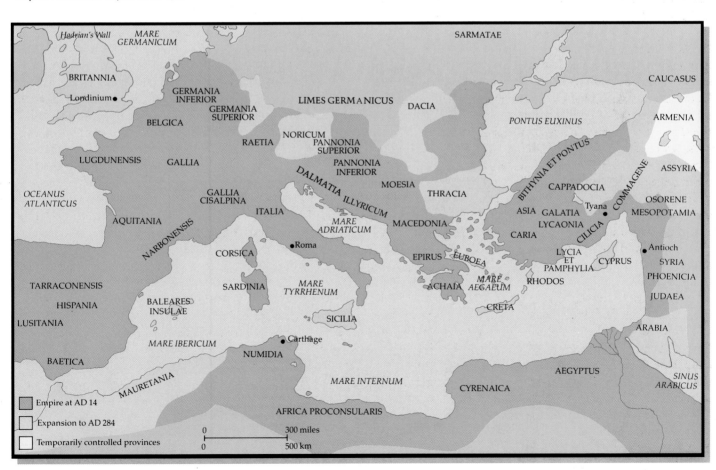

hand. Octavian split with his former allies, especially with Mark Antony, who was now Cleopatra's lover. In a climactic naval battle at Actium in 31 B.C., Octavian defeated Mark Antony. Antony's death and Octavian's victory effectively ended the Roman Civil War. In the thirty-seventh poem in his first book of *Odes*, the poet Horace wrote in response: *Nunc est bibendum nunc pede libero pulsanda tellus!* ("Now is the time for drinking, now, with unshackled foot, for dancing!") Octavian took power, and Horace hailed him as "Caesar," which, for the first time, became an honorific title.

Gaius Julius Caesar Octavianus held both military command (*imperium*) and tribunician power (spokesperson for the people); he was both chief priest (*pontifex maximus*) and first citizen (*princeps*). He was also politically astute enough to adorn reality with palatable outward forms, replacing democracy with autocracy in a way that did not antagonize the public. He called on the services of culture, religion, literature, architecture, and the visual arts to help create a new picture of the world,

with the result that there was a politically inspired aesthetic revolution, which led to the legalization of absolute power. In 27 B.C., Octavian formally divested himself of all authority. In response, the Senate and the people promptly gave it back to him, voting him the title Augustus (the Fortunate and Blessed). Although he was never officially "emperor" of Rome at all, within four years he had assumed complete power—including the right of veto over any law. The Republic was formally dead.

During the forty-five years that Augustus ruled (31 B.C.–A.D. 14), the Senate and popular assemblies continued to meet. However, the election of consuls, proconsuls, tribunes, and other officials required his blessing, the Senate was filled with Augustus' friends, and the popular assemblies seem to have lost all political function. As commander of the armies, he ruled all the vast territories of an empire that reached to the Rivers Rhine and Danube in what is now Germany. He commanded in the name of his uncle, Julius Caesar, and on the basis of his own military victories, claiming that he brought peace and order after a

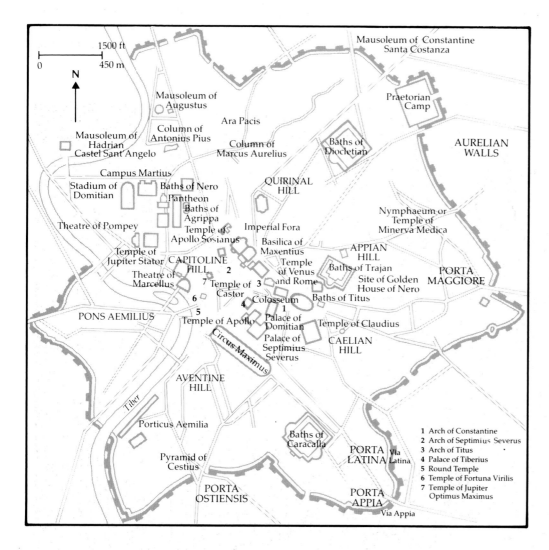

4.8 Imperial Rome.

century of civil wars. He rebuilt temples to the Olympian gods, the "divine" Julius Caesar, and to "Rome and Augustus." He built roads, bridges, and aqueducts, established a sound currency, nurtured honest government, and maintained peace, which lasted nearly two hundred years.

Pax Romana

"The Roman Peace" (*Pax Romana*) brought under a single government a huge geographical area (Map **4.2**). The Augustan heritage was carried forward during the first and second centuries by a number of excellent emperors—for example, Claudius, Trajan, Hadrian, and Marcus Aurelius. The city of Rome spread out across its "seven hills" (Fig. **4.8**) and Roman citizenship was granted to the peoples of Italy (Map **4.3**) and the far-flung provinces, which meant that they were equal to their conquerors and could serve in the army, the bureaucracy, and higher levels of government. Roman administration and Roman law kept order, prosperity, and peace intact. The Roman administrative system developed a closely supervised hierarchy of professional officials, who made the machinery of day-to-day living work for the people. At its height, the Roman Empire covered more than 3 million square miles (7.78 million square kilometers): just slightly less than the size of the United States of today. The population was approximately 80 million. The entire empire was linked by a system of roads reaching out from a central hub at Rome. Wherever the Romans went, they took their culture. Roman theatres, for example, were built in Orange, France, and Sabratha in North Africa.

The age was not entirely free of calamities and tyrants—in the modern sense of the word. Along with good emperors came the insane Caligula (kuh-LIG-yoo-luh) and Nero, who crucified Christians and drove Gaul to revolt. It was a time in which anyone who took up arms against Rome had their right hand severed as punishment. Overall, however, it was a time of peace and prosperity (Fig. **4.9**).

The best of times ended at the end of the reign of Marcus Aurelius (MAHR-kuhs oh-REEL-ee-uhs; A.D. 161–180), called the Stoic emperor (see p. 122). In A.D. 180 the army seized power and, to all intents and purposes, central authority in Rome collapsed. Emperors came and went, largely at the whim of the army. Standards of living declined precipitously as the population moved from the countryside to cities that became bloated by the

4.9 Scale model of ancient Rome. Museo della Civiltà Romana, Rome.

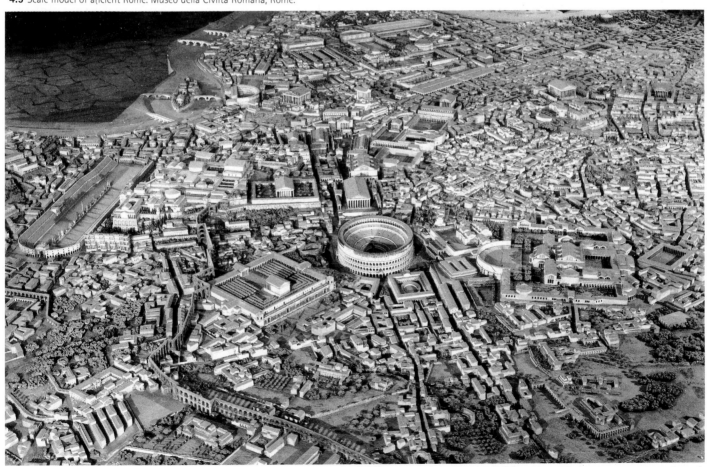

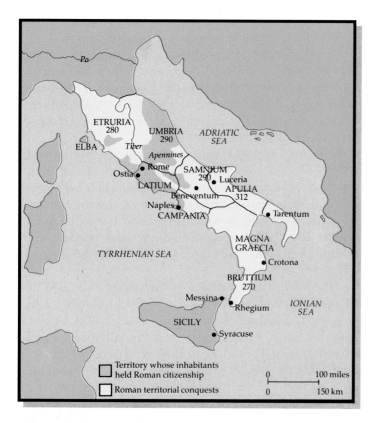

Map 4.3 Italy during the Roman Empire A.D. 14–284, showing dates (B.C.) conquered.

poor living on public charity. Taxes rose and the middle class shrank. New pressures along the borders further destabilized the empire. Although, as we shall see in the next chapter, the empire survived for another century, with a brief resurgence under Diocletian and Constantine, Rome was in its death throes as an empire.

Roman Law

Probably the most influential concept developed by the Romans in any field was the technique for deciding how general laws could be applied to specific cases (jurisprudence). This question was dealt with by legal experts—jurisconsults—who were not part of the state machinery, but who had special knowledge of the meanings of laws. Judges were able to choose only from opinions they submitted; the jurisconsults, in effect, became the lawmakers.

Thus a knowledge of the law and a body of expert opinion on its interpretation was established and handed down. Legal knowledge replaced family and position as a requisite for the practice of law.

Roman law was transformed from a set of isolated instances into a legal system by applying philosophical methods to legal cases: drawing out similarities and differences between them. General principles could thus be laid down. These showed how laws should be applied consistently, thereby making the law predictable and the same for all.

Philosophy

Seneca

The changes wrought on Stoicism by the Romans and the general nature of the times are illustrated by the writings of the Roman philosopher, dramatist, and statesman, Seneca (SEN-uh-kuh; 8 B.C.–A.D. 65). "Austere and somewhat sanctimonious by nature, he was given to deploring human weakness and to bewailing the vanity and wickedness of the world, from which he professed himself to await impatiently release in a happier home beyond the grave."[2] He was not, however, averse to success in his own life. His business sense was shrewd, and he was tireless in his attempts to increase the considerable fortune he had inherited. While the Epicureans deprecated wealth, Seneca staunchly defended the "righteousness of great wealth" in his philosophical sermons. He believed that reason was bankrupt, and late Stoicism saw sentimental and moral needs as sufficient grounds for religious convictions.

Marcus Aurelius and Epictetus

By the time of Augustus Caesar (63 B.C.–A.D. 14), Stoicism had gained popularity among the masses as well as the upper classes, by accepting popular religion as an allegory of the truth. But by the time of Nero (A.D. 37–68), who sought to suppress all freedom of thought, Stoicism, which propounded free inquiry and discussion, had fallen on hard times. It was seen as a threat to the state, and many of its leaders were executed or exiled.

Stoicism reemerged as a central doctrine under the Stoic Emperor Marcus Aurelius (A.D. 121–80), who, along with the slave Epictetus (eh-pik-TEE-tuhs), gave final definition to the revived philosophy. The *Discourses* and the *Manual* of Epictetus and the *Meditations* of Marcus Aurelius show us a somewhat old-fashioned Stoicism, leaning toward austerity and concerned mainly with moral and religious rules of behavior. Stoicism now appealed to the moral sense rather than to the intellect, and it turned people to the "way that led to happiness and peace." Salvation lay in cultivating independence from external circumstances, enriching oneself by religious sentiment, and having faith in "an assurance that all is for the best." Central to the thinking of both Marcus Aurelius and Epictetus was the idea that all people are the "children of

4.10 *Hercules and Telephos*, Roman copy of a Greek work of the second century B.C. Wall painting from Herculaneum, 5 ft 7½ ins (1.71 m) high. Museo Archeologico Nazionale, Naples, Italy.

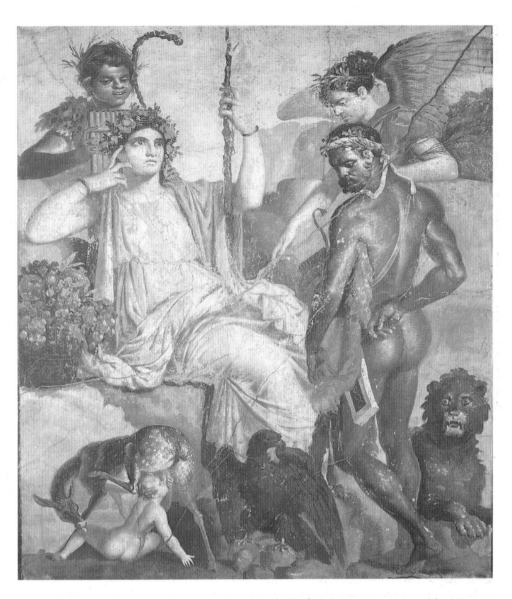

one Father." Thus, everyone, regardless of age or status, should be loved uncritically, as one loves one's family.

Above all, the world was seen as rationally ordered. Everything was an expression of a divine reason. Death was the end of the individual, merging each of us with that from which we sprang, and reuniting our reason with the *logos* of which it was a part. Death was therefore to be neither feared nor desired: it was merely to be accepted. After Marcus Aurelius' death, however, Stoicism lost ground to the emerging Christianity.

Plotinus: Beauty and Symbol

Plotinus (ploh-TY-nuhs; c. 205–270) was an Egyptian-born philosopher and the greatest exponent of the neo-Platonist school: that is, a partial return to Platonic doctrines with additions from Stoic and Epicurean teachings.

According to Plotinus, beauty in art and nature reflect a unified universe—individual beauty is a reflection of harmony in the universe and a higher "reality" on which all experiences of beauty depend. As a result, artists' products are valuable because they are symbols of a higher order of existence. Plotinus was the first philosopher to treat art in a comprehensive manner. In the *Ennead*, Plotinus uses dance as a symbol of how nature has harmony and exists as a "living whole." He also reasons that a universal "Good" is the source of all "Beauty"; artworks—that is, man-made objects of beauty—thus imitate the universal "Beauty" and, in so doing, imitate the "Good." In addition, the arts are able to perfect the incomplete beauty of natural objects. As a result, for Plotinus, artworks occupy a special place in human experience because they form a bridge between incomplete natural objects and the universal concept of beauty, and, therefore, good: art raises the mind to a higher moral plane. An artwork can thus be seen as symbolic in two senses: it symbolizes the natural world, but perfected; and it

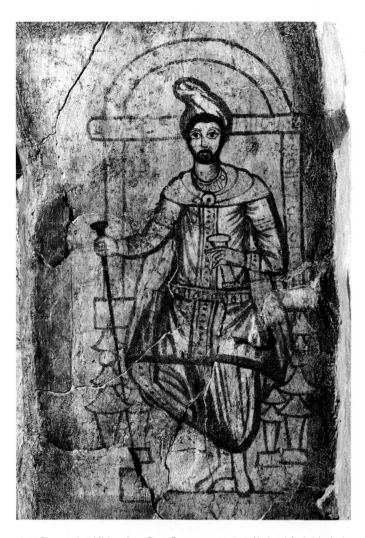

4.11 The prophet Mithra, from Dura-Europos, c. A.D. 245. National Archeological Museum, Damascus, Syria.

symbolizes ultimate reality in the only way comprehensible to human minds.

Religion

By the end of the first century A.D., the most formidable religious cult in the empire was the Persian mystery-cult of Mithra (MITH-ruh), which took root in Rome and was carried by the Roman legions to the far corners of the empire. Roman monuments to Mithra can be found at the borders of Scotland, the shores of the Black Sea, and the frontiers of the Sahara Desert in Africa. Mithraism particularly appealed to soldiers, for it encouraged military virtues, imposed severe self-discipline, abstinence, and control of the passions, and imparted a sense of brotherhood. Mithra was not the supreme god in Mithraism; rather, he was the mediator between an unknowable and unreachable god who dwelt in eternal spheres and a suffering and struggling human race.

Mithra is pictured as constantly engaged in a struggle against the powers of evil (Fig. **4.11**). He had been compelled to catch a bull and, after a struggle, to slay him. From the body of the slaughtered bull came all plants and useful animals. Dogs, scorpions, and other creatures were considered malevolent, and it was with these creatures that Mithra did battle. Mithra also presided over the judgment of souls after death and guided them to their celestial homes, where he received them like children returning from a long voyage. Although Mithra was the god of light, his worship was carried on in underground temples. Those who sought membership of the cult were required to endure a long, painful course of preparation, after which the initiate took an oath called *sacramentum*. The initiate was eventually allowed to participate in a sacred rite in which a loaf of bread and a cup of wine and water were placed before the priest, who pronounced a sacred formula over it. By partaking of the mystical food, the new convert gained power to combat evil spirits and to gain immortality.

Two-Dimensional Art

Although it is less well known than Pompeii (pohm-PAY-ee), the city of Herculaneum (hur-kyoo-LAY-nee-uhm) provides us with excellent examples of wall painting from the Roman Empire period, which were preserved by the ash and lava of Mount Vesuvius' cataclysmic eruption in A.D. 79. In these works, as well as in works from Pompeii, we see that, as in wall painting from the Republican era, brightly colored frescoes were the order of the day. These works also share the naturalism of their predecessors. The wall painting *Hercules and Telephos* (TEL-eh-fohs; Fig. **4.10**) uses highlight and shadow to create marvelously rendered flesh and musculature as well as intricately detailed fabric in the Hellenistic style. Here the subject matter is mythical and heroic: Hercules' discovery of the infant Telephos in Arcadia. Hercules, the dynamic figure on the right, reveals warm flesh and sinewy musculature, full of life and warmth. In contrast, the personification of Arcadia, the semireclining figure, seems distant and remote—as cold as a piece of sculpture. The lion is rendered with quick, rough brushstrokes, which stand in stark contrast to the smooth, delicate treatment of the doe in the lower left. Above Arcadia, a playful Pan with his pipes shows an almost offhand treatment, as flippant as his smirk.

A second example from Herculaneum (Fig. **4.12**) exemplifies the Roman taste for forceful colors and the painted "architectural structuring" of large areas. Paintings are a permanent part of the wall and are "framed" with painted architectural detail. This particular painting was a shrine devoted to the cult of the emperor, and the central panel, which depicts the introduction of Hercules into Olympus in the presence of Minerva and Juno, is a metaphor for the divinity of the emperor.

All the illustrations of Roman wall decoration in this chapter, whether of the earlier Republican or of the Imperial period, demonstrate the colorfulness of Roman interior design. The style of the painting is certainly theatrical, but it has a permanence, not only in that it forms an integral part of the wall, but also in that each panel contains an architecturally complete composition enclosed in a painted "frame." This approach is very different from that of later periods, in which pictures are separate framed entities, and can be moved from place to place.

Sculpture

The straightforward naturalism of the Roman Republic was modified during the Augustan period. Although Hellenistic influence had become strong by the late first century B.C., Greek classical influence always predominated in some quarters, but with a Roman—that is, a more practical and individual—flavor. By the time of the Empire, classical influence had gained precedence, returning sculpture to the idealized character of that of Periclean Athens. Augustus (Fig. 4.13) boasted that when he came to power, Rome was a city of sundried bricks, and that when he left it, it had become a metropolis of marble. Greek classical form in sculpture was revived and translated into vital forms for the Romans. The Greek concept of the "perfect body" held sway. It was common for a sculptor to copy the idealized body of a well-known Greek statue and add to it a portrait head of a contemporary Roman. Other figures after the Greek style were similarly Romanized. A male nude might be draped in a toga; another might be made to represent Augustus in armor. The aesthetics of sculptural depiction thus remained Greek, with Roman clothing added. The pose, rhythm, and movement of the body originated in the past.

At this time much sculpture portrayed the emperor. Emperors had been raised to the status of gods, perhaps because in so far-flung an empire it was useful for people to revere their leaders as superhuman.

Other sculptures told the story of a leader's accomplishments. Trajan's (TRAY-juhn) Column, erected in the Emperor's Forum, rose 128 feet (39 meters) above the pavement on an 18-foot (5.5-meter) base. Atop the 97-foot (30-meter) column stood a more than twice lifesize statue of Trajan (Fig. 4.15). (Trajan's statue was later replaced by a figure of St Peter.) Inside the column, a staircase winds upward to the top. On the outside, from bottom to top, a

spiral band of relief sculpture (Fig. 4.16) depicts the campaign in which Trajan defended Rome. Trajan himself appears ninety times in the narration, each appearance marking the start of a new episode.

The sculpture relies on symbolism and convention. Water is represented by a waving line; mountains, by jagged lines. Proportions are not lifelike, and perspective is irrational. However, the intent and effect are clear. Trajan's story unfolds in a form to be "read" by the man and woman in the street.

We have touched already on the death mask as Roman funerary art. The intricate relief sculpture which decorated Roman SARCOPHAGI (sahr-KAWF-uh-jy) shows the way that Roman art reflected private life. This type of sculpture emerged early in the second century A.D., when the practice of cremation fell out of favor. Marble sarcophagi were adorned with rich and varied relief decoration. There were three major centers of sarcophagus production—Athens, Asia Minor, and Rome—and sarcophagi were often exported before completion and finished at the site. Attic sarcophagi had decoration on all four sides, with scenes drawn from Greek mythology. They were typically carved in high relief, with a somber tone. Sarcophagi from Asia Minor had figures carved almost in the round, against a background of architectural detail. Roman sarcophagi were carved on three sides, with the fourth side designed to sit against a wall. The front typically showed a mythological scene, while the ends were carved with decorative motifs in low relief (Fig. 4.17).

Architecture

In the Augustan age at the beginning of the imperial period, Roman architecture, like contemporary sculpture, was refashioned in Greek style. This accounts to a large extent for the dearth of surviving buildings from previous eras since old buildings were replaced with new ones, in the new style. Temples were built on Greek plans, but the proportions were significantly different from those of the classical Greek.

The first through the fourth centuries A.D. brought what is now typically identified as the "Roman style." The most significant characteristic of this style is the use of the arch as a structural element, in ARCADES and TUNNEL and GROIN VAULTS (Figs. 4.18 and 4.19; see also Fig. 0.11). The Colosseum (Figs. 4.20 and 4.21), the best-known of Roman buildings and one of the most stylistically typical, could seat 50,000 spectators. Combining an arcaded exterior with vaulted corridors, it was a marvel of engineering. The circular sweep of its plan and the curves of the arches are countered by the vertical lines of the engaged columns flanking each arch. The columns at each level are of

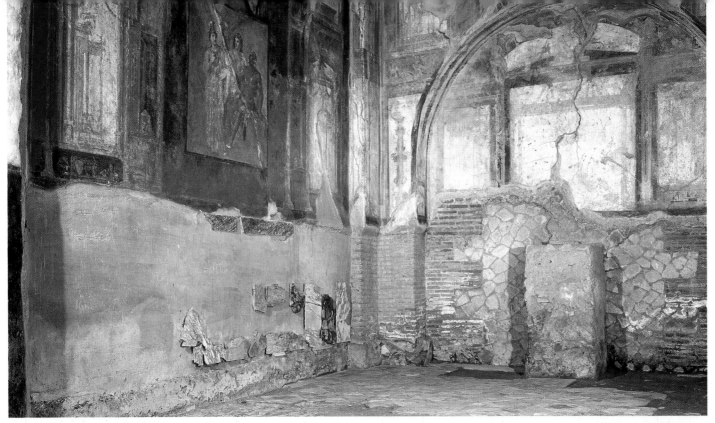

4.12 Wall decoration, c. A.D. 70–79. Wall painting, room dimensions 14 ft 2 ins × 13 ft 4 ins (4.32 × 4.06 m). Collegium of the Augustales, Herculaneum, Italy.

4.13 Augustus in armor, Villa of Livia, Prima Porta, c. 20 B.C. Marble, 6 ft 8 ins (2.03 m) high. Vatican Museums, Rome.

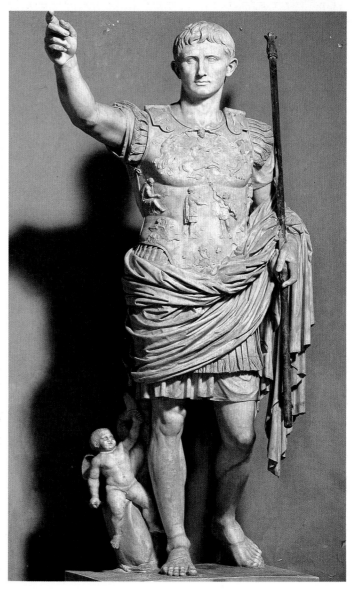

different orders, and progress upward from heavy Doric columns, to Ionic ones, to lighter Corinthian ones at the top level.

Placed in the center of the city of Rome, the Colosseum was the site of gladiatorial games and other spectator sports. Emperors competed with their predecessors to produce the most lavish spectacles there. The Colosseum was a new type of building, called an AMPHITHEATRE, in which two semicircular theatres are combined, facing each other, to form an arena surrounding an oval interior space. Originally, a system of poles and ropes supported awnings to shade spectators. The space below the arena contained animal enclosures, barracks for gladiators, and machines for raising and lowering scenery.

Roman triumphal arches are also impressive architectural monuments. The Roman classical style survives in a memorial to Titus (TY-tuhs), which was raised by his younger brother, Domitian (doh-MIH-shun).

OUR DYNAMIC WORLD

Chinese Painting

At almost the same time as the Roman Empire, the Han dynasty gave China a great empire in the East. The two empires had much in common—both covered vast areas and contained tremendous populations, and in each power was concentrated in the hands of an emperor and an immense, centralized bureaucracy. Like Rome, China perceived itself as the only true civilization, surrounded by barbarians, and in both cases, a significant breakdown of authority occurred early in what we call the Christian era. Interestingly, the two great empires knew of, and, indirectly, traded with, each other.

The Han dynasty produced remarkable scholarship and artistry. Three styles of painting existed during the period of the Han dynasty that spanned the first century A.D. The first style was a rather formal and stiff style, very geometric and HIERATIC, in which the figures were flat and outlined. In contrast, the second style depicted lively action and deep space. The third was midway between the two previous styles, being more painterly and exhibiting movement and lively depictions of, for example, mythic beings, dragons, and rabbits. As can be seen in Figure **4.14**, a tile taken from the lintel and pediment of a Han tomb, masterfully rendered figures are drawn with brushstrokes that suggest liveliness and movement. The figures appear in three-quarter poses, which gives the painting a sense of depth and action, and the active line, with its diagonal sweeps, adds to the sense of action. The poses of the people suggest character—that is, the psychology of the figure portrayed—but although the use of pose and direction reflects a sophisticated approach and technique, the figures remain on the same baseline, with no sense of placement in deeper space.

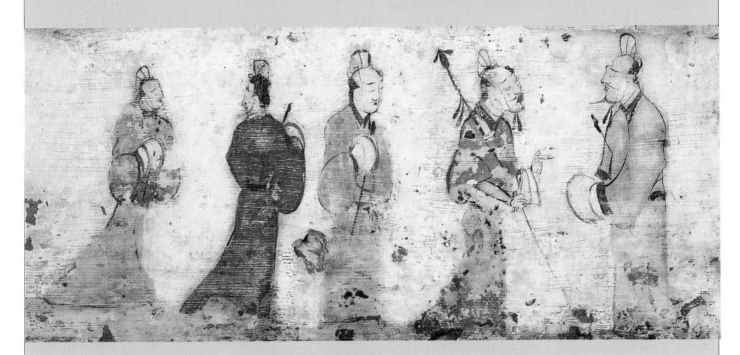

4.14 Lintel and pediment of tomb, Han dynasty, 50 B.C.–A.D. 50. Earthenware, hollow tiles painted in ink and colors on a whitewashed ground, 29 × 80½ ins (73.8 × 204.7 cm). Museum of Fine Arts, Boston (Denman Waldo Ross Collection). (Gift of C.T. Loo).

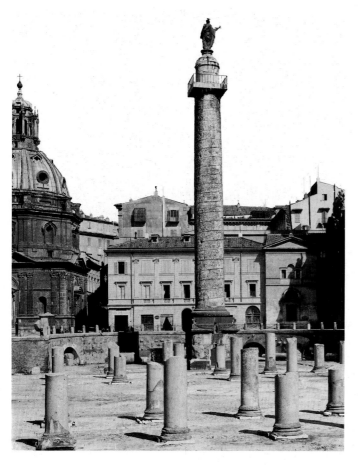

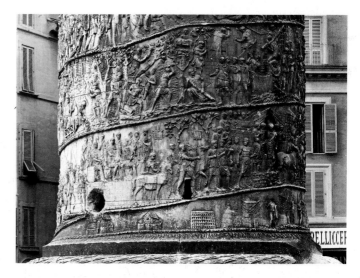

4.16 (*below*) Trajan's Campaign against the Dacians, detail of Trajan's Column, A.D. 106–113. Marble, frieze band 4 ft 2 ins (1.27 m) high.

4.15 Apollodorus of Damascus, Trajan's Column and ruins of Basilica Ulpia, Rome. Trajan's Column, A.D. 106–113. Marble, base 18 ft (5.49 m) high, column 97 ft (29.57 m) high.

4.17 Roman sarcophagus, showing Dionysus, the Seasons, and other figures, c. A.D. 220–230. Marble, 7 ft 3³/₄ ins (2.23 m) long. Metropolitan Museum of Art, New York (Purchase, Joseph Pulitzer Bequest, 1995).

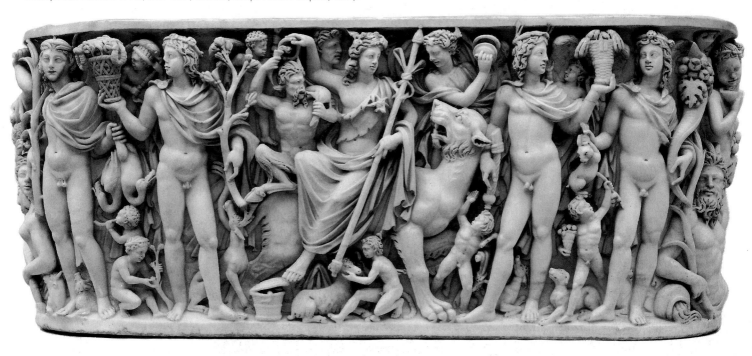

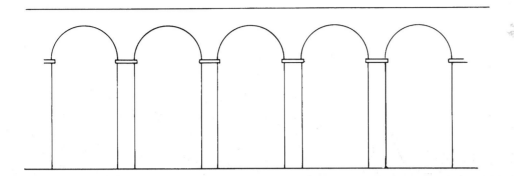

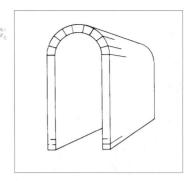

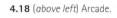

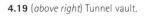

4.18 (*above left*) Arcade.

4.19 (*above right*) Tunnel vault.

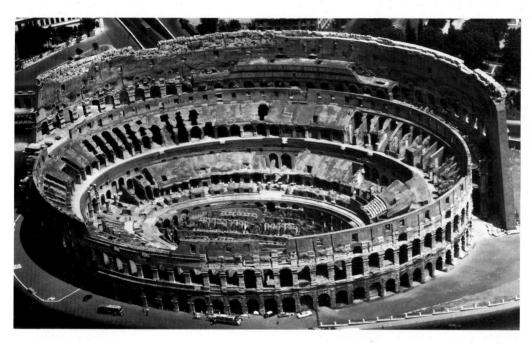

4.20 (*above*) Colosseum, Rome, c. A.D. 70–82. Stone and concrete, 159 ft (48.5 m) high.

4.21 (*right*) Colosseum, interior 616 ft 9 ins (188 m) long; 511 ft 10 ins (156 m) wide.

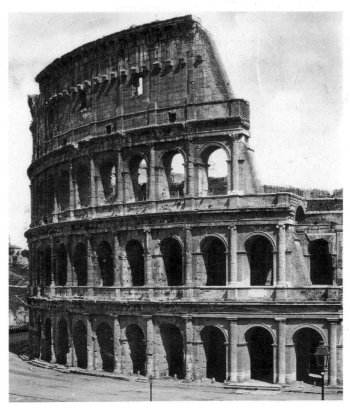

MASTERWORK

The Pantheon

As its name suggests, the Pantheon (PAN-thee-ahn; Figs. **4.22**, **4.23**, and **4.24**) was designed and built, by Hadrian, to honor all the gods. The structure brought together Roman engineering, practicality, and style in a domed temple of unprecedented scale.

Until the mid-nineteenth century, only two buildings had equalled the span of its dome, and during the Middle Ages, it was suspected that demons might be holding up the roof of this pagan temple. Around the circular interior statues of the gods stood in NICHES (NIHCH-ehz) in the massive walls. Corinthian columns add grace and lightness to the lower level. Heavy horizontal moldings accentuate the feeling of open space under the huge dome. The dome itself is 143 feet (44 meters) in both diameter and height (from the floor to the OCULUS, or eye, the round opening at the top of the dome). The circular walls supporting the dome are 20 feet (6 meters) thick and 70 feet (21 meters) high. Square COFFERS on the underside of the dome give an added sense of lightness and reflect the framework

into which concrete was poured. Originally the dome's interior was gilded to suggest "the golden dome of heaven."

In both plan and CROSS-SECTION the Pantheon is designed on a perfect circle: the dome is a hemisphere (Fig. **4.23**). From the exterior, we see a simple, sparsely adorned cylinder capped by a gently curving dome. The entrance is via a porch in the Hellenistic style with graceful Corinthian columns. Originally the porch was approached by a series of steps and a rectangular forecourt, so what remains is only part of a larger, more complex original design.

Inside, both the scale and the detail are overwhelming, but the way in which practical problems have been solved is equally impressive. The drum and dome consist of solid monolithic concrete reinforced with bands of vitrified tile. The vertical gravity loads are collected and distributed to the drum by arches incorporated in the concrete. The wall of the 20-foot-thick drum has alternating rectangular and curved niches cut into it, thus forming a series of massive

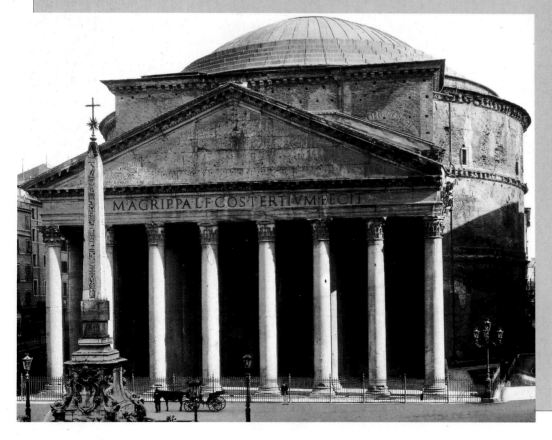

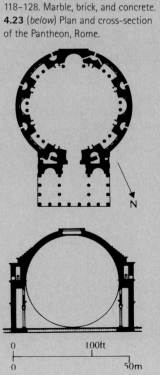

4.22 (*left*) Pantheon, Rome, c. A.D. 118–128. Marble, brick, and concrete. **4.23** (*below*) Plan and cross-section of the Pantheon, Rome.

radial buttresses. Drains cut into the slightly concave floor of the building carry away any rain that falls through the oculus above.

What captures our immediate attention is the sense of space. In most Egyptian and Greek architecture, the focus is on mass—the solids of the buildings. Here, despite the scale and beauty of the solids, it is the vast openness of the interior that strikes us. This is Roman inventiveness and practicality at its best, yet the atmosphere of the building is not one of practical achievement but of sublimity.

How could the Romans build such a colossal structure? Some historians argue that the key lies in a new building technology made possible by concrete containing a specific kind of cement newly developed near Naples. The secret, however, may lie in the mysterious rings around the dome. As a study at Princeton University suggests, they probably "perform a function similar to the buttresses of a Gothic cathedral.... The extra weight of the rings ... helps stabilize the lower portion of the dome. Rather than functioning like a conventional dome, the Pantheon behaves like a circular array of arches, with the weight of the rings holding the end of each arch in place."[3]

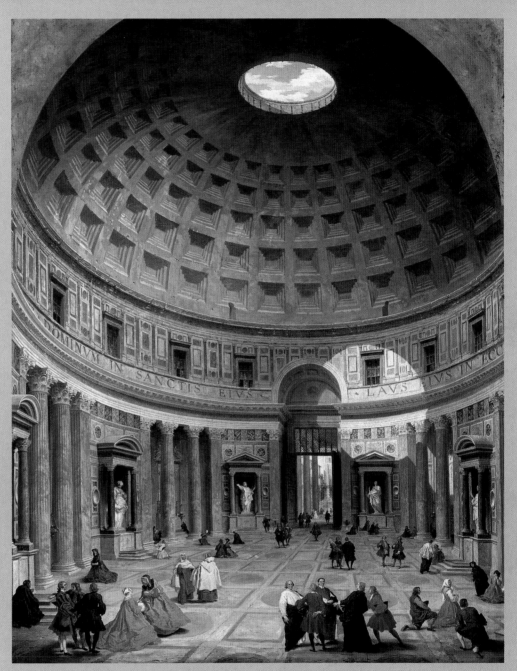

4.24 Giovanni Paolo Panini, *Interior of the Pantheon*, c. 1740. Oil on canvas, 4 ft 2 ins × 3 ft 3 ins (127 × 99 cm). National Gallery of Art, Washington D.C. (Samuel H. Kress Collection).

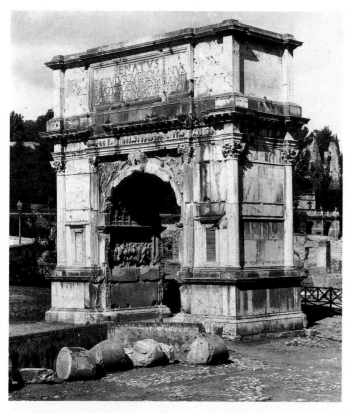

The Arch of Titus (Fig. **4.25**) was a political gesture of homage to the accomplishments of Titus and his father, Vespasian, during the conquest of Jerusalem. The reliefs on the arch illustrate allegories rather than actual historical events. Titus appears as *triumphator*, along with figures such as the *genius Senatus*, or spirit of the Senate, and the *genius populi Romani*, or spirit of the people of Rome. The richly and delicately ornamented FAÇADE of this arch stands in marked contrast to its massive internal structure. This is an important characteristic of Roman architecture, which distinguishes it from Greek principles, in which the structure can always be seen.

Roman engineering not only made heating and cooling possible within homes, but it also created huge MASONRY structures for channeling water tremendous distances. Aqueducts such as that of the Pont du Garde at Nîmes in France (Fig. **4.26**) remind us of just how ingenious and practical the Romans were.

4.25 Arch of Titus, Roman Forum, Rome, c. A.D. 81. Marble, about 50 ft (15 m) high.

4.26 Roman aqueduct at the Pont du Garde, Nîmes, France. Photo: © Paul M.R. Maeyaert, Mont de l'Enclus (Orroir), Belgium.

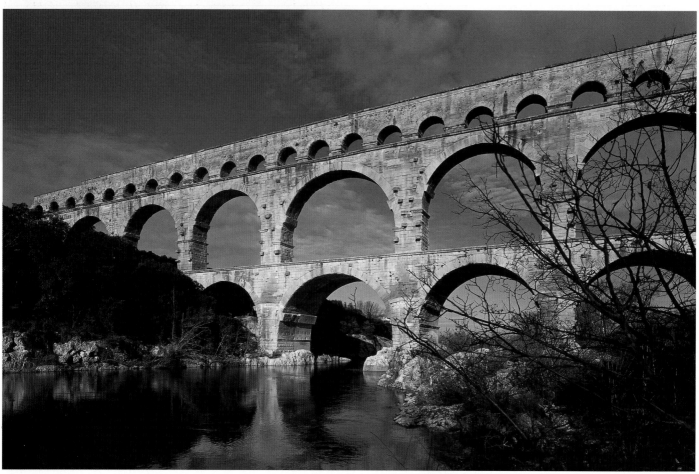

TECHNOLOGY: PUTTING DISCOVERY TO WORK

Cement

In their rapid conquests, the Romans learned quickly to appreciate and to copy other people's mechanical devices. The major contribution to technological development made by the Romans was probably their ability to absorb ideas and then to provide the administrative underpinnings to allow those ideas to be used to their fullest. Many technological practices are credited to Rome, but, in fairness, a large number of these had been invented and practiced elsewhere before the Romans acquired them. Even aqueducts, a much-vaunted Roman innovation, had seen predecessors in Greece, Assyria, Babylonia, Persia, and Egypt, and the same was true of drainage systems, which, as we noted, were part of the technology of Minoa. Roman roads were no better than those in Greece and Persia.

One of the truly original contributions of Rome to technology was the introduction of cement. In addition to its uses as a bonding material, the Romans discovered that it could be used in the making of concrete, which, when combined with a brick facing, allowed them to construct solid arches, thus eliminat-

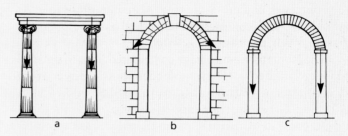

4.27 Diagram showing the stresses involved in (a) the Greek post and lintel; (b) a true arch; and (c) the Roman arch.

ing the need for buttressing (Fig. **4.27**). This type of arch was seen most frequently in the construction of aqueducts, but the development of the brick-and-concrete arch may also be considered a major Roman contribution to technology. Essentially, this consisted of a brick arch reinforced with a heavy infill of concrete. Once the concrete set, the arch became a vast lintel that exerted little lateral pressure. Thus, the pillars that supported it required no supporting buttresses.

Music

Music was very popular among the Romans. Contemporary reports describe festivals, competitions, and virtuoso performances. Many Roman emperors were patrons of music, and Greek music teachers were popular and very well paid. Large choruses and orchestras performed regularly, and the *hydraulos* (hy-DRAWL-ohs), or water organ, was a popular attraction at the Colosseum (Fig. **4.28**). The *hydraulos* was apparently so loud that it could be heard a mile away, and the fact that it provided "background music" for the spectacles in which Christians were fed to lions meant that it was banned from Christian churches for centuries.

Aristotle had deplored professionalism in the pursuit of music. Music, he believed, existed for its own aesthetic qualities and as a moral force in character development. It was a measure of intelligence. The pragmatic Romans did not see it this way. Professional dexterity and *virtuosity* were social assets, and meaningless accomplishments, such as blowing the loudest tone or holding the longest note, were rewarded with great acclaim. Musical entertainment

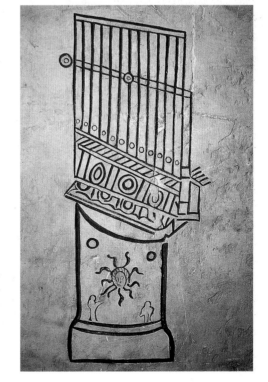

4.28 Roman *hydraulos*, copy of graffito in the church of St Paul, Rome, fourth century A.D. Photo: C.M. Dixon.

did fulfill an important social and political function for the Romans, however. As more and more people flocked to Rome from conquered territories, the numbers of the poor grew. The state began to provide entertainments to keep them occupied and under control. "Bread and circuses" became the answer to the dissatisfactions of the poor and the oppressed, and music also played an important role. As a result, music became less an individual pastime and more an exclusively professional activity.

The Romans seem to have contributed little to musical practice or theory. They took their music direct from Greece after it became a Roman province in 146 B.C., adopting Greek instruments and theory. But they did invent some new instruments, principally brass trumpets and horns for military use.

Literature

The practical early Romans did not produce any remarkable literature. When literature as an art form did become reasonably popular, it was Greek slaves who nurtured it.

The first literary works were imitations of Greek works, and they were written in Greek. Latin was initially considered a peasant language, with few words capable of expressing abstract notions. A Latin prose style and vocabulary for the expression of philosophical ideas had to wait.

During the reign of Augustus, the poets Horace and Vergil were commanded to write verses glorifying the emperor, the origins of Rome, the simple honesty of rural Roman life, patriotism, and the glory of dying for one's country. Livy set about retelling Roman history in sweeping style. Vergil's *Aeneid*, an epic account of the journey of Aeneas from the ruins of Troy to the shores of Italy, far surpasses mere propaganda.

Vergil makes Aeneas the founder of Roman greatness by making him the founder of Lavinium, the parent town of Alba Longa and Rome. Aeneas had been told, as he left the burning ruins of Troy, that he was fated to found a new city with a glorious destiny in the west.

In Book I, Aeneas, traveling to his fated destination, runs into foul weather which forces him to land his fleet on the coast of Libya, where he is welcomed by the widowed Dido, queen of Carthage. In Books II and III, Aeneas tells Dido of the natural and supernatural events that led him to

PROFILE

Vergil (70–19 B.C.)

Rome's greatest poet, Publius Vergilius Maro, loved the rural countryside. He was born a peasant, and he focused the central force of his poetry on people. His writings also reveal his thorough education in Cremona, Milan, and Rome and the influence of the Epicureans and Stoics, who were central to the rhetoric and philosophy of his studies. Shy and retiring, he seems never to have participated in politics or the military; he was a poet first and foremost. Nevertheless, he kept in close contact with current events, and his works often reflect an overview of contemporary Roman life.

His first work, the *Eclogues* (EK-lawgs), brought him immediate recognition and access to the exclusive literary circles of Rome. The following years, 37–30 B.C., were spent writing the *Georgics*, and the remainder of his life was occupied by the *Aeneid* (i-NEE-id), which is to Rome what the *Iliad* and the *Odyssey* are to Greece (see p. 72).

The twelve books of the *Aeneid* tell the story of Rome, and in them Vergil sought to hold up to his readers the qualities of Roman character and Roman virtues that had made the city great. The first six books tell the story of Aeneas' wanderings—as Homer had told of Ulysses' travels in the *Odyssey*—and the final six books set the scenes of battle—as Homer did in the *Iliad*. Further internal similarities exist as well.

Vergil's influence on literature and Western thought is probably greater than any other classical poet. His poetry reflects consummate skill in the use of diction, rhythm, and word music. Above all, he captures a quality of the human condition, elevated to a grand scale, with which every human being can identify. At the time of his death, Vergil was highly troubled by the imperfections he found in the *Aeneid*, and he wanted to burn it. However, the Emperor Augustus refused to allow the work to be destroyed and had it published, with some minor revisions, two years after the poet's death.

her shore. In Book IV, Dido confesses her love for Aeneas. Aeneas, however, regretting his fate, must set sail again—forced to do so by the gods. Dido prepares to kill herself. Book V finds the Trojans journeying to Sicily, where they engage in a series of contests to commemorate the death of Aeneas' father, Anchises. Then they cast off again. Book VI tells of Aeneas' journey to the underworld and Elysium, where he meets the ghosts of Dido and Anchises. Aeneas learns of the destiny of Rome. In Books VII through XII, the Trojans reach the Tiber River and are received by Latinus, the king of the region. Spurred by the gods, other Latins resent Aeneas and the Trojans' arrival and the proposed marriage of Aeneas to Lavinia, daughter of Latinus. War ensues, but the Trojans, with the help of the Etruscans, emerge victorious. Aeneas marries Lavinia and founds Lavinium.

Here is a brief excerpt from the beginning of Book I:

Arms and the man I sing, who first made way
Predestined exile, from the Trojan shore
To Italy, the blest Lavinian strand.
Smitten by storms he was on land and sea
By violence of Heaven, to satisfy
Stern Juno's sleepless wrath; and much in war.
He suffered, seeking at the last to found
The city, and bring o'er his fathers' gods
To safe abode in Latium; whence arose
The Latin race, old Alba's reverend lords,
And from her hills wide-walled, imperial Rome.[4]

Horace (b. 65 B.C.) was an outstanding Latin lyric poet and satirist. The most frequent themes of his *Odes* and verse *Epistles* are love, friendship, philosophy, and the art of poetry. Son of a former slave, Horace was educated in Rome and traveled to Athens, where he attended lectures at the Academy. In the *Odes*, Horace represented himself as heir to earlier Greek lyric poets but displayed a sensitive, economical mastery all his own.

Little is known about Livy's life, and nothing about his family background. Probably he spent most of his life in Rome, and attracted the attention of Augustus while he was fairly young. Livy's lifework was the composition of his history of Rome, composed of 142 Books. Unfortunately, only Books 21–45 survive, along with summaries of the books after Book 45. Unique among Roman historians, Livy took no part in politics. Thus, his writing seeks no historical explanations in political terms. He saw history in terms of human personalities and representative individuals rather than partisan politics. Together with Cicero and Tacitus (TAS-ih-tuhs), Livy set a new standard for Roman literary style by writing in Latin rather than Greek.

On the other hand, Plutarch (PLOO-tahrk; c. A.D. 46–after 119) wrote in Greek and strongly influenced the evolution of the essay, biography, and historical writing in Europe between the sixteenth and nineteenth centuries. Plutarch's literary output was immense, but his popularity rests on his *Parallel Lives*, a series of biographies of famous Greeks and Romans, an example of which follows. We can see a visual representation of the story in a painting by Poussin from the seventeenth century (see Fig. **13.15**).

Phocion
402?–317 B.C.
Translated by John Dryden

. . . Although he was most gentle and humane in his disposition, his aspect was stern and forbidding, so that he was seldom accosted alone by any who were not intimate with him. When Chares once made some remark on his frowning looks, the Athenians laughed at the jest. "My sullenness," said Phocion, "never yet made any of you sad, but these men's jollities have given you sorrow enough." In like manner Phocion's language, also, was full of instruction, abounding in happy maxims and wise thoughts, but admitted no embellishments to its austere and commanding brevity. Zeno said a philosopher should never speak till his words had been steeped in meaning; and such, it may be said, were Phocion's, crowding the greatest amount of significance into the smallest allowance of space. And to this probably, Polyeuctus, the Sphettian, referred, when he said that Demosthenes was, indeed, the best orator of his time, but Phocion the most powerful speaker.

His dead body was excluded from burial within the boundaries of the country, and none of the Athenians could light a funeral pile to burn the corpse; neither durst any of his friends venture to concern themselves about it. A certain Conopian, a man who used to do these offices for hire, took the body and carried it beyond Eleusis, and procuring fire from over the frontier of Megara, burned it. Phocion's wife, with her servant-maids, being present and assisting at the solemnity, raised there an empty tomb, and performed the customary libations, and gathering up the bones in her lap, and bringing them home by night, dug a place for them by the fireside in her house, saying, "Blessed hearth, to your custody I commit the remains of a good and brave man, and, I beseech you, protect and restore them to the sepulchre of his fathers, when the Athenians return to their right minds."

And, indeed, a very little time and their own sad experience soon informed them what an excellent governor, and how great an example and guardian of justice and of temperance they had bereft themselves of. And now they decreed him a statue of brass, and his bones to be buried honourably at the public charge.

Catullus (b. c. 84 B.C.) was a poet whose expressions of love and hatred are generally considered the finest lyric poetry of ancient Rome. The facts of Catullus' life are few, but the poet Ovid states that Catullus died young. His poetry reflects strong emotion and twenty-five of his poems portray an unhappy love affair with a woman named Clodia. Most of the poems are written in forms that served for inscriptions and dedications and as verse of light occasions, satirical comment, and elegant sentiment.

Here is one example:

—15—

If man can find rich consolation, remembering his
    good deeds and all he has done,
if he remembers his loyalty to others, nor abuses his
    religion by heartless betrayal
of friends to the anger of powerful gods,
then, my Catullus, the long years before you shall
    not sink in darkness with all hope gone,
wandering, dismayed, through the ruins of love.
All the devotion that man gives to man, you have
    given, Catullus,
your heart and your brain flowed into a love that
    was desolate, wasted, nor can it return.
But why, why do you crucify love and yourself
    through the years?
Take what the gods have to offer and standing
    serene, rise forth as a rock against darkening
    skies;
and yet you do nothing but grieve, sunken deep in
    your sorrow, Catullus,
for it is hard, hard to throw aside years lived in
    poisonous love that has tainted your brain
and must end.
If this seems impossible now, you must rise
to salvation. O gods of pity and mercy, descend and
    witness my sorrow, if ever
you have looked upon man in his hour of death, see
    me now in despair.
Tear this loathsome disease from my brain. Look, a
    subtle corruption has entered my bones,
no longer shall happiness flow through my veins like
    a river. No longer I pray
that she love me again, that her body be chaste, mine
    forever.
Cleanse my soul of this sickness of love, give me
    power to rise, resurrected, to thrust love aside.
I have given my heart to the gods. O hear me,
    omnipotent heaven,
and ease me of love and its pain.

A moralizing Stoicism runs throughout the literature of the Augustan period. In poetry, this Stoicism was expressed through satire, which allowed writers to combine morality with popular appeal. Martial and Juve-

nal used satire to attack vice by describing it in graphic detail. Petronius produced satirical PICARESQUES in verse and prose that were as readable as Martial's and Juvenal's work, but free of their moralizing.

Finally, Apuleius (ap-yuh-LEE-uhs) and Lucan (LOO-kuhn) followed in the same tradition. Apuleius' *Golden Ass* is one of the earliest precursors of the novel. The author creates a fictional biography that describes how the central character is tried and condemned to death for the murder of three wineskins. He is brought back to life by a sorceress, but as he tries to follow her in the form of a bird, he is changed instead into an ass. The only cure for this affliction appears to be the procurement of some rose leaves, and in his search for these, he has bizarre and fantastic adventures.

Dance

One of Rome's significant legacies was the unique dance form of pantomime. Pylades of Cilicia (PY-luh-deez; sil-IH-shuh) and Buthyllus (boo-THY-luhs) of Alexandria are credited with the invention of pantomime, around 22 B.C. They brought together a number of dance elements, some of which dated to prehistoric Greece. Although the words "mime" and "pantomime" are sometimes used interchangeably in our vocabulary, they were very different art forms. Pantomime was serious and interpretative. Some pictorial evidence suggests that a single dancer portrayed many roles by changing costumes and masks. Wind, brass, and string instruments played as the dancer leapt, twisted, and performed acrobatic feats. The interpretation of delicate emotions also played a part. Pantomimes often had tragic themes, apparently taken from Greek and Roman tragedies and mythology. But many pantomimes also had a distinctly sexual orientation that some sources call pornographic.

This dance form fell into disfavor as its lewdness increased. Treated comically, lewdness may have been tolerable, even endearing. The same subject matter treated seriously, however, may have become tedious or obnoxious, even to the pragmatic (and decadent) Romans. The more notorious emperors, such as Nero and Caligula, apparently loved pantomime, as did certain of the populace. Eventually, however, pantomimists were forced out of the major cities to the provinces. These itinerant entertainers may have helped to keep theatrical dance alive through the Middle Ages and into the Renaissance.

Focal Point
Augustus—Classical Visions

The aesthetic revolution at the start of the Roman Empire saw a shift in the purpose of art toward propaganda. One of the artistic ramifications of Augustus' new political order was the emergence of the NEO-ATTIC style.

Sculptural works, with their new emphasis on portraying the emperor, can be divided into three main types. These are differentiated by scholars primarily by hairstyle, while facial features remain recognizably the same. In the first type (Fig. **4.29**), before Octavian was made emperor, his hair is shown in disorder. The second type (Fig. **4.30**) depicts the same man (now called Augustus) as emperor, with a more refined, nobler face and the hair divided into two strands above the right eyebrow. In the third type (Fig. **4.31**), the forelock is gone, and the hair is combed to the side.

The essence of Roman neo-Attic sculpture, however, is to be found in the statue of Augustus shown in Figure **4.13**. The portrait head of the Emperor sits on an idealized, youthful body like that Polyclitus made for his *Lance Bearer* (see Fig. **3.7**). Unlike the lance bearer, however, Augustus reaches outside his cube of compositional space,

and the final effect is much less introspective and more dignified than that of its prototype.

The Forum of Augustus in Rome (Figs **4.32** and **4.33**) exemplifies monumental Imperial art at its classical grandest. In both its conception and its dimensions, it speaks of greatness. Constructed from war booty, the Forum honors Mars the Avenger, to whom Octavian had made a vow during his wars against the assassins of Julius Caesar. The Forum's style reflects Augustus' view that in all the arts the Greeks had achieved perfection in the classical style. All this served to establish Augustus as the greatest among *summi viri*, or the greatest "among all the great men of Roman history."[5]

Vergil's *Aeneid* tells not only the story of the legendary founding of Rome by Aeneas of Troy, but, further, as a kind of dual birth, the Roman unification of the world by Augustus—both events viewed as extraordinary tasks, glorious achievements, and divinely ordained necessities.

Finally, we turn to a "jewel" of Augustan classicism, the *Ara Pacis*, or Altar of Peace (Fig. **4.34**). It is representative of a movement toward a saturating symbolism, in

4.29 Octavian, copy of a type created in 31 B.C. Marble, 14⅝ ins (37.2 cm) high. Museo Capitolino, Rome.

4.30 Augustus, copy of a type created in 27 B.C. Bronze, 16⅞ ins (42.9 cm) high. British Museum, London.

4.31 Augustus, final type before 12 B.C. Marble, 12 ins (30.5 cm) high. Museum of Fine Arts, Boston (Gift of Edward W. Forbes).

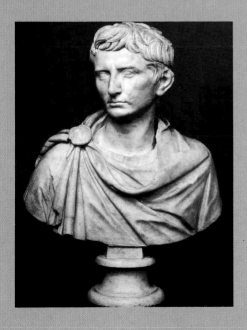

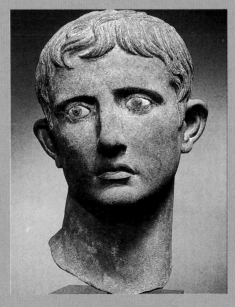

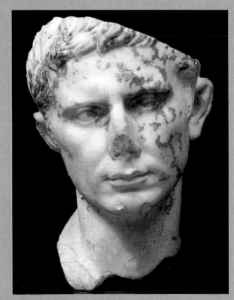

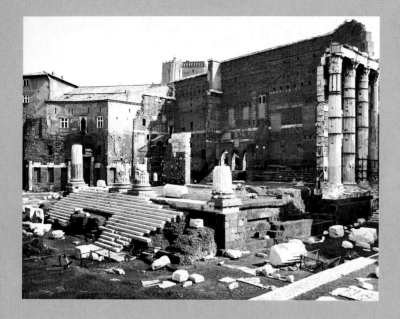

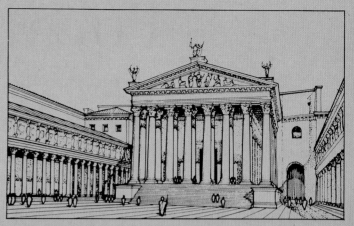

4.32 (*left*) Temple of Mars the Avenger, Forum of Augustus, Rome, from the south, dedicated 2 B.C. Marble facing over stone and concrete.

4.33 (*above*) Temple of Mars the Avenger, Forum of Augustus, reconstructed view.

4.34 *Ara Pacis* (Altar of Peace), Rome, 13–9 B.C. Marble. Outer wall about 34 ft 5 ins × 38 × 23 ft (10.5 × 11.6 × 7 m).

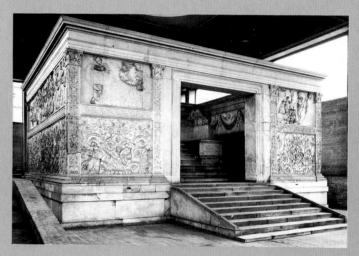

which every detail was intended to convey meaning. Here, even apparently decorative elements are symbolic: the garlands, or swags, strung from ox-skulls represent peace, while the fact that they are composed of varieties of fruit which do not ripen together symbolizes the unending nature of this peace. The figures themselves, though their poses are perfectly natural, exude royal dignity and nobility, characteristics that Augustus sought to emphasize in the popular conception of himself. The whole altar, dedicated to peace, thus serves as an image of the golden age of Augustus—that is, an era of peace and prosperity whose source was the emperor himself.

Monumentality, symbolism, practicality, and a resurrection of Greek classicism adapted to Roman tastes—these are the hallmarks of the Augustan age. Taken together, they describe what we have come to know as Roman classicism, and they reflect the quintessence of Roman life, as the Romans themselves saw it.

CHAPTER REVIEW

Critical Thought

Remarkably, the Roman genius for organization created a system that, although it certainly did not foster a cultural ethos like that of the Hellenes, nonetheless worked efficiently enough to ensure that, under a single government, the world knew relative peace and prosperity. Augustus Caesar was one of the cleverest politicians of all history. In addition to knowing how to manipulate public opinion in order to achieve his own ends, he knew the power of art and literature in shaping a public persona and public opinion, much as today's media consultants and "spin-doctors" do. Augustus used art and literature to invent not only his own aura but that of Rome itself.

If we walk the streets of Rome today, we see a curious amalgam of the old and the new. The Colosseum's tattered remains rise shakily above a heavily traveled thoroughfare, and across the street we walk through the Roman Forum, whose fragmented remains surround us like giant tombstones in a quiet cemetery. In other places, we can look down into the ruins of the Empire and marvel at how high the current street is above the ground of 2,000 years ago. Elsewhere, Imperial ruins have simply been incorporated into later construction to create a curious timewarp.

The ruins of Pompeii and Herculaneum, as well as Rome, tell us that life—at least for some—during the Roman Empire must have been fairly pleasant. In the mild Mediterranean climate, homes of marble, centered on an open courtyard and richly decorated with wall paintings, would be inviting and comfortable, even by modern standards. The solid proportions of classical Greece must have suggested to Romans a sense of order and stability that seemed eternal. Of course, it was not—but then, neither were they. Were they aware of the subtle changes taking place around the edges of their society? Were they able to compare it with what it once was? Were they able to grasp when the zenith had been reached?

Summary

After reading this chapter you should be able to:

- Characterize Roman Republican art and architecture and compare them with those of the Roman Empire.
- Discuss Roman theatrical, musical, and dance forms.
- Explain the philosophies of Seneca, Marcus Aurelius, Epictetus, and Plotinus.
- Identify the various aspects of Roman religions and cults.
- Describe the main directions of Roman literature and its writers.
- Apply the elements and principles of composition to analyze and compare individual works of Roman art and architecture.

CHAPTER FIVE

Judaism and Early Christianity

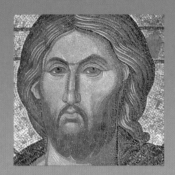

OUTLINE

THE PEOPLE OF ISRAEL
The Patriarchs
The Ten Commandments
Conquest and the Judges
The United Monarchy
The Divided Kingdom and Exile
The Post-Exilic Period and Beyond
  PROFILE: Solomon
The Hebrew Bible
Jewish Art and Architecture
  MASTERWORK: The Temple of
  Jerusalem

CHRISTIANITY
  OUR DYNAMIC WORLD: Shinto
  Sculpture in Japan
Jesus Christ and His Teachings
The Apostolic Mission
The Early Christian Church

**CHRISTIANITY AND THE LATE
ROMAN EMPIRE**
Diocletian
Constantine

**LATE ROMAN AND EARLY
CHRISTIAN ART**
The Visual Arts and Architecture
Literature
Music
  TECHNOLOGY: Matches

FOCAL POINT: ST PAUL AND THE
WESTERNIZATION OF
CHRISTIANITY

VIEW

THE JUDEO-CHRISTIAN HERITAGE

The chapters of this textbook unfold more or less chronologically. At this point in our journey, however, we must halt our forward momentum to backtrack, because during the Roman Imperial period a different heritage—the Judeo-Christian—made a new and significant impact on Rome and on Western civilization. Judaism was already an important religion and culture in the Mediterranean, but it was, essentially, an Eastern religion. Out of it came a new religion, Christianity, whose translation by the Apostle Paul into terms compatible with Greek thinking spread it throughout the Roman Empire, profoundly changing the course of Roman and European history. To pull these relationships together, we must return to the Middle East, some two thousand years before Augustus Caesar, and work our way forward again.

A relationship exists between Judaism and Christianity. As we will see, in the early years their worship forms were indistinguishable, and many Christians believed that becoming a Christian meant first converting to Judaism.

Above Detail of Fig. **5.14**.

5.1 The apse, S. Apollinare in Classe, c. A.D. 540–47. Ravenna, Italy.

KEY TERMS

Some of the basic terms and concepts we will encounter in this chapter include the following:

Torah, "The Teaching," the Old Testament books of Genesis, Exodus, Leviticus, and Deuteronomy, which include statements of Jewish doctrine, practice, religion, and morals.

Neoplatonism was a philosophy and religious system developed in the third century A.D., based on the doctrines of Plato and other Greek philosophers, and combined with elements of Oriental mysticism, and some Judaic and Christian concepts.

Affective means related to feelings and emotions as opposed to facts.

Rebus, a riddle composed of symbols suggesting the sounds they represent.

Clerestory, a row of windows in the upper part of a wall.

Basilica is a term that in Roman times referred to building function, usually a law court; it was later used by Christians to refer to church buildings and to a specific form of church buildings.

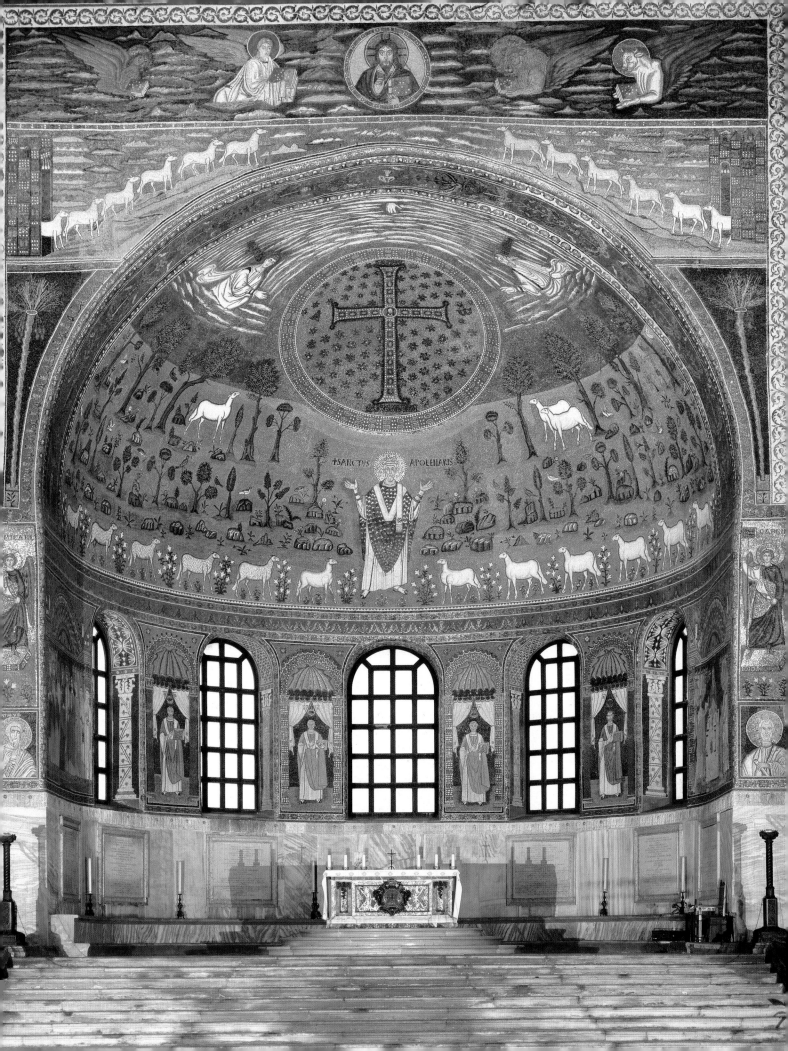

The story of Israel is an unbroken chain of development from which came a new religion and perhaps the most fundamental force in the shaping of the Western world—that is, Christianity. Christianity overlaps the Roman Empire, and at the time that the Empire was in its nadir, Christianity was in its ascent. In actual terms, Christianity and the Roman Empire overlapped for nearly five hundred years, but it was not until the late third century that, as strong forces, they intertwined significantly. Thus, it is now appropriate that in our chronological development of Western culture, we take up the subject of the final years of the Roman Empire and the development of Christianity.

In order to do so, however, we must backtrack not only through the previous three centuries of Rome to the Caesar Augustus who appointed King Herod of Judea and ordered all the world to be taxed, thus bringing Joseph and a pregnant Mary to Bethlehem, but also through history to a time in the second millennium B.C. when the "father of nations," Abraham, began a chain of events that led to Judaism, Christianity, and Islam.

THE PEOPLE OF ISRAEL

The Patriarchs

Abraham

The ancestors of Israel were seminomadic peoples from Mesopotamia. The Israelites traced their history back to a patriarch named Abram (later Abraham) who lived in "Ur of the Chaldees" in the second millennium B.C.

5.2 *The Sacrifice of Isaac.* Mosaic. Beth-Alpha Synagogue.

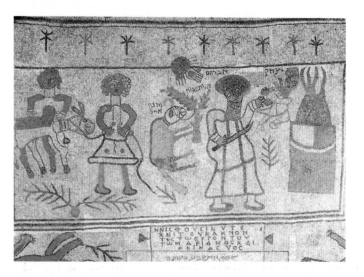

Abram took his wife and household from the heathen environment of Haran and traveled to Canaan. Canaan held a particular spiritual appeal to Abram, because he believed that the land there was suitable for the fulfillment of a destiny to which he had been appointed by God. Canaan (KAY-nuhn) was a secluded hill country, which made it possible for Abram and his people to practice their religion in relative peace and isolation. On the other hand, Canaan lay quite close to important trade routes of the ancient world, and was thus in a good position for spreading the new religion (Map **5.1**). Because they came from the other side of the Euphrates (yoo-FRAY-teez), Abram and his family were known as Hebrews, from a word meaning "the other side." Abram had a son, Isaac, through whose line of descent God's promises were seen to continue. As a boy, Isaac was nearly sacrificed by Abram at God's command (Genesis, chapter 22; Fig. **5.2**).

Moses

In the fifteenth century B.C. when the Hebrews were in slavery in Egypt, there arose a national liberator named Moses. During one particularly cruel oppression, the Pharaoh ordered the slaughter of all Hebrew children. To avoid this, the mother of the infant Moses made a basket of bulrushes and set the baby afloat in the Nile near where Pharaoh's sister bathed. The princess found the baby, adopted him, and brought him up in the royal court. However, when Moses killed an Egyptian who was abusing an Israelite, he was forced to flee the country to Midian, east of Egypt, where he became a shepherd.

One day, while he was tending his flocks in the Sinai wilderness, he came to Mount Horeb, and there heard the voice of God coming from a burning bush that was not consumed by the fire. God ordered him to return to Egypt to deliver his brethren from bondage and lead them to the land of promise. Moses returned to Egypt in approximately 1450 B.C. The enslaved Hebrews soon recognized Moses' message as authentic, but convincing the ruling Pharaoh was another matter entirely. However, after a series of divine visitations, known as the ten plagues, Pharaoh's heart was softened and he allowed the people of Israel to depart from Egypt, by biblical reckoning, approximately 1250 B.C. (Fig. **5.3**).

Moses led his people from Egypt toward the Sinai wilderness by way of the Red Sea, which they crossed by a miraculous parting of the waters (Fig. **5.4**). Pharaoh had changed his mind, and the Egyptian army was in hot pursuit when they were swallowed up as the sea crashed in upon them. The result of the miracle gave Moses' people a greater sensitivity to divine promise and action and inspired their faith to new heights. The God of their fathers was seen as he who saved them from bondage and would spare them from the hands of their enemies.

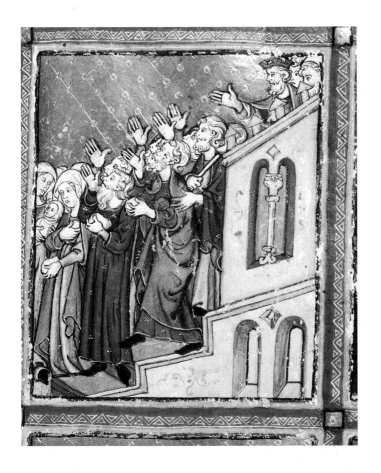

The Selection of Israel

In the third month after their escape from Egypt, the Israelites arrived at Sinai, a burning desert with steep cliffs and volcanic mountains. Here, they made a covenant with their God, Yahweh (YAH-way): He would be their God, and they would be his people. The Sinai covenant had its roots in Yahweh's covenant with Abraham, which, in turn, could be traced to the covenant with Noah, and, thereby, to a framework in which humanity, made in the image of God, must conform to the character of God. Because God is a creating God, humankind must also create and work with God in maintaining and developing the work God had committed, in the creation of the world, into human care. Obedience to God must express itself in obedience to his moral law—that is, *justice* and *righteousness*. Thus, the selection of Israel as a people formed an important moment of universal history in the eyes of the Judaic tradition.

Ratification of God's covenant with Abraham came in a covenant with Israel at Sinai, expressed in the giving of the Ten Commandments, or Decalogue.

5.3 Miniature from the *Golden Haggadah* (Spanish), fourteenth century A.D. The Jews are portrayed leaving Egypt "with a high hand"—a Hebrew expression meaning "triumphantly," but here illustrated literally. British Museum, London.

Map 5.1 Lands of the Bible.

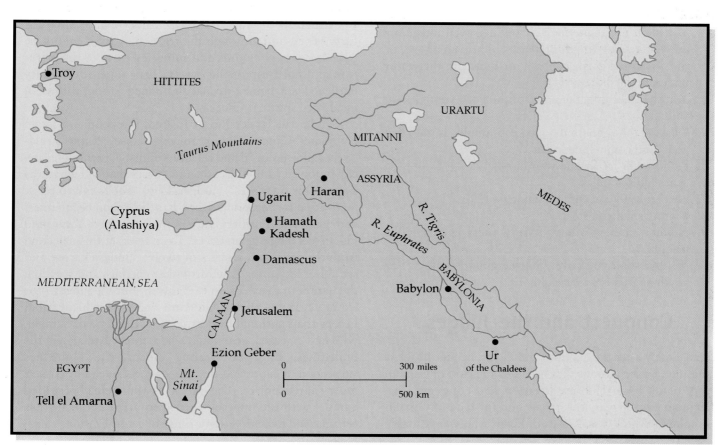

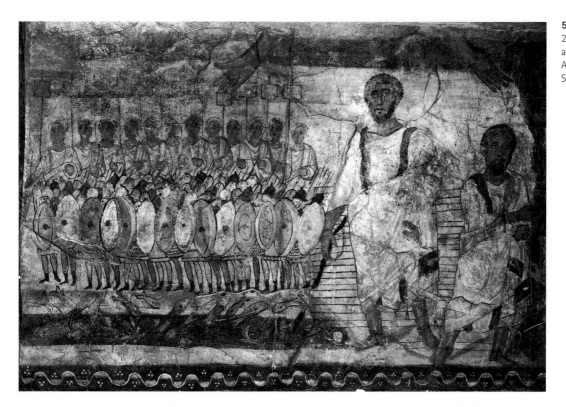

5.4 *Crossing the Red Sea*, c. A.D. 245. Fresco from the synagogue at Dura-Europos. National Archeological Museum, Damascus, Syria.

The Ten Commandments

(Deuteronomy 5:6–21)
1. You shall have no other gods before me.
2. You shall not make for yourself a graven image, or any likeness of any thing that is in heaven above, or that is on the earth beneath, or that is in the water under the earth. . . .
3. You shall not take the name of the Lord your God in vain. . . .
4. Observe the sabbath day, to keep it holy, as the Lord your God commanded you. . . .
5. Honor your father and your mother. . . .
6. You shall not kill.
7. Neither shall you commit adultery.
8. Neither shall you steal.
9. Neither shall you bear false witness against your neighbor.
10. Neither shall you covet your neighbor's wife . . . or anything that is your neighbor's.

Conquest and the Judges

Immediately after the exodus from Egypt, neither Israel as a nation nor the nations that occupied the land of Canaan were ready for a Hebrew invasion and conquest. The Egyptian empire was still strong, and the land of Canaan contained several vassal kings of Egypt who were capable of banding together to resist such an invasion. As a people fresh from servitude, the Israelites had not yet progressed to a point of unification and cohesion, but were still an undisciplined, spiritually immature, and fractious group. They therefore wandered in the wilderness of Sinai for forty years, and although the route they took cannot be traced, it was circuitous and subjected them to the privation and hardship of the desert. That time of difficulty hardened Israel into a strong, disciplined nation, with well-inculcated spiritual values.

Under the leadership of Joshua, the people of Israel conquered Canaan and organized themselves into a relatively stable political and religious entity. A period of anarchy followed Joshua's death, and "every man did what was right in his own eyes" (Judges 17:6). Too weak to resist infiltration by bordering tribes, Israelites soon began intermarrying with outsiders and turning away from Yahweh to idolatrous religious practices. To counteract this defection from the covenant, a series of twelve "Judges" arose and set about liberating Israel from her enemies and recalling the nation to the worship of Yahweh. But the judges—for example, Deborah and Gideon—were more local tribal heroes than national leaders, and by the time of Samuel, who had emerged as a judge, a new threat had arisen: the Philistines. In a devastating defeat, the Philistines succeeded in capturing the Ark of the Covenant, Israel's most sacred object. The shock of this defeat provided Samuel with the impetus needed to bring about further reforms and to achieve some sense of centralization, which

	GENERAL EVENTS	LITERATURE & PHILOSOPHY	VISUAL ART & ARCHITECTURE	PERFORMING ARTS
2000 B.C.				
	Patriarchs in Canaan			
1700 B.C.				
	Jacob's descendants in Egypt			
1500 B.C.				
	Moses Exodus	Ten Commandments		
1200 B.C.				
	Invasion of Canaan Period of Judges Saul			
1000 B.C.				
	David Solomon	First Bible	Temple of Solomon (5.7–5.11)	
900 B.C.				
	Divided Kingdom			
800 B.C.				
	Isaiah			
700 B.C.				
	Fall of Samaria			
600 B.C.				
	Destruction of Jerusalem Exile First exiles return		Rebuilding of Temple	
500 B.C.				
	Judea under the Seleucids Maccabean rebellion			
100 B.C.				
	Roman capture of Jerusalem Herod the Great			
0 B.C./A.D.				
	Jesus Christ St Paul	Synoptic Gospels		
A.D. 100				
	Emperor Domitian		Catacomb painting (5.22, 5.23)	
A.D. 200				
		Tertullian	Synagogue of Dura-Europos (5.6) SS. Pietro e Marcellino (5.15, 5.23)	
A.D. 300				
	Emperor Diocletian Constantine Constantinople founded		Baths of Diocletian (5.25) Basilica of Constantine (5.26, 5.27) St Peter's Basilica (5.28) The Good Shepherd (5.21) Chi-Rho (5.18)	Christian hymnody
		St Augustine	Sarcophagus of Bassus (5.24) San Paolo Fuori le Mura (5.29)	
A.D. 400				
	Christianity a state religion Fall of Rome			

Timeline 5.1 Judaism and early Christianity.

led, in turn, to a great clamor for the appointment of a king. After initial resistance by Samuel and the careful delineation of the powers of the king, Saul was chosen by common consent of the people, and became probably the first constitutional king in history.

The United Monarchy

Although he was unable to meet all the demands placed on him, Saul was able to free Israel from the Philistines and to unify the nation. It lay to David, however, to consolidate the monarchy. The prophet Samuel chose David as the instrument of Yahweh, and at first David was Saul's comforter and right arm, but he was also immensely popular with the people, which made Saul jealous and vengeful. In the ensuing struggle, David became king, and Israel's golden age began. He unified the tribes of Israel and extended the kingdom from Phoenicia in the west to the Arabian Desert in the east, and from the River Orontes in the north to the Gulf of Aqaba in the south. He ultimately captured the Canaanite stronghold of Jerusalem, where he established a national and religious capital in which his son Solomon built the great Temple.

The Divided Kingdom and Exile

Following the death of Solomon, a dispute over succession split the nation into Northern and Southern Kingdoms, with Jerusalem remaining the capital of the Southern Kingdom. The division left the nation weakened, and in the eighth century B.C. the Northern Kingdom fell to the Assyrians. The period between Solomon and the Assyrian conquest of the Northern Kingdom, which was called Samaria, gave rise to the great prophet Isaiah. Subsequently, the exile and dispersion of the Northern peoples led to their being called the "Lost Tribes of Israel." In 587 B.C., the Babylonians conquered the Southern Kingdom, now called Judah, destroyed Solomon's Temple, and carried the people into the Babylonian Captivity.

The Post-Exilic Period and Beyond

At the end of the sixth century, Cyrus the Great led the Persian Empire to dominion in the Middle East. After conquering the Babylonians, Cyrus freed the Jews, as they were now called, and in 538 B.C. the first exiles were able to return from Babylon. In 515 the Temple was rebuilt, and the next hundred years witnessed the building projects and leadership of Nehemiah (nee-eh-MY-uh) and Ezra. It

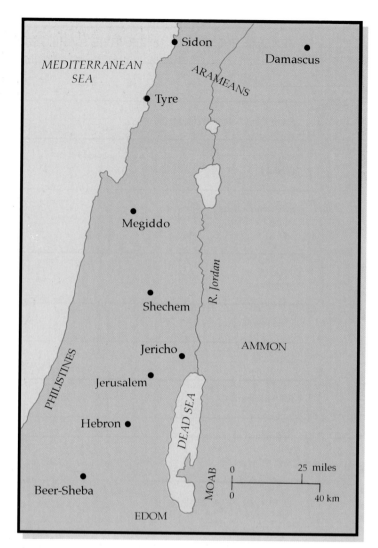

Map 5.2 Palestine.

was a time of spiritual revival and the renewal of religious rites and practices for the Jews, who believed that their God had rescued them. As a result, they established a theocracy—that is, a government ruled by those who are believed to have special divine approval and direction. Although many exiles returned to their homeland, many did not, and these Jews, who remained outside their homeland, became known as Jews of the Diaspora—that is, the Dispersion. A group called the Pharisees (FAIR-i-seez), mistakenly confused with the Sadducees (SA-jyoo-seez) in the New Testament, were responsible for the preservation and codification of Jewish religious practice (the "Mishnah"), which had been centered, by law, around the Temple.

In 332 B.C., Alexander the Great conquered the region. After his death, the Hellenistic Empire was divided and Judah fell under a series of foreign rulers. At this time, Jewish visions of the apocalypse were popularized. Antiochus IV (an-TY-oh-kuhs), a descendant of the Seleucid (suh-LOO-sid) kings who ruled this part of the Hellenistic

PROFILE

Solomon (c. tenth century B.C.)

Solomon, son of David and Bathsheba, ruled Israel for forty years during the second third of the tenth century B.C. In Hebrew the name meant "Yahweh's beloved," as indicated in the biblical book of Samuel II, 12:25. While David still ruled, he affirmed his commitment to make Solomon his successor. The priest Zadok, with the assistance of the prophet Nathan, installed Solomon as co-regent until David's death, when Solomon's brother Adonijah sought Bathsheba's support in his request to marry Abishag, who had served David in his old age. Regarding this move as a threat, Solomon had Adonijah executed, and others, who were seen as accomplices, were expelled from Jerusalem.

Solomon effected a political consolidation of Israel and created administrative districts that cut across old tribal lines. He also expanded Israel's international affairs, and his empire included trade routes that linked Africa, Asia, Arabia, and Asia Minor. Solomon's political and commercial activities brought much wealth and a cosmopolitan sophistication to the kingdom, and his wisdom "surpassed the wisdom of all the people of the east, and all the wisdom of Egypt" (1 Kings 4:30, Hebrews 5:10). The Bible ascribes seven hundred wives to Solomon, including many whom he undoubtedly married as part of political alliances. Solomon's extensive building program included stone cities as well as fortifications, and in Jerusalem, he built an elaborate palace complex and a temple. His reign brought the promises made to the patriarchs of Israel to fruition. On the other hand, the influx of foreign practices marks the beginning of a religious decay that increased internal dissent and external enemies.

Empire after Alexander the Great's death, singled out and banned Jewish practice and culture in 168–167 B.C. As a result, a group of peasants, known as the Hasmoneans (haz-MOHN-ee-uhns), started a mini-rebellion. Two conflicting accounts of the period occur in Maccabees I and II. Initially regarded as saviors, the Hasmoneans soon became even more of a threat to Jewish religious practice than even Antiochus IV had been.

A brief uprising by the Maccabees under Judas Maccabeus (JOO-duhs mac-uh-BAY-uhs) brought a short period of independence around 165 B.C. Within a century, Israel fell under the rule of Rome. In A.D. 70, after an uprising in Jerusalem, the Romans sacked the city and destroyed the Temple. A small band of rebels held off the Romans for two years at a mountain fortress called Massada until it, too, fell in A.D. 73. The destruction of the Temple of Jerusalem meant the destruction of Israel and the Judaic nation.

The Hebrew Bible

The word "bible" comes from the Greek word for book, and it refers to the town of Byblos, which exported the papyrus reed used in the ancient world for making books. The Jews compiled the history of their culture and religion into a collection of sacred writings called scriptures. The compilation grew from the oral traditions of the Hebrew people and took shape over a period of years as it was assembled, transcribed, and verified by state officials and scholars. The Bible has been handed down in a variety of forms. The Hebrew Bible, often called the Masoretic Text (MT), is a collection of twenty-four books written in Hebrew, with a few passages in Aramaic.

The earliest written Bible probably dates to the United Monarchy in the tenth century B.C. It is composed of an assemblage of history, songs, stories, and prophecy. After the Babylonian Captivity, in the fifth century B.C., Jewish religious leaders and scholars carefully scrutinized the body of writings and established a canon—that is, an officially accepted compilation—that was believed to be divinely inspired. The first canon consisted of the Torah or the Pentateuch, the first five books of the current Bible. The current Hebrew Bible was canonized by the Council of Jamnia in A.D. 90. It contained three parts: The Law (Torah), the Prophets, and the Writings.

During the Hellenistic period major centers of Judaism existed in Syria, Asia Minor, Babylonia, and, particularly, in Alexandria, Egypt. Here, the Jewish Canon was translated into Greek and called the Septuagint, meaning "seventy" from the seventy scholars who were supposed to have worked on it.

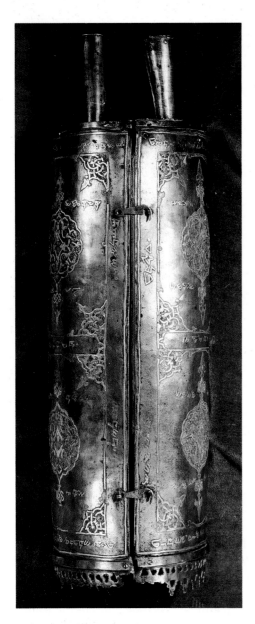

5.5 Joseph (maker, first name), Torah case from Damascus, Syria, 1565. Copper inlaid with silver, 32 ins (81.3 cm) high. Jewish Museum, New York.

The Torah

The Torah (TOH-ruh), meaning "the teaching," includes doctrine and practice, religion, and morals. It contains the books of Genesis, Exodus, Leviticus, and Deuteronomy. The commandments, in addition to the Decalogue, were designed to prepare Israel for a holy mission that the nation would be called upon to undertake in order to become "holy unto God." The preparation entails a separation from all that is opposed to the will of God and a dedication to his service. Thus, holiness meant religion and morality. In religion, the holiness of Israel meant abhorring idolatry and its associated practices, such as human sacrifice, sacred prostitution, divination, and magic. It also meant adopting a cult and ritual that were ennobling and elevating. In morals, holiness meant resisting the urges of nature that were self-serving and adopting an ethic in which service to others lay at the center of life. Consequently, the Torah, as given to Israel, prescribes two sets of laws that connect religion and morality—that is, belief and practice. In their positive nature, they are intended to carry a dynamism that can transform individuals and, therefore, societies. Disregard of the law thus becomes not an individual but a social offense.

Fundamental to moral law in the Torah are the two principles, mentioned earlier, of justice and righteousness. These lie at the heart of humankind's creative cooperation with God. Justice meant the recognition of six fundamental rights: the right to live; the right of possession; the right to work; the right to clothing; the right to shelter; and the right of the person, which includes the right to leisure and liberty and the prohibition to hate, avenge, or bear a grudge. Righteousness manifested itself in the acceptance of duties—for example, concern for the poor, the weak, and the helpless, whether friend or foe—and although possession of earthly goods was a right, it was also a divine trust.

The Torah constitutes the uniqueness of the religion of Israel (Fig. 5.5). The distinct approach of the Torah to the conduct of human behavior is by way of the heart. It speaks to the mind concerning duties, but applies itself to the heart in terms of the perversities of vices and evil. Torah embraces all of life and, thus, becomes a means for strengthening the supremacy of holy will and bringing all life into relationship with serving God. In the Torah we find, for example, the stories of the Creation, Adam and Eve, Noah and the Flood, Joseph and the Coat of Many Colors, the Ten Commandments, and the law of "an eye for an eye."

The Prophets

The Prophets include the Former Prophets—that is, Joshua, Judges, Samuel, Kings—and the Latter Prophets—that is, Isaiah, Jeremiah, Ezekiel (y-ZAY-uh; Jair-uh-MY-uh; ih-ZEEK-ee-uhl), and the twelve minor prophets. These books record the history of Israel and Judah and further develop Hebrew concepts of God, his nature, and the Hebrews' relationship to him. They tell the story of the conquest of Canaan, the Judges, and the United Monarchy, and describe the development of the theocratic state in the post-Babylonian Captivity period. They also tell the stories of the battle of Jericho (JAIR-ih-koh), Samson and Delilah, Daniel and the lions' den, King Saul, David and Goliath, and King Solomon and the Temple of Jerusalem. They contain the well-known images from Isaiah of the "suffering servant" and the saying, "They shall beat their swords into plowshares." Of course, this is more than history. The prophets speak with the authority of God. We tend to think of a prophet as one who predicts the future, but such was not the case with the Hebrew prophets. The Prophets did speak of a coming time of peace and justice when the Messiah would come, but their principal message was one of reconciliation of the Hebrew people with their God. The prophets called upon the people of Israel to return to the ways of the covenant with God and pointed out exactly how they had fallen short of the expectations of that covenant. In a sense, the prophets were social critics. They admonished the people of Israel to remember the Law, which requires justice and decent treatment of the poor, and called on them to turn away from the self-indulgences of the current generation and to return to the compassionate behavior called for in the Torah.

Unlike the Levites (LEE-vyts)—that is, the priestly tribe—whose divine function came as a result of their birth into the tribe of Levi, prophets were individuals called directly by God to preach his word to the nation. The life of a prophet was not an easy one, and prophets like Isaiah often resisted their initial calling. Accepting God's prophetic ministry often meant a violent death—railing against contemporary practice has never been popular.

The Writings

The writings, which contain a variety of literary forms, including poetry and apocalyptic visions, are made up of the biblical books of Psalms, Proverbs, Job, Song of Songs, Ruth, Lamentations, Ecclesiastes (ih-kleez-ee-AS-teez), Esther, Daniel, Ezra, Nehemiah, and Chronicles. The story of Job, for example, tells the story of a righteous man who is beset with calamity so that God can show Satan how a truly righteous man will respond to adversity. Satan maintains that a good man like Job is good only because he is blessed. Take away his comfort and he will curse God. The tale, like many, illustrates the qualities of righteous behavior more than it details the nature of God—although that is present as well. In the book of Ruth we learn of the qualities of love, devotion, and loyalty: "Where you go, I will go. And where you lodge, I will lodge. Your people shall be my people, and your God, my God; where you die, I will die, and there I will be buried. May the Lord do so to me and more also if even death parts me from you" (Ruth 1:16–17). Certain texts within the Writings purport to be from the time of Solomon, but are actually products of the Hellenistic age. These texts include, among others, Song of Songs and Ecclesiastes. These contain words and concepts which would have been completely foreign to Jews from Solomon's time—for example, philosophy, chance/luck, and wisdom ("hachmah").

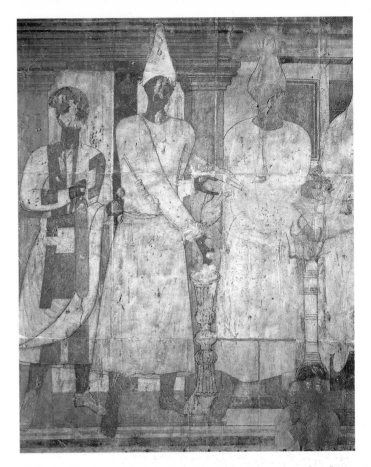

5.6 *The Sacrifice of Conon*, from the assembly hall of the synagogue at Dura-Europos, A.D. 245–256. Mural. National Museum, Damascus, Syria.

Jewish Art and Architecture

Visual Art

The biblical injunction against graven images means that there is little significant Jewish sculpture or painting. Occasionally, however, the injunctions were relaxed sufficiently to allow decoration, and the assembly hall wall of the synagogue at Dura-Europos is one such example (Fig. **5.6**). Dating to approximately A.D. 250, this richly detailed account tells the history of the Chosen People and their covenant with the Lord, and is an attempt to put into pictures the traditions previously restricted to words. Unlike most paintings, there appears to be no unifying relationship among the details of this decoration. Animals, humans, buildings, and cult objects are all exquisitely portrayed, but we find nothing that would tell us how they relate to each other. It is as if the artist assumed that the viewer would understand how these objects coalesce. Nevertheless, if the meaning is hidden, the execution is explicit, and we can find pleasure in the luster of the execution and the sophisticated depiction of details. Although it is less naturalistic than the Roman wall decoration we have previously examined, these depictions reveal a concern with PLASTICITY—that is, three-dimensional space. Human

MASTERWORK

The Temple of Jerusalem

The Temple of Jerusalem was the symbol of Israel's faith as early as its third king, Solomon, son of David (c. 1000 B.C.). Described in 1 Kings 5–9, the Temple of Solomon was primarily the house of the Lord God—Yahweh—as opposed to a place to which common people came to worship. In fact, the general populace had access to only the Temple courts and not to the inside of the structure itself. Even the clergy did not have free access to the building. The inner sanctum remained off limits to everyone except the chief priest, and to him only on the Day of Atonement. Although the public did not have access to the Temple, it was very much a public building in all senses, including politically and economically. Ancient Israel, although a monarchy, remained a theocracy, and the Temple played an important role in the organization and administration of the national community.

Two major rebuilding projects took place between its construction under Solomon and its ultimate destruction by the Romans in A.D. 70 (Fig. **5.9**), and we often find reference to the First, Second, and Third Temples. The Temple of Solomon is the First Temple, and we know it primarily from the description in 1 Kings 6–8 and a parallel account in 2 Chronicles 2–4. No trace of the first Jerusalem Temple exists archeologically. The basic shape of the Jerusalem Temple (Figs. **5.7** and **5.8**) was a rectangle subdivided laterally into three sections, each with the same interior width—20 cubits. The building was 60 cubits long and 30 cubits high. A cubit equals approximately 20.9 inches (53 centimeters), so the Temple was approximately 105 feet (32 meters) long, 35 feet (10.7 meters) wide, and 52 feet (15.8 meters) high. These are internal measurements given in 1 Kings, but the biblical book of Ezekiel gives a different set of dimensions—100 by 50 cubits. These, however, are probably external dimensions and include subsidiary rooms built around the Temple.

The Temple stood on a 6-cubit-high platform with a dominating entrance of huge wooden doors flanked by two bronze pillars, 18 cubits high, situated at the top of the ten stairs. The doors were decorated with carved palms, flowers, and cherubim—that is, guardian winged beasts sometimes shown with human or animal faces. To enter the Temple, one passed through the first of its three sections, variously referred to as a "vestibule," "porch," "portico," or "entrance hall." The second section of the Temple was its main or largest room, measuring 40 by 20 cubits and reaching a height of 30 cubits. The Hebrew word *hikhal* or *hekal* means that this room—the Temple's largest—was a "great house" or "holy place," and it signifies that the Temple was the "house of the Lord," an earthly dwelling place of the deity. A large, elaborate cypresswood doorway carved with cherubim and palm trees and overlaid with gold provided entry. Walls paneled with cedarwood exhibiting rich floral carvings had small rectangular windows at the top, through which light

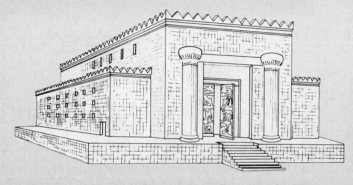

5.7 Reconstruction drawing of Solomon's Temple. The significance of the two bronze pillars is uncertain, but some scholars suggest that they may have represented the twin pillars of fire and smoke that guided the Israelites during their wanderings in the desert after the Exodus from Egypt.

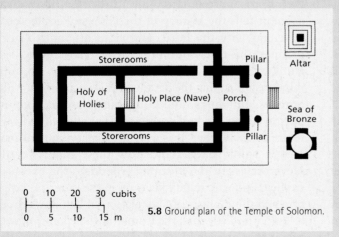

5.8 Ground plan of the Temple of Solomon.

entered the space. In the room itself were various sacred furnishings—ten large golden lampstands, an inlaid table for priestly offerings, and a cedarwood altar covered with gold.

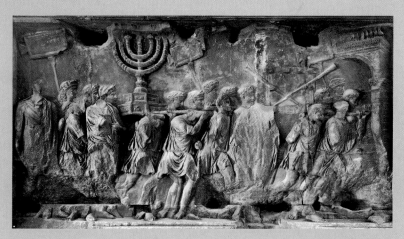

5.9 (*above*) Destruction of the Temple, a detail from the Arch of Titus, showing the menorah procession, A.D. 81. (A menorah is a ceremonial seven-branched candelabrum of the Jewish temple symbolizing the seven days of the creation). Marble, arch 47 ft 4 ins (14.43 m) high. Rome.

5.10 The third (Herod's) Temple, 20 B.C. (reconstruction). Jerusalem, Israel.

From a staircase behind the altar one entered the Holy of Holies, the most sacred part of the Temple. This was a windowless cubicle, 20 by 20 by 20 cubits, which contained the Ark of the Covenant, the symbol of God's presence, which the Jews had carried with them from the wilderness. The Ark was flanked by two large cherubim.

The symbolic nature of the Temple as a residence for God went beyond providing assurance to the Israelites that God was with them. Construction of the Temple was anticipated by David, who brought the Ark of the Covenant to Jerusalem and began assembling materials. Solomon gave great priority to completing the Temple. He assembled an enormous workforce and completed the job in a remarkably short time: seven years.

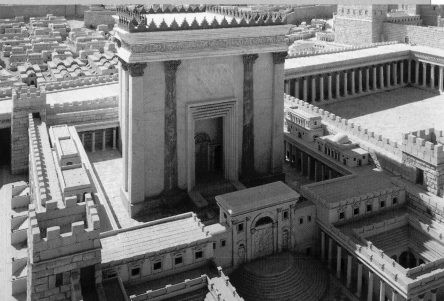

5.11 (*below*) Reconstruction of the third Temple.

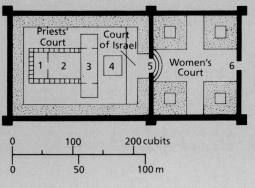

1 Holy of Holies

2 Holy Place (Nave)

3 Porch

4 Altar

5 Nicanor Gate

6 Beautiful Gate

Construction of the Temple coincided with the institution of the monarchy and the emergence of Israel, for the only time in its existence, as an independent and dominant political power in the region. Thus, the Temple symbolized not only the presence of the Lord God, but also Israel's very national identity.

The Temple was extended extravagantly by Herod beginning c. 20 B.C. (Fig. **5.11**); a reconstruction can be seen in Jerusalem (Fig. **5.10**).

and animal forms are shaded and detailed in such a way as to give fullness to form and a sense of action and character.

Music and Dance

References to music and dance occur frequently in the Jewish scriptures. Genesis 4:21 refers to those who play the "lyre and the pipe." In Exodus 15:20–21:

> Miriam the prophetess, the sister of Aaron, took a timbrel in her hand; and all the women went after her with timbrels and with dances.
>
>   And Miriam answered them, Sing ye to the Lord, for he hath triumphed gloriously; the horse and his rider hath he thrown into the sea.

The musicianship of David is documented in 1 Samuel 16:23. When King Saul was tormented, "David took the lyre and played it with his hand; so Saul was refreshed, and was well, and the evil spirit departed from him."

CHRISTIANITY

Rooted in Judaism's post-exilic Messianic hopes, Christianity arose in what its central personage and its later believers professed was God's intervention in human history to establish a new covenant to supplant the covenant established with Moses. Jesus of Nazareth was the Christ—Messiah. As Christianity spread through the Roman world after the death of Jesus, Christology became an important and divisive issue among Christians. Exactly what was the nature of Jesus Christ: Man or God or some combination? And what was the relationship of God, Christ, and the Holy Spirit, about whom Jesus preached? These and other fundamental concepts brought Judaism, Rome, and the Western world together in a manner that has shaped humankind in the two thousand years since.

Jesus Christ and His Teachings

What we know of Jesus Christ comes from later writings called the gospels, the first four books of the New Testament of the Christian Bible. Jesus' early life remains unknown. The gospel of St Matthew includes a long genealogy tracing Jesus' ancestry to King David, and provides a number of stories about Jesus' birth, the Wise Men, the flight to Egypt, the slaughter of the innocents, the return to Israel, and the residence in Nazareth, but these provide few details of Jesus' life. In the gospel of St Luke (Fig. 5.13) we find a poetic narration of the birth and connection between Jesus and John the Baptist through their mothers, Mary and her cousin Elizabeth, and we find

OUR DYNAMIC WORLD

Shinto Sculpture in Japan

Unlike the monotheism of Judaism, Shinto, or "Way of the Gods," Japan's indigenous religion, was a polytheistic nature cult without dogmas, scriptures, or images. At the same time as the late Roman Empire the graves of Japanese rulers were surrounded by moats and topped by huge burial mounds. One burial site near Osaka covers nearly 277 acres (112 hectares) in area and rises to a height of 110 feet (33.5 meters). Around the tombs, Shinto devotees erected terracotta tubes called *haniwa*. These stood 2 feet (61 centimeters) tall and were topped with human figures or heads or figures of animals. Tradition indicates that they were substitutes for real humans who at one time had been slaughtered at the chieftain's funeral. The figure shown in Figure **5.12** reveals high stylization. There is absolutely no attempt to portray anatomically correct details. The effect is one of exaggeration for visual effect. As in the pictograms of Japanese writing, the ebbing and flowing of curvilinear line is most important. Unlike the carefully detailed naturalism of Roman wall painting and sculpture, Shinto sculpture of the period shows a logical simplicity that draws attention to materials and overall form rather than on internal compositional particulars.

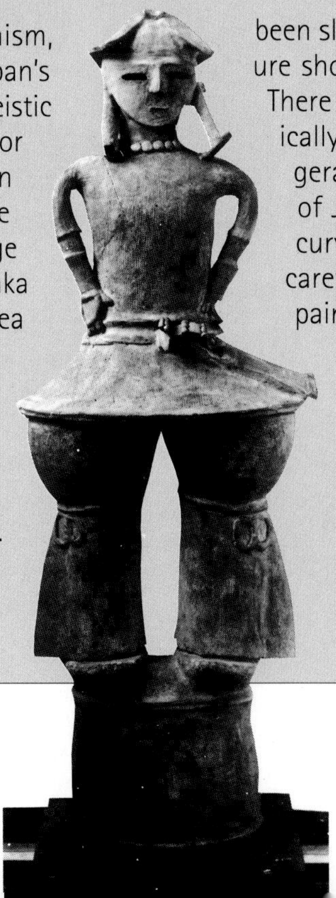

5.12 *Haniwa* figure, c. A.D. 300–600. Terracotta, about 2 ft (61 cm) high. Musée Guimet, Paris.

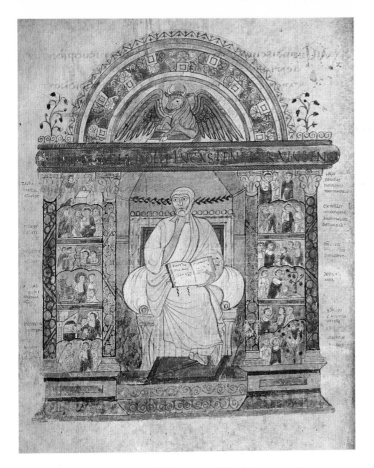

5.13 St Luke, from the presumed St Augustine Bible, sixth century. Corpus Christi College, Cambridge, England.

The core of Jesus' teaching was the Kingdom of God. Although the significance of the Kingdom with regard to human activity is strong, Jesus used the symbol as a means for revealing God himself. Through it, Jesus evokes God's active involvement in saving humankind and in establishing a reign of justice and peace. Above all, it reveals God's steadfast love and grace, which is offered to humankind without precondition. One of the most interesting aspects of this complex teaching is the step it takes away from conventional Jewish thought in regard to the judgment of God on the human race—the end of the world or the Time of Tribulation in Jewish theology—which it says has already begun. The central focus of Jesus' ethic is love, based on the Judaic commandment: "Thou shalt love the Lord thy God with all thy heart, soul, mind, and strength, and thy neighbor as thyself." The call for repentance, like that of the Old Testament prophets, presupposes that there is a tremendous distance between God and the daily life of his people. Hence, the need to repent, not just to polish up a few sinful acts, but to have a fundamental change of heart.

The gospels portray Jesus as a teacher, miracle worker, and friend of sinners (Fig. **5.14**). He goes out of his way to

5.14 Christ as Pantocrator, Kariye Church, Istanbul, Turkey. Christ as Pantocrator (or Pantokrator) indicates Christ as judge of the world.

historical figures such as King Herod, Caesar Augustus, Quirinius (kwir-IN-ee-uhs), governor of Syria, and a specific reference to Caesar's "first" enrollment. Correlating Herod's actual death in 4 B.C., Augustus' reign, and Jesus' birth story, and accommodating changes and corrections to the calendar that have occurred since, we get a birth date for Jesus at somewhere around 4 B.C.

With the exception of the story of Jesus in the Temple as a youth, no further information is available about him until he began his public ministry when he was thirty years old. The gospel of St Mark is vague about whether Jesus was a carpenter—the reference could apply to Joseph, his father—and although he appears to have been a "teacher," no indication exists of his formal education. He had close associations with women, which would have been unusual for a Jewish teacher at that time, and we conclude that he must have had a relatively normal and typical home life in his formative years.

The actual beginnings of Jesus' ministry are also vague. He was baptized by John the Baptist, whom the gospels portray as a harbinger of Jesus, and he shared John's message that the people of Israel must "repent" and return to the ways of God. During his ministry, Jesus called twelve disciples to share his teaching and healing ministry. The symbolic link with the twelve tribes of Israel undoubtedly was intentional.

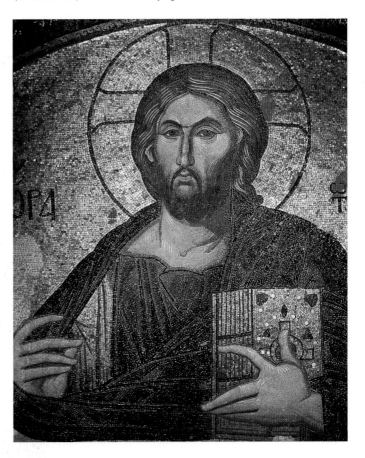

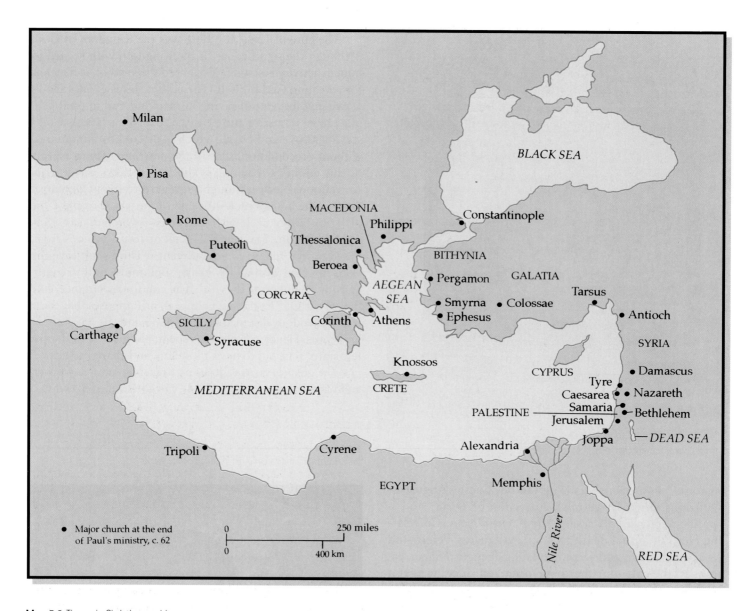

Map 5.3 The early Christian world.

associate with the poor, the downtrodden, and the socially unacceptable. His ministry proclaims that such people, not the righteous, are the special objects of God's love and care.

Jesus' message was revolutionary. What he said and did—while not illegal by either Jewish or Roman standards—was cause for concern because it created unrest in the population. That, in first-century Palestine, was dangerous, and Jesus was put to death in the Roman custom—crucified with other criminals on a hill called Golgotha (the place of the skull) outside the city of Jerusalem.

All four gospels maintain that on the third day after his death, Jesus rose from the dead and, at various times, appeared to his disciples—not as a spirit, but in a solid body—before ascending into heaven. The resurrection becomes for Christians not only a miracle, but also God's redeeming act in the salvation of the world.

The Apostolic Mission

Christianity spread principally because Jesus commanded his followers to carry on his commission from God. In the Synoptic Gospels—Matthew, Mark, and Luke—the charge is direct. After the Resurrection, Jesus appears to the disciples and tells them: "All authority in heaven and on earth has been given to me. Go therefore and make disciples of all nations, baptizing them in the name of the Father and of the Son and of the Holy Spirit, teaching them to observe all that I have commanded you" (Matthew 28:18a–20a). Implicit in this commission is the assumption that the Way, as the followers called themselves immediately after the resurrection, would spread beyond the confines of Judaism and include the Gentile world as well. Within a generation, the new name, Christian, had appeared, and an organized movement with appointed leaders took shape. We should note that in the beginning Jews and Jewish Christians (so-called "Nazarenes") were indistinguishable in religious practice and places of worship. The Romans, in fact, made no distinction between the two groups. Pointedly, one of the early divisions among Christians concerned the issue of whether or not one could become a Christian without first converting to Judaism.

Critical to the spread of Christianity was its own written canon. Serious questions about exactly who Jesus was and what the faith entailed needed to be settled, and divisions within early Christianity were many. The Bible of the earliest Christians was the Old Testament—the Jewish canon—and this was supplemented in Christian worship by oral apostolic accounts of the words of Jesus, interpretations of his person and significance for the life of the Church. This was soon to change.

5.15 *St Peter*, third-century A.D. Wall painting from a catacomb of SS. Pietro e Marcellino, Rome.

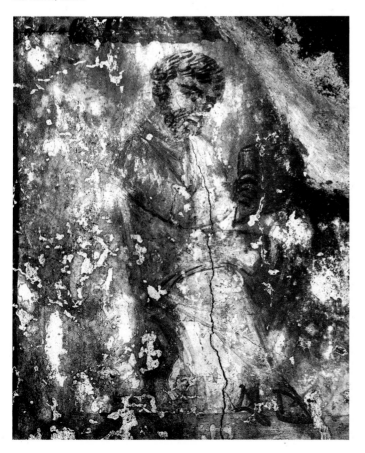

The books of the New Testament, which were later adopted as the Christian canon (KAN-uhn), were written within a period of less than one hundred years. They fall into four different literary forms. Four of them are "Gospels," so-called because they tell the "good news" of Jesus Christ. Early Church history occurs in the Acts of the Apostles, which is an account of the spread of the Christian faith during the first thirty years after the Resurrection. Twenty-one of the books are epistles, or letters, written to various churches and individuals by the early evangelists. The last book of the New Testament (the book of Revelation) is an apocalypse—that is, a revelation of God's will for the future.

The earliest of the four gospels was written by John Mark around the year A.D. 70. According to tradition, John Mark was a disciple of the Apostle Peter (Fig. **5.15**). The Gospels of Matthew and Luke use Mark as a source (each appeared ten to twenty years later than Mark), and because they have so much in common, they are called the Synoptic Gospels—from the Greek word *synopsis*, a seeing together. Unlike the Synoptics, which tell mainly of Jesus' public teaching and ministry, the Gospel according to John contains information concerning Jesus' early Judean ministry and extensive discussions with the disciples about the union of the Church with Christ. None of the parables of the Synoptics appear in John.

Much of basic Christian theology emerges from the letters section of the New Testament, much of which is attributed to St Paul. Probably the most important promulgator of Christian thought, Paul shaped the eastern tone of Judaic Christianity into the logical, intellectual patterns of the Greek-thinking world of the Roman Empire.

The book of Revelation, or Apocalypse, closes the Christian scriptures, and its last chapters portray the fulfillment toward which the entire biblical message of redemption is focused. It contains powerful poetic imagery that appeals to the imagination. It represents a vision of its author, whose name was John. Probably, parts of the book were written before the fall of Jerusalem in A.D. 70, but the book apparently achieved its final form on the rocky island of Patmos (PAT-mohs), to which the author had been exiled by the Emperor Domitian (A.D. 81–96). Over the centuries the Revelation to John has proved to be one of the most difficult and inspiring representations of God ever written.

The Early Christian Church

Like most emerging religions, Christianity felt an intense need to create institutions. Christianity was loosely organized and totally different in its theology from the religions around it. It needed a united front in order to grow and to make its way in a suspicious, pagan world. In the first centuries of its existence, Christians had shed each other's blood as various sects battled over questions of dogma, and this had to stop if the Church were to survive. In the thrust and counterthrust of all this, however, the emerging Church was a force coming together in a world that was mainly falling apart.

Why and how did Christianity survive? Its monotheism was an extension of the Jewish heritage. The historical immediacy of its founder and the doctrines he taught appealed to men and women of the late Roman and post-Roman periods. In its extreme simplicity on the one hand and its subtlety on the other, Christianity had a multi-faceted appeal that made it acceptable to the most lowly and illiterate people as well as those of sophistication and schooling.

Little is known about the spread of Christianity through the Roman Empire. Conversions among the aristocracy and upper classes enhanced its chances of survival substantially, and by the end of the third century, Christians were numerous enough to count as a political force. Every city of consequence had a Christian community presided over by a bishop who was assisted by priests and deacons. Regarded as successors of the original apostles, bishops were chosen by their communities, and theological disputes were decided in councils of bishops.

Christianity encountered varying degrees of tolerance from the Roman state. In general, the Imperial government treated all the various religious practices in its diverse empire with an even hand. Occasionally, however, Christians suffered fierce persecution, mainly because they refused to worship the emperor as a divine being. In addition, their secret meetings and rites troubled the authoritarian government. Christians also abhorred violence and refused to serve in the Roman army, which was very difficult for the besieged state to tolerate.

As we shall see, the last great persecution occurred under Diocletian (dy-uh-KLEE-shun) in 303. Shortly afterward, Constantine transformed Christianity into a favored religion in the Roman state. According to the bishop Eusebius (yoo-SEE-bee-uhs), Constantine reported that he had had a dream prior to the battle of Milvian Bridge against his co-ruler, the tetrarch Maxentius, in which he was told to send his soldiers into battle carrying standards marked with Christian symbols. Constantine did so, won the battle, and was converted to Christianity. He later claimed that he was "brought to the faith by God to be the means of the faith's triumph." Christianity soon became the official religion of the empire.

Numerous privileges came with this new status. The Church could receive legacies, its clergy were exempt from taxation, and bishops were permitted to settle disputes of law in all civil cases in which a Christian was a party. In addition, the Church obtained the rights of sanctuary for its buildings—that is, they became places where a criminal was safe from arrest or punishment.

After Constantine's conversion, the Church began to build up its own administration, adopting a structure similar to that of the civil bureaucracy. By the fourth century, each province was divided into bishoprics, with an archbishop at its head. There was, however, no centralized administration for the whole Church comparable to the Imperial government. The bishops of the four great cities of Rome, Jerusalem, Antioch, and Alexandria claimed special privilege because the Church in each of those cities was founded by the apostles. Rome, however, claimed supremacy both because it was founded by St Peter, to whom Jesus had entrusted the building of the Church, and because it was the capital of the empire.

Yet the opportunities presented by the conversion of emperors to Christianity were to some extent offset by problems that stemmed from the same source. In return for championing the faith, the emperor expected the bishops to act as loyal servants of the Imperial crown. When theological disputes arose, the emperor often insisted on deciding the matter himself.

The Popes

References to the primacy of Rome can be found as early as the letters of St Ignatius in 110 and St Irenaesis around 185. The claim of the medieval popes to exercise complete authority over all of Christendom was developed slowly, however. The bishops of Rome claimed supremacy because they were the heirs of St Peter and because their city was the capital. Other arguments included the sanctification of Rome by the blood of martyrs and its freedom from the contamination of the heresies that had touched other churches. Specific acknowledgement of Rome's supremacy by a Church council first came in 344 from the Council of Sardica. The Council of Constantinople placed the bishop of Constantinople second after the bishop of Rome "because Constantinople is the New Rome." A series of strong and able bishops of Rome consolidated the move toward Rome's supremacy during the next century.

The argument put forward by the bishops of Rome in support of their case came to be known as the "Petrine theory," and perhaps its clearest formulation came from Pope Leo 1 (r. 440–61), a man with considerable administrative ability who played a significant role in civil affairs as well as religious ones. Leo was twice called on by the emperor to negotiate with the leaders of the barbarian armies that invaded Italy in 453 and 455. He affirmed that because all other apostles were subordinate to Peter, all other bishops were subordinate to the bishop of Rome, who had succeeded to Peter's see at Rome. In fact, nearly all Western Christians came to acknowledge the pope of Rome as head of the whole Church. What remained unclear was the actual extent of his authority in temporal affairs and in affairs of Church governance.

Early Christian Thought

Tertullian and Legalism

The study of medieval thought of the first millennium is really the study of Christian thought. In order to understand the men and women of the early Middle Ages—how they might have seen the universe, and how that viewpoint was translated into art—it is important to examine some of early Christian thought. Two of its most important thinkers were Tertullian (tuhr-TUL-ee-uhn) and Augustine (aw-GUS-tuhn), and our examination focuses on them.

In the early years of the Middle Ages, the West depended for its culture on the East. Its art, literature, and philosophy tended to be derivative rather than original. On the other hand, the prevailing interests of the West differed significantly from those of the East. Reflecting the West's Roman heritage, they concentrated on the functional, practical, and ethical. Law and government, the sovereignty of the state, institutions and tradition, were social preoccupations, and they also affected Western Christianity. The functions and authority of the Church as an institution were of prime importance. Duty, responsibility, sin, and grace were all topics of great interest.

The main contribution of Tertullian (c. A.D. 160–230) to Christian thought lies in two areas. He founded the language of the Western Church, and he enunciated those aspects of its theology that marked a break with the East. His writings were highly influential, and continued to be so even after his defection to Montanism destroyed his standing as a Catholic Father.

Probably the most important of Tertullian's writings is an elaborate analysis of the soul. His arguments lean heavily on Stoicism (see p. 118). He believed that the soul has length, breadth, and thickness, and although it is not identical with the body, it permeates all its parts, with its center lying in the heart. The soul controls the body, using the body as it wills. Yet, the soul remains spiritual, not material. For Tertullian, spirit and matter were two substances, different in nature but both equally real. Spirit, being indivisible, was therefore indestructible.

His notion of God and the Trinity was based on legal concepts. When Tertullian says that God has three parts, he means that God is "three persons in the legal sense, that is, three persons who share or own in common one substance or property."[1] God is a personal sovereign, to whom all people are subject. Independent and omnipotent, God created the world out of nothing. On the question of one's proper relationship to God, Tertullian was precise in defining God as an authority figure whom one approaches with humility and fear. "The fear of man is the honor of God. . . . Where there is no fear there is no amendment. . . . How are you going to love unless you are afraid not to love?" Virtue is thus obedience to divine law springing from fear of punishment if the law is broken. In this and many other areas, Tertullian's legal training is clear. He also formulated an elaborate list of sins, including the seven deadly sins of idolatry, blasphemy, murder, adultery, fornication, false witness, and fraud.

By the time of Tertullian, the Church had begun to see this life as a mere probation for the life to come. Earthly life was without value in itself and possessed meaning only in that it provided the opportunity to lay up rewards in the life beyond the grave. Tertullian believed the supreme virtues were humility and the spirit of otherworldliness, by which Christians could escape the perils of this life and be assured of enjoying the reward prepared for the saints in heaven.

St Augustine and Neo-Platonism

St Augustine (354–430) did not receive the sacrament of baptism until he was an adult. His mother, who was a Christian, believed that if he were baptized as a child, the healing virtue of accepting the faith would be destroyed by the lusts of youth. Nonetheless, after a period of skepticism, and adherence to Manichaeism (MAN-ik-ee-iz-uhm)—a philosophy that combined Christianity with elements from other religions of the time—he was baptized into the Christian faith. He later became bishop of Hippo, in Asia Minor. A prolific writer, his works greatly influenced developing Christian thought. The *Confessions* and *City of God* are the best known of his works.

Apparently Augustine found great inspiration in the writings of Plotinus (see p. 123), but he was also highly influenced by Platonic and neo-Platonic thought. He recoiled from Tertullian's emphasis on the senses and the body, but shared Tertullian's belief in intuition as the source of knowledge concerning God, although Augustine's concept of intuition had an intellectual cast. The senses, he believed, give us unreliable images of the truth. Instead, our intuition, our AFFECTIVE thinking, has a certainty which springs from "the fact that it is of the very nature of reason to know the truth."[2] Knowledge is an inner illumination of the soul by God. Whatever we find intelligible is, therefore, certain. Knowledge comes from intuition and "confirms and amplifies the certainty of faith."[3]

Augustine argued that to doubt the existence of the soul is in fact to confirm its existence: in order to doubt we must think, and if we think, we therefore must be thinking beings, and therefore souls. Unlike Tertullian, Augustine thought the soul immaterial, that is, a purely spiritual entity. This spiritual character, as well as its immortality, is demonstrated by our power to grasp eternal and immaterial essences.

His concept of original sin, as developed in *City of God*, held that all people are born to sin because of Adam's fall from grace when he disobeyed God in the Garden of Eden. Thus, we are "punished by being born to a state of sin and death, physical and spiritual, from which only Christ's passion and saving grace can redeem us." Augustine held that people were inherently bad and therefore did bad things.

Augustine attacked the question of predestination and divine foreknowledge—that is, whether God's omniscience robs humans of free will. His conclusion, that free will is not a certainty, influenced later contributors to the debate, which continues among Christian theologians today.

Augustine's philosophy of art represents a radical shift from that of Plato and Aristotle, especially in the principles of art evaluation. Plato and Aristotle approach art from political and metaphysical points of view. Augustine approaches the subject from a Christian point of view. Scripture, not philosophy, is his guide. Augustine considers the production and consumption of art to hold the interest for the Church that Plato felt they held for the polis. The Christian and the pagan face the same questions about the function and purpose of art. Augustine, however, finds the answers in a strictly Christian context, in the teachings of scripture and tradition. For him, the answers are found in

an understanding of God's relationship with the world, and in the mission of the Church in dealing with art. Augustine untiringly attempted to satisfy the requisites of faith while doing justice to the natural pleasures that art can provide.

Even when the basic conflict is resolved, Augustine still has a problem in the immediate sensuous gratification of art. Although "divine order and harmony" are reflected in nature and to a degree in art, "perceptual objects tie the senses down to earthly things and prevent the mind from contemplating what is eternal and unchanging."[4] Art and beauty are thus guides for the soul. Those arts that depend least upon the senses best mirror the divine order.

The best teacher of all, however, is scripture. Properly interpreted, scripture provides the most direct knowledge of God's purpose and order, although the arts can contribute to our understanding as well. As long as art agrees with the tenets of faith and reflects the harmony of divine creation, it is justified.

CHRISTIANITY AND THE LATE ROMAN EMPIRE

Christianity spread to Rome early in the first century, brought there by nameless individuals who benefited from the freedom of travel that existed throughout the Empire

Map 5.4 Europe and North Africa in the late Roman period.

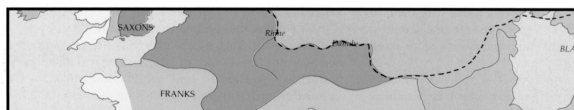

during the *Pax Romana*. While the Romans tolerated the Jews—despite their occasional rebellions in Palestine—Christians suffered repeatedly and perhaps grew stronger because of it.

Diocletian

The Roman Empire's crisis of the third century, which we discussed in Chapter 4, ended with the reforms brought about by two emperors, Diocletian and Constantine (KAHN-stuhn-teen), who also changed the fortunes of Christianity. Diocletian (r. 284–305) was born in the Balkans and rose to power through the ranks of the Roman army. He was strong-willed, insisting on divine status, and he took the image of emperor to grandiose heights—whenever he was in the presence of his subjects, for example, he separated himself from them by a wall of curtains. His self-image must have reflected the larger-than-life portrait that was necessary for him to cope with all the problems of the far-flung empire, in which anarchy was rampant, barbarians threatened every border, and the army turned rebellious.

Nonetheless, Diocletian attacked the problems with a creative and organized plan that, eventually—if only temporarily—brought some stability and reasonable prosperity. He restructured the empire by installing a Tetrarchy, wherein imperial power was shared among four rulers: two senior Augusti supported by two junior Caesars. Diocletian reformed and strengthened the imperial bureaucracy, reformed taxation to effect greater equality, and attempted to control wages and prices. His most ambitious undertaking was to split the empire into two halves, east and west, with each half administered by an Augustus and a Caesar. He also divided the provinces into dioceses. The cumulative effect of splitting the empire and restructuring the provinces was to centralize the state and to create an awkward and increasingly large class of bureaucrats.

In his last years Diocletian embarked on a major persecution of the Christian Church, whose expanding power he regarded as a threat to the hierarchy of the state. The persecution lasted for a period of eight years, extending beyond Diocletian's reign, which ended with his retirement in 305. The persecution, which was given official status by a series of edicts, was intended to eliminate Christianity

Map 5.5 The Roman Empire in the fourth century.

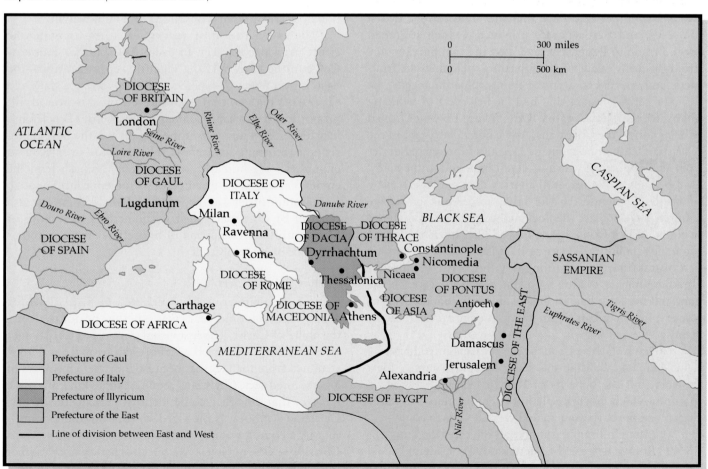

159

altogether by forbidding Christians to worship, destroying their churches and books, and arresting their bishops. Anyone suspected of being a Christian was forced to make a sacrifice to the emperor, which amounted to a repudiation of their faith, and failure to do so was punishable by death. In 311 the persecution ceased. Its purpose had been to stamp out Christianity, but its effect, by creating martyrs, was just the opposite. Christianity won many new converts on the strength of the faith of those who died rather than renounce.

Constantine

The Tetrarchy (teh-TRARK-ee) collapsed after Diocletian, and a series of civil wars between the tetrarchs broke out. Eventually, Constantine (r. 306–337), son of one of the tetrarchs, fought his way to power as sole emperor of Rome, and carried Diocletian's reforms to even greater lengths. Constantine established two capitals—one in Rome, the other in Byzantium, later named Constantinople in his honor—thereby creating two Roman empires, one in the West and one in the East. The latter lasted for another thousand years, the former for barely a century.

Constantine arranged an elaborate administrative system, split into four huge imperial prefectures, a dozen dioceses, and 120 separate provinces, which stretched from Britain to Egypt. He separated the civil bureaucracy from the army, which he reformed to strengthen the frontiers, and in order to keep the empire afloat financially, he levied a series of taxes that had the net effect of reducing many to near-slave status. One group, however, loved Constantine—the Christians. As we noted, he legalized the Christian Church in Rome in 313, and it prospered under this new opportunity. Priests could be found in the army, and bishops at the imperial court. Constantine, who saw himself as defender of the faith, undertook an active campaign to increase the flock and to enhance its material welfare. When Constantine moved his capital to Byzantium, he rebuilt the old city as a Christian center, renaming it Constantinople, and filling it with Christian churches and monuments. All the following emperors were Christian, and the faith had an unshakable hold on all levels of society, from peasant to aristocrat, the bureaucracy to the army.

The cumulative effects of the reforms introduced by Diocletian and Constantine enabled Rome to survive for a century, but the benefits of Roman rule had reached a point at which most people in the empire may well have welcomed the barbarian incursions that were to come.

The Roman Empire did not fall on a specific date, but by 406 Roman defenses had deteriorated considerably, and a mixed horde of Germanic peoples, mostly Vandals, surged into the empire and made their way through Gaul into Spain. Capitalizing on the situation. Alaric attacked Italy and succeeded in sacking Rome itself in 410.

LATE ROMAN AND EARLY CHRISTIAN ART

The Visual Arts and Architecture

Visual Art

Late Roman Art

Roman visual art of the period continued the practice of Augustan times in the celebration of emperors. Diocletian's Tetrarchy was represented in sculptural solidity (Fig. 5.16), with the figures clasping shoulders to further signify the steadfastness of imperial rule. The figures here are squat and stylized, as opposed to the naturalism of earlier Roman sculpture, although this may partly stem from the need to place this particular piece within the framework of the building to which it is attached, a feature found in later, Romanesque sculpture. The compactness of the composition does create a sense of solidity and immovability.

The exaggeration of anatomical form for symbolic effect may also be seen in a colossal bust of Emperor Constantine (Fig. 5.17), a gigantic representation—the head is over 8 feet (2.4 meters) tall—exhibiting a stark and expressive realism that is countered by caricatured, ill-proportioned intensity. Coming as it does after Diocletian's insistence on being worshipped as divine, the bust represents a returning awareness that people—even Roman emperors—are humans and not gods. Nonetheless, the empire needed to see its emperor as someone large enough to maintain order and prosperity. This likeness is not a portrait of Constantine—it is the artist's view both of Constantine's presentation of himself as emperor and of the office of emperor itself.

Early Christian Art

One of the major questions debated by Christians for nearly eight hundred years was whether or not to depict the figure of Christ. The first visual symbols of Christianity were symbolic rather than representational, and they stemmed from the fact that because they were members of a persecuted sect, Christians required some kind of arcane imagery that only they could identify. Perhaps the earliest Christian symbol was the *Chi-Rho* (ky-roh) monogram—that is, a combination of the first two letters of the word *Christos*—XP—in Greek. We see an artistic elaboration of the sign in Figure 5.18, which is taken from a fourth-

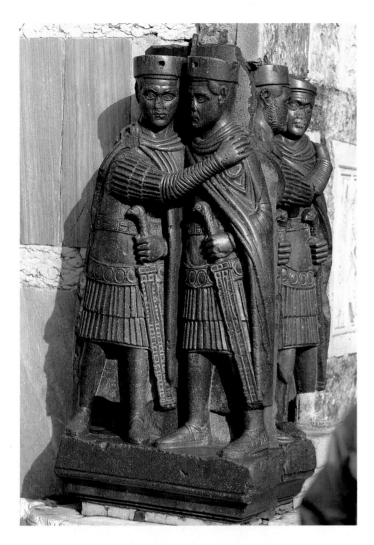

5.16 Diocletian's Tetrarchy, fourth century. St Mark's Cathedral, Venice, Italy.

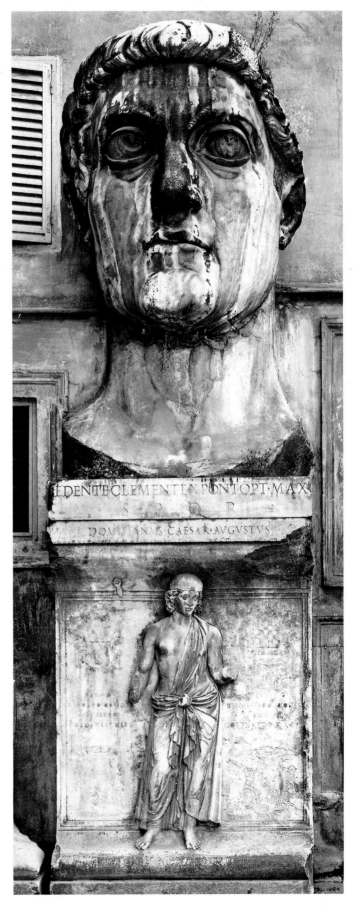

5.17 Head of Constantine the Great (originally part of a colossal seated statue), A.D. 313. Marble, 8 ft 6³⁄₈ ins (2.61 m) high. Palazzo dei Conservatori, Rome.

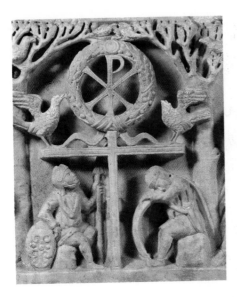

5.18 *Chi-Rho* monogram, detail of a sarcophagus, c. A.D. 340. Museo Pio Cristiano, Vatican Museums, Rome.

century sarcophagus. The *Chi-Rho* symbol stands at the center of a Roman triumphal wreath and above a cross. Doves, a symbol of the Holy Spirit and a reference to Jesus' baptism by John the Baptist, surround the monogram, which indicates the triumph of Christ over death, as two Roman soldiers, present at the crucifixion, sit below.

In addition to the *Chi-Rho*, Christians used a number of other visual symbols—for example, the fish and the lamb. The fish was a *rebus*—that is, a riddle composed of symbols suggesting the sound of the words they represent. The Greek word for fish, *icthus*, provided the initials for the formula "Jesus Christ Son of God, Saviour." The rebus of two curved, intersecting lines, created a means by which two Christians could secretly identify each other. One would trace a curve in the dirt. The other, if a Christian, would respond to create the sign of the fish (Fig. **5.19**).

The lamb as a symbol referred to the metaphor used by John the Baptist, who described Christ as the "Lamb of God, which taketh away the sins of the world." Christ described himself as the "Good Shepherd" that "giveth his life for his sheep." The symbol of the lamb had been used in pagan art to represent benevolence or philanthropy, but it took a new meaning in Christianity and became one of the earliest artistic symbols in the faith (Fig. **5.20**). In this early depiction of the Trinity, the diadem and *chlamys*

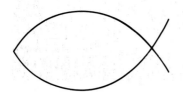

5.19 The "fish" rebus for "Jesus Christ Son of God, Savior." Early Christian symbol.

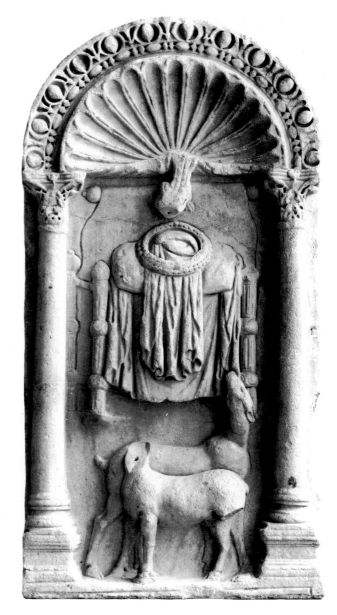

5.20 The Throne of God as a Trinitarian image, probably Constantinopolitan c. A.D. 400. Marble 65²/₃ × 33 ins (167 × 84 cm). Stiftung Preussisches Kulturbesitz, Berlin-Dahlem, Germany.

(KLAH-mihs; a Greek mantle worn pinned at the shoulder) represent Christ the Son, the empty throne represents God the Father, and the dove represents the Holy Spirit. It is probable that in this depiction, the lambs symbolize the classic virtue of beneficence rather than Christ.

The same is true of a beautifully detailed statue entitled *The Good Shepherd* (Fig. **5.21**). According to some scholars, depictions such as this, based on the injunctions we noted earlier, were not supposed to represent Christ but acquired Christian meaning only from their context in

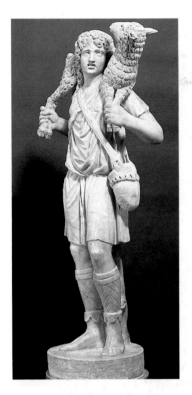

5.21 *The Good Shepherd*, c. A.D. 300. Marble, 36 ins (92 cm) high. Vatican Museums, Rome.

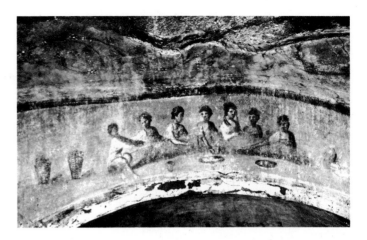

5.22 *The Breaking of Bread*, late second century A.D. Wall painting in the catacomb of Priscilla, Rome.

Christian tombs. In this particular case, the influence of classical Greek sculpture is clear right down to the Praxitelean "S" curve that forms the axis of the figure. The dress is classic Greek, and the detailing is skillful and naturalistic, with the clothing hanging like real fabric rather than decoration.

The earliest Christian painting is found in the catacombs of Rome. The catacombs served as underground cemeteries, for both Christians and Jews avoided public burial places that were dedicated to pagan deities. In addition, belief in the resurrection of the body meant that early Christians eschewed cremation, which was the norm for ordinary citizens in Rome. Wall paintings similar to that seen in Figure **5.22** often had multiple meanings. This work, which depicts men and women sitting at table with bread and wine, could represent the early Christian "love feast" (*agape*; AH-guh-pay), or it may represent Christ's first miracle—the wedding feast at Cana at which he turned water into wine. The obvious meaning was that of the sacrament of Holy Eucharist—that is, the reenactment of the Last Supper.

The catacombs reveal much about early Christian thought and communal spirit. An otherworldly outlook can be seen in the example shown in Figure **5.23**, although here, again, the art itself has pre-Christian influences. In

this case, the ceiling is divided into compartments, as we witnessed in earlier Roman wall painting (see Fig. **4.4**). However, the artist, who was of only modest ability, translates old forms into new meanings: the great circle represents the dome of heaven inscribed with the cross; the symbol of the good shepherd with a sheep on his shoulders, similar to the statue in Figure **5.21**, adorns the central panel; and the semicircular panels tell the story of Jonah. The standing figures represent members of the Church, their hands raised in prayer for divine assistance.

The spread of Christianity among the ruling classes in Rome gave rise to personal expressions in Christian art, as

5.23 Painted ceiling, fourth century. Catacomb of SS. Pietro e Marcellino, Rome.

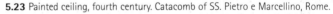
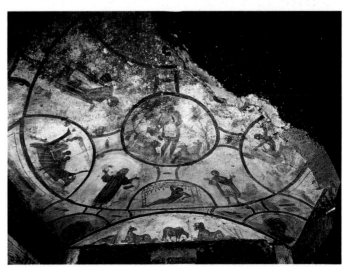

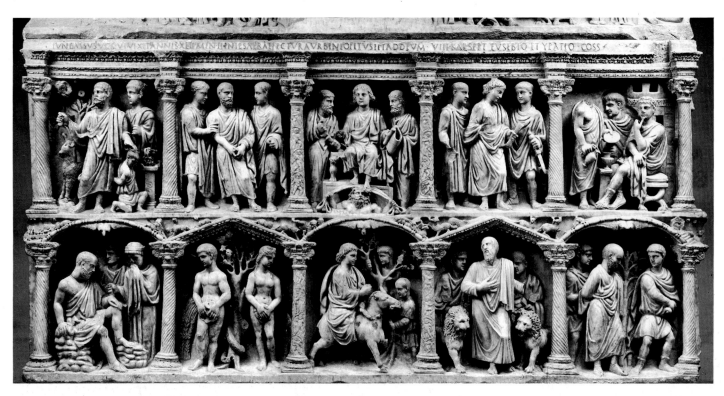

5.24 Sarcophagus of Junius Bassus, A.D. 359. Grottoes of St Peter, Vatican Museum, Rome.

can be seen in the sarcophagus of Junius Bassus (Fig. **5.24**). Bassus was a prefect of the city of Rome, and his burial vault reflects a carefully designed, classically inspired creation. Two separate, elaborate arcades tell a variety of biblical stories, including those of the Hebrew children in the fiery furnace, the baptism of Christ, and the raising of Lazarus. The composition itself represents a sophisticated intricacy of high artistic quality. In the first place, the figures, although small, are carved with delicate attention to naturalistic detail. They stand away from the background, creating a sense of deep space between the COLON-NETTES, and this gives each scene an individual identity, while the overall composition of the sarcophagus is maintained by the continuing linearity of the upper and lower architrave and the colonnade. Curiously, the heaviest architectural representation is on the top—that is, the post-and-lintel structure of the upper band looks heavier than the alternating arches and pediments of the lower band. One would expect the opposite. The detailing on the colonnettes also reveals the artist's skill. The middle scenes create a central axis, which is balanced by symmetrical treatments on either side. The central axis is identified by pairs of colonnettes, whose detailing differs from the two pairs that flank them. However, in order to create maximum variety and interest, the artist has reversed the angles of diagonal banding on these outer sets of colonnettes.

In addition, the scenes themselves balance themati-cally. For example, at either end of the lower register, we find an afflicted Job and St Paul being led to execution. These parallel treatments not only represent redemption through suffering but also refer to Christ's suffering for the redemption of humankind. Christ himself occupies the central focal points of both registers. On the bottom, he is shown in his triumphal entry into Jerusalem; on the top, he is enthroned between St Peter and St Paul. The enthronement signifies his regal triumph. Christ's feet rest on a canopy supported by the Roman sky god Coelus.

Architecture

By the third century A.D., Rome may have been in decline, but the opposite may be said for the ornateness of its architecture. Opulent buildings with excessive decoration arose throughout the Roman Empire, especially in Egypt, Syria, and Asia Minor, where Hellenistic architectural principles were revised to reflect Roman ideals—for example, axial symmetry (equality of form around a central axis) and logical sequence. Size and scale were the order of the day.

Even though much of the political power of the empire was moving toward the East, Roman emperors still built their most lavish monuments in Rome. The best examples of Roman monumentality in architecture are the *thermae* or baths, and one of the most grandiose of these is the Baths of Diocletian (Fig. **5.25**). The interior proportions of the tepidarium or hall enclosed over 16,000 square feet

(1,486 square meters). The space we see today has been diminished because of a later renovation that converted the building to a church and raised the floor by 7 feet (2.1 meters). In its original form, the tepidarium contained huge openings that made it possible to see into adjacent spaces. The walls and ceilings were covered with mosaics and marble, which reflected light entering the space through high windows, but the renovation replaced the reflective surfaces with plaster and paint and closed in the openings. Nonetheless, we can appreciate the vastness of this work, which is supported by 50-foot-high (15-meter) columns of Egyptian granite, supported by eight huge concrete piers.

Another building based on the shape of the Roman baths, particularly that of Diocletian, is the Basilica of Constantine, whose scale exceeded even Diocletian's Baths. In its time, it probably was the largest roofed building in Rome (Figs **5.26** and **5.27**) but only the north aisle remains. The three groined vaults covering the NAVE and directing the thrust of force outward to four corners, made it possible to erect upper walls into which openings called CLERESTORY (KLIR-stohr-ee) windows could be cut to

5.25 Tepidarium of the Baths of Diocletian, Rome, c. A.D. 298–305. (Converted by Michelangelo and others into the church of S. Maria degli Angeli.)

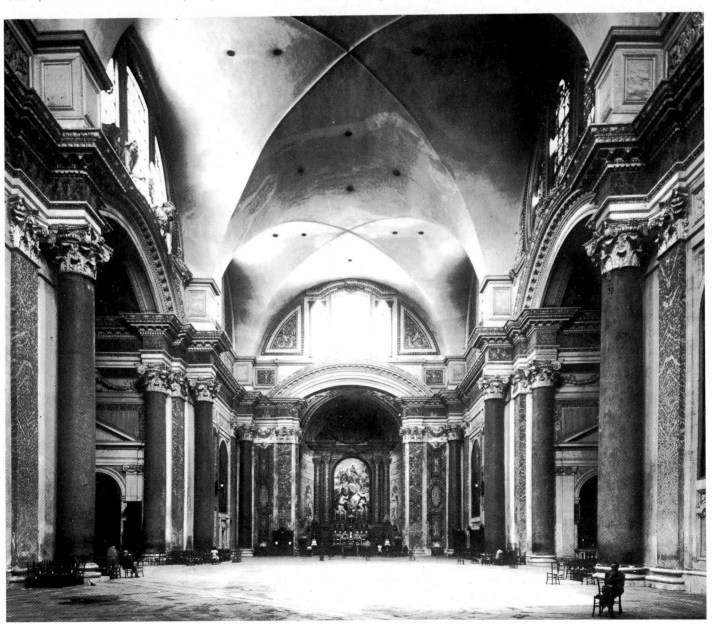

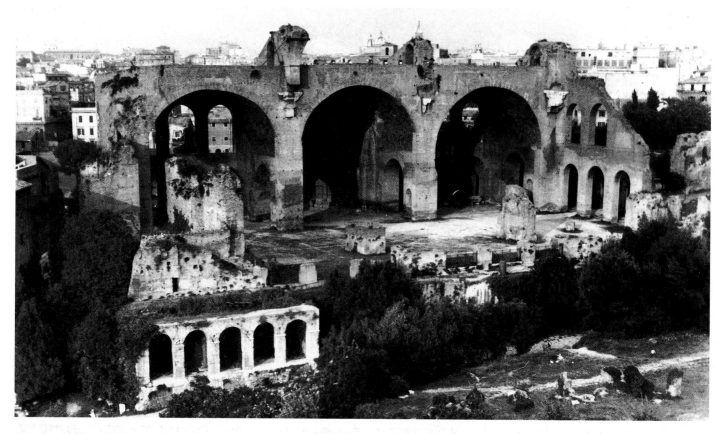

5.26 The Basilica of Constantine, Rome, c. A.D. 310–20.

allow light into the space. Thus, despite its tremendous size, the building must have had a light and airy atmosphere. This detail of design was used extensively from the Middle Ages onward.

When Christianity became a state religion in Rome, an explosion of building took place to accommodate the need for places to worship. Previously, small groups of the faithful had gathered as inconspicuously as possible wherever it was practical and prudent for them to do so. Even had it been safe to worship publicly, there was no need for a building of any size to house so few people. Respectability changed all that.

Early Christian architecture was, like painting, an adaptation of existing Roman style. For the most part, churches took the form of the Roman BASILICA. We tend to think of the word "basilica" as referring specifically to Christian structures, as in St Peter's Basilica in Rome. The term originally referred to Roman law courts, whose form the first large Christian churches took.

The original basilica had a specific architectural design, to which Christian architects made some simple alterations. Roman basilicas had many doors along the sides of the building to facilitate entrances and exits. Church ritual required the altar to be the focal point, and so the entrance to the Christian basilica was moved to the end of the building, usually at the western end, to focus attention down the long, relatively narrow nave to the altar at the far end. Often the altar was set off by a large archway reminiscent of a Roman triumphal arch, and elevated to enhance sightlines from the congregation, who occupied a flat floor space.

5.27 Reconstruction drawing of the Basilica of Constantine (after Huelsen).

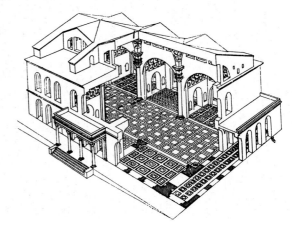

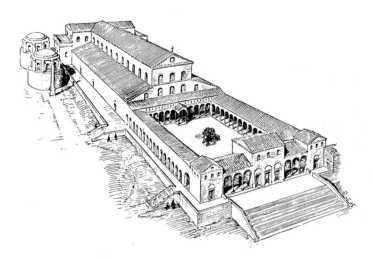

5.28 Old St Peter's Basilica, Rome, c. A.D. 333. Reconstruction by Kenneth J. Conant, Francis Loeb Library, Harvard University, Cambridge, MA.

5.29 Interior of San Paolo Fuori le Mura, Rome, late fourth century. Engraving by Giovanni Battista Piranesi (1720–78).

The basic structure of a basilica (Figs. **5.28** and **5.29**) has two or four long, parallel rows of columns, or piers, surrounded by an outer wall that is separated from the columns by an aisle. The central space, or nave, was heightened by a clerestory and a beam or simple truss roof describing an isosceles triangle of fairly low pitch. Low-pitched roofs covered the side aisles. The basilica was reasonably easy to build, yielding a nave width of 70 or 80 feet (21 or 24 meters). In contrast to later church styles, the basilica was not monumental by virtue of its height, although its early association with the law courts gave it an air of social authority. Interior parts and spaces were clearly defined, and this form was stated in simple structural terms.

Another change occurred in the treatment of interior space as different from the exterior shell. In architectural design, there are two approaches to the interior–exterior problem. Either the exterior structure expresses and reveals the nature and quality of interior space and *vice versa*, or the exterior shell is just that—a shell—in many instances obscuring what lies inside. The basilica exemplified the latter style. Whether intentionally or not, it thus symbolizes the difference between the exterior world of the flesh and the interior world of the spirit.

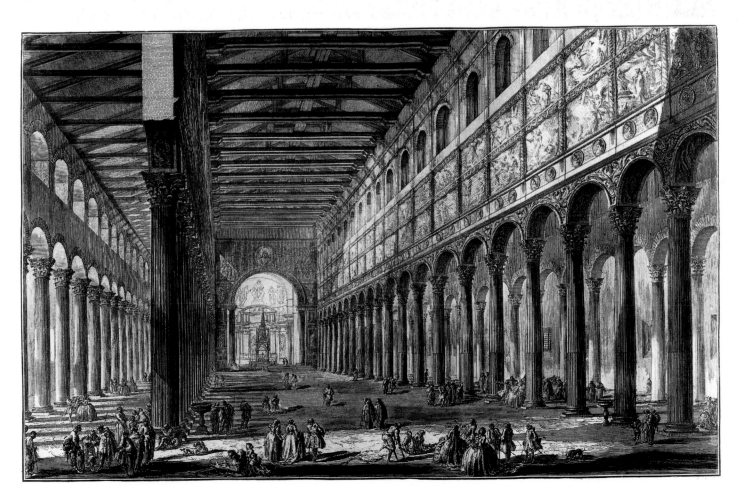

Literature

The literature of the late Roman Empire reflected a dispirited decline, parallel to that of the Empire in which it existed. Compared with earlier times, little work of any quality was produced—there was no experimentation with new forms, nor a major production of old forms—and it seemed as if the only writers whose outlook was to the future and optimism were the Christians.

The Bible, which was not widely available until 313, emerged as the most significant literature of the period. By the mid-second century, Irenaeus, a bishop of Lyon, had put forward a canon of twenty-one of the present twenty-seven books—the inclusion of Revelation raised considerable disagreement—and some books not at present in the Bible were often included. Church councils in Hippo (393) and Carthage (397) recognized the twenty-seven-book canon.

Although the Bible speaks to Judaic and Christian religious needs, it also contains some of the most vibrant literature of all time. Certainly, its poetry is without peer, even though it comes to us in translation. Later, we will witness the epistolary form of Paul's letters, but one of the most beautiful hymns ever written is the Magnificat of Mary, which is found in the Gospel of St Luke. This is Mary's response to God's plan for her to bear his son, and it is an example of the kind of obedience deemed righteous by both Jews and Christians. The passage is steeped in the Old Testament, and is especially akin to Hannah's song of praise in 1 Samuel 2:1–10. Some commentators have seen the Magnificat as a revolutionary document because it speaks of three revolutions of God. First, it speaks of a moral revolution, because God will scatter the proud in the plans of their hearts. A basic tenet of Christianity is the death of pride, and seeing oneself in the light of Christ is a death blow to pride. Second, it speaks of a social revolution: "He casts down the mighty—he exalts the humble." Prestige and social labeling have no place in the new covenant. Third, it speaks of an economic revolution: "He has filled those who are hungry . . . he sends away empty those who are rich." There is no room here for an acquisitive society—that is, one in which people are out for as much as they can get. What the Magnificat argues for is a society in which no one dares to have too much while others have too little.[5]

Thus, within this poetry, there is a powerful upheaval—a revolution of thinking that is as applicable today as it was two thousand years ago. In Luke 1:46–56:

And Mary said, "My soul magnifies the Lord, and my spirit has exulted in God, my Saviour, because he looked graciously on the humble estate of his servant. For—look you—from now on all generations shall call me blessed, for the Mighty One has done great things for me and his name is holy. His mercy is from generation to generation to those who fear him. He demonstrates his power with his arm. He scatters the proud in the plans of their hearts. He casts down the mighty from their seats of power. He exalts the humble. He fills those who are hungry with good things and he sends away empty those who are rich. He has helped Israel, his son, in that he has remembered his mercy—as he said to our fathers that he would—to Abraham and to his descendants forever."

Music

As with almost everything else we have noted, music in the late Roman period reflected Roman decline and Christian ascension. Just as St Paul took the Judaic and Eastern mystical traditions of Christian thought and shaped them into the logical processes of the Greco-Roman world, so early Christian music began to combine the music of Jewish worship with forms from the classical heritage. Most of the music from the Greek, Hellenistic, and Roman traditions was rejected by the early Christian Church, while music that was cultivated simply for enjoyment together with any music or musical instrument associated with activities objectionable to the Church, was considered unsuitable. The *hydraulos* (see Fig. **4.28**), for example, was banned. On the whole, the music of the classical West was simpler than the more ornate elaborations of liturgical texts in the East, especially in congregations with a large Jewish contingent. The consequent intermingling of the two styles resulted in a rich pastiche of hymnody and liturgy that was both vocal and instrumental. There was, nevertheless, a deep suspicion of instrumental music in many quarters and an outright rejection of it in others, because it was reminiscent of pagan customs. Disapproval of Roman or Greek music did not reflect a negative attitude toward music itself as much as a need to break ties with pagan traditions.

There was also a reaction against the use of trained choruses, initially instituted to help lead congregations who were unfamiliar with the chanting of psalms. When trained choruses were used, the congregation tended to sing less and the chorus more. In turn, this led to more complex music, which church leaders eventually found undesirable. In 361 the Provincial Council of Laodicea (lay-oh-di-SEE-uh) ruled that each congregation could have only one paid cantor or performer. In responsorial PSALMODY, the leader sang a line of the psalm, and the congregation sang a second in response. The melody began with a single note for the first few words, changing for the final words to a HALF CADENCE. The congregation then sang the beginning of the response on the same note, concluding with a CADENCE. The early Church also used an

TECHNOLOGY: PUTTING DISCOVERY TO WORK

Matches

The year 577 marked the invention of an item that today we take for granted—the match. In 950, in a book entitled *Records of the Unworldly and the Strange*, the Chinese author T'ao Ku writes: "An ingenious man devised the system of impregnating little sticks of pinewood with sulfur and storing them ready for use. At the slightest touch of fire, they burst into flame." Actually, T'ao Ku was wrong. Matches were a Chinese invention, but credit must go to some impoverished court ladies, who, during a military siege in the shortlived kingdom of the Northern Ch'i, were so short of tinder that they could not start fires for cooking and heating. They therefore devised a means of making it possible to start fires in a more opportune fashion. As T'ao Ku indicates, they devised a means of impregnating little sticks of pinewood with sulfur. The marvelous invention was initially called a "light-bringing slave," but it rapidly became an article of commerce, and its name was changed to "fire inch-stick."

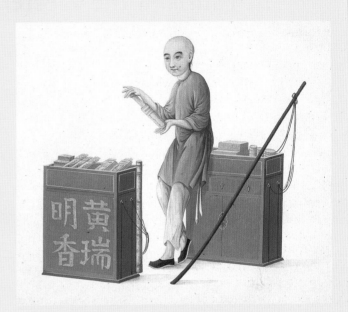

5.30 Pu Qua workshop, *A Boy Selling Pipe Lighters and Matches* (?), c. 1790. Watercolor on paper, 14⅛ × 17¼ ins (36 × 44 cm). Victoria & Albert Museum, London.

ANTIPHONAL (an-TIF-oh-nuhl) psalmody, in which singing alternated between two choruses.

We know that from earliest times music played a role in Christian worship, and because Christian services were modeled on Jewish synagogue services, it is likely that any music in them was closely linked to liturgical function. In Rome, Christian liturgy (literally, "the work of the people") included only chants and unaccompanied singing. In Antioch, however, a new form, HYMNODY, emerged via the Jewish synagogue and its songs. The hymn, a song of praise to God, quickly spread throughout the Christian world as part of the liturgy that comprised the worship service, or Mass, in which the eucharist was the focus.

Hymns were introduced into the Western Church early in the fourth century. Some sources credit St Ambrose for this innovation, others credit Hilary, bishop of Poitiers.

Early hymns had poetic texts consisting of several verses, all of which were sung to the same melody, which may have been taken from popular secular songs. The hymns were mostly syllabic (sil-A-bik)—that is, each syllable was sung on a single note—and they were intended to be sung by the congregations, not by a choir or a soloist. In style and content, early Church hymns tended to express personal, individual ideas, although other sections of the liturgy were more formal, objective, and impersonal.

Another type of Church music at this time was the *alleluia*, which presented an interesting contrast in style to the hymn. The *alleluia* was melismatic in style—that is, there were many notes for each syllable of text—and it was sung after the verse of a psalm. The last syllable of the word was drawn out "in gladness of heart." Eastern in influence and emotional in appeal, the *alleluia* came to the Christian service directly from Jewish liturgy.

Focal Point

St Paul and the Westernization of Christianity

In this section we look at one of the most influential Christian figures, St Paul (Fig. 5.31). Although Constantine cleared the way for Christianity to proceed without overt persecution, it was undoubtedly St Paul who made it palatable to the more logical inclinations of the Roman Empire, whose heritage lay in Greek classical thought. Paul carried the Christian gospel into Greece, and his interpretation of the Christian message and the nature of Christ were singularly successful in adapting what, basically, was an Eastern, mystical religion into a Western, intellectual one. Because Paul represents the transition of Judeo-Christian culture successfully into the Greco-Roman culture, he provides us with a picture of how these two cultures coalesced, to the point that soon one would supplant the other.

The Apostle Paul was the most effective missionary of early Christianity and its first theologian. He is sometimes called the "second founder" of Christianity, having written more than one-fourth of the New Testament and having been responsible for translating Christianity into terms that could be accepted by the Greek-thinking people of the Roman Empire. His theology emerges from the many letters he wrote to the young churches throughout Asia Minor and Greece, but his Letter to the Romans probably stands as the greatest systemization of Christian theology ever produced. Although generally not a systematic theologian, Paul uses the Letter to the Romans as a means for establishing Christian dogma. While acknowledging his theological debt to Judaism, including his concept of righteousness, his cosmology—that is, his philosophy about the origin and shape of the universe—reflects that of the Hellenistic world. His belief that improper participation in the Lord's Supper causes sickness and death is not unlike ideas found in some of the Hellenistic cults. Above all, however, Paul is a biblical theologian, and his basic purpose was to interpret the revelation of the God of the Old Testament in the death and resurrection of Jesus Christ.

One of the central premises in Pauline theology is the concept of justification through faith. He presents this view in the Letters to the Romans and Corinthians, in which he argues that God moved first to save humankind and that nothing that humans can do—except believing in Jesus Christ as Lord—can earn them salvation. Also central to Paul's thinking is a kind of apocalyptic mysticism—that is, an emphasis on the coming of the end of history. In this view, Paul accepts and affirms the ultimate triumph of God over evil.

All of this rests, of course, on the assumption that Jesus is Lord and Messiah, and, because Messiah has come, the end is at hand. The decisive event has occurred in the crucifixion and resurrection of Christ, and the cross becomes a central force in Paul's Christology—that is, his definition of Christ. Through the crucifixion, God reveals his love for humankind and uses it as a propitiation for all sin. However, Paul's theology includes God's judgment. Humankind has failed to follow the word of God and lives enslaved by sin, which leads to death. The Law is insufficient for redemption. Only God's grace, with its consequent gift of righteousness, can lead to eternal life. In Christ, God reveals his mercy to those who respond in faith.

Paul's theology is far more complex than this brief description can encompass, but his systematic explanation of who Christ is and what God intended in Christ has underpinned Christian thought and belief for nearly two thousand years. Paul explained his theology in a series of occasional letters written to specific local churches undergoing specific local problems. They were intended to be read to the entire congregation and are structured according to the letter-writing standards of the day. They begin with an introductory salutation, followed by a statement of thanksgiving; then comes the main body of the letter, which addresses the major points of concern. Paul first treats questions of doctrine, then he uses persuasive exhortation in order to move the congregation to the action he desires of them, before ending the letter with a statement of his travel plans, a greeting, and benediction. The letters were arranged in their current form after their collection toward the end of the first century. They represent the heart of Christian doctrine as it was shaped into canon by the early Church, and it is through Paul's inspiration and interpretation that the Christian world has viewed the events described in the Gospels and chronicled in the Acts of the Apostles.

Paul's favorite form is the Hellenistic discourse known

5.31 Juan Fernández de Navarrette, *St Peter and St Paul*, 1577. Oil on canvas, 7 ft 6½ ins × 6 ft (2.3 × 1.8 m), The Escorial.

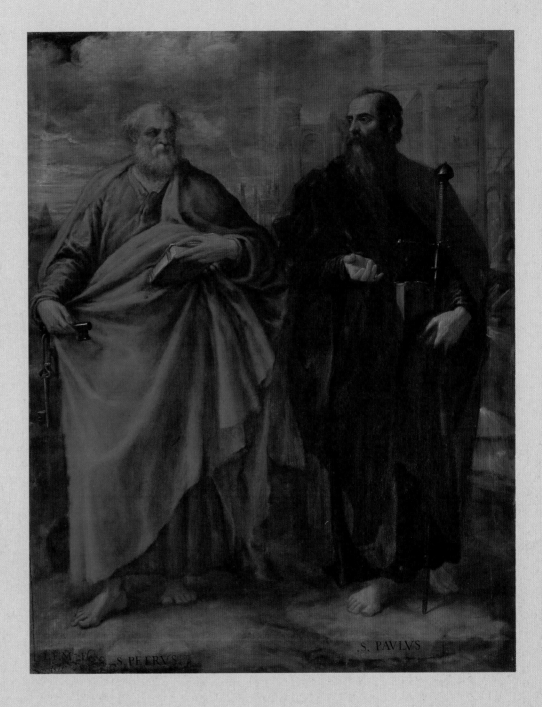

as the *diatribe*. In this argumentative structure, the correspondent raises a series of questions and then answers them. Because Paul dictated his letters, their style is often awkward and, occasionally, difficult to comprehend. Complex sentences, which never seem to end, are not infrequent, and thoughts are often truncated or expressed in incomplete sentences. When they are placed in the framework of modern practice, his cultural assumptions sometimes cause problems—for example, his comments in the Letters to the Corinthians about restricting the role of women. Scholars and clerics have been dealing with these issues for two millennia, but it is important to remember that the letters were written to address specific circumstances in specific locations. It has, for example, been suggested that the comments about women in Corinthians were made in response to the fact that some women in Corinthian society were especially disruptive, and applying Paul's comments in general distorts their original intention.

Paul sees women in a role of equality: "Let the husband give to the wife all that is due to her; and in the same way let the wife give to the husband all that is due to him. A wife is not in absolute control of her own body, but her husband is. In the same way a husband is not in absolute control of his own, but his wife is. Do not deprive each other of each other's legitimate rights, unless it be by common agreement" (1 Corinthians 7:3–7).

The letters were arranged in their current form after their collection toward the end of the first century. They represent the heart of Christian doctrine as it was shaped into canon by the early Church, and it is through Paul's inspiration and interpretation that the Christian world has viewed the events described in the Gospels and chronicled in the Acts of the Apostles.

During his second missionary journey, Paul, accompanied by Silas and Timothy, went to Thessalonica, the capital of Macedonia, where, for three successive Sabbaths, he preached in the Jewish Synagogue, proclaiming Jesus as Messiah and using scripture to prove the necessity of Jesus' death and resurrection. Many Jews, including recent Hellenistic converts to Judaism, were converted to Christianity by Paul, and as a result the leaders of the synagogue accused him of sedition, making it necessary for Paul and Silas to be spirited out of town by their friends. Concerned for the young Christian community in Thessalonica, which had been deprived of its leadership, persecuted by the synagogue, and subjected to some scurrilous attacks on Paul's character, motives, and authority, Paul sent Timothy to strengthen and encourage the Thessalonican church. When Timothy returned with good news about the faith and loyalty of the Christians in Thessalonica, Paul wrote the first letter to that congregation. He expresses his gratitude and joy at their perseverance, exhorts them to Christian conduct, and answers two questions that concerned them: Is a Christian deprived of the blessings of the kingdom if he dies before the second coming of Christ? and When will Christ come in glory?

The earliest of Paul's correspondence, the letter was written from Corinth around A.D. 50.

Among Paul's admonitions and theology come some truly great poetic passages that have endured the test of time and endeared themselves to millions. Perhaps the best example is the "Hymn of Love" from 1 Corinthians 13:

> I may speak with the tongues of men and of angels, but if I have not love, I am become no more than echoing brass or a clanging cymbal. I may have the gift of prophecy, I may understand all sacred secrets and all knowledge, I may have faith enough to remove mountains, but if I have not love I am nothing. I may dole out all that I have, I may surrender my body that I may be burned, but if I have not love it is no good to me.
>
> Love is patient; love is kind; love knows no envy; love is no braggart; it is not inflated with its own importance; it does not behave gracelessly; it does not insist on its rights; it never flies into a temper; it does not store up the memory of any wrong it has received; it finds no pleasure in evil-doing; it rejoices with the truth; it can endure anything; it is completely trusting; it never ceases to hope; it bears everything with triumphant fortitude.
>
> Love never fails. Whatever prophecies there are, they will vanish away. Whatever tongues there are, they will cease. Whatever knowledge we have, it will pass away. It is only part of the truth that we know now and only part of the truth that we can foretell to others. But when that which is complete shall come, that which is incomplete will vanish away. When I was a child I used to speak like a child; I used to think like a child; I used to reason like a child. When I became a man I put an end to childish things. Now we see only reflections in a mirror which leaves us with nothing but riddles to solve, but then we shall see face to face. Now I know in part; but then I will know even as I am known. Now faith, hope, love remain—these three; but the greatest of these is love.

CHAPTER REVIEW

Critical Thought

Judaism followed a challenging course from the Patriarchs through the Judges to the Monarchy. The story is one of a people to whom God revealed himself, with whom he made a covenant, and whom he led to nationhood. It also is the story of a recurring cycle of disobedience, contrition, and forgiveness centering on the constant struggle of humankind to follow its own dictates rather than those of a divine being—even one who performed mighty acts to show his power and his steadfast love for his chosen people. There is much to find in the story of the Hebrews about theology and the emergence of monotheism, about the nature of revealed truth, about human obstinacy and self-will, and about the consequences of disobedience.

The theme of obedience moves from Judaism to Christianity in the first century, and we have seen it expressed beautifully in the Magnificat of Mary. The concept of obedience has proved difficult not only for devoted Christians; it is problematic in general, for it raises the question of the fundamental nature of the individual and of his or her "freedom" or "rights" to pursue individual happiness. Under what conditions should individuals submit to authority—religious or secular?

Summary

After reading this chapter, you should be able to:

- Describe the history of the Jewish people, the rise of Christianity, and the impact of Judeo-Christian culture and religion on the Roman Empire.
- Discuss the major divisions of the Bible and relate them to the basic story and beliefs of Judaism and Christianity.
- Compare Augustine with Tertullian on the nature of the soul, and with Plato and Aristotle on the nature of art.
- Identify the reforms of Diocletian and Constantine and explain how these reforms rejuvenated the late Roman Empire and affected the spread of Christianity.
- Explain the relevance of the "Petrine Theory" to the development of the Western Christian Church.
- Identify and characterize Judaic, Christian, and late Roman art, architecture, and music.
- Apply the elements and principles of composition to describe, analyze, and compare individual works of art illustrated in the chapter.

CHAPTER SIX

Byzantium and the Rise of Islam

OUTLINE

BYZANTIUM
Justinian
The Isaurian Emperors and
Iconoclasm
From Rise to Fall (867–1453)
Byzantine Intellectualism
The Arts of Byzantium
MASTERWORK: The *Harbaville
Triptych*
OUR DYNAMIC WORLD: Chinese
Theatre

THE RISE OF ISLAM
The Religion of Islam
PROFILE: Muhammad
The Spread of Islam
Islamic Style in the Arts

FOCAL POINT: IN PRAISE OF THE
EMPEROR—THE MARK OF
JUSTINIAN
PROFILE: Anthemius of Tralles
TECHNOLOGY: Spanning Space
with Triangles and Pots

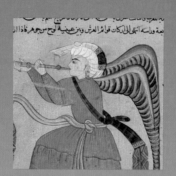

VIEW

CHURCH AND STATE

A number of critical issues will be explored in this chapter. These include major early factors that caused the split between the Eastern and Western Empires of Rome. Implicit in that split, although we sometimes barely acknowledge its importance, was the split of the Christian Church into Roman Catholicism and Eastern Orthodoxy. The split of the Roman Empire into East and West had profound implications for both the Christian religion and secular politics. Central to it all was Byzantium or Constantinople. Later, Byzantium would connect not only East and West but also Christianity and Islam—in a geographical sense, if not a theological one. Byzantium occupies a pivotal geographical location, as critical today as it was one thousand years ago. It is the place where Islam, Eastern Orthodoxy, and Roman Catholicism meet. The overlapping and conflicts among Orthodox Christianity, Roman Catholicism, and Islam are as old as Byzantium and as recent as today's newscast.

Above Detail of Fig. **6.19**.

6.1 Empress Theodora and attendants, c. 547. Detail of wall mosaic. San Vitale, Ravenna, Italy.

KEY TERMS

Some of the basic terms and concepts we will encounter in this chapter include the following:

Orthodoxy means the practice of adhering to the accepted, traditional, and established religious, in this case Christian, faith.

Humanism is a philosophy concerned with human beings, their achievements, and interests, as opposed to abstract beings and problems of theology.

Mosaic, a decorative work for walls, vaults, floors, or ceilings, composed of pieces of colored material set in plaster or cement.

Hieratic style is an artistic style of depicting sacred persons or offices: it means "holy" or "sacred" and its treatment of the proportions of the human body is elongated as opposed to naturalistic.

Apse, a large niche or niche-like space projecting from and expanding the interior space of a building.

Hajj, a Muslim's sacred pilgrimage to Mecca.

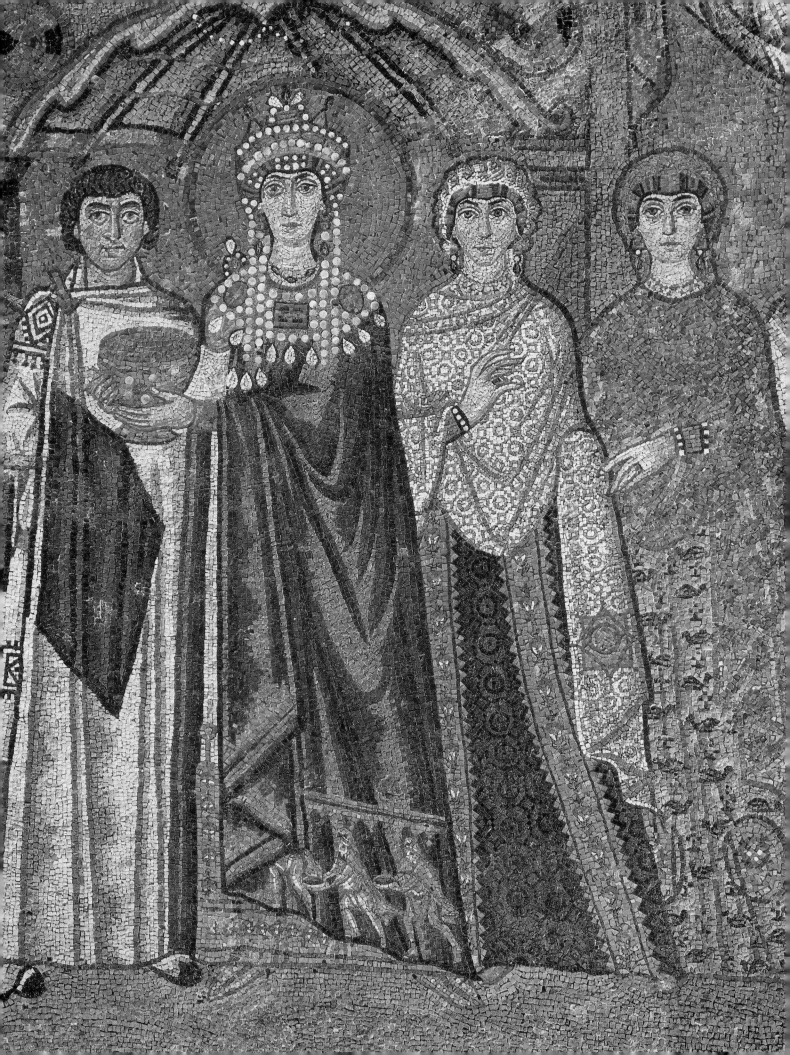

BYZANTIUM

Astride the main land route from Europe to Asia and its riches, the city of Byzantium had great potential as a major metropolis. The city's defensible deep-water port, which controlled the passage between the Mediterranean and the Black Sea, and agriculturally fertile environs, made it into an ideal "New Rome." And this was precisely the objective of the Emperor Constantine when he dedicated his new capital in A.D. 330 and changed its name to Constantinople (it is now known as Istanbul). The city prospered, becom-

ing the center of Christian Orthodoxy and the source of a unique and intense style in the visual arts and architecture. When Rome fell to the Goths in 476, it had long since handed the torch of its civilization to Constantinople, where the arts and learning of the classical world were preserved and nurtured, while Western Europe suffered the turmoil and destruction of wave upon wave of barbarian invasion.

Although the Eastern Empire of Byzantium is geographically considered part of the Eastern world, its relationship with and influence on Western thought and art were highly significant. Here we examine the history and

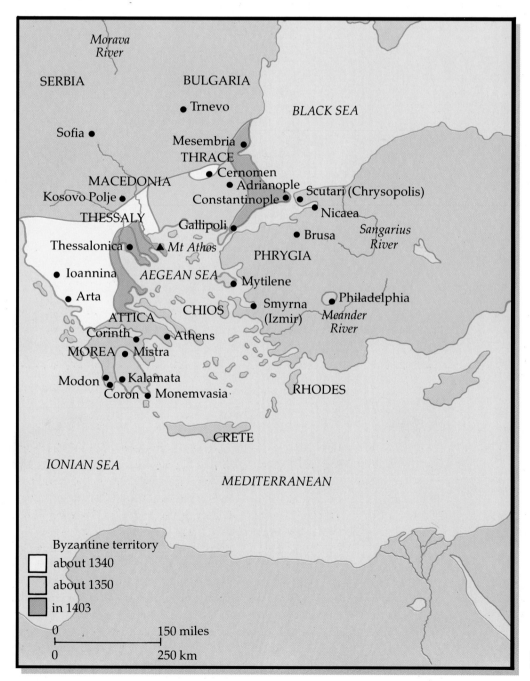

Map 6.1 The Byzantine Empire 1340–1403.

	GENERAL EVENTS	LITERATURE & PHILOSOPHY	VISUAL ART & ARCHITECTURE	PERFORMING ARTS
300				
	Constantinople founded Eastern and Western Empires split	Early hagiography	Theodosian obelisk (6.10)	
400				
	Fall of Rome			
500				
	Reign of Justinian	Justinian legal code Procopius of Caesarea Anthemius of Tralles Isidorus of Miletus	*Barberini Ivory* (6.11) San Vitale, Ravenna (6.1, 6.3, 6.27, 6.28, 6,29, 6.32) St Sophia (6.30, 6.33, 6.34, 6.35, 6.36) Mosaics (6.3, 6.4, 6.5, 6.6)	
600				
	Death of Muhammad Isaurian rulers Spread of Islam Battle of Poitiers		Dome of the Rock (6.23, 6.24) Great Mosque, Damascus (6.25, 6.26) Silk textile art (6.9)	
800				
	Charlemagne unifies Western Empire End of iconoclast struggle		*Raising of Lazarus* (6.8) *Vision of Ezekiel* (6.7) *Virgin and Child* (6.12) *Harbaville Triptych* (6.13)	Kanones
1000				
	Comneni rulers Muslim conquest in west Africa	Revival of Platonism Prodromic poems	St Theodosia (6.16) St Luke and the Virgin (6.17)	
1200				
	Fourth Crusade Constantinople sacked by Frankish invaders		St Mary Pammakaristos (6.18) *Dormition of the Virgin* (6.2)	
1400				
	Fall of Constantinople to the Ottoman Turks			

Timeline 6.1 Byzantium and the rise of Islam.

culture of the capital city of the Eastern Roman Empire from the year 330 until its conquest by the Muslim Turks in 1453. Parallel developments in the West are covered in Chapters 7, 8, and 9.

The Byzantine Empire was founded on 11 May 330. On that day, Constantine made Byzantium the second capital of the Roman Empire, and renamed it Constantinople. The geographical location of the city, at the bridging point between Europe and Asia, made it an ideal center for trade, governance, and the development of the arts. The culture of the region at that time was based upon a mixture of Hellenistic tradition and Christian thought.

The separation of the Eastern Roman Empire from Rome and the Western Roman Empire became fact in the year 395. Emperor Theodosius the Great died in that year, and he divided his empire between his two sons, Arcadius and Honorus. While Eastern in many respects, Constantinople maintained its Roman traditions after the fall of the Roman Empire in 476 until the end of the sixth century. From then on, it followed its own independent course.

Two crises contributed to the distinctive character of the Eastern Empire. First, barbarians invaded Europe in the fifth century—the Visigoths, led by Alaric; the Huns, led by Attila; and the Ostrogoths, led by Theodoric. The barbarians were successful in carving up the Western Empire, yet they were unable to make more than superficial inroads into the East. This gave the New Rome political supremacy. The second crisis was religious. During the fourth and fifth centuries, the Eastern Empire was the seedbed of several "heresies" in the Christian Church. True to its Greek spirit, the Eastern Orthodox Church reveled in subtle theological metaphysics. This characteristic led to the development of ideas that conflicted with the official theology of the Church in Italy and eventually caused a schism between the Eastern and Roman Church establishments that persists to this day. Out of this schism emerged the important concept of a purely Eastern Empire. Its system of government was an absolute monarchy in the Eastern tradition. Its Church used the Greek language in its writings and rituals, and it was closely linked with the government that ruled it.

Justinian

The movement toward total separation from the Western Empire lost some momentum under the rule of the Emperor Justinian (juhs-TIN-ee-uhn; 527–65). He aspired to be Roman emperor as well as emperor in the East, and tried to promote both imperialism and Christianity. He claimed to be heir to the Caesars, and his great ambition was to re-establish Roman unity. This ambition was partly achieved as he reconquered Africa, Italy, Corsica, Sardinia, the Balearic Islands, and part of Spain (Map 6.2). The Frankish kings of Gaul recognized his suzerainty, and as head of the Eastern Empire, he was also revered as Vicar of God on earth and champion of Orthodoxy.

In an attempt to hold his reconstructed empire together, Justinian sought a close alliance with the Roman papacy. As he concentrated on the West, however, he left the Eastern Empire vulnerable to hostile forces from the East, who tried to exploit this weakness over the following two centuries.

A major factor in Justinian's rule consisted of the role played by his wife, Empress Theodora (thee-oh-DOHR-ah; c. 500–548), whom some sources call "joint ruler." In his unreliable *Secret History*, Procopius of Caesarea (proh-COH-pee-uhs; seh-zuh-REE-uh) alleges that before her marriage to Justinian in 525 she had been an actress and prostitute. There is some credence in the former assertion, at least, as we will note later in the section on theatre. Her charms and personality undeniably exerted great influence over Justinian. During the Nika (NEE-kuh) Rebellion (532), her intervention prevented him from fleeing the capital and probably saved his crown, although there is scholarly dissension about her popularity and acceptance.

The Nika (the word means conquer) Rebellion was an uprising of thousands of citizens that occurred when two factions of soldiers, who were rival horseracing charioteers known as the blues and the greens, united to oppose Justinian's policies. It was Theodora who refused to yield, and at

her instigation, a young general named Belisarius led troops in a massacre of thousands in the Hippodrome. Although parts of the city were destroyed in this rebellion, Justinian's (or Theodora's) victory ushered in a new era of absolute imperial rule.

Theodora, further, moved decisively on other public policy issues. In one instance she tried, with only partial success, to secure her husband's tolerance of Monophysitism (mahn-oh-FIHZ-ih-tiz-uhm)—a Christian heresy in which its adherents claimed that Jesus' nature was strictly divine, as opposed to the orthodox belief that Jesus was both human and divine. Justinian, who advocated *caesaro-papism*—that is, the supremacy of Emperor even over Church—called the Second Council of Constantinople (553) in an unsuccessful attempt to reconcile the Monophysites to the Church. After Theodora's death, Justinian's rule lost intensity and purpose.

Justinian's greatest legacy lies not in his brief reconstruction of the Roman Empire, however, but in the enormous work of recodifying the outmoded and cumbersome apparatus of Roman law. The result was the *Corpus Juris Civilis* (KOR-puhs JOOR-is si-VIL-is), which reduced the reference books needed by a Roman lawyer from 106 volumes to six. This recodification of the law greatly influenced Justinian's own and succeeding centuries.

Because Justinian's power was concentrated, his abilities great, and his spending extravagant, his death left the Eastern Empire severely weakened, both economically and militarily. It was not until the advent of the Isaurian emperors in 717 that Byzantium recovered, but critical changes resulted. All political power was invested in the military leaders. Latin was replaced by Greek, and literary forms began to take on Eastern characteristics. Orthodox Christianity, with its emphasis on monastic retreat from worldly life, strengthened its hold on public affairs. In all areas of life, the breach with the Roman legacy widened. Out of all this arose a truly Eastern and enduring empire, militarily strong and efficiently organized.

The Isaurian Emperors and Iconoclasm

The task of stabilizing the Eastern Empire fell to the first oriental rulers to take control. These were the Isaurian (i-SOR-ee-uhn) emperors, who ruled from 717 to 867. They had originally come from the distant mountains of Anatolia. The first ruler of the Isaurian dynasty, Leo III, drove the Arabs from Constantinople in 717. His successor, Constantine V, re-established control over important territories in Asia Minor, and fortified and consolidated the Balkan frontier. As they tried to minimize internal strife, the Isaurians concerned themselves with administrative order and the general welfare of their subjects. The bureaucracy of the Empire thus became more closely associated with the imperial palace.

An even briefer legal code, called the *Ecloga*, replaced Justinian's *Corpus*. The *Ecloga* (ehk-LOHG-uh) limited the traditional authority of the Roman *paterfamilias*, the male head of the household, by increasing rights for women and children. This was a concept new to Christian society: marriage was no longer a dissoluble human contract, but, rather, an irrevocable sacrament. The oriental punishment of mutilation replaced the death penalty in criminal justice, reflecting at least some concern for rehabilitation.

The period of Isaurian rule saw violent conflict within the Christian Church, however. The causes of this conflict, known as the "iconoclastic controversy," have been variously interpreted. In the preface to the *Ecloga*, the emperor's duties were cast in terms of a divine mandate:

Since God has put in our hands the imperial authority . . . we believe that there is nothing higher or greater that we can do in return than to govern in judgment and justice those who are commited by Him to our care.[1]

In his self-appointed role of king–priest, Leo III entered the controversy, which concerned the use of ICONS in the Eastern Church. Icons, or images, depicting the saints, the blessed Virgin, and God himself, by now occupied a special place in Orthodox churches. From the sixth century onward, these paintings and mosaics had been extremely important in Orthodox worship and teaching, but in the eighth century, their use was questioned, and those who were opposed to them maintained that icons were idols—that is, they had become objects of worship in themselves, perverting the worship of God. They demanded the removal of icons, and on many occasions they used force to impose their will, hence the name "iconoclast," or "icon-destroyer."

Leo III favored the iconoclasts, and, in 730, issued a proclamation forbidding the use of images in public worship. One reason for the edict appears to have been Leo's belief that the Arab invasions and volcanic eruptions at the time indicated God's displeasure with Orthodox practices. The iconoclast movement reached its peak under Constantine V and was formally approved by the council of bishops in 754. Over the next century, icons remained at the center of controversy, and their use ebbed and flowed, depending on the current emperor. Gradually, however, the "iconophiles," or "icon-lovers," gained ground. Persecution was relaxed, and on the first Sunday of Lent in 843, a day still celebrated as an Orthodox feast-day, icons were permanently restored to their place in Eastern worship.

The resolution of the iconoclastic struggle and the establishment of a united empire under Charlemagne in the West in 800 finally set Byzantium on its own course. By the time of the Emperor Theophilus (thee-AH-fil-uhs; 829–92), the Byzantine court rivaled any in the world. The University of Constantinople was reorganized, in about 850, by Caesar Bordas, and it became a great intellectual center. The triumph of the iconophiles in 843 united the Orthodox Church, and strengthened its influence and character. The 150 years that followed the reign of Theophilus were a period of great prosperity and brilliance.

From Rise to Fall (867–1453)

Nothing in the West during this period remotely resembled the splendor and sophistication of Byzantium. In the East, unlike the West, religious and secular life were closely intertwined. The visual arts flourished, and the subject matter was almost without exception religious. The Church calendar was inseparable from the court calendar. Moreover, the spectacle of court and Church ritual had a theatrical splendor, which reinforced the majesty of the empire and the place of the emperor as the vice-regent of God. Even the emperor's public appearances were staged. Seated behind a series of heavy curtains which were raised one by one, he was revealed only when the final curtain was lifted. Yet despite its strong economic and commercial base, and its military strength, Constantinople was unable to withstand the trials ahead.

A slide into chaos was checked for a time under the rule of the Comneni (kuhm-NEE-nee) emperors. The Comneni dynasty, which lasted until 1185, succeeded in ridding Greece of the Normans and defending the Empire against the Petchenegs, a group of southern Russian nomads. Venice had supplied naval assistance, however, and in return demanded important commercial concessions. Venetian influence and power increased immensely, while Byzantium could not recover its former strength, and internal struggles and conflicts proliferated.

In 1203 a crusade set out from the West for the Holy Land, but the Venetian contingent diverted it instead to Constantinople, whose wealth Venice was keen to plunder. In 1204 a riot provided the Crusaders with an excuse for sacking the city. This delivered the fatal blow to the Empire. The treasures of the city—books and works of art centuries old—were almost all destroyed or carried off. Central organization collapsed. Trying to preserve themselves, parts of the empire broke away. The Crusaders had stripped the empire of its strength, and it lay defenseless against the Ottoman Turks when they overran it in 1453.

The importance of the sack of Constantinople cannot be overemphasized. Two major results occurred: (1) the terrible slaughter of innocents stained the Crusades in the

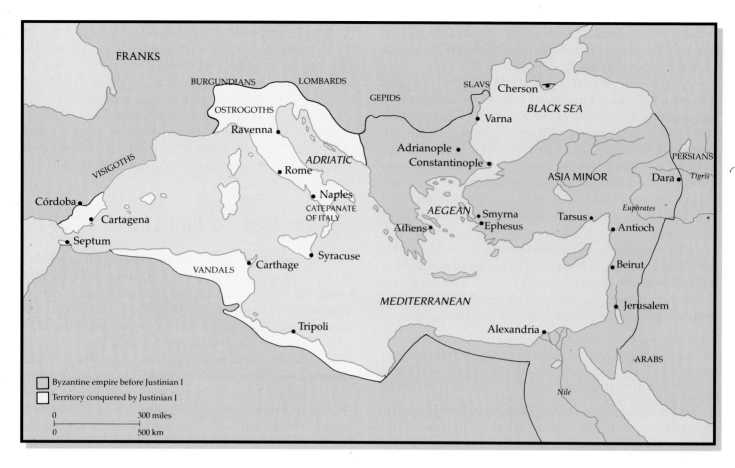

Map 6.2 The empire of Justinian I.

eyes of all Orthodox Christians—a further exacerbation of the rift between Eastern and Western Christianity; (2) the booty taken from Constantinople to Europe—especially to Venice—contained such value and quality that it formed the foundation for the Renaissance, providing models for artists across Europe—particularly in northern Italy.

Byzantine Intellectualism

Nowhere in the medieval world was the classical tradition better preserved than in Constantinople. Although it was heir to the Roman Empire, the Eastern Empire was directly descended from classical Greece. The Greek cities of Athens, Antioch, and Alexandria all lay within its borders. Constantinople itself was to all intents and purposes a Greek city. Its native language was Greek—at a time when no nation of the Western Empire even spoke the language—and so its citizens were better versed in Greek classicism than anyone else. Eastern libraries overflowed with treasured classical texts. Greek literature formed the basis of Byzantine education. Homer, Hesiod, Aristophanes, Aeschylus, Plato, and Aristotle were widely read among the cultured classes. At the University of Constan-

tinople, the "consuls of the philosophers" and the "masters of the rhetoricians" found inspiration in classical traditions. The same love of antiquity seems also to have been felt by private individuals. Even at its very lowest ebb, Constantinople never fell into a cultural dark age.

The study of history took pride of place in Byzantine thought. In the sixth century great historians arose, who were without equal in the Western world. They understood both politics and human psychology and their writings display superb composition and style. Although some, such as Anna Comnena, imitated the ancients so faithfully that their style became cramped and involved, she and others, such as Nicephorus Bryennius, were inspired to make the historian's task a true art, rather than a sterile recitation of events.

Theology held the second highest place among Eastern intellectual pursuits. The proliferation of theological literature was undoubtedly fueled by the seemingly endless heresies that troubled Byzantium and required defenses of Orthodoxy. Numerous works were devoted to scriptural commentary, and the development of monasticism produced a new genre: mystical literature. Classical rhetoric influenced religious speaking, which became very popular.

In the realm of philosophy, Platonic thought re-emerged in the University of Constantinople during the eleventh century. The intellectual accomplishments of the Eastern Empire influenced the West considerably. The Byzantine conception of Imperial power, which derived from the Justinian Code, had a profound effect on emerging Western ideas of absolute monarchy. The law of Justinian was brought to Italy, and by the eleventh century, law schools in Rome, Ravenna, and Bologna were teaching its doctrines. Here Frederick Barbarossa (bahr-buh-ROH-suh) found strong arguments for establishing his Imperial claims in the middle of the twelfth century. In the thirteenth century, scholars in Bologna provided the bases on which the Emperor Frederick II Hohenstaufen (HOH-en-shtow-fen) proclaimed himself "law incarnate upon earth," and justified "his right to order ecclesiastical affairs as freely as the secular interests of his empire."[2] In the same tradition, the king of France was later declared "above the law."

Theological accomplishment in the Eastern Orthodox Church was superior to that in the West, at least until the twelfth century. Its influence can be seen in the works of many Western theologians, among them Thomas Aquinas (uh-KWY-nuhs). French literature and legend also display strong links with Byzantine sources, and particularly its hagiography, or descriptions of lives of the saints.

Other Byzantine legacies included the promulgation of Aristotelian philosophy and a strong current of HUMANISM, both of which figured prominently in the Renaissance of the mid-fifteenth century in Western Europe, centered on Italy. Platonic doctrine had taken a place of honor in the University of Constantinople in the eleventh century, and it was from there that Platonic thought spread, first to Florence, in Italy, and then to the rest of Europe. The Greek scholars who left Constantinople after its sack and came to Italy brought Byzantine humanism with them. Humanism enjoyed great currency during the thirteenth and early fourteenth centuries in Europe. These scholars also brought many important Greek manuscripts, and rekindled an appreciation of Greek intellectual accomplishment in the West.

The Arts of Byzantium

Two-Dimensional Art

Fundamental to the visual art of the Eastern Empire is the idea that art can be used to interpret as well as to represent its subject matter. Byzantine art was conservative, and, for the most part, anonymous and impersonal. The artist was clearly subordinate to the work. Much of Byzantine art remains undated, and questions about how styles developed and where they came from are unresolved. We can,

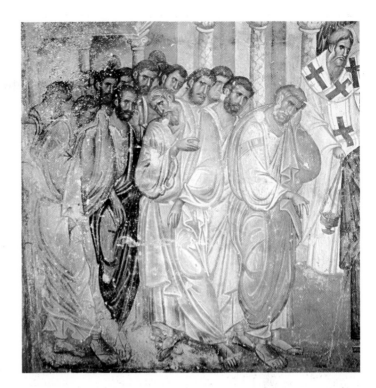

6.2 *Dormition of the Virgin* (detail), 1258–64. Fresco. Church of the Trinity, Sopoćani, Yugoslavia.

however, draw a few general conclusions with regard to Byzantine art (which, we must remember, encompasses nearly a thousand years of history and, thereby, several shifts in style). First, the **content** of Byzantine art focuses on human figures. Those figures reveal three main elements: (1) *holy figures*—Christ, the Virgin Mary, the saints, and the apostles with bishops and angels portrayed in their company; (2) *the emperor*—believed to be divinely sanctioned by God; (3) *the classical heritage*—images of cherubs, mythological heroes, gods and goddesses, and personifications of virtues. In addition, the **form** of Byzantine two-dimensional art increasingly reflected a consciously derived spirituality.

The ostentation of the Imperial court influenced artistic style, and Christ and the saints were depicted as frozen in immobile poses and garbed in regal purples. Lacy ornamentation ended what was left of classical purity in the sixth century.

The period of Justinian marks an apparently deliberate break with the past. What we describe as the distinctly "Byzantine style," with its characteristic abstraction and its focus on spirituality, began to take shape in the fifth and sixth centuries. (If the classical Hellenistic tradition survived at all, it was only as an undercurrent.) Throughout the seventh century, classicism and decorative abstraction intermingled freely.

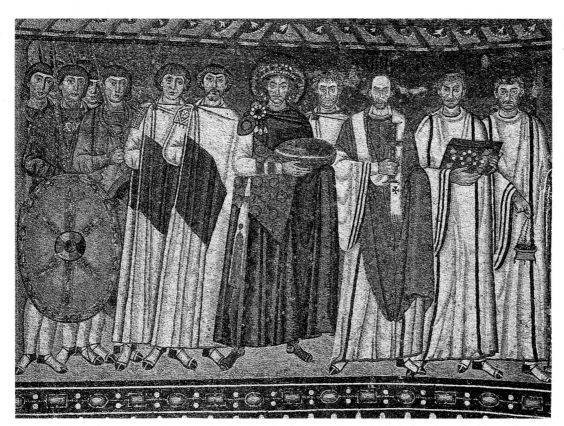

6.3 *Emperor Justinian and his Court*, c. 547. Wall mosaic, San Vitale, Ravenna, Italy.

By the eleventh century, Byzantine wall painting and mosaics had developed a hierarchical (hy-er-ARK-i-kuhl) formula. There was reduced emphasis on narrative. The Church represented the kingdom of God, and as one moves up the hierarchy, one encounters figures ranging from human to the divine. Placement of figures in the composition depended upon religious, not spatial, relationships. Figures are strictly two-dimensional, but portrayal is elegant and decorative. In twelfth- and especially in thirteenth-century art, this approach intensifies, detailed with architectural backdrops, flowing garments, and elongated but dynamic figures (Fig. **6.2**). The fourteenth century produced small-scale, crowded works that are highly narrative. Space is confused by irrational perspective, and figures are distorted, with small heads and feet. The effect is of intense spirituality.

Hieratic Style

In the middle centuries of the Empire, a style known as *hieratic* (hy-er-AT-ik), meaning here "holy" or "sacred," emerged, consisting of formal, almost rigid images. (Do not confuse this style with the hierarchical formula just discussed.) It was less intended to represent real life than to inspire reverence and meditation. The canon of proportion of the hieratic style ordained that a man should measure nine heads in height (seven heads gives a lifelike proportion). The hairline was one nose length above the forehead.

In addition, "if the man is naked, four noses' lengths are needed for half his width."

By the thirteenth century, mosaics had returned to more naturalistic depictions, but they did not lose the clear sense of the spiritual that was apparent in the much earlier Ravenna mosaic of Emperor Justinian and his court (Fig. **6.3**). The hieratic style also occurs in other media, for example, in the *Harbaville Triptych* (TRIP-tik; see Fig. **6.13**) and *Virgin and Child* ivories (see Fig. **6.12**). In both, we see the formality, frontal poses, and slight elongation of forms that are typical of this style.

When the emperor was depicted in Byzantine art, we may note any of several characteristics. The emperor may be shown in the presence of Christ to validate his supreme powers. One or several exclusive attributes of the emperor may be present—for example: (1) red shoes decorated with jewels; (2) a long purple robe over which is worn a scarf covered with jeweled patterns; (3) a crown from which a strand of pearls is suspended on each side of the face (called a *pendulia*); (4) a scepter.

Mosaic

Covering a period of a thousand turbulent years, Byzantine art contains a complex repertoire of styles. When Constantine established his capital at Constantinople, a group of artists and craftsmen, trained in other centers, was already there. When these people set to work on

Constantine's artistic projects, they naturally rendered their subjects in a manner quite different from the Roman style.

One of the earliest examples of two-dimensional art is a MOSAIC floor in the Imperial Palace of Constantinople. Mosaic was a characteristic Byzantine medium, and Figures **6.4**, **6.5**, and **6.6** show examples whose finely detailed execution allows for an essentially naturalistic style. The mosaics depict figures, buildings, and scenes, unconnected with each other, presented against a white background. The grandeur and elegance of these works reveal Greek classical influence. Although the figures are fairly naturalistic, the absence of background and shadow indicates that pictorial verisimilitude was neither intended

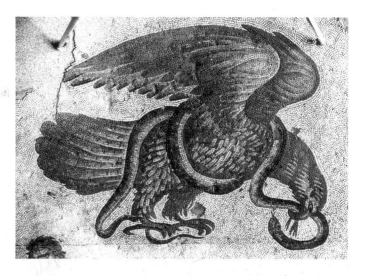

6.4 Eagle and serpent.

6.5 A seated "philosopher," early sixth century. Floor mosaic, Imperial Palace, Istanbul, Turkey.

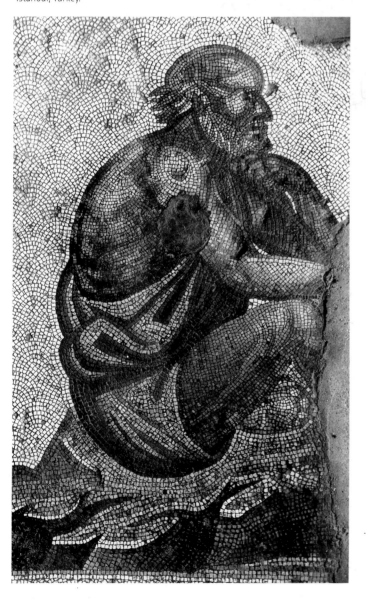

nor important. Rather, each figure has a mystical, abstract feel that is clearly unclassical.

The palette is rich and varied. The fragment shown in Figure **6.6** is representative of one important development in the use of color. The hair of the head which forms part of the decorative border as it intermingles with the foliage is green in places, while the mustache is blue. Yet the overall effect remains quite lifelike—a curious mix of the vividness and stylization that would later typify Byzantine art.

Manuscript Illumination

In addition to the mosaics that decorated palaces and the wealthier churches, manuscript ILLUMINATION and wall

6.6 Border, detail of head.

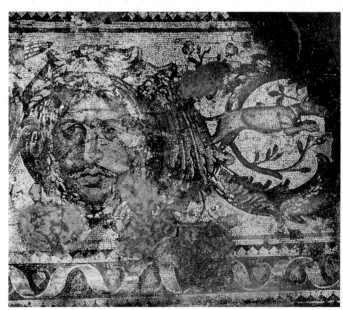

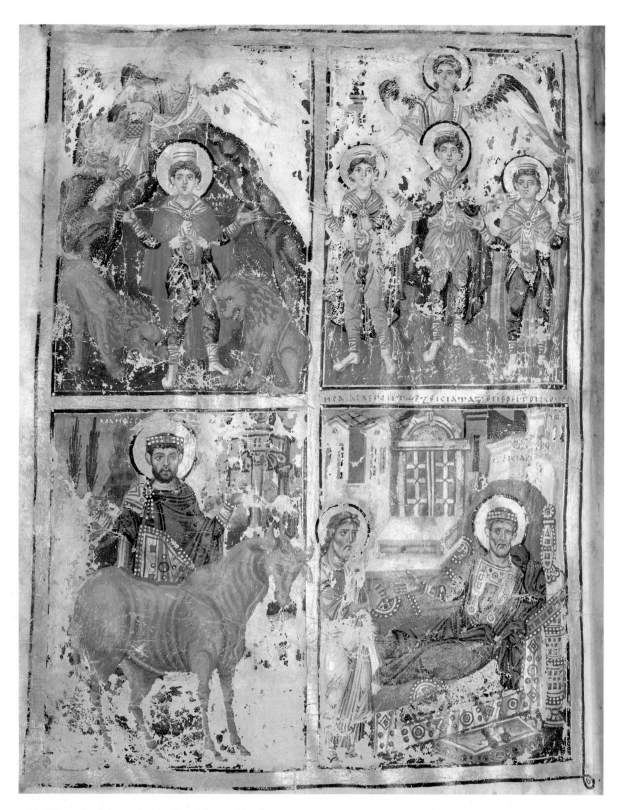

6.7 *The Vision of Ezekiel*, from the Homilies of Gregory Nazianzus, 867–87.
Bibliothèque Nationale, Paris.

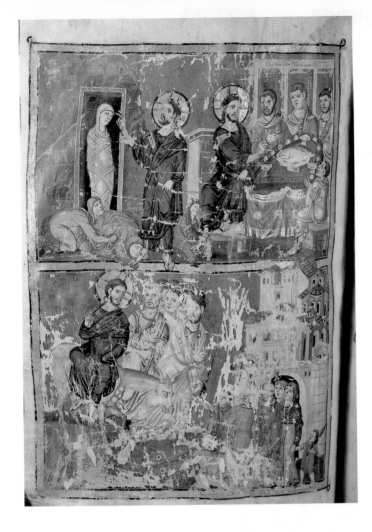

painting were also important in Byzantine art. From the period immediately after the iconoclastic controversy come exquisite manuscript illuminations. The rich colors are handled with masterful control and delicacy, to give assured shading and elegant detail.

The scenes shown in Figures **6.7** and **6.8** tell stories. *The Vision of Ezekiel* (Fig. **6.7**) treats the story from the Old Testament in four separate panels. Continuity is established by some part of each scene (except the last) breaking through its border into the neutral space between the panels. In the upper right corner, one picture actually breaks into the adjoining scene. Figure **6.8** unfolds its narrative in two registers, depicting the New Testament stories of Jesus raising Lazarus from the dead, and of his entry into Jerusalem shortly afterward. The technique is called "continuous narration," with the episodes laid out across the top, and then continuing in the bottom register. There is much in these works that is classically derived, and yet the treatment of space, with its crowded figures, its concentration on the surface plane, and lack of rational linear perspective, is entirely Byzantine.

Figure **6.9** shows the use of figure reversal and repetition. The central, repeated figure of the design is probably Samson, whose struggle with a lion is recounted in the Old Testament Book of Judges. The borders are composed of representational and geometric elements.

6.8 *The Raising of Lazarus and the Entry into Jerusalem*, from the Homilies of Gregory Nazianzus, 867–86. 16¹/₈ × 12 ins (41 × 30.5 cm). Bibliothèque Nationale, Paris.

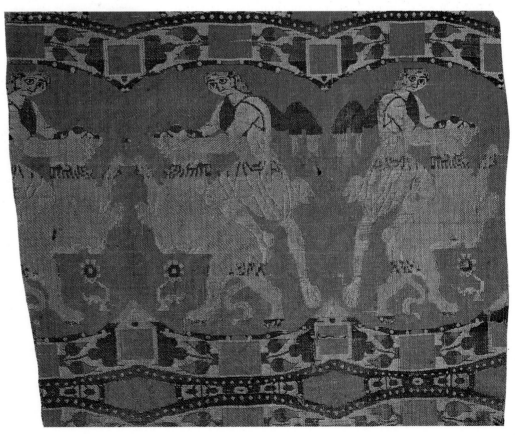

6.9 A lion strangler (Samson?), eighth century. Silk textile, 15¹/₂ × 12¹/₄ ins (39.5 × 31 cm). Victoria & Albert Museum, London.

Sculpture

Sculpture developed in the same historical context as the two-dimensional arts. Early works include sculptural vignettes illustrating Old and New Testament themes of salvation and life after death. For two centuries or so, the old art of Roman portrait sculpture held sway. But by the end of the fourth century, styles had begun to change. In Figure **6.10**, the base of an obelisk set up by Theodosius I, the frontal poses of figures, the ranks in which they are grouped, and the large, accentuated heads reflect oriental influence. Oriental and classically inspired works existed alongside each other in this period. Large-scale sculpture virtually disappeared from Byzantine art after the fifth century. Small-scale reliefs in ivory and metal continued in abundance, however. The clear-cut, precise style of Greek carving later became an outstanding characteristic of Byzantine sculpture. As in painting, sculpture took a classical turn after the iconoclastic struggle, but with an added awareness of the spiritual side of human beauty.

Ivory, traditionally a precious material, was always very popular in Byzantium. The number of carved works in different styles provides evidence of the various influences and degrees of technical ability in the Eastern Empire. Many of the ivories are *diptychs* (DIP-tiks), that is, in two panels. The *Barberini Ivory* (bahr-bair-EE-nee; Fig. **6.11**) is a work of five separate pieces, one of which is missing. At the center, an emperor is depicted on horseback. To the side is a consul in military costume, and above is a bust of Christ with winged victories on either side. The long panel at the bottom depicts Gothic emissaries on the left side and emissaries from India on the right; interestingly, the latter are portrayed carrying elephant tusks—the source of the artist's material. The rounded features and brilliant high-relief technique are typical of the period. The portrait of the emperor is individualized and recognizable. Later ivories show a more delicate elegance and a highly finished style.

The only known Byzantine freestanding sculpture in ivory is the tenth-century *Virgin and Child* (Fig. **6.12**). The drapery falls exquisitely and the surface is highly finished. The facial features, hands, and torsos display characteristic hieratic elongation.

Literature

The literature of Byzantium is often thought of as Greek literature. That is true of the majority of Byzantine literary works, and certainly of the literature coming out of Constantinople. But the Eastern Empire of Byzantium was not confined to Constantinople. The literature of the Empire in fact includes works in Latin, Syriac, Coptic, Church Slavonic, Armenian, and Georgian.

Byzantine literature in Greek, however, does comprise a vast quantity of works. Much from the early period has

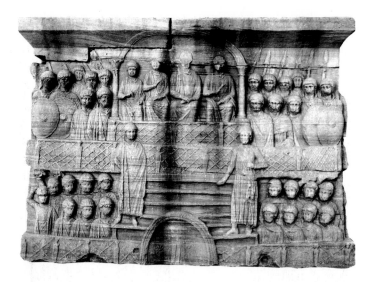

6.10 Base of the Theodosian obelisk, c. 395. Marble, about 13 ft 11 ins (4.2 m) high. Hippodrome, Istanbul, Turkey.

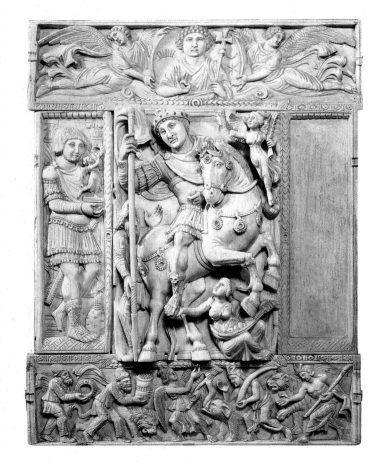

6.11 *Barberini Ivory*, showing a mounted emperor, c. 500. Ivory, 13½ × 10½ ins (34.1 × 26.6 cm). Louvre, Paris.

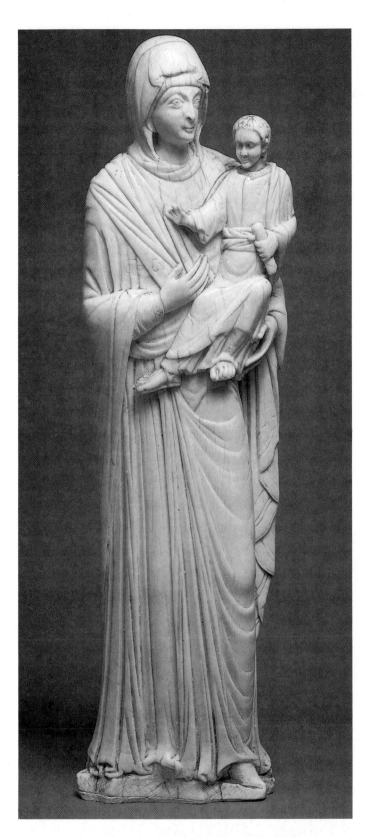

6.12 *Virgin and Child*, tenth century. Ivory, 12⁷/₈ ins (32.5 cm) high. Victoria & Albert Museum, London.

unfortunately been lost, and much remains unpublished, in manuscript form. Most of Greek Byzantine literature is on religious subjects, and much of it is hagiographic—that is, covering the life stories of saints and other religious figures. In addition, there are sermons, liturgical books, poetry, theology, devotional works, scriptural commentaries, and so on. Of the thousands of volumes that have survived, only a few hundred are secular.

To understand Byzantine literature, we need to know something about Byzantine aesthetic taste, which was quite different from our own. Modern readers do not obtain much pleasure from Byzantine literature, because we expect to find quite different qualities in what we read: we like originality of thought and expression. Educated Byzantines did not wish to be surprised. They liked clichés. Where we value clarity and directness, they admired elaboration and verbiage.

The Greek language itself had gone through several stages: an epic stage (the language of Homer and Hesiod); a literary stage (the Attic of the fifth and fourth centuries B.C.), and a New Testament Greek stage, which Byzantine scholars considered decadent. Sensitive to the rhetorical excesses of the past, churchmen admired only humble Byzantine speech and rejected "the fine style of the Hellenes," which they compared "to the proverbial honey that drips from the mouth of a whore." They would have considered that using the epic meters of the past was "an insult to Christ and the apostles."[3] As a result, each generation of Byzantine authors resisted the influence of its predecessors, going directly to ancient models. Many Byzantine works, therefore, exist in a sort of stylistic vacuum, without an acknowledged author, without contemporary references, and without place.

Byzantine literature falls into three principal genres. The first is historiography. This is not the history we speak of when we refer to a chronicled record of events, which was a separate activity in Byzantium. Historiography is, rather, a specific literary genre, related to rhetoric. It is written in ancient Greek, in imitation of ancient models, and interprets events and their influence on each other. As Theophanes Continuatus wrote: "The body of history is indeed mute and empty if it is deprived of the cause of actions." Probably the best-known of the Byzantine historiographers was Procopius of Caesarea. His broad, sweeping narratives, which were known for their objectivity and accuracy, were modeled on the work of the Athenian historian Thucydides.

The bulk of Byzantine literature belongs to the second genre, hagiography. Many of these texts on the lives of the saints survive, most of them written in ecclesiastical Greek. They consist of anecdotes about the saints, as well as full life-histories, which had been preserved by Egyptian monks. The anecdotal accounts were first circulated by

MASTERWORK

The *Harbaville Triptych*

The tenth and eleventh centuries have left us the greatest number of ivory objects, many decorated with small, elegant reliefs. In secular art, ivory caskets covered with minute carvings were the most popular form. Byzantine ivory carvers of the time showed remarkable ease and skill in imitating classical models. The same technique was used for small-scale reliefs of religious subjects. The *Harbaville Triptych* (Fig. **6.13**) is an exquisite example.

The TRIPTYCH was probably intended as a portable altar or shrine. The two wings folded shut for traveling, across the center panel. In the top center Christ is enthroned and flanked by John the Baptist and the Virgin Mary, who plead for mercy on behalf of all humanity. Five of the apostles appear below. The two

registers of the central panel are divided by an ornament repeated, with the addition of rosettes at the bottom border, and three heads in the top border. On either side of Christ's head appear medallions depicting angels holding symbols of the sun and moon. The figures have hieratic formality and solemnity, yet the depiction exhibits a certain softness that may result from a strong classical influence.

The figures stand on a plain, flat ground, ornamented only by the lettering of their names beside the heads. The side wings contain portraits of four soldier saints and four bishop saints. Between the levels are bust-length portraits of other saints. All the saints wear the dress of various civilian dignitaries. The triptych thus aligns the powers of Church and State, within the hierarchical formula of Byzantine art: each personage has his or her own place in the divine hierarchy, with Christ at the top.

This work and others from the same period belong to a class of works known as "Romanus," after a plaque in the Bibliothèque Nationale in Paris that shows Christ crowning the Emperor Romanus IV and his empress, Eudocia. The works of this Romanus school of ivory carvers are identifiable by style but they also have a particular ICONOGRAPHIC peculiarity. The cross in Christ's NIMBUS, or halo, shows the usual rectangular outline, but a pearled border has been added to both cross and nimbus. Similarly fine workmanship is found in the mosaics and painting of the time; in fact, stylistic developments in the ivories were closely associated with those in painting.

6.13 The *Harbaville Triptych*, interior, late tenth century. Ivory, 9½ ins (24.2 cm) high, central panel 5⅝ ins (14.2 cm) wide. Louvre, Paris.

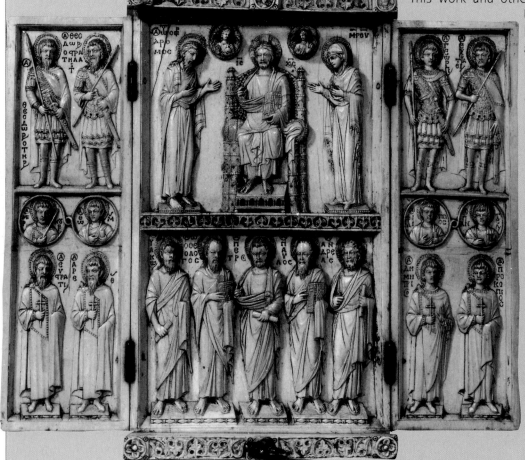

word of mouth, then collected in books. The stories told of supernatural deeds attributed to monks, and stressed the moral precepts they followed in their lives. Principally designed to praise the behavior of its subject, a "life" usually follows a specific rhetorical format. The writer first proclaims embarrassment at undertaking a task so great; then the birthplace (if it is worthy of note) or the nation in which the subject was born is described and praised; next comes a description of the family, but only if it is glorious; then the subject's birth and any miraculous signs accompanying it, real or invented, are noted; finally, in carefully organized subdivisions, physical appearance, education, upbringing, deeds, and so on, are described. This outline, or SCHEMA, made it easy to develop biographies of saints about whom little was known or who may never have

existed. The "lives" are interesting and readable, if somewhat predictable, and they provided heroes and heroines for the medieval world. Written in simple language, they were intended for as wide an audience as possible.

The third genre was literature written in the vernacular, or language of the common people. The earliest works of this sort, the Prodromic poems, date to the first half of the twelfth century. They are attributed to the court poet Theodore Prodromos, although they may have been written by several authors.

These poems employ a popular verse-form based on fifteen syllables and are written as complaints directed to the Emperors John II and Manuel I and other members of the Comneni family. One of the poems tells the story of a hen-pecked husband; another, the story of the father of a

OUR DYNAMIC WORLD

Chinese Theatre

At the time that East was separating from West in Rome, Confucius put to death an entire troupe of actors who took part in a play that violated his teaching.

Chinese drama forbade women on stage. All female roles in Chinese theatre were played by men, who mimicked the teetering style of walking that resulted from the practice of footbinding among the upper classes, and utilized a device called *tsai jiao* (tsy-jow) to keep the actor "on point"—in the balletic sense—throughout the performance.

Costume and makeup played a significant and symbolic role in Chinese theatre. Color, especially, portrayed emotion and social standing. Chinese theatrical costume, like its scenery, did not attempt to depict historical accuracy. Styles and periods mixed freely so as to create dramatic effect and reinforce nuances. Like the American movie genre the Western, in which the "good guys" wore white hats, and the "bad guys" black ones, in Chinese theatre, the good guys wore square hats, and the bad guys, round ones.

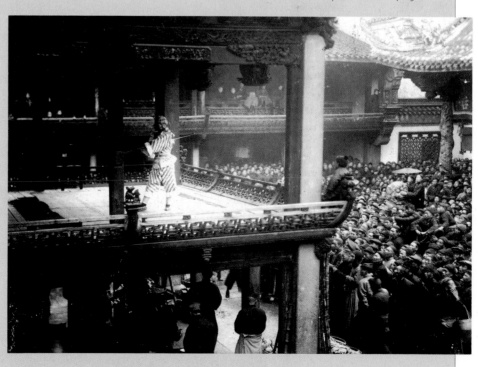

6.14 Chinese theatre performance in progress.

large family who cannot make ends meet on his small salary. These works are largely humorous, with a tendency to monotony and repetition and the coinage of bizarre words. Romances of chivalric knights, maidens, witches, and dragons in the fashion of the Western Empire were also popular. Epic poems that told heroic tales of the eastern border between Byzantium and the Arabs in the ninth and tenth centuries also found favor.

Much of Byzantine literature, however, is solemn, even somber in mood. Its writers seem most at home with themes of calamity, death, and the precariousness of human existence.

Theatre, Music, and Dance

The Byzantines were undoubtedly familiar with theatre. Ruins of Hellenistic theatres have been found throughout the Eastern Empire. Justinian's wife, Theodora, was an actress, and theatrical spectacles surrounded the life of the Imperial court. There are references to an exodus of actors and playwrights from Byzantium at the time of the Turkish conquest.

But what of theatre itself? The period between the fall of Rome and the late Middle Ages witnessed the virtual extinction of theatre in both East and West, except in its most rudimentary form. The Byzantine preference for artistic anonymity might account for the absence of dramas, and the literature of Byzantium certainly excluded drama from its priorities. In a society dominated by the Christian Church, the kind of debased spectacles popular in the late years of the Roman Empire were undoubtedly frowned upon. Such was the moral tone of the time that senators were barred by law from marrying actresses: Justinian had to change this law in order to marry Theodora. We hear of professional actors in Byzantium as late as the seventh century, but after that formal theatre performances seem to have disappeared. As one commentator puts it, "In the East problems more serious soon set people thinking of things sterner than merry supper-parties with groups of dancing girls."[4]

Throughout the Middle Ages, critical remarks to the effect that it was "better to please God than the actors" suggest that some form of performance art continued,

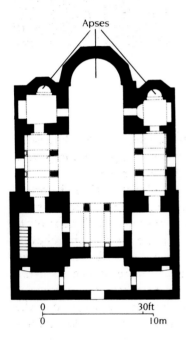

6.15 (*above*) Ground plan of the church of St Clement, Ankara.

6.16 (*right*) St Theodosia, Istanbul, Turkey, c. 1000.

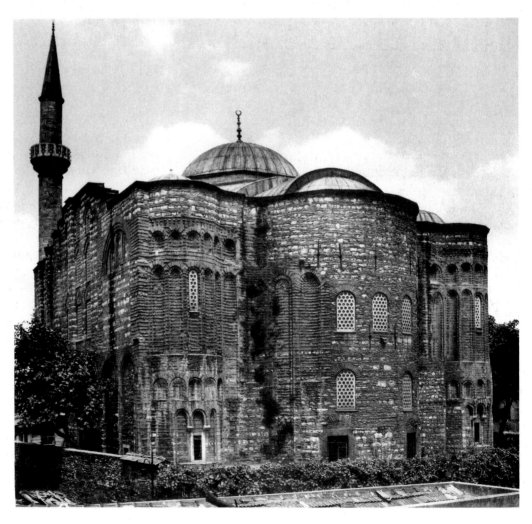

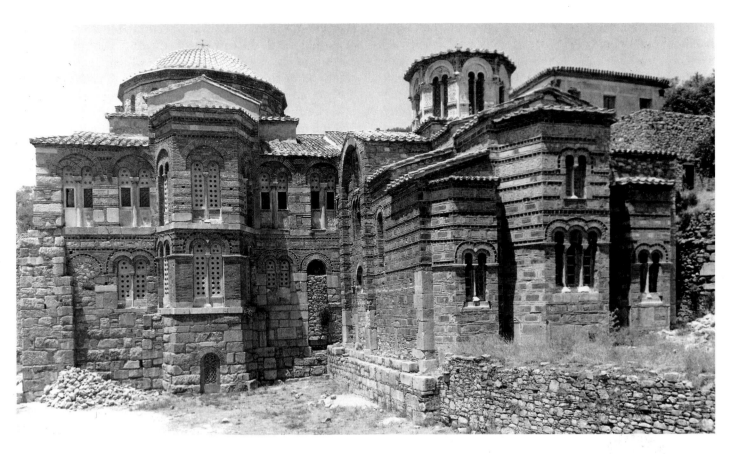

6.17 Churches of St Luke and the Virgin, Stiris, Turkey, eleventh century.

6.18 St Mary Pammakaristos, Istanbul, Turkey, thirteenth century.

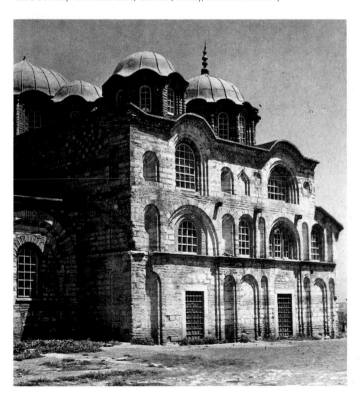

however, and it is not unlikely that this was also the case in Byzantium. Mime, and some form of pantomime, were probably the only forms of theatrical activity.

Before reaching Europe, the Christian Church spread throughout Asia Minor, accumulating musical elements on its way. Byzantium appears to have acquired much of its musical heritage from the monasteries and churches of Syria, where the development of antiphonal psalmody and the use of hymns originated. Clear evidence of hymn singing can be found in the New Testament, both in the Gospels and in the letters of Paul and James, and in the writings of Pliny the Younger in Bithynia and Asia Minor in the second century. Some early Christian hymns were probably sung to folk melodies. Thus there seem to have been both Eastern and Greek influences on early Christian music.

Although no music manuscripts survive from this period, the strong traditions of the Greek Orthodox, Russian, and other Eastern Churches still preserve what must be a flavor of the Byzantine chants that served as their models. Based on Syrian melodies and incorporating short responses between verses of the psalms, an independent hymnody gradually developed. Byzantine hymns had an elaborate structure, which stood in contrast to the simple hymns of the Western Church.

One type, developed in the eighth to tenth centuries, was based on sixth-century hymns and was called *kanones* (kuh-NAHN-ehs). Its texts were commentaries based on passages from the Bible. Its melodies, also not entirely original, were constructed on a principle common to Eastern music but were unfamiliar in the West. Rather than building a new melody from the tones in a scale, Eastern singers constructed melody out of a series of short given motifs, which they chose and combined. Some motifs were designed for beginnings, some for middles, some for endings, and some for links. There were also standard ornamental formulas, and originality in performance depended on the combination, variation, and ornamentation of the motifs. Byzantine music had eight forms, or *echoi* (EHK-oy). These *echoi* played a fundamental part in the development of Western music. Our knowledge of them is limited, however, by the fact that in the Byzantine Church music was passed on by oral tradition for centuries before being written down.

Undoubtedly Eastern music had a contemplative, even mystical, character and a degree of complexity that was quite in keeping with the character of Eastern thought.

References to dance occur from time to time throughout this period. Whether we should consider Byzantine dance as an artistic form is problematical, however. Two situations, at least, in which dance occurred are known. Some form of dancing apparently took place as part of religious services, but we do not know any details of its content or purpose. A second form of dancing provided entertainment. This was probably a vestige of the Roman pantomime (see p. 136), in which case it would have exhibited subtlety of movement and expression. Pantomime was mounted throughout the Byzantine Empire, either as solo performances at fairs and village festivals or using small traveling bands.

Architecture

The architecture of the early years of the Eastern Empire was dominated by the personality and objectives of the Emperor Justinian. It was an age in which royal patronage encouraged artistry, but the arts clearly reflected the source of that encouragement. Justinian's purpose was to glorify Justinian, and, in a remarkably creative way, the arts and architecture of the age succeeded in doing just that. The results of his efforts can be seen both in the West (see Figs. 6.3 and 6.32) and in the East (see Figs. 6.30, 6.33–6.36).

After Justinian's death, the construction of public churches all but ceased. The palace was the only important building project. Yet the churches that were built at this time became models for later Byzantine architecture. The general form of these early churches, such as that of St

Clement in Ankara, consists of a central dome and a group of three APSES at the east end (Fig. 6.15). The entire space describes a cross-in-square layout, which, again, can be seen in later churches. The cross-in-square is outlined on the ground plan: look outward from the center to the end of each of the transverse arms, the lower arm of the nave, and the upper arm just to the edge of the circular apse at top center.

The churches constructed in the two or three centuries after St Clement's employed the classical principles of harmony among their parts, and composition to express human aspirations (Fig. 6.16). The three apses just described point toward the viewer, and the dome above the central pavilion is visible at the top. The church's vertical striving and precise symmetry give it an elegant solidity. Delicate, arched niches and grilled windows tend to counter the heaviness of the walls.

As Byzantine power waned, the vigor and scale of new church construction reduced. The ground plans became smaller, and in partial compensation, height was increased. Greater emphasis was also placed on the appearance of the exterior, with decorative surface treatment of the brickwork or masonry of the walls (Figs. 6.17 and 6.18). Another characteristic of later church building was the addition of churches or chapels to existing ones, creating very different forms from the organized massing of the single-domed church. The elaborate detail and frequent changes of plane that these additions created give us a fascinating surface with which to interreact, as the churches of St Luke and the Virgin illustrate (Fig. 6.17). Here, verticality or upward striving line is much less apparent—the strength of horizontal elements and the shorter apses give the impression that the building is much more squat.

The interiors of these churches are elegant, jewel-like, sumptuous, glowing with color, and heavily decorated. They are reached through NARTHEXES, and sometimes side porches, that create a spatial and visual transition from the outside world to the interior. The spaces of the church flow smoothly from one to another and are carefully designed to meet liturgical needs. A deep, vaulted sanctuary and apse house the altar. Chambers adjoin the apse on either side. Just beyond the eastern columns, a screen painted with icons stands across the sanctuary. The entire effect of the mosaic-covered vaults, elaborate ecclesiastical vestments, chants, ancient rites, and incense sought to create for the worshipper the spiritual and physical sense of another world.

Byzantine Art and Culture

In summary, we can make the following observations about the relationship between Byzantine art and Byzantine culture. (1) The power and expressiveness of the figures in Byzantine art suggest the strength and vitality of Byzantine traditions. (2) Rich materials, such as gold, indicate a culture of great wealth. (3) The great variety in subject matter, media, and types of art reveal a culture of taste and sophistication as well as tremendous artistic skill among artists themselves. (4) The presence of classical themes and style prove the importance of the classical heritage to Byzantine culture. (5) The presence of Byzantine artistic style in cultures as far removed as Russia, Europe, and the Middle East indicates the vast expanse of Byzantine cultural influence.

THE RISE OF ISLAM

The Religion of Islam

The Islamic tradition springs from the religion of Islam, of which Muhammad (c. 570–632) was the prophet. The latest of the three great monotheistic religions, it drew upon both Judaism and Christianity. When Muhammad, the prophet of Islam, was called to preach, the conditions included great suffering among the poor—notably in the city of Mecca in southwestern Arabia. Most of the people worshiped a variety of gods and prayed to various idols and spirits. Muhammad taught that there was only one God and that this God requires people to make Islam—that is, submission—to him.

Muhammad began preaching in Mecca around A.D. 610, but, as noted in the Profile on p. 195 that follows, his teachings were not immediately accepted. However, by the time of his death in 632 he was acknowledged as Prophet. His companions preserved his revelations and combined them to form the holy book of the Muslims, the Koran. The word Koran (koh-RAN) means "recitation," and Muslims consider the Koran to contain the words of God himself, spoken to Muhammad by an angel. Parts of the Koran resemble the Hebrew Bible and contain many stories about the prophets who appear in the Old Testament. The Koran also has stories from the New Testament about Jesus, whom it calls the "Word of God." The strictures of the Koran prohibit usury, games of chance, and the consumption of pork and alcohol. Like the Bible, it forbids lying, stealing, adultery, and murder, but it does not require "an eye for an eye." Instead, the offender can pay "blood money" and is urged to seek forgiveness. The Koran permits slavery but urges that slaves be treated with kindness and freed. Polygamy—up to four wives—is permitted under some conditions.

In the religion of Islam, there is one absolute and all-powerful God, known as Allah. He is the creator of the universe, and is just and merciful. God desires that people repent and purify themselves so that they can attain Paradise after death. God communicates with the human race through prophets, and the predecessors of Muhammad were the Old Testament prophets and Jesus. Muhammad was the last of the prophets. Muslims respect Muhammad, but they do not worship him.

Like Judaism and Christianity, the Islamic faith teaches that parents should be honored, orphans and widows protected, and charity given to the poor. It proclaims faith in God, kindness, honesty, industry, courage, and generosity. An Islamic wife has rights against her husband to protect her from abuse. Islam also teaches that life on earth is a period of testing in preparation for an afterlife. Angels keep a record of individual good and bad deeds, and God's justice determines a person's reward. Death is the gateway to eternal life, and at the last day, judgment will occur. The record book of each individual will be placed in the right hand of those who will go to heaven and in the left hand of the wicked who will go to hell. The description of the agonies and tortures of hell are similar to those in the Bible, while heaven is a garden with flowing streams, delicious fruit, richly covered furniture, and beautiful maidens.

Five duties are prescribed for every Muslim, the last being that he must, if he can, once in his life make the pilgrimage, or Hajj (hahj), to Mecca (MEHK-uh). This last provision has made the pilgrimage the greatest in the world and a great unifying force in Islam. The other duties are profession of God and the prophethood of Muhammad, prayer, almsgiving, and fasting.

Muslims pray five times daily: at dawn, noon, in the afternoon, in the evening, and at nightfall. A crier or muezzin (myoo-EZ-in) announces prayer time from a tower, or minaret, in the mosque, the Muslim place of worship, meaning a place of kneeling. Noon prayer is expected to be performed in the mosque. Immediately before prayer, Muslims wash their face, hands, and feet. Friday is a day similar to the Jewish Sabbath and the Christian Sunday. During prayer, the leader faces Mecca, and the men stand in rows behind him, with women standing behind the men. Prayers include bowing from the hips and kneeling with one's face to the ground. Friday prayers include a sermon. Islam does not have an organized priesthood—any virtuous and able Muslim can lead prayers—but most mosques have an imam, or leader, who is the chief officer of the mosque and leads the people in prayer.

Early in its history, Islam split between the Sunnites (SOON-yts) and Shiites (SHEE-yts), and this split has persisted. The original split was over the caliphate, which was the crowning institution of the theocratic structure of Islam—that is, the placement of both religious and political leadership in the hands of a single ruler. The caliphs were the successors, or deputies, of Muhammad, and their claim to authority rested on their descent from the families

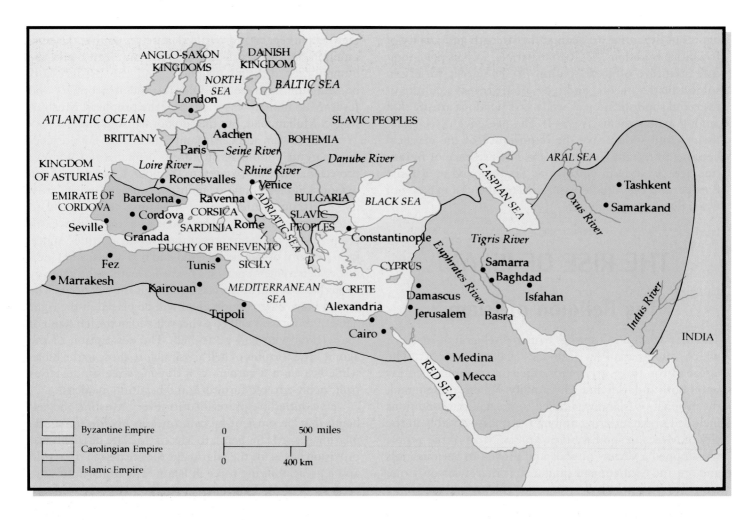

Map 6.3 The Byzantine, Carolingian, and Islamic Empires c. 814.

of the Prophet or his early associates. Although secularism has modified the unity somewhat, in theory the civil law in Muslim countries is not separate from religious law; religion governs all aspects of life. There have developed some four different systems of interpretation of the law in Sunnite Islam, all regarded as orthodox. Islamic philosophy is in effect part theology; rationalism and mysticism both grew up in Islam, but were equally absorbed.

The Spread of Islam

Islam spread rapidly throughout the Middle East and North Africa in the seventh and eighth centuries, beginning with conquests launched from Mecca and Medina (Map **6.3**). After Muhammad's death, the Caliph Abu Bakr (KAYL-if AHB-oo BAHK-uhr) and his successors encouraged jihad, or holy war, in order to expand the faith's sphere of influence. Within a century, an Islamic empire stretched from northern Spain to India, engulfing much of the Byzantine and Persian empires, and the Muslims threat-

ened to overrun Europe until they were defeated by Charles Martel (mahr-TEL) at the battle of Poitiers (Tours) in 732.

A religion that was originally spread "by the sword," Islam's appeal lay in its openness to everyone. It stresses the brotherhood of the faithful before God, regardless of race or culture, although the Arab warriors who started out to conquer the world for Allah did not expect to make converts of conquered peoples—they expected the unbelievers to be obedient to them, the servants of the One True God. The Koran was not translated into any languages because it was dictated by God to Muhammad in Arabic. Converts were expected to become Arabs, and they had to submit to the social and legal precepts of the Muslim community (Fig. **6.20**). As a result, the conquering Arabs resisted the usual fate of conquerors—being absorbed into the culture of the conquered.

During the early Middle Ages in Europe, the Muslims were responsible for transmitting much of the classical knowledge of the ancient world. They were proficient mathematicians and scientists, as well as artists, writers, and architects.

PROFILE

Muhammad (c. 570–632)

The name Muhammad means Praised One, and there are several common spellings of the name, including Mohammed and Mahomet. Muhammad was born in Mecca, but his father died before he was born, and his mother died shortly thereafter. Raised under the guardianship of his grandfather and, later, his uncle, Muhammad lived for a while with a desert tribe tending sheep and camels. Tradition maintains that he went with his uncle on caravans throughout Arabia and to Syria.

When he was twenty-five years old, Muhammad went to work for a wealthy widow who was fifteen years older than he was and whom he later married. They had two sons and four daughters, and although the sons died young, one of the daughters, Fatima (FAT-i-muh), married Ali, son of Abu Talib. Many Muslims trace their ancestry to Muhammad through his daughter in a genealogy called the Fatamid dynasty.

When Muhammad was thirty-five years old and living in Mecca, a flood damaged the most sacred shrine, the Kaaba (KAH-uh-buh). Because of his moral excellence, Muhammad was selected to put the sacred stone back into place. The angel Gabriel later appeared to Muhammad in a vision and called him to serve as a prophet to proclaim God's message to his people. Although he was at first unsure of the vision, he was convinced of its validity by his wife, who became his first disciple. However, no further visions occurred, and Muhammad grew disheartened. Then, Gabriel appeared again and told him: "Arise and warn, magnify thy Lord . . . wait patiently for Him."

Muhammad began to preach periodically in public, and although, at first, most of the people who heard him ridiculed him, he gained a few followers. He continued preaching in Mecca until both his wife and son-in-law died, but the people of Mecca persecuted him for his claims and attacks on their way of life. In A.D. 622, therefore, he fled to Medina in the north. That emigration is called the *Hegira* (huh-JY-ruh), and Muslims date their calendar from this year. In Medina he found a welcome, and most of the population became his followers. He eventually became both head of a religion and a political leader—his religious message became law, and he made a variety of changes in

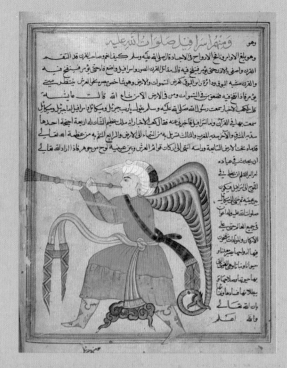

6.19 The Archangel Gabriel. British Library, London.

the legal system and customs to conform to the precepts of Islam.

At first it seems as though Muhammad expected Christians and Jews to recognize him as a prophet. He was benevolent to them and decreed that Jerusalem was to be faced in prayer. However, a conspiracy among Jews in Medina and Muhammad's enemies in Mecca caused him to drive them from the city and to organize a strictly Muslim society. In order to recognize the independence of the religion, he decreed that from that time onward his followers face Mecca in prayer, a practice still observed.

In 630 Muhammad and his followers attacked Mecca and successfully destroyed all the idols in the Kaaba, turning it into a mosque. In a gesture of reconciliation, Muhammad offered to pardon the people of Mecca, who accepted Islam and acknowledged Muhammad as a prophet. The two cities of Medina and Mecca became the sacred cities of the religion. Muhammad died in Medina (muh-DEE-nuh) two years later, and his tomb is in the Prophet's Mosque there.

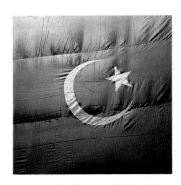

6.20 Symbol of Islam on Pakistan's national flag.

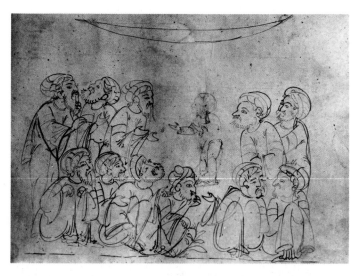

6.21 Al-Qasim ibn 'Ali al-Hariri, *Maqamat al-Hariri* (a book of stories), 1323. Mesopotamian manuscript, Oriental Collection, British Library, London.

Islamic Style in the Arts

Visual Art

Theoretically, all human and animal figures are prohibited from Islamic art, but in reality, images are widespread: the only prohibition seems to have been on those objects intended for public display. In the courts of the caliphs, for example, images of living things were commonplace. They were considered harmless if they did not cast a shadow, were small in scale, or appeared on everyday objects.

A continuity of visual art seems to have occurred during the early years of Islam through the illustration of scientific texts. The Arabs obtained manuscripts from Byzantium, and were tremendously interested in Greek science. The result was a plethora of texts translated into Arabic. Illustrations from original Greek works also were copied. Typical of the illustration drawn in Arab manuscripts is a pen-and-ink sketch, perhaps from a Mesopotamian manuscript of the fourteenth century (Fig. **6.21**). The drawing has a clear presentation, with many of the strokes seeming to act as accents. The lines flow freely in subtle curvilinear movements to establish a comfortable rhythm across the page. In very simple line, the artist is able to capture human character, thus showing a strong observational ability. The witty flavor of the drawing goes far beyond mere illustration.

Even before Islam, Arab traders had penetrated the Far East, and as a result Chinese influence can be seen throughout the Middle East. This is particularly true in the emergence of religious subjects for visual art. The Mongol rulers were very familiar with the Buddhist tradition in Chinese art, and brought that interest to Islamic art—ignoring their predecessors' reluctance to pictorialize Muhammad. Thus, in the fourteenth century painting that depicted narratives about Muhammad became quite common. Chinese influences are strongly at work in an Islamic manuscript illustration from sixteenth-century

Persia. *The Ascension of Muhammad* (Fig. **6.22**) tells the story from the Koran, in which Muhammad ascends into Paradise after "a journey by night . . . to the remote place of worship." The reference in the Koran was later expanded upon: Muhammad ascended from Jerusalem under the guidance of the Angel Gabriel, rising through seven heavens and meeting Adam, Abraham, Moses, and Jesus before coming into the presence of God.

The images in the painting are fascinating. Muhammad rides a curiously oriental centaur—a mythological beast with a horse's body and the head of a man. The surrounding angels have oriental faces, and the composition seems to divide along the diagonal axis—also similar to some oriental works. The crescent-shaped figures appear to swirl in an elliptical path around Muhammad, and the artist shows a sophisticated color composition by carrying the predominant colors of one section into another section—for example, the white of the clouds carries into the upper parts of the painting in small details of trim and in the lighter flesh tones; reds that provide an encircling motif in the upper portion are carried into the lower section, where they accent rather than dominate.

Literature

Probably the most familiar Islamic literature, aside from the Koran, is a collection of tales called *The Arabian Nights* or *The Thousand and One Nights*. These tales accumulated during the Middle Ages, and as early as the tenth century they were part of the oral traditions of Islam in the Near East. Over the years more tales were added,

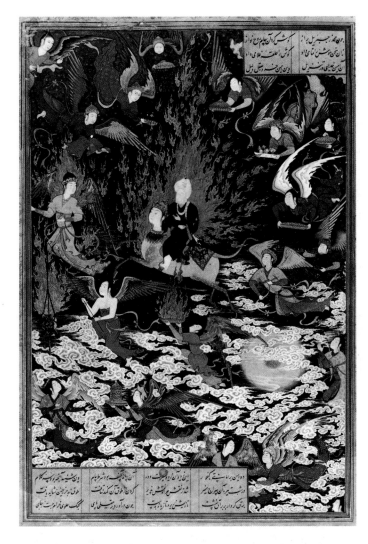

6.22 Unknown illustrator, *The Ascension of Muhammad*, 1539–43. Persian manuscript. Oriental Collection, British Library, London.

including a unifying device called a FRAMING TALE, which placed all the separate stories within a larger framework. By around 1450, the work had assumed its final form.

The framing tale recounts the story of a jealous Sultan who, convinced that all women were unfaithful, married a new wife each evening and put her to death the following morning. A new bride, Shaharazad, or Scheherazade, gained a reprieve by beginning a story on her wedding night and artfully maintaining the Sultan's curiosity. She was able to gain a reprieve for one thousand and one nights—during which she produced three male heirs—after which the Sultan abandoned his original practice. The tales capture the spirit of Islamic life, its exotic setting, and sensuality. Although no particular moral purpose underlies the stories, there is a moral code within the

fantasies. The tales cover a variety of subjects and range from fact to fiction. They include stories of camel trains, desert riders, and insistent calls to prayers. They are supernatural, aristocratic, romantic, bawdy, and satiric.

Architecture

The first major example of Islamic architecture did not appear until A.D. 691, when work began on the Dome of the Rock in Jerusalem (Fig. **6.23**). Built near the site of the Temple of Solomon, it was begun by Islamic emperors who were direct descendants of the Prophet's companions. Shaped as an octagon, it was designed as a special holy place—not an ordinary mosque. Inside, it contains two concentric ambulatories, walkways, surrounding a central space capped by the dome. The mosque sits on a site revered by Jews as the tomb of Adam and the place where Abraham prepared to sacrifice Isaac. According to Muslim tradition, it is also the place from which Muhammad ascended into heaven. Written accounts suggest that it was built to overshadow a sacred temple of similar construction on the other side of Jerusalem—the Holy Sepulchre. Calif Abd al-Malik (AHB-uhd al-mah-leek) wanted a monument that would outshine the Christian churches of the area, and, perhaps, the Kaaba in Mecca. The exterior was later decorated with the glazed blue tiles that give the façade its dazzling appearance; the inside glitters with gold, glass, and mother-of-pearl, in multicolored mosaics. A detail of the richly intricate mosaics of the Dome of the Rock in Jerusalem can be seen in Figure **6.24**. This symmetrical pattern in deep red and gold, highlighted with accents of white and purple, illustrates the skill and delicacy that Muslim artists brought to this form. Undoubtedly, the Dome of the Rock was intended to speak to Christians as well as Muslims, distracting the former from the splendor of Christian churches. Inside the mosque is an inscription: "The Messiah Jesus Son of Mary is only an apostle of God, and His Word which he conveyed into Mary, and a Spirit proceeding from Him. Believe therefore in God and his apostles and say not 'Three.' It will be better for you. God is only one God. Far be it from his glory that He should have a son."

Another excellent example of Islamic architecture is the Great Mosque of Damascus (Fig. **6.26**). When the Muslims captured Damascus in 635, they adapted the precinct of a pagan temple, which had been converted into a Christian church, into an open-air mosque. Seventy years later, al-Walid demolished the church and set about building the largest mosque in Islam. The only feature of the original buildings left standing was the Roman wall, although the four original towers were metamorphosed into the first minarets, from which the faithful were called to prayer. Unfortunately, the centuries have not been kind to the Great Mosque. Sacked a number of times, much of

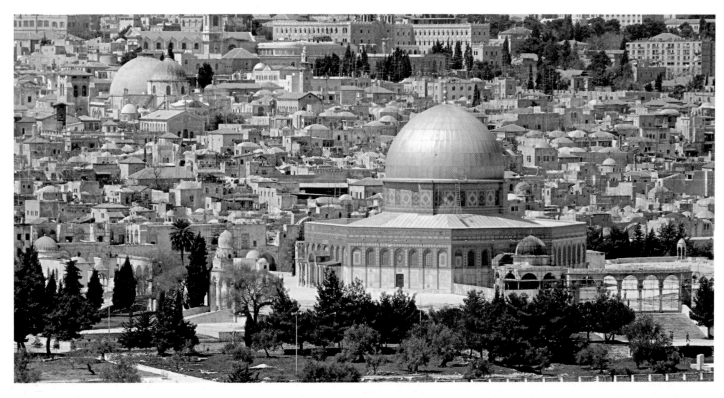

6.23 Dome of the Rock, Jerusalem, late seventh century.

6.25 Details of mosaic decoration, Great Mosque, Damascus, c. 715.

6.24 Details of mosaic decoration, Dome of the Rock, Jerusalem, Israel, 691–692.

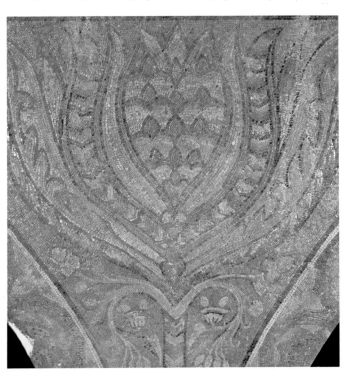

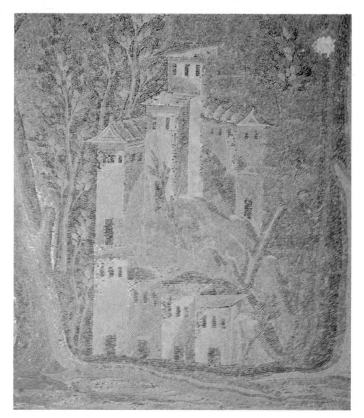

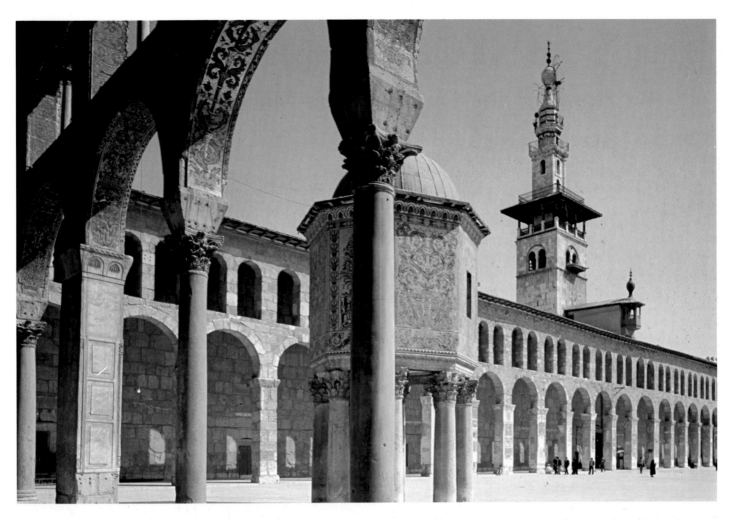

6.26 Great Mosque, Damascus, Syria. Courtyard looking west, c. 715.

the splendor of its lavish decorations has been lost. However, some of its grandeur can be seen in the arcaded courtyard, with fine, gold-inlaid detailing visible in the returns of the arches (Fig. **6.26**). Inside, colorful mosaics (Fig. **6.25**) express great subtlety of detail and texture. These works rank among the most accomplished of mosaics and were probably produced by Byzantine craftsmen.

Focal Point

In Praise of the Emperor—the Mark of Justinian

Our Focal Point material for this chapter comes from the individual who tried to reunite the Eastern and Western Empires. Like Augustus Caesar, he saw art as a way of perpetuating his image as an emperor, although a Christian one. We draw the focus by examining two great edifices, the church of San Vitale (sahn vee-TAH-lay) in Ravenna and the monumental Hagia Sophia (HAH-juh soh-FEE-uh), Church of St Sophia, in Constantinople. We have to imagine the Church of St Sophia without its four minarets. These were added after the Muslims conquered Byzantium and converted the building to a mosque. Today St Sophia is a museum, and there is no picture that can prepare you for the breathtaking nature of its scale. After nearly fifteen hundred years, its dome still represents one of the greatest engineering feats of human history. Thus, these two edifices, one in the East and one in the West—reflecting the persona of the emperor who would reunite East and West

and altered by Islamic minarets—give us a closing overview of Byzantium, the crossroads of Europe and Asia, Roman Catholicism, Eastern Orthodoxy, and Islam.

The portraits of Justinian that appear in mosaics—such as that in Figure 6.3—reveal a man who does not look like an emperor. He was of average height and build, and had dark hair and a ruddy complexion. He was clean shaven, and every portrait shows a slight smile. However, despite his unexceptional appearance, he was a brilliant thinker who possessed enormous talents. He apparently liked the role of emperor and played it to the hilt, but he seems to have been likeable, in spite of his vigor and arrogance.

San Vitale in Ravenna (Figs. 6.27 and 6.28) is the major Justinian monument in the West. It was probably built as a testament to the power of Orthodoxy in the declining kingdom of the Ostrogoths.

PROFILE

Anthemius of Tralles (c. sixth century)

It may seem strange to include a profile about someone like Anthemius of Tralles (an-THEE-mee-us), about whom virtually nothing is known. However, the fact that we know his name at all is a testament to the vision and profound quality of his architectural work. During this period of history, individual artists—especially architects—did not gain fame. Their work was an expression, usually religious, that glorified God, the emperor, or the Church, and individualism, as we know it, in artistic work had ceased. However, we know of Anthemius. Although Anthemius was not an architect or master mason by training, he wrote a treatise on the geometry of conical sections, had a knowledge of projective geometry, and was familiar with the mechanical inventions of Archimedes (ark-ih-MEE-deez), a Greek mathematician, physicist, and inventor who lived in the third century B.C.

Anthemius' lasting fame, however, came as a

result of his design for what was at the time, and still remains, one of the greatest architectural accomplishments of history—the church of St Sophia in Constantinople. Commissioned by the Emperor Justinian, Anthemius designed a building that, according to Justinian's court historian, Procopius, "through the harmony of its measurements . . . is distinguished by indescribable beauty." Inasmuch as Anthemius was a mathematician, it does not surprise us to discover that he and his partner, Isidorus of Miletus (also a mathematician), based the design for St Sophia on a sphere standing upon a circle. To Anthemius, architecture was the "application of geometry to solid matter," and his designs brought to Constantinople an entirely new approach to architecture by showing an inventive structure of form that stood entirely outside the Roman tradition. Such a departure reveals a profound intellect and great courage.

The church consists of two concentric octagons (see Fig. 6.28). The hemispherical dome, 100 feet (30 meters) above the floor, rises from a drum above the inner octagon, which is pierced with windows that flood the interior with light. Below, eight large piers alternate with columned niches to define precisely the central space and to create an intricate, many-layered design. The narthex is placed at an odd angle. There are two possible explanations for this: the practical one is that the narthex paralleled a then-

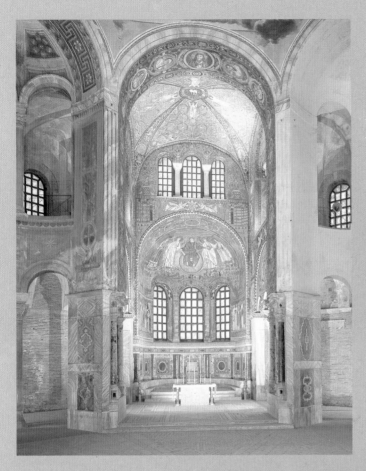

6.27 San Vitale, Ravenna, Italy, 526–547. Interior, looking east.

6.28 (*right*) Plan and transverse section of San Vitale, Ravenna, Italy.

6.29 *Abraham's Hospitality and the Sacrifice of Isaac*. Wall mosaic, San Vitale, Ravenna, Italy.

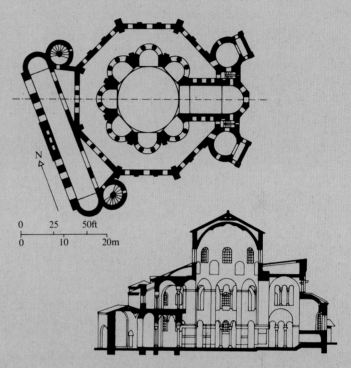

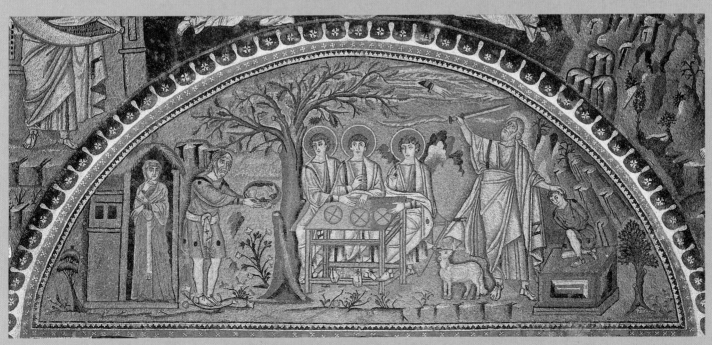

existing street; a more spiritual one is that the narthex was so designed in order to force worshippers to reorient themselves on entering, thereby facilitating the transition from the outside world to the spiritual one.

On the second level of the ambulatory was a special gallery reserved for women—a standard feature of Byzantine churches.

The internal spatial design is intricate. The visitor experiences an ever-changing vista of arches within arches, linking flat walls and curved spaces. All the aisles and galleries contrast strikingly with the calm area under the dome. The clerestory light reflects off the mosaic tiles with great richness. In fact, new construction techniques in the vaulting allowed for windows on every level and opened the sanctuary to much more light than had previously been possible.

The sanctuary itself is alive with mosaics of the Imperial court and of sacred events. The difference in style between two mosaics in the same church is particularly fascinating. *Abraham's Hospitality and the Sacrifice of Isaac* (Fig. **6.29**) demonstrates what is, by Byzantine standards, a relaxed naturalism. The mosaic showing Justinian and his court (see Fig. **6.3**), on the other hand, demonstrates the orientalized style, more typically Byzantine, with the figures posed rigidly and facing forward. The mosaics clearly link the church to the Byzantine court, reflecting again the connection of the emperor to the Faith, of Christianity to the State, and, indeed, the concept of the "Divine Emperor." Justinian (see Fig. **6.3**) and Theodora (see Fig. **6.1**) are portrayed very much like Christ and the Virgin. The two mosaics face each other behind the high altar of San Vitale. In Figure **6.3** the emperor has a golden halo with a red border, he wears a regal purple robe, and he is shown presenting a golden bowl to Christ, who is pictured in the SEMIDOME above the mosaic (see Fig. **6.27**).

If San Vitale praises the emperor and Orthodoxy in the West, St Sophia is a crowning monument to his achievement in the East (Figs. **6.30**, **6.33–6.36**). Its architect, Anthemius, was a natural scientist and geometer from Tralles in Asia Minor. St Sophia is characteristic of the Justinian Byzantine style in its use of well-rehearsed Roman vaulting techniques combined with Hellenistic principles of design and geometry. The result is a building in an orientalized, antique style.

6.30 Anthemius of Tralles and Isidorus of Miletus, St Sophia, Istanbul, Turkey, 532–537.

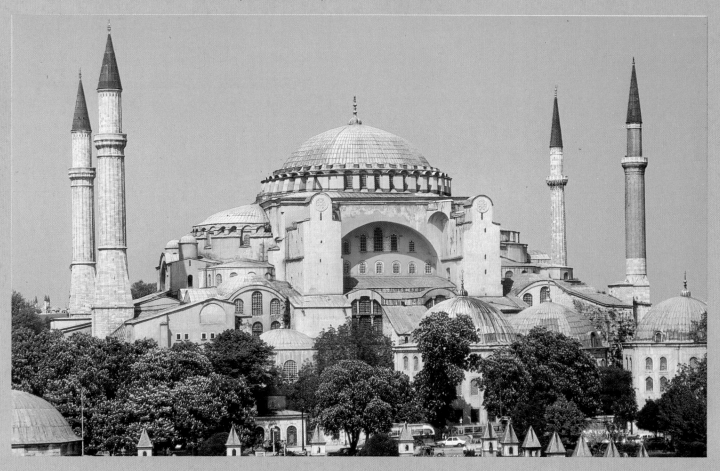

TECHNOLOGY: PUTTING DISCOVERY TO WORK

Spanning Space with Triangles and Pots

The ingenuity of human achievement is often revealed in the subtleties of invention that have allowed architects to create great open spaces under remarkably heavy materials such as stone and cement. We have seen this in the great dome of the Pantheon of Rome, and now we see it in what is still the largest dome ever created, St Sophia in Constantinople. It is a reminder that what was best in the West came from the uninterrupted Roman building tradition of that city. In 537, when Western Europe was at its most barbaric, Justinian's great brickwork cathedral was dedicated. What made it remarkable was the invention of a device to transfer the weight of a great dome downward—not on a cylindrical tub as in the Pantheon, but through a triangular device called a PENDENTIVE (pehn-DEHN-tihv; Fig. **6.31**)—to the corners of a square tower, 180 feet (55 meters) above the ground. Dedicated to the Divine Wisdom, St Sophia illustrates the sublime ingenuity of humankind.

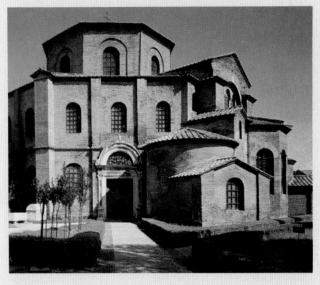

6.32 Façade of San Vitale, Ravenna, Italy.

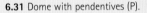
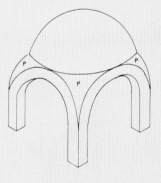

6.31 Dome with pendentives (P).

In another of Justinian's marvels, as we have noted, Byzantine influence and technological creativity reflects itself in the church of San Vitale in Ravenna (Fig. **6.32**). Here, in order to compensate for the potentially crushing weight of a solid dome, the architect used hollow earthenware pots for construction. Thus, space was enclosed without utilizing a base so cumbersome as to ruin the aesthetic considerations of lightness and beauty. Whether in soaring domes or towers that reach 110 stories into the air, technological inventiveness has always lain at the heart of new dimensions in architecture. None has superseded the marvels of Byzantium, where, in addition to unsurpassed domes, stone was jointed with such precision that some buildings did not require mortar.

Built to replace an earlier basilica, St Sophia was for a long time the largest church in the world. It was completed in only five years and ten months, between 532 and 537. The speed of the work, together with Byzantine masonry techniques, in which courses of brick alternate with courses of mortar as thick as, or thicker than, the bricks, caused great weight to be placed on insufficiently dry mortar. As a result, arches buckled, and buttresses had to be erected almost at once. The additional effects of two earthquakes caused the eastern arch and part of the dome itself to fall in 557.

The flatness of a dome so large—110 feet (33.5 meters) in diameter—remains unique, and the delicate proportioning of the vaults that support such great weight is also remarkable. Basic to the conception is the elevated central area, with its picture of heaven in the dome and its large, open, and functional spaces. The building could hold large numbers of worshippers in a transcendental environment,

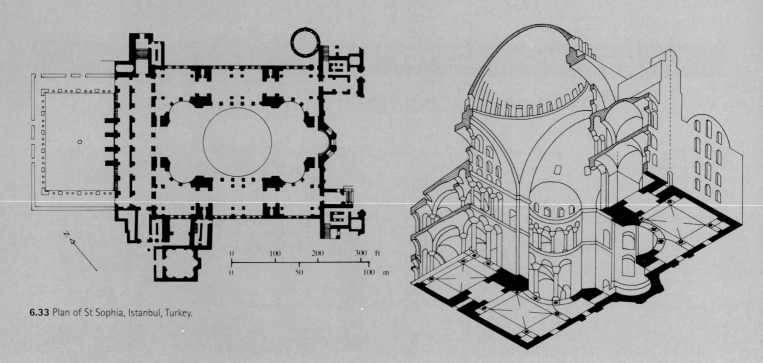

6.33 Plan of St Sophia, Istanbul, Turkey.

6.35 Axonometric section (perspective view) of St Sophia, Istanbul, Turkey.

6.34 St Sophia, Istanbul, interior.

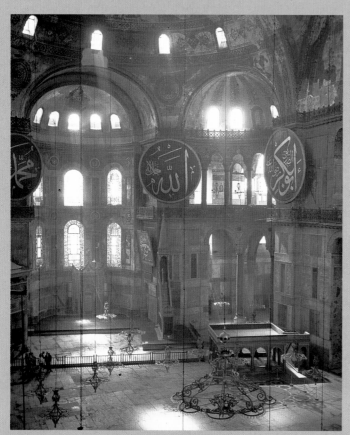

6.36 Capitals in St Sophia, Istanbul, Turkey.

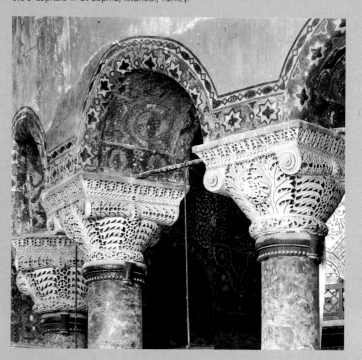

where thoughts at once rise to a spiritual sphere. "It seemed as if the vault of heaven were suspended above one," wrote Procopius.

The capitals of the columns in St Sophia (Fig. **6.36**) illustrate a style that is totally Byzantine. The deeply undercut ornament shows originality and technical mastery. Classical elements, such as volutes and leaves like those on Corinthian capitals, are subsumed into the vigorous decoration. This is in no way a dilution of classicism, but the birth of a new style. Justinian's other buildings show work of the same type, but that in St Sophia represents the highest quality.

Justinian's reign inaugurated the style called "Byzantine," blending traces of previous styles, Eastern and Western, to form a new style. The hieratic art from the reign of Justinian expresses the relationship between God and the State. With the emperor governing by, and for, the will of God, all reality—political, philosophical, and artistic—became spiritualized.

CHAPTER REVIEW

Critical Thought

Looking at a map of the region, we get a clear picture of Byzantium's pivotal location—it is the point where, today, Islam, Roman Catholicism, and Eastern Orthodoxy touch and where the Middle East, Europe, and Asia meet. Byzantium, because of that location, became a vital center for creative ingenuity and artistic vitality, producing, at the same time as it nurtured Greek and Roman classicism, a new and distinct approach to art—an approach whose uniqueness renders it easily recognizable and powerful a thousand years after the fact.

Byzantium also has been a flashpoint. Islam, Christianity, and Judaism trace their heritages to a common ancestor. Judaism is fundamental to Christianity, and Jesus plays a prominent role in the Islamic faith, especially its view of the end of the world. Islam, Christianity, and Judaism rest on the premise of "revealed truth"—a set of holy scriptures in which the single God of the universe is claimed to have revealed his nature and his will directly to an individual or individuals who have, then, passed that revealed truth on to others. Why is it that "revealed truth" appears to cause such discord among cultures that value so many basic principles, including peace, in common?

Summary

After reading this chapter, you should be able to:

- Relate the history of Byzantium to Eastern Orthodoxy, Greek classicism, and intellectual development in the West.
- Identify and describe the basic characteristics of Byzantine art, architecture, literature, theatre, music, and dance.
- Explain the basic precepts and spread of Islam.
- Discuss Islamic art and architecture and relate them to the tenets of the faith.
- Define hieratic style and characterize its qualities in two- and three-dimensional art.
- Apply the elements and principles of composition to analyze and compare the works of art and architecture illustrated in this chapter.

CHAPTER SEVEN

The Early Middle Ages
The Monastic and Feudal Romanesque Period

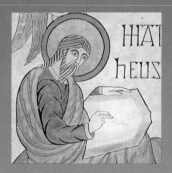

OUTLINE

THE MIDDLE AGES

THE MEDIEVAL CHURCH
Devils and Division
The Roman Papacy
Monasticism
  PROFILE: Pope Gregory I, the
    Great

CHARLEMAGNE'S EMPIRE

FEUDALISM
Feudal Lords
Serfs and Women
  TECHNOLOGY: The Viking Ships

THE VISUAL ARTS
Manuscript Illumination and
  Sculpture
Romanesque Style in Architecture
  and Sculpture
MASTERWORK: The Bronze Doors of
  Hildesheim Cathedral
OUR DYNAMIC WORLD: Igbo-Ukwu

MUSIC
Sacred Music
  PROFILE: Hildegard of Bingen
Secular Music

LITERATURE

THEATRE

DANCE

FOCAL POINT: THE CAROLINGIAN
RENAISSANCE

VIEW

CARPE DIEM
Pope Gregory I, the Great, believed that the world would not last much longer. Thus he saw his decisions as affecting only the immediate future. What is the best timescale in which to view decisions? Some people say, "*carpe diem*," meaning "seize the day!"—that is, today may be the only day we have, so we should make the most of it. The critical phrase is, of course, "make the most," and our reaction hinges on how we define "most." One person's interpretation of *carpe diem* might be "eat, drink, and be merry, for tomorrow you may die," but to another, making the most of a day may mean doing as much good as we can for others. In the early Middle Ages, people slaved for the lord of the manor in a system called feudalism. Although feudalism may have disappeared, feudal thinking has not. Many have world-views centered only on themselves and events immediate to them.

Above Detail of Fig. **7.8**.

7.1 Scenes from the life of St Paul, from the Bible of Charles the Bald, c. 875–877. San Paolo Fuori le Mura, Rome.

KEY TERMS

Some of the basic terms and concepts we will encounter in this chapter include the following:

Middle Ages, the time in Western European history that occurred between Antiquity (Chapters 1–5) and the Renaissance (Chapters 10–13), from approximately 476 A.D.

Feudalism was a political and economic system in Europe from the ninth to about the fifteenth century, based on the relation of lord to vassal.

Monasticism (from the Greek *monos*, meaning "single" or "alone") usually refers to a way of life in which an ideal of perfection or a higher level of religious experience is pursued through living together in a community.

Romanesque style flourished throughout Western Europe from about 1050 to about 1200. The word Romanesque originally meant "in the Roman manner."

Gregorian Chant, Plainsong, or Plainchant is the name commonly given to the monodic (single melodic line) vocal liturgical music of the Christian Catholic churches.

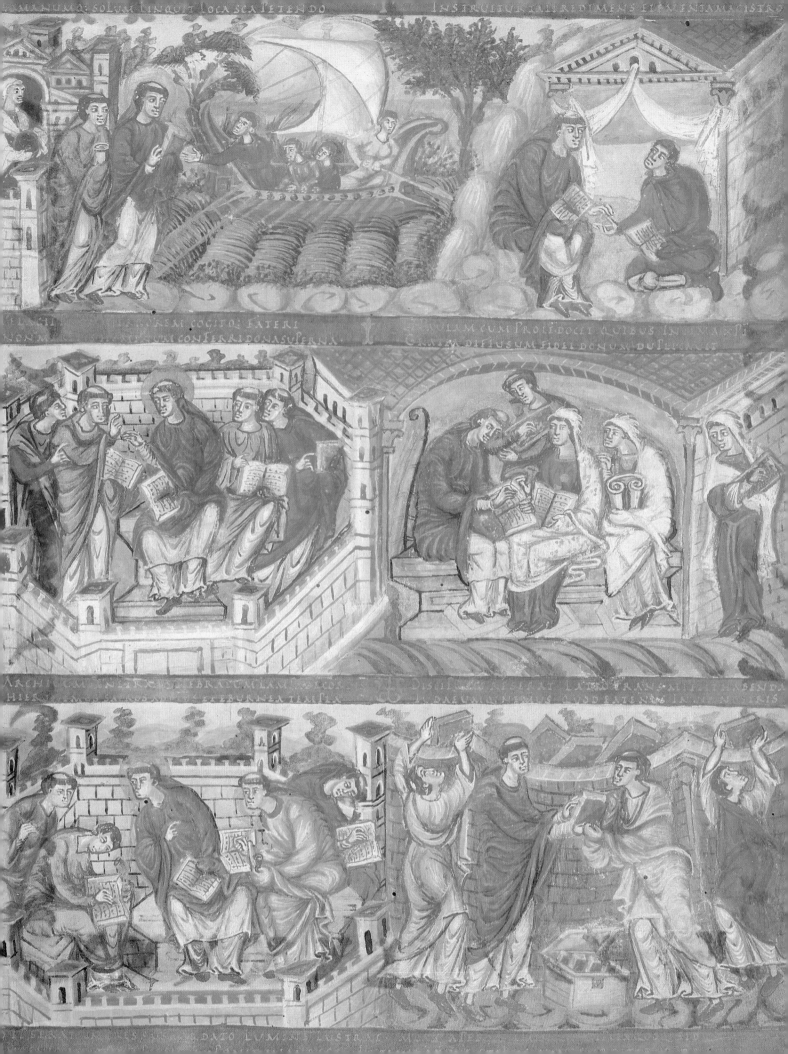

THE MIDDLE AGES

We have come to use the name the Middle Ages for the period that began with the fall of Rome and closed with the Renaissance in Italy. The years from around A.D. 200 to the middle of the sixth century are often called the *Early Christian* period. We have already looked at part of this period, and our examination continues in this chapter. The term *Dark Ages* is occasionally used to describe the years between 550 and 750. The *Carolingian and Ottonian* period occurred from 750 to 1000; the *Romanesque*, from 1000 to 1150; and the *High Gothic*, from 1150 to 1400. The *late Gothic* period from 1300 to 1500 overlaps High Gothic, and was a time of transition when the flower of the Renaissance began to bloom. This chapter will take us from approximately 500 to 1150, or from the Dark Ages through to the artistic style called Romanesque.

The thousand years between the fifth and the fifteenth centuries have been called the Middle Ages or medieval period on the theory that nothing—or worse than nothing—happened between the classical perfection of Greece and Rome and the revival of classical humanism in the fifteenth century.

Pessimism and disillusionment had increased in ancient Rome, and this mood, summed up in a well-known epitaph—"I was not; I was; I am not; I care not"—continued into the Middle Ages. Civic, secular government had all but ceased to exist. When Constantine I founded the second capital of the Roman Empire at Constantinople, he set in motion a division that became permanent in 395. In the West, the cloak of internationalism, which had loosely united the Mediterranean world since Alexander, fell apart. It became a case of "every locality and every people for themselves." Nations as we know them did not exist. Borders changed from day to day as one or another people wandered into the nebulously defined territory of its neighbors, bringing confusion and war.

Timeline 7.1 The early Middle Ages.

	GENERAL EVENTS	LITERATURE & PHILOSOPHY	VISUAL ART & ARCHITECTURE	PERFORMING ARTS
400				
		First Latin Bible of St Jerome		
500				
	Gregory I, the Great sends St Augustine to England	St Benedict *Book of Pastoral Care*		Gregorian chant
600				
	Sutton Hoo burial ship Buddhism established	Lindisfarne Gospels (7.8)		Troubadours
700				
	Charles Martel in France	*Beowulf* Gospel of Godescale (7.22) Dagulf Psalter (7.26)		
800				
	Charlemagne Earliest dated book printed in China Viking explorations	Gospel of St Médard (7.23) Lorsch Gospels (7.27) Carolingian Renaissance	Palatine Chapel, Aachen (7.28, 7.29)	
900				
	Sung dynasty in China (until 1279)		*Gero crucifix* (7.10)	Hrosvitha
1000				
	Norman invasion of England 1066	*Nibelungenlied* *Song of Roland*	Hildesheim Cathedral (7.12) St Sernin (7.11, 7.13) Cluny III (7.14, 7.15, 7.16) Autun Cathedral (7.18) Ste-Madeleine (7.19) St Albans Cathedral (7.17)	Hildegard of Bingen
1300				

THE MEDIEVAL CHURCH

Devils and Division

The devil, as a symbol of the powers of darkness and evil, was a strong force in medieval thinking, and the Church manipulated those fears as it sought, often fanatically, to convert the pagan world of the early Middle Ages. The promise of heaven and the prospect of the fires of hell were constant themes of the times. Ever-present devils and demons fostered a certain fascination as well as fear—as we shall see in medieval theatre, for example, the devil often had the best part.

The Church was itself divided, however, and it did little to reduce the isolation and ignorance of its followers. Very early, the clergy separated into two groups, one consisting of the regular clergy, monks, and others who preferred to withdraw into a cloistered life—a lifestyle that greatly appealed to many intellectuals as well—and the other consisting of the secular clergy—that is, the Pope, bishops, and parish priests who served in society at large. The overall effect of this division was to confine learning and philosophy to monasteries, and to withhold intellectual activity from the broader world. Inquiry among both groups was rigidly restricted. Detailed and unquestioned dogma was deemed essential to the Church's mission of conversion—and, indeed, to its very survival—and as a result, the medieval world was one of barricades, physical, spiritual, and intellectual. Each man, woman, and institution retreated behind whatever barricade he, she, or it found safest.

The Roman Papacy

By the middle of the sixth century, it appeared likely that the Roman Church and its pope would simply become tools of Byzantine Imperial policy. Rome appeared to have been demoted to a peripheral status as a mere center of Catholic Christianity, with little actual power or influence. Rome was rescued from potential demise by one of the greatest pontiffs in the history of the Roman Church, Gregory I (the Great), who was pope between 590 and 604. Gregory showed great abilities as a ruler and teacher that significantly affected numerous aspects of the Church and society. His land reforms and his administration of estates that had been given to the Church revitalized Church income, relieved famine, and provided money for churches, hospitals, and schools. His influence spread from Rome to the rest of Italy and beyond. One of the most important tasks he undertook was the sponsorship of St Augustine in his mission to convert England in 597. The most significant of Gregory's written works was his *Book of Pastoral Care*, in which he spoke idealistically of the way a bishop should live and how he should care for his flock.

As a result of Gregory's efforts, Rome regained its position of primacy among the Western Christian Churches. Despite the long-term results of Gregory's actions, he did not himself consider that he was building for the future. He believed that the Second Coming of Christ was near, and he merely did what he thought had to be done in what little time remained. Thus, unintentionally, he built a base for an enduring Church and a dominant papacy of wealth and prestige.

Monasticism

Seeking refuge from the temptations and tribulations of the medieval world, monks, nuns, some aristocrats, and others sought refuge behind the walls of perhaps the most

7.2 Monks in choir. Illustration from Cotton Domitian, A XVII, folio 122v. British Library, London.

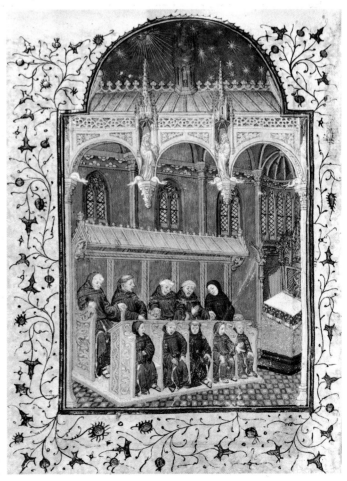

PROFILE

Pope Gregory I, the Great (540–604)

Nothing is known about Pope Gregory's early years and education. He rose to the position of prefect of the city of Rome, but left politics and founded the Monastery of St Andrew in Rome. Pope Pelagius II sent Gregory to Constantinople—then the seat of Roman Imperial government—as ambassador, and his experiences and the contacts he made over six years in that position proved invaluable. When Pelagius died in 590, Gregory was elected pope when he was fifty years old.

One of the major difficulties confronting the new pope lay in the conflict over the Roman ideology of emperor as divinity on earth. In such a scheme, the pope was merely another patriarch. While he had served as ambassador in Constantinople, Gregory had gained a realistic understanding of the political situations of the day, and he recognized

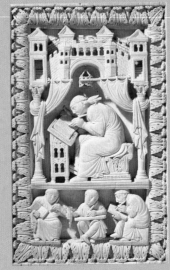

7.3 Pope Gregory I, the Great (540–604).

the delicacy of the pope's relationship to the secular, imperial government. Gregory wisely turned his attention to Western Europe, a domain that lay outside imperial jurisdiction, where he could push the claim of the supremacy of the Church of Rome without any interference from Constantinople.

One of his major missionary achievements was the conversion of England, which began in 597 with the mission of St Augustine. Gregory also supported St Benedict, leading to the development of Benedictine monasticism. His extraordinary administrative abilities brought most of Europe and North Africa under Roman papal authority, and he provided the driving force in the unification of much of Church doctrine and practice, exercising in all these ways a tremendous influence throughout the Western world.

---

typical example of medieval life—the monastery and the convent, which were outposts of order and charity. Often, too, they were well-organized and productive centers of agriculture. Monasteries and nunneries were established in the centers of non-Christian populations as means of converting pagans to Christianity. If monastery life offered an escape from some of the tribulations of the secular world, it did not permit an escape from rigor and hard work. Pious men and women of the monastic communities combined labor in the fields with religious thought, meditation, prayer, and other activities, such as copying sacred scripts and creating beautiful manuscript illuminations. Monks, who took vows of poverty, chastity, and obedience, renouncing all worldly goods, family life, and the pleasures of the senses, owned nothing—not even their own wills. They were subject to a strict discipline under the authority of the abbot and the will of God (Fig. 7.2).

Within the walls of the monastery, everything that was necessary for bodily and spiritual existence was provided, and the objective of the monastery was to be fully independent from all secular authority and life. In the monastery, a fine example being the great monastery at Cluny (see Figs. 7.14, 7.15, and 7.16), the ascetic world and the secular

world often rubbed shoulders, however. In addition to clerics and contemplatives, Cluny, for example, often harbored criminals seeking refuge from secular authorities.

Life for the Cluniac monk exemplified life in the cloistered communities of Europe in general. Religious contemplation alternated with other religious duties, and the abbey church witnessed prayer and worship day and night. Prayers were held according to the appointed hours of liturgy, running from sunrise to sunset in a form similar to the following:

2:00 a.m. Rise
2:10–3:30 Nocturns (matins). The first office of prayer
3:30–5:00 Individual study and contemplation
5:00–5:45 Lauds (morning prayer)
5:45–8:15 Prime (an office of prayer); private reading;
  Mass; or breakfast, depending on the season
8:25–2:30 Work, separated by the offices of Tierce,
  Sext, and None (third, sixth, and ninth hours)
2:30–3:15 Dinner
3:15–4:15 Private reading and contemplation
4:15–4:45 Vespers; Compline (night prayers)
5:15–6:00 Retire for the night

The daily schedule, or *horarium* (hohr-AR-ee-uhm), changed somewhat for Feast Days and to allow for the longer days of the summer months.

Many monasteries were also centers for pilgrimages, and travelers as well as pious pilgrims came for veneration and overnight accommodation to those monasteries that contained sacred relics. A hospice, or guest house, provided lodging, especially for visitors during the pilgrimage season, and barns, stables, and places for blacksmithing were often among the components of a monastic community.

The way of the monk and nun was the way of *asceticism* (eh-SEHT-i-sihz-uhm)—that is, a life of austerity and self-discipline. Reflecting religious thought of the time, monks and nuns considered earthly life to be a mere preparation for the eternal life to come, and in order to develop the thoughts and actions required for the life to come, they renounced the distractions of the world, seeking instead a disciplined but rich inner life of the spirit that, they believed, could come only through poverty, chastity, and humility.

The earliest communal monasteries preceded the fall of the Western Roman Empire. St Martin founded Ligugé in 360. But the greatest influence of all was that of St Benedict of Nursia (c. 480–550), who formulated the most widely adopted of all monastic rules, the Benedictine.

CHARLEMAGNE'S EMPIRE

In 732, the threat of Islam and the Moorish conquest was repelled by Charles Martel at the battle of Poitiers (pwah-TYAY) in France. The succeeding Carolingian period,

Map 7.1 Europe in the ninth century.

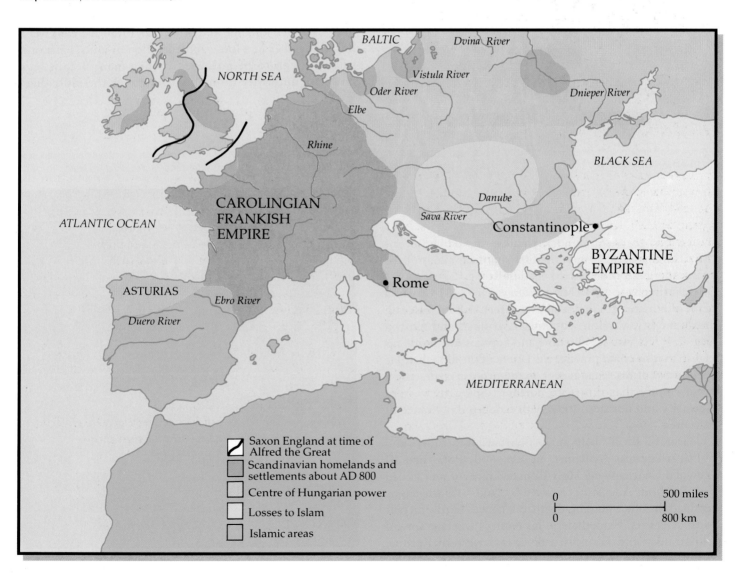

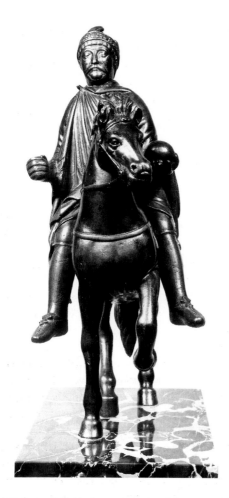

7.4 So-called *Statuette of Charlemagne*, c. 860–870. Bronze cast and gilt, 9¼ ins (23.5 cm) high. Louvre, Paris.

Despite his own lack of learning, he briefly revived interest in art, antiquity, and learning, as we shall see in the Focal Point section at the end of this chapter.

Charlemagne's reign succeeded in slowing—perhaps halting—the long decline of Europe, and it illumined a pathway whereby peace and prosperity might be restored. However, the heir to the Carolingian throne did not have Charlemagne's physical strength or his strength of will. Less than thirty years after his death, his grandsons divided the kingdom into three.

FEUDALISM

Feudal Lords

Perhaps the main reason why centralized authority had difficulty taking hold in the Middle Ages was a societal system called *feudalism* (FYOO-duhl-iz-uhm). The real political powers in Europe in the Middle Ages were the dukes, counts, knights, and other warrior lords, who were linked together in a loose confederation of units, each one small enough to be governed by one man. Because no powerful authority ultimately controlled the individual

7.5 The girding-on of swords, part of an increasingly formalized ritual associated with the making of a knight. MS D XI fol 134 vi. British Library, London.

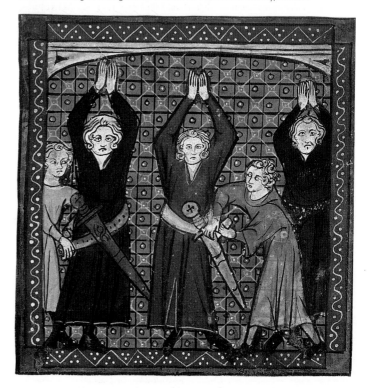

under his grandson Charlemagne—the name means "Charles the Great"—saw the first significant centralized political organization since the fall of Rome.

Charlemagne (SHAHR-luh-mayn; 768–814) was a giant of a man, standing well over 6 feet (1.8 meters) tall, and a mighty warrior, womanizer, drinker, and glutton (Fig. 7.4). He was semiliterate, and kept a slate beside his bed so that he could practice the letters of the alphabet. He spent most of his reign at war, in the process coalescing a large empire that ran from northern Spain to western Germany and northern Italy, with modern-day France as its center.

Grateful for his help against barbarian intruders and political enemies in Rome, in A.D. 800, Pope Leo III crowned Charlemagne Holy Roman Emperor and hailed him as "Pious Augustus, crowned by God." Charlemagne retained the office until his death, but he was hardly an heir to the Caesars. Nonetheless, his endless warfare spread Christianity and Frankish rule across western Europe.

parts, the system encouraged bloodshed and warfare as feudal lords continually raided each other to increase their wealth and property.

Feudalism was a system of military service and land ownership that created a pyramid of political and military power. Under this system, the less powerful knights sought protection and economic support from more powerful knights who, thus, became their feudal lords, or *seigneurs* (sehn-YUHR), and who required military service, money, and political support from their vassals. Although feudalism was based on a system of vassalage, by which barons were responsible to, or vassals of, kings, sufficient power to effect real control rarely existed at any level above the individual landholder.

The *oath of fealty* was performed at a solemn and symbolic ceremony. The vassal knelt, put his hands between those of his lord, and pledged allegiance to the lord, promising a certain number of days of military service each year and specific sums of money on occasions such as the knighting of the lord's son (Fig. **7.5**) or the marriage of the lord's daughter, or ransom for the lord himself if he were captured by his enemies. To complete the ceremony, the lord would present to the vassal a piece of earth or a sprig from a tree to symbolize the lord's grant of a fief—that is, a parcel of land including villages of serfs to work it.

Serfs and Women

Feudal society comprised a thick network of contractual relationships that linked the highest to the lowest in the realm. The lowest in the realm was a serf, whose life was one of ignorance and destitution, and of subservience to the manor's lord. Serfs did the work of the manor, and in return paid the lord for the privilege. All law enforcement and punishment occurred within the manor, and no serf could marry without the lord's consent. In the strictest sense of the ancient world, serfs were not slaves, but they were bound to the land of the estate for life, and, bound to the land, they were bound to the lord of the manor for as long as the lord owned it. In return, the lord was obliged to provide guardianship for his serfs—that is, provide basic necessities and care for them in their old age, should they reach it.

Drudgery marked the daily life of the village. People lived in one-room, sparsely furnished huts with earthen floors. They shared the hut with members of the family, chickens, and whatever other animals may have been theirs, and at night the entire family slept huddled together on straw bedding. In the spring, life took a decided turn for the worse, for typically the fall's harvest barely lasted the winter, and it was too early in the growing season for new

crops to mature. As a result, starvation in the springtime provided a constant threat, as did raids by other, equally hungry, people who formed raiding parties of barbarians or other local barons. Disease was a constant companion, and there were no doctors (Fig. **7.6**). All told, the medieval serf could only resign himself to his fate and trudge on from day to day, hopeful that death would release him into a better condition.

Women played a central role at every level of medieval society. In the manor house as well as the village hut, the family was the core of the social order, and among serfs, it also provided the central production unit. Women shared the burdens of daily existence, caring for children and animals and working small vegetable plots near the hut. They prepared food, made clothing, and helped with the harvest. Their life expectancy was short.

On the other hand, women of the manor often shared ruling functions and responsibilities. The power structure, again, was based on the family, and one was born into the aristocracy. The system depended on inheritance and marriage, and because women could inherit, they often owned vast estates. As wives of feudal barons, women were often faced with the necessity of managing the manor in its entirety while the lord was away for long periods, fighting wars on behalf of his liege lord.

Women could also find individual identity and authority in the Church. If the burdens of secular life proved overpowering, women could "take the veil" by entering a convent. A wealthy woman could establish her own convent and become a mother superior or abbess, wielding absolute authority over her subservient nuns. A woman who so devoted her life to the Church and worked diligently on behalf of it and her fellow humans could dream of sainthood—an honor bestowed by the Church after death—which would place her at the right hand of God for eternity.

THE VISUAL ARTS

Manuscript Illumination and Sculpture

Early Christian painting adopted local styles. The tomb paintings in the catacombs of Rome were, for example, Roman in style but incorporated Christian symbolism. Roman Christians were converted Roman pagans, and their paintings had a frankly practical intent. In its earliest phases, before Constantine, Christian painting was a secret art in a secret place, and its function was simply to affirm the faith of the follower on his or her tomb.

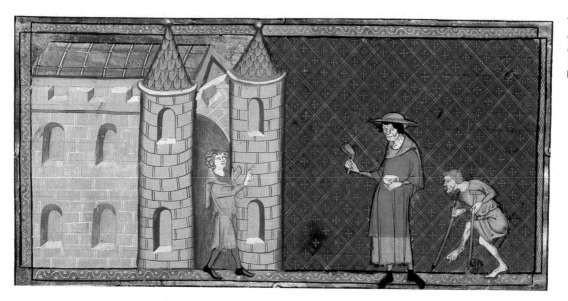

7.6 Leprosy, from the manuscript *Miroir historial de Vincent de Beauvais*, trans. by Jean de Vignay, 1330–50. Bibliothèque Nationale, Paris.

Map 7.2 Europe in the early twelfth century.

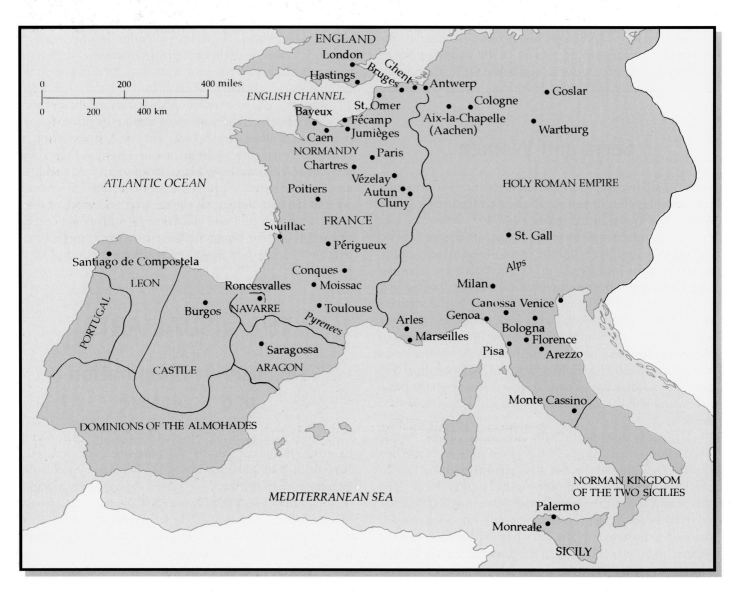

One often finds in early Christian painting a primitive quality; it is probably more a reflection of lack of technical ability than anything else. The need to pictorialize the faith was foremost. Artistic skill was not important.

Christian painting developed in several stages. From the beginning, it reflected the absolute belief in another, superior, existence in which individual believers retained their identity. Painting was a tangible expression of faith. Later, it was used to make the rites of the Church more vivid. Its final role was that of depicting and recording Christian history and tradition. Inherent from the start was a code of symbolism whose meaning could be grasped only by a fellow Christian.

As the Roman world first split and then fell apart, plunging the West into chaos, painting became once again a private art, more an intellectual pursuit than an inspiration to the faithful. A new and exquisite form of two-dimensional art emerged, not on canvases or church walls, but on the beautifully illustrated pages of scholarly Church manuscripts. By the time Christianity had sufficient status to come into the open, a dramatic change had occurred in the format of written texts. Rolls of papyrus had been replaced by more convenient and durable parchment pages bound together between hard, protective covers, known as a *codex*. Although scrolls continued to be used for special occasions throughout the Middle Ages, they were now made of stitched parchment.

The only illustrated manuscript of the New Testament in Latin to survive from this early period is a copy of the Gospels that probably came to England in 597 with St Augustine, the first archbishop of Canterbury and a missionary from Pope Gregory the Great. (This Augustine (aw-GUHS-tuhn) is not to be confused with the earlier St Augustine of Hippo.) Only two full-page miniatures

TECHNOLOGY: PUTTING DISCOVERY TO WORK

The Viking Ships

While feudal Europe struggled and while Charlemagne was emerging as Holy Roman Emperor, the Vikings of Scandinavia were sailing as far as the shores of North America, preceding Columbus to the New World by more than six hundred years. Their means of transport was the Viking ship (Fig. **7.7**), and its construction and use prove that these hearty and hardy peoples were as skillful in their technology as they were warlike and adventurous. The vessel had a true keel, a single steering-oar with a tiller handle, well-raked—that is, angled—stem- and stern-posts, sixteen rowing ports cut into each side, and a square-sail rigged on a single mast amidships. Light and buoyant, they were called long-ships because their length was such a striking feature, exceeding the beam by more than five to one. In time, the Viking ships grew until they had thirty and even sixty oars to a side. It was in these large vessels that the Vikings made their raids, conquests, and far-reaching explorations to Russia and America.

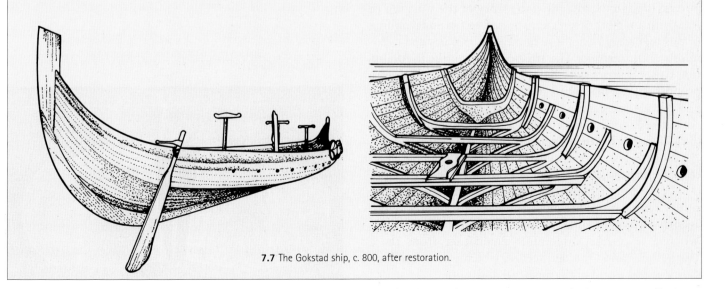

7.7 The Gokstad ship, c. 800, after restoration.

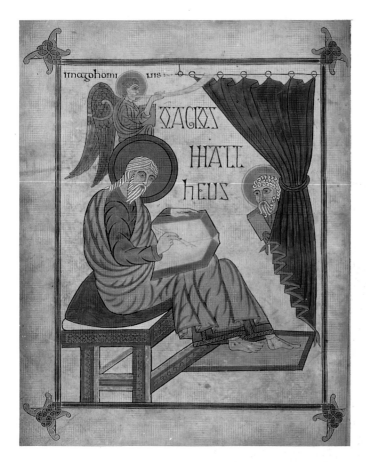

7.8 St Matthew, from the Lindisfarne Gospels, before 698. 13¹/₂ × 9³/₄ ins (34.3 × 24.8 cm). British Library, London.

survive, one of which (see Fig. **5.13**) shows St Luke and twelve scenes from his Gospel. It is a full-page frontispiece. We see the saint seated in the foreground within an arched border. In the sides of the frame are little compartments portraying events, including the story of the washing of feet, with an unbearded Peter. The rich colors and detailing of this miniature rival those of the wall mosaics and decorations of Byzantium. The artistic quality of the St Augustine Gospels is not very high, however, in that the figure proportions are inaccurate, the medium is handled loosely, and details are carelessly executed. Perhaps it was not considered worthwhile to send a more valuable book to the still largely heathen England.

Nonetheless, this work is an interesting example of an early *picture cycle*, and it typifies certain stylistic qualities that became more marked in medieval painting and sculpture. Compositions are close and nervous: figures bump against each other amid an atmosphere of frenetic energy. We feel a certain discomfort emanating from these "walled-in" and crowded scenes, which perhaps mirror the closed-in world of the medieval illustrator.

An Irish contribution to medieval manuscript illumination appears in Figure **7.8**. Here the figures are flat and almost ornamental, though they are precisely and delicately rendered. Highlight and shadow give a sense of depth in the curtain, and space is suggested by the oblique treatment of the bench. Accurate linear perspective is unknown to these artists. Colors are few and subtle. Of note here is the frontal treatment of the angel's eye, in contrast to the head, which is in profile. Outlining adds to the stylization. The picture is carefully composed, with both color and form controlled to achieve a pleasing balance.

From the fifth to the eleventh centuries, a tremendous wealth of artistic work emerged in several nontraditional areas. Life was generally in a state of flux throughout Europe in the early Middle Ages, and it was to ordinary and portable media that nonmonastic nomadic people turned much of their artistic energy. Clothing, jewelry, and ships, for example, all exhibited the artistry of the Germanic, Irish, and Scandinavian peoples (Fig. **7.9**).

Emotionalism in art increased as the approach of the millennium sounded its trumpet of expected doom. The fact that the world did not end on 1 January 1001 reduced this feeling only slightly. Emotionalism was strengthened further by an influx of Eastern art when Otto II married a Byzantine princess. A combination of Roman, Carolingian, and Byzantine characteristics typify Ottonian manuscript illustration. Despite the crowding and an inherent appeal to feeling, such work testifies to the increasingly outward-looking approach of the early years of the second millennium.

Sculpture played only a very minor role in the centuries between the collapse of the Roman Empire and the rise of the Romanesque style in the eleventh century. The fact that

7.9 Hinged shoulder clasp from the ship burial at Sutton Hoo, England, seventh century. Gold decorated with garnets, mosaic, glass, and filigree. British Museum, London.

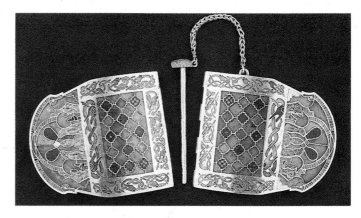

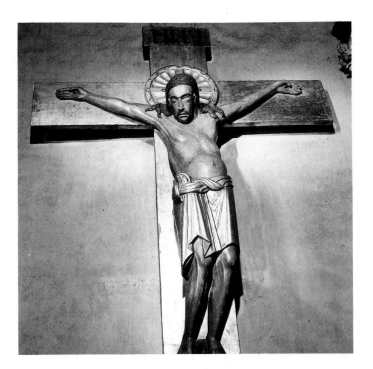

7.10 *Gero crucifix*, 969–976. Oak, 6 ft 1⅝ ins (1.87 m) high. Cologne Cathedral, Germany.

Romanesque Style in Architecture and Sculpture

As Charlemagne's empire in the ninth century, and then the tenth century, passed, a new and radical style in architecture emerged. Unlike its counterparts in painting and sculpture, Romanesque architecture had a fairly identifiable style, despite its diversity. The Romanesque took hold throughout Europe in a relatively short period of time. When people of the Renaissance saw its curved arches over doorways and windows throughout Europe, they saw a style that was pre-Gothic and post-Roman—but like the Roman. Therefore, they called it "Romanesque." With its arched doorways and windows, this style was massive, static, and comparatively lightless, which seems further to reflect the barricaded mentality and lifestyle generally associated with the Middle Ages.

The Romanesque style nonetheless exemplified the power and wealth of the Church militant and triumphant. If the style mirrored the social and intellectual system that produced it, it also reflected a new religious fervor and a turning of the Church toward its growing flock. Romanesque churches were larger than earlier ones; we can see their scale in Figures **7.11** and **7.13**. St Sernin (san

7.11 St Sernin, Toulouse, France, c. 1080–1120.

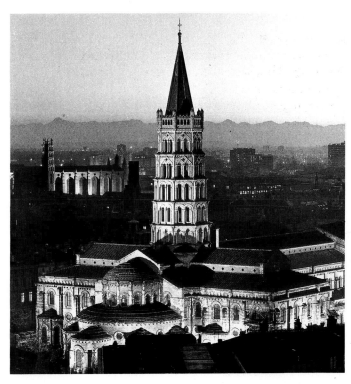

the Old Testament prohibited graven images may have been partly responsible for this. The association of statuary with pagan societies, notably Rome, was fresh in the memory of the Church. Thus, when Christian sculpture emerged, it was largely funerary and not monumental. The earliest examples are all sarcophagi.

Some of the most beautiful sculptural work of the Christian era after Constantine resembles manuscript illumination in its small-scale, MINIATURE-like detail. Its restless, linear style is eloquent with emotion, and it is very precise in its detail.

Especially poignant is the *Gero* (GAIR-oh) *crucifix* (Fig. **7.10**). The realism of the crucified Christ, whose downward- and forward-sagging body pulls against the nails, and the emotion with which it is rendered, are very compelling. The muscle striations on the right arm and chest, the bulging belly, and the rendering of cloth are particularly expressive. This work has a hardness of surface. The form is human, but the flesh, hair, and cloth do not have the soft texture we might expect. The face is a mask of agony, but no less full of pathos for that. An intense spirituality reflects the mysticism prevalent in the early Middle Ages. The *Gero crucifix* depicts a suffering Christ whose agony parallels the spirit of the times. This portrayal contrasts markedly with the *Christus Rex* crucifixes that became popular later and are frequently seen today, in which Christ on the cross is a victorious, resurrected King.

MASTERWORK

The Bronze Doors of Hildesheim Cathedral

During Bernard of Hildesheim's years as bishop (993–1022), the city of Hildesheim became a center for manuscript painting and other arts. Bernward's patronage, however, was largely confined to the area of metalwork, in particular, the bronze doors of the Hildesheim (hil-duh-SHYM) Cathedral (Fig. 7.12). These doors were cast by the *cire-perdue* (sihr-pair-DOO), or LOST-WAX, process.

The building of the Abbey Church of St Michael at Hildesheim was part of Bishop Bernward's plan to make the town a center of learning. The doors for the south portal of St Michael's were completed in 1015 and they were probably installed before 1035. Apparently cast in one piece, Hildesheim's doors are the first in a succession of figured bronze doors throughout the Middle Ages and the Renaissance, a tradition that culminated in Ghiberti's *Gates of Paradise* for the Baptistery in Florence (see p. 303). The massive doors of Hildesheim also represent a return to larger scale sculpture that was to become typical of the Romanesque period.

The scenes portrayed on Bernward's doors tell biblical stories in a carefully arranged order. The number of scenes depicted—sixteen—is an example of medieval number symbolism. (Sixteen is the number of the Gospels multiplied by itself.) Reading from top to bottom, the scenes are paired, so that the left door unfolds the Old Testament story of the fall, and the right, the New Testament story of the redemption. For example, *The Temptation of Adam and Eve* (third from the top, left), which depicts the fall from grace, is purposely aligned with the *Crucifixion* (third from the top, right), which illustrates the redemption of humankind.

The scenes are highly reminiscent of manuscript illustration, and they tell their stories with a simple directness. In the fourth panel from the top on the left, an angry God reproaches Adam and Eve. His angry glare is heightened by his accusatory, pointing finger, and Adam and Eve cower under his condemnation. As the sinners try to shield their nakedness, Adam points to Eve, passing to her the blame for his transgression; she, in turn, looks downward, and with her left hand points an accusing finger at the serpent.

What is striking about all the scenes is the strong sense of composition and physical movement. Every set of images, against a plain background of open space, speaks forcefully in dumb show. The doors tell their story in medieval fashion, as a vivid but silent drama, effectively communicating the message of the Christian faith to a largely illiterate public. Replace these simple scenes with a clergy-actor, and you have the beginnings of liturgical drama (see the theatre section below). Just as the mystics of the Middle Ages understood communication through the intuition and nonrational emotions, so the artists of the period understood the raw power and effectiveness of the simple nonverbal image.

7.12 Doors of Hildesheim Cathedral, 1015. Bronze, 16 ft 6 ins (5.03 m) high. Hildesheim, Germany.

Sair-NAN) reflects a heavy elegance and complexity we have not previously seen. The plan of the church describes a Roman cross, that is, a cross with the lower staff longer than the arms. (Recall the cross-in-square, or Greek cross design, of Byzantine churches in Chapter 6.) The side aisles extend beyond the crossing to create an ambulatory, or walking space. This was so that pilgrims, most of whom were on their way to Spain, could walk around the altar without disturbing the service.

One additional change is worth noting. The roof of this church is made of stone, whereas earlier buildings had wooden roofs. As we view the magnificent vaulted interior, we wonder how successfully the architect reconciled the conflicts between engineering, material properties, and aesthetics. Given the properties of stone and the increased force of added height, did he try to push his skills to the edge, in order to create a breathtaking interior? Did he aim to reflect the glory of God or the ability of humanity?

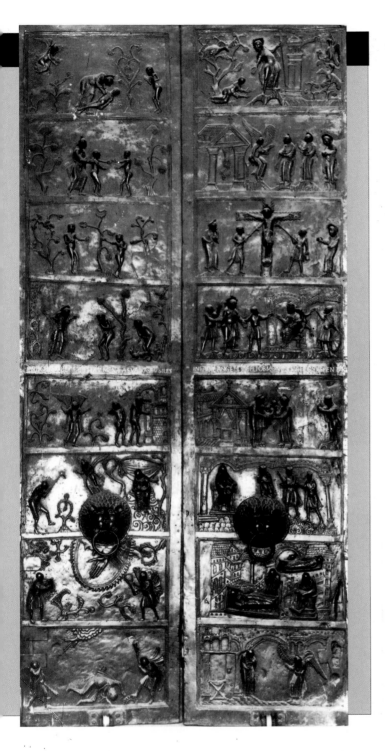

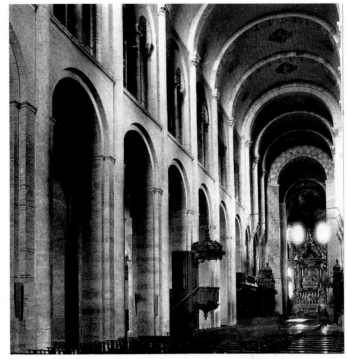

7.13 Interior of the nave at St Sernin, Toulouse, France, c. 1080–1120.

Returning to the exterior view, we can see how some of the stress of the high vaulting was diffused. In a complex series of vaults, transverse arches, and bays, the tremendous weight and outward thrust of the central vault were transferred to the ground, leaving a high and unencumbered central space. If we compare this structural system with post-and-lintel structure and consider the compressive and tensile properties of stone, we can see why the arch is superior as a structural device for creating open space. Because of the weight and the distribution of stress in this style, only very small windows were possible. So, although the fortress-like, lightless qualities of Romanesque architecture reflect the spirit of their time, they also had a practical explanation.

The tenth-century church of Cluny, known as Cluny II, inspired numerous buildings throughout the West in the eleventh century. When it became too small, a new church, Cluny III, was begun in 1088. It remained the largest church in Christendom until St Peter's in Rome was rebuilt in the sixteenth century. Although Cluny III (Figs. **7.14**, **7.15**, and **7.16**), was badly damaged during the French Revolution, we know that the nave, which had double aisles, the double transepts, and the choir with an ambulatory were all enormous in scale. The arcades of the nave had pointed arches, and the interior housed magnificent wall paintings. Protruding apses and numerous towers adorned the exterior.

The Norman Romanesque style of building, with its accent on rounded arches, was loosely based on the classical architecture of Roman times. It is, therefore, covered by the broad umbrella term, "Romanesque style." Norman style came to England from western Europe even before the Norman invasion of 1066 and flourished alongside the earlier Saxon architecture. Norman style, however, became firmly established in the flurry of building—especially

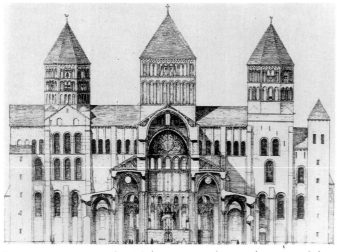

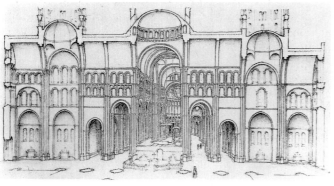

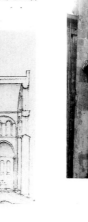

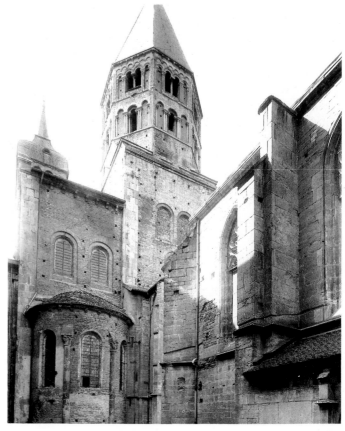

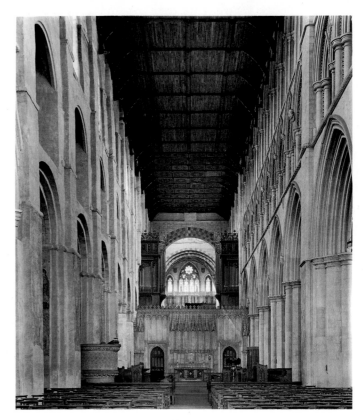

7.14 (*top*) Transverse section of the nave, and west elevation of the great transept of the Abbey Church, Cluny III, France, 1088–1130.

7.15 (*middle*) Transverse section of the transept. Drawing by Kenneth J. Conant. Frances Loeb Library, Harvard University, Cambridge, MA.

7.16 (*top right*) Exterior of southwest transept of Cluny III.

7.17 (*right*) St Albans Cathedral, England, the nave facing east, c. 1280–90.

church building and rebuilding—that followed the Conquest and continued until around 1190. Its impact was especially noticeable on the larger churches. Small parish churches adopted the changes more slowly.

Most Norman churches were built of stone cut into square blocks, although when stone was not readily available, bricks and cut flints were also used. In the Abbey Church of St Alban (Fig. **7.17**) bricks and cut flints from Roman ruins served for the building. The Roman bricks were thinner than our bricks—about the size and shape of paving stones. The massive piers of St Albans—nearly 6 feet (1.8 meters) thick at the tower ceiling level—are constructed of rubble faced with Roman bricks. The walls of the nave were plastered over and painted white.

Norman arches were often decorated with carvings of various designs. At St Albans, the Roman brickwork proved too hard to carve and so the arches of the nave were brightly painted in typical Norman linear designs. Ribbed vaulting (see Introduction), which was introduced late in the Norman period, proved stronger and more attractive than groin vaulting. The earliest known Norman ribbed vaults appear in Durham Cathedral in England, and date from approximately 1095.

Like the architecture of the period, sculpture of the eleventh and early twelfth centuries is also called Romanesque. In the case of sculpture, the label refers more to an era than to a style. Examples of sculpture are so diverse that we probably could not group them under a single label, were it not for the fact that most of them take the form of decorative elements attached to Romanesque architecture. We can, however, draw some general conclusions about Romanesque sculpture. First, it is associated with Romanesque architecture; second, it is stone; third, it is monumental. The last characteristic represents a distinct departure from previous sculptural style. Monumental stone sculpture had all but disappeared in the fifth century. Its reemergence across Europe at the end of the eleventh century over such a short period was remarkable. The emergence of sculptural decoration indicated at least the beginning of dissemination of knowledge from the cloistered world of the monastery to the general populace. Romanesque sculpture was applied to exteriors of buildings where the lay worshipper could see it and respond to it. The relationship of this artistic development to the increase in religious zeal among the laity was probably strong. In works such as the *Last Judgment* TYMPANUM (TIM-puh-nuhm) of Autun (Fig. **7.18**), the illiterate masses could now read the message of the Church, an opportunity previously reserved for the clergy. The message of this carved scene is quite clear. In the center of the composition, framed by a Roman-style arch, is an awe-inspiring figure of Christ. Next to him, malproportioned figures writhe in various degrees of torment. The inscription of the artist, Gislebertus (jis-ul-BAIR-tuhs), tells us that their purpose was "to let this horror appal those bound by earthly sin." Evil was still central to medieval thought, and devils share the stage with Christ, attempting to tip the scales of judgment in their favor and gleefully pushing the damned into the flaming pit.

Another Romanesque tympanum comes from the central portal of the narthex of the abbey and pilgrim church of Sainte-Madeleine, Vézelay (vay-zeh-LAY), in Burgundy (Fig. **7.19**). The story depicts the mission of the apostles and became especially meaningful to medieval

7.18 Gislebertus, *Last Judgment* tympanum, west porch, c. 1130–35. Autun Cathedral, France. Photo: © Paul M.R. Maeyaert, Mont de l'Enclus (Orroir), Belgium.

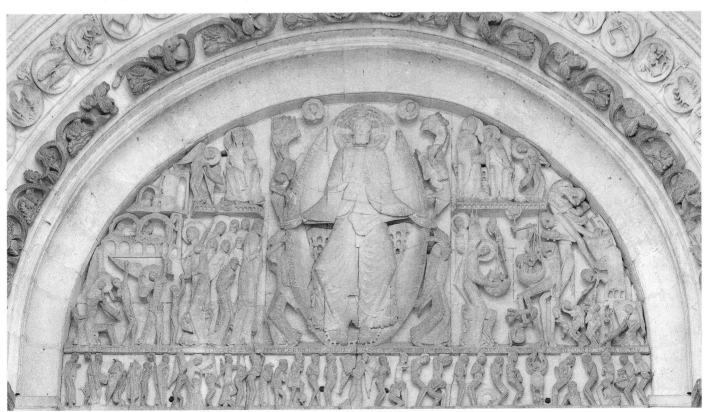

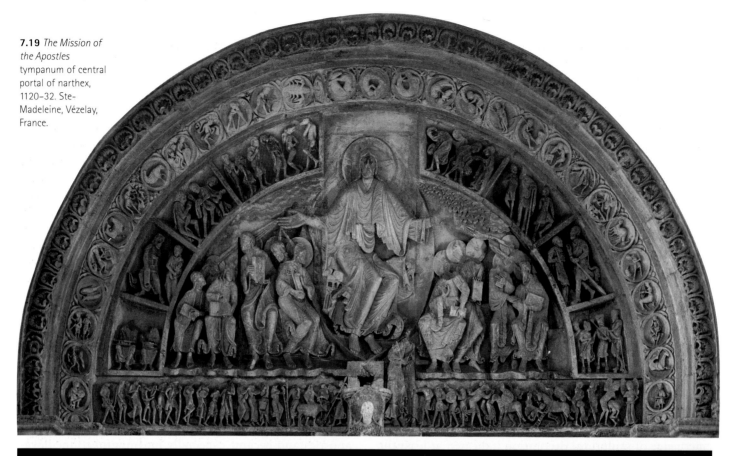

7.19 *The Mission of the Apostles* tympanum of central portal of narthex, 1120–32. Ste-Madeleine, Vézelay, France.

OUR DYNAMIC WORLD

Igbo-Ukwu

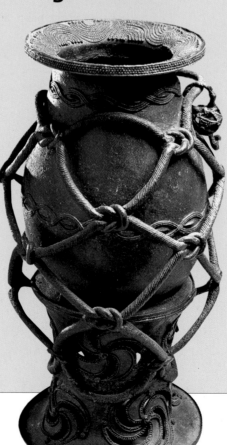

During Europe's early Middle Ages, African artists and artisans not only used but mastered bronze, and a remarkable example of that mastery is in a ritual water-pot found in the village of Igbo-Ukwu in eastern Nigeria (Fig. **7.20**).

The level of skill achieved by ninth- and tenth-century Africans in this object is astounding. In the first place, it was cast using the same sophisticated *cire-perdue* (lost-wax) method employed in casting the bronze doors of Hildesheim Cathedral (Fig. **7.12**). This method involves the making of a wax model around which a mold is placed. The mold is heated, the wax melts and runs out of the

mold, and the void is then filled with the molten metal that forms the finished work. This leaded bronze artifact has amazing virtuosity. The ritual water-pot stands enclosed in a net of simulated rope. The knots and delicate striations are perfect, and the graceful design of its recurved lines and flaring base by themselves are exquisite. This is a design and execution of immense sophistication of both technique and vision.

7.20 Roped pot on a stand, from Igbo-Ukwu, ninth to tenth centuries. Leaded bronze, 12½ ins (32 cm) high. National Museum, Lagos, Nigeria.

Christians at the time of the crusades (see Chapter 8). Here the artist proclaimed the duty of every Christian to spread the gospel to the ends of the earth. At the center of the tympanum, a rather elongated figure of Christ spreads his arms, from which emanate the rays of the Holy Spirit, empowering the apostles, who carry the scriptures as tokens of their mission. Around the border is a plethora of representatives of the heathen world. The arch is framed by the signs of the zodiac and labors appropriate to the months of the year, stressing that the preaching of the faith is an ongoing, year-round responsibility without end.

MUSIC

Sacred Music

Gregorian Chant

By around the year 500, a body of sacred—that is, religious—music called chant, *plainchant*, or *plainsong*, had been developed for use in Christian worship services. (The terms, along with Gregorian chant, are commonly used as synonyms, although detailed study reveals differences.) Chant was vocal and took the form of a single melodic line (*monophony*; muh-NAH-foh-nee) using notes relatively near each other on the musical scale. The haunting, undulating character of early chant possibly points to Near Eastern origins. Chants were sung in a flexible tempo with unmeasured rhythms following the natural accents of normal Latin speech. There were two types of chant settings. In one, called *syllabic*, each syllable of the chant was given one note. In the other, called MELISMATIC (mehl-iz-MAT-ik), each syllable was spread over several notes. The selection "Kyrie: Hodie Christus Resurrexit" (CD track 4) lets us sense the flavor of the undulating and ethereal melody of the melismatic type. The Kyrie is one of the five parts of the *mass ordinary*—texts that remain the same from day to day throughout most of the church year. The other parts of the Mass are the *Gloria* (Glory be to God on high), *Credo* (I believe . . .), *Sanctus* (Holy, holy, holy, Lord God of Hosts), and *Agnus Dei* (O Lamb of God that takest away the sins of the world). The Kyrie entreats, "Kyrie eleison" (Lord have mercy upon us), "Christe eleison" (Christ have mercy upon us), "Kyrie eleison" (Lord have mercy upon us). These sections, sung by the choir, are alternated with the affirmation, "Hodie Christus Resurrexit" (Today Christ is Risen), sung by a soloist, which gives the piece an ABABA structure.

Plainchant is often called Gregorian chant because Pope Gregory I (540–604) supervised the selection of melodies and texts he thought most appropriate and compiled them for Church services. Although Pope Gregory did not invent plainchant, his contributions of selection and codification were such that it acquired his name.

Polyphony: Organum

At some time between the eighth and tenth centuries, monks in monastery choirs began to add a second melodic line to the chant. At first, the additional line paralleled the original at the interval of a fourth or a fifth. Medieval music that consists of Gregorian chant and an additional melodic line (or lines) is called *organum* (OHR-guh-nuhm). Between the tenth and the thirteenth centuries, organum became truly POLYPHONIC. As time progressed, the independent melodies became more and more independent of each other and differed rhythmically as well as melodically.

Secular Music

The Middle Ages also witnessed a growth in secular music—that is, not related to the Church. As might be expected, secular music used vernacular texts—that is, texts in the language of the common people, as opposed to the Latin of church music. The subject matter mostly concerned love, but other topics were also popular. Medieval secular song was probably mostly STROPHIC (STROHF-ik) (composed of several stanzas that were sung to the same melody).

Musical instruments of this era (Fig. **7.21**) included the lyre, the harp, and a bowed instrument called the vielle or

7.21 *Medieval Minstrel playing to Nobleman*, MS. Fr 13096 fol 46. Bibliothèque Nationale, Paris.

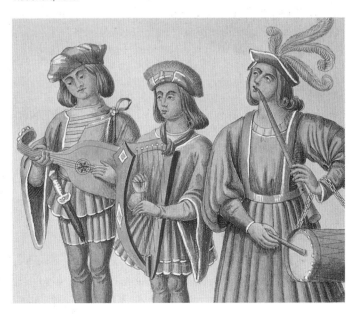

fiedel, (the viol, or fiddle). The psaltery, which was similar to a zither, the lute, the flute, the shawm, which was a reed instrument like an oboe, trumpets, horns, drums, and bagpipes were all popular. Small, portable organs were also popular, despite the instrument's unpleasant associations with the Roman persecution of Christians, and the organ eventually found its way into the medieval church.

LITERATURE

It seems clear that in the early Middle Ages—with the notable exception of the Carolingian court—the politically powerful cared little for culture, and for the most part could neither read nor write. Thanks to the efforts of the monastic community, and particularly the Benedictine monks, however, important books and manuscripts were preserved and copied. St Benedict (c. 480–c. 550) was one of the few great scholars of the Dark Ages.

The Muslims had come into contact with Greek culture when they invaded Egypt, and they brought it with them to Spain, where literature flourished. The schools they set up in Cordoba studied Aristotle and Plato alongside the Koran. Toledo and Seville were also centers of learning. It was biblical literature, however, that became the central focus during the early Middle Ages.

St Jerome (c. 342–420) was a contemporary of St Augustine of Hippo, and his writings assumed a position of primary importance in the last years of the Roman Empire. St Jerome was familiar with the classical writers, and the style of the scriptures seemed somewhat crude to him. He had a dream, however, in which Christ reproached him and accused him of being more a Ciceronian than a Christian. As a result, Jerome resolved to spend the rest of his life in the study of the sacred books. He made a famous translation of the Bible into Latin, and assisted by Jewish scholars, he also translated the Old Testament from the Hebrew.

Another major literary accomplishment of the early Middle Ages, one with a completely different subject matter, was the German *Nibelungenlied* (nee-beh-LUNG-en-leet; "Song of the People of the Mists," meaning the dead). These early hero-stories of northern peoples, which took their final shape in southeast Germany c. 1200, are a rich mixture of history, magic, and myth. There are ten complete and twenty incomplete manuscripts of the *Nibelungenlied*, folk tales of thirty-nine adventures, commencing with that of the hero Siegfried, son of Siegmund, king of the Netherworld.

The poem begins by introducing Kriemhild (KREEM-hilt), a Burgundian princess of Worms, and Siegfried (SEEG-freed), a prince from the lower Rhine who is deter-mined to woo her. When he arrives in Worms, he is identified by Hagen (HAHG-ehn), a henchman of Kriemhild's brother King Gunther. Hagen then recounts Siegfried's earlier heroic deeds, including his acquisition of a treasure. When the Danes and Saxons declare war, Siegfried leads the Burgundians and distinguishes himself in battle. Upon his return, he meets Kriemhild, and their affections develop during his residence at court.

Hearing of the contest for Brunhild, a queen of outstanding strength and beauty who may be won only by a man capable of matching her athletic prowess, Gunther decides to woo her. He enlists the aid of Siegfried, to whom he promises the hand of Kriemhild if successful. By trickery the two men defeat Brunhild, and she accepts Gunther as her husband. Siegfried and Kriemhild are then married as promised, but Brunhild is suspicious. The two queens soon quarrel, and Kriemhild reveals how Brunhild was deceived. Hagen sides with Brunhild and kills Siegfried.

During these events, Brunhild drops almost unnoticed out of the story. Siegfried's funeral is conducted with great ceremony, and the griefstricken Kriemhild remains at Worms, though for a long time estranged from Gunther and Hagen. Siegfried's treasure is brought to Worms, but Hagen sinks the treasure in the Rhine.

The second part of the poem deals principally with the conflict between Hagen and Kriemhild and her vengeance against the Burgundians. Etzel (Attila), king of the Huns, asks the hand of Kriemhild, who accepts. After many years, she persuades Etzel to invite her brothers and Hagen to his court. Though Hagen is wary, they all go, and carnage ensues. Kriemhild has Gunther killed and then, with Siegfried's sword, she slays the bound and defenseless Hagen. Kriemhild herself is slain by a knight named Hildebrand.

The favorite Old English epic, *Beowulf* (BAY-oh-wuhlf; c. 725), is the earliest extant poem in a modern European language. Composed by an unknown author, it falls into separate episodes that incorporate old legends. The poem is written in unrhymed alliterative verse. Its three folk stories center on the hero, Beowulf, and his exploits against the monster Grendel (GREHN-duhl), Grendel's mother—a hideous water hag—and a fire-breathing dragon. In the poem, the "battle-brave" Beowulf crosses the sea from "Geatland" (possibly Sweden) to the land of the Danes and frees that country from a terrible ogre, Grendel. In revenge, the ogre's mother carries off a king's councillor. Beowulf follows her to her lair under the waters of a lake and slays her. Beowulf becomes king of the Geats and rules for half a century. He is fatally wounded when he battles a fire-breathing dragon. Mourned by his subjects, he is buried under a great barrow, or mound.

Another popular poem, the *Chanson de Roland* or "Song of Roland," tells of Charlemagne. The poem proba-

Hildegard of Bingen (1098–1179)

One of the significant musical and literary figures of the time, Hildegard of Bingen was educated at the Benedictine cloister of Disibodenberg and became prioress there in 1136. Having experienced visions since she was a child, at age forty-three she consulted her confessor, who in turn reported the matter to the archbishop of Mainz. A committee of theologians subsequently confirmed the authenticity of her visions, and a monk was appointed to help her record them in writing. The finished work, *Scivias* (1141–52), consisted of twenty-six visions, prophetic, symbolic, and apocalyptic in form. About 1147, she left Disibodenberg to found a new convent, where she continued to prophesy, to record her visions in writing, and perform her musical plays.

Hildegard is the first composer whose biography is known. She wrote music and texts to her songs, mostly liturgical plainchant honoring saints and the Virgin Mary. She believed that music was the means of recapturing the original joy and beauty of paradise and that music was invented and musical instruments made in order to worship God appropriately. She wrote in the plainchant tradition of a single vocal melodic line that we have just discussed. She wrote seventy-seven chants and the first musical drama in history, which she entitled "The Ritual of the Virtues."

Hildegard of Bingen's music was written for performance by the nuns of the convent she headed. She combined all her music into a cycle called "The Symphony of the Harmony of the Heavenly Revelations," from which the "Lauds of Saint Ursula" ("O Ecclesia" excerpt, CD track 5) is one example. This music is sung by three sopranos accompanied by an instrumental drone, which serves as a sustained bass above which the voices soar in the chantlike melody. It celebrates St Ursula who, according to legend, was martyred with eleven thousand virgins in Cologne.

Hildegard believed that many times a day, humans fall out of sorts and lose their way. Music was the sacred technology that could best redirect human hearts toward heaven. It could integrate mind, heart, and body and heal discord.

Hildegard's numerous other writings include a morality play, a book of saints' lives, two treatises on medicine and natural history, and extensive correspondence, in which are to be found further prophecies and allegorical treatises. Her lyrical poetry, gathered in "The Symphony of the Harmony of the Heavenly Revelations" (*Symphonia armonie celestium revelationum*), consists of seventy-seven poems (all with music), and together they form a liturgical cycle.

---

bly dates to around 1100. Its author was probably a Norman poet named Turold, whose name is mentioned in the last line of the poem. It is the story of the historical battle of Roncesvalles, which was fought in 778 between the armies of Charlemagne and the Saracens of Saragossa in the Pyrenees mountains between France and Spain. In reality, the battle was little more than a skirmish against the Basques, but the poet turns the event into a heroic encounter on the level of the Greek battle of Thermopylae, which we studied earlier.

In style, the poem is direct and sober. It focuses on the clash between the recklessly courageous Roland and his more cautious friend Oliver, a conflict that illustrates divergent views of feudal loyalty.

The poem begins as Charlemagne, having conquered all of Spain except Saragossa, receives overtures from the Saracen king. In response, Charlemagne sends the knight Ganelon to negotiate peace terms, but Ganelon, Roland's stepfather, is angry because Roland proposed him for the dangerous task, and he conspires with the Saracens to achieve Roland's death. On his return to Charlemagne's camp, Ganelon ensures that Roland will command the rear guard of the army as it withdraws from Spain. As the army crosses the Pyrenees, the rear guard is surrounded at the pass of Roncesvalles by an overwhelming Saracen force.

The headstrong Roland, preoccupied with valor, rejects his friend Oliver's advice to blow his horn and summon help from the rest of Charlemagne's army. The battle ensues, and the valiant French soldiers fight until only a handful remain alive. Finally, the horn is sounded, but it is too late to save Oliver or Roland, who is fatally wounded in error by a blow from a blinded Oliver. However, it is not too late for the arriving army to avenge the heroic vassals.

When Charlemagne returns to France, he breaks the news to Aude, Roland's fiancée and Oliver's sister, who falls dead at the news. The poem ends with the trial and execution of Ganelon.

THEATRE

Scholars used to argue that theatre ceased to exist in the Western world for a period of several hundred years. However, two pieces of evidence certainly suggest that theatrical productions continued. One is the presence of wandering entertainers (see Chapter 8). In this tribe of entertainers were mimists, jugglers, bear baiters, acrobats, wrestlers, and storytellers. The propensity of human beings for acting out or mimicking actions and events is too compelling to deny its existence amid the entertainments we know existed in this era. We do not know, however, how such entertainments were presented during the early Middle Ages. They may have consisted simply of the acting out of a story silently or the reading of a play script, rather than the formal presentations we call "theatre."

Our second piece of evidence proves more conclusively that theatre existed. Writings from north Africa argue that mime continued there and it is probable that if it still existed in north Africa, it also existed in Europe. The king of Spain in the seventh century refers to the popularity of old Roman festival plays at marriages and feasts, adding that members of the clergy should leave when these were performed. In France in the ninth century, the Council of Tours and the Council of Aix-la-Chapelle (EKS-lah-shah-PEHL) ruled that the clergy should witness neither plays nor the obscenities of actors. These railings of the Church against the theatre certainly suggest that it existed. Charlemagne added his powerful backing in defense of the clergy by ruling that no actor could wear a priest's robe under penalty of corporal punishment or banishment. This edict has been taken by some as evidence of theatrical presentation and also, perhaps inaccurately, as evidence of the beginnings of liturgical drama. If this were the case, the prohibition would imply the use of actors other than the clergy in church drama.

In the tenth century, the German nun Hrosvitha (hrohs-VEET-ah) is known to have written six plays based on comedies by Terence. We do not know if Hrosvitha's plays were performed, but if they were, the audience would have been restricted to the other nuns in the convent.

We are sure, however, that liturgical drama began as an elaboration of the Roman Catholic Mass, probably in France. These elaborations were called tropes, and they took place on ceremonial occasions, especially at Easter, the dramatic highlight of the Church year. Records at Winchester in southern England dating from the late tenth century tell of a trope in which priests acted out the discovery of Jesus' empty tomb by his followers on Easter morning.

The first dramatic trope was the "Quem Quaeritis" trope. This earliest Easter trope dates from 925, and the dialogue was:

> *Angels*: Whom seek ye in the tomb, O Christians?
> *The Three Marys*: Jesus of Nazareth, the crucified, O Heavenly Beings.
> *Angels*: He is not here, he is risen as he foretold. Go and announce that he is risen from the tomb.

So theatre, along with all the other arts, except dance, was adopted by the Church and became an instrument of God in an age of faith and demons.

DANCE

Dancing did not surrender to the dictates of Christianity in the early Middle Ages. Church writings continue to condemn dancing from Constantine's time to the eleventh century and beyond. St Augustine complained that it was better to dig ditches on the Sabbath than to dance a "Choric Reigen" (RY-gehn; a type of "round dance").

Bitter conflict understandably characterized a previously pagan world in an age of expanding Church influence. A religious philosophy in which all pleasures of the flesh were evil clashed with a pagan belief to which fertility rites, including wild dances and orgies, were central. History records many examples of masked pagan dancers attempting to invade churches. Even when Christianity gained a firm hold, it was impossible to eradicate ritualistic dancing completely. It appears that a certain unspoken compromise was reached. Dancing continued because people will continue to do what gives them pleasure, Church or not, the threat of damnation notwithstanding. But the pagan contexts of dance were put aside. The Christian Church made many such compromises with life as it found it.

Any dance in this period, however, was largely spontaneous and took no account of a performer/audience relationship. Such dancing was a response to a chaotic and frightening world in which people were reduced to their baser selves. Later, demonic dances, dances of death, and animal mummeries would take on a more formal, presentational character—Death as a dancer was a frequent medieval image.

Theatrical dance remained alive, however, through successors to the Roman pantomimes. Dancers appeared at fairs and festivals, performing nearly always for the peasants—rarely for the nobility.

Focal Point
The Carolingian Renaissance

On few occasions in history have individuals been able to put their individual temperament on so many aspects of society and art as did Charlemagne. His reign was so all-encompassing and his interest in all the aspects of life so wide that the word "renaissance" has been applied to the time of his rule. As we will see, the Carolingian renaissance had its limits, but, given its time and circumstances, it truly was remarkable.

When Pepin III died in 768, he was succeeded by his two sons, Charles and Carloman. Carloman died three years later, and Charles, denying the succession of Carloman's infant sons, acquired for himself the entire Frankish Empire. Carrying on the work of his father and grandfather, Charlemagne set about subduing the Frankish peoples and other tribes throughout Europe. He ruled over a vast empire of many nations, and became protector of

7.22 St Mark and St Luke, from the Gospel Book of Godescale, 781–783. Vellum, 12¼ × 8¼ ins (31.3 × 21 cm). Bibliothèque Nationale, Paris.

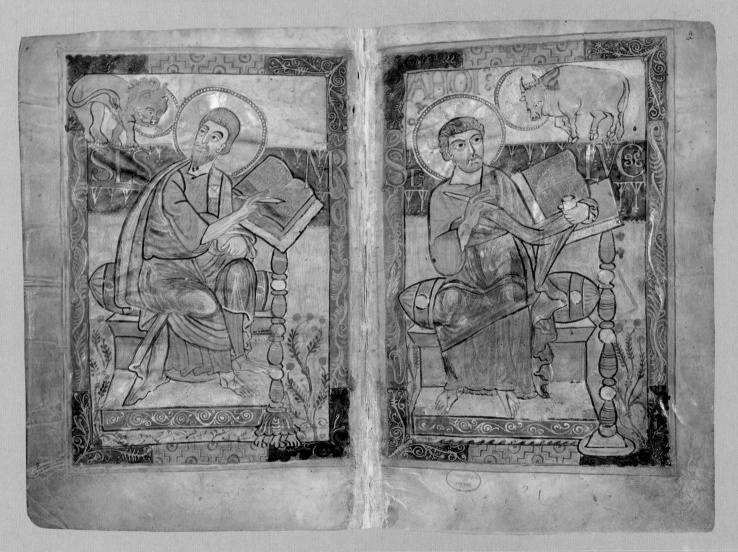

Pope Leo III in Rome. On Christmas Day in the year 800, as Charlemagne knelt in prayer before the altar in the old church of St Peter, Pope Leo suddenly placed a crown on his head, and the people acclaimed him as emperor.

Perhaps his greatest contributions to European civilization lay in his support of education, reform of the Church, and cultivation of the liberal arts. Under the leadership of Alcuin (AL-kwin) of York, scholars were assembled from all parts of the West to reunite the scattered fragments of the classical heritage. The classical revival initiated by Charlemagne was part of his attempt to revive the Roman Empire.

Manuscript Illumination and Wall Painting

Carolingian manuscript illuminations are striking examples of early medieval painting. As an official court art, book illumination was promoted by the king, his relatives, associates, and officers of state. One exemplary product of

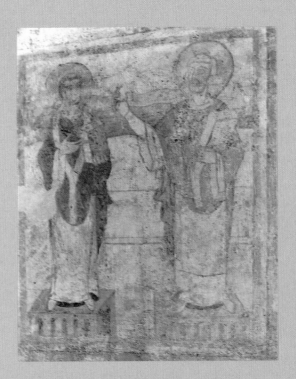

7.24 The crypts at St-Germain, Auxerre, France, ninth century.

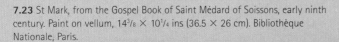

7.23 St Mark, from the Gospel Book of Saint Médard of Soissons, early ninth century. Paint on vellum, 14³/₈ × 10¹/₄ ins (36.5 × 26 cm). Bibliothèque Nationale, Paris.

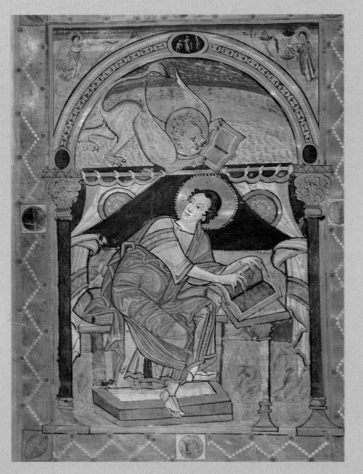

the time was the Gospel Book of Godescale (Fig. 7.22). The models for this work were probably Byzantine: the evangelists have lean, bearded faces, and the cloth of their garments reveals a rudimentary attempt at modeling, with light and dark stripes representing the highlight and shadow of the folds. Unlike the Gospel Book of Godescale (GOHD-uhs-kal), the Gospel Book of Saint-Médard of Soissons (san-may-DARD; swah-SAWN; Fig. 7.23) displays a definite classicism in its arches complete with columns, intricate architecture, and frames adorned with pictures containing tiny figures. Nonetheless, there is confusion in the plethora of detail and a crowded nervousness characteristic of medieval work.

Wall paintings were a highly original feature of Carolingian art and architecture. Although few examples remain, evidence suggests that Carolingian palaces and churches were brightly painted in a style not unlike that of the Romans. For example, three-dimensional architectural detail is presented in a highly lifelike fashion on a two-dimensional surface. Large frescoes depicting the history of the Franks were also typical. In many cases, the inscriptions accompanying these frescoes reflect the scholarship of Alcuin and others. The lifesize figures of several bishops of Auxerre (oh-SAIR) found in the crypts there (Fig. 7.24) show a great deal of originality. Clearly the mural painters of the period possessed great skill and imagination. In the

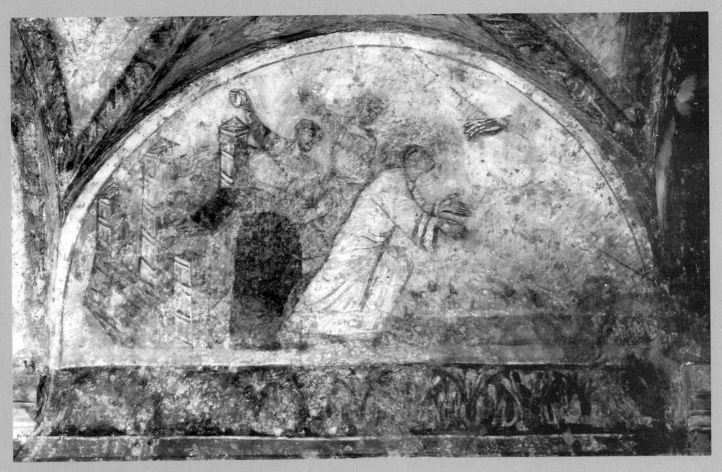

7.25 (*above*) *The Stoning of St Stephen at the Gate of Jerusalem*, ninth century. Wall painting. Crypts of St-Germain, Auxerre, France.

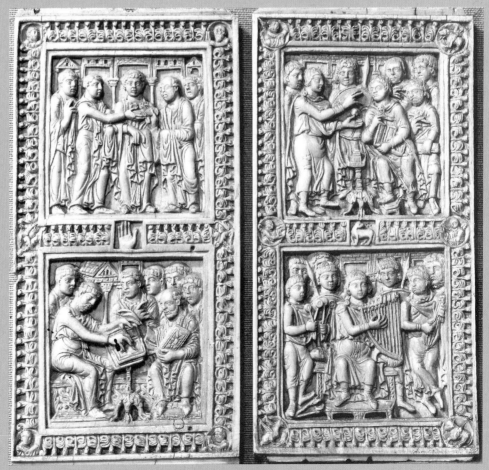

7.26 (*right*) Cover of the Dagulf Psalter, showing David in various scenes, 783–95. Ivory, each leaf 6⅝ × 3¼ ins (16.8 × 8.3 cm). Louvre, Paris.

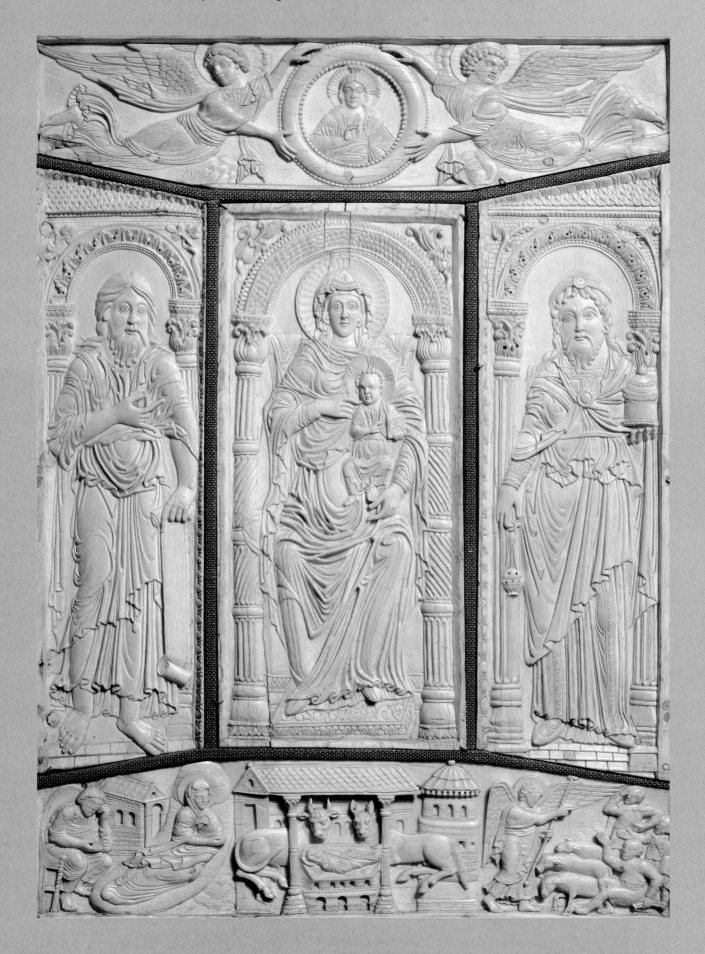

segment depicting the stoning of St Stephen (Fig. 7.25), all of the important vertical lines of the painting conform to a mathematical formula based on a grid created from the half-square in which the arch bordering the painting is framed.

Sculpture

The works of the palace school at Charlemagne's court also reflect an effort to revive classical style by copying sculpture from the late antique period. Classical influence continued to be nurtured, perhaps because Charlemagne's political opposition to the Byzantine Empire led him to reject its artistic style as well. The so-called *Statuette of Charlemagne* (see Fig. 7.4), for example, clearly imitates a classical model.

It is, however, the ivories of this period that most clearly show both the classicizing trend and the artistry of the time. Although derived from antique models, these works are highly individual. The ivory covers of the Dagulf Psalter (Fig. 7.26) bear a close resemblance to Roman work. Commissioned as a gift for Pope Adrian I, the figures and ornamentation on this cover are stilted and life-less. There is little attempt at creating three-dimensional space, although the figures themselves appear in high relief. Composition in each panel appears to be organized around a central area, to which interior line directs the viewer's eye. This focus is reinforced by the direction in which the figures themselves are looking. The scenes are crowded, but not frenetic. The figures have strange proportions, almost dwarf-like, with heavy rounded heads, long torsos, and short legs. Hairstyles reflect the late Roman Imperial period.

The ivory cover of the ninth-century Lorsch (lohrsh) Gospels (Fig. 7.27), on the other hand, is an exact replica of a sixth-century design. The images in the upper register, the layout, and the rounded faces in the figure depiction clearly show its kinship with the *Barberini Ivory* (see Fig. 6.11). The Roman arches in each of the three middle panels testify to the classical derivation of the Lorsch Gospels. In the center panel sits the Virgin Mary, enthroned, with the infant Christ and surrounded by saints. The face of the Christ child is that of a wise adult, a common medieval practice. The risen Christ appears encircled in the top register and flanked by heraldic angels. The lower register shows scenes from the nativity. So the Gospel cover reads chronologically from birth to Resurrection in *hierarchical* fashion (see Chapter 6).

7.27 (*opposite*) Back of the Lorsch Gospels, showing the Virgin and Child between Zacharias and John the Baptist, c. 810. Ivory, 15¹⁄₈ × 10⁵⁄₈ ins (38.4 × 27 cm). Victoria & Albert Museum, London.

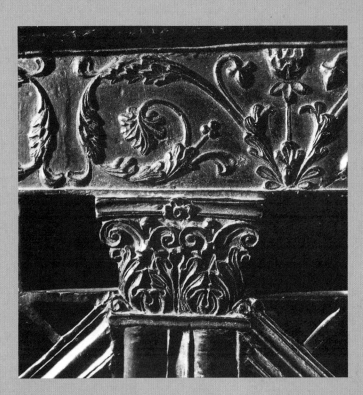

7.28 Detail of the parapet railings in the Tribune of the Palatine Chapel, Aachen, Germany, 792–805.

Architecture

Architecture, like painting and sculpture, was ruled by the political goals of the Carolingian court. Clearly artists of the period could reproduce capitals and friezes from classical antiquity accurately, as Figure 7.28 illustrates. Charlemagne carefully chose bishops for his kingdom who would assist in the building program he envisaged, and almost immediately new construction began across the empire.

He returned to his capital, Aachen, or Aix-la-Chapelle, from visits to Italy not only with visions of Roman monuments, but also with a belief that majesty and permanence must be symbolized in impressive architecture.

The realization of these dreams, however, was tempered by some of the difficult architectural facts of life. Charlemagne took as his model the church of San Vitale in Ravenna (see Figs. 6.27, 6.28, and 6.32), built by Justinian in the Byzantine style. All Charlemagne's materials, including columns and bronze gratings, had to be transported over the Alps from Italy to Aachen in Germany. Skilled stonemasons were few and far between, but the task was, nevertheless, accomplished.

The Palatine Chapel at Aachen (Fig. 7.29), built to be Charlemagne's tomb-house, became the jewel in his crown. The interior reveals the grandeur and style of this

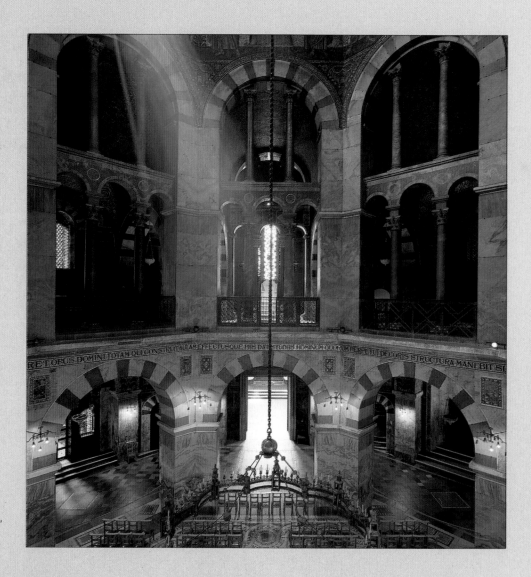

7.29 Palatine Chapel of Charlemagne, Aachen, Germany 792–805. Photo: © Steffans/SOA Photo Agency, London.

building. Designed by a Frankish architect, Odo of Metz, the Palatine Chapel has very little of the spatial subtlety of San Vitale, however. There is less mystery, and the space itself seems more constricted, with the emphasis on verticality rather than openness. The rounded arches and thick, rectangular pillars supporting the dome create massiveness, which cannot be offset by slender, decorative columns. Part of the building's sense of massiveness comes from its material: rubble faced with stone for the vault.

Charlemagne's throne was placed in the first gallery above the door and looked down and across the central space to the altar.

During Charlemagne's reign, then, we find a true renaissance, modified as it may have been to serve the grand design and political ambitions of the emperor. The recreation of antiquity in the arts and humanities made visible and intelligible the dream of a resurrected Roman Empire, with Charlemagne at its head.

CHAPTER REVIEW

Critical Thought

Debates often arise about questions such as these: Does art really mirror its times, or is it purely a result of some internal necessity of the artist? Should it be useful or does it exist for its own sake? In this chapter we have made more than a little of the relationships between the barricaded mentality of the political times and the nervous and crowded spaces of the visual art and the heavy fortress-like nature of architecture. Can you think of examples of how visual art, music, drama, and architecture of our time makes similar statements? What is your viewpoint on art as a reflection of society?

Summary

After reading this chapter, you should be able to:

- Identify and define the divisions of the Middle Ages.
- Describe the role of the Christian Church and monasticism in the life of the times.
- Characterize the music of the early Middle Ages, identify its forms, and discuss the role of Pope Gregory I in its development.
- Understand how the Carolingian renaissance affected politics, religion, and the arts and architecture of the period.
- Discuss feudalism as a social system.
- Explain the nature of theatre, dance, and literature and cite specific writers and works with regard to literature.
- Characterize the Romanesque style in visual art and architecture.
- Apply the elements and principles of composition to analyze and compare specific works of art and architecture illustrated in this chapter.

CHAPTER EIGHT

The High Middle Ages

The Gothic Age

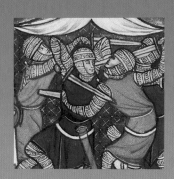

OUTLINE

THE SOCIAL ORDER OF THE HIGH MIDDLE AGES
The Rise of Cities
The Middle Class
 TECHNOLOGY: A Better Horse
  Collar
Feudal Monarchs and Monarchies
Chivalry

THE CHRISTIAN CHURCH
Reform in the Christian Church
St Bernard of Clairvaux and
 Mysticism
The Crusades

PHILOSOPHY AND THEOLOGY
The Rise of Universities
Abelard and Realism
St Thomas Aquinas and
 Aristotelianism
 PROFILE: St Francis of Assisi

LITERATURE
Courtly Romances
Dante and the *Divine Comedy*

GOTHIC STYLE
Architecture
 MASTERWORK: Suger and the
  Abbey Church of Saint-Denis
Sculpture
Painting
 OUR DYNAMIC WORLD: Japanese
  Sculpture
Theatre

FOCAL POINT: CHARTRES
CATHEDRAL

VIEW

INDIVIDUALISM

We all desire to be thought of as individuals of worth and to have some semblance of control in our lives. It should come as no surprise that the people of the Middle Ages had similar desires. In the twelfth century, humankind found a new interest in themselves as individuals: individuals who had some further purpose on earth than merely getting through this "vale of tears" and into the eternal happiness of heaven beyond the grave. People began to see themselves as being important and as having a relationship with the world of the past. New "personalist" elements entered devotion, philosophy, theology, and literature. Individualism meant a degree of control over one's existence and the sphere around it.

Such drift was especially true of the ongoing conflict between the Church and secular leaders, but it had an interesting twist. In our society, we find the issue of separation of Church and state essentially one of keeping the Church out of the affairs of state. In the Middle Ages, the reverse was true: the local secular rulers wanted to oversee the Church.

Above Detail of Fig. **8.18**.

8.1 Salisbury Cathedral, England, from the southwest, begun 1220.

KEY TERMS

Some of the basic terms and concepts we will encounter in this chapter include the following:

Chivalry, a more feminine point of view in ethics and personal conduct as compared to feudalism.

Realism, a belief, as championed by Abelard, that objects, as we know them, have real individuality, which makes each object a substance in its own right.

Stigmata, the appearance of wounds, from no discernible cause, that resemble the crucifixion wounds of Jesus Christ.

Allegory is expression by means of symbols to make a more effective generalization or moral commentary about human existence than could be achieved by direct or literal means.

Gothic style, a synthesis of medieval intellect, spirituality, and engineering—in architecture characterized by the pointed arch.

Measured rhythm, music employing definite time values and precise meters.

Mystery play, a medieval religious play produced by occupational guilds.

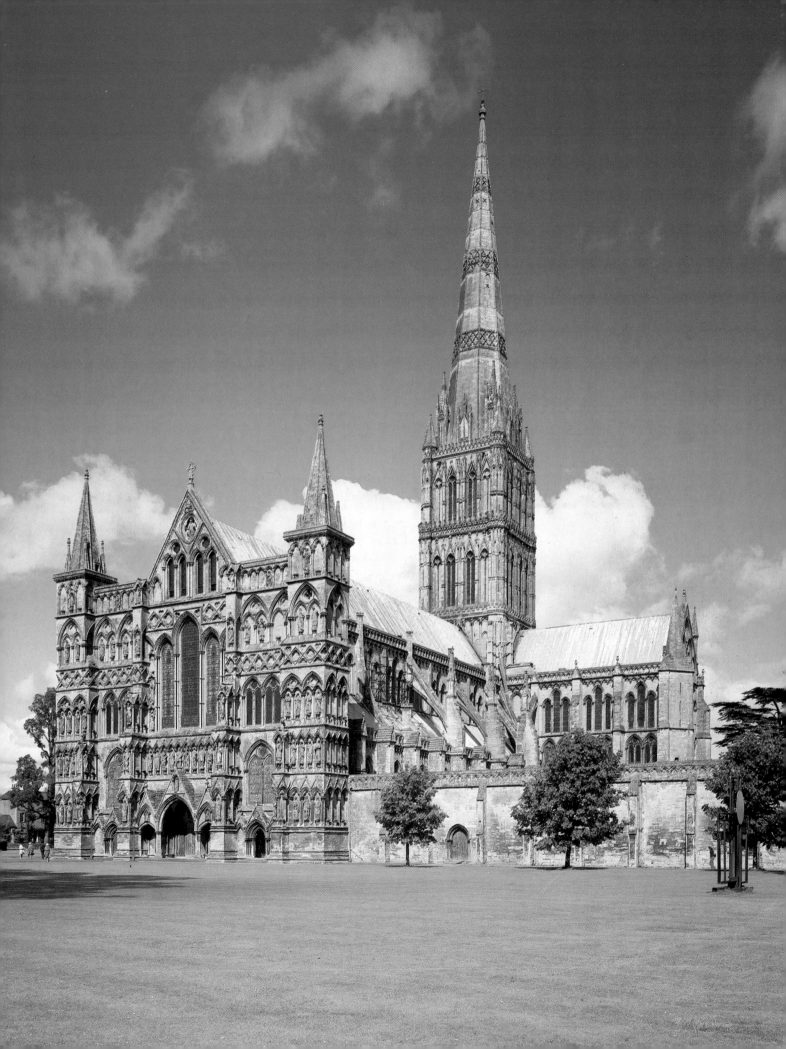

THE SOCIAL ORDER OF THE HIGH MIDDLE AGES

The Rise of Cities

Humanity in the late Middle Ages seemed to undergo a spiritual and intellectual revival that had a profound influence on the creative spirit.

In the year A.D. 1000, Europe consisted of stone fortresses on hills and muddy huts in cramped villages. Two centuries later, the world had been transformed. This transformation of medieval society sprang largely from the resurgence of cities, for which three main factors were responsible—agricultural improvements, population growth, and the revival of trade.

Primitive as the manor system of feudalism was, it did produce a number of important agricultural improvements. One of these was a three-field system of crop rotation. After the year 1000, the amount of land under cultivation increased tremendously. An increase in the food supply meant an increase in the general population of Europe.

However, the primary cause of the rebirth of cities was revival of trade in the eleventh, twelfth, and thirteenth centuries. Soldiers returning from the crusades brought tales of the East and of marvelous fabrics and goods that caught the fancy of nobles and commoners alike.

Merchant and craft guilds—that is, trade associations of dealers in, or makers of, particular products from cloth to metals—dominated trading cities. As time progressed, cities developed independent political authorities—for example, magistrates and city councils—although these political authorities were elected only by business people. At the heart of the city lay the doers of business—crafts guilds, their masters, assistants, and apprentices; merchants who required stevedores, porters, and muleteers, and so on. In addition, priests, students, lawyers, runaway serfs, and others were drawn to the city in search of protection and employment. The city offered a new hope of escape from slavery to the land, and thousands flocked there.

TECHNOLOGY: PUTTING DISCOVERY TO WORK

A Better Horse Collar

In the Middle Ages, the horse came into its own as a technological tool. Horsepower was the most universally available source of power known to humankind, although in the medieval period, the horse was seen primarily as a means of carrying knights and their retinue. However, the horse offered potential for both transportation and agriculture. The first horse harnesses unsuccessfully used the ox yoke as a model, but horses do not have the prominent and powerful shoulders of the ox. The next step consisted of a breast-band, which held the harness down by means of a strap passing between the legs to a girth-band. This device chafed the horse, and, when heavy loads were pulled, the breast-band caused choking pressure on the horse's neck and windpipe. Even the ingenious Romans had not been able to invent a useful means for hitching a horse to wagon or plow. In the twelfth century, however, three main improvements occurred. Shafts, which could be attached well down the breast-band, came into common use. Next, traces—that is, side straps or chains to connect the animal to what it is pulling—served in the same way as shafts to bring the pressure to the middle of the breast-band, and made it possible to use horses in file, as opposed to side by side. However, the most important invention was that of the padded horse collar. This stiff apparatus replaced the breast-band and made it possible for the horse's power to be multiplied by as much as five times over the old method. Thus, the horse came into its own as a technological device. Modern horse carts were developed in France, and the horse replaced the ox for pulling plows and carriages. As a result, effective agriculture and land-based trade were just a step away.

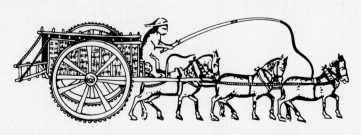

8.2 Two-wheeled cart, from the Luttrell Psalter.

	GENERAL EVENTS	LITERATURE & PHILOSOPHY	VISUAL ART & ARCHITECTURE	PERFORMING ARTS
1000				
	Monastic reform			
1050				
	Norman Conquest of England	Anselm		
	Cistercians founded			
	First Crusade			
1100				Mystery, miracle, and morality plays
	Investiture Controversy	Peter Abelard	Abbey Church of Saint-Denis (**8.7, 8.8, 8.15, 8.16**)	
		St Bernard of Clairvaux		
1150				Troubadours and *jongleurs*
	Eleanor of Aquitaine			Courtly tradition
	Second Crusade			Pérotin
	Muslims conquer Jerusalem			Léonin
	Third Crusade	Chrétien de Troyes		
1200				
	Fourth Crusade	St Francis of Assisi	Chartres Cathedral (**8.24–8.30**)	
	Franciscans founded	Thomas Aquinas		
	Dominicans founded		Notre Dame (**8.9, 8.10**)	
		Psalter of St Louis	Amiens Cathedral (**8.12**)	
	Louis IX	Douce Apocalypse	Salisbury Cathedral (**8.13, 8.14**)	
		Dante		

Timeline 8.1 The High Middle Ages.

The Middle Class

As the commercial class grew richer, it also gained power, filling a vacuum between nobility and peasantry. However, no order gives up power easily, and struggles, sometimes violent, pitted burgher against nobleman. The crusades ruined many feudal landholders, and a taste of potential power and wealth strengthened the resolve of the "middle-class" citizens. They needed a more dynamic society than feudalism could offer, so they threw their weight and power into strengthening monarchies that favored them. Thus, an emerging middle class played a vital role in a changing social order that would see more centralized administration, stabilization, and rudimentary democracy.

Feudal Monarchs and Monarchies

The explosion of economic activity led to the reestablishment of centralized power in the hands of medieval kings. Under their aegis a new form of government itself evolved. The basic problem for the medieval monarch was the need to replace feudal law with royal law and to tax what

amounted to a nation. For such problems to be solved, compromises had to be made, and where the monarchies were most successful—in England and France—the monarchs paid for their growing power by granting rights to representative bodies that spoke for the primary classes of medieval society—that is, the nobility, the Church, and the wealthy new cities and towns.

Some monarchs were more successful than others at statecraft. Probably the most notable of the medieval monarchs was Duke William, the Bastard of Normandy, who invaded and conquered England in 1066, thus gaining for himself the name William I the Conqueror (1066–87). As king of England, he gave the country greater centralized government than it had ever known, and under his successors, Henry I and Henry II, England developed its system of common law, the royal council, and the exchequer (treasury). By the end of the twelfth century, England had the strongest monarchial government in Europe.

France had two significant monarchs during the High Middle Ages. The first was Philip Augustus (1180–1223). Although not particularly inspiring physically, Philip proved to be France's most successful medieval monarch. He used his position to gain power over the nobility and to develop an effective, independent royal administrative system that included a strengthened legal system. Unlike

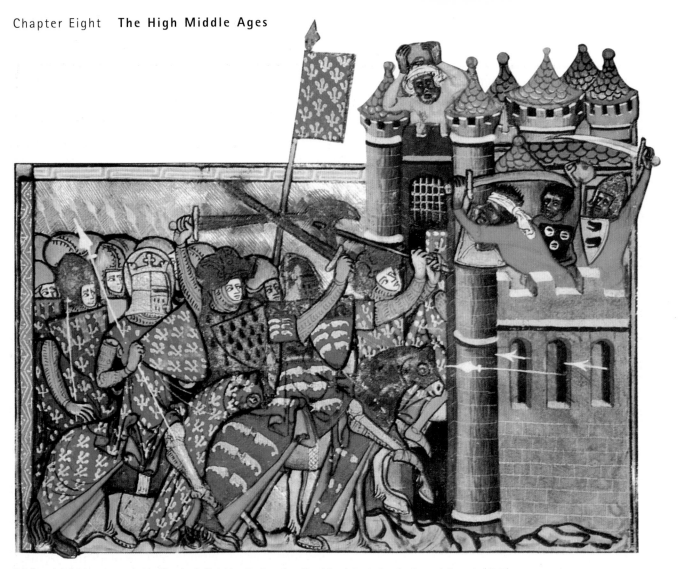

8.3 French knights, commanded by King Louis XI, taking the Egyptian city of Damietta during the Seventh Crusade (1249). MS Fr. 13568. Fol. 83. Bibliothèque Nationale, Paris.

William I of England, Philip Augustus did not conquer any foreign lands. However, he did conquer rebellious feudal barons in the south of France, and he won from Henry II of England parts of western France that had been under English rule since the time of William the Conqueror. Thus, under his rule, France tripled in size and replaced the Holy Roman Empire as the most powerful entity in Europe.

The strong but pious Louis IX (1215–70), who reigned from 1226, gave France the prestige of a saint in its royal lineage. Although Louis did not hesitate to increase royal power, to issue royal edicts without consultation, or to tamper with the legal system, he possessed great strength of character and medieval Christian virtue. He had such a reputation for justice, which he often meted out sitting under an oak tree, that he was known as Louis the Just. Among the acts for which he was canonized only thirty years after his death was the washing of lepers' feet. His saintly life did much to solidify his power.

Chivalry

At the same time, another medieval phenomenon was born of a change in attitude that permeated society and the arts. Feudalism was a masculine, "men-at-arms" code of behavior. But by the twelfth century, a distinctly feminine point of view ruled ethics and personal conduct—that of *chivalry* and the courtly tradition. Men were away from their homes or castles for long periods of time, whether they were off trading or off warring, and it fell to women to run their households and control domestic matters and manners. If Eleanor of Aquitaine (AH-kwih-tayn; 1122–1204) is a representative example, women managed this very well. Society thus took on a gentler, more civil tone than under the rough code of feudalism, and elaborate codes of conduct and etiquette emerged, which culminated in "courts of love," and gave rise to a literary form called the Romance (see p. 244), whose subject matter treated chivalric adventure and religious allegories.

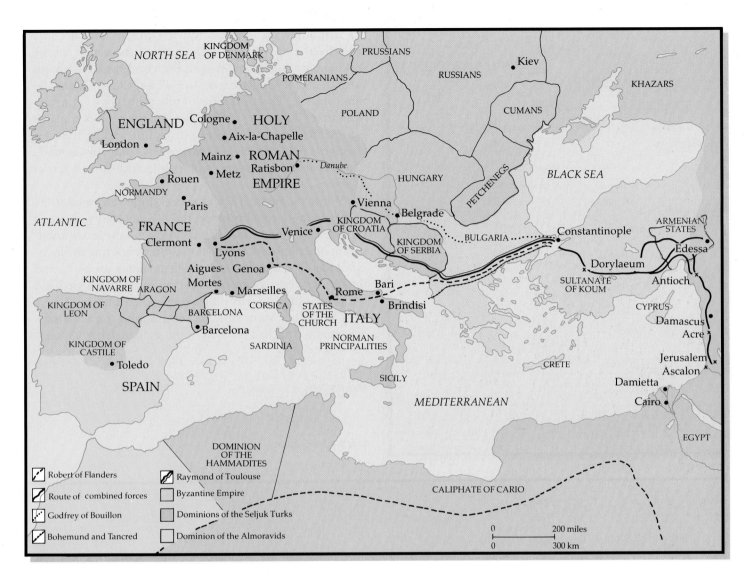

Map 8.1 Europe at the time of the First Crusade.

The courtly tradition had an important impact on religious philosophy. The early Middle Ages were fixated on devils and death, faith notwithstanding. As time passed, however, we find a warmer feeling, a quality of mercy. Christ the Savior and Mary, his compassionate mother, became the focal points of the faith. This change in viewpoint is reflected very clearly in the arts of the time.

Although chivalry introduced a "feminine" ethos into the High Middle Ages, and although some important women such as Eleanor of Aquitaine emerged, in general, women lost many of the independent opportunities and positions of authority they had earlier enjoyed.

In its earliest formulation, chivalry meant mostly the virtues of war—that is, courage, skill with weapons, fairness to one's foes, and loyalty to one's liege lord (Fig. 8.3). However, under the guidance of medieval women, the chivalric code, as we have just noted, turned to a code of courtly love. The truly chivalrous knight was encouraged

to protect women *and* to love, serve, and revere a particular lady, although from afar. Women paid for the services of minstrels and troubadours, and these wandering entertainers were suited to the tastes of their benefactresses. They composed and sang songs of love, praising knights who served their ladies well.

THE CHRISTIAN CHURCH

Reform in the Christian Church

The development of Western culture, including its artistic institutions in the late Middle Ages, was profoundly affected, if not controlled, by the Christian Church. By the middle of the eleventh century, the Church had become extremely powerful.

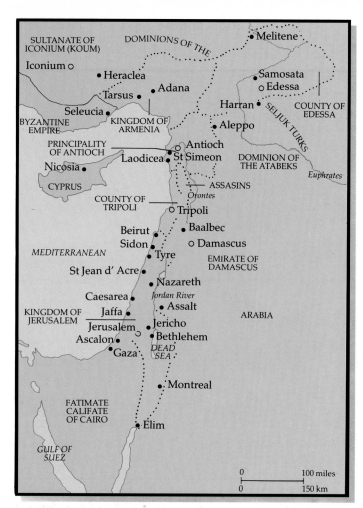

Although the tenth-century Church had become feudalized and corrupt, with many of its secular clergy seeking only wealth and power, this corruption did not go unchallenged. Cries for reform came loudest from the monasteries. The founding of the Abbey of Cluny by William of Aquitaine in 910 signaled the start of a major reform movement. The strict discipline and high moral standards of Cluny's Benedictine monks and abbots made Cluny a model of reform, and its influence spread across Europe.

While monastic life was successfully reformed to its original standards, however, the secular clergy changed their behavior very little. Feudal lords and the lesser nobility appointed priests and bishops, often choosing the highest bidder. Bishoprics were treated as family property, and the secular clergy, many of whose priests were married, did not place a high priority on their religious duties.

Conditions were ripe for reform, and the reformers vehemently attacked the evils of the secular clergy. Circum-

Map 8.2 Areas of the Crusades.

Map 8.3 The Crusades.

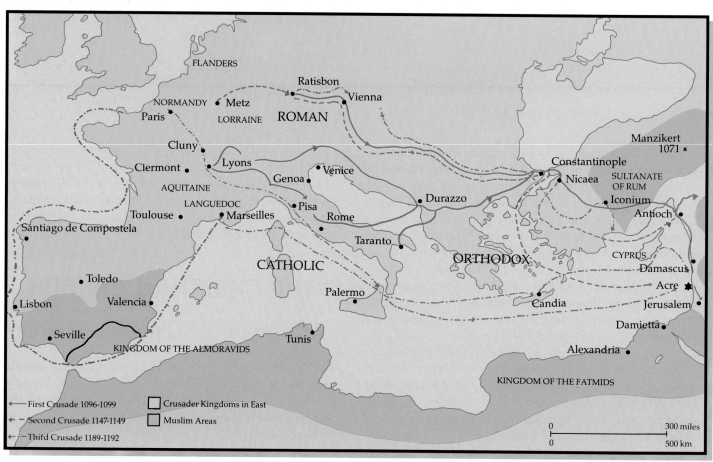

stances changed in 1046 under Emperor Henry III of Germany. Henry championed the cause of the reformers, and in 1049 he appointed Pope Leo IX, who ruled until 1054. During those five years, Leo introduced a brilliant ecclesiastical reorganization, including the creation of a body of cardinals. Creation of the rank of cardinal made it possible for the papacy to exercise control over those bishops who had been named by lay rulers. After a series of synods in Rome, Leo made a personal tour of the empire, during which he publicized his reforms. As he put them into practice, he both consolidated his program and rid the clergy of many of its most offensive bishops.

Conflict between papacy and laity over the investiture of ecclesiastical office was not solved so easily, however. At the heart of the matter lay the issue of the basis of royal authority. The resulting struggle became known as the "Investiture conflict." Through a series of negotiated settlements with the various monarchs of Europe, the relationships between nobility and clergy, and clergy and papacy, were stabilized. The outcome was a compromise in which kings gave up their ancient claims to represent God's will in appointing senior clergy. They did continue to nominate bishops, but they had greater difficulty in presenting candidates considered unsuitable by the Church. From the twelfth century onward, the quality of ecclesiastical appointments improved substantially.

The papacy emerged from the conflict with greatly enhanced prestige, and the importance of the Church in medieval affairs, artistic and otherwise, continued to grow.

St Bernard of Clairvaux and Mysticism

Many new religious orders were founded during this period. The Virgin Mary assumed a new importance in religious life, and the cult of Mary Magdalene spread through Europe. A key figure in the changing religious thought was a young nobleman, Bernard of Clairvaux (klair-VOH; 1090–1153), who entered the order of Cîteaux (sih-TOH), or the Cistercians, the most influential new monastic movement of the twelfth century.

Bernard was an enthusiast, perhaps even a fanatic, having no doubt in his own mind that his views were correct. He entered into eager combat with anyone who disagreed with him, and those individuals included the most influential clerics and philosophers of the times, men such as the scholar and theologian Peter Abelard (AB-uh-lahrd), the monk and abbot Suger (soo-ZHAY), of Saint-Denis, and the entire order of Cluny. At the same time, Bernard could show great patience and common sense. He treated his monks with patience and forgiveness, and

reportedly turned down the duke of Burgundy's request to become a monk by saying that the world had many virtuous monks but few pious dukes.

His religious teaching set a new tone for twelfth-century Christianity through its emphasis on a more mystical and personal sense of piety than had existed previously. In his writings he described a way of "ascent to God," consisting of four stages of love by which a soul could gain union with God. In his sermons for the common people, he treated more ordinary themes and vividly retold familiar stories from the New Testament. Rather than treating Jesus, Mary, and the apostles as remote images, Bernard described them as living personalities. Bernard's preaching was an important stimulant for the spread of the Mary cults.

The Crusades

Many have the notion that the Crusades featured knights in shining armor setting out on glorious quests to free the Holy Land from Infidels. The Crusades were far from a romantic quest, however. Instead, they illustrate clearly a new and practical energy and optimism in Europe in a new millennium and a new era.

As early as the tenth century, popes had led armies against the Saracens in Italy. By the end of the eleventh century, the Church was able to put forward several reasons why a Christian army might march against the Muslims. Constantinople had been rescued from the Turks, and a healing of the east–west schism seemed possible. Furthermore, pilgrimages to the Holy Land as a form of penance had become increasingly popular in this age of religious zeal, and the safety of these pilgrims was ample reason for interference by the popes. A more practical benefit closer to home was the removal of troublesome nobles from the local scene. An opportunity came in 1095 at the Council of Clermont. When envoys of the eastern emperor Alexius Comnenus supposedly asked Pope Urban II for aid, Urban set about mounting a crusading army. The response to his call was astonishing. Thousands came forward to take up the cross. Men, women, and children— even those who were disabled—clamored to take part, and the aforementioned nobles also went riding off to war.

The reasons for the First Crusade (Map 8.1) went beyond its political and military objectives. Its impetus came from the religious enthusiasm of those who made up the crusading army. These people were ready to make significant sacrifices for their faith. The idea of a Crusade generated such a tremendous emotional response that even the Pope could not control it. Itinerant preachers heralded an upcoming Crusade in their revival meetings. No one cared about the practical problems—it was an act of faith and piety. The infidels would scatter in fear before the banner of the cross. The walls of fortresses would tumble down like those of Jericho. The First Crusade ultimately led to the capture of Jerusalem and a bloody massacre. The Second Crusade set out in 1147, but ended in disarray and defeat. After that, Europe lost its enthusiasm for such ventures, for a generation.

The Muslims gathered their forces and set about driving out the Christians. On 3 October 1187, led by Saladin, the Muslims conquered Jerusalem, ending eighty-three years of Christian rule. The news shocked Europe, and again the pope took the opportunity to attempt to make peace among warring nobles in Europe by sending them on a crusade. Henry II of England and his son Richard, Philip Augustus of France, and Frederick Barbarossa of Germany all took up the cross. Well-planned, well-financed, and led by the most powerful rulers of Europe, the Third Crusade set off in high spirits, with high expectations. But one disaster after another befell the crusaders. Their major accomplishment was the capture of Acre after a two-year siege.

PHILOSOPHY AND THEOLOGY

The twelfth century has often been called an "age of humanism." The wave of religious enthusiasm that swept Europe from the second half of the eleventh century to the middle of the twelfth coincided with a burst of cultural activity and a zestful interest in learning. The writers of the twelfth century seem more like real persons—much more so than those of the earlier Middle Ages. There was a revival of classical literary studies, a vivid feeling for nature in lyric poetry, and a new naturalism in Gothic art. With these exciting intellectual and ecclesiastical developments, new humanist or "personalist" elements in religious devotion, theology, and philosophy also took hold.

Aristotle was rediscovered and his works introduced throughout Europe. As intellectual walls broke down, light and fresh air flooded into Western culture. New freedoms, new comforts, both physical and spiritual, and a new confidence in the future pervaded every level of society.

The Rise of Universities

Many universities gained their charters in the twelfth and thirteenth centuries—for example, Oxford University in England, the University of Salamanca in Spain, the University of Bologna in Italy, and the University of Paris in France. Many had existed previously in association with

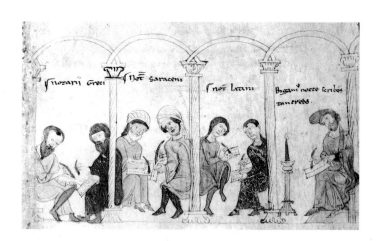

8.4 Medieval scholars studying in Latin, Hebrew, and Arabic at a school in Sicily, c. 1200.

monasteries, but their formal chartering made the public more aware of them.

Medieval universities were not like today's institutions. They had no buildings or classrooms; instead, they were guilds of scholars and teachers who gathered their students together wherever space permitted. Students came from all over Europe, for example, to hear the lectures at the University of Paris by teachers such as William of Champeaux (1070–1121) and, later, Peter Abelard. University life spawned people with trained minds who sought knowledge for its own sake and who could not accept a society that walled itself in and rigidly resisted any questioning of authority. In Paris, by the late twelfth century, the arts became a prelude to the study of theology.

The rise of universities at this particular time came as a result of a number of factors. This was a time of rediscovery and publication of many of the texts of the classical world, especially the works by Aristotle, which came to the West through Muslim sources in Spain (Fig. 8.4). There was also a large amount of mathematical and scientific material coming to the attention of European scholars, again, largely through contact with Muslim scholars. In addition, for example in Bologna, legal studies received new impetus. All of this, coupled with the exploding population of the new cities and the consequent complexity of life, created a demand for a new, intellectual class who could bolster the cultural and socioeconomic foundations of medieval society.

Abelard and Realism

One member of such a class was Peter Abelard (1079–1142), a figure of both philosophy and romance. His lifelong correspondence and late-in-life love affair with

PROFILE

St Francis of Assisi (1181/2–1226)

Francis (Fig. **8.5**) was baptized Francesco di Pietro di Bernardone (fron-CHAY-scoe dee pee-AY-troe dee bur-nahr-DOE-nay), the son of a cloth merchant. He learned to read and write Latin as a child and later learned to speak some French. In 1202 he participated in the war between Assisi and Perugia, was taken prisoner, and held for nearly a year. On his release, he was seriously ill, but he recovered and sought to serve in the army again in late 1205. However, after a vision told him to return to Assisi and await a call to a new kind of knighthood, he devoted himself to solitude and prayer in order to know the will of God. This began his conversion, which consisted of a number of episodes. He renounced material goods and family ties and embraced a life of poverty.

Although he was a layman, he began to preach the gospel. He attracted a number of disciples and devised a rule of life for them, based on the Gospel of Matthew: "Take no gold, nor silver, nor money in your belts, no bag for your journey" (Matthew 10:9–11). When the number of disciples, called friars, reached twelve, they went to Rome, where Pope Innocent III gave his blessing to their rule of life. This event, on 16 April 1209, marked the formal beginning of the

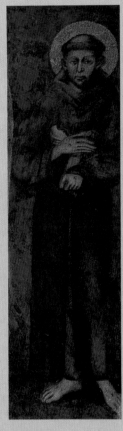

8.5 Cimabue, *Enthroned Madonna with St Francis* (detail), 1280. Fresco, lower church of San Francisco, Assisi, Italy.

Franciscan order. The Franciscans preached in the streets and, gradually, the order grew and spread throughout Italy.

Perhaps the most powerful experience of Francis' life occurred in the summer of 1224, when he went to the mountain retreat of La Verna to celebrate the feast of the Assumption of the Virgin and to prepare for St Michael's day with a forty-day fast. He prayed that he might know how best to please God. Opening the Gospels to find an answer, he came three times to the Passion of Christ. Then, as he prayed, he saw a figure coming toward him from heaven. It had the form of a seraph and smiled at him. Francis felt both joy and deep sorrow because of Christ's crucifixion. He understood that by God's providence he would be made like the crucified Christ through conformity of mind and heart. After the vision was over, Francis was marked with the *stigmata* of the Crucified—Francis' body actually showed marks resembling the wounds on the body of Christ. Francis tried to hide the marks for the remainder of his life. He lived for only another two years, and was blind and in constant pain. After his death, his stigmata were announced to the order by letter. One of the most venerated religious figures of his time, he was made a saint on 15 July 1228.

Héloïse accounts for the romantic element. As for the philosophy, Abelard denied that objects are merely imperfect imitations of universal ideal models to which they owe their reality. Instead, he argued for the concrete nature of reality. That is to say, objects as we know them have real individuality which makes each object a substance "in its own right."

Abelard went beyond this, to argue that universals do exist, and comprise the "form of the universe" as conceived by the mind of God. These universals are patterns, or types, after which individual substances are created and which make these substances the kinds of things they are.

Abelard has been called a "moderate realist," or, sometimes, a "conceptualist," even though that term is usually applied to later teaching. His views were adopted and modified by St Thomas Aquinas, and in this revised form they constitute part of Roman Catholic Church dogma today. Abelard believed that philosophy had a duty to define Christian doctrine and to make it intelligible. He also believed that philosophers should be free to criticize theology and to reject beliefs that are contrary to reason.

Abelard regarded Christianity as a way of life, but he was very tolerant of other religions as well. He considered Socrates and Plato to have been "inspired." The essence of Christianity was not its dogma, but the way Christ had lived his life. Those who lived prior to Jesus were, in a sense, already Christians if they had lived the kind of life Christ did. An individual act should be understood as good or evil "solely as it is well or ill intended," he argued in his treatise *Know Thyself*. However, lest anyone excuse acts on the basis of "good intentions," Abelard insisted that there should be some sort of standard for judging whether intentions were good or bad. Such a standard existed in a natural law of morality, "manifested in the conscience possessed by every man, and founded upon the will of God." When opinions differed over the interpretation of the law of God, he said, each person must obey his or her own conscience. Therefore, "anything a man does that is against his own conscience is sinful, no matter how much his act may commend itself to the consciences of others."[1]

St Thomas Aquinas and Aristotelianism

The rediscovery of Aristotle in the thirteenth century marked a new era in Christian thought. With the exception of Aristotle's treatises on logic, called the *Organon*, his writings were inaccessible to the West until the late twelfth century. Their reintroduction created turmoil. Some centers of education, such as the University of Paris, forbade Aristotle's metaphysics and physics. Others championed Aristotelian thought. These scholars asserted the eternity of the world and denied the existence of divine providence and the foreknowlege of contingent events. In the middle were thinkers such as Albertus Magnus, who, though orthodox in their acceptance of the traditional Christian faith, regarded the rediscovery of Aristotle in a wholly positive light. Magnus' first pupil was Thomas Aquinas (1227–74).

In his youth, Aquinas joined the newly formed mendicant Order of Preachers, the Dominican Order. This led him to Paris to study with Magnus, who was the master teacher of the Dominicans. A prolific writer, Aquinas produced philosophical and theological works and commentaries on Aristotle, the Bible, and Peter Lombard. Aquinas, like Magnus, was a modernist, and he sought to reinterpret the Christian system in the light of Aristotle—in other words, to synthesize Christian theology and Aristotelian thought. He believed that the philosophy of Aristotle would prove acceptable to intelligent men and women, and further, that if Christianity were to maintain the confidence of educated people, it would have to come to terms with and accommodate Aristotle. Nonetheless,

Aquinas was a very devout and orthodox believer. He had no wish to sacrifice Christian truth, whether to Aristotle or any other philosopher.

In dealing with God and the universe, Aquinas carefully defined the fields of theology and philosophy. Philosophy was limited to whatever lay open to argument, and its purpose was to establish such truth as could be discovered and demonstrated by human reason. Theology, on the other hand, was restricted to the "content of faith," or "revealed truth," which is beyond the ability of reason to discern or demonstrate, and "about which there can be no argument." There was, nonetheless, an area of overlap.

Aquinas concentrated upon philosophical proofs of God's existence and nature. The existence of God could be proved by reason, he thought, and Aristotle had inadvertently done just that. The qualities, to which Aristotle reduced all the activities of the universe, become intelligible "only on the supposition that there is an unmoved ... self-existent ... form of being whose sheer perfection sets the whole world moving in pursuit of it."

LITERATURE

Courtly Romances

The change in outlook that accompanied the code of chivalry brought with it a new, popular form of poetry called the *romance*. These romances were long narratives whose subjects were knights and ladies. The name itself, like Romanesque, comes from a later age that mistakenly thought that these poems sought to imitate Roman literary forms. Chivalric and sentimental, the romance often drew its subjects from classical legends, from Celtic myths of King Arthur and the knights of the Round Table, and the exploits of Charlemagne and his knights.

Perhaps the first treatment of Arthur and Camelot came from Chrétien de Troyes (krayt-YEN duh TWAH-yuh; c. 1148–c. 1190). In this prototype, the simple story we know from the musical *Camelot* is elaborated through many episodes and complicated with religious and courtly themes. In the end, Lancelot rescues Guinevere but, *en route*, suffers through misadventure after misadventure, from which he learns humility in order to love Guinevere with absolute obedience. The fact that Chrétien clearly parallels Lancelot's adventures with the suffering and death of Jesus, gives the work a disturbing character that borders on sacrilege. Also troubling for many is the moral neutrality with which the author treats Guinevere's adultery—a deadly sin in the eyes of the medieval Church. That Chrétien's perspective was unacceptable to some can be seen in a later, English, version of the story, Thomas

Mallory's *Le Morte d'Arthur*, in which the collapse of Arthur's court is blamed directly on Lancelot and Guinevere's passions.

Dante and the *Divine Comedy*

Undoubtedly, the greatest poet of the age was Dante Alighieri (ah-lee-GYAY-ree; 1265–1321). Dante wrote a few lyric poems and told the story of his passion for his unattainable love, Beatrice, in *La Vita Nuova*, but the *Divine Comedy* was the major work of his life. Its description of heaven, hell, and purgatory is a vision of the state of souls after death told in an ALLEGORY—that is, a dramatic device in which the superficial sense is accompanied by a deeper or more profound meaning. It works on several levels to demonstrate the human need for spiritual illumination and guidance. On a literal level, it describes the author's fears as a sinner and his hopes for eternal life. On deeper levels, it represents the quandaries and character of medieval society faced with, for example, balancing classicism and Christianity. Part of Dante's significance lies in the fact that he elevated vernacular Italian to the status of a rich, expressive language that was suitable for poetry. It was no longer necessary for writers to use Latin.

Dante, an aristocrat, was educated in both classical and Christian works. As with many Florentine officeholders and literati, Dante suffered exile when his political allies fell from power. In 1301 he was banished from Florence for life. During the years of his exile, in which he suffered deprivation and poverty, he composed *The Comedy (Commedia)*. Actually, Dante gave the work a particularly personal title: *The Comedy of Dante Alighieri, A Florentine by Birth but not in Behavior*. He called it a comedy because, according to him, it had a happy ending and was written in the language of the people. Recognition of the superb character of the work caused later admirers to affix the word "Divine," which has remained since. The poem is divided into three book-length parts, detailed in Figure 8.6.

In the *Comedy*, Dante narrates his fictional travels through three realms of the Christian afterlife, beginning on Good Friday 1300. For the first two parts of the journey, he is accompanied by the Roman poet Vergil, from whose work *The Aeneid* Dante drew considerable inspiration. Vergil represents human reason and the classical culture. In the first part, Dante descends into Hell, where he hears the damned tell of their sins against God and moral law. In the second part, Dante stands in Purgatory, where lesser sinners do penance while awaiting their entrance into heaven. In Purgatory, Vergil turns over Dante's guidance to Beatrice (Italian for "blessing"), Dante's symbol of the eternal female and of spiritualized

---

DANTE'S *COMEDY*

HELL
The Anteroom of the Neutrals
Circle 1: The Virtuous Pagans (Limbo)
Circle 2: The Lascivious
Circle 3: The Gluttonous
Circle 4: The Greedy and the Wasteful
Circle 5: The Wrathful
Circle 6: The Heretics
Circle 7: The Violent against Others, Self, God/Nature/and Art
Circle 8: The Fraudulent
Circle 9: The Lake of the Treacherous against kindred, country, guests, lords, and benefactors

PURGATORY
Ante-Purgatory: The Excommunicated/The Lazy/The Unabsolved/Negligent Rulers
The Terraces of the Mount of Purgatory
1. The Proud
2. The Envious
3. The Wrathful
4. The Slothful
5. The Avaricious
6. The Gluttonous
7. The Lascivious
The Earthly Paradise

PARADISE
1. The Moon: The Faithful who were inconstant
2. Mercury: Service marred by ambition
3. Venus: Love marred by lust
4. The Sun: Wisdom; the theologians
5. Mars: Courage; the just warriors
6. Jupiter: Justice; the great rulers
7. Saturn: Temperance; the contemplatives and mystics
8. The Fixed Stars: The Church Triumphant
9. The Primum Mobile: The Order of Angels
10. The Empyrean Heavens: Angels, Saints, The Virgin, and the Holy Trinity

8.6 The structure of Dante's *Divine Comedy*.

love and Christian culture. She also represents divine revelation, and is, therefore, superior to Vergil. She guides Dante into Paradise, where he finds the souls of the saved divided into three groups: lay people, the active, and the contemplative. Nine categories of angels inhabit the closest circles to the throne of God.

As occurs often in medieval arts, Dante's *Comedy* contains symbolic numbers. The structure of the work breaks into one hundred cantos. The first canto serves as an introduction, and the three major parts each have thirty-three cantos. Three is a common symbol for the Christian Trinity (Father, Son, and Holy Spirit). The poem is written in a three-line verse form called *terza rima*, which uses an interlocking rhyme scheme in three-line stanzas—for example *aba, bcb, cdc, ded*, and so on, ending in a rhymed couplet. Multiples of three occur in the nine regions, plus a vestibule of Hell and Purgatory. Paradise contains nine heavens plus the highest heaven (*Empyrean*; ehm-PEER-ee-ahn). In Hell, the damned are divided into three groups: those who sinned by incontinence, by violence, or by fraud. In Purgatory, those who wait are divided in three ways depending on how they acted in relation to love. Paradise contains nine categories of angels. Here is a short selection from *Inferno*:

(Circle Two) Canto V

The Carnal

So we went down to the second ledge alone;
  a smaller circle of so much greater pain
  the voice of the damned rose in a bestial moan.

There Minos sits, grinning, grotesque, and hale.
  He examines each lost soul as it arrives
  and delivers his verdict with his coiling tail.

That is to say, when the ill-fated soul
  appears before him it confesses all,
  and that grim sorter of the dark and foul

decides which place in Hell shall be its end,
  then wraps his twitching tail about himself
  one coil for each degree it must descend.

GOTHIC STYLE

Architecture

Gothic style in architecture took many forms, but we know it best through the Gothic cathedral. In its synthesis of intellect, spirituality, and engineering, the cathedral perfectly expresses the medieval mind. Gothic style was widespread in Europe, but, like the other arts, it was not uniform in application, nor was it uniform in date. Initially a very local style on the Île de France (eel duh frahns) in the late twelfth century, it spread outward to the rest of Europe. It had died as a style in some places before it was adopted in others.

The cathedral was, of course, a church building whose purpose was the service of God. However, civic pride as well as spirituality inspired the cathedral builders. Local guilds contributed their services in financing or in building the churches, and guilds were often memorialized in special chapels and stained-glass windows. The Gothic church occupied the central, often elevated, area of the town or city—like the acropolis of ancient Greece. Its position symbolized the dominance of the universal Church over all human affairs, both spiritual and secular. Probably no other architectural style has exercised such an influence across the centuries. The story of the Gothic church is an intricate and fascinating one, only a few details of which we can highlight here.

8.7 Exterior of the Abbey Church of Saint-Denis, near Paris, 1137–44.

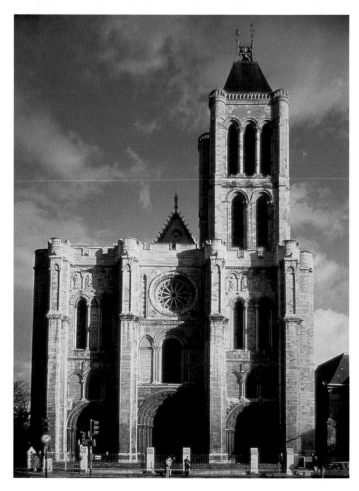

ground through a delicate network of ribs, vaults, and FLYING BUTTRESSES (see Fig. **8.10**). Every detail of the decorative tracery is carefully integrated into a system that emphasizes mysterious space.

The beginnings of Gothic architecture can be pinpointed to between 1137 and 1144, in the rebuilding of the royal Abbey Church of Saint-Denis, near Paris (Figs. **8.7, 8.8, 8.15, 8.16**).

In preparing for the reconstruction of Saint-Denis, Abbot Suger visited artists throughout Europe. He believed that the church should offer attainment of outward splendor, spectacles offered to God and humankind, and light to lead the dull mind from the material to the immaterial, and that he was translating a godly philosophy into stone, glass, precious metals, and jewels. He summoned the best artists and artisans, and his administrative skills made it possible to handle the finances to attract the best. He guaranteed funds that put no limitations on their work, so an international gathering of artists and craftsmen translated Suger's ideas.

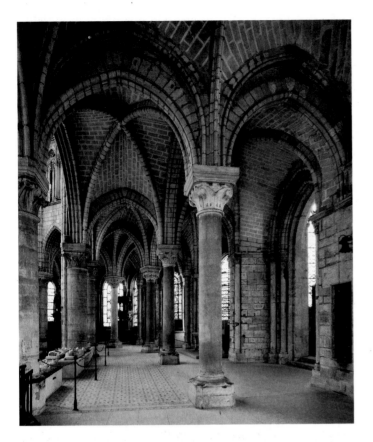

8.8 Interior of the Abbey Church of Saint-Denis.

8.9 Notre Dame, Paris, west front, 1163–1250.

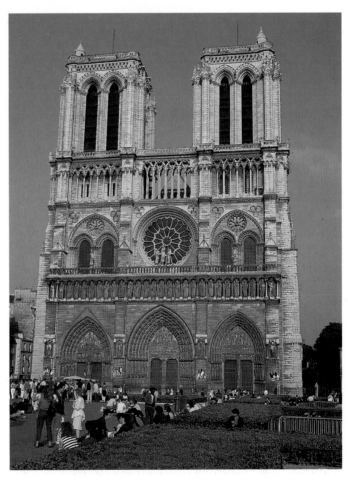

Gothic cathedrals use refined, upward-striving lines to symbolize humanity's upward striving to escape the bounds of earth and enter the mystery of space (the kingdom of heaven). The pointed arch is the most easily identifiable characteristic of this style. It represents not only a symbol of Gothic spirituality, but also an engineering practicality. The round arch of the previous eras places tremendous pressure on its keystone (see Chapter 7), which then transfers thrust outward to the sides, but the pointed arch redistributes the thrust of downward force in more equal, controllable directions. It controls thrust by sending it downward through its legs, and it makes design flexibility possible. The Gothic arch also increases the sense of height in its vaults. Some have said that Gothic structure actually made increased heights possible, but this is not quite correct. Some Romanesque churches had vaults as high as Gothic churches. It is the possibility of changing the proportion of height to width that increases the apparent height of the Gothic church.

Engineering advances implicit in the new form made possible larger clerestory windows, which let in more light (see Fig. **8.11**). And more slender ribbing placed greater emphasis on space as opposed to mass. On the exterior, the outward thrust of the vaults is carried gracefully to the

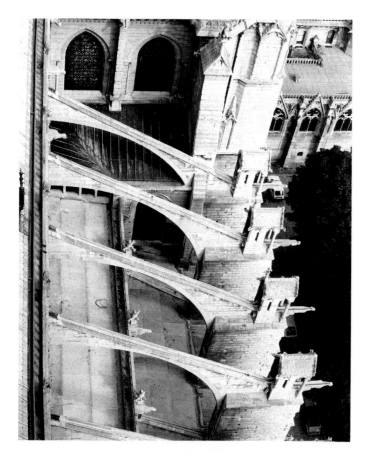

8.10 Notre Dame, Paris, flying buttresses, 1163–1250.

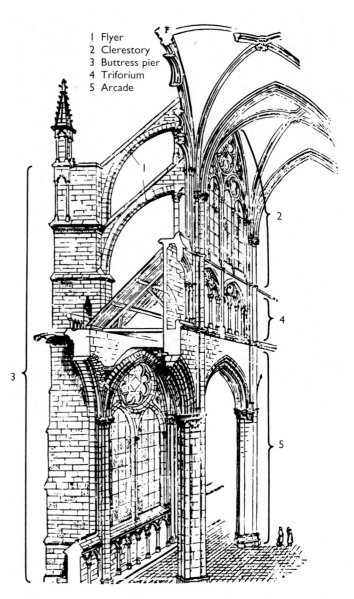

1 Flyer
2 Clerestory
3 Buttress pier
4 Triforium
5 Arcade

8.11 Principal features of a typical Gothic church.

The façade at Saint-Denis, unlike that of many churches, is not merely an exterior embellishment. The Norman towers are set back on the entrance bays so that they become an integral part of the western structure (see Fig. **8.16**). The bays have two stories with upper chapels, which function independently from the rest of the building. This is symbolic of royal, secular authority, as distinct from the authority of the church, which is presided over by the clergy at the high altar and chapels at the eastern end of the building.

The four-square power of Notre Dame de Paris (Figs. **8.9** and **8.10**) reflects the strength and solidity of an urban cathedral in Europe's greatest city of the age. Its careful design is highly mathematical—each level is equal to the one below it, and its three-part division is clearly symbolic of the Trinity. Arcs (whose radii are equal to the width of the building) drawn from the lower corners meet at the top of the circular window at the second level. The effect of this design is to draw the eye inward and slowly upward.

The Cathedral at Amiens (ah-mee-EN; Fig. **8.12**) is similar to Notre Dame in scale and proportion. Rather than creating a sense of power, however, it has a delicate feel. Amiens Cathedral illustrates late developments in Gothic style and also provides, in contrast with Notre Dame, an important lesson in the ways design can be used to elicit response. Amiens is less stolid than Notre Dame, and this feeling is enhanced by the greater detail that focuses our attention on space rather than flat stone. Both cathedrals are divided into three very obvious horizontal and vertical sections of roughly the same proportion. Notre Dame appears to rest heavily on its lowest section, the proportions of which are apparently diminished by the

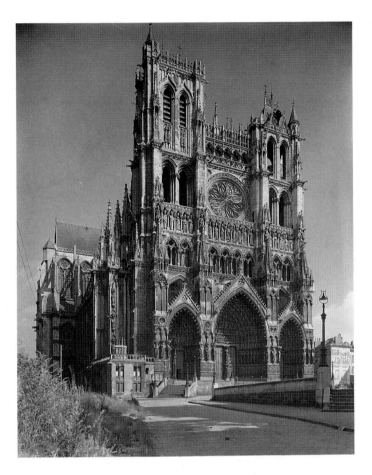

8.12 Amiens Cathedral, France, west front, c. 1220–59.

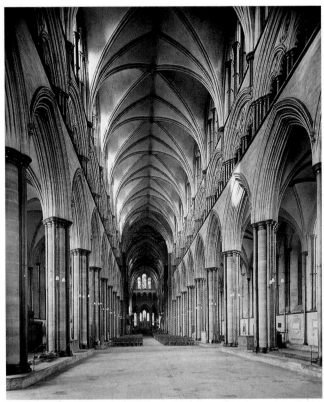

8.13 Salisbury Cathedral, England, nave and choir.

horizontal band of sculptures above the portal. Amiens, on the other hand, carries its portals upward to the full height of the lower section. In fact, the lines of the central portal, which is much larger than the central portal of Notre Dame, combine with the lines of the side portals to form a pyramid whose apex penetrates into the section above. The roughly similar size of the portals of Notre Dame reinforces its horizontality, and this is what gives it stability. Every use of line, form, and proportion in Amiens reinforces lightness and action. Everything about the appearance of Notre Dame reinforces stability and strength. One design is no better than the other, of course. Nevertheless, both cathedrals are unquestionably Gothic, and the qualities that make them so are easy to identify.

The Cathedral Church of the Blessed Virgin Mary at Salisbury in England (Figs. **8.1** and **8.13**) is famous more for its beauty than for its historical associations. Its breathtaking spire nearly caused the building to collapse when it was added. A graceful work of architecture, it has been celebrated widely, especially in the paintings of John Constable.

With the exception of St Paul's Cathedral in London, Salisbury is the only English cathedral whose entire interior structure was built to the design of a single architect and completed without a break. This was accomplished in 1265. What is perhaps the most perfect part of the cathedral, however, took another fifty-five years to complete. The famous spire, built between 1285 and 1310, added an additional 404 feet (123 meters) to a very squat tower, which rose only a few feet above the nave. The spire thus

8.14 Plan of Salisbury Cathedral, England.

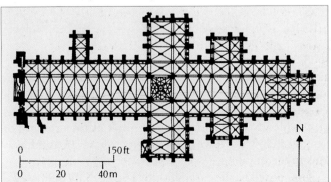

MASTERWORK

Suger and the Abbey Church of Saint-Denis

Between 1135 and 1137, Suger, abbot of Saint-Denis, began to rebuild the royal abbey church. That undertaking changed architecture for all time. The ancestry of every Gothic church in the world owes its existence to it. Unlike any other artistic style, the beginning of Gothic style can be pinpointed to the planning and construction of this one building.

Suger, a man blessed with personal charm and great talent, was abbot of Saint-Denis from 1122 to 1151. He was born in 1081 in humble circumstances, but by the time he died, he was known as "father of his country."

Suger was a champion of the monarchy, which he invested with religious significance. The Abbey Church of Saint-Denis benefited from Suger's politics and from its own history. It was the shrine of the apostle of France, the sacred protector of the realm, and the chief memorial of the Carolingian dynasty: Charlemagne and his father, Pepin, had been consecrated there, and it was the burial place of Charles Martel, Pepin, and Charles the Bald. Suger wanted to

make the abbey the spiritual center of France, a center of pilgrimage and the center of religious and patriotic emotion. To meet such ends, the church needed to be enlarged. His chronicles of the planning and goals of that project have given us a clear picture of the nature and scope of Gothic architecture itself.

8.15 (*below*) Plan of the ambulatory and radiating chapels of choir at Saint-Denis, Paris, 1140–44.

8.16 (*right*) Reconstruction of the west façade of Saint-Denis as envisaged by Abbot Suger. Drawn by Gregory Robeson.

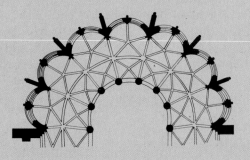

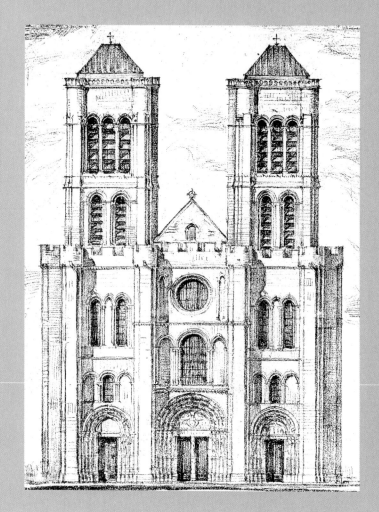

became the highest in England and the second highest in Europe. Unfortunately, the piers and foundations were not designed to carry the additional 6,400 tons, and masons were forced to add a strong stone vault at the crossing of the nave below the tower, one of the few stylistic modifications in the building.

Compared to the cathedrals of France, Salisbury seems long, low, and sprawling. The west front functions more as a screen wall, wider than the nave, whose horizontal bands of decoration further emphasize the horizontal thrust of the building. The plan of the cathedral (Fig. **8.14**), with its double transept, is reminiscent of the earlier Romanesque style. The same emphasis on the horizontal appears in the interior, where the nave wall looks more like a succession

Sculpture

Gothic sculpture again reveals the changes in attitude of the period. It portrays serenity, idealism, and simple naturalism. Gothic sculpture, like painting, has a human quality. Life now seems to be more valuable. The vale of tears, death, and damnation are replaced by conceptions of Christ as a benevolent teacher and of God as awesome in his beauty rather than in his vengeance. There is a new order, symmetry, and clarity. Visual images carry over a distance with greater distinctness. The figures of Gothic sculpture are less entrapped in their material and stand away from their backgrounds.

Schools of sculpture developed throughout France. Thus, although individual stone carvers worked alone, their links with a particular school gave their works the character of that school. The work from Reims, for example, had an almost classical quality; that from Paris was dogmatic and intellectual, perhaps reflecting the role of Paris as a university city. As time went on, sculpture became more naturalistic. Spiritual meaning was sacrificed to everyday appeal, and sculpture increasingly reflected secular interests, both middle-class and aristocratic.

Compositional unity also changed over time. Early Gothic architectural sculpture was subordinate to the overall design of the building. Later work began to claim attention on its own.

The content of Gothic sculpture is also noteworthy. Like most church art, it was *didactic*, or designed to teach. Many of its lessons are straightforward. The Last Judgment tympanum above the central western door of Saint-Denis illustrates this (Fig. 8.17).

Christ the Judge dominates everything. He reveals his two natures as Son of God and Son of Man. As judge, Christ summons the dead to appear from the grave, which is depicted in the lintel below his feet. He is also depicted at the moment of his crucifixion with outstretched arms and his right side bared showing the mark of the spear. Surrounding the central figure are angels, trumpeting the awakening of the dead, scenes of heaven and hell awaiting the blessed and the damned, and the Apostles, seated together to represent the Last Judgment. They are conversing with each other in their role as teachers.

Other lessons of Gothic cathedral sculpture are more complex and less obvious. According to some scholars, much of this art was created according to specific conventions, codes, and sacred mathematical calculations. These formulas govern positioning, grouping, numbers, and symmetry. For example, the numbers three, four, and seven (which often appear as groupings in compositions of post-Gothic periods) symbolize the Trinity, the Gospels, the sacraments, and the deadly sins (the last two both number seven). The placement of figures around Christ shows their

In reality, none of the individual elements of Saint-Denis was completely new. Apses with radial chapels had been built as early as St Sernin (see Figs. **7.11** and **7.13**). However, at Saint-Denis, the plan allowed space to flow around them, uninterrupted by walls (Fig. **8.15**). Pointed arches and ribbed vaults also had been used before, but never in such a way that the heaviness of Romanesque style was transformed into the lightness of slender supports and bearing walls that occurred here. The revolution represented at Saint-Denis was one of structural relationships rather than of forms. It took existing ideas and transformed them into something new and enduring.

An additional revolution occurred in the transformation of the interior. As Suger wrote, the entire church shone "with the wonderful and uninterrupted light of most luminous windows, pervading the interior beauty." The architectural forms seem graceful and weightless, and the windows cease to be openings and become translucent walls in themselves. All this is possible because of the accommodation of the active thrust of the high arches through buttresses. The weight of the whole structure is transferred through them, and, thus, the interior space becomes open and clean, and the structural system is visible only from outside.

The result is a new dimension, a new spirit. Suger's emphasis was on strict geometric planning and a search for luminosity. Suger continually insists that his design placed the highest value on harmony—that is, the perfect relationship among parts in terms of mathematical proportions—as the source of beauty. Harmony for Suger represents the "Divine Reason" by which the universe has been constructed. The light that floods the interior is "Light Divine," a mystic revelation of God's spirit.

of arches and supports. Typical of Early English Gothic, the nave vaults curve steeply with their ribs extending down to the TRIFORIUM level, thereby tucking the clerestory windows into the vaults. Also characteristic of the Early English style is the use of dark marble for the colonnettes and capitals. The building is free of tracery, and the LANCET WINDOWS are grouped in threes and fives.

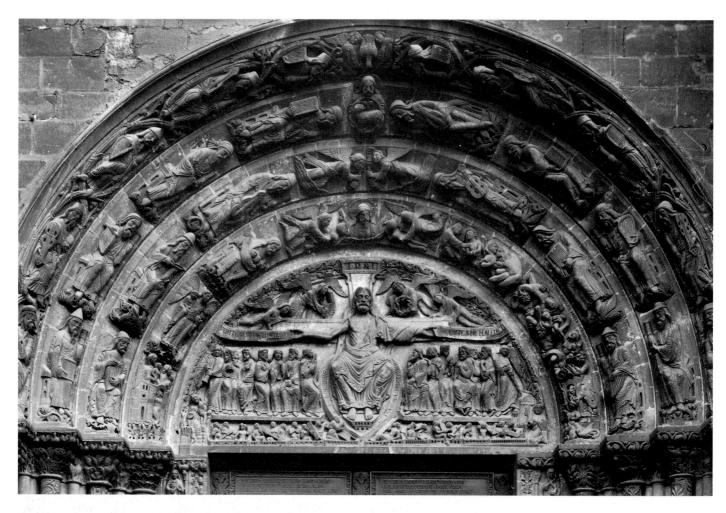

8.17 The tympanum of the west portal, west façade, Saint-Denis. (All heads are nineteenth-century restorations).

relative importance with the position on Christ's right being the most important. These codes and symbols, consistent with the tendency toward mysticism, and finding allegorical and hidden meanings in holy sources, became more and more complex.

Painting

In the twelfth and thirteenth centuries, traditional fresco painting returned to prominence. Manuscript illumination also continued. Two-dimensionality flowed from one style into another without any clearly dominant identity emerging. Because this period is so closely identified with Gothic architecture, and because painting found its primary outlet within the Gothic cathedral, however, we need to ask what qualities identify a Gothic style in painting. The answer is not as readily apparent as it is in architecture and sculp-

ture, but several characteristics can be identified. One is the beginnings of three-dimensionality in figure representation. Another is a striving to give figures mobility and life within three-dimensional space. Space is the essence of Gothic style. Gothic painters and illuminators had not mastered perspective, and their compositions do not exhibit the spatial rationality of later works. But if we compare these painters with their medieval predecessors, we discover that they have more or less broken free from the frozen two-dimensionality of earlier styles. Gothic style also exhibits spirituality, lyricism, and a new humanism. In other words, it favors mercy over irrevocable judgment. Gothic style is less crowded and frantic—its figures are less entangled with each other. It was a changing style with many variations.

The Gothic style of two-dimensional art found magnificent expression in manuscript illumination. The Court Style of France and England is represented by some truly

8.18 *Gideon's Army Surprises the Midianites,* from the Psalter of St Louis, c. 1250. 4³/₄ × 3⁵/₈ ins (12.1 × 9.2 cm). Bibliothèque Nationale, Paris.

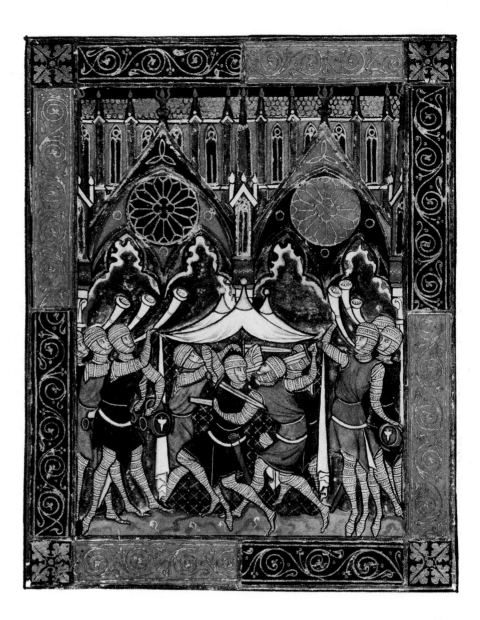

exquisite works. The Psalter of St Louis (Fig. **8.18**) was produced for King Louis IX of France in about 1250. It was a lavish book containing seventy-eight full-page pictures of scenes from the Old Testament. The figures are gracefully elongated and delicate. Set against gold backgrounds, the compositions are carefully balanced and, while somewhat crowded, show a relaxed comfort in their spatial relationships. Precision and control characterize the technique. Colors are rich. Human figures and architectural details are blended in the same manner that church sculpture both decorated and became a part of its architectural environment.

The artists who made these works were professionals living in Paris. They were influenced by Italian style, and they clearly had a new interest in pictorial space, which begins to distinguish them from their predecessors. This Parisian style, in turn, influenced English manuscript illu-

mination. Figure **8.19** of *St John on Patmos* was painted for Edward, son of Henry III, and his wife Eleanor of Castile. The elongated figures and small heads reflect the French court influence, as does the heavy drapery. The English painters, however, frequently differed from their French models, by treating drapery folds with greater angularity and giving human subjects exaggerated poses.

The same characteristics can be seen in Figure **8.20**, *David Harping.* The curious proportions of face and hands, as well as the awkward linear draping of fabric juxtaposed against the curved forms of the harp and chair, create a sense of tension. The layout of the background screen is almost careless. The upward curving arcs at the top are intended to be symmetrical, despite the imprecise diamond shapes. A touch of naturalism appears in the curved harp string which David is plucking. A rudimentary use of highlight and shadow gives basic three-

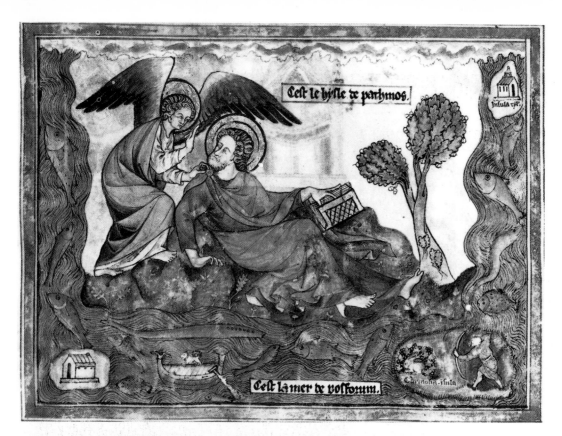

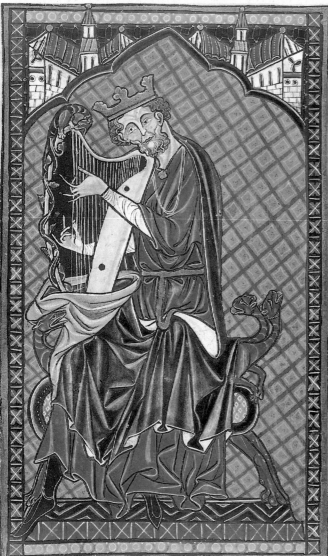

dimensionality to cloth and skin, and although it is out of balance in its interior space, the figure does not appear to crowd the borders. It has space in which to move.

MUSIC

Perhaps in response to the additional stability and increasing complexity of life, music gradually became more formal in notation and in structure, and also increased in textural complexity. Improvisation had formed the basis of musical composition. Gradually musicians felt the need to write down compositions—as opposed to making up each piece anew along certain melodic patterns every time it was performed.

Usually, music was transmitted from performer to performer or from teacher to student. Standardized musical notation, however, made it possible for the composer to transmit ideas directly to the performer. The role of the performer thus changed, making him or her a vehicle of transmission and interpretation in the process of musical communication.

In the twelfth century, as Gothic architecture spread out from the Île de France, composers in Paris developed innovations in rhythm. Two composers, Leonin (leh-oh-NEHN) and Perotin (peh-roh-TEHN), employed *measured rhythm*, which had definite time values and precise meter. Perotin (c. 1200) was the first known composer to use more than two voices in his compositions. We can find in Perotin's work the use of a *cantus firmus*, or

OUR DYNAMIC WORLD

Japanese Sculpture

In contrast to European sculpture, in the thirteenth century in Japan, sculpture reached a new maturity, turning to simple works that stressed strength and virility. A series of civil wars had led to the military dictatorship of the shoguns and their samurai (warriors) and to a wider-based feudal regime. This was reflected in the works of sculptors, such as Unkei, whose demonic and colossal wooden Buddhist deities (Fig. **8.21**) guard the entrance to the Todaiji Temple at Nara. We are drawn by both the statue's power, expressed in the fierce facial expression and forbidding hand, and by its simplicity, through the clean lines of the swirling fabrics.

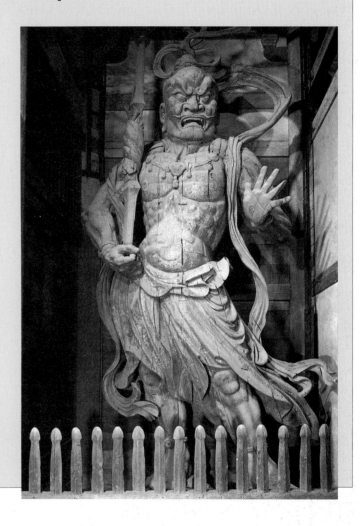

8.21 Unkei, *Nio*, 1203. Wood, 26 ft 6 ins (8 m) high. Todaiji Temple, Nara, Japan.

fixed melody—a chant used as the basis for polyphony. Above the fixed melody might be found two additional lines moving much more rapidly, with many notes sung against one long, sustained tone in the chant.

Music was affected by the same change of attitude as two-dimensional art and sculpture—a more rational, as opposed to emotional, underlying approach and feeling. Alongside sacred music existed secular songs such as BALLADES (bahl-LAHD) and RONDEAUX (rohn-DOH). These were vernacular songs in set forms, usually easy to listen to and direct in appeal. Some were dancelike, often in triple meter. The tradition of the troubadour and the wandering entertainer continued, and the courtly approach found in music and poetry an exquisite forum for its love-centered philosophy.

THEATRE

As the Middle Ages progressed, drama associated with the Church followed the example of painting and included more and more Church-related material. Earliest Church drama, that is, the *trope*, was a simple elaboration and illustration of the Mass. The subject matter of later drama included Bible stories (mystery plays), lives of the saints (miracle plays), and didactic allegories (morality plays), which had characters such as Lust, Pride, Sloth, Gluttony, and Hatred.

Mystery plays take their name from the Latin word meaning "service" or "occupation" rather than from the word for "mystery." The designation probably refers to the production of religious plays by the occupational guilds of the Middle Ages rather than the "mysteries" of revelation. Dating from the twelfth century, *The Representation of Adam* is the oldest known French mystery play. There were three parts, each with written dialogue: The Fall of Adam and Eve, the Murder of Abel, and the Prophecies of Christ. Latin instructions, which indicated scenery, costumes, and even actors' gestures, were written into the play: "Paradise shall be situated in a rather prominent place, and is to be hung all around with draperies and silk curtains."

Miracle plays presented a real or fictitious account of the life, miracles, or martyrdom of a saint. Almost all the surviving miracle plays concern either the Virgin Mary or St Nicholas, the fourth-century bishop of Myra in Asia Minor, both of whom had active cults during the Middle Ages. The Mary plays consistently involve her coming to the aid of all who invoke her, be they worthy or wanton. The Nicholas plays are similar, usually chronicling the deliverance of a crusader or the conversion of a Saracen king. We will discuss morality plays in the next chapter (see p. 284).

Tropes were performed in the church sanctuaries, using niches around the church as specific scenic locations. On special occasions, cycles of plays were performed, and the congregation moved to see different parts of the cycle. These dramatizations quickly became very popular.

Over the years, production standards for the same plays changed drastically. At first, only priests performed the roles; later, laymen were allowed to act in liturgical drama. Female roles were usually played by boys, but some evidence suggests that women did participate occasionally. The popularity of church drama soon made it impractical, if not impossible, to contain the audience within the church building. Evidence also suggests that as laymen assumed a greater role, certain vulgarities were introduced. Comedy and comic characters appeared, even in the Easter tropes. For example, on their way to Jesus' tomb, the three Marys stop to buy ointments and cloths from a merchant. This merchant developed into one of the earliest medieval comic characters. The most popular comic character of all, of course, was the devil.

Church drama eventually moved outside the sanctuary. As medieval drama moved out of the church—first to the west porch of the church and then to the city squares—various production practices developed. In France and Italy, the stationary stage decoration of the church interior became a *mansion stage* (Fig. 8.22), so-called because the different areas represented "mansions," or houses. The specific configuration of the mansion stage differed from location to location. In Italy, it was rectangular and linear, designed to be viewed from one or two sides. In some parts of France, *arena staging*, in which the audience completely surrounded the stage area, was introduced. Whatever the

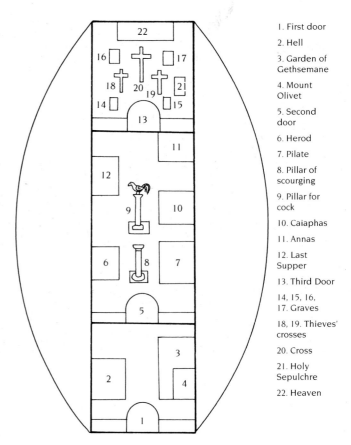

8.22 Plan of a medieval mansion stage, showing the mansions in the Donaueschingen Mystery Play, Germany.

1. First door
2. Hell
3. Garden of Gethsemane
4. Mount Olivet
5. Second door
6. Herod
7. Pilate
8. Pillar of scourging
9. Pillar for cock
10. Caiaphas
11. Annas
12. Last Supper
13. Third Door
14, 15, 16, 17. Graves
18, 19. Thieves' crosses
20. Cross
21. Holy Sepulchre
22. Heaven

specific application, the mansion stage had a particular set of aesthetic conventions. The individual mansions depicted their locations realistically. At the same time, areas between the mansions could serve as any location. When the action of a play moved away from a specific mansion, the aesthetic became conventional, just as we saw in classical Greek theatre. That is, the stage could represent any place, as opposed to the representation of place found in the mansion. The text of the play told the audience where the action was supposed to occur, and the audience then imagined that locale.

The most interesting depiction on the medieval stage was that of hell, or hellmouth—the mouth of hell into which sinners were cast. Audiences demanded more and more realism and complexity in the depiction of hellmouth. Descriptions of devils amid smoke and fire, pulling sinners into the mouth of hell, often the jaws of a dragon-like monster, are common (Fig. 8.23). One source describes a hellmouth so complicated that it took seventeen people to operate it. Some plays, *Antecriste* and *Domes Daye*, for example, were clearly intended to be frightening. But in the late Middle Ages, even vividly

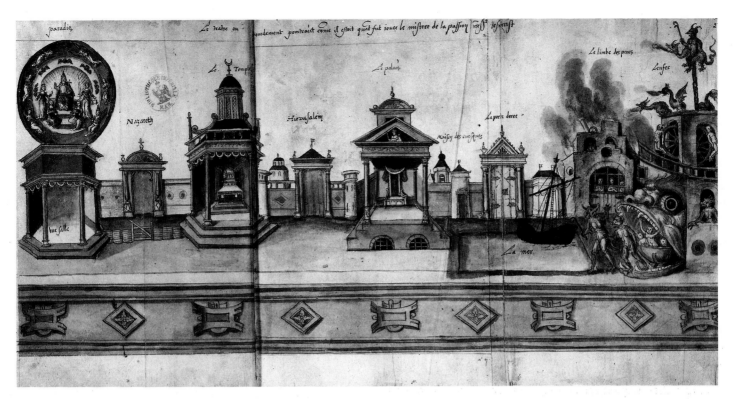

8.23 The Valenciennes Mystery Play, 1547. Contemporary drawing. Bibliothèque Nationale, Paris.

depicted hellmouths seem to have been comic in their intentions, rather than fearsome. Plays of the period are humorous and compassionate, clearly reflecting the cultural change in attitude.

In England and parts of France and the Netherlands, another staging style developed. Rather than move the audience or set up all the locations in different places on a mansion stage, theatre was brought to the audience on a succession of pageant wagons, like the floats of a modern parade. Each wagon carried the set for a specific part of the play cycle. Many of these wagons were very elaborate, two stories tall, and curtained for entrances and exits like a modern theatre. In some cases, a flat wagon was combined with an elaborate background wagon to provide a playing area. This type of production was mostly used in cities where narrow wagons were needed to negotiate narrow streets. At intersections where there was more space, wagons were coupled and crowds gathered to watch a segment of the play. When the segment finished, the wagon moved on, and was shortly replaced by another wagon, which served as the setting for another short play in the cycle.

Focal Point

Chartres Cathedral

Chartres (SHAHRT-ruh) Cathedral (Figs. 8.24–8.30) is a country cathedral that rises above the center of a small city. Its sculptures illustrate a progression of style (Figs. 8.27 and 8.29), and so does its architectural design. At first glance, we wonder why its cramped entry portal is so small in comparison with the rest of the building. The reason is that Chartres was not built all at once. Rather, it was built cumulatively over many years, as fire destroyed one part of the church after another. The main entry portal and the windows above it date back to its Romanesque beginnings.

8.24 Chartres Cathedral, France, west front, 1145–1220.

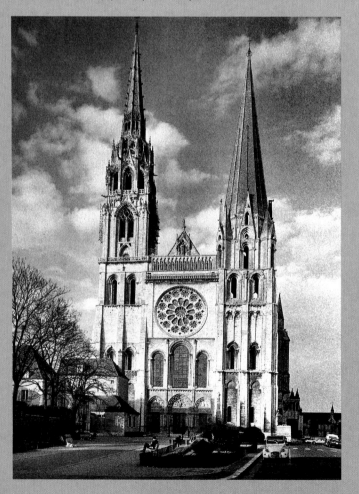

The porch of the south transept (Fig. 8.25) is much larger and more in harmony with the rest of the building.

Our biggest question, however, concerns the incongruity of the two unmatched spires. Again, fire was responsible. The early spire, on the right, illustrates faith in its simple upward lines rising, unencumbered, to disappear at the tip into the ultimate mystery of space. The later spire is more ornate and complex—the eye travels up it with increasing difficulty, its progress halted and held by decoration and detail.

A major difference between the Gothic style and the Romanesque lies in the FENESTRATION (fen-uh-STRAY-shuhn). Gothic-style walls are pierced by windows that take the form of sparkling jewels of stained glass, such as the *Notre Dame de Belle Verrière* ("Our Lady of the Beautiful Window"; Fig. 8.26). Stained-glass windows replaced the wall paintings of the Romanesque and the mosaics of the Byzantine style. Their ethereal, multicolored light further mysticized the spiritual experience of the medieval worshipper. Light now became an additional property for artistic manipulation and design. The loveliness and intricacy typical of the art of medieval stained glass can also be seen in the magnificent rose window of the north transept of Chartres Cathedral (Fig. 8.28). In the center, the Virgin Mary sits with the Christ Child on her knee. Around her, panels are grouped together in series of twelve, an important symbolic number in the Middle Ages. Angels, archangels, and four white doves represent the gospel and the Holy Spirit. In the squares appear the kings of Israel, named by St Matthew as the ancestors of Joseph, while the prophets sit on the outer edge of the window. Every element in the design leads the eye to the focal center, the Virgin and Child, and, thereby, draws together the Old and New Testaments.

The importance of stained-glass windows in Gothic cathedrals cannot be overemphasized. They carefully control the light entering the sanctuary, and the quality of that light reinforces a marvelous sense of mystery. With the walls of Romanesque style replaced by the space and light of the Gothic style, these windows take the place of wall paintings in telling the story of the Gospels and the saints.

The sculptures of Chartres Cathedral, which bracket nearly a century from 1145 to 1220, illustrate clearly the

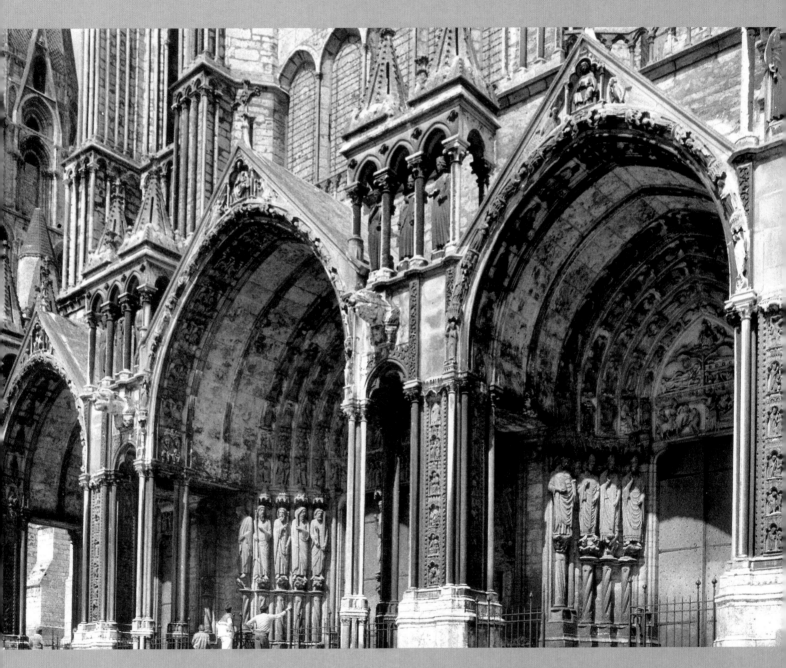

8.25 Chartres Cathedral, France, south transept porth, c. 1205–50.

transition from early to High Gothic. The attenuated figures of the JAMB statues in Figure **8.27**, from the middle of the twelfth century, display a relaxed serenity, idealism, and simple naturalism. They are an integral part of the portal columns, but they also emerge from them, each in its own space. Each figure has a particular human dignity despite its idealization. Cloth drapes easily over the bodies. Detail is somewhat formal and shallow, but we now see the human figure beneath the fabric, in contrast to the previous use of fabric merely as surface decoration.

As human as these figures may appear, this quality is even more pronounced in the figures from less than a century later (Fig. **8.29**). Here we see the characteristics of the High Gothic style, or Gothic classicism. These figures have only the most tenuous connection to the building. Proportions are more lifelike, and the figures are carved in subtle S-curves rather than as rigid perpendicular columns. The drape of the fabric is much more natural, with deeper and softer folds. In contrast to the idealized portraits of the earlier period, these figures have the features of specific

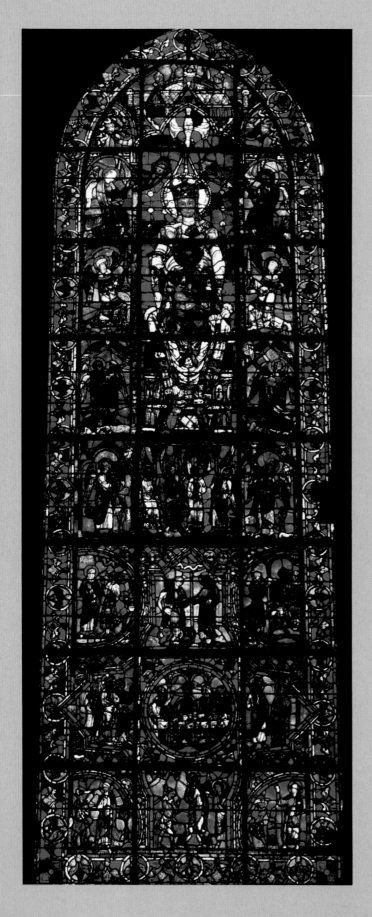

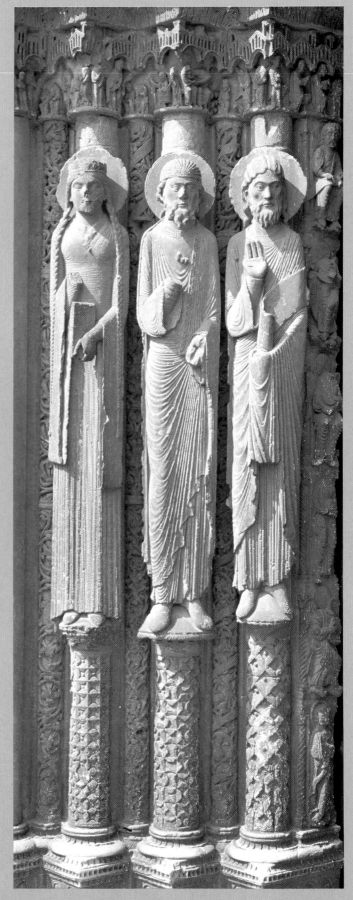

8.26 (*opposite left*) *Notre Dame de Belle Verrière*, Chartres Cathedral, France.

8.27 (*opposite right*) Chartres Cathedral, France, jamb statues, west portal, c. 1145–70.

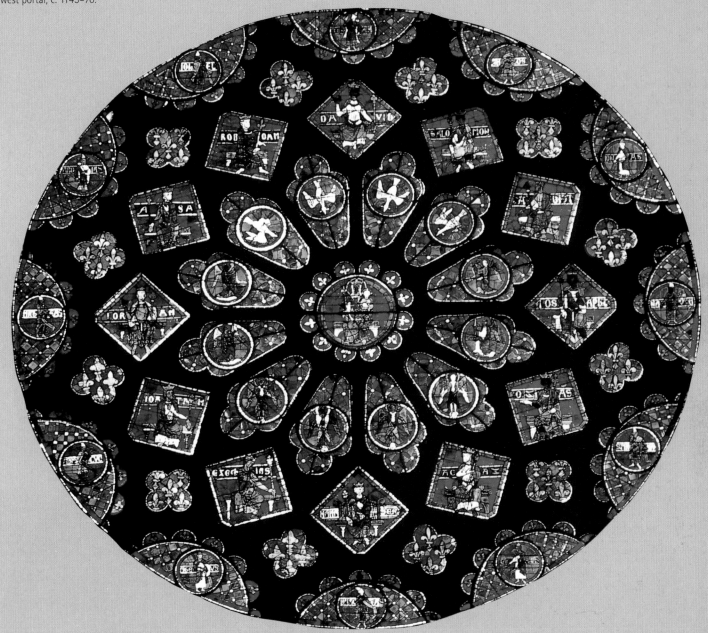

8.28 Chartres Cathedral, France, rose window, north transept, c. 1230. 42 ft 8 ins (13 m) in diameter.

individuals, and they express qualities of spirituality and determination.

The didactic quality of Gothic sculpture is present here as well. Above the main doorway, Christ appears as a ruler and judge of the universe, along with a host of symbols of the apostles and others (Fig. 8.30). The portal sculptures are the prophets and kings of the Old Testament, and they proclaim the harmony of secular and spiritual rule, thus suggesting that the kings of France are spiritual descendants of biblical rulers.

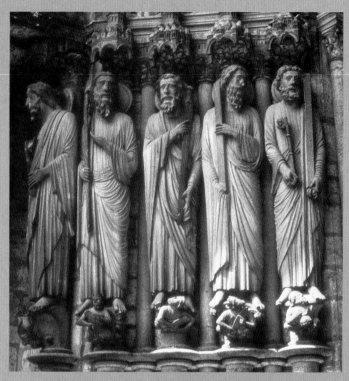

8.29 Chartres Cathedral, France, jamb statues, south transept portal, c. 1215–20.

8.30 Chartres Cathedral, France, central tympanum, west portal, c. 1145–70.

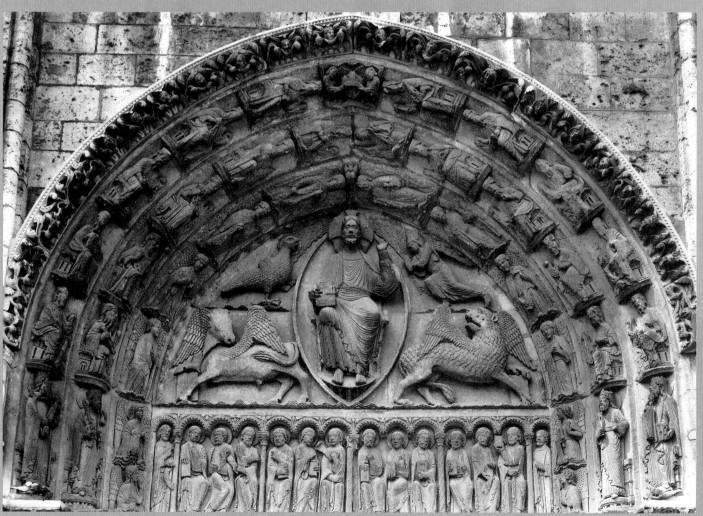

CHAPTER REVIEW

Critical Thought

During the High Middle Ages, profound changes took place in Europe, not only in its institutions but also in the way it viewed matters both earthly and eternal. As we have seen, several reforms affected the Christian Church: the rise of mysticism and the crusades. Philosophy, theology, and literature shaped the ideas and directions of intellectual and cultural life even as they do today. This was a time of flux. Barricades were coming down and light flowed into every corner of human existence. Universities were born, and people such as Abelard and St Thomas Aquinas remolded and shaped the tenets of Christian faith. Literature gave birth to a new genre, called "courtly romance," and a major poet, named Dante.

Like the Greek temple, Gothic architecture—particularly the Gothic cathedral—has come to symbolize an entire era and to form an important prototype for building not only churches but also other structures in our contemporary world. With similar characteristics in line, form, balance, and unity, Gothic sculpture and two-dimensional art mirror their architectural kindred. Music and theatre embarked on new paths as well, as the "old" gave way to the "new."

Summary

After reading this chapter, you should be able to:

- Explain the changes affecting secular and religious life in the High Middle Ages by citing specific individuals, trends, and conditions.
- Compare and contrast the philosophies of Abelard and St Thomas Aquinas.
- Describe the literature of the period, including the courtly romance and Dante's *Divine Comedy*.
- Understand and discuss the attitudes, reflections, and general characteristics of Gothic architecture, painting, and sculpture, including how Gothic style differs from Romanesque and how Gothic style changed from early to late.
- Characterize the theatre and music of the High Middle Ages, including their forms and presentation.
- Apply the elements and principles of composition to analyze and compare works of art and architecture illustrated in this chapter.

CHAPTER NINE

The Late Middle Ages

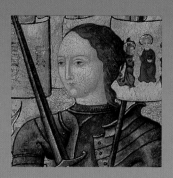

OUTLINE

THE END OF THE MIDDLE AGES
Secularism and Transition
The Hundred Years' War
  PROFILE: Joan of Arc
The Secular Monarchies
The Plague
Economics and Industrialization
Religion and the Great Schism
  TECHNOLOGY: Keeping Time

LITERATURE
Petrarch and Boccaccio
  PROFILE: Geoffrey Chaucer
Froissart's Chronicles
Christine de Pisan

ART AND ARCHITECTURE
Late Gothic Architecture
Late Gothic Sculpture
Painting
  MASTERWORK: Giotto—*The Lamentation*

MUSIC
Ars Nova

THEATRE
  OUR DYNAMIC WORLD: Noh Theatre of Japan

DANCE

FOCAL POINT: WOMEN MYSTICS OF THE LATE MIDDLE AGES

VIEW

LEADERS AND DISAPPOINTMENT

The condition of the Christian Church and political Europe in the fourteenth century may remind us of the all-too-human nature of those who undertake leadership in any institution. The nobility or goodness of the institution itself seems irrelevant when humans struggle for power, and the person in "control" often appears to be more important—especially to him- or herself—than the institution. When abuse becomes virulent, cries for "reform" are heard throughout the land, but, even then, often the cries turn into cynicism when the individuals who must carry out the reforms recognize the cost to themselves that "doing the right thing" entails; then the cycle begins again.
If the foregoing paragraph sounds like a reflection on a particular event in today's political or religious life, it is only because such comments really do reflect the nature of humankind. So, when it seems as if all our leaders have "gone south" when it comes to showing courage and moral fiber, it's nothing new.

KEY TERMS

Some of the basic terms and concepts we will encounter in this chapter include the following:

Secularism is the rejection of religion and religious considerations.

Schism is a separation into divisions or factions, especially within a Church.

Humanism, a philosophy concerned with human beings, their achievements, and interests, as opposed to abstract beings and problems of theology.

Duomo, the Italian word for cathedral: usually the central architectural feature of a city or town.

Pietà, a sculpture or painting of the dead Christ supported by Mary.

Ars Nova, "New Art," referring to changes in music occurring in the fourteenth century.

Hallenkirche, a German interpretation of Gothic style in which the aisles and nave are the same height.

Above Detail of Fig. **9.3**.

9.1 Giovanni Pisano, Pulpit, begun 1297. Marble, Sant'Andrea, Pistoia, Italy.

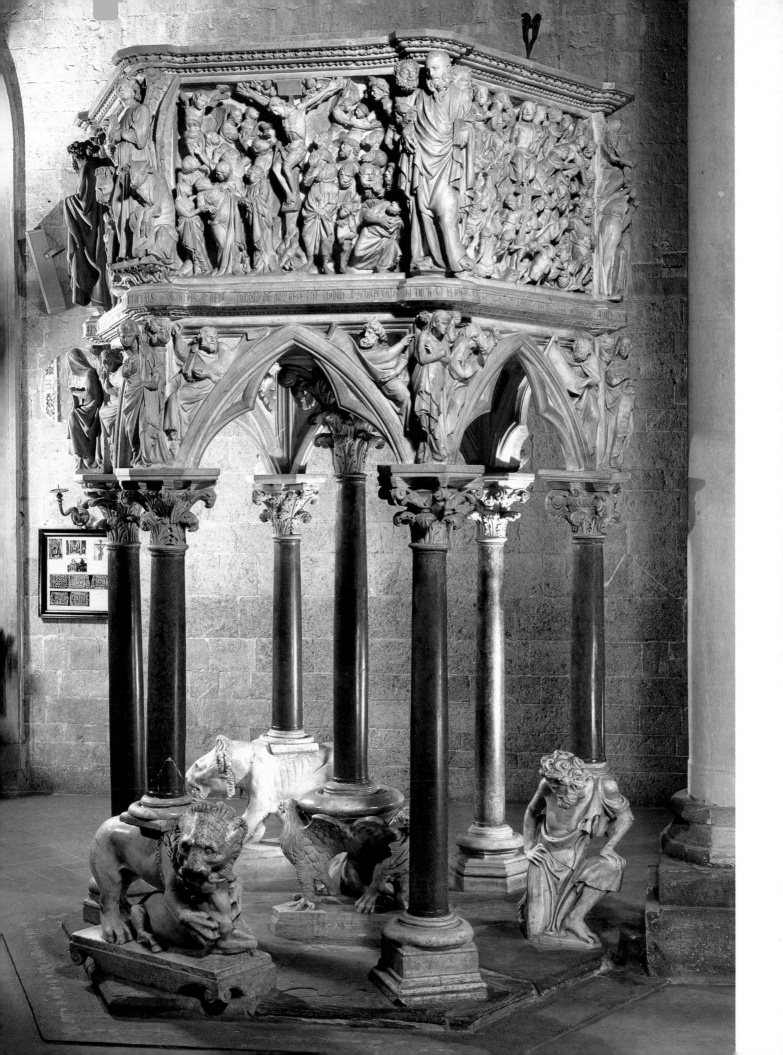

THE END OF THE MIDDLE AGES

Secularism and Transition

By the fourteenth century, revelation and reason, and God and the State, were considered to be separate spheres of authority, neither subject to the other. Such a separation, of what had previously been the full realm of the Church, was the beginning of secularism—that is, a rejection of religion and religious considerations. Individual nations—rather than feudal states or holy empires—had arisen throughout Europe, although it would be misleading to say that religion and matters of State were entirely divorced. As we shall see, they intermingled freely when it was convenient; but they clashed severely when questions of power and authority were at stake. However, amid the conflict of secular and Church interests, two events had a catastrophic impact on Europe. The year 1338 marked the beginning of what came to be known as the Hundred Years' War, and, early in that, the plague (1348–51) further disrupted the relative prosperity of the High Middle Ages. During this time, secular arts gradually gained prominence, respectability, and significance, reflecting a shifting emphasis rather than an outright reversal of values.

The Hundred Years' War

The Hundred Years' War really lasted more than one hundred years. It consisted of an intermittent struggle between England and France which involved periodic fighting over the question of English fiefs in France, fighting that had begun in the twelfth century. The series of ongoing battles concerning a number of issues, including the rightful succession to the French crown, traditionally began in 1337 and lasted until 1453.

In the medieval world, one king might, in fact, be the vassal of another king if the first king inherited land that lay within the claim of the second king. Such was the condition of Europe, and such was the situation that had existed in England and France since William I, the Conqueror, who was duke of Normandy, had conquered and become king of England in 1066. William's successor English kings laid claim to portions of France, and marriages and other alliances complicated the picture. The ensuing conflict was called the Hundred Years' War.

As in modern warfare, medieval wars occasionally consisted of massed armies pitted in battles, a victory in which might prove decisive. More often, however, they consisted of lengthy and expensive sieges of important

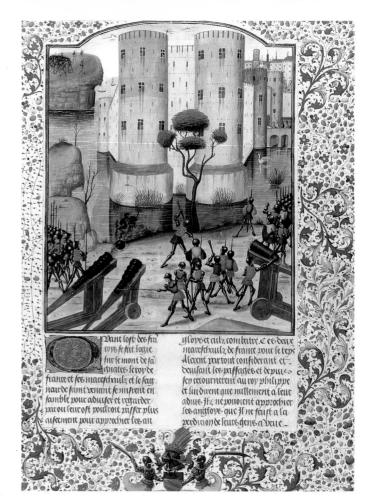

9.2 Jean de Wavrin, *Chroniques d'Angleterre*, showing cannons used as siege weapons, fifteenth century. Bibliothèque Nationale, Paris.

fortified cities (Fig. **9.2**). For approximately twenty-seven years from 1337, the English kept a military presence in France, but did not gain much territory in the process, although they won some battles—for example, at Crécy (kray-SEE) in 1346 and Poitiers (pwah-tee-AY) in 1356. The French then offered a settlement to the English granting full sovereignty over lands formerly held.

In 1429, inspired by Joan of Arc, the French broke the English siege of Orléans (see Profile, p. 268). When the English became embroiled in the War of the Roses at home, France conquered Normandy and Aquitaine, and by 1453, Calais remained as the only English territory in France, and that was relinquished in 1458. The end of the Hundred Years' War heralded the end of English adventurism on the Continent and contributed to a new sense of national identity in western Europe.

The Secular Monarchies

Amazingly, both France and England seem to have emerged as more stable countries as a result of the Hundred Years' War. In France, the period following the

	GENERAL EVENTS	LITERATURE & PHILOSOPHY	VISUAL ART & ARCHITECTURE	PERFORMING ARTS
1300				
	Papacy to Avignon Hundred Years' War begins		Pisano (**9.1, 9.14**) Cimabue (**9.15**) Duccio (**9.16**) Giotto (**9.17, 9.18**) Florence Cathedral (**9.9**) Jean Pucelle (**9.20**) Doge's Palace (**9.11**) Lorenzetti (**9.19**)	Philippe de Vitry
1350				

	Black Death or plague in
	   Europe
	Battle of Poitiers
	Ming Dynasty in China
	   (until 1644)
		Petrarch
		Boccaccio
		John Wycliffe
			Hallenkirchen, St Sebald (**9.8**)	Danse macabre
				
				de Machaut

1375				
	Great Schism Hanseatic League controls Baltic Mechanical clocks	Chaucer Froissart Julian of Norwich John Huss	Sluter (**9.13**) Milan Cathedral (**9.10**)	*Ars nova* Francesco Landini
1400				
	Joan of Arc Wars of the Roses	Christine de Pisan		

Timeline 9.1 The late Middle Ages.

Map 9.1 France in 1429.

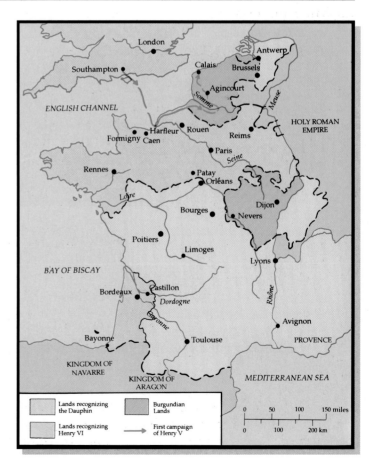

war saw the establishment of a strengthened absolute monarchy, which reached its zenith under Louis XIV in the seventeenth century (see Chapter 13).

In England at this time there were disputes and a power struggle between the kings and an increasingly influential Parliament. In 1485, after the Wars of the Roses, a new dynasty, the Tudors, founded by Henry VII (1485–1509), placed the king and Parliament in less of an adversarial relationship, and managed to avoid most of the issues that had caused friction between previous kings and the legislative body. As a result, England experienced a new centralization of monarchial power, and Henry's political acumen moved Parliament to an increasingly peripheral role. In the end, England emerged with as strong a central monarchy as had been established in France.

The Plague

Known as the Black Death, the catastrophic plague that ravaged Europe between 1348 and 1350 was a combination of bubonic and pneumonic plagues. The epidemic, which eventually claimed more than 25 million lives,

Joan of Arc (1412–31)

It is fair to say that Christianity was the heart of medieval European culture, and the life and death of Joan of Arc (Fig. **9.3**) illustrate that circumstance poignantly. Born in a small village in northeastern France, St Joan was a pious but illiterate woman growing up in the middle of the Hundred Years' War. When she was seventeen years old, she began to hear heavenly voices telling her to save her country from the unending ravages of war. With childlike belief and obedience, she left home and family and traveled to the court of King Charles VII. The king was a particularly uninspiring presence—and, at the time, uncrowned—but somehow Joan was able to pick him out of the hundreds of his courtiers. Her simple faith and straightforwardness convinced the unhappy monarch that she should be allowed to join the French army, which was massing for a major battle with the English.

Her presence among the troops lifted their morale and inspired them to victory after victory, from breaking the siege at Orléans to the battle of Reims. After the victory at Reims, Charles was formally crowned at the cathedral there in 1429. Victories inspired by The Maid, as she was universally called, provided a focus for the French, who rallied to the support of the newly crowned and anointed king. After Charles' coronation,

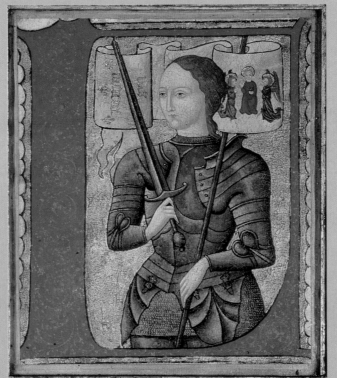

9.3 Joan of Arc (1412–31).

Joan ceased hearing her voices. That, for her, meant that her mission had ended, and she wished to return home. The king, however, recognized the powerful symbol she represented and kept her in his service, sending her to lead the French troops marching on Paris, which was still held by the English. The attack failed, and Joan was captured by England's Burgundian allies and sold to the English. She was tried for witchcraft by an ecclesiastical court subservient to the English, found guilty, and burned at the stake in Rouen in 1431.

Although her public career lasted only two years, half of which was spent in prison after her capture, Joan remains one of the most potent symbols of the age: mystical, charismatic, faithful, courageous, and enigmatic. Although she did not actually command troops, she knew exactly when and where to make her appearance felt in order to inspire and turn the tide of battle. She believed completely in her voices—St Catherine and the archangel Michael—and obediently followed their commands, regardless of the circumstances. In many ways, this obedience to the faith was typical of the times. She said that her voices called her a "daughter of God," and no one questioned the powers that drove her, although the English called her "a disciple and limb of the Fiend."

originated in China and spread to Europe probably by traders. The first cases of the disease occurred in the Crimea, then in Mediterranean ports in Sicily, north Africa, Italy, Spain, and France, before engulfing the European continent and England. Although it officially came to an end after three years, outbreaks recurred for the next fifty years.

There seemed to be no logic to the disease's devastation. Some areas—for example, Milan and Flanders—suffered little, while others, such as Tuscany and Aragon, were decimated. Those areas with the densest populations—for examples, large cities and monasteries—suffered most. Neither rank nor station offered sanctuary—kings, queens, princes, and archbishops felt the sting of the plague's effects as much as peasants and merchants. In total, nearly one-third of the entire population of Europe died from the disease in the three-year period. By 1400, for example, the population of England had declined to one-half of what it had been a century before, and chroniclers estimated that a thousand English villages were completely wiped out.

The effects of the plague were many. Commerce slumped temporarily, but more importantly, the death of so many people made cultivation of land nearly impossible. In order to stay afloat, many landowners had to begin to pay wages and to substitute money rents in lieu of labor services. The shortage of workers thus led to an increase in wages for both peasants and artisans and tended to break down the previous stratification of society.

Economics and Industrialization

The drastic reduction of population resulting from wars and the plague changed the basic shape of the European economy. Wages rose, production declined, and the cost of goods spiraled upward. Consumers and landowners suffered from inflationary pressures, encouraging many landowners to turn to less labor-intensive use of their lands, such as raising sheep rather than growing crops. Governments across Europe attempted to control the situation by imposing price and wage controls.

The precarious living conditions fomented violent class struggles, conflicts between peasants and landowners, clashes between craft guilds and merchants, and anticlerical outbursts as well. The Church occupied a privileged position—not only did it pay no taxes, but the clergy benefited through the payment of tithes—and was widely resented. Although social unrest accomplished little—those protesting had little power and were easily subdued by a well-armed officialdom—the unheavals ultimately created a better standard of living for everyone. Workers earned higher wages, merchants benefited from higher

prices, and landowners profited from new uses of their resources. A new class of entrepreneurs also emerged, who established more effective business practices and encouraged innovation and mechanization (Fig. 9.4). The textile industry, for example, changed significantly. Previous textile centers, such as Flanders, were cut off from their sources and faced new competition from Germany and Poland, while England stopped exporting raw wool and began to export finished cloth.

In many spheres—mining, metallurgy, printing (Johann Gutenberg—c. 1400–c. 1468—introduced the printing press with movable type around 1450), and shipbuilding, for example—industry became more efficient because of the switch from labor-intensive practices to technology. Demand for iron products—especially

9.4 Banking scenes, miniature from *De septem vitiis*, Italian, late fourteenth century. British Museum, London.

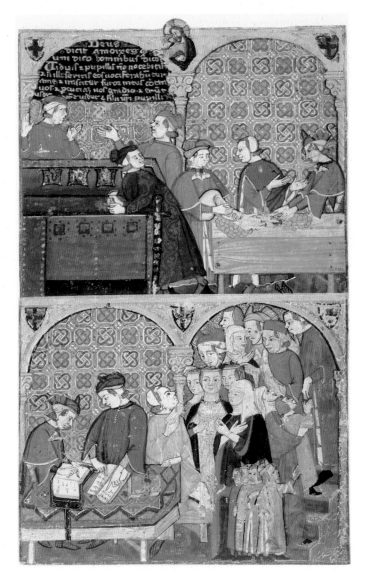

TECHNOLOGY: PUTTING DISCOVERY TO WORK

Keeping Time

The measurement of time presented humankind with tremendous difficulties until the late Middle Ages. Records of time were among the earliest uses of writing, and the Egyptians had established a relatively accurate calendar by 3500 B.C., but for primitive people, work began at sunrise and ended at dusk, and the divisions of time between were of little interest. A seasonal calendar, on the other hand, was of prime importance. The first attempt to divide daylight into units was probably the shadow-clock, which was developed in Egypt around 1450 B.C., with later developments including water clocks and sandglasses. It was not until the thirteenth century, however, that mechanical clocks were invented to bring consistent accuracy into the telling of time. The first mechanical clocks (Fig. **9.5**) were driven by falling weights, and spring-driven mechanisms, which made watches possible, came into being in the fifteenth century.

The accurate measurement of time must be based on some repetitive movement that occurs with com-

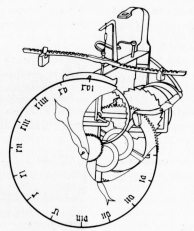

9.5 Early alarm clock, c. 1390.

plete regularity. The earliest mechanism, called a verge, had a pair of pallets attached to an oscillating arm, which engaged alternately with cogs on a wheel rotated by a falling weight. The earliest surviving clock of this type, in Salisbury Cathedral (see p. 249), dates from around 1386. Although it worked perfectly satisfactorily, the verge was friction-driven and not, therefore, wholly accurate. The spring made it possible to construct more compact mechanisms, but required a device to compensate for the diminishing force of the spring as it uncoiled. This problem did not exist with weight-driven mechanisms, because the force exerted by the weight at the end of the descent is the same as at the beginning. To compensate, spring-driven mechanisms employed a fuse—that is, a conical drum with a helical groove—cut so that, as the spring uncoiled, the connecting cord exerted greater pressure on the shaft.

Early clocks often had only a single hand to indicate the hours. Soon, however, a face to indicate quarter hours became common, as did a minute hand.

weapons, armor, and horseshoes—provided a spur to that industry. Rag paper, which had been invented by the Chinese and perfected by the Arabs, was manufactured in Spain and distributed widely. All these conditions drastically changed the course of events in Europe. Printing and publishing industries arose, profoundly changing literature and education. Of course, these developments depended on the extent of the plague's devastation. In some places—for example, Germany and eastern Europe—the plague had little impact, and the old feudal order remained as strong as it had ever been.

Religion and the Great Schism

By the end of the Black Death, it was not uncommon to find religious penitents walking along the roads, flagellat-

ing each other and prophesying the end of the world. It was the time of the *dance of death* (see p. 284), with skeletal figures leading knights, burghers, and peasants to the grave. The increasing secularism in government, which separated the Church from the European monarchies, did not diminish the weight of medieval Christianity on the lives of individuals. The simple faith of someone like Saint Joan stood side by side with the fanaticism of the Inquisition and the burning of witches and heretics. Pogroms against Jews and the persecution of all individuals believed to be in league with Satan were common. Charged with maintaining the purity of Christian thought, the Holy Office of Inquisition used any means necessary—including torture—to obtain confessions from all those accused of heresy. Anyone found to be an enemy of Christ and unrepentant was given over to the civil authorities to be burned alive.

These excesses went hand in hand with sincere and deep, mystical faith among the laity. By this time, the creeds of the Christian Church were well established and much more elaborate than the simple virtues of Pauline Christianity (faith in Christ, hope of salvation, and charity towards one's fellow human beings). The Medieval Church recognized seven deadly sins: pride, greed, envy, sexual self-indulgence, violence, laziness, and gluttony. Religious duties were essential. The sacraments brought the Church into the events of everyday life (for example baptism, confirmation, marriage, and death). They also provided penance and absolution for sins, conferred spiritual powers on ordained clergy, and celebrated the communion of believers with their savior in the central Christian mystery of the Mass.

In the fourteenth century, the papacy fell to its nadir. The once mighty and independent popes came under the influence of the French kings, who moved the papal see to Avignon (ah-veen-YOHN) in southern France. The office of pope was humiliated under the force of the French monarchs and further weakened by what is called the Great Schism in 1378. During the Schism, groups supporting diverse claimants to the papal throne fought each other, and for several decades, there were two and even three aspirants to the papacy, each excommunicating the others in what bewildered lay people saw as a complete degradation of the Church. In 1417 the Council of Constance, convened by the Holy Roman Emperor, deposed three pretenders and reunified the papal see at Rome.

The tragedy of what was called the Babylonian Captivity—a term paralleling the Avignon papacy with the Hebrews' captivity in Babylon—and the Great Schism brought increased demands for reform, especially to free the papacy from the control of French monarchs. In England between approximately 1320 and 1384, the reformer John Wycliffe (WY-klif) sought to cleanse the church of its worldliness. He argued for abolition of all church property, the subjugation of the Church to secular authority, and the denial of papal authority, although his greatest achievement was the inspiration of a scholarly translation of the first Bible in English. Wycliffe's followers were branded as heretics and were persecuted and punished by the secular authorities. Wycliffe's influence extended as far as Bohemia via reformers in the Holy Roman Empire who had met him at Oxford. In the hands of pietistic Christians and evangelical preachers and theologians such as John Huss (huhs; c. 1369–1415), the reform movement spread. Huss, to whom modern-day Moravian Brethren trace their heritage, accepted some of Wycliffe's teachings and rejected others. He was present at the Council of Constance, but his ideas were viewed as heretical and condemned, and he was burned at the stake. His martyrdom inspired his followers, many of whom were wealthy nobles, and they, in turn, used his beliefs as a vehicle for Czech nationalism against the German emperors and the Roman Church.

LITERATURE

Petrarch and Boccaccio

It is fair to say that the late Middle Ages—especially the fourteenth century—provided a transition between medieval thought and the Renaissance that was to come. In literature, especially, occurred stirrings of ideas that are more Renaissance than medieval. In the fourteenth century, Italian writers such as Petrarch (PEE-trahrk) and Boccaccio (boh-KAH-choh) began to take the works of ancient writers in a new direction. They borrowed ideas, stories, figures of speech, and general style, and tried to recreate ancient poetic and prose styles. In so doing, they provided a more penetrating investigation and analysis of ancient literature and art than their medieval predecessors had achieved, and achieved an ordered plan, integrated structure, symmetry, and lofty style, which fourteenth-century writers believed represented classical beauty. Various rules emerged—for example, the epic must begin in the middle of the plot, must contain supernatural elements, and must end with a victory for the hero.

Petrarch

The Italian poet Petrarch (1304–74) wrote in both Latin and his native Tuscan dialect and is a key figure in the transition from medieval to Renaissance thought. His writings are very different from those of Dante, for example, and are filled with complaints about "the dangers and apprehensions I have suffered." Contrary to what he wrote, however, he enjoyed the favor of the great men and women of his day. He flourished at the papal court at Avignon. Petrarch was unable to reconcile his own conflicting aspirations and interests into a workable existence: he desired solitude and quiet, but was continually active. Although he adored being a celebrity, he attacked the superficiality of the world around him and longed for the monastic life.
He is well known for his love poems to Laura, written over a period of about twenty years. Petrarch wrote more than 300 Italian *sonnets* to Laura (the *sonnet* is a fixed verse form consisting of fourteen lines), as well as other short lyrics and one long poem. They treat a variety of moods and subjects, but particularly his intense psychological reactions to his beloved. As he wrote in Sonnet CCXXV, Canzone XXI, To Laura in Life: "I know and love the good, yet, ah! The worst pursue."

Canzone VI
So Wayward is the madness of Desire

Petrarch
Translated by Joseph Auslander

So wayward is the madness of desire
In following her who turns from me in flight,
And who, at liberty, like air or light,
My love-encumbered chase eludes like fire,

That when the more I call, the more aspire
To point the safer path by left or right,
The less it heeds; to curb or to excite
Avails not: Love drives faster, fiercer, higher!

Thus, the triumphant bit between its teeth,
I must remain incapable and mute,
That while against my will it speeds my death

Straight to that laurel whose most fatal fruit,
Instead of healing, spreads its bitter breath
And nourishes the pain it should uproot.

Petrarch's real love was learning, for which he earned the title "Father of Humanism," and he made a significant impact on those who followed. He rejected medieval philosophy and also found science wanting as a way toward a "happy life." He had a passion for classical literature and Roman antiquity, but although he was a classical scholar, his religious thought was thoroughly medieval. He felt guilty about admiring the things learned from pagan philosophers, and he could not accept Dante's connection between the good of this world and that of the next. He rejected the intellectual tradition of the Middle Ages but clung tenaciously to its moral code.

Boccaccio

Giovanni Boccaccio (1313–75), a lifelong friend of Petrarch, was, in contrast, a man of the world. Much of his early work was inspired by, and dedicated to, his consuming passion, Fiammetta, but this was completely overshadowed by the *Decameron*, which was completed in 1358. In the framing tale, ten young people flee from the plague in Florence in 1348 to sit out the danger in the countryside. To amuse themselves, they tell one hundred stories. The first tale from Day One tells of a lively day spent in witty conversation. Days Two and Three are tales of adventure. Day Four presents unhappy love, and Day Five treats the same subject in a somewhat lighter vein. Day Six returns to the happiness of Day One, and Days Seven, Eight, and Nine cover laughter, trickery, and license. Day Ten ties the foregoing themes together in a conclusion. In total, the *Decameron* extols the virtue of humankind, proposing that to be noble, one must accept life as one finds it, with-

out bitterness. Above all, one must accept the responsibility for, and consequences of, one's own actions.

Froissart's Chronicles

A popular genre of literature during this period was the *medieval chronicle*. A chronicle is history told in a "romantic" way, and in the contemporary language of the country. The *Chronicles of England, France, and Spain* by the French writer Jean Froissart (fwah-SAHR; c. 1333–c. 1400) is an outstanding example of this genre. Froissart's work covers the history of the fourteenth century and the wars between England and France. It was not written as a factual account but, in the words of its author, "to encourage all valorous hearts and to show them honorable examples."

Froissart loved the ideals of knighthood and its heroic deeds, and his sympathies were always with the lordly knights. In his "history," however, he allowed his imagination free rein to fill in details where facts were missing. He never let accuracy stand in the way of a good story. To collect his tales, he wandered on horseback throughout Europe, his trusty greyhound tagging along behind. He talked to squires, knights, heralds, and pages, gathering their recollections and sometimes fanciful tales of the court and the battlefield.

Christine de Pisan

Christine de Pisan (pee-ZAHN; c. 1365–c. 1463) was a prolific and versatile French poet and author whose diverse writings include numerous poems of courtly love and several works championing women. Her father was astrologer to Charles V, and Christine spent her childhood at the French court. She was married at age fifteen to Estienne de Castel, who became court secretary. Ten years later, after his death, she began writing in order to support herself and her three young children. Her first poems were ballades of lost love written in memory of her husband. Immediately successful, she continued writing in a variety of forms, expressing her feelings with grace and sincerity (Fig. **9.6**). In total, she wrote ten volumes in verse, including "Letter to the God of Loves" (1399), in which she defended women against the attacks of Jean de Meun in his satire *Roman de la Rose*.

Christine's prose works include *The Book of the City of Ladies* (1405), in which she described women known for their heroism and virtue. Another prose work, *The Book of Three Virtues* (1405), was a sequel to *The Book of the City of Ladies*, which classified women's roles in medieval society and detailed moral instructions for women in various social circumstances. Her life's story,

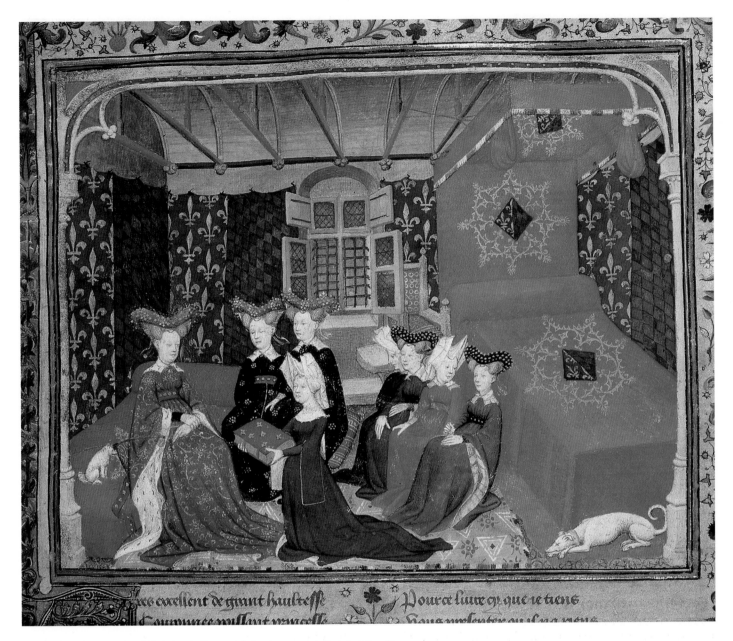

9.6 Illuminated manuscript of Christine de Pisan presenting her poems to Isabel of Bavaria.
MS. Harl. 4431 fol. 3. Min. The British Library.

L'Avision de Christine (1405), was an allegorical reply to her detractors. At the request of the regent, she wrote a biography of the deceased king (*Book of the Deeds and Good Morals of the Wise King Charles V*). It was a first-hand view of the king and his court. This and her eight other prose works revealed her outstanding breadth of knowledge.

Her final work, written in 1429, was a lyrical and joyous piece inspired by the victories of Joan of Arc. It is the only such French-language work written during Joan's lifetime.

ART AND ARCHITECTURE
Late Gothic Architecture

We should be aware by now that broad categorizations about places as diverse as Europe and timespans as broad as two hundred years do not always apply uniformly. In Germany, for example, Gothic style in architecture took much longer to gain a foothold than in other parts of Europe, and most characteristic of the German interpreta-

PROFILE

Geoffrey Chaucer (c. 1340–1400)

Born in London, Geoffrey Chaucer (CHAW-sir) came from a prosperous family of vintners who were occasionally connected to the King's court (Fig. **9.7**). We know little of his education, although we do know that he learned Latin and French. Although we know him as a writer, he appears mainly to have been a successful government employee with a long career as courtier, diplomat, and public servant. In 1359 he was captured and held for ransom while on a military expedition to France. He married in 1366. He traveled in Spain, and entertained in song, stories, and music at the court of the king of England. Traveling to Italy on the King's business he encountered the works of Dante and Boccaccio, and these probably influenced his poetry, especially *The Canterbury Tales*.

Between 1374 and 1386, he created three major works: *The House of Fame*, *The Parliament of Fowls*, and *Troilus and Criseyde*. His best-known work, *The Canterbury Tales*, was written over a period of years, mostly after 1387. The large scheme for this work included a band of thirty pilgrims on a journey from the Tabard Inn in Southwark, a suburb of London, to the shrine of Thomas à Becket in Canterbury and back again. Each pilgrim was to tell two stories when going and two while returning, but the final work included only twenty-four stories, some of which remain unfinished. The tales are funny, satirical, ironic, insightful, and individualistic in character development; some are philosophical, some are thoughtful, and others are serious. Altogether, they paint a broad portrait of fourteenth-century life and expectations. The framework resembles that of Boccaccio's *Decameron*, with which Chaucer was familiar, but Chaucer's cultivated irony and robust comedy are unprecedented.

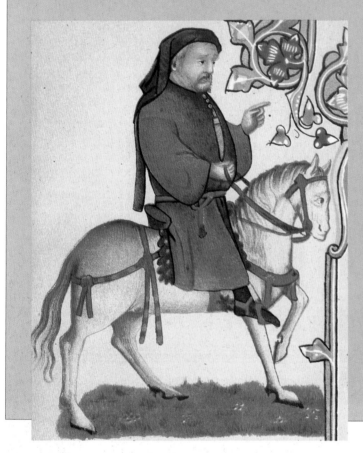

9.7 Geoffrey Chaucer (c. 1340–1400).

tion of Gothic style is a form known as the hall church or Hallenkirche (HAHL-ehn-kersh), in which the aisles and the nave are the same height, unlike the more traditional Gothic style, in which the nave is high and the aisles lower in order to allow for clerestory windows in the nave. The *Hallenkirche* approach is, in reality, similar to Romanesque. The large hall choir added to the church of St Sebald in Nuremberg (Fig. **9.8**) is a typical example. Here graceful bundles of columns rise toward pointed arches, flaring outward at the last second into a series of ribs. Space is light and airy, with tall lancet windows adding delicacy to the feeling of openness that results from the slender columns and seemingly unimpeded space. The tone of the design is simple. Nothing interrupts the eye as it travels up the unadorned vertical line to narrow vaults that belie the unencumbered expanse below.

In Italy we find another variation on the Gothic theme in the Florence Cathedral or *Duomo* (Fig. **9.9**). Although the architect's primary concern was an impressive interior, our view of this church tends to focus on the impressive dome (see Fig. **10.7**), which was added later by the Renaissance architect Brunelleschi (broo-nel-LES-kee) in an imitation of classical forms.

As we look at Florence Cathedral from any angle on

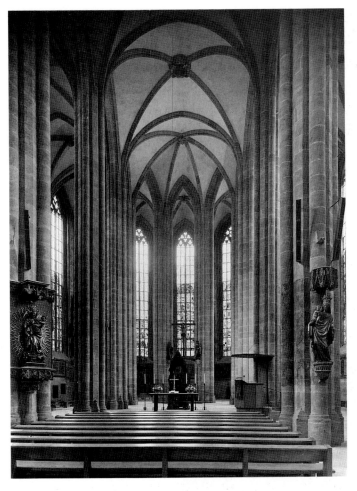

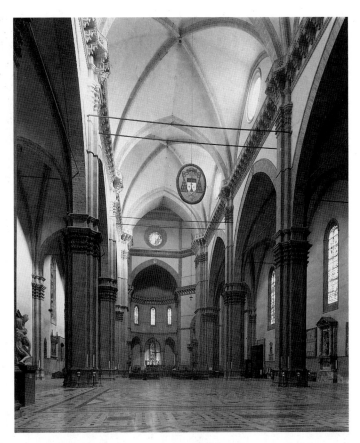

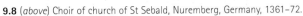

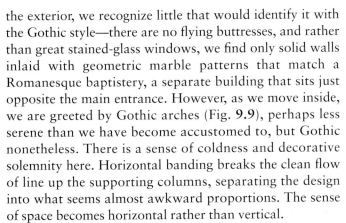

9.8 (*above*) Choir of church of St Sebald, Nuremberg, Germany, 1361–72.

9.9 (*above right*) Nave and choir, Florence Cathedral, Italy, begun 1296.

9.10 (*right*) Apse of Milan Cathedral, Italy, begun 1386.

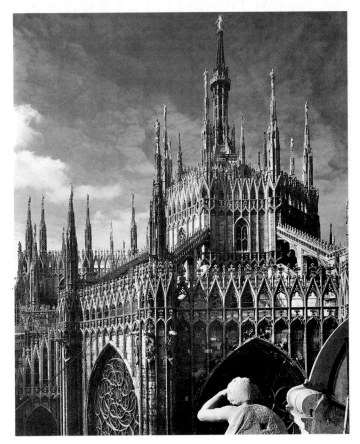

the exterior, we recognize little that would identify it with the Gothic style—there are no flying buttresses, and rather than great stained-glass windows, we find only solid walls inlaid with geometric marble patterns that match a Romanesque baptistery, a separate building that sits just opposite the main entrance. However, as we move inside, we are greeted by Gothic arches (Fig. **9.9**), perhaps less serene than we have become accustomed to, but Gothic nonetheless. There is a sense of coldness and decorative solemnity here. Horizontal banding breaks the clean flow of line up the supporting columns, separating the design into what seems almost awkward proportions. The sense of space becomes horizontal rather than vertical.

On the other hand, Milan Cathedral (Fig. **9.10**), the largest of Italy's Gothic churches, is, with its delicate traceries, pure late Gothic. Although it was begun in 1386, it

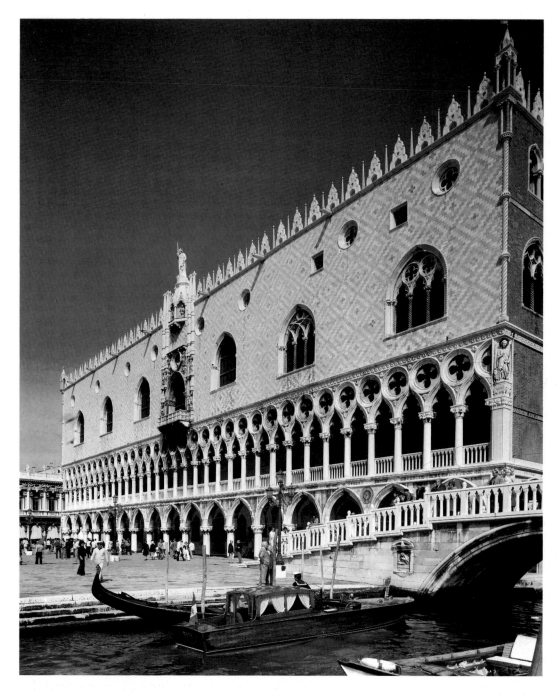

9.11 The Doge's Palace, Venice, Italy, c. 1345–1438.

was completed only in 1910. Its flamboyance lends the façade a lightness that the somewhat horizontal sprawl of the building would not otherwise achieve. Needlelike spires reach above the roof line to lift the spirit from earth into the mystery of space.

Gothic style was also used in secular buildings, and we capture glimpses of this late application, typical of the spirit of the age, in Venice, where a unique version of the style developed in the fourteenth century and was used in particular for nonreligious buildings. One of the most delightful examples is the Doge's (dohzh) Palace (Fig. **9.11**), which represents a direction in architecture devel-

oped specifically for the palaces of the rich and powerful merchant class. Begun in the 1340s, the palace was designed to serve as a large meeting hall for the *Maggior Consiglio*, the elective assembly of the Republic of Venice. Remarkable for this period is the building's sense of openness and tranquility, and the absence of features for fortification reflects the relative peace that the republic enjoyed at the time. The solidity of the upper stories above the open colonnades gives an almost top-heavy appearance, and the rather squat proportions of the lower arcade detract from the delicacy of the overall design. Eastern influences join gracefully with Gothic arches in the patterned brickwork.

The result illustrates a particularly Venetian inventiveness seen often in the city, as European and Moorish influences intermix.

Late Gothic Sculpture

In general, we may say that Gothic sculpture took the traditional themes of Christian art and gave them emotional appeal, and toward the end of the thirteenth century, that tendency was applied to objects designed to enhance private worship. This type of object is often called *Andachtsbild* (AHN-dahkts-bihlt), because Germany played a leading role in its development, and it was best exemplified by the PIETÀ, which derives from the Latin word *pietas*, meaning both "pity" and "piety"; its main visual representation was a grieving Virgin Mary holding the dead Christ in her arms. The pietà offers a symmetrical balance to the Madonna and Child depictions that were always popular, although nothing in scripture suggests that the Virgin Mary ever held the body of the crucified Christ in her arms. This tragic scene—full of deep emotion—is a complete invention of the time. The emotion typical of this genre of sculpture stands out poignantly in a German pietà

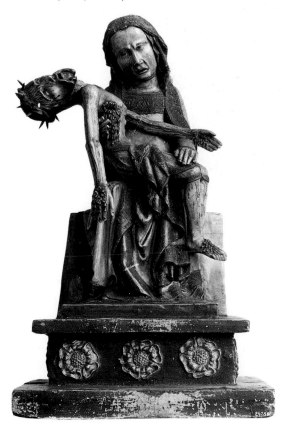

9.12 *Pietà*, early fourteenth century. Wood, 34¹/₂ ins (87.5 cm) high. Provinzialmuseum, Bonn, Germany.

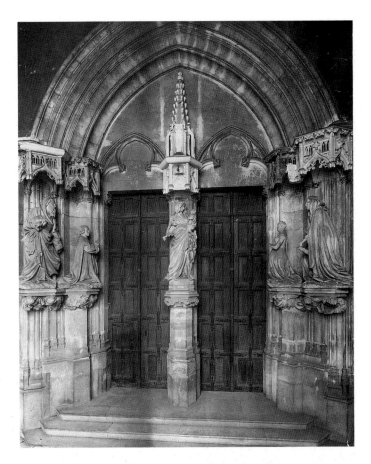

9.13 Claus Sluter, portal of the Chartreuse de Champol, Dijon, France, 1385–93. Stone.

from the early fourteenth century (Fig. **9.12**). In a move away from the emerging naturalism we have seen previously, this work subordinates lifelikeness to powerful emotion, which is achieved through stylization and exaggeration. The forms of Mary and Jesus look remarkably like puppets, and Christ's wounds are exaggerated to grotesque proportion for emotional effect. The work clearly asks the viewer to identify with the horror and grief felt by the Mother of God.

In the north of Europe, reaching a climax around the year 1400, the *International style* found its greatest exponent in the Flemish sculptor Claus Sluter (SLOO-tur; c. 1350–1405), who worked for the duke of Burgundy in Dijon. Sluter's work, as evidenced by the portal of the Chartreuse de Champol at Dijon (Fig. **9.13**) commands the space, seeming to be affixed to the portal rather than growing from it as did earlier medieval sculptures such as those at Chartres (see Figs. **8.27** and **8.29**). The figures are large, bold, and nearly full-round. The dynamic quality of the work is intensified by the fact that the figures of Duke Philip the Bold and his wife, who are accompanied by their patron saints, turn inward to direct attention to the central

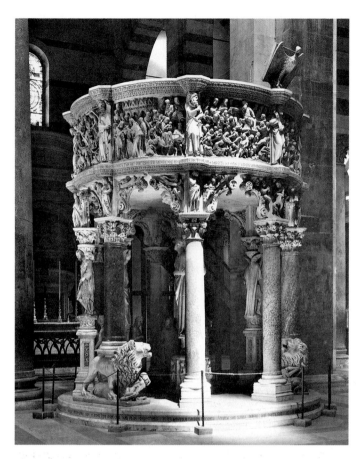

9.14 Giovanni Pisano, pulpit, 1302–10. Marble. Pisa Cathedral, Italy.

figure of the Madonna. Thus, rather than a series of separate jamb statues, like those at Chartres, this grouping forms a single statement—it is a single work composed to highlight a central focal area.

In sculpture as in architecture, Italy stood apart from the Gothic style found in the rest of Europe. Although the Gothic emotionalism we have previously noted is present, the figures of Italian Gothic sculpture have a more classical sense than their northern counterparts. Figures have a roundness that has been tied not only to classicism but also to Byzantium. We can see this tendency in the work of Giovanni Pisano (c. 1250–c. 1320), the son of the famous Tuscan sculptor, Nicola Pisano (pee-ZAHN-oh; c. 1225–c. 1284) whose works reflect the same tendencies. On visits to the Cathedral at Pisa, care must be taken to note which Pisano's works one is viewing. Nicola carved a pulpit in the Baptistery; his son, a pulpit in the cathedral proper, and it is this work that draws our attention here (Fig. **9.14**). Done in marble, Giovanni's figures reflect delicacy and a flowing line. The young Pisano's work reflects the elegance found earlier in Gothic sculpture in Paris. Giovanni's figures have great depth in their dimensionality, in which space becomes as important as the forms themselves (see Fig. **9.1**).

Painting

Italy

The end of the thirteenth century produced an outburst of creative activity in Italy destined profoundly to influence future painting. When the Fourth Crusade sacked Constantinople in 1204, it reinvigorated Byzantine influence in Italian painting that had stayed alive throughout the medieval period, although never straying further north. The "neo-Byzantine" style, or "Greek manner," prevailed in Italy throughout the thirteenth century, and when the Gothic style of northern Europe mixed with the "Greek manner," it produced a revolutionary approach exemplified by Giotto, as we shall see momentarily.

9.15 Cimabue, *Madonna Enthroned*, c. 1280–90. Tempera on wood, about. 12 ft 7¹⁄₂ ins × 7 ft 4 ins (3.84 × 2.24 cm). Uffizi Gallery, Florence, Italy.

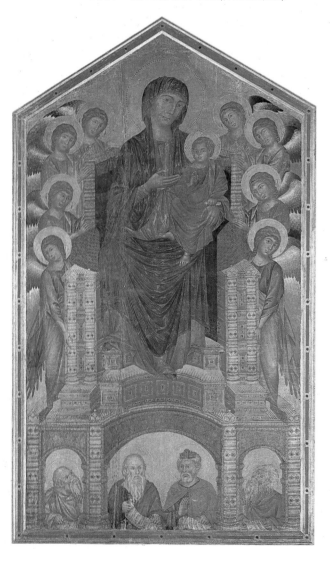

Cimabue

Among the artists of the Greek manner, one of the most famous was Cimabue (chee-mah-BOO-ay), who may have been Giotto's teacher. Cimabue (c. 1250–c. 1302) created very large tempera panels. Tempera is a painting medium in which egg yolk acts as a binder for the pigment, and it was usually applied to panels that had been prepared with a coating of gesso, a smooth mixture of ground chalk or plaster and glue. An application of gold leaf and an under-painting in green or brown preceded the application of the tempera paint. Cimabue's panels were larger than anything that had been attempted in the East, and they further differed from Byzantine works in the severity of their design and expression. The very form of *Madonna Enthroned* (Fig. **9.15**) embodies an upward-striving monumentality, and the gabled shape is quite unlike anything done in Byzantium. Designed for the high altar of the church of Santa Trinità, the work rises over 12 feet (3.7 meters) in height. Its *hierarchical* design places the Virgin Mary at the very top center, surrounded by angels, with the Christ Child supported on her lap. Below her elaborate throne, four half-length prophets display their scrolls.

The verticality of the composition is reinforced by rows of inlaid wood in the throne and by ranks of angels rising, one behind the other, on either side. The figures in the top rank bend inward to reinforce both the painting's exterior form and the focus on the Virgin's face. The delicate folds of the blue mantle and dark red robe, which are highlighted with gold, encircle the upper torso, drawing attention to the Madonna's face and to the Child. In a convention appropriate to the theology of the time, the Christ Child is depicted as a wise and omniscient presence, with a patriarchal face older than his infant years. The clean precision of the execution gives the work a fineness and lightness that recall the exquisiteness of Byzantine mosaics.

Duccio

A quarter century later, the Italian artist Duccio (c. 1255–c. 1319) portrayed the same subject matter in a similar scheme but with significant differences (Fig. **9.16**). Duccio (DOOT-choh) softens the frozen, Byzantine linearity of Cimabue—his roundness of form and treatment of fabric reflecting Roman characteristics—and gives it a Gothic three-dimensionality. The tender emotion exchanged between mother and child stands in contrast with Cimabue's formal, outward stares of the principal figures. The Sienese called this painting the *maestà* or "majesty," thus identifying the Virgin's role as Queen of Heaven. Unlike Cimabue's vertical composition, Duccio's work flows outward in a horizontal format, increasing the size of the celestial court and adding small compartments with scenes from the lives of Christ and the Madonna. The composition itself reflects a new treatment of space, giving

9.16 Duccio, *Madonna Enthroned*, center of the *maestà* altar, 1308–11. Tempera on panel, 6 ft 10½ ins (2.1 m) high. Museo dell' Opera del Duomo, Siena, Italy.

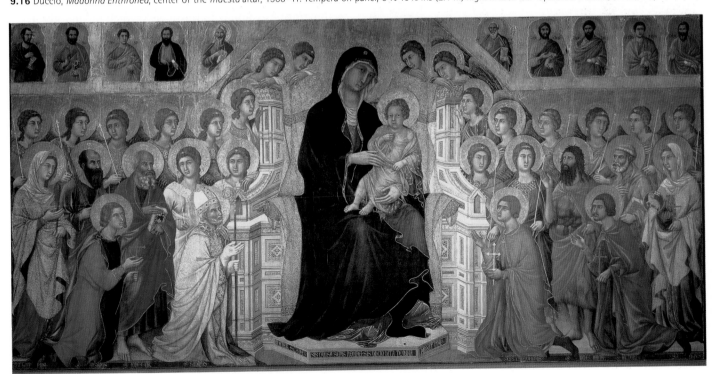

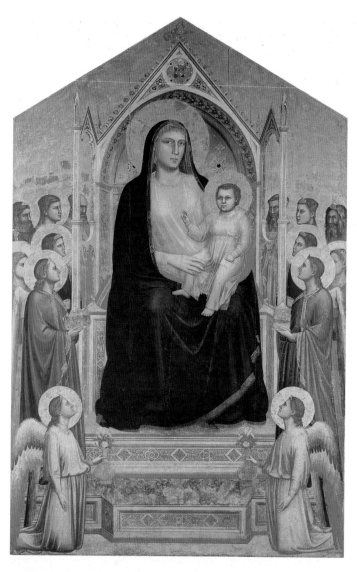

9.17 Giotto, *Madonna Enthroned*, c. 1310. Tempera on panel, 10 ft 8 ins × 6 ft 8 ins (3.3 × 2 m). Uffizi Gallery, Florence, Italy.

us the sense that the figures are enveloped by space rather than sitting on the front edge of a two-dimensional plane.

Giotto

Despite the advances of Cimabue and Duccio, it remained for Giotto (c. 1266–1336/7) to take far bolder and more dramatic steps. Perhaps less close to the Greek manner than his predecessors, Giotto (JAH-toe) undertook wall painting on a monumental scale. He also painted in tempera on panel. Giotto's treatment of the same subject as Duccio and Cimabue—that is, *Madonna Enthroned* (Fig. 9.17)—gives us another means by which we can learn to

identify the subtleties of style that differentiate one artistic vision from another. In the first place, we find in Giotto's treatment a greater simplification of the subject matter and supporting details. The central focus is even more human, warm, and three-dimensional than in the two earlier works, and it has a sense of drama, heightened by the fact that Giotto's viewpoint is lower than Duccio's or Cimabue's—that is, the viewpoint of the observer relative to the space in the painting. Giotto innovates by defining the actual confines of the painting more by the figures than by the architectural details, and although such a perspective tends to lessen depth of space, it nevertheless gives a more dynamic quality to it. The figures come to life for the viewer, as Giotto's genius gives painting a previously unknown liveliness and brings painting to a par with sculpture.

Giotto did not attempt merely to transfer Gothic sculpture into paint. Rather, by creating what amounted to an entirely new treatment of space, he gave the surface of the painting a new appearance. In the past, composition tended to lead the eye from one specific detail to another. Giotto, on the other hand, takes our eye and allows us to grasp the entire work at one time, and the composition has an inner unity achieved by strong, simple groupings of figures. The throne, based on Italian Gothic architecture, encloses the Madonna and cuts her off from the background. In another innovation, Giotto takes great pains to create a fake texture in the colored marble surfaces. The creation of false textures had not been used in painting since early Christian times, and Giotto's reintroduction of this approach attests to his familiarity with ancient Roman wall paintings, similar to those we studied in Chapter 4.

Pietro Lorenzetti

One of those who followed Giotto and succeeded in creating his own revolutionary approach to space was Pietro Lorenzetti (pee-AY-troh loh-rehn-ZEHT-ee; d. 1348?). *The Birth of the Virgin* (Fig. **9.19**) is a bold attempt to solve the problems of space and to create a unified and flowing compositional picture. In contrast to Giotto's sculptural space, we find a new sense of architectural picture space. The figures are lifelike, and highlight and shadow flesh out their faces and garments, with the treatment of draping fabric in the gowns in the right panel showing precise attention to detail. We have a sense of looking in on a scene in progress, rather than at a flat, frozen rendering. The scene has a relaxed atmosphere, and the eye is drawn across the work in a lyrical sweep. The groups of figures are spaced comfortably, and the whole picture, which continues behind the columns separating the panels, spreads throughout the triptych—that is, a devotional picture with a central panel and two flanking hinged wings.

MASTERWORK

Giotto—*The Lamentation*

A new sense of space, three-dimensionality, and mobility are clear in Giotto's masterpiece *The Lamentation* (Fig. **9.18**). The figures are skillfully grouped in a simple, coherent scene. Giotto's fabrics retain a decorative quality from an earlier time, but they also show an increased realism. Although the figures are crowded, they still seem free to move within the space. For all its emotion and intensity, the fresco remains human, individualized, and controlled. What makes the fresco so compelling is Giotto's unique mastery of three-dimensional space. He employs AERIAL PERSPECTIVE—that is, the use of haze and indistinction to create a sense of distance—for the background, but unlike other painters, who created deep space behind the primary focal plane, Giotto brings the horizon to our eyelevel. As a result, we can move into a three-dimensional space that also moves out to us.

In summary, Giotto was a radical innovator whose dramatic departures made him among the giants of visual art and overshadowed those who followed immediately in his footsteps.

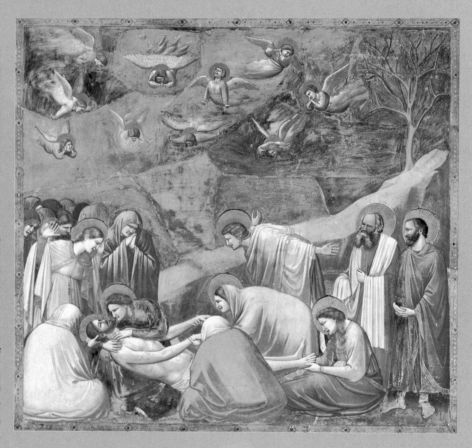

9.18 Giotto, *The Lamentation*, 1305–6. Fresco, 7 ft 7 ins × 7 ft 9 ins (2.31 × 2.36 m). Arena Chapel, Padua, Italy.

Pucelle

In the later years of the period, French and Italian manuscript illuminators also experimented with three-dimensional space. The work of Jean Pucelle (zhahn poo-SEHL; 1300?–1355?) graphically demonstrates this change in the *Book of Hours of Jeanne d'Evreux* (Fig. 9.20) through his treatment of space and architectural framework. However, Pucelle's treatment of picture space must accommodate the confines of a manuscript rather than a panel, and as a result, the Virgin floats on the page without a background.

MUSIC

Ars Nova

The fourteenth century witnessed a distinct change in musical style. This new style was called *ars nova* or "new art," from the title of a book by Philippe de Vitry (1291–1361). Music of the *ars nova* was more diverse than past music in its harmonies and rhythms. By the early fourteenth century, a new system of musical notation had

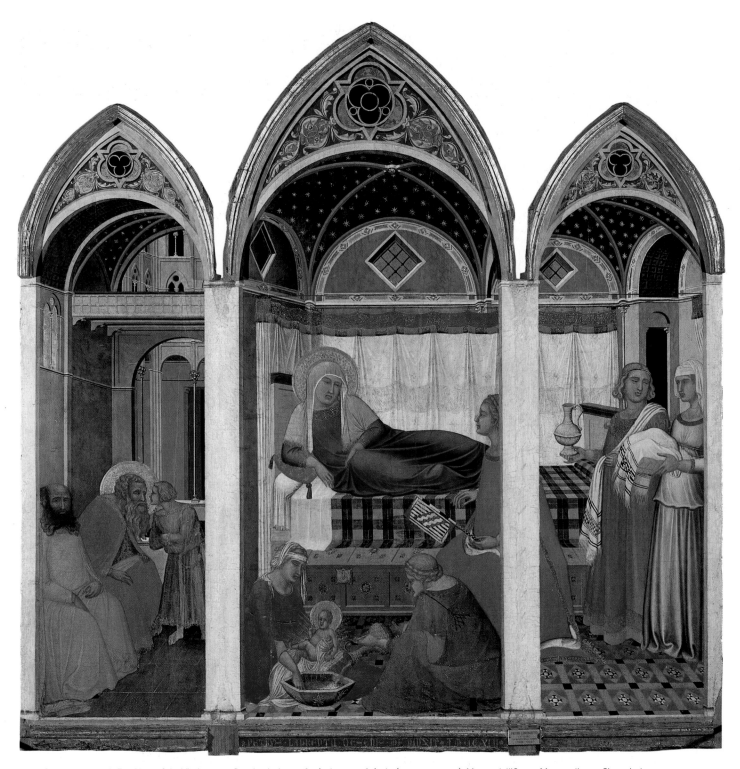

9.19 Pietro Lorenzetti, *The Birth of the Virgin*, 1342. Panel painting, 6 ft 1¹/₂ ins × 6 ft ¹/₂ in (1.87 × 1.84 m). Museo dell'Opera Metropolitana, Siena, Italy.

emerged that allowed a composer to specify nearly any rhythmic pattern. Beats could be subdivided into two as well as three, and SYNCOPATION took on an important role.

Ars nova was primarily a secular movement. The characteristics of its rhythmic vibrancy did not meet the

Church's expectations for worship, and early in the century, the Church forbade any musical elaboration of the Mass that might alter the character of the chant, and this had the effect of stifling polyphonic development in sacred music.

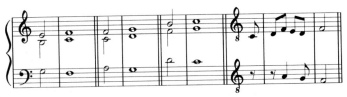

9.21 Examples of cadences.

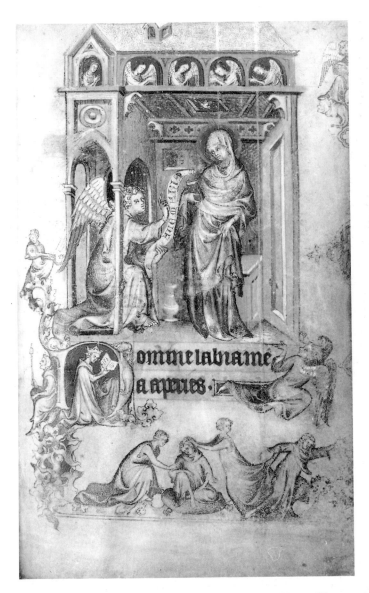

9.20 Jean Pucelle, *The Annunciation*, from the *Book of Hours of Jeanne d'Evreux*, 1325–8. Grisaille and color on vellum, 3¹/₂ × 2⁷/₁₆ ins (8.9 × 6.2 cm). Metropolitan Museum of Art, New York, (Cloisters Collection, 1954).

Guillaume de Machaut

Nonetheless, the first great exponent of *ars nova* was the French composer Guillaume de Machaut (gee-YOHM-duh mah-SHOH; 1300–77); priest, poet, and composer, who served King John of Bohemia. Machaut's music in the new style had a smoothness and sweetness, and made increasing use of polyphony. He also used a new structural form that gave his compositions unity of style. One of the features Machaut used to achieve unity was *isorhythm*, in which phrases are repeated in their rhythm, but not necessarily in their melody. He also used short fragments of melody to create unity. This technique provided the structural underpinnings for his *Notre Dame* Mass for four voices, written c. 1364. It is the first complete polyphonic setting of the Mass ordinary by a known composer.

In addition, because his music had a fundamental smoothness and consonance, Machaut was able to use dissonance as an emotional effect. For example, as the words of the Mass describe the crucifixion, the composer underscores them with discordant notes, thereby creating not only beauty but emotional expressiveness.

Machaut also wrote secular poems, often with music. His characteristic texture was that of a solo voice with two instrumental parts forming an accompaniment. Each of his phrases comes to a definite end, called a *cadence*. Some of these are simple, and some are quite ornamental, as an example from one of his *virelais* illustrates (Fig. **9.21**).

Machaut was an inventive craftsman and the sound of the music mattered as much to him as its structure. His watchwords were beauty and feeling, and he once indicated that words and music without true feeling were merely false.

Francesco Landini

The most celebrated Italian composer of the fourteenth century was Francesco Landini (lan-DEE-nee; d. 1397). Blind from childhood, he was a famous organist, poet, and scholar. Landini illustrates the new secular impetus of the time. His compositions are exclusively Italian songs for two or three voices that deal with subjects as diverse as nature, love, morality, and politics. His composition *Ecco la primavera* (Spring has Come) is a *ballata*, an Italian poetic and musical form that originated as a dance-song. The text speaks of the joys of springtime, and its lively rhythms result from the use of syncopation.

THEATRE

The characteristics of theatre we noted in the last chapter continued throughout the late medieval period. Theatre is often a static art, far more resistant to change than the other arts, which tend to evolve around the vision of a single artist. Theatre, more a group expression, gets caught in its own inertia, and that, certainly, was the case in the late Middle Ages. However, one of the most enduring

OUR DYNAMIC WORLD

Noh Theatre of Japan

Japanese Noh drama came of age in the four-teenth century. Buddhist monks used it as a teaching tool in much the same way as the Christian Church used medieval miracle, mystery, and morality plays. Slowly it became more and more secularized.

Noh drama is performed on a simple, almost bare stage and, like classical Greek tragedy (see Chapter 3), uses only two actors. Also, as in classical Greek drama, actors wear elaborate masks and costumes, men play women's roles (Fig. **9.22**), and a chorus functions as a narrator. Actors chant the highly poetic dialogue to orchestral, musical accompaniment. All the actions suggest rather than depict, which gives the drama its sense of stylization and conventionality, and symbolism and restraint characterize both acting and staging.

The tone of the plays tends to be serious. The plays are usually short, and an evening's performance encompasses several plays interspersed with comic burlesques called *Kyogen* ("crazy words").

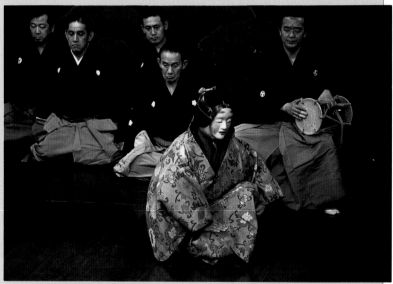

9.22 Performance at the Noh Theatre of the Kongo School, Kyoto.

plays, which is still performed and enjoyed in modern times, came out of this era. No one knows for certain when it originated, because it circulated through the oral tradition before it was finally put into print. Nonetheless, the most famous play of this era—indeed, of the entire Middle Ages—is *Everyman*, an anonymous morality play.

Death summons Everyman to his final judgment. Everyman then seeks, as companions on his journey to judgment, the qualities (characters) of Fellowship, Kindred, Cousin, and Goods. Each refuses to join him. He finally asks Good Deeds, but Good Deeds is too weak from neglect to make the journey. Seeking advice from Knowledge, Everyman is told to do penance—an act that revives Good Deeds, who then takes up the journey with Everyman. Along the way, Five Wits also deserts him as he nears the grave. Good Deeds, however, stays with him until the end, and so is welcomed to Heaven.

DANCE

Dance was part of medieval religious and secular activity, but with the exception of pantomime, examples of which

have perished, theatre dance was less important than forms of group dancing. Fascinating illustrations survive of the "ring dance," for example, in which twelve dancers representing the apostles and the zodiac danced in a circle. Amid the ravages of the plague, the *danse macabre* (dahns mah-CAHB), or dance of death, appeared. Whipped by hysteria, people danced in a frenzy until some dropped dead of exhaustion. *Choreomania*, an English version of the *danse macabre*, seems to have expressed a kind of group psychosis in the throes of which the participants engaged in all kinds of demented behavior, including self-flagellation. Numerous folk and court dances also existed.

Within the courtly tradition, theatre dance was reborn. Dances done at court were performed to instrumental accompaniment. A certain degree of expressiveness and spontaneity marked these court dances, but increasingly they conformed to specific rules. Dance that was performed in the course of court theatricals employed professional entertainers. These performances depended to a large degree upon the guiding hand of the dancing master, who was perhaps more like a square-dance caller than a ballet master or choreographer.

Focal Point

Women Mystics of the Late Middle Ages

Despite a growing secularization in society, the mysticism of the earlier Middle Ages remained very much alive, as Joan of Arc demonstrated, and we can see it clearly in the lives and works of four women.

Marguerite Porète (d. 1306) wrote *Le Miroir des simples âmes* (*Mirror of Simple Souls*) sometime between 1296 and 1306. Her verse and commentary form a dialogue between Love, Reason, and the Soul and suggest that the individual moves through seven stages of spiritual growth as it progresses toward union with God. Porète argues that in the last stage the soul need not concern itself with masses, penance, sermons, fasts, or prayer. Her book was condemned in 1306 and was burned in her presence.

Two years later, she was accused of continuing to make copies of her book available to others. She was imprisoned in Paris, tried for heresy, and burned at the stake.

The Mirror of Simple Souls is sprawling and episodic, changing quickly from narrative to dialogue. The main speakers, personifications of "Love," "Reason," and "the Soul," discuss sublime matters as one might hear lively discussions on the street: "Oh, for god's sake, love, what are you saying?"; "Reason, you'll always be half-blind"; "Oh, you sheep, how crude is your understanding!"

The Mirror of Simple Souls (excerpt)

Introduction:

You who would read this book,
if you indeed wish to grasp it,
think about what you say,
for it is very difficult to comprehend;
humility, who is keeper of the treasury of
    knowledge
and the mother of the other Virtues,
Must overtake you.

Theologians and other clerks,
you will not have the intellect for it,
no matter how brilliant your abilities,
if you do not proceed humbly
and make Love and Faith, together,
cause you to rise above Reason
[since] they are the ladies of the house.

...

Humble, then your wisdom
which is based on Reason,
and place all your fidelity
in those things which are given
by Love, illuminated through Faith.
And thus you will understand this book
which makes the Soul live by love.

Margery Kempe (c. 1373–c. 1440) was one of the Middle Ages' most profound mystics and visionaries. Born in Bishop's Lynn, in Norfolk, England, she saw herself as a saint who claimed to be on terms with God. Her writings, however, indicate that she had normal conversations with her neighbors and friends.

She was a pilgrim and made numerous trips abroad. Although she was illiterate and did not keep any notes or diaries until the end of her life, she possessed an incredible memory, but sometimes she would mistake the sequence of certain events. Her writings contain valuable insights into the details of everyday life in medieval Europe.

The England Margery knew was economically and politically corrupt. The aristocracy lived in incredible luxury while the remainder of English society dwelt amid filth and rubbish. The plague was endemic, and everyone, including the wealthy, suffered the ills of lice, fleas, mites, bedbugs, internal parasites, and rats.

Margery lived during the period of Chaucer and Froissart, but there is no evidence she had even heard of them. When she was about twenty, she married the burgess of Lynn, John Kempe, also in his twenties. John Kempe was the son of a successful merchant and public official. He was also said to be very charming and affectionate. She bore him fourteen children.

Margery was a pilgrim who made numerous contacts with notable people throughout Europe. People began to hear about her visions and ideologies. She had even been accused of heresy, but her powerful friends backed her during heresy trials. As time passed, Margery was continually harassed as a heretic. She and her husband spent much time moving around and enduring one heresy trial after another. This all changed during the Great Fire of Lynn in 1421. The town was threatened with total destruction.

Priests and other religious figures said that if Margery was indeed under the care of God, then she could save Lynn. Three days later a blizzard came, putting the fire out. She was no longer persecuted after this miracle.

In 1431, Margery followed the news of the trial of Joan of Arc, and only the illness of her husband kept her from going to Joan's aid.

Catherine of Siena (1347–80; Fig. **9.23**) was an Italian Dominican, mystic and diplomat, Doctor of the Church. In response to a vision she entered public life and in 1376 influenced Pope Gregory XI to end the Babylonian Captivity of the papacy (see p. 271) and return to Rome. She was later papal ambassador to Florence. Catherine caused a spiritual revival almost everywhere she went, and her mysticism contains an overwhelming love of God and humanity. *The Dialogue* is a remarkable mystical work.

The Dialogue of the Seraphic Virgin Catherine of Siena

Dictated by her, while in a state of ecstasy,
to her secretaries, and completed
in the year of our lord 1370

Translated by Algar Thorold and modernized by
Harry Plantinga

A Treatise of Prayer
Of the means which the soul takes to arrive at pure and generous love; and here begins the Treatise of Prayer. "When the soul has passed through the doctrine of Christ crucified, with true love of virtue and hatred of vice, and has arrived at the house of self-knowledge and entered therein, she remains, with her door barred, in watching and constant prayer, separated entirely from the consolations of the world. Why does she thus shut herself in? She does so from fear, knowing her own imperfections, and also from the desire, which she has, of arriving at pure and generous love. And because she sees and knows well that in no other way can she arrive thereat, she waits, with a lively faith for my arrival, through increase of grace in her. How is a lively faith to be recognized? By perseverance in virtue, and by the fact that the soul never turns back for anything, whatever it be, nor rises from holy prayer, for any reason except (note well) for obedience or charity's sake. For no other reason ought she to leave off prayer, for, during the time ordained for prayer, the Devil is wont to arrive in the soul, causing much more conflict and trouble than when the soul is not occupied in prayer. This he does in order that holy prayer may become tedious to the soul, tempting her often with these words: 'This prayer avails you nothing, for you need attend to nothing except your vocal prayers.' He acts thus in order that, becoming wearied and confused in mind, she may abandon the exercise of prayer, which is a weapon with which the soul can defend herself from every adversary, if grasped with the hand of love, by the arm of free choice in the light of the Holy Faith."

Julian of Norwich (1342–1416) was a celebrated

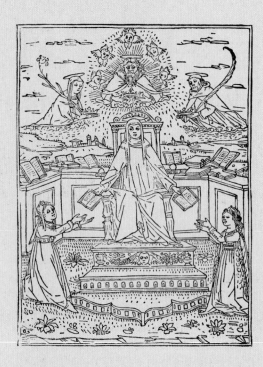

9.23 St Catherine of Siena (1347–80).

mystic, whose *Revelations of Divine Love* provide one of the most remarkable insights into the medieval religious experience. According to her report, on 13 May 1373, she was healed of a serious illness after experiencing a series of visions of Christ's suffering and of the Blessed Virgin, about which she wrote two accounts; the second version was composed twenty or thirty years after the first. *The Revelations* treats some of the most profound mysteries of Christianity: predestination, foreknowledge of God, and the existence of evil. Clear and deep in its perception, the work possesses beautiful sincerity and expression.

Revelations of Divine Love

Recorded by Julian, anchoress at Norwich
Anno Domini 1371

In lumine tuo videbimus lumen.

First Revelation—Of His precious crowning with thorns; and therewith was comprehended and specified the Trinity, with the Incarnation, and unity betwixt God and man's soul; with many fair shewings of endless wisdom and teachings of love: in which all the Shewings that follow be grounded and oned.

Second Revelation—The changing of colour of His fair face in token of His dear worthy Passion.

Third Revelation—That our Lord God, Almighty Wisdom, All-Love, right as verily as He hath made everything that is, all-so verily He doeth and worketh all-thing that is done.

Fourth Revelation—The scourging of His tender body, with plenteous shedding of His blood.

Fifth Revelation—That the Fiend is overcome by the precious Passion of Christ.

Sixth Revelation—The worshipful thanking by our Lord God in which He rewardeth His blessed servants in Heaven.

Seventh Revelation—[Our] often feeling of weal and woe; with ghostly understanding that we are kept all as securely in Love in woe as in weal, by the Goodness of God.

Eighth Revelation—Of the last pains of Christ, and His cruel dying.

Ninth Revelation—Of the pleasing which is in the Blissful Trinity by the hard Passion of Christ and His rueful dying: in which joy and pleasing He willeth that we be solaced and mirthed with Him, till when we come to the fulness in Heaven.

Tenth Revelation—Our Lord Jesus sheweth in love His blissful heart even cloven in two, rejoicing.[1]

CHAPTER REVIEW

Critical Thought

The struggle between Church and State that occurred in the late Middle Ages broke the hold of the Roman Catholic Church on the general social order and created an increasingly secular society. At the same time, war, disease, and economics changed the basic conditions of human life. Society in Europe moved into a new era, with national interests rising. Several interesting personalities emerged, and feudalism and Church authority took a back seat to emerging secular monarchs who ruled large, nationally homogeneous populations that were beginning to approximate what we recognize today as "countries." All this occurred while nearly half the population of Europe and England succumbed to the plague.

However bleak it may have been, life under the monolithic control of feudal lords and a central Church must have been fairly simple and straightforward. As society changed during the late Middle Ages, things got more complicated, and, as if to mirror the life around it, art reflected that increased complication with an emerging ornateness and emotionalism. The theme of increased complication permeated painting, sculpture, architecture, literature, theatre, and dance. All the while, humankind kept its good humor—perhaps the best solution of all to all the affairs of life.

Summary

After reading this chapter, you should be able to:

- Explain how theatre, dance, and painting reflected their social and religious contexts.
- Characterize late Gothic sculpture and architecture including specific characteristics such as *Andachtsbild*.
- Describe *ars nova* and its principal exponent.
- Identify the major writers of the time and their works, including general characteristics and themes.
- Discuss the effects of the plague and the Hundred Years' War, the rise of secular monarchies, and the Great Schism on European society, commerce, and religion.
- Apply the elements and principles of composition to analyze and compare individual works of art illustrated in this chapter.

CHAPTER TEN

The Early Renaissance

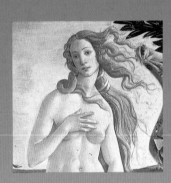

OUTLINE

THE RENAISSANCE

THE RENAISSANCE VIEWPOINT
Antiquity Revisited and Measured
   Humanism
   PROFILE: Niccolò Machiavelli
Capitalism
Discovery
The Papal States
Italian City-States
   TECHNOLOGY: Flywheels and
      Connecting Rods

**THE BEGINNINGS OF
RENAISSANCE ARCHITECTURE**
Alberti
Brunelleschi

SCULPTURE
Donatello
Ghiberti

PAINTING
Masaccio
   MASTERWORK: Masaccio—*The
      Tribute Money*
The Heritage of Masaccio
Lyrical Poetry in Painting
   OUR DYNAMIC WORLD: Chinese
      Painting

MUSIC

THEATRE

DANCE

FOCAL POINT: FLORENCE IN THE
QUATTROCENTO

VIEW

THE BEST OF TIMES?

The people of the Renaissance saw themselves as witnessing the rebirth of what was the best of culture—the classical—after a long darkness that they labeled the "Middle Ages." Humans like to think highly of themselves and their ideas, and they like to classify other humans by fitting them into generalized, neat little boxes.

A common human tendency that ties us to our ancient predecessors is the tendency of the elderly to look back to "the good old days," to bemoan the disrespect shown by youth, and to see the circumstances of youth as the forerunners of doom and disaster. Equally commonly, youth tend to see the values and activities of their elders as stuffy, old-fashioned, and hopelessly ridiculous. Undoubtedly, no age has been the "best of times," as some maintain, nor has any age been the "worst of all worlds" that others bemoan. Perhaps it is healthy to believe that the world has "progressed" beyond the previous generation. What is not healthy is for one generation to discount the value of another and to fail to learn from it. When we cease to learn, we die.

Above Detail of Fig. **10.25**.

10.1 Andrea Mantegna, detail of the ceiling of the Camera degli Sposi, 1474. Fresco. Ducal Palace, Mantua, Italy.

KEY TERMS

Some of the basic terms and concepts we will encounter in this chapter include the following:

Renaissance, which includes among its many possible meanings, "rebirth."

Capitalism is an economic system pursuing market freedom.

Verisimilitude is lifelikeness or the nearness to truth.

Sottie, a bawdy burlesque type of theatrical performance.

Farce, a type of low comedy characterized by slapstick.

Perspective, the rational portrayal of depth in a work of art either through linear or atmospheric means.

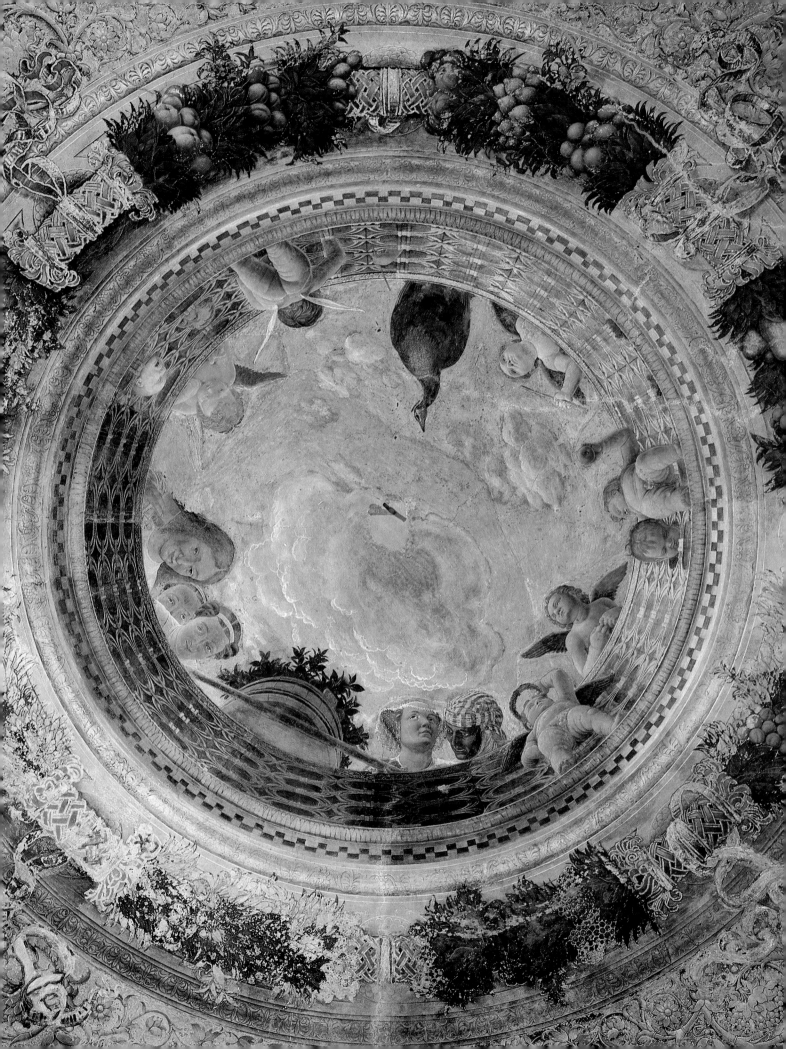

THE RENAISSANCE

The Renaissance was explicitly seen by its leaders as a rebirth of our understanding of ourselves as social and creative beings. "Out of the sick Gothic night our eyes are opened to the glorious touch of the sun," was how the writer Rabelais (RAB-uh-lay) expressed what most of his educated contemporaries felt. Florence, the crucible of the Renaissance in Italy, was called the "New Athens," and it was here that the fine arts, or "liberal arts," were first redefined as art, in contrast to their status as crafts in the Middle Ages. Now accepted among the intellectual disciplines, the arts became an essential part of learning and literary culture. Artists, architects, composers, and writers gained confidence from their new status and from the technical mastery they were achieving. For the first time, it seemed possible not merely to imitate the works of the classical world, but to surpass them.

Definitions of the Renaissance have been debated for centuries. The word certainly describes a new sense of self and self-awareness felt by western European people, who had come to see themselves as no longer part of the "Middle Ages." But deciding where and how the Renaissance began, and what specifically it was, is as difficult as answering the question of where and how it ended—if it ended at all.

In the middle of the nineteenth century, a Swiss historian, Jacob Burckhardt, began what is formally known as Renaissance studies. He maintained—thus agreeing with fifteenth-century Italians—that an actual rebirth of ideas began in the 1400s after centuries of stagnation, and asserted that in Italy during the fourteenth century, there was a new spirit of inquiry and understanding in which the classical world of Greece and Rome again became the inspiration for a superior civilization.

However, many scholars in the mid-twentieth century felt that Burckhardt's viewpoint was over-simplistic, and that the period was nothing more than a natural extension of the previous times—that is, the clear break identified by Burckhardt had not occurred. The apparent change that took place in the fifteenth century was more of a shift in cultural and educational emphasis than it was a new discovery of the past. In addition, the Renaissance, rather than being a monolithic period, was really three or more periods, each with its own circumstances and—to a large degree—its own characteristics. That is, we can identify an early Renaissance, particularly that occurring in Florence; a High Renaissance, specifically in Rome and Venice; and a Renaissance that occurred outside Italy, particularly in the northern European states, and that was highly influenced by—or at least related to—the Protestant Reformation.

In the last thirty years, a third viewpoint has emerged, which attests that the word "Renaissance" is strictly an educational and artistic label and is not particularly applicable to politics and society at large. According to this viewpoint, any label such as "Renaissance" does not do justice to the complex issues and circumstances that arose in such a diverse area as Europe over a period as long as two hundred years.

Whatever the circumstances, we will examine the Renaissance in three chapters: the early Renaissance in this chapter, the High and late Renaissance and Mannerism in Chapter 11, and the Renaissance in the North in Chapter 12.

THE RENAISSANCE VIEWPOINT

Antiquity Revisited and Measured

In the Renaissance, as in other times, attitudes and events are interrelated in complex ways, and if certain aspects of society—for example, politics, religion, and the arts—are treated separately, as they are in these chapters, it does not mean that they were isolated from each other.

The revived interest in antiquity that is normally associated with the Renaissance was not its first revival. As seen in Chapter 7, Charlemagne had already rekindled an interest in antiquity, and indeed, in some quarters, such an interest had never been extinguished. For example, as we also noted, the German nun Hrosvitha had access to Terence and used his works as models for her plays, and scholars had studied Aristotle in the late Middle Ages. However, fifteenth-century interest in classical antiquity was more intense and widespread than before, and these men and women felt that they had found kindred spirits in the Greeks and Romans. They were, after all, interested in things of this world. The Roman emphasis on civic responsibility and intellectual competence helped revivify the social order, and there was a desire to reinterpret the ancient writings, which many believed had been corrupted in the service of Church dogma.

Aristotle's work offered an appealing balance of active living and sober reflection, and the Greeks of Periclean Athens gave an idealized model of humankind that could, for example, be expressed in painting and sculpture. These ideals of nobility, intellect, and physical perfection led to new conceptions of what constituted beauty. As scholars pursued an understanding of classical art and architecture, they became enamored of measuring things. "True proportions" were revealed when *De Architectura*, by the Roman architect Vitruvius, was rediscovered in 1414 (Fig. **10.2**). Scientific curiosity and concern for detail led to a fascination with anatomy, and scientific investigation led to a new system of mechanical perspective. All this measuring and codifying produced a set of rules of proportion and balance, and unity, form, and perfect proportion were codified as a set of laws, to which Michelangelo, as we shall see in Chapter 11, objected strongly.

Humanism

The roots of humanism can be traced to the slowly developing separation of organized religion and the State in the fourteenth century. Its specific origins can be found in Italy

10.2 Leonardo da Vinci, *Vitruvian Man*, c. 1485–90. Pen and ink, 13$\frac{1}{2}$ × 9$\frac{5}{8}$ ins (34.3 × 24.5 cm). Academy, Venice, Italy.

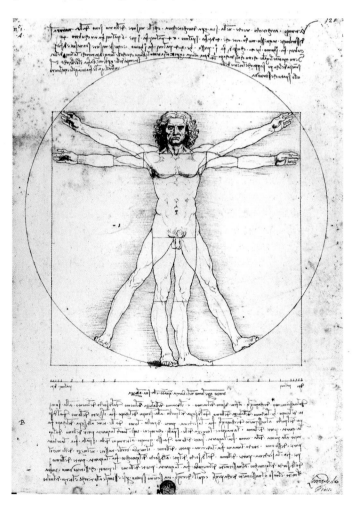

in the writings of Petrarch around 1341. Petrarch is a key figure in the transition from medieval to Renaissance thought, and, as we noted in Chapter 9, his writings are very different from those of Dante. He rejected medieval philosophy and found the science of the time wanting as a way toward a "happy life." Although he had a passion for classical literature and Roman antiquity, he clung to the religious thought of the Middle Ages. He felt guilty about admiring the things learned from pagan philosophers, and he found Dante's connection between the good of this world and that of the next impossible. On the other hand, his real love of learning made him reject the intellectual tradition of the Middle Ages, for which he was given the title Father of Humanism. From Italy, Petrarch's ideas spread throughout the Western world.

Humanism as a philosophy was not, as some have ventured, a denial of God or faith. Rather, it was an attempt to discover humankind's own earthly fulfillment, and was perfectly expressed in the biblical idea: "O Adam, you may have whatever you shall desire." The medieval view of life as a vale of tears, with no purpose other than preparing for salvation and the afterlife, gave way to what was viewed as a more liberating ideal of people playing important roles in this world.

Concern for diversity and individuality had emerged in the late Middle Ages, when expanding horizons and the increasing complexity of life provoked a new debate about human responsibility for a stable moral order and for the management of events. Such a discussion yielded a philosophy consistent with Christian principles, which focused on the dignity and intrinsic value of the individual. Human beings were both good and ultimately perfectible. They were capable of finding worldly fulfillment and intellectual satisfaction. Humanism developed an increasing distaste for dogma, and embraced a figurative interpretation of the scriptures and an attitude of tolerance toward all viewpoints.

When Constantinople fell to the Ottomans in 1453, an influx of Byzantine scholars carrying with them precious manuscripts made Italy a center for the study of Greek literature, language, and philosophy, especially of Platonic and neo-Platonic philosophy. Cosimo de' Medici (MEH-deh-chee) established the Platonic Academy at one of his villas near Florence, and, under the direction of Marsilio Ficino (fee-CHEE-noh; 1433–99), this academy set about the examination of Platonic thought and the reinterpretations of Plato, called neo-Platonism, that earlier had influenced Christian theology. Our understanding of the originality of Italian humanism and the new direction it gave the arts is enhanced by Ficino's commentary on Plato's *Symposium*. It demonstrates the interest in interpeting ancient texts, myths, and stories according to an elaborate allegorizing.

PROFILE

Niccolò Machiavelli (1469–1527)

Italian political philosopher, statesman, poet, playwright, and thinker Niccolò Machiavelli (nee-coh-LOH mah-kee-ah-VAY-lee) earned an undeservedly unsavory reputation because of his insights on political power and human nature. Born into a wealthy and important Florentine family, Machiavelli was taught from an early age "to do without before he learned to enjoy," as he later wrote. Although he did attend the local school, he remained essentially self-taught through reading the books in the family's extensive library.

When he was twenty-nine years old, he held an important public appointment as secretary to the magistracy—that is, the agency that directed foreign affairs and defense. At the time, Europe, especially Italy, was in political turmoil, and during much of the time that Machiavelli spent in public office, Florentine political policy centered on the conquest of Pisa. He therefore spent a great deal of his time traveling to various Italian city-states on diplomatic missions, through which he gained significant firsthand information about military tactics. He came to know the Italian rulers, spending many weeks with the unscrupulous Cesare Borgia (CHAY-zuh-ray BOHR-zhuh), and thus becoming an eyewitness to Borgia's vicious handling of those who stood in his way.

In 1512 the Medici family returned from exile to power in Florence, and Machiavelli lost his public position. He was accused of complicity in an ill-conceived coup attempt and was imprisoned and tortured. On his eventual release, his movements and residence were severely restricted, and so, living in poverty and unhappiness, he retired to a small property he had inherited from his father in San Caciano. Forbidden to enter politics, this genius, who had previously reorganized the Florentine military and introduced conscription, began to write. By 1513 he had completed his most famous and influential work, *The Prince*, and other works followed over a thirteen-year period. In 1526, following another exile of the Medici, Pope Clement VII restored Machiavelli to favor. He died a year later in Florence.

The Prince represents Machiavelli's political theory. Written in the form of advice to a new ruler, it tells how to found a state and to maintain himself in

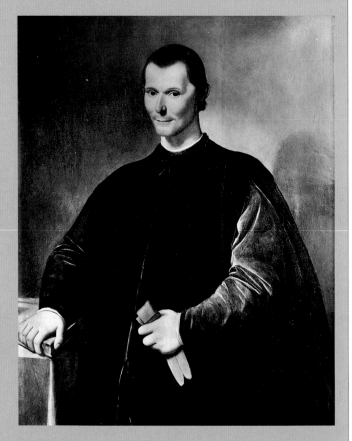

10.3 Niccolò Machiavelli (1469–1527). Painting by Santi di Tito. Palazzo Vecchio, Florence, Italy.

power. The blunt nature of the maxims has given Machiavelli a reputation for immorality but many find in his theories merely a sense of the reality of humans and their political situations. These theories do not deal with life as it should be; rather, within the framework of their objectives, they describe life as Machiavelli saw it. It seems likely that he was not the cold, cynical, and irreligious man he is often accused of being. Above all, his theories seek the good of the public. He dreamed and hoped for the ideal prince who could rescue and restore Italy from the conflagration in which the times and the people of those times had embroiled it. The prince to whom Machiavelli directs his theoretical advice would have to deal with human nature and harsh realities as Machiavelli found them in Renaissance Italy.

	GENERAL EVENTS	LITERATURE & PHILOSOPHY	VISUAL ART & ARCHITECTURE	PERFORMING ARTS
1400			Masaccio (**10.18, 10.19**)	Mummeries
	Council of Constance Battle of Agincourt			
1420	Henry the Navigator		Ghiberti (**10.15, 10.16, 10.17**) Brunelleschi (**10.7, 10.9, 10.10, 10.14**) Donatello (**10.11, 10.12, 10.13, 10.29**) Fra Angelico (**10.20**)	
1450	Fall of Constantinople Hundred Years' War ends Cosimo de' Medici	Marsilio Ficino	Alberti (**10.6**) Uccello (**10.21**) Mantegna (**10.1, 10.25**)	*Maître Pierre Pathelin*
1475	Spanish Inquisition begins Lorenzo de' Medici Columbus Vasco da Gama	Pico della Mirandola	Botticelli (**10.22, 10.25**)	
1500		Machiavelli		

Timeline 10.1 The early Renaissance.

Map 10.1 Renaissance Italy.

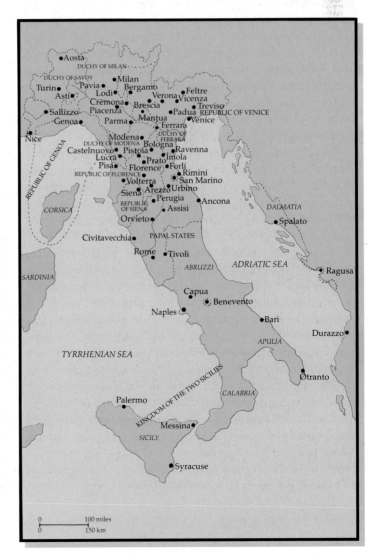

Ficino's student Pico della Mirandola (PEE-koh DEL-lah mee-RAHN-doh-lah; 1463–94), produced one of the Renaissance's most important documents of humanist thought, *De hominis dignitate oratio* ("Oration on the Dignity of Man"). This work reflected Pico's syncretistic method of taking the best elements from other philosophies and combining them in his own work. A brilliant but precocious child and the son of a prince of the small territory of Mirandola, Pico received a thorough humanistic education at home. He was convinced that all human knowledge could be combined into basic truths, and he set out to master all forms of knowledge. He mastered the Greek and Latin classics and Aristotelian philosophy, and learned the Hebrew, Aramaic, and Arabic languages. After being introduced to the Hebrew kabbala (cabbala), an occult theosophy based on an esoteric interpretation of Hebrew scriptures and widely transmitted in medieval Europe, he became the first Christian scholar to use kabbalistic doctrine in support of Christian theology. When he was twenty years old, he proposed nine hundred theses—intellectual propositions—that, he asserted, quantified all human knowledge, and in 1486 he invited scholars from all of Europe to Rome for a public disputation, for which he composed his celebrated *Oratio*. However, a papal commission pronounced thirteen of his theses as heretical and the assembly was forbidden by Pope Innocent VIII.

Despite producing an *Apologia* for the theses, Pico prudently fled to France, whereupon he was arrested. After a brief period in prison, he returned to Florence, where he became affiliated with the Platonic Academy and lived under the protection of the Florentine prince Lorenzo de Medici. In 1492 he was absolved of the charge of heresy by Pope Alexander VI, and toward the end of his life fell under the influence of the orthodox Christian monk Savonarola, the enemy of Lorenzo and, later, a martyr.

Pico began an unfinished treatise against the enemies of the church, which included a critique of the deficiencies of astrology. Religious rather than scientific, it nevertheless influenced the seventeenth-century scientist Johannes Kepler, whose studies of planetary movements proved basic to modern astronomy.

Capitalism

In all facets of society, the Renaissance placed new emphasis on the individual and on individual achievement. The rising middle classes, with their new-found wealth and power, were not long in discovering that, salvation or not, life was a great deal more worth living if one had a good house, good clothes, good food, and reasonable control over one's own existence. Such comfort seemed to stem directly from material wealth, and so, amid all other aspects of Renaissance life and perfectly in tune with them, there developed a new economic system of *capitalism*, or mercantilism. To a large degree, capitalism pursued wealth and power as its goals. In its broadest, and perhaps lowest form, it is a corporate endeavor with goals that can never be satisfied. The corporation is not an individual, but an extension of one, and therefore it is not constrained by individual needs or by limitations on the consumption of wealth.

Capitalism was only starting during the Renaissance, and it did not develop fully. It was, however, based on the tenets of pursuing wealth and power as ends in themselves. In contrast to medieval feudalism, capitalism offered a person reasonable freedom to pursue a better material standard of living to the extent of his or her wits and abilities. Capitalism challenged Renaissance men and women to pursue their own individual goals. As a result, there was an explosion of economic activity in the trading of goods and services previously unavailable or unheard of.

Capitalism depends on the creation of markets as well as the supply of goods, in contrast with the guild system, which produced only what was necessary. Therefore, it encouraged an increasing diversification of occupations and social positions. It flourished best in urban settings,

and home and the workplace now tended to become separate. Expansion of trade, capitalism, and commerce in the fourteenth and fifteenth centuries brought high prosperity to four locations in western Europe in particular—northern Italy, southern Germany, the Low Countries (now Belgium and the Netherlands), and England (Map **10.2**).

Discovery

To the already complex Renaissance social order was now added a thirst for new discovery of all kinds, scientific, technological, and geographic. The dream of human flight was explored in Leonardo da Vinci's remarkable designs for complex flying machines. Renaissance scholars sought the answers to all questions, and they took empirical approaches to their inquiry rather than using the tools of faith and philosophy. As a result, conflicts between forward-looking science and backward-looking traditional values were common. Spirited inquiry often raised more questions than it could answer, and the questions and conflicts that flowed from this inquiry had unsettling and destabilizing effects.

Technology significantly changed the character of this era. The printing press allowed the writings of the humanists as well as the literature of Greece and Rome to be rapidly and widely disseminated. Availability of textbooks at reasonable prices revolutionized education and gave rise to *scholas*, which were similar to our public schools. This brought a higher level of education to a wider segment of society.

Technology, science, curiosity, and increased individual self-confidence took humankind to the furthest reaches of the globe. Renaissance explorers vastly increased the geographical knowledge of the age. In 1486, Bartolomeu Diaz (DEE-ahz) sailed down the coast of Africa, ending the isolation of the Mediterranean world. Six years later, Columbus sailed to the West Indies. In 1499, Vasco da Gama completed a two-year voyage around the horn of Africa to India. At the turn of the sixteenth century Balboa reached the Pacific Ocean.

The Papal States

After the Council of Constance ended the Great Schism (see Chapter 9), the papacy made a concerted effort to regain its power and control. By the middle of the fifteenth century it had succeeded, and a large area of central Italy was known as the Papal States (Map **10.1**). Three popes in particular—Nicholas V (r. 1447–55), Pius II (r. 1458–64), and Sixtus IV (r. 1471–84)—as well as their successors, who were called the Renaissance popes, expended great time, wealth, and energy in consolidating the Papal States.

This often included diplomacy and war, and such activities brought the Church directly down to the level of the world around it. The Renaissance popes filled their treasuries with art—in fact, they were great patrons of Renaissance artists and ideas—and they did all they could to ensure the power of the papacy by filling papal offices with loyal self-seekers, usually their relatives. There is little question that, although some benefits did come to humanity through the intrigues and escapades of these popes, the benefits were mostly in worldly realms rather than in spiritual ones. For example, Nicholas V founded the Vatican Library, filled it with priceless manuscripts, brought major scholars to Rome, and supported their research. He also rebuilt most of the city.

Classical scholarship was also the forte of Pius II, and his renown as a poet contributed significantly to his election. He was also a clever politician, who understood the dynamics of power and intrigue. However, his accomplishments as pope seem limited to the ability to fill Rome with intellectuals and artists.

Less intellectual and learned than his immediate predecessors, Sixtus IV, likewise, made his mark in other than spiritual areas. Nonetheless, this skilled intriguer, who actively engaged in the feud between the Medicis and Pazzis (PAHT-zees) in Florence and the plot to kill Lorenzo de' Medici, did manage to oversee the construction of the Sistine Chapel. His active patronage of art and architecture helped to turn Rome into one of the most beautiful cities of the world.

Italian City-States

Like Greece in earlier times, Italy did not have a national political identity but consisted of a collection of independent city-states that were forever at war with each other. In the north were the Republic of Venice, the Duchy of Milan, and the Republic of Florence. In the south was the Kingdom of Naples, which included the island of Sicily. In between lay the Papal States. Of course, there were other important states, such as Ferrara, Savoy, Genoa, Urbino (Fig. 10.4), and Modena, but the five states just mentioned dominated the political and cultural map (see Map 10.1).

At about the same time as the Hundred Years' War came to an end and Constantinople fell—and probably in response to the threat from outside that these two events presaged—the northern states of Florence, Venice, and Milan achieved a significant, if fragile, peace accord in the Peace of Lodi (1454). When Naples joined the pact, Italy gained nearly half a century of relative peace.

However, while the agreement at Lodi may have brought peace among the city-states, it did not necessarily create peace within them. The second half of the fifteenth

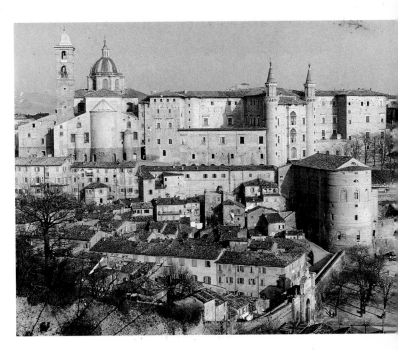

10.4 Luciano Laurana and Francesco di Giorgio, Palazzo Ducale, Urbino, Italy, 1466–c. 1481.

century saw the fall of more republican forms of government and the rise of autocracy, principally in the guise of ruling families. The story of Florence, in our Focal Point section at the end of this chapter, illustrates the perfidy and turmoil that beset all of Italy at this time. One of the most ironic outcomes of the context of the period is the cultural outpouring of art and architecture that exhibits peace and stability, totally belying its milieu.

THE BEGINNINGS OF RENAISSANCE ARCHITECTURE

In the early fourteenth century, a new style of art arose among artists in Florence. This style sought to capture the forms and ideas of the ancient Greeks and Romans, and it was a style dedicated to human principles and potentials rather than to ecclesiastical ones. There were three significant stylistic departures from medieval architecture. First, architects became concerned with reviving classical models, but they did so along mechanical lines. They measured ruins of Roman buildings and translated the proportions into Renaissance buildings, so that, for example, Roman arches became geometric devices by which formally derived designs could be superimposed on new buildings. Second, decorative detail—that is, nonstructural

TECHNOLOGY: PUTTING DISCOVERY TO WORK

Flywheels and Connecting Rods

The development of the machine and belief in its almost infinite possibilities represent one of the fundamental characteristics of the Renaissance. The most brilliant minds of the time went to work to invent machinery for industrial purposes, for games, and for war, and an interesting aspect of such development is that it lay principally in the realm of speculative thinking. Even before practical applications were discovered, machines were created for the pure joy of inventing them and of solving difficult problems. Nonetheless, practical applications came close on the heels of speculative thinking, and perhaps the most important mechanical development of the fifteenth century was the invention of the crank-and-connecting-rod system. Unknown in the medieval period, this system allows the transformation of continuous circular movement into straight-line, alternating, back-and-forth movement (Fig. **10.5**).

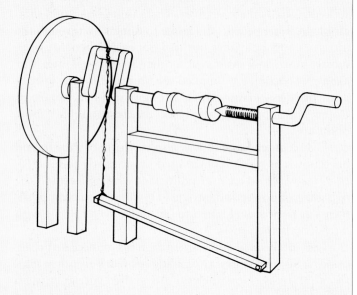

10.5 A lathe, designed by Leonardo da Vinci, c. 1500.

ornamentation—on the façades of buildings now came into favor. Third, there was a radical change in the outer expression of structure. The outward form of a building had previously been closely related to its structural systems—that is, the structural supports of the building—but in the Renaissance, supporting elements, such as posts and lintels, masonry, and arches, were hidden from view. External appearance was no longer subordinated to structural concerns, and it took on a life of its own.

Alberti

First among the formulators of the theoretical principles of the new style was Leon Battista Alberti (al-BAIR-tee; 1404–72), whose books were written some twenty years after the innovations began to be used. Alberti, a scholar, writer, architect, and composer, dominated the second half of the fifteenth century. His treatise *Concerning Architecture* was based on Vitruvius, and it provided a scholarly approach to architecture that influenced Western building for centuries. His scientific approach to sculpture and painting, as well as to architecture, encompassed theories on Roman antiquity and tended to reduce aesthetics to rules.

The problems confronting Renaissance architects were different from those facing their predecessors, however. There was an expanding range of types of buildings—for example, townhouses, hospitals, and business establishments—for which classical forms had to be adapted to meet specific practical needs. Alberti claimed that art was easier for the ancients because they had models to imitate and from which they could learn. Therefore, he asserted, the fame of Renaissance artists ought to be that much greater if they discovered unheard-of and never before seen arts and sciences without benefit of models or teachers.

In meeting these new needs, Renaissance architects applied classical detail to a wide range of forms and structures, many of which were basically nonclassical. For example, Alberti, himself, used a system of classical details on a nonclassical building in his design of the Palazzo Rucellai (puh-LAHT-zoh roo-CHAYL-y; Fig. **10.6**), which reminds us of the Roman Colosseum in its alternating arches and attached columns of changing orders. However, his system is academic in its effect rather than being individual.

For Alberti, the supreme example of the new art was the dome of the Cathedral of Florence (Fig. **10.7**), then being completed by Filippo Brunelleschi (fee-LEEP-poh broo-nuhl-ES-kee; 1377–1446). Its great dome had been appended to a Gothic building. According to Alberti, the construction of such a great dome, without great quantities of wood, seemed impossible even for that time and, thus, surely "unknown and unthought of among the Ancients."

Brunelleschi

As we will discuss at the end of the chapter, Brunelleschi's dome rose amid the most turbulent of times, dominating the skyline of Florence and the surrounding valley of the River Arno. After studying the remains of ancient architecture in Rome, Brunelleschi returned to Florence with his own ideas on how to utilize ancient elements in contemporary ways. Actually, Brunelleschi had been involved, at least peripherally, in the design of the original building at the turn of the fifteenth century, for in 1417 he had been hired as an advisor to the building committee and spent three years building a model to complete the project. The model was accepted, and the task of finishing the project began. Brunelleschi was limited by the nature of the existing structure. The overall plan of the cathedral, begun in the fourteenth century, could not be changed, and this included an octagonal base for the dome itself, whose shape has an immense tension that resembles a Gothic arch

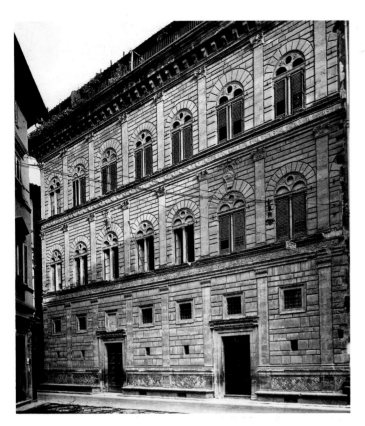

10.6 Leon Battista Alberti, Palazzo Rucellai, c. 1452–70.

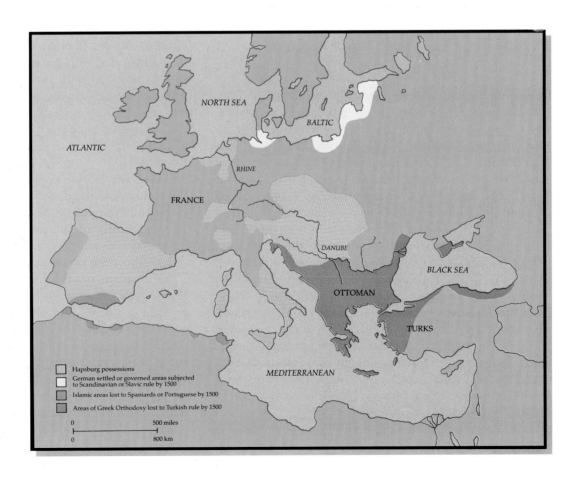

NORTH SEA

BALTIC

ATLANTIC

RHINE

FRANCE

DANUBE

BLACK SEA

OTTOMAN

TURKS

MEDITERRANEAN

☐ Hapsburg possessions
☐ German settled or governed areas subjected to Scandinavian or Slavic rule by 1500
☐ Islamic areas lost to Spaniards or Portuguese by 1500
☐ Areas of Greek Orthodoxy lost to Turkish rule by 1500

0   500 miles
0   800 km

Map 10.2 Renaissance Europe.

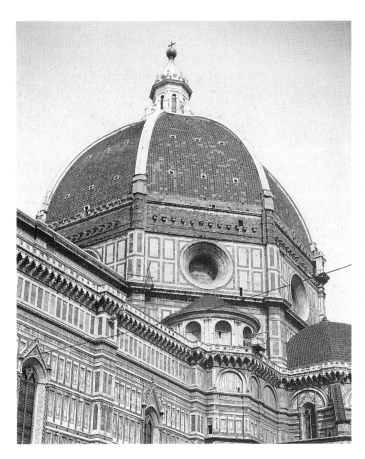

10.7 Filippo Brunelleschi, dome of Florence Cathedral, Italy, 1420–36.

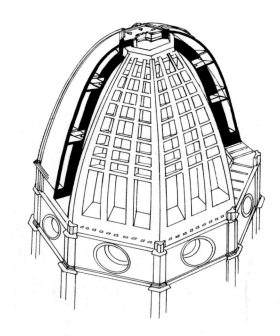

10.8 Schematic of Brunelleschi's dome.

more than a classical dome. Eight massive ribs (Fig. **10.8**), like the spokes of an umbrella, seem to be held together at the top by the marble lantern, designed to admit light into the interior. Construction began in 1420 and was completed in 1436, but the lantern was not completed until late in the century. Instead, an octagonal oculus or "eye," like that of the Pantheon (see Fig. **4.24**), sufficed temporarily. Brunelleschi's dome rises 180 feet (55 meters) into the air and its height is apparent from both the outside and inside. If we compare it with the Pantheon, Brunelleschi's departure from tradition becomes clearer. The dome of the Pantheon is impressive only from the inside of the building, because its exterior supporting structure is so massive that it clutters the visual experience. The phenomenal height of Brunelleschi's dome is apparent because the architect has hidden the supporting elements, such as girdles and lightweight ribbing. The result is a clear statement that visual experience is foremost, and structural considerations are subordinate. Thus, the dome becomes related to a work of sculpture.

One of the most striking examples of Brunelleschi's exploration of the new style in architecture is the Hospital of the Innocents, or Foundling Hospital (Ospedali degli Innocenti), in Florence (Fig. **10.9**). The very existence of the new building tells us something about the human flavor of the times. Although orphanages existed, the Republic of Florence decided to provide care for a growing number of foundlings from infancy to the age of eighteen, and this care included housing, food, education, and vocational training. Sitting on one side of an open square, even today it is a refreshing sight with its harmonious arcade of Roman arches supported by Corinthian columns. In its graceful simplicity the design of the façade reflects Brunelleschi's science of measure and proportion. The unbroken entablature reinforces the horizontal placidity of the composition and is aided by the curvilinear arches, carried into the wall of the building itself, and by the circular medallions of infants placed between each arch. Symmetry is enhanced and elegance added by the windows that sit above the keystone of each arch.

The plan of the building, which, incidentally, Brunelleschi drew for the builders—something never done previously—instead of using a model, is based on two geometric forms: the cube and the hemisphere. The distance between the centers of the columns is equal to that between the center of a column and the wall of the building. The same distance equals the height from the floor of the loggia (LOH-gee-uh; a roofed open arcade) to the point where two arches meet. All these measurements were precisely calculated and even dealt with the difficult factor of π that needed to be accommodated in measuring circles.

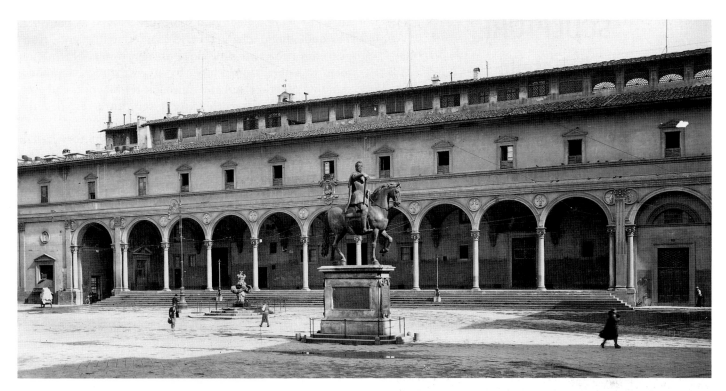

10.9 Filippo Brunelleschi, Foundling Hospital, Florence, Italy, designed 1419, built 1421–44.

The distance from the cornice, on which the windows rest, to the base of the architrave equals the distance from the base of the architrave to the junction point of the arches. Half this distance established the width of the smaller doors and windows. Every relationship in the building is calculated mathematically, based on the proportions of one to two, one to five, and two to five. The symbolism of Christ, the second member of the Trinity, the five wounds of Christ, and the Ten Commandments is obvious.

The culminating achievement of Brunelleschi's career, although it was not finished until after his death, was the intimate and lovely chapter house of Santa Croce (KRO-chay), known as the Pazzi Chapel because it was commissioned by the rich and powerful Pazzi family (Fig. **10.10**). The chapel again illustrates the use of classical ornamentation, and although small in scale, its walls serve as a plain background for a wealth of surface decoration. Concern for proportion and geometric design is clear, but the overall composition is not enslaved by arithmetical considerations. Rather, the Pazzi Chapel reflects Brunelleschi's classical aesthetics. It is a rectangular structure, three stories tall, twice as long as it is wide, which served as a meeting place for the Franciscan chapter of Santa Croce. The second story contains the arches and pendentives that support a star-vaulted dome, which culminates in a temple lantern.

10.10 Filippo Brunelleschi, Pazzi Chapel, Santa Croce, Florence, Italy, c. 1440–61.

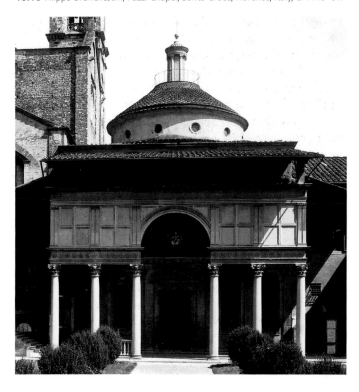

SCULPTURE

Donatello

The essence of European sculpture in the early Renaissance can, once again, best be examined by looking to fifteenth-century Florence. Early Renaissance sculptors had developed the skills to create images of great VERISIMILITUDE, but their goal was not the same as that of the Greeks, who idealized the human form. Renaissance sculptors found their ideal in individuality—the glorious individual, even if not quite the perfect individual—and sculpture of this style presented a particularly clear-eyed and uncompromising view of humankind: complex, balanced, and full of action.

While relief sculpture, as we shall see, found new ways of representing deep space through the systematic use of perspective, freestanding sculpture, long out of favor, now returned to dominance. Scientific inquiry and an interest in anatomy were reflected in sculpture as well as painting. The nude, full of character and charged with energy, reappeared for the first time since ancient times. The human form was approached layer by layer, through an understanding of its skeletal and muscular framework, and even when clothed, fifteenth-century sculpture revealed the body under the surface.

The greatest masterpieces of fifteenth-century Italian Renaissance sculpture came from the unsurpassed master of the age, Donatello (dah-nuh-TEL-oh; 1386–1466). Donato di Niccolò Bardi, known later as Donatello, saw life and reality in terms much different from his predecessors and contemporaries. He did not share Brunelleschi's

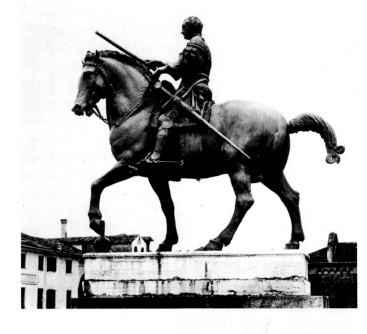

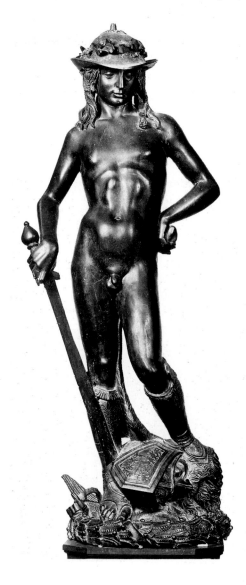

10.11 (*left*) Donatello, *David*, dated variously 1430–40. Bronze, 5 ft 2¼ ins (1.58 m) high. Museo Nazionale del Bargello, Florence, Italy.

10.12 (*above*) Donatello, *Equestrian Monument to Gattamelata*, 1445–50. Bronze, about 11 × 13 ft (3.4 × 4 m). Piazza del Santo, Padua, Italy.

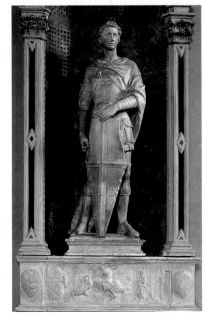

10.13 (*right*) Donatello, *St George*, 1415. Marble, 3ft 7½ ins × 2 ft 3 ins (109 × 67 cm). Museo Nazionale del Bargello, Florence, Italy.

concern for proportion. He was fascinated by the optical qualities of form and by the intense inner life of his subjects, and, as a result, produced amazingly dramatic and forceful works. His new approach is seen vividly in the statue of *St George* (Fig. **10.13**). Carved for a guild of armorers and sword makers, who could not afford a work cast in bronze, *St George* was intended to look very different from the way we now see it in the Bargello Museum. Originally, the figure bore evidence of the products of the guild—that is, a helmet and jutting sword—which were attached to the statue by holes drilled in the back of the head and a socket attached to the right hand. Nevertheless, as it now stands, the figure reveals a tautness of line in the pointed shapes of the shield, armored feet, and drapery. The facial expression reflects a lifelike human quality—not idealism. Sensitivity, reflectiveness, and delicate features make this figure a hero of everyday proportions and not a godlike warrior out of mythology. This is humanism at work in art, illustrating how flesh and blood people react in crisis.

Over the next twenty years, Donatello's style was refined, and from that refinement came his magnificent *David* (Fig. **10.11**), the first freestanding nude since classical times, although, like most classical figures, *David* is partially clothed. The figure exhibits a return to classical *contrapposto* stance in its refined form, but the armor and helmet, and the bony elbows and adolescent features, invest him with a highly individual presence. The work symbolizes Christ's triumph over Satan, and the laurel crown on the helmet and the laurel wreath on which the work stands allude to the Medici family, in whose palace the statue was displayed in 1469.

Perhaps Donatello's greatest achievement is the *Equestrian Monument to Gattamelata* (Fig. **10.12**). In this larger-than-life monument to a deceased general, we see the influence of Roman monumental statuary, and, in particular, the statue of *Marcus Aurelius on Horseback*, but Donatello creates a unique concentration on both human and animal anatomy. The viewer's focus is directed not to the powerful mass of the horse, however, but to the overpowering presence of the person astride it. The triangular composition anticipates the geometric approach to sculpture in the High Renaissance.

Ghiberti

In 1401 the Opera, the Board of Works, of the Baptistery of Florence's Cathedral conducted a competition for relief sculptures for the north doors of the Baptistery. Seven sculptors were chosen to compete, including Filippo

10.14 Filippo Brunelleschi, *Sacrifice of Isaac*, 1401. Gilt bronze, 21 × 17½ ins (53 × 44 cm). Museo Nazionale del Bargello, Florence, Italy.

10.15 Lorenzo Ghiberti, *Sacrifice of Isaac*, 1402. Gilt bronze, 21 × 17½ ins (53 × 44 cm). Museo Nazionale del Bargello, Florence, Italy.

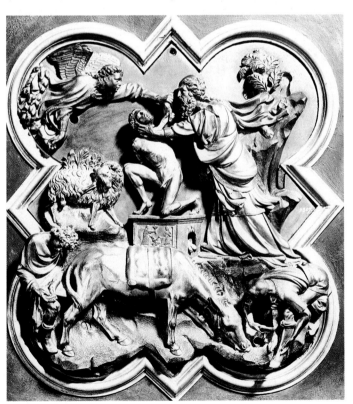

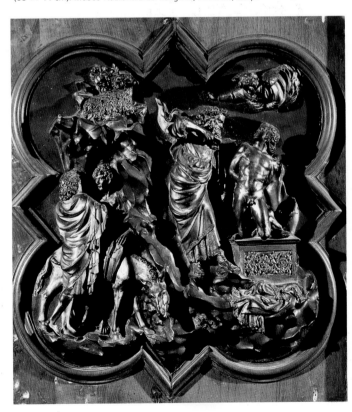

Brunelleschi and Lorenzo Ghiberti (gee-BAIR-tee; 1381?–1455), a contemporary of Donatello. The award went to Ghiberti, who was only twenty years old at the time, and the disappointment and humiliation of the defeat caused Brunelleschi to abandon sculpture for the rest of his life, although, as we have seen, his devotion to architecture made such abandonment fortuitous for history. We are fortunate in that the models submitted by both Brunelleschi and Ghiberti have been saved (Figs **10.14** and **10.15**). The subject is the sacrifice of Isaac by his father, Abraham, at the Lord's command, and both reliefs explore the same moment—that is, Isaac is kneeling on the altar with Abraham ready to put the knife to his throat. The archangel intervenes, and the ram that the Lord provides as a substitute sacrifice is clearly visible. The two servants and the ass drinking water from a rock are also present. The theme of both works is the divine intervention that delivers the Chosen People from catastrophe, including the substitute victim and the miraculous appearance of water.

Brunelleschi's treatment of the subject (Fig. **10.14**) is full of lifelike detail, from the scrawny, screaming boy to the dramatic imposition of the angel, who grabs the wrist of Abraham at the very last moment. Abraham twists the boy's head melodramatically. There is high drama here, but the rhythms seem awkward and disjointed. Line moves in fractured angles, refusing to carry through the work and, thus, create the overriding symmetry and balance we see in Brunelleschi's architecture.

Ghiberti's story, on the other hand, flows with sweeping curves, drawing its emotion from inference rather than contortion (Fig. **10.15**). Abraham reaches around his son and grasps him by the left shoulder. The boy gazes expectantly at his father, while the angel remains in the heavens, not touching the obedient patriarch. The emphases are spiritual rather than physical, while the overtones of the work give us a sequence of curvilinear rhythms in which the principal axis runs across the diagonal to provide energy and tension. The way in which the two artists treat the human figure provides a further contrast. Brunelleschi uses anatomically correct details awkwardly, while Ghiberti infuses them with what scholars called *natura naturata*—that is, transfigured nature. Ghiberti was trained as a painter and had not yet joined any guild—especially not the metalworkers' guild—but his handling of the metal is profound and sophisticated. The project occupied Ghiberti from 1403 until 1424, and in the process, the Opera changed its mind about the subject matter, and Ghiberti found himself faced with the task of depicting the New Testament. The subject of Abraham and Isaac had to wait for the third set of doors.

Perhaps the major breakthrough of Renaissance art came in the discovery of principles for depicting perspective mechanically and, thus, naturalistically. This new means of spatial representation produced a visually convincing and attractive means of depicting objects in space and imbuing them with qualities that gave their relationship to the distant horizon rationality. We can see these principles at work in Ghiberti's, *The Gates of Paradise* for the east doors of the Florence Baptistery (Fig. **10.17**). Commissioned in 1425, these great doors bear ten scenes. Each square is totally gilded, and the sculptor freely uses each as if it were the canvas of a painting. In so doing, Ghiberti employed perspective to bring to relief sculpture a totally new sense of deep space. The title of the doors apparently comes from the fact that they open on the *paradiso* (pahr-uh-DEE-soh), the area between the Baptistery and the entrance to the Cathedral. Michelangelo is said to have remarked that the doors were worthy to be the Gates of Paradise, and the name stuck.

Each panel depicts an incident from the Old Testament. The perspective is so rational and the relief so defined, that the scenes take on a remarkable sense of space in which the picture plane seems almost to be fully round and free of the background. For example, in *The Story of Jacob and Esau* (Fig. **10.16**) Ghiberti created beautiful surfaces with delicate and careful detail, and used receding arcades to portray depth and perspective. Every detail is exact, and the bold relief of these scenes took Ghiberti twenty-one years to complete.

10.16 Lorenzo Ghiberti, *The Story of Jacob and Esau*, panel of *The Gates of Paradise*, c. 1435. Gilt bronze, 31¼ ins (79.4 cm) square. Baptistery, Florence, Italy.

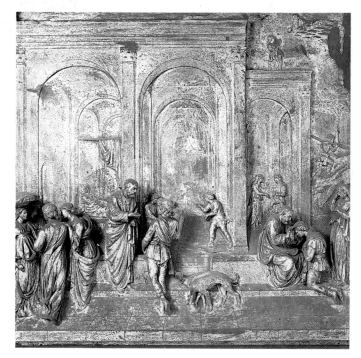

10.17 Lorenzo Ghiberti, *The Gates of Paradise*, 1424–52. Gilt bronze, about 17 ft (5.2 m) high. Baptistery, Florence, Italy.

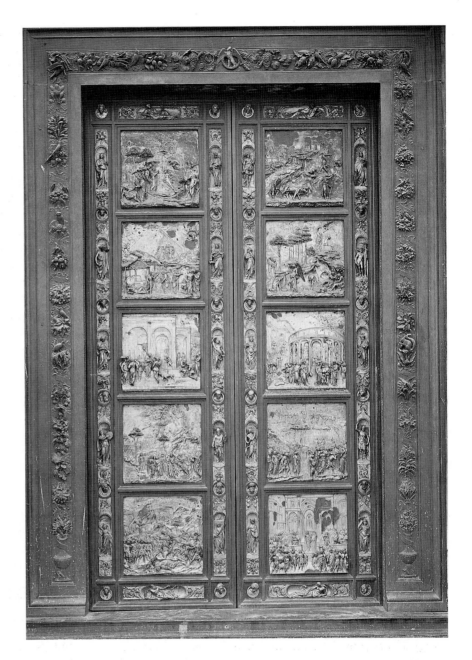

PAINTING

Masaccio

Tommaso di Giovanni, better known as Masaccio (mah-ZAH-coh or mah-ZAHT-choh; 1401–29), joined the painters' guild in Florence in 1422, where he worked for four years, before moving to Pisa for two years, and then to Rome, where he died, probably of malaria, in 1429. The hallmark of Masaccio's invention and development of a "new" style lies in the way he employs deep space and rational foreshortening or perspective in his figures. In collaboration with the Florentine artist Masolino (c.

1383–c. 1432), Masaccio was summoned in 1425 to create a series of frescoes for the Brancacci Chapel of the Church of Santa Maria del Carmine in Florence. Among these works were Masaccio's acknowledged masterpiece, *The Tribute Money* (Fig. **10.18**).

Masaccio's works have a gravity and monumentality that make them larger than lifesize. The use of deep perspective, plasticity, and modeling to create dramatic contrasts gives solidity to the figures and unifies the paintings. Atmospheric perspective enhances the deep spatial naturalism. Figures are strong, detailed, and very human. At the same time, the composition carefully subordinates the parts of the painting to the whole.

The maturation of Masaccio's style can be seen in a

MASTERWORK

Masaccio—*The Tribute Money*

Masaccio's perception of the universe exploded into life in the decoration of the chapel of the Brancacci family in the Church of Santa Maria del Carmine in Florence. Late Renaissance artists such as Michelangelo came to view these frescoes and to study the new art developed by Masaccio.

The most famous of these frescoes is *The Tribute Money* (Fig. **10.18**). Its setting makes full use of the new discovery of linear perspective, as the rounded figures move freely in unencumbered deep space. *The Tribute Money* employs continuous narration, where a series of events unfolds across a single picture. Here Masaccio depicts a New Testament story from Matthew (17:24–27). In the center, Christ instructs Peter to catch a fish, whose mouth will contain the tribute money for the tax collector. On the far left, Peter takes the coin from the fish's mouth; on the right he gives it to the tax collector. Masaccio has changed the story somewhat, so that the tax collector appears directly before Christ and the apostles, who are not "at home," but in a landscape of the Arno Valley. Masaccio's choice of subject matter may relate to a debate over taxation going on at the time in Florence. A contemporary interpretation of the fresco held that Christ had instructed all people, including clerics, to pay taxes to earthly rulers for the support of military defense.

The presentation of the figures in this fresco is remarkably accomplished. They are like "clothed nudes," dressed in fabric which falls like real cloth. Weight and volume are depicted in an entirely new way. Each figure stands in classical *contrapposto* stance, and although the sense of motion is not particularly remarkable, the accurate rendering of the feet and the anatomically correct weight distribution make these the first painted figures to seem to stand solidly on the ground. The narrative comes across through pantomimic gestures and intense glances. Nonetheless, the figures do encapsulate an astonishing energy and reality. Comparing these figures with those of Botticelli, later in the chapter, we will see that while Botticelli reveals form and volume through line, Masaccio uses the play of light and shade on an object—that is, by modeling. The key to this is the artist's establishment of a consistent source for the light, inside or outside the painting, which strikes the figures. That source might be the sun or a candle, for example, but the artist must then render the objects in the painting so that all highlights and shadows occur consistently as if caused by that single light source. Masaccio does not include a light source in the fresco itself; instead, he uses a window in the nearby chapel to act as a light source, and the highlights and shadows are rendered accordingly (compare Rembrandt's *The Night Watch*, Fig. **13.26**). In addition, the figures form a circular and three-dimensional grouping rather than a flat line across the surface of the work. Even the haloes of the apostles appear in the new perspective and overlap at odd angles.

Any expectation of historical accuracy in works of art was unknown to Masaccio. Masaccio's setting is local and his figures are clothed in Italian Renaissance

second work, *The Holy Trinity* (Fig. **10.19**), which is in the Church of Santa Maria Novella in Florence. Here, Masaccio states the central doctrine of Christianity in a full-frontal, single vanishing point perspective rendering, which places the crucified Christ at the center of the statement. The fresco uses the viewer's eye level as the horizontal line, and the coffered barrel vault of the painted niche therefore recedes dramatically, as if we were gazing up into actual three-dimensional space. The linear angles of the T-shaped cross and the body and outstretched arms of Christ stand in dramatic juxtaposition to the rounded arch of the architectural frame and the ceiling of the vault itself.

Masaccio carries the blood red colors of the architrave and cornice down through the arch, its capitals, the undergarment of God, and the figures at the lower corners, thereby achieving a unification and central focal area by virtue of this encirclement of color. The symbolism reflects the dead Christ (*Christus mortus*), sacrificed for humankind by God, who stands behind His son, steadying the cross with His hands while staring out at the rest of the universe. The dove of the Holy Spirit floats between the heads of Father and Son. Mary, the mother of Christ, looks out at us and gestures to us, indicating the sacrifice of her son. St John, the only disciple present at the Crucifixion, looks on, lost

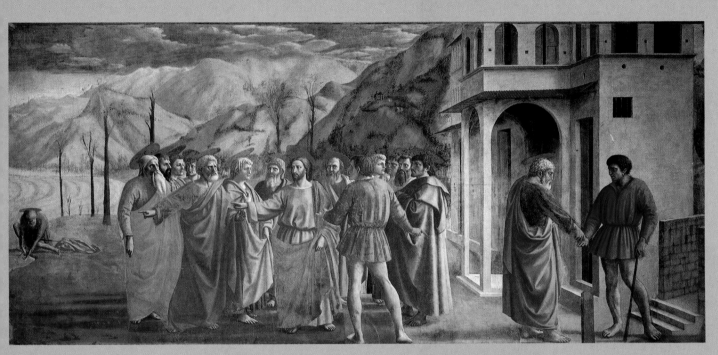

costume. Until the eighteenth century, history was considered irrelevant to art. The apostles appear as Florentine "men in the street," and they have sympathetic and human features.

Compositionally, the single vanishing point, by which the linear perspective is controlled, sits at the head of Christ. In addition, Masaccio has rediscovered aerial perspective, in which distance is indicated through diminution of light and blurring of outlines. We can also see Masaccio's skill in handling landscape as well as figures. There is a previously unknown skill and seldom rivaled grandeur about this. As one art historian describes it:

10.18 Masaccio, *The Tribute Money*, c. 1427. Fresco (after restoration 1989), 8 ft 4 ins × 19 ft 8 ins (2.54 × 5.9 m). Santa Maria del Carmine, Florence, Italy.

The background is filled with soft atmosphere. Misty patches of woodland are sketched near the banks. Masaccio's brush moves with an ease and freedom unexampled in Italian art since ancient Roman times. It represents not hairs but hair, not leaves but foliage, not waves but water, not physical entities but optical impressions. ... Each stroke of Masaccio's brush, in fact, is equivalent to a separate reflection of light on the retina.[1]

in the mystery. The figures at the lower corners, outside the niche, may be contemporary Florentines, and their coloration gives Masaccio a way of interjecting diagonal line to increase the sense of dynamics in the work. Black robes tie Mary and the feminine figure together, as do the red robes of the gentleman and St John. Thus, two, crossing, implied diagonals join at the feet of Christ.

The entire painting is executed with deliberate concern for verisimilitude. Even the nails of the cross protrude according to the perspective of the chapel. Masaccio renders each body part with absolutely precise anatomical detail and accuracy.

The Heritage of Masaccio

However revolutionary and important Masaccio may have been in retrospect, his influence on his contemporaries appears to have been relatively modest. His ideas did, however, strike a spark in some—for example, Fra Filippo Lippi and Fra Angelico—and Italian painting moved in the 1430s, 1440s, and 1450s toward a more common Renaissance style, called the second Renaissance style. This was the era of the Medicis, as we will see at the end of this chapter. The time was one of humanistically oriented

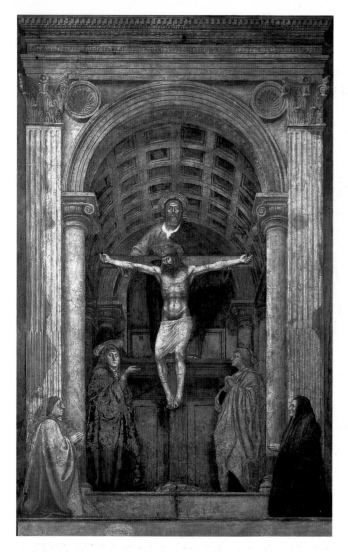

10.19 Masaccio, *The Holy Trinity*, c. 1426–7. Fresco, 21 ft 10½ ins × 10 ft 5 ins (6.67 × 3.17 m). Santa Maria Novella, Florence, Italy.

in this book (see Chapter 5), we will examine it (Fig. **10.20**). The work dates to the 1430s and was created as the altarpiece for San Domenico, Cortona, and its intent—or perhaps inspiration—should be seen within the context of monastic setting and contemplation. It now hangs in a museum in Cortona.

A portico of slender Corinthian columns provides the setting as the angel comes to Mary. The delicacy of the columns and the simplicity of the capital details lend delicacy and classical appropriateness to the simple faith and obedience of the Virgin. Angelico divides the canvas into thirds. The arches on the picture plane occupy two-thirds of the work; the receding arcade occupies the remainder. Mary is seated on a chair decorated with gold brocade, and the angel, genuflecting before the seated presence, enters the portico. Fra Angelico prints the angel's words so that they appear to come out of his mouth, running from left to right. Mary's reply—"Behold the handmaiden of the Lord; be it unto me according to thy word" (Luke 1:38)—is written upside down, so that it must be read from Mary toward the angel. The dove of the Holy Spirit floats directly above Mary's head under a blue, star-filled ceiling. The prophet Isaiah looks down from a medallion above the column that separates the two figures. The garden at the left is a symbol of Mary's virginity and also represents the Garden of Eden, from which a weeping Adam and Eve are being politely expelled at the rear. There is logic to the inclusion of the Eden scene here, because, according to Christian prophecy and doctrine, Christ would become the "new Adam" and Mary would be the second Eve.

The figures of Adam and Eve are fully clothed in the garments God gave them, and the entire scene lacks the dramatic power we have seen before. Fra Angelico's figures are rendered three-dimensionally, but barely. The highlight and shadow contrasts remain subdued, and the scene takes on an ethereal lightness as Mary crosses her hands over her breast in acceptance of God's request. Nonetheless, the rendering speaks of plasticity—however refined—even if the celebrated human anatomy of Renaissance depiction does not show through the clothing. There is deep space here, as the arcade recedes to a vanishing point on an imagined horizon drawn across the center of the picture. Fra Angelico has captured the spiritual beauty of the moment with a simple and delicate use of line, form, and color. The perfectly drawn hands of the angel, for example, give us a taste of the mastery of medium and execution that accompany the profound simplicity of the story.

patrons of art who commissioned buildings, statues, portraits, and altarpieces to fit their new classical tastes. The laws of Florence forbade luxury and display in personal finery, but the tone was set for a new life of ease and grace.

Fra Angelico

Fra Angelico (frah ahn-JAY-lee-koh; c. 1400–55) lived a life of piety and humility. He was born Guido di Pietro and appears to have become an accomplished painter before taking vows in the Dominican Order as Fra Giovanni da Fiesole. Once he had become a monk, he served his order as a prolific artist in San Domenico, Fiesole, and in San Marco, Florence. Eventually, he became prior of San Marco, and before his death he was widely known as "the angelic painter"—hence the name by which we know him, Fra Angelico. We have such a wealth of work from this amazing monk that it is difficult to choose one as illustrative. However, his *Annunciation* appears to be his most popular and best-known, and, since we have told the story

Paolo Uccello

Another important exemplar of the second Renaissance style is Paolo di Dono, known as Paolo Uccello (oot-CHEL-loh; 1397–1475), whose work is representative of the fascination with the new understanding of perspective

Focal Point

Florence in the Quattrocento

If you walk through the streets of Florence today, you are able to see almost all the important cultural accomplishments of the Renaissance, which had its beginnings here in the fifteenth century, a century the Italians called the Quattrocento (kwaht-troh-CHEN-toh)—that is, simply, the 1400s. Almost everywhere you go, you can look up and see Brunelleschi's great dome above the Duomo. You can walk around the Baptistery and marvel at Ghiberti's doors or across the famous Ponte Vecchio bridge to the rather humble-looking Santa Maria del Carmine church and gaze in awe at Masaccio's *The Tribute Money* in the Brancacci Chapel. In fact, there is hardly any church that does not contain some masterpiece of the Quattrocento, and a day in the Uffizi Gallery will leave you numb.

But Florence is and was more than a living museum. It is and was a city as human and individualistic as its Quattrocento humanist philosophy. If we are to understand these magnificent works as something other than artifacts, we must know something about Florence in the Quattrocento: a city of people who were probably not much different from you or me in their needs and desires. Who were the Florentines of the Quattrocento and how did they

come to be the world's most famous and productive culture?

In the very early Middle Ages, the *piazza* or town center consisted of a mass of small houses and public buildings. In the fourth century, the church of Santa Reparata was built over the foundations of an older building, and three centuries later a Baptistery was added, and the area began to be the center of Florentine religious life. Santa Reparata became a cathedral in 1128, but it quickly outgrew its size, as its role and importance grew greater as Florence's population continued to increase. In 1289 the Commune decided to enlarge the cathedral as part of a massive building project that involved new and more extensive city walls, a new Prior's Palace (now the Palazzo Vecchio), and alterations to other existing buildings and churches. Wishing the city to be new but harmonious, the city fathers hired one man, Arnolfo di Cambio, to direct and coordinate the work. A great architect and sculptor, he demolished houses, raised the level of the piazza, and began to build the new cathedral, for which he planned a dome and external decoration to match the Baptistery. He died in 1302, but the work continued with the construc-

10.27 Francesco Rosselli, *View of Florence*, c. 1490. Watercolor after an engraving. Museo dell' Opera del Duomo, Florence, Italy.

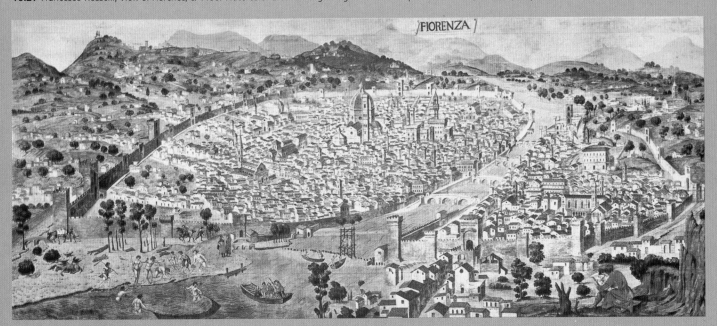

tion of the bell tower under the direction of Giotto (see Chapter 9). With a population of approximately 50,000, Florence now stood on the threshold of the Quattrocento (Fig. **10.27**).

A population of 50,000 may not seem large by today's standards, but at the time, Florence was the most populous city in Europe. Before the Black Death, it had a population of 100,000, and at the time, London and Paris contained roughly 20,000 people each. Florence was a city founded on commerce, and at the heart of its political and commercial life lay the guilds, which ruled the city. The guilds were self-regulating and subject to a single political party, the Guelph party. However, it was a democracy, and one that was far more advanced than Europe had seen since Pericles.

Despite almost constant war and tribulation, during the first quarter of the Quattrocento Florence acquired the ports of Pisa and Livorno, important inland cities such as Arezzo and Cortona, and controlled all of Tuscany, from Lucca to Siena. It was the time of Masaccio, Donatello, Ghiberti, and Brunelleschi, but the source of greatest pride to the Florentines was its republicanism. The city's constitution was designed to spread political power among a large group of responsible citizens, and it contained legal devices to prevent political parties from developing or a single family from becoming dominant.

Cosimo de' Medici

Notwithstanding the city's constitution, a mere six years later, Cosimo de' Medici (1389–1464), a middle-aged banker with scholarly tendencies, returned to Florence from a year's exile in Venice, and he received a welcome from the city, a welcome that Machiavelli saw almost in military terms. Cosimo was saluted as the benefactor of the people and the father of the country (Fig. **10.28**). The impossible had happened—a single, previously unremarkable, family created a party and produced a leader whose legacy, although occasionally interrupted, produced a hereditary chain of almost absolutist power.

The Medici were a family of bankers with bases in Venice, Rome, and Naples. Cosimo's father, Giovanni, had become chief papal banker in Rome in 1413, and by 1420, he had become predominant. Giovanni did not wish to appear politically ambitious, however, and he kept a reasonably low profile, although he had served in the *signoria* (seen-YOHR-ee-uh; an elected ruling body) and as a Florentine representative in Venice and Rome. Skillfull and clever, Giovanni built the Medici fortune and laid its power base while staying in the good graces of the population. On Giovanni's death in 1429, his entire inheritance went to Cosimo, whom Giovanni had married to the daughter of the reputable Bardi family.

Cosimo's scholarly qualities did much to endear him to

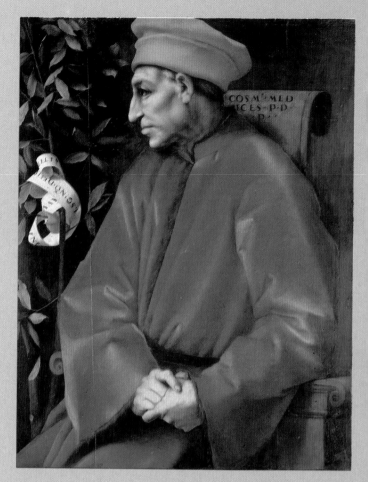

10.28 Cosimo de' Medici (1389–1464). Painting by Jacopo Pontormo, c. 1518–19. Uffizi Gallery, Florence, Italy.

the people of Florence and to mitigate any rough edges of political intrigue and ambition. He was a patron of art—a trait he learned from his father, who had been on the panel that chose Ghiberti to design the Baptistery doors and who had been instrumental in hiring Brunelleschi to design the dome of the Duomo, with sculptural additions from Donatello. He also donated the money to build the Duomo's sacristy.

By the time of Giovanni's death, the Medici interests were actively pursued by a Medici political party formed from various branches of the family and bolstered by its wealth and careful marriages with several poorer, but more prestigious families. Although family pride and advancement were more or less a hallmark of the age and certainly a reminder of feudal times, the actual fostering of family interests in political terms ran foul of Florentine law. For example, it was illegal to solicit votes, and other practices, if less problematical, were nonetheless corrupt. Again, for example, the Medici did everything they could to put their own family members in positions of political power; they offered loans to members of the party who were in financial difficulty; and they offered advice on financial and legal matters, all actions that were just within the law. Opposition to the Medici came from a larger but less unified old guard of the city.

In 1433, those who were opposed to the Medici managed a one-vote majority in the *signoria*, and Cosimo was summoned and imprisoned. The opposition tried valiantly to have him condemned to death as a traitor who planned to overthrow the government, but instead Cosimo was banished to Padua for ten years. In August 1434 the *signoria* election produced a pro-Medici majority, which promptly relinquished all power of the *signoria* to an open assembly of all Florentine males, called a *parliamento*, asking it to steer the city out of its present crisis. This was ostensibly a democratic device to allow the people to act in the face of political deadlock, but worked to tilt the power directly to one side or the other. In this case, power went to the Medici, and Cosimo returned in triumph, barely ten months after his original sentence.

Cosimo proved to be a new kind of leader, who drew his power from banking and his political principles from

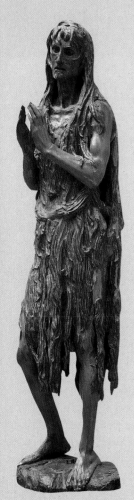

10.29 Donatello, *Mary Magdalen*, c. 1455. Wood, painted, 6 ft 3¼ ins (1.88 m) high. Museo dell' Opera del Duomo, Florence, Italy.

the Roman Republic. He had never been in war, and he had no royal blood or famous ancestors. All his influence came from his extensive banking interests, but through these he was able to make his city prosperous. He was also a learned man, and he founded an Academy for the study of Plato, whose head was Marsilio Ficino. He actively supported the arts, and artists such as Donatello were free to pursue their new artistic style, one that, in Donatello's case, progressed from the *St George* and *David* we considered earlier to the modernly expressionistic portrayal of *Mary Magdalen* (Fig. **10.29**). He also collected Roman coins and prints, and loved gardening.

For thirty years, until his death in 1464, Cosimo de' Medici was the most influential man in Florence. His wealth increased through the banks that he opened throughout Italy and Europe. Although he was under some pressure to assume complete power in Florence, as he undoubtedly could have done, he remained an ordinary citizen all his life. He held high office often, but no more often than any other leading citizen.

Piero de' Medici

Cosimo's son Piero (1418–69) inherited his father's fortune, palace, and villas, and it seemed likely that he would inherit his father's influence as well. However, to the Florentines of the time, the inheritance of a position that had depended so much on the personal qualities of Cosimo was not a foregone conclusion, and it appeared, two years later, that Piero would follow his father into exile. For the next five years, he lived in his father's shadow and was destined to shrink in the light of his even more famous son, Lorenzo. Nonetheless, he did manage to overcome a Florentine constitutional crisis in 1465–6 and thus make sure that the Medici were given the opportunity to become a dynasty of princes.

Nicknamed *Il Gottoso*, "the Gouty," Piero inherited his father's uricemia and, crippled and bedridden much of the time, he was carried about in a litter. Despite his unimpressive appearance, he remained a man of no mean accomplishment in many ways. He had been thoroughly educated, and had mastered Latin. He collected manuscripts, coins, and cameos, and, even before his father's death, had become a significant patron of art. Thus, whereas Cosimo built, Piero decorated. It is, for example, speculated that Piero ordered Uccello's battle scenes (see Fig. **10.21**) for the Medici palace. He was perhaps petty and a spendthrift, but he proved an active and helpful patron.

When it was audited, the Medici bank proved to be seriously overextended, because Cosimo had patiently overlooked many debts in order to gain political advantage. When Piero, needing to retrench, called them in, it created a storm of resentment. Florence was in something of financial panic because of the wars between Venice and the Turks, which had compromised important Florentine trade with Venice and the eastern Mediterranean, and Piero's retrenchment was seen—unfairly perhaps—as a threat. Even his own son Lorenzo complained of his father's temperament and its cost in friends. Voices of discontent were heard, including cries for open elections to the *signoria* and a broadened base of those eligible. The deference accorded Cosimo in similar circumstances did not extend to his son. However, Piero weathered the storm, showing skill and resolution, and actually emerged even more influential as the controlling voice in Florentine governmental decisions. By his death in 1469, however, many were thinking of change because Piero's heir, Lorenzo, was only twenty and was of unknown character.

Lorenzo de' Medici

While the Florentines respected Cosimo and accepted Piero, they felt more affection for Lorenzo (1449–92). He had a natural charm and dashing style, which appealed to the people of Florence, and was a well-educated youth, fluent in the classics, who loved art as well as sport (Fig. 10.30). Although it was still a democracy at heart, Florence gave Lorenzo an influence that occasionally upset the balance of the State. His period of influence coincided with a military threat from Naples and Rome and with economic decline, which hit the Medici hard personally, forcing Lorenzo to close branches of the bank in Milan and Bruges. Lorenzo moved to strengthen Florence's government and did so by resurrecting his grandfather's idea of a Senate. As a result, a Council of Seventy assumed power in Florence, its members holding their position for life. Although Lorenzo proposed the council, the Florentines themselves approved it, hoping that it would provide a decision-making body that would prove equal to the needs of the times.

One of the council's first acts was to institute progressive taxation, which hit the rich very heavily. Lorenzo's taxes amounted to double those disproportionate taxes that Cosimo had paid. Looking back on Lorenzo's place in the political scheme of Florence, one finds that, even though he was sometimes called a "tyrant," there were real limits to his power. He certainly had considerable personal influence—his diarist described him as a man who "with a single gesture was able to bend all the other citizens to his will"—but he seems never to have stepped beyond constitutional bounds. When another plot to assassinate him was uncovered in 1481, however, the *signoria* passed a law making any attempt on Lorenzo's life a crime against the state.

Perhaps the most important factor in his rise to power was the role he inherited in foreign policy. Good personal relationships with other rulers had been one of his grandfa-

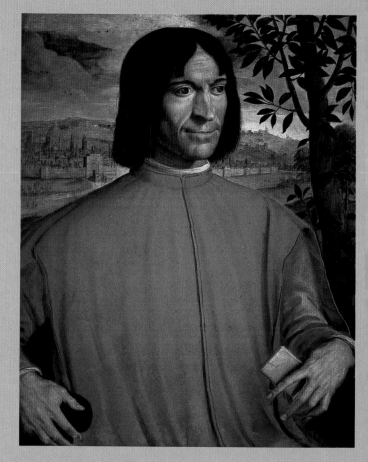

10.30 Lorenzo de' Medici (1449–92).

ther's strengths, and it was misjudgment in this area that led to Lorenzo's son's exile in 1494 and the family's temporary decline. Lorenzo had met and favorably impressed many heads of state in Italy, a large number of whom assumed that Lorenzo had more power than, in fact, he did. He had to tread a delicate path in all his relationships, both domestic and foreign, and his diplomacy was often hampered by his insecure position as a banker. The family's political prestige made it uniquely liable to requests from rulers for loans, and although his fortunes were not totally dependent on the bank, Lorenzo had less access than his father or grandfather to free money by which to extend his influence. His whole political career was marked by intrigues and difficult situations—including major confrontations with Pope Sixtus IV.

Lorenzo the man, as distinct from Lorenzo the politician, now draws our attention, however. He undertook a staggering range of activities, in addition to his political activities—he ran the largest international bank in Europe, managed four country estates and a townhouse, planted botanical gardens, raised cows, bred racehorses, looked after his children's education, did charitable work for the church, read Plato, bought art, played the lyre and the organ, possessed a theoretical and practical knowledge of architecture, and wrote music and poetry. Some of his friends thought that he was a better poet than Dante and Petrarch, because, as a Platonist, he had a deeper insight into the nature of love and reality.

CHAPTER REVIEW

Critical Thought

Without doubt the world was changing, although it is equally certain that no one woke up one morning and said, "Today is the dawn of the Renaissance!" Evaluations that categorize times usually come with the vision of hindsight, which we, of course, have. Looking back on the Renaissance, we have the luxury to speculate on whether or why we should call it the Renaissance and to examine changes that occurred in how people lived, in the way the political map was drawn, and in how people went about doing business and exploring their world. One of the ways in which things were different was in the sheer amount of activity occurring, coupled with the manner in which men and women pushed open the frontiers of their spiritual, psychological, and physical worlds.

There definitely was a tremendous outpouring of creative activity and it was clearly marked by new ways of exploring subject matter in visual art, and expressing form and structure in architecture. Dance entered the scene as an art rather than an activity, and theatre found itself mired in the old while puttering with the new.

Understanding Renaissance art means understanding the work of its artists. It means being able to look at the work of one artist and compare its qualities with that of other artists of the same or other periods and of other styles. For example, we should be able to point out the characteristics that differentiate the east doors of the Baptistery of the Florence Cathedral from the bronze doors of Hildesheim Cathedral (Fig. **7.12**) and to understand why Masaccio and Botticelli, for example, reflect new ways of painting, compared to Giotto.

Summary

After reading this chapter, you should be able to:

• Describe specific qualities that represent Renaissance art and architecture, identify the individual artists who contributed to the tradition, and explain how, within the artworks themselves, artists applied those innovations.
• Identify new forms and plays in Renaissance theatre.
• Discuss the rise of dance from a group activity to a formal art, with specific references to the individual responsible.
• Explain the geographical, economic, political, and philosophical circumstances of the Renaissance—as well as understanding the implications of the term "Renaissance" itself.
• Apply the elements and principles of composition to analyze and compare specific works of art and architecture illustrated in the text.

CHAPTER ELEVEN

The High Renaissance and Mannerism

OUTLINE

THE HIGH RENAISSANCE

SOUTHERN EUROPE IN THE SIXTEENTH CENTURY
The Expanding World
  OUR DYNAMIC WORLD: Painting in India
The Ottoman Turks
The Papal States
  TECHNOLOGY: Leonardo: Turning the Screw
Spain's Golden Century

THE VISUAL ARTS
The High Renaissance
  PROFILE: Michelangelo
  MASTERWORK: Michelangelo—
    David
Mannerism

ARCHITECTURE

THE PERFORMING ARTS
Music
Theatre

LITERATURE
Baldassare Castiglione
Ludovico Ariosto

FOCAL POINT: PAPAL SPLENDOR—THE VATICAN

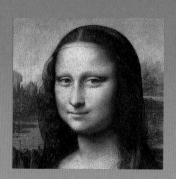

VIEW

HOW TO BE REMEMBERED

When we use the word Renaissance, which of course includes the High Renaissance, on which we focus in this chapter, we identify an important historical period by the nature of its art and ideas. Isn't it interesting that the means by which we identify historical periods often have to do with art and culture? No one discounts the importance of areas such as business, medicine, science, and so on, but rarely do we identify historical eras by material pursuits of this sort.

When we look at the remarkable accomplishments of human history, regardless of the field in which they occurred, we inevitably encounter individuals who possess qualities that place them outside the ordinary. These are people who have something to "say" and who "say" it well. They avow the unique rather than the cliché, and they know that being remembered requires something more than outlandish behavior and good PR.

Above Detail of Fig. **11.11**.

11.1 Michelangelo, *David*, 1501–4. Marble, 14 ft 3 ins (4.1 m) high. Academy, Florence, Italy. Photo: © Studio Fotografico Quattrone.

KEY TERMS

Some of the basic terms and concepts we will encounter in this chapter include the following:

Terribilità, genius, an awesome force, a concept akin to sublimity, a supreme confidence.

High Renaissance, the time from around 1495 until around 1520, primarily in Rome and characterized by the works of Michelangelo, Raphael, and Leonardo da Vinci.

Conquistadors (conquerors), the early Spanish explorers of the New World.

Sfumato is a blending of light and shadow practiced by Leonardo da Vinci.

Mannerism is a movement in art characterized by a "mannered" or affected appearance of subjects.

Commedia dell'arte, a Renaissance theatre type performed by troupes of actors wearing masks and employing improvised plots and stock characters.

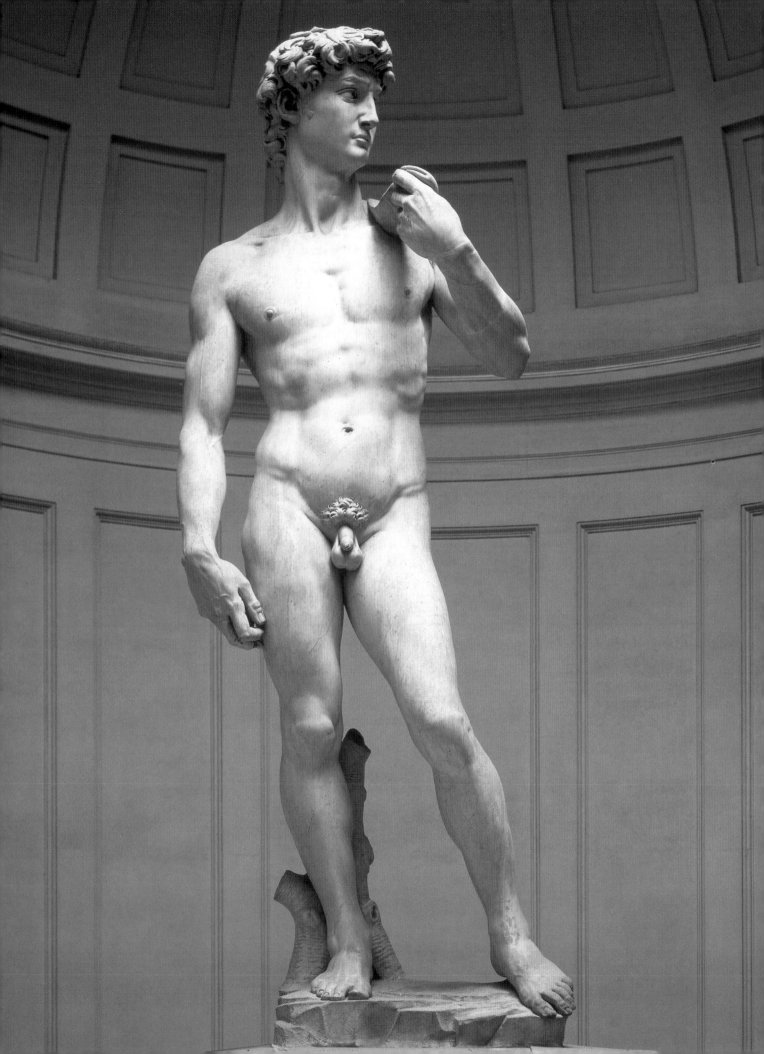

THE HIGH RENAISSANCE

As important and revolutionary as the fifteenth century or Quattrocento was, the high point of the Renaissance came in the early sixteenth century, as papal authority was reestablished and artists were called to Rome. The importance of this brief period, occurring from approximately 1495 until 1527 in Rome and exemplified by Michelangelo and Raphael, has led scholars to call it the High Renaissance. However, as we shall see, it began earlier in Florence with the work of a man very much ahead of his time: Leonardo da Vinci (VIN-chee). It also involved locations other than Rome—for example, the great city of Venice.

Especially important to an understanding of the High Renaissance is a new concept—the concept of genius. In particular, we might argue that everything done in the visual arts in Italy between 1495 and 1520 was subordinate to the overwhelming genius of two men, Leonardo da Vinci and Michelangelo Buonarroti (bwoh-nuh-ROHT-ee). In fact, such was the achievement of these two men that many have argued that the High Renaissance in visual art was a new kind of art entirely.

Whatever may be the case, by 1500 the courts of the Italian princes had become centers of cultural activity and important sources of patronage. Machiavelli, who thought the leaders of these centers soft and effeminate, accused them of deliberately living in an unreal world. However, the Italian courtiers needed artists, writers, and musicians to pursue their lofty ideals of beauty. They now regarded the arts of the early Renaissance as vulgar and naive, and they demanded a more aristocratic, elegant, dignified, and lofty art, and this accounts, at least in part, for the new style found in the works of playwrights and painters. The wealth of the popes and their desire to rebuild and transform Rome on a grand scale also contributed to the shift in style and the emergence of Rome as the center of patronage. Music came of age as a major art form. Ancient Roman sculptural and architectural style was revived. There were also important discoveries of ancient sculptures, such as the *Apollo Belvedere* and the *Laocoön* (see Fig. 3.30), and because the artists of this period had such a rich immediate inheritance from the early Renaissance, but felt that they had developed even further, they considered themselves to be on an equal footing with the artists of antiquity. Their approach to the antique in arts and letters was, therefore, different from that of their early Renaissance predecessors. So was their world.

SOUTHERN EUROPE IN THE SIXTEENTH CENTURY

The Expanding World

In July 1497, Vasco da Gama sailed from Lisbon, Portugal, with two well-armed ships. In November 1497, he rounded the Cape of Good Hope, the southern tip of

Timeline 11.1 The High Renaissance and Mannerism.

	GENERAL EVENTS	LITERATURE & PHILOSOPHY	VISUAL ART & ARCHITECTURE	PERFORMING ARTS
1400				
	Ferdinand and Isabella of Spain			
1475				
			Leonardo (**11.7, 11.9, 11.10**)	
	End of Wars of Roses			
1500				
	Pope Julius II		Bramante (**11.25, 11.40**)	
	Brazil discovered	Ariosto	Raphael (**11.18, 11.19, 11.34, 11.43**)	
	Cortes conquers Aztecs	Castiglione	Michelangelo (**11.1, 11.12, 11.14, 11.16,**	
	Charles V of Spain		**11.17, 11.36, 11.39, 11.41, 11.42**)	
	Suleiman I, the Magnificent		Titian (**11.20**)	
	Jesuits founded		Lescot (**11.26**)	
	Founding of Mughal Dynasty		Bronzino (**11.22**)	
			Serlio (**11.31**)	
1550				
	Inquisition		Tintoretto (**11.21**)	Madrigals
			da Bologna (**11.24**)	Palestrina
			Palladio (**11.27**)	Commedia dell'arte
				Teatro Olimpico

Africa. By May of 1498, he had reached India, where he found people living in rich principalities and used to trading with Persian and Arab merchants. Despite difficulties, he managed to load his ships with spices and precious stones and to return to Portugal. Although he lost half his fleet and men on the way, he proved beyond doubt that a sea route to India existed and that it could be exploited practically and profitably. Less than a year later, Pedro Alvares Cabral left Portugal with fifteen heavily armed ships and 1,500 men, determined to make Portugal a major trading power in the Indian Ocean. However, on his way down the coast of Africa, he sailed too far west and ended up on the coast of Brazil, which he promptly claimed for Portugal.

By 1515 Portugal dominated the main spice-producing region of the world, and Portuguese sailors found their way to Japan as well. In the wake of the traders were Christian missionaries, and in 1559 a Jesuit mission was welcomed to the Japanese imperial capital at Kyoto. In 1569 a powerful Christian convert gave the Jesuits the town of Nagasaki, which became their major base. By the end of the century, there were over 300,000 Christians in Japan, and although Portuguese attempts to gain entry into China were not successful, by the mid-sixteenth century, Portugal had established a tremendous commercial empire stretching across four continents.

After Christopher Columbus had shown the way, the rate of exploration of the world increased rapidly. Among those who descended on the Americas were restless men and ex-soldiers looking for easy wealth and fame. Such an individual was Vasco de Balboa, who, after leading a revolt against the governor of a new settlement on the coast of South America, set out up the coast and, crossing the Isthmus of Panama, sighted the Pacific Ocean in 1515.

Also among the footloose adventurers of the time was Hernando Cortés (kohr-TEHZ), who was typical of the early explorers and *conquistadors* (conquerors). He had heard stories of a rich and mighty kingdom and was determined to find it. He founded the settlement of Veracruz ("True Cross"), now in Mexico, and received a commission to continue his search for the mysterious kingdom. He set out in 1519 with six hundred men, sixteen horses, ten small guns, and thirteen muskets, determined to attack and overthrow the Aztec empire, in which he was helped by the native peoples who had been conquered by the Aztecs and who turned on the Aztec ruler, Montezuma. Cortés seized Montezuma, who had welcomed the Spaniards and heaped gifts upon them, and thus caused a riot in which the Aztec ruler was killed and the Spanish were driven from Tenochtitlán, a city of 300,000 residents. But Cortés was not deterred, and, aided by his native allies, he laid

11.2 *Indians Giving Cortés a Neckband,* illustration from Diego Duran, *Historia de las Indias.* Biblioteca Nacional, Madrid.

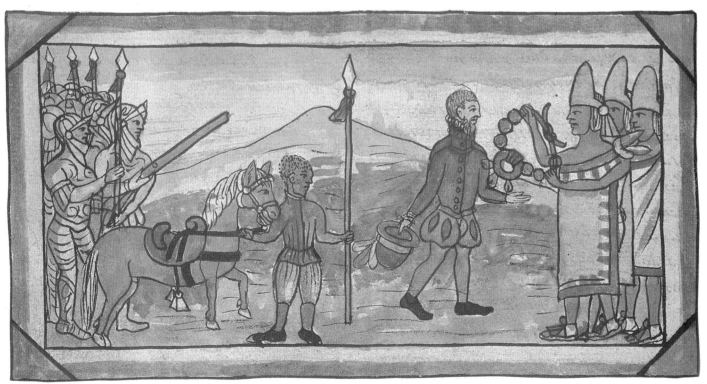

siege to the city. Eighty days later, it surrendered, and Cortés was master of Mexico (Fig. **11.2**).

In a few short years, therefore, curiosity and individual self-confidence had taken humankind to the furthest reaches of the planet to explore and exploit it for the benefit of the kingdoms of Europe. The full implications of the fact that the world was, indeed, round fell upon Renaissance men and women in 1522, when Magellan completed his three-year voyage around the world.

The Ottoman Turks

In essence, the powers of Europe in the early sixteenth century were disunited and in conflict. The Ottoman Turks, on the other hand, represented a united and formidable fighting force. Their major asset was a well-disciplined army, which struck fear into the hearts of the opposition, but the army also showed one of the major characteristics of the Turks—toleration. Most of the peoples in the Ottoman Empire were Jewish or Christian, and they were left to the unhindered practice of their own religions, provided that they paid tribute money for the sultan's military campaigns and turned over their male children to his service. The conscripted children were raised as Muslims, trained for the army, and then sent throughout the Empire.

The sultan to whom fell this dynamic and, perhaps, overextended empire was Suleiman (SOO-lay-mahn) I, the Magnificent (1494–1566). He succeeded his father in 1520 and became one of the greatest rulers of the sixteenth century (Fig. **11.3**). He was a warrior, but also a cultured and learned man, a lover of the arts, and a lawgiver. One of his first acts as sultan was to demand tribute from young King Louis II of Bohemia (now part of the Czech Republic) and Hungary. When Louis refused, Suleiman invaded Hungary and captured Belgrade. In a later offensive in 1526, the Turks defeated Louis's forces at Mohacs, and reached the border of the Hapsburg Empire (the Hapsburgs were an aristocratic German family who, at this time, ruled the Austrian and Holy Roman Empires). Louis was drowned in the fight, and Suleiman prepared to assault the Hapsburg capital, Vienna. The Turks were beaten back, and the onset of winter, overextended Turkish supply lines, and trouble elsewhere caused the Turks to retreat, and in 1533 to agree to a truce. Because of renewed conflict over the succession to the throne of the buffer state of Transylvania, the Turks succeeded in consolidating their hold on the Balkans and two-thirds of Hungary. By the middle of the century, the Ottoman Empire was secure, and by the time Suleiman died in 1566, it extended unbroken from the Black Sea to the Persian Gulf. Despite continued conflicts with the Hapsburgs and with Spain, the Ottoman Empire changed little in the rest of the century.

The Papal States

Having been a plaything of the great powers of Europe, the Church wished to secure independence by increasing its temporal and political strength. It looked for leadership not among saints and scholars, but among administrators and politicians, seeking worldly men of powerful personality and toughness who could make quick decisions. The power of the Papacy began to grow through worldly measures—such as war and diplomacy—and that reinforced the need for popes who could maintain such domin-

11.3 Suleiman I, the Magnificent (1494–1566). British Library, London.

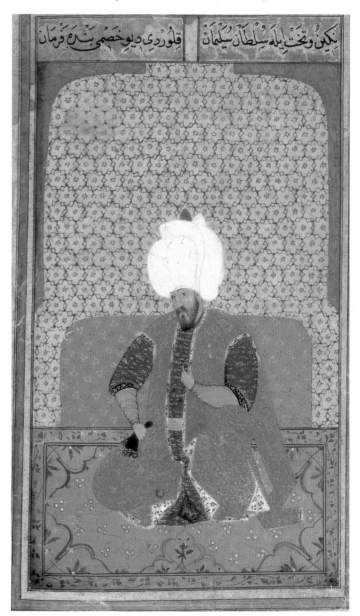

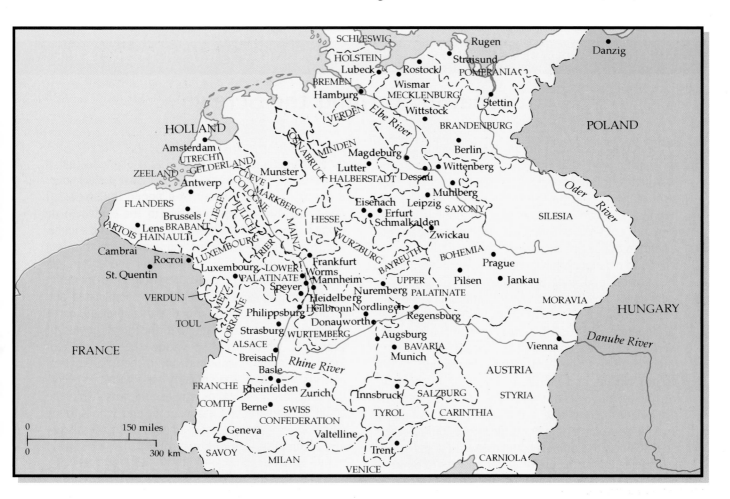

Map 11.1 The Holy Roman Empire.

ions. Popes such as Alexander VI and Julius II came to power. Alexander VI, whose lusts were repellent even in an age renowned for toleration, proved a hard-knuckled diplomat and an excellent administrator in the dogged pursuit of policies that he believed were necessary for the Church—that is, temporal power expressed in dominion over central Italy.

Even as pope, Julius II loved war, often mounting his horse in full armor to hear the bloody sounds of battle. The Renaissance popes were tough, practical, worldly men, who were concerned with power. Like their secular counterparts, they did not wish to be outdone in the display of their wealth and greatness. They spent lavishly to construct vast churches, huge palaces, and magnificent fountains, and hired the best artists and artisans, collected the best antiques, the most expensive jewels, and the most remarkable books and manuscripts. Such things, like armies, were the necessities of State—whatever the cost.

Perhaps the triumph of the Renaissance papacy came in the coronation of Lorenzo de' Medici's son Giovanni as Leo X in 1513. He was subtle, intuitive, sophisticated,

charming, generous, and affable. He was discreet in his private life and maintained a wide variety of intellectual interests. Raised in the luxury of the Medici at their peak, he had no qualms about displays of riches and pageantry. Rome increased in splendor, the pope increased in majesty, and all around, violence, turmoil, and intrigue abounded among the French, the Milanese, and the Spanish. However, the Church was now dependent on vast influxes of money to support its extravagance and required new taxes, the worst of which was the sale of indulgences, which would become one of the many causes that led to the Reformation in northern Europe that we will discuss in Chapter 12.

The Spanish invasion of Rome in 1527 (the "Sack of Rome") effectively brought the extravagances of the Renaissance to an end. The invasion, mounted by Charles V, Holy Roman Emperor (whom we discuss momentarily), was part of Charles' grand scheme to enlarge the influence of the Spanish Empire, then the largest in the world. The rise of Protestantism and the shock of the devastation of Rome led to a sterner spirit in the Church and Papacy.

TECHNOLOGY: PUTTING DISCOVERY TO WORK

Leonardo: Turning the Screw

Leonardo's notebooks mark the beginning of scientific work that had conspicuous results at the hands of Galileo and Kepler (see Chapter 13). They also mark the beginning of modern treatises on hydraulics and applied mechanics. Although new ideas were not confined to Leonardo, his lifetime represents a definite transition, and his efforts contributed significantly to change. Graphic record became his consuming passion, and important notes and trivial jottings went down on paper, often on the same sheet. The earliest material we have dates from 1488, and thereafter he apparently kept all his ideas in notebooks, which were a complete record of his mental activity and were intended to be a series of treatises: on painting, on the nature, weight, and motion of water, on impacts, on weight, on moments of energy, and on the elements of machinery. There is also material on human anatomy and the anatomy of the horse, and notes on a treatise on machinery, including a complete series of mills with arrangements for the use of all the sources of power—wind, water, horses, treadmills, and cranks turned by men. There are drawings of all forms of pumps and hydraulic apparatus, containing many new features for the application of power. There is a fairly comprehensive series of drawings of machinery for the textile industry and the manufacture of metals.

In essence, the notebooks are a record of existing apparatus and of Leonardo's attempts to apply the principles known to him to new problems. Thus, Leonardo left a record highly characteristic of an inventor: positive accomplishments, complete projects, and rough sketches of new mechanical concepts not carried through to completion.

We tend to think of Leonardo's notebooks as containing lofty and imaginative ventures well ahead of their time, and, indeed, many were. However, they also contain down-to-earth ideas—for example, Leonardo invented simple and practical devices for cutting screws and nuts. The notebooks contain sketches for three distinct sets of apparatus: two sets designed for cutting screws on wooden spindles or in wooden nuts and one piece of apparatus designed for preparing molds for casting and polishing bronze screws. The most interesting of these devices (Figs. **11.4** and **11.5**) involves the process of cutting the nut and the spin-

dles. To cut the nut, a hole is made in a block (*m*) the gross diameter of the screw. A strip of metal (*ab*) is nailed over one end of the hole so that it projects over it by one-half the breadth of a finger. The screw (*rf*) must then be cut appropriately to the thread to be made in the nut, and a steel point is set in the spindle. The thread of the screw turning against the strip (*ab*) draws the spindle into the nut and the cutter (*cd*) makes the thread in the nut. Describing the operation of the spindle cutter is even more complicated and arcane, and so we will suffice with appreciating the basic design and the fact that the great genius of Leonardo, which could envisage the elements of flight—although he could not bring them to practical conclusion—could also concern itself with the everyday practicality of cutting screws and nuts—which he could bring to practical usage. In the end, who is to say which may have been more important to the history and accomplishment of humankind?

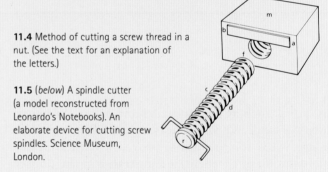

11.4 Method of cutting a screw thread in a nut. (See the text for an explanation of the letters.)

11.5 (*below*) A spindle cutter (a model reconstructed from Leonardo's Notebooks). An elaborate device for cutting screw spindles. Science Museum, London.

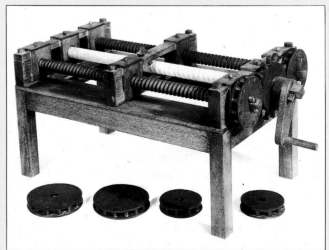

Spain's Golden Century

Ferdinand and Isabella may be the best-known sovereigns of Spain because they financed the voyage of Christopher Columbus. In Spanish history, however, they are the rulers who finally expelled the Moorish conquerors of Spain, unified the country, and made it one of the great powers of Europe. By asserting Italian territorial claims, negotiating a French alliance, and marrying their children into the royal houses of England and the Holy Roman Empire, they made their country by the end of the fifteenth century one of the most powerful in Europe. In the following century, the Spanish Empire was the largest in the world.

The sixteenth century is called the *siglo de oro* ("golden century"), and it owed much of its glitter to the Americas—although it was really silver, not gold, that underlay its richness. Charles V (r. 1516–56), the grandson of Ferdinand and Isabella, was Holy Roman Emperor, king of Spain, and lord of the Netherlands, much of Italy, Mexico, Peru, and elsewhere, and he was undoubtedly the most powerful ruler in Europe. Yet, by the end of his life, he had retired to a monastery, a broken old man who had

failed to achieve his purpose, for which there were three principal reasons.

The first of these was the Protestant Reformation, which disrupted Germany. The second was the Ottoman invasion, which caused the Hungarian monarchy to collapse and gave Charles an eastern warfront, thus drawing his attention and his resources away from France and Italy. The third reason for his failure was the constant conflict with France, which persisted in its vain attempts to conquer Italy and entered into an alliance with the enemies of Christendom, the Turks. Nonetheless, Charles did win the domination of Italy and fought the Turks to a standstill, while France fell victim to its own internal religious wars between Catholics and Huguenots (HYOO-guhnawts; French Protestants). However, in his own eyes, Charles had failed to make the Holy Roman Empire the undisputable power he had hoped, and he was ashamed of the behavior of his troops when they conquered Rome. In October 1555 he abdicated the Spanish throne, and transferred the administration of his Spanish possessions to his son Philip. The following year, he resigned the Imperial Crown to his brother Ferdinand, and retired to Spain.

Philip II (r. 1556–98) had even greater ambitions than

11.6 Hendrik Cornelisz Vroom, *The Sea Battle*, c. 1600. Oil on canvas, 3 ft 1¼ ins × 5 ft 1⅛ ins (91 × 153 cm). Landesmuseum Ferdinandeum, Innsbruck, Austria.

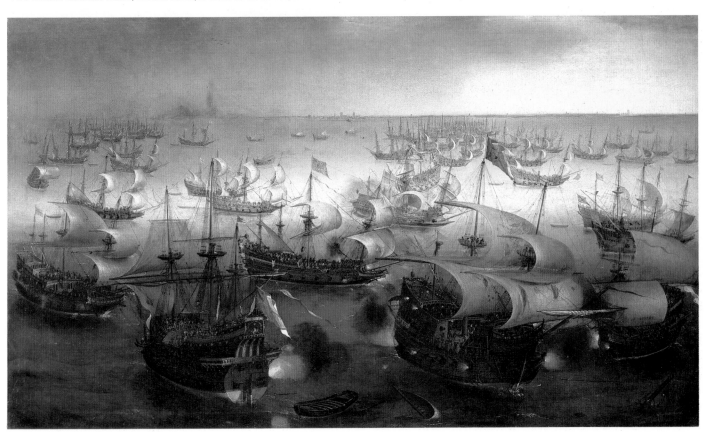

his father. A fervent Catholic, he made Spain the sword and shield of the Counter-Reformation. An autocrat by temperament, he tried to impress his will on the vast Spanish Empire, and, as he inherited the best armies in Europe and the largest revenues in the world, it appeared that, unlike his father, he would succeed in dominating the entire Western world. It did not happen.

The growing Protestant powers of Europe allied themselves against him: England under Elizabeth I, the French Huguenots, and the Netherlands. As we shall see in Chapter 12, the cause was as much political as religious. Although Philip had some military successes, especially against the Turks, his critical battles were failures—for example, the attempted invasion of England that led to the catastrophic defeat of the Spanish Armada (Fig. **11.6**). His attempts to crush a revolt in the Netherlands ended in 1609 with Dutch independence. Thus, in one generation, the most powerful empire in the world went from ascendancy to eclipse, and by the end of the sixteenth century, Spain had gone from a Golden Age into an insignificant footnote to subsequent European history.

THE VISUAL ARTS
The High Renaissance

High Renaissance painting sought a universal ideal achieved through impressive themes and styles. Tricks of perspective or stunning renditions of anatomy were no longer enough. Figures became types again, rather than individuals—godlike human beings in the Greek classical tradition. Artists and writers of the High Renaissance sought to capture the essence of classical art and literature without resorting to copying, which would have captured only the externals. They tried to emulate rather than imitate. As a result, High Renaissance art idealizes all forms and delights in composition. Its impact is one of stability without immobility, variety without confusion, and definition without dullness. High Renaissance artists carefully observed how the ancients borrowed motifs from nature, and then set out to develop a system of mathematically defined proportion and compositional beauty emanating from a harmony of parts. This faith in harmonious proportions reflected a belief among artists, writers, and composers that the world of nature, not to mention the universe, also possessed perfect order.

This human-centered attitude also included a certain artificiality and emotionalism that reflected the conflicts of the times. High Renaissance style departed from previous styles in its meticulous composition, which was based almost exclusively on geometric devices. Compositions

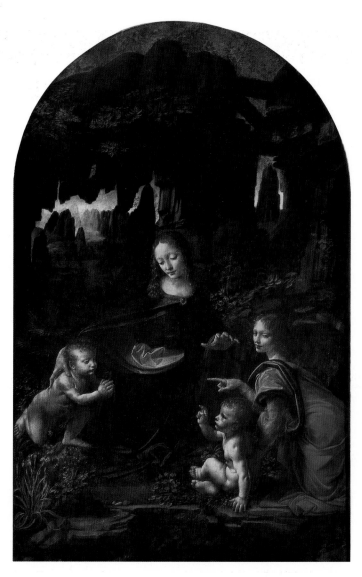

11.7 Leonardo da Vinci, *The Madonna of the Rocks* (*Virgin of the Rocks*), c. 1485. Oil on panel, 6 ft 3 ins × 3 ft 7 ins (1.91 × 1.09 m). Louvre, Paris.

were closed—that is, line, color, and form kept the viewer's eye continually redirected into the work, as opposed to leading the eye off the canvas—and the organizing principle of a painting was usually a geometric shape, such as a triangle or an oval.

Leonardo da Vinci

The work of Leonardo da Vinci (1452–1519) has an ethereal quality which he achieved by blending light and shadow, a technique called SFUMATO (sfoo-MAHT-oh). His figures hover between reality and illusion as one form disappears into another, with only the highlighted portions emerging. In *The Madonna of the Rocks* (Fig. **11.7**),

OUR DYNAMIC WORLD

Painting in India

An example of painting from India's Mughal Dynasty of the sixteenth century gives us a good comparison with Western art of the High Renaissance. Our example comes from a major manuscript, *The Romance of Amir Hamza*, which was produced during the reign of the great Islamic Mughal ruler Akbar (1542–1605). These paintings, done on fine linen, unify Persian and Indian images into a Mughal style. Typical of Indian art, they depict their subjects in fairly lifelike detail, with bold colors and dynamic composition. The hero of *Alam Shah Closing the Dam at Shishan Pass* (Fig. **11.8**) takes the predominant position at the top of the work. Indian painting makes little use of natural perspective that was so critical to Renaissance painting. This painting exists solely on the surface plane, but although the images are fragmented, the composition balances psychologically. A strong diagonal, moving from upper left to lower right, counters an opposite diagonal from lower left to upper right. Each segment of the painting carries its own narrative content, and the pieces of the composition fit together like multicolored tiles of a mosaic. The work is unified by its underlying and framing use of gold, and the "frame" is part of the painting itself.

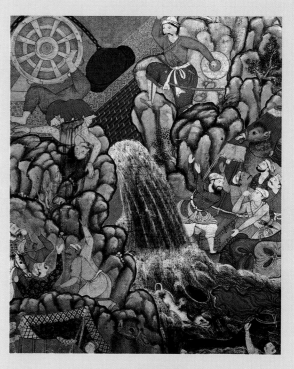

11.8 *Alam Shah Closing the Dam at Shishan Pass* (leaf from *The Romance of Amir Hamza*), Mughal, c. 1570. Color and gold on cotton, 27$\frac{1}{8}$ × 20$\frac{1}{2}$ ins (69 × 52.2 cm). Cleveland Museum of Art (Gift of George P. Bickford).

Leonardo interprets the doctrine of the Immaculate Conception, which proposed that Mary was freed from original sin by the Immaculate Conception in order to be a worthy vessel for the incarnation of Christ. Mary sits in the midst of a dark world and shines forth from it. She protects the Infant Christ, who blesses John the Baptist, to whom the angel points. The gestures and eye direction create movement around the perimeter of a single central triangle outlined in light. Leonardo takes the central triangle and gives it enough depth to make it a three-dimensional pyramid of considerable weight. Light and shade are delicately used, even though the highlights and shadows do not flow from a consistent light source. The portrayal of rocks, foliage, and cloth displays meticulous attention to detail.

It is difficult to say which of Leonardo's paintings is the most admirable, but certainly *The Last Supper* (Fig. **11.9**) ranks among the greatest. It captures the moment at which

the apostles are responding with disbelief to Christ's prophecy that "one of you shall betray me." Leonardo's choice of medium proved most unfortunate because, unlike fresco, his own mixtures of oil, varnish, and pigments were not suited to the damp wall. The painting began to flake, and was reported to be perishing as early as 1517. Since then it has been clouded by retouching, defaced by a door cut through the wall at Christ's feet, and bombed during World War II. Miraculously, it survives.

In *The Last Supper*, human figures, not architecture, are the focus. Christ dominates the center of the painting. All lines, actual and implied, lead outward from his face, pause at various subordinate focal areas, reverse direction at the edges of the work, and return to the central figure. Various postures, gestures, and groupings of the disciples direct the eye from point to point. Figures emerge from the architectural background in strongly accented relief; it is surprising how much psychological drama the mathemati-

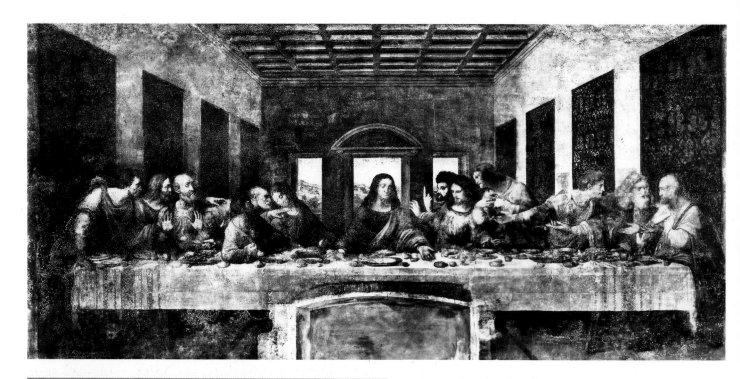

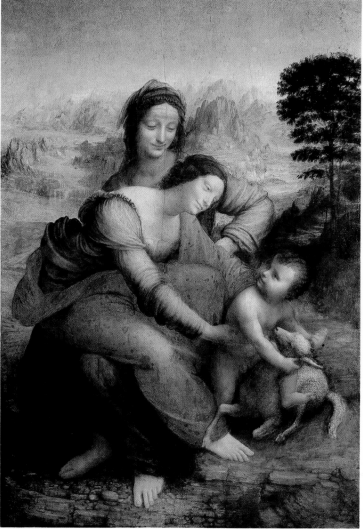

11.9 Leonardo da Vinci, *The Last Supper*, c. 1495–8. Mural painting, 15 ft 1¹/₈ ins × 28 ft 10¹/₂ ins (4.6 × 8.56 m). Santa Maria delle Grazie, Milan, Italy.

11.10 (*left*) Leonardo da Vinci, *Virgin and Child with St Anne*, 1508–10. Oil on panel, 5 ft 6¹/₈ ins × 4 ft 3¹/₄ ins (1.68 × 1.3 m). Louvre, Paris.

cal format allows. Yet, despite the drama, the mood in this work and others is calm, belying the turbulence of Leonardo's own personality and his times.

Leonardo reverts to the pyramid as the basis of the composition in his *Virgin and Child with St Anne* (Fig. **11.10**). The Virgin Mary sits on the lap of her mother, St Anne. St Anne becomes the apex of the triangle whose right side flows downward to the Christ Child, who embraces a lamb, symbolic of his sacrificial death. The famous *Mona Lisa* (Fig. **11.11**) was painted at about the same time as the *Virgin and Child with St Anne*. We are drawn to this work not so much by the subject as by the background. As if to emphasize the serenity of the subject, and in common with the *Virgin and Child with St Anne*, the background reveals an exciting mountain setting, full of dramatic crags and peaks, winding roads which disappear, and exquisitely detailed natural forms receding into the mists. The composition is unusual in its treatment of the full torso with the hands and arms pictured, completing the unity of the gentle spiral turn. Three-quarters of the figure is pictured, not just a bust. This marked a new format in

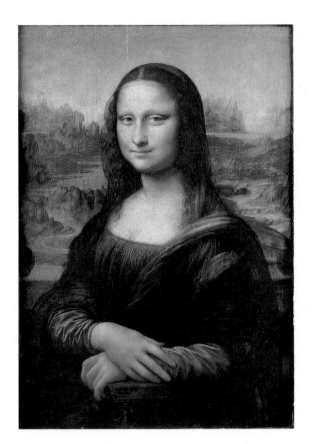

11.11 Leonardo da Vinci, *Mona Lisa*, c. 1503–5. Oil on panel, 30 × 21 ins (76.2 × 53.3 cm). Louvre, Paris.

11.12 Michelangelo, *The Creation of Adam*, detail from the Sistine Chapel ceiling, 1508–12. Fresco. Vatican, Rome.

Italian portraiture and provided a model which has been followed ever since. The result is a larger, grander, and more natural portrait, in keeping with the new sense of human dignity implicit in Renaissance idealism.

Michelangelo

Perhaps the dominant figure of the High Renaissance was Michelangelo Buonarroti (1475–1564). Michelangelo was entirely different in character from Leonardo. Leonardo was a skeptic, while Michelangelo was a man of great faith. Leonardo was fascinated by science and natural objects. Michelangelo showed little interest in anything other than the human form.

Michelangelo's Sistine Chapel ceiling (Figs. **11.12**, **11.14**, and **11.15**) perfectly exemplifies the ambition and genius of this era. In each of the triangles along the sides of the chapel, the ancestors of Christ await the Redeemer. Between them, amid *trompe l'oeil* architectural elements, are the sages of antiquity. In the corners, Michelangelo depicts various biblical stories, and across the center of the ceiling he unfolds the episodes of Genesis. The center of the ceiling captures the creation of Adam at the moment of fulfillment (Fig. **11.12**). The human forms display sculpturally modeled anatomical detail. God stretches outward from his angels to a reclining, but dynamic Adam, awaiting the divine infusion, the spark of the soul. The fingers do not touch, but we can anticipate the electrifying power of God's physical contact with a mortal man.

The Sistine Chapel ceiling creates a breathtaking visual panoply. It is impossible to get a comprehensive view of the whole of the ceiling from any point in the chapel.

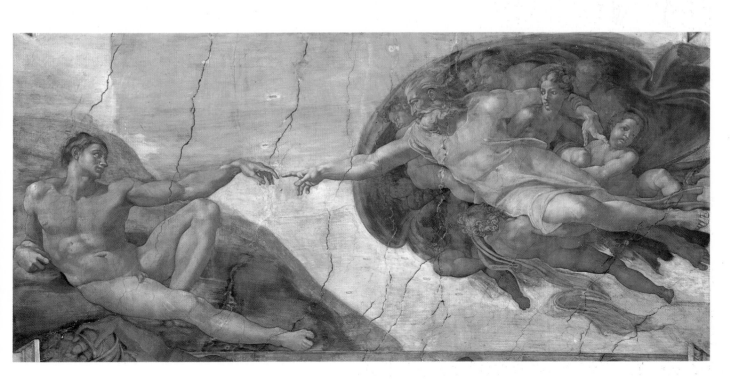

PROFILE

Michelangelo (1475–1564)

Sculptor, painter, architect, and poet, Michelangelo was one of the world's greatest artists. Born Michelangelo Buonarroti, he came from a respectable Florentine family and when he was twelve years old he was apprenticed to the Florentine painter Domenico Ghirlandaio. Even before his apprenticeship had ended, Michelangelo turned away from painting to sculpture, and he gained the attention of Florence's ruler, Lorenzo de' Medici, the Magnificent, who invited the young Michelangelo to stay at his palace. During these early years, Michelangelo became a master of anatomy.

In 1494, after the Medici fell from power, Michelangelo traveled. He spent five years in Rome and enjoyed his first success as a sculptor with a life-size statue of the Roman wine god, Bacchus. He carved his magnificent *Pietà*—that is, the dead Christ in the lap of his mother—when he was twenty-three years old (see Fig. **11.17**), and this larger-than-lifesize work established him as a leading sculptor of his time.

He returned to Florence for four years in 1501, and there met Leonardo da Vinci. Both artists were commissioned to work on large battle scenes for the walls of the city hall. Leonardo never finished his scenes, and Michelangelo's are lost, and we know of them only through sketches and copies made by other artists. According to some sources, during this time Michelangelo learned from Leonardo how to depict flowing and active movement in the human form, and the style developed during these years in Florence stayed with him for the rest of his life.

By 1505 Michelangelo was back in Rome, beginning a series of grand, large-scale works under the patronage of Pope Julius II. Over the next forty years he struggled unsuccessfully to complete the first of these colossal endeavors, Pope Julius' tomb. The second, the Sistine Chapel in the Vatican (Figs. **11.12**, **11.15**, and **11.39**) became Michelangelo's most famous work, with *David* (see Fig. **11.16**) a close second.

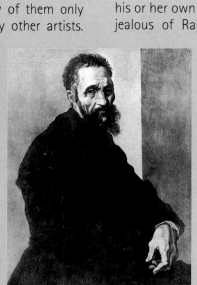

11.13 Michelangelo (1475–1564). Painting by Giuliano Bugiardini. Uffizi Gallery, Florence, Italy.

Between 1515 and 1534 he was back in Florence, working for the Medici, who had returned to power. There, he designed and sculpted tombs for two Medici princes and began the Medici chapel in which the tombs were placed. He left Florence and the unfinished chapel in 1534. Returning to Rome, he painted the fresco *The Last Judgment* for Pope Paul III on the altar wall of the Sistine Chapel, and the pope appointed him supervising architect of St Peter's Church in Rome. Earlier in this period he designed a square for the civic center of Rome, which symbolized Rome as the center of the world.

During the last years of his life, Michelangelo's religious faith deepened, and he produced not only the complicated and somber frescoes of the Pauline Chapel in the Vatican but also a considerable amount of poetry. Among the few sculptural works attempted in his late years was a *pietà*, which he designed for his own tomb. After his death in 1564, his body was returned to Florence for burial.

Michelangelo's ideal was the full realization of individuality—a reflection of his own unique genius. He epitomized the quality of *terribilità*, a supreme confidence that allows a person to accept no authority but his or her own genius. Critical of his own work, he was jealous of Raphael, disliked Leonardo, and clashed constantly with his patrons, yet in his letters he expresses a real sympathy and concern for those close to him. His works reveal a deep understanding of humanity and reflect a neo-Platonic philosophy. He captures the Platonic idea of potential energy, imprisoned in the earthly body, and he believed, as did Plato, that the image from the artist's hand must spring from the idea in his or her mind. The idea is the reality, and it is revealed by the genius of the artist. The artist does not create the ideas, but finds them in the natural world, which reflects the absolute idea: beauty. Thus, to the neo-Platonist, when art imitates nature, it reveals truths hidden within nature.

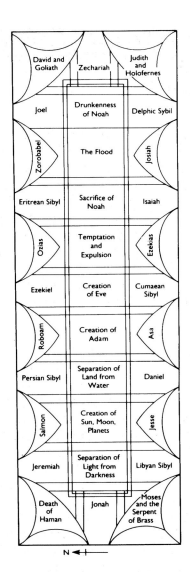

11.14 Diagram of scenes from the Sistine Chapel ceiling.

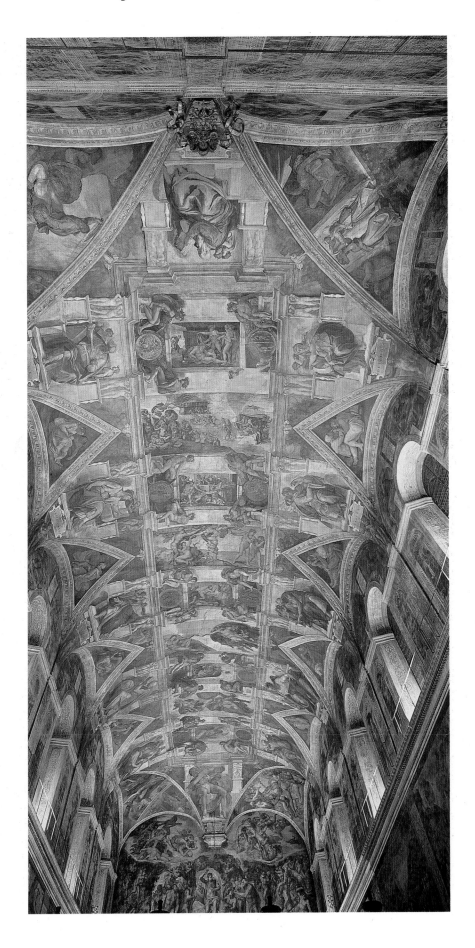

11.15 Michelangelo, Sistine Chapel ceiling, 1508–12.
Fresco, 44 × 128 ft (13.41 × 39 m). Vatican, Rome.

Michelangelo—*David*

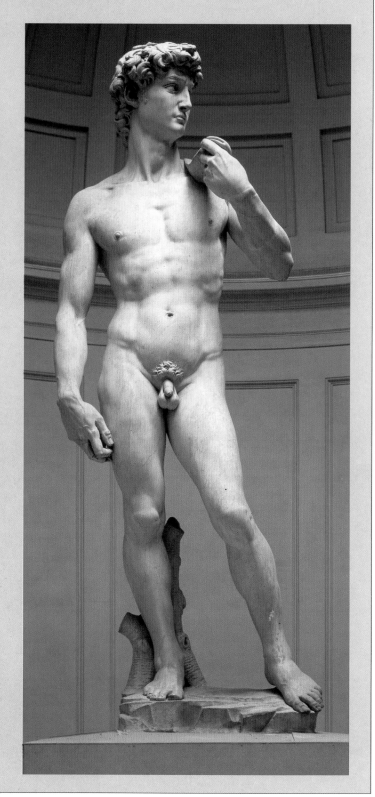

Towering some 18 feet (5.5 meters) above the floor, Michelangelo's *David* awesomely exemplifies *terribilità*. This nude champion exudes a pent-up energy, as the body seems to exist merely as an earthly prison for the soul. The upper body moves in opposition to the lower. The viewer's eye is led downward by the right arm and leg, then upward along the left arm. The entire figure seeks to break free from its confinement through thrust and counter-thrust.

Much of the effect of the *David*—the bulging muscles, exaggerated rib cage, heavy hair, undercut eyes, and frowning brow—may be due to the fact that these features were intended to be read from a distance. The work was originally meant to be placed high above the ground on a buttress for Florence Cathedral. Instead, the city leaders, believing it to be too magnificent to be placed so high, put it in front of the Palazzo Vecchio (pah-LAHT-soh VEHK-kee-oh). It also had to be protected from the rain, since the soft marble rapidly began to deteriorate.

The political symbolism of the work was recognized from the outset. The *David* stood for the valiant Florentine Republic. It also stood for all of humanity, elevated to a new and superhuman power, beauty, and grandeur. However, its revolutionary "total and triumphant nudity," which reflected Michelangelo's belief in the divinity of the human body, kept it hidden from the public for two months. When it did appear, a brass girdle with twenty-eight copper leaves hung around the waist.

Inspired by the Hellenistic sculptures he had seen in Rome, Michelangelo set out in pursuit of an emotion-charged, heroic ideal. The scale, musculature, emotion, and stunning beauty and power of those earlier works became a part of Michelangelo's style. In contrast to the Hellenistic approach, in which the "body 'acts' out the spirit's agony" (compare the *Laocoön*, by Hagesandrus, Polydorus, and Athenodorus shown in Figure **3.30**), *David* remains calm and tense.

11.16 Michelangelo, *David*, 1501–4. Marble, 14 ft 3 ins (4.1 m) high. Academy, Florence, Italy.

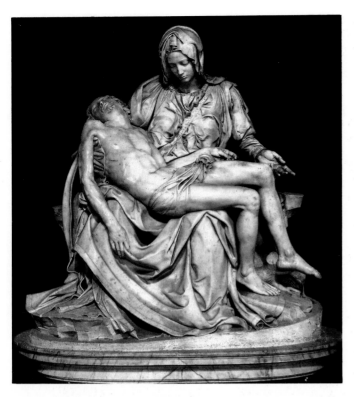

11.17 Michelangelo, *Pietà*, 1498–99. Marble, 5 ft 9 ins (1.75 m) high. St Peter's, Rome.

ment. He believed that measurement and proportion should be kept "in the eyes." This rationale for genius to do what it would, free from any pre-established "rules," enabled him to produce works such as *David* (Fig. **11.16**), a colossal figure and the earliest monumental sculpture of the High Renaissance. Its impact on the viewer is as overpowering today as it was then.

In contrast to the energy of *David* is the quiet simplicity of the *Pietà* (Fig. **11.17**). This is the only work Michelangelo ever signed. Here High Renaissance triangularity contrasts with what many believe to be a late medieval subject matter and figure treatment. The size of the Madonna compared to Jesus reflects the cult of the Virgin characteristic of the late medieval period.

Beyond these considerations, however, lies the absolute perfection of surface texture. Michelangelo's polish has so enlivened the marble that it seems to assume the warmth of real human flesh. Skin becomes even more sensuous in its contrast to rough stone. Cloth has an exquisite softness, and the expressive sway of drape reinforces the compositional line of the work. Emotion and energy are captured within the contrasting forces of form, line, and texture.

If we look upward and read the scenes back toward the altar, the prophets and sibyls appear on their sides. If we view one side as upright, the other appears upside down. These opposing directions are held together by the structure of simulated architecture, whose transverse arches and diagonal bands separate the painted vault compartments. Nudes appear at the intersections and tie the composition together because they can be read either with the prophets and sibyls below them or with the Genesis scenes, at whose corners they appear. We thus see a prime example of the basic High Renaissance principle of composition unified by the interaction of component elements.

Michelangelo broke with earlier Renaissance artists in his insistence that measurement was subordinate to judg-

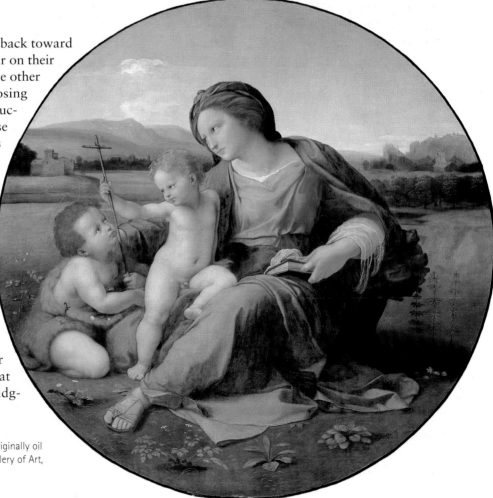

11.18 Raphael, *The Alba Madonna*, c. 1510. Canvas (originally oil on panel), 37¼ ins (94.5 cm) in diameter. National Gallery of Art, Washington D.C. (Andrew W. Mellon Collection).

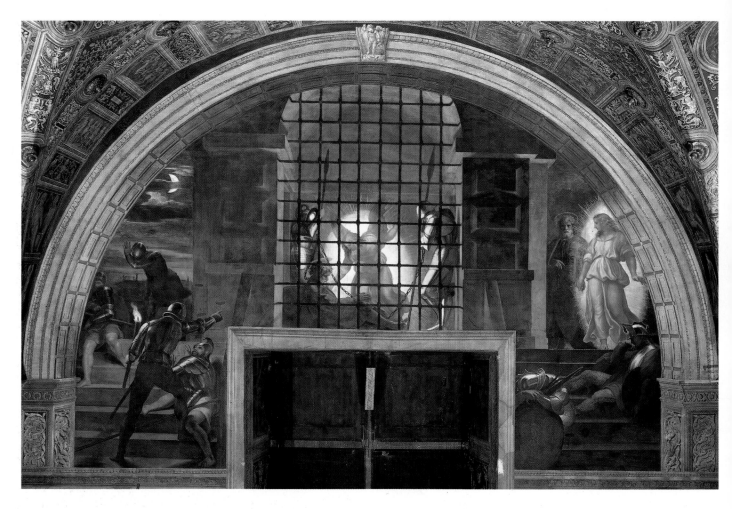

11.19 Raphael, *The Deliverance of St Peter*, 1512–14. Fresco. Stanza dell'Eliodoro, Vatican, Rome.

Raphael

Raphael (rah-fah-EL; 1483–1520) is generally regarded as the third painter in the High Renaissance triumvirate, although it has been argued that he did not reach the same level of genius and accomplishment as Leonardo and Michelangelo. In *The Alba Madonna* (Fig. **11.18**), the strong central triangle appears within the geometric parameters of a TONDO, or circular shape. The tendency of a circle to roll (visually) is counteracted by strong, parallel horizontal lines. The solid baseline of the central triangle is described by the leg of the infant John the Baptist (left), the foot of the Christ Child, the folds of the Madonna's robes, and the rock and shadow at the right. The left side of the central triangle comprises the eyes of all three figures and carries along the back of the Child to the border. The right side of the triangle is created by the edge of the Madonna's robe, joining the horizontal shadow at the right border.

Within this formula, Raphael depicts a comfortable, subtly modeled, and idealized Mary and Christ Child. The textures are soft and warm, and Raphael's treatment of skin creates an almost tactile sensation—we can almost discern the warm blood flowing beneath it, a characteristic relatively new to two-dimensional art. Raphael's figures express lively power, and his mastery of three-dimensional form and deep space is unsurpassed.

In *The Deliverance of St Peter* (Fig. **11.19**) Raphael again accepted the challenge of a constraining space. To accommodate the intrusion of the window into the semi-circular area of the wall, Raphael divided the composition into three sections representing the three phases of the miracle of St Peter's escape from prison. The intense light shining from the center section emphasizes the expressiveness of this depiction.

Titian and Tintoretto: The High Renaissance in Venice

Tiziano Vecelli, known in English as Titian (TISH-uhn; 1488?–1576), made one of the most crucial discoveries in the history of art. The art historian Frederick Hartt describes it this way: "He was the first man in modern times to free the brush from the task of exact description of tactile surfaces, volumes, and details, and to convert it into a vehicle for the direct perception of light through color and for the unimpeded expression of feeling."[1] This new type of brushwork is present in the *Assumption of the Virgin* (Fig. **11.20**) but is restricted to the background. Long before he died, he used the technique on entire paintings, and so did most other painters in Venice.

Part of Titian's unique technique lay in the way in which he built up pigment from a reddish ground through many layers of glaze, which lent warmth to all the colors of the painting. The glazes were used to tone down colors that the artist believed were too demanding and to give depth and richness to the work. Glazing made many of the colors and shadows seem "miraculously suspended." If Titian himself is a reliable source, he may have used as many as thirty or forty layers of glaze on a single painting.

Assumption of the Virgin exudes an almost fiery glow from the underpainting, and our eyes are led upward from the base of the picture, where our eye level is, to a hovering Madonna lifted on a cloud by a host of PUTTI or cherubs. Above her, emerging from a flaming yellow and orange sky, boiling in undulating brushstrokes and angelic faces, is the figure of God. The circular sweep of the painting's arched top and the encircling angels separate the Virgin from the outstretched hands of the apostles by compositional psychology as well as space, which is almost breached by the raised arm of the foreground figure.

As Titian grew old, the Venetian School produced another claim for leadership in Jacopo Robusti, called Tintoretto (teen-toh-RET-toh; 1518–94), who took his name from his father's trade as a dyer. In many respects, Tintoretto bridges the time from Renaissance to baroque. It is said that Tintoretto worked in Titian's studio as a boy until Titian saw one of his drawings and ejected him from his house, never to return. Nonetheless, Tintoretto always admired Titian. He was impetuous as an artist and a man. For example, when he was competing for the commission to paint the ceiling of the Scuola San Rocco in Venice, Tintoretto reportedly sneaked into the school in the middle of the night and affixed his full-scale painting to the ceiling. That and other impetuous acts did not endear him to everyone, but his behaviour succeeded in gaining important commissions, which he finished with tremendous speed. It was, in fact, that spontaneous rapidity that characterized his style—he worked rapidly and with great passion, capturing the essences of the forms in opposition to the careful detail of others.

Darkness seems always to dominate the tone of his paintings, because he began his works with a dark underpainting, and the resulting tone can be seen in his first masterpiece, *St Mark Freeing a Christian Slave* (Fig. **11.21**). This depiction tells the story of the legend of a

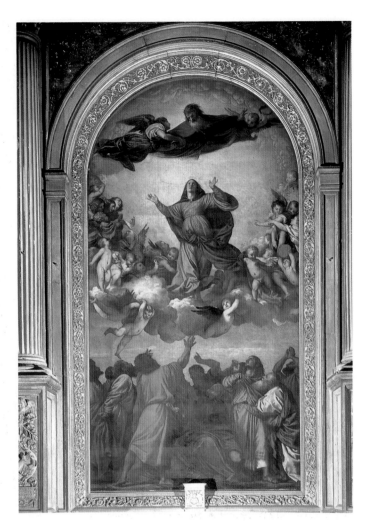

11.20 Titian, *Assumption of the Virgin*, 1516–18. Panel, 22 ft 6 ins × 11 ft 10 ins (6.9 × 3.6 m). Santa Maria Gloriosa dei Frari, Venice, Italy.

slave of a French knight who slipped away to go to Alexandria to venerate the bones of St Mark. When he returned, his master decided to punish him by gouging out his eyes and breaking his legs with hammers. However, St Mark descends from heaven and intercedes to end the torment and free the slave, whom we see at the base of the painting in dramatic CHIAROSCURO and perspective foreshortening. Broken hammer handles lie around him and, in a curious counterpoint to the line of the painting, extend upward in the hands of the turbaned executioner. The golden cape of St Mark draws the eye powerfully and makes the viewer acutely aware of the disjointed emotionalism of the composition as a jumble of figures, formed from broken lines and competing colors, and throws the surface of the work into turmoil. This twisted and turning whirlpool effect of figures around a central point appears in many of

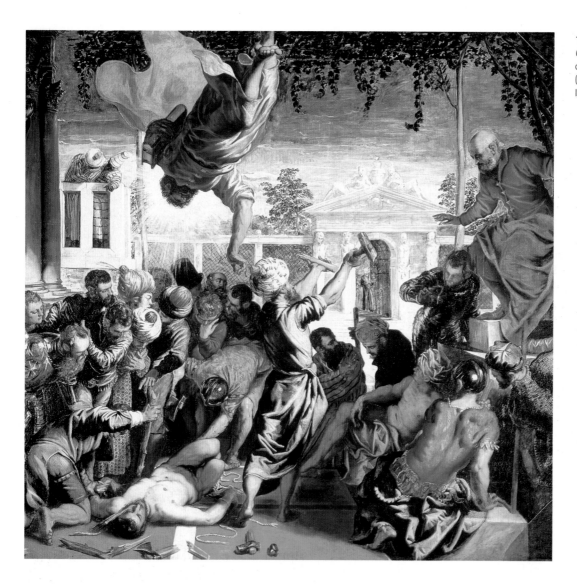

11.21 Tintoretto, *St Mark Freeing a Christian Slave*, 1548. Oil on canvas, 13 ft 10 ins × 18ft ⅛ in (4.15 × 5.41 m). Academy, Venice, Italy.

Tintoretto's works, and gives them their characteristic frenetic appearance. Despite the darkened underpainting, the colors are vibrant and gleaming. Faces reflect deep human emotion and psychological insight. Originally intended as a ceiling painting in an octagonal space, the strong diagonal figures run parallel with or at right angles to the corners.

Mannerism

Papal patronage had assembled great genius in Rome at the turn of the sixteenth century. It had also ignited and supported a brilliant fire of human genius in the arts. The Spanish invasion and Sack of Rome doused the flame of Italian art in 1527 and scattered its ashes across Europe, contributing to the disillusionment and turmoil of religious and political strife that marked the next seventy years.

Considerable debate exists about the nature of the style or trend occurring around the clearly developed style of the High Renaissance and lasting until the baroque style of the next century. The prevalent view today is positive, rather than dismissing it as a decadent and affected imitation of the High Renaissance.

The name attached to this trend, if not style, is Mannerism. The term originates from the mannered, or affected, appearance of subjects in paintings. These works are coldly formal and inward-looking. Their oddly proportioned forms, icy stares, and subjective viewpoint can be puzzling yet intriguing when they are seen out of context. Nevertheless, we find an appealing modernism in their emotional, sensitive, subtle, and elegant content. At the same time, Mannerism has an intellectual component that distorts reality, alters space, and makes often obscure cultural allusions. Anti-classical emotionalism and the abandonment of classical balance and form, alongside of form and color in Parmigianino's (pahr-mee-jah-NEE-noh) *Madonna with the Long Neck* (Fig. **11.23**). This striking work was commissioned in 1534 for the Church of the Servi in Bologna but was never delivered. What captures us is exactly that quality of elongation that is associated with Mannerism. The line, color, and proportions of the painting have an exotic, ethereal, and almost "other-worldly" appearance, especially the Christ Child. If we hearken back to the basic triangle of High Renaissance composition, we find none of that here. The long, exposed leg at the painting's left border creates a disjointed angle as it meets the foot of Jesus. Simplicity of composition has

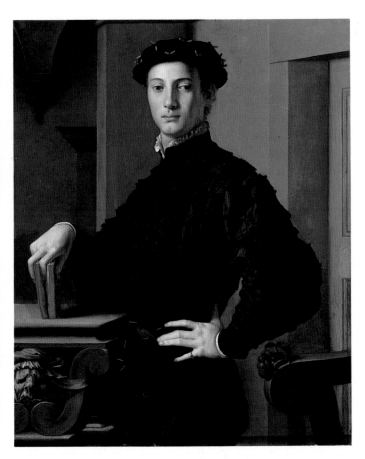

11.22 Bronzino (Agnolo di Cosimo di Mariano), *Portrait of a Young Man*, c. 1535–40. Oil on wood, 37⅝ × 29½ ins (95.6 × 73 cm). Metropolitan Museum of Art, New York (Bequest of Mrs. H.O. Havemeyer, 1929).

11.23 Parmigianino, *Madonna with the Long Neck*, c. 1534. Oil on canvas, 7ft 1 in × 4 ft 4 ins (2.16 × 1.32 m). Uffizi Gallery, Florence, Italy. Photo: © Studio Fotografico Quattrone.

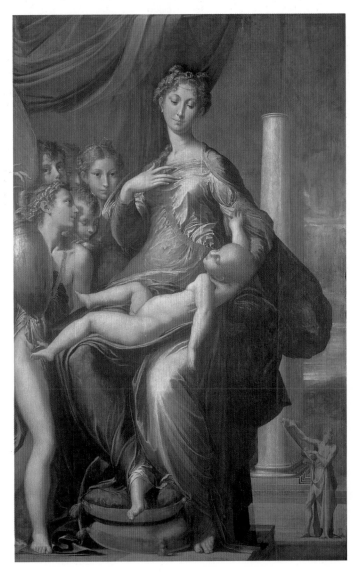

clear underpinnings of formality and geometry, suggest the troubled nature of this style and the times in which it flourished.

Bronzino's (brahn-ZEEN-oh) *Portrait of a Young Man* (Fig. **11.22**) makes the point. A strong High Renaissance central triangle dominates the basic composition of this work. Its lines, however, have a nervous and unstable quality—incongruous, juxtaposed rectangular and curved forms create an uneasy feeling. The greens and blacks of the painting are very cold, and the starkness of the background adds to the feeling of discomfort. Shadows are harsh, and skin quality is cold. Light and shade create some dimension, but the absence of perspective brings background objects inappropriately into the forward plane of the picture. The human form is attenuated and disproportionate. The young man's head is too small for his body, and particularly for his hands. Finally, his pose and affected stare are typical of the artificiality that gave this movement its name. We can see a clearly similar treatment

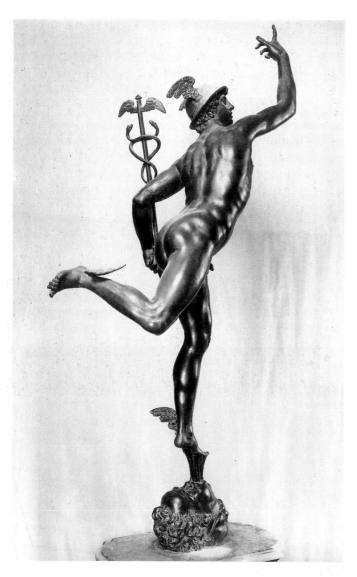

11.24 Giovanni da Bologna, *Mercury*, c. 1567. Bronze, 5 ft 9 ins (1.75 m) high. Museo Nazionale del Bargello, Florence, Italy.

ARCHITECTURE

At the turn of the sixteenth century, architecture saw Christian and classical ideas come into balance. At the same time, it moved away from its insistence on decorative surface detail and toward a greater concern for space and volume. The shift of patronage from the local rulers to the Roman Catholic Church, which drew visual artists—painters, sculptors, and architects—to Rome, also brought to architecture a more formal, monumental, and serious style.

A perfect early example of High Renaissance architecture is Bramante's (brah-MAHNT-ay) Tempietto (temp-ee-YET-toh) or "little temple" (Fig. **11.25**). Pope Julius II wanted all Roman basilica-form churches replaced by magnificent monuments that would overshadow the remains of Imperial Rome, and the Tempietto was built as part of this plan. The building was authorized in 1502, to be set on the spot where St Peter was believed to have been crucified. However, the work was not completed until after 1511.

In contrast to the Corinthian and Ionic details that had been popular, Bramante chose for the Tempietto the more severe Doric order. The circular plan, however, gave him a new flexibility. The culmination of this style appears in Bramante's design for St Peter's, a design later revised by Michelangelo and finished, later still, by Giacomo della Porta (JAH-coh-moh day-lah-POHR-tah; see Figs. **11.36**, **11.40**, **11.41**, and **11.42**). The geometrical and symmetrical design of St Peter's was based on the circle and the square, over which perched a tremendous dome surrounded by four lesser domes.

By the late sixteenth century, architecture had taken on Mannerist tendencies, especially in France under King Francis I. The Lescot (lehs-KOH) wing of the Louvre Palace (Fig. **11.26**) has a discomfiting design of superficial detail and unusual proportions, with strange juxtapositions of curvilinearity and rectilinearity. Here we find a continuation of decorative detail applied to exterior wall surfaces in the Renaissance fashion. However, careful mathematical proportions have been replaced by a flattened dome and dissimilar treatments of the shallow arches. The helmet-like dome stands in awkward contrast to the pediment of the central section and wears a sort of crown, perched nervously on top. The relief sculptures of the top level of the central section are far too large to be comfortable in their architectural context.

In this same period, another style sprang up that would significantly influence later eras. Andrea Palladio (pahl-LAH-dee-oh; 1518–80) designed villas and palaces which reflected his clients' individuality and pride in their worldly possessions. The Villa Rotonda in Vicenza (Fig. **11.27**)

been replaced by a myriad of detail so complex that every square inch of the painting reveals something intriguing and captivating.

The late sixteenth century produced relatively little sculpture of major significance. The twisting, elongated form of *Mercury* (Fig. **11.24**) by Giovanni da Bologna (joh-VAHN-ee dah boh-LOH-nyuh; 1529–1608), however, shows us qualities that are equivalent to the Mannerist tendencies in painting of the same era. The affected pose, the upward-striving line, the linear emphasis, and the nearly total detachment from earth suggest tension and nervous energy. Mercury races through the air seeking the escape of flight, supported by a puff of breath from a mask symbolizing the wind.

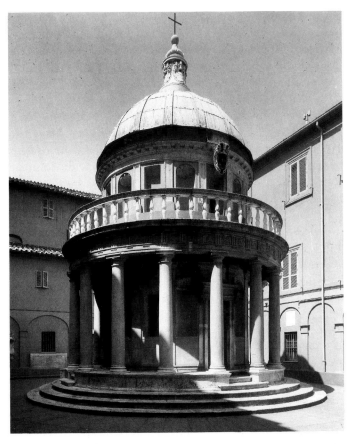

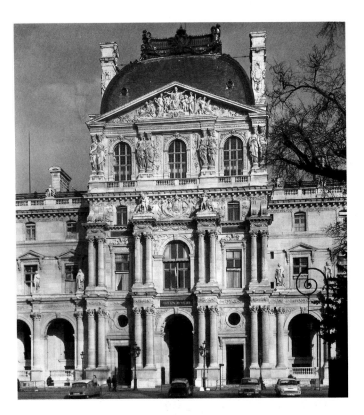

11.26 Pierre Lescot, exterior façade of the Square Court of the Louvre, Paris, begun 1546.

11.25 Donato Bramante, the Tempietto, authorized 1502, completed after 1511. San Pietro in Montorio, Rome.

11.27 Palladio, Villa Rotonda, Vicenza, Italy, begun 1567–9.

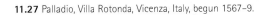

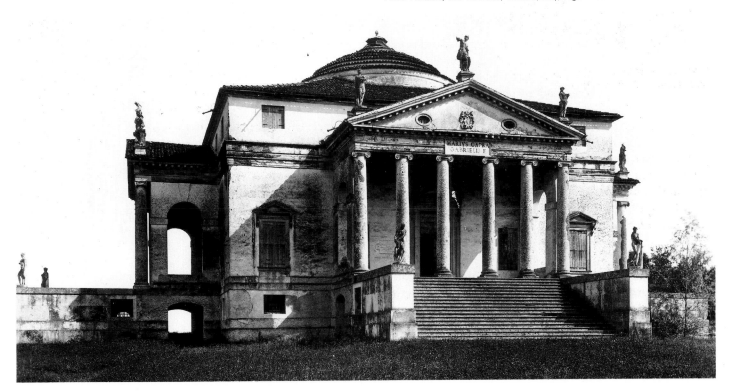

shows strong classical influences, combining Greek and Roman details. The porticos carry freestanding Ionic columns, and the dome is reminiscent of the Pantheon. The rooms of the villa are arranged symmetrically around the central rotunda. Palladio's mathematical combination of cubes and circles is characteristic of the Renaissance, but he has cleansed the exterior surfaces of detail, placing the decorative sculpture above, in anticipation of baroque treatments. Palladio explained his designs in *Four Books on Architecture*, which were highly influential in establishing canons later used in various "revival" periods. Thomas Jefferson's Monticello in the United States is one such example (see Fig. **14.22**).

THE PERFORMING ARTS
Music

Renaissance music differed from the late medieval style particularly in features such as greater melodic and rhythmic integration, a more extended range, broader texture, and subjection to harmonic principles of order. In the sixteenth century, this integrated style produced distinct vocal and instrumental idioms, and vocal music, under the influence of humanism, became increasingly intent on expressing a text. In fact, vocal music, because of the humanistic interest in language, was a more important musical idiom than instrumental music. Renaissance composers tried to enhance the meaning and emotion of the written text. In doing so, they often used what is called *word painting*—for example, if a text described a descent, then the music might utilize a descending melodic line. In sum, however, and despite the increased sense of emotion, Renaissance music remained restrained and balanced: avoiding extreme contrasts in dynamics, tone color, or rhythm.

The texture of Renaissance music was mostly polyphonic, with imitation among the voices being fairly common. There was also homophony, especially in light music such as dance. In addition, the musical texture of a piece might vary, with the contrast used to highlight the particular emotion of the composition.

Sacred Music
Although the Sack of Rome by Charles V destroyed the city, its musical traditions survived, and the Papal chapel continued as one of the central musical forces in Europe. There, the career of Giovanni Pierluigi da Palestrina (pal-es-TREEN-uh; 1526?–1594) flourished. Palestrina (Fig. **11.28**) enjoyed the grace and favor of popes and cardinals. Director of the Julian Chapel Choir from 1551 to 1555, he

became a singer in the pontifical choir in the latter year and began to compose for the papal chapel. Because he was married, however, he was forced to leave his post when Pope Paul IV imposed a stricter discipline in choral appointments.

Palestrina's works are exclusively vocal and almost totally liturgical, the only exceptions being a single book of madrigals and a collection of spiritual madrigals. He wrote 105 masses and became the most celebrated composer of his time, and his name became synonymous with Counter-Reformation polyphony. (We will discuss the Counter-Reformation in Chapter 13.)

Palestrina's *Pope Marcellus* Mass is his most famous. It was dedicated to Pope Marcellus II, who reigned briefly in 1555, when Palestrina sang in the Papal Choir. The Mass is written for six voice parts (*a cappella*—that is, without accompaniment): soprano, alto, two tenors, and two basses. Earlier we examined a *Kyrie* from Gregorian chant (CD track 4). Let's now examine the Kyrie from Palestrina's *Pope Marcellus* Mass (CD track 7; Fig. **11.29**).

The Kyrie has a rich, polyphonic texture, in which the six voices imitate each other. The melodic contours are

11.28 Giovanni Pierluigi da Palestrina.

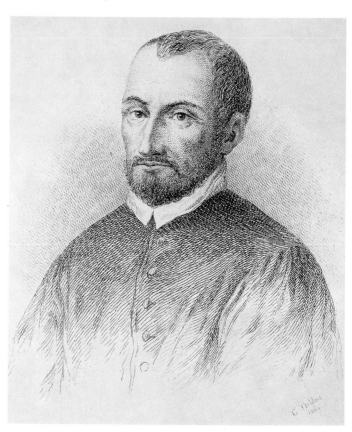

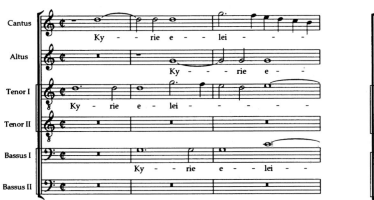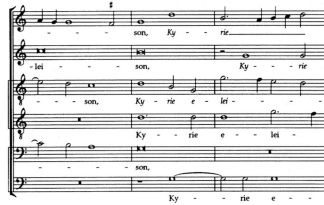

11.29 Giovanni Pierluigi da Palestrina, Kyrie from the *Pope Marcellus* Mass (published 1567).

rounded, evoking images of the Gregorian chant. The melody is in the top voice, the *cantus* or soprano line. The Kyrie is in the traditional three sections we discussed in Chapter 7:

1. *Kyrie eleison.*   Lord, have mercy upon us.
2. *Christe eleison.*   Christ, have mercy upon us.
3. *Kyrie eleison.*   Lord, have mercy upon us.

The words of this brief text are repeated with different melodic treatments and express calm supplication. Each section ends with all voices coming together on sustained chords.

Another important form of Renaissance sacred music is the *motet*, which is like the Mass in style, but shorter. The Renaissance motet is a polyphonic choral work set to a Latin text other than the ordinary of the mass. We will examine the motet in greater detail, along with its most prominent composer, Josquin des Prez, in the next chapter.

Secular Music

The sixteenth century witnessed the development of previous forms into the *madrigal*, a setting of lyric poetry for four or five voices. Madrigal is the name given to two important types of secular vocal music. One type was cultivated exclusively in fourteenth-century Italy; the other developed anew and flourished in Italy during the sixteenth century during an explosion of Italian poetry. Poetically, the sixteenth-century madrigal normally comprises a text of from three to fourteen lines (of seven and eleven syllables in no particular order) arranged in a rhyme scheme of the poet's choosing. The musical setting emphasizes the mood and meaning of individual words and phrases of the text rather than formal structure.

Madrigals were composed for as few as three and as many as eight parts, although, in general, before 1650 a four-part texture was preferred. After that, a five-part texture predominated. Madrigals were often sung by solo voices, one per part, but also were performed with instruments substituting for some of the voices or doubling the various parts. By the second half of the sixteenth century, the madrigal had become established as the dominant form of secular music in Italy and the rest of Europe.

Instrumental Music

In the sixteenth century, musical instruments rose above their old role of merely reinforcing voice parts, and instrumental music developed an independence from vocal music (although instrumental music still remained subordinate to vocal music). Previously, instruments tended to accompany voices or to play music originally intended for the voice. In the sixteenth century, more music was written expressly for instruments, and music was written to exploit the qualities of individual instruments. Much instrumental music was written for dancing, an extremely popular form of entertainment (see the Dance section of Chapter 10).

A new treatment of instrumental sound can be heard in music written for the *vihuela*, a type of guitar, and the harpsichord. The lute (a guitar-like instrument with a pear-shaped body) also was a popular instrument. In the later part of the century, Mannerism reacted against the complicated texture of polyphony and sought to revive Greek musical practice with its emphasis on simplicity.

Renaissance musicians differentiated between two general types of instruments: soft, indoor instruments—such as the lute and the recorder (an early flute)—and loud, outdoor instruments—such as trumpets and the shawm (a predecessor of the oboe). Interestingly, Renaissance composers did not indicate which instruments they desired, and the same work might be played by one set of instruments on one occasion and by something quite different on another.

Theatre

Renaissance drama in Italy, like painting, tended not to reflect the discordant political cloak-and-dagger atmo-

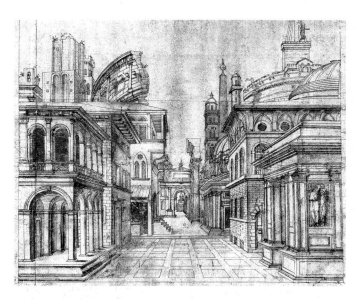

11.30 Baldassare Peruzzi, stage design, probably for *La Calendria*, 1514.

sphere of its surroundings. Italian playwrights chose mostly to write tender, sentimental, pastoral comedies, in a graceful, witty, and polished style, and the drama was theatre of the aristocracy, produced with elaborate trappings and usually at court (Fig. **11.30**), although sometimes in public squares under courtly sponsorship. No permanent theatres existed at the time, and the surviving Roman theatre buildings were in such disrepair that they were unusable. When, rather late in the day, the theatre of the late Renaissance era finally caught the Renaissance spirit, it developed in ways that had a great impact on theatre in every part of Europe.

In Italy, where the Renaissance was largely in the visual arts, two important developments occurred. One was a new form of theatre building, and the other was painted scenery. Both contributed to changing aesthetics and style in formal theatre production. Vitruvius, the Roman architect and historian, was the source of plans for new theatre buildings in Italy.

The discovery of mechanical perspective found its way into the theatre in the sixteenth century. The designs of Sebastiano Serlio (SAIR-lee-oh; Fig. **11.31**) illustrate some of this new painted scenery. Just as in early Renaissance paintings, the visual effect of falsified perspective "tricks" is based on mechanical principles. From a point slightly upstage of the actual playing area, the scenery gets smaller and smaller to an imaginary vanishing point. The effect induces a sense of great depth when, in reality, the set recedes only a few feet. Of course, the actors were restricted to a narrow playing area adjacent to the full-size downstage wings. If the actors had moved upstage, they would have towered over the buildings. Stage settings

became more and more elaborate, and a new "opening" usually brought an audience to see not a new play, but, rather, the new accomplishments of the set designer.

Palladio's Teatro Olimpico (tay-AHT-troh oh-LIM-pee-koh; Fig. **11.32**) was once thought to be the model for modern theatre, but scholars now believe that our theatre derived from the Teatro Farnese at Parma. The most significant change in the theatre of this era was a move to enclose the dramatic action within a "picture frame," or *proscenium*, so that the audience sat on only one side of the stage and watched the action through a rectangular or arched opening. The term "picture-frame stage" is particularly appropriate, in respect of both what it resembled and of the painting traditions of the era.

Commedia dell'arte

Also competing for the attention of the public was Italy's unique COMMEDIA DELL'ARTE (kohm-MAY-dee-ah del AHR-tay). This theatrical form developed parallel to the traditions of the regular theatre, and it enjoyed tremendous popular support. Most singularly, it featured the actor rather than the script.

Commedia dell'arte could be identified by four specific characteristics. The first was improvisation. Even though fully fledged productions had plots and subplots, dialogue was completely improvised within the plot outline, or *scenario*. A few works were serious, and some pastoral,

11.31 Sebastiano Serlio, stage setting from *D'Architettura*, 1540–51.

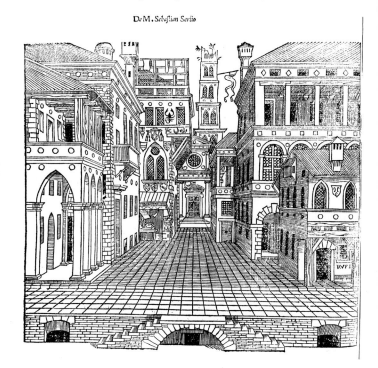

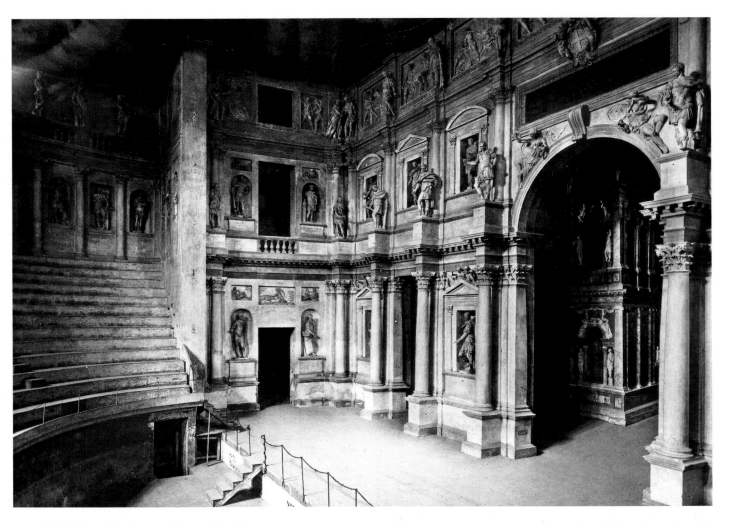

11.32 Palladio, Teatro Olimpico, stage, Vicenza, Italy, 1580–4.

but most were comic. The acting style appears to have been natural, though the actors needed good entrance and exit lines as well as repartee.

The second characteristic was the use of stock characters—young lovers, old fathers, braggart soldiers, and comic servants, or *zanni* (ZAH-nee). All wore stock costumes, which the audience could easily identify. Actors portraying these roles required great skill, physical dexterity, and timing, since much of the humor was visual. The famous actor who played Scaramouche, Tiberio Fiorilli, could apparently still box another actor's ears with his foot at the age of eighty-three. Actors in the commedia also had to dance, sing, and do acrobatics. Somersaulting without spilling a glass of wine, for example, seems to have brought down the house.

A third characteristic was the use of mime and pantomime. All characters except the lovers and the serving maid wore masks, and attitudes were communicated through gestures (Fig. **11.33**).

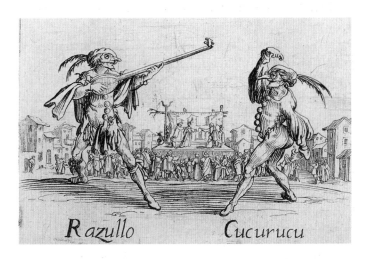

11.33 Two figures from the commedia dell'arte, copy of an etching by the engraver Jacques Callot.

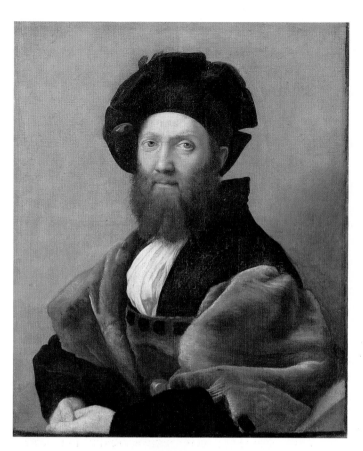

11.34 Raphael, *Count Baldassare Castiglione*, 1514. Oil transferred from wood to canvas, 2 ft 9³/₄ ins × 2 ft 3¹/₂ ins (82 × 66 cm). Louvre, Paris.

Finally, commedia actors traveled in companies, and each member of the company played the same role over and over again. The practice was so pervasive that actors often lost their own identities. Many actors even changed their original names to those of the stage personages they portrayed.

From the mid-sixteenth to the mid-seventeenth centuries, troupes of commedia actors traveled throughout Europe. Their influence and popularity were tremendous, but commedia remained an Italian form, although its characters and situations found their way into the theatre of other nations. By the end of the seventeenth century, commedia had, to all intents and purposes, disappeared. One final fact must be noted: commedia dell'arte introduced women into the theatre as equals. Their roles were as important as, and often more important than, those of men; women, not boys, played the female parts.

LITERATURE

The sixteenth century witnessed the climax and close of what amounted to an Italian monopoly in Renaissance literature. The influence of the Italian Renaissance spread to the rest of Europe, reaching France in the middle third of the century and England in the last third of the century. The common factor everywhere was imitation of the classics. In Italy the writers of the High Renaissance were apparently indifferent to the tragic social and political events to which they bore witness. In the last chapter, we noted something of Machiavelli's view—that of limited hope—but others reacted with bland unconcern and ironic humor. Most, like Castiglione, chose to ignore what was going on. However, it is reasonably clear that after the Spanish Sack of Rome in 1527, literature, with perhaps the exception of Torquato Tasso, slipped into mediocrity.

Baldassare Castiglione

In essence, the Renaissance state was monarchial. In fact, the whole movement of the Renaissance was toward monarchial government, as we have seen in France and Spain and will see in England in Chapter 12. In Italy, it may have seemed less so, but it was nonetheless the case in the petty duchies and principalities, and the gentlemen and ladies of the Renaissance were courtiers. The Conte Baldassare Castiglione (bahl-dahs-SAH-ray kahs-teel-YOH-nay; 1478–1529) was himself the perfect courtier (Fig. **11.34**), and his book *Il Cortegiano* or *The Courtier* became a universal guide to "goodly manners" and "civil conversation" of the court of the duchy of Urbino. In effect, he was the arbiter of courtly behavior for all of Europe. In this influential work, Castiglione suggests, through an imagined dialogue, a picture of an artistically ordered society, in which cultivated Italians regard social living as a fine art.

Castiglione was raised at the court of Duke Sforza of Milan. He studied Greek, Latin, and Italian poetry, music, painting, and horsemanship. As his portrait reveals, he was a handsome, intelligent man, who entered the service of the duke of Urbino in 1504, thereby entering an environment with a fabulous library that was the rendezvous of European scholars and artists. As a diplomat, he visited England, became an advisor of Pope Leo X, and papal nuncio of Pope Clement VII to the court of the Holy Roman Emperor Charles V. When the Emperor's troops sacked Rome, Castiglione became the subject of numerous rumors of treason.

The particular character of *The Courtier* lies in the realistic manner in which the conversations are handled and the way in which the various opinions of the participants are introduced. Above all, *The Courtier* propounds the humanist's ultimate ideals—of men and women of intellectual refinement, cultural grace, moral stability, spiritual insight, and social consciousness. It provided a model of the ideal Renaissance society, but its values are timeless: true worth is determined "by character and intellect rather than by birth." The excerpt that follows, although brief, illustrates both the context of the time and the content of Castiglione's work.

The Courtier
Baldassare Castiglione

On Women

Leaving aside, therefore, those virtues of the mind which she must have in common with the courtier, such as prudence, magnanimity, continence and many others besides, and also the qualities that are common to all kinds of women, such as goodness and discretion, the ability to take good care, if she is married, of her husband's belongings and house and children, and the virtues belonging to a good mother, I say that the lady who is at Court should properly have, before all else, a certain pleasing affability whereby she will know how to entertain graciously every kind of man with charming and honest conversation, suited to the time and the place and the rank of the person with whom she is talking. And her sense and modest behavior, and the candor that ought to inform all her actions, should be accompanied by a quick and vivacious spirit by which she shows her freedom from boorishness; but with such a virtuous manner that she makes herself thought no less chaste, prudent and benign than she is pleasing, witty and discreet. Thus she must observe a certain difficult mean, composed as it were of contrasting qualities, and take care not to stray beyond certain fixed limits. Nor in her desire to be thought chaste and virtuous, should she appear withdrawn or run off if she dislikes the company she finds herself in or thinks the conversation improper. For it might easily be thought that she was pretending to be straitlaced simply to hide something she feared others could find out about her; and in any case, unsociable manners are always deplorable.

Ludovico Ariosto

A second major literary figure of the time was Ludovico Ariosto (loo-doh-VEE-koh ah-ree-AWS-toh; 1474–1533). Ariosto was a courtier of the house of Este at Ferrara, and was in the civil and diplomatic service, as well as court poet. Classically trained, he wrote most of his work in Latin until he was twenty-five years old. His father died when he was twenty-six, and he assumed responsibility for providing for his four brothers and five sisters. He spent fourteen years as confidential secretary to Cardinal d'Este, and during this time he traveled throughout Italy on political missions. In 1518, he entered the service of the cardinal's brother, the duke of Ferrara, eventually becoming the duke's director of entertainment. Under Ariosto's supervision, the court enjoyed pageants and dramatic productions, Ariosto himself designing the theatre and scenery and writing a number of the plays. As early as 1505 he began his masterpiece, *Orlando Furioso*, forty cantos (sections) of which were published in 1516. For nearly thirty years he continued to revise the work, which became one of the most influential poems of the Renaissance. *Orlando Furioso* ("Roland in a Mad Fury") is a romantic epic—its forty-six cantos total over 1,200 pages—of "Loves and Ladies, Knights and Arms ... Of Curtesies, and many a Daring Feat." Ariosto depended heavily on the Greco-Roman tradition of Homer and Vergil, and borrowed incidents, character types, and rhetorical devices, such as the catalogue of troops and extended simile. Designed for a sophisticated audience, it employs an ottava rima (a stanza of eight lines rhyming abababcc), and it has a polished, graceful style. It became a bestseller throughout Europe.

Orlando Furioso captivated its sixteenth-century readers with its elements of supernatural trips to the moon, allegorical incidents that taught modesty and chastity, and romantic adventure. However, the characters are shallow and two-dimensional, for Ariosto made no attempt to probe the depths of human behavior or to tackle important issues. Nonetheless, individual incidents are worked out with care and carried through to a climax, after which the next is taken up, and all the loose threads are tied together at the end. *Orlando Furioso* served the Renaissance as a model of the large-scale narrative poem that was written with technical skill, smoothness, and the gracefulness typical of the classics. Ariosto spent most of his adult life writing and revising this masterpiece.

Focal Point

Papal Splendor—The Vatican

In this chapter, our Focal Point demonstrates the visual art and architecture that sought to make Rome and the Renaissance popes magnificent: the art of the Vatican.

Here for almost 2,000 years has been the center of a spiritual communion; in countries all over the world, Christians aspire to achieve a community of spirit with the successor to St Peter. By comprehending this significance of the Vatican, we can also understand what it was that led Roman Catholicism to embellish the center of its spiritual power with the diversity of human knowledge, including the arts.[2]

The Vatican owes most of its splendor to the Renaissance, and particularly the High Renaissance, when the popes called all great artists to Rome. The papacy as a force and the Vatican as the symbol of that force represent a synthesis of Renaissance ideas and reflections. Rome was the city devoted to the arts in the fifteenth and sixteenth centuries. The artists of the age rediscovered classical antiquity and emulated what they found. Imitation was frowned upon, and the classical quality of Renaissance art lies in its expressiveness, which is indeed comparable to that of Greece and Rome. St Peter's and the Vatican also have earthly and heavenly qualities that reflect the reality of the Church on earth and the mystery of the spiritual Church of Christ.

The magnificence of the Vatican lies in its scale, its detail, and, above all, in the enormous dome of St Peter's (Figs. **11.35** and **11.36**), the focal point as seen from the outside. Renaissance domes were intended to provide large sculptural forms against the skyline, so architects raised them on tall cylinders and often placed large central lanterns at their tops. The dome of St Peter's, a double shell of brick and stone, weighs hundreds of tons and caused critical structural problems. St Peter's lacks the solid surrounding walls of the Pantheon, and the supporting structure does little to stop the outward spread as the weight of the dome pushes downward and outward. Cracking occurred almost immediately, and a series of massive chains was placed around the base of the dome to hold it in position.

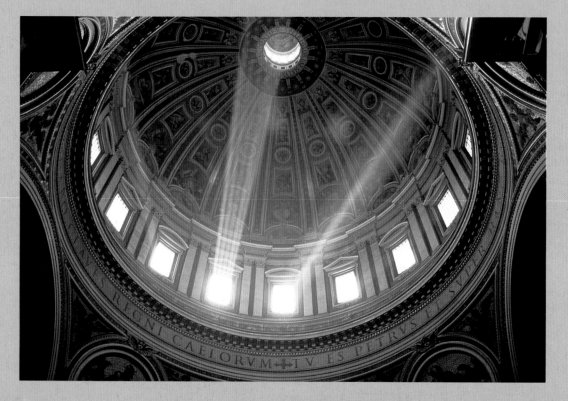

11.35 Interior of the dome of St Peter's, Rome.

The entire complex of the Vatican, with St Peter's as its focal point, is a vast scheme of parks, gardens, fountains, and buildings (Fig. **11.37**). The colonnades of St Peter's Square are decorated with 140 majestic statues of popes, bishops, and apostles by Bernini (Fig. **11.38**). Larger than life and harmonious in design, these works reach upward and create a finishing touch to the square, the façade, and the dome.

Plans for replacement of the original basilica of Old St Peter's were made by Nicholas V (r. 1447–55) in the fifteenth century, but it was Julius II (r. 1503–13) who decided actually to put those plans into effect. Julius commissioned Donato Bramante to construct the new basilica. Bramante's design called for a building in the form of a GREEK CROSS (Fig. **11.40**). The work was planned as "an harmonious arrangement of architectural forms" in an "image of bright amplitude and picturesque liveliness."

When Bramante died in 1514, two of his assistants and Raphael continued his work. However, liturgical considerations required an elongated structure, and these and other changes were made by additional architects, whose designs were severely criticized by Michelangelo. Following the death of the last of these architects, Pope Paul III (r. 1534–49) persuaded Michelangelo to become chief architect. Michelangelo set aside liturgical considerations and returned to Bramante's original conceptions, which he described as "clear and pure, full of light … whoever distances himself from Bramante, also distances himself from the truth" (Fig. **11.41**). Michelangelo's project was completed in May of 1590, as the last stone was added to the dome, and a High Mass was celebrated. Work on the thirty-six columns continued, however. This was completed by Giacomo Della Porta and Domenico Fontana after Michelangelo's death. Full completion of the basilica as it stands today had to wait for the direction of yet more architects, including Carlo Maderno. Maderno was forced to yield to the wishes of the cardinals and to change the original form of the Greek cross to a LATIN CROSS (Fig. **11.42**). As a result, the Renaissance design of Michelangelo and Bramante, with its central altar, was put aside. It was replaced by Maderno's design of a TRAVERTINE façade of gigantic proportions and sober elegance. His

11.36 Michelangelo, St Peter's, Rome, from the west, 1546–64 (dome completed by Giacomo della Porta, 1590).

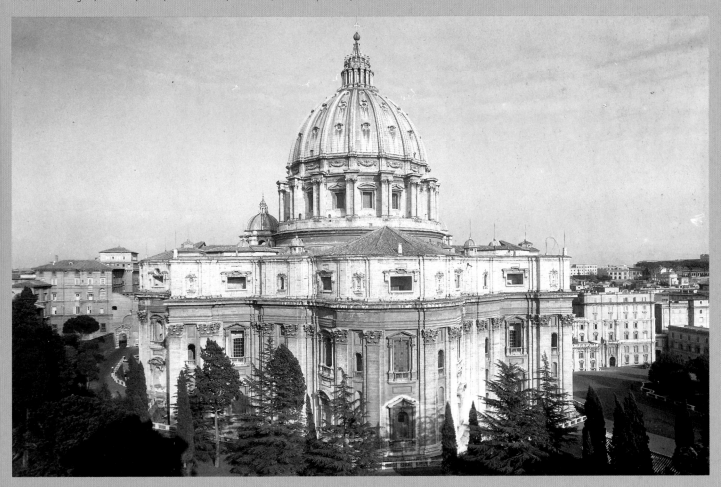

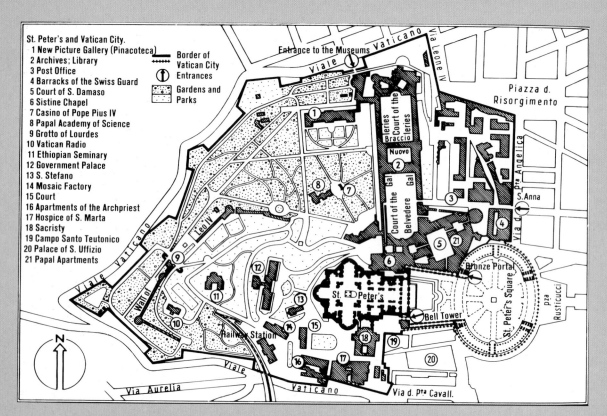

11.37 Plan of the Vatican and St Peter's, Rome.

St. Peter's and Vatican City.
1 New Picture Gallery (Pinacoteca)
2 Archives; Library
3 Post Office
4 Barracks of the Swiss Guard
5 Court of S. Damaso
6 Sistine Chapel
7 Casino of Pope Pius IV
8 Papal Academy of Science
9 Grotto of Lourdes
10 Vatican Radio
11 Ethiopian Seminary
12 Government Palace
13 S. Stefano
14 Mosaic Factory
15 Court
16 Apartments of the Archpriest
17 Hospice of S. Marta
18 Sacristy
19 Campo Santo Teutonico
20 Palace of S. Uffizio
21 Papal Apartments

Border of Vatican City
Entrances
Gardens and Parks

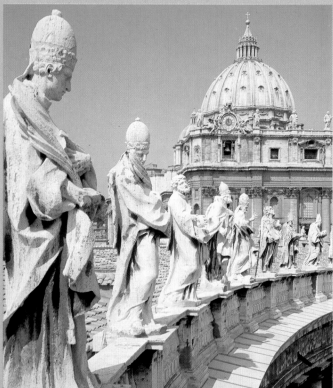

11.38 Gian Lorenzo Bernini, statues on the colonnade of St Peter's Square, Rome; colonnade designed 1657.

11.39 (*opposite*) Michelangelo, Sistine Chapel, Vatican, Rome, showing the ceiling (1508–12) and *Last Judgment* (1534–41).

extension of the basilica was influential in the development of baroque architecture. The project was finally completed in 1615.

Throughout the Vatican complex there are magnificent paintings and sculptures of Renaissance, High Renaissance, Counter-Reformation, and baroque styles. Raphael's Loggia (LOH-jah; Fig. **11.43**) forms part of the Vatican Palace apartments. Based on Raphael's study of ancient Rome and its buildings, the Loggia's theme is one of delight in seemingly inexhaustible inventiveness. Flowers, fruit, vegetables, bizarre animal figures, and winged putti appear throughout. On the ceiling vault is a series of frescoes devoted to Old Testament themes called *Raphael's Bible*. Raphael's *The Deliverance of St Peter* (see Fig. **11.19**) is also found in these apartments.

The Vatican is a rich complex that fully reflects its times and the power and wealth of the Church and the papacy. Perhaps its crowning jewel is the Sistine Chapel (see Figs. **11.12**, **11.14**, and **11.15**), with its magnificent ceiling. But the ceiling is only part of a whole. It is the entirety of the Sistine Chapel (Fig. **11.39**) that is a supreme recreation of classical harmony.

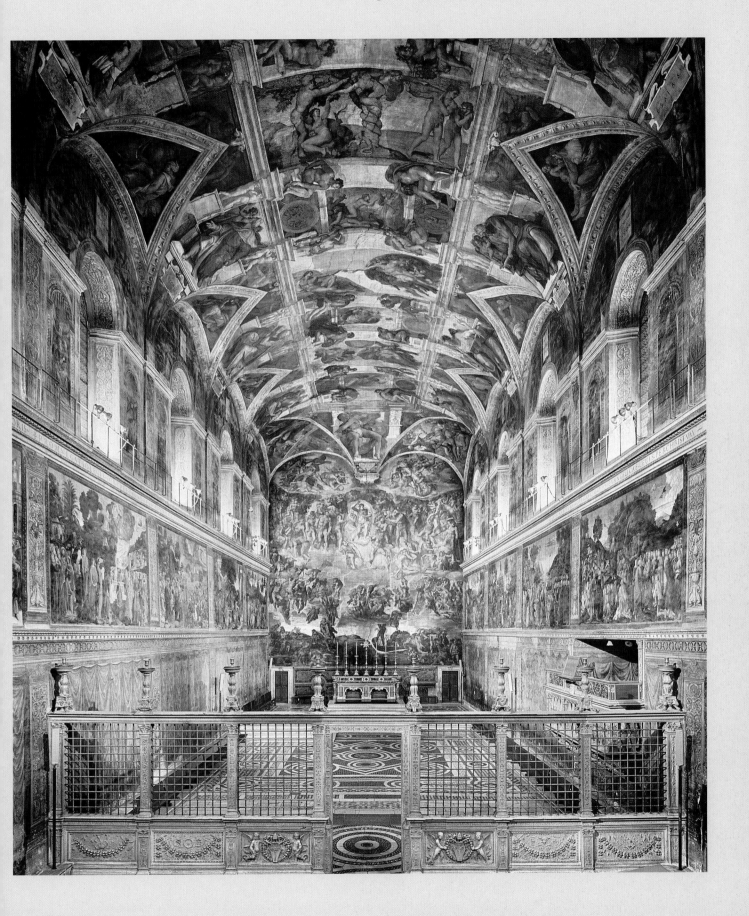

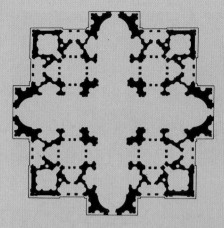

11.40 Bramante's design for St Peter's, 1506.

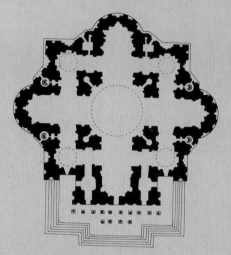

11.41 Michelangelo's design for St Peter's, 1547.

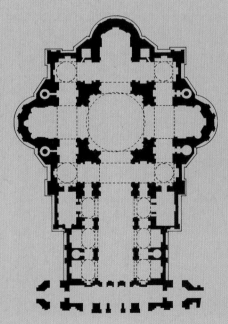

11.42 Plan of St Peter's as built to Michelangelo's design, with alterations by Carlo Maderno, 1606–15.

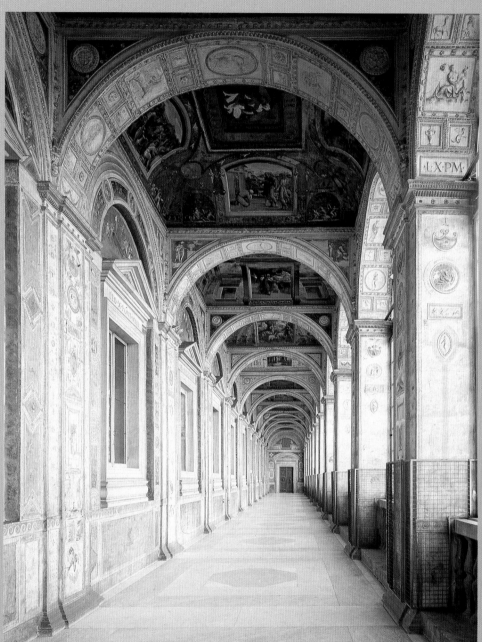

11.43 Raphael's Loggia, Vatican, Rome, c. 1516–19.

CHAPTER REVIEW

Critical Thought

In the Introduction to this book, we talked about two qualities we could examine in judging the quality of a work of art. One of them was craft: how well the artwork was made. The second was the uniqueness of its message or vision. In previous chapters we have seen many superbly crafted and profoundly communicative works of art. Among the makers of these works, arguably, Michelangelo and Leonardo da Vinci rank at the top. If you have mastered the material of this text, you ought to be able to support the previous assertion—whether you agree with it or not—citing specific qualities of communication and craftsmanship as well as comparative examples well sprinkled with the proper terminology from the Introduction to underscore your argument.

Finally, let's consider the larger question of art and its context. We look at the magnificent accomplishments of the artists of the High Renaissance and place them in the context of political events. If art is the mirror of its time, how do these artistic accomplishments reflect the social and political environment that gave them birth?

Summary

After reading this chapter, you should be able to:

- Characterize the world of the sixteenth century and identify individuals and accomplishments that shaped it.
- Compare the qualities and characteristics that define High Renaissance art and architecture and contrast those with the qualities and characteristics of Mannerism.
- Describe the literary works of Castiglione and Ariosto.
- Identify the major musical developments of the era and describe the work of Palestrina.
- Discuss the theatre of the High Renaissance, relating specifically the nature and qualities of commedia dell'arte.
- Apply the elements and principles of composition to analyze and compare works of art and architecture illustrated in this chapter.

CHAPTER TWELVE

Renaissance and Reformation in Northern Europe

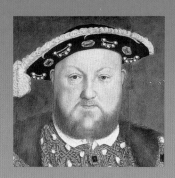

OUTLINE

THE REFORMATION
The Background
Erasmus and Christian Humanism
Martin Luther
Ulrich Zwingli and Zurich
John Calvin and the New
  Jerusalem

SCIENCE AND THE INTELLECT
The Scientific Revival
  TECHNOLOGY: Naval Artillery
Michel de Montaigne

**THE VISUAL ARTS AND
ARCHITECTURE**
Flanders
The Netherlands
Germany
France
  OUR DYNAMIC WORLD: Ming
    Dynasty Porcelain

MUSIC
The Renaissance Style in Flanders
Lutheranism and *Lieder*
Parisian Chanson

DANCE

FOCAL POINT: THE GREAT AGE
OF THE TUDORS
  PROFILE: William Shakespeare
  MASTERWORK: Shakespeare—
    Hamlet

VIEW

RELIGION AND POLITICS

As seems clear from contemporary events in the United States, politics and religion are hardly ever easy to separate. Part of the Reformation of the sixteenth century had to do with questions of the mix of civil and religious authority, and the theocracies of Switzerland illustrate the solution proposed by some who wanted separation from the authority of the Roman Church. In places such as Germany, things were less certain. Some areas remained loyal to Rome, while others found it expedient in a more secular realm to do away with Roman authority. In England there was no Reformation in the strict sense of the word, merely a semantic argument over who was head of the Church. As we will see, however, the Reformation, like much of the crusading religion seen today, has, perhaps, more to do with power and politics than with faith.

Above Detail of Fig. **12.24**.

12.1 Lucas Cranach the Younger, *Martin Luther and the Wittenberg Reformers* (detail), c. 1543. Oil on wood, 27⅝ × 15⅝ ins (70 × 40 cm). Toledo Museum of Art, Toledo, Ohio.

KEY TERMS

Some of the basic terms and concepts we will encounter in this chapter include the following:

Aerial perspective, the use of atmosphere to create a sense of deep space in a painting.

The Reformation, political and religious conflicts that led to the establishment of Protestant sects in the Christian Church.

Theocracy is government run by religious leaders.

Transubstantiation is the belief in the Roman Catholic Church that the communion elements of bread and wine actually become the body and blood of Christ.

Deposition scene, a work of art portraying the removal of Christ's body from the cross.

Diptych, a form in which two images (usually paintings on panel or reliefs) are hinged together.

Woodcut, a block of wood with an engraved design, and a print made from such a block.

Chorale, a hymn tune.

Lieder, German secular songs.

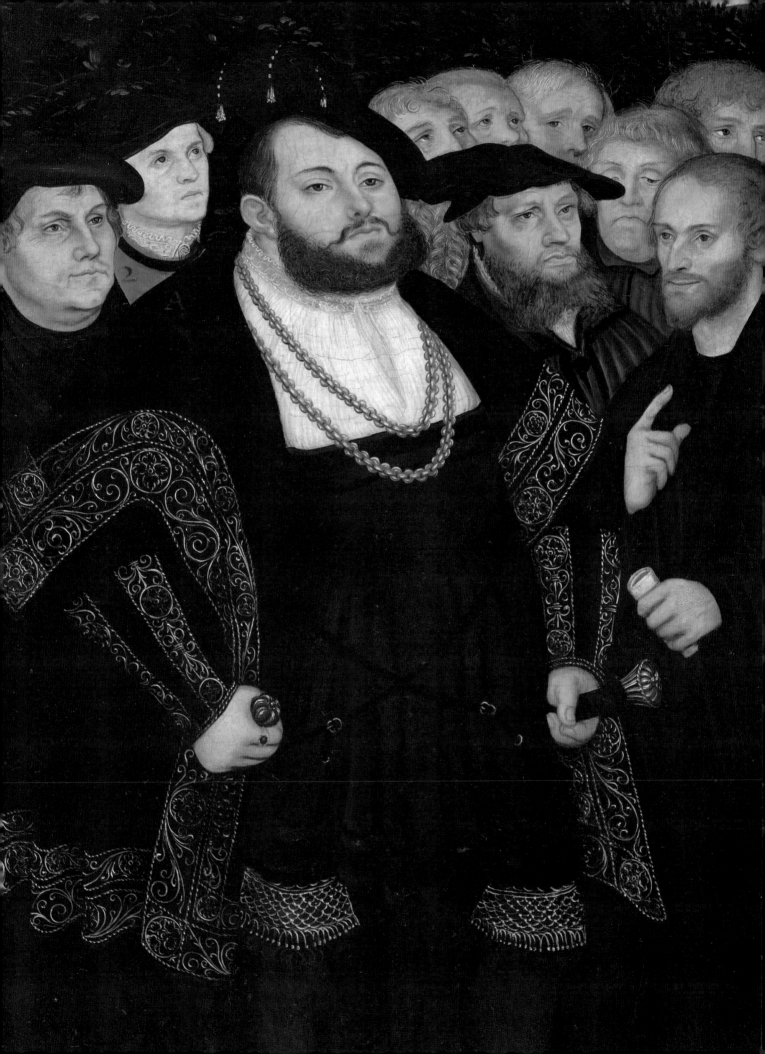

THE REFORMATION

The Background

In this chapter we turn our attention to the north of Europe and examine roughly the same time in history that we pursued in Chapters 10 and 11. What we are about to see represents a confluence of economic, political, and religious conflicts that, for ease of reference, we call the Reformation. It took place at the same time as the "Renaissance" and represented the most shattering and lasting blow the Christian Church has perhaps ever experienced. Of course, it did not just appear out of the blue, but was, rather, the climax of centuries of sectarian agitation—in the fourteenth century, for example, English cries for reform and resentment of papal authority led to an English translation of the Bible. But reform and separation are worlds apart, and it is important to realize that the Reformation did not begin as an attempt to start a new branch of Christianity, but as a sincere attempt to reform what were perceived as serious religious problems in the Roman Catholic Church.

Throughout Roman Catholic Europe, the huge body of clergy had amassed considerable tax-free wealth, at which secular governments chafed, particularly because the Church, in return, taxed the secular sector heavily. Widespread popular resentment of central ecclesiastical authority strengthened from political stability, even in areas still essentially feudal. In addition, many people found existing Church dogma indefensible. As we noted in Chapter 9, some early opposition occurred among the followers of John Huss. A break with Rome—political rather than religious—occurred in England under Henry VIII, and resulted in the confiscation of all Roman Church property in the Act of Dissolution (1536).

Erasmus and Christian Humanism

Humanism did much to prepare the way for the Reformation, although the two should not be identified too closely. The influence of the humanists can be seen most clearly in their techniques of studying language, which they gained through their interest in classical literature, and in their work on the Bible and texts by the Church Fathers. They compared the contemporary Church unfavorably with early Christianity, noting the hair-splitting of scholars, the hierarchical structure, and the secular activities of the clergy, and they campaigned for reform, seeking a return to the simple good news of the Gospel for moral living and

Timeline 12.1 Renaissance and Reformation in northern Europe.

	GENERAL EVENTS	LITERATURE & PHILOSOPHY	VISUAL ART & ARCHITECTURE	PERFORMING ARTS
1400			van Eyck (**12.8**) van der Weyden (**12.9**)	Dufay
1500	Pope Leo X Francis I of France Luther	Erasmus	Dürer (**12.12, 12.13, 12.14**) Grünewald (**12.15**) Altdorfer (**12.16**) Bosch (**12.10**) Clouet (**12.18**)	Josquin des Prez
1525	Henry VIII of England Dissolution of the monasteries in England Copernicus Vesalius Mary Tudor	Zwingli Thomas More (*Utopia*) Calvin	Holbein (**12.24, 12.25**) Cranach (**12.3**)	Clement Janequin
1550	Edward VI of England Elizabeth I of England	Montaigne Philip Sidney Edmund Spenser	Smythson (**12.23**) Bruegel (**12.11**) Hilliard (**12.26**)	Caroso Morley Marlowe Shakespeare Byrd
1600				

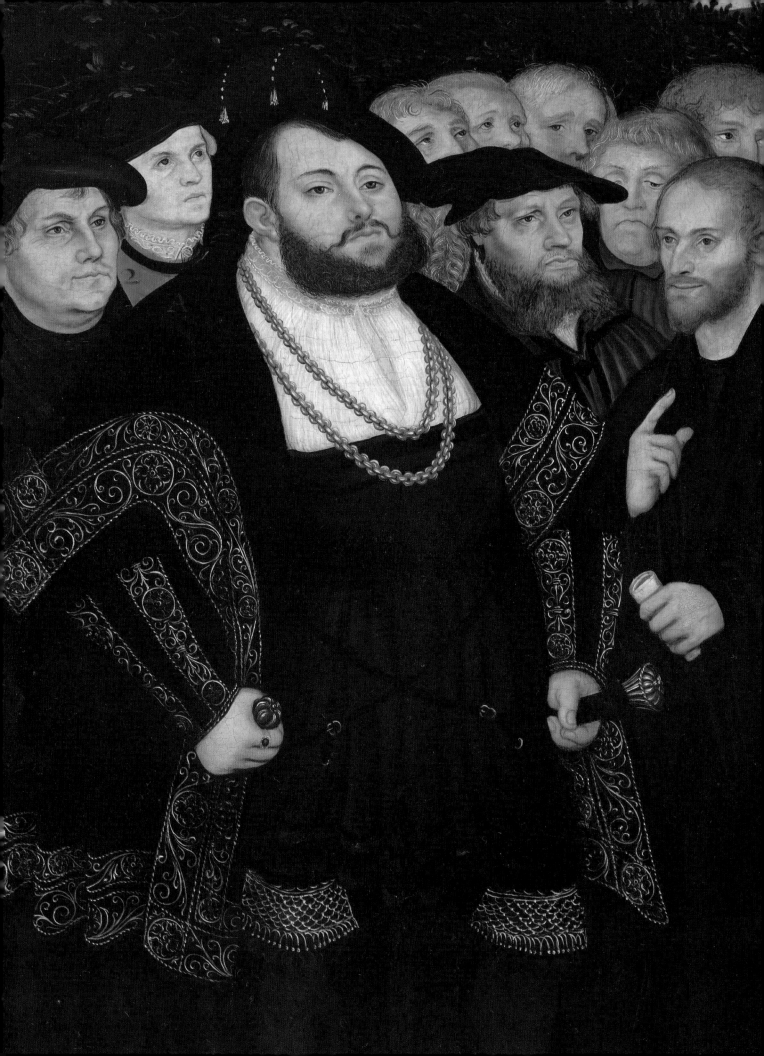

THE REFORMATION

The Background

In this chapter we turn our attention to the north of Europe and examine roughly the same time in history that we pursued in Chapters 10 and 11. What we are about to see represents a confluence of economic, political, and religious conflicts that, for ease of reference, we call the Reformation. It took place at the same time as the "Renaissance" and represented the most shattering and lasting blow the Christian Church has perhaps ever experienced. Of course, it did not just appear out of the blue, but was, rather, the climax of centuries of sectarian agitation—in the fourteenth century, for example, English cries for reform and resentment of papal authority led to an English translation of the Bible. But reform and separation are worlds apart, and it is important to realize that the Reformation did not begin as an attempt to start a new branch of Christianity, but as a sincere attempt to reform what were perceived as serious religious problems in the Roman Catholic Church.

Throughout Roman Catholic Europe, the huge body of clergy had amassed considerable tax-free wealth, at which secular governments chafed, particularly because the Church, in return, taxed the secular sector heavily. Widespread popular resentment of central ecclesiastical authority strengthened from political stability, even in areas still essentially feudal. In addition, many people found existing Church dogma indefensible. As we noted in Chapter 9, some early opposition occurred among the followers of John Huss. A break with Rome—political rather than religious—occurred in England under Henry VIII, and resulted in the confiscation of all Roman Church property in the Act of Dissolution (1536).

Erasmus and Christian Humanism

Humanism did much to prepare the way for the Reformation, although the two should not be identified too closely. The influence of the humanists can be seen most clearly in their techniques of studying language, which they gained through their interest in classical literature, and in their work on the Bible and texts by the Church Fathers. They compared the contemporary Church unfavorably with early Christianity, noting the hair-splitting of scholars, the hierarchical structure, and the secular activities of the clergy, and they campaigned for reform, seeking a return to the simple good news of the Gospel for moral living and

Timeline 12.1 Renaissance and Reformation in northern Europe.

	GENERAL EVENTS	LITERATURE & PHILOSOPHY	VISUAL ART & ARCHITECTURE	PERFORMING ARTS
1400			van Eyck (**12.8**) van der Weyden (**12.9**)	Dufay
1500	Pope Leo X Francis I of France Luther	Erasmus	Dürer (**12.12, 12.13, 12.14**) Grünewald (**12.15**) Altdorfer (**12.16**) Bosch (**12.10**) Clouet (**12.18**)	Josquin des Prez
1525	Henry VIII of England Dissolution of the monasteries in England Copernicus Vesalius Mary Tudor	Zwingli Thomas More (*Utopia*) Calvin	Holbein (**12.24, 12.25**) Cranach (**12.3**)	Clement Janequin
1550	Edward VI of England Elizabeth I of England	Montaigne Philip Sidney Edmund Spenser	Smythson (**12.23**) Bruegel (**12.11**) Hilliard (**12.26**)	Caroso Morley Marlowe Shakespeare Byrd
1600				

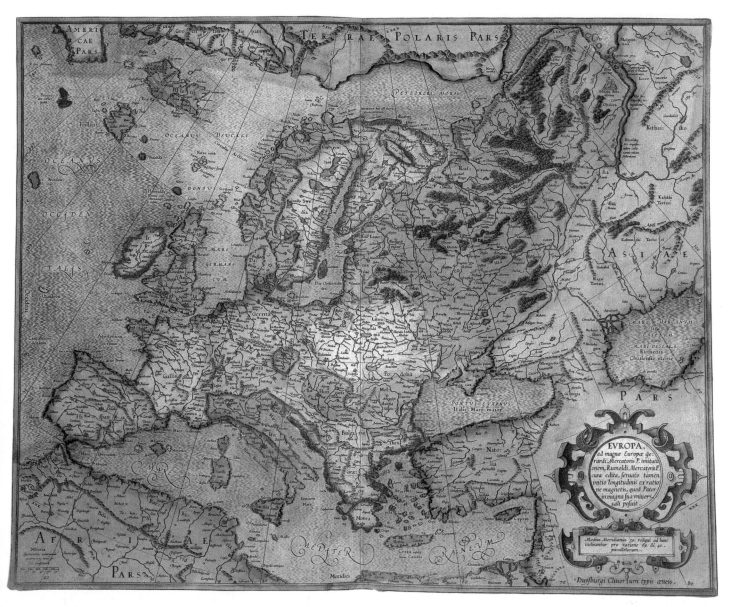

Map 12.1 A contemporary map of Europe in the 1590s.

for peace. Humanism was primarily an intellectual movement, whose followers preferred religious contemplation to political action.

There was one major doctrinal difference between the humanists and the reformers, however: humanists believed in the fundamental goodness of the human race and ignored Augustine's teaching on original sin, and they were, therefore, positive about human development based on a combination of Christianity and the classics. Luther, on the other hand, emphasized faith as the way to salvation from sin, while Calvin focused on predestination—that is, God chose those whom he would save. Another point of great significance to the humanists was the inwardness of religion. They regarded the external aspects

of worship, such as festivals, sacraments, music, and imagery, as less important than inner belief. For example, long before Luther raised the issue, Erasmus (ir-AZ-muhs) expressed doubt about whether the sacraments of bread and wine actually turned into the body and blood of Jesus in the service of the Mass or simply represented them, although he distanced himself from the Protestant reformers so as not to endanger the unity of the Christian Church.

Desiderius Erasmus (1469–1536) was born in Rotterdam, and he became the greatest scholar of the northern Renaissance (Fig. 12.2). He was the first editor of the New Testament and an important writer on classical literature. The illegitimate son of a priest and a physician's daughter, he found an opening for his talents in the Church like

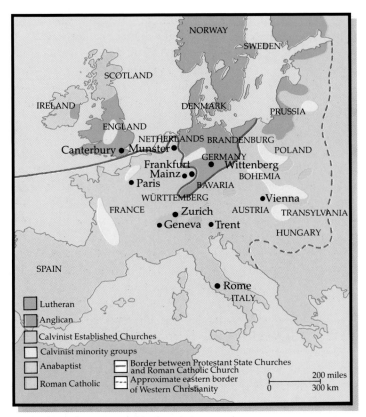

Map 12.2 Religious divisions in sixteenth-century Europe.

Greek New Testament, he openly attacked what he called "schoolmen" and their sterile "scholasticism." Following the example of other humanists, he called for new techniques of critical study to obtain a more profound understanding of the Bible and the early Church Fathers.

Erasmus believed that the Bible was essentially simple, and that he had so much difficulty with scholars because they turned it into an involved puzzle to which they alone claimed the key—thereby barring ordinary men and women from direct inspiration from the scriptures. Erasmus wanted the Bible to be translated into the vernacular so that all literate people could read it for themselves. Erasmus wanted to see a massive program of education from which, he believed, would come a universal Christian community. It was a gigantic task, but because the Church was rich, Erasmus believed the task could be accomplished if the Church rethought its priorities and cut waste. To accomplish his goals, Erasmus appealed to the princes of Europe to take the lead in reforming the Church wherever

12.2 Hans Holbein the Younger, *Erasmus of Rotterdam*, 1523. Oil on wood, 17¼ × 13⅛ ins (43 × 33 cm). Louvre, Paris.

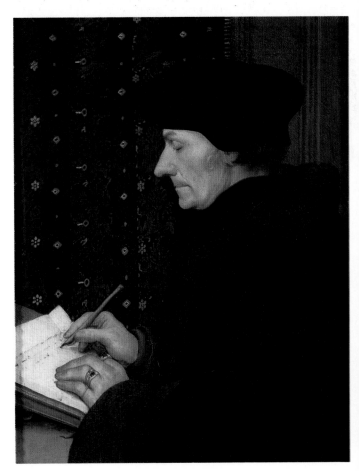

many able boys from poor backgrounds. He became an Augustinian canon and was ordained a priest in 1492. He was given the opportunity to study the classics and granted leave to study in Paris, where he came into contact with humanist groups and learned to dislike scholastic theology.

While Erasmus was in Venice, he became a member of the informal academy around the printer Aldus Manutius and deepened his knowledge of Greek and Latin classical literature. He began to write, and books such as the *Adages*, a collection of several thousand pithy sayings drawn from the classics, and *In Praise of Folly*, a satire on the affectations and vices of contemporary society, gained him a reputation throughout Europe. In 1516 his edition of the Greek New Testament accompanied by his own Latin translation was published. This was a landmark in biblical studies because, for the first time, it gave scholars the original text of the Church's fundamental document. His efforts were not universally well received, however, and scholars of the old school—that is, those who studied the Bible only at second hand through various commentaries and glossaries of theologians—considered him a threat to their authority. Their feelings were well founded, because, in 1519, in the preface to the second edition of his

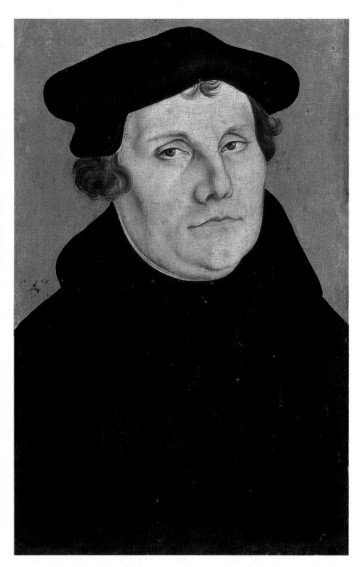

12.3 Lucas Cranach the Elder, *Martin Luther*, 1529. Oil on wood, 14³/₄ × 9 ins (37 × 23 cm). Uffizi, Florence, Italy.

stronghold of those "schoolmen" whom Erasmus so detested. These scholars believed that there was an uncrossable gap between reason and revelation and that human limitation and finite knowledge could never understand the divine. Knowledge of God could be obtained only by revelation, the main source of which was the Bible. Luther, who was obsessive about his own sinfulness, was particularly responsive to the idea of the apartness of God. In 1505 he entered the Augustinian friary at Erfurt, whose friars kept a strict discipline. Even in this dedicated order, Luther distinguished himself by his extreme asceticism— that is, the renunciation of the comforts of society and austere self-discipline—even though he found little peace in rigorous discipline and confession. He had been brought up to believe that humans could gradually make themselves acceptable to God through the sacraments and the performance of good works, but he believed that God could never love such a sinful creature as himself, and he grew to hate a God who demanded love but made it impossible for his children to approach Him without fear and awe.

For the next six years he lectured and preached, and gradually came to realize that humankind could not possibly draw near to God of their own free will, because human nature had been corrupted by original sin and, thus, was driven irrevocably toward evil. To Luther, a human being trying to attain salvation through his or her own efforts was like a badly made clay pot trying to reshape itself. The potter—that is, God—must intervene. Humans could do little but wait for the divine spark to set them alight and burn out their sin. God could not be forced to intervene, but because God had sent Christ into the

the Church was unwilling to reform itself. He also urged the princes to stay out of war, which bred unChristian attitudes, such as anger and cruelty, and wasted huge sums of money that could better be spent on education.

Martin Luther

The son of a copper miner from Saxony, in what is now Germany, Luther (1483–1546; Fig. **12.3**) was born into a family in which money was always tight. In 1497 he was sent to a school in Magdeburg that was run by the Brethren of the Common Life, and in 1505 he earned a Master of Arts degree from Erfurt University. Erfurt was a

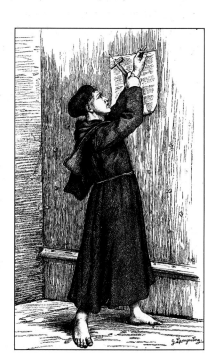

12.4 Luther nailing his Theses to the church door. Engraving.

world, there was hope for all sinners. Faith was essential, and through faith came salvation. In effect, Luther had rediscovered St Paul (see Chapter 5) and St Augustine (see Chapter 7), but his discovery made him aware that the Holy Spirit was at work and that his self-loathing was the first step in his regeneration.

Amid all this came Luther's reaction to the sale of indulgences, a lucrative Church business based on the belief that the Church had built up a "surplus of merits" which it could sell to the truly penitent to release them from part of their required penance, an outward sign of their inward repentance. He was incensed that people such as Prince Albert Hohenzollern (HOH-en-tsohl-urn), acting on behalf of the pope, were persuading credulous men and women that the purchase of an indulgence would buy pardon from sin. To Luther, the Church was denying its very reason for existence by selling indulgences. God could not be fooled nor the Last Judgment averted by the possession of a piece of paper with a papal seal on it.

In October 1517, Luther fastened what have come to be known as the Ninety-five Theses to the door of the town church in Wittenberg, where they would be seen by all visitors (Fig. 12.4). Although he made his opinions clear, he avoided making a direct attack on papal authority. Rather, he blamed the local emissary who was selling the indulgences, indicating that if the pope knew of the tricks being used to sell the indulgences, he would let St Peter's collapse rather than use tainted money to build it.

The Theses were quickly translated from their original Latin and disseminated throughout Germany. Again, the printing press contributed in spreading material that would earlier probably have gone unnoticed. The reaction surprised Luther, and he tried to withdraw the Theses. But they were now public property, and he was called to Rome to answer charges of heresy and rebellion against ecclesiastical authority.

Although he did not want an open break with Rome, he was absolutely convinced of the rightness of his own arguments and caught up in the outpouring of emotion that they had stirred up. Politics came to Luther's aid. Emperor Maximilian died in 1519, and for the next six months, until the election of Charles V, the Elector of Saxony was a much-courted man. He was also Luther's protector, and managed to enable Luther to escape any judgment. In the meantime, Luther became something of a national hero, against whom any German ruler would have had great difficulty taking action.

The die was cast, and over the next year, Luther put his thoughts into a program of fundamental reform in several widely selling works. These included *Sermon on the Mass*, in which he argued that Christ's sacrifice on the cross had been made once and for all, and there could, therefore, be no re-enacting it, as priests claimed took place in the Mass.

At issue here was the fact that priests offered the sacrifice by communing with both bread and wine, whereas the laity were restricted to bread alone. He amplified some of these themes in *An Appeal to the German Nation*, in which he made a call to national and anti-clerical feeling, arguing that if the Church were the community of all believers and not merely the ordained minority, secular authority had a duty to intervene and redress abuses if the Church refused to do so. Because the Bible made no mention of popes or papal taxes, there was no need to submit to the former nor pay the latter. He also went on to consider the issues of monasticism, spiritually empty pilgrimages, and clerical celibacy, all of which stood outside scripture.

In June 1520 Pope Leo X condemned a number of Luther's beliefs and threatened to excommunicate him if he did not recant. Luther responded by burning the letter and all the books of canon law. In January 1521 Pope Leo excommunicated Luther and called on Emperor Charles V to take necessary action. However, despite being a devout Catholic, Charles did not wish to enrage his new German subjects. He was too aware of Luther's immense popularity, not only among the people at large but also with the German princes. Charles issued a proclamation condemning Luther's ideas and forbidding their publication, but he granted Luther a safe-conduct pass to Worms to defend himself publicly before the Diet that was due to assemble there.

The emperor hoped that Luther would either submit to the display of authority at Worms or be so intemperate in his reply that public opinion would turn against him. Luther did neither. His response to the charges against him was so temperate and well reasoned that he came away in public triumph, deeply impressing people with his appeals to conscience. He replied to his inquisitors with the famous words: "Here I stand—I cannot do otherwise." Nonetheless, the emperor was under obligation to ban Luther, which would be enforced by edict. Luther left Worms hurriedly and was promptly "kidnapped" by his old protector, the elector of Saxony, who had him taken to Wartburg Castle so that he could deny any knowledge of him and escape the need to enforce the emperor's edict. The wheels of revolution had begun to spin and would not be stopped. Religious protest turned into political revolt.

Ulrich Zwingli and Zurich

Ulrich Zwingli (TSVING-lee; 1484–1531), who was born in Switzerland, had studied at humanist universities in Basel and Vienna before accepting the position of parish priest in the principal church of Zurich (Fig. **12.5**).

For Zwingli, true faith demanded active commitment, and he believed his task was to preach and teach the pure

gospel as he saw it. He came to these conclusions even before he heard of Martin Luther, whose stand against indulgences Zwingli approved. After studying writings by both Luther and Huss, Zwingli launched his own reform movement, beginning with all the practices of the Church that were not specifically authorized in the Bible. In 1523 he published a series of articles condemning *transubstantiation*, pilgrimages, fasts, and papal supremacy. The city council of Zurich was so impressed by his logic that it ordered a public debate between Zwingli and a representative of the Catholic Church. Zwingli carried the day, and the council ordered public Bible reading and vernacular prayers. They denounced clerical celibacy, dissolved all religious houses, and abolished the Mass, replacing it with a simple communion service in which preaching and prayers played the major role.

Zwingli also found no biblical authority for ritual and images, and here he differed with Luther, who believed that the physical and spiritual were two aspects of the same divine nature. In his *Commentary on the True and False*

12.5 Ulrich Zwingli (1484–1531).

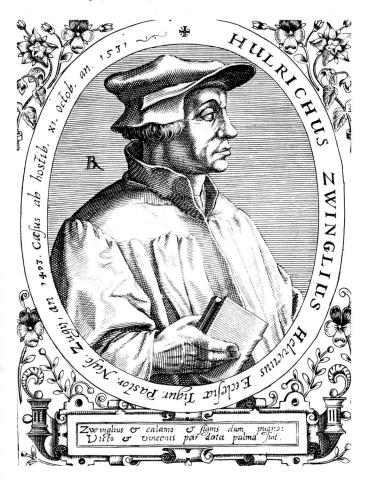

Religion Zwingli asserted that: "Body and spirit are such essentially different things that whichever one you take, it cannot be the other." That is, he contended that there was no trace of the real presence of God in the consecrated sacraments and that communion was merely the commemoration of Christ's sacrifice. Any hint that the real presence of Christ existed in the elements—whether asserted by the Catholic Church or Luther—was pure superstition. Zwingli's theology admitted the need for grace, but it put greater emphasis on the law of God that was revealed in the Bible and that Christ gave humankind the will to obey. Therefore, not only the Church but also the State must create the necessary conditions for Christian life. Zwingli believed in a *theocracy*—that is, a merger of the Church and State in which the State became the guardian of public conduct, and the government of Zurich established a court of morals to oversee public conduct and punish any backsliders. In the end, Zwingli's major contribution to the Protestant Reformation was the evangelical reform of individual lives, effected under the aegis of the civil government.

In 1529, five of the Swiss cantons that had remained loyal to the Catholic Church formed a coalition to bring the Protestant rebellion to a close by force. The original conflict was shortlived, but fighting erupted two years later. Zwingli, who had no qualms about fighting force with force, accompanied the Protestant army as chaplain. He was wounded, taken prisoner, and executed.

John Calvin and the New Jerusalem

Probably the most famous reformer of the generation after Luther was John Calvin of Geneva (1509–64), who came to prominence in the 1530s. Calvin was a very different character from Luther. A sophisticated Frenchman, trained in humanism and law in addition to theology, Calvin lacked Luther's passion and eloquence but instead had shrewd organizational abilities and a careful logic. While Luther was corpulent, Calvin was the picture of a fanatical ascetic, with a thin face, hollow eyes, and long, scraggly beard.

Like Zwingli, Calvin succeeded in establishing a Swiss Protestant theocracy in the city–state of Geneva, and his militant preaching inspired Protestants all over Europe. In terms of theology, Calvin was very close to Luther, the differences between them being more matters of emphasis than of substance. Calvin stressed the omnipotence of God, and he placed the doctrine of predestination of souls to Heaven or Hell at the center of his belief system. Salvation came through faith alone, but because faith was a gift of God, it was not given to all but only to those whom God

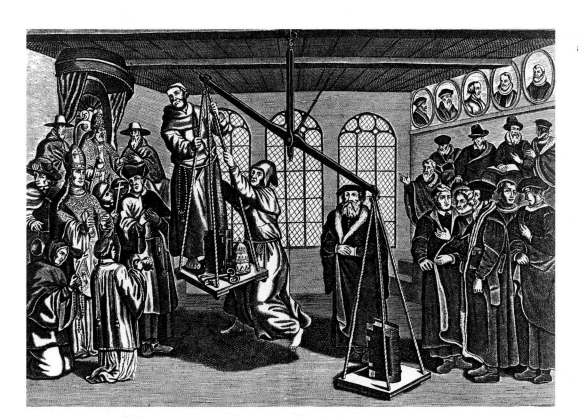

12.6 Calvin weighing the Bible against Popish pomp.

had predestined for eternal life. He declared that the scriptures were the only source of guidance on matters of faith and that errors in the Church remained errors regardless of how much tradition they had behind them. Calvin believed in only two sacraments—baptism and eucharist (YOO-kuh-rist)—because these were the only ones found in the Bible. Like Zwingli and Luther, he rejected transubstantiation, but he was closer to Luther than to Zwingli because he believed that some sort of "real presence" existed in the eucharist. Most of his theology was recorded in his great book *The Institutes of the Christian Religion*, which was first published in 1536 and revised in later editions to contain more emphasis on the organization of the Church. It was read by Protestants everywhere, and Geneva was seen as the Protestant ideal of a Christian community.

Geneva had just overthrown the dukes of Savoy, but had not joined the Swiss confederation. Calvin's zealots gained political power and, like Zurich, Geneva became a theocracy, ruled by Calvinist pastors, who, in turn, were ruled by Calvin. Life in Geneva was austere and rigorous. It was governed by puritanical, moral legislation, and sermons were the staple of life, which reflected Calvin's rather inflexible vision of a world divided into the saved and the damned. Church attendance was mandatory and heresy was punishable by death. Calvinist Protestants were seen as the builders of the New Jerusalem on earth, and the Pope was the Antichrist (Fig. **12.6**). The fervency of such crusading faith fueled religious revolutions across Europe,

and it spread to the Huguenots in France and the Dutch Reformed church in the Netherlands. Its successors could be found in English Puritans, such as Oliver Cromwell in the seventeenth century, and the fiery Scottish Presbyterian followers of John Knox. It even spread across the Atlantic ocean to the early Puritan settlers of America.

Calvin's ultimate influence went beyond the bounds of religion to economics. His call for a capitalistic spirit based on unceasing labor in gainful pursuits for the glory of God may well have inspired the disciplined, rigorous drive that made Calvinist Huguenots and Puritans among the most successful businessmen in France and England, respectively. It has been suggested that Calvinism may have been an important cause in the growth of the capitalist system in the West.

SCIENCE AND THE INTELLECT

The Scientific Revival

Into the religious upheaval of the late Renaissance and its human-centered universe burst the revelations of scientific discovery. This scientific revival, which came hard on the heels of religious reformation, revealed itself in two differ-

TECHNOLOGY: PUTTING DISCOVERY TO WORK

Naval Artillery

A major technological change in the fifteenth century was the improvement of cannons and the development of lighter weapons, which, in particular, benefited naval artillery. However, the evolution of naval artillery depended on another peculiar factor on board ship. The first cannons, which were iron, were placed on a wooden cradle, and sailing ships were able to carry these cannons because they had space along the decks. Cannons were placed in a pivoting form (Fig. **12.7A**) attached to the framework of the bulwarks. These small-caliber guns were used to attack personnel on the deck and castles of an enemy ship, but they were not sufficiently powerful to damage the hull of a ship. The tops of ships could be equipped with as many as 200 cannons, and such large numbers often proved of great menace to the crew and the rigging. Larger caliber cannons that were capable of attacking the hulls of ships, demolishing their tops, and sinking them, were so heavy that placing them on the deck or castles made the ships unstable. Sailing vessels are stable only when their weight topside is compensated for by ballast in the hold. Heavy cannons on deck would have required massive amounts of ballast.

At the beginning of the sixteenth century, the plan of merchant ships was altered to produce a warship capable of supporting the weight of the artillery, counterbalanced by ballast. Around 1500 a man from Brest named Descharges had the idea of placing the cannon on a lower deck and opening gunports for the artillery. Positioning guns in this way shielded them from the firing of lighter deck cannon on an opposing ship (Fig. **12.7B**). Thus, the beginning of the sixteenth century marks a turning point in naval warfare, and eighty-eight years later, one of the most significant naval battles of all time—that is, the defeat of the Spanish Armada by the English—brought this development to a new level of importance.

12.7 A Deck cannon mounted on pivoting form.
B Cannon placed on lower deck, behind closable gunports.

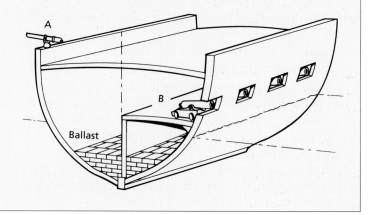

ent forms represented in two different books, both published in 1543. Both books and their authors, however dissimilar, had a decisive impact on the scientific movement. The first was *On the Fabric of the Human Body* by a Fleming, Andreas Vesalius (vuh-SAY-lee-uhs; 1514–64). Its significance lies in its descriptive reporting and skillful illustrations, which render the structures of the human body in space in a way that represents the first step towards photographic realism in science. Vesalius was an ambitious and popular teacher at the University of Padua, which at the time was becoming increasingly important as a center for the teaching of medicine, and his impact on science was as the founder of a method of investigation. Vesalius greatly improved the range and precision of knowledge of the structure of the human body. He had explored the body more thoroughly than anyone before, and that exploration proved to be an essential foundation for the rational physiology that followed in the seventeenth century.

The second book to be published in 1543, *On the Revolutions of the Celestial Orbs*, was by Nicholas Copernicus (1473–1543), of Poland. It was a work of philosophy and technical mathematics. Copernicus was an ecclesiastical administrator who had nurtured his great idea for nearly forty years. He did not make observations himself and did not use others' observations, nor did he aim at predictive accuracy. His impact lay in the way he exploited a great new principle—that in the system of the heavens there is a perfect reciprocity between sun-centered systems and earth-centered systems. Copernicus believed in a sun-centered system not because he observed it or drew his conclusions by scientific evidence, but rather because he believed that the Earth was associated with a number of planets for reasons of simplicity, order, and harmony. The

conclusions in his book had actually existed for nearly a generation, but merely as an elegant but inherently implausible mathematical model. Copernicus was not, in fact, interested in the practical reform of astronomy nor in making new discoveries in the heavens. He was a mathematician and made no claim for himself other than the right to philosophize about what is more or less likely to be "real." His "discovery" was a theoretical one, totally without a factual basis. It was nonetheless, accurate. Although it was not immediately accepted, Copernican theory—the formulation of a *heliocentric*, or sun-centered, universe—transformed the world and humankind's perception of itself and its God, and devastated those whose view of reality placed humankind as the ultimate being in an earth-centered universe.

Michel de Montaigne

As the Reformation raged on, a new assault on religion came from Michel de Montaigne (mee-SHEL duh mohn-TAYN; 1533–92). He was born at his family's ancestral castle in southwestern France, and as soon as he could talk, he was placed under the tutelage of a German preceptor, who knew no French and who was required to use Latin exclusively when instructing his infant pupil. As Montaigne matured, he derived his philosophy from the classical forms of self-discipline he found in Socrates and the Stoics. After studying law, he served in the Parliament of Bordeaux, and when he was thirty-seven he retired to the château of Montaigne to write his *Essays*, the first two books of which appeared in 1580. After travels to Rome and a period as mayor of Bordeaux, he again retired to the château to write. A third edition of the *Essays* appeared posthumously in 1595.

Montaigne found religions of worship and mystical revelation incomprehensible, whether Greek or Christian. On the other hand, he granted the mind and body "their ordinary comforts." Sobriety, self-control, and the acceptance of reason were the basis of his outlook, and his skepticism was the result of his observation that humans are essentially changeable, "undulating and diverse" individuals, incapable of attaining truth. Neither science, nor reason, nor philosophy can guide humankind, which is the obedient servant of customs, prejudices, self-interest, and fanaticism. Men and women are the victims of circumstances and of the impressions that circumstances make. Such a view of humankind is found throughout the essays and constitutes their central theme.

According to Montaigne, the ultimate goal of education is to enable humans to understand themselves and things as they are and to live more harmoniously. His morality lay outside the conventions of the times, because

he drew most of it from Seneca and Plutarch, who treated ethical and moral questions in an easy-going manner. The core of Montaigne's character was a "congenital dislike of straining." His ninety-five essays drift from one topic to another, with no discernible order, and the titles include "On Fleas" and "On the Habit of Wearing Clothes." Emerson, in his *Representative Men*, summed up Montaigne's appeal: "There have been men with deeper insight; but, one would say, never a man with such abundance of thoughts: he is never dull, never insincere, and has the genius to make the reader care for all that he cares for." Montaigne's book inaugurated the term *essay* for the short prose composition treating a given subject in a rather informal and personal manner.

THE VISUAL ARTS AND ARCHITECTURE

Flanders

Van Eyck and van der Weyden

Flemish painting of the fifteenth century was revolutionary. Flemish painters achieved pictorial verisimilitude through rational perspective. Line, form, and color were painstakingly controlled to create subtle, varied, three-dimensional representations.

Part of the drastic change in Flemish painting stemmed from a new development in painting media—oil paint. The versatile properties of oil paints gave Flemish painters new opportunities to vary surface texture and brilliance, and to create far greater subtlety of form. Oils allowed the blending of color areas because they remained wet and could be worked on the canvas for a while. Egg tempera, the earlier medium, dried almost immediately upon application.

Gradual transitions between color areas made possible by oil paints allowed fifteenth-century Flemish painters to refine AERIAL PERSPECTIVE—that is, the increasingly hazy appearance of the objects farthest from the viewer. This helped them to control this most effective indicator of deep space. Blending between color areas also helped them achieve realistic MODELING, or light and shade, by which all objects assume three-dimensionality. Without highlight and shadow, the appearance of life-like relief disappears. Early fifteenth-century Flemish painters used sophisticated light and shade, not only to heighten three-dimensionality, but also to achieve perceptual unity in their compositions. Pictures without consistent light sources or without natural shadows on surrounding objects create very strange effects, even if they depict individual forms very accurately. The new skill in creating natural three-dimen-

sionality separated fifteenth-century Flemish style from the Gothic style and tied it to the Renaissance.

"The prince of painters of our age," was the way one of his contemporaries described Jan van Eyck (yahn vahn-YKE; c. 1390–1441), whose work advances the new naturalism of the age. Although little is known about his life, he seems to have been an active and highly placed functionary of the duke of Burgundy. On one of his trips in the duke's service, van Eyck visited Italy, where he met Masaccio and other Florentine artists. Without doubt, van Eyck was one of the greatest artists of any age, and he brought a new "reality" to painting. Jan van Eyck's *The Arnolfini Marriage* (ahrn-ohl-FEEN-ee; Fig. **12.8**) uses strong perspective in the bedroom to create a sense of great depth. All forms achieve three-dimensionality through subtle color blending and softened shadow edges. Natural highlights originate from the window, and this ties the figures and objects together.

As naturalistic as this painting appears, however, it is a selective portrayal. It is an artist's vision of an event, a portrayal clearly staged for pictorial purposes. The location of objects, the drape of fabric, and the nature of the figures themselves are beyond reality. Van Eyck's work achieves what much art does—that is, it gives the surface appearance of reality while revealing a deeper essence of the scene or the subject matter, in this case, man, woman, marriage, and their place within Christian society and philosophy.

The case has been made many times that this work contains an elaborate symbolism commenting on marriage and the marriage ceremony. The artist has signed the painting in legal script above the mirror "Johannes de Eyck fuit hic, 1434" (Jan van Eyck was here, 1434), and in fact, we can see the artist and another witness reflected in the mirror. The burning candle is part of the oath-taking ceremony and symbolizes marriage, the dog represents marital faith, and the figure on the bedhead is of St Margaret, the patron saint of childbirth. There is considerable debate about the accuracy or appropriateness of all these symbols and on whether the bride is pregnant or not. Inasmuch as clothing design and posture of the period emphasized the stomach, most experts agree she is not.

Although slightly different in style from van Eyck's work, Rogier van der Weyden's (VY-duhn) *The Descent*

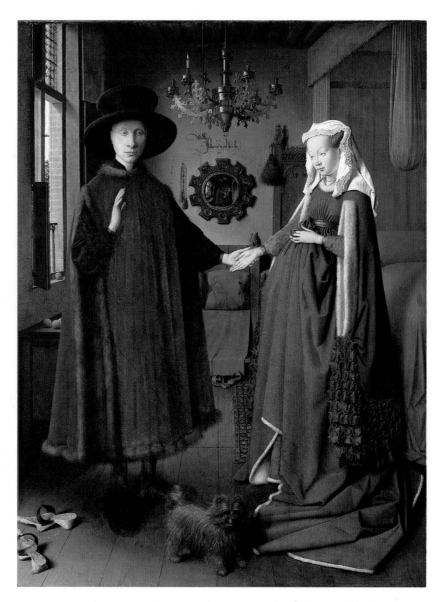

12.8 Jan van Eyck, *The Arnolfini Marriage (Giovanni Arnolfini and his Bride)*, 1434. Oil on panel, 33 × 22¹/₂ ins (83.8 × 57.1 cm). National Gallery, London.

from the Cross (Fig. **12.9**) displays softly shaded forms and three-dimensionality. Its surface naturalism is quite unlike that of Gothic style. Carefully controlled line and form create soft, undulating S-curves around the borders and diagonally through the center. The painter explores the full range of the color spectrum, from reds and golds to blues and greens, and the full extent of the value scale from dark to light. Composition, balance, and unity are extremely subtle. The figures are depicted almost in the manner of statues, yet the shallow drapery folds exhibit a nervous broken linearity.

363

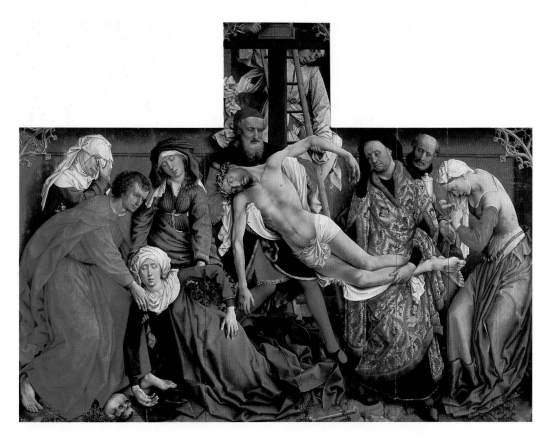

12.9 Rogier van der Weyden, *The Descent from the Cross*, c. 1435. Oil on panel, 7 ft 2⅝ ins × 8 ft ⅞ ins (2.2 × 2.46 m). Museo del Prado, Madrid.

The striking feature in this painting, however, is its individualized presentation of human emotion. Each character displays a particularized reaction to the emotion-charged situation. These figures are not types—they are individual people so fully portrayed that we might expect to encounter them on the street.

The Netherlands

Hieronymus Bosch

Around 1500 the tradition started by Jan van Eyck diminished as ideas were brought to the Netherlands, with trade, from Italy. It became a period of crisis and change for painters, and both the grand style of the High Renaissance and the emotional Mannerist movement that followed made strong inroads into the art of the country. However, the two greatest painters of the time in the Netherlands seem to have remained solidly apart from the styles of sixteenth-century Italy. The first of these painters was Hieronymus Bosch (hay-RAW-nee-mus bawsh or baws; c. 1450–1516). His fantastic works are all we know about him, and we do not even know when they were painted. Bosch has been an intriguing figure for a number of different reasons. First, as we noted, is the total lack of informa-

tion about him as a human being. Second, is the amazing likeness of his work to the images of the twentieth-century surrealists whom we will encounter in Chapter 17. Third, is the fact that his imagery lends itself to fascinating psychological probing and speculation. Fourth, the complexity and imagery of his most famous work *The Garden of Earthly Delights* (Fig. **12.10**) has fueled almost feverish rumors of some connection with heretical sects. However, what little evidence there is suggests that Bosch was an orthodox Roman Catholic, and we do know that his work was admired by the Catholic monarch Philip II of Spain.

Bosch was clearly a man of tremendous imaginative powers. Had that not been the case, he could not have created the truly fantastic depictions present in *Garden of Earthly Delights*. What we see in this illustration is the central panel of a three-panelled work. The left panel, called *The Creation of Eve*, is a fairly straightforward portrayal, but, like the central panel, it contains images that might remind us of Dr Seuss. However, the large central panel, measuring more than 7 feet (2.1 meters) by more than 6 feet (1.8 meters), takes us into a much more complex and mystifying world. Without exaggeration, we could probably spend the remainder of this book trying to describe each of the little scenarios present in this

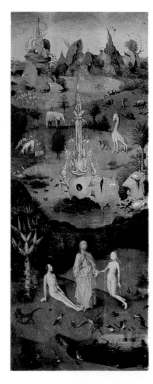
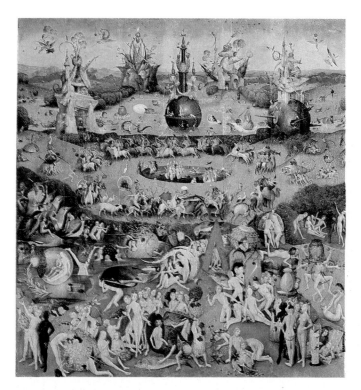
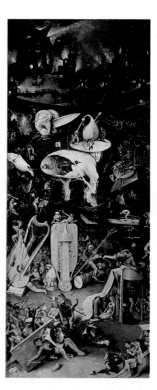

12.10 Hieronymus Bosch, *The Garden of Earthly Delights*, triptych, left panel *Garden of Eden*, center panel *The World Before the Flood*, right panel *Hell*, c. 1505. Side panels 86 × 36 ins (218.5 × 91.5 cm), center panel 86 × 76 ins (218.5 × 195 cm). Museo del Prado, Madrid.

portrayal. Bosch's choice of color alone would lead us into a miasma of analysis and speculation. The vibrant pinks played against darkened blues draw the picture together and give emphases that run throughout. Of course, the figure groupings fascinate, too. They consist of youthful, thin, muscle-less individuals frolicking naked amid gigantic fruits, clams, fish, and so on. Other animals parade in line around the work. Although no explicit sexual activity is shown, the images are clearly erotic and have sexual connotations in several languages. But what is probably most arresting about the work is the collection of strange "machines" such as the one that sits in the center of the lake in the background. What could Bosch have had in mind here? Is he depicting a paradise in which everyone may freely engage in their sexual fascinations, or is he making a statement about earthly life wherein sexual desire is the central force in human thought? One reading of the painting is a condemnation of erotic activity—but all the while one wonders about Bosch's obvious fascination with it.

Pieter Bruegel The Elder

The second Netherlandish painter of note is the sixteenth-century master Pieter Bruegel (PEE-tuhr BROY-guhl) the Elder (c. 1525/30–69). After traveling extensively in Italy,

where he developed a deep love for the beauty of the southern Italian countryside as well as a mastery of Italian painting styles, and France in the 1550s, Bruegel worked in Antwerp and Brussels. A close follower of Bosch, he was influenced by Bosch's pessimism and fantasy, and although his work avoided the nudes of Renaissance Italian art, it captured its harmony of space and form and infused it with a northern European perspective on life. We can see the Italian influence in the colorful *Landscape with the Fall of Icarus* (IK-uh-ruhs; Fig. **12.11**). The painting tells the story of Icarus, who, against the advice of his father, flew so high that the wax of his wings was melted by the sun. Icarus was a popular symbol in Italian art partly because it represented unbridled ambition and partly because it gave artists an opportunity to depict the human body in flight or falling. In Bruegel's portrayal, Icarus is hardly more than a sidebar. In fact, were it not for the title of the painting, we probably would barely notice him at all. His only manifestation in the painting is his legs, about to submerge with the rest of him under the water at the lower right. Instead, Bruegel gives us a warm and comfortable depiction of a farmer plowing his field, a singing shepherd, and an elegant ship, its sails billowing in the freshening breeze. Mountains the color of huge icebergs reach into a bright sky at the far horizon, and, as in Altdorfer's *Battle* (see Fig.

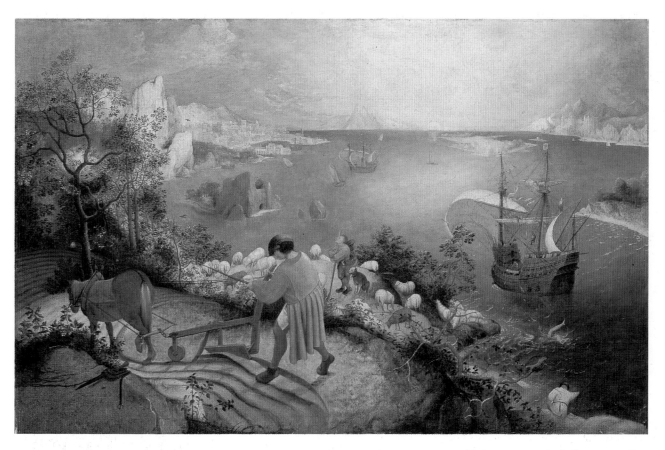

12.11 Pieter Bruegel the Elder, *Landscape with the Fall of Icarus*, c. 1554–5. Oil on panel (transferred to canvas), 2 ft 5 ins × 3 ft 8⅛ ins (74 × 112 cm). Musées Royaux des Beaux-Arts, Brussels.

12.16), we see the earth's curvature from our elevated vantage point.

The fact that no one pays the slightest attention to Icarus probably relates to an old German and Netherlandish proverb that says "When a man dies no plow stops." It may be that Bruegel was reflecting the belief of a group of Antwerp humanists—to which he reportedly belonged—that humans are driven to sin by foolishness, and to try to escape the inevitable cycle of nature is folly.

Although Bruegel pursues Italian ambience and, in his deep perspectives, Italian spatial interests, there is still a lack of the fully rounded, human figures of the Renaissance in this portrayal. The folds of the plowman's tunic are stiff and elementary, the furrows of the field lie flattened like steps in the sunbaked ground, and the trees are stylized with minimal chiaroscuro and painterly foliage applied by stippling—that is, dabbing with the point of the brush. Overall, the work is closer to Bosch than to anything Italian. If we were to examine more of Bruegel's works, we would conclude that his delights in flights of fantasy in his images draw him even closer to Bosch, and that he has a sense of macabre pessimism.

Germany

As early as the late Middle Ages, southern Germany was positioned at the center of a thriving trade axis that connected the Netherlands with Italy. This economic activity gave rise to rich merchant oligarchies and semi-independent city–states modeled on the Italian pattern. Throughout Europe, much of the wealth created in centers such as the Netherlands and Germany was used for the encouragement of arts and letters. By the late fifteenth century important artists such as Albrecht Dürer were following the trade routes back and forth to Italy, and helping to bring the Renaissance to northern Europe.

Albrecht Dürer

Albrecht Dürer (AHL-brekt DYUR-ur; 1471–1528), whom many regard as Germany's greatest artist, could be viewed as the Leonardo of the northern Renaissance (Fig. **12.12**). Both were transitional figures and, at the same time, innovators. Dürer shared Leonardo's deep curiosity about the natural world, a curiosity that is expressed especially in his drawings, which explore the human figure and

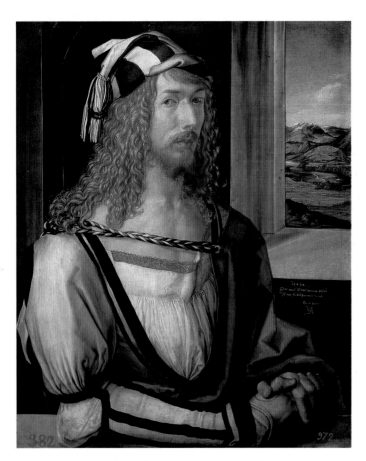

12.12 Albrecht Dürer, *Self-portrait*, 1498. Oil on wood, 20³/₄ × 16¹/₈ ins (52 × 41 cm). Museo del Prado, Madrid.

der Weyden, however, Dürer's works reflect the tensions present in northern Europe at the end of the fifteenth century and in the early sixteenth century. The emotion of *The Four Horsemen of the Apocalypse* (Fig. **12.13**), for example, and its medieval preoccupation with superstition, famine, fear, and death typify German art of this period, and it places Dürer at the pivot point between medieval and Renaissance styles. *The Four Horsemen of the Apocalypse* is the fourth work in a series of woodcuts. This print presents a frightening vision of doomsday and the omens leading up to it, as described in the Revelation of St John, the last book of the Bible. In the foreground, Death tramples a bishop, and working toward the background, Famine swings scales, War brandishes a sword, and Pestilence draws a bow. Underneath, trampled by the horses' hoofs, lies the human race. The crowding and angularity of shapes are reminiscent of late Gothic style,

12.13 Albrecht Dürer, *The Four Horsemen of the Apocalypse*, c. 1497–8. Woodcut, 15²/₅ × 11 ins (39.2 × 27.9 cm). Museum of Fine Arts, Boston (Bequest of Francis Bullard).

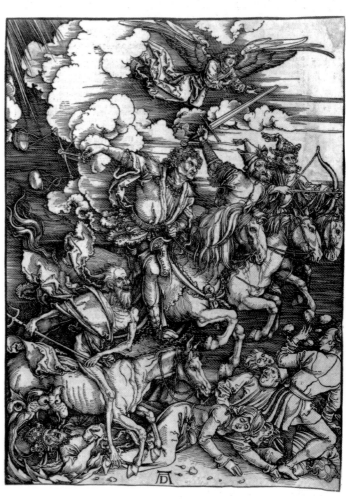

physiognomy, animals, plants, and landscapes. Like Leonardo, Dürer explored aesthetic theory and wrote a treatise on proportion. Also like Leonardo, Dürer was gracious, handsome, famous, courted throughout Europe, and respected by his fellow artists. Unlike Leonardo, however, Dürer worked principally as an engraver and was tortured by religious problems.

The son of a Nuremberg goldsmith, Dürer became the pupil of Michael Wolgemut (VOHL-ge-moot; 1434–1519), whose studio produced a large number of altarpieces, portraits, and woodcuts for book illustration. It was here that he gained his grounding in drawing and painting, and in the techniques of woodcut and copperplate engraving in which he achieved his greatest works. These media allowed his work to be widely distributed and purchased by individuals of modest means, a process that made Dürer rich.

Rogier van der Weyden's deposition scene, *The Descent from the Cross* (see Fig. **12.9**), uses a linear style that greatly influenced Dürer—especially his masterly woodcuts and engravings. In contrast to the works of van

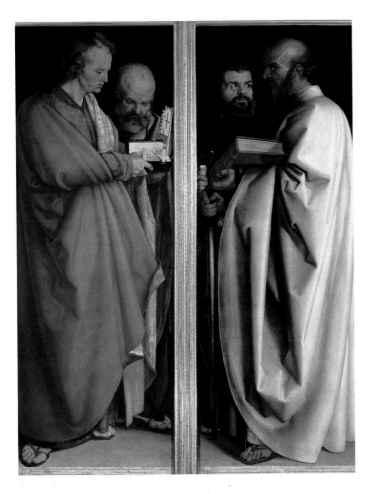

12.14 Albrecht Dürer, *Four Apostles*. Oil on wood, each panel 7 ft 2 ins × 2 ft 6 ins (215 × 76 cm). Altepinakothek, Munich, Germany.

and yet the perspective foreshortening and three-dimensionality of figures reflects the influence of the Italian Renaissance. We can read human character and emotion in the faces of the figures, which humanize them and give them a sense of reality and a proximity to life that adds depth to the meaning of the work.

The technique of the woodcut gives the work its particular quality. The picture is created by building up individual lines, formed when the artist cuts into the block of wood, leaving only exposed edges to which ink will be applied and then pressed onto the paper. Dürer shows remarkable skill in creating lines of tremendous delicacy, which combine into a poignantly complex picture. Notice in particular his treatment of the horses—Death rides an emaciated old nag, while the other three horsemen are astride powerfully muscular steeds. The power of the print emerges from both its technical and aesthetic aspects—the complexity of the linear expression of the woodcut gives the work some of its frenetic quality, but powerful diago-

nal sweeps add to the composition, as does the raw emotional terror of the human elements.

Dürer's last major work was a painting entitled the *Four Apostles* (Fig. **12.14**). It is a diptych—that is, two panels—portraying John and Peter in the left panel and Mark, who was not an apostle, and Paul in the right. The panels were originally intended as the wings of a triptych, of which the central panel would show the Madonna and Child with saints. However, the effects of the Reformation made such a rendering impossible in Nuremberg in 1526, and so the piece was never completed. When Dürer presented the panels to the city council, he gave them inscriptions of Luther's translation of the New Testament that warned all who read them not to confuse human error for the will of God. Dürer enthusiastically supported the Lutheran Reformation, agreeing with Luther's views on papal supremacy, but he found equally repugnant some of the extreme positions of those Protestants who advocated radical experiments, including polygamy.

Matthias Grünewald

Matthias Grünewald (mah-TEE-ahs GRUN-eh-vahlt; c. 1475–1528), Dürer's contemporary, was deeply affected by Luther's reformation. His real name is believed to have been Mathis Gothardt Neithardt, and the name "Grünewald," by which he will always be known, was given to him by his first biographer, the seventeenth-century writer Joachim von Sandrart. As well as an artist, Grünewald was also an architect and hydraulic engineer. Unlike Dürer, he never went to Italy. Second only to Dürer among Germany's great artists, Grünewald, unlike Dürer, remained relatively faithful to earlier traditions. He apparently knew of Dürer, and some of Dürer's influence can be seen in Grünewald's work. For example, the figure of the Virgin in the Isenheim altarpiece (IHZ-en-hym; Fig. **12.15**) recalls a famous watercolor by Dürer. Nonetheless, although Grünewald retains the emotional expressiveness of the medieval period, he did learn how to handle space and perspective and how to treat flesh from the Italians of the Renaissance. The Isenheim altarpiece, Grünewald's greatest work, was painted between 1512 and 1515 for the church of the Hospital of Saint Anthony in Isenheim near Colmar, France. It takes the form of an elaborate series of painted wings for a carved wooden shrine. The *Crucifixion* occupies the outermost wings and is visible when the altarpiece is closed. The picture's tragic intensity is amplified by the stark roughness of the cross itself: two freshly hewn logs. We can feel the weight of the body of Christ and the agony of pain in the grotesquely upraised fingers and the bending of the crossbar under the weight of the inert body of the dead Christ. Everything about the rendering puts us in mind of the torment of such a death—the arm bones seem almost torn from their sockets, and the crown of

12.15 Matthias Grünewald, *Crucifixion*, central panel of the Isenheim altarpiece, c. 1513–15. Oil on wood, 8 ft × 10 ft 1 in (2.44 × 3.07 m). Unterlindenmuseum, Colmar, France.

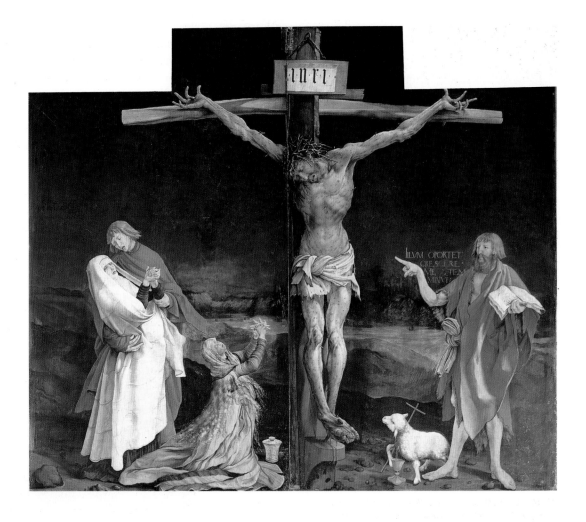

thorns, unlike the neat circular arrangements often depicted, is a misshapen mass of thorns thrust down over the entire head. Christ's face is a ghastly grayish-green: the pallor of death. The body is a mass of scars and scratches exuding deep red drops of blood, and the feet have been punctured by a giant spike.

The figure of Christ is accompanied by John the Baptist, above whose pointing finger appear the words "He must increase, but I must decrease" (John 3:30). Next to John stands the Lamb of God, holding a cross and pulling a chalice to its breast. Mary Magdalene throws herself at the feet of the cross, while St John the Evangelist holds the Virgin Mary, who has fainted from grief. Grünewald sets the figures of the scene in stark contrast to a greenish-black sky. The emotionalism of the painting must have been particularly moving to the patients of the hospital, who were brought before it daily and who must have recognized in it the message that Christ understood their suffering because of the extreme nature of his own. In this painting, Grünewald has raised the grotesque to the level of the tragic and, as a result, has created a painting of great appeal and beauty.

Albrecht Altdorfer

Similar to Grünewald in imaginative power was the painter Albrecht Altdorfer (AHLT-dorf-ur; 1480–1538). Born in Regensburg, a beautiful Bavarian city on the Danube, Altdorfer had a special gift and affinity for landscape. In his most famous painting, *Battle of Alexander and Darius on the Issus* (Fig. **12.16**), we find the ancient battle between Darius III of Persia and Alexander the Great in 333 B.C. depicted as if it were a modern battle, probably the battle of Ravenna in 1512 or the battle of Pavia in 1525. What is most striking in this particular work is the fact that Altdorfer has painted thousands of individual soldiers in a space barely 5 feet (1.5 meters) high and 4 feet (1.2 meters) wide.

In contrast with some of the massive perspectives of the Italian Renaissance that we have examined, Altdorfer takes us up high for our perspective vantage point. From here we get a bird's eye glimpse of the solid mass of soldiers coming towards us out of a fantasy landscape that recedes without benefit of atmospheric perspective to the edge of the earth, whose very curvature we can see, almost as if we were astronauts gazing at earth from space. Our eyes are

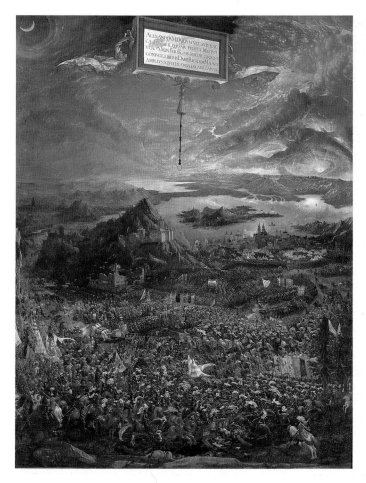

12.16 Albrecht Altdorfer, *Battle of Alexander and Darius on the Issus*, 1529. Oil on wood, 5 ft 3¼ ins × 4 ft (1.58 × 1.20 m). Altepinakothek, Munich, Germany.

free to drift from point to point, for there is very little in the subject of the painting—that is, the battle—to hold our attention. A few fluttering flags create focal points, but the human element is lost in the swarm of thousands of indistinguishable bodies. Much more interesting than the human spectacle, massive though it is, is the glorious landscape and its rugged mountains, alpine lakes, swirling clouds, and glowing sunrise. A tablet with a lengthy Latin inscription and unfurling pennant floats over the scene, hung theatrically and magically in the sky. The stunning effect of the overall work stems from its absolute graphic clarity and accuracy. Each detail emerges crystal clear from foreground to background, and the perspective depiction of castles and armies winding away from us is nothing short of remarkable.

France

In Chapter 11, touching on the style known as Mannerism, we briefly considered architecture in France in an examination of the Lescot Wing of the Louvre (see Fig. **11.26**). We

12.18 Jean Clouet, *Francis I*, c. 1525–30. Tempera and oil on wood, 38¼ × 29½ ins (96 × 74 cm). Louvre, Paris.

12.17 Exterior of the Château of Chambord, France, begun 1529.

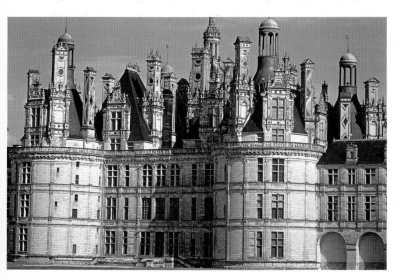

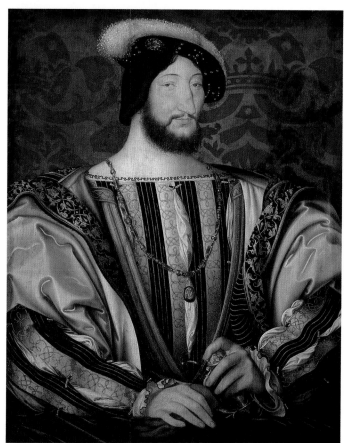

Ming Dynasty Porcelain

At the time of the Western Reformation, the Ming dynasty in China produced exquisite porcelain, by which the dynasty is primarily known today. The classic period of the familiar blue-and-white porcelains was between the years 1426 and 1435, and the style was characterized by clarity of detail and variety of shapes. Over the next one hundred years, works were enriched by adding multicolored enamels to the basic blue. The result of this development, which occurred in the late sixteenth century, can be seen in a five-color enamel jar (Fig. **12.19**) from the reign of Wan Li (1573–1619). The complex process of adding layers of color called for refined designs and repeated firings in the kiln.

The white ground and blue designs came first and were glazed and fired. Over this fired glaze, the decoration was completed in red, green, yellow, and brown, and the work was then refired. The entire process required several firings and resulted in a rich, delicate ceramic. The freely painted narrative scenes and floral compositions have charm, grace, and appeal. Their shapes tend to be slightly irregular, which gives a uniqueness and human quality that adds warmth to their otherwise perfect execution.

12.19 Covered jar, mark of Wan Li, c. 1600. Porcelain, 4 ins (10.2 cm) high. Cleveland Museum of Art (John L. Severance Fund).

now return to that country for more exploration of the sixteenth century to see how the Renaissance outside Italy affected the artistic qualities of this country.

The impetus of the Italian Renaissance came to France, at least in part, from the insistence of King Francis I (r. 1515–47), who greatly admired the achievements of Italian Renaissance art. He invaded Italy—with only modest success and a disastrous ending—and had a continuing confrontation with the forces of Charles V of Spain and the Holy Roman Empire, but this did open France to the ideas of the Italian Renaissance. Francis tried to coax Italian artists to his court, and Leonardo da Vinci actually spent two years there towards the end of his life. Francis wanted his patronage of the arts to rival that of the greatest Italian princes, but in fact, all the Renaissance that Francis got was its successor, Mannerism, and the results are what is known as the School of Fontainebleau (fohn-ten-BLOH), named after the grand palace southeast of Paris.

Although Italian ideas were introduced, they were strangely interpreted by French artisans, as may be seen in the Château of Chambord (shahm-BOHR; Fig. **12.17**), which took over thirty years to build, so it is possible that the original intent got lost over that time. Designed by the Italian Domenico da Cortona, the completed château, which has over four hundred rooms and fifty staircases, is peculiarly medieval, with its pinnacles and rounded turrets. The most Italian parts of the building are the central keep and exterior decoration. Within the central block and concentrated on a corner tower lie self-sufficient apartments. There is a complex double central staircase, whose spirals intertwine so that those going up cannot see those coming down.

There were no artists of great stature in France in the sixteenth century. However, the best portraitists of the court of Francis I were French, and the best of these was Jean Clouet (KLOO-ay; c. 1485–1541). Clouet's portrait of the king (Fig. **12.18**), done between 1525 and 1530, shows a self-indulgent, calculating character—Francis was, in fact, notorious for his sexual affairs—but the likeness is stiff and formal, with the same kind of distorted, mannered appearance that we saw in Bronzino's *Portrait of a Young Man* (see Fig. **11.22**). The line and form of the foreground clash with the decor of the background, and the brocade and stripes of the costume lead the eye downward to focus on the king's left hand, which seems to toy nervously with his poniard.

MUSIC

The Renaissance Style in Flanders

Like their Italian counterparts, the aristocracy of Flanders were active patrons of the arts, and the painter Jan van Eyck, for example, benefited greatly from their patronage. As part of their courtly entourage, the courts retained a group of musicians to provide entertainment and chapel music. Musicians were frequently imported from elsewhere, thus contributing to the cosmopolitan character of the Flemish courts and disseminating Flemish influence throughout Europe.

Flemish composers were widely educated and thoroughly aware of the world around them. In their Masses and motets, they made significant contributions to the development of FOUR-PART HARMONY. They gave greater independence to the lower lines, in particular. The bass part was independent for the first time, and this became a typical feature of this style of composition. By the end of the Renaissance, it was normal for all parts to imitate each other using consistent, measured rhythm. They came together only at the ends of sections for cadences, the musical equivalents of punctuation marks, so that, for the first time in history, Flemish music used a true four-part texture.

Guillaume Dufay and Josquin des Prez were its most prominent composers. Dufay (1400–74) had been a member of the Papal Chapel at Rome and Florence, and he had traveled extensively throughout Europe. Thus he brought to Flanders a wealth of knowledge and experience. Within his lifetime, he was hailed as one of the great composers of the era. He wrote prolifically, and a wealth of his work has been published in modern editions. His style is striking for its relative straightforwardness as compared with the complexity of much late Gothic music. Dufay's sacred motets, based on the chant *Salve regina* (sahl-vay ray-JEEN-uh), formed the basis for numerous later polyphonic settings of the Mass. He also wrote many secular songs in the standard medieval forms, such as rondeaux and ballads, of which about eighty have survived.

Patronage and secular influence on music continued. The printing press enabled music, like the written word, to be transmitted easily. More music than ever before was composed, and people started to identify composers as individuals. Composers strove to achieve an "ideal" sound, by which they meant four or more voice lines of similar and compatible timbres (as opposed to the contrasting timbres of earlier periods). Small groups of singers on each part replaced the earlier soloists. Composers concentrated on making each work a unified

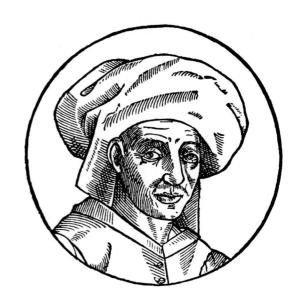

12.20 Josquin des Prez. Photo: Corbis-Bettmann, London.

whole. The practice of combining texts in different languages within one piece died out. Much more attention was given to the relationship of music and text, and clarity of communication became one of the objectives of music. According to the values of the day, the ideal vehicle for musical communication was an unaccompanied vocal ensemble.

Perhaps the most influential and widely published composer of the early sixteenth century, however, was Josquin des Prez (zhohs-KAN day PRAY; c.1440–1521; Fig. **12.20**). Trained in Milan, Rome, and Florence, among other places, Josquin brought to Flanders a rich Renaissance heritage. Compared to Michelangelo and called the "father of musicians," he wrote about seventy secular songs of a light, homophonic nature, but his chief contribution lay in the development of polyphony, especially in his masses and motets. Imitation became an important structural feature—that is, for each group of words, a short musical theme would be presented in one voice and then be restated (imitated) in the other voices. Another structural device he sometimes used was the repetition of sections of music, in which an opening section (A) is followed by new material (B), and then is restated in a third section (A). This became known as ABA form. Josquin's music flows freely with varied rhythms and a full, rich sound. Above all, emotion shines through.

We find a typically skillful example of Josquin's composition in the motet *Ave Maria . . . Virgo Serena* ("Hail, Mary . . . Serene Virgin;" 1502; CD track 6) The text is a prayer to the Virgin, and a short melodic phrase begins in the soprano voice (Fig. **12.21**). Then the alto,

tenor, and bass voices, in turn, imitate the soprano line. The next phrase of text, *gratia plena* ("full of grace") employs a different melody, again imitated among the voices. Note that each voice enters in the middle of the phrase by the previous voice. This pattern gives a richer texture to the piece and contributes to a sense of ongoing flow in the music. At points in the piece we find imitation between two voices, and at other times there is imitation between pairs of voices: duets between the upper two voices are imitated by the lower two voices. There are also changes in meter from duple to triple, and for a moment the tempo adopts a great sense of agitation. Then the piece returns to duple meter and a more peaceful mood. The composition ends with slow chords that reinforce the textual entreaty: "O Mother of God, remember me. Amen."

Lutheranism and *Lieder*

Unlike Zwingli and Calvin, who either removed music from worship entirely or severely limited its use, Martin Luther saw music as an integral part of liturgical worship. As we saw, the hallmark of the Reformation was the primacy of the Word of God, as revealed in the Bible, which was to be heard, obeyed, and incorporated into daily life. The Swiss reformers distrusted music because it had a power of its own that they believed could subvert the Word of God. Music also had secular connections—often with immoral connotations—that made Zwingli and Calvin nervous. Luther, on the other hand, saw music in a more positive light and believed that it could be used for the glorification of God. He found in music a connection to the prophets, who he believed used music to proclaim truth through psalms and song.

The Lutheran Reformation, therefore, brought many changes to Church music. Even after the separation, Lutheran music continued to have many Roman Catholic characteristics, including some Latin texts and plainsong chants. However, the most important contribution of the Lutheran Reformation was the *chorale* or hymn tune. Modern hymns, many of which date back to Martin Luther for both text and tune, illustrate this form. Our four-part harmonies are a later modification. Originally, the chorale was a single melody, stemming from the chant or folk song, and a text. Congregational singing was in unison and without accompaniment. The liturgical experience that developed in Lutheran churches, particularly in Wittenberg under Luther's leadership, contributed a rich and varied combination of Latin and German, traditional monody and contemporary polyphony, the music of Catholic and Lutheran composers, and choral and organ music, all held together by congregational hymnody.

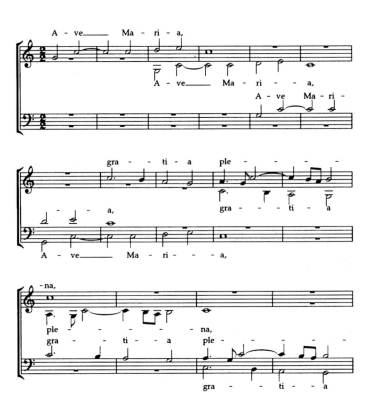

12.21 Josquin des Prez, *Ave Maria...Virgo Serena*, 1502.

Lutheranism also contributed a considerable body of polyphonic choral settings, many from Luther's principal collaborator, Johann Walter (VAHL-tuhr; 1496–1574). These settings vary tremendously in style and source, some being based on German *Lieder* (LEE-duhr; secular songs) and some on Flemish motets. Polyphony, a complex texture, is not, however, ideal for congregational singing, and polyphonic settings were uniformly reserved for the choir. By the end of the sixteenth century, Lutheran congregational singing had changed again, with the organ being given an expanded role. The congregation sang the melody, but was no longer unaccompanied—an organ played harmonic parts.

Also in Germany in the late fifteenth century, the Renaissance spirit, with its secular traditions, produced polyphonic *Lieder*. These predominantly three-part secular songs provided much of the melodic basis for the church hymns of Lutheranism after the Reformation. Heinrich Isaac (1450–1517) was probably the first and most notable German *Lied* composer of this era. The frequent usage and refashioning of this type of composition can be seen in one of Isaac's most famous works, "Innsbruck, I Must Leave Thee." The song was originally a folk love song, but Isaac changed the song into a polyphonic piece with words by the Emperor Maximilian. Later, he used the melody in his own sacred work, the

Missa Carminum. The song then became widely known in another adaptation under the sacred title, "O World, I Now Must Leave Thee." Even Johann Sebastian Bach used the *Innsbruck Lied* in the *St Matthew Passion*.

Parisian Chanson

Paris retained its importance as a musical center for centuries. By the mid-sixteenth century, a new French style of music had emerged. In the late 1520s, again thanks to mass printing, vast quantities of music, written by composers living and working in and around Paris and representing a markedly different style, began to appear. One of the greatest French composers of the time was Clément Janequin (ZHAN-nih-kan; c. 1485–c. 1560), associated with a new kind of chanson (song), known as the Parisian chanson, which represented a genre that perfectly captured the elegant simplicity and rational spirit of French musicians.

Janequin's works typically express the vivacious and irreverent side of the French character. Today, Janequin is best remembered for his long descriptive chansons—for example, *Le chant des oiseaux* (*The Song of the Birds*)—in which he explored a particular theme—in this instance bird songs, but also battles, hunts, street cries, and ladies' gossip—that allowed him to make a virtuoso display of onomatopoeia (words that sound like their reference). *The Song of the Birds* uses a series of slow-moving chords to frame a rich jumble of elaborate animal noises which make up the central point of this amusing piece.

DANCE

European indoor court entertainments of the early and mid-sixteenth century often took the form of "dinner ballets." These entertainments were long and lavish, with interludes called *entrées*, between the courses. Often the mythological characters in these *entrées* (ahn-TRAYZ) corresponded to the dishes served in the meal. Poseidon, god of the sea, for example, would accompany the fish course.

Courtly dancing in Europe, and especially in Italy, became more and more professional in the late sixteenth century. Skilled professionals performed on a raised stage, then left the stage to perform in the center of the banquet

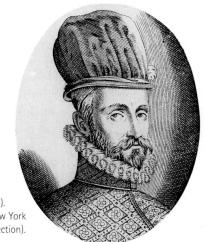

12.22 Fabrizio Caroso (b. c. 1553). Contemporary engraving. The New York Public Library. (Cia Fornaroli Collection).

hall, joined by members of court. During this period, dancing technique improved and more complicated rhythms were introduced. All of these changes were faithfully recorded by Fabrizio Caroso (fahb-REET-zee-oh kah-ROH-soh; Fig. **12.22**).

Formal ballet came of age as an art form under the aegis of the powerful Catherine de' Medici (1519–89), great-granddaughter of Lorenzo the Magnificent. Love of spectacle permeated the French court, and lavish entertainments, some of which nearly bankrupted the shaky French treasury, marked important events, such as the marriage of Catherine's eldest son, Francis II, to Mary, Queen of Scots. Although sources vary on just how these spectaculars developed into the ballet, we can be sure that either *Le Ballet de Polonais* (1572) or the *Ballet Comique de la Reine* (1581) marked the real beginning of formal Western ballet tradition.

Le Ballet de Polonais, the "Polish Ballet," was produced in the great hall of the Palace of the Tuileries on a temporary stage with steps leading to the hall floor. The audience surrounded three sides of the stage and joined the dancers at the end of the performance in "general dancing." Music was composed by Orlando di Lasso.

This extravaganza had a mixture of biblical and mythological sources. It had original music, poetry, and song, and Italian Renaissance scenic devices overwhelmed the audience with fountains and aquatic machines. Over ten thousand spectators witnessed this event, which cost 3.5 million francs. It ran from ten in the evening to four the next morning. Probably the most significant aspect of the *Ballet Comique* was its use of a single dramatic story line throughout.

Focal Point

The Great Age of the Tudors

In 1485 the Wars of the Roses came to an end, and Henry VII, the first Tudor, became king. His son Henry VIII succeeded, at the height of the humanist Renaissance and the Lutheran Reformation, in asserting the national, independent character of the English throne. Whether through desire for a son and heir or from pure ambition, Henry VIII came in conflict with Rome over the pope's refusal to grant him a divorce, eventually rejecting Rome and proclaiming himself head of the Church of England. The turmoil with Rome took a heavy toll: in 1533 Henry was excommunicated, and two years later Henry's close advisor and a staunch Roman Catholic, Sir Thomas More, was executed for treason. Between 1536 and 1539 the Act of Dissolution dissolved all monasteries and created a nobility based on the wealth of those who were loyal to the state. After Henry's death in 1547, a period of instability followed, with Edward VI (r. 1547–53) supporting the Reformation, and Mary Tudor (r. 1553–8) instituting a "Spanish-style" Catholic reaction. Elizabeth I, who became queen in 1558, ended the uncertainty. She consolidated the Acts of Supremacy and Uniformity by which her father and brother had broken from Rome, and she stood firm against both foreign "Papists" and rebellious Puritans at home. The 1534 Act of Supremacy had made the king head of the Church of England, and the 1559 Act of Uniformity made Elizabeth I head of the episcopal hierarchy of the new Church of England. She instituted a national religion, later called "Anglicanism," that, in effect, represented a compromise between Protestant dogmatism and episcopal discipline and hierarchy. For this reason, Anglicanism may accurately be seen as not a Protestant faith. The Anglican Church is based on two documents, the Thirty-nine Articles and the *Book of Common Prayer*.

Elizabeth "allowed" her rival to the throne, Franco-Scottish Mary Stuart, Queen of Scots, to be executed in 1587, and her rule was further strengthened by the catastrophic destruction of the Spanish Armada in 1588. The forty-five years of Elizabeth's reign consolidated an English national identity and gave birth to a magnificent cultural Renaissance, especially in literature and theatre, with

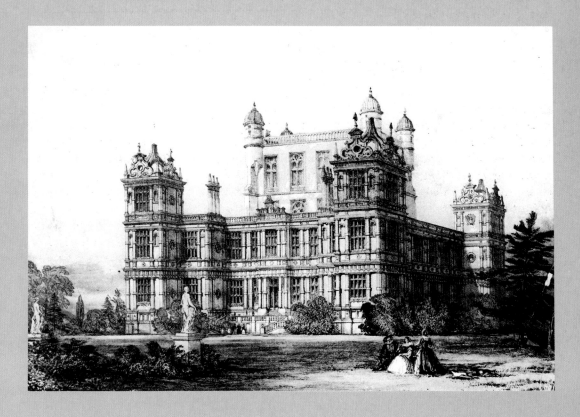

12.23 Exterior of Wollaton Hall, Nottingham, UK, 1588.

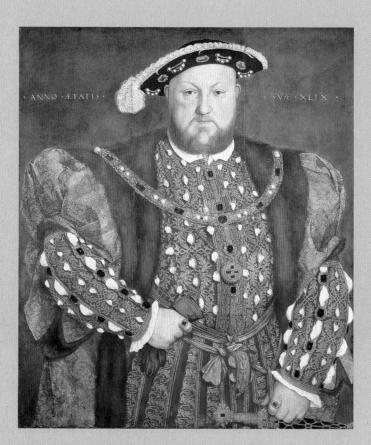

12.24 Hans Holbein the Younger, *Henry VIII in Wedding Dress*, 1540. Oil on panel, 35¹/₂ × 30 ins (89 × 75 cm). Galleria Nazionale d'Arte Antica, Rome.

Spenser, whose fantasy in the epic poem *The Faerie Queene* we will note later in this chapter. Like Spenser's poetry, Wollaton Hall, whose first two stories would leave it sufficient, rises up in dream-like majesty.

A German painter whose work in London made him the favorite of Henry VIII, Hans Holbein (HOHL-byn) the Younger (c. 1497–1543), came from a family of Augsburg painters, all of whose reputations he eclipsed. He traveled widely in France and Italy and was strongly influenced by the work of Mantegna and Leonardo (see Chapter 11). It is possible that Holbein's letter of introduction to Henry VIII came from Erasmus, who was impressed by the young artist's promise. Erasmus did provide Holbein a letter of introduction to Sir Thomas More, who became the artist's principal patron and protector during his first visit to England, when Holbein undertook an ambitious portrait of Sir Thomas More and his family, a work that has not survived. Shortly after arriving in England for the second time in 1532, Holbein became court painter to Henry VIII, who set him up in a studio in St James's Palace. Holbein painted a series of portraits of the king, including that seen in Figure **12.24**. There is such control of technique here that Henry almost comes to life in all his obesity and obsessive temperament. Equally sensitive is the portrayal of Jane Seymour (Fig. **12.25**), and the artist's vibrancy, control,

lesser accomplishments in music, visual art, and architecture. It was a time of empire, with Sir Francis Drake leaving in 1577 to circumnavigate the globe.

Visual Art and Architecture

The pre-eminent English architect of the period was Robert Smythson (c. 1535–1614). One of his most famous houses is Wollaton Hall, near Nottingham (Fig. **12.23**). Designed for the sheriff of Nottingham, Sir Francis Willoughby, and completed in 1588, it shows Italian influences dating to Serlio (see Chapter 11), but is a unique application of the style. The tall, forceful central hall is illuminated by clerestory windows and topped by a turreted chamber that rises above the ornamented façade like an overweight crown—compare the Lescot façade of the Louvre, Figure **11.26**. The proportions established by such a design are totally without precedent. The central hall is flanked by equally fanciful toppings on the wings, whose gables resemble the façades of Renaissance Italian churches and the bell gables of the Netherlands. One might conclude that there is as much fantasy in Smythson's designs as there is in Bosch and Bruegel, and we must remember that in England this was the time of Edmund

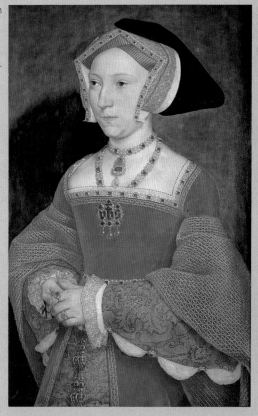

12.25 Hans Holbein the Younger, *Jane Seymour*, 1536. Oil on wood, 26³/₄ × 19 ins (66 × 48 cm). Kunsthistorisches Museum, Vienna.

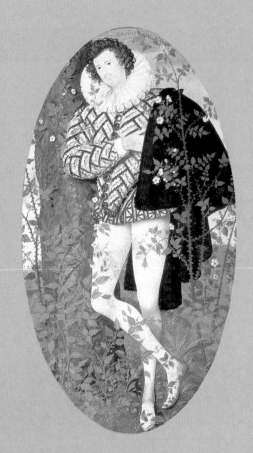

12.26 Nicholas Hilliard, *A Youth Leaning Against a Tree with Roses*, c. 1590. Parchment, 5³/₈ × 2³/₄ ins (14 × 7 cm). Victoria & Albert Museum, London.

umbers of the tree, the young man's hair, and the elongated rose stems in graceful curves to balance the elliptical outline of the painting itself.

Literature and Drama

In England, Renaissance literature and drama flowered during the last quarter of the sixteenth century. After the seemingly interminable Wars of the Roses and the turbulence of the Reformation, under Elizabeth I England entered a period of political and social stability that engendered a mood of optimism and readiness to experiment in cultural matters.

Lyric poetry enjoyed wide popularity, and the ability to compose a sonnet or to coin an original and witty phrase was regarded as essential in any courtier, while the growing and increasingly prosperous middle class—no longer confined to the large towns, but extending throughout the shires and country towns—demanded increasingly sophisticated entertainment. At the same time, a large and educated readership, women as well as men, also developed. Writers and booksellers quickly responded to this new market. An early and notable testament to this upsurge in interest came in Sir Philip Sidney's *A Defense of Poesie* (published posthumously in 1595), a brilliant and forceful polemic, which laid claim to the cultural high ground for verse. Sidney (1554–86), in many ways the model English Renaissance courtier and man of letters—that is, considered the ideal gentleman of his day— had read widely and judiciously in ancient Italian and French literature. His sonnets, best represented in *Astrophel and Stella*, perfectly embodied the delicacy, elegance, wit, and expressiveness of contemporary writing.

The mantle of Elizabethan poetry falls, however, on the shoulders of Edmund Spenser (c. 1552–99). Born in London to middle-class parents, he was well educated in humanist disciplines and the classics, and he also studied English composition and drama. He received two degrees from Cambridge University, where he developed a deep love of poetry and made a wide group of friends who turned out to be both intellectually stimulating and politically useful. Although he enjoyed aristocratic patronage, poetry, although popular, was not at the time a particularly desirable career, and his first work *The Shepheardes Calendar*, dedicated to Philip Sidney, was published under a pseudonym in 1579. Meticulously symmetrical, it reveals Spenser's impulse toward experimentation in verse types. The result is a quaint and moderately charming poem, in which a group of shepherds, representing Spenser and his friends, reveal their ideas about love, poetry, and religous feeling. Writing did not give Spenser a steady income, and in 1580 he took a position in Ireland as private secretary to the new governor, Lord Grey of Wilton. Spenser lived in Ireland for the rest of his life, regarding himself as an exile

and acute observation give us the sense that we know this person, who appears almost ready to leave the canvas and join us in polite conversation. There is such delicacy in the portrayal of details that the textures seem to lift off the surface. The harmony and symmetry of the pose gives the painting a quiet and yet strong elegance that marks Holbein's style.

The second half of the sixteenth century gave England its first native Renaissance master in the area of painting. Nicholas Hilliard (HIL-yurd; c. 1547–1619) is best known for his miniatures and small portraits, such as that of the unidentified *Youth Leaning Against a Tree with Roses* (Fig. **12.26**). This miniature, barely 5 inches by 3 inches (14 × 7 centimeters), is done in watercolor on parchment. Apart from the rather dreamy expression of its subject and the romanticized setting, the work tells us more about the costume of the period than anything else, but we can sense Hilliard's delicate touch and command of fine detail, which is often more difficult in small scale than it is in large. Hilliard also shows a clear sense of balance and color quality, as he encircles the young man with green leaves, which pull the floor of the painting up to its apex, and carries the

PROFILE

William Shakespeare (1564–1616)

The greatest literary genius of all was William Shakespeare (1564–1616), most of whose work was for the theatre, but who also left a remarkable sequence of sonnets in which he pushed the resources of the English language to breathtaking extremes. In his works for the theatre, Shakespeare represents the Elizabethan love of drama, and the theatres of London were patronized by lords and commoners alike. They sought and found, usually in the same play, action, spectacle, comedy, character, and intellectual stimulation deeply reflective of the human condition. Thus it was with Shakespeare, the pre-eminent Elizabethan playwright. His appreciation of the Italian Renaissance can be seen in the settings of many of his plays. With true Renaissance breadth, Shakespeare went back into history, both British and classical, and far beyond, to the fantasy world of *The Tempest*. Like most playwrights of his age, Shakespeare wrote for a specific professional company, of which he became a partial owner. The need for new plays to keep the company alive from season to season provided much of the impetus for his prolific output.

Although we know only a little of his life, the principal facts are well established. He was baptized in the parish church of Stratford upon Avon on 26 April 1564, and probably attended the local grammar school. We next learn of him in his marriage to Ann Hathaway in 1582, when a special action was necessary to allow the marriage without delay. The reason is clear—five months later, Ann gave birth to their first daughter, Susanna. The next public mention comes in 1592, when his reputation as a playwright was sufficient to warrant a malicious comment from another playwright, Robert Greene. From then on, there are many records of his activities as dramatist, actor, and businessman. In addition to his steady output of plays, he also published a narrative poem entitled *Venus and Adonis*, which was popular enough to have nine printings in the next few years. His standing as a lyric poet was established with the publication of 154 sonnets in 1609.

In 1594 he was a founder of a theatrical company called the Lord Chamberlain's Company, in which he functioned as shareholder, actor, and playwright. In 1599, the company built its own theatre, the Globe, which came directly under the patronage of James I when he assumed the throne in 1603. Shakespeare died in 1616, shortly after executing a detailed will. Although more is known about Shakespeare than the few facts mentioned here, playwrights were not held in high esteem in England in the sixteenth century, and there was virtually no reason to write about them. We do, in fact, know more about Shakespeare than we do most of his contemporaries.

and having little sympathy with the Irish. He approved of Lord Grey's cruel policy of military plunder and portrayed him sympathetically in *The Faerie Queene* and a report on the *View of the Present State of Ireland*.

The *Faerie Queene*, which was circulated in manuscript form long before it was published, was widely admired. In 1589 Spenser returned to London with Sir Walter Raleigh, who had read *The Faerie Queene* and who represented for Spenser a way to patronage and position. When the first parts were published in 1590, the work was dedicated to the "most mighty and magnificent" Empress Elizabeth, "the greatest Gloriana," the heroine of the poem. The work made Spenser famous, and he gained a small pension from it. However, he failed to gain either an important position or a patron, and he returned to Ireland disillusioned. Over the years, he published many more poems and enjoyed great fame, but had little material benefit.

In the summer of 1598 the Irish rebelled against England. Spenser's home was burned and ransacked, and he barely escaped to England with his wife and four children. He died soon after, an emotional and physical wreck. Even in death, the ironic juxtaposition of fame and ill-fortune continued, for while poets accompanied his body to burial in Westminster Abbey, a monument ordered by Queen Elizabeth was never erected.

Although his own generation revered his great skill in fashioning a new literature from the classics, Chaucer, and the French and Italian Renaissance poets, today Spenser remains one of the least-read of the great English poets.

The dramatist William Shakespeare's plays fall into three genres: comedies, tragedies, and histories. The third category represents a particularly Elizabethan type. England's prosperity and rising greatness, accentuated by the defeat of the Spanish Armada, led to a tremendous

MASTERWORK

Shakespeare—*Hamlet*

*H*amlet, Shakespeare's most famous play, was first performed in 1601 and published in 1603. The Hamlet story was a widespread legend in northern Europe, and Shakespeare's source for the play may have been Belleforest's *Histoires Tragiques* (1559). Shakespeare's play may also have used as a source a lost play supposedly by Thomas Kyd, usually referred to as the *Ur-Hamlet*. Shakespeare's *Hamlet*, however, has its own unique central element in Hamlet's tragic flaw, his hesitation to avenge his father's murder.

At the beginning of the play, Hamlet mourns the death of his father, who has been murdered, and also laments his mother's marriage to his uncle Claudius within a month of his father's death. Hamlet's father's ghost appears to Hamlet, telling him that he was poisoned by Claudius and asking him to avenge his death. Hamlet hesitates, requiring further evidence of foul play. His uncertainty and hesitancy make him increasingly moody, and everyone believes that Hamlet is going mad. The pompous old courtier Polonius believes Hamlet is lovesick over his daughter Ophelia.

Despite Claudius' apparent guilt, Hamlet still cannot act. Nevertheless, he terrorizes his mother and kills the eavesdropping Polonius. Fearing for his life, Claudius sends Hamlet to England with his friends Rosencrantz and Guildenstern, who have orders to have Hamlet killed. Discovering the orders, Hamlet arranges to have his friends killed instead. Returning to Denmark, Hamlet learns that Ophelia has killed herself, and her brother Laertes has vowed vengeance on Hamlet for Polonius' death. Claudius happily arranges the duel. Both Hamlet and Laertes are struck by the sword that Claudius has had dipped in poison. Gertrude mistakenly drinks from the cup of poison intended for Hamlet. Before Hamlet dies, he fatally stabs Claudius.

In the play, Shakespeare appears to suggest that traditional beliefs about revenge are over-simplified, arguing that revenge does not solve evil if evil lies in a complex situation: "The time is out of joint; O cursed spite/That ever I was born to set it right" (V.i.189–90). He also seems to maintain that revenge itself is morally wrong. In *Hamlet*, as well as the other tragedies (*Othello*, *King Lear*, and *Macbeth*), Shakespeare explores with great psychological subtlety how the personality flaws in the protagonist lead almost inevitably to his own destruction and the destruction of those around him.

Hamlet
William Shakespeare
Act 3, Sc. 1

Hamlet:
> To be, or not to be: that is the question:
> Whether 'tis nobler in the mind to suffer
> The slings and arrows of outrageous fortune,
> Or to take arms against a sea of troubles,
> And by opposing end them? To die: to sleep:
> No more; and by a sleep to say we end
> The heartache and the thousand natural shocks
> That flesh is heir to,—'tis a consummation
> Devoutly to be wish'd. To die, to sleep;
> To sleep: perchance to dream: ay, there's the rub:
> For in that sleep of death what dreams may
>   come,
> When we have shuffled off this mortal coil,
> Must give us pause: there's the respect
> That makes calamity of so long life;
> For who would bear the whips and scorns of
>   time,
> The oppressor's wrong, the proud man's
>   contumely,
> The pangs of despised love, the law's delay,
> The insolence of office and the spurns
> That patient merit of the unworthy takes,
> When he himself might his quietus make
> With a bare bodkin? Who would fardels bear,
> To grunt and sweat under a weary life,
> But that the dread of something after death,
> The undiscover'd country from whose bourn
> No traveller returns, puzzles the will
> And makes us rather bear those ills we have
> Than fly to others that we know not of?
> Thus conscience does make cowards of us all;
> And thus the native hue of resolution
> Is sicklied o'er with the pale cast of thought,
> And enterprises of great pith and moment
> With this regard their currents turn awry,
> And lose the name of action.

popular interest in English history, and Shakespeare's history plays are large-scale dramatizations and glorifications of events that took place between 1200 and 1550. An occasional tragedy—*Julius Caesar*, for example—was based on history, and he often set his comedies in Renaissance Italy—for example, *The Taming of the Shrew*—but the true "histories" have a particular flavor and type and are identified by titles referring to English kings—for example, *Richard II*, *Henry V*, and so on. King Lear was a mythical English king, but the play of that title is a tragedy rather than a "history."

There is a robust, peculiarly Elizabethan quality in Shakespeare's plays. The ideas expressed in them have a universal appeal because of his understanding of human motivation and character, and his ability to probe deeply into emotion. The plays reflect life and love, action and nationalism, and they present those qualities in a magnificent poetry that explores and expands the English language in unrivaled fashion. Shakespeare's use of tone, color, and complex or new word meanings gives his plays a musical as well as dramatic quality, which appeals to every generation.

The English dramatist Christopher Marlowe was an important contemporary of Shakespeare. He was the son of a Canterbury shoemaker, and he obtained a bachelor's degree from Corpus Christi College, Cambridge, in 1584, progressing to the master's degree after some difficulty about irregular attendance and a letter from the Privy Council certifying the worthwhileness of his government employment, part of which had taken him abroad as a member of the Queen's secret service. Thereafter, he resided in London and wrote actively for the theatre. Unorthodox in religious belief and behavior, he was attacked as an atheist and also sentenced to prison for a brawl in which someone was killed. He was himself killed in a quarrel over a tavern bill on 1 May 1593, at the age of twenty-nine.

Marlowe wrote a number of plays, two of which have earned acclaim—*Tamburlaine* (TAM-buhr-layn) *the Great* and *Doctor Faustus* (FOW-stuhs). His earliest play, *Tamburlaine the Great* (1587), established blank verse as the convention for later Elizabethan and Jacobean playwrights. This verse form consists of nonrhyming lines of iambic pentameter—that is, lines of five metrical feet in which each foot has two syllables, the second one generally bearing the rhythmic stress. The play itself is in two parts, the second part—as Marlowe explains in its prologue—having been written as a result of the popularity of the first. The play tells the story of Tamburlaine's quest for power and luxury and possession of beauty, as he rises from being an obscure shepherd to a powerful conqueror. By Part II, the fairly sympathetic hero of Part I becomes cruel and obsessed with power; he succumbs to a fatal illness, a victim of his own weakness. In this tale, Marlowe paints an amazingly three-dimensional picture of grandeur and impotence.

Marlowe's most famous play, first published in 1604, is *The Tragical History of the Life and Death of Doctor Faustus*, or simply *Doctor Faustus*. The story tells the tale of human temptation, fall, and damnation in richly poetic language.

Marlowe's source appears to have been an English translation of the German legend of Faustus that appeared in England at that time. The plot centers on the scholar Faust, who despairs of the limitations of his own learning and of all human knowledge. He turns to magic, and makes a contract with Mephistophilis, a minor devil. They agree that Mephistophilis will assist Faust and be his slave for twenty-four years. After that, Mephistophilis will claim Faust's soul, and Faust will be damned for eternity. So for twenty-four years, Faust uses his powers to the full, from playing practical jokes to calling back Helen of Troy. On the last night, he waits in agony and terror. In the end, Mephistophilis comes and carries him off to hell. Marlowe's love of sound permeates his works, and if his character development is occasionally weak, the heroic grandeur of his action has the universal qualities of Aeschylus and Sophocles.

Ben Jonson's comedy stands in contrast to Marlowe's heroic tragedy. The play *Every Man in his Humor* documents the lives of a group of Elizabethan eccentrics. Jonson's wit and pen were sharp, and his tolerance was low. His plays were often vicious caricatures of contemporary individuals.

The Elizabethan Playhouse

The structure of Elizabethan theatre buildings is familiar, even though documentation is fairly sketchy (Fig. **12.27**). In general, we assume that the audience surrounded the stage on three sides, an inheritance from earlier times when stages were erected in the enclosed courtyards of inns. By 1576 buildings housing the professional theatre existed in London. They were round or octagonal in shape ("This wooden O," according to Shakespeare in *Henry V*). A cross-section of society attended them, from commoners in the "pit," or standing area around the stage, to nobility in the galleries, a seating area under a roof. Situated against one wall of the circular building, the stage may or may not have been protected by a canopy, but the great spectacle of Elizabethan drama was, by and large, an outdoor event. Theatres were constructed of wood; fire was a constant threat and a frequent reality. Johannes de Witt, from whose accounts of a trip to London in 1596 we derive nearly all our knowledge of the physical theatre of the era, claimed that the Swan Theatre could seat 3,000 spectators.

12.27 The second Globe Theatre, as reconstructed, c. 1614.

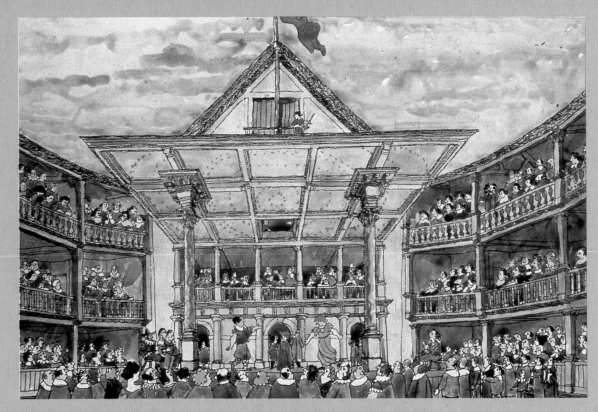

Music

In sixteenth-century England, nothing compared to London, especially in music. The capital city afforded the opportunity for all kinds of musical composition and performance; it was the center of music printing, and it was the home of foreign and domestic musicians and instrument makers. In addition, London was the location of the court of the monarch, whose patronage was of the utmost importance, and the sovereign supported the best musicians both secular and sacred.

In the field of sacred music, the dominant force was the Chapel Royal, although during the early and mid-sixteenth century, the liturgical tradition in the Chapel was unstable. As we have noted, the Church of England's formal separation from the Roman Catholic communion in 1534 under Henry VIII had political rather than doctrinal causes, and there was, therefore, no immediate change in liturgy or music. In 1544, Archbishop Thomas Cranmer published an English version of the litany in which the traditional chants were adapted to the vernacular, and a second version of the service, published in the same year, had settings of the chants for five voices. Between the reigns of Henry VIII and Elizabeth I—that is, during the brief but tempestuous reigns of Edward VI and Mary Tudor—great doctrinal swings took place. In 1549, shortly after Edward VI became king, the Act of Uniformity decreed that the liturgy as prescribed in the *English Book of Common Prayer* should be used in all services. A year later John

Merbecke issued his *Booke of Common Praier*, which included traditional chants and new monophonic music for the service. These compositions contained melodies that nicely matched the English words.

The reign of Mary Tudor saw the re-establishment of Roman Catholicism, but the accession of Elizabeth I in 1558, and the return of the Puritan faction, brought the restoration of English rites, and the Church of England acquired its present form. In Elizabeth's time, a period when church music was bitterly attacked by the English followers of John Calvin, the Chapel Royal remained the most important bastion of elaborate ritual. However, the Chapel Royal reflected the monarch's will, and there was little the reformers could do, as the monarch was head of the English Church. During Elizabeth I's reign, therefore, the Chapel Royal stabilized as an institution, and what is known as the Elizabethan "golden age of church music" began. Elizabeth was clearly more drawn to the elaborate ritual of Catholicism than to the austerity of the Puritans, recognizing perhaps that ceremony and trappings could glorify not only God but also the supreme Head of the Church of England as well. There were, in addition, political reasons for maintaining some vestiges of Catholicism rather than adopting wholeheartedly the simplicity of the Calvinists, for the powerful Catholic monarchies of Europe were reassured by the appearance, at least, that England had not been totally subverted by the Reformers.

Elizabeth I specifically allowed Latin to continue to be

used in those collegiate chapels and churches where the language was familiar to the congregations. However, the result of her influence was the creation of an entirely new body of English church music. During the first years of her reign, an attempt was made to build a more impressive repertory than had existed previously, and the burden of that task fell on the shoulders of the composer William Byrd (1543–1623). Byrd displayed a multifaceted musical personality, and his range, versatility, and superb quality set him apart from his contemporaries. He excelled in virtually every form—Latin Masses, motets, English anthems and services, songs and madrigals, and music for stringed and keyboard instruments. He was a pivotal figure in English music—at the same time the last great composer in the rich tradition of Catholic polyphony and the first of the Elizabethan golden age. He is the originator of the English verse anthem.

Byrd spent most of his professional life as organist for the Chapel Royal, and served the court for nearly fifty years. Interestingly, he remained a Catholic all his life, surviving in a Protestant country that was, at times, vigorously hostile to his religion. Nonetheless, he felt secure enough to compose and publish music for the Catholic liturgy even as he maintained an important position in the Anglican church and provided music for its services. His settings were often grave, penitential, and supplicatory. Earlier English composers—such as Byrd's predecessor as organist at the Chapel Royal, Thomas Tallis—used imitative techniques and laid out their points in perfectly symmetrical patterns. Byrd adopted more flexible procedures and introduced successive voices irregularly, to give his counterpoint greater interest and complexity. Many of his motets are unusually long, and this allowed him to expand his themes and show them off in various combinations. His later motets incorporated a wide range of textures and styles, with a greater use of chromaticism and antiphonal effects, and livelier, more varied rhythms.

Some of Byrd's finest music includes complete services for the Anglican church, including settings of the morning and evening canticles and the communion service. Byrd's services employed the note-against-note counterpoint that Archbishop Thomas Cranmer had recommended to Henry VIII as the only appropriate style for church music. They also used florid counterpoint and explored fully the possible combinations of its two five-voiced choirs. The rich density and imitative texture of his Great Service make it one of the greatest in the Anglican tradition.

At the same time, another English composer, Thomas Morley (1557–1603) excelled in a type of Renaissance secular music called the *ballett* (or *fa-la*), a simpler type of composition than the madrigal (see p. 341). The ballett was a dancelike song for several solo voices. Mostly homophonic (in contrast to much Renaissance music, which was polyphonic), the ballett had the melody in the highest voice. It repeated the same music for each stanza of the poem and used the syllables *fa-la* as a refrain. Morley's *Now is the Month of Maying* (CD track 8) is one of the most widely performed of all the balletts. It describes courtship and flirtation during the springtime:

> Now is the month of maying,
> When merry lads are playing, fa la.
> Each with his bonny lass
> Upon the greeny grass. Fa la.
>
> The spring, clad all in gladness,
> Doth laugh at winter's sadness, fa la.
> And to the bagpipe's sound
> The nymphs tread out their ground. Fa la.
>
> Fie then! why sit we musing,
> Youth's sweet delight refusing? Fa la.
> Say, dainty nymphs and speak,
> Shall we play barley break? Fa la.

Most of the piece is homophonic in texture, but the *fa-la* section ending the second part of each verse has very graceful polyphonic imitation among the voices.

CHAPTER REVIEW

Critical Thought

When we survey the religious map of the world today, we find that Roman Catholicism is, by far, the largest Christian sect. In many countries, however, the Roman Catholic Church represents a small minority of those people who call themselves Christian. The pain and separation of the Reformation remain as strong a schism today as it was in the sixteenth century. Divisions between Protestants and Catholics have been eased by the ecumenical movement of the last thirty years, but some Protestant denominations remain as anti-Catholic as ever.

As we have seen, the Reformation was a complex affair, often religious, but equally often political, that went far beyond the simple corruption of the Roman Catholic hierarchy during the Renaissance and revealed some truly profound divisions involving important issues of dogma. We spent a good deal of space on the personages and issues of the Reformation, and we should understand the fundamental, driving circumstances as well as the eventual outcomes. We also witnessed a new force arising and putting a new spin on events of the sixteenth century; that force is science in the modern sense of the word. Finally, as always, we examined art, architecture, music, dance, and theatre as they developed in parallel with the events and arts we examined in the last two chapters. Again, our movement through our textbook has become sideways rather than forward.

Summary

After reading this chapter, you should be able to:

- Identify and explain the political and religious conditions that led to the Reformation, including the theological and dogmatic contentions of Erasmus, Luther, Zwingli, Calvin, and Montaigne.
- Discuss the contributions to science of Vesalius and Copernicus.
- Characterize the work of Dürer, Grünewald, Altdorfer, Hieronymus Bosch, and Pieter Breugel the Elder.
- Explain the music of Flanders and Lutheranism, *Lieder* and the Parisian chanson.
- Detail the rise of courtly dance and ballet.
- Trace the Tudor heritage in England by discussing its history, visual art, architecture, theatre, and music.
- Apply the elements and principles of composition to analyze and compare individual works of art and architecture illustrated in this chapter.

The Baroque Age

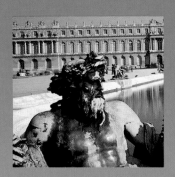

OUTLINE

SCIENTIFIC REVOLUTION AND SYSTEMATIC RATIONALISM
Francis Bacon
Galileo Galilei
Johannes Kepler
René Descartes
Isaac Newton

PHILOSOPHY
Thomas Hobbes
John Locke

THE COUNTER-REFORMATION
The Council of Trent
The Wars of Religion

ABSOLUTISM

THE VISUAL ARTS AND ARCHITECTURE
Baroque Style
Counter-Reformation Baroque
Aristocratic Baroque
Bourgeois Baroque

LITERATURE
Poetry and Satire
The Rise of the Novel

MUSIC
Baroque Style
Instrumental Music
Vocal Music

FRENCH NEOCLASSICAL THEATRE

DANCE

FOCAL POINT: ENGLISH BAROQUE – SEVENTEENTH-CENTURY LONDON

VIEW

LOGICAL THOUGHT

Induction and *deduction* are two means of developing logical conclusions. Both are rational—that is, they rely on systematic order and progression—but they approach the development of conclusions from opposite directions. Induction begins with specifics and deduces generalities. Deduction relies on intuitive thinking. In other words, it intuits that some general condition exists, then the observer investigates to see if that general condition can be supported by sufficient details to be conclusive.

In both cases—induction and deduction—the conclusions will stand the test of replication—that is, when the hypothesis is retested, the conclusions come up the same. Induction and deduction re-emerged in the seventeenth century as bases for drawing conclusions. They form the foundation of logical thought and remain as important today as they were four hundred or two thousand years ago. Without the ability to draw logical conclusions from the evidence at hand, we cannot solve problems. It's as simple as that.

Above Detail of Fig. **13.19**.

13.1 Gian Lorenzo Bernini, *Baldacchino* in St Peter's, Rome, 1624–33. Gilded bronze, about 100 ft (30 m) high.

KEY TERMS

Some of the basic terms and concepts we will encounter in this chapter include the following:

Systematic Rationalism is an attempt to provide an unchanging fabric to life whose relevance to particulars could be deduced by inquiry.

Induction is a mode of inquiry that reaches conclusions by moving from specifics to generalities.

Deduction is a mode of inquiry that reaches conclusions by moving from generalities to specifics.

Counter-Reformation, an internal reform based on the desire for spiritual regeneration in the Roman Catholic Church from the mid-sixteenth to the early seventeenth centuries.

Absolutism, government with power vested in the hands of an absolute monarch.

Baroque Style, a pluralistic style in the arts that exhibited, among other characteristics, ornateness and emotionalism.

Opera, a type of music/drama.

Neoclassicism, a variety of styles that borrow classical themes and motifs. In the seventeenth century it manifested itself in French theatre.

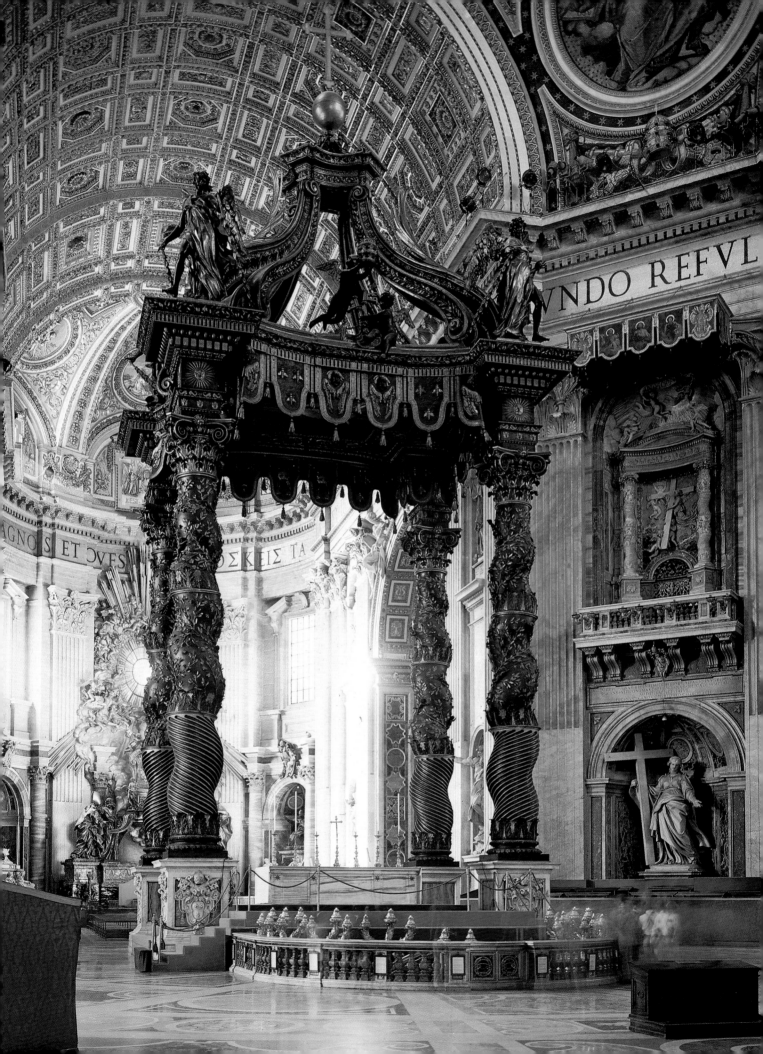

SCIENTIFIC REVOLUTION AND SYSTEMATIC RATIONALISM

The latter part of the sixteenth century marked the dissolution of what we can call the Aristotelian consensus. Since the fourth century B.C., Aristotle's views on the natural world had served as the basic model, but the revival in science that we noted in Chapter 12 with the works of Copernicus and Vesalius gathered strength in the seventeenth century with the first public teaching of modern natural philosophy, accompanied by experimental demonstrations, at the University of Utrecht in 1672. This was a generation after the first discussions of a philosophy that reoriented much of scientific method.

Francis Bacon

The English writer Francis Bacon (1561–1626) reflected the Renaissance hope that humankind could discover all there was to know about the universe through the use of reason, which, he believed, was the path to knowledge. Knowledge, in turn, was power, and the ultimate power was human domination of nature, which would be achieved through an understanding of natural laws. Bacon was one of the first to describe the modern scientific method. He saw that it was based on *induction*—that is, the progression from specifics to generalities. Fundamental to this process are the examination of negative instances and a critical spirit, which will prevent the inquirer from jumping to unwarranted conclusions. The verification of conclusions by continual observation and experiment is also essential. The task of science, Bacon believed, was to conquer nature by obeying it, while the task of poetry was to conquer nature by freeing the mind from obedience to nature and releasing it into its own world where the mind reshapes nature. In Bacon's own words in the *Advancement of Learning* (1605): "Therefore, poetry was ever thought to have some participation of divineness, because it doth raise and erect the mind by submitting the show of things to the desires of the mind, whereas reason doth buckle and bow the mind unto the nature of things." Here we have as good a statement as any of the dichotomy between the intellect and the imagination, the separation of ways of knowing that has obsessed artists and thinkers ever since.

Bacon was a prolific writer, and his talents ranged from the scientific to the poetic. His *Essays* are masterpieces of English literature, and his philosophy employs a methodology that anticipated modern inquiry. He was born into a family that had access to power and prestige, and after studying law, he entered politics and became a member of the English Parliament, becoming attorney general and lord chancellor under King James I. In 1618 he was raised to the peerage. He was not above treachery, however, and he fell from grace as rapidly as he had risen.

Galileo Galilei

Galileo (ga-lih-LAY-oh; 1564–1642), an Italian astronomer and physicist, emphasized the characteristics of mathematics, believing that the "Book of Nature" was written in the language of geometry. In his view, the mathematical proof of a proposition was the best proof there is. These kinds of assertions were new, for although the ancients had regarded mathematical reasoning as valid, they considered it to be inappropriate outside strictly mathematical contexts. Recognizing that mathematical principles were no better than the physical premises on which they were based, the ancients rejected mathematics as a guide to truth. Galileo did much to establish not only the mathematical approach to discovery but also the sound premises that could strengthen conclusions.

Galileo made other significant scientific advances. For example, he built the first astronomical telescope and observed for the first time the mountains on the moon, sunspots, the rings of Saturn, the moons of Jupiter, and the stellar composition of the Milky Way. He also made earthly discoveries—for example, the law of the acceleration of falling bodies and the principle of the pendulum. Unfortunately for Galileo, the Church, which still supported the Aristotelian concept of a fixed earth, objected to his experiments and conclusions, and in 1633 he was arrested by the Inquisition and charged with false teaching. Under threat of torture, Galileo recanted his discoveries and was released. He died a broken man.

Johannes Kepler

The German mathematician Johannes Kepler (1571–1630) added to the scientific revolution by proposing the three laws of planetary motion. He had devoted himself to the study of the heliocentric universe, and his first treatise, *On the Motion of Mars*, propounded his solution as to what kept planets in their orbits. It was here that he proposed his first planetary law: planets move around the sun in elliptical orbits rather than circles. His second law, given in precise mathematical formulae, accounted for the variable speed of planetary motion by asserting that nearness to the sun affected speed: the closer to the sun, the faster the speed. A few years later, he published his third law of planetary motion: the squares of the length of time for each planet's orbit are in the same ratios as the cubes of their respective mean distances from the sun. Thus, he affirmed the conclusion that the solar system was regular and organized by mathematically determined relationships.

René Descartes

The French philosopher and mathematician René Descartes (ren-AY day-KART; 1596–1650), who created a metaphysical theory and complete system of nature that explained all phenomena, promised an unfailing method of discovery (Fig. **13.2**). He opposed the belief that experimental method led to knowledge, arguing instead for a purely mathematical approach in science. His insights in the field of biology serve as an illustration. For two thousand years, the question of what makes the body internally active, able to respond, to move, to speak, and so on, had been answered by "the spirits," with much elaboration on the three basic spirits of natural, vital, and animal. Descartes held that the principle of movement lay in motion, of which an unending and unchanging quantity resided in the universe. Some of the constancy of motion that Descartes found in the universe was obvious in the apparently perpetual motion of large bodies such as planets, but he also found it in the invisible motions of the smallest particles of matter. Thus, for Descartes, understanding the physical make-up of the universe began with concepts about matter. The primary belief about matter was that it occupied time and space. The Descartian or *Cartesian* (kahrt-EEZH-uhn) model universe suggested that planets, being solidified minor stars, were a closed system—that is, original matter had changed in form, but no matter or motion had ever been added. Descartes's laws of nature were arrived at *deductively*—that is, they moved from the general to the particular, with their conclusions following necessarily from the premises. His scientific system began with the certainty of the existence of mind and of God, and then worked outward to embrace universal truths or laws of nature that could be detected by reason. His entire system was both rational and systematic: it aimed to provide an unchanging fabric whose relevance to particulars could be deduced by inquiry. This means that not only may one expect the universe to be rationally ordered but that this rationality may be mathematically realized. In essence, Descartes laid the foundations for an age of systematic rationalism and encapsulated it in a statement, the gist of Cartesianism: "I think, therefore I am."

In his *Discourse on Method* (1637), he postulated four steps for approaching knowledge: (1) accept nothing as true unless it is self-evident; (2) split problems into manageable parts; (3) solve problems by starting with the

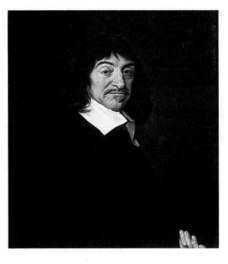

13.2 Frans Hals, *René Descartes*, after 1649. Oil on canvas, 30³/₄ × 26³/₄ ins (78.1 × 67.9 cm). Louvre, Paris.

simplest and moving to the most complex; and (4) review and re-examine the solutions.

Isaac Newton

The English mathematician Sir Isaac Newton (1642–1727) tied together the emerging scientific discoveries into a coherent whole (Fig. **13.3**). At the center of his theory lay the law of universal gravitation: every particle of matter in the universe, from planets in their orbits to falling bodies on earth, attracts every other particle of matter with a force called gravity. In his *Mathematical Principles of Natural Philosophy* (1687), Newton asserted that gravitational force varies directly with the sum of the mass of objects and inversely with the square of the distance between them. In Newton's scheme, the sun held each of its

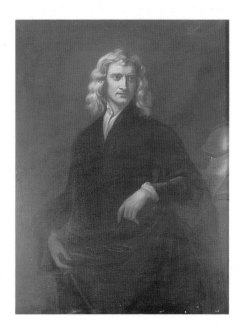

13.3 Anonymous, *Sir Isaac Newton*. Trinity College, Cambridge, UK.

	GENERAL EVENTS	LITERATURE & PHILOSOPHY	VISUAL ART & ARCHITECTURE	PERFORMING ARTS
1540				
	Founding of Jesuits Council of Trent Elizabeth I of England Philip II of Spain		della Porta (**13.11, 13.12**) Caravaggio (**13.6, 13.7**)	
1600				
		Francis Bacon Descartes Cervantes Metaphysical poets	El Greco (**13.8**) Bernini (**13.1, 13.9, 13.10**) Rubens (**13.13, 13.14**) Poussin (**13.15**)	Monteverdi
	Thirty Years' War Galileo Kepler Civil War in England Oliver Cromwell	 Milton	Taj Mahal (**13.24**) Houasse (**13.21**) Rembrandt (**13.26, 13.27**)	Buxtehude Corneille Molière
1650				

	Restoration of monarchy
	  (Charles II) in England
	Louis XIV of France
	Plague and fire of London
		Hobbes
		
		Dryden
		
		Locke
			van Ruisdael (**13.28**)
			Puget (**13.16**)
			Coysevox (**13.17**)
			Le Brun, Le Vau and Hardouin-Mansart
			  (**13.19, 13.20**)
			Vermeer (**13.29**)
			Wren (**13.35, 13.37, 13.38, 13.39**)
				Racine
				Alessandro Scarlatti
				Pierre Beauchamps

1700				
	Newton	Defoe		Purcell Vivaldi Handel J.S. Bach

Timeline 13.1 The Baroque age.

planets in its gravitational pull and each, in turn, influenced, however lightly, the sun and the other planets. Similarly, the earth interacted with its moon. The effect was a harmonious system, in which each body attracted the others.

One of the important characteristics of Newton's system lay in his refusal to speculate on why the universe operated as it did. Thus, he effectively separated science from metaphysics or theology, two areas previously intertwined with "scientific" matters. The publication of his *Principia*, the familiar title of *Mathematical Principles*, made him the world's authority, and it represented the culmination of the scientific revolution that brought the world into the modern age.

PHILOSOPHY

The revolution in science had a profound influence on wider issues of society, and two men influenced by the new science provided the world with a new philosophy of social living. Contradictory in conclusions, they represent the political drift of Europe in the seventeenth century, a drift that contrasted rising democracy with strengthening monarchial absolutism.

Thomas Hobbes

Thomas Hobbes (1588–1679) attempted to synthesize a universal philosophy based on geometric design. His best-known work, *Leviathan* (1651), espoused a rather pessimistic theory of government based on the assumption that humans are driven by two forces: the fear of death, and the quest for power. Hobbes believed that unless some overarching supreme power restrained humans against these two drives, life would deteriorate into a short, ugly circumstance. His ultimate solution was a civil society under the rule of one man, and he thought that once humans saw the awfulness of their situation, they would willingly agree. In order to bring about such a society, the first step lay in achieving a social contract, drawn up between the ruler and his subjects. In such a contract, the

TECHNOLOGY: PUTTING DISCOVERY TO WORK

Standardized Measurement

The standardization of measures had interested several scientists whose attention had been attracted by Galileo's observations on the pendulum. The phenomenon inspired them to choose the length of the pendulum that beats the second as a "natural and universal" unit of measure, but before they could do so, it was necessary to determine that the amplitude of oscillations did not vary from place to place. This concern led to the painstaking construction by the abbot Gabriel Mouton, the permanent priest of the Church of Saint-Jean at Lyon in France, of a system of measurement based on the unit of linear measure related to the size of the earth. He borrowed the definition of this unit from the thousandth part of the angular minute—that is, from the thousandth part of the nautical mile of 1,852 millimeters. This unit was called the *virga* (Fig. **13.4**).

In addition, Abbot Mouton subjected the multiples and submultiples of the unit to decimal division. The idea had considerable scope, and the introduction of decimal numeration into the metric system played a vital role in its expansion throughout the world. Although Mouton's terminology was never accepted into the metric system, the concept of a universal unit was continued into the eighteenth century, and the actual creation of a decimal metric system finally occurred in 1790.

In the seventeenth century, scientists were conscious of the importance of standardized units of measure in their research, and they recognized the need to increase the precision of the results of measurement. Although we take such precision for granted, they had to define new units of measurement previously unknown: measurements of time, temperature, pressure, and so on. Revolutionary views gradually gained ground, but only when there was a unified system of measurement could such a basic concept become an effective instrument of the scientific and technological revolution.

Centesima						
10	*Decima*					
100	10	*Virgula*				
1,000	100	10	*Virga*			
10,000	1,000	100	10	*Decuria*		
100,000	10,000	1,000	100	10	*Centuria*	
1,000,000	100,000	10,000	1,000	100	10	*Milliare*

13.4 Mouton's table of standard measurement terminology.

subjects would give up all claims to sovereignty, while absolute power would be in the hands of the ruler, whose commands would be carried out by all under his authority, including religious and civic leaders. In return, the sovereign would keep peace at home and protect his country from outside enemies.

Although Hobbes' formula appears to argue for an absolute monarchy, that was not necessarily his aim. He cared little about the exact form of an authoritarian government—the result of his social contract could, in fact, be a commonwealth—because his concern was that enough power be vested in a central figure to contravene the negative forces and self-destructive inclinations he found in human nature.

John Locke

Championing the opposite point of view and doing so in response to Hobbes' published philosophy was another Englishman, John Locke (1632–1704). Unlike Hobbes, Locke believed that humankind was essentially good and that humans were capable of governing themselves. Locke, the founder of the *liberal* school of thought, laid out his principles in two *Treatises of Government*, both published anonymously in 1690. The first treatise argues against the theory of the divine right of kings; the second constructs a model for popular self-government. Locke's ideal political system had a government limited by laws, subject to the will of the people, and serving to protect life and property.

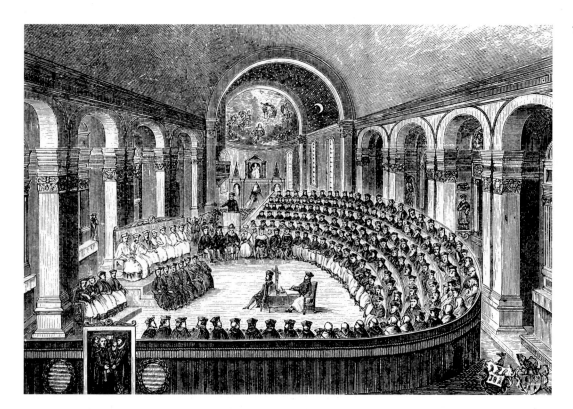

13.5 The Council of Trent, 1545.

Locke shared Hobbes' view of the necessity of some form of social contract in order to counter the violent and disorderly forces that were inevitable in the natural state of things. However, he rejected the idea that people should abrogate their sovereignty to an absolute ruler, arguing instead that humans, who are reasonable by nature, should maintain their basic rights, including life and property, and enter into contracts with each other to create a limited form of government that had no other purpose than the protection of life and property. This would work, in Locke's view, because humans are, he thought, basically decent and law-abiding.

Locke would give individuals the right to choose their rulers and to expect that the rulers would govern justly. If they did not, the governed reserved the right to remove them by whatever means necessary and reclaim their natural rights. In addition, no ruler should have absolute authority. All authority should be held in check by a separation of powers and a series of balances within the government. We can, of course, recognize in Locke's thinking many of the bases of government that would emerge in the next century in the United States.

In the same year that he published his *Treatises*, Locke also published *An Essay Concerning Human Understanding* in which he considered more philosophical questions along the lines of Descartes, and his views provide a contrast with Cartesian philosophy that gives us a convenient means by which to draw the opening sections of this chapter together in summary. Descartes believed in a universal truth that was inborn—that is, people were born knowing basic truths. The application of systematic, intellectual thought processes could bring forth these truths without allowing them to be corrupted by the senses. In contrast, Locke believed that the mind at birth was a *tabula rasa* (TAHB-yoo-luh RAHS-uh)—that is, a clean slate or "erased table." Whatever humans knew came from the senses and made its imprint on their minds. By using methods such as evaluation, manipulation, and so on, raw data and abstract concepts were formed in the mind, and the use of reason and experience allows humans to understand the universe and discern what is real.

THE COUNTER-REFORMATION

The Council of Trent

The desire for spiritual regeneration in the Roman Catholic Church in the late fifteenth and early sixteenth centuries eventually led to internal reform. This process is often called the Counter-Reformation, because its characteristics took shape in the 1540s and 1550s in apparent opposition to Protestant doctrines and practices. There was, however, more to the Catholic Reformation than a mere reaction against Protestantism, for the impulse for renovation and purification had existed for more than half a century before it transformed the papacy and made possible the codification of doctrine and discipline by the Council of Trent. We should remember that Erasmus and the Christian humanists whom we studied in Chapter 12 sought Catholic reform. There were others, who held closely to the older traditions, who wished the Catholic Church to make a positive contribution to the contemporary age. Catholic theologians, dating back to St Augustine (see Chapter 7) and St Thomas Aquinas (see Chapter 8), had tried to reconcile the omnipotence of an Almighty God and human free will, and the Catholic Reformation also drew some of its inspiration from late medieval mysticism. Thus, the spirit of renewal was at work among those who would remain loyal to the ongoing institution of Roman Catholicism. The desire for a more spiritual, more relevant, and less worldly religion affected Catholic and Protestant alike, and at first it was not entirely clear that the result would lead to the split that followed. However, as the gap between the two points of view widened in the 1550s, attitudes became more entrenched, open conflict occurred, and differences rather than similarities were emphasized. By the time of the Council of Trent, Roman Catholicism set out to make the definition of doctrine between Catholics and Protestants as clear as possible, and in so doing, many aspects of Catholicism were themselves obviated with the result that, between 1550 and 1650, orthodoxy was placed above universality—an outcome that was probably necessary if the Church were to survive.

The reformation of the Catholic Church depended on a change in the papacy, since, given its structure and hierarchy, the pope was the only possible source of the necessary leadership. During the pontificate of Paul III (r. 1534–49) the papal court was reformed, and reformers gained commanding positions in the Church, from which they and their successors were able to guide the Catholic Reformation. Pope Paul reinstituted the medieval Inquisition and established a board of censors, the Index of Forbidden Books, by means of which he hoped to meet the Protestant threat head on. He also recognized a new order, called the Society of Jesus, the Jesuits. Organized in 1540 by a Spanish knight and future saint, Ignatius Loyola (ig-NAY-shuhs loy-OH-luh; 1491–1556), the friars of this order became the Church's most militant agents of the Counter-Reformation, and the order proved to be the greatest missionary order in the history of the Church. However, the most important action taken by Paul III was the calling of the Council of Trent, which met off and on for twenty years in the 1540s, 1550s, and 1560s (Fig. **13.5**).

Pope Paul began the council at the cathedral in the city of Trent, a small imperial city deep in the southern Alps, in 1542. Some thirty bishops and fifty theologians assembled for the opening ceremony in December 1545, and although the pope took no active part, his views were well known and fully represented. The papal secretariat provided continuity to the council, whose participants, by the time it recessed, numbered around 270. One of the important agreements of the council was the reaffirmation that the pope outranked the general council, with the result that none of its resolutions could take effect until they were approved by the pope. Ultimately, the Council of Trent carried the reforming impulse from the pope to the church at large, with decrees on doctrine and discipline providing stiff penalties for immorality and corruption. The council formed new seminaries in order to produce a better educated priesthood, and it also reaffirmed traditional Catholic views on all the theological points the Protestants had attacked.

The final session of the Council of Trent took place in 1562–3. Its main achievement was the emphasis it placed on the quality of the clergy and the role of bishops, which was in contrast to the Protestants, who, with their belief in the priesthood of all believers, downgraded the role of clergy and either did away with bishops altogether or severely limited their functions. The Counter-Reformation strengthened both clergy and bishops so that they could give leadership to the laity. And herein lies the fundamental difference between the two stands. Protestants put individual conscience and the Bible first. Catholics insisted that conscience and the Scriptures must be interpreted by the Church in light of its own traditions and understanding. Although the Council of Trent did not transform the Catholic Church immediately, it did mark a turning point, and the combination of new religious orders, the Inquisition, and a spiritually regenerated papacy gave Catholics a new certainty of belief and practice that had been lacking previously.

The Wars of Religion

Unfortunately, the clash of theological ideas and their casting in the political crucible of the time created one of the bloodiest periods in European history. Religious wars began in the sixteenth century in such conflicts as the Peasants' War in Germany, and they recurred with varying degrees of intensity in the Thirty Years' War in central Europe and in the seventeenth-century English Puritan Revolution. However, the height of the violence came between 1560 and 1600, when there was a bitter war in the Netherlands between Calvinist Protestants and Spanish Catholics, an equally horrific conflict in France between the Huguenots and the Catholic League, and the global Anglo-Spanish naval war. During these passionate unheavals, Protestant mobs vandalized Catholic cathe-

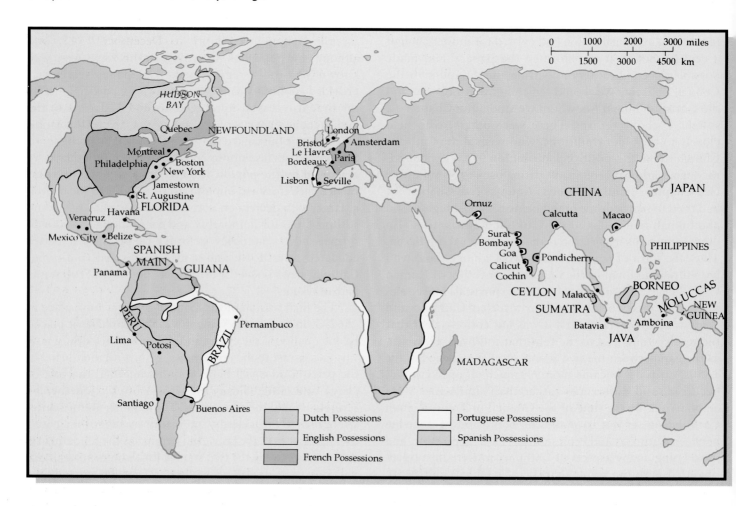

Map 13.1 Colonial possessions at the end of the seventeenth century.

drals, the Inquisition tortured and burned at the stake anyone deemed heretical, Luther approved the execution of the extremist Anabaptists, and Calvin martyred the religious eccentric Michael Servetus. These religious wars between Protestants and Catholics continued into the 1600s, lasting into the middle of the century, when they, at last, burned themselves out.

ABSOLUTISM

One important aspect of political life in the seventeenth and early eighteenth centuries was absolutism. Although some democratic ideals existed, the major force in European national life was the absolute monarch, who received a mandate from God, according to "divine right." Strong dynasties controlled Europe. England passed its crown through the Tudors from Henry VII to Elizabeth I (r. 1558–1603). The monarchy as an institution survived the reign of her successor, the Stuart James I, but his son

Charles I, and the monarchy, were toppled by Cromwell in 1642. However, Charles II was restored in 1660, and the country returned to continental style and elegance. This elegant opulence, which was perhaps the hallmark of the age, was personified in France's Louis XIV, the Sun King (r. 1643–1715). His court made any previous Roman Catholic encouragement of the arts look meager by comparison.

The first half of the seventeenth century saw the consolidation of secular control over religious affairs in the European states. Absolutism made it difficult to envisage a society that did not follow the religion of its sovereign and it was politically advantageous for rulers to clothe themselves with divine right. The Protestant movements, which taught that truth and sovereignty lay in the Bible alone, continued nonetheless to defy the state Churches. In states where royal power proved strongest, dissent went underground or into asylum elsewhere, and yet, in all cases, religious dissent became a powerful force, especially in countries such as Germany, where it was coupled with social, political, and economic forces.

Even where Catholicism remained as the state religion, power struggles between absolute monarchs and popes continued to rage. It seems clear that by 1650 the papacy no longer exercised authority over international affairs. During the rule of Pope Innocent X (r. 1644–55), the European states refused to comply with papal demands that no peace be made with the Protestants.

The triumph of the absolutist state over the Church is best seen in France. Jean Armand du Plessis, duke of Richelieu (ree-shel-YOO), and a cardinal, held the post of chief minister to Louis XIII (r. 1610–43) from 1624 to 1642. Richelieu sought to strengthen the monarchy, and, after a bitter conflict, he succeeded in subduing the Huguenots (French Protestants) in 1628. The Peace of Alais in 1629 concluded the last of the religious wars, and deprived the Huguenots of their political and military rights, although their civil and religious rights remained protected under the Edict of Nantes (NAHNT). Thereafter, the Huguenots were strong supporters of the monarchy. The grip of royal absolutism continued to tighten under Cardinal Mazarin, chief minister of Louis XIV from 1643 to 1661. The upper nobility tried to break its hold, but, partially because of the refusal of the Huguenots to participate, their attempts failed. When Mazarin died in 1661 at the end of the war with Spain, Louis XIV assumed complete control of France. Armed with the spirit of "one God, one king, one faith," he took the Jesuits' advice and, in a swift reversal, initiated a program of persecuting the Huguenots. In 1685, he revoked the Edict of Nantes, thereby forcing them either to become Catholics or leave the country.

When Louis XIV came into conflict with the papacy, it looked as if he would respond by establishing a national church in France, similar to that established by Henry VIII in England. However, Louis found it to his advantage not to break with Rome, and he pulled back. Articles drawn up to limit the authority of the pope in France were not enforced, although they remained part of the law.

THE VISUAL ARTS AND ARCHITECTURE

Baroque Style

Painting in the baroque style appealed to the emotions and to a desire for magnificence through opulent ornamentation. At the same time, it adopted systematic and rational composition in which ornamentation was unified through variation on a single theme. Realism (lifelikeness using selected details) replaced beauty as the objective for painting. Color and grandeur were emphasized, as was dramatic use of light and shade (chiaroscuro). In much of baroque art, sophisticated organizational schemes carefully subordinate and merge one part into the next to create a complex but unified whole. Open composition symbolizes the notion of an expansive universe: the viewer's eye travels off the canvas to a wider reality. The human figure, as an object or focus in painting, could be monumental in full Renaissance fashion, but it could also now be a minuscule figure in a landscape, part of, but subordinate to, a vast universe. Baroque style often exhibited intensely active compositions that emphasized feeling rather than form, and emotion rather than the intellect. Like its cousin of the nineteenth century, Romanticism, the baroque (buh-ROHK) exalted intuition, inspiration, and the genius of human creativity as reactions against the rationalistic classicism of Renaissance and High Renaissance styles. Having said that, however, we must caution that baroque art was also diverse and pluralistic. Its artworks do not conform to a simple mold, as the examples that follow illustrate.

Baroque painting is readily identifiable, even though it had a variety of applications. It glorified the Church and religious sentiment, both Catholic and Protestant; it portrayed the magnificence of secular wealth, both noble and bourgeois; and it stressed the themes of absolutism and individualism as well. Virtuosity emerged, as each artist sought to establish a personal style. But as a general phenomenon, the baroque style spread widely throughout the continent, and it was used by most European artists during the period 1600 to 1725.

Counter-Reformation Baroque

Counter-Reformation baroque art pursued the objectives and visions of the Roman Catholic Church after the Council of Trent.

Caravaggio

In Rome—the center of the early baroque—papal patronage and the spirit of the Counter-Reformation brought artists together to make Rome the "most beautiful city of the entire Christian world." Caravaggio (kah-rah-VAHJ-joh; 1569–1609) was probably the most significant of the Roman baroque painters, and in two of his works we can see his extraordinary style, in which verisimilitude is carried to new heights. In *The Calling of St Matthew* (Fig. 13.6), highlight and shadow create a dramatic portrayal of the moment when the future apostle is touched by divine grace. This religious subject is, however, depicted in contemporary terms. The painter turns away from idealized forms, and instead presents us with a mundane scene. The call from Christ streams, with dynamic chiaroscuro,

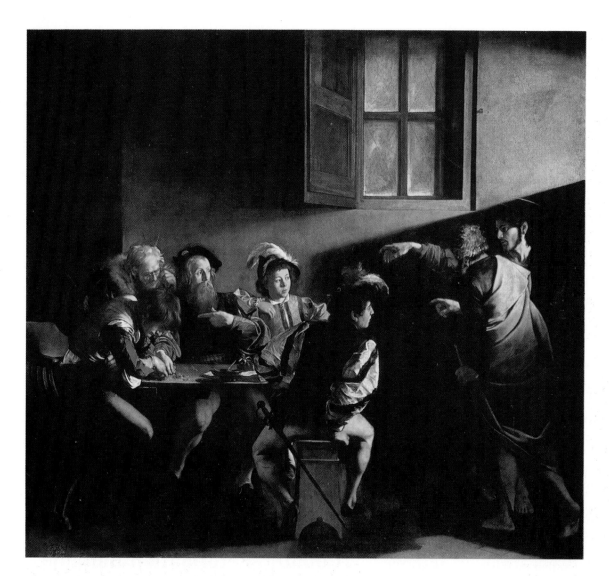

13.6 Caravaggio, *The Calling of St Matthew*, c. 1596–8. Oil on canvas, 11 ft 1 in × 11 ft 5 ins (3.38 × 3.48 m). Contarelli Chapel, San Luigi dei Francesi, Rome.

across the groups of figures, emphasized by the powerful gesture of Christ to Matthew. This great painting expresses one of the central themes of Counter-Reformation belief: that faith and grace are open to all, and that spiritual understanding is a personal, and overpowering, emotional experience.

We see the same emotional dynamism in *The Death of the Virgin* (Fig. **13.7**). Here again, the painter depicts real, almost common people, rather than idealized figures. The picture shows the corpse of the Virgin Mary, surrounded by the mourning disciples and friends of Christ. She is laid out awkwardly and unceremoniously, with all the grim reality of death apparent. Her feet are left uncovered, which was considered indecent in the early seventeenth century. A curtain drapes over the entire scene, as if to frame it like a theatrical setting. As in *The Calling of St Matthew*, a harsh light streams across the tableau, emphasizing the figure of the Virgin and creating dynamic broken patterns of light and shade.

Caravaggio had frequent conflicts with the Church, and, in the case of *The Death of the Virgin*, the Roman parish of Santa Maria del Popolo rejected the painting. The duke of Mantua then purchased the work, on the advice of Rubens, who was court painter. Before it was taken from Rome, however, it was put on public display for a week so that all Rome could see it.

El Greco

Although sometimes identified with Mannerism, El Greco (el GREHK-oh; 1541–1614), a Spanish painter born in Crete (hence the name El Greco, "the Greek"), exemplified the intense, inward-looking subjectivity and mysticism of the Counter-Reformation. In his *St Jerome* (Fig. **13.8**), space seems to be compressed. Forms are piled on top of each other in two-dimensional, as opposed to deep, space. Rather than having the subject complete and framed within the composition, as was usual in the High Renaissance, here the picture is cut by the frame. The emotional the work. As in painting, sculpture directed the viewer's vision inward and invited participation rather than neutral observation. Feeling was the focus. Baroque sculpture tended to treat space pictorially, almost like a painting, to describe action scenes rather than single sculptural forms. To see this, we can focus on the work of Gian Lorenzo Bernini (jahn lohr-EHN-zoh buhr-NEEN-ee; 1598–1680).

Bernini's *David* (Fig. 13.9) exudes a sense of power and action as he curls to unleash the stone from his sling to hit Goliath, who is outside the statue's space. Our eyes sweep upward along a diagonally curved line and are propelled outward in the direction of David's concentrated expression. Repetition of the curving lines carries movement throughout the work. The viewer participates emotionally, feels the drama, and responds to the sensuous

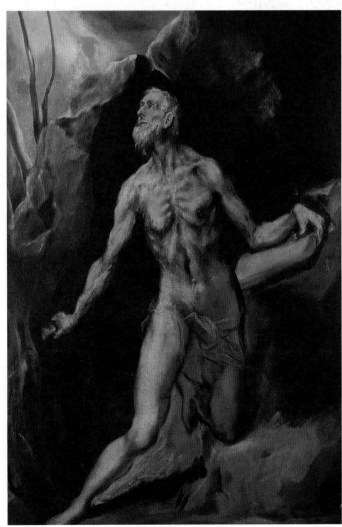

13.8 El Greco (Domenikos Theotokopoulos), *St Jerome*, c. 1610–14. Oil on canvas, 5 ft 6¼ ins × 3 ft 7½ ins (1.68 × 1.11 m). National Gallery of Art, Washington D.C. (Chester Dale Collection). © 1998 Board of Trustees, National Gallery of Art, Washington D.C.

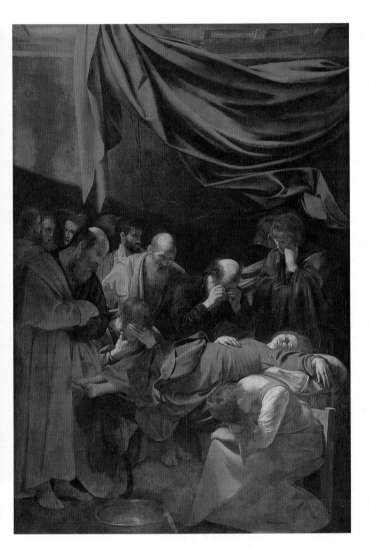

13.7 Caravaggio, *The Death of the Virgin*, 1605–6. Oil on canvas, 12 ft 1 in × 8 ft ½ in (3.69 × 2.45 m). Louvre, Paris.

disturbance this suggests is further heightened by the attenuated form of St Jerome himself.

El Greco's predominantly monochromatic shades of red-brown in this painting belong to the "warm" end of the color spectrum. However, his characteristic use of strongly highlighted forms—the highlight is pure white, as opposed to a higher value of the base hue—sharpens the contrasts, and this, too, intensifies the emotional tone of the work. The obvious brushwork in many places encourages the viewer to look beneath the surface reality of the painting into a special truth within.

Sculpture

The splendor of Counter-Reformation baroque was particularly apparent in sculpture. Forms and space were charged with an energy that carried beyond the confines of

13.9 Gian Lorenzo Bernini, *David*,
1623. Marble, 5 ft 7 ins (1.70 m)
high. Galleria Borghese, Rome.
© Araldo de Luca, Rome.

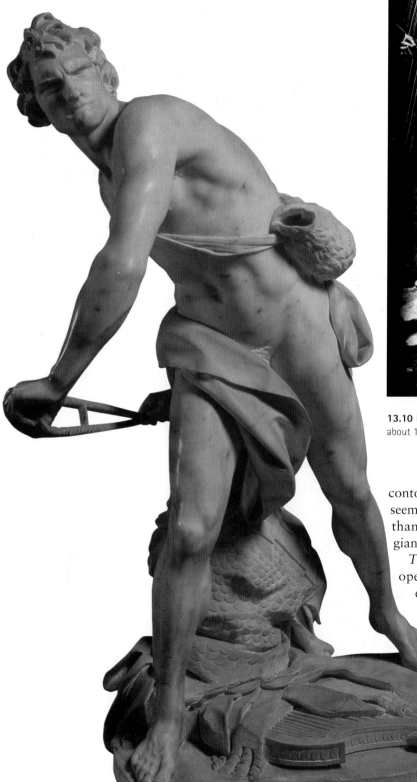

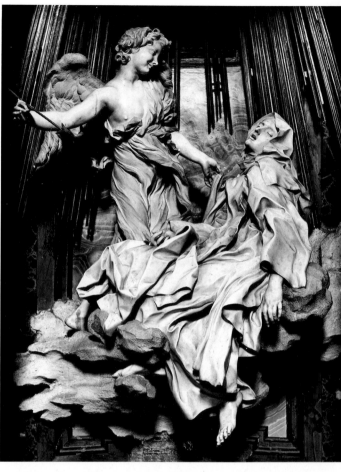

13.10 (*above*) Gian Lorenzo Bernini, *The Ecstasy of St Theresa*, 1645–52. Marble,
about 11 ft 6 ins (3.5 m) high. Cornaro Chapel, Santa Maria della Vittoria, Rome.

contours of the fully articulated muscles. Bernini's David
seems to flex and contract in the moment of action, rather
than expressing the pent-up energy of Michelangelo's
giant-slayer (see Fig. **11.16**).

The Ecstasy of St Theresa (Fig. **13.10**) is a fully developed "painting" in sculptural form. It represents an
experience described by St Theresa, one of the saints
of the Counter-Reformation, of an angel piercing
her heart with a golden flaming arrow: "The pain
was so great that I screamed aloud; but at the
same time I felt such infinite sweetness that I
wished the pain to last forever." Accentuated by golden rays, the figure embodies
St Theresa's ecstasy. Typical of baroque
sculptural design, the lines of the
draperies swirl diagonally, creating
circular movement. Each element
slips into the next in an unbroken chain, and every aspect of
the work suggests motion.

Figures float upward and draperies billow from an imaginary wind. Deep recesses and contours establish strong highlights and shadows, which further heighten the drama. The "picture" forces the viewer's involvement in an overwhelming emotional and religious experience. Bernini's Baldichino (bahl-dih-KEEN-oh) and the interior of St Peter's Cathedral also illustrate the ornate and complex forms of the Counter-Reformation baroque style (see Fig. **13.1**).

Architecture

The baroque style in architecture emphasized the same contrasts between light and shade and the same action, emotion, opulence, and ornamentation as the other visual arts of the period. Because of its scale, however, the effect was one of dramatic spectacle. There were many excellent baroque architects, among them Giacomo della Porta (JAH-koh-moh dehl-lah-POHR-tah; 1540–1602; Figs. **13.11** and **13.12**). His Church of Il Gesù (eel jay-ZOO),

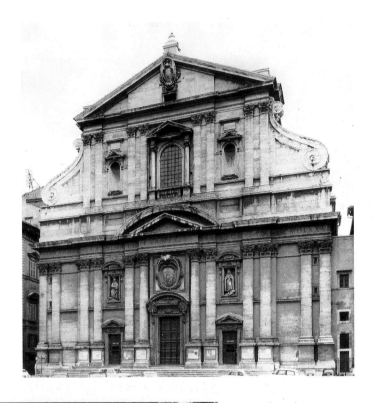

13.11 (*above*) Giacomo della Porta, west front of Il Gesù, Rome, 1568–84.

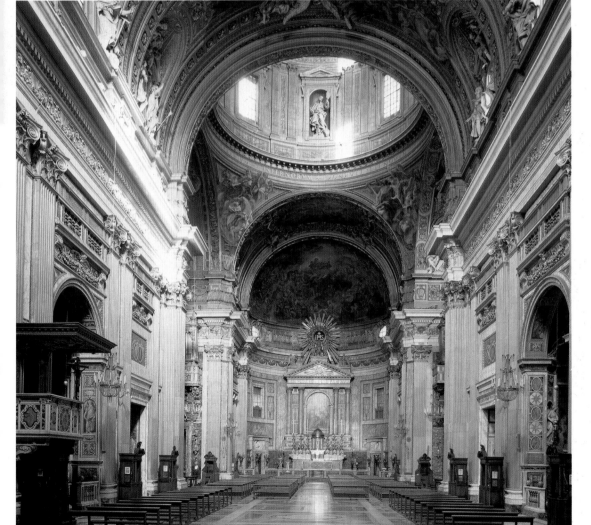

13.12 Giacomo della Porta, interior of Il Gesù, Rome, 1568–84.

397

although not the most ornate example of the style, is the mother church of the Jesuit order, which was founded in 1534, and it had a profound influence on later church architecture, especially in Latin America. This church truly represents the spirit of the Counter-Reformation. Il Gesù is a compact basilica. By eliminating side aisles, the design literally forces the congregation into a large, hall-like space directly in view of the altar. Della Porta's façade (Fig. **13.11**) boldly repeats its row of double pilasters on a smaller scale at the second level. Scroll-shaped buttresses create the transition from the wider first level to the crowning pediment of the second. The design reflects the influences of Alberti, Palladio, and Michelangelo, but in its skillful synthesis of these influences it is unique.

Aristocratic Baroque

The term "aristocratic baroque" describes art generally in the baroque style that reflected the visions and purposes of an aristocracy that at this time had become increasingly aware that its power was threatened by the growing bourgeoisie or middle class.

Rubens

Peter Paul Rubens (ROO-behns; 1577–1640) is noted for his vast, overwhelming paintings and fleshy female nudes (Fig. **13.13**). In 1621–5 he painted a series of works as a commission from Maria de' Medici, widow of the French King Henry IV and regent during the minority of her son Louis XIII. *Henry IV Receiving the Portrait of Maria de' Medici* (Fig. **13.14**) is one of twenty-one canvases that give an allegorized version of the queen's life. In this painting, we see Rubens' ornate, curvilinear composition, lively action, and complex color. It is rich in detail, but each finely rendered part is subordinate to the whole. Typical of Rubens are the corpulent cupids (*putti*; poot-tee) and female flesh, which has a sense of softness and warmth that we find in the work of few other artists, and the colors are warm, with deep, rich blues pulled throughout the picture. The composition sweeps from upper left to lower right, circling around the rectangular frame of Maria's portrait at the juncture of the vertical, horizontal, and diagonal axes. There is a strong contrast, making for enhanced dynamics between lights and darks, and between lively and more subdued tones. The painting seems to swirl before our eyes, and Rubens leads the eye around the painting, upward, downward, inward, and outward, even occasionally escaping the frame altogether. Nevertheless, Rubens' sophisticated composition, beneath all this complexity, holds the base of the painting solidly in place and leads the eye to the smiling face of its subject. The overall effect of this painting is of richness, glamor, and optimism, and

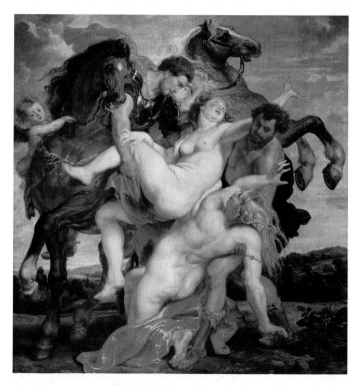

13.13 Peter Paul Rubens, *Rape of the Daughters of Leucippus*, c. 1648. Oil on canvas, 7 ft 3 ins × 6 ft 10 ins (2.21 × 2.08 m). Alte Pinakothek, Monaco.

its appeal is directly to the emotions rather than to the intellect.

The classical allegory of the painting has the aging king, whose helmet and shield are being stolen by the cupids, being advised by the mythical Minerva to accept the Florentine princess as his second bride. Maria's portrait is presented by Mercury, and Juno and Jupiter look on approvingly. The painting depicts happy promises of divine intervention, radiant health, and grandeur.

Rubens produced works at a great rate, primarily because he ran what was virtually a painting factory, with numerous artists and apprentices assisting in his work. He priced his paintings on the basis of their size and according to how much actual work he did on them personally. Nevertheless, his unique style emerges from every painting, and even an observer untrained in art history can easily recognize his works. Clearly, artistic value here lies in the conception, not merely in the handiwork.

Poussin

Nicolas Poussin (poo-SAHN; 1593–1663) often chose his subjects from the literature of antiquity. In *Landscape with the Burial of Phocion* (Fig. **13.15**), he takes a theme from Plutarch's story (see p. 135) about an ancient Athenian hero who was wrongly put to death but then given a state

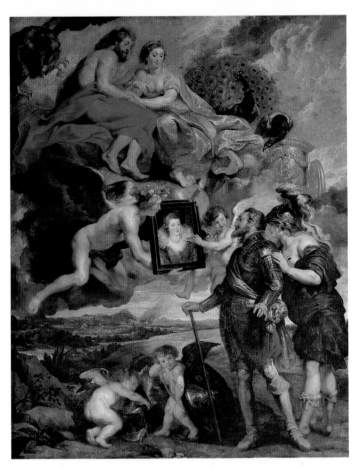

funeral. In the foreground, the hero's corpse is being carried away, having been denied burial on Athenian soil.

The landscape overpowers the human forms here. Isolated at the bottom of the picture, perhaps symbolizing his isolation and rejection in the story, the hero seems a very minor focus. Instead, the eye of the viewer is drawn up and into the background, an overwhelming stretch of deep space, depicted with intricate and graphic clarity as far as the eye can see. Poussin uses no atmospheric perspective here. The objects farthest away are as clearly depicted as those in the foreground. The various planes of the composition lead the viewer methodically from side to side, working toward the background one plane at a time. The composition is rich in human, natural, and architectural details that please the eye.

Although the *Landscape with the Burial of Phocion* is more subdued than Rubens' work, in every way the details in this painting are no less complex. The scheme is one of

13.14 Peter Paul Rubens, *Henry IV Receiving the Portrait of Maria de' Medici*, 1622–5. Oil on canvas, 13 ft × 9ft 8 ins (3.96 × 2.95 m). Louvre, Paris.

13.15 Nicolas Poussin, *Landscape with the Burial of Phocion*, 1648. Oil on canvas, 5 ft 10 ins × 3 ft 11 ins (1.78 × 1.2 m). Louvre, Paris.

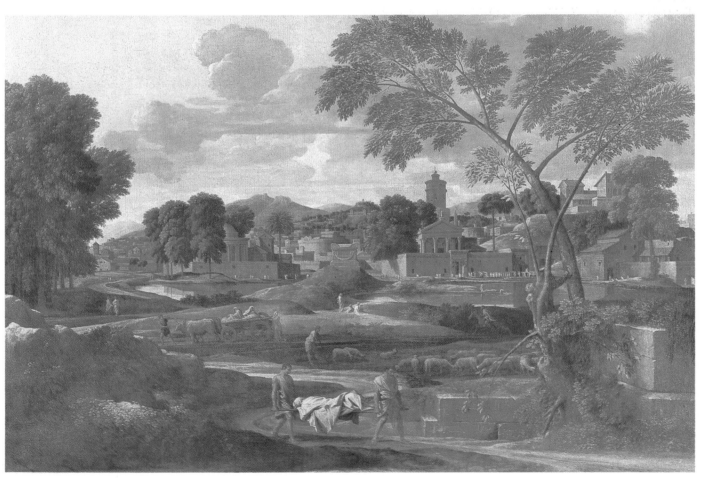

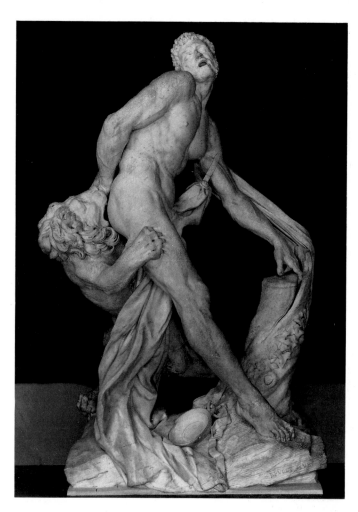

13.16 Pierre Puget, *Milo of Crotona*, 1671–83. Marble, 8 ft 10½ ins (2.71 m) high. Louvre, Paris.

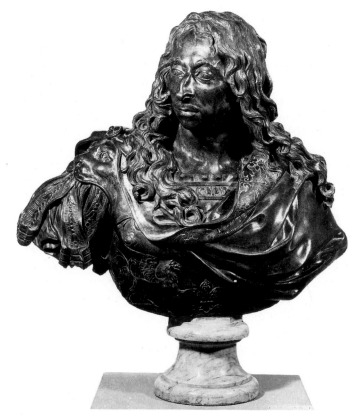

13.17 Antoine Coysevox, *The Great Condé*, 1688. Bronze, 23 ins (58.4 cm) high. Louvre, Paris.

systematically interrelated pieces, in typically rational baroque fashion. Also typical of the baroque is the play of strong highlight against strong shadow. Although the picture does not show a real place, Poussin has depicted the architecture very precisely. He studied Vitruvius, the Roman architectural historian, and Vitruvius' accounts are the source of this detail.

Sculpture

Pierre Puget's (pue-ZHAY; 1620–94) *Milo of Crotona* (Fig. **13.16**) seems possessed by its own physical strength. The statue depicts Milo, the Olympic wrestling champion, who challenged the god Apollo. His punishment for daring to challenge the gods was death. The powerful hero, with his hand caught in a split treestump, is held helpless as he is mauled by a lion. Neither classical idealism nor reason has any part in this portrayal—it is pure physical pain and torment. The figure is caught in the violent agonies of pain and imminent death. The skin is about to tear under the

pressure of the lion's claws—in an instant it will split open. The sweeping and intersecting arcs of the composition create intense energy of a kind that recalls the Laocoön group (see Fig. **3.30**).

Portrait busts of the period, such as those by the French sculptor Antoine Coysevox (kwahz-VOH; 1640–1720), also attempt an emotional portrayal of their subjects. *The Great Condé* (Fig. **13.17**) uses dynamic line and strong and emphatic features to express the energy of the sitter.

Architecture

Probably no monarch better personified the baroque era than Louis XIV, and probably no work of art better represents the magnificence and grandeur of the aristocratic baroque style than the grand design of the Palace of Versailles (vair-SY), along with its sculpture and grounds. The great Versailles complex grew from the modest hunting lodge of Louis XIII into the grand palace of the Sun King over a number of years, involving several architects.

The Versailles château was rebuilt in 1631 by Philibert Le Roy (luh WAH). The façade was decorated by Louis Le Vau (luh VOH; 1612–70) with bricks and stone, sculpture, wrought iron, and gilt lead. In 1668 Louis XIV ordered Le

Vau to enlarge the building by enclosing it in a stone envelope containing the king's and queen's apartments (Fig. **13.18**). The city side of the château thus retains the spirit of Louis XIII, while the park side reflects classical influence. François d'Orbay (dohr-BAY) and, later, Jules Hardouin-Mansart (ar-DWAN mahn-ZAHR; 1646–1708) expanded the château into a palace whose west façade extends over 2,000 feet (610 meters) (Fig. **13.19**). The palace became Louis XIV's permanent residence in 1682. French royalty was at the height of its power, and Versailles was the symbol of the monarchy and of the divine right of kings. As a symbol and in practical fact, Versailles played a fundamental role in keeping France stable. Its symbolism as a magnificent testament to royal centrality and to France's sense of nationalism is fairly obvious. As a practical device, Versailles served the purpose of pulling the aristocracy out of Paris, where they could foment discontent, and isolated them where Louis XIV could keep his eye on them and keep them busy. Versailles further served as a giant economic engine to develop and export French taste and the French luxury trades.

As much care, elegance, and precision were employed on the interior as on the exterior. With the aim of supporting French craftsmen and merchants, Louis XIV had his court live in unparalleled luxury. He also decided to put permanent furnishings in his château, something that was unheard of. The result was a fantastically rich and beautiful interior. Royal workshops produced mirrors (Fig. **13.20**), tapestries, and brocades of the highest quality, and

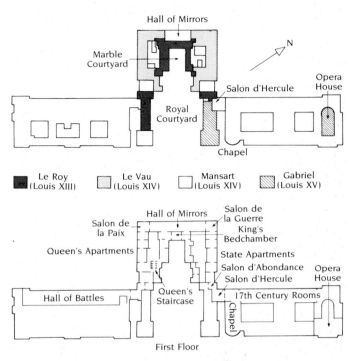

13.18 Plans of the Palace of Versailles, 1669–85.

13.19 Louis Le Vau and Jules Hardouin-Mansart, garden façade. Palace of Versailles, 1669–85.

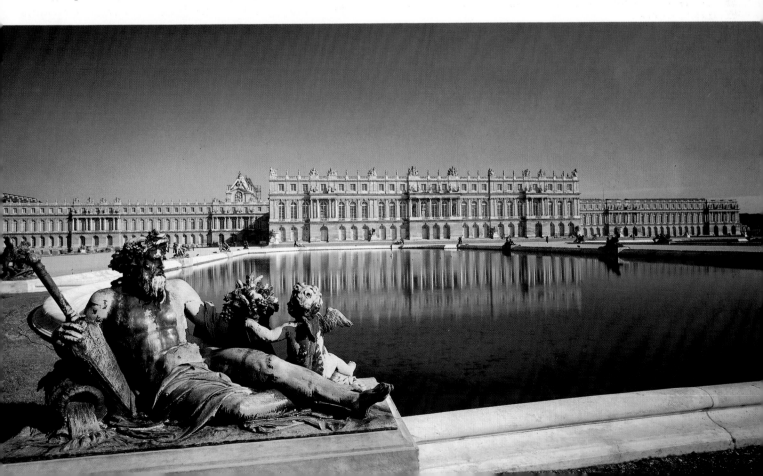

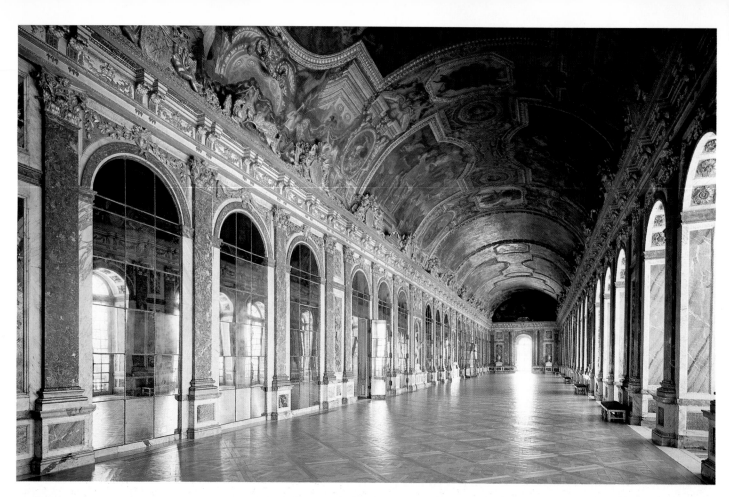

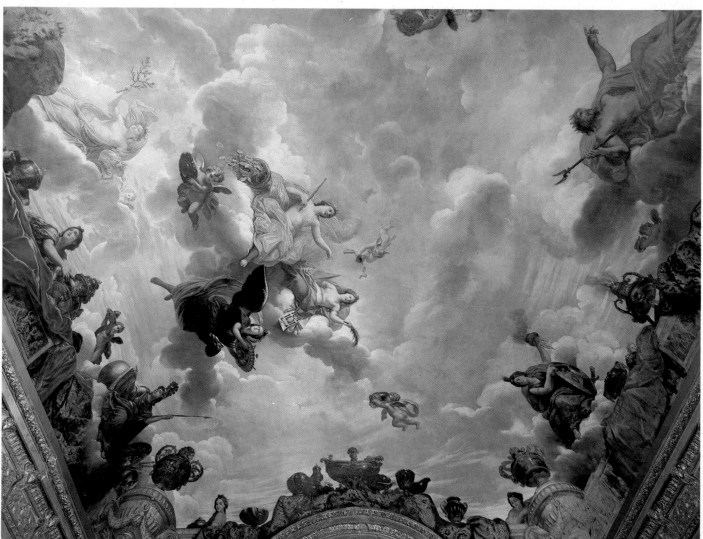

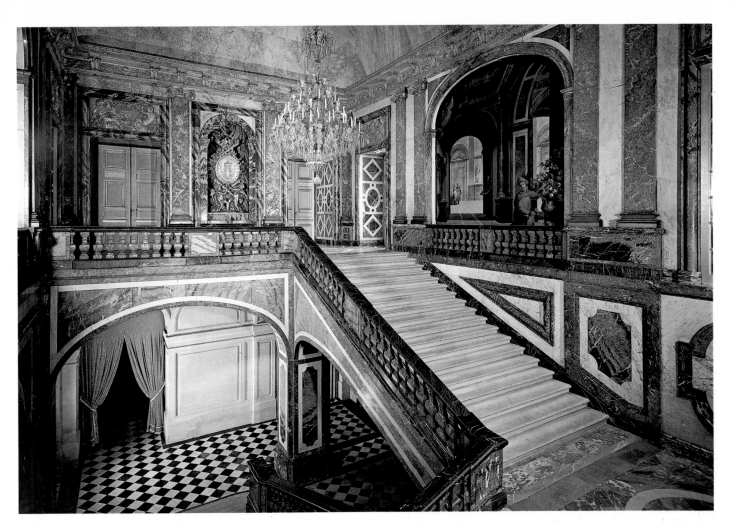

13.20 (*opposite, above*) Jules Hardouin-Mansart and Charles Le Brun, Hall of Mirrors, Palace of Versailles, begun 1678.

13.21 (*opposite, below*) René-Antoine Houasse, *Royal Magnificence*, ceiling of the Salon d'Abondance, Palace of Versailles.

13.22 (*above*) The Queen's Staircase, Palace of Versailles.

13.23 (*below*) The Parterre du Midi, Palace of Versailles.

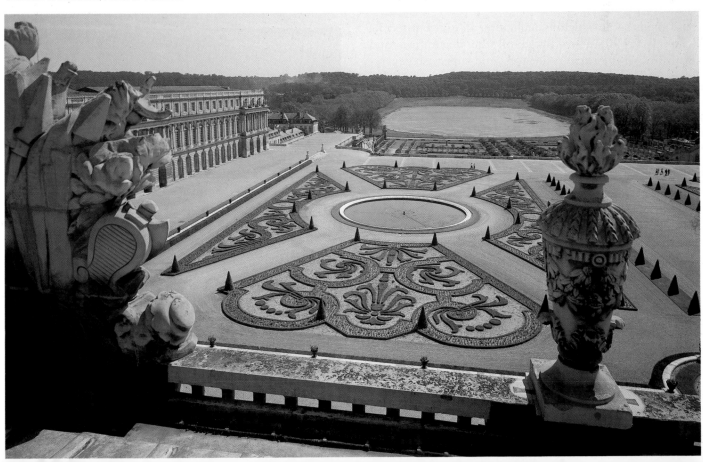

OUR DYNAMIC WORLD

The Taj Mahal

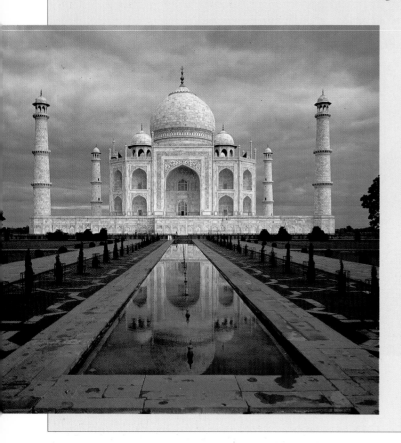

Like Louis XIV, the Islamic Mughal (moo-GAHL) emperors of India were patrons of architecture, and the most famous of all Indian architectural accomplishments also qualifies as an example of splendid aristocratic art—the Taj Mahal at Agra (Fig. **13.24**). However, the Taj Mahal blends Islamic and indigenous Indian styles. The tomb, built by Shah Jahan as a mausoleum for his favorite wife, Mumtaz Mahal (1593–1631), was entirely without precedent in Islam, and it is possible that the building also was intended as an allegory of the day of Resurrection, for the building is a symbolic replica of the throne of God. Four intersecting waterways in the garden by which one approaches the Taj symbolized the four flowing Rivers of Paradise as described in the Koran. The scale of the building is immense, yet the details are exquisitely refined, and the proportions are well balanced and symmetrical. The effect of this huge, white octagonal structure with its impressive dome and flanking minarets is nothing short of breathtaking.

13.24 Ustad Ahmad Lahori (architect), the Taj Mahal, Agra, India, 1632–48.

these goods became highly sought after all over Europe. Le Brun (1619–90) coordinated all the decoration and furnishing of the royal residences, and supervised everything for the state apartments, such as the statues, the painted ceilings, and the silver pieces of furniture.

The apartments of the palace boast a splendor and wealth previously unseen. Each room was dedicated to one of the planetary gods. The Salon d'Abondance (Fig. **13.21**) was not considered a part of the state apartments until the north wing was built. The ceiling here shows an allegorical figure of Magnificence, whose scepter and cornucopia are symbols of the royal prerogatives of power and provision. Around Magnificence are Immortality and the Fine Arts, symbolized by a winged figure.

The Queen's staircase (Fig. **13.22**) leads to a suite created by Le Vau for Queen Marie-Thérèse. It comprises

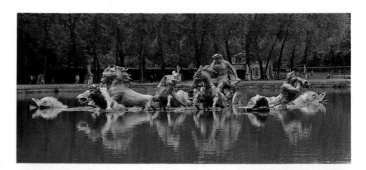

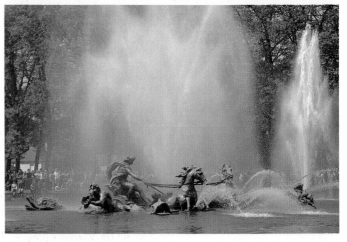

13.25 The Fountain of Apollo, Palace of Versailles.

four large rooms whose windows open to the plantings on the Parterre du Midi (Fig. **13.23**). The grounds here and elsewhere are adorned with fountains and statues. The magnificent Fountain of Apollo by Tuby (too-BEE; Fig. **13.25**), which sits astride the east-west axis of the grounds, was originally covered with gold. The sculpture was executed from a drawing by Le Brun and inspired by a painting by Albani. It continues the allegorical glorification of *Le Roi Soleil* (luh WAH soh-LAY), representing the break of day, as the sun-god rises in his chariot from the waters. Apollo was the perfect symbol for the Sun King, who reigned, it was thought, at God's behest and in his stead, in glorious baroque splendor, surrounded by art that was rational yet emotional, opulent in tone, and complex in design.

Bourgeois Baroque

Art in the bourgeois baroque style reflected the visions and objectives of the new and wealthy middle class. The wealth and opulent lifestyle of the bourgeoisie sometimes exceeded that of the aristocracy. As a result, a power struggle was at hand.

Rembrandt

Born in Leiden, Rembrandt van Rijn (REM-brant fahn RYN; 1606–69) trained under local artists and then moved to Amsterdam. His early and rapid success gained him many commissions and students—more, in fact, than he could handle. In contrast to the work of Rubens, Rembrandt's art is by, for, and about the middle class. Indeed, Rembrandt became what could be called the first

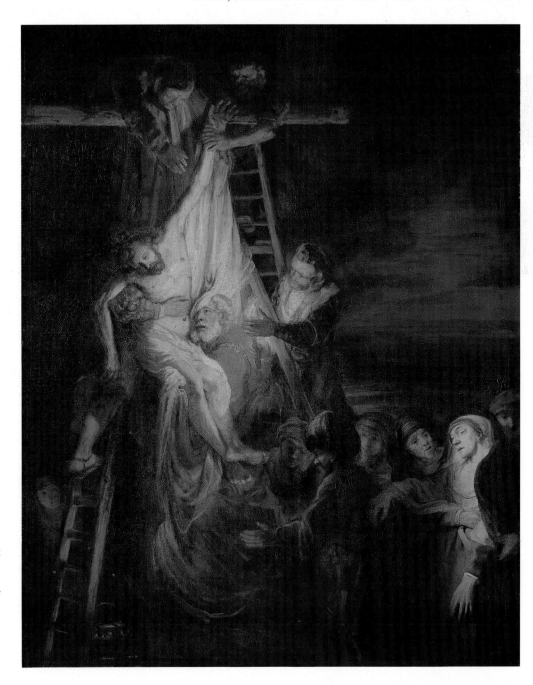

13.26 After Rembrandt van Rijn, *The Descent from the Cross*, c. 1652. Oil on canvas. 4 ft 8¼ ins × 3 ft 7¾ ins (1.43 × 1.11 m). National Gallery of Art, Washington D.C. (Widener Collection). © 1998 Board of Trustees, National Gallery of Art, Washington D.C.

Rembrandt—*The Night Watch*

The huge canvas now in the Rijksmuseum in Amsterdam is only a portion of the original group portrait *The Night Watch* (Fig. **13.27**), which was cut down in the eighteenth century to fit into a space in Amsterdam Town Hall. So it happens that it no longer shows the bridge over which the members of the watch were about to cross.

Group portraits, especially of military units, were popular at the time. Usually the company posed in a social setting, such as a gathering around a banquet table, but Rembrandt chose to break with the norm and portrayed the company, led by Captain Cocq, as if it were out on duty. The result was a scene of great vigor and dramatic intensity, true to the baroque spirit.

As a dramatic scene, the painting is a virtuoso performance of baroque lighting and movement. There is nothing regular or mechanical about it. The result, however, angered the members of Captain Cocq's company. They had paid equally, and expected to be treated equally in the portrait, but they are not. Some of the figures fade into the shadows. Others are hidden by the gestures of those placed in front of them.

Cleaning revealed the vivid color of the original. The painting is now a good deal brighter than when it was named in the nineteenth century. Yet its dramatic highlights and shadows reflect no natural light source whatsoever, and no analysis of the light can solve the problem of how the figures in the painting are supposed to be illuminated. It has been suggested that perhaps the painting depicts a "day watch," with the intense light at the center of the work being morning sunlight. An examination of the highlights and shadows in the painting, however, shows that Rembrandt has used light for dramatic purposes only. While the figures are rendered realistically, no such claim can be made for the light sources.

Rembrandt's genius lay in depicting human emotions and characters. He suggests detail without including it, and we find him taking this approach in *The Night Watch*. Here he concentrates on atmosphere and implication. As in most baroque art, the viewer is invited to share in an emotional experience, to enter in, rather than to observe.

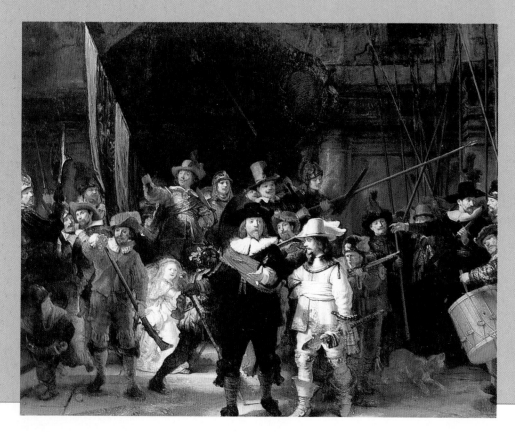

13.27 Rembrandt van Rijn, *The Night Watch* (*The Company of Captain Frans Banning Cocq*), 1642. Oil on canvas, 12 ft 2 ins × 14 ft 7 ins (3.7 × 4.45 m). Rijksmuseum, Amsterdam.

"capitalist" artist. The quality of art could be gauged, he believed, not only on its own merits but also by its value on the open market. He is reported to have spent huge sums of money buying his own works in order to increase their value.

Rembrandt's genius lay in delivering the depths of human emotion and psychology in the most dramatic terms. Unlike Rubens, for example, Rembrandt uses suggestion rather than great detail. After all, the human spirit is intangible—it can never be portrayed, only alluded to. Thus in Rembrandt's work we find atmosphere, shadow, and implication creating emotion.

Rembrandt's DEPOSITION scene, *The Descent from the Cross* (Fig. **13.26**) has a certain sense of richness. Rembrandt uses only reds, golds, and red-browns: except for the robe of the figure pressing into Christ's body, the painting is nearly monochromatic. Contrasts are provided

and forms are revealed through changes in value. The composition is open—that is, lines escape the frame at the left arm of the cross and in the half-forms at the lower right border. The horizontal line of the darkened sky is subtly carried off the canvas, middle right. A strong central triangle holds the composition together. From a dark, shadowed base, which runs the full width of the lower border, it is delineated by the highlighted figure on the lower right and the ladder at the lower left. Christ's upstretched arm completes the apex of the triangle.

Van Ruisdael

Rembrandt's emotional subject matter was probably hard for most collectors to cope with. More to the taste of the new, general marketplace were the subjects of the emerging landscape painters. *The Jewish Cemetery* (Fig. **13.28**), a painting by Jacob van Ruisdael (ROYS-dahl; 1628–82),

13.28 Jacob van Ruisdael, *The Jewish Cemetery*, c. 1655. Oil on canvas, 4 ft 8 ins × 6 ft 2¼ ins (1.42 × 1.89 m). Detroit Institute of Arts (Gift of Julius H. Haass, in memory of his brother Dr Ernest W. Haass).

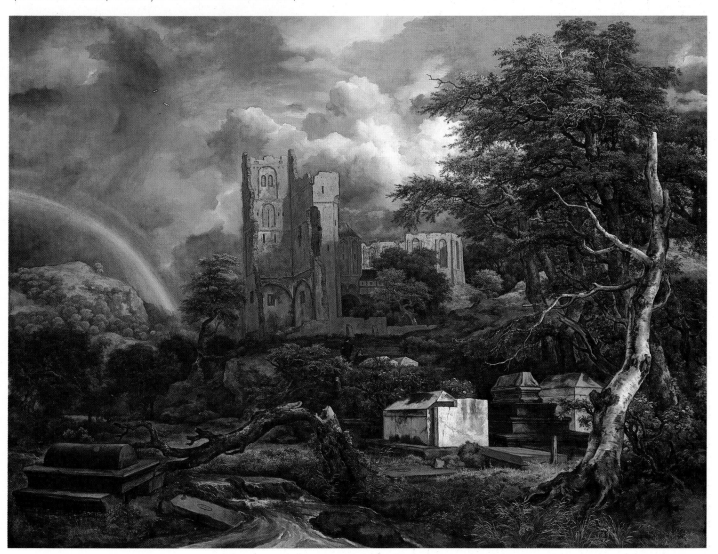

appeals to the emotions with its rich detail and atmosphere, light and shade, and grandiose scale.

The painting is large, nearly 5 feet (1.5 meters) high and more than 6 feet (1.8 meters) wide. The graveyard itself, along with the medieval ruins, casts a melancholy spell over the work. The absence of human life in the painting suggests its insignificance in the universe. The ruins suggest that even the traces of human presence shall also pass away. Highlight and shadow lead the eye around the composition, but not in any consecutive way. The eye's path is broken, or at least disturbed, by changes of direction, for example, in the tree trunk across the stream and in the stark tree limbs. Nature broods over both the scene and the wider universe outside the frame.

Vermeer

Virtually forgotten until the nineteenth century, Jan Vermeer (vuhr-MIHR; 1632–75), like Rembrandt, probed great depths of feeling in his works with masterful control of light and shade. His painting *The Girl with a Red Hat* (Fig. **13.29**) not only creates plasticity—that is, three-dimensionality—but also heightens the dramatic effect of a rather simple subject. Vermeer takes CHIAROSCURO (Italian for "light and shade") and develops strong value contrasts that are not only emotional but compositional as well. The highlights, falling as they do, establish a basic compositional triangle extending from shoulder to cheek, down to the hand, and then across the sleeve and back to the shoulder. A dynamic flare of red encircles the subject's face with a feathery nimbus (halo) that draws our attention, surprisingly, not to the red hat, but to the eyes and liquid, half-opened mouth: as if she were about to speak to us.

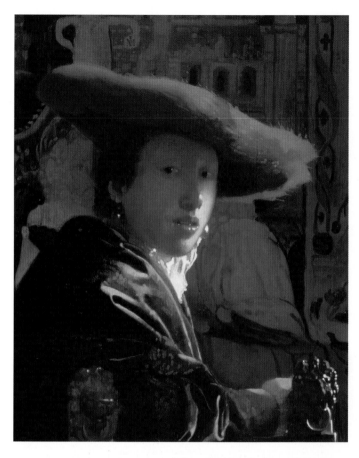

13.29 Jan Vermeer, The *Girl with a Red Hat*, c. 1665. Oil on panel, 9$\frac{1}{8}$ × 7$\frac{1}{8}$ ins (23 × 18 cm). National Gallery of Art, Washington D.C. (Andrew W. Mellon Collection). © 1998 Board of Trustees, National Gallery of Art, Washington D.C.

LITERATURE

Poetry and Satire

After the golden age of the late sixteenth century, the mood in England darkened noticeably with the death of Queen Elizabeth in 1603. Political instability and economic difficulties threatened, and the finest writing turned away from love—almost the exclusive theme of the Elizabethans—to an often anguished inner questioning.

The work of John Donne (duhn; 1573–1631), a cleric who became dean of St Paul's, demonstrates this sea-change. Donne's early love sonnets are among the most urgently erotic poems in the language, but the work of his later years relentlessly explores the meaning of an intelligent person's relationship with the soul and with God. Donne was among the leading figures in a group that has since become known as the Metaphysical poets, after their concern with "first and last things." Their often intensely private writing is characterized by deliberate and rich ambiguity of word structures and imagery.

Death, Be Not Proud
John Donne

Death, be not proud, though some have callèd thee
Mighty and dreadful, for thou art not so;
For those whom thou think'st thou dost overthrow
Die not, poor Death, nor yet canst thou kill me.
From rest and sleep, which but thy pictures be,
Much pleasure; then from thee much more must
  flow,
And soonest our best men with thee do go,
Rest of their bones, and soul's delivery.
Thou'rt slave to fate, chance, kings, and desperate
  men,
And dost with poison, war, and sickness dwell;
And poppy or charms can make us sleep as well
And better than thy stroke; why swell'st thou then?

One short sleep past, we wake eternally,
And death shall be no more: Death, thou shalt die.

Holy Sonnet X

The poems of George Herbert (1593–1633)—never meant for publication—exemplify this movement at its best. Herbert was a devout clergyman and a religious poet of great intellect and passion.

Love Bade Me Welcome
George Herbert

Love bade me welcome; yet my soul drew back,
   Guilty of dust and sin.
But quick-eyed Love, observing me grow slack
   From my first entrance in,
Drew nearer to me, sweetly questioning
   If I lacked any thing.

"A guest," I answered, "worthy to be here";
   Love said, "You shall be he."
"I the unkind, ungrateful? Ah my dear,
   I cannot look on thee."
Love took my hand, and smiling did reply,
   "Who made the eyes but I?"

"Truth, Lord, but I have marred them: let my shame
   Go where it doth deserve."
"And know you not," says Love, "who bore the
   blame?"
    "My dear, then I will serve."
"You must sit down," says Love, "and taste my
   meat."
   So I did sit and eat.

Many of the methods of the Metaphysical poets were further developed by Andrew Marvell (1621–78), a poet as public as they had been private. He wrote at the time of, and in the period immediately after, the English Civil War, and his *Horatian Ode* in praise of Oliver Cromwell marks the return of poets and poetry to the political stage. His contemporary John Milton (1608–74) was also deeply committed to the parliamentarian cause, and his early works reflect his humanist education and his belief in the importance of the classical cultural and political heritage. In old age, blind, solitary, and disappointed by the failure of his political ideals, he wrote his masterpiece, *Paradise Lost*. This monumental verse account of the fall of Satan and of Adam and Eve has been described as the literary equivalent of the baroque style in the visual arts. His richly Latinate language is deeply musical, confident, and powerful. His themes are epic, tragic, and uncompromisingly Protestant.

With the Restoration of Charles II, in 1660, which had so embittered Milton, the seriousness and quality of poetic output declined. Cynical and licentious verse became typical of these shallow years. The Glorious Revolution of 1688, when a new royal family came over from the Low Countries, marked a decisive change. At this point, the middle classes had broken the power of the absolute monarch and the influence of the court. The confidence and pragmatism of this new "Augustan" age found a voice in John Dryden (1631–1700), whose satirical *Absalom and Achitophel* marked a new role for the poet as a witty and entertaining critic of his age.

The Rise of the Novel

This period also saw the development of the novel. An early form of this genre had been in existence in Elizabethan England, but it was Miguel Cervantes (sair-VAHN-tays; 1547–1616) in Spain who first exploited its full potential. Cervantes' novel *Don Quixote* (don kee-HOH-tay) recounts the adventures of a comically self-deluded knight. The novel is a parody of the chivalric romances of an earlier age, but also an eloquent lament for a lost time of innocence and moral clarity.

Writers in both France and England began to experiment with the versatile new form, which, because of its extended length and realistic language, seemed ideally suited to the treatment of contemporary and everyday themes. The Englishman Daniel Defoe (dee-FOH; 1660–1731) set the direction that the European novel would take. His *Robinson Crusoe* is widely read to this day, and his *Moll Flanders* defined the novel's voice and audience for the age. Subsequent novels were imaginary biographies or autobiographies set in contemporary society. The central figure would be a man or, more commonly, a woman, with whom the reader (usually female) would identify. So it was that the great age of poetry came to a close with the rise of the novel.

MUSIC

Baroque Style

The term *baroque* refers to music written during the period extending approximately from 1600 to 1750. The term itself originally referred to a large, irregularly shaped pearl of the kind often used in the extremely fanciful jewelry of the post-Renaissance period, and music of this style was as luscious, ornate, and emotionally appealing as were its siblings of painting, sculpture, and architecture.

Baroque composers began to write for specific instruments, or for voices, in contrast to earlier music that might be either sung or played. They also brought to their music new kinds of action and tension, for example, quick, strong contrasts in tone color or volume, and strict rhythms juxtaposed against free rhythms. Gradually during the time of this style, a system evolved whereby the relationship between keys was established in an orderly way. Thus, the baroque era in music was crucial to the development of the modern musical language.

Instrumental Music

As baroque composers began to write specifically for individual voices and instruments, instrumental music assumed a new importance. A wide range of possibilities for individual instruments was explored, and the instruments themselves underwent technical development. For one thing, instruments had to be made so they could play in any key. Before the baroque era, an instrument such as the harpsichord had to be retuned virtually each time a piece in a new key was played. Equal TEMPERAMENT established the convention we accept without question, that each half-step in a musical scale is equidistant from the one preceding or following it. This was not immediately seen as desirable, and Johann Sebastian Bach (bahk) composed a series of two sets of preludes and fugues in all possible keys (*The Well-Tempered Clavier* (klah-VEER), Part I, 1722; Part II, 1740) to illustrate the virtues of the new system.

As a result of these developments, a wealth of keyboard music was composed in this era. The FUGUE, with its formal structure and strict imitation, best demonstrates the complexity and virtuosity of this music, and the highest point in its development came, once again, in the work of J.S. Bach, the leading composer of the baroque age. His instrumental compositions range from simple dances, arranged into groups as SUITES, to the famous pieces for solo violin and solo cello, which to this day are some of the most complex and technically challenging works in the repertoire. As we noted, Bach was a prolific composer: his keyboard music alone includes over six hundred organ pieces based on chorale tunes, and hundreds of other harpsichord and organ works in all the contemporary instrumental forms.

Concerto

Another of the forms contributed to Western music by the baroque age was the CONCERTO. In this musical form, two or more dissimilar musical forces are used—for example, one or more soloists playing opposite an orchestra. Basically, three types of concerto emerged from the early seventeenth century, when the concerto became largely an orchestral form: (1) the *orchestral concerto*, in which differences in texture or treatment mark the different

groups of instruments; (2) the *concerto grosso*, in which a small group called the *concertino* stand out from the main force, called the *tutti* or *ripieno* (meaning "remainder" or "filling"); (3) the *solo concerto*, for one instrument and orchestra.

One of the masters of the concerto was Antonio Vivaldi (vee-VAHL-dee; 1669–1741), who composed for specific occasions and usually for a specific company of performers. He wrote prolifically: approximately 450 concertos, twenty-three sinfonias, seventy-five sonatas, forty-nine operas, and numerous cantatas, motets, and oratorios. About two-thirds of his concertos are for solo instrument and orchestra and one-third are concerti grossi.

Probably his most familiar solo concerto is "Spring," one of four works in Op. 8 *The Seasons* (1725). *The Seasons* is an early example of PROGRAM MUSIC, written to illustrate an external idea, in contrast with ABSOLUTE MUSIC, which presents purely musical ideas. In "Spring," (CD Track 11) a series of individual pieces interlock to form an ornate whole. In the first movement (allegro), Vivaldi alternates an opening theme (A) with sections that depict bird song, a flowing brook, a storm, and the birds' return (ABACADAEA). Theme A is known as a *ritornello* (ri-tohr-NEL-loh), from the Italian "to return," and this alternating pattern is called RITORNELLO FORM. Within the solo part there is elaborate melodic ornamentation. For example, on a simple ascending scale of five notes, the composer added ornamental notes, and thus the ascending scale becomes a melodic pattern of perhaps as many as twenty tones—a musical equivalent of the complex ornamental visual detail seen in baroque painting, sculpture, and architecture.

Sonata

The term "sonata" (suh-NAHT-uh) comprises one of the most elastic terms in music and has been used to denote many different musical forms. We will confine our discussion to its place in the baroque era. The word itself comes from the Italian *sonare* (to sound), and came into use during the baroque era to indicate any piece played on instruments, as distinct from the vocal *cantata* (kuhn-TAHT-uh), which means "sung." Its most popular treatment during the seventeenth century became known as the *trio sonata*, with two high, intertwining parts for violins or flutes, or oboes, played above a bass part for cello or bassoon. Usually an organist or harpsichordist played along to reinforce the bass and fill in harmonies indicated by symbols written in the bass part (a practice called "figured bass").

The violin came to the fore in the baroque era, replacing the viol, which had previously been the primary bowed string instrument. The violin was fully explored as a solo

MASTERWORK

Bach—Fugue in G Minor

Bach's organ compositions are famous for their drama, bold pedal solos, and virtuoso fingerwork. The Fugue in G minor, or "Little Fugue," is a characteristic example.

A fugue is a polyphonic piece for one or more instruments or a group of singers. It develops at least two musical themes, the first called the subject and the second called the countersubject. The word "fugue" takes its name from the Latin *fuga*, which means "flight," and a typical fugue has a fairly rapid tempo and a crisp feeling. As a musical form, a fugue embodies development through imitative counterpoint, alternating with contrasting "episodes."

The subject of Bach's Fugue in G minor is typical in that the thematic material is based around the tones of two common chords, and it begins with longer note values and gradually gains impetus. This fugue has four voices—the melodic lines are called voices although they are, of course, played in this instance. The main subject, which falls into two parts, is first stated in the soprano (top) voice (Fig. **13.30**), then answered by the alto voice (the second voice from the top).

The texture of the composition builds up: at the beginning we hear only one voice, thereafter two or more independent voices play at the same time, in counterpoint. The opening section of the fugue—the

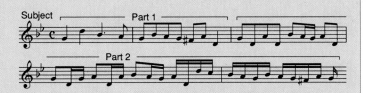

13.30 J.S. Bach, Fugue in G minor, first statement of subject.

EXPOSITION—states the subject in each of the four voices. As each new voice enters, the previous one takes up a second theme, or countersubject.

Once that has been accomplished, Bach inserts a brief episode based on two short motifs taken from the subject. The rest of the structure is built around various key changes, which introduce a new level of contrast. Bach also continues to alternate episodes and statements of the subject. Beneath the complex texture of the fugue, a sustained bass tone sometimes appears; this is called a pedal point. The final episode of the piece is an intricate development which moves to a climax that we can hear in a rising chromatic scale, or series of half-steps. The final statement of the subject appears in the bass line, and the fugue ends with a strong cadence back in the original key of G minor.

---

instrument, and it was also perfected physically. From the late seventeenth and early eighteenth centuries came the greatest violins ever built. Made of maple, pine and ebony by such craftsmen as Antonio Stradivari (strah-dee-VAH-ree; 1644–1737), these remarkable instruments fetch enormous sums of money today. Despite our best scientific attempts, they have never been matched in their superb qualities, the secrets of which died with Stradivari. Not only is a violin similar to the human voice in timbre, but a well-made violin has an individual personality. It assumes certain qualities of its environment and of the performer. It responds sensitively to external factors such as temperature and humidity, and getting the best from it depends upon care from its owner, not to mention skill and musicianship.

The baroque age in music was a magnificent one. To all intents and purposes, in its harmonies, structures, and forms, it laid the groundwork for the music of the eras that were to come, and its legacy can still be heard today.

Vocal Music

Cantata

As we just noted, the Italian word CANTATA denotes "sung." It comprises vocal compositions with instrumental accompaniment, with several movements based on related text segments. It developed from monody, or solo singing with a predominant vocal line, centering on a text, to which the music was subservient. These works, which

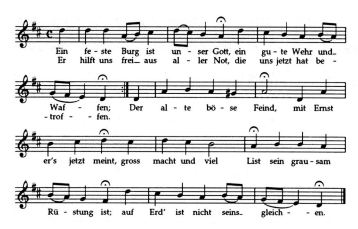

13.31 J.S. Bach, *Ein feste Burg ist unser Gott*, from Cantata xlo. 80.

consisted of many short, contrasting sections, were far less spectacular than opera, and they were designed to be performed without costumes or scenery. Most cantatas were written for solo soprano voice, although many used other voices and groups of voices. Two types of cantatas existed during the baroque era, the secular and the religious. The secular Italian cantata had become, by 1650, a piece alternating two or three RECITATIVES and ARIAS, usually for soprano voice and accompaniment.

The high point of the Italian cantata came in the works of Alessandro Scarlatti (skar-LAT-ee; 1660–1725), who composed more than six hundred of them. Typically Scarlatti's cantatas begin with a short "arioso" section, that is somewhere between recitative and ARIA (a set-piece song). A recitative follows, then a full aria, a second recitative, and a final aria in the opening key. Scarlatti's moods tended to be melancholic and tender, and his composition elegant and refined. The theme of almost all of his works is love, and particularly its betrayal.

In Germany, the cantata was a sacred work that grew out of the Lutheran chorale. Its most accomplished composers were Johann Sebastian Bach (1685–1750) and Dietrich Buxtehude (BUHKS-te-hoo-de; c. 1637–1707), of whom Bach is by far the greater. As a choirmaster, Bach was under a professional obligation to compose a new cantata weekly, and between 1704 and 1740, he composed more than two hundred. His cantatas were primarily contrapuntal in texture, usually written for up to four soloists and a four-part chorus.

Bach's work is one of the great responses of Protestant art to the challenge of the Counter-Reformation. His sacred music achieves extraordinary power as a humane, heartfelt expression of faith. Never theatrical, its drama derives from an inner striving, a hard-won triumph over doubt and death.

An excellent example, whose basic theme is well known, is Cantata No. 80: *Ein feste Burg ist unser Gott* ("A Mighty Fortress is our God"). The chorale on which the cantata is based was written by Martin Luther (Luther probably wrote both words and music), and the chorale is a centerpiece of Protestant hymnology. Luther's words and melody are used in the first, second, fifth, and last movements. Salomo Franck, Bach's favorite librettist, wrote the remainder of the text. The first movement (Fig. **13.31**) , a choral fugue, states the familiar theme and text:

> A mighty fortress is our God,
> A good defense and weapon;
> He helps free us from all the troubles
> That have now befallen us.
> Our ever evil foe,
> In earnest plots against us,
> With great strength and cunning
> He prepares his dreadful plans.
> Earth holds none like him.

The final movement (CD track 9) rounds off the cantata. Luther's chorale is now sung in Bach's own four-part harmonization. Instruments double each voice, and the simple, powerful melody stands out against the lower parts:

> Das Wort, sie sollen lassen stehen
> und kein Dank dazu haben.
> Er ist bei uns wohl auf dem Plan
> mit seinem Geist und Gaben.
> Nehmen sie uns den Leib,
> Gut, Her, Kind und Weib,
> lass fahren dahin
> sie haben kein Gewinn
> das Reich muss uns doch bleiben.

> Now let the Word of God abide
> without further thought.
> He is firmly on our side
> with His spirit and strength.
> Though they deprive us of life,
> Wealth, honor, child, and wife,
> we will not complain.
> It will avail them nothing
> For God's kingdom must prevail.

Opera

The word *opera* means "work" in Italian and is short for the Italian *opera in musica*. An opera is a drama set to music. It may have some spoken dialogue but more often than not, the music is continuous, with set pieces (solos, duets, etc.) designed to dramatize the action and display the vocal skills of the singers. Opera exemplifies the baroque spirit in many ways. Whether we consider it to be music with theatre or theatre with music, opera combines a

Johann Sebastian Bach (1685–1750)

Although currently considered one of the giants of music, Johann Sebastian Bach was considered old-fashioned during his lifetime, and his works lay virtually dormant after his death. Not until the nineteenth century did he gain recognition as one of the greatest composers of the Western world. He was born in Thuringia, in what is now Germany, and when he was ten years old both his parents died. His oldest brother, Johann Christoph, took responsibility for raising and teaching him, and Johann Sebastian became a choirboy at the Michaelskirche in Luneburg when he was fifteen. He studied the organ and was appointed organist at Neukirche in Arnstadt, where he remained for four years. Then he took a similar post at Muhlhausen at about the same time as he married his cousin Maria Barbara Bach. One year later, he took the position of court organist at Weimar, remaining there until 1717, when Prince Leopold of Kothen hired him as his musical director. While he was serving as musical director to Prince Leopold, Bach completed the Brandenberg Concertos in 1721.

In 1720 Bach's wife died, and one year later he married Anna Magdalena Wilcken. In 1723 he moved to Leipzig as the city's musical director at the school attached to St Thomas' Church, and among his responsibilities to the city, was the supply of performers for four churches. In 1747 he played at Potsdam for Frederick II the Great of Prussia but shortly thereafter his eyesight began to fail, and he went blind just before his death in 1750.

Bach's output as a composer was prodigious but also required as part of his responsibilities, especially at Leipzig. Over his career, he wrote more than two hundred cantatas, the *Mass in B Minor*, and three settings of the Passion story, works that illustrate Bach's deep religious faith. His sacred music allowed him to explore and communicate the profound mysteries of the Christian faith and to glorify God. His cantatas typify the baroque exploration of wide-ranging emotional development. They range from ecstatic expressions of joy to profound meditations on death. *The Passions*, of which the *St Matthew Passion* is typical, tell the story of the trial and crucifixion of Jesus. Written in German rather than the traditional Latin, the Passions express Bach's devotion to Lutheranism.

In addition to his sacred works, Bach wrote a tremendous amount of important music for harpsichord and organ, including the forty-eight Preludes and Fugues, called *The Well-Tempered Clavier*, and the *Goldberg Variations*. In the fugues, he develops a single theme, which is then imitated among the polyphonically developed voices of the composition (see the Masterwork section on the *Fugue in G Minor*, p. 411). Among his many instrumental works are twenty concertos and twelve unaccompanied sonatas for violin and cello.

---

number of complex art forms into one big, ornate, and even more complex system which is greater than and different from the sum of its parts: music, drama, dance, visual art (scenery and costumes), and architecture (since an opera house is a unique architectural entity). And in particular, in true baroque spirit, opera is primarily an overwhelming emotional experience. The earliest operas included roles for *castrati* (kuh-STRAHT-ee), male singers who had been castrated in boyhood so their voices would remain in the soprano and contralto range. This created adult voices of unusual strength and clarity, and castrati played many male heroic roles.

Opera began in Italy in musical discussions among a small group of nobles, poets, and composers who began meeting regularly in Florence around 1575. This group,

known as the *Camerata* (meaning "fellowship" or "society"), wished to develop a new vocal style based on the music of ancient Greek tragedy. Inasmuch as no Greek examples had survived, they based their theories on literary accounts, suggesting that Greek dramas had been sung in a style halfway between singing and speech. The Camerata wanted their new style to resemble the intonations and rhythms of speech, and so the new style was called *recitative* ("recited").

The operas themselves grew out of late fifteenth-century madrigals. Many of these madrigals, some called "madrigal comedies" and some called *intermedi*, were written to be performed between the acts of theatre productions. They were fairly dramatic, and included pastoral scenes, narrative reflections, and amorous adventures. They gave rise to a new style of solo singing, as opposed to ensemble singing. In 1600, an Italian singer–composer, Jacopo Peri (YAH-koh-poh PAY-ree; 1561–1633), took a contemporary pastoral drama, *Eurydice* (yoo-RID-i-see) and set it to music. Peri's work is the first surviving opera. It was sparely scored, and consisted primarily of recitative, or sung monologue reflecting the pitches and rhythms of speech, over a slow-moving bass. Peri's opera, however, was weak, both musically and theatrically.

It was Claudio Monteverdi (mohn-tay-VAIR-dee) who took a firmer hand to the new art form. In *Orfeo* (OHR-fay-oh; 1607), he expanded the same mythological subject matter, the story of Orpheus and Eurydice, into a full, five-act structure—five acts were considered classically "correct"—and gave it richer, more substantial music. The emotional effect was consequently much stronger. The mood swung widely through contrasting passages of louds and softs. (In baroque music, quick shifts in volume, speed, and expression are the musical equivalents of the strong contrasts in light and shade in baroque painting and sculpture). Monteverdi added solos, duets, ensemble singing and dances. *Orfeo*'s melodic lines were highly embellished and ornamental. The orchestra consisted of approximately forty instruments, including brass, woodwind, strings, and CONTINUO. The grandiose scenic designs of the great Bibiena family, one of which appears in Figure **13.32**, suggests the spectacular staging of this and other baroque operas. Monteverdi's innovation was the dramatic prototype of

what we know today, and he is rightly called the "father of opera."

By the second half of the seventeenth century, opera had become an important art form, especially in Italy, but also in France, England, and Germany. A French national opera was established under the patronage of Louis XIV. French opera included colorful and rich ballet and cultivated strong literary qualities using the dramatic talents of playwrights such as Corneille and Racine, of whom we will speak momentarily. In England, the court masques of the late sixteenth century led to fledgling opera during the suspension of the monarchy, when Cromwell's zealots shut down the theatres. Indeed, English opera probably owed more to a desire to circumvent the prohibition of stage plays than anything else. In Germany, a strong Italian influence spurred on opera in the courts. This German tradition led to one of the most astonishing eras in opera, during the mid-nineteenth century.

Another important form of baroque music, ORATORIO, is discussed in the Focal Point section at the end of the chapter.

FRENCH NEOCLASSICAL THEATRE

Between the years 1550 and 1720, France developed a significant theatrical tradition that scholars have called

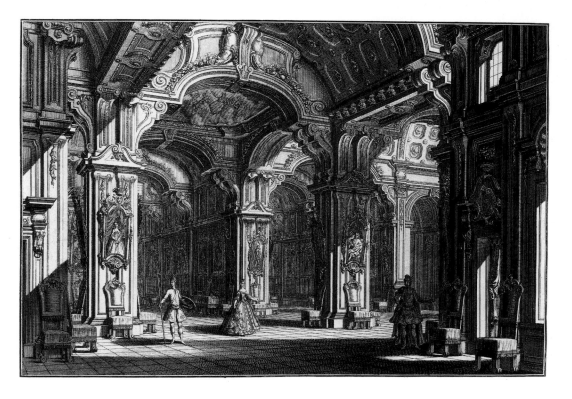

13.32 Giuseppe Galli de Bibiena, design for an opera, 1719. Contemporary engraving. Metropolitan Museum of Art, New York (The Elisha Whittelsey Collection, The Elisha Whittelsey Fund, 1951).

"French neoclassicism." (Remember that labels are sometimes confusing. French neoclassicism in the theatre is related, especially in its later years, to the baroque style in music and visual art. The labels "classicism" and "neoclassicism" also describe later developments in both music and the visual arts, and it is important to keep all this straight.)

We have already noted in the previous chapter the support that Francis I gave to Renaissance ideas. Despite this, French theatre remained essentially medieval until after he died in 1547. In 1548, however, a strange combination of Protestant and Catholic attitudes resulted in the legal suppression of all religious drama. Freed from its religious competition, secular drama turned to Renaissance classicism. The French also rediscovered Sophocles, Euripides, Aristophanes, and Menander, and this return to the ancients fostered specific rules for "acceptable" drama. In the French theatre, plays had to fit a structural and spatial mold called, after Aristotle's formula, "the Unities." The spirit of classical drama was now lost as its substance was forced into artificial confines of time and space. The academies found no play acceptable unless it conformed to two specific rules: the action had to occur in a single location and to encompass no more than twenty-four hours. Had French antiquarians studied classical Greek dramas, of course, they would have discovered many violations of the Unities. Perhaps as a result of this rulemaking, little French tragedy of consequence was written during the period of England's great dramatic achievement. But, as in Italy and England, this era was rich in scenic invention and extravagant productions.

Pierre Corneille (kohr-NAY; 1606–84) managed to conform somewhat to these arbitrary and misinterpreted conventions and yet write great plays. In 1635 he produced a masterpiece, *Le Cid* (luh SEED). His characterizations were original, his themes were grand and heroic, and his language was richly poetic. However, he violated the Unities, and Cardinal Richelieu, France's official arbiter of taste, and the subservient Académie Française, condemned the play. Corneille continued to write, and his late work served as a vehicle for imported Italian scenery and stage machinery. The form and quality of Corneille's tragedies strongly influenced a second important playwright of this era, Jean Racine (rah-SEEN; 1639–99). *Phèdre* (FED-ruh), perhaps his best work, illustrates the tragic intensity, powerful but controlled emotion, compressed poetry, subtle psychology, and carefully developed plots that mark the best examples of French neoclassical drama.

Molière (1622–73) provided a comic counterpoint to the great achievements of the French tragedians. Early in his career he joined a professional company, a family of actors named Béjart. His earliest productions took place in indoor tennis courts, whose size and shape made them easily adaptable to theatre (hence the term "tennis-court theatre"). For over thirteen years, Molière toured France with the Béjarts (bay-ZHAHR), as an actor and manager, until a crucial appearance before Louis XIV launched his career as a playwright.

Tartuffe (see the Introduction), *The Misanthrope*, and *The Bourgeois Gentleman* brought new esteem to French comedy. Highly regarded comedy is rare in the history of the theatre. Molière's instinct for penetrating human psychology, fast-paced action, crisp language, and gentle but effective mockery of human foibles earned him a foremost place in theatre history. Not only were Molière's comedies dramatic masterpieces, but they also stood up to the potentially overpowering baroque scenic conventions of Louis XIV's theatre at Versailles. His plays challenged the painted backgrounds and elaborate machinery of Italian scene designers and emerged triumphant.

DANCE

During the reign of Henry IV (1589–1610), over eighty ballets were performed at the French court. In a ballet in 1615, "30 genii, suspended in the air, heralded the coming of Minerva, the Queen of Spain. . . . Forty persons were on the stage at once, 30 high in the air, and six suspended in mid-air; all of these dancing and singing at the same time."[1] Later, under Louis XIII, a fairly typical ballet of the period, the *Mountain Ballet*, had five great allegorical mountains on stage: the Windy, the Resounding, the Luminous, the Shadowy, and the Alps. A character, Fame,

13.33 Jean-Baptiste Lully (1632–87), costume designs for the Ballet de Cour from *Oeuvres Complètes*. Contemporary sepia drawing. The New York Public Library.

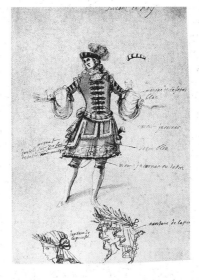
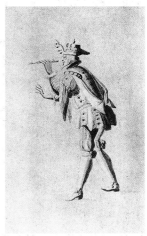

disguised as an old woman, explained the story, and the "quadrilles of dancers," in flesh-colored costumes with windmills on their heads (representing the winds), competed with other allegorical characters for the "Field of Glory." Such work typically consisted of a series of dances dramatizing a common theme.

By the late seventeenth century, baroque art was consolidated in the court of Louis XIV (Fig. **13.33**). A great patron of painting, sculpture, theatre, and architecture, Louis also brought ballet into full participation in the splendor of the era. An avid dancer, Louis studied for over twenty years with the dancing master Pierre Beauchamps (boh-SHAHMP), who is credited with inventing the basic dance positions of classical ballet. Louis's title, *Le Roi Soleil* or the "Sun King," certainly indicates his behavior and his political philosophy, but it actually derived from his favorite childhood role, that of Apollo the sun-god in *Le Ballet de la Nuit*, which he danced at the age of fourteen. Mazarin (MA-zah-rehn), Louis's first minister, exploited this splendid dance role to promote the young monarch.

Louis employed a team of professional artists to produce ballet and opera at court, and the playwright Molière was active in these grand collaborative efforts. Usually the plots for French ballets came from classical mythology and the works themselves were a series of verses, music, and dance. The style of dancing, at least in these works, appears to have been fairly simple and controlled. Gestures were symmetrical and harmonious. The theatrical trappings were opulent. The emotionality of the baroque style precludes neither formality nor restraint. One must also bear in mind that the costume of the era included elaborate wigs. Any movements that threatened to knock one's wig askew would, after all, have been impractical and awkward.

Ballet became formally institutionalized when Louis XIV founded the Académie Royale de Danse in 1661. Thirteen dancing masters were appointed to the Académie to "reestablish the art in its perfections." Ten years later, the Académie Royale de Danse was merged with a newly established Académie Royale de Musique. Both schools were given the use of the theatre of the Palais Royal, which had been occupied by Molière's company. Its proscenium stage altered forever the aesthetic relationship of ballet and its audience. Choreography had to be designed for an audience on one side only. Such designs focused on the "open"

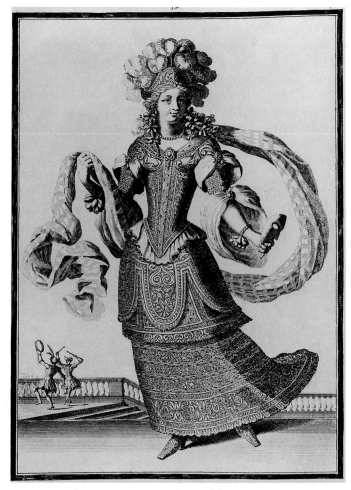

13.34 Jean Louis Bérain (1638–1711), *Dame en habit de ballet.* Contemporary engraving. The New York Public Library.

position, and that is still basic to formal ballet choreography today.

Establishment of the Royal Academy of Dance led to prescribed "rules" for positions and movements. It also led to the full art form, in which women took the stage as professional ballerinas for the first time in 1681 (Fig. **13.34**). The stage of the Palais Royal, which did not allow access to the auditorium, placed the final barricade between the professional artist and the "noble amateur" of the previous eras. As the baroque era came to a close in the early eighteenth century, the foundations of ballet as a formal art were firmly in place.

Focal Point

English Baroque—Seventeenth-Century London

Our Focal Point discussion takes us again to England. A new dynasty of rulers has taken over, and things are in turmoil. Nonetheless, some important things take place, not the least of which is a new English Bible, the King James Version. It is a time of great art and artists: Sir Christopher Wren and George Frederick Handel, for example. We choose it because all the components of baroque art were there, and because its baroque examples are closer to us than any other representations: Christian or not, most people have heard Handel's *Messiah* or some portion thereof, and almost everybody knows about the King James Bible, whether or not they have ever read it. The favorite foreign city for Americans is London, and every visitor to London has at least seen one Wren building, probably St Paul's Cathedral.

The year 1603 marked the change of a dynasty: Elizabeth I had died, leaving no heirs to maintain the Tudor line, and her successor was James I of the Stuart line. James was the king of Scotland and son of Mary, Queen of Scots. He was also the patron of the King James version of the Bible. Nonetheless, his explicit absolutism and the financial disorder he created exasperated both the country gentry and the city bourgeoisie, who held power in the House of Commons ("God's Elect"), and in London the word "reform" was on everyone's lips. However, when James died in 1625, the succession went to the next Stuart, Charles I. Absolutist in the French fashion, Charles did nothing to lessen the cries for reform, and the pressure mounted, as Parliament demanded a share in decision-making. The Petition of Right was punished by eleven

13.35 Christopher Wren, garden façade of Hampton Court Palace, UK, c. 1690.

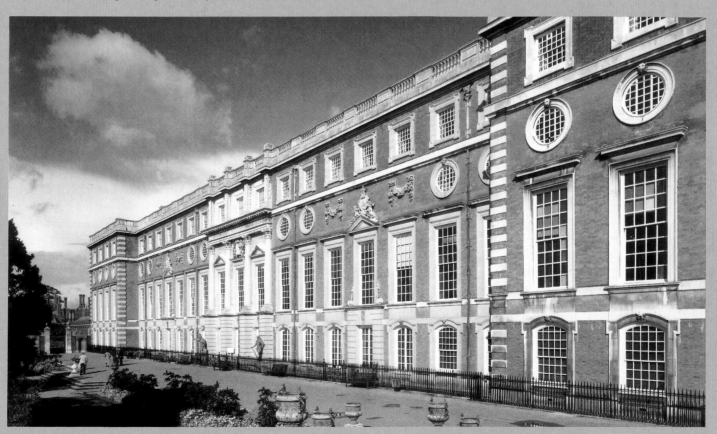

Sir Christopher Wren (1632–1723)

Sir Christopher Wren was a child prodigy in mathematics and natural science. By the time he was twenty-one, he had earned a master's degree from Oxford and spent three years studying and researching astronomy. He spent the years from 1657 to 1673 as professor of astronomy, first at Gresham College, London, and then at Oxford.

His first architectural designs came in 1663, when he designed the chapel at Pembroke College, Cambridge, and the Sheldonian Theatre, Oxford. In the same year, he was appointed to advise on the repair of old St Paul's Cathedral (see Masterwork, p. 420). Essentially self-taught as an architect, he used a nine-month visit to France in 1665–6 as a sabbatical for future architectural preparation. The Great Fire of London in 1666 left not only St Paul's Cathedral available for his talents but also destroyed three-fourths of London, and he responded to the challenge with an extensive plan for rebuilding the City—that is, the central, one-square-mile heart of contemporary London. He was appointed as surveyor-general of works for the City, and, although his plan for rebuilding the City was not accepted, he was put in charge of all royal and governmental building in England. He either drew up or authorized plans for rebuilding fifty-two London churches. The major project was, of course, the rebuilding of St Paul's Cathedral, from 1673 to 1710. He also designed the palaces at Winchester and Kensington and oversaw the rebuilding of Hampton Court (see Fig. **13.35**). His style finds its roots in the Italian Renaissance and reflects the classical restraint that characterizes English baroque style and separates it from the more flamboyant baroque of the European continent.

Knighted in 1673, Wren also served as a member of Parliament in 1685–7 and 1701–2.

---

years of tyranny in which both crown and Anglican clergy joined forces. The king's failure to extend Anglicanism to Calvinist Scotland unleashed revolution in 1640, and the key word was now not "reform" but "revolt." Under great financial pressure, the king accepted the remonstrances of parliament, which voted to "extirpate" (pull up by the roots) the bishops and the courts. In Ulster, the Catholics revolted, and the violation of the immunity of the Commons provoked civil war. When the New Model Army of the independent parliamentarian Cromwell had crushed the Royalists in 1645, freedom seemed won. Parliament judged the King and condemned him to death for having violated the political contract. A republic was proclaimed and affirmed the personal power of the Lord Protector of the Commonwealth—that is Oliver Cromwell—but when he died in 1558, there was turmoil for two years, and Parliament invited the executed king's son, Charles II, to return from exile. The monarchy was reinstituted—in the Restoration—in 1660.

In a framework of economic vitality, with both papists and dissidents removed, the Restoration witnessed an exchange of power between the Whig and Tory parties. When Charles II died, he was succeeded by his brother, James II, a Catholic. James had apparently learned little from the traumas of his father, and his absolutist three-year reign ended in his exile in 1688 in what the English call the Glorious Revolution. For the next monarch, Parliament turned to James' daughter Mary, who with her husband, the stadholder of Holland, William of Orange, were invited to be crowned monarchs on the basis of a contract by which the king was to be controlled "in Parliament." Two years later, John Locke produced his *Treatises of Government* (see p. 389), justifying the events of 1688.

English Baroque Architecture

The baroque influence of the court of Louis XIV came to England with the Restoration of Charles II. Over the next fifty years, London witnessed numerous significant building projects directed by its most notable architect, Christopher Wren (rehn; 1632–1723). Two of these projects, St Paul's Cathedral and Hampton Court, illustrate the intricate but restrained complexity of English baroque style. The impact of Wren's genius, obvious in his designs, is attested to in an inscription in St Paul's: "If you seek a monument, look around you." On a smaller scale than St Paul's but equally expressive of the English baroque is Wren's garden façade for Hampton Court Palace (Fig. **13.35**). His additions to this Tudor building, which was built by Cardinal Wolsey (WOHL-zee) in the sixteenth century, were intended to make it a rival of Louis XIV's

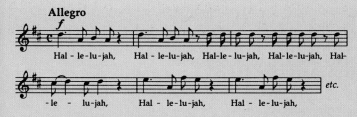

13.36 G.F. Handel, *Hallelujah Chorus.*

Palace of Versailles. In comparing the two, we conclude that the English approach to the style yields a more restrained result. The seemingly straightforward overall design of this façade, which was commissioned in 1689, during the reign of William and Mary, is actually a sophisticated interrelationship of merging patterns and details. The lines are clean, and the silhouette lacks the visual interruption of statuary present in the Versailles palace. Line, repetition, and balance in this façade not only create a pleasing impression, they also form a perceptual exercise. Wren chose red brick to harmonize with the original palace, while contrasting dressed stone emphasizes the central features of the façade and creates richness and variety. Wren's use of circular windows was unusual—it probably reflects French influence.

English Baroque Music

George Frederick Handel

A major development in seventeenth-century music was the *oratorio*, which combined a sacred subject with a narrative poetic text. Like the opera, it was broad in scale, highly dramatic, and used soloists to portray specific characters. Like the cantata, it was designed for concert performances, without scenery or costume.

Oratorio began in Italy in the early seventeenth century, but all accomplishments pale in comparison with the works of the greatest master of the oratorio, George Frederick Handel (HAHN-duhl; 1685–1759). Although Handel was German by birth, he lived much of his life in England and wrote his oratorios in English. His works continue to enjoy wide popularity, and each year his *Messiah* has thousands of performances around the world.

Most of Handel's oratorios are highly dramatic in structure, containing exposition, conflict or complication, and *dénouement* (day-noo-MAWN) or resolution sections. All but two, *Israel in Egypt* and *Messiah*, could be staged in full operatic tradition. The most popular of all oratorios, Handel's *Messiah*, was written in 1741, in twenty-four days. The work is divided into three parts: the birth of Jesus; Jesus' death and resurrection; and the redemption of humanity. The music comprises an overture, choruses,

recitatives, and arias, and is written for small orchestra, chorus, and soloists. The choruses provide some of the world's best-loved music, including the famous *Hallelujah Chorus* (CD Track 10).

The *Hallelujah Chorus* comprises the climax of the second part (Fig. **13.36**). The text proclaims a victorious Lord, whose host is an army with banners. Handel creates infinite variety by sudden changes of texture among monophony, polyphony, and homophony. Words and phrases are repeated over and over again. In unison the voices and instruments proclaim, "For the Lord God Omnipotent reigneth." Polyphony marks the repeated exclamations of "Hallelujah" and yields to homophony in the hymn-like *The kingdom of this world*.

Henry Purcell

Perhaps the greatest English composer, Henry Purcell (c. 1659–95) was born in London. His father was one of King Charles II's household musicians. At twenty, Henry Purcell became organist at Westminster Abbey. His compositions run the gamut of types required by all his appointments: orchestral suites and dances, chamber music for royal enjoyment, odes and other ceremonial pieces for state occasions, anthems and other works for the Church. His great love, however, was theatre. During Cromwell's Commonwealth government, all the London theatres were closed. When Charles II took the throne an explosion of theatre works occurred. Dozens of new plays and operas were performed each year. In the last fifteen years of his life (he died at age thirty-six), Purcell wrote a dozen large-scale music-theatre works, incidental music for more than forty plays, and hundreds of individual songs and dances. His opera *Dido and Aeneas* (1689), based on the *Aeneid* of Vergil (see p. 134), is quite different from the recitative-and-aria Italian operas of the time. It is shorter, has deeper characterizations, very breezy choruses, and a spectacular "Sorceress Scene."

English Baroque Theatre

The scenic simplicity of Elizabethan theatre—all acting was done in front of an unchanging architectural façade—gave way to the opulent spectaculars of English court masques (mahsks) during the reign of Charles I in the early years of the seventeenth century. Essentially, the court masque was a game for the nobility, an indoor extravagance which had developed earlier in the sixteenth century, probably influenced by its visually resplendent cousins in Italy. Short on literary merit, the English masque was nevertheless a dramatic spectacle that reflected monarchial splendor.

Banqueting halls of palaces were often redesigned to accommodate the scenic complexities and large stages of the masques. These stages allowed manipulation of

MASTERWORK

Wren—St Paul's Cathedral

Christopher Wren was invited to restore old St Paul's Cathedral, a Gothic structure to which Wren intended to affix a mighty dome, before the Great Fire of London. After the fire, however, only a small part of the nave remained, and even Wren's genius could not save the old church. Wren, who was surveyor-general of London and responsible for the cathedral as well as the king's palaces and other government properties, set about the task of designing a new St Paul's (Figs. **13.37**, **13.38**, and **13.39**).

His first plan was rejected outright by the authorities as too untraditional. For example, it had no aisles to the choir, or eastern arm, and no proper nave. Wren had attempted in this first design to come up with a cathedral which would be inexpensive and yet handsome, but the authorities insisted that the country's prestige was at stake and no expense should be spared. A second, more ambitious design followed a classical pattern, crowned with a huge dome. Charles II approved this plan but the commissioners did not. A third design barely gained their approval. Here Wren used the traditional Latin cross plan, with the nave longer than the choir, two short transepts, and a dome and spire atop the crossing (Fig. **13.37**). Once approved, with allowances for "modifications," the entire project ground to a halt because of the difficulty of demolishing the pillars of the old church. After unsuccessful attempts to blast them down with gunpowder, Wren finally resorted to the battering ram technique used against castles in the Middle Ages. After a day of "relentless battering," the old church succumbed, and in November 1673 work began on the new building.

The new cathedral has an overall length of 515 feet (157 meters) and a width of 248 feet (76 meters). Its dome measures 112 feet (34 meters) in diameter and stands 365 feet (111 meters) tall at the top of the cross. The lantern and cross alone weigh 700 tons while the dome and its superstructure weigh 64,000 tons. Like the architects of the Pantheon and St Peter's in Rome, Wren faced seemingly endless problems with supporting the tremendous load of the dome. His solution was ingenious: he constructed the dome of nothing more than a timber shell covered in lead, supported by a brick cone. This lightened the weight of the dome to a fraction of what it would have been and allowed Wren to create a wonderful silhouette on the outside, while an inner dome gave the correct proportion to the interior (Fig. **13.39**). It was a solution never before used.

Renaissance geometric design and Greek and Roman detail all mark the cathedral. The drum of the dome echoes Bramante's Tempietto (see Fig. **11.25**) in the arrangement of its columns, and reflects Michelangelo's St Peter's in its verticality. The exterior façade has a subtle elegance, with ornate detail but an absence of overstatement or clutter. Yet, at the same time, the scale of the dome and of the building as a whole is overpowering. The many imitations of Wren's design in Europe and the United States attest to its genius. The interior, as in all of Wren's designs, emphasizes linear, structural elements such as arches, frames, and circles. Somewhat cold in comparison with baroque churches of the continent, St Paul's Anglican heritage is clear in its refusal of extensive ornamentation and gilding. The nave has a strong sense of movement that draws the worshipper forward toward the high altar. At the very center of the cathedral (the Crossing) the eye rises to the underside of the great dome, which is decorated with monochrome paintings by Sir James Thornhill depicting incidents in the life of St Paul. Wren opposed the decision to paint the dome. He wanted it decorated with brilliant mosaic like St Peter's in Rome.

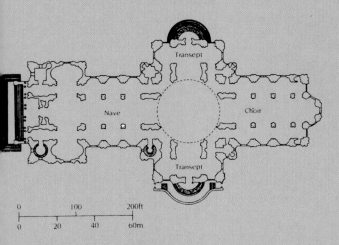

13.37 Plan of St Paul's Cathedral, London.

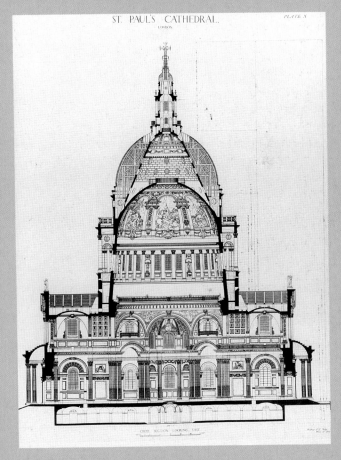

13.39 Christopher Wren, St Paul's Cathedral, London, 1675–1710. Cross-section looking east.

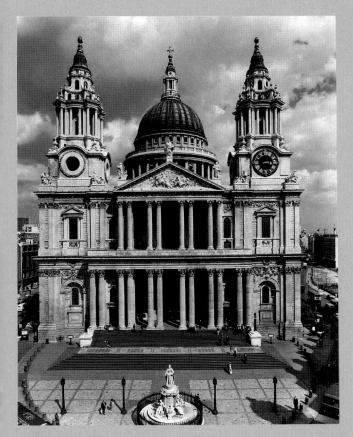

13.38 Christopher Wren, St Paul's Cathedral, London, 1675–1710. Façade.

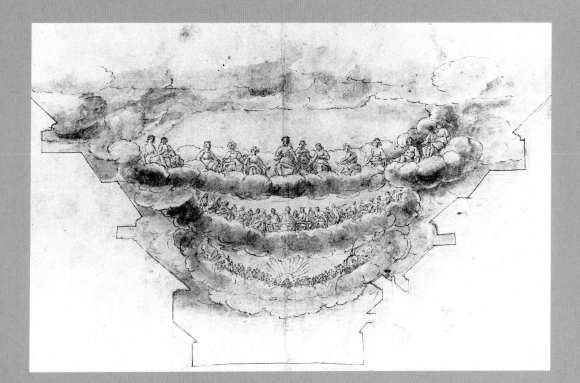

13.40 Inigo Jones, "The Whole Heaven" in *Salmacida Spolia*, 1640. Collection of the Duke of Devonshire, Chatsworth, UK.

scenery from below. The actors played on a protruding area in front of (as opposed to amid) the drops and wings (a type of staging called forestage-façade). The English court masque had direct links with the scenic style of Palladio and Serlio in Italy. The architect Inigo Jones (1573–1652) was the most influential English stage designer of the time, and he freely imitated Italian perspective, using elaborate stage machines and effects (Fig. **13.40**).

This "baroque-like" style in English theatre ended when Cromwell's zealots overthrew the monarchy in 1642. Theatres were closed and productions forbidden until the Restoration of Charles II in 1660. (Opera provided a handsome substitute, however, as we noted.) When Charles returned from exile in France, he brought with him the continental style current in the French court. One result was a sophisticated comedy of manners known as "Restoration comedy," which focused on the adventures of "people of quality" and reflected their intrigues, manners, and idiosyncratic dispositions. The verbal wit of this style of comedy often satirized the morality of the bourgeoisie.

CHAPTER REVIEW

Critical Thought

When we listen to a musical piece by J. S. Bach, we hear exactly what it means to be "baroque." It seems as if the composer uses more notes per second than we have ever heard before. If he wants to go from one tone to another, he takes five tones to get there—Mozart, whom we will meet in the next chapter, would take only one—but that is precisely what baroque style is all about: it is big, it is ornate, and it is emotional, cramming everything possible into the smallest possible space. Yet at the same time, it does so in an extremely rational way—it is emotional, but it is not irrational—which takes us back to one of the principles we noted briefly at the beginning of the chapter, and that is, systematic rationalism. It sounds almost like a contradiction to assert that something can be intensely emotional and free, yet also be controlled and rational. The ornately decorous details of baroque art and music fit within a complex but rational organization. It is all carefully thought out—that is, systematic—and the rational organization is what allows the emotional content to mean something to us. If it were all emotion, we would get lost, because the work would be chaotic and unable to communicate.

Summary

After reading this chapter, you should be able to:

- Understand and differentiate between the theories and discoveries of Francis Bacon, Galileo, Kepler, Descartes, and Isaac Newton.
- Describe and contrast the philosophies of Thomas Hobbes and John Locke, and contrast Locke and Descartes on the nature of knowledge of truth.
- Relate the Counter-Reformation, Council of Trent, religious upheaval, and the rise of absolutism in Europe.
- Characterize baroque art, sculpture, and architecture by defining major divisions such as "aristocratic baroque" and identifying major artists, architects, and their works.
- Discuss baroque music, theatre, and dance, including major forms, composers, playwrights, and performance conditions.
- Apply the elements and principles of composition to analyze and compare works of art and architecture illustrated in this chapter.

CHAPTER FOURTEEN

The Enlightenment

OUTLINE

THE ENLIGHTENMENT
Technology
  TECHNOLOGY: James Watt and the
    Steam Engine
Philosophy
The Philosophes
  PROFILE: Voltaire
Economics and Politics
  PROFILE: Maria Theresa
Aesthetics and Classicism

**THE VISUAL ARTS AND
ARCHITECTURE**
Rococo Style
Humanitarianism and Hogarth
Landscape and Portraiture
Genre
Neoclassicism
  MASTERWORK: David—*The Oath of
    the Horatii*

LITERATURE
Rococo
Pamphlets and Essays
Genre
The Pre-Romantics

MUSIC
Pre-Classical
Expressive Style
Classical Style

THEATRE
Britain
America
  OUR DYNAMIC WORLD: Japanese
    Kabuki Theatre
France

DANCE

FOCAL POINT: THE ENLIGHTENED
DESPOT—FREDERICK THE GREAT

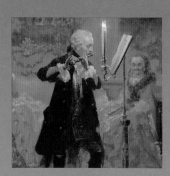

VIEW

SWINGING BETWEEN TWO POLES

The eighteenth century represents the insurgence of the common people. Government, social policy, intellectual matters, and the arts took the masses into account, which had not previously been the case. Aristocrats fell from favor, and a new social fabric and way of looking at life emerged with the new republics of Europe and America. Even classical music turned toward mass audiences.
Something like modern society emerged.
We now have come far enough in our journey to recognize a trend—not only social but artistic as well. The social, to which we alluded in the previous paragraph, swung between the poles of monarchial—if beneficent—absolutism and rudimentary democracy (between the ideas of Locke and Hobbes discussed in the last chapter); the artistic swung between classicism and anti-classicism. At one pole, classicism, form, and content lean toward intellectual restraint and careful order, and at the other pole, toward emotionalism: "form versus feeling" as it has been described. The pendulum now swings toward classicism, away from the anti-classicism of the baroque. Very soon, it will reverse once more.

KEY TERMS

Some of the terms and concepts we will encounter in this chapter include the following:

Enlightenment, a faith in science, in human rights arising from natural law, in human reason, and progress.

Enlightened despotism, rule by an "absolute" monarch who holds "enlightened" views regarding his or her relationship to his or her subjects.

Philosophes, popularizers who culled thought from great books and translated it into simple terms.

Rococo style, a decorous and sensitive style in the arts.

Genre is a term usually meaning "type," but in the eighteenth century it refers to works of art dealing with mundane subjects.

Classical style, in music refers to the works and style of Mozart and Haydn, particularly.

Pre-Romantic style, a style in literature referring to the works of Henry Fielding, Jean-Jacques Rousseau, Goethe, and others who anticipated the anti-classical literary style of the next century.

Above Detail of Fig. **14.36**.

14.1 Jean-Honoré Fragonard, *The Swing*, c. 1768–9. Oil on canvas, 32 × 25¹/₂ ins (83 × 66 cm). Wallace Collection, London.

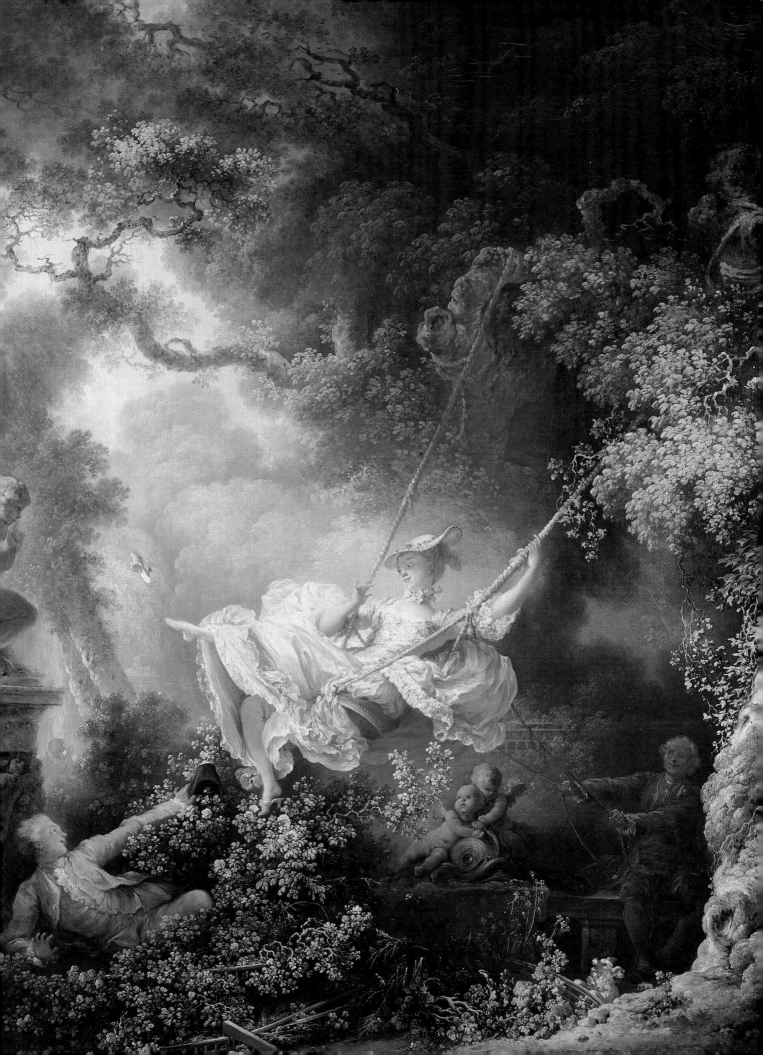

THE ENLIGHTENMENT

The eighteenth century has often been called the "Age of Enlightenment," but, as we noted in Chapter 13, century marks are arbitrary boundaries that tell us very little about history or art. Styles, philosophies, and politics come and go for a variety of reasons. We have already pushed halfway through the eighteenth century in some areas, without encountering any natural barriers—J.S. Bach, for example, lived and worked until 1750. The best we can say, then, is that eighteenth-century enlightenment grew out of various seventeenth-century ideas that fell on more or less fertile soil at different times in different places.

Seventeenth- and eighteenth-century thought held that people were rational beings in a universe governed by some systematic natural law. Some believed that law to be an extension of God's law. Others held that natural law stood by itself. Natural law was extended to include international law, and accords were formulated in which sover-eign nations, bound by no higher authority, could work together for a common good.

Faith in science, in human rights arising from the natural law, in human reason, and in progress, were touch-stones of eighteenth-century thought. The idea of *progress* was based on the assumption that the conditions of life could only improve with time and that each generation made life even better for those following. Some scholars—the "ancients"—held that the works of the Greeks and Romans had never been surpassed. Others—the "moderns"—held that science, art, literature, and the inventions of their own age were better since they were built upon the achievements of their predecessors.

Enlightenment, reason, and progress are secular ideas, and the age became increasingly secular. Politics and business superseded religion, wresting leadership away from the Church, of whatever denomination. Toleration increased and persecution and the imposition of corporal punishment for religious, political, or criminal offenses became less common as the era progressed.

Timeline 14.1 The Enlightenment.

	GENERAL EVENTS	LITERATURE & PHILOSOPHY	VISUAL ART & ARCHITECTURE	PERFORMING ARTS
1700				
		Alexander Pope	Watteau (14.5)	Beginning of American theatre
	Humanitarianism		de Cuvilliès (14.10)	Couperin
1725				
	Herculaneum excavated	Swift	Hogarth (14.11, 14.12)	
	Frederick the Great		Chardin (14.15)	
	Maria Theresa of Austria		Pesne (14.35)	Gay
	War of Austrian Succession	Fielding	Krohne (14.9)	Camargo
	Pompeii excavated		von Knobelsdorff (14.37, 14.38, 14.40)	
1750				
	Encyclopédie published	Johnson	Boucher (14.6)	Garrick
	Industrial Revolution begins	Rousseau		
		Hume		
		Kant		
		Diderot		
		Voltaire		
	George III of England	Baumgarten		C.P.E. Bach
		Goldsmith	Fragonard (14.1)	
	Watt's steam engine	Winckelmann		
		Herder		
1775				
	American Revolution	Schiller	Clodion (14.8)	
	First iron bridge	Adam Smith	Houdon (14.16, 14.17)	
	Louis XVI	Paine	Falconet (14.7)	Beaumarchais
	French Revolution	Wollstonecraft	Gainsborough (14.13, 14.14)	Haydn
		Goethe	David (14.19, 14.20)	Mozart
1800				
			Jefferson (14.21, 14.22)	Beethoven
			Canova (14.18)	

TECHNOLOGY: PUTTING DISCOVERY TO WORK

James Watt and the Steam Engine

Strictly speaking, the work of James Watt (1736–1819) on the steam engine was more a critical revision and study of an existing machine than a new composition. However, his scientific and critical innovations were so significant that science views it as a strategic invention. Watt's specific contribution lay in the concept of a separate condensing chamber for an engine invented by Thomas Newcomen and the problem of heat loss through the cooling and heating of the cylinder. The primary concept of a condensing chamber came to Watt on his regular Sunday walk. He saw that steam was an elastic body, which would rush into a vacuum, and if there were a connection between the cylinder and an exhausting vehicle, the steam would rush into it and be condensed without cooling the cylinder. He began testing his possible solution to the problem the next day with the apparatus shown in Figure **14.2**. His model proved highly efficient and demonstrated the soundness of the fundamental principles.

Watt worked rapidly from that point, refining his basic design in larger models, until he had developed a steam engine in the accurate sense of the word, and the result became a well-designed machine based on a sound scientific perception of the properties of steam. Watt's concept of the engine quickly carried him beyond the limits of current facilities for machine building, and many of the parts he required presented problems that no existing ironmakers could solve. Consequently, the attempt to build a working steam engine was postponed until after Watt secured a patent for it in 1769. Even with financial assistance, however, Watt was unable to pay for the construction of the engine and he was forced into bankruptcy.

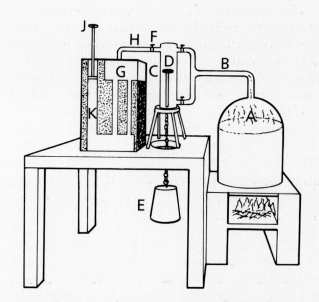

14.2 James Watt's experimental condensing chamber. Water heated in a closed container (A) produced steam, which traveled through tubes (B and H) into chambers (C and K), moderated by valves (F), to create force to move pistons (D and J) and raise weight E.

The rapid increase in scientific discovery that followed Newton's work resulted in the development of new disciplines. Physics, astronomy, and mathematics remained primary, but fragmented inquiry was replaced by quiet categorizing. The vast body of information gathered during the late Renaissance period needed codification. The new sciences of mineralogy, botany, and zoology developed. First came classification of fossils, then classification of rocks, minerals, and plants. Carolus Linnaeus, the botanist, and Georges Buffon, the zoologist, were pioneers in their fields. Antoine Lavoisier correctly explained the chemical process of combustion. In addition, he isolated hydrogen and oxygen as the two component elements of water, and he also postulated that although matter may alter its state, its mass always remains the same.

Technology

Science went hand in hand with technology. Telescopes and microscopes were improved. The barometer and the thermometer were invented, as were the air pump and the steam engine. By 1796, James Watt had patented a steam engine reliable enough to drive a machine. The invention of the steam engine gave rise to other machines, and paved the way for the Industrial Revolution at the end of the century.

The use of coal fuel in place of charcoal to smelt iron revolutionized metallurgy in the early eighteenth century. Strong coke fuel tremendously increased the capacity of blast furnaces. Coke-smelted iron initially proved to be more impure than charcoal-smelted iron, but the puddling furnace solved that problem. Around 1740 Benjamin

Huntsman invented the crucible melting and casting process. Using hard coke as fuel achieved higher temperatures, and a greater blast could be gained using tall chimneys instead of bellows. A new understanding of the properties of oxygen and chemical reagents created further advances. These improvements in metallurgy made possible the later use of iron and steel as structural elements, first in bridges and later in buildings. They also enhanced the development of new machinery for the manufacture of yet other machinery, tools, and finely constructed hardware and instruments.

Scientific and medical inquiry in the seventeenth and eighteenth centuries created a demand for precise instruments. It is important to note here that new technology resulted from the demand created by inquiry, and not the other way around. A need for greater precision in observation and measurement led to the development of improved surveying, astronomical, and navigation instruments, and the thermometer and the barometer were refined. Advances were also made in the skills and materials used in the manufacture of instruments, resulting in greater specialization and the creation of craft shops. These included advances in making optical glass, which, in turn, led to the development of better lenses for use in telescopes and compound microscopes.

Improvements in precision tooling affected clockmaking and tools such as the lathe. The introduction of cams and templates allowed even greater accuracy and intricacy in production. An instrument called the dividing engine made it possible to graduate a circle by mechanical means, and to graduate scales on surveying and navigational instruments accurately.

The field of engineering in the seventeenth and eighteenth centuries saw advances in hydraulics, road building, and bridge construction. The control of water flow in canals was aided by the development of an extremely accurate bubble-tube leveling device. The surveyor's level with a telescopic sight was another productive invention. Bridge building was improved by modifications to the construction of pier foundations, and the first iron bridge was erected at Coalbrookdale, England, in 1779.

The introduction of power machinery revolutionized the English textile industry in the late eighteenth century, but the steam engine was undoubtedly the most significant invention of the period. In replacing human, animal, wind, and water power with machine power, it changed the course of history. The first full-scale steam engine had been developed in England in 1699, and early steam engines were used to drain mine shafts. By the mid-eighteenth century, some wealthy people were using steam engines to pump domestic water supplies, but James Watt's invention of the separate condenser in 1769 brought steam engines to new levels of practicality and productivity. Further

modifications primed the engine for its role as cornerstone of the Industrial Revolution. In 1800, when the patent for Watt's engine expired, new high-pressure steam engines were applied to a variety of tasks, most notably in the first successful steam locomotive in 1804. By 1820, the steam engine could generate an estimated 1,000 horsepower, and the Industrial Revolution was at hand.

Philosophy

To understand the philosophy of the eighteenth century, we must retrace our steps to the Middle Ages. In the medieval period, philosophy was closely linked to theology. As we noted in the last chapter, Descartes (1596–1650) had peeled philosophy away from theology and allied it with the natural sciences and mathematics. Reason was supreme, and Descartes called for rejection of all that could not be proved. Descartes's philosophy is known as "Cartesianism," and it is based on the contention that human reason can solve every problem that the mind can entertain.

We have also seen how John Locke (1632–1704) challenged the Cartesian idea that knowledge stemmed from the intellect. Locke argued that knowledge derives first from the senses. He redirected philosophical energies from the vast metaphysical systems of pure rationalism to a more practical, earthbound sphere. Locke's philosophy was grounded in reason, but because he stressed sensations and experience as the primary sources of knowledge, he is known as a "sensualist" or an "empiricist."

Empiricism became the predominant philosophy of the late eighteenth century, although it was not without its critics. Locke's approach formed the basis for the later philosophical thought of Hume (hyoom) and Kant (kahnt). David Hume (1711–76), a Scotsman, differed from Locke in his assertions that the mind is incapable of building up knowledge from sensations, and that the world we live in consists only of probabilities. Hume maintained that not only philosophy, but also natural science, existed in a cloud of doubt. Mathematics was the only true and valid science.

Hume was not the only skeptic of the age, and his philosophy might have been disregarded, were it not for the German philosopher Immanuel Kant (1724–1804). Kant's major contribution to late eighteenth-century thought was his distinction between science and philosophy and his attribution to each of separate functions and techniques. For Kant, science was concerned with the phenomenal world, or the world of appearances, which it describes by general propositions and laws. Science must not go beyond the world of appearances to concern itself with the reality beyond. That reality, the "noumenal" world, is the realm of philosophy. Kant's division of science and philosophy succeeded in giving a much-needed assurance to both philosophy and science allowing both to move forward.

The Philosophes

The Enlightenment was concerned with more than philosophy and invention. Enlightened thought led to an active desire, called humanitarianism, to raise the downtrodden from the low social circumstances into which ignorance and tyranny had cast them. All men and women had a right, as rational creatures, to dignity and happiness. This desire to elevate the social circumstances of all people led to an examination and questioning of political, judicial, economic, and ecclesiastical institutions.

The ideas of the Enlightenment spread largely through the efforts of the *philosophes* (FIL-oh-sawf; Fig. **14.3**). Although this term suggests philosophy, the philosophes were not philosophers in the usual sense of the word. Rather, they were popularizers or publicists. They were men of letters who culled thought from great books and translated it into simple terms that could be understood by a reading public. In France, the most serious of all the philosophe enterprises was the *Encyclopedia*, edited by Denis Diderot (deed-ROH; 1713–84). The seventeen-volume *Encyclopedia*, which took from 1751 to 1772 to complete, was a compendium of scientific, technical, and historical knowledge, incorporating a good deal of social criticism. Voltaire and Rousseau were among its contributors.

No philosophe undertook such a vocal or universal attack on contemporary institutions as Voltaire (1697–1778; his name was originally François-Marie Arouet), about whom we will have more to say shortly. It is easy to see Voltaire as an aggressive, churlish skeptic, who had nothing positive to offer as a substitute for the ills he found everywhere. In fact, his championship of DEISM contributed greatly to improved religious toleration. His stinging wit broadened awareness of and reaction against witch-burnings, torture, and other such abuses of human rights. Without question, his popularizing of knowledge and his broad program of social reform helped to bring about the French Revolution, which cast out the old absolutist order once and for all.

Another influential figure in the mid-eighteenth century was Jean-Jacques Rousseau (roo-SOH; 1712–72). Rousseau propounded a theory of government so purely rationalistic that it had no connection whatever with the experience of history. To Rousseau, human beings were essentially unhappy, feeble, frustrated, and trapped in a social environment of their own making. He believed people could be happy and free only in a "state of nature," or, at most, in a small and simple community. Such a philosophy stands completely in contrast to that of Diderot, who held that only accumulated knowledge would liberate humanity.

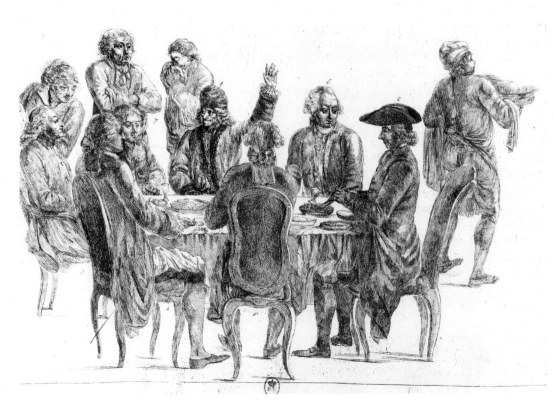

14.3 Jean Huber, *The Philosophes at Supper*, c. 1750. Engraving. Bibliothèque Nationale, Paris.

PROFILE

Voltaire (1694–1778)

Voltaire (vohl-TAIR) ranged widely through French literature during the years of the Enlightenment and leading up to the French Revolution. Born into a middle-class Parisian family, he lost his mother when he was seven and believed that his real father was not his legal one. A rebel from authority, he grew up in the company of his freethinking godfather, the Abbé de Châteauneuf, and always maintained a clear sense of reality and a positive outlook. His schooling, at the Jesuit College of Louis-le-Grand in Paris, nurtured his love of literature, theatre, and social life, but the school's religious instruction left him skeptical. The period around 1709 saw the last years of Louis XIV accompanied by military disasters and religious persecution, events that left an indelible impression on the young Voltaire, although he continued to admire Louis XIV and to believe that kings were agents of progress.

His wit and desire to pursue a career in literature, coupled with the peculiar circumstances of the years after Louis XIV, in which the literary salon was the center of French society, soon brought Voltaire into social prominence. However, when he mocked the Regent, he found himself imprisoned for a year in the Bastille. Nonetheless, he saw himself as the Vergil of French literature and set about the serious task of writing, and he was soon back in favor. A two-year visit to England made him acquainted with the writings of Sir Isaac Newton and John Locke and gave him a greater appreciation of English literature, and he returned to France determined to use England as a model for his compatriots. Careful investments made Voltaire rich, and this allowed him to proceed on literary and social ventures of his choice. He wrote several mediocre tragedies before turning to writing history. His histories read like novels, and as he wrote, he increasingly began to insert philosophy into his texts.

However, his profound insights were not appreciated by his contemporaries, and a warrant was issued for his arrest. He retreated to the château of Madame du Chatelet, with whom he spent the next several years. He also was a companion of the enlightened Prussian despot Frederick II, the Great, and frequently visited Frederick's palace at Sans Souci (see p. 459).

However, the French court remained hostile. Voltaire committed several personal indiscretions and some of his plays failed miserably, and he was forced to lead a restless existence that eventually made him ill. In despair after the death of Madame du Chatelet, he returned to Germany at the invitation of Frederick II. Controversy seemed to follow him, however, and by 1753 he was out of favor with Frederick and forbidden to return to Paris. He retired to Geneva, where he completed two major historical studies but also became embroiled in religious controversy with the Calvinists (see p. 359). During this time, he wrote his most famous work, *Candide* (1758). Then he purchased an estate on the French–Swiss border, which afforded him safe haven from whichever police were after him at the moment. This began the most active period of his life. Although he was constantly embroiled in minor feuds over everything from land titles to liberation for the serfs, he was world-famous and the constant host for international celebrities. He used his fame to speak out on anything and everything—especially the Church—and he fought vigorously for religious toleration, material prosperity, respect for the rights of all humans, and the abolition of torture and useless punishments. He continued to write for the theatre, and it was the theatre that brought about his triumphant return to Paris in 1778. However, the excitement proved too great, and his health suffered irreparably. He died on 30 May that same year.

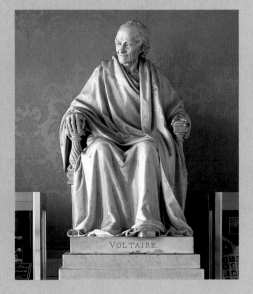

14.4 Jean-Antoine Houdon, *Voltaire*, 1781. Marble, 20 ins (51 cm) high. Victoria & Albert Museum, London.

Maria Theresa (1717–80)

Maria Theresa, like her nemesis, Frederick the Great, an enlightened despot, was the daughter of Emperor Charles VI. In 1740 she succeeded to the Hapsburg lands. Her succession was contested in the War of the Austrian Succession, in which she lost Silesia to Prussia but secured the election of her husband as emperor. She carried out agrarian reforms and centralized the administration. During her reign, Vienna developed as a center for music and the arts. Called "the most human of the Hapsburgs," Maria Theresa was a key figure in the complex politics of Europe in the 1700s. Her father, the Holy Roman Emperor Charles VI, tried to ensure her succession to his domains, and she devoted much of her life to the fight to keep her lands.

Maria Theresa was born in Vienna on 13 May 1717. At the age of twenty-three she became archduchess of Austria and queen of Bohemia and Hungary. She also inherited outlying possessions of the house of Austria in Italy and the Netherlands. Various powers hoped to add to their territories at the expense of the inexperienced queen. Most determined of all her enemies was young Frederick II, king of Prussia.

Maria Theresa's father was the last of the direct male line of the Austrian Hapsburgs. He had no sons, and the Hapsburg law forbade women to inherit Hapsburg lands. In order to secure his oldest daughter's succession, he drew up a revision of the law, called the Pragmatic Sanction. After long negotiations, he persuaded all the major powers of Europe—including Prussia—to agree to this international treaty. Before coming to the throne, Maria Theresa married Duke Francis of Lorraine. Maria Theresa had been on the throne only two months when Frederick marched his army southward into Silesia, the fertile valley of the Oder River that stretched southeastward from his own Brandenburg. Her Hungarian subjects failed in their attempts to expel Frederick from Silesia.

Maria Theresa's pride and her devout Roman Catholicism made her determined to recover her lost province from Protestant Prussia. She formed an alliance with Russia and then set about to win France as an ally against Prussia. To continue this complicated exchange of allegiances, Frederick then entered into an alliance with Great Britain.

Among Maria Theresa's sixteen children were Emperor Joseph II and Leopold II. To strengthen the alliance with France, she married her youngest daughter, Marie Antoinette, to the heir to the French throne. Her oldest son, Joseph II, assisted her in the government after the death of her husband. She carried out many reforms to strengthen the unity of her lands. She ruled as an absolute monarch, but she was one of the enlightened despots of the eighteenth century. She died in Vienna on 28 November 1780. Joseph II succeeded her.

Indeed, it was an age of contrasts. Rousseau was an anarchist, and did not believe in government of any kind. He wrote on politics, therefore, not because he was trying to improve government, but because he lived in an age of political speculation and believed he had the power to deal with every problem. His *Social Contract* (1762) was utterly rationalistic. It reasserted Locke's propositions about the social contract, sovereignty of the people, and the right of revolution. More importantly, he took Locke's concept of primitive humanity and converted such people into "noble savages" who had been subjected to progressive degradation by an advancing civilization. In an age turning to rational, intellectual classicism, Rousseau sowed the seeds of Romanticism, which were to flower in the next century. He also sounded the call for revolution: the opening sentence of the *Social Contract* reads, "Man is born free and everywhere he is in chains," a thought that predates Karl Marx by about a century.

Economics and Politics

The same spirit of challenge and questioning was also applied to economics. Critics of mercantilistic government regulation and control were called "physiocrats," from the Greek *physis*, meaning "nature," because they saw nature as the single source of all wealth. Agriculture, forestry, and mining were of greater importance than manufacturing. Physiocratic theory also advocated a *laissez-faire* (LEHS-say-FAIR) approach to economic endeavor. In other

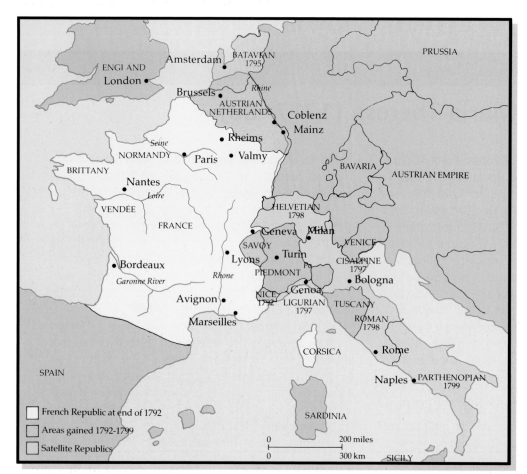

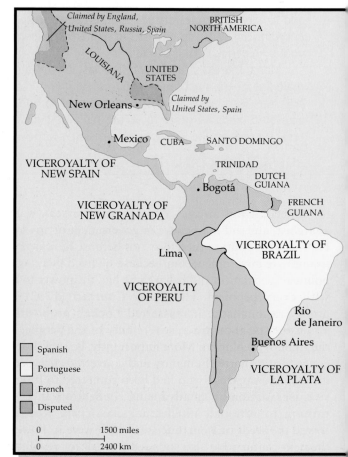

Map 14.1 Europe in the eighteenth century.

Map 14.2 America in the eighteenth century.

words, physiocrats believed that production and distribution were best handled without government interference. Government supervision should be abandoned so that nature and enterprising individuals could co-operate in the production of the greatest possible wealth. General physiocratic ideas were refined and codified in Adam Smith's *Wealth of Nations* (1776). Smith (1723–90), a Scotsman, argued that the basic factor in production was human labor (rather than nature). He believed that enlightened self-interest, without government intervention, would be sufficient to inspire individuals to produce wealth on an unheard-of scale.

On the political scene, the German states were in turmoil and flux in the eighteenth century. In 1701 Frederick I (1657–1713) became King in Prussia (the word "in" rather than "of" was used to placate Poland, which occupied West Prussia). Frederick's major political stronghold lay in a small area called Brandenburg. However, Frederick's family, the Hohenzollern (HOH-hen-tsohl-uhrn), soon came to dominate the whole of Prussia. Frederick's son, King Frederick William I (r. 1713–40), perfected the structure of the army and the German civil service.

Frederick William was a notable eccentric. For example, anyone he suspected of having wealth was compelled to build a fine residence to improve the appearance of his city. He also had a craze for tall soldiers, whom he recruited from all over Europe, thereby making his palace guard a cadre of coddled giants. Frederick William's son, who would become Frederick II, the Great, was given a rigorous training in the army and civil service.

When Frederick the Great (1712–86) assumed the throne on his father's death in 1740, he brought to it a detailed knowledge of the Prussian service, together with an intense love of arts and literature. He was a person of immense ambition, and he turned his sights very quickly on neighboring Austria. Austria's House of Hapsburg was ruled by Charles VI, who died in 1740. His daughter, the Archduchess Maria Theresa, became ruler of all the Hapsburg territories, many of which were the subject of disputed claims of possession. Scenting opportunity, Frederick the Great promptly marched into Austrian territory. A tug-of-war-and-peace between Austria and Prussia followed. Both countries emerged from these hostilities strong and socially stable, and both became centers of artistic, literary, and intellectual activity in the second half of the eighteenth century.

Frederick the Great was an "enlightened" and humanitarian ruler, a "benevolent despot." He championed thinkers throughout Europe and reformed German institutions so that they were better able to render service to all classes of society, especially the poor and oppressed (in strong contrast to Louis XV and XVI of France). When he died in 1786, he left behind a strong country.

In Austria under the Hapsburgs, too, constant warfare did not interfere with internal order and enlightened reform. Maria Theresa's husband became Emperor Francis I in 1745. He was followed, in 1765, by their son, Joseph II. Ruling jointly with his mother from 1765 to 1780 and alone until his death in 1790, Joseph II was also an enlightened monarch. He unified and centralized the Hapsburg dominions and brought Austria into line with the economic and intellectual conditions of the day.

Meanwhile, in England, King George III (1738–1820; r. 1760–1820), and in France, Louis XV (1710–74; r. 1715–74) and his grandson, Louis XVI, along with his wife, Marie Antoinette (1755–93), saw revolution overtake their colonies or their country. The events and ramifications of the American Revolution are already familiar. The complexities of the French Revolution (1789), which are beyond our scope here, led from wars throughout Europe and a second revolution in 1792, through an "Emergency Republic," the "Terror," the Directory, Napoleon's *coup d'état* (koo-day-TAH) in 1799, to a new and politically explosive century in Europe.

Aesthetics and Classicism

The death of Louis XIV in 1715 brought to a close a magnificent French courtly tradition that had championed baroque art (although the German baroque continued well into the eighteenth century). The French court and aristocracy moved to more modest surroundings, to intimate, elegant townhouses and salons, a milieu entirely different from the vastness and opulence of the Palace of Versailles. Charm, manners, and finesse replaced previous standards of social behavior. Enlightenment society sought refinement of detail and décor, and delicacy in everything. "Sociability" became the credo of early eighteenth-century France and the rest of Europe.

Classical influences dating from the Renaissance continued to be important, principally because a "classical education" was considered essential for all members of the upper classes. The excavation of the ruins of the Roman city of Pompeii, found virtually intact, in 1748 caused a wave of excitement. The ancient city of Herculaneum (hur-kyoo-LAYN-ee-uhm) had been partly excavated in 1738. Amid this revived interest came Gottlieb Baumgarten's significant book, *Aesthetica* (1750–8). For the first time the word "aesthetics" was used to mean "the study of beauty and theory of art." Then, in 1764, came Johann Winckelmann's (VING-kuhl-mahn) *History of Ancient Art*, in which the author described the essential qualities of Greek art as "a noble simplicity and tranquil loftiness ... a beautiful proportion, order, and harmony."

These values brought the arts of the eighteenth century out of the baroque era. Herculaneum, Pompeii, aesthetic theory, and a return to antiquity and the simplicity of nature, closed a century marked by war and revolution, rationalism, and skepticism.

THE VISUAL ARTS AND ARCHITECTURE

Rococo Style

The change from the splendor of courtly life to the style of the small salon and the intimate townhouse was reflected in a new style of painting called "rococo (ruh-KOH-koh or roh-kuh-KOH)." Often rococo is described as an inconsequential version of baroque, and there is some justification for such a description. Some paintings of this style display fussy detail, complex composition, and a certain superficiality. To dismiss early eighteenth-century work thus would be wrong, however.

Rococo was a product of its time. It is essentially decorative and nonfunctional, like the declining aristocracy it represented. Its intimate grace, charm, and delicate superficiality reflect the social ideals and manners of the age. Informality replaced formality in life and in painting. The

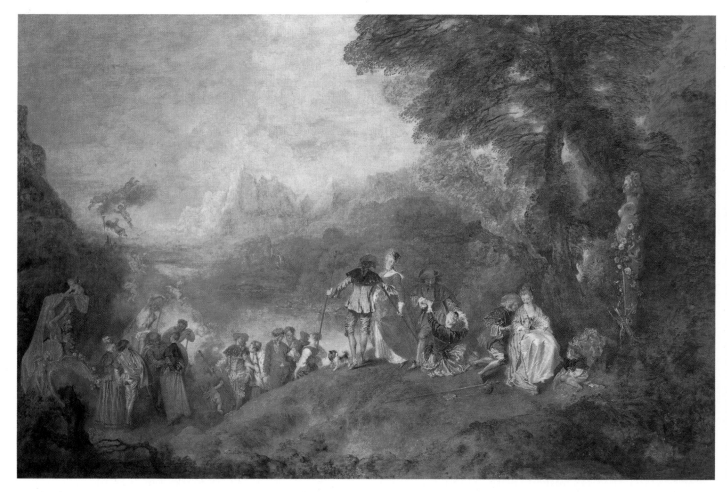

14.5 Antoine Watteau, *Embarkation for Cythera*, 1717. Oil on canvas, 4 ft × 3 ins × 6 ft 4¹/₂ ins (1.29 × 1.94 m). Louvre, Paris.

heavy academic character of the baroque of Louis XIV was found lacking in feeling and sensitivity. Deeply dramatic action was now transmuted into lively effervescence and melodrama. Love, friendship, sentiment, pleasure, and sincerity became predominant themes. None of these characteristics conflicts significantly with the overall tone of the Enlightenment, whose major goal was refinement. The arts of the period could dignify the human spirit through social and moral consciousness as well as through the graceful sentiments of friendship and love. Delicacy and informality did not have to imply limp or empty sentimentality.

The rococo paintings of Antoine Watteau (wah-TOH; 1683–1721) are representative of many of the changing values of the aristocracy. Watteau's work is largely sentimental, but it is not particularly frivolous. *Embarkation for Cythera* (Fig. **14.5**) idealizes the social graces of the high-born classes. Cythera is a mythological land of enchantment, the island of Venus, and Watteau portrays aristocrats idling away their time in amorous pursuits as they wait to leave for that faraway place.

Soft color areas and hazy atmosphere add the qualities of fantasy to the landscape. An undulating line underscores the human figures, all posed in slightly affected attitudes. Each group of doll-like couples engages in graceful conversation and amorous games. An armless bust of Venus presides over the delicate scene. Watteau's fussy details and decorative treatment of clothing contrast with the diffused quality of the background. But underlying this fantasy is a deep, poetic melancholy.

The slightly later work of François Boucher (boo-SHAY; 1703–70) continues in the rococo tradition. His work even more fully exemplifies the decorative, mundane, and somewhat erotic painting popular in the early and mid-eighteenth century. As a protégé of Madame de Pompadour, the mistress of King Louis XV, Boucher enjoyed great popularity. His work has a highly decorative surface detail and portrays pastoral and mythological settings such as *Venus Consoling Love* (Fig. **14.6**). Boucher's figures almost always appear amid exquisitely detailed drapery. His technique is nearly flawless, and,

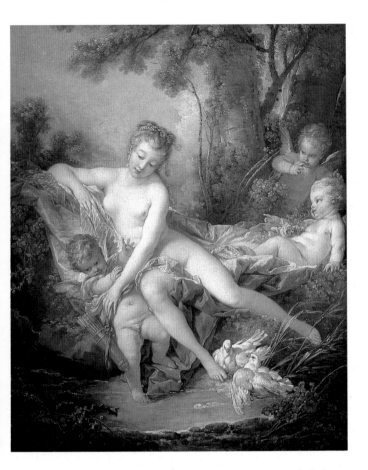

14.6 François Boucher, *Venus Consoling Love*, 1751. Oil on canvas, 3 ft 6⅛ ins × 2 ft 9⅜ ins (1.07 × 0.85 m). National Gallery of Art, Washington D.C. (Chester Dale Collection). © 1998 Board of Trustees, National Gallery of Art, Washington D.C.

Sculpture struggled as an art form in the eighteenth century. The Academy of Sculpture and the French Academy in Rome encouraged the copying of antique sculpture, and resisted any changes in style. Most sculpture thus continued in a derivative baroque style.

Rococo style did find expression in the sculpture of Falconet (fahl-koh-NAY; 1716–91) and Clodion (klawd-YOHN; 1738–1814). Their works feature decorative cupids and nymphs, motifs that recur in painting of this style. Venus appears frequently, often in the form of a thinly disguised prominent lady of the day. Madame de Pompadour, who epitomized love, charm, grace, and delicacy for the French, appears often as a subject in sculpture as well as in painting.

Rococo sculpture did not have the monumental scale of its predecessors. Rather, in the spirit of decoration that marked the era, sculpture often took the form of graceful porcelain and metal figurines. Falconet's *Madame de Pompadour as the Venus of the Doves* (Fig. **14.7**) fully captures the erotic sensuality, delicacy, lively intelligence, and charm of the rococo heritage. The unpretentious nudity indicates the complete comfort and naturalness the eighteenth century found in affairs of the flesh. Rococo

14.7 Étienne-Maurice Falconet, *Madame de Pompadour as the Venus of the Doves*, 1782. Marble, 29½ ins (75 cm) high. National Gallery of Art, Washington D.C. (Samuel H. Kress Collection). © 1998 Board of Trustees, National Gallery of Art, Washington D.C.

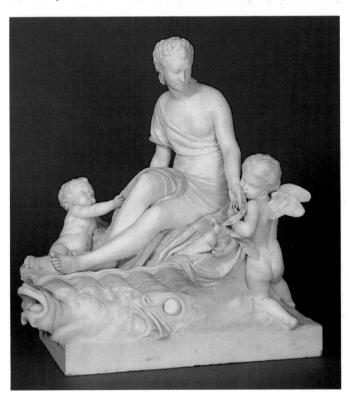

with his painterly virtuosity, he creates fussily pretty works, the subjects of which compete with their decorative backgrounds for attention. Compared with the power, sweep, and grandeur of baroque painting, Boucher's work is gentle and shallow. Here, each of the intricate and delicate details takes on a separate focus of its own and leads the eye in a disorderly fashion first in one direction and then another.

Characteristic of later rococo style, *The Swing* (see Fig. **14.1**) by Jean-Honoré Fragonard (frah-goh-NAR; 1732–1806) is an "intrigue" picture. A young gentleman has enticed an unsuspecting old cleric to swing the gentleman's sweetheart higher and higher so that he, strategically placed, can catch a glimpse of her exposed limbs. The young lady, perfectly aware of his trick, gladly joins in the game, kicking off her shoe toward the statue of the god of discretion, who holds his finger to his lips in an admonishment of silence. The scene is one of frivolous naughtiness and sensuality, with lush foliage, foaming petticoats, and luxurious colors.

techniques for conveying surface textures, detail, and line in sculpture display mastery of the medium. If this style, and the society it exemplifies, is found wanting in profundity, it must be admired for its technical achievement.

Claude Michel, known as Clodion, created dynamic miniatures such as the *Satyr and Bacchante* (Fig. **14.8**). His groups of accurately modeled figures in erotic abandon are made all the fresher and more alluring by his knowing use of pinkish terracotta as if it were actually pulsating flesh, rendering each incipient embrace "forever warm and still to be enjoyed."

Unlike most previous architectural styles, rococo was principally a style of interior design. Its refinement and decorativeness applied to furniture and décor more than to exterior structure or even detail. By now, even the aristocracy lived in attached row houses, and townhouses quite simply have virtually no exteriors to design. Attention turned to interiors, where the difference between opulence

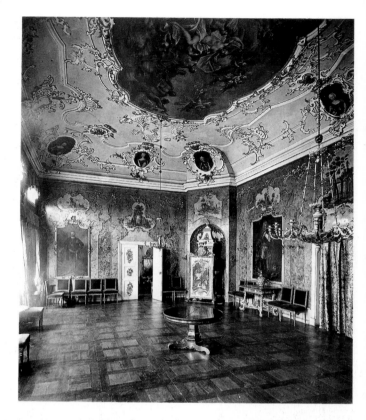

14.8 Clodion (Claude Michel), *Satyr and Bacchante*, c. 1775. Terracotta, 23¼ ins (59 cm) high. Metropolitan Museum of Art, New York (Bequest of Benjamin Altman, 1913).

14.9 G.H. Krohne, music room, Thuringer Museum, Eisenach, Germany, 1742–51.

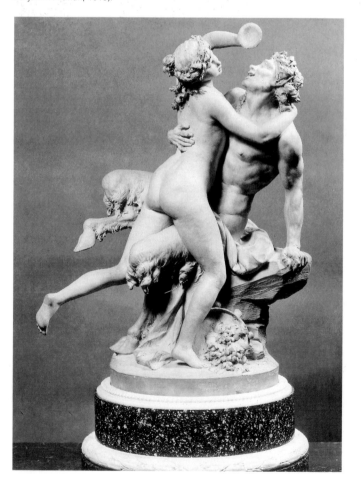

and delicacy was apparent. Figure **14.9** shows a polygonal music room characteristic of German rococo. Its broken wall surfaces display stucco decoration of floral branches that creates a pseudonatural effect. In Venice, curved leg furniture, cornices, and gilded carvings were the fashion. French designer Jean François de Cuvilliès (kue-vee-ES; 1695–1768) combined refinement, lightness, and reduced scale to produce a pleasant atmosphere of grace and propriety (Fig. **14.10**).

English architecture of the early eighteenth century shared in these rococo refinements, but its style differed in many ways from that of the continent. The late seventeenth and early eighteenth centuries in England produced a so-called "Georgian style"—the name refers to Kings George I, II, and III, whose reigns the style partially encompassed. Georgian style was a kind of vernacular neoclassicism. Its relationship to rococo can be seen mainly in its refinement and delicacy. Georgian architecture developed from the English baroque style of Christopher Wren, which had also been more restrained and classical than the florid baroque style of the continent. Georgian architecture was particularly popular in the American South.

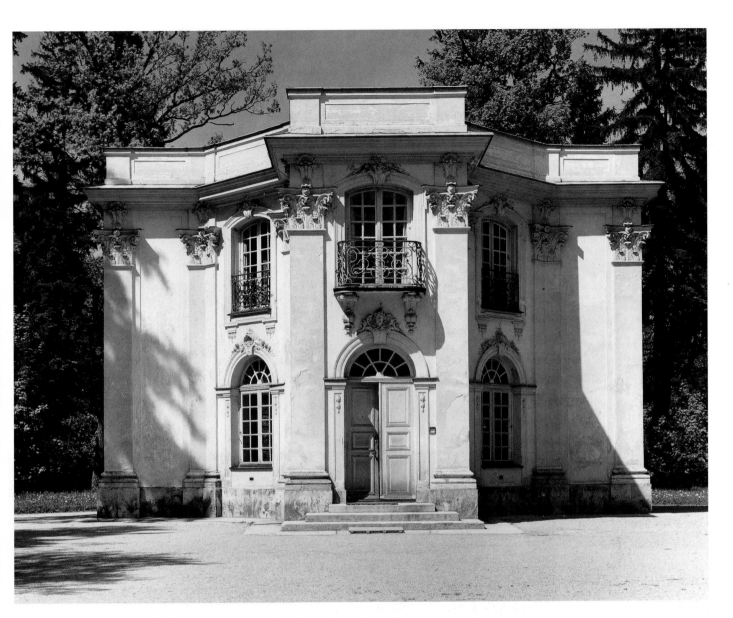

14.10 Jean François de Cuvilliès, The Pagodenburg, c. 1722. Schloss Nymphenburg, Munich, Germany.

Humanitarianism and Hogarth

The aristocratic frivolity of rococo style was heavily counterbalanced by the biting satire and social comment of enlightened humanitarians such as William Hogarth (1697–1764). In England during the 1730s, Hogarth portrayed dramatic scenes on moral subjects. His *Rake's Progress and Harlot's Progress* series are attempts to correct raging social ills and to instill solid middle-class values. Hogarth attacked the foppery of the aristocracy, drunkenness, and social cruelty. In *The Harlot's Progress* series (Fig. **14.11**), the prostitute is a victim of circumstances. She arrives in London, her employer seduces her,

and she ends up in Bridewell Prison. Hogarth blames her final fate more on human cruelty than on her sins. The same may be said of *The Rake's Progress*, which in a series of six tableaux, portrays the downfall of a foolish young man from comfortable circumstances. This series moves through several views of the young man as he sinks lower and lower into corruption (Fig. **14.12**) until he ends up in the Bedlam insane asylum.

Hogarth's criticism of social conditions is clear in his paintings, intended as an incitement to action, a purpose characteristic of eighteenth-century humanitarians. The fact that his paintings were made into engravings and widely sold to the public as prints illustrates just how popular were attacks on the social institutions of the day.

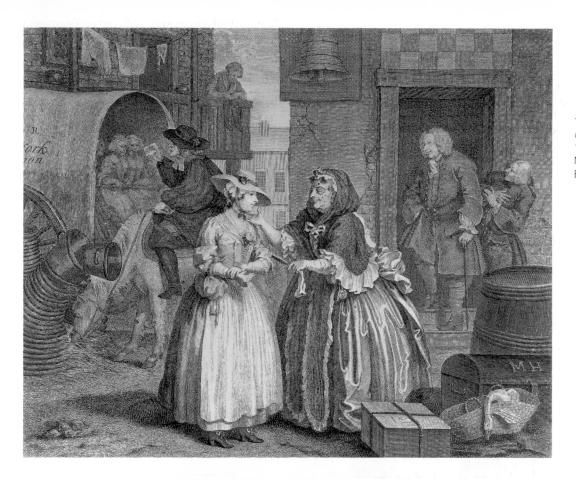

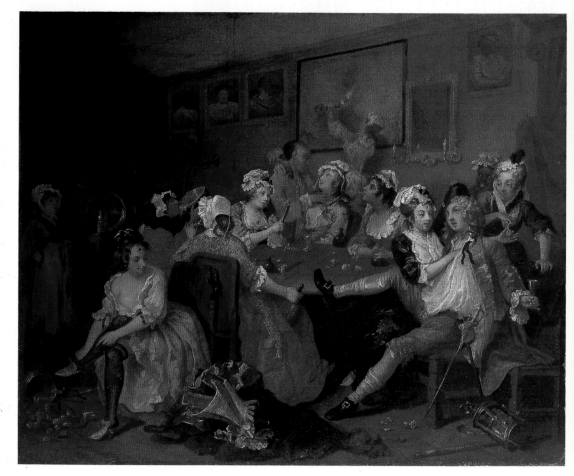

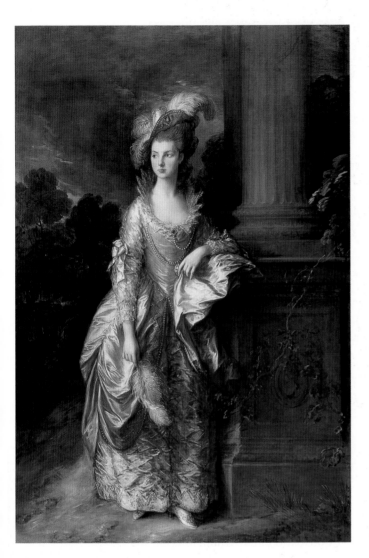

14.13 Thomas Gainsborough, *The Hon. Mrs Graham*, c. 1777. Oil on canvas, 7 ft 9³/₈ ins × 5 ft ³/₄ in (2.37 × 1.54 m). National Gallery of Scotland.

Landscape and Portraiture

The popularity of portraiture and landscape also increased in the eighteenth century. One of the most influential English painters of the time was Thomas Gainsborough (1727–88). His landscapes bridge the gap between the baroque and Romantic styles, and his portraits exhibit sensitive elegance. Gainsborough's full-length portraits of lords and ladies (Fig. **14.13**) have a unique freshness and lyric grace. Occasionally art critics object to the lack of structure in his attenuated, almost weightless figures; however, such objections fade away when confronted by the beauty of Gainsborough's color and the delicacy of his touch.

His landscapes reveal a freshness typically associated with the English approach to painting. In *The Market Cart*

(Fig. **14.14**) we find a delicate use of wash reminiscent of Watteau. Here the painter explores tonalities and shapes that express a deep and almost mystical response to nature. Although the subject is pastoral, the composition has an unusual energy that derives from its diagonal composition. The tree forms on the right border are twisted and gnarled: the foremost tree leads the viewer's eye up and to the left, to be caught by the downward circling line of the trees and clouds in the background and returned on the diagonal. The human figures in the picture are not of particular interest—although they are warmly rendered, they are not individuals, and their forms remain indistinct. We see them, rather, as subordinate to the forces of nature which ebb and flow around and through them.

Genre

A fresh bourgeois flavor could be found in the mundane subjects of France's Jean-Baptiste Siméon Chardin (shahr-DAN; 1699–1779), whose paintings show an interest in the servants and life "below stairs" in well-to-do households. He was the finest STILL LIFE and *genre* painter of his

14.14 Thomas Gainsborough, *The Market Cart*, 1786–7. Oil on canvas, 6 ft ¹/₂ in × 5 ft ¹/₄ in (1.84 × 1.53 m). Tate Gallery, London.

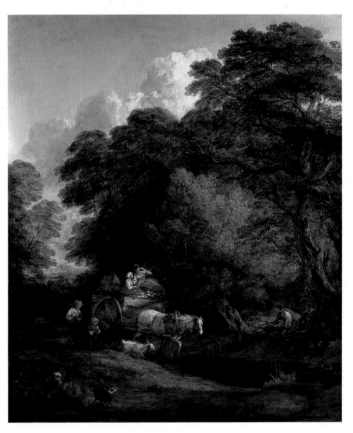

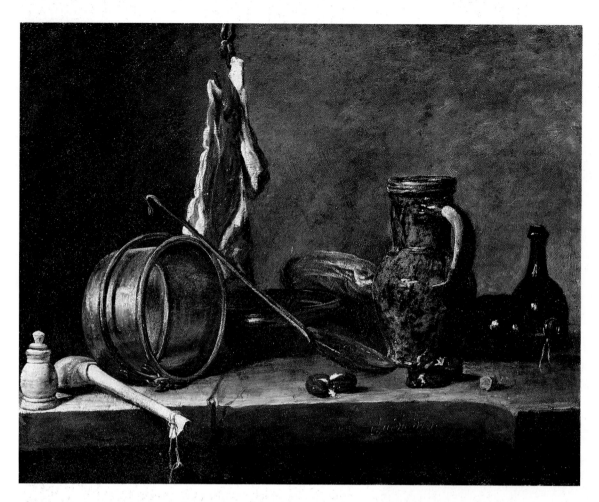

14.15 Jean-Baptiste Siméon Chardin, *Menu de Gras*, 1731. Oil on canvas, 13 × 16¹/₈ ins (33 × 41 cm). Louvre, Paris.

time, and can be seen to continue the tradition of the Dutch masters of the previous century. His early works are almost exclusively still-lifes, and *Menu de Gras* (men-oo-duh grah; Fig. **14.15**) illustrates how everyday items could be raised to a level of unsuspected beauty.

The artist invests each item—cooking pot, ladle, pitcher, bottles, cork, a piece of meat, and other small things—with intense significance, as richness of texture and color combined with careful composition and the use of chiaroscuro make these humble items somehow noble. The eye moves slowly from point to point, carefully directed by shapes and angles, color and highlight. The work itself controls the speed at which we view it. Each new focus demands that we pause and savor its richness. Chardin urges us to look beneath our surface impressions of these objects into their deeper reality.

Neoclassicism

The discovery of the ruins of Pompeii, Winckelmann's interpretation of Greek classicism, Rousseau's "noble savage," and Baumgarten's aesthetics sent the interests of late eighteenth-century artists and thinkers back into antiquity, and in particular, into nature.

A principal proponent of *neoclassicism* in painting was Jacques-Louis David (dah-VEED; 1748–1825). His works illustrate the newly perceived grandeur of antiquity, and this is reflected in his subject matter, composition, and historical accuracy. Propagandist in tone—he sought to inspire French patriotism and democracy—his paintings have a strong, simple compositional unity. In both *The Death of Socrates* (see Fig. **14.19**) and *The Oath of the Horatii* (see Fig. **14.20**), David exploits his political ideas using Greek and Roman themes. In both cases, the subjects suggest a devotion to ideals so strong that one should be prepared to die in their defense. David's values are made dramatically clear by his sparse, simple composition.

The neoclassicism of David and others was, of course, not a simple matter of copying ancient works. Classical detail and principles were used selectively and frequently adapted to suit the artist's own purposes.

During the years just prior to the French Revolution, Jean-Antoine Houdon (oo-DOHN; 1741–1828) created portrait busts of children, such as those of Alexandre and Louise Brongniart (Figs. **14.16** and **14.17**), which show

14.16 (*right*) Jean-Antoine Houdon, *Alexandre Brongniart*, 1777. Marble, 15³/₈ ins (39.2 cm) high. National Gallery of Art, Washington D.C. (Widener Collection). © 1998 Board of Trustees, National Gallery of Art, Washington D.C.

14.17 (*far right*) Jean-Antoine Houdon, *Louise Brongniart*, 1777. Marble, 14¹/₈ ins (37.7 cm) high. National Gallery of Art, Washington D.C. (Widener Collection).

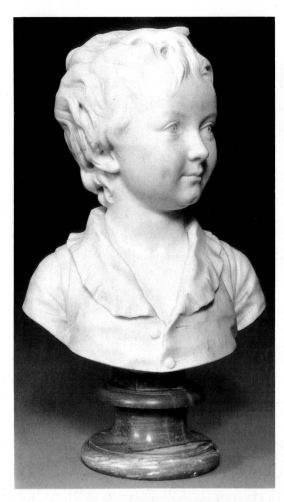

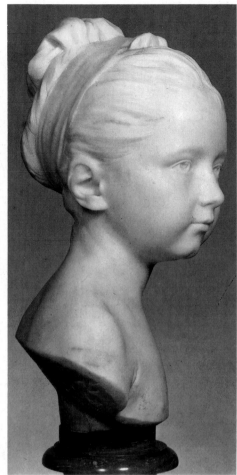

14.18 Antonio Canova, *Pauline Borghese as Venus Victrix*, 1808. Marble, lifesize. Galleria Borghese, Rome.

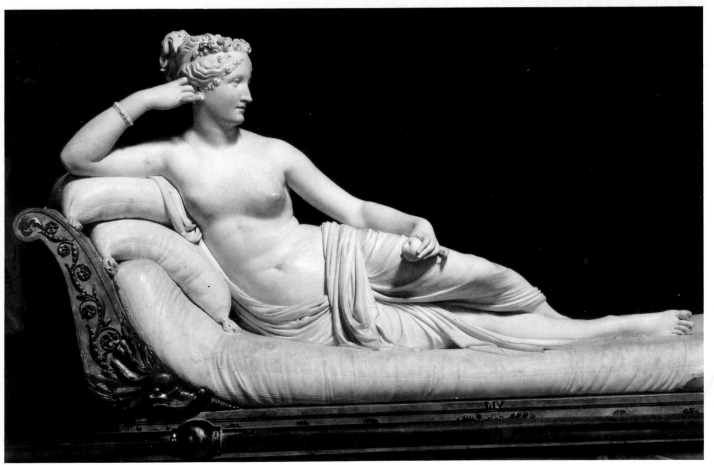

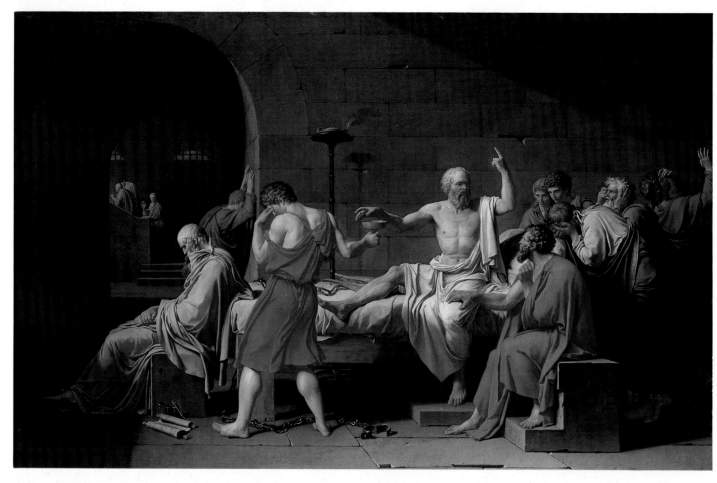

14.19 Jacques-Louis David, *The Death of Socrates*, 1787. Oil on canvas, 4 ft 3 ins × 6 ft 5¼ ins (1.29 × 1.96 m). Metropolitan Museum of Art, New York (Wolfe Fund, 1931. Catherine Lorillard Wolfe Collection).

acute psychological observation as well as accurate technical execution. Houdon's works distill the personality of his subjects, and his busts of American revolutionary figures, such as Washington, Jefferson, John Paul Jones, and Benjamin Franklin, are revealing character portraits, as is his portrait of Voltaire (see Fig. **14.4**). Houdon's work seems to belong to the emerging eighteenth-century neoclassical style. The lifelikeness and truth that Houdon puts into his individual characters are much more akin to the ideals of neoclassicism than to those of the rococo.

Antonio Canova (kah-NOV-ah; 1757–1822) was the ablest of the neoclassical sculptors, and his works also show influences of the rococo style. *Pauline Borghese as Venus Victrix* (Fig. **14.18**), for which Napoleon's sister was the model, uses a classical pose and proportions. Line, costume, and hairstyle reflect the ancients, but sensuous texture, individualized expression, and fussy lifelike detail suggest other approaches. At the same time, this work is almost two-dimensional. Canova seems unconcerned with the sculpture from any angle other than a straight-on view.

In the mid-eighteenth century, the aims of architecture altered to embrace the complex philosophical concerns of the Enlightenment. The result was a series of styles and sub-styles broadly referred to also as "neoclassical." Excavations at Herculaneum and Pompeii, philosophical concepts of progress, the aesthetics of Baumgarten, and the writings of Winckelmann all expressed and created a new view of antiquity. Neoclassicism was thus a new way of examining the past: rather than seeing the past as a single, continuous cultural flow broken by a medieval collapse of classical values, theoreticians of the eighteenth century saw history as a series of separate compartments—Antiquity, the Middle Ages, the Renaissance, and so on.

Three important approaches emerged as a result of this new idea. The archeological school saw the present as continually enriched by persistent inquiry into the past. In other words, history was the story of progress. The second approach was eclectic. It saw the artist as someone who could choose among styles, or, more importantly, combine elements of various styles. A third, modernist, approach

David—*The Oath of the Horatii*

David's famous painting *The Oath of the Horatii* (Fig. **14.20**) concerns the conflict between love and patriotism. In legend, the leaders of the Roman and Alban armies, on the verge of battle, decide to resolve their conflicts by means of an organized combat between three representatives from each side. The three Horatius brothers represented Rome; the Curatius sons represented the Albans. A sister of the Horatii was the fiancée of one of the Curatius brothers. David's painting depicts the Horatii as they swear on their swords to win or die for Rome, disregarding the anguish of their sister.

The work captures a directness and an intensity of expression that were to play an important role in Romanticism. But the starkness of outline, the strong geometric composition (which juxtaposes straight line in the men and curved line in the women), and the smooth color areas and gradations hold it to the more formal, classical tradition. The style of *The Oath of the Horatii* is academic neoclassicism. The scene takes place in a shallow picture box, defined by a severely simple architectural framework. The costumes are historically correct. The musculature, even of the women, is devoid of warmth or softness.

It is ironic that David's work was admired and purchased by King Louis XVI, against whom David's revolutionary cries were directed and whom David, as a member of the French Revolutionary Convention, would sentence to death. Neoclassicism increased in popularity and continued through the Napoleonic era and into the nineteenth century.

14.20 Jacques-Louis David, *The Oath of the Horatii*, 1784–5. Oil on canvas, about. 14 × 11 ft (4.27 × 3.35 m). Louvre, Paris.

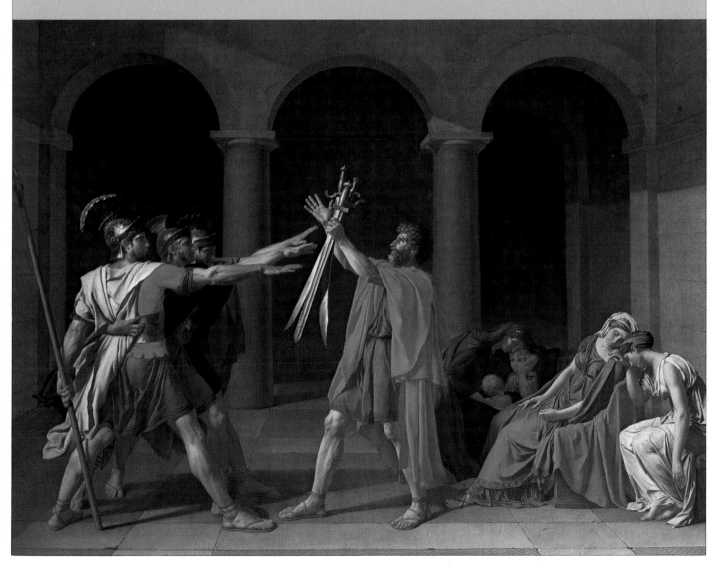

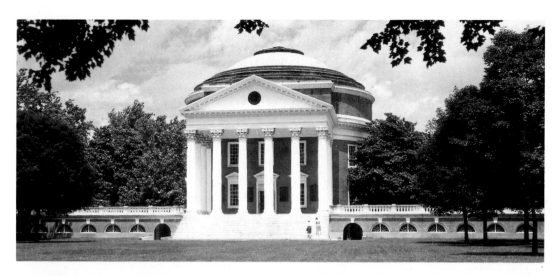

14.21 Thomas Jefferson, Rotunda of the University of Virginia, 1819–28.

14.22 Thomas Jefferson, Monticello, Charlottesville, Virginia, 1770–84; rebuilt 1796–1800.

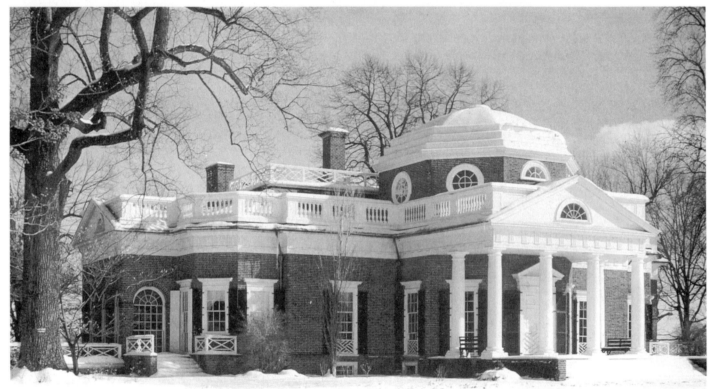

viewed the present as unique and, therefore, capable of expression in its own terms. Each of these three concepts profoundly influenced eighteenth-century architecture and bore importantly on the other arts. From this time forward, the basic premises of art were fundamentally changed.

Neoclassicism in architecture alludes to all three concepts, and encompasses a variety of treatments and terminologies. The identifiable forms of Greece and Rome are basic to it, of course. It also took considerable impetus from the *Essai sur l'architecture* (1753) by the Abbé Laugier (ah-BAY lo-ZHAY). Laugier's strictly rationalistic work expressed neoclassicism in a nutshell. Discarding all

architectural language developed since the Renaissance, he urged the architect to seek truth in the architectural principles of the ancient world and to use those principles to design modern buildings. Laugier's neoclassicism descended directly from the Greeks, with only passing reference to the Romans.

In Italy, the architect Giambattista Piranesi (pee-rahn-AY-zee; 1720–78) was incensed by Laugier's arguments, which placed Greece above Rome. He retaliated with an overwhelmingly detailed work, *Della Magnificenza ed Architettura dei Romani*, which professed to prove the superiority of Rome over Greece. This quarrel aside, both Piranesi and Laugier were instigators of the neoclassical tradition, and in general, this revival of classicism in architecture, with its high moral seriousness, was seen in many quarters as a revolt against the frivolity of the rococo.

In America, neoclassicism had special meaning, as the colonies struggled to rid themselves of the monarchial rule of George III of England. For the revolutionary colonists, classicism meant Greece, and Greece meant democracy. The designs of colonial architect Thomas Jefferson (Figs **14.21** and **14.22**) reflect the ideas of this period. Jefferson was highly influenced by Palladio (see p. 338), whose popularity had soared during the significant period of English villa architecture, between 1710 and 1750. In a uniquely eighteenth-century way, Jefferson looked at architecture objectively, within the framework of contemporary thought. Strongly influenced by Lockean ideas of natural law, Jefferson believed that the architecture of antiquity embodied indisputable natural principles, and he made Palladian reconstructions of the Roman temple the foundation for his theory of architecture. His country house, Monticello, consists of a central structure with attached Doric porticos, or porches, and short, low wings attached to the center by continuing Doric entablatures. The simplicity and refinement of Jefferson's statement here goes beyond mere reconstruction of classical prototypes, and appeals directly to the viewer's intellect and sensibilities.

Throughout the United States, and particularly in the South, the classical revival found frequent expression. In Charleston, South Carolina, the Miles Brewton House provides us with one of the finest examples of American Georgian architecture (Fig. **14.23**). The large pedimented portico, supported by Ionic columns, indicates the boldness of American neoclassicism.

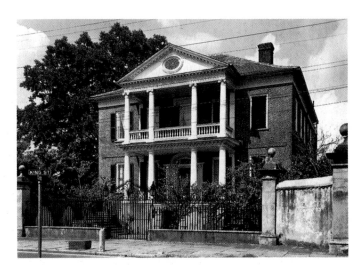

14.23 Miles Brewton House, Charleston, South Carolina (architect unknown), c. 1769.

LITERATURE

Rococo

Alexander Pope (1688–1744) gave new meaning to the term "wit." The most brilliant satirist of an age in which satire was a major art form, his rhymed couplets hit home, in poems such as *The Rape of the Lock*, with devastating poise and accuracy. Pope's idolatry of classical values and his contempt for a society that fell short of them led him to write a mock-heroic poem, *The Dunciad*, an epic on dunces, and he filled it with profound moral anger.

Pope's name is often linked with that of Jonathan Swift (1667–1745), an Anglo-Irish satirist and churchman who shared many of his concerns. Swift was, if anything, even more bitter than Pope. *Gulliver's Travels* mocked pompous pragmatism and woolly-headed idealism equally.

Another famous prose work, *A Modest Proposal*, took satire to the very edge of horror. Here Swift argues with chilling mock-seriousness that the English should solve the "Irish problem" by eating the babies of the Irish poor.

Pamphlets and Essays

In an age of enlightenment, humanitarianism, democratic ideals, moral reformation, and broad mass appeal, pamphlets and essays became vital forces in literary endeavors. In the American colonies, Thomas Paine (1737–1809) turned his energies to writing pamphlets in support of the libertarian ideals of the times. An Englishman, he worked for the American movement toward independence, and later wrote *The Rights of Man* (1792) in support of the French Revolution. He was banished from Britain, imprisoned in France, and died in poverty in the United States.

English pamphleteer and novelist Mary Wollstonecraft (1759–97) was notable for her outspoken views on the role of women in society and on the role education played in oppressing women. She set out her ideas in the pamphlet *Thoughts on the Education of Daughters* (1787). Her most famous work, *A Vindication of the Rights of Women* (1792), stands as one of the major documents in the history of women's writing. She attacked the "mistaken notion of female excellence" she saw in contemporary attitudes about "femininity," and she argued that women were not naturally submissive, but taught to be so, confined to "smiling under the lash at which [they] dare not snarl."

The mid-eighteenth century is often called the "Age of Johnson." Samuel Johnson (1709–84) began his literary career as a sort of odd-job journalist, writing for a newspaper. His principal achievements were as a lexicographer and essayist: the 208 *Rambler* essays cover a huge variety of topics, including "Folly of Anger: Misery of a Peevish Old Age" and "Advantages of Mediocrity: an Eastern Fable." These essays promoted the glory of God and the writer's salvation. In 1758, Johnson began the *Idler Essays*, a weekly contribution to a newspaper called the *Universal Chronicle*. In these essays we find the moralistic, reforming tone still present, but with an increasingly comic element.

Genre

Contemporary literature also reflected the eighteenth-century focus on the commonplace that we saw in the genre paintings of the day. Common ordinary occurrences are frequently used as symbols of a higher reality. The work of Oliver Goldsmith (1730–74), the prominent British eighteenth-century poet and playwright, illustrates this quite clearly. Goldsmith grew up in the village of Lissoy, where his father was vicar, and *The Deserted Village*, written in 1770, describes the sights and personalities of Lissoy:

> Sweet Auburn! Loveliest village of the plain
> Where health and plenty cheered the laboring swain;
> Where smiling spring its earliest visit paid,
> And parting summer's lingering blooms delayed.
> Dear lovely bowers of innocence and ease,
> Seats of my youth, where every sport could please;
> How often have I loitered o'er thy green,
> Where humble happiness endeared each scene!

Goldsmith's portrait of the old village parson includes a lovely simile.

> To them his heart, his love, his griefs were given,
> But all his serious thoughts had rest in heaven.
> As some tall cliff that lifts its awful form,
> Swells from the vale, and midway leaves the storm,
> External sunshine settles on its head.

Finally, there is great tenderness in the way he describes his dream of ending his life amid the scenes in which it had begun.

> In all my wanderings round this world of care,
> In all my griefs—and God has given my share—
> I still had hopes, my latest hours to crown,
> Amid these humble bowers to lay me down,
> To husband out life's taper at the close,
> And keep the flame from wasting by repose. . . .

> And as an hare whom hounds and horns pursue,
> Pants to the place from which at first she flew,
> I still had hopes my long vexations past,
> Here to return—and die at home at last.

The Pre-Romantics

Here we face one of the challenging issues of the entire classical/romantic relationship. As we stated very early in this book, history has seen a swinging back and forth between classicism and what we, for want of better terms, called "anti-classicism," one of whose forms is Romanticism. Things in the arts and life in general, however, rarely prove simple, and the relationship between classical ideals—form—and anti-classical ideals—feeling—proves the point. As we already have witnessed, the words themselves have diverse aspects and uses. In point of fact, in art the form of a work can be classical while the content and expression reflect romantic ideas. As we previously stated, just because a work is "classical" does not make it void of emotion. Likewise, because a work may be classified as "Romantic" or "baroque" (both fundamentally anti-classical in spirit) does not rob it of logical organization.

In addition, the term "romanticism," as we suggest in the next chapter, can refer to a specific compositional style c. 1830, but it also refers to a longlived cultural movement that began in the eighteenth century and of which some scholars now see "neoclassicism" as a sub-category.

From roughly the 1740s to the 1780s, the pre-Romantic movement shifted public taste away from the grandeur, austerity, nobility, idealization, and elevated sentiments of neoclassicism toward a simpler, more sincere, and more natural form of expression.

The decline of drama and the rise of the novel in the eighteenth century marked a significant shift in literature. The life of Henry Fielding (1707–54) mirrored this transition as he moved from a distinguished career in the theatre—he had written about twenty-five plays, mostly satirical and topical comedies—to become a pre-eminent novelist. His first full novel, *Joseph Andrews* (1742), portrays one of the first memorable characters in English fiction—an idealistic and inconsistent hero who constantly falls into ridiculous adventures. Fielding called his novel a "comic prose epic," and it is remarkable for its structure as well as its humor and its satire. His most famous novel remains *Tom Jones* (1749), a splendid romp which ranks among the greatest works in English literature.

One of the most influential of the pre-Romantic writers in France was Jean-Jacques Rousseau. He placed a new emphasis on emotion rather than reason, on sympathy rather than rational understanding. Other English pre-Romantics included the novelists Horace Walpole

(1717–97) and Mrs Radcliffe (1764–1823), who catered to the public taste for Gothic tales of dark castles and shining heroism in medieval settings.

The German Johann Gottfried von Herder (HAIR-dur; 1744–1803) also contributed to the Pre-Romantic movement. Herder's essays, *German Way and German Art* (1773), have been called the "manifesto of German *Sturm und Drang*" ("storm and stress"). In his greatest work, *Ideas on the Philosophy of the History of Mankind* (1784–91), he analyzed nationalism and prescribed a way of reviving "a national feeling through school, books, and newspapers using the national language." Among the major exponents of *Sturm und Drang* were Johann Wolfgang von Goethe (GUHR-tuh) (1749–1832) and Friedrich von Schiller (SHIL-ur; 1759–1805). They advocated freedom and a return to nature, and took Shakespeare and Jean-Jacques Rousseau as their models. They exalted the individual, personal experience, genius, and creative imagination.

Goethe was, perhaps, the most influential man of letters of his era. In 1773 he provided the *Sturm und Drang* movement with its first major drama, *Götz von Berlichingen* (gehrts fon BAIR-lik-ing-uhn), which Goethe wrote in conscious imitation of Shakespeare. He followed with the movement's first novel, *Die Leiden des jungen Werthers* (dee LY-ten des YOONG-en VAIR-tuhrs; "The Sorrows of Young Werther"). In Werther, a sensitive, ill-fated protagonist, Goethe created the prototype of the Romantic hero. Goethe also chronicled the Faust legend (see p. 380) for a discussion of Christopher Marlowe's treatment of the Faust story). Part I of Goethe's sweeping, two-part dramatic poem *Faust* was published in 1808 and Part II in 1832, after the author's death. *Faust* constituted the supreme work of Goethe's later years and is sometimes considered Germany's greatest contribution to world literature.

Part I details the magician Faust's despair, his pact with Mephistopheles, and his love for Gretchen. Part II covers Faust's life at court, the wooing and winning of Helen of Troy, and his purification and salvation. Occasionally described as formless because of its array of lyric, epic, dramatic, operatic, and balletic elements, the work was probably conceived not as a play but as a dramatic poem. As theatre, it is virtually impossible to stage, although some have tried. Part I offers possibilities, being the more realistic of the two parts. Part II is highly symbolic and defies theatrical production.

Goethe's friendship and correspondence with the poet Friedrich von Schiller solidified his aesthetic theories. Schiller, in his plays, examined the inward freedom of the soul that enables the individual to rise above physical frailties and the pressure of material conditions. His first poetic drama, *Don Carlos* (1787), helped establish blank verse as the recognized medium of German poetic drama. He gave jubilant expression to a mood of contentment in his hymn "Ode to Joy," which Ludwig von Beethoven used for the choral movement of his Ninth Symphony. Schiller wrote extensively on the character of aesthetic activity, its function in society, and its relation to moral experience in essays on moral grace and dignity and on the sublime, as well as an essay on the distinction between two types of poetic creativity.

MUSIC

Pre-Classical

As French court society and its baroque arts slipped from favor, the ornamentation, delicacy, prettiness, and pleasant artificiality of the rococo style came to music as well as to painting and sculpture. Musicians improvised "decorations" in their performances, and the practice was so common that many composers purposely left their melodic lines bare in order to allow performers the opportunity for playful trills and other ornaments. The purpose of music was to entertain and to charm.

François Couperin (koo-pur-AN; 1668–1733) exemplified the musical spirit of his time, but he also retained sufficient of his baroque roots to avoid excessive sentimentality or completely artificial decoration. Nevertheless, his works are appropriate to salon performance, and do not limit any one piece or movement to one emotion. He shows a pleasant blending of logic and rationality with emotion and delicacy, in true rococo fashion.

Couperin was part of a uniquely French school of keyboard music, which specialized in long dance suites, so-called "genre pieces," contrapuntal works with highly ornamented introductions, and overtures similar to those found in French opera. Many of the pieces are miniatures, and the grand sweep of the baroque era is replaced by an abundance of short melodic phrases with much repetition and profuse ornamentation.

Expressive Style

A second style of music, the *Expressive style*, paralleled the rococo style and formed a transitional stage between baroque and classical. This Expressive style (more literally, "sensitive" style), or *empfindsamer Stil* (emp-finnt-ZAH-mair shteel), came from Germany. It permitted a freer expression of emotions than the baroque, largely by allowing a variety of moods to occur within a single movement. Polyphonic complexities were reduced, and different themes, with harmonic and rhythmic contrasts, were introduced. Expressive style was thus simple and highly original. Composers had the freedom to use rhythmic contrasts, original melodies, and new nuances and shading of loud and soft. Yet the goal was a carefully proportioned, logical, unified whole, whose parts were clear and carefully articulated.

The principal exponent of the *empfindsamer Stil* was Carl Philipp Emanuel Bach (1714–88), one of J.S. Bach's sons. His position between the baroque and classical styles has led some scholars to call him the "founder" of the classical style. For many years he was court harpsichordist to Frederick the Great, and it is his keyboard works that are generally considered his most important compositions. He understood music to be an art of the emotions, and believed it very important that the player be involved personally in each performance.

Classical Style

In 1785 Michel Paul de Chabanon (shahb-ah-NOHN) wrote: "Today there is but one music in all of Europe." What he meant was that music was being composed to appeal not only to the aristocracy but to the middle classes as well. Egalitarian tendencies and the popular ideals of the philosophes had also influenced artists, who now sought larger audiences. Pleasure had become a legitimate artistic purpose. Eighteenth-century rationalism saw excessive ornamentation and excessive complexity (both baroque characteristics) as not appealing to a wide audience on its own terms. Those sentiments, which coincided with the discoveries of Pompeii and the ideas of Winckelmann and Baumgarten, prompted a move toward order, simplicity, and careful attention to form. We call this style in music *classical* (the term was not applied until the nineteenth century), rather than neoclassical or classical revival, because although the other arts returned, more or less, to Greek and Roman prototypes, music had no known classical antecedents to revive. Music thus turned to classical ideals, though not to classical models.

The classical style in music had, among others, five basic characteristics. The first of these is variety and contrast in *mood*. In contrast to the baroque style, which typically deals with a single emotion, classical pieces typically explore contrasts between moods. There may be contrasting moods within movements and also within themes, as well. Changes in mood may be gradual or sudden; they are, however, as one might expect of a style called "classical," well controlled, unified, and logical.

A second characteristic of classical style is flexibility of *rhythm*. Classical music explores a wide variety of rhythms, utilizing unexpected pauses, syncopations, and frequent changes from long to shorter notes. As in mood, changes in rhythm may be sudden or gradual. A third characteristic of classical style is a predominantly homophonic *texture*. Nonetheless, texture also is flexible, with sudden and gradual shifts from one texture to another.

A fourth characteristic is memorable *melody*. The themes of classical music tend to be very tuneful, and often have a folk or popular flavor. Classical melodies tend toward balance and symmetry, again what one would expect of "classical" works as we have seen them since the Athenian Greeks. Frequently, classical themes have two phrases of equal length. The second phrase often begins like the first but ends more decisively.

A fifth characteristic of classical style is gradual changes in *dynamics*, in contrast to baroque music, which employs sudden changes in dynamics (*step dynamics*). One of the consequences of this direction in composition was the replacement of the harpsichord with the piano, which was more capable of handling the subtlety of classical dynamic patterns.

The Classical Sonata and Sonata Form

As we noted in the last chapter, "sonata" has been used to denote many different musical forms, from a short piece for a single instrument to complex works in many sections or movements, for a large ensemble. By the middle of the eighteenth century, however, the sonata for one or two keyboard instruments, or for another instrument accompanied by keyboard, was utilized as an instrumental genre comparable to the symphony, which we discuss momentarily. These genres share a flexible multi-movement design that music analysts call the *sonata cycle*. The term *sonata form* refers to the form of a *single movement* and should not be confused with the term *sonata*, which describes a composition made of several movements. The sonata form, the most important musical structure of the classical period, was used in symphonies, sonatas, and other genres mostly in the first movement, although sometimes in other movements as well. Sonata form has three main sections: *exposition* (where themes are presented), *development* (where themes are treated in new ways), and *recapitulation* (where the themes return). These three sections often are followed by a concluding section, the *coda* (Italian for "tail"). The three main sections comprise an ABA design.

The Classical Symphony

The word "symphony" comes from the Latin *symphonia* (based in turn on a Greek word), meaning "a sounding together." In practical terms, a symphony is an extended, ambitious composition typically lasting between twenty and forty-five minutes and exploring the broad range of tone colors and dynamics of the classical orchestra. Franz Josef Haydn (see below) began composing symphonies in the classical sense about 1757. In his long life he solidified and enriched symphonic style, culminating in a set of twelve works composed for London in 1791–5 (called the "Salomon Symphonies," after the German impresario J.P. Salomon, who, in 1790, persuaded Haydn to go to England). Haydn wrote 104 symphonies (some scholars put the number higher), which were widely performed and imitated during his lifetime. Wolfgang Amadeus Mozart wrote forty-one symphonies, and his last six—No. 35 in D ("Haffner"), No. 36 in C ("Linz"), No. 38 in D ("Prague"), No. 39 in E flat, No. 40 in G Minor, and No. 41 in C ("Jupiter")—are complex in design and rich in orchestration, wedding formal perfection and expressive depth. Ludwig van Beethoven wrote only nine symphonies (1800–24), but in them he greatly increased the form's weight and size.

The classical orchestra, which performed the classical symphony, was typified by the supreme orchestra of the time, the court orchestra at Mannheim (mahn-HYM), Germany, which flourished in the third quarter of the century. It had approximately thirty string players and helped to standardize the remaining instrumental complement, specifically, two flutes, two oboes, two bassoons, two horns, two trumpets, two kettledrums, and a new instrument, the clarinet. Beethoven increased the technical demands on every instrument and occasionally enlarged the classical orchestra by writing parts for piccolo, trombones, and contrabassoon. The finale of his Symphony No. 9 also requires triangle, cymbals, and bass drum (in addition to choral voices).

Other Classical Forms

Although the sonata and symphony were the most important musical forms of this period, there were others. One form, called *theme and variations*, was widely used as an independent piece or as one movement of a symphony, sonata, or string quartet. In a theme and variations the theme (a basic musical idea) is repeated over and over, each time with some change—for example, mood, rhythm, dynamics and so on.

A form known as *minuet and trio*, or just *minuet*, often occurs as the third movement of a symphony, string quartet, or other work. The form originated as a stately dance, but in classical music it is designed purely for listening. It has triple meter and, usually, a moderate tempo. Its ABA form consists of a minuet (A), trio (B), and minuet (A). The trio (B) section utilizes fewer instruments than the minuet (A) sections. Another musical form that was popular in the classical time was the *rondo*. This features a melodic main theme (A) that returns several times, alternating with other themes. Other forms, for example the concerto, witnessed their own transformation into classical characteristics.

Haydn

The Austrian-born Franz Josef Haydn (1732–1809) pioneered the development of the symphony from a short, simple work into a longer, more sophisticated one. Haydn's symphonies are diverse and numerous. Some are light and simple, others are serious and sophisticated.

Many of Haydn's early symphonies use the preclassical, fast-slow-fast three-movement form. These usually consist of an opening *allegro*, followed by an *andante* in a related key, and close with a rapid dance-like movement in triple meter. Other early works use four movements, the first of which is in a slow tempo. In contrast, the Symphony No. 3 in G major (c. 1762) has a typical four-movement structure beginning with a fast tempo: I *allegro*, II *andante moderato*, III minuet and trio, and IV *allegro*. The third movement, the minuet and trio, is a new feature, found in nearly every classical symphony. Haydn's minuets contain very charming music, often emphasizing instrumental color in the trio.

Among his late works is his most famous symphony, No. 94 in G major (1792), commonly known as the "Surprise" Symphony. Its second movement contains a simple, charming theme and the dramatic musical surprise that gives the work its popular name. The movement is in a theme and variations form (AA'A"A'")—the apostrophes represent a VARIATION of the original material. The tempo is *andante*, and the orchestra begins with a soft statement of the theme. After presenting the theme a second time, even more quietly, Haydn inserts a tremendous *fortissimo* (very loud) chord. This is the surprise that makes those who are unfamiliar with the work jump out of their skin. With the exception of the "surprise," this movement is typical in its use of a melody based on the two main harmonies of Western music, the TONIC or home chord, and the dominant chord.

In the opening movement of this four-movement work, Haydn uses sonata form. This is preceded by a pastoral introduction, marked *adagio cantabile*, that is, in a slow, singing style, in triple meter. The introductory material alternates between the strings and the woodwind.

The tempo switches to *vivace assai*, that is, very fast, and the strings quietly introduce the first theme in G major (Fig. **14.24**).

The last note of the theme is marked *f*, or *forte* (loud). At this point, the full orchestra joins the violins in a lively

14.24 Franz Josef Haydn, Symphony No. 94 in G major, first theme of first movement.

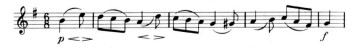

Prefatory Phrase

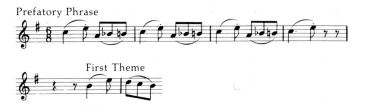

First Theme

14.25 Franz Josef Haydn, Symphony No. 94 in G major, prefatory phrase, first movement.

Allegro molto

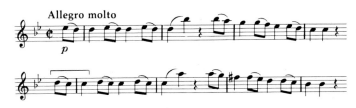

14.26 Wolfgang Amadeus Mozart, Symphony No. 40 in G minor, first theme of first movement.

section. Just before a pause, the orchestra plays a short prefatory phrase which will recur throughout the movement (Fig. **14.25**):

The first theme then reappears, with a slightly altered rhythmic pattern. This marks a bridge, or transition passage, to a new key, the dominant, D major. A quick series of scales in the violins and flutes leads to the introduction of the second theme, a lyrical theme with trills and a falling motif. The exposition section closes with a short scale figure and repeated notes, and then the entire exposition is repeated.

The development section opens with a variation of the first theme and then goes through a series of key and dynamic changes.

The recapitulation starts—as recapitulations always do—with a return to the first theme in the original key. A passage based on motifs from the first theme, a repeat and brief development of the first theme, a pause, and finally, another repeat of the first theme follow. Then the second theme appears again, now in the home key, and the movement closes with a short scale passage and a strong cadence.

Mozart

Wolfgang Amadeus Mozart (1756–91), also an Austrian, had performed at the court of Empress Maria Theresa at the age of six. As was the case throughout the classical period, aristocratic patronage was essential for musicians to earn a living, although the middle classes provided a progressively larger portion of commissions, pupil fees, and concert attendance. Mozart's short career (he died at the age of thirty-five) was dogged by financial insecurity.

His early symphonies were simple and relatively short, like those of Haydn, while his later works were longer and more complex. His last three symphonies are generally regarded as among his greatest masterpieces, and Symphony No. 40 in G minor is often referred to as the typical classical symphony. This work, along with Nos. 39 and 41, have clear order and restraint, yet they exhibit a tremendous emotional urgency, which many scholars cite as the beginning of the Romantic style.

The first of the four movements of Symphony No. 40,

written in sonata form, begins *allegro molto*. The violins state the first theme above a soft chordal accompaniment, which establishes the tonic key of G minor (Fig. **14.26**). Three short motifs are repeated throughout the piece.

The restlessness of the rhythm is accentuated by the liveliness of the lower strings. The second theme in the woodwinds and strings provides a relaxing contrast. It is in a contrasting key, the relative major, B flat, and it flows smoothly, each phrase beginning with a gliding movement down a chromatic scale. A codetta echoes the basic motif on various instruments and finishes with a cadence in B flat major. In most performances the entire exposition section is repeated, giving the movement an AABA form.

The development section concentrates on the basic three-note motif and explores the possibilities of the opening theme. This section is somewhat brief, but full of drama.

The recapitulation restates the first theme in the home key, and then the second theme, also in G minor rather than in the original major. This gives the ending a more mournful character than the equivalent section in the exposition. A coda in the original key ends the movement.

The second movement, *andante*, in E flat major, also uses sonata form. The first theme of the movement is passed successively among the violas, second violins, and first violins. The horns provide a rich background. Unlike the first movement, there is no strong contrast between the first and second themes. They are presented in E flat major and B flat major—the standard contrast of keys in a movement that starts in a major key. The development changes key further, moving into the minor, then returns to the home key with a dialogue among the woodwinds. This movement features many graceful embellishments, which were popular with the Austrian court.

The third movement, *allegretto*, returns to G minor and the emotional tension of the first movement. The meter is triple—it is a minuet and trio, which is typical for the third movement. This is a lively piece with symmetrically arranged phrases and strong cross-rhythms. The trio changes key to G major and has a more relaxed mood.

The finale, *allegro assai*, uses a compact sonata form. The violins state the subject in G minor and create a

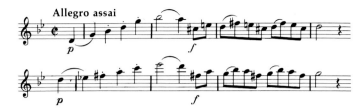

14.27 Wolfgang Amadeus Mozart, Symphony No. 40 in G minor, first theme of fourth movement.

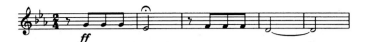

14.29 Ludwig van Beethoven, Symphony No. 5, first theme of first movement.

"rocket theme," that is, an upward thrusting arpeggio (Fig. **14.27**).

The violins play the second, contrasting theme in the related key of B flat major, and the woodwinds pick it up and embellish it. The development in this movement is very dramatic. The rocket motif bounces from instrument to instrument, creating a highly complex texture, which is increased by rapid modulation through several remote keys. The recapitulation returns, of course, to the home key of G minor, with subtle restatement and variation.

In a totally different vein, the final movement of Mozart's Sonata No. 11 for piano in A (CD track 12) has always been a popular favorite. Called the "Turkish Rondo," it has an exotic or "Turkish" character underlined by the main theme in A minor (Fig. **14.28**) that reappears throughout the rondo, softly:

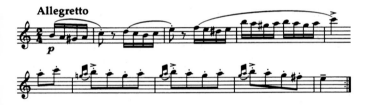

14.28 Wolfgang Amadeus Mozart, Sonata No. 11 for piano in A (K. 331) ("Turkish Rondo").

Beethoven

Ludwig van Beethoven (1770–1827) is often considered a singular transitional figure between classicism and Romanticism, and we might easily consider him in the next chapter. Beethoven wanted to expand the classical symphonic form to accommodate greater emotional character. The typical classical symphony has movements with contrasting and unrelated themes. Beethoven moved toward a single thematic development throughout, thereby achieving a unity of emotion in the whole work.

Beethoven's works differ significantly from those of Haydn and Mozart. They are more dramatic, and they use changing dynamics for starker emotional effects. Silence is used to pursue both dramatic and structural ends. Beethoven's works are also longer. He lengthened the development section of sonata form and did the same to his codas, many of which take on characteristics of a second development section.

He also changed traditional numbers of and relationships among movements, especially in the unusual Symphony No. 6, which has no break between the fourth and fifth movements. In the Symphony No. 5, no break occurs between the third and fourth movements. In some of his four-movement works, he changed the traditional third movement minuet and trio to a scherzo and trio of significantly livelier character. Beethoven's symphonies draw heavily on imagery, for example heroism in Symphony No. 3 and pastoral settings in Symphony No. 6. The famous Symphony No. 5 in C minor, for example, begins with a motif that Beethoven described as "fate knocking at the door" (Fig. **14.29**). The first movement (*allegro con brio*) develops according to typical sonata form (CD Track 13), the second and contrasting movement (*andante con moto*) is in theme-and-variation form, and the third movement (*allegro*) is a scherzo and trio in triple meter. Movement number four returns to *allegro* and to sonata form.

Beethoven's nine symphonies became progressively more Romantic, and the Ninth is a gigantic work of tremendous power. Its finale includes a chorus singing the text of Schiller's *Ode to Joy*.

Undoubtedly one of Beethoven's loveliest and most popular works is the Piano Sonata in C minor, Op. 13 (the "Pathétique"), published in 1799. The work is in three movements. The first movement is marked *grave; allegro di molto e con brio*, and is in sonata form. The strong tempo contrast between the opening *grave* (very slow) passages and the *allegro* heightens the drama of the movement. The second movement is marked *adagio cantabile*, a slow, singing style, in the contrasting key of A flat major.

The third movement is in the home key of C minor and is structured ABACABA. This is known as RONDO form— that is, it has a recurrent theme, and is similar in structure to baroque ritornello form. It opens its first, or A, section with a lively theme in duple meter (Fig. **14.30**).

Classical style may have had a simpler character and a more symmetrical structure than baroque style, but it did not sacrifice any of its energy or quality. In the same way

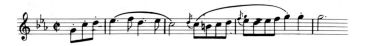

14.30 Ludwig van Beethoven, Piano Sonata in C minor, Op. 13, first theme of third movement.

that Greek simplicity in architecture, for example, kept its sophistication and interest in pursuing mathematical form and symmetry, so classical music kept its dynamism and sophistication in its pursuit of form and reason. As classical style was shaped by its practitioners, it moved as comfortably toward Romanticism as it had moved away from baroque.

THEATRE

Despite the shift of interest to the novel, the eighteenth century saw the growth of a remarkable nationalism in the theatre. Britain, France, and the United States each contributed.

Britain

The character of British audiences was changing, and the theatre changed with it. Queen Anne did not care for the theatre, and George I, who was German and did not speak English well, could not understand it. Audiences in England increasingly tended to be made up of well-to-do middle-class tradespeople. One effect of this was the shift in emphasis of comedy toward sentiment.

Undoubtedly the most popular theatre form in early eighteenth-century London was the *ballad opera*. The best of these was unquestionably John Gay's *Beggar's Opera* (1728). The story caricatured a bribery scandal involving the British prime minister Sir Robert Walpole, and it created a social scandal. *The Beggar's Opera* was not the only theatrical piece to burlesque the corruption of Walpole, and as a result of these attacks, Walpole successfully convinced Parliament to institute the Licensing Act of 1737. This act limited legal theatrical production to three theatres, Drury Lane, Covent Garden, and Haymarket, and gave the Lord Chamberlain the right to censor any play.

Production style remained refined, however, and the theatre in London retained its elegant but intimate physical size and scale, in contrast to the mammoth opera houses that flourished elsewhere. The playing area consisted of a forestage, the sides of which contained doorways for entrances and exits by the actors. Above these were boxes for spectators. Wing and drop scenery—flat, painted pieces used strictly as background—was placed upstage, behind a proscenium arch. Lighting consisted of wax candles in chandeliers over the audience. As might be expected, fire was a constant danger, and smoke from the candles was an irritating nuisance.

America

In colonial America, the arts, and the theatre especially, came up squarely against unbending Puritan austerity. Sometime between 1699 and 1702, however, Richard Hunter gained permission from the acting governor of the province of New York to present plays in the city of New York. In 1703, an English actor named Anthony Ashton landed at Charleston, South Carolina. He was "full of Lice, Shame, Poverty, Nakedness, and Hunger," and to survive became "Player and Poet." Eventually he found his way to New York, where he spent the winter "acting, writing, courting, and fighting." Perhaps as a consequence, the Province forbade "play acting and other forms of disreputable entertainment" in 1709.

Notwithstanding this inauspicious start, American theatre struggled forward. The first recorded theatre was built in Williamsburg, Virginia, in 1716, and housed a performing company for the next several years. For the most part, theatre in America was merely an extension of the British stage, and English touring companies provided most of the fare. Theatres themselves appear to have been small and closely modeled upon provincial English theatres with their RAKED stages, proscenium arches, painted scenery, and apron forestages flanked by entrance doors. Four hundred seats seems to have been about average. The front curtain rose and fell at the beginning and end of each act, but the numerous scene changes within the acts were executed in full view of the audience.

Companies from London, usually comedy troupes, came to Williamsburg annually for an eleven-month season. By 1766, touring British companies played the entire eastern seaboard from New York, Philadelphia, and Annapolis to Charleston. A milestone was passed on 24 April 1767, when the American Company, which was, in fact, British, presented Thomas Godfrey's *The Prince of Parthia*, the first play written by an American to receive a professional production.

France

French drama had one final blaze of brilliance before the Revolution, in the plays of Pierre de Beaumarchais (boh-mahr-SHAY; 1732–99). His two most famous works, *The Barber of Seville* (1775) and *The Marriage of Figaro*

OUR DYNAMIC WORLD

Japanese Kabuki Theatre

Like Western theatre, Japanese Kabuki theatre (originating approximately 400 years ago) has changed significantly over the centuries because of its ability to adapt and incorporate aspects of other theatre traditions (Fig. **14.31**). It has borrowed freely from Noh drama (see p. 284), and from the popular Japanese puppet theatre. Kabuki originated as middle class theatre and was held in contempt by Samurai and the court.

The earliest Kabuki plays were simple sketches. Two-act plays did not appear until the mid-seventeenth century. By the mid-eighteenth century plays had grown to eleven acts, and took an entire day to perform. Productions continue to be lengthy, although the practice of the day-long performance of the eighteenth century has been pared back to two five-hour performances per day.

Kabuki plays tend to be melodramas focusing on climactic moments as opposed to plots, and in that sense, Kabuki has a strong parallel with the "sensation-scene" focus of the Western melodramas of the nineteenth century. However, the connections between scenes in Kabuki plays tend to be rather vague—in contrast to the Western melodrama, whose development follows a causal scheme. Because actors do not speak, a narrator and chorus play predominant roles in Kabuki productions. The narrator describes the scene, comments on the action, and even speaks portions of the dialogue. Every location is portrayed scenically, and scenery is changed in full view of the audience.

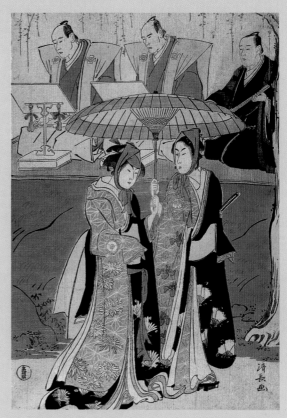

14.31 Torri Kayonaga, *Kabuki Scene with Part of Chorus*, c. 1783. Color woodblock print, 10 × 14½ ins (25.5 × 36.5 cm). British Library, London.

(1784), are entertaining comedies built upon the traditions of neoclassicism dating back to Corneille's tragedy *Le Cid* (1636). In fact, at the last moment Beaumarchais expanded *The Barber of Seville* into a neoclassical five-act structure, which only added ponderousness to a fine play. However, criticism on the opening night caused him to rewrite it with four acts, which restored the play's original sparkle. The plots of both *The Barber of Seville* and *The Marriage of Figaro* presaged the coming Revolution, and the nine years between the works saw a dramatically changed audience perception of this message. *The Barber of Seville* was enjoyed and received calmly but, by 1784, France was well aware of what was going on. The criticisms directed against the characters in the play were taken seriously as an indictment of society as a whole. When the Revolution came, its horrors left the French stage bare during the final ten years of the eighteenth century.

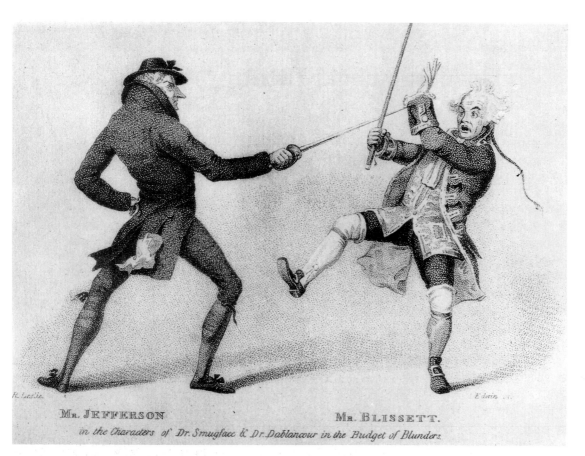

Mr. JEFFERSON   Mr. BLISSETT.

in the Characters of Dr. Smugface & Dr. Dablancour in the Budget of Blunders.

14.32 Joseph Jefferson and Francis Blissett in *The Budget of Blunders*, at the John Street Theatre, c. 1796. Contemporary engraving. The New York Public Library.

DANCE

"The only way to make ballet more popular is to lengthen the dances and shorten the *danseuses*' [female dancers'] skirts." This opinion was attributed to the composer Campra. With the courtly splendor of Louis XIV's Versailles left behind, one of the most significant obstacles to the further development of the ballerina's art was costume. Floor-length skirts were not conducive to freedom of movement, and, as a result, *danseurs* (male dancers) played the prominent roles at the turn of the eighteenth century (Fig. **14.33**). In 1730, one of those curious accidents of history occurred, which helped to change the course of ballet and bring the ballerina into pre-eminence.

Marie Anne Cupis de Camargo (kahm-ar-GOH; 1710–70) was a brilliant dancer, so much so that her mentor, Mademoiselle Prevost, tried to keep her hidden among the *corps de ballet*. During one particular performance, however, a male dancer failed to make his entrance, and Camargo quickly stepped forward to dance his role—superbly. Her footwork was so dazzling that, in order to feature it more fully, she raised her skirts a discreet inch or two above the ankle! Her forte was the *entrechat* (ahn-trah-SHAHT), a movement in which the dancer jumps

straight up and rapidly crosses the legs or at least beats the feet together, as many times as possible, while in the air. The move is still a technical achievement especially favored by male dancers. Voltaire indicated that Camargo was the first woman to dance like a man, that is, the first ballerina to display the technical skills and brilliance previously associated with *danseurs*.

Another significant stylistic change came about through the ballerina, Marie Sallé (sah-YAY; Fig. **14.34**). Her studies in mime and drama led her to believe that the style prevalent in Paris was too formal and repetitious. So, in the early 1730s, she broke her contract with the Paris Opéra (an act punishable by imprisonment), and took up residence in London. Her style was expressive, rather than a series of "leaps and frolics," and in 1734, in her famous *Pygmalion*, she wore simple draperies rather than the traditional panniers (wide extensions of the skirt at the hips), and her hair flowed freely rather than being piled up on top of her head. The contrast between the styles of Camargo and Sallé was an early example of how instantly changeable balletic style is. A flashy technique that becomes boring can quickly be relieved by a shift to expressiveness. When emotion becomes melodramatic, the pendulum can swing back to technique.

14.33 Jean Baptiste Martin, *Apollo*, 1760. Engraving. The New York Public Library.

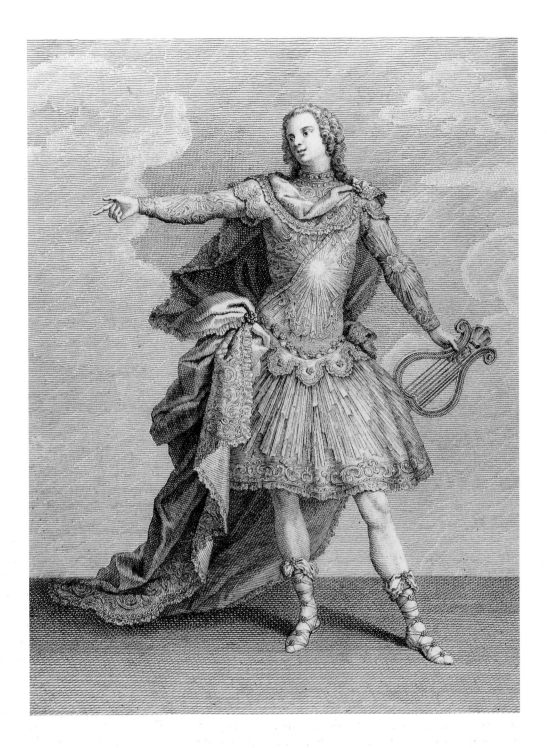

We have no way of identifying the technical characteristics of eighteenth-century ballet, but its mythological subject matter in the first half of the century is consistent with that of painting, sculpture, and music. Significant in earlier works, most of which were produced in London by the dancing master John Weaver, was the use of movement to communicate a story. These early attempts to integrate movement and dramatic content brought forth *ballet d'action* (bah-LAY dahk-SHOHN) in the last half of the century. Its popularity helped to separate this form from the sprawling *ballet à entrée*. It also reinforced ballet's independence from opera and drama. *Ballet d'action* contained an evolving classical concern for unity. Its emphasis on drama stood in contrast to the focus on display of *ballet à entrée*.

The primary moving force in this new form was Jean-Georges Noverre (noh-VAIR; 1727–1810). In his influential *Letters on Dancing and Ballets* (1760), he wrote that ballets should be unified works in which all elements contribute to the main theme. For Noverre, ballet was a

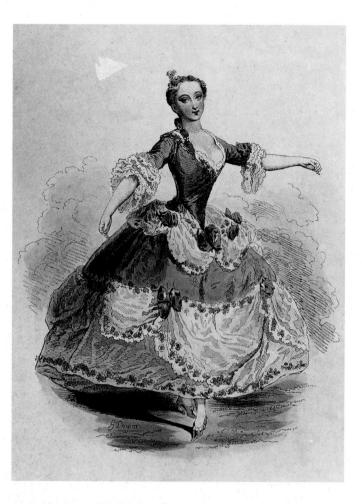

14.34 After Lancret, *Marie Sallé*, 1730. Engraving. The New York Public Library.

dramatic spectacle, a play without words. Its content was communicated through expressive movement. Music should be "written to fit each phrase and thought," and technical virtuosity for its own sake, or for the purposes of display, should be discouraged. Noverre thought that ballet should study other arts and draw upon natural forms of movement in order to be "a faithful likeness of beautiful Nature." He also argued for costumes that enhanced rather than impeded movement, and his ballets were considered excellent examples of "psychological realism."

Along with other arts, ballet became more popular, and, by 1789, ballet themes, like those of painting, began to include subjects beyond mythology. Ordinary country life provided topics for rustic ballets. These attempts at realism undoubtedly left much to be desired. They do serve, however, to illustrate trends toward egalitarianism in France and England, especially.

As the eighteenth century came to a close, Charles Didelot (deed-LOH; 1767–1837) changed the course of ballet forever. First, he introduced tights, which simplified the line and form of dance costume. Next, he set the ballet world on its ear by attaching ballerinas to wires in *Zephyr and Flora* (1796) and flying them in and out of the scene. According to some sources, Didelot's wires allowed ballerinas to pause, resting effortlessly on the tips of their toes. The new line of the body created by that single effect instantly creates a dramatic change in the aesthetics of a dance. That change was as obvious then as it is now. Soon ballerinas were dancing *en pointe* without using wires. With this change, an entirely new age in dance had begun.

Focal Point

The Enlightened Despot—Frederick the Great (1712–86)

We have already discussed the concepts of Enlightenment and talked about government by rulers, enlightened and absolute, in contrast with government by constitutional monarchy or republican in form. Our Focal Point in this chapter highlights the one shining example of a monarch who ruled with the best interests of the people in general at heart. It is likely the "enlightened" state of Frederick the Great's reign kept him in power when the monarchs of Europe were having their powers curtailed, as in England, or were being beheaded, as in France. Thus, in the Age of Enlightenment, this enlightened despot (Fig. **14.35**) becomes a representation of the age.

"The philosopher of Sans Souci (sahn soo-SEE)," as Frederick the Great was known (his palace, Sans Souci, is discussed below), gloried in his reputation as a reformer. The result of his labors was a system of practical administrative reforms known as the "Prussian General Law." In all areas of Prussian life, whether in criminal law, agriculture, the Church, schools, forestry, mining, manufacturing, trade, or shipping, through skillful manipulation of his administrators, he carried out reforms true to the enlightened spirit of the age. His insight, vision, and flexibility made his government dynamic and responsive. Such genius undoubtedly kept Frederick clear of the troubles that beset Marie Antoinette and Louis XVI of France.

Frederick II began a long career as a patron of the arts as soon as he came to the throne. He sent Karl Heinrich Graun to Italy to hire singers, and an envoy to Paris to hire dancers. He wrote to Voltaire in order to secure a troupe of French actors. While he was still a prince, Frederick had developed plans for a new opera house. Once he was king, work immediately began on the Berlin Opera. But after a feverish start, construction soon slowed down when the site had to be leveled.

But Frederick wanted an opera to be produced fairly soon, and he clearly could not depend upon the completion of this building. An existing theatre was rigged for the production of opera. On 13 December 1741, the first opera opened.

A comment from the time indicates that:

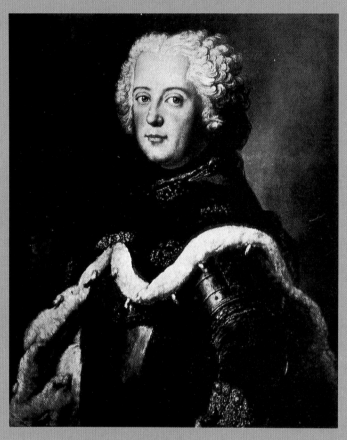

14.35 Antoine Pesne, *Frederick the Great as a Young Monarch*, 1739. Oil on canvas, 30³/₄ × 24³/₄ ins (78 × 63 cm). Gemäldegalerie, Berlin.

For the beginning there was a symphony in which fiery and gentle sections were opposed. This was such a masterpiece of full, pure harmony, such a many-sided, artful mixture of tunes, that it seemed as if the Muses and the Graces had united to draw Frederick out of his own heroic sphere and to themselves, where he could be held back from the rude cares of war. The bewitching voices of the singers, the naturalness and beauty of the action—everything was captivating to eye and ear. The whole spectacle, brought to such artistic perfection and executed with such skill, was received by the Monarch with

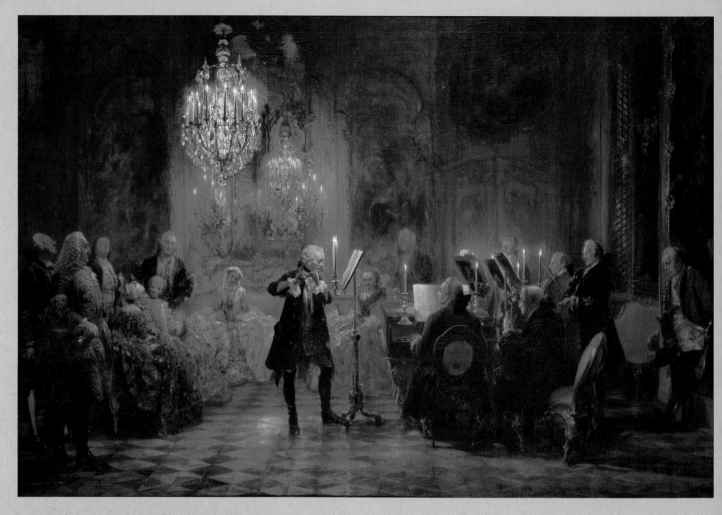

14.36 Adolf von Menzel, *Frederick's Flute Concert at Sans Souci*, 1852. Oil on canvas, 4 ft 7⅞ ins × 6 ft 8¾ ins (1.42 × 2.05 m). Staatliche Museen Preussischer Kulturbesitz, Nationalgalerie, Berlin.

high approval, and the public went forth from the theatre lost in enchantment.[1]

The new and impressive opera house finally opened on 7 December 1742, but even then, the building was not complete. Exterior decoration lay unfinished, and the audience had to pick its way through debris and piles of building materials. The building bore the inscription FREDERICK REX APOLLONI ET MUSIS ("King Frederick, Dear to Apollo and the Muses"). The immediate surroundings of the opera house were also magnificent. A large square next to the opera house could hold one thousand carriages. An intricate arrangement of plumbing was planned around a 9-foot (2.7 meters) deep canal that ran under the theatre, providing water for fountains and jets, as well as for dousing the entire theatre in case of fire. By means of an elaborate system of pneumatic jacks, the entire floor of the theatre could be raised to stage level, and the scenery could be replaced by sculptured fountains made of marble, thus creating an elaborate, three-part rococo ballroom. At the time, it was the largest theatre in the world.

On the instructions of the king, the audience was admitted free of charge to the operas. Anyone wearing acceptable clothing could get into the pit and stand for the entire performance. Performances began with pomp and ceremony upon the king's entrance at six o'clock, and usually lasted until nearly eleven. Afterwards, an invited group dined in a room adjacent to the theatre, then returned to participate in an extravagant opera ball.

The members of Frederick's local musical entourage, poorly paid and out of the limelight while imported stars enjoyed the fanfare, may in fact have made the most lasting contributions to musical development. Nonetheless, Frederick's achievements were notable, and his enthusiasm and musical sophistication created an atmosphere in which music could flourish. He held auditions, commissioned composers, evaluated compositions, and decided artistic policy. His spirit of *Aufklärung* (OWF-klahr-oong), or

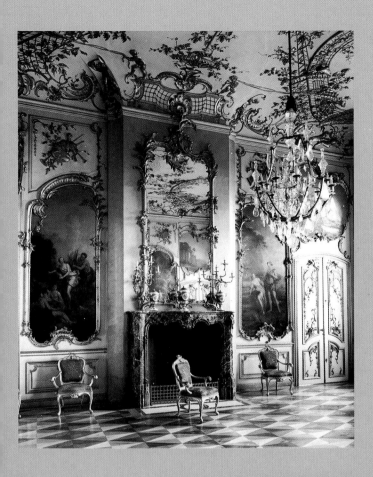

14.37 Georg Wenzelaus von Knobelsdorff, interior of music room, Sans Souci, Potsdam, Germany, 1745–7.

Enlightenment, set the intellectual tone in Berlin, and stimulated a tremendous amount of writing and discussion of music and musical theory. He also exerted considerable influence on composers such as J.S. Bach and C.P.E. Bach.

Frederick the Great often held concerts at his grand Sans Souci Palace in Potsdam (Fig. **14.36**). It represents a new stylistic phase of eighteenth-century German art (Figs. **14.37–14.40**). Designed by Knobelsdorff, the architect of Frederick's opera house, the palace indicates both an increasing German receptivity to French rococo style and an amplification of Italian baroque style. Planned as a retreat for a philosopher-king, Sans Souci, which means "carefree," was Frederick's summer palace where he could work, think, and entertain the intellectual élite of Europe in seclusion and privacy. Voltaire was one of his guests.

14.38 Georg Wenzelaus von Knobelsdorff, garden front of Sans Souci.

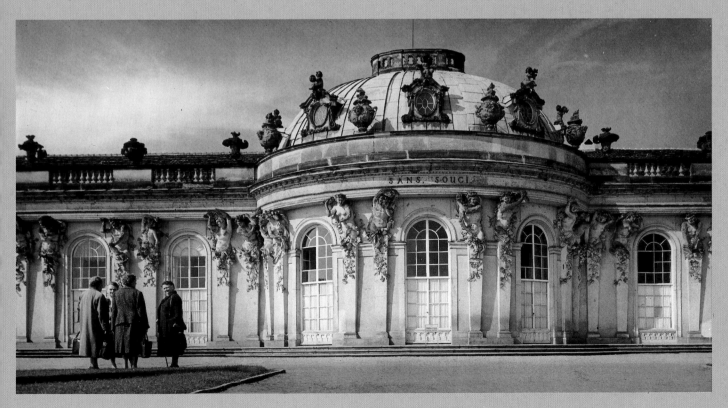

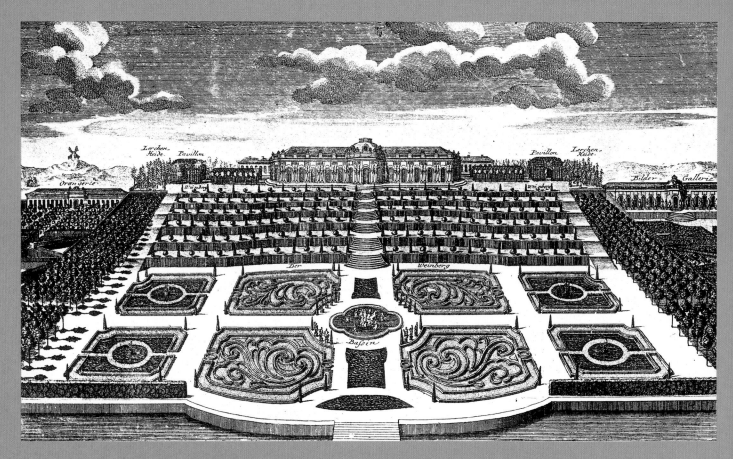

14.39 Garden front of Sans Souci soon after completion. Contemporary engraving.

14.40 (*right*) Georg Wenzelaus von Knobelsdorff, entrance hall, San Souci.

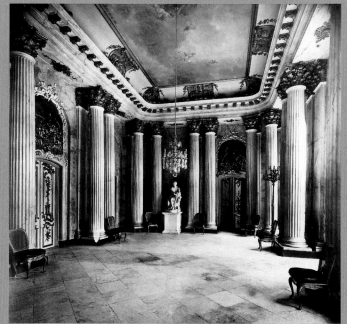

Like Versailles, San Souci had a formal design, as an engraving of the garden front illustrates (Fig. **14.39**). The original plan was Frederick's, and it included terraces faced with glass houses curved to catch the sun's rays from different angles. The entrance way and entrance hall of the palace interior show a return to classical tradition with their curving colonnades and Corinthian columns (Fig. **14.40**). These classical features provide a curious counterpoint to the richness and delicacy of the rococo interior. Sans Souci is a monument to the vision of an enlightened monarch who reflected eighteenth-century ideals. Although a critic of his own German culture, he nonetheless brought about a rich period of German artistry.

Critical Thought

The concept of the "enlightened despot" is an important one with regard to this period. As we noted in the Focal Point section, this century did away with the "absolute monarchs," although the "enlightened despots" survived. The concept describes a condition of social order that seemed to work—at least at the time. Power, although not absolute, rested in a monarch: therefore, things got done. The enlightened attitude of the monarch, however, made it possible to meet the needs of even the lowest, most humble individual in society— order was kept, and the basic conditions and rights of humans were respected and maintained. Life seemed pretty good on the whole—at least in the German states in the eighteenth century. In France, on the other hand, the roughshod ways of absolute monarchy caused a mass uprising in which the aristocracy was not only overthrown but exterminated under the guillotine. Once the mob controlled France, however, conditions got even worse, and chaos reigned. Eventually this rude sort of democracy led to the emergence, not of a king, but of a dictator—Napoleon—leading some to speculate that enlightened despotism was a better form of government than democracy. Where do the "rights" of individuals stop and the "rights" of society begin?

Summary

After reading this chapter, you should be able to:

- Relate the politics, economics, and technology of the eighteenth century to the condition of the general social order in Europe and America.
- Describe the philosophes and the nature of philosophy during the Enlightenment.
- Discuss the prevalent aesthetics of the time and apply specific events, publications, and people to your discussion.
- Characterize the rococo, neoclassical, and other approaches to visual art and architecture with specific reference to individual artists and works of art.
- Identify individual writers of the Enlightenment period and their works.
- Define classical style and its antecedents in music with reference to particular developments, forms, composers, and works.
- Explain the nature of theatre and dance during the eighteenth century by outlining specific conditions and developments, as well as individuals.
- Apply the elements and principles of composition to analyze and compare individual works of art and architecture illustrated in this chapter.

CHAPTER FIFTEEN

The Romantic Age

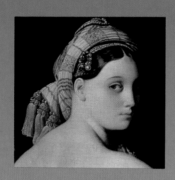

OUTLINE

THE AGE OF INDUSTRY
Technology
  TECHNOLOGY: Exact Tolerance
Social Changes
Marxism
Science
Philosophy
Internationalism
Patronage

ROMANTICISM IN THE VISUAL ARTS AND ARCHITECTURE
  MASTERWORK: Géricault—*The Raft of the "Medusa"*
  PROFILE: Rosa Bonheur
  OUR DYNAMIC WORLD: Japanese Painting

ROMANTICISM IN LITERATURE
Wordsworth
Jane Austen
  MASTERWORK: Austen—*Pride and Prejudice*
Other Nineteenth-Century Romantics

ROMANTICISM IN MUSIC
Lieder
Piano Works
Program Music
Symphonies
Trends
Choral Music
  PROFILE: Johannes Brahms
Opera

ROMANTICISM IN THEATRE
Popularism and Historical Accuracy
Melodrama

ROMANTICISM IN DANCE

FOCAL POINT: THE VICTORIANS

VIEW

VALIDATING SUBJECTIVE EXPERIENCES

"The Romantic Age," the title of this chapter, refers to the style and direction of art, literature, and philosophy of the late eighteenth and nineteenth centuries, and, in this context, the word Romantic has a different connotation from our customary use. Of course, the word means "having to do with romance"—that is, a love affair—but it also has to do with a romance, which is a long narrative story dealing with the exploits of a chivalrous hero. Romantic also means "having to do with romanticism," an assertion of subjective experience and feeling in opposition to the form and objectivity of classicism. Thus, when we speak of the Romantic age, we speak of living, thinking, perceiving, and communicating with a focus on subjectivity rather than objectivity. We are about to watch the classical/anti-classical pendulum swing again, and this time it will swing further than ever toward emotionalism. The temperament of the artist becomes a filter through which the world is viewed, and the only limits placed on art are the practicalities of the artistic disciplines themselves.

Above Detail of Fig. **15.4.**

15.1 Caspar David Friedrich, *The Wanderer above the Mists*, c. 1817–18. Oil on canvas, 29½ × 37¼ ins (74.8 × 94.8 cm). Kunsthalle, Hamburg, Germany.

KEY TERMS

Some of the basic terms and concepts we will encounter in this chapter include the following:

Industrial Revolution, social and economic changes brought about when extensive mechanization resulted in a shift from home manufacturing to large-scale factory production.

Idealism, a philosophy contending that the nature of reality is the nature of the mind—that is, ideal.

Romanticism, a literary and artistic movement that sought to assert the validity of subjective experience.

Marxism, the body of ideas developed by Karl Marx, forming the basic tenets of modern socialism and communism.

Program music, musical works built around a non-musical story.

Melodrama, a type of theatre characterized by sensationalism and sentimentality.

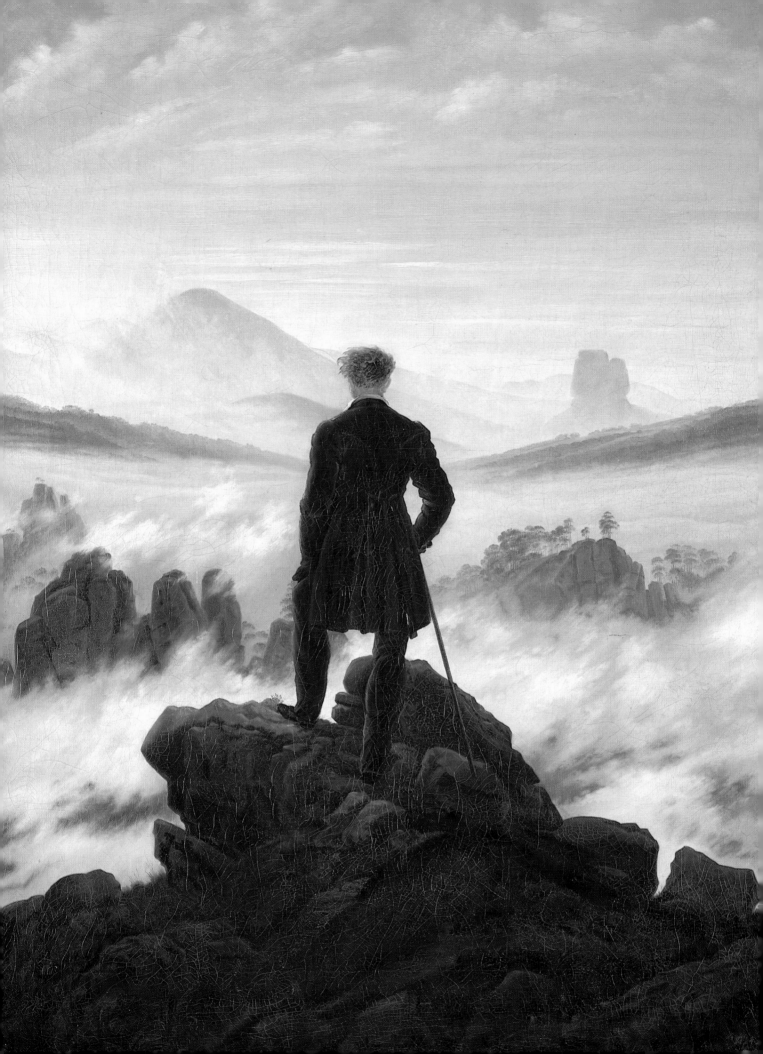

THE AGE OF INDUSTRY

The major social development since the Middle Ages had been the rise of the middle class. Until the French Revolution, the British middle class had reaped the greatest benefit from changing circumstances. Capitalism had gradually replaced the guild system, and individual initiative fostered a spirit of invention.

The first major industry to profit from the new inventions was the textile industry, which was fundamental to the requirements of society. Cumulative inventions revolutionized the British textile industry to the point where one worker with a machine could do as much work in a day as four or five people had previously accomplished. The increased production capacity meant more cotton could be planted in Britain's colonies in the southern United States, and now more cotton could be processed, because Eli Whitney's cotton gin could replace a dozen slaves.

Technology

The early years of the nineteenth century saw wide experimentation with sources and uses of energy. Gas was generally used as a fuel and for illumination. Yet the pursuit of technological efficiency was so effective that gas was replaced by electricity before the century was over.

Important developments in engine design took place in the first two decades of the nineteenth century. The early steam engine could generate only enough steam pressure to drive one cylinder at one pressure, and although water turbines were much more efficient, they could be installed only near moving water. It took only a few years to find the path to a more efficient engine, however, and by the second decade of the century, a successful compound engine had been developed. The principal use of the compound steam engine was in ocean-going ships, and because the engine required less fuel, the cargo capacity of the ships was proportionately increased. Later developments included steam turbines and internal combustion engines.

By the mid-nineteenth century, the world's entire transportation system had undergone a complete revolution. Steam engines ran sawmills, printing presses, pumping stations, and hundreds of other kinds of machinery, and further inventions and discoveries followed on the heels of steam power. Electricity, too, was in fairly wide use before the century was over, at least in the urban centers. The discovery of electricity made the telegraph possible in 1832. Telegraph lines spanned continents and, in 1866, joined them via the first transatlantic cable. The telephone was invented in 1876, and by 1895, radio-telegraphy was ready for twentieth-century development.

Mining production increased when new explosives, based on nitroglycerine, and more powerful hoisting and pumping equipment were introduced, making ore extraction and separation more efficient. These improvements were eclipsed, however, by the flotation method devised by the Bessel brothers in 1877. Significant improvements in smelting furnaces, such as the blast furnace and the "wet process" of Joseph Hall, along with Nasmyth's steam hammer, improved production of iron and steel.

In America, a new process for producing what became known as "Bessemer steel" soon made wrought iron obsolete and provided high-quality steel for rails, ships and, late in the century, building beams and girders. Further refinements of the "open hearth" steel process produced even higher quality, more economical steel. The development of the rolling mill made possible more and more applications, including cable for suspension bridges. The most famous use of suspension cable at the time was in the Brooklyn Bridge in 1883.

A major problem in food distribution had been the shipment and storage of perishables. Natural ice was used worldwide for large-scale refrigeration early in the nineteenth century, but shortly after the middle of the century, the development of ice cabinets the size of railroad cars and improved tools for harvesting ice meant that perishable goods could be refrigerated, and frozen goods could even be shipped across the American continent.

At the mid-point of the century, the process of pasteurization was discovered, eliminating several milk-borne diseases. Largely as a result of the experiments of Nicholas Appert, early in the nineteenth century, the use of heat in preserving food gave rise to the canning industry, and by the late 1840s, hermetic sealing was widespread.

Another major aspect of the technological revolution was the harnessing of electricity. By the nineteenth century, the wet battery provided a source for the continuous flow of current. Electrical energy was gradually applied to heating, lighting, and mechanical energy. Experiments produced a practical filament for an incandescent light bulb. The electric-powered streetcar rendered horsecars obsolete by 1888. By 1895 Niagara Falls had been harnessed for hydroelectric power. Elsewhere, long transmission lines and transformers carried electrical power throughout the Western world. By the turn of the twentieth century, the Western world had been fully mechanized.

Social Changes

The Industrial Revolution began in Britain and, at the conclusion of the Napoleonic wars in 1815, spread to France and the rest of Europe. It gained momentum as it spread, and irrevocably altered the fabric of civilization.

By 1871, the year of the first unification of Germany, major industrial centers had been established all over Europe.

Coal and iron production gave Britain, Germany, France, and Belgium the lead in European industry. But vast resources of coal, iron, and other raw materials, more than all Europe had, soon propelled the United States into a position of economic dominance. Throughout the Western world, centers of heavy industry grew up near the sources of raw materials and transportation routes. Colonial expansion provided world markets for new goods. Wealth increased enormously, and although the effects of investment were felt at every level of society, the principal effect of industrialization was to centralize economic control in the hands of a relatively small class of capitalists. Populations grew as the mortality rate went down. A new class of machine workers, "blue-collar workers," or labor, emerged.

Drawn from pre-industrial home industries and farms, the new machine-worker class lived and worked in deplorable conditions. No longer their own masters, they became virtual slaves. Unable to help themselves, they were subject to severe organizing restrictions, hampered by lack of education, and threatened constantly by the prospect of unemployment. Slums, tenements, and horrifying living conditions awaited them. The middle classes, caught up in their own aspirations to wealth and political power, largely ignored their plight.

The middle class now turned toward Liberalism, a political program dedicated to advancing religious toleration and reducing the authority of a dominant Church, reducing the power of the monarch or the aristocracy through constitutional means, and removing provincial economic barriers through nationalism. In other words, Liberalism built its political program on those movements that would enhance middle-class power. It gained widespread support, and became the political watchword of the age. Part of the middle-class program was a *laissez-faire*, or "Let people do as they please," economic policy.

A new code of morality stressed individual freedom. The "free man" became the model of what one could achieve only by standing on one's own feet and creating one's own destiny. Individual freedom was achieved by struggle and eventual triumph. The unfit—the degraded masses—perished; the fit—a few rugged individuals—survived.

The masses, however, wanted to count too. In order for them to do so, two conditions had to be met. They needed a basic education, and they needed basic confidence in themselves. Only in Prussia was there a public school system that provided mass education. Britain and France did nothing about this until the 1870s and 1880s. In the United States local support for public education began as early as the 1820s, but even the concept of mass education did not take root until mid-century, and compulsory elementary education was not introduced until toward the end of the nineteenth century.

Many different solutions to the working-class problem were proposed—philanthropy, utopianism, and, most important of all, the socialism of Karl Marx (1818–83). Gradually, and not without bloodshed, workers acquired the right to form unions. But it was only in the second half of the nineteenth century that laborers began to unionize, and thereby to promote their own interests.

Marxism

Karl Marx (marks; 1818–83), a German economist, philosopher, and revolutionist, developed the body of ideas known as Marxism, and together with Friedrich Engels (ENG-els), he formed the basic tenets of modern socialism and communism. As a university student, Marx was strongly influenced by the ideas of Hegel and by a group of radical students who tried to use Hegelian thought in a movement against organized religion and the Prussian aristocracy. Later, Marx turned to a book called *The Essence of Christianity*, written by Ludwig Feuerbach, and adapted its central thesis—that if religion were abolished, human beings could overcome their alienation—to argue for the abolition of private property. According to Marx, private property caused humans to work only for themselves, not for the good of their species. He further argued that alienation had an economic base, and he called for a communist society to overcome the dehumanizing effect of private property. Still later, with the collaboration of his friend Engels, Marx declared in *The Communist Manifesto* (1848) that all history was the history of class struggles. Under capitalism, the conflict between the working class and the business class would end in a new, communist society. In 1867, Marx published the first volume of *Das Kapital* (the second through fourth volumes were published after Marx's death), a monumental politico-economic study arguing that all history was determined by humanity's relationship to material wealth and that governments served only the interests of the ruling class. He reiterated his prediction of revolution ending first in socialism and then communism. *Das Kapital* became the theoretical basis for modern socialism and communism.

Science

Scientific attention turned both to investigating the atom and formulating theories of evolution. Evolution as a unifying concept in science dated back to the Greeks, but now, Sir Charles Lyell (1797–1875) became the first to

	GENERAL EVENTS	LITERATURE & PHILOSOPHY	VISUAL ART & ARCHITECTURE	PERFORMING ARTS
1800				
	Napoleon Bonaparte Battle of Waterloo Congress of Vienna	Wordsworth Coleridge Scott Austen Byron Shelley Keats Hegel	Goya (15.5) Friedrich (15.1) Ingres (15.4) Géricault (15.6) Hokusai (15.14) Nash (15.11) Delacroix (15.8)	Schubert Mendelssohn Marie Taglioni Berlioz Chopin Rossini
1835	Queen Victoria in Britain	Brontë Balzac Schopenhauer Poe	Corot (15.10) Landseer (15.24) Turner (15.7)	Meyerbeer
	Year of revolutions (1848) in Europe	Comte Dickens	Bonheur (15.9)	Hugo
1850	Milling machine Internal combustion engine US Civil War Transatlantic cable Vatican Council	Darwin Whitman Marx Flaubert Baudelaire	Creswick (15.26) Barry and Pugin (15.12) Paxton (15.13) Dadd (15.25)	Tchaikovsky Offenbach Thomas Liszt Petipa Gounod Verdi Wagner
1875		Spencer James		Brahms Strauss

Timeline 15.1 The Romantic age.

coordinate earth studies, and his *Principles of Geology* (1830) provided an important base for evolutionary thinking. In 1859 Charles Darwin (1809–82) put forward the concept of natural selection as the explanation of species development in *The Origin of Species*. Darwin's theories were given a practical base when Gregor Mendel's (MEHN-duhl) work on inheritance, originally done in 1866, was rediscovered and developed in 1900. Evolution was established as the framework that the science of biology would use for the foreseeable future.

A clash between evolution and Christianity was inevitable. After the initial shock, many Protestant denominations were able to come to grips with the principles of evolution. This was easier for Protestants than for Roman Catholics because, essentially, Protestants recognized the right of individuals to make private judgments, while Catholics had to accept doctrinal control. At the same time that evolutionary doctrine was first being propounded, some Protestant scholars were acknowledging the Bible as

a compilation of human writings over a period of time, written under real, historical circumstances and not dictated, word for word, by God. Of course, some Christian groups condemned these notions as just as evil as Darwinism. Nevertheless, Protestantism, in general, gradually arrived at a "modern" outlook. Pope Pius IX, on the other hand, rejected evolution in his *Syllabus of Errors* (1864), and the Vatican Council of 1870 declared papal infallibility. The Church maintained a position of intransigence on the subject of evolution throughout the papacy of Leo XIII (1878–1903).

Philosophy

Idealism

In the late eighteenth century, Immanuel Kant put forward a dualistic metaphysics that distinguished between a knowable world of sense perceptions and an unknowable

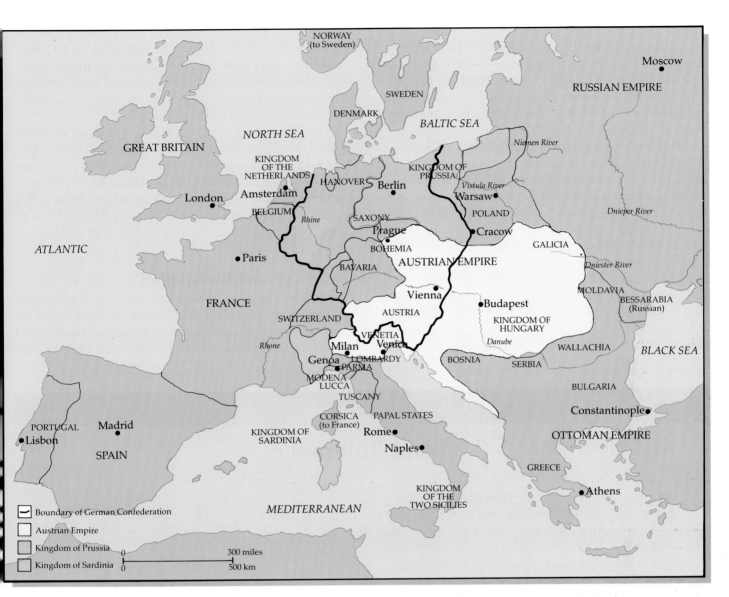

Map 15.1 The industrialized world in the nineteenth century.

world of essences. This reconciliation of philosophical extremes led to a nineteenth-century philosophy focused on the emotions. According to Kant, the real world, so far as humans could possibly rationalize it, is a mental reconstruction, an ideal world of the understanding; thus, the nature of reality is of the nature of the mind—that is, ideal. Hence the doctrines were called *Kantian idealism.*

Such an idealistic appeal was also called *Romanticism,* and this reaction against eighteenth-century rationalism permeated both philosophy and the arts. Other German idealists—Johann Fichte (FIK-te; 1762–1814) and Friedrich Schelling (1775–1854), for example—rejected Kant's dualism, and developed an absolute system, based on emotion, that asserted the oneness of God and nature. However, nineteenth-century idealism, or Romanticism, culminated in the work of Georg Wilhelm Friedrich Hegel

(HAY-gul 1770–1831), who believed that both God and humankind possessed unfolding and expanding energy. Hegelian philosophy combined German idealism with a belief in evolutionary development and viewed the course of human history optimistically.

Hegel's Aesthetic Theory

Hegel's philosophy viewed "reality" as spirit, or mind. Hegel believed art to be *one* ultimate form, but not *the* ultimate form, of mind. Philosophy was the final form, while art was a preliminary "step toward truth."

According to Hegel, the objective of art is beauty, which is, in turn, a means for expressing truth. He defined beauty as the "sensuous appearance of the Idea, or the show of the Absolute Concept. The Concept which shows itself for itself is art."[1] Hegel believed classical art was the format whereby the ideal content "reaches the highest level that sensuous, imaginative material can correctly express." Classical art comprises the perfection of artistic beauty, and the essence of classical art, for Hegel, is sculpture. Hegel conceived of sculpture in the same way as the classical Greeks did—that is, as the expression of the human form which alone can "reveal Spirit in sensuous fashion."

This assertion goes back to the ideas of Kant and Winckelmann. Kant maintained that human beings alone are capable of an ideal of beauty, and Winckelmann saw Greek sculpture as the perfection of beauty. Hegel went beyond Kant and Winckelmann to suggest that "Greek religion realized a concept of the divine which harmonized the ethical and the natural. Hence the Greek gods, the subject of Greek sculpture, are the perfect expression of a religion of art itself."

Finally, Romantic art evolves content to such a degree that it contains "more than any sensuous imaginative material can expressly embody." Being subjective, the content of Romantic art is the "Absolute that knows itself in its own spirituality." As Hegel attempts to reconcile this concept with the Christian concept of God, he ranks Romantic art in three progressively more spiritual forms. First comes painting, second is music, and third is poetry, the most spiritual and universal of all the arts, which includes within itself all the others.

The idealism of Schelling, Fichte, and Hegel was challenged by Artur Schopenhauer (SHOH-pen-how-uhr; 1788–1860), who saw the world as a gigantic machine that was operating according to its unchanging law. Schopenhauer recognized no Creator, no benevolent Father, only a tyrannical and unfathomable First Cause. If Hegel was an optimist, Schopenhauer was a pessimist of the highest order.

Positivism and Materialism

Unlike the Germans, who were intent on coping with metaphysical issues, the British and French focused on philosophical explanations of the emerging, mechanized world. To them, what was beyond this world was beyond

TECHNOLOGY: PUTTING DISCOVERY TO WORK

Exact Tolerance

All areas of industry saw the invention and design of new machines and machine tools throughout the century. One of these was the milling machine (Fig. **15.2**), whose rotary cutting edges made possible the manufacture of parts of exact tolerance that could be interchanged in a single product. This idea of interchangeable parts is called the "American System," and is generally attributed to Eli Whitney. The armaments industry also began to use a new grinding machine that enabled machinists to shape metal parts as opposed to merely polishing or sharpening them. Further experiments refined the accuracy of grinding wheels and improved their abrasive surfaces. A new turret lathe made it possible to use several tools on a workpiece. Advances of this sort made possible a "second generation" of machine tools in the industrialized West.

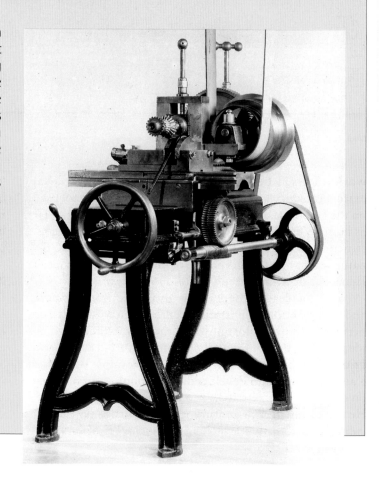

15.2 F.A. Pratt and Amos Whitney, the Lincoln Miller, 1855. Smithsonian Institution, Washington D.C.

knowledge and, therefore, inconsequential. For philosophers such as the Frenchman Auguste Comte (kohnt; 1798–1857), the nineteenth century was an era of science; Comte saw philosophy's task as the sorting out of factual details of worldly existence rather than the solution of riddles of an unknown universe. Comte's philosophy was called "positivism," and his approach formed the basis for the science of sociology.

Across the channel in Britain, Herbert Spencer (1820–1903) expounded a philosophy of evolutionary "materialism," in which evolution provided the framework. He also believed that a struggle for existence and survival of the fittest were fundamental social processes, and that the human mind, ethics, social organization, and economics were "exactly what they ought to be."

Internationalism

Mechanization, especially in transportation and communications, made the nineteenth century an international age while, at the same time, nations strove for individual power. Communications networks bridged distances, and there were increasing numbers of international agreements. All this was set against fierce and imperialistic competition for raw materials and marketplaces. The nations of the Western world depended upon armaments to secure and protect their advances. In the late nineteenth century, various pragmatic alliances and treaties were forged under the guise of cooperation, but, in fact, they cast the die for war.

War was an ever-present specter in European existence. At the close of the eighteenth century, as France struggled to emerge from the chaos of its Revolution, Napoleon Bonaparte maneuvered his way to power. He skillfully planned his rise from first consul to dictator behind a screen of hand-picked legislators. War with Britain and Austria persisted, and Napoleon set about resolving things in France's favor. The battle of Marengo in 1800 gave France all of Italy and crushed the Austrians at a single stroke. The Peace of Amiens with Britain in 1802 left Napoleon free to concentrate on rebuilding France. But the Franco-British War was renewed in 1803. With Napoleon's rise to emperor in 1804, his armies swept across Europe.

After Napoleon's defeat at Waterloo in 1815, the Congress of Vienna attempted to arrange the affairs of Europe (Fig. 15.3). In essence, the Congress, which was controlled by factions of the old aristocracy, gave legitimacy to the restoration of dynasties that had been displaced by the Revolution, and it returned Europe to pre-Revolution boundaries. War and revolution continued to sweep through Europe in 1820, 1830, and 1848. A new

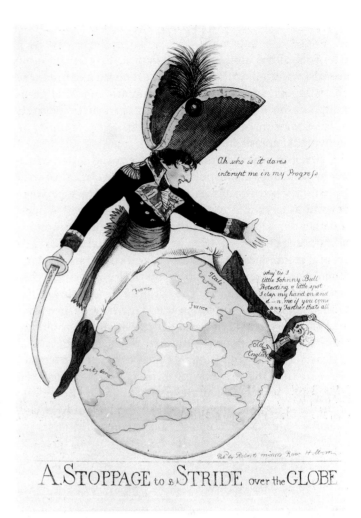

15.3 Anonymous cartoon, "A stoppage to a stride over the globe," showing Napoleon's expansion checked by the English, c. 1810.

Napoleon emerged in 1849—Louis, who later became Napoleon III. War hovered around the edges of Europe in 1854, then returned in full force in 1859.

The times were full of turbulence and frustration. France, for example, had an entire generation of young men raised in an era of patriotic and military fervor under Napoleon. After his defeat, they were left to vegetate in a country ruined by war and controlled by a weak, conservative government. Feelings of isolation and alienation increased. The suffering, isolated, sensitive youth, personified by Goethe's Werther (see p. 447), became the Romantic hero. Curiosity about the supernatural was rampant. Escape to Utopia was a common goal. Those who saw salvation in a "return to nature" saw nature, on the one hand, as the ultimate source of reason, and, on the other, as a boundless, completely free environment in which all emotions could be freely expressed. This latter idea became a core for Romanticism.

Patronage

The role of the artist changed significantly in the nineteenth century. For the first time, art could exist without the support of significant aristocratic and religious commissions and patronage. In fact, artists deliberately resisted patronage, which imposed unwelcome limits on individual expression.

Artists enjoyed a new place in the social order. Much art became individualistic and increasingly critical of society and its institutions. A huge gap opened up between rebellious personal expression and established values, whether of a critic or of society at large, and this prompted some artists to try out increasingly personal and experimental techniques. In many cases, artists, and particularly visual artists, were barred from the world with which they needed to communicate. The traditional academies that controlled formal exhibitions would not hang their works, and commercial galleries, and hence the public, would not buy them. As a result, many artists became the social outcasts, the starving Romantic heroes, of public legend. We can find these "starving artists"—a poet, painter, philosopher, and musician—explored in Puccini's opera *La Bohème* (The Bohemians), and the "bohemian lifestyle" remains a phrase that connotes such a way of living.

ROMANTICISM IN THE VISUAL ARTS AND ARCHITECTURE

Many painters willingly championed the cause of Romanticism. The Romantic style had an emotional appeal, and its subjects tended toward the picturesque, including nature, Gothic images, and often, the macabre. In seeking to break the geometric principles of classical composition, Romantic compositions moved toward fragmentation of images, with the intention of dramatizing, personalizing, and escaping into imagination. Such painting strove to subordinate formal content to expressive intent, and to express an intense introversion. As the writer Émile Zola said: "A work of art is part of the universe as seen through a temperament." Many Romantic painters are worthy of note, but a look at the work of seven painters should provide a general overview of what the movement was all about.

In many ways, Jean-Auguste-Dominique Ingres (ANG-gruh; 1780–1867) pursued the physical and intellectual perfection initiated by David (see p. 440). Ingres's work illustrates the complex relationships and occasional

15.4 Jean-Auguste-Dominique Ingres, *La Grande Odalisque* (*Harem Girl*), 1814. Oil on canvas, 36¼ × 63¼ ins (92 × 160.6 cm). Louvre, Paris.

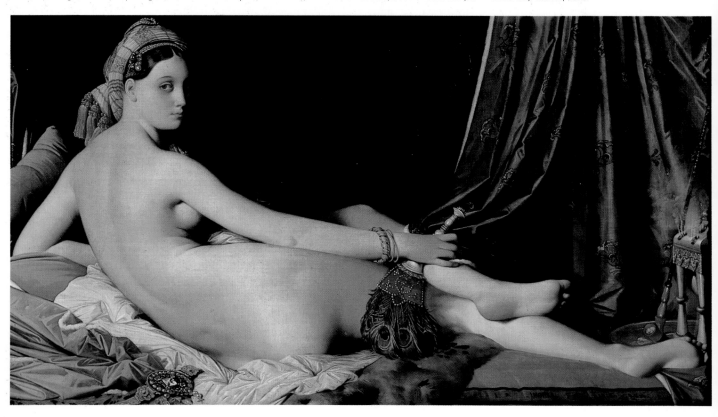

conflicts between neoclassicalism and Romanticism, as we mentioned in the last chapter. Painted in 1814, Ingres's *La Grande Odalisque* or *Harem Girl* (Fig. **15.4**) has been called both neoclassical and romantic, and in many ways it represents both styles and their relationships. Ingres professed to despise Romanticism, and yet the proportions he gives his subject matter, and the subject matter itself, exude individual style and a Romantic longing for exotic times and places. His textures, too, are sensuous and emotional, yet his line is simple, his palette, cool, and his spatial effects, geometric. The linear rhythms of this painting are very precise and calculated and, perhaps, classical in their appeal.

Théodore Géricault (tay-oh-DOHR zhay-ree-KOH; 1791–1824) was an important early French Romantic. His life offers us a fully developed example of the Romantic hero: he was a brilliant prodigy, he was a champion of the downtrodden, and he died extremely young. He was a Romantic in his art as well. Although greatly influenced by David, Géricault departed drastically from his master in his brushwork. David insisted that the surface of a painting

should be smooth and that the brushwork should not show. Géricault uses the visual impact of the strokes themselves to communicate mood. He accepted the heroic view of human struggle that characterized this period, and his paintings frequently treat the human struggle against the violent forces of nature. His famous painting *The Raft of the "Medusa"* (see Fig. **15.6**) is much like Michelangelo's work in its turbulence and grandeur.

The Spanish painter and printmaker Francisco de Goya (frahn-THEES-koh day GOY-ah; 1746–1828) used his paintings to attack the abuses perpetrated by governments, both the Spanish and the French. His highly imaginative and often nightmarish works capture the emotional character of humanity and nature, and frequently their malevolence.

The Third of May 1808 (Fig. **15.5**) tells a true story. On that date, the citizens of Madrid rebelled against the invading army of Napoleon. People were arbitrarily arrested and summarily executed. Using compositional devices even more fragmented than those of Géricault, Goya captured the climactic moment in the story. It is

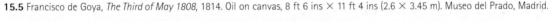

15.5 Francisco de Goya, *The Third of May 1808*, 1814. Oil on canvas, 8 ft 6 ins × 11 ft 4 ins (2.6 × 3.45 m). Museo del Prado, Madrid.

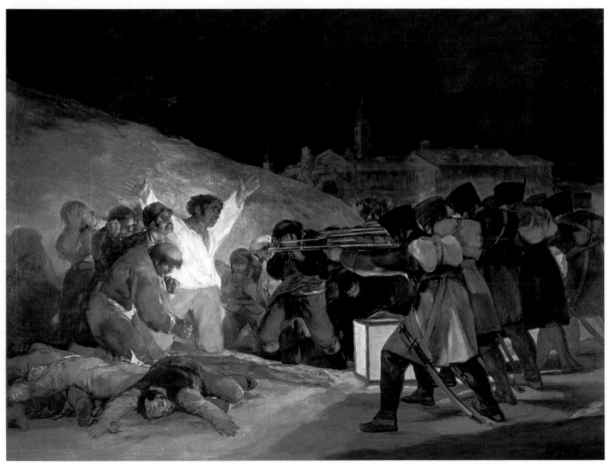

MASTERWORK

Géricault—*The Raft of the "Medusa"*

*T*he Raft of the "Medusa" (Fig. **15.6**) by Théodore Géricault illustrates both an emerging rebellion against classicism in painting and a growing criticism of social institutions in general. The painting tells a story of governmental incompetence that resulted in tragedy. In 1816, the French government allowed an unseaworthy ship, the *Medusa*, to leave port, and it was wrecked. Aboard a makeshift raft, the survivors endured tremendous suffering, and were eventually driven to cannibalism. In preparing for the work, Géricault interviewed the survivors, read newspaper accounts, and went so far as to paint corpses and the heads of guillotined criminals.

In contrast to David's ordered, two-dimensional paintings, for example, Géricault used complex and fragmented compositional structures. For example, he chose to base the design on two triangles rather than a strong central triangle. In *The Raft of the "Medusa"* the left triangle's apex is the makeshift mast, which points back toward despair and death. The other triangle moves up to the right to the figure waving the fabric, pointing toward hope and life as a rescue ship appears in the distance.

Géricault captures the precise moment at which the rescue ship is sighted. The play of light and shade heightens the dramatic effect, and the composition builds upward from the bodies of the dead and dying in the foreground to the dynamic group whose final energies are summoned to support the figure waving to the ship.

15.6 Théodore Géricault, *The Raft of the "Medusa"*, 1819. Oil on canvas, 16 ft × 23 ft 6 ins (4.91 × 7.16 m). Louvre, Paris.

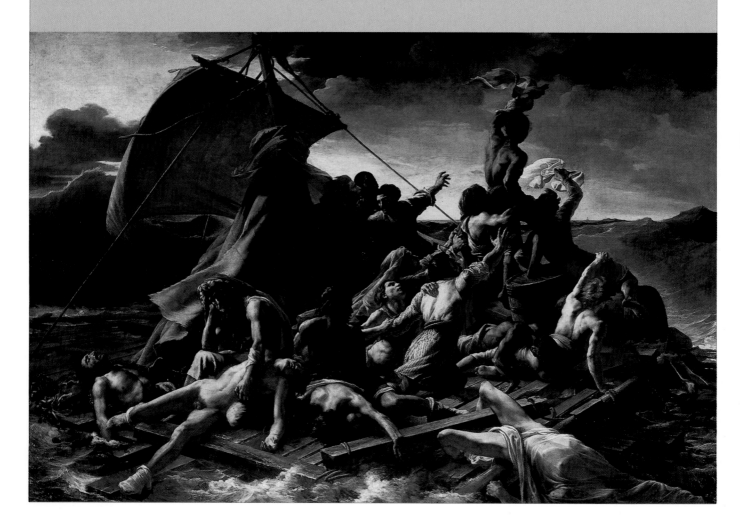

impossible to escape the focal point of the painting, the man in white who is about to die. Goya's strong value contrasts force the eye back to the victim; only the lantern behind the soldiers keeps the composition in balance.

Goya leads us beyond the death of individuals here. These figures are not naturalistically depicted people. Instead, Goya makes a powerful social and emotional statement. Napoleon's soldiers are not even human types. Their faces are hidden, and their rigid, repeated forms become a line of subhuman automatons. The murky quality of the background strengthens the value contrasts in the painting and this charges the emotional drama of the scene. Color areas have hard edges, and a stark line of light running diagonally from the oversized lantern to the lower border irrevocably separates executioners and victims. Goya has no sympathy for French soldiers as human beings here. His subjectivity fills the painting, which is as

emotional as the irrational behavior he wished to condemn.

The Englishman J.M.W. Turner (1775–1851) indulged in a subjectivity even beyond that of his Romantic contemporaries, and his work foreshadows the dissolving image of twentieth-century painting. The Romantic painter John Constable described Turner's works as "airy visions painted with tinted steam." *The Slave Ship* (Fig. **15.7**) visualizes a passage in James Thomson's poem *The Seasons* which describes how sharks follow a slave ship in a storm, "lured by the scent of steaming crowds of rank disease, and death." The poem was based on an actual event, where the captain of a slave ship dumped his human cargo into the sea when disease broke out below decks.

Turner's work demonstrates the elements of Romantic painting. His disjointed diagonals contribute to an overall fragmentation of the composition. His space is deeply

15.7 Joseph Mallord William Turner, *The Slave Ship* (*Slavers Throwing Overboard the Dead and Dying, Typhoon Coming On*), 1840. Oil on canvas, 35³⁄₄ × 48¹⁄₄ ins (90.8 × 122.6 cm). Museum of Fine Arts, Boston (Henry Lillie Pierce Fund).

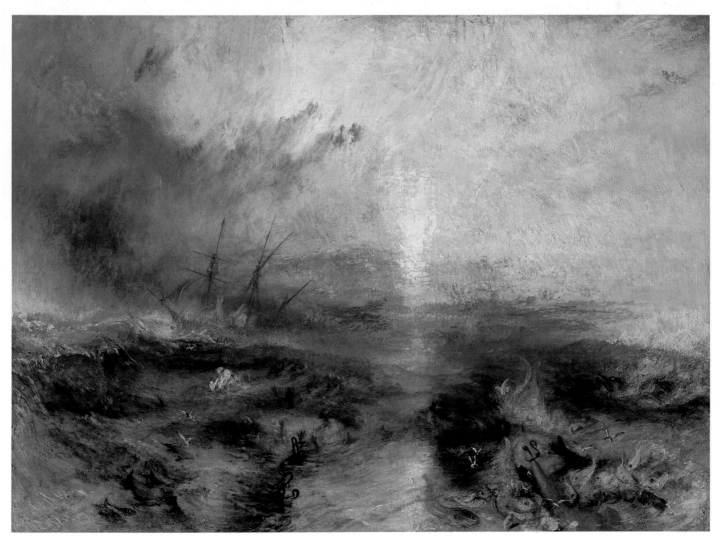

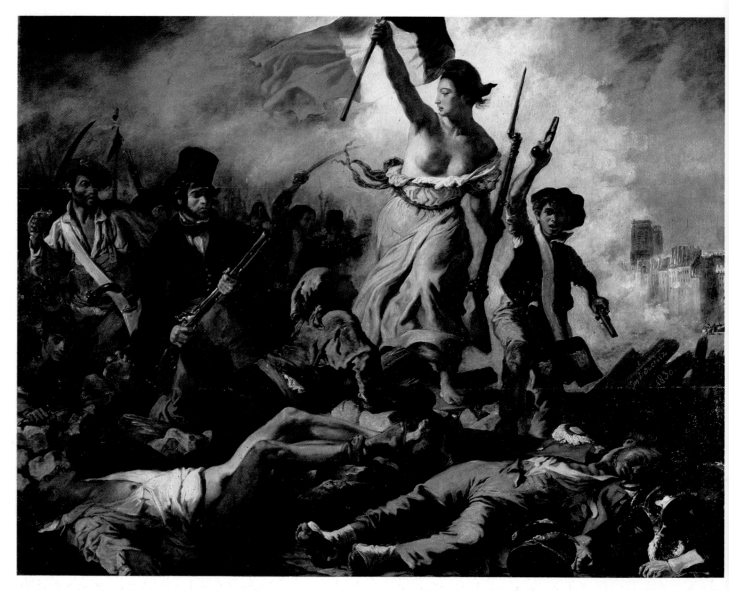

15.8 Eugène Delacroix, *The 28th July: Liberty Leading the People*, 1830. Oil on canvas, 8 ft 6 ins × 10 ft 7 ins (2.59 × 3.25 m). Louvre, Paris.

three-dimensional. The turbulence of the event pictured is reflected in the loose painting technique. The sea and sky appear transparent, and the brushstrokes are energetic and spontaneous. Expression dominates form and content, and a sense of doom prevails.

Eugène Delacroix (duh-lah-KWAH; 1798–1863) employed color, light, and shade to capture the climactic moments of high emotion. In *The 28th July: Liberty Leading the People* (Fig. **15.8**), Delacroix shows the allegorical figure of Liberty bearing aloft the tricolor flag of France and leading the charge of a freedom-loving common people. Lights and darks provide strong and dramatic contrasts. The red, white, and blue of the French flag symbolize patriotism, purity, and freedom, and as

Delacroix picks up these colors throughout the work, they also serve to balance and unify the scene.

The approach of Jean-Baptiste-Camille Corot (koh-ROH; 1796–1875) is often described as "Romantic naturalism." Corot was among the first to execute finished paintings out-of-doors rather than in the studio. He wanted to recreate the full luminosity of nature and to capture the natural effect of visual perception, that is, how the eye focuses on detail and how peripheral vision actually works. In *Volterra* (Fig. **15.10**), he strives to this true-to-life visual effect by reducing the graphic clarity of all details except those of the central objects which he presents very clearly, just as our eyes perceive clearly only those objects on which we are focusing at the moment, while

PROFILE

Rosa Bonheur (1822–99)

One of the most significant and prominent women artists of the time, Rosa Bonheur focused her artistic attention almost solely on animals. Born in Bordeaux, France, she was the eldest of four children of an amateur painter. After early instruction from her father, she studied with Léon Cogniet at the École des Beaux-Arts in Paris, and rather early on began to specialize in animal subjects, studying them wherever she could. Her early paintings won awards in Paris, and in 1848, she won a first-class medal for *Plowing in the Nivernais* (Fig. **15.9**). By 1853 her work had reached full maturity, and she received high acclaim in Europe and the United States. Her paintings were much admired and became widely known through engraved copies. She was also well known as a sculptor, and her animal subjects led to her success among contemporary French sculptors.

Rosa Bonheur had an independent spirit and fought to gain acceptance on a level equal to that of male artists of the time. Her ability and popularity earned her the title of Chevalier of the Legion of Honor in 1865, and she was the first woman to receive the Grand Cross of the Legion. Befriended by Queen Victoria of Britain, who became her patron, Bonheur became a favorite among the British aristocracy, although her last years were spent in France, and she died near Fontainebleau in 1899.

15.9 Rosa Bonheur, *Plowing in the Nivernais*, 1849. Oil on canvas, 5 ft 9 ins × 8 ft 8 ins (1.75 × 2.64 m). Musée Nationale du Château de Fontainebleau, France.

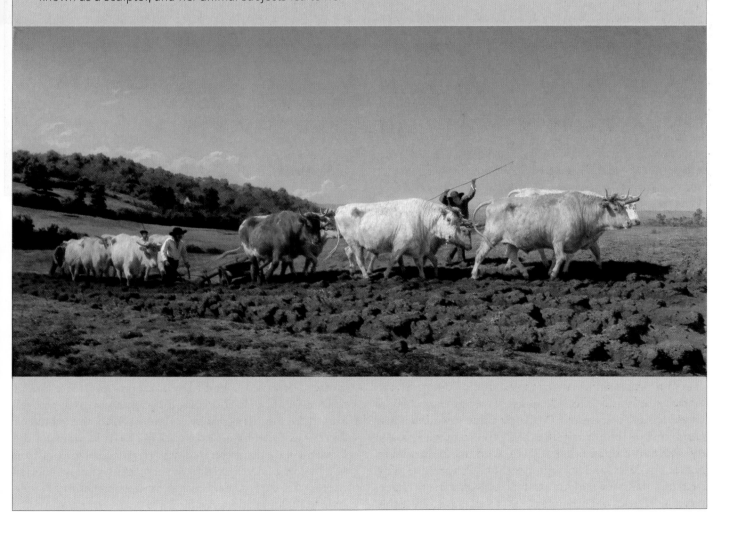

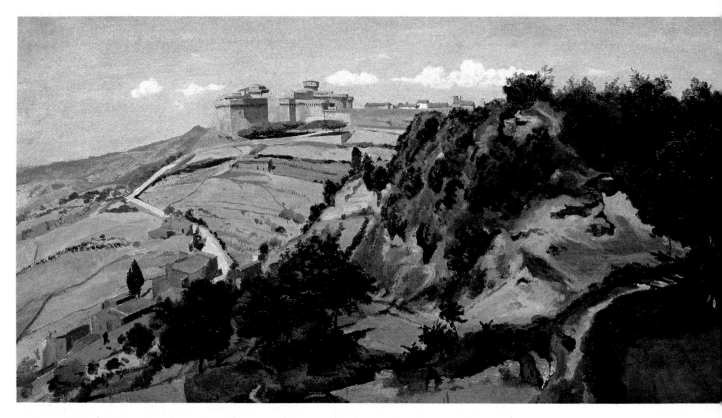

15.10 Jean-Baptiste-Camille Corot, *Volterra*, 1843. Oil on canvas, 18¹/₂ × 32¹/₄ ins (47 × 82 cm). Louvre, Paris.

everything else in our field of vision is relatively out of focus. Corot's works are spontaneous and subjective, but he retains a formal order to balance that spontaneity.

Rosa Bonheur (bawn-UR; 1822–99), certainly the most popular woman painter of her time, has been labeled both a "realist" and a "Romantic" in style. Her subjects were mostly animals and their raw energy. "Wading in pools of blood," as she put it, she studied animal anatomy even in slaughter houses, and was particularly interested in animal psychology. *Plowing in the Nivernais* (nee-vair-NAY; see Fig. **15.9**) captures the tremendous power of the oxen on which European agriculture had depended before the Industrial Revolution. The beasts appear almost monumental, and each detail is precisely executed. The painting clearly reveals Bonheur's reverence for the dignity of labor and her vision of human beings in harmony with nature.

Romantic architecture also borrowed styles from other eras and produced a vast array of buildings that revived Gothic motifs and reflected fantasy. This style has come to be known as "picturesque." Eastern influence and whimsy abounded in John Nash's Royal Pavilion in Brighton, in the south of England (Fig. **15.11**), with its onion-shaped domes, minarets, and horseshoe arches. "Picturesque" also describes the most famous example of Romantic architecture, the Houses of Parliament (Fig. **15.12**), a building that

demonstrates one significant architectural concept that can be described as "modern." The exterior walls function simply as a screen, and have nothing to say about structure, interior design, or function. The inside has absolutely no spatial relationship to the outside. The strong contrast of forms and asymmetrical balance also suggest the modern.

If the nineteenth century was an age of industry, it was also an age of experimentation and new materials. In architecture, steel and glass came to the fore. At first, an architect needed much courage actually to display the support materials as part of the design itself. The Crystal Palace in London (Fig. **15.13**) exemplified the nineteenth-century fascination with new materials and concepts. Built for the Great Exhibition of 1851, this mammoth structure was completed in the space of nine months. Space was defined by a three-dimensional grid of iron stanchions and girders, designed specifically for mass production and rapid assembly. (In this case, disassembly was also possible—the entire structure was disassembled and rebuilt in 1852–4 at Sydenham.) Like the Houses of Parliament, the Crystal Palace demonstrated the divergence of the function of a building (as reflected in the arrangement of its interior spaces), its surface decoration, and its structure. A new style of building had arrived.

15.11 John Nash, Royal Pavilion, Brighton, England, remodeled 1815–23.

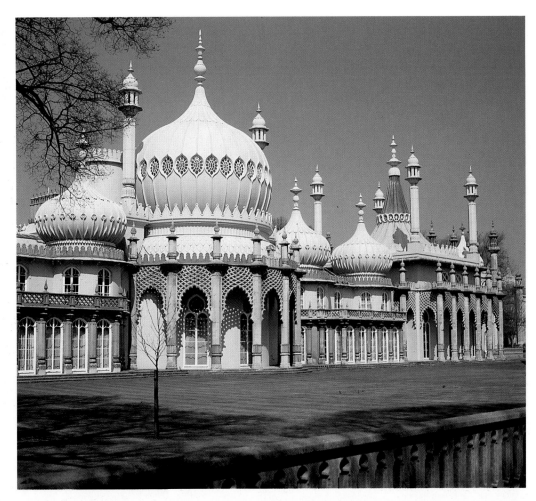

15.12 Sir Charles Barry and Augustus Welby Northmore Pugin, Houses of Parliament, London, 1839–52.

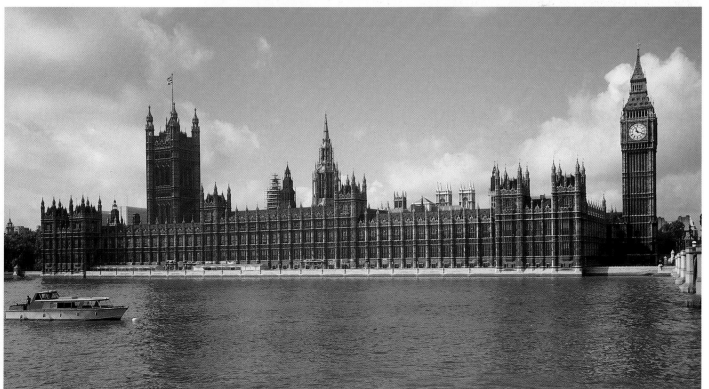

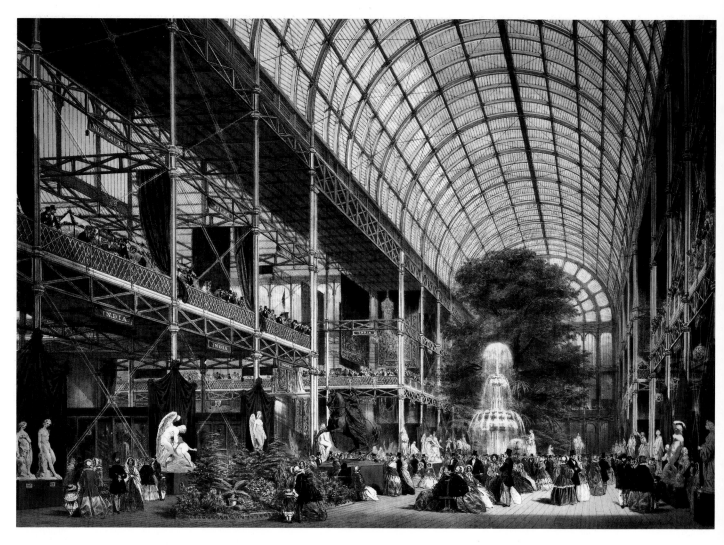

15.13 Sir Joseph Paxton, Crystal Palace, London, 1851.

ROMANTICISM IN LITERATURE

The main phase of Romantic literature probably began around 1790. In the United States the Romantic spirit found among its champions Edgar Allan Poe (1809–49) and Walt Whitman (1819–92). Poe's Romantic poetry is very distinguished, but he is most remembered for his horror stories based on the Gothic novel. Whitman's writings encompass a wide range of subjects—he intended to celebrate everything. Nothing was beneath the quest for his senses. Out of the Civil War came an unexpected author, whose contributions were oratorical, but which, because of their importance, have become part of the important canon of literature; these are the speeches of Abraham Lincoln.

Romantic writers tended to form groups or partnerships. In Britain, Wordsworth and Coleridge were also close colleagues, and Byron, Shelley, and Keats knew and criticized each other's work.

Wordsworth

William Wordsworth (1770–1850) saw transcendental and often indefinable significance in commonplace and everyday things. His worship of nature and the harmony he felt existed between people and nature led him to create a new and individual world of Romantic beauty.

In 1795 he met Samuel Taylor Coleridge (1772–1834), another British poet, and in working with Coleridge, Wordsworth found that his life and writing suddenly opened up. Out of this relationship came the Lyrical Ballads, which Wordsworth published anonymously along

OUR DYNAMIC WORLD

Japanese Painting

In the nineteenth century, as Japan began to look westward, the style of the country's two-dimensional art began to evolve, and the style has emotional similarities to European Romanticism. Illustrative is the work of Katsushika Hokusai (hoh-KU-sy; 1760–1849). In the landscape *The Great Wave off Kanazawa*, for example (Fig. **15.14**), Hokusai produces a boldly colored rendering that is neither naturalistic nor idealized. While Mount Fuji reposes calmly in the background, the great wave breaks over the boats with raging fury, and the foam reaches out like grasping fingers to crash down on the fragile craft. There is a new sense of directness here. Hokusai's response to natural forms has a romantic sweep although his decorative patterning rests firmly within the traditions of Japanese art.

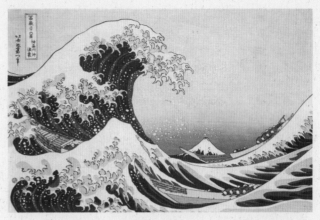

15.14 Katsushika Hokusai, *The Great Wave off Kanazawa*, 1823-9. Polychrome woodblock print, 10 × 14³/₄ ins (25.5 × 37.5 cm). Victoria & Albert Museum, London.

with four poems by Coleridge. Among these ballads, *Tintern Abbey* describes Wordsworth's love of nature most explicitly. That love is first presented as the animal passion of a wild young boy, then as a restorative and moral influence, and finally as a mystical communion with an eternal truth.

Lines Composed a Few Miles above Tintern Abbey
(excerpt)
William Wordsworth

Five years have passed; five summers, with the length
Of five long winters! and again I hear
These waters, rolling from their mountain-springs
With a sweet inland murmur.—Once again
Do I behold these steep and lofty cliffs,
Which on a wild secluded scene impress
Thoughts of more deep seclusion; and connect
The landscape with the quiet of the sky.
The day is come when I again repose
Here, under this dark sycamore, and view
These plots of cottage-ground, these orchard-tufts,
Which, at this season, with their unripe fruits,
Are clad in one green hue, and lose themselves
Mid groves and copses. Once again I see
These hedge-rows, hardly hedge-rows, little lines
Of sportive wood run wild; these pastoral farms
Green to the very door; and wreathes of smoke

Sent up, in silence, from among the trees,
With some uncertain notice, as might seem,
Of vagrant dwellers in the houseless woods,
Or of some hermit's cave, where by his fire
The hermit sits alone.

Jane Austen

Jane Austen (1775–1817) lived and worked in the high years of the major English Romantics, but she shunned the Romantic cult of personality and remained largely indifferent to Romantic literature. She looked back to neoclassicism and the comedy of manners as her sources, and her work portrays middle-class people living in provincial towns and going about the daily routine of family life—a life of good breeding, wit, and a reasonable hope that difficulties can be resolved in a satisfactory manner. She occasionally portrayed disappointments in love and threatened or actual seduction, but, somehow, these seem less important than the ongoing and routine conversations and rituals of daily life. Merely because she portrayed a quiet form of life does not mean, however, that her characters lack depth or interest. She explored human experience deeply and with humor. She proved that one does not require spectacular events in order to provide engaging art.

Her early years produced a variety of works that parody the sentimental and romantic clichés of popular

MASTERWORK

Austen—*Pride and Prejudice*

Pride and Prejudice (1813) contains little of the satire of works of the same period, but an ironic and sympathetic view of human nature and its propensity for comic incongruity. The narrative, which Austen originally titled "First Impressions," describes the clash between Elizabeth Bennet, the daughter of a country gentleman, and Fitzwilliam Darcy, a rich and aristocratic landowner. Austen reverses the convention of first impressions: "pride" of rank and fortune, and "prejudice" against Elizabeth's inferiority of family, hold Darcy aloof; while Elizabeth is equally fired both by the pride of self-respect and by prejudice against Darcy's snobbery. Ultimately they come together in love and self-understanding.

In the story, as summarized in *The Bloomsbury Guide to English Literature* (Prentice Hall, 1990), Mr and Mrs Bennet belong to the minor gentry and live at Longbourn, near London. Mr Bennet is witty and intelligent, and bored with his foolish wife. They have five daughters, whose marriage prospects are Mrs Bennet's chief interest in life, since the estate is 'entailed'—i.e. by the law of the period it will go on Mr Bennet's death to his nearest male relation, a sycophantic clergyman called Mr Collins. The main part of the story is concerned with the relationship between the witty and attractive Elizabeth Bennet and the haughty and fastidious Fitzwilliam Darcy, who at first considers her beneath his notice and later, on coming to the point of asking her to marry him, finds that she is resolutely prejudiced against him.

Elizabeth is subjected to an insolent offer of marriage by Mr Collins and the arrogant condescension of his patroness, Lady Catherine de Bourgh, Darcy's aunt. In the end, chastened by finding in one another a fastidiousness and pride that equal their own and despite a family scandal, they are united.

The central comedy of *Pride and Prejudice* lies in the fully developed character that reveals a sense of human realities and values. For example, in the character of Mr Bennet, Austen made a symbolic comment on intelligence that exists without will or drive. In her two opposing protagonists, Darcy and Elizabeth, who reflect the title of the book, Austen revealed character overlaid with class superciliousness and character abounding in independence and sharpness of mind that acts with prejudgment, wrong-headedness, and self-satisfaction. In all situations, Jane Austen remained detached, witty, and good-humored. The disturbances that upset things in the worlds Austen creates are, in sum, minor intrusions in an unshakable moral universe in which one can point out an entire range of human frailties and yet not despair.

---

fiction. In her second period of writing, from 1810 on, she crowned her career with works such as *Emma* (1815), *Persuasion* (1818), and *Mansfield Park* (1813). *Emma* shows Austen's ability to remain detached from her heroine, Emma Woodhouse, who represents self-deception, as she misreads evidence, misleads others, and discovers her own feelings only by accident. In her other works, Austen portrayed many gentle and self-effacing characters in the mode of her earlier masterpiece *Pride and Prejudice* (1813).

Other Nineteenth-Century Romantics

The life and works of Wordsworth's friend Coleridge more closely resembled the temperament of German Romanti-cism. He is best remembered for his long poem *The Rime of the Ancient Mariner*, which exemplifies the mystery and wonder of the Romantic spirit. Walter Scott (1771–1832) was also influenced by German Romanticism. His romances have an easy, fluent style, color, and a lack of depth. Like many nineteenth-century artists, Scott delighted in the romance of history, and he was fond of evoking the charms of the Middle Ages and of the Renaissance.

Lord Byron (1788–1824), was the Romantic poet *par excellence* with his colorful and dramatic private life, his support of the nationalist aspirations of the Greeks, and his energetic verse. *Don Juan*, a richly ironic ramble through human frailties, is probably his best poem. Percy Bysshe Shelley (1792–1822) wrote in a more meditative and more lyrical vein, and the passions of Romanticism are never far below the surface. The greatest of English

Romantics, however, was John Keats (1795–1821). The best of his poems, such as *Ode on a Grecian Urn* and *Ode to a Nightingale*, are essentially lyric meditations on an object or quality that prompts the poet to confront the conflicting impulses of his inner being and to reflect upon his own longings and their relations to the wider world around him.

Emily Brontë (BRAHN-tee; 1818–48) wrote the stormily romantic *Wuthering Heights*, while her sister Charlotte (1816–55) produced the more sophisticated *Jane Eyre*. New possibilities for the novel were opened up by the French writer Honoré de Balzac (oh-nohr-AY duh bahl-ZAHK; 1799–1850), whose great cycle of novels, part of his projected and only partially completed *Comédie Humaine*, sought to survey contemporary society from the palace to the gutter. The heroes and heroines of Balzac's works are figures whose experiences reveal how society really works. Charles Dickens (1812–70) had a similar aim in his novels. The best of them, such as *Bleak House*, deliver up a cross-section of the teeming society of Victorian England. His best-known works, of course, include *A Tale of Two Cities*, *Oliver Twist*, and *A Christmas Carol*. Dickens's plots are dazzlingly ingenious and entertaining in their own right. But this complexity also captures the interdependence of rich and poor, and the endless ramifications of every individual act. The naturalism of writers such as Gustave Flaubert (floh-BAIR; 1821–80) and Émile Zola (zoh-LAH; 1840–1902), which developed out of this tradition, closely parallels realism in painting.

An interest in the morbid, the pathological, and the bizarre also developed, and the "decadent" poems of Charles Baudelaire (bohd-LAIR; 1821–67), especially in his *Les Fleurs du Mal* (*Flowers of Evil*), typify this trend. The paths of poetry and the novel now diverged, poetry moving into symbolism, while the novel, in the hands of writers such as Henry James (1843–1916), became more psychological as it explored the interior life and the nature of consciousness.

ROMANTICISM IN MUSIC

In an era of Romantic subjectivity, music provided the medium in which many found an unrivaled opportunity to express emotion. In trying to express human emotion, Romantic music made stylistic changes to classical music, and although Romanticism amounted to rebellion in many of the arts, in music it involved a more gradual and natural extension of classical principles.

As in painting, spontaneity replaced control, but the primary emphasis of music in this era was on beautiful, lyrical, and expressive melody. Phrases became longer, more irregular, and more complex than they had been in classical music. Much Romantic rhythm was traditional, but experiments produced new meters and patterns. Emotional conflict was often suggested by juxtaposing different meters, and rhythmic irregularity became increasingly common as the century progressed.

Romantic composers emphasized colorful harmonies and instrumentation. Harmony was seen as a means of expression, and any previous "laws" regarding key relationships could be broken to achieve striking emotional effects. Harmonies became increasingly complex, and traditional distinctions between major and minor keys were blurred in chromatic harmonies, complicated chords, and modulations to distant keys. In fact, some composers used key changes so frequently that their compositions are virtually nothing but whirls of continuous modulation.

As composers sought to disrupt the listener's expectations, more and more dissonance occurred, until it became a principal focus. Dissonance was explored for its own sake, as a strong stimulant of emotional response rather than merely as a decorative way to get to the traditional tonic chord. By the end of the Romantic period, the exhaustion of chromatic usage and dissonance had led to a search for a completely different type of tonal system.

Exploring musical color to elicit feeling was as important to the Romantic musician as it was to the painter. Interest in tonal color, or timbre, led to great diversity in vocal and instrumental performance, and the music of this period abounds with solo works and exhibits a tremendous increase in the size and diversity of the orchestra. We have many options in how we might go about exploring Romantic music, none of which we could pursue exhaustively. We will proceed by isolating some major genres and, within them, noting major composers as we pass.

Lieder

In many ways, the "art song," or *Lied*, characterized Romantic music. A composition for solo voice with piano accompaniment and poetic text allowed for a variety of lyrical and dramatic expressions and linked music directly with literature.

The burst of German lyric poetry in this period encouraged the growth of *Lieder*. Literary nuances affected music, and music added deeper emotional implications to the poem. This partnership had various results: some *Lieder* were complex, others were simple; some were structured, others were freely composed. The pieces themselves depended on a close relationship between the piano and the voice. In many ways, the piano was an inseparable part of the experience, and certainly it served as more than accompaniment, for the piano explored mood and established rhythmic and thematic material, and sometimes had solo passages of its own. The interdependency of the song and its accompaniment is basic to the art song.

The earliest, and perhaps the most important, composer of *Lieder* was Franz Schubert (SHOO-bairt; 1797–1828). Schubert's troubled life epitomized the Romantic view of the artist's desperate and isolated condition. Known only among a close circle of friends and musicians, Schubert composed almost one thousand works, from symphonies to sonatas and operas, to Masses, choral

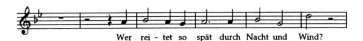

15.15 Franz Schubert, from *The Erlking*.

compositions, and *Lieder*. None of his work was publicly performed, however, until the year of his death. He took his *Lieder* texts from a wide variety of poems, and in each case the melodic contours, harmonies, rhythms, and structures of the music were determined by the poem.

Schubert's song *Der Erlkönig* (The Erlking, 1815; CD track 14; Fig. **15.15**) provides an excellent example both of Schubert's work and of Romantic music in general. The song consists of a musical setting of a poem about the supernatural by Goethe (see p. 447). Schubert uses a through-composed setting—that is, he writes new music for each stanza—in order to capture the poem's mounting excitement. The piano plays the role of an important partner in transmitting the mood of the piece, creating tension with rapid octaves and menacing bass motif. Imaginative variety in the music allows Schubert's soloist to sound like several characters in the dramatic development.

> Who rides so late through the night and the wind?
> It is the father with his child;
> He folds the boy close in his arms,
> He clasps him securely, he holds him warmly.
>
> "My son, why do you hide your face so anxiously?"
> "Father, don't you see the Erlking?
> The Erlking with his crown and his train?"
> "My son, it's a streak of mist."
>
> "Dear child, come, go with me!
> I'll play the prettiest games with you.
> Many-colored flowers grow along the shore;
> My mother has many golden garments."
>
> "My father, my father, and don't you hear
> The Erlking whispering promises to me?"
> "Be quiet, stay quiet, my child;
> The wind is rustling in the dead leaves."

> "My handsome boy, will you come with me?
> My daughters shall wait upon you;
> My daughters lead off in the dance every night,
> And cradle and dance and sing you to sleep."
>
> "My father, my father, and don't you see there
> The Erlking's daughters in the shadows?"
> "My son, my son, I see it clearly;
> The old willows look so gray."
>
> "I love you, your beautiful figure delights me!
> And if you are not willing, then I shall use force!"
> "My father, my father, now he is taking hold of me!
> The Erlking has hurt me!"
>
> The father shudders, he rides swiftly on;
> He holds in his arms the groaning child,
> He reaches the courtyard weary and anxious:
> In his arms the child was dead.
>
> Translated by Philip L. Miller

Piano Works

The development of the art song depended in no small way on nineteenth-century improvements in piano design. The instrument for which Schubert wrote had a much warmer, richer tone than earlier pianos, and improvements in pedal technique made sustained tones possible and gave the instrument greater lyrical potential.

Such flexibility made the piano an excellent instrument for accompaniment, and, more importantly, made it an almost ideal solo instrument. As a result, new works were composed solely for the piano, ranging from short, intimate pieces, similar to *Lieder*, to larger works designed to exhibit great virtuosity in performance. Franz Schubert wrote such pieces, as did Franz Liszt (frahnts list; 1811–86). Liszt was one of the most celebrated pianists of the nineteenth century and one of its most innovative composers. He enthralled audiences with his expressive, dramatic playing, and taught most of the major pianists of the next generation. He also influenced Richard Wagner and Richard Strauss. His piano works include six *Paganini Études* (1851), concertos, and twenty *Hungarian Rhapsodies* based on Hungarian urban popular music rather than folk music. The technical demands of Liszt's compositions, and the rather florid way he performed them, gave rise to a theatricality, the primary purpose of which was to impress audiences with flashy presentation. This fitted well with the Romantic concept of the artist as hero.

The compositions of Frédéric Chopin (shoh-PAN; 1810–49) were somewhat more restrained. Chopin wrote almost exclusively for the piano. Each of his ÉTUDES, or studies, explored a single technical problem, usually set around a single motif. More than simple exercises, these

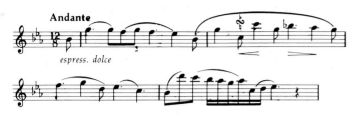

15.16 Frédéric Chopin, Nocturne in E flat major, Op. 9, No. 2, first theme.

works explored the possibilities of the instrument and became short tone poems in their own right. A second group of compositions included short intimate works such as preludes, nocturnes, and impromptus, and dances such as waltzes, polonaises, and mazurkas. (Chopin was Polish but lived in France, and Polish folk music had a particularly strong influence on him.) A final class of larger works included scherzos, ballades, and fantasies. Chopin's compositions are highly individual, many without precedent. His style is almost totally without standard form. His melodies are lyrical, and his moods vary.

Chopin's nocturnes, or night pieces, are among his most celebrated works. His Nocturne in E flat major Op. 9, No. 2 (CD Track 15; 1833) illustrates the structure and style of this sort of mood piece well. It has a number of sections, with a main theme alternating with a second until both give way to a third. The piece has a complex AA'BA"BA'"CC' structure. The nocturne is in *andante* tempo, a moderate, walking speed, and begins with the most important theme (Fig. **15.16**).

The melody is very graceful and lyrical over its supporting chords. The contours of the melody alternately use pitches that are close together and widely spaced. The theme is stated, then immediately repeated with ornamentation. The second theme begins in the dominant key of B flat major and returns to E flat for a more elaborate repeat of the first theme. The second theme is restated, and followed by an even more elaborate restatement of the first theme, leading to a dramatic climax in the home key. A third theme is presented and then repeated more elaborately in the tonic key. The work ends with a short cadenza, which builds through a crescendo and finishes pianissimo, very softly.

Program Music

One of the new ways in which Romantic composers structured their longer works was to build them around a nonmusical story, a picture, or some other idea. Music of this sort is called "descriptive." When the idea is quite specific and closely followed throughout the piece, the music is called "programmatic" or "program music."

These techniques were not entirely new—we have already noted the descriptive elements in Beethoven's "Pastoral" Symphony—but the Romantics found them particularly attractive and employed them with great gusto. A nonmusical idea allowed composers to rid themselves of formal structure altogether. Of course, actual practice varied tremendously—some used programmatic material as their only structural device, while others subordinated a program idea to formal structure. Nevertheless, the Romantic period has become known as the "age of program music." Among the best-known composers of program music were Hector Berlioz (BAIR-lee-ohz; 1803–69) and Richard Strauss (strows; 1864–1949).

Berlioz's *Symphonie Fantastique* (1830) employed a single motif, called an IDÉE FIXE (ee-DAY feex), to tie the five movements of the work together. The story on which the musical piece is based involves a hero who has poisoned himself because of unrequited love. However, the drug only sends him into semi-consciousness, in which he has visions. Throughout these visions the recurrent musical theme (the *idée fixe*) symbolizes his beloved. Movement 1 consists of "Reveries" and "Passions." Movement 2 represents "A Ball." "In the Country" is movement 3, in which he imagines a pastoral scene. In movement 4, "March to the Scaffold," (Fig. **15.17**; CD Track 16) he dreams he has killed his beloved and is about to be executed. The *idée fixe* returns at the end of the movement and is abruptly shattered by the fall of the axe. The final movement describes a "Dream of a Witches' Sabbath" in grotesque and orgiastic musical imagery.

Not all program music depends for its interest upon an understanding of its text. Many people believe, however, that the tone poems, or symphonic poems, of Richard Strauss require an understanding of the story. His *Don Juan* (dahn whahn), *Till Eulenspiegel* (tihl oil-ehn-SHPEEG-ehl), and *Don Quixote* (dohn kee-HOH-tay) draw such detailed material from specific legends that

15.17 Hector Berlioz, from the *Symphonie Fantastique*, fourth movement: A. "March to the Scaffold;" B. *idée fixe*.

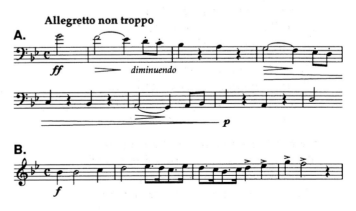

program explanations and comments are integral to the works and help to give them coherence. In *Till Eulenspiegels lustige Streiche* (*Till Eulenspiegel's Merry Pranks*), Strauss tells the legendary German story of Till Eulenspiegel and his practical jokes. Till is traced through three escapades, all musically identifiable. He is then confronted by his critics and finally executed. Throughout, the musical references are quite specific.

Symphonies

Beethoven's powerful symphonies strongly influenced nineteenth-century composers. Schubert, whom we just discussed as a composer of *Lieder*, wrote eight symphonies, one of which, the so-called "Unfinished" (B Minor) has a darkly romantic style. Hector Berlioz's *Symphonie Fantastique* (see above) illustrated that a symphony could be written in an entirely different manner from Beethoven's. Felix Mendelssohn (MEN-dehl-suhn; 1809–47) followed classical tradition in most of his symphonies, but we should note that although classical form was followed in many Romantic symphonies, the form was employed more as a means to a Romantically expressive end and not for its own sake.

An outstanding example of the Romantic symphony is Brahms' (brahmz) Symphony No. 3 in F major (1883). Composed in four movements, the work calls for pairs of flutes, oboes, clarinets, a bassoon, a contrabassoon, four horns, two trumpets, three trombones, two timpani, and strings—not an adventurous grouping of instruments for the period. Composed in sonata form, the first movement is *allegro con brio* (fast with spirit), and begins in F major (Fig. **15.18**).

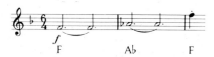

15.18 Johannes Brahms, Symphony No. 3 in F major, opening motif of first movement.

The exposition section closes with a return to the opening motif and meter, employing rising scales and arpeggios. Then, following classical tradition, the exposition is repeated.

The development section uses both the principal themes, with changes in tonal colors, dynamics, and modulation.

The recapitulation opens with a forceful restatement of the opening motif, followed by a restatement and further development of materials from the exposition. Then comes a lengthy coda, again announced by the opening motif, and

based on the first theme. A final, quiet, restatement of the opening motif and first phrase of the theme brings the first movement to an end.

Trends

The Romantic period also gave birth to new trends in music. The roots of such movements went deep into the past, but composers also wrote with the political circumstances of the century in mind. Folk tunes appear in these works as themes, as do local rhythms and harmonies. The exaltation of national identity was consistent with Romantic requirements, and it occurs in the music of nineteenth-century Russia, Bohemia, Spain, Britain, Scandinavia, Germany, and Austria.

Of all the composers of the Romantic period, the Russian Peter Ilyich Tchaikovsky (chy-KAWF-skee; 1840–93) has enjoyed the greatest popularity with his "1812 Overture" perhaps topping the list, followed closely by his *Nutcracker* ballet. In his First Symphony, he imitates the lyricism of Russian folk song, and the traits of the nineteenth-century Russian salon song can be found in his Fifth and Sixth Symphonies.

The *symphonic poem*, an offshoot of the symphony proper, was a term invented by Franz Liszt to describe a series of orchestral works he wrote which take their musical form and rhetoric from nonabstract ideas, some of them poetic and others visual. Other composers followed Liszt's lead, and the model proved especially popular in topics stemming from nationalistic sources, among them Smetana (SMET-ah-nah; *My Country*), Dvořák (DVOR-zhahk; *The Noonday Witch*), Borodin (bor-oh-DEEN; *In the Steppes of Central Asia*), Sibelius (sib-AYL-ee-us; *Tapiola*), and Elgar (EL-gahr; *Falstaff*).

Choral Music

Vocal music ranged from solo to massive ensemble works. The emotional requirements of Romanticism were well served by the diverse timbres and lyricism of the human voice. Almost every major composer of the era wrote some form of vocal music. Franz Schubert is remembered for his Masses, the most notable of which is the Mass in A flat major. Felix Mendelssohn's *Elijah* stands beside Handel's *Messiah* and Haydn's *Creation* as a masterpiece of oratorio. Hector Berlioz marshaled full Romantic power for his *Requiem*, which called for 210 voices, a large orchestra, and four brass bands.

One of the most enduringly popular choral works of the Romantic period is Brahms' *Ein Deutsches Requiem* (*A German Requiem*). Based on selected texts from the

PROFILE

Joannes Brahms (1833–97)

Although he was born into an impoverished family, Johannes Brahms appears to have had a relatively happy childhood. His father was an itinerant musician, who eked out a meager living playing the horn and double bass in taverns and night clubs. The family lived in the slums of Hamburg, Germany, but despite their economic hardships, they retained close and loving family relationships. Early in life, Johannes showed evidence of considerable musical talent, and the eminent piano teacher Eduard Marxsen agreed to teach him without pay.

By the time he was twenty, Brahms had gained acclaim as a pianist and accepted an invitation to participate in a concert tour with the Hungarian violinist Eduard Remenyi. The event was invaluable to the young Brahms, because it introduced him to Franz Liszt and Robert Schumann, and through Schumann's efforts Brahms was able to publish several of his compositions, which opened the door to the wider artistic world and launched his prolific career. Brahms gained experience as musical director at the little court of Detmold and as founder and director of a women's chorus in Hamburg, for which he wrote several choral works. His musical creativity showed a deep love of folk music and a sensitivity of

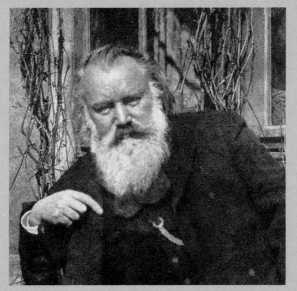

expression. He mastered German *Lieder* (see page 481) and remained devoted to the Romantic style throughout his career, notwithstanding his fondness for clarity of structure and form based in the classical style of the previous century.

Although Brahms wanted to stay in Hamburg, he was passed over for a position, and, feeling betrayed and neglected by his native town's rejection, he moved to Vienna. That city's rich musical ambience enriched his talent and experience, and he gained tremendous success, serving as director of the Vienna Singakademie and as conductor of the Society of Friends of Music. In 1875, he resigned his positions and spent the rest of his days in creative endeavors. For the next twenty-two years, he sacrificed his personal life in pursuit of his career, and the results gained him—in his own lifetime—recognition as one of the world's greatest artists.

His work spanned several idioms, from solo piano compositions and chamber music to full orchestral works. He was never interested in music for the stage nor in program music, but he reveled in symphonic compositions ruled by purely musical ideas (absolute music). See page 484 for a discussion of Brahms' Symphony No. 3 in F major.

15.19 Johannes Brahms in 1894.

Bible, in contrast with the Latin liturgy of traditional requiems, Brahms' work is not so much a Mass for the dead as a consolation for the living. It is principally a choral work—the solos are minimal: two for baritone and one for soprano—but both vocal and instrumental writing are very expressive. Soaring melodic lines and rich harmonies weave thick textures. After the chorus sings "All mortal flesh is as the grass," the orchestra suggests fields of grass moving in the wind. The lyrical movement, "How lovely is thy dwelling place," soars with emotion.

Brahms' *Requiem* begins and ends with moving passages aimed directly at the living: "Blest are they that mourn." Hope and consolation underlie the entire work.

An important factor in Brahms' music is its lyricism and its vocal beauty. Brahms explored the voice as a human voice, and not as another instrument or some other mechanism unaffected by any restrictions, as other composers have done. His parts are written and his words chosen so that no voice is ever required to sing outside its natural range or technical capacity.

Opera

The spirit and style of Romanticism are summed up in that perfect synthesis of all the arts, opera. Three countries, France (especially Paris), Italy, and Germany, dominated the development of opera.

Paris occupied an important position in Romantic opera during the first half of the nineteenth century. The spectacular quality of opera and the size of its auditoriums had made it an effective vehicle for propaganda during the Revolution, and as an art form, opera enjoyed great popular appeal among the rising and influential middle classes.

A new type of opera, called "grand opera," emerged early in the nineteenth century, principally through the efforts of Louis Veron, a businessman, the playwright Eugène Scribe (screeb), and Giacomo Meyerbeer (JAH-koh-moh MY-ur-bair), a composer. These three broke away from classical themes and subject matter and staged spectacular productions with crowd scenes, ballets, choruses, and fantastic scenery, written around medieval and contemporary themes. Meyerbeer (1791–1864), a German, studied Italian opera in Venice and produced French opera in Paris. *Robert the Devil* and *The Huguenots* typify Meyerbeer's extravagant style; they achieved great popular success, although the composer Schumann called *The Huguenots* "a conglomeration of monstrosities." Berlioz's *The Trojans*, written in the late 1850s, was more classically based and more musically controlled. At the same time, Jacques Offenbach (AW-fen-bahk; 1819–80) brought to the stage a lighter style, in which spoken dialogue was mixed with the music. This type of opera, called *opéra comique*, is serious in intent despite what the French word *comique* might suggest. It is a satirical and light form of opera, using vaudeville humor to satirize other operas, popular events, and so forth. In between the styles of Meyerbeer and Offenbach there was a third form of Romantic opera, lyric opera. Ambroise Thomas (1811–96) and Charles Gounod (goo-NOH; 1818–93) turned to Romantic drama and fantasy for their plots. Thomas's *Mignon* contains highly lyrical passages, and Gounod's *Faust*, based on Goethe's play, stresses melodic beauty.

Early Romantic opera in Italy featured the BEL CANTO style, which emphasizes beauty of sound, and the works of Gioacchino Rossini (rohs-SEE-nee; 1792–1868) epitomize this feature. Rossini's *The Barber of Seville* takes melodic singing to new heights with light, ornamented, and highly appealing work, particularly for his soprano voices.

Great artists often stand apart from or astride general stylistic trends while they explore their own themes. Such is the case with the Italian composer Giuseppe Verdi (VAIR-dee; 1813–1901). With Verdi, opera is truly a human drama, expressed through simple, beautiful melody.

In what might be described as typical of Romanticism, Verdi dared to make an operatic hero out of a hunchbacked court jester—Rigoletto—whose only redeeming quality seems to be his great love for his daughter, Gilda. Rigoletto's master is the licentious duke of Mantua, who, while posing as a poor student, wins Gilda's love. When the duke seduces the innocent girl, Rigoletto plots his death. Despite the seduction, Gilda loves the dissolute duke and ultimately gives her life to save his. Virtue does not triumph in this opera.

Act Three contains one of the most popular of all operatic arias, *La donna è mobile* ("Woman is fickle"; Fig. **15.20**; CD Track 17):

Woman is fickle
Like a feather in the wind,
She changes her words
And her thoughts.
Always a lovable
And lovely face,
Weeping or laughing,
Is lying.
Woman is fickle, etc.
The man's always wretched
Who believes in her,
Who recklessly entrusts
His heart to her!
And yet no one who never
Drinks love on that breast
Ever feels
Entirely happy!
Woman is fickle, etc.

Late in his career, Verdi wrote works such as *Aïda* (1871), grand operas of spectacular proportions built upon tightly woven dramatic structures. Finally, in a third phase, he produced operas based on Shakespearean plays. *Otello* (1887) contrasts tragedy and *opera buffa*—comic opera, not *opéra comique*—and explores subtle balances among voices and orchestra, together with strong melodic development.

15.20 Giuseppe Verdi, *La donna è mobile*, from *Rigoletto* (1851).

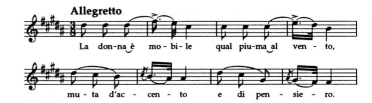

Richard Wagner (REEK-art VAHG-nuhr; 1813–83) was one of the masters of Romantic opera. At the heart of Wagner's artistry lay a philosophy that has affected the stage from the mid-nineteenth century to the present day. His ideas were laid out principally in two books, *Art and Revolution* (1849) and *Opera and Drama* (1851). Wagner's philosophy centered on the *Gesamtkunstwerk* (geh-ZAMT-koonst-VAIRK), a comprehensive work of art in which music, poetry, and scenery are all subservient to the central generating idea. For Wagner, the total unity of all elements was supremely important. In line with German Romantic philosophy, which gives music supremacy over the other arts, music has the predominant role in Wagner's operas. Dramatic meaning unfolds through the LEITMOTIF, for which Wagner is famous, although he did not invent it. A *Leitmotif* (LYT-moh-TEEF) is a musical theme that is tied to an idea, a person, or an object. Whenever that idea, person, or object appears on stage or comes to mind in the action, that theme is heard. Juxtaposing *Leitmotifs* gives the audience an idea of relationships between their subjects. *Leitmotifs* also give the composer building blocks to use for development, recapitulation, and unification. The sweeping strains of an excerpt (*Liebestod*) from the opera *Tristan und Isolde* (CD track 18) can only suggest to us the power of Wagner's music.

Each of Wagner's magnificent operas deserves detailed attention. Anything we might say here by way of description or analysis would be insignificant compared to the dramatic power these works exhibit in full production. Even recordings cannot approach the tremendous effect of these works on stage in an opera house.

ROMANTICISM IN THEATRE

"The play-going world of the West End is at this moment occupied in rubbing its eyes, that it may recover completely from the dazzle of Thursday last, when, amid the acclamations of Queen Victoria's subjects, King Richard the Second was enthroned at the Princess's Theatre." Thus began the reviewer's comments in *The Spectator*, 14 March 1857. The dazzle of scenery, revivals, and a potpourri of uncertain accomplishments helped a stumbling theatre to keep up with the other arts that flourished through the early years of the nineteenth century.

Popularism and Historical Accuracy

Romanticism as a philosophy of art was its own worst enemy in the theatre. Artists sought new forms to express great truths, and they strove to free themselves from neoclassical rules and restraints. They did, however, admire Shakespeare as an example of new ideals and as a symbol of freedom from structural confinement. Intuition reigned, and the artistic genius was set apart from everyday people and above normal constraints. As a result, Romantic writers had no use for any guide but their own imagination.

Unfortunately, the theatre operates within some rather specific limits. Many nineteenth-century playwrights penned scripts that were unstageable and/or unplayable, and great writers could not or would not abide by constraints of the stage, while the hacks, yielding to popular taste, could not resist overindulgence in phony emotionalism, melodrama, and stage gimmickry. As a result, the best Romantic theatre performances came from the pen of William Shakespeare, whose work was revived in a great rush of nineteenth-century antiquarianism.

Poor as it may have been in original drama, however, the Romantic period did succeed in loosening the arbitrary rules of neoclassical convention. Thus, it paved the way for a new theatrical era in the later years of the century.

The audiences of the nineteenth century played a significant part in determining what took the stage. Royal patronage was gone, and box office receipts were needed to pay the bills. A rising middle class had swelled the eighteenth-century audience and changed its character. Then, in the nineteenth century, the lower classes began attending the theatre. The Industrial Revolution had created larger urban populations and expanded public education to a degree. As feelings of egalitarianism spread throughout Europe and America, theatre audiences grew, and theatre building flourished. To appeal to this diverse audience, theatre managers had to put on plays for the popular as well as the sophisticated taste if they wanted to make money, so to offer something for everyone, an evening's theatre program might contain several types of fare and last over five hours. The consequence was predictable. Fewer and fewer sophisticated patrons chose to attend, and the quality of the productions declined.

By 1850, theatres began to specialize, and sophisticated playgoers came back to certain theatres, although the multipart production remained typical until nearly the turn of the twentieth century. Audience demand was high, and theatre continued to expand.

The early nineteenth-century theatre had some very particular characteristics. First of all, there was the repertory company, with a set group of actors, including stars, which stayed in one place and staged several productions during a given season. (That is quite unlike contemporary Broadway professional theatre, in which each play is produced and cast independently and runs for as long as it shows a profit.) Gradually, better-known actors capitalized on their reputations and began to go on tour, starring in local productions and featuring their most famous roles. A craze for visiting stars developed, and the most famous actors began to make world tours. This increase in touring stars led to an increase in touring companies, and, in the United States especially, these companies, with their star attractions and complete sets of costumes and scenery, became a regular feature of the landscape. By 1886 America could boast 282 touring companies. At the same time, local resident companies became less popular, except in Germany, where a series of local, state-run theatres was established.

After the Civil War a number of African American theatre companies emerged, featuring artists such as Anna and Emma Hyers, classically trained actors from California. In 1884, J.A. Arneaux founded the Astor Place Company of Colored Tragedians, who performed a repertory of Shakespearean plays. By the turn of the twentieth century, African Americans had made notable contributions to straight drama in the works of such playwrights as William Edgar Easton, who wrote historical plays.

Although theatre design was by now very diverse, some general similarities existed. Principally, the changes in nineteenth-century stages and staging were prompted by increased interest in historical accuracy and popular demand for depiction rather than convention. Before the eighteenth century, history had been considered irrelevant to art. Knowledge of antiquity that began with archeological excavations in Pompeii, however, aroused curiosity, and the Romantic dream of escape to the long ago and far away suggested that the stage picture of exotic places

should be somehow believable. At first, such detail was used inconsistently, but, by 1823, some productions claimed that they were entirely historical in every respect. Attempts at historical accuracy had begun as early as 1801, and in France, Victor Hugo (HUE-goh or yoo-GOH) and Alexandre Dumas (due-MAH) *père* insisted on historically accurate settings and costumes during the early years of the century. However, it was Charles Kean (1811–68) who brought the spectacle of antiquarianism in the London theatre to fruition in the 1850s (Fig. **15.21**).

The onset of accuracy as a standard for production led to three-dimensionality in settings and away from drop and wing scenery to the box set. The stage floor was leveled—since the Renaissance it had been raked—and new methods of shifting and rigging were devised to meet specific staging problems. Over a period of years, all elements of the production became integrated, much in the spirit of Wagner's totally unified artwork, the GESAMTKUNSTWERK. The distraction of numerous scene changes was eliminated by closing the curtain.

Melodrama

On the popular side, nineteenth-century theatre developed a Romantically exaggerated form called "melodrama." Typically this kind of theatre is characterized by sensationalism and sentimentality. Characters are stereotyped, and everything and everyone tends to be all good or all evil. Plots are sentimental and the action is exaggerated. Regardless of circumstances, good must be rewarded and evil punished. There was often also some form of comic relief, usually through a minor character. The action of melodrama progresses at the whim of the villain, and the hero is forced to endure episode after episode of trial and suffering. Suspense is imperative, and a reversal at the end is obligatory.

The term "melodrama" implies music and drama, and, in the nineteenth century, these plays were accompanied by a musical score tailored to the emotional or dynamic character of the scene. In practice, this was very similar to the way music is used in films and television programs today, with the added attractions of incidental songs and dances that were used as curtain raisers and *entr'acte* entertainment.

Melodrama was popular throughout Europe and the United States. *Uncle Tom's Cabin*, based on the novel by Harriet Beecher Stowe (1852), took the stage by storm. The stage version was opposed by Stowe, but copyright laws did not exist to protect her. The play does retain her complex themes of slavery, religion, and love. The action involves a number of episodes, some of which are rather loosely connected. Characteristic of melodrama, *Uncle*

15.21 Charles Kean's production of Shakespeare's *Richard II*, London, 1857. Between Acts III and IV, the Entry of Bolingbroke into London. Contemporary watercolor by Thomas Grieve. Victoria & Albert Museum, London.

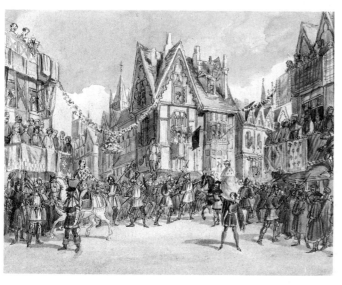

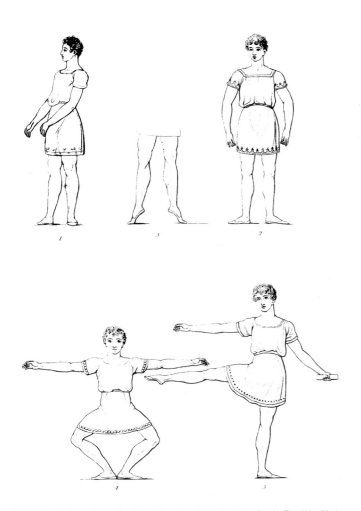

15.22 Illustrations from *The Art of Dancing*, 1820, by Carlo Blasis. The New York Public Library.

Tom's Cabin places considerable emphasis on spectacle, the most popular of which at the time was Eliza's crossing of the ice with mules, horses, and bloodhounds in pursuit.

ROMANTICISM IN DANCE

In a totally unrehearsed move, a ballerina leaped from the tomb on which she posed and narrowly escaped a piece of falling scenery. This and other disasters plagued the opening night performance of Meyerbeer's *Robert the Devil* in 1831. The novelty of tenors falling into trapdoors, and falling stagelights and scenery, however, was eclipsed by the startling novelty of the choreography for this opera. Romantic ballet was at hand. To varying degrees, all the arts turned against the often cold formality of classicism and neoclassicism. The subjective (not the objective) viewpoint and feeling (rather than reason) sought release.

Two sources are helpful in understanding the Romantic ballet, the writings of Théophile Gautier (tay-oh-FEEL goh-tee-AY) and Carlo Blasis (BLAH-zees). Gautier (1811–72) was a poet and critic, and his aesthetic principles held first of all that beauty was truth, a central Romantic conception. Gautier believed that dance was visual stimulation to show "beautiful forms in graceful attitudes." Dancing for Gautier was like a living painting or sculpture—"physical pleasure and feminine beauty." This exclusive focus on ballerinas placed sensual enjoyment and eroticism squarely at the center of his aesthetics. Gautier's influence was significant, and it accounted for the central role of the ballerina in Romantic ballet. Male dancers were relegated to the background, strength being the only grace permissible to them.

The second general premise for Romantic ballet came from *Code of Terpsichore* by Carlo Blasis (1803–78). Blasis was much more systematic and specific than Gautier—he was a former dancer—and his principles covered training, structure, and positioning. Everything in the ballet required a beginning, a middle, and an ending. The basic "attitude" in dance, which was modeled on Bologna's statue of *Mercury* (see Fig. **11.24**), was to stand on one leg with the other brought up behind at a 90-degree angle with the knee bent. The dancer needed to display the human figure with taste and elegance. If the dancer trained each part of the body, the result would be grace without affectation. From Blasis comes the turned-out position, which is still fundamental to ballet today (Fig. **15.22**). These broad principles provided the framework, and, to a great extent, a summary, of objectives for Romantic ballet: delicate ballerinas, lightly poised, costumed in soft tulle, and moving *en pointe*, with elegant grace.

The first truly Romantic ballet, *Robert the Devil* told the story of Duke Robert of Normandy, his love for a princess, and an encounter with the devil. The ballet contains ghosts, bacchanalian dancing, and a spectral figure who was danced by Marie Taglioni (tahl-ee-OHN-ee; Fig. **15.23**).

Taglioni went on to star in perhaps the most famous of all Romantic ballets, *La Sylphide* (lah sihl-FEED; 1832). Here the plot centered on the tragic impossibility of love between a mortal and a supernatural being. A spirit of the air, a sylph, falls in love with a young Scot on his wedding day. Torn between his real fiancée and his ideal, the sylph, he deserts his fiancée to run off with the spirit. A witch gives him a scarf, and, unaware that it is enchanted, he ties it around the spirit's waist. Immediately her wings fall off and she dies. She drifts away to sylphs' heaven. The young man, disconsolate and alone, sees his fiancée passing in the distance with a new lover on the way to her wedding. The Scottish setting was exotic, at least to Parisians. Gaslight provided a ghostly, moonlit mood in the darkened auditorium. Taglioni danced the role of La Sylphide like "a creature of mist drifting over the stage" (assisted by flying

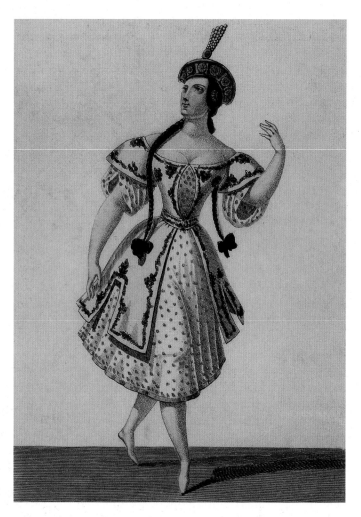

15.23 Marie Taglioni (1804–84). Engraving, 1834. The New York Public Library.

machinery). Her lightness, delicacy, and modest grace established the standard for Romantic style in dancing. The story, exotic design, and mood-evoking lighting completed the production style, a style that prevailed for the next forty years—"moonbeams and gossamer," as some have described it.

Choreographers of Romantic ballet sought magic and escape in fantasies and legends. Ballets about elves and nymphs enjoyed great popularity, as did ballets about madness, sleepwalking, and opium dreams. Unusual subject matter came to the fore. For example, harem wives revolt against their oppressors with the help of the "Spirit of Womankind" in Filippo Taglioni's *The Revolt in the Harem*, possibly the first ballet about the emancipation of women. Women appeared not only as performers and as subjects of the dance, however. They also began to come to prominence as choreographers.

The ballet *Giselle* (zhee-ZEL; 1841) marks the height of Romantic achievement. With its many fine dancing

roles, both for women and for men, it has been a favorite of ballet companies since its first production.

The ballet has two acts; Act I is in sunlight, and Act II in moonlight. During a vine festival in a Rhineland village, Giselle, a frail peasant girl in love with a mysterious young man, discovers that the object of her affection is Albrecht, Count of Silesia. Albrecht is already engaged to a noblewoman. Giselle is shattered. She goes mad, turns from her deceitful lover, tries to commit suicide, swoons, and falls dead. In Act II, Giselle is summoned from her grave, deep in the forest, by Myrthe (MUHR-te), Queen of the Wilis (VIHL-ihs), spirits of women who, having died unhappy in love, are condemned to lead men to destruction. (The word *wili* comes from a Slavic word for "vampire.") When a repentant Albrecht comes to bring flowers to Giselle's grave, Myrthe orders her to dance him to his death. Instead, Giselle protects Albrecht until the first rays of dawn break Myrthe's power.

In St Petersburg, Russia, in 1862, an English ballet called the *Daughter of Pharaoh*, choreographed by Marius Petipa (mahr-ee-OOS peh-tee-PAH), sent Russian audiences into rapture. Petipa had come to Russia from France in 1842, and he remained a central figure in Russian ballet for almost sixty years. By the middle of the nineteenth century, ballet companies were flourishing in Moscow and St Petersburg. Dancers enjoyed positions of high esteem in Russia, as they did not in the rest of Europe.

In Russia, the influence of Petipa carried Russian ballet forward in a quasi-Romantic style. He shared the sentimental taste of his time, but his works often contained very strange elements and numerous anachronisms. Minor characters might wear costumes suggesting period or locale, but the stars wore conventional garb, often of classical derivation. Prima ballerinas often appeared in stylish contemporary coiffures and jewels, even when playing the role of a slave. *Divertissements* (dee-vair-TEES-mawn)—light entertainments—were often inserted into a ballet. Petipa included many different kinds of dance in his ballets—classical, character, and folk dance. His creative approach more than compensated for his anachronisms. As some have said in his defense, "No one criticized Shakespeare for having Antony and Cleopatra speak in blank verse."

From this Russian school came the ever-popular *Nutcracker* and *Swan Lake*. The scores for both were composed by Tchaikovsky. *Swan Lake* was first produced in 1877 by the Moscow Bolshoi (BOHL-shoy or buhl-SHOY) and *Nutcracker* in 1892. *Swan Lake* popularized the *fouetté*, or whipping turn, introduced by the ballerina Pierina Legnani in Petipa's *Cinderella* and incorporated for her in *Swan Lake*. In one scene, Legnani danced thirty-two consecutive *fouettés*, and to this day that number is mandatory.

Focal Point

The Victorians

The Romantic Age, also known as the Age of Industry, is also known as the Victorian Age, referring to Britain's Queen Victoria, who reigned through most of the period. Thus, because of the importance of Britain in the Industrial Revolution, the Romantic style in the arts, and the morals and mores that have become associated with the nineteenth century and Victorian England, we return to England once more for our Focal Point. In it we see the tremendous diversity that Romanticism made possible by freeing painters to follow the subjective impulses of their emotions.

15.24 Sir Edwin Landseer, *Dignity and Impudence*, 1839. Oil on canvas, 35 × 27½ ins (89 × 70 cm). Tate Gallery, London.

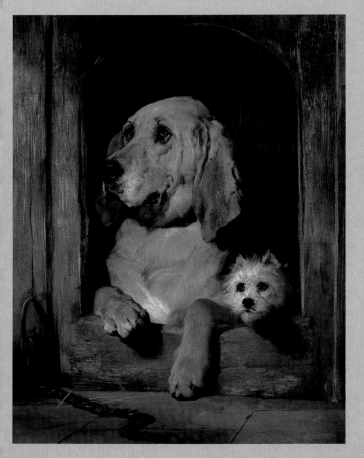

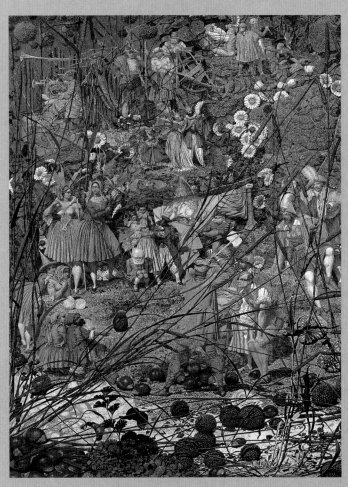

15.25 Richard Dadd, *The Fairy Feller's Master Stroke*, 1855–64. Oil on canvas, 21¼ × 15¼ ins (54 × 38.5 cm). Tate Gallery, London.

British confidence soared to great heights in the middle decades of the nineteenth century. That was when the British began to use the term "Victorian" to describe the era in which they were living, demonstrating their consciousness that their values dominated a distinct period. New technologies and new economics combined with social stability and traditional values. Parliament and the monarchy symbolized continuity, stability, and tradition in changing times. The new Parliament buildings (see

491

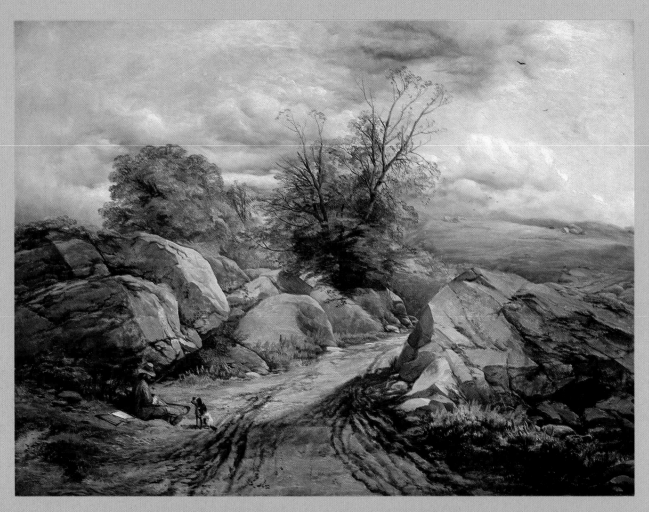

15.26 Thomas Creswick, *Landscape*, c. 1851. Oil on canvas, 27 × 35 ins (68.5 × 89 cm). Royal Academy of Arts, London.

Fig. 15.12) reflected the antiquity of the institution of Parliament in their mock-medieval architecture. The revolutionary nature of the era was hidden behind a cloak of custom and tradition. When Victoria ascended to the throne in 1837, the British monarchy could trace its ancestry back further than any other European political institution apart from the papacy. Victoria and Albert raised the monarchy to new heights of public esteem.

The character and essence of Victorianism can be clearly seen in the single discipline of painting, which reveals a remarkable complexity and scope. "There were contradictions, movements and countermovements; endless and labyrinthine courses were explored, false gods pursued. . . . If the period produced few artists of world stature, this was balanced by the cumulative effect of the rich diversity of high talent, occasionally bordering on greatness."[2] The Victorian age was compulsively multidisciplinary. G.K. Chesterton described it as "a world in which painters were trying to be novelists, and novelists

trying to be historians, and musicians doing the work of school-masters, and sculptors doing the work of curates." Although official patronage had more or less disappeared, state support of artists did exist, and there was some increase in private patronage. Support groups for artists were first set up during this period, among them, Morris and Company (1861), the Art Workers Guild (1884), and the New English Art Club (1885). The Royal Academy, which had been founded in 1769, also supported artistic endeavors. On the one hand, it provided a focus for artistic activity, but on the other, it was seen as an established institution against which rebellious artists could react. The age produced historical painters, landscape painters, marine painters, sporting painters, animal painters, genre painters, fairy painters, nude and still-life painters, neoclassical painters, portrait painters, and the Pre-Raphaelites.

The Victorian love of animals is legendary, and owning bizarre, wild, and exotic pets became the rage, a development perfectly consistent with the Romantic tendency and

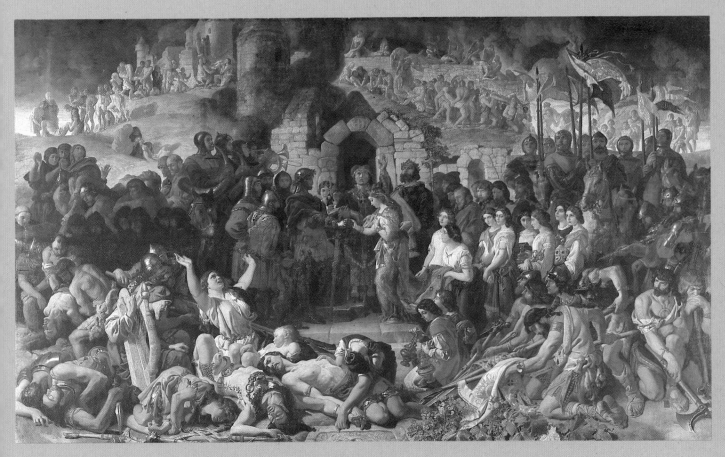

15.27 Daniel MacLise, *The Marriage of Eva and Strongbow*, first exhibited 1854. Oil on canvas, 10 ft 2 ins × 16 ft 7 ins (3.09 × 5.05 m). National Gallery of Ireland, Dublin.

outlook. In the jubilee year of 1887, thousands of prisoners all over the British Empire were released. The only criminals not released were those convicted of cruelty to animals, which Queen Victoria regarded as "one of the worst traits of human nature." In *Dignity and Impudence*, Edwin Landseer (1802–73) (Fig. **15.24**) anthropomorphizes two dogs (that is gives them human attributes).

Highly controversial, the Pre-Raphaelites appear to have exercised significant influence on later movements away from naturalism. They formed themselves into a group in 1848. The Pre-Raphaelites had a significant influence on art and design because of their ability to envision and paint with detailed skill and their use of a wide range of symbolism. They returned to the direct symbolism, frank naturalism, and poetic sentiment previously found in medieval art, prior to the Renaissance painter Raphael—hence the name. To such medieval qualities they added a modern analysis and profound and intellectual study of art and nature. They loved detail, and their works abound with painstaking attention to it.

Escape to legend and literature, along with a strong interest in the occult and spiritualism, led to an English fascination with fairy tales. As Charles Dickens wrote in *Household Words* (vol. 8), "In a utilitarian age, of all other times, it is a matter of grave importance that fairy tales should be respected." Fairy tales were subject matter understood and shared by artist and viewer alike. The art that emerged represents a unique, Victorian contribution to art.

The fascinating painting *The Fairy Feller's Master Stroke* (Fig. **15.25**) took the artist, who was suffering from schizophrenia, nine years to complete. Richard Dadd (1817–87) had been among the founders of a group of painters called "the Clique," and his early works had been undistinguished attempts at landscape, marine, and animal painting. After returning from an extensive trip to the Middle East and Italy, and after being rejected in the competition for the decoration of the Houses of Parliament, he stabbed his father to death. Fleeing to France, he planned to assassinate the emperor of Austria. Captured after stabbing a passenger at Fontainebleau, he spent his remaining years institutionalized in Bedlam, or the Hospital of St Mary of Bethlehem. He was provided with painting materials, and his subsequent works have an insistent supernatural quality, as we can see in Figure **15.25**. The flat coloring and obsessive detail have been explained as a reflection of certain symptoms of schizophrenia. The main event in the painting is placed in the center, and the myriad details that surround it seem to be nothing more than highly imaginative decoration.

Victorian landscape painters produced a prodigious quantity of "pretty, undisturbed scenes" which were designed for a growing picture-buying public. The themes were mostly superficial, emotional, and repetitive, and yet for the most part the genre is highly pleasing. The genius of John Constable (1776–1837) was the guiding light as well as the shadow over other Victorian landscape artists. Constable's "chiaroscuro of nature" lent itself to easy adaptation, and his naturalistic style permeated the genre. *Landscape* (Fig. **15.26**) by Thomas Creswick (1811–69) has much in common with the work of Corot (see Fig. **15.10**), displaying a careful treatment of rocks, trees, and foliage.

Interest in history, both as a backdrop for Utopian escape and for antiquarianism, colored the arts as well as philosophy. Images of heroism and sublimity caught the imagination of the Romantic painters. Scale as well as attitude found its way onto the canvas. *The Marriage of Eva and Strongbow* (Fig. **15.27**) by Daniel MacLise (1806–70), which covers a canvas 10 feet 2 inches by 16 feet 7 inches (3.09 × 5.05 meters), depicts the twelfth-century marriage of Richard Strongbow, second earl of Pembroke and Strigul, to Eva, eldest daughter of Dermot. Complex and busy, the work elicits an emotional response and captures a climactic moment. Strong contrasts in tones compete with many different focal areas for the viewer's attention. The central situation is played out while everything around it is in confusion. The coloring is harsh, and the facial expressions not very real.

Victorian painting, with all its diversity, complexity, contradictions, and often mediocre quality, very effectively represents the remarkable lot of Romantics, realists, and jacks-of-all-trades who rode the crest of the first wave that swept us into our modern world.

CHAPTER REVIEW

Critical Thought

Many people believe that the Romantic age has never ended and point to the self-centered, nonrationalistic emotionalism of today's attitudes and arts. We might wish to test that assertion, or at least check its partial validity on things we contact daily. For example, how about a daily soap opera, a favorite song (rock or otherwise), or even a TV talk show? If we take the situation apart and describe its component parts, moods, and attitudes, do we come up with something restrained, idealized, simple, and carefully structured, or do we end up with unrestrained emotions, complexity, lifelikeness, and fragmentation? Are we riding a pendulum on one end of the classical/anti-classical spectrum, or are we hanging on somewhere in the middle, swinging toward one extreme or the other?

Summary

After reading this chapter, you should be able to:

- Understand the impact of technology on the social setting of the nineteenth century.
- Discuss the philosophies of Kant and Hegel, illustrating why they are called "idealist."
- Characterize the art and architecture of the Romantic style with references to specific qualities in specific works and artists' visions.
- Describe the literary works of major writers of the Romantic age.
- Identify general characteristics of Romanticism in music and apply them to specific musical genres and composers.
- Explain the conditions of theatre and dance in the Romantic age, including genres, theories, and specific artists and works.
- Apply the elements and principles of composition to analyze and compare individual works of art illustrated in this chapter.

CHAPTER SIXTEEN

The Beginnings of Modernism

OUTLINE

THE WORLD IN TURMOIL

PHILOSOPHY AND PSYCHOLOGY

THE VISUAL ARTS AND ARCHITECTURE
Realism
Impressionism
Post-Impressionism
Experimentation and Art Nouveau
Cubism
Mechanism and Futurism
Expressionism
Fauvism

LITERATURE
Realism
Naturalism
Symbolism

MUSIC
Impressionism
Naturalism in Opera
Nontraditional Transitions
Jazz

THEATRE
Realism and Naturalism
Symbolism

FILM: ART AND MECHANIZATION

DANCE
Ethnic Foundations
Diaghilev and the *Ballets russes*
Duncan and the Modern Dance Movement

FOCAL POINT: AMERICA'S GILDED AGE

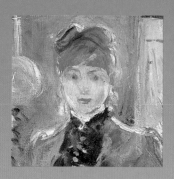

VIEW

ART FOR ART'S SAKE

In the early nineteenth century, the French philosopher Victor Cousin (koo-ZEN) coined the slogan, *l'art pour l'art* (literally, "art for art"). By the late nineteenth century, that phrase came to express the belief held by many writers and artists, especially those associated with Aestheticism, that art needs no justification, that it need serve no political, didactic, or other end. It exists for the sake of its beauty alone. This was a reaction to the utilitarianism (a philosophical doctrine that considers utility as the criterion of action and usefulness as good or worthwhile) of the industrial revolution and its social fabric, and it built on ideas amplified by Goethe and the philosophies of Kant, who argued for an autonomous standard for art.

Freed from the constraints of patronage and their traditional roles as "documentors" (because of the invention of photography), artists could work for themselves and for their own sake.

Above Detail of Fig. **16.12**.

16.1 Claude Monet, *Rouen Cathedral, the Portal, Morning Sun, Harmony in Blue*, 1893. Oil on canvas, 35¹/₂ × 24¹/₂ ins (91 × 63 cm). Musée d'Orsay, Paris.

KEY TERMS

Some of the basic terms and concepts we will encounter in this chapter include the following:

Realism, an artistic and literary style based on the theory that the method of presentation should be true to life.

Naturalism, an even more faithful and unselective representation of reality than realism.

Impressionism, applying to art, music, and literature, implies an approach that evokes subjective and sensory impressions, including mood.

Post-impressionism, a diverse art style in which the essentials of perception are portrayed through concentration on light, atmosphere, and color.

Cubism, a style that violates the usual concepts of two- and three-dimensional space and involves the use of geometric shapes to represent objects and figures.

Expressionism, a style in visual and performing arts that seeks to express the artist's emotions rather than accurately represent line or form.

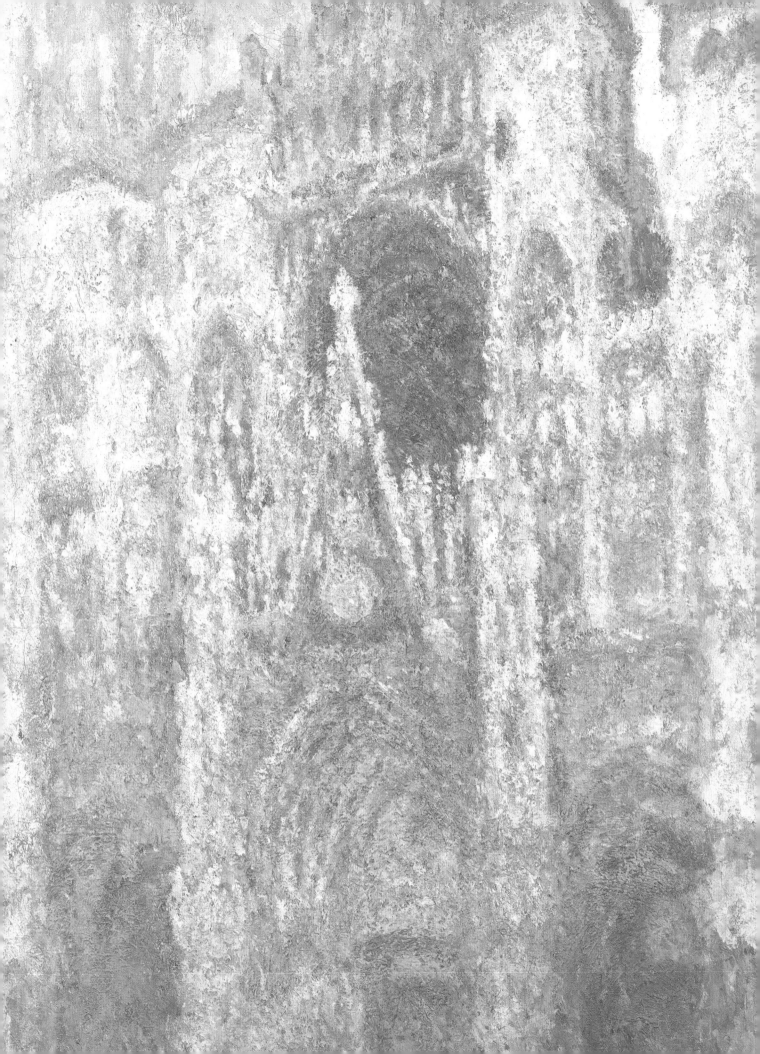

As the nineteenth century wears on, the pace quickens. Turmoil and flux increase as Europe's population leaves in droves for other corners of the globe. Business and industry continue their technological and industrial revolution, and individual workers strive for greater rights and rewards. Nationalism rises, and science explodes. Philosophy and psychology take fire and influence the arts, whose reactions against Romanticism turn particularly "modernist."

THE WORLD IN TURMOIL

European Migration

During the eighteenth and nineteenth centuries seventy million people emigrated from Europe to other continents, mostly to North America, but also to Siberia, Latin America, and Australia. By 1900 the total European population outside of Europe numbered approximately 560 million

and represented more than one-third of the world's entire population. Not all European countries participated in this migration equally—for example, France, which early adopted birth control practices, barely reproduced at replacement level, but the declining death rate resulting from better medicine and a number of other factors, allowed France's population to grow. Nevertheless, it contributed little to the great movement of European migration.

The populations of most other European countries, on the other hand, exploded and led to migration on a massive scale. Among the first to contribute to the emigration were the British and the Irish. In the mid-nineteenth century, Ireland was contributing nearly half of the immigrants to the United States, and in four successive waves (1850, 1870, 1885, and 1910) thirteen million English and Scots left their native lands. Two-thirds of them came to the United States, half that many to Canada, and the remainder to Australia and South Africa. In the same period six million Germans left home (most of them for the United States), and two million Scandinavians did the same. Sixteen million Italians left Italy—nearly 750,000

Timeline 16.1 The beginnings of modernism.

	GENERAL EVENTS	LITERATURE & PHILOSOPHY	VISUAL ART & ARCHITECTURE	THEATRE & CINEMA	MUSIC & DANCE
1850					
	Emigration from Europe Unification of Germany	Zola	Courbet (16.6)		
			Millet (16.7)		
		Dostoyevski	Hiroshige (16.18)		
			Rodin (16.15)		
			Manet (16.8)		
			Daumier (16.9)		
1875					
		La Flesche	Renoir (16.13)	Ibsen	Bizet
	Brooklyn Bridge		Tanner (16.10)	Chekhov	Debussy
	Hydroelectric power		Morisot (16.12)		Moscagni
	Pasteurization	Nietzsche	Cassatt (16.14)		Puccini
	Radio-telegraphy		Monet (16.1, 16.11)		Leoncavallo
	Discovery of radium		Gauguin (16.19)		
	Renault makes cars		van Gogh (16.20, 16.21)		
			Burnham and Root (16.22)		
			Seurat (16.16)	Maeterlinck	
			Hunt (16.39)	Lumière brothers	
1900					
	Rise of nationalism in Europe	Freud	Sullivan (16.23)	Shaw	Ravel
		Proust	Cézanne (16.17)	Armat	Diaghilev
	Genetics		Gaudí (16.24)	Méliès	Stravinsky
	Einstein		Picasso (16.25, 16.26)	Porter	Schoenberg
	Superconductivity		Boccioni (16.28)	Pathé	Duncan
			Matisse (16.30)	Sennet	Jazz
			Duchamp (16.27)	Griffith	
			Beckmann (16.29)	Chaplin	
1925					

people in 1913 alone—half going to North and South America and the other half to other parts of Europe. Central and Eastern Europeans contributed nine million people to the waves of emigration. By the end of the nineteenth century, Europeans had, literally, populated the globe.

Business and Industry

During the nineteenth century, industrial civilization changed from a system of production based on iron and coal to one based on the technology of electricity, the internal combustion engine, and the chemistry of synthetic materials. The turning point came in the 1890s, when technological development accelerated exponentially. An overview of industrial and technological development isolates three principal periods. The first began in the late eighteenth century in Britain and had moved, by the first half of the nineteenth century, to France, Belgium, Switzerland, and the United States. However, with the exception of the United States, the industrial explosion slowed in these countries after the 1860s—between 1875 and 1913, on the other hand, the United States' share of world industrial output had climbed from 23 percent to 36 percent. The second period of industrial development, which occurred between 1840 and 1873, witnessed the first real world boom in railway construction and the widespread industrialization of the remainder of Europe, particularly Germany, where a much greater economic transformation took Germany to a position as the world's second largest industrial producer by the end of the century. The last wave of industrial expansion came at the very end of the nineteenth century and encompassed Russia, the Scandinavian countries, Italy, parts of Eastern Europe, and Japan. By 1913, Europe and North America represented 82 percent of the world's industrial production—down by 4 percent from 1870.

The growth and spread of industry and technology created fundamental changes in the organization of the system of production. Until the 1870s the capitalist system underpinned economic activity in Europe. The social dynamic centered on the family, and its system of organization rested on the authority of one man, the omniscient entrepreneur. It was the age, as we will see in the Focal Point section at the end of this chapter, when great personal fortunes were amassed by individual businessmen. Gradually, however, especially in the United States and Germany, business and industry placed at their center the concept of continuous production and mass distribution. The change, which might be defined as a shift from the "visible" hand of an integrated company to the "invisible" hand of the market, coincided with a growing concentration of businesses that tended to bring together in one unit the activities of production, marketing, and research. Thus, the world began to see huge corporations with multi-functional hierarchical structures. Some companies retained a family structure, but others moved toward a managerial model, with decision-making placed in the hands of salaried executives, and at the same time, the concept of marketing networks created more and more mergers and larger and larger corporations. In addition, the marketplace experienced a dynamic increase in new business centered on new products that emerged from new technologies—for example, automobiles, bicycles, the cinema, and, later, airplanes.

Workers and Socialism

Among the major results of industrialization were the growth of the working class, the development of its organizational forms, and its links to other elements in society who were, to varying degrees, unwilling to integrate with bourgeois society (Figs. **16.2** and **16.3**). The organization of the working class came in three spurts. The first, from 1864 to 1893, witnessed powerful popular movements and brutally repressed mass strikes. During this period, the International Working Men's Association (1864) and the socialist International (1889–93) were formed. The second spurt, which occurred between 1893 and 1905, saw the rise of trade unions and the emergence of nation-states of political parties. The last spurt, from 1905 until World War I, included a general expansion of the labor and socialist movements.

The International Working Men's Association was founded in London in 1864, and it drew much support across Europe. It was intended to be a worldwide workers' party through which workers could derive a sense of solidarity in their struggle to improve their conditions. The movement split in 1869, with the followers of Karl Marx going in one direction, and the others, known as the "anti-authoritarian faction," going in another. Within twenty years, the movement had splintered into national groups, for the simple reason that the different forms of action and militancy could not develop according to a single model. The movement polarized around two centers: unions and political parties.

The socialist creed continued to be spread through the organization of the Second International in 1889–91, a loose federation of organizations. According to its agenda, in order to be called a socialist, an individual had to work for the collective ownership of the means of production and to recognize the need for political and parliamentary action. Strikes became the main weapon of the union movement in Europe, but by the beginning of the twentieth

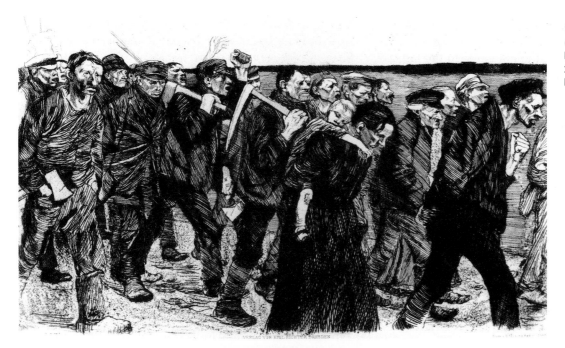

16.2 Käthe Kollwitz, *The Weaver's Cycle: March of the Weavers*, 1897. Etching, 8³/₈ × 11⁵/₈ ins (21.3 × 29.5 cm). University of Michigan Museum of Art. © DACS 1999.

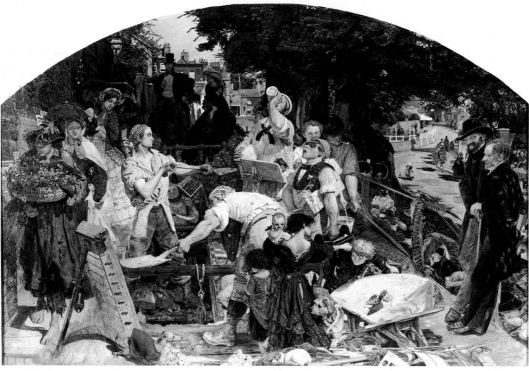

16.3 Ford Madox Brown, *Work*, 1852–65. Oil on canvas, 4 ft 6¹/₂ ins × 6 ft 5¹/₈ ins (1.38 × 1.96 m). Manchester City Art Gallery, UK.

century, the labor movement in Europe proved relatively impotent in the face of rising nationalism and imperialism, central to which was the German Reich—or state.

The German Reich

As we have seen in preceding chapters, unlike much of the rest of Europe, Germany remained a series of independent states under individual rule. However, on 18 January 1871, twenty-five German states, including three city-states, joined together to create a unified German Reich (state) with William I, King of Prussia, as Kaiser (KYZ-er). It was an authoritarian state, whose government was not responsible to the parliament. The previous state of Prussia dominated the remaining members of the Reich, and that gave the new state a particular civilization and type of government—that is, a conservative business class and the domination of the civil service by a powerful professional military. Bismarck, the prime minister of the Reich, was a Prussian, and he began a *Kulturkampf* (campaign for secularization), which attacked Catholics, expelled the Jesuits, and placed controls on the Roman clergy. However, because such a campaign also alarmed the Protestants, it did not succeed. After two attempts were made to assassinate the Kaiser, Bismarck dissolved the Reichstag (parliament) and instituted anti-socialist laws. Despite the crash of the Viennese stock market, German industrial expansion continued, and heavy industry became more highly concentrated. The country became more and more urban, and the population grew quickly. Agriculture was modernized, and Germany, practicing a form of state capitalism, became the second most powerful nation on earth. The German aristocracy joined forces with the richest industrialists against socialism and trade unionism.

Bismarck's foreign policy sought to consolidate Germany's position in Europe by forging a set of contra-

dictory treaties. In 1879 Germany entered an alliance with Austria-Hungary, in 1881 Bismarck engineered the Three Emperors' League, and in 1882 he produced the Triple Alliance among Germany, Austria-Hungary, and Italy. German nationalism strengthened when Kaiser William II took the throne in 1888 and began his search for Germany's "place in the sun." However, during this time, socialist influence increased and, in 1912, the Social Democratic Party (SPD) became the largest group in the Reichstag. Among its major objectives, which it tried to accomplish by demonstrations and strikes, was universal suffrage in those areas of Germany where three classes—aristocracy, bourgeoisie, and workers—still existed. This demand proved an important point in the SPD's acceptance of Germany's entry into World War I under a government of national unity on 4 August 1914. The "Great War" was expected to last for three or four months and be over by Christmas. It wasn't.

Map 16.1 Political frontiers and national communities in Europe, 1848.

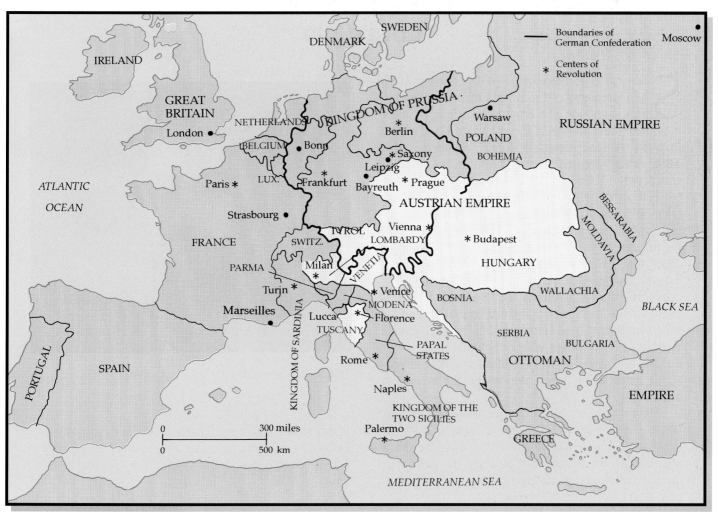

A Scientific Explosion

Physics

So much happened in science in the last quarter of the nineteenth century and the first decade of the twentieth century that a mere scratching of the surface is all that a book that is primarily about art and culture can manage.

In 1900, no law had been discovered to account for the phenomenon of heat and light radiation by a solid, white-hot body. In that year, Max Planck (plahnk; 1858–1947) guessed that radiation did not occur in a continuous fashion but in small discrete units, separate quantities or quanta. This theory, which enabled scientists to explain heat radiation, turned physics upside down. Building on this theory, Albert Einstein (YN-styn; 1879–1955) explained in 1905 the photoelectric effect, by showing that light, which comprises both waves and particles, moves by quanta—that is, tiny packets of light, which were later called photons. Nils Bohr (1885–1962) used this quantum theory to build a model of an atom, in 1911, describing the movement of electrons within an atom. This model enabled him to achieve remarkable results in the fields of the spectroscopy of gaseous matter and of X-ray physics.

In September 1895, Wilhelm Conrad Röntgen (also spelled Roentgen; pronounced RENT-guhn; 1845–1923) discovered X-rays—he called the rays "X" because their nature was then unknown. It was not defined until 1912, when Max von Laue (LOW-eh; 1879–1960) managed to diffract the rays through a lattice of crystal. X-rays are electromagnetic waves with very short wavelengths that pass through material that is normally opaque to light, and their discovery gained Röntgen a Nobel Prize for Physics in 1901. In 1911 Heike Kamerlingh Onnes (HY-kuh KAH-mur-ling OH-nes) of the Netherlands discovered superconductivity—that is, the property of certain metals or alloys, at very low temperatures, to lose their resistance to electricity. It took until 1986 for research in superconductivity

---

TECHNOLOGY: PUTTING DISCOVERY TO WORK

Coca-Cola

Sugar, caffeine, and vegetable extracts are some of the ingredients of the world's most popular soft drink, although the exact proportions of these ingredients remain one of the corporate world's most jealously guarded secrets. Dr John S. Pemberton (Fig. **16.4**) never patented his original formula, which he concocted in 1886 in Atlanta, Georgia.

Pemberton, a pharmacist, developed a variety of chemical compounds for treating various human ailments—for example, Globe of Flower Cough Syrup, Indian Queen Hair Dye, and Triplex Liver Pills—and he spent much of his time in his chemical laboratory looking for new flavors to make his pharmaceutical products more tasty. Around 1880 he began to experiment with a "soft" drink that could be sold at the food soda fountain of drug stores. In 1886 he discovered a syrup that, when mixed with carbonated water, made a thirst-quenching drink. He added caffeine and vegetable extracts, for flavor, and mixed the brew in a brass kettle.

The first person to test the new drink was William Venable, the resident "soda jerk" of Jacob's Drugstore in Atlanta. Apparently, Venable liked what he drank and bought the mix on a trial basis. His customers loved it, and wanted to ask for it by name. One of

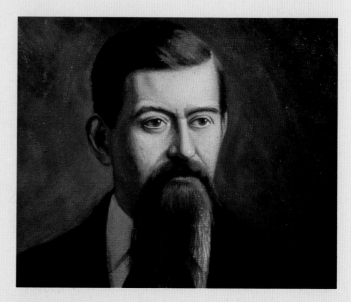

16.4 Dr John S. Pemberton of the Coca-Cola corporation.

Pemberton's partners, Frank Robinson, suggested Coca-Cola, and the next day, an elaborate script logo was produced. It and the product remain the same today.

to lead to the development now being seen in contemporary physical processes.

Biology

In 1865, the Moravian-born botanist Gregor Johann Mendel (MEN-dul; 1822–84) demonstrated that hereditary characteristics are transmitted via distinct elements, which are today called genes. Mendel's findings, the discovery of chromosomes in 1888 and of mutations in 1901, founded the science of genetics. The gene itself emerged in 1909, when the Danish botanist Wilhelm Johannsen (1857–1927) coined the name "genes" for the hereditary units that produce the physical characteristics of an organism.

In microbiology, the second half of the century produced the work of Frenchman Louis Pasteur (1822–95), who explained the fermentation process as the result of the action of microscopic living organisms. Pasteur extended his research to include bacteria, thus beginning the field of bacteriology, and he promulgated the idea that living beings contain in themselves the means of fighting disease. Thus, the immune system became a serious subject for scientific study. Birth itself emerged from scientific experimentation in the early twentieth century, when *in vitro* cultivation—that is, a method in which a living organism is sustained outside of its natural environment—was invented in 1907.

PHILOSOPHY AND PSYCHOLOGY

Friedrich Nietzsche

If science experienced an explosion, then we might characterize approaches to philosophy and psychology in the late nineteenth century as a firestorm. The provocative German thinker, philosopher, and poet Friedrich Nietzsche (NEE-che; 1844–1900) illustrates this. Nietzsche was a classical philologist, and he voiced the sentiments of the radical moralist. He attacked all the accepted ideas of his time and argued for a revision of all values. He attacked rationalism and contemporary morality, characterizing Christianity and other religions as contributors to the formation of a "slave morality." He saw contemporary democracy and its sympathy for the weak and helpless as rule by mass mediocrity. Instead, he championed the "superman," the superior individual with the vision and courage to produce a "master" morality.

Nietzsche was raised after his father's death by his religious female relatives, and, according to some, this accounted for the attacks on religion and women that he made in his writings. His brilliance brought him the appointment as professor of Greek at the University of Basel in 1869, but ten years later he resigned the post because of poor health and, for the next ten years, led a mostly solitary life. In January 1889 he suffered a complete mental collapse from which he never recovered, although he lived for another eleven years.

Soon after going to Basel, he published an intuitive philosophical investigation of the spiritual background of Greek tragedy, entitled *The Birth of Tragedy from the Spirit of Music* (1872). Three years later he wrote *Untimely Opinions* in which he attacked the smug conceit of Bismarck's Germany. Perhaps his best-known work is *Thus Spake Zarathustra* (1883–92), a series of rhapsodical sermons by an imaginary prophet and written in poetic prose modeled after the Bible.

Many of his ideas are clearly fascistic, and the followers of Adolf Hitler claimed him as their inspiration and prophet. Perhaps there is an irony in the fact that Nietzsche himself opposed nationalism, armies, the German Empire, politics, and racism, especially anti-Semitism. Understanding and interpreting Nietzsche were made exceedingly difficult by the fact that he often wrote in hyperbole—that is, by overstating his case in order to get a reaction—and whatever he wrote, he wrote with verve and caustic wit. He reportedly warned a friend that it was not desirable for his readers to agree with him. He accepted the idea of human helplessness in a mechanical world operating under inexorable law, but he rejected Schopenhauer's pessimism. Instead, he preached courage in the face of the unknown and found this to be humanity's highest attribute. After a long selective process, Nietzsche was certain that courage would produce a race of supermen and superwomen.

Sigmund Freud

One of the towering figures of modern times, the Austrian Sigmund Freud (froyd; 1856–1939) was the first to develop what he called "psychoanalysis"—that is, the probing of the human "unconscious"—in the study of human behavior by exploring the world of dreams (Fig. 16.5). Psychoanalysis is a method of understanding psychological and psychopathological phenomena, and at the same time a method of treating mental illness. Freud developed his theories around 1885 in Vienna, and although he did not invent the idea of the psychic unconscious, he undertook a systematic exploration of it. At first his ideas were met with considerable skepticism because of their novel propositions regarding sexuality. However, psychoanalysis gradually gained an important place in medicine and psychology.

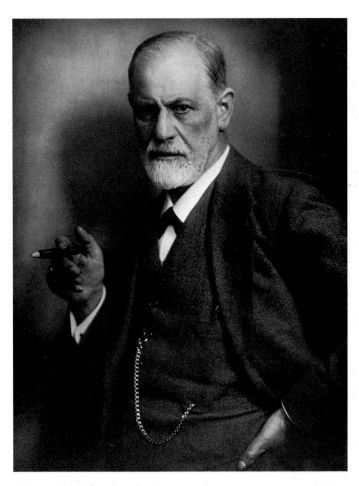

16.5 Max Halberstadt, photograph of Sigmund Freud, c. 1926. Courtesy of W. Ernest Freud, by arrangement with Mark Patterson and Associates and the Freud Museum, London.

Freud's principal work was *The Interpretation of Dreams* (1900), in which he showed that the discoveries of psychoanalysis about dreaming and using symbols can be applied to literature as well as to psychology and psychiatry. His ideas significantly influenced twentieth-century literature, and some of the misinterpretations of his ideas led to the exploration of the creative imagination.

Freud's impact on literature falls into three areas. The first, called literary surrealism, is based on the idea of breaking human psychological defenses and giving uncensored expression to the irrational symbolic modes of the unconscious. The second area concerns an aspect of what, in the Introduction to this text, we called "contextual criticism." Here, biographers and critics "psychoanalyze" writers, and other artists, in order to explain literary works in terms of the writer's "conditioning." The final area consists of writers, particularly novelists and dramatists, conceiving and presenting their characters in psychoanalytical terms. This is especially true of the "stream-of-consciousness" school, in which the character's inner

monologue imposes on the reader the job of finding the person in the midst of the material comprising his or her personal experience.

THE VISUAL ARTS AND ARCHITECTURE

Realism

The style that is referred to as "realism" ran through the 1840s, 1850s, and 1860s, and its central figure was Gustave Courbet (koor-BAY; 1819–77). Courbet was influenced by the innovations of Corot in terms of the play of light on surfaces. But, unlike Corot, his aim was to make an objective and unprejudiced record of the customs, ideas, and appearances of contemporary French society. *The Stone Breakers* (Fig. **16.6**) was the first painting to display his philosophy to the full. Courbet painted two men as he had seen them working beside a road. The work is lifesize, and, while the treatment seems objective, it makes a sharp comment on the tedium and laborious nature of the task. A social realist, Courbet was more intent on social message than on meditative reaction. Therefore, his work is less dramatic and nostalgic than that of others.

Jean-François Millet (mee-LAY; 1814–75) was one of a group of painters called the Barbizon School, which focused upon a realistic-Romantic vision of landscape, and typically used peasants as its subject matter. The Barbizon School did not espouse socialism, but it did exalt the honest, simple life and work on the land, as contrasted with the urban bourgeois life. In Millet's *Woman Baking Bread* (Fig. **16.7**) these themes are apparent, and the peasant emerges as an heroic figure. This quality is enhanced by the vantage point the painter has chosen. Seen from slightly below, the peasant woman has an added height and dominance which emphasize her grandeur.

Edouard Manet (mah-NAY; 1832–83) strove to paint "only what the eye can see." Yet his works go beyond a mere reflection of reality to a larger artistic reality, one which suggests that a painting has an internal logic different from the logic of familiar reality. Manet liberated the painter's art from competition with the camera. *Déjeuner sur l'herbe* (Fig. **16.8**), in which Manet sought to "speak in a new voice," shocked the public when it was first shown at the Salon des Refusés in 1863. The setting is pastoral, like one we might find in Watteau, for example, but the people are real and identifiable: Manet's model, his brother, and the sculptor Leenhof. The apparent immorality of a naked frolic in a Paris park outraged the public and

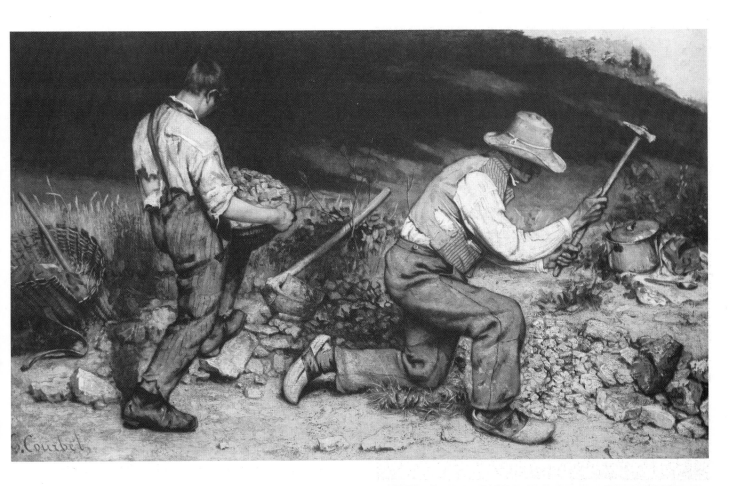

16.6 Gustave Courbet, *The Stone Breakers*, 1849. Oil on canvas, 5 ft 3 ins ×
8 ft 6 ins (1.6 × 2.59 m). Formerly Gemäldegalerie, Dresden, Germany
(destroyed 1945).

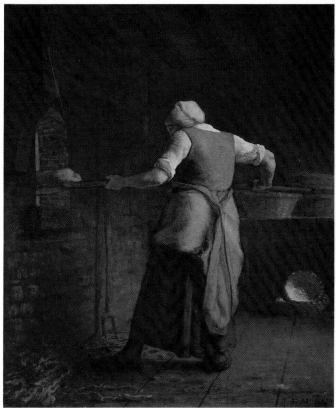

16.7 Jean-François Millet, *Woman Baking Bread*, 1853–4. Oil on canvas, 21³/₄ ×
18 ins (55 × 46 cm). Collection, State Museum Kröller-Müller, Otterlo, The
Netherlands.

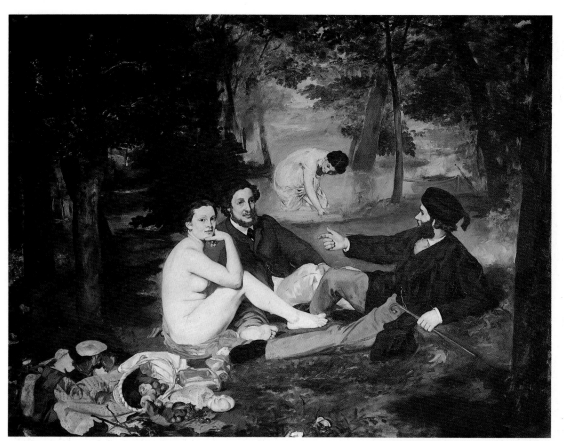

16.8 Edouard Manet, *Déjeuner sur l'herbe* (*The Picnic*), 1863. Oil on canvas, 7 ft × 8 ft 10 ins (2.13 × 2.69 m). Louvre, Paris.

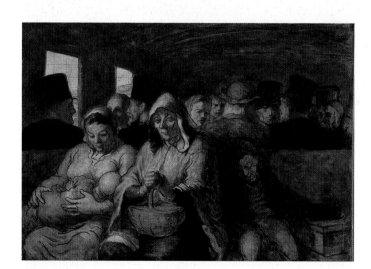

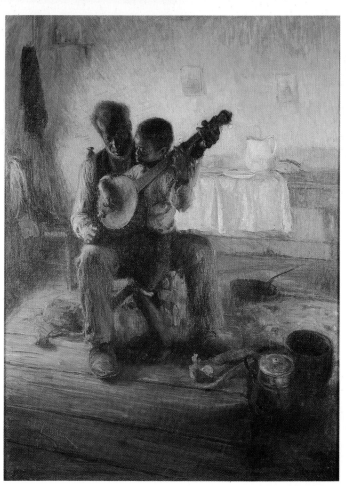

16.9 (*above*) Honoré Daumier, *The Third-Class Carriage*, c. 1862. The National Gallery of Canada.

16.10 (*right*) Henry O. Tanner, *The Banjo Lesson*, c. 1893. Oil on canvas, 48 × 35 ins (122 × 89 cm). Hampton Institute, Hampton, Virginia.

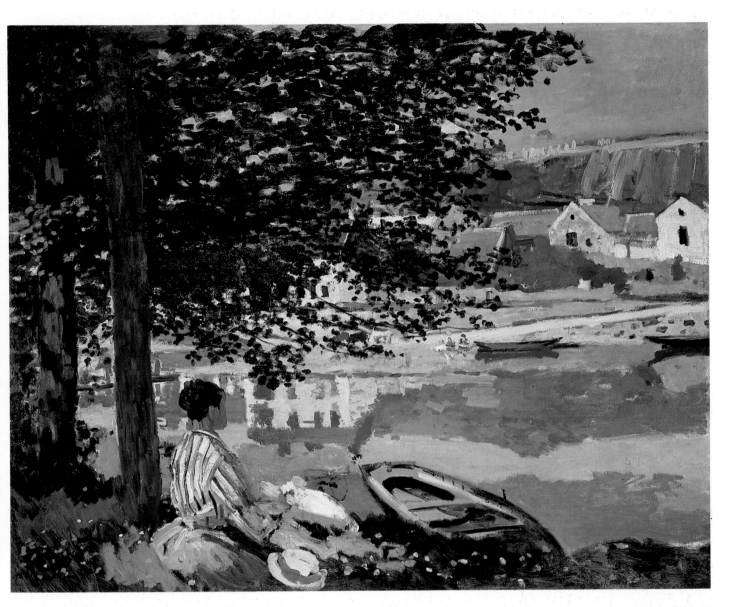

16.11 Claude Monet, *On the Seine at Bennecourt*, 1868. Oil on canvas, 31⁷/₈ × 39¹/₂ ins (78.5 × 100.5 cm).
Courtesy of The Art Institute of Chicago (Mr. & Mrs. Potter Palmer Collection). Photo: © 1998 The Art Institute of Chicago. All rights reserved.

the critics. Had his figures been classical nymphs and satyrs, all would have been well. But the intrusion of reality into the sacred mythical setting, not to mention the nudity of a common woman while her male companions have their clothes on, proved unsettling for the public.

Honoré Daumier (1808–79) often depicted urban scenes, for example *The Third-Class Carriage* (Fig. **16.9**). The painting shows the interior of a large, horse-drawn bus in Paris. Daumier puts the viewer in the seat opposite a grandmother, her daughter, and two grandchildren. Together, they form a strong compositional triangle that contrasts them with the people behind them. Some scholars suggest that the painting is a comment on urban alienation, which became an important topic in art after 1880.

The first important African American painter, Henry O. Tanner (1859–1937), although somewhat later, painted in a similar style (Fig. **16.10**). He studied at the Philadelphia Academy of Fine Arts with the American realist painter Thomas Eakins (1844–1916), who encouraged both African Americans and women at a time when professional careers were essentially closed to them. *The Banjo Lesson* presents its images in a strictly realistic manner, without sentimentality. The painting's focus is achieved through the contrast of clarity in the central objects and less detail in the surrounding areas. In many respects this technique follows Corot. Tanner skillfully captures an atmosphere of concentration and shows us a warm relationship between teacher and pupil.

507

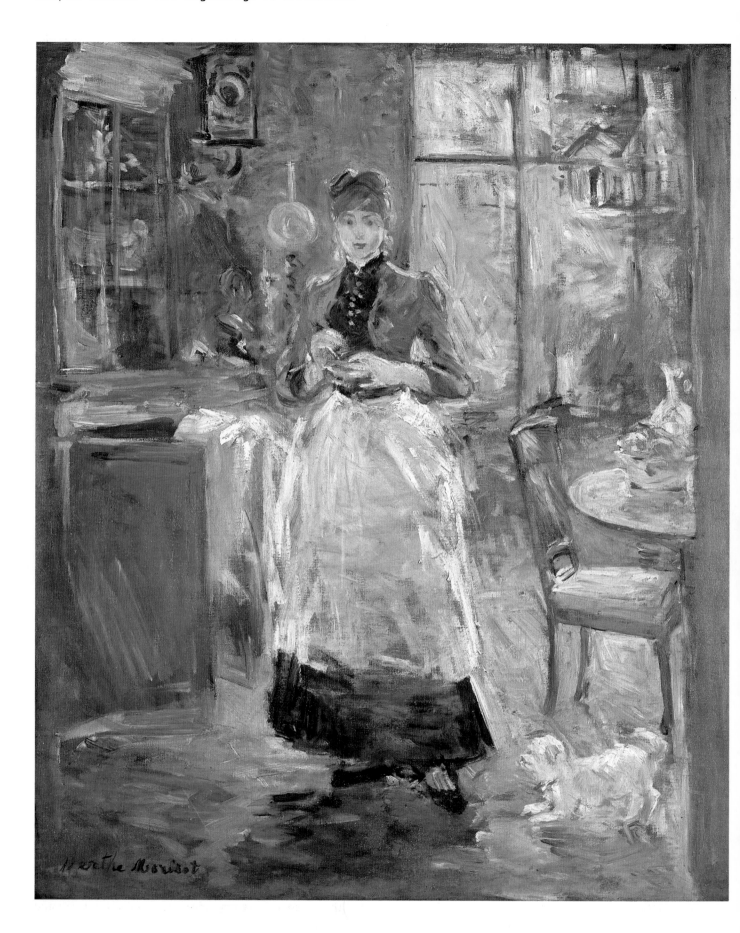

Impressionism

The realists' search for spontaneity, harmonious colors, subjects from everyday life, and faithfulness to observed lighting and atmospheric effects led to the development of a style used by a small group of painters in the 1860s, and described by a hostile critic in 1874 as "impressionism." The "impressionists" created a new way of seeing reality through color and motion. Their style emerged in competition with the newly invented technology of the camera, and these painters tried to outdo photography by portraying those essentials of perception that the camera cannot capture. They emphasized the presence of color within shadows and based their style on an understanding of the interrelated mechanisms of the camera and the eye: vision consists of the result of light and color making an "impression" on the retina.

The style lasted only fifteen years in its purest form, but it profoundly influenced all painting that followed. Working out-of-doors, the impressionists concentrated on the effects of natural light on objects and atmosphere. Their experiments resulted in a profoundly different vision of the world around them and way of rendering that vision. For them, the painted canvas was, first of all, "a material covered with pigments"—small "color patches," which together create lively, vibrant images.

Impressionism was as collective a style as any we have seen thus far. In an individualistic age, this style reflected the common concerns of a relatively small group of artists who met frequently and held joint exhibitions. The subjects painted are impressions of landscapes, rivers, streets, cafés, theatres, and so on.

Two individuals, Claude Monet (klohd moh-NAY) and Pierre-Auguste Renoir, brought impressionism to its birth. They spent the summer of 1866 at Bougival on the River Seine, working closely together, and from that collaboration came the beginnings of the style. In his paintings, Claude Monet (1840–1926) tried to find an art of modern life by recording everyday themes with on-the-spot, objective observations. He sought to achieve two aims: representation of contemporary subject matter and optical truth—that is, the way colors and textures really appear to the eye. Monet's paintings reflect an innocent joy in the world around him and an intensely positive view of life. He had no specific aesthetic theory—in fact, he detested theorizing—but he did seek to bring realism to its peak. His work encompasses scientific observation, the study of optics, and other aspects of human perception. Monet translated objects into color stimuli.

Monet's *On the Seine at Bennecourt* (Fig. **16.11**) illustrates these concerns. It conveys a pleasant picture of the times, an optimistic view rather than the often pessimistic outlook of the Romantics. This was a new tone for a new era. Although the scene is a landscape panorama, lack of atmospheric or linear perspective brings the entire painting to the foreground without deep space. The scene is bright, alive, and pleasant. We are comfortable in its presence.

One of the original group of impressionists was Berthe Morisot (bairt mohr-ee-ZOH; 1841–95). Her works have a gentle introspectiveness, often focusing on family members, and her view of contemporary life is edged with pathos and sentimentality. In *In the Dining Room* (Fig. **16.12**), she gives a penetrating glimpse into psychological reality. The servant girl has a distinct personality, and she stares back at the viewer almost impudently. The painting captures a moment of disorder—the cabinet door stands ajar with what appears to be a used table cloth flung over it. The little dog playfully demands attention. Morisot's brushstrokes are delicate, loose, and casual.

In 1877, another woman joined the impressionists. Mary Cassatt (kuh-SAT; 1845–1926) came to Paris from Philadelphia, a minor center for artists at the time. Thanks to her financial independence, she was able to override her family's objections to a career deemed unsuitable for a woman, especially a woman of wealth. In fact, it was her wealth and connections with wealthy collectors in the United States that helped the impressionists gain exposure and acceptance in this country. In *The Child's Bath* (Fig. **16.14**), she depicts her favorite subjects—women and children. In this painting, Cassatt's brushwork is far less obvious than that in other impressionist works, and this helped conventional viewers to understand the work and relate closely to the scene. Painted in clear, bright colors, Cassatt's subjects do not make eye contact with the viewer. Their forms are purposeful, and they awaken interest, rather than emotions.

The surface and textural concerns of the impressionist can be seen in the work of the century's most remarkable sculptor, Auguste Rodin (roh-DAN; 1840–1917). Although his style is not easy to classify, we find plenty of idealism and social comment—for example, in his powerful work *The Burghers of Calais* (kah-LAY; Fig. **16.15**). Commissioned by the city of Calais, France, as a public monument, the work honors six leading citizens (burghers) who, in 1347, offered themselves as hostages to the English King Edward III, who had laid siege to the city. The burghers were ready to sacrifice their lives if the city would

16.12 Berthe Morisot, *In the Dining Room*, 1886. Oil on canvas, 24¹/₈ × 19³/₄ ins (61 × 50 cm). National Gallery of Art, Washington D.C. (Chester Dale Collection). © 1998 Board of Trustees, National Gallery of Art, Washington, D.C.

MASTERWORK

Renoir—*Le Moulin de la Galette*

The impressionist Pierre-Auguste Renoir (ren-WAHR; 1841–1919) specialized in painting the human figure and sought out what was beautiful in the body. His paintings sparkle with the joy of life. In *Le Moulin da la Galette* (Fig. **16.13**), he depicts the bright gaiety of a Sunday afternoon crowd in a popular Parisian dance venue. The artist celebrates the liveliness and charm of these everyday folk as they talk, crowd the tables, flirt, and dance. Warmth infuses the setting. Sunlight and shade dapple the scene and create a sensation of floating in light.

There is a casualness here, a sense of life captured in a fleeting and spontaneous moment, and of a much wider scene extending beyond the canvas. This is no formally composed scene like that in David's *Oath of the Horatii* (see Fig. **14.20**). Rather, we are invited to become a part of the action. People are going about their everyday lives with no sense of the painter's presence. As opposed to the realism of the classicist who seeks the universal and the typical, the realism of the impressionist seeks "the incidental, the momentary, and the passing."

Le Moulin de la Galette captures the enjoyment of a moment outdoors. The colors shimmer, and although Renoir skillfully plays off highlights against dark tones, the uniform hue of the lowest values is not black but blue. In short, the beauty of this work exemplifies Renoir's statement, "The earth as the paradise of the gods, that is what I want to paint."

16.13 Pierre-Auguste Renoir, *Le Moulin de la Galette*, 1876. Oil on canvas, 4 ft 3½ ins × 5 ft 9 ins (1.31 × 1.75 m). Louvre, Paris.

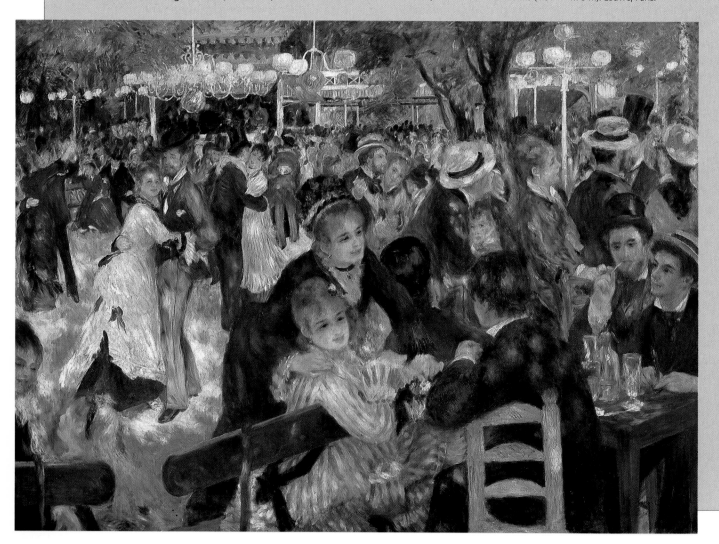

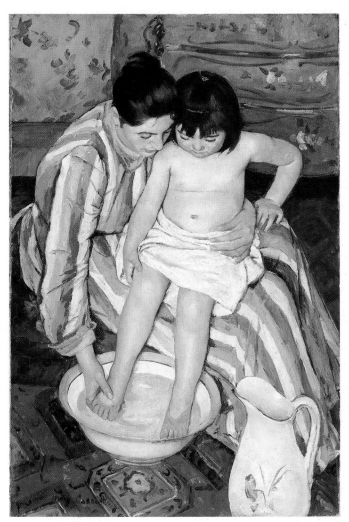

16.14 Mary Cassatt, *The Child's Bath*, 1891. Oil on canvas, 39¹/₂ × 26 ins (100 × 66 cm). The Art Institute of Chicago (Robert A. Waller Fund). Photo: © 1998 The Art Institute of Chicago. All rights reserved.

be spared. Edward III was so impressed with their courage that he spared both the burghers and Calais. Rodin's textures are impressionistic: his surfaces appear to shimmer as light plays on their irregularities, but they are more than reflective surfaces. They give his works dynamic and dramatic qualities. Although Rodin worked fairly realistically, he nevertheless created a subjective reality beyond the surface, and the subjectivity of his viewpoint is even more clear and dramatic in his pessimistic later sculptures.

Post-Impressionism

In the last two decades of the nineteenth century, impressionism evolved gently into a collection of rather disparate styles called simply "post-impressionism." In subject matter, post-impressionist paintings were similar to impressionist paintings—landscapes, familiar portraits, groups, and café and nightclub scenes—but the post-impressionists gave their subject matter a complex and profoundly personal significance.

The post-impressionists were deeply concerned about capturing sensory experience. They maintained the contemporary philosophy of art for art's sake and rarely attempted to sell their works. They did wish to share their subjective impressions of the real world, but moved beyond the Romantic and impressionistic world of pure sensation. They were more interested in the painting as a flat surface carefully composed of shapes, lines, and colors, an idea that became the foundation for most of the art movements that followed.

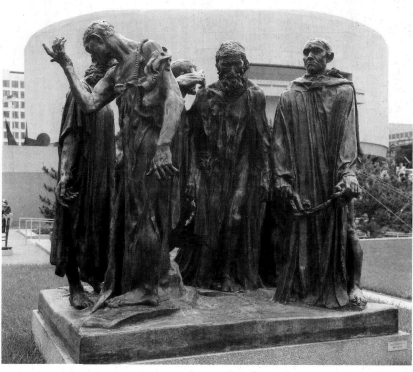

16.15 Auguste Rodin, *The Burghers of Calais*, 1866. Bronze, 6 ft 10¹/₂ ins (2.1 m) high. Hirshhorn Museum and Sculpture Garden, Smithsonian Institution, Washington D.C.

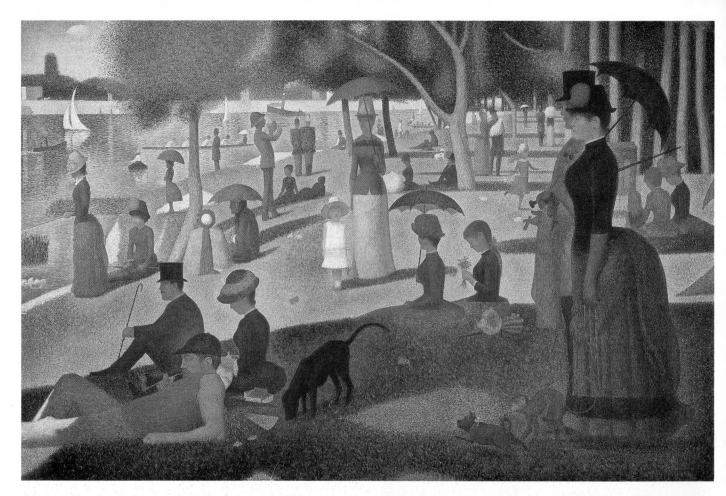

16.16 Georges Seurat, *A Sunday Afternoon on the Island of La Grande Jatte*, 1884–6. Oil on canvas, 6 ft 9¹/₂ ins × 10 ft ³/₈ ins (2.06 × 3.06 m). Courtesy of the Art Institute of Chicago (Helen Birch Bartlett Memorial Collection).

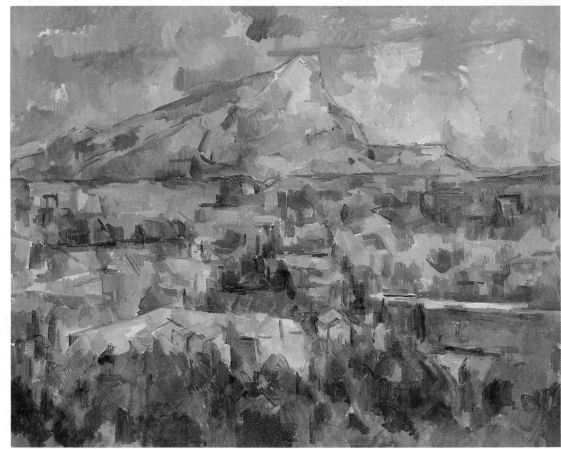

16.17 Paul Cézanne, *Mont Sainte-Victoire seen from Les Lauves*, 1902–4. Oil on canvas, 27¹/₂ × 35¹/₄ ins (69.8 × 89.5 cm). Philadelphia Museum of Art (George W. Elkins Collection).

The post-impressionists called for a return to form and structure in painting, characteristics they believed were lacking in the works of the impressionists. Taking the evanescent light qualities of the impressionists, they brought formal patterning to their canvases. They used clean color areas, and applied color in a systematic, almost scientific manner. The post-impressionists sought to return painting to traditional goals while retaining the clean palette of the impressionists.

Georges Seurat (sur-AH; 1859–91), often described as a "neo-impressionist"—he called his approach and technique "divisionism"—departed radically from existing painting technique with his experiments in optics and color theory. His patient and systematic application of specks of paint is called POINTILLISM, because paint is applied with the point of the brush, one small dot at a time. *A Sunday Afternoon on the Island of La Grande Jatte* (Fig. **16.16**) illustrates both his theory of color perception and his concern for the accurate depiction of light and colorations of objects. The composition of this work shows attention to perspective, and yet it willfully avoids three-dimensionality. Japanese influence is apparent here,

as it was in much post-impressionist work. Color areas are fairly uniform, figures are flattened, and outlining is continuous. Throughout the work we find conscious systematizing. The painting is broken into proportions of three-eighths and halves, which Seurat believed represented true harmony. He also selected his colors by formula. For Seurat, the painter's representation of physical reality was simply a search for a superior harmony, for an abstract perfection.

Paul Cézanne (say-ZAHN; 1839–1906), considered by many to be the father of modern art, illustrates concern for formal design, and his *Mont Sainte-Victoire seen from Les Lauves* (Fig. **16.17**) shows a nearly geometric configuration and balance. Foreground and background are tied together in a systematic manner so that both join in the foreground to create patterns. Shapes are simplified, and outlining is used throughout. Cézanne believed that all forms in nature are based on geometric shapes—the cone, the sphere, and the cylinder. Employing these forms, he sought to reveal the enduring reality that lay beneath surface appearance. Cézanne tried to invest his paintings with a strong sense of three-dimensionality. His use of

OUR DYNAMIC WORLD

Japanese Painting

The flat color areas that provided the Japanese influence on post-impressionism can be seen in a work from the mid-nineteenth century by Andō Hiroshige (hee-roh-SHEE-gee), *Maple Leaves at Mama, Tekona Shrine and Mama Bridge* (Fig. **16.18**). In this strongly colored landscape, Hiroshige shows deep space in a novel fashion, using the foreground to "frame" the distance. Hiroshige uses neither linear nor atmospheric perspective to achieve the illusion of deep space, and yet the portrayal appears rational. Hiroshige uses a clever manipulation of hue, value, and contrast to keep interest and control. By using complementary colors of red in the leaves and green in the distance, Hiroshige strikes a harmonious visual chord, and creates a counterpoint to hold our vision stable in the center of the work.

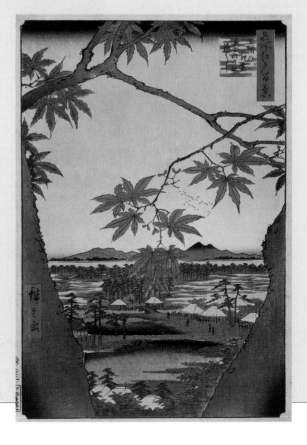

16.18 Andō Hiroshige, *Maple Leaves at Mama, Tekona Shrine and Mama Bridge.* Series: *Meisho Edo Hyakkei (100 Views of Edo)*, No. 94, c. 1856–9. Polychrome wood-block print, 13³/₄ × 9³/₄ ins (35 × 24 cm). British Museum, London.

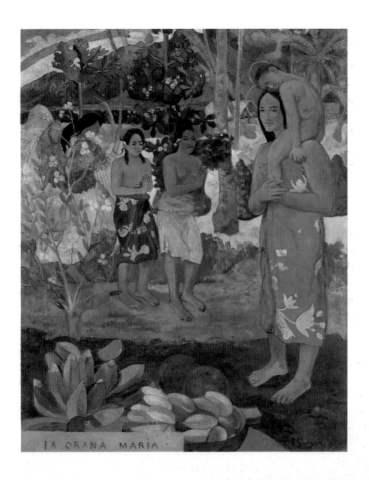

colored planes is much like Seurat's use of colored dots. He took great liberty with color and changed traditional ways of rendering objects, utilizing the cones, cylinders, and other geometric shapes just mentioned.

Paul Gauguin (goh-GAN; 1848–1903) brought a highly imaginative approach to post-impressionist goals. An artist without training, and a nomad who believed that European society and all its works were sick, Gauguin devoted his life to art and to wandering, spending many years in rural Brittany and the end of his life in Tahiti and the Marquesas Islands. The first picture Gauguin painted in Tahiti was *la Orana Maria* ("We Hail Thee Mary"; Fig. **16.19**). In this portrayal, Mary is a strong Polynesian woman, and the Christ Child is a completely relaxed boy of perhaps two or three years of age. In Tahiti, Gauguin believed he could re-enter the Garden of Paradise, and the rich, warm colors and decorative patterns suggest that life in this "uncivilized" world is, indeed, sweet and innocent. The table piled high with fruit illustrates that the people of this garden, like Adam and Eve in the Garden of Eden, need only pick the fruit off the trees. The table is the closest object to the viewer, and it, and its promise, appear to invite the viewer to leave the industrialized world for a more peaceful one.

Vincent van Gogh (1853–90) took yet another approach. His intense emotionalism in pursuing form was

16.19 Paul Gauguin, *La Orana Maria* ("We Hail Thee Mary"), c. 1891–2. Oil on canvas, 44³/₄ × 34¹/₂ ins (113.7 × 87.7 cm). The Metropolitan Museum of Art, New York. Bequest of Samuel A. Lewisohn, 1951.

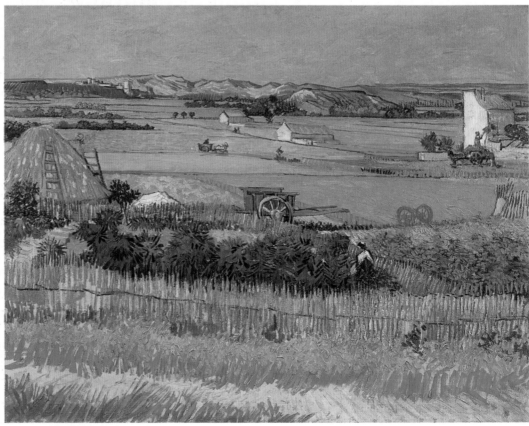

16.20 Vincent van Gogh, *Harvest at La Crau* ("The Blue Cart"), 1888. Oil on canvas, 28¹/₂ × 36¹/₄ ins (72.5 × 92 cm). Rijksmuseum Vincent van Gogh, Amsterdam, Netherlands.

unique. Van Gogh's turbulent life included numerous short-lived careers, impossible love affairs, a tempestuous friendship with Gauguin, and, finally, serious mental illness. Biography here is essential because Van Gogh gives us one of the most personal and subjective artistic viewpoints in the history of Western art. Works such as *Harvest at La Crau* ("The Blue Cart"; Fig. **16.20**), which Van Gogh produced in his Arles period, reflects an interest in *complementary colors* (colors on opposite sides of the color wheel—see the Introduction). Unlike Seurat, for example, who applied such colors in small dots, van Gogh, inspired by Japanese prints, placed large color areas side by side. Doing so, he believed, expressed the quiet, harmonious life of the rural community. Notice that the brushwork in the foreground is active while the fields in the background are smooth. Subtle diagonals break the predominantly horizontal line of the work, giving the painting, overall, a tranquil atmosphere.

Frenetic energy explodes from his brushwork in paintings such as *The Starry Night* (see Fig. **16.21**). Flattened forms and outlining also reflect Japanese influence. Tremendous power surges through the painting, especially in focal areas, and we can sense the dynamic, personal feeling and mental turmoil barely contained by the painting's surface. This work represents one of the earliest and most famous examples of *expressionism*, a style we will examine momentarily.

Experimentation and Art Nouveau

A new age of experimentation also took nineteenth-century architects in a different direction—upward. Late in the period, the skyscraper was designed in response to the need to create additional commercial space on the limited land space in burgeoning urban areas. Burnham and Root's Monadnock Building in Chicago (Fig. **16.22**) was

16.21 Vincent van Gogh, *The Starry Night*, 1889. Oil on canvas, 29 × 36¼ ins (74 × 92 cm). Collection, Museum of Modern Art, New York (acquired through the Lillie P. Bliss Bequest).

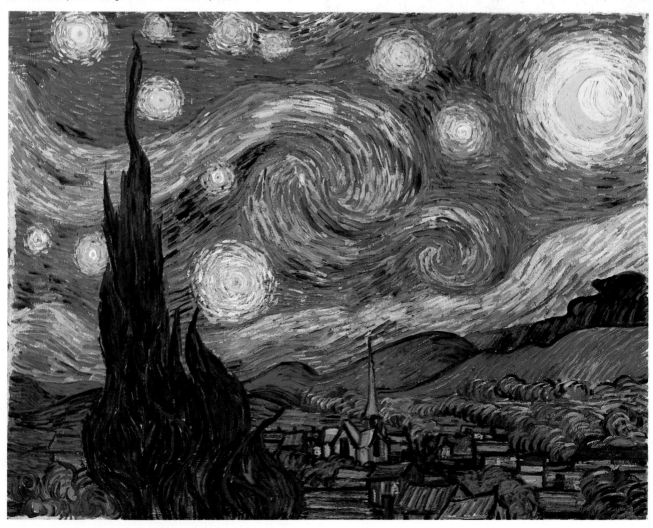

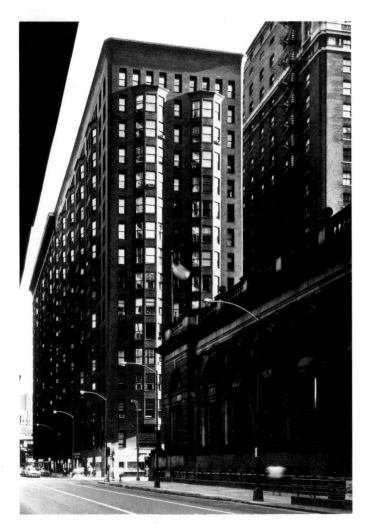

16.22 Daniel Hudson Burnham and John Wellborn Root, the Monadnock Building, Chicago, 1889–91.

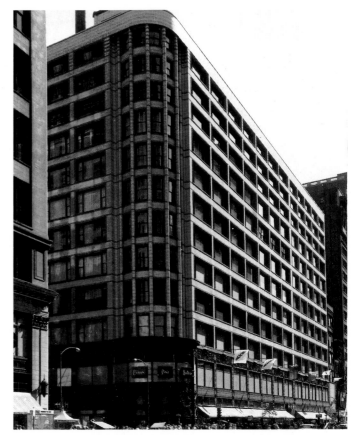

16.23 Louis Henry Sullivan, Carson, Pirie, and Scott Department Store, Chicago, 1899–1904.

16.24 Antoni Gaudí, Casa Batlló, Barcelona, Spain, 1904–6.

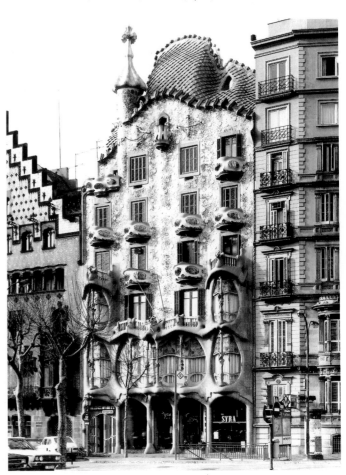

an early example. Although this prototypical "skyscraper" is all masonry—that is, it is built completely of brick and requires increasingly thick supportive walls toward its base—it was part of the trend in architecture to combine design, materials, and new concepts of space.

When all these elements were finally combined, the skyscraper emerged, almost exclusively in America. Architects erected buildings of unprecedented height without increasing the thickness of lower walls by using structural frameworks—first of iron, later of steel—and by treating walls as independent partitions. Each story was supported on horizontal girders. The concept of the skyscraper could not be realized comfortably, however, until the invention of a safe and reliable elevator.

One of the most influential figures in the development of the skyscraper and philosophies of modern architecture was Louis Sullivan, the first truly modern architect. Working in the last decade of the nineteenth century in Chicago, then the most rapidly developing metropolis in the world, Sullivan designed buildings of great dignity, simplicity, and strength. Most important, however, he created a rubric for

Louis Sullivan (1856–1924)

Born in Boston, Louis Sullivan became one of the leaders in modern architectural design in the United States. He studied briefly at the Massachusetts Institute of Technology and worked for W. le Baron Jenney, an architectural pioneer in the use of the steel skeleton type of building construction, before finishing his education at the École des Beaux-Arts in Paris.

When he was twenty-five years old, Sullivan entered into a partnership with the engineer Dankmar Adler (1844–1900) in Chicago, and the next fourteen years, in partnership with Adler, were the most productive period of Sullivan's career. Between 1886 and 1890 he redesigned the interior of the huge masonry Auditorium building in Chicago, and over the next four years, Sullivan designed two buildings—the Wainwright Building in St Louis and the Guaranty Building in Buffalo—in which he initiated a new set of aesthetics for tall, steel-frame office buildings.

Sullivan rejected historic styles and proposed organically designed buildings that were as expressive of their nature and function as living things are of theirs, and his philosophy was summarized in the phrase "form follows function." His pioneering work made him the father of the modern skyscraper, and, although his designs thrust upward in vertical composition, he embellished them with lively, plantlike ornament very much like art nouveau (noo-VOH; see below).

By 1893, however, his star had begun to fade. His colorful Transportation Building at the Columbian Exposition of that year brought little praise, and at the same time, the country experienced a depression, and Sullivan ended his partnership with Adler. Uncompromising in attitude, Sullivan received very few commissions after the dissolution of the partnership. Nonetheless, he built the Carson, Pirie and Scott Department Store in Chicago (1899–1904; Fig. **16.23**), replete with strong verticals and horizontals contrasting with lush cast iron foliage, and he also designed a few midwestern banks. He died in poverty in Chicago on 24 April 1924, but his influence continued in the twentieth century, principally through the success of his young pupil Frank Lloyd Wright.

modern architecture with his theory that form flowed from function. As Sullivan said to an observer of the Carson, Pirie, and Scott building (Fig. **16.23**): "It is evident that we are looking at a department store. Its purpose is clearly set forth in its general aspect, and the form follows the function in a simple, straightforward way."

In the final years of the nineteenth century, a new style of architectural decoration evolved, called ART NOUVEAU. It is not primarily an architectural mode but, like rococo, which it resembles, it provides a decorative surface—one that is closely associated with graphic art—that imparts a unique character to any building.

Art nouveau is connected in some ways with the doctrines of nineteenth-century artistic symbolism, and its identifying characteristic is the lively, serpentine curve, known as the "whiplash." Art nouveau incorporates organic and often symbolic motifs, usually languid-looking flowers and animals, and treats them in a flat, linear, and relief-like manner.

One of the greatest exponents of Art nouveau, which continued into the early years of the twentieth century, was Antoni Gaudí (gow-DEE; 1852–1926). Gaudí designed a number of important buildings in Spain, including town-houses. At Casa Batlló (baht-LOH; Fig. **16.24**) in Barcelona he refaced an older building with colored tiles, adding a steep but undulating roof that flows from orange to blue-green. The bay windows, rippling stone entrance, and sinister balconies are his too.

At the same time, widespread experimentation with new forms and materials continued. Many attempts have been made to categorize general tendencies and to label specific ones. But attempts at far-ranging categorizing have not met with universal acceptance. Terms such as "rational," "functional," and "international" have been suggested, but perhaps only the vague term "modern" covers most cases. Rather than pursue such categories, we shall, instead, focus as much as possible on individual architectural work. It was individualism, after all, that was the hallmark of the arts in the twentieth century.

Cubism

The years between 1901 and 1912 witnessed an emerging approach to pictorial space, called CUBISM. Cubist space violated all usual concepts of two- and three-dimensional perspective. Until this time, the space within a composition

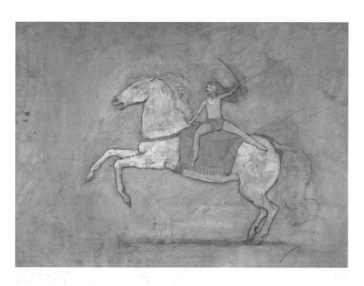

16.25 Pablo Picasso, *Youth Riding*, 1905. Sketch. Private collection.
© Succession Picasso/DACS 1999.

had been thought of as an entity separate from the main subject of the work—that is, if the subject were removed, the space would remain, unaffected.

Pablo Picasso (1881–1973) and Georges Braque (1882–1963) changed that relationship. In their view the artist should paint "not objects, but the space they engender." The area around an object became an extension of the object itself, and if the object were removed, the space around it would collapse. Cubist space is typically quite shallow and gives the impression of reaching forward out of the frontal plane toward the viewer.

Essentially, the style developed as the result of independent experiments by Braque and Picasso with various ways of describing form. Newly evolving notions of the time–space continuum were being proposed by Albert Einstein at this time. We do not know whether the Theory of Relativity influenced Picasso and Braque, but it was being talked about at the time, and it certainly helped to make their works more acceptable. The results of both painters' experiments brought them to remarkably similar artistic conclusions.

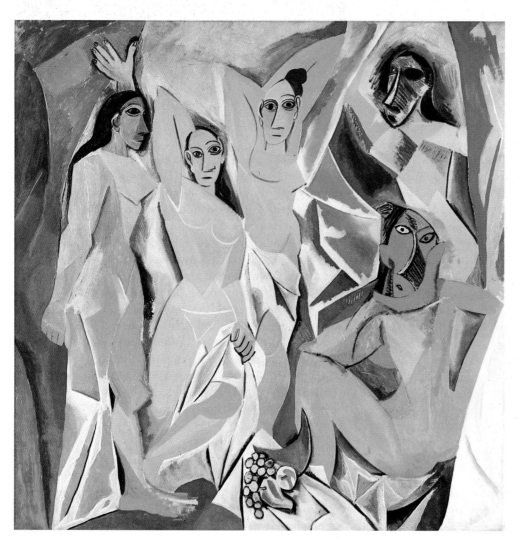

16.26 Pablo Picasso, *Les Demoiselles d'Avignon*, 1907. Oil on canvas, 8 ft × 7 ft 8 ins (2.44 × 2.34 m). The Museum of Modern Art, New York (acquired through the Lillie P. Bliss Bequest). Photo: © 1998 The Museum of Modern Art, New York. © Succession Picasso/DACS 1999.

Picasso influenced the arts of the twentieth century more than any other painter. Born in Spain, in 1900 he moved to France, where he lived for most of his life. In Paris he was influenced by Toulouse-Lautrec (too-LOOZ loh-TREK) and the late works of Cézanne, particularly in organization, analysis of forms, and use of different points of view. Very early on Picasso began to identify deeply with society's misfits and cast-offs. In the period from 1901 until around 1904 or 1905, known as Picasso's Blue Period, these oppressed subjects appear in paintings, in which blue tones predominate. In his Rose Period (Fig. 16.25), from 1904 to 1906, he became more concerned with make-believe, which he expressed as portraits of circus performers, than with the tragedy of poverty. *Les Demoiselles d'Avignon* (Fig. 16.26) has become the single most discussed image in modern art. Its simplified forms and restricted color were adopted by many cubists, as they reduced their palettes in order to concentrate on spatial exploration. A result of personal conflicts on the part of the artist, combined with his ambition to be recognized as the leader of the AVANT-GARDE, the painting deliberately breaks with the traditions of Western illusionistic art. The painter denies both classical proportions and the organic integrity and continuity of the human body.

Les Demoiselles d'Avignon (Avignon in the title refers to a street in Barcelona's red-light district) is aggressive and harsh, like the world of the prostitutes who inhabit it. Forms are simplified and angular, and colors are restricted to blues, pinks, and terracottas. Picasso breaks his subjects into angular wedges which convey a sense of three-dimensionality. We do not know whether the forms protrude out or recess in. In rejecting a single viewpoint, Picasso presents "reality" not as a mirror image of what we see in the world, but as images that have been re-interpreted within the terms of new principles. Understanding thus depends on knowing rather than seeing. The large canvas measures 8 feet by 7 feet 8 inches (2.44 × 2.34 meters)—and its effect suggests great violence.

Like Picasso, Braque took a new approach to spatial construction and reduced objects to geometric shapes, drawing upon the ideas of Cézanne. It was from Braque's geometric forms that the term "cubist" first came. Unfortunately, the label has led many observers to look for solid cubic shapes rather than for a new kind of space "which was only visible when solid forms became transparent and lost their rigid cubical contours."[1]

Mechanism and Futurism

Themes dealing with mechanism proved to be popular in the early twentieth century, as life became more and more dominated by machines. A brief movement in Italy, mecha-

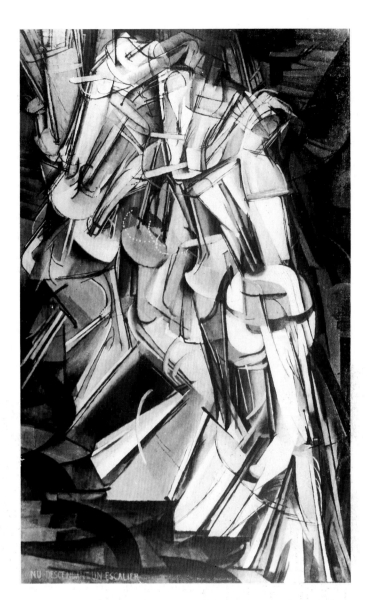

16.27 Marcel Duchamp, *Nude Descending a Staircase, No. 2*, 1912. Oil on canvas, 58 × 35 ins (147 × 89 cm). Philadelphia Museum of Art (Louise and Walter Arensberg Collection). © Succession Marcel Duchamp/DACS 1999.

nism, sought to express the spirit of the age by capturing speed and power through representation of vehicles and machines in motion. Mechanistic themes can be seen clearly in the works of Marcel Duchamp (doo-SHAWM; 1887–1968), who is often associated with the dada movement (see p. 553) and whose famous *Nude Descending a Staircase*, No. 2 (Fig. **16.27**) is sometimes called "proto-dadaist." To Duchamp, apparently, men and women were machines that ran on passion as fuel. Like those of the dadaists, many of Duchamp's works also exploit chance and accident.

Sculptors now turned to further explorations of three-dimensional space and what they could do with it. Technological developments and new materials also encouraged among Italian sculptors. In searching for new dynamic qualities, the Italian futurists in the visual arts found that many new machines had sculptural form. Their own sculptures followed mechanistic lines and included representations of motion.

Umberto Boccioni's (boh-CHOH-nee) *Unique Forms of Continuity in Space* (Fig. **16.28**) takes the mythological subject of Mercury, messenger of the gods (compare Bologna's *Mercury*, Fig. **11.24**), and turns him into a futuristic machine. The overall form is recognizable and the outlines of the myth move the viewer's thoughts in a particular direction. Nonetheless, this is primarily an exercise in composition. The intense sense of energy and movement is created by the variety of surfaces and curves that flow into one another in a seemingly random, yet highly controlled, pattern. The overall impression is of the motion of the figure rather than of the figure itself.

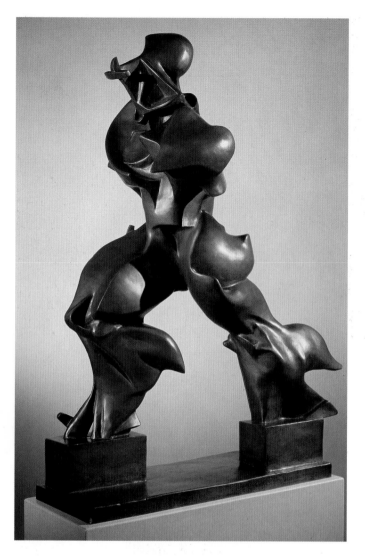

16.28 Umberto Boccioni, *Unique Forms of Continuity in Space*, 1913. Bronze (cast 1931), 3 ft 7⁷/₈ ins (1.1 m) high. Tate Galley, London.

16.29 Max Beckmann, *Christ and the Woman Taken in Adultery*, 1917. Oil on canvas, 4 ft 10¹/₄ ins × 4 ft 1¹/₈ ins (1.49 × 1.27 m). Saint Louis Art Museum (Bequest of Curt Valentin). © DACS 1999.

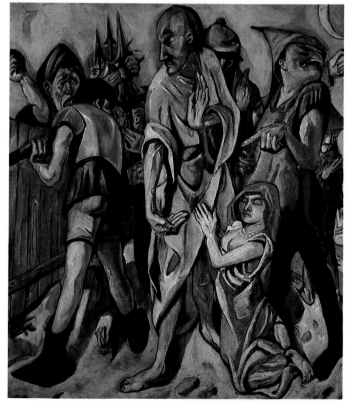

the search for new forms to characterize the age. This search resulted in a style called "futurism," which was really more of an ideology than a style. Futurism encompassed more than just the arts, and it sought to destroy the past—especially the Italian past—in order to institute a totally new society, a new art, and new poetry. Its basis lay in "new dynamic sensations." In other words, the objects of modern life, such as "screaming automobiles" that run like machine guns, have a new beauty—speed—that is more beautiful than even the most dynamic objects of previous generations. Futurists found in the noise, speed, and mechanical energy of the modern city a unique exhilaration that made everything of the past drab and unnecessary. The movement was particularly strong in Italy and

16.30 Henri Matisse, *Blue Nude* (*Souvenir de Biskra*), 1907. Oil on canvas, 3 ft ¼ in × 4 ft 7¼ ins (92.1 × 140.4 cm). Baltimore Museum of Art (The Cone Collection, formed by Dr Claribel Cone and Miss Etta Cone of Baltimore, Maryland). © Succession H. Matisse/DACS 1999.

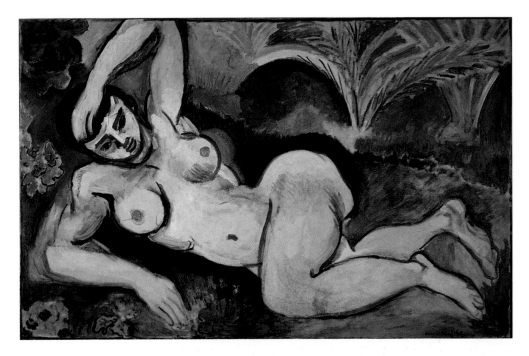

Expressionism

"Expressionism" traditionally refers to a movement in Germany between 1905 and 1930. Broadly speaking, however, it includes a variety of approaches, mostly in Europe, that aimed at eliciting in the viewer the same feelings the artist felt in creating the work—a sort of joint artist/viewer response to elements in the work of art. Any element—line, form, color—might be emphasized to elicit this response. The subject matter itself did not matter (see Fig. **16.21**). What mattered was that the artist consciously tried to stimulate in the viewer a specific response similar to his or her own. The term EXPRESSIONISM as a description of this approach to visual art and architecture first appeared in 1911. It emerged following six years of work by an organized group of German artists who called themselves *Die Brücke* ("The Bridge"). Trying to define their purposes, the painter Ernst Ludwig Kirchner (KIRSH-nur; 1880–1938) wrote: "He who renders his inner convictions as he knows he must, and does so with spontaneity and sincerity, is one of us." The intent was to protest against academic naturalism. They used simple media such as woodcuts and created often brutal, but nonetheless powerful effects that expressed inner emotions.

The early expressionists maintained representationalism to a degree, but later expressionist artists, for example those of the Blue Rider group between 1912 and 1916, created some of the first completely abstract or nonobjective works of art. Color and form emerged as stimuli extrinsic to subject matter, and without any natural spatial relationships of recognizable objects, paintings took a new direction in internal organization.

In Max Beckmann's *Christ and the Woman Taken in Adultery* (Fig. **16.29**), the artist's revulsion against physical cruelty and suffering is transmitted through distorted figures crushed into shallow space. Linear distortion, changes of scale and perspective, and a nearly Gothic spirituality communicate Beckmann's reactions to the horrors of World War I. In this approach, the meaning of the painting—that is, the painter's meaning—is carried by very specific visual communication.

Fauvism

Closely associated with the expressionist movement was the style of the *fauves* (the French word for "wild beasts"). The label was applied in 1905 by a critic in response to a sculpture which seemed to him "a Donatello in a cage of wild beasts." Violent distortion and outrageous coloring mark the work of the fauves, whose two-dimensional surfaces and flat color areas were new to European painting.

The best-known artist of this short-lived movement was Henri Matisse (mah-TEES; 1869–1954). Matisse tried to paint pictures that would "unravel the tensions of modern existence." In his old age, he made a series of very joyful designs for the Chapel of the Rosary at Venice, not as exercises in religious art but as expressions of joy and the nearly religious feeling he had for life.

The Blue Nude (Fig. **16.30**) illustrates the wild coloring and distortions in the paintings of Matisse and the other fauves. The painting takes its name from the energetically applied blues, which occur throughout the figure as

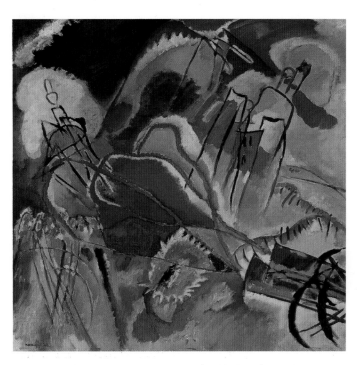

16.31 Vasily Kandinsky, *Improvisation No. 30 (Warlike Theme)*, 1913. Oil on canvas, 43 × 43¼ ins (109.2 × 109.9 cm). The Art Institute of Chicago (Arthur Jerome Eddy Memorial Collection). © ADAGP, Paris and DACS, London 1999.

dark accents. For Matisse, color and line were indivisible devices, and the bold strokes of color in his work both reveal forms and stimulate a purely aesthetic response. Matisse literally "drew with color." His purpose was not, of course, to draw a nude as he saw it in life. Rather, he tried to express his feelings about the nude as an object of aesthetic interest. Thus Matisse, along with the other fauve painters, represents one brand of expressionism. There were others, including the Bridge and Blue Rider groups, and artists such as Kandinsky (kuhn-DEEN-skee; Fig. **16.31**), Rouault (roo-OH), and Kokoschka (koh-KOHSH-kuh).

LITERATURE

Realism

We have seen how realism took hold as a style in painting, and we shall see it again later in the chapter. Realism as a literary style held that the purpose of art is to depict life with absolute honesty—that is, to show things "as they really are." In pursuit of that goal, realists look for specific, verifiable details rather than for sweeping generalities, and

they value impersonal, photographic accuracy more than the individual interpretation of experience. The triumph of realism, which began in the eighteenth century, came to full flower in the nineteenth and early twentieth centuries, and it was influenced by the growth of science and by a revolt against the sweeping emotionalism of Romanticism. Because realists sought to avoid idealism and Romantic "prettifying," they tended to stress the commonplace and, often, sordid and brutal aspects of life.

Considered the father of the modern novel, Russian novelist Feodor Dostoyevski (dohs-tuh-YEF-skee; 1821–81) was born and raised in Moscow. Both his parents died while he was in his teens—his father was murdered by his own serfs—and although he was interested in literature early on, he did not begin writing until he had finished military school and a two-year stint in the army. In 1846 he published a short story, "Poor Folk," which made him an instant success. He then became associated with a group of political revolutionaries and utopian reformers, and when the group was arrested, Dostoyevski was sentenced to death, being pardoned by the Czar at the last moment. Apparently, the Czar had planned to pardon the prisoners all along, but he let the matter proceed, right up to the point where they stood before the firing squad, more as a whimsical joke than anything else. Dostoyevski was sent to Siberia for five years and then forced back into the army. In 1859 he was finally pardoned, but these experiences, plus the fact that he suffered from epilepsy, left him bitter. He believed that his imprisonment gave him an opportunity to expiate his sins, and his beliefs that humans required penitence and that salvation comes through suffering reached the point of obsession and recur constantly in his novels. Like Nietzsche, he believed that European materialism had led to decadence and decline.

We know Dostoyevski best for two works from among his many: *The Brothers Karamazov* and *Crime and Punishment*. *Crime and Punishment* (1866) is a psychological novel that explores multiple personality—that is, the hidden and confused motivations of human behavior—and its constant theme is moral redemption through suffering. Perhaps the most outstanding characteristic of the novel is its capacity to force the reader to think seriously about the many problems it presents. Dostoyevski accomplishes this by refusing to allow us to confuse oversimplification with deep thought. For example, in tackling the issue of distinguishing between morality and respectability, Dostoyevski gives us one truly good character, the prostitute Sonia, who at the same time is the most openly disreputable, and contrasts her with a truly evil character, Raskolnikov's sister, who is the most respectable of the characters. Thus, he forces us to see that morality consists of what a person is, while respectability is the front that we put up in public, and that there need not be any connection between the two. He also shows that morality and respectability are not opposites, because, that, too, would be an oversimplification. The work forces us, through the objectively detailed manner of the realist, to think seriously about money, social position, sanity and insanity, and, above all, about crime and punishment. Dostoyevski presents these issues with such compelling insight that we cannot escape them or explain them away with superficial responses.

In addition to great writers such as Dostoyevski, fiction writing appeared in more humble surroundings in the late nineteenth and early twentieth centuries. Literacy among Native Americans began to take hold in the late eighteenth century as the result of missionary activity, particularly that of the Methodists and Presbyterians, and a century later increased interest in America's heritage gave rise to the publication of tribal histories written by Native Americans.

Fiction writing among Native Americans appeared as early as 1823, but between 1870 and 1920 Native American culture underwent tremendous change: tribal autonomy decreased, and all tribes within the territory of the United States were confined to reservations. By the end of 1870, the federal government had become actively involved in Native American education, and a subsequent increase in literacy produced what may be called a tribal intellectual elite. As a result, numerous authors emerged, many of them women, one of whom was Susette La Flesche. Her story "Nedawi" was first published in 1881 in a popular magazine for children, and it probably represents the first short story written by a Native American that is not a reworking of a legend. The author's gender testifies to the prominence of women in Native American—as well as in American—literature, and the story, subtitled "An Indian Story from Real Life," is representative of much Native American fiction prior to 1920.

Naturalism

The tradition of realism in literature was extended by a movement called naturalism, which aimed at an even more faithful, unselective representation of reality, presented without moral judgment. Naturalism differed from realism in its assumption of scientific determinism, which led naturalistic authors to emphasize the accidental, physiological nature of their characters rather than their moral or rational qualities. The naturalists saw individual characters as helpless products of heredity and environment, motivated by strong instinctual drives from within, and assaulted by social and economic pressures from without.

Naturalism began in France, where the leading exponent of the movement was Emile Zola (zoh-LAH; 1840–1902), whose essay "Le roman expérimental" ("The Experimental Novel"; 1880) became the manifesto for the movement. Unable to pass his *baccalauréat* examination, Zola spent two years unemployed. Eventually he secured a clerical post in a shipping firm, which he hated, and in 1862 he moved to the sales department of the publishing house of Louis-Christophe-François Hachette. Hachette encouraged Zola in his writing. Zola's first book, published in 1864, was a collection of short stories. In 1865, he wrote a sordid autobiographical novel, *La confession de Claude*, which landed him in trouble with the police and led to his departure from Hachette.

Zola put his "scientific" theories into practice in a gruesome novel, *Thérèse Raquin* (1867), but it was his *L'Assommoir* ("The Drunkard"; 1877), a study of alchoholism, that made him the best-known writer in France. Zola held a credulous faith in science and accepted scientific determinism as fact. He argued that naturalism was indigenous to French life and believed that human nature was completely determined by heredity. He died under mysterious circumstances, overcome by carbon monoxide fumes in his sleep.

Symbolism

Another literary movement of the late nineteenth century was symbolism, a conscious and deliberate attempt to use symbols because, as its proponents believed, the transient objective world is not true reality but a reflection of the invisible absolute. Symbolists rebelled against the techniques of the realists, which were designed to capture the transient world, believing instead that the inner eternal reality could only be suggested. They achieved intensity and complexity by using condensed syntax and minor images centered around one main METAPHOR, so that one sense impression was translated into another and both became symbols of the original impression. Although their writing was often as arcane as that assertion, that was acceptable to them, because they wished their writing to be "an enigma for the vulgar." They rejected sociological and ethical themes, and held that art pursues sensations of beauty that are quite separate from moral or social responsibility. The symbolists subscribed to the theory of "art for art's sake"—any theme or perception was appropriate as long as it captured the writer's subtle intuitions and contributed to an overall design. They were contemptuous of their environment and middle-class morality, often flaunting their perversions and despair, but they freed literature from its conventional subject matter and emphasized technique. Of those who used symbolist techniques, Marcel Proust stands out.

French novelist Marcel Proust (proost; 1871–1922) was a legend in French literary circles. Reclusive, frail, and asthmatic, he was allergic to noise, to light, and to dust, and he kept his room soundproofed, overheated, and in semi-darkness. He spent long periods in bed, during which he wrote the long novels on which he thrived. He was, in fact, a bold literary experimenter, who was able to put in writing remarkable sensory and imaginative experience. His magnum opus was *Remembrance of Things Past*, published in sixteen volumes between 1913 and 1927, in which Proust sought to write the past—time lost and apparently irrecoverable—into permanence. He is preoccupied with time, which becomes an ever-present fact as the memory of the narrator shuttles back and forth without regard for chronology. Proust explores the distinctions between mechanical and psychological time by drawing upon his own past experiences, and as he juxtaposes past against present, he shows us the fraudulent values of high society and strips away its glitter. Proust uses the techniques of the symbolists to achieve his ends—that is, metaphor, symbol, and image—as he tries to recreate the atmosphere of the mind, and thus we find his main themes—love, art, human ways of seeing and feeling life, homosexuality, rituals of the aristocracy, and architecture. In a sense, all of civilization trudges across his pages.

MUSIC

Impressionism

The anti-Romantic spirit also produced a style of music analogous to that of the impressionist painters. A free use of chromatic tones marked later nineteenth-century style, even among the Romantics. However a parting of the ways occurred, the effects of which still permeate contemporary music. Some composers made free use of chromatic harmony and key shifts but stayed within the parameters of traditional major/minor tonality. Others rejected traditional tonality completely, and a new ATONAL harmonic expression came into being. This rejection of traditional tonality led to impressionism in music.

Impressionist music can best be found in the work of its primary champion, the Frenchman Claude Debussy (deh-BYOO-see; 1862–1918), although he did not like to be called an "impressionist"—the label, after all, had been coined by a critic of the painters and was meant to be derogatory. Debussy maintained that he was "an old Romantic who has thrown the worries of success out the window," and he sought no association with the painters. There are, however, similarities. His use of tone color has been described as "wedges of color," much like those the painters provided with individual brushstrokes. Oriental

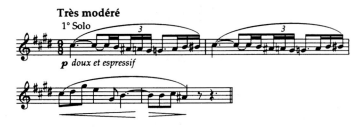

Très modéré

16.32 Claude Debussy, *Prelude to The Afternoon of a Faun*, opening theme.

influence is also apparent, especially in Debussy's use of the Asian six-tone scale. He wished above all to return French music to fundamental sources in nature and move it away from the heaviness of the German tradition. He delighted in natural scenes, as did the impressionist painters, and he sought to capture the effects of shimmering light in music.

Unlike his predecessors, Debussy reduced melodic development to limited short motifs, and in perhaps his greatest break with tradition he moved away from traditional progressions of chordal harmonies. Debussy considered a chord strictly on the merits of its expressive capabilities, apart from any idea of tonal progression within a key. As a result, gliding chords, that is, the repetition of a chord up and down the scale, became a hallmark of musical impressionism. DISSONANCE and irregular rhythm and meter further distinguish Debussy's works. Here, again, form and content are subordinate to expressive intent. His works suggest rather than state, leaving the listener only with an impression, perhaps even an ambiguous one.

Freedom, flexibility, and nontraditional timbres mark Debussy's compositions, the most famous of which is *Prélude à l'après-midi d'un faune* ("Prelude to The Afternoon of a Faun"; a faun is a mythological creature with the body of a man and the horns, ears, tail, and sometimes the legs, of a goat) based on a poem by Mallarmé (mah-larh-MAY). The piece uses a large orchestra, with emphasis on the woodwinds, most notably in the haunting theme running throughout (Fig. **16.32**; CD Track 19). Two harps also play a prominent part in the texture, and antique cymbals are used to add an exotic touch near the end. Although freely ranging in an irregular $\frac{9}{8}$ meter and having virtually no tonal centers, the *Prélude* does have the traditional ABA structure.

Naturalism in Opera

Romanticism in all the arts saw many counter-reactions, and late nineteenth-century opera was no exception. In France, an anti-Romantic movement called "naturalism" developed. It opposed stylization, although it maintained exotic settings, and included brute force and immorality in its subject matter. The best operatic example of naturalism is Georges Bizet's (bee-ZAY) *Carmen* (1875). Unlike earlier Romantic operas, the text for *Carmen* is in prose rather than poetry. Set in Spain, its scenes are naturalistic, and its

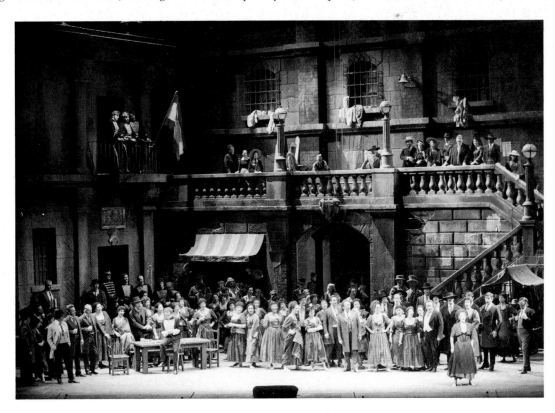

16.33 Georges Bizet, *Carmen*, 1875. José Carreras as Don José and Agnes Baltsa as Carmen in this 1986–7 New York production.

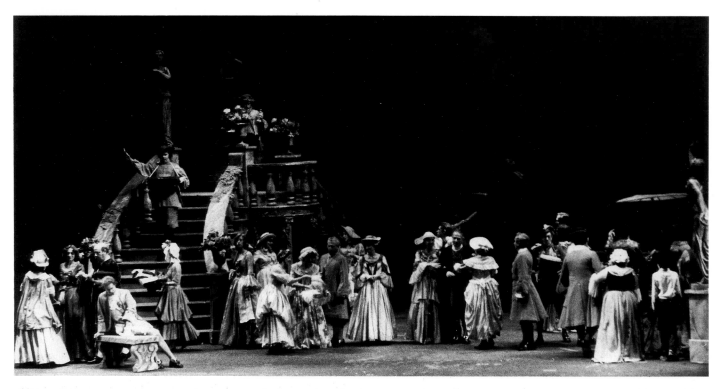

16.34 Giacomo Puccini, *Manon Lescaut*, 1893. Opera Company of Philadelphia.

music is colorful and concise. The libretto comes from a literary classic, a story by Prosper Mérimée, whose heroine, Carmen, is a seductive employee in a cigarette factory in nineteenth-century Seville (Fig. **16.33**). She flirts with Don José, a soldier, and so enraptures him that he deserts from the army to follow her to her haunt, a disreputable tavern, and then to a mountain pass where gypsy smugglers have their hideout. Carmen soon tires of Don José, however, and becomes interested in the toreador Escamillo. On the day of a bullfight in Seville, Carmen arrives with Escamillo, who is welcomed as a hero. After Escamillo enters the bullring, Don José is seen, dishevelled and distraught. He pleads with Carmen to return to him, and when she refuses, he stabs her with a dagger. Emerging from his bullfight, Escamillo finds Don José weeping over Carmen's dead body.

Carmen began as *opéra-comique*. When Bizet first wrote his score, he used spoken dialogue, and this is the way *Carmen* was heard at the Opéra-Comique in Paris on 3 March 1875, and, incidentally, the way it is still played in that house. Elsewhere, however, dialogue was replaced by recitatives prepared by another composer. As we now hear it, *Carmen* differs in a further way from the way it was introduced—today a number of ballet sequences, using background music from other Bizet compositions, are interpolated. As an *opéra-comique* in 1875, *Carmen* had no ballets.

Carmen herself is a fascinating character. Bizet uses her

as a symbol of "Woman," and every passage he gave her to sing is a new mask, mirroring the man she is addressing. Bizet's sympathetic portrayal shows uncanny naturalism in her change of tone as she addresses the passers-by, José, the smugglers, and Escamillo. To each of the men she is a different woman, changing the sound of her voice, the character of her melody, her mood, her tempo.

There was much in *Carmen* to disturb audiences in 1875. The vivid portrayal of a character as immoral as Carmen was shocking. Never before had an opera presented girls onstage smoking cigarettes, and some listeners objected to the music, thinking it was too Wagnerian, because Bizet assigned such importance to the orchestra and occasionally used a *leitmotif* technique. Nevertheless, *Carmen* was by no means the total failure that some of Bizet's early biographers suggested. Some critics hailed it, a publisher paid a handsome price for the publication rights, and the opera company kept it in its repertory the following season.

Bizet's naturalism was similar to that of Italian *verismo* (vair-EEZ-moh) opera, which emerged at the turn of the twentieth century. The spirit of *verismo*—that is, of verisimilitude or true-to-life settings and events—is the same hot-blooded vitality that was implicit in Pietro Mascagni's statement about his new opera *Il Piccolo Marat* (1921): "I have written the opera with clenched fists, like my spirit! Do not look for melody; do not look for culture: in *Marat* there is only blood!" The works of

Mascagni, Puccini (poo-CHEE-nee; Fig. **16.34**), Leoncavallo (lay-ohn-kah-VAHL-loh), and others exemplify this *verismo* tradition in musical drama, which concentrates on the violent passions and common experiences of everyday people. Adultery, revenge, and murder are frequent themes. Mascagni's *Cavalleria Rusticana*, Leoncavallo's *I Pagliacci*, and to some extent Puccini's *Tosca* are the best-known examples of this style.

Nontraditional Transitions

If painting and sculpture took a path that diverged radically from their heritage, so did music. Its new directions parted with past traditions in three ways.

The first was rhythmic complexity. Since the Middle Ages, tradition had emphasized the grouping of beats together in rhythmic patterns, called "meter." The characteristic accents of double and triple meters helped to unify and clarify compositions, as well as to give them certain flavors. For example, triple meter, with its one-two-three, one-two-three accent patterns, created lilting dance rhythms, of which the waltz was characteristic. The alternating accents of double meter, one-two, one-two, or one-two-three-four, suggested the regularity of a march. But modern composers did away with these patterns and the regularity of accents, choosing instead to employ complex, changing rhythms in which it is often virtually impossible to determine meter, or even the actual beat.

The second change consisted of a focus on dissonant harmonies. Before the late nineteenth century, CONSONANCE was the norm, and dissonances were expected to be brief and passing, then return to consonance. In the late nineteenth century there was significant tampering with that principle, however. By the twentieth century, composers were using more and more dissonance, and not necessarily resolving it.

A third change involved a rejection of traditional TONALITY, or sense of key, altogether. Traditional thinking held that one note, the *doh*, or tonic, of a scale, was the most important. All music was composed in a specific key. Modulations into distant or related keys occurred, but the tonic of the basic key was the touchstone to which everything related. Many composers now chose to pursue other paths. One was to get rid of any tonal center. Thus, no one tone was more important than the others. All twelve semitones of the chromatic scale in effect became equal. The systems that resulted from this new tonality were called TWELVE-TONE composition.

Another path, of German-Italian influence, built upon the works of Richard Wagner and was called the "cosmopolitan" style. The principal composer in this group was César Franck (frahnk; 1822–90). The works of Camille Saint-Saëns (ka-MEE san-SAHNS; 1835–1921)

represent the more classically oriented style that continued into the twentieth century.

The French composer Maurice Ravel (rah-VEL; 1875–1937) began as an impressionist, but his style became more and more classical as years went by. Even in his earlier works, however, Ravel did not adopt Debussy's complex sonorities and ambiguous tonal centers. Ravel's *Boléro* (1928) exhibits strong primitive influences and the relentless rhythm of certain Spanish dance music. More typical works of Ravel—for example, his Piano Concerto in G—use Mozart and traditional classicism as their models. Thus, some composers stayed completely within established neo-classical conventions of Western music well into the twentieth century.

Stravinsky

Another nontraditionalist, Igor Stravinsky (struh-VIN-skee; 1882–1971), came to prominence with *The Firebird* (1910). *The Rite of Spring* (1912–13) created an even greater impact. Both works were ballets. *The Firebird* was a commission for the Russian impresario Serge Diaghilev, and it was premièred successfully at the Paris Opéra. Another commission, *The Rite of Spring*, created a riot because of its revolutionary orchestrations and driving, primitive rhythms.

Why was *The Rite of Spring* so controversial? The third of his ballet commissions for Diaghilev, it is subtitled "Pictures of Pagan Russia," and it depicts the cruel rites of spring that culminate in the sacrifice of a virgin, who dances herself to death accompanied by frenetic music. It is those compelling rhythms (CD Track 20) that give the work its impressive character. Rapid, irregular mixtures of very short note values create an almost intolerable tension, or at least a tension that was intolerable to the public of that day. The melodic material is quite unconventional—short driving motifs that stop short of thematic fulfillment. Such melodies as there are are short and fragmentary.

Schoenberg

The movement that drew the most attention in the first half of the twentieth century grew out of German Romanticism, but it took a radical turn into atonality. At the root of the movement was Arnold Schoenberg (SHURN-bairk; 1874–1951). Between 1905 and 1912 Schoenberg moved away from the gigantic post-Romantic works he had been composing and began to adopt a more contained style, writing works for smaller ensembles, and treating instruments in a more individual manner. His orchestral works of this period display swiftly alternating timbres, in contrast with the massive orchestral texture of earlier works. They also employ increased complexity in their rhythms, harmonies, and fragmented melodies.

Although the word "atonality," meaning without

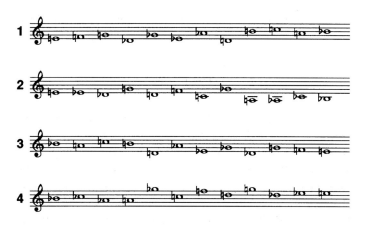

16.35 Tone Row from Schoenberg's *Piano Suite*, Op. 25 (1); shown in inversion (2); retrograde (3); and retrograde inversion (4).

tonality, is used to describe Schoenberg's works, he preferred the term "pantonality"—that is, inclusive of all tonalities. In his compositions Schoenberg used any combination of tones without having to resolve chord progressions, a concept he called "the emancipation of dissonance." In 1912 Schoenberg created one of his most famous works, *Pierrot Lunaire (Moonstruck Pierrot)*, a cycle of twenty-one songs based on French surrealist poems translated into German. The cycle uses a female solo voice accompanied by various instruments, and important in this work is the stylized use of the speaking voice, *Sprechgesang* (SPREHK-geh-zahng).

By 1923 Schoenberg was composing in *twelve-tone* technique. This involves "tone rows." A tone row presents the twelve semitones of a chromatic scale only once, in an order chosen by the composer. This series of notes can be used in various ways—as melodies and harmonies, upside down, backward, upside down and backward—that is, in whatever order or form the composer chooses. Figure **16.35** illustrates the tone row Schoenberg used in the first movement of his *Piano Suite* Op. 25. No. 1 is the row itself; No. 2 shows No. 1 in *inversion*—that is, the notes have the same distance of separation but go in the opposite direction, down as opposed to up and vice versa; No. 3 illustrates the row in *retrograde*—that is, backward; and No. 4 places the original row in an inversion of the retrograde or *retrograde inversion*. The structure of this technique is fairly mathematical and formal, but a good composer can maintain a balance between emotion and mechanics. The important thing to understand about these works is that they are specifically and logically organized so as to be completely atonal. When the listener knows the concepts behind them, Schoenberg's dramatic and experimental compositions can be heard as artistic entities just as much as more traditional music can.

Jazz

Undoubtedly the most significant African American contribution to American music, and, in turn, a uniquely American contribution to the world of music, jazz began near the turn of the century, and from there went through many changes and forms. Jazz includes many sophisticated and complicated styles, but all of them feature improvised variations on a theme.

The earliest form, *blues*, went back to the rhythmic music of the slaves, and consisted of a repeated line, with a second, concluding line (AAB). This was music of oppression, and early singers, such as Bessie Smith (1894–1937), evoked an emotional quality which the instruments tried to imitate.

At approximately the same time came ragtime, a piano style with a strict, two-part form. Syncopation played an important role in this style, whose most famous exponent was Scott Joplin (1868–1917). New Orleans, the cradle of jazz, also produced traditional jazz, which featured improvisational development from a basic, memorized chordal sequence. All this was followed in the thirties and forties by swing, bebop, and cool jazz.

THEATRE
Realism and Naturalism

In line with trends in philosophy and the other arts, a conscious movement toward realism in the theatre emerged around the middle of the nineteenth century, and by 1860 dramatic literature strove for truthful portrayal. Objectivity was stressed, and knowledge of the real world was seen as possible only through direct observation. (Corot's approach to painting was based on a similar viewpoint, as was the realism of writers such as Dostoyevski.) Thus, everyday life, with which the playwright was directly familiar, became the subject matter of drama. Interest shifted from the past to human motives and experience, or, more likely, idealized versions of these. Exposure to such topics on the stage was not particularly pleasant, and many play-goers objected that the theatre was turning into a "sewer or a tavern." Playwrights countered the criticisms by saying that the way to avoid such ugly depictions on the stage was to change society.

The acknowledged master of realist drama was Norway's Henrik Ibsen (1828–1906). Ibsen built powerful problem-dramas around carefully selected detail and plausible character-to-action motivations. His plays usually bring to conclusion events that began well in the past, with meticulous exposition. Ibsen's concern for detail carries to the scenery and costumes, and his plays contain detailed descriptions of settings and properties, all of which are essential to the action. The content of many of Ibsen's plays was controversial, and most deal with questions about moral and social issues that remain difficult today. In his late plays, however, Ibsen abandoned realism in favor of symbolist experiment.

Realism spread widely, finding expression in the work of Anton Chekhov (CHEHK-hawf; 1860–1904), although, like Ibsen, Chekhov incorporates symbolism into his works. Many people regard him as the founder of modern realism. He drew his themes and subject matter from Russian daily life, and they are accurate portrayals of frustration and the depressing nature of existence. His structures flow in the same apparently aimless manner as the lives of his characters. While short on theatricality and compact structure, his skillfully constructed plots give the appearance of actuality.

The Irish writer George Bernard Shaw (1856–1950) embodied the spirit of nineteenth-century realism, although his career overlapped the nineteenth and twentieth centuries. This witty, brilliant artist was above all a humanitarian, and although many Victorians considered him a heretic and a subversive (because of his devotion to socialism), his faith lay in humanity and its infinite potential.

Shaw's plays deal with the unexpected, and they often appear contradictory and inconsistent in characterization and structure. His favorite device was to build up a pompous notion and then destroy it. For example, in *Man and Superman*, when a respectable Victorian family learns that their daughter is pregnant, they react with predictable indignation. A character who appears to speak for the playwright comes to the girl's defense, attacking the family's hypocrisy and defending the girl. She, however, explodes in anger, not against her family, but against her defender. She had been secretly married all the time, and, as the most respectable of the lot, she condemns her defender's (and possibly the audience's) freethinking.

Shaw opposed the doctrine of "art for art's sake," and he insisted that art should have a purpose. He believed that plays made better vehicles for social messages than speeches or pamphlets. Although each play usually has a character who acts as the playwright's mouthpiece, Shaw does more than sermonize. His characters probe the depths of the human condition, often discovering themselves through some lifelike crisis.

Naturalism, a style closely related to realism, also flourished in the same period. Émile Zola (1840–1902), was a leading proponent, although he was more a theoretician and novelist than a playwright. Both realism and naturalism insisted on a truthful depiction of life, but naturalism went on to insist on the basic principle that behavior is determined by heredity and environment. Absolute objectivity, not personal opinion, was the naturalistic goal.

Symbolism

To amplify our earlier discussion, late in the nineteenth century, and very briefly, there was an anti-realistic literary movement called "symbolism," also known as "neo-Romanticism," "idealism," or "impressionism." Symbolism was briefly popular in France, and it has recurred occasionally in the twentieth century. The idea behind symbolism is that truth can be grasped only by intuition, not through the senses or rational thought. Thus, ultimate truths can be suggested only through symbols, which evoke in the audience various states of mind that correspond vaguely with the playwright's feelings.

One of the principal dramatic symbolists, the Belgian Maurice Maeterlinck (mah-tur-LANK; 1862–1949), believed that every play contains a "second level" of dialogue that speaks to the soul. Through verbal beauty, contemplation, and a passionate portrayal of nature, great drama conveys the poet's idea of the unknown. Therefore, plays that present human actions can only, through symbols, suggest higher truths gained through intuition. The symbolists did not deal at all with social problems. Rather, they turned to the past and tried to suggest universal truths independent of time and place, as Maeterlinck did, for example, in *Pelléas and Mélisande* (1892).

FILM: ART AND MECHANIZATION

On 23 April 1896, at Koster and Bial's Music Hall in New York, the Leigh Sisters performed their umbrella dance. Then the audience was astonished to see waves breaking upon the shore. Thus was launched a new process for screen projection of movies—the Vitascope. Invented by Thomas Armat (although Thomas Edison has received much of the credit), the Vitascope was the latest in centuries of experiments on how to make pictures move. Relying on the "persistence of vision"—that is, the continuance of a visual image on the retina for a brief time after the removal of the object—and basic photographic techniques, the Vitascope captured real objects in motion and presented those images on a screen.

Technological experiments in rapid-frame photography were common in the last half of the nineteenth century, but it remained for Thomas Armat and others to perfect a stop-motion device essential to screen projection. Two Frenchmen, the Lumière (loo-mee-AIR) brothers, are

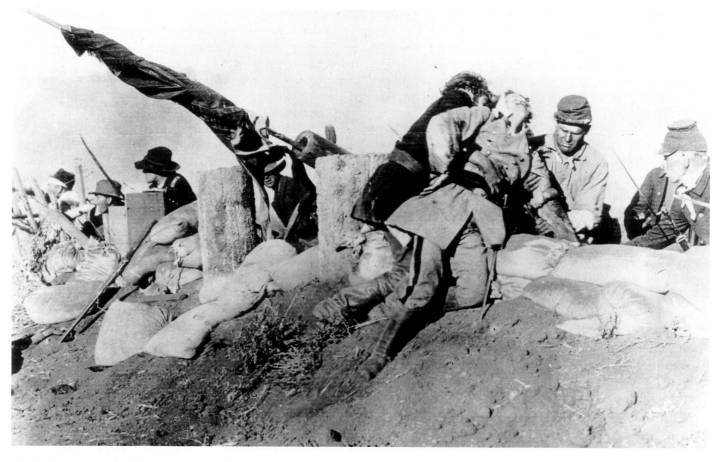

16.36 D.W. Griffith, *The Birth of a Nation*, 1915.

usually credited with the first public projection of movies on a large screen in 1895. By 1897, the Lumières had successfully exhibited their *cinématographie* all over Europe, and their catalogue listed 358 films. They opened in America three months after the première of the Vitascope. Later that year, the American Biograph made its début using larger film and projecting twice as many pictures per minute, creating the largest, brightest, and steadiest picture of all.

At that point, movies did nothing more than record everyday life. It took Georges Méliès (may-lee-ES; 1861–1938) in France and Edwin S. Porter (1870–1941) in the United States to demonstrate the narrative and manipulative potential of the cinema. Between 1896 and 1914, Méliès turned out more than a thousand films. Edwin S. Porter, who was in charge of the Edison Company Studios, studied the narrative attempts of Méliès. Then, acting as his own scriptwriter, cameraman, and director, he spliced together old and freshly shot film into *The Life of an American Firefighter*. In 1903 Porter made *The Great Train Robbery*, the most popular film of the decade. It ran a total of twelve minutes. The popular audience was entranced, and flocked to electric theatres to see movies

that could excite and thrill them with stories of romance and adventure. The movies were a window to a wider world for the poor of America.

By 1910, the young film industry counted a handful of recognized stars who had made more than four hundred films for the screen's first mogul, Charles Pathé (pah-TAY). Short films remained the staple of the industry, but there was a growing taste for more spectacular fare, especially in Europe. The Italian film *Quo Vadis* was produced in 1912, complete with lavish sets, chariot races, Christians, lions, and a cast of hundreds. A full two hours long, it proved a huge success.

Lawsuits over patents and monopolies marked the first decade of the century. In order to escape the constant badgering of Thomas Edison's lawyers, independent filmmakers headed west to a sleepy California town called Hollywood, where, among other things, the weather, the natural light, and the exotic, varied landscape were much more conducive to cinematography. By 1915 over half of all American movies were made in Hollywood.

That year also witnessed the release of D.W. Griffith's *The Birth of a Nation* (Fig. **16.36**), which ran for three hours. Popular and controversial, the film was destined to become a landmark in cinema history. It unfolds the story of two families during the Civil War and the Reconstruction period. Now condemned for its depiction of leering, bestial blacks rioting and raping white women, and for the rescue of whites by the Ku Klux Klan, the film is nonetheless a work of great artistry. Griffith defined and refined nearly every technique in film-making: the fade-in, fade-out, long shot, full shot, close-up, moving camera, flashback, CROSSCUTTING, and juxtaposition. In addition, Griffith virtually invented film editing and preshooting rehearsals.

As if *The Birth of a Nation* were not colossal enough, Griffith followed it in 1916 with *Intolerance*, a $2 million epic of ancient Babylon, biblical Judea, sixteenth-century France, and contemporary America. As the film progressed, brilliant crosscutting increased at a frantic pace to heighten suspense and tension. However, audiences found the film confusing. It failed miserably at the box office, and the failure ruined Griffith financially.

The same era produced the Mack Sennet comedies, which featured the hilarious antics and wild chase scenes of the Keystone Kops. Sennet was one of Griffith's partners in the Triangle Film Company. A third partner was Thomas Ince, who brought to the screen the prototypical cowboy hero, William S. Hart, in such works as *Wagon Tracks*.

Nothing better represents the second decade of the twentieth century, however, than the work of the genius Charlie Chaplin, the "little fellow." Chaplin's characters represent all of humanity, and he communicates through the silent film as eloquently and deeply as anyone ever has. In an era marked by disillusionment, Chaplin represented resilience, optimism, and an indomitable spirit. By the end of World War I Chaplin shared the limelight with that most dashing of American heroes, Douglas Fairbanks.

DANCE

Ethnic Foundations

At this point we must take a pause in our heretofore chronological development of what we call *theatre dance* to inject a brief examination of *ethnic* and *folk* dance (see the Introduction). The need for a diversion occurs because at the point in history treated by the current chapter, the folk tradition emerged as a fundamental element in dance directions for the twentieth century.

An expression in rhythmic movement, dance can be an individual experience, a group experience, and also a cultural mirror. When dance as a simple emotional expression develops into a design—a planned pattern of rhythms,

steps, gestures, and so on—it becomes a specific dance. Several dances of the same type become a dance form such as ballet. In general, we can divide dance into two broad categories, *communal dance* and *theatre dance*, and we have already seen how the former can develop into the latter. The dance we discussed relative to ancient Greece reflected more a communal type of dance called *ritual dance*, a planned and conscious effort organized for a specific purpose. Later, in Renaissance France, we saw how another form of communal dance, *social dance*, actually became a form of theatre dance, the ballet. A third type of communal dance, which we discussed in the introduction, called *folk dance*, predominated in the Middle Ages.

Folk dance might be seen as the basis of all other dance forms, including ballet and *modern dance*, which we discover emerging momentarily. Intermingling with folk dance, and technically a variant, is *ethnic* dance. Both folk and ethnic dance share peasant culture origins, but ethnic dance reflects more selectivity and artistic consciousness than folk dance. Perhaps the oldest and most illustrative example of ethnic dance in the West, a theatre dance form that has retained its folkloric base, is *Spanish* dance. Here we find a physical expression of the sensuality of love and its passions. In Spanish dance, the footwork takes center stage: the striking of the toe, the heel, and the full sole in a variety of tonic and rhythmic combinations, accented by clicking castanets and guitar. Proud carriage of the head and torso, as much as movements, project essential emotions. Ethnic and folk traditions such as Spanish dance—and, indeed, many others—played a vital role in the emergence of much of twentieth-century dance, beginning with the Russian traditions of Diaghilev's *Ballets russes*.

Diaghilev and the *Ballets russes*

Two major revolutions in dance occurred in the early twentieth century. Sergei Diaghilev (DYAH-gee-lef; 1872–1929) was largely responsible for one of them. When Diaghilev arrived in St Petersburg, Russia, in 1890 to study law, he soon became friends with several artists. In 1898, Diaghilev's artist friends launched a new magazine, *World of Art*, and appointed him editor. His entrepreneurial and managerial talents made the venture a success.

Thus began a career in artistic management that would shape the ballet world of the twentieth century. In producing outstanding works that employed the finest choreographers, Diaghilev played a tremendously important role in bringing the art of Paris and Munich to Moscow and St Petersburg and vice versa.

Once Diaghilev had successfully produced opera outside of Russia, he was encouraged to take Russian

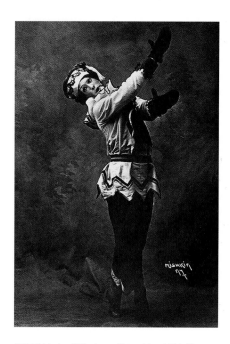

16.37 Vaslav Nijinsky as Petrushka, 1911. The New York Public Library.

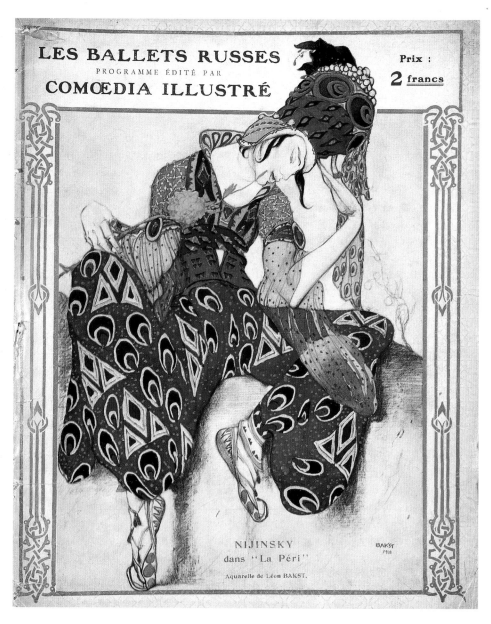

16.38 Leon Bakst, costume design, *Les Ballets russes—Comœdia Illustré*, "Nijinsky dans La Péri," 1911. Victoria & Albert Museum, London.

ballet to Paris. In 1909, he opened the first of his many *Ballets russes*. The dancers included the greatest dancers of Russia, among them Anna Pavlova and Vaslav Nijinsky (Fig. **16.37**). For the next three years, Diaghilev's ballets were choreographed by Mikhail Fokine (foh-KEEN), whose original approach stood in marked contrast to the evening-long spectaculars of Petipa (see p. 490). Fokine's work was in line with the theatrical and musical theories espoused by Wagner and others. That is, he too believed in the artistic unity of all production elements—costumes, settings, and music, to which, of course, he added dancing. Dancing, in turn, he felt, should blend harmoniously with the theme and subject of the production.

Success was due as much to the integration of superb music, costume, and set design as it was to Fokine's choreography. Leon Bakst's costumes and sets were works of consummate artistry, as their exquisite line and style, shown in Figure **16.38**, demonstrate. Bakst's vibrant colors and rich textures greatly influenced fashion and interior decoration of the period.

Diaghilev was not content to allow Nijinsky to remain just his *premier danseur*. He insisted that Nijinsky be a choreographer as well, which partially accounted for Fokine's departure. In 1912 Nijinsky (ni-ZHIN-skee) choreographed the controversial *Prélude à l'apres-midi d'un faune* with music by Debussy. The choreography was rife with sexual suggestion, and the "obscenity" of the performance caused an uproar. Nijinsky's choreography was strangely angular in contrast to Debussy's music. The dancing suggested the linear qualities of a Greek frieze. A year later, the unveiling of Nijinsky's choreography of Stravinsky's *Rite of Spring* caused an actual riot, as mentioned previously.

Although the controversy had more to do with the music than with the dancing, the choreography was also shocking, hinting at deep primordial forces, especially in the scene in which a virgin dances herself to death to satisfy the gods. Nijinsky's decision to marry in 1913 caused a rift with Diaghilev, who was homosexual, and Nijinsky was dismissed from the company.

Diaghilev's new choreographer, Léonide Massine (lay-oh-NEED mah-SEEN), took the company (and ballet in general) in new directions. Previously the *Ballets russes* had featured picturesque Russian themes. Now it turned to themes emerging in the visual arts, to cubism and surrealism. *Parade* in 1917 found dancers in huge skyscraper-like cubist costumes designed by Pablo Picasso. The music, by Eric Satie (1866–1925), included sounds of typewriters and steamship whistles.

In 1924, Diaghilev hired a new choreographer who was to be a force in ballet for the next 60 years. George Balanchine came to Diaghilev from St Petersburg and choreographed ten productions for him over the next four years. Two of these continue to be danced—*The Prodigal Son*, composed by Prokofiev, and *Apollo*, composed by Stravinsky. When Diaghilev died in 1929, his company died with him, and an era ended. Ballet had been reborn as a major art form, a blending of choreography, dancing, music, and visual art—a rival to opera as a "perfect synthesis of the arts."

Duncan and the Modern Dance Movement

While Diaghilev continued within balletic traditions, others did not. The most significant of these was the remarkable and unrestrained Isadora Duncan (1878–1927). By 1905, Duncan had gained notoriety for her barefoot, deeply emotional dancing. She was considered controversial among balletomanes and reformers alike, but even Fokine saw in her style a confirmation of his own beliefs.

Although an American, Isadora Duncan achieved her fame in Europe. Her dances were emotional interpretations of moods suggested to her by music or by nature. Her dance was personal. Her costume was inspired by Greek tunics and draperies, and, most significantly, she danced in bare feet. This break with convention continues to this day as a basic condition of the modern dance tradition she helped to form.

Focal Point

America's Gilded Age

Despite the conditions we loosely refer to as "democracy" in the United States and Europe, society, even without a powerful aristocracy, tended to be two-tiered. In the United States, a new class of super-rich separated themselves from the remainder of society. The worlds represented by these differences were as apart as earth and moon, and those worlds did not include the African American, who, although "free" because of the Civil War, lived in a state of cultural limbo, or many immigrants, exploitation of whom ran rampant in the North.

To focus on what was happening in society, we turn to the world of the wealthy and the homes they built. These homes bring together in a physical location, the general conditions of society in America at the time. As you read about these homes and the individuals who built them, compare them with current housing directions in the United States. In the period after World War II, the typical suburban house had about 1,200 square feet (110 square meters) of space and contained as many as four bedrooms. Today a typical suburban home has 3,000 square feet (280 square metres) of space and the same number of bedrooms.

After the Civil War (1861–5), America boomed economically as it had never done before. The United States expanded westward and reached out across the oceans to secure its share of the world's trade and empire. However, viewed from the vantage point of history, the

16.39 Richard Morris Hunt, The Breakers, Newport, Rhode Island, 1893–5.

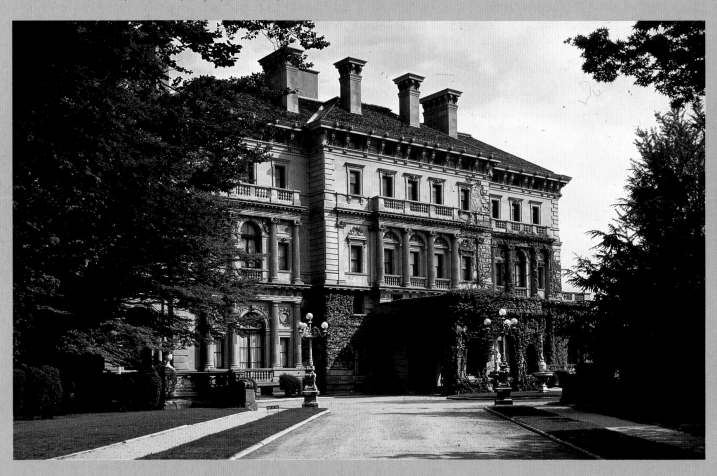

period was not an honorable one—political corruption reigned among ineffectual presidents, state political machines, big-city bosses, and legislators whose votes were for sale to the highest bidder.

Reconstruction in the South soon saw the return of the white aristocracy, and African Americans, free but without land, were forced to become sharecroppers for landowners who demanded higher and higher portions of the crops they grew. African Americans remained second-class citizens who were discriminated against and denied the right to vote. While farmers' organizations agitated for reform, and labor unions struggled to gain a foothold, the overall economic picture was, nevertheless, rosy. The nation grew rapidly, the population doubling every twenty-five years, and its resources seemed endless. Europe provided the United States with an almost inexhaustible supply of capital and people, and the nation benefited from rapid technological advances. There was a spirit in the land that anyone could go from rags to riches if they steadfastly applied entrepreneurial energy.

Railroads stretched across the continent—the United States had more miles of railroad than all of Europe—and between 1877 and 1892 the output of American factories tripled. By the end of the century the United States led the world in both agriculture and industry. Big business devel-oped with huge corporations emerging and hiring. The boom produced America's legendary financial and corporate giants—for example, J. Pierpont Morgan, Andrew Carnegie, John D. Rockefeller, Cornelius Vanderbilt, and Henry Flagler. To the reformers of the time, these were the "robber barons" of the United States, men who seemed able, through all kinds of conditions, to manipulate and, through ruthlessness, to build their personal empires to phenomenal heights. They were symbols of monopoly and exemplars of what Americans considered to be the "American Dream"—that is, success. It was the Gilded Age of America—before income and inheritance taxes despoiled personal fortunes—and the homes of these members of America's aristocracy, which was of money, not birth, symbolize and synthesize the opulent, overindulgent ostentation of the time.

The Breakers

During this golden period, the burning ambition of those who had access to power and money was to be accepted in high society, and they would go to almost any lengths to achieve this aim. The acknowledged leaders of New York society were Mr and Mrs Cornelius Vanderbilt. Cornelius Vanderbilt (1843–99) was president of the New York Central Railroad, and, in 1893, one year after his brother,

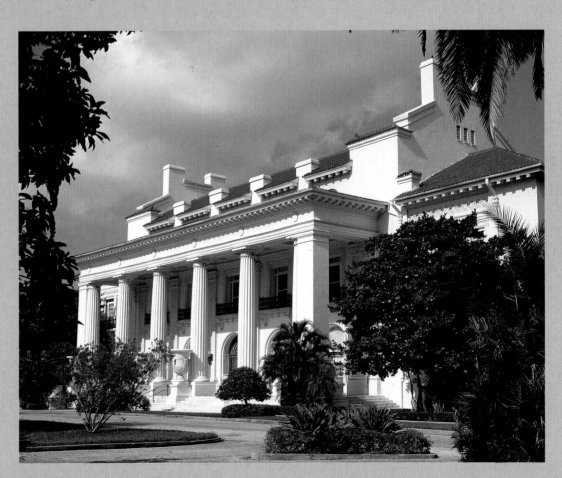

16.40 Carrère and Hastings, Whitehall, Palm Beach, Florida, 1900–01.

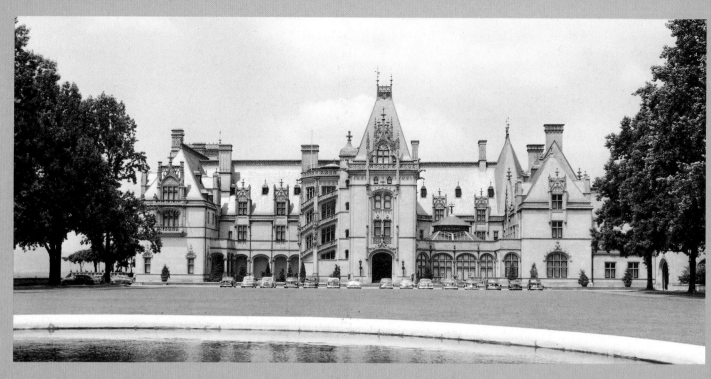

16.41 Hunt and Olmstead, Biltmore House, Asheville, North Carolina, 1895.

William, had built an unrivaled statement about his own power—a mansion called Marble House—Cornelius engaged Richard Morris Hunt to build The Breakers. His vision was a sixteenth-century Italian palace, and money was no object. The house had to be fireproof, to be finished quickly, and to be the finest house in all of Newport. Workers from all over the world worked day and night for two years to create an exquisite seventy-room, $7 million palace (Fig. **16.39**). Unique among American homes, it was equipped with electricity and with gas, in case the new power source should fail, and the structure integrated steel framing, which represented a major departure in construction techniques. It was a house perfectly suited to the grand style of entertaining that the Vanderbilts enjoyed.

The interior boasted an enclosed courtyard with a ceiling painted to resemble the sky, complete with wind-swept clouds. The dining room, which covered 2,400 square feet (222 square meters), sat thirty-four, and was adorned with two Baccarat crystal chandeliers. The house is an example of social ritual, with particular spaces divided to provide specific activities representing the structured daily and nightly life of the social elite. The exterior landscape was also designed for social ritual, with acres of formal gardens, for which the sod was imported from Britain.

Whitehall

Henry Flagler was a visionary who had made his millions in partnership with John D. Rockefeller in the Standard Oil Company. He went to Florida in 1877, at a time when the state was little more than a wilderness, and saw its potential. Beginning with the Ponce de Leon Hotel in St Augustine, Flagler spent the next twenty-five years building hotels throughout Florida, transforming the state from swampland to playground. Called the Taj Mahal of North America, Flagler's home, Whitehall (Fig. **16.40**), became the envy of America's social elite. It contained seventy-three rooms on 6 acres (2.4 hectares) overlooking Lake Worth in Palm Beach. It was a castle worthy of a king, and 71-year-old Flagler and his 35-year-old third wife ruled Palm Beach society.

Construction began in 1900 and took a mere eighteen months to complete. As many as a thousand workmen created elaborate marble designs with wooden accents. Each of the rooms reflects a different European style, and the house features treasures from around the world. Despite the $4 million spent on building and the further $1.5 million for interior furnishings, Whitehall was used for only two months of the year, January and February. It was an entertainment pavilion designed to impress, and, unlike The Breakers, it was not a home.

Biltmore House

Without doubt, the grandest house from this period is George Vanderbilt's ultimate dreamhouse, Biltmore House (Fig. **16.41**). The grandson of Commodore Vanderbilt, George had traveled the world and seemed to disdain the kind of ostentation that typified his family's palaces in Newport. Nonetheless, in the mountains of North Carolina, on 125,000 acres (50,590 hectares), George built a 225-room palace that is still America's largest private home. During his travels George had come to admire the country estates of the European nobility, and Biltmore House was built to realize a dream. It was to be a self-sustaining working estate, on which all the necessary provisions for the house—everything from beef to agricultural crops and forestry—could be produced to support the house and its guests. The entire project was the responsibility of two friends of the Vanderbilt family, architect Richard Morris Hunt, who had designed The Breakers, and landscape architect Frederick Law Olmstead, who designed New York's Central Park (a smaller project than Biltmore House). At the time Biltmore House was built, both architects were very old, and neither lived to see the completion of the project.

The work took five years to complete, and employed thousands of people. The house, completed in 1895, occupied 4 acres (1.6 hectares) of floor space and had sixty-five fireplaces. The gallery, 90 feet (27 meters) long, contains three huge sixteenth-century tapestries representing the victory of virtue over vice. Rich furnishings and magnificent art grace every room, and over ten thousand books occupy the shelves of the library. The medieval banquet hall covers more than 3,000 square feet (910 meters), with a 70-foot arched ceiling, and a triple fireplace at one end. It had an indoor pool, a gym, and a bowling alley. Although all but 8,000 acres (3,240 hectares) have been sold to become the Pisgah National Forest, Biltmore House remains a private estate today.

CHAPTER REVIEW

Critical Thought

One of the ways we can identify how the arts interrelate is to take examples from more than one general grouping and compare them. For example, we have become accustomed in this text to referring to painting, sculpture, and architecture not only by their individual names but also by the term "visual arts." Another grouping of arts, called the "performing arts," includes music, theatre, dance, and film. In these arts, the basic visions of composer, playwright, and choreographer are interpreted and performed by other artists, who lend some of their own vision to the artwork. Thus, we can find a useful means of comparison if we take an example of visual art and compare it with an example of performing art. Perhaps groupings such as "visual" and "performing" can assist us to master the complexities of a chapter containing so many diverse styles.

Summary

After reading this chapter, you should be able to:

- Understand how styles such as impressionism, expressionism, and realism are applied to visual and performing arts.
- Characterize the ideas of Nietzsche and Freud.
- Describe the social, political, and economic condition of the world at the end of the nineteenth century.
- Explain how realism, naturalism, and symbolism manifested themselves in theatre and literature.
- Discuss the state of film and dance at the end of the nineteenth century by citing specific individuals, events, and characteristics.
- Apply the elements and principles of composition to analyze and compare individual works of visual art illustrated in this chapter.

CHAPTER SEVENTEEN

Modernism

OUTLINE

THE MODERN WORLD IN CONFLICT

BETWEEN THE WARS

WORLD WAR II

SCIENCE AND WAR

PHILOSOPHY

LITERATURE
Fiction
Poetry

THE VISUAL ARTS AND ARCHITECTURE
Abstraction
Dada
Fantasy and Surrealism
American Painting
African and Primitive Influences
Architectural Modernism

MUSIC
Modern Traditionalism
Departures

THEATRE
Expressionism
Epic Theatre
Absurdism

MODERN DANCE
Native American Dance

PHOTOGRAPHY

FILM
European Film
The Rise of the Studio
New Genres
Social Commentary

FOCAL POINT: THE BAUHAUS—INTEGRATION OF THE ARTS

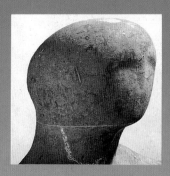

VIEW

DREAMS AND EXPECTATIONS

Probably every generation experiences deprivations, uncertainties, anxieties, and what it believes is a collapse of its expectations. Of course, different generations have different expectations, especially about what constitutes deprivation and/or needs. In most cases, collapsing dreams result from two tendencies recognized thousands of years ago as primary obstacles to healthy living: self-pity and fear. Both the Old and New Testaments of the Bible point out those conditions, and Aristotle spoke of them when he described the desired outcomes of Greek tragedy—that is, the purgation of pity and fear. Many dreams collapsed with the onset of World War I in 1914, and expectations collapsed again with the stock market crash of 1929, which gave rise to the Great Depression, whose deprivations, in turn, did much to cause World War II. Reactions to these shattered dreams took artistic, as well as political form: specifically, art that denied art and art that emphasized shock. The modern age had arrived.

KEY TERMS

Some of the basic terms and concepts we will encounter in this chapter include the following:

Pragmatism, a philosophy for which the criterion for truth consists in the workability of an idea.

Existentialism, a philosophical doctrine and literary and dramatic movement that insists on the existence of individuals as basic and important.

Abstract art, abstraction, nonrepresentationalism; art which depicts the essence of a thing rather than its actual appearance.

Dada, an artistic and literary movement emphasizing the discovery of reality through the abolition of traditional cultural and aesthetic forms. Derision, shock, irrationality, and chance play major roles.

Surrealism, an artistic style emphasizing discovery of reality through reliance on the subconscious.

Absurdism, a style dealing with life's apparent meaninglessness and the difficulty or impossibility of human communication.

Above Detail of Fig. **17.24.**

17.1 Frida Kahlo, *The Broken Column*, 1940. Oil on canvas, 15³/₄ × 12¹/₄ ins (40 × 31 cm). Museo Dolores Olmedo Patiño, Mexico.

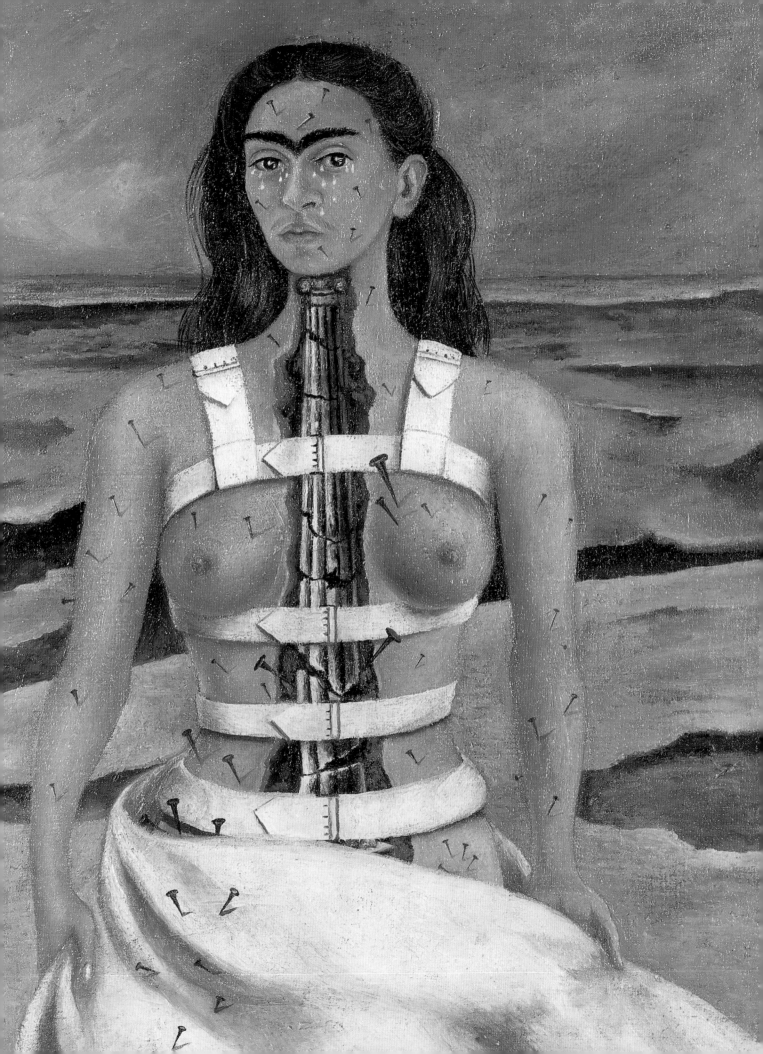

"Make it new," said the poet Ezra Pound, and the one constant in the arts of the early part of the turbulent twentieth century was a seemingly inexhaustible quest for originality and freshness. The age witnessed the worst and the best that humanity is capable of (Fig. **17.2**). In the aftermath of World War I, many believed that any culture that could produce the wanton destruction wrought by the war must be abandoned, if not destroyed, and the appeal of communism as an alternative to capitalistic democracy captivated many liberals. The conflicts and unresolved issues resulting from "the peace" soon, however, led the world into another war.

Some time before 1914, Europe and the rest of the Western world seem to have gone astray. Societies believed they were approaching the best that science and invention could offer, and that competitive struggle would produce desirable, positive results. The war changed that.

THE MODERN WORLD IN CONFLICT

Toward World War I

We noted in Chapter 16 the way in which Germany developed during the last quarter of the nineteenth century under Chancellor Bismarck and Kaiser William II. One of Bismarck's main policies was to maintain the balance of power in Europe. France, which had been isolated and weakened in the last quarter of the century, was not a threat, but Bismarck saw that the major danger to European stability was in the two multinational empires—that is, the Ottoman Empire and the Austro-Hungarian Empire. The Turks controlled part of the Balkans, and both Austria-Hungary and Russia wanted this area in their hegemony. In Austria-Hungary, the Slav minority, discreetly supported by the Russians, pushed for independence. Through diplomatic maneuvering, Bismarck was able to keep the lid on any potential confrontation between Austria-Hungary and Russia, but in 1890 William II forced Bismarck to resign and broke with Bismarck's policies, forging an alliance with Austria-Hungary, as we noted in Chapter 16. In response, Russia, which needed French capital to develop its industries, formed an alliance with France.

Europe now found itself split into two camps. Germany joined with Austria-Hungary and Italy to form the Triple Alliance, which held a military advantage over the other camp, the Triple Entente (the Allies) of Great Britain, France, and Russia, which were unable to coordinate their military affairs. The Triple Alliance stepped up the pressure on its temporarily weaker opponent, particularly in Morocco, where the Kaiser wanted to stop French advancement, and at the same time Austria-Hungary, with

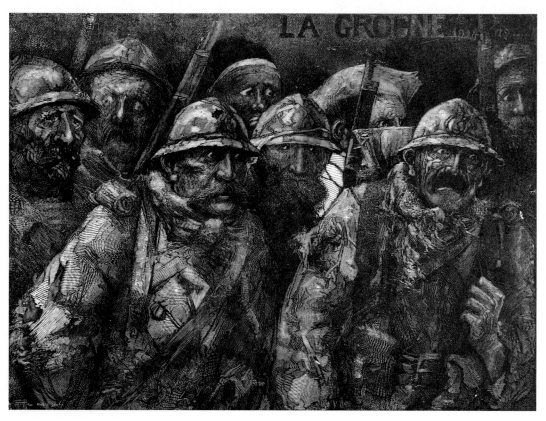

17.2 L. Ruffe, *La Grogne* (*Grumbling*), c. 1917. Wood-engraving of World War I soldiers.

	GENERAL EVENTS	LITERATURE & PHILOSOPHY	VISUAL ART & ARCHITECTURE	THEATRE & CINEMA	MUSIC & DANCE
1900					
	Triple Entente	Dewey		Strindberg	
	Balkan wars	Yeats	Gilbert (17.28)	Toller	
	Women's suffrage (USA)		de Chirico (17.12)	Wiene	
	World War I	Gide	Lipchitz (17.23)		
	Russian Revolution		Malevich (17.8)	Rice	
	Treaty of Versailles	Frost			Ives
1920					
	League of Nations	Joyce	Ernst (17.10)	Eisenstein	
		Hughes	Davis (17.15)		William Schuman
	German rearmament	Lawrence	O'Keeffe (17.14)	Brecht	
		Kafka	Stieglitz		
	Japanese invasion of	Mann	Mondrian (17.9)	Lang	Prokofiev
	Manchuria	Faulkner	Wood (17.16)		
		Woolf	Lange (17.32)	Pirandello	
		Eliot	Brancusi (17.21, 17.22)		Bartók
	Great Depression	Pound	Wright (17.25, 17.26)	DeMille	
		Auden	Gropius (17.34)		
			Rivera (17.19)	Vidor	Hindemith
			Dalí (17.11)		
			Kahlo (17.13)	Disney	
			Douglas (17.17, 17.18)		Berg
			Le Corbusier (17.27)		Webern
			Moore (17.24)		
1940					
	World War II			Ford	
	Pearl Harbor	Hemingway		Welles	Copland
		e.e. cummings	Adams (17.31)		Graham
	First computers			Camus	
				Sartre	
	Nuclear weapons				
1950					

Timeline 17.1 Modernism.

the unconditional support of the Kaiser, decided to extend its territory and influence in the Balkans.

At the beginning of 1914, the Balkans remained the sole sensitive area of Europe. Russia had one ally left in the area, the Serbs, and she gave them her unconditional support. The Austro-Hungarian Empire, encouraged by the Bulgarians, was looking for a pretext to remove the one final obstacle to its own interests in the Balkan peninsula. Ten years of tension had caused all the powers to increase their armed forces and to align themselves in such a way that any confrontation would lead to an irreversible chain reaction. War was not imminent, but the precarious alliances and interests of the two coalitions made it impossible to stop the mobilization process if something might occur to set it in motion.

That something occurred on 28 June 1914. An Austrian archduke was assassinated in Sarajevo, and Austria-Hungary held the Serbs responsible. William II promised to support the Austro-Hungarians in case of war.

One month later, on 28 July, Austria-Hungary declared war on Serbia. On 1 August Germany declared war on Serbia's ally, Russia. On 3 August Germany declared war on France and invaded Belgium. On 4 August Britain declared war on Germany.

The Great War

Between 1914 and 1918 the military commands of both sides changed strategies repeatedly. On one hand, they would pursue a "strong point" strategy, in which they attacked the enemy in order to break its resistance, then they would switch to a "weak point" strategy, which aimed to disorganize the enemy and reduce the number of its allies. All of which resulted in three years of bloody trench warfare with little resolution.

The situation began to change in 1917. What had been a European conflict took on global dimensions when

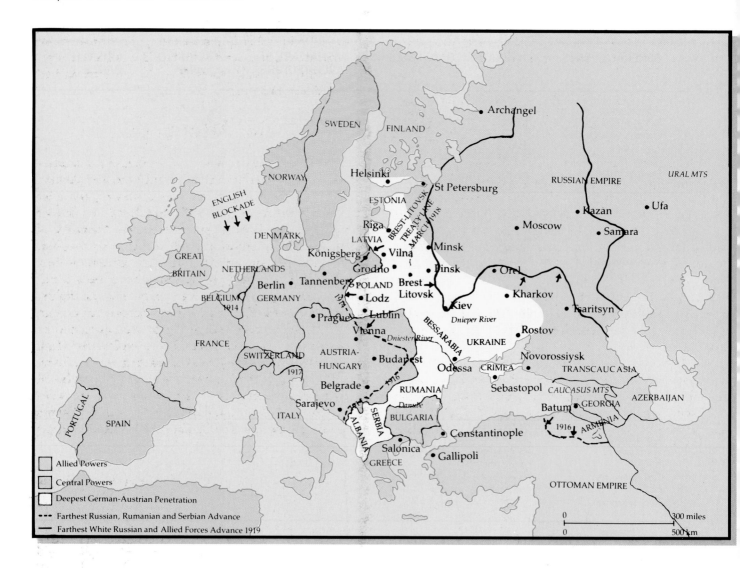

Map 17.1 World War I and its aftermath in Europe.

Britain mounted offensives in Egypt, Iraq, and elsewhere in the Arab world. Then Japan and China entered the conflict. Finally, Germany's submarine attacks, which came as a result of its policy of unrestricted naval warfare, brought the United States into the war on 6 April 1917.

Both sides used strategies designed to disrupt the other side's efforts. This, as we noted, comprised the "weak point" strategy. The main thrust of the Triple Alliance Powers (Germany, *et al*.) consisted of trying to provoke non-Russian nationalities into rebelling against the Czarist empire. The Allies pursued the same strategy by promising independence (on victory) to every oppressed minority in central Europe—for example, the Croats, Slovenes, Czechs, and Slovaks—which weakened enemy morale somewhat, but proved not to be much of a factor, although it was more effective against the Ottoman Empire. In Armenia, nearby Russian advances led to a massacre that killed over a million people in 1915, and Arab uprisings

led by the Englishman T.E. Lawrence, Lawrence of Arabia, eventually led to the reconstitution of Syria—a nation that had been fragmented for several centuries.

The Allies attempted to destroy the Triple Alliance's seaborne trade and thus to destroy the foundations of their economies: a strategy that provoked Germany into unlimited submarine warfare. This in turn had the unfortunate effect of provoking the United States into entering the war on the side of the Allies. In the end, the effects of the weak point strategy were difficult to evaluate, although it does appear to have caused the United States to enter the war, which proved decisive in an Allied victory. The deterioration of the Russian economy and the resultant shortages played a major role in the Russian Revolution in 1917. Eventually, however, the war was won by military rather than economic means. In 1917 things began to go badly for Germany and her partners on the western front, and by 1918 the Germans realized that they could no longer hope to turn things in their own favor. The first armistices were signed at the end of October and in November 1918.

Revolution and Civil War in Russia

A combination of military defeats, shortages, and hatred of the aristocracy made an explosive combination for Russia, and in an uprising that lasted for five days in Petrograd, the revolution triumphed and Czar Nicholas II abdicated. Power was shared by a government made up of former members of the Russian Duma (parliament) and a Soviet of Workers and Soldiers' Deputies (Fig. 17.3). Under the leadership of Alexander Kerensky, this alliance between the bourgeois and proletarian revolutions proved incapable of either winning or ending the war and unable to put into effect the necessary reforms to transform the social order.

The revolution, which had both political and social consequences, gave a temporary incentive for states of the old empire to seek independence, something that the Bolsheviks hinted at in a declaration of the people's right to self-determination. Once the revolution had succeeded,

however, Lenin and Stalin put the clamps on the nationalist movements, and at the end of the world war and the revolution, only the Baltic States, Poland, and Finland had preserved their independence.

The Aftermath

After months of negotiations, a series of agreements called the Treaty of Versailles formally ended the war. Almost immediately, these agreements were contested, and after twenty years the treaty was totally repudiated. It failed for four reasons. The first reason was called the "principle of nationalities." For centuries, the three great empires—that is, the Austro-Hungarian, Russian, and Ottoman—had within them groups of oppressed minorities under a dominant community that gave them only minimal rights. These groups had tried to gain independence throughout the nineteenth century, and during the war, as part of its weak point strategy, the Allies tried to exploit this ideal. However, within the empires, the minorities were intermingled, and it proved impossible to draw up political borders that were also ethnic ones. In one case, the problem was resolved by a massive repatriation: 400,000 Turks moved from Macedonia to Turkey, and 1,300,000 Greeks

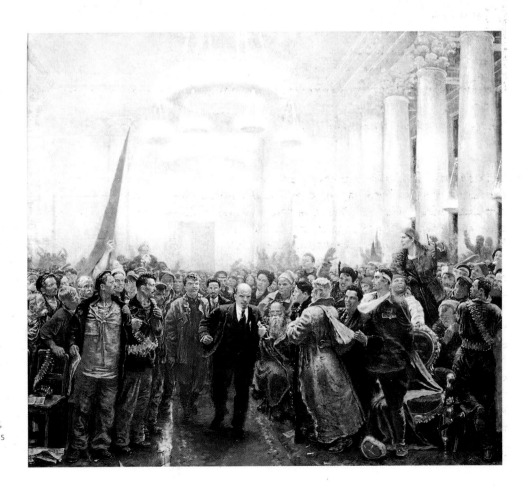

17.3 Alexandr Nikolayevich Samochvalov, *V.I. Lenin Entering the Second All Russian Congress,* 1940. Oil on canvas, 11 ft 7³/₈ ins × 9 ft 3³/₈ ins (3.54 × 2.83 m). Russian State Museum, St Petersburg. © DACS 1999.

moved from Asia Minor to Greece. That did little to dampen Greek and Turkish ill-feeling, and elsewhere ethnic populations simply stayed put. Large German populations became included in Czechoslovakia, and others found themselves in Poland. This "principle of nationalities" later gave Hitler one of his most effective propaganda themes.

The second reason the treaty failed had to do with the problem of non-European territories. German colonies and non-Turkish territories of the Ottoman Empire were divided up between the victors, and from that time onward, the Middle East became a thorn in the side of both France and Britain.

The third reason had to do with Germany itself. Judged responsible for the war, she was disarmed and condemned to pay reparations. A set of fifty-year payment plans was established, and then revised and abandoned. Even though the Allies had not come close to invading

Germany, the Treaty of Versailles regarded Germany as the guilty party. That label and the crippling reparations were seen by all Germans as unfair, and the rejection of the Versailles *diktat* would be the Nazis' first priority.

Finally, there was no way that the territorial divisions stipulated in the treaty and the payment of reparations could be enforced. The United States refused to ratify the treaty, and the new League of Nations, the forerunner of the United Nations, had no means of external action. As early as 1920 the Turks rebelled against the terms of the treaty and forced a revision, called the Treaty of Lausanne. Between 1935 and World War II, Hitler did everything he could simply to abolish the treaty unilaterally. He reintroduced military service, remilitarized the left bank of the Rhine River, annexed the German border region of Bohemia, and made a claim on the Polish corridor. The spirit of the Versailles Treaty was simply anathema to the Nazis.

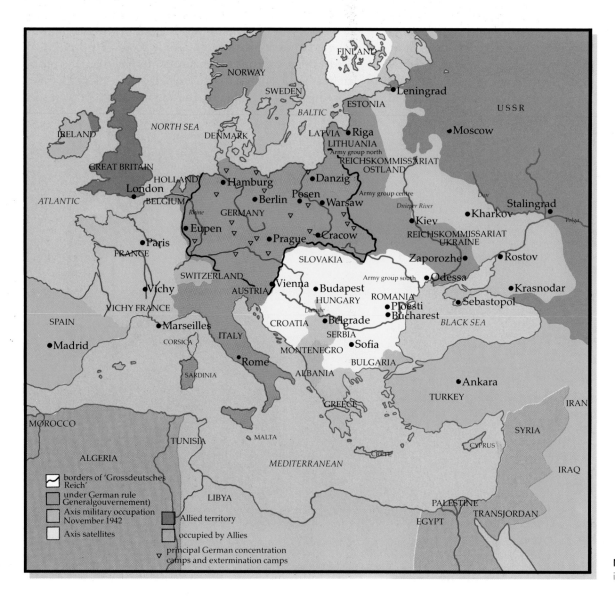

Map 17.2 World War II in Europe.

17.4 Wall Street, during the collapse of share prices on the New York Stock Exchange, 25 October 1929 (Black Friday).

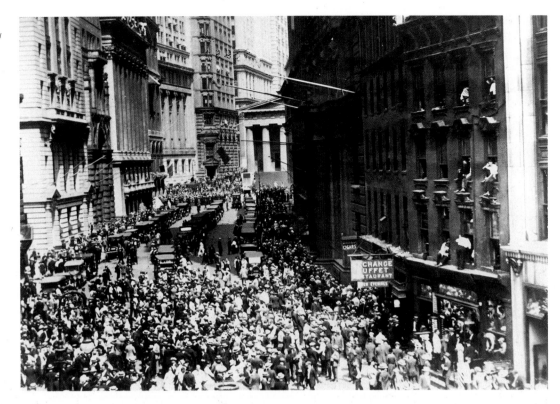

BETWEEN THE WARS
The Great Depression

The crisis that began in the United States reflected not only the deep strains and stresses in world capitalism, but also a continuation of problems occurring in Europe since the second half of the nineteenth century. Low consumer spending, currency crises, and credit and international trade problems combined in a sequence of events that accelerated after the end of the Great War. Inflation, which had been spectacular in Germany, ruined people almost everywhere. International currencies were extremely fragile, and the power of banks increased. Then, a wave of speculation on Wall Street caused the stock market to crash on 24 October 1929 (Fig. **17.4**), and stocks and shares plummeted until 1932.

The crisis spread throughout the world, and bankruptcies mushroomed in any country whose credit system had ties to the United States. The crisis in business and banking caused an industrial crisis, which, in turn, affected agriculture. Agricultural prices fell by 50 percent in the United States. In 1932 alone, forty million people were out of work and on the dole, and the lack of any social security system in many countries increased human tragedy.

Social and political unrest increased. Around the world there were protest marches and uprisings by people who could not understand a system by which, for example, corn was burned to maintain prices while children starved. Confidence in the "free enterprise" system was deeply shaken, and a call to get the economy moving at any cost reverberated around the world. New political forces came to power, and government intervention was demanded by businessmen, farmers, and workers.

Spurred on by violence in the streets, different countries adopted different solutions, depending on the depth of the crisis and the influence and make-up of the various factions in society. The United States witnessed the New Deal; Germany saw Nazism; France and Spain experienced the Popular Front. Many countries returned to protectionism, and devalued their currencies. Nothing, however, seemed to work. Wealthier nations then turned to public works, as in the United States, increases in wages, as in France, or closer links with colonies, as in Britain, while countries such as Italy, Germany, and Japan chose the path of rearmament and preparation for war, which seemed to some countries the only logical way out of the crisis.

Hitler's Conquests

On 30 January 1933, Adolf Hitler (1889–1945) became chancellor of Germany. It took less than a year for him to have his party declared the only legal one and to bring all sectors of public life into line through an orchestrated

Map 17.3 World War II in the Pacific.

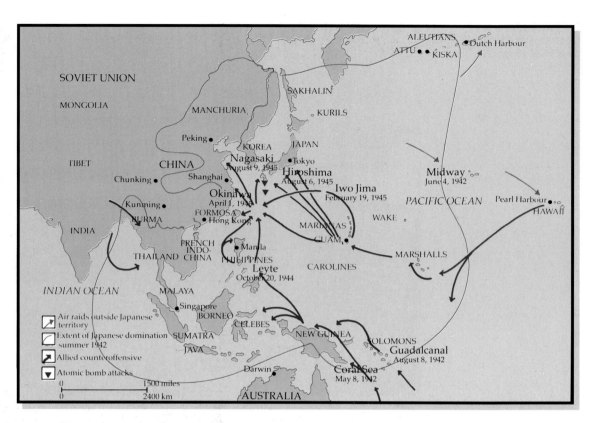

17.5 Nazi Party labor convention at Nuremberg, 7–13 September 1937.

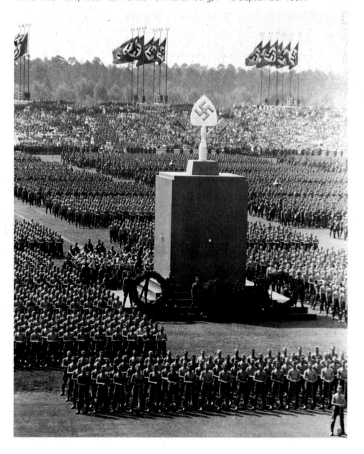

campaign of intimidation and violence (Fig. **17.5**). Once assured of compliance at home, Hitler had the means to effect the final blows against the hated Treaty of Versailles. He reintroduced compulsory military service and rearmed the Rhineland. Making such a show of strength enabled Hitler to assess the lack of resolve on the part of France and Britain and to achieve a *rapprochement* (rah-prohsh-MAHW) with the states of central and southeastern Europe. He also aided Franco's forces in the Spanish Civil War and formalized an Axis with Benito Mussolini ("Il Duce") and Italy.

Although supposedly disarmed, Germany was actually militarily superior to the rest of Europe, and Hitler was, therefore, able to effect a solution to what he saw as the "problem of Greater Germany." The first step meant annexation of lands inhabited by Germans, and in the spring of 1938 the Wehrmacht, Germany's war machine, moved into Austria, earning only a mild rebuke from Paris and London. In the classic act of "appeasement," British prime minister Neville Chamberlain negotiated the Munich Agreement, which effectively dismantled Czecho-slovakia and added the Sudetenland to Hitler's growing list of annexations to the Reich. In March 1939 Bohemia–Moravia disappeared from the map of Europe, and Germany grew accordingly. Hitler had completed the second stage of his campaign for *Lebensraum* (living room) in the east.

TECHNOLOGY: PUTTING DISCOVERY TO WORK

Computers

Early in the 1930s, a German engineer named Konrad Zuse made computers that operated in binary mode. This was called the Z1, and it was followed by Z2 and Z3, a relay computer that could perform a multiplication in three or four seconds. Hindered by the slowness of his machines, Zuse suggested to the German government that electromechanical relays should be replaced by electronic tubes, but Hitler, bent on winning the war, reduced funds to the project, which Zuse continued working on until 1944, when all his machines were destroyed in the bombing of Berlin.

The first true binary computer was made in 1939 at the Bell Laboratories in the United States by a mathematician, George R. Stibitz. Called the Model 1 Relay Computer or Complex Number Calculator, it consisted of a logical mechanism in which the data output consisted of the sum of the data entered. Telephone relays in the computer functioned in the binary "all or nothing mode"—that is, it used only the digits 1 and 0. Stibitz assembled the computer in a weekend using a few discarded relays, two lightbulbs, and fragments of a tobacco jar.

In the same year, an Iowa State College professor, John Atanasoff, applied the principles of vacuum tubes to digital calculation. The result, designed to solve the complex equations used in physics, became known as the ABC (Atanasoff Berry Computer). However, neither Atanasoff nor Iowa State registered a patent; thus, the invention of the tube computer was long attributed to J. Presper Eckert for his ENIAC (Electronic Numerical Integrator and Calculator).

The first fully automatic calculator was Harvard Mark 1, at that time called the IBM Automatic Sequence Controlled Calculator (Fig. **17.6**). Financed by IBM and developed by Howard Aiken of Harvard University, it weighed five metric tons and contained 500 miles (805 kilometers) of wire. It included a clock to synchronize sequences and registers—that is, a device used by the computer to store information for high-speed access.

17.6 The Harvard Mark I calculator (1944) from the IBM Corporation.

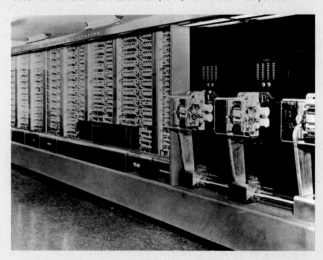

When Hitler turned toward Poland, however, neither Paris nor London could retreat for fear of losing further face with the threatened smaller countries of Europe. Britain joined France in guarantees to Poland, and the Soviets were also included. Poland balked at the prospect of Soviet forces within its borders, and the negotiations ground on. Meanwhile, talks began in Moscow that led to a secret Nazi–Soviet non-aggression pact, which effectively divided Poland between Germany and the Soviet Union. Hitler offered an agreement to Britain in which they would divide the world between them, but the British refused. On 1 September 1939, Hitler invaded Poland, and war again engulfed Europe. Three years later, Japan attacked Pearl Harbor, and World War II reached around the globe.

WORLD WAR II

Europe and Africa

After success in Poland, Germany launched a *Blitzkrieg* (BLITS-kreeg; "lightning war") in the spring of 1940, in which it seized the Danish straits, the Norwegian coast, the Netherlands, Belgium, and France in a period of six weeks. After heavily bombing Britain, Hitler turned his focus to the Mediterranean and the Balkans. In a fateful move, Operation Barbarossa, the German invasion of the Soviet Union, began on 22 June 1941. Despite the tremendous amount of territory involved and the severity of the Russian winter, German forces continued to advance until November 1942, when they had reached the Caucasus Mountains and the River Volga.

Depending on a number of factors—for example the Nazis' racial doctrines that led to the Holocaust—conquered areas suffered under varying degrees of oppression and economic exploitation. Millions of individuals, including some six million Jews, died in the Reich's concentration camps.

At the end of 1942, fortunes began to change. British and American forces landed in North Africa, and British Field Marshal Montgomery won an important victory at El Alamein. At the same time, Hitler's General Paulus was forced to surrender at Stalingrad. The war on several fronts gave the Allies superiority, and Hitler's decision to break his treaty with Stalin and invade Russia ultimately proved catastrophic. Using north Africa as a base, the Allies invaded Italy and brought about the fall of Hitler's henchman, the Italian dictator Benito Mussolini. The Red Army began counterattacking, and the draining of German forces to the eastern front left Hitler vulnerable to a European invasion that commenced on D-Day, 6 June 1944. By the fall of that year, Germany's Fortress Europe was crumbling, and many of its allies had been forced to sign armistices.

Hitler's scientists had made enormous strides in rocketry, and the unmanned rocket-bombs the V1 and V2 had rained terror on Britain from Belgium. However, even these, and German counteroffensives in the Ardennes and Budapest, could not halt the Allied advance, and Germany collapsed from both east and west as the Allies and Soviets headed through Germany toward Berlin. On 30 April 1945, Hitler committed suicide in his Berlin bunker. The task of negotiating with the Allies fell to Admiral Doenitz, and unconditional surrender occurred on 8 May 1945.

The Pacific

The Japanese attack on Pearl Harbor on 7 December 1941 illustrates the eagerness with which the Japanese approached war with the United States, which had opposed the Japanese invasion of China. In addition, the Japanese were determined to seize the resources of Indochina and the Dutch East Indies after their rulers had fallen to Germany in 1940. In moves as swift and decisive as the German *Blitzkrieg*, the Japanese swept through the eastern Pacific and threatened India and Australia. Perhaps expecting the United States to seek a peaceful solution, the Japanese got, instead, an all-out response that included the bombing of Tokyo as early as 1942. Decisive United States' victories at Midway and the Coral Sea weakened the Japanese forces to the point that the overextended commu-

nications and forces of the "Empire of the Sun" were unable to prevent a three-year pincer movement, as American forces strategically leap-frogged Japanese concentrations and worked their way toward the Philippines. Japanese resistance was stubborn and fanatic, however: *Kamikaze* (kah-mih-KAH-zee) pilots committed suicide by crashing their planes into American ships, and ground forces fought to the death rather than be dishonored by surrender. At the beginning of 1945, American forces had inched their way to Iwo Jima and Okinawa, where they won strategic victories and gained bases from which bombers could reach Japan for saturation bombing, and ships could intercept supplies heading to Japan.

Nonetheless, Japan refused to surrender, and it still held Indochina, the Dutch East Indies, and the coast of China. The American high command did not expect to be able to launch an invasion of Japan until 1946, and believed that such an invasion would cost the lives of a million American men. Resolution came when President Truman decided to drop two atomic bombs: one on Hiroshima on 6 August 1945, and one on Nagasaki on 9 August 1945. In the meantime, Russia entered the war in Asia and invaded the Japanese-held areas of Manchuria and Korea. Emperor Hirohito intervened personally and forced his ministers and military leaders to accept surrender. The surrender document was signed on the deck of the battleship *Missouri* in the Bay of Tokyo on 2 September 1945. World War II had ended.

SCIENCE AND WAR

The possibilities of a nuclear bomb and its world-changing consequences came as a result of a number of factors and individuals. In the 1930s, the situation across the world was, as we have already discussed, in flux, and in different parts of Europe and in America, physicists worked separately, but aware of each other's progress, to find ways to split the atom and so create large quantities of energy. Later, during World War II, in Germany and the United States, these scientists worked feverishly against each other to create an atomic bomb.

The British scientist Sir James Chadwick discovered the neutron in 1932. He was able to split this electrically charged neutral particle in the atom by bombarding it with alpha rays from radium. The Italian-born Enrico Fermi (FAIR-mee) continued the work on nuclear fission, and was able to split uranium. In 1938 Fermi won the Nobel Prize, and was sent to Sweden by Mussolini. However, Fermi defected to the United States, where he continued his work to create an atomic pile that could sustain a chain reaction and create a constant flow of energy.

In 1939 three physicists, including Albert Einstein, wrote to President Roosevelt to warn of Germany's progress toward developing a nuclear reactor. As a result, the United States government supported Fermi's research, and in 1942, the first nuclear reaction occurred. It lasted twenty-eight minutes. From that point, a team of scientists, including Fermi, worked at Los Alamos, New Mexico, and by August 1945, Fermi's nuclear reactor had become the world's most destructive bomb. After the war, Fermi's discovery was harnessed to create energy, nuclear devices for medicine, and other peaceful applications.

PHILOSOPHY
Pragmatism

Philosophy had lost credit in the nineteenth century. Unlike their former colleagues in the sciences, philosophers came to be seen as useless appendages to social progress. People began to believe that sensory and intellectual powers could not solve the problems posed by philosophy.

Early in the twentieth century, a reorientation occurred. A new philosophy, *pragmatism*, emerged in America, championed by John Dewey (1859–1952). Pragmatism abandoned the search for final answers to great problems, such as the existence of immortality, and instead contented itself with more modest goals in the realm of social experience. Pragmatism pursued such issues as what moral and aesthetic values might be in a democratic, industrialized society, and how one might achieve the highest personal fulfillment through education.

Dewey's concept of "art as experience" is enlightening, challenging, and sometimes frustrating. "Experience" is fundamental to Dewey's philosophy in all areas, but it appears most significant in his philosophy of aesthetics. Human experience, as interpreted by his aesthetics, presents a significant challenge to philosophy. According to Dewey, the philosopher needs to go to aesthetic experience in order to understand experience in general. Dewey is building on Hegel's concept of truth as a whole here, and he shares Schelling's belief that aesthetic intuition is "the organ of philosophy," and so aesthetics is "the crown of philosophy." For the pragmatist, the criterion for truth consists of the workability of an idea. If an idea works, it is true. The truth of an idea, then, can be tested by its consequences; an idea void of results is inconsequential, thus meaningless. Pragmatism ignores ideas that are so metaphysical that they contain no practical value. If an idea has no *cash value*, as the philosopher William James put it—that is, no practical aspect or useful consequential element—then it must be repudiated.

Existentialism

Existentialism is a philosophical doctrine that insists on the actual existence of individuals as basic and important—that is, rather than relying on theories and abstractions. The idea itself is relatively ancient, but it was shaped into a modern statement by Sören Kierkegaard (SUR-en KYAIR-kuh-gawr; 1813–55). Philosophers such as Karl Jaspers and Martin Heidegger (HY-deg-ur) worked with the idea, and it can be seen in the writings of Feodor Dostoyevski, for example (see Chapter 16), and Franz Kafka (see p. 550). Existentialism became associated with a literary school in the 1940s with the writings of Jean-Paul Sartre (SAHR-truh) among others (see p. 569).

The central doctrine of existentialism is that human beings are what they make of themselves. They are not predestined by God, society, or biology, but have free will and the responsibility that goes with it. If people refuse to make choices or allow outside forces to determine them, they are regarded as contemptible. Existentialists stress humankind's basic elements, such as the irrationality of unconscious and subconscious acts, and they consider life to be dynamic and in a constant state of flux. Human life is not an abstraction but a series of consecutive movements. Existentialists insist on the concrete rather than the abstract, on existence itself rather than the idea of existence. Christian existentialism holds that the positive act of the will is a matter of religious choice and must ultimately lead to God.

Existentialism inspired a large body of imaginative literature, and the existentialist writers are characterized by their concern with "being" which contrasts not only with "knowing" but also with abstract concepts, which cannot fully capture what is individual and specific. Jean-Paul Sartre (1905–80) illustrates and provides us a transition into the Literature section which, in this chapter, we have divided into genres rather than styles.

As a student, Sartre formed with Simone de Beauvoir, another important existentialist writer, a romantic and intellectual union that remained a partnership for life. His first novel, *La Nausée* ("Nausea") was published in 1938. In it, he used the *phenomenological* method, which proposes careful, unprejudiced description rather than deduction. His later novel *L'Etre et le néant* ("Being and Nothingness"; 1943) more fully expressed his philosophical system.

Sartre places human consciousness, or no-thingness, in opposition to being, or thingness. Consciousness, as not-matter, escapes determinism and thus is the source of freedom. With freedom comes the responsibility for giving meaning to human endeavor, which otherwise remains futile.

LITERATURE

Fiction

Between 1914 and 1939, the novel came to the fore as a literary medium. The economic, moral, and intellectual chaos of the interwar period required complex literary forms to express it. The novel—"fiction in prose of a certain extent," as the French critic Abel Chevally and, later, the British writer E.M. Forster called it—proved adaptable enough to handle a multitude of ideas and experiences, and thus became a catch-all form, which replaced tighter mediums of expression such as the drama, the essay, and the epic poem. Improving standards of education created a new reading public that was receptive to fiction "of a certain extent." In an age of revolt against old certainties, the novel seemed immune to rules and restrictions.

As a result, subject matter was enriched, and so was technique. Novelists now challenged the traditional forms of the novel as well as traditional concepts of time and space. Edouard, a character in *The Counterfeiters* (1925) by André Gide (zheed; 1869–1951) says: "My novel hasn't got a subject . . . 'slice of life,' the naturalistic school used to say. The great defect of that school is that it always cuts its slice in the same direction; in time, lengthwise. Why not in breadth? Or in depth? As for me, I should not like to cut it at all. Police notwithstanding, I should like to put everything in my novel."

The interwar period produced an Irish novelist of extraordinary quality, James Joyce (1882–1941). Like Gide's Edouard, Joyce in *Ulysses* did "put everything in [his] novel." In this case, however, the police *were* a factor to be reckoned with. The serial publication of *Ulysses* in the United States was stopped by the American courts, although the finished work appeared in Paris in 1922. It was banned by the British authorities until 1941. Using STREAM OF CONSCIOUSNESS methods new to fiction, Joyce spins out actions and thoughts in great detail. The whole novel is the account of a single day in the life of Leopold Bloom. While the overall form is epic, virtually all other conventions of the novel are broken down, parodied, and recombined. Joyce also explored the unconscious mind in greater depth in *Finnegans Wake* (1939), a work of dazzling originality and great difficulty, in which the English language is replaced by a kind of polyglot punning.

The novels of D.H. Lawrence (1885–1930), such as *Sons and Lovers* and *Women in Love*, were more traditional in technique. His rejection of contemporary mass culture and the materialistic society that produced it, together with his messianic faith in "natural" (which included "sexual") things, links him strongly with the Romantics of the nineteenth century. The novels and short stories of Virginia Woolf (1882–1941) painstakingly explore the inner landscape of feeling and emotion, particularly that of women.

Woolf, who committed suicide during World War II, was one of the most gifted and innovative of the stream of consciousness writers. Her explorations are intensely subjective, and she worked toward high condensation and glimpses of moments of experience rather than attempting the illusion of a total picture. She advocated freedom for the novelist to capture the "shower of atoms" and the discontinuity of experience, and she pictured men and women as enclosed in their "envelope" of consciousness from birth to death. In *A Room of One's Own* (1929) she spoke out for women's liberation.

The German writer Thomas Mann (mahn; 1874–1955) created a richly symbolic picture of the fatal contradictions that beset European intellectuals between the wars in his masterpiece, *The Magic Mountain* (1924). The Austrian novelist Franz Kafka (KAHF-kuh; 1883–1924) lived and wrote in Prague, of the Austro-Hungarian Empire. Although he finished law school, he did not practice, but took a minor clerical position in the department of workmen's compensation, which made him tremendously aware of the bureaucracy and red tape in which life can become entangled. He never developed the ability to assert himself (writing but never publishing), and he could not bring himself to marry even though he was engaged several times. His early death resulted from tuberculosis, and he directed his executor to destroy all his manuscripts. Instead, his executor published them. Kafka never finished any of his novels, but even in their incomplete state, they captured the fancy of Europeans caught in a world of rising dictatorships. *The Trial* (1925) and *The Castle* (1926) portray an incomprehensible world of authority—for example, when the hero finds himself unexpectedly arrested. Unlike the stream of consciousness writers, Kafka explored the intangible inner world as if it were an outward reality. It is never clear whether what takes place in the story is actual reality or merely part of the character's fantasy. He portrays guilt-obsessed people who trip themselves up and are never aware of their identity or relation to authority.

What all these writers had in common was a certain dissatisfaction with their times and a sense of alienation from them. In America, the response was different. Powerful, vital novels of social realism began to appear. William Cuthbert Faulkner (1897–1962) wrote both novels and short stories, and in 1929, he published his most admired work, *The Sound and the Fury*, in which he made use of the stream of consciousness technique. His methods of narration included moving from the present to the past and presenting two or more seemingly unrelated stories juxta-

PROFILE

Langston Hughes (1902–67)

Langston Hughes is often referred to as the "poet laureate of Harlem." He portrayed the life of the ordinary African American in the United States, and his poetry is particularly meaningful to young people. He speaks of the basic qualities of life—love, hate, aspirations, and despair—yet he writes with a faith in humanity in general. He interprets all life as it is experienced in the real world as well as in idealism. At the same time, some of his work contains militant ideas that carry broad socio-political implications. He struggled within himself between what he wanted to write and what his audience expected him to write.

He was born in Joplin, Missouri, and soon after his birth his parents separated, his father, embittered by racial discrimina-tion, moving to Mexico where he practiced law and pursued other business ventures. Langston was raised by his mother and grand-mother. After his grandmother's death, he and his mother moved frequently, finally living in Cleveland, where he finished high

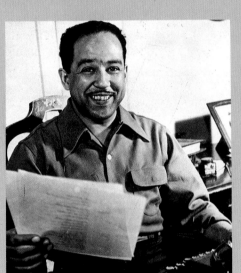

17.7 Langston Hughes (1902–67).

school. An unhappy year with his father in Mexico fol-lowed, as did a year at Columbia University. Then he traveled in West Africa and Europe, finished a degree at Lincoln University in 1929, and settled in Harlem, which he called the "great dark city."

Hughes received considerable attention as a poet as early as 1921 with his poem "The Negro Speaks of Rivers." His poetry and his involvement in social causes often intertwined, but although he is sometimes identified with the political left, his works often defy political interpretation. He experimented with numerous lit-erary forms, and his collected works comprise thirty-two books, including poetry, short stories, an autobiography, drama, and history. His fictional character Jesse B. Simple, revealing the uncensored thoughts of a native young urban youth, became a legend among African Americans. In his novel *Not Without Laughter*, —his first prose work—Hughes created a brilliant portrayal of an African American's passage into manhood.

posed against each other. He wrote more than twenty novels based on characters in the imaginary Southern Yoknapatawpha County.

Ernest Hemingway (1898–1961), American novelist, short-story writer, and Nobel Prize winner, erased the dividing line between journalism and literature. His style is characterized by the terse representation of simple acts, sparse dialogue, and understatement of emotion. His themes emphasize the sensual side of life, with overassertive males and two-dimensional women who exist for the pleasure of men.

The period from 1870 to 1920 produced a profound change in Native American culture and circumstances. Confinement to reservations and an increase in formal education changed both the Indian way of life and its tradi-tion of oral transmission of culture. The perception of

Indian and white cultures as being incompatible was a frequent issue for both cultures, and these conflicts were a common preoccupation and central theme for Indian writ-ers, many of whom were "half-breeds" and the products of the white man's education. "Half-breeds" were popular subjects in the nineteenth and early twentieth centuries, and writers who focused on transculturation give us a profound insight into the Native American mind.

Gertrude Bonnin, a South Dakota Yankton Sioux, who had a full-blooded mother and an Anglo-American father, wrote under the penname of Red Bird (Zitkala-Sa). The mixed-blood protagonist of "The Soft-Hearted Sioux," a short story published in 1901, reflects the conflicts of the Native American caught between cultures. Unable to func-tion in either world, he is given no alternative but to face a violent death. Here is a short excerpt:

On the day after my father's death, having led my mother to the camp of the medicine-man, I gave myself up to those who were searching for the murderer of the paleface.

They bound me hand and foot. Here in this cell I was placed four days ago.

The shrieking winter winds have followed me higher. Rattling the bars, they howl unceasingly: "Your soft heart! your soft heart will see me die before you bring me food!" Hark! something is clanking the chain on the door. It is being opened. From the dark night without a black figure crosses the threshold. . . . It is the guard. He tells me that tomorrow I must die. In his stern face I laugh aloud. I do not fear death.

Yet I wonder who shall come to welcome me in the realm of strange sight. Will the loving Jesus grant me pardon and give my soul a soothing sleep? or will my warrior father greet me and receive me as his son? Will my spirit fly upward to a happy heaven? or shall I sink into the bottomless pit, an outcast from a God of infinite love?

Soon, soon I shall know, for now I see the east is growing red. My heart is strong. My face is calm. My eyes are dry and eager for new scenes. My hands hang quietly at my side. Serene and brave, my soul awaits the men to perch me on the gallows for another flight. I go.[1]

Poetry

The Negro Speaks of Rivers
Langston Hughes

I've known rivers:
I've known rivers ancient as the world and older
    than the flow of human blood in human veins.

My soul has grown deep like the rivers.

I bathed in the Euphrates when dawns were young.
I built my hut near the Congo and it lulled me to
    sleep.
I looked upon the Nile and raised the pyramids

    above it.
I heard the singing of the Mississippi when Abe
    Lincoln went down to New Orleans, and I've
    seen its muddy bosom turn all golden in the
    sunset.

I've known rivers:
Ancient, dusky rivers.

My soul has grown deep like the rivers.

Bold new directions were also taken in poetry. Among the numerous important poets of the early twentieth century we must certainly mention the Irish William Butler Yeats (1865–1939) and the American Robert Frost (1874–1963), both of whom brought their own individual touch to an age of ever-expanding and experimental styles.

The most famous work of T.S. Eliot (1888–1965), *The Waste Land* (1922), marked the full emergence of modernism in poetry. Here Eliot cast aside traditional meters and rhymes in favor of free verse. This new kind of writing needs to be read with great care if it is to make any sense at all. The *Cantos* of Ezra Pound (1885–1972) and the works of e. e. cummings took this approach even further. Not all poets, however, responded to the complexity of their times by pursuing this strenuous route. W.H. Auden (1907–73), for example, reflected the mood of the 1930s in rhymed, epigrammatic satirical poetry that harked back to the eighteenth century.

The African American poet Langston Hughes caught with sharp immediacy and intensity the humor, pathos, irony, and humiliation of being black in America. As early as 1921, Hughes received considerable attention with his poem "The Negro Speaks of Rivers," written the summer after his graduation from high school.

THE VISUAL ARTS AND ARCHITECTURE

Abstraction

The phrase "dissolving image" describes tendencies in nineteenth-century visual art to move away from recognizable, or objective, reality. This is what most people think of when they describe "modern" art as ABSTRACT art. A more precise term, however, is NONREPRESENTATIONAL art. All art is abstract, of course—that is, it is not the real thing itself, but a representation of something made from a distance, literally, "standing apart from it." Thus, paintings, sculptures, plays, and symphonies are abstractions, regardless of how "realistic" they are.

Abstract or nonrepresentational art, however, contains minimal reference to natural objects—that is, objects in the world we perceive through our senses. In many ways, abstract art stands in contrast to impressionism and expressionism in that the observer can read little or nothing in the painting of the artist's feelings for anything outside the painting. Abstract art seeks to explore the expressive qualities of formal design elements and materials in their own right. These elements are assumed to stand apart from subject matter. The aesthetic theory underlying abstract art maintains that beauty can exist in form alone and that no other quality is needed. Many painters explored these approaches, and several subgroups, such as *de Stijl* (duh styl), the suprematists, the constructivists, and the Bauhaus painters, have pursued its goals. The works of Piet Mondrian (peet MOHN-dree-ahn) and Kasimir

17.8 Kasimir Malevich, *Suprematist Composition: White on White*, c. 1918. Oil on canvas, 31¼ × 31¼ ins (79.4 × 79.4 cm). Museum of Modern Art, New York. Photo: © 1998 Museum of Modern Art, New York.

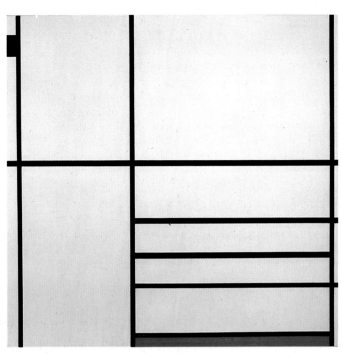

17.9 Piet Mondrian, *Composition in White, Black, and Red*, 1936. Oil on canvas, 3 ft 4¼ ins × 3 ft 5 ins (1.02 × 1.04 m). Museum of Modern Art, New York (Gift of the Advisory Committee). Photo: © 1998 Museum of Modern Art, New York.

Malevich (mahl-YAY-vich) illustrate many of the principles at issue in abstract painting.

A work such as *Suprematist Composition: White on White* (Fig. **17.8**) by Kasimir Malevich (1878–1935) seems simple but confusing, even by abstract standards. For Malevich, such works go beyond reducing painting to its basic common denominator of oil on canvas. Rather, he sought basic pictorial elements that could "communicate the most profound expressive reality."

Mondrian (1872–1944) believed that straight lines and right angles represented the fundamental principles of life. A vertical line signified activity, vitality, and life, while a horizontal line signified rest, tranquility, and death. The crossing of the two in a right angle expressed the highest possible tension between these forces, positive and negative. Mondrian's exploration of this theory in *Composition in White, Black, and Red* (Fig. **17.9**) is typical of all his linear compositions. The planes of the painting are close to the surface of the canvas, creating, in essence, the shallowest space possible. The palette is restricted to three hues. Even the edges of the canvas take on expressive possibilities as they provide additional points of interaction between lines. Mondrian believed that he could create "the equivalence of reality" and make the "absolute appear in the relativity of time and space" by keeping visual elements in a state of constant tension.

Dada

The horrors of World War I caused tremendous disillusionment. One expression of this was the birth of a movement called "dada." (Considerable debate exists about when and how the word "dada"—it is French for "hobbyhorse"—came to be chosen. The dadaists themselves accepted it as two nonsense syllables, like one of a baby's first words.) During the years 1915 and 1916, many artists gathered in neutral capitals in Europe to express their disgust at the direction Western societies were taking. Dada was thus a political protest, and in many places the dadaists produced more left-wing propaganda than art.

By 1916, a few works of art began to appear, many of them FOUND OBJECTS and experiments in which chance played an important role. For example, Jean Arp (1888–1966) produced collages that he made by dropping haphazardly cut pieces of paper onto a surface and pasting them down the way they fell. Max Ernst (1891–1976) juxtaposed strange, unrelated items to produce unexplainable phenomena. This use of conventional items placed in circumstances that alter their traditional meanings is characteristic of dadaist art. Irrationality, meaninglessness, and harsh, mechanical images are typical effects, as shown in *Woman, Old Man, and Flower* (Fig. **17.10**). This is a

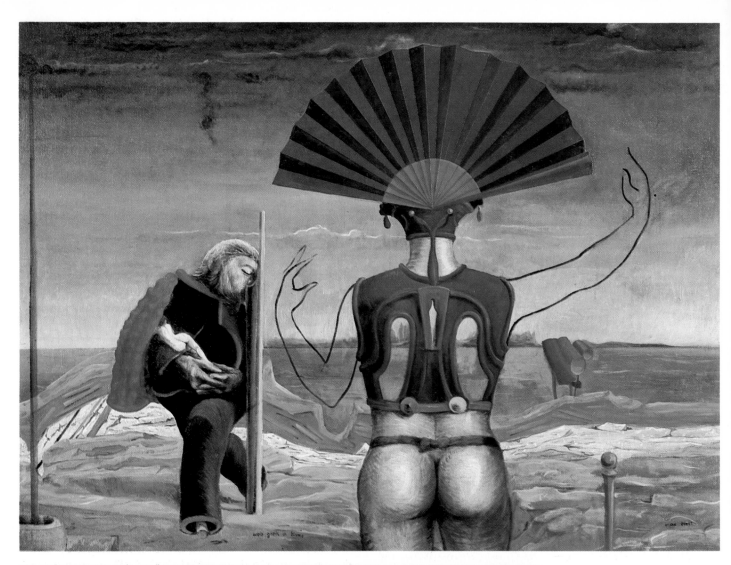

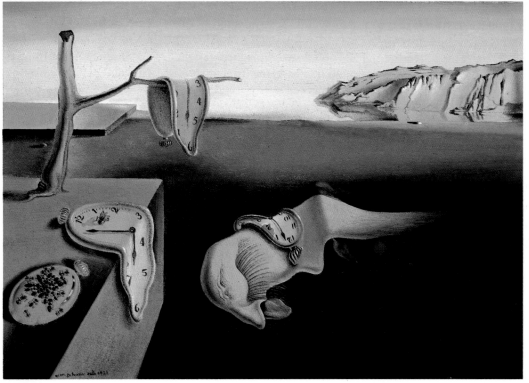

17.10 Max Ernst, *Woman, Old Man, and Flower*, 1923–4. Oil on canvas, 3 ft 2 ins × 4 ft 3¹/₄ ins (96.5 × 130.2 cm). Museum of Modern Art, New York. Purchase. Photo: © 1998 Museum of Modern Art, New York. © ADAGP, Paris and DACS, London 1999.

17.11 Salvador Dalí, *The Persistence of Memory*, 1931. Oil on canvas, 9¹/₂ × 13 ins (24 × 33 cm). Museum of Modern Art, New York. Given anonymously. Photo: © 1998 Museum of Modern Art, New York. © Salvador Dalí–Foundation Gala–Salvador Dalí/DACS 1999.

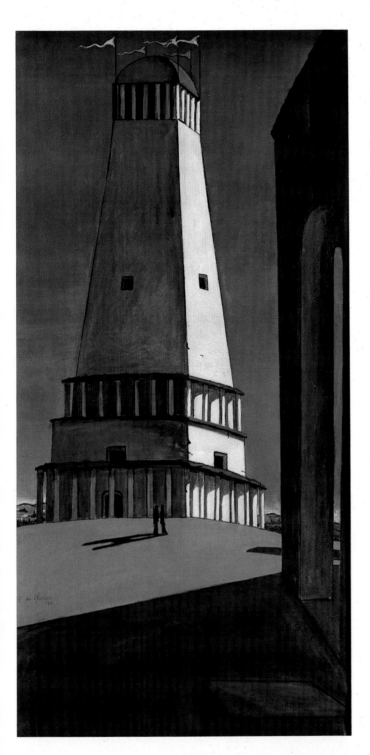

17.12 Giorgio de Chirico, *The Nostalgia of the Infinite*, c. 1913–14, dated 1911 on painting. Oil on canvas, 4 ft 5¼ ins × 2 ft 1½ ins (135.2 × 64.8 cm). Museum of Modern Art, New York. Photo: © 1998 Museum of Modern Art, New York. © DACS 1999.

nonsensical world in which pseudo-human forms with their bizarre features and proportions suggest a malevolent unreality. Dada emphasizes protest and leads to the idea that one element of the arts must be to shock. Perhaps the most vivid exponent of Dada was Marcel Duchamp, whose proto-dadaist expressions of futurism we have already seen in *Nude Descending a Staircase* (see Fig. **16.27**).

Fantasy and Surrealism

As the work of Sigmund Freud became popular, artists became fascinated by the subconscious mind. By 1924, a surrealist manifesto stated some specific connections between the subconscious mind and painting. Surrealist works were thought to be created by "pure psychic automatism." Its advocates saw surrealism as a way to discover the basic realities of psychic life by automatic associations. Supposedly, a dream could be transferred directly from the unconscious mind of the painter to canvas without control or conscious interruption.

The metaphysical fantasies of Giorgio de Chirico (KEE-ree-koh; 1888–1978) have surrealist qualities. In works such as *The Nostalgia of the Infinite* (Fig. **17.12**), strange objects are irrationally juxtaposed: they come together as in a dream. These bizarre works reflect a world that human beings do not control. In them, "there is only what I see with my eyes open, and even better, closed."

Surrealism is probably more accurately represented by the paintings of Salvador Dalí (dah-LEE), however. Dalí (1904–89) called his works, such as *The Persistence of Memory* (Fig. **17.11**), "hand-colored photographs of the subconscious," and the almost photographic detail of his work, coupled with the nightmarish relationships of the objects he pictures, has a forceful impact. The whole idea of time is destroyed in these "soft watches" (as they were called by those who first saw this work) hanging limply and crawling with ants. And yet the images are strangely fascinating, perhaps in the way we are fascinated by the world of our dreams.

Perhaps the most celebrated female painter of the early twentieth century was the Mexican Frida Kahlo (1907–54). Her works (more than one third are self-portraits) reflect what she called the "two great accidents" of her life: a bus crash that left her crippled at age eighteen and her marriage to Mexican mural painter Diego Rivera (see p. 559). Her paintings are studies in pain and suffering, both physical and mental. The lingering results of her accident required more than thirty surgeries and ultimately the loss of her right leg. She suffered repeated miscarriages and was never able to bear a child. But her art also reflects Mexican folk culture and her deep feeling for the power

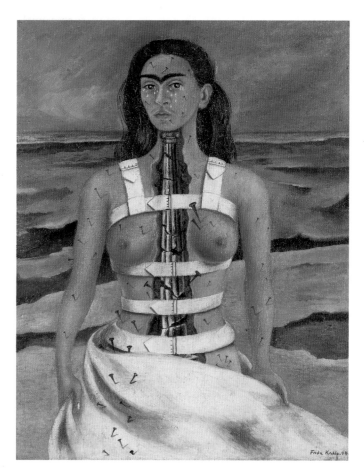

17.13 Frida Kahlo, *The Broken Column*, 1940. Oil on canvas 15³/₄ × 12¹/₄ ins (40 × 31 cm). Museo Dolores Olmedo Patiño, Mexico.

and beauty of folk art. In *The Broken Column* (Fig. **17.13**), we sense a myriad of emotions, as she appears as both sufferer and savior.

American Painting

Until the early twentieth century, painting in the United States had done little more than adapt European trends to the American experience. Strong and vigorous American painting emerged in the early twentieth century, however, and it encompasses so many people and styles that we will have to be content with only a few representative examples.

An early group called "the Eight" appeared in 1908 as painters of the American "scene." They were Robert Henri, George Luks, John Sloan, William Glackens, Everett Shinn, Ernest Lawson, Maurice Prendergast, and Arthur B. Davies. These painters shared a warm and somewhat sentimental view of American city life, and they

presented it both with and without social criticism. Although uniquely American in tone, the works of the Eight often revealed European influences, for example, of impressionism.

The modern movement in America owed much to the tremendous impact of the International Exhibition of Modern Art (called the Armory Show) in 1913. There, rather shocking European modernist works, such as Duchamp's *Nude Descending a Staircase, No. 2* (see Fig. **16.27**) and the cubist work of Braque and Picasso (see Fig. **16.26**), were first revealed to the American public.

Georgia O'Keeffe (1887–1986), an American, proved to be one of the most original artists of the century. Her imagery draws on a wide variety of objects that she abstracts in a uniquely personal way. She takes, for example, an animal skull and transforms it into a form of absolute simplicity and beauty. In *Dark Abstraction* (Fig. **17.14**) an organic form becomes an exquisite landscape which, despite the modest size of the painting, appears monumental. Her lines flow gracefully upward and outward with a skillful blending of colors and rhythmic

17.14 Georgia O'Keeffe, *Dark Abstraction*, 1924. Oil on canvas, 24⁷/₈ × 20⁷/₈ ins (63 × 53 cm). St Louis Art Museum (Gift of Charles E. and Mary Merrill). © ARS, New York and DACS, London 1999.

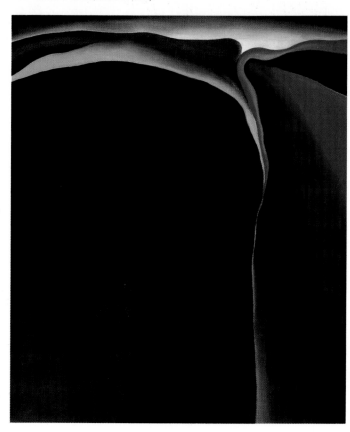

grace. The painting expresses a mystical reverence for nature, whatever we take its subject matter to be. O'Keeffe creates a sense of reality that takes us beyond our usual perceptions into something much deeper.

Precisionists, such as Stuart Davis (1894–1964), took real objects and arranged them into abstract groupings, as in *Lucky Strike* (Fig. **17.15**). These paintings often use the strong, vibrant colors of commerical art (and are much like those of pop art in the 1960s). At every turn, this subject matter surprises us. At first we wonder at the frame within the frame. The gray textured border provides a strong color contrast to the interior form, which, were it not for the curved form at the top, would look very much like a window. The curve is repeated in reverse near the bottom of the picture, and the slight slant of these two opposing lines is encountered by the reverse slant of the white and black arcs. The strength of this work lies in the juxtaposition of complementary colors, rectilinear and curvilinear forms, and opposing values, that is, lights and darks.

The *realist* tradition continued in the works of Grant Wood (1892–1942). The painting *American Gothic* (Fig. **17.16**) is a wonderful celebration of the simple, hardwork- ing people of America's heartland. There is a lyric spirituality behind the façade of this down-home illustration. The elongated forms are pulled up together into a pointed arch which encapsulates the Gothic window of the farmhouse and escapes the frame of the painting through the lightning rod (just as the Gothic spire released the spirituality of the earth into heaven at its tip). Rural American reverence for home and labor is celebrated here with gentle humor.

The Harlem Renaissance

From 1919 to 1925, Harlem, a neighborhood in upper Manhattan, became the international capital of African American culture. "Harlem was in vogue," wrote the poet Langston Hughes. African American painters, sculptors, musicians, poets, and novelists joined in a remarkable artistic outpouring. Some critics at the time attacked this work as isolationist and conventional, and the quality of the Harlem Renaissance still stirs debate.

The movement took up several themes: glorification of the black American's African heritage, the tradition of black folklore, and the daily life of black people. In exploring these subjects, Harlem Renaissance artists broke with

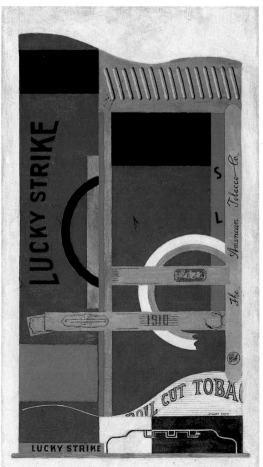

17.15 (*left*) Stuart Davis, *Lucky Strike*, 1921. Oil on canvas, 33¼ × 18 ins (84.5 × 45.7 cm). Museum of Modern Art, New York (Gift of the American Tobacco Company, Inc.). Photo: © 1998 Museum of Modern Art, New York. © Estate of Stuart Davis/VAGA, New York/DACS, London 1999.

17.16 (*right*) Grant Wood, *American Gothic*, 1930. Oil on beaver board, 29⅞ × 24⅞ ins (79 × 63.2 cm). Friends of American Art Collection, courtesy of The Art Institute of Chicago and VAGA. Photo: © 1998 The Art Institute of Chicago.

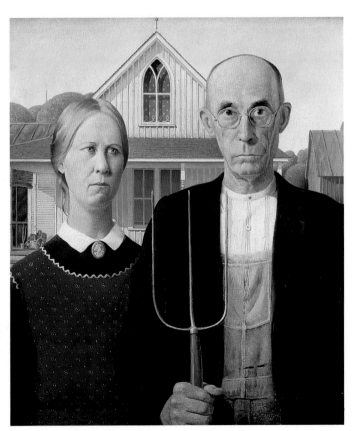

previous African American artistic traditions. But they celebrated black history and culture and defined a visual vocabulary for black Americans.

African American intellectuals such as W.E.B. Du Bois (doo-BOYS; 1868–1963), Alain Locke (1886–1954), and Charles Spurgeon spearheaded the movement. Among the notable artists were social documentarian and photographer James van der Zee (1886–1983), painter William Henry Johnson (1901–70), painter Palmer Hayden (1890–1973), painter Aaron Douglas (1899–1979), and sculptor Meta Vaux Warrick Fuller (1877–1968).

Aaron Douglas was arguably the foremost painter of the Harlem Renaissance. In his highly stylized work, he explores a palette of muted tones. Douglas was particularly well known for his illustrations and cover designs for many books by African American writers. His portrait of *Aalta* (Fig. **17.17**) is warm and relaxed, and its color and line express dignity, elegance, and stability. *Aspects of the Negro Life* (Fig. **17.18**), at the New York Public Library's Cullen branch, documents the emergence of an African American identity in four panels. The first portrays the African background in images of music, dance, and sculpture. The next two panels bring to life slavery and emancipation in the American South and the flight of blacks to the cities of the North. The fourth panel returns to the theme of music. The master of many styles, Douglas was extremely effective in his realistic work.

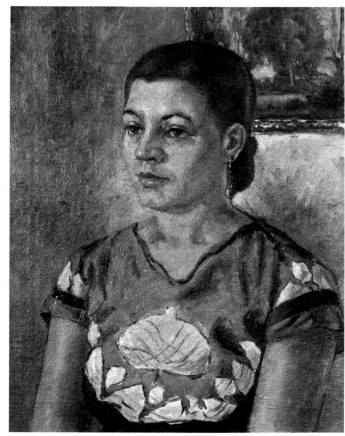

17.17 Aaron Douglas, *Aalta*, 1936. Oil on canvas, 18 × 23 ins (45.7 × 58.4 cm). African American Collection of Art, The Carl Van Vechten Gallery of Fine Arts, Fisk University, Nashville, Tennessee.

PROFILE

Georgia O'Keeffe (1887–1986)

American painter Georgia O'Keeffe was born near Sun Prairie, Wisconsin. She grew up on the family farm in Wisconsin before deciding that she wanted to be an artist. She spent 1904–5 at the Art Institute of Chicago and 1907–8 at the Art Students League of New York, then supported herself by doing commercial art and teaching at various schools and colleges in Texas and the South. Her break came in 1916, when her drawings were discovered and exhibited by the famous American photographer Alfred Stieglitz, who praised and promoted her work vigorously. They maintained a lifelong relationship, marrying in 1924, and O'Keeffe became the subject of hundreds of Stieglitz's photographs. After meeting Stieglitz, O'Keeffe spent most of her time in New York, with occasional periods in New Mexico, but she moved permanently to New Mexico after her husband's death in 1946.

Her early pictures lacked originality, but by the 1920s she developed a uniquely individualistic style. Many of her subjects included enlarged views of skulls and other animal bones, flowers, plants, shells, rocks, mountains, and other natural forms. Her images have a mysterious quality about them, with clear color washes and a suggestive, psychological symbolism that often suggests eroticism. Her rhythms undulate gracefully. The works bridge the gap between abstraction and biomorphic form (see Fig. **17.14**).

Perhaps her best-known work was created in the 1920s, 1930s, and 1940s, but she remained active as a painter almost until her death in 1986. Her later works exalt the New Mexico landscape which she loved.

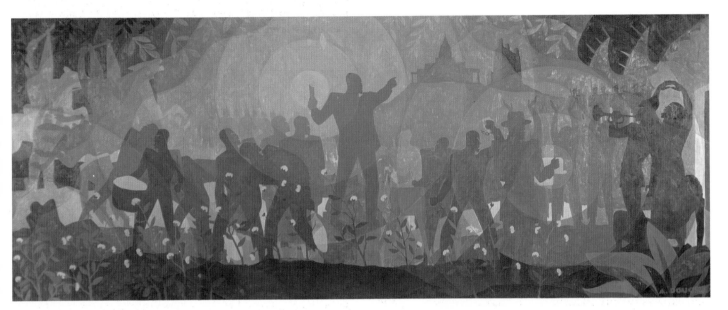

17.18 Aaron Douglas, *Aspects of the Negro Life* (detail), 1934. Oil on canvas, entire work 5 ft × 11 ft 7 ins (1.52 × 3.53 m). Schomburg Center for Research in Black Culture, New York Public Library, Astor, Lenox and Tilden Foundations.

Central American Painting

Diego Rivera (ree-VAY-rah; 1886–1957) revived the fresco mural as an art form in Mexico in the 1920s. Working with the support of a new revolutionary government, he produced large-scale public murals that picture contemporary subjects in a style that blends European and native traditions. The fresco painting *Enslavement of the Indians* (Fig. **17.19**) creates a dramatic comment on that chapter in Mexican history. The composition is not unlike that of Goya's *The Third of May 1808* (see Fig. **15.5**). A strong diagonal sweeps across the work, separating the oppressed from the oppressor, and provides a dynamic movement stabilized by the classically derived arcade framing the top of the composition.

African and Primitive Influences

The direct influence of African art can be seen in the sculptures of Constantin Brancusi (BRAHN-koosh; 1876–1957; Figs. **17.21** and **17.22**). Yet beyond this, the smooth, precise surfaces of much of his work seem to have an abstract, machined quality. Brancusi's search for essential form led to very economical presentations, often ovoid and simple, yet animate. Certainly, great psychological complexity exists in *Bird in Space* (Fig. **19.22**). Its highly polished surface and upward striving line has a modern sleekness, and yet somehow its primitive essence remains, reminding us of the work of African or aboriginal tribes. Brancusi's *Mlle Pogany* (Fig. **17.21**), despite the superbly polished surface and accomplished curves which lead the

17.19 Diego Rivera, *Enslavement of the Indians*, 1930–1. Fresco. Palace of Cortez, Cuernavaca, Mexico.

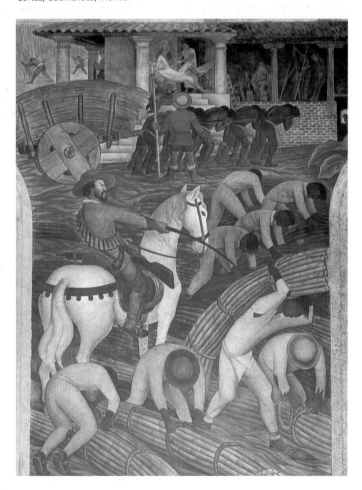

OUR DYNAMIC WORLD

African Masks

Headdress masks are important in African ritual, and we can see the influence of this style in the work of some Western artists in the twentieth century. In Figure **17.20** we see an Igbo face mask from eastern Nigeria. This mask was created by the same tribe that made the *Igbo-Ukwu* roped pot on a stand (see Fig. **7.20**), some thousand years earlier. The ritual mask of Figure **17.20** is realistically styled and represents a beautiful and refined spirit. It could be one of a great group of spirits represented in Igbo masquerades. It has a shiny surface and careful detailing, and its patina comes from the process of smoking. Each element of facial tattoos, anatomical parts, and headdress shows care and skill in execution.

17.20 Igbo face mask from eastern Nigeria, twentieth century. Wood with smoke patina. Photo: Eric Robertson.

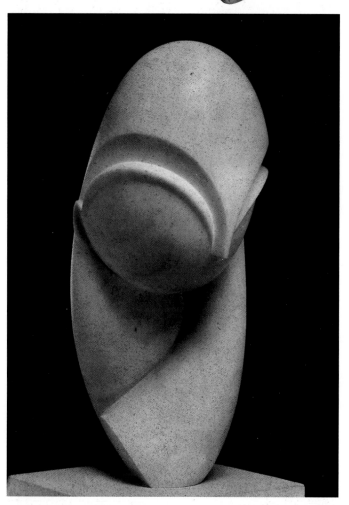

eye inward, has an enigmatic character that is reminiscent of an African mask.

In 1925, Jacques Lipchitz (leep-SHEETS; 1891–1973) created a series of "transparents" made from cardboard cut and bent to approximate the cubism of Picasso's paintings. He thus opened up the interiors of these works, to achieve a radical new understanding of space: interior spaces need not be voids, but, rather, could become integral parts of the sculptural work itself. Thus, he arrived at the concept of NEGATIVE SPACE, which played an important role in sculpture, especially in the work of Henry Moore.

Lipchitz's *Man with a Guitar* (Fig. **17.23**) predates his discovery of negative space, but clearly it reflects his interest in form, space, cubism, and archaic and primitive art. Here, these influences appear in the way forms are combined to create a multifaceted shape that has the appearance of being viewed from several directions at once. At the same time, the work has an archaic, geometric solidity. The primitive influence is apparent in its proportions—an elongated torso and head and shortened legs. The interaction of angles and curves draws the viewer in to examine the work from many different observation points.

17.21 Constantin Brancusi, *Mlle Pogany*, 1931. Marble on limestone base, 19 ins (48 cm) high. Philadelphia Museum of Art (Louise and Walter Arensberg Collection). © ADAGP, Paris Send DACS, London 1999.

17.22 (*opposite left*) Constantin Brancusi, *Bird in Space*, c. 1928. Bronze (unique cast), 4 ft 6 ins (1.37 m) high. Museum of Modern Art, New York. Given anonymously. Photo: © 1998 Museum of Modern Art, New York. © ADAGP, Paris and DACS, London 1999.

17.23 (*opposite right*) Jacques Lipchitz, *Man with a Guitar*, 1915. Limestone, 38¼ ins (97.2 cm) high. Museum of Modern Art, New York (Mrs Simon Guggenheim Fund) (by exchange). Photo: © 1998 Museum of Modern Art, New York. © Estate of Jacques Lipchitz/VAGA, New York/DACS, London 1999.

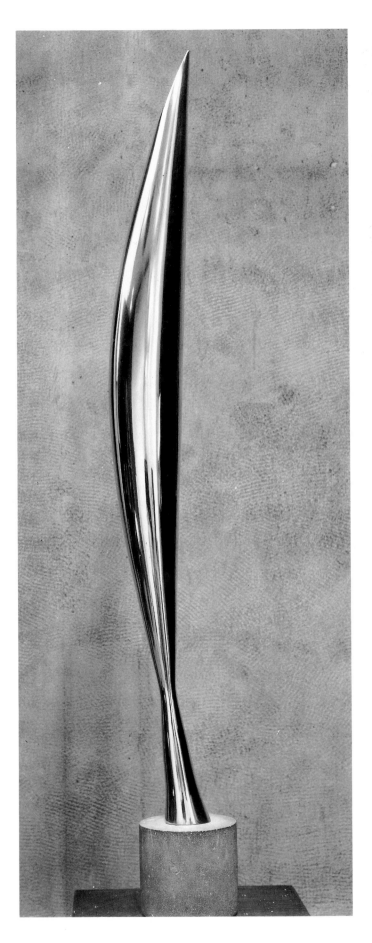

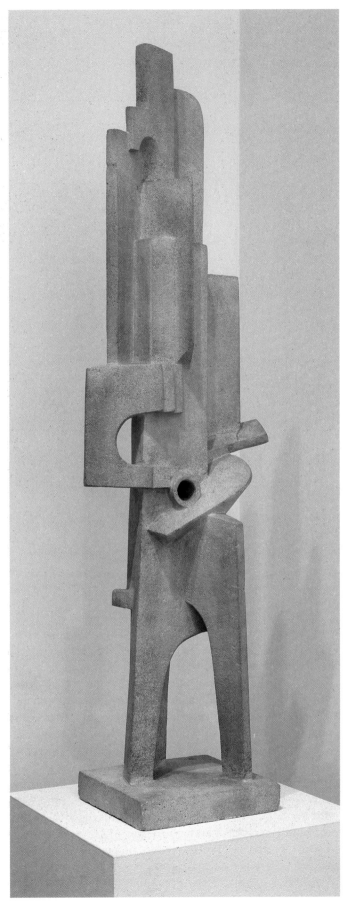

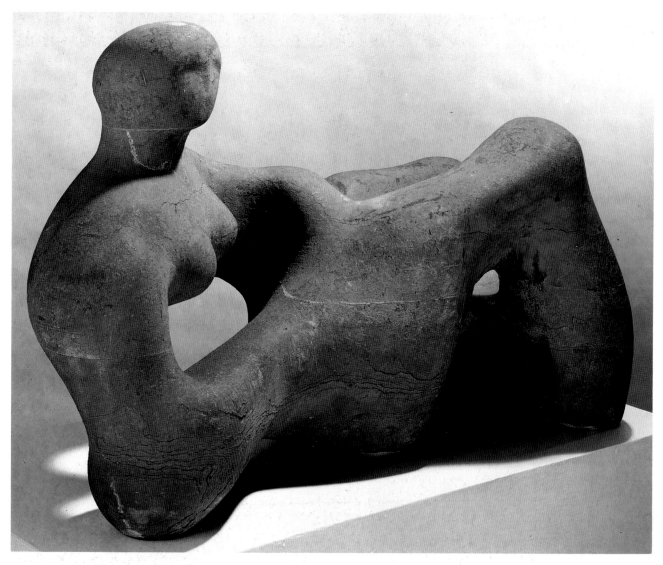

17.24 Henry Moore, *Recumbent Figure*, 1938. Green Hornton stone, 4 ft 7 ins (1.4 m) long. Tate Gallery, London.

The British sculptor Henry Moore (1898–1986) explored many ways of depicting the human figure. These various treatments are unified by a deep feeling for the dignity of the human form, however. In *Recumbent Figure* (Fig. **17.24**), the humanity of the piece emerges perhaps more strongly than it would in a purely naturalistic expression.

Moore's work reflects the "primevalism" inherent in some sculpture even today, and his early work was influenced by the monoliths of Stonehenge. However, *Recumbent Figure* also displays a certain classicism. The sense of the resting form recalls that of Dionysus in the sculptures from the pediment of the Parthenon (see p. 87). In a very modern way, the stone is not disguised, but rather profoundly exploited. Perhaps the most famous features of Moore's sculptures are the holes, or "negative spaces," that he inserts. The negative space provides a counterpoint to the interlocking shapes of the solids in his work.

Architectural Modernism

Frank Lloyd Wright (1867–1959) was one of the most influential and innovative architects of the twentieth century. He wished to initiate new traditions. One such new tradition was the prairie style, which Wright developed around 1900. In creating these designs, Wright drew on the flat landscape of the midwest as well as the simple horizontal and vertical accents of the Japanese style. Wright followed Louis Sullivan in his pursuit of form that expressed function, and he took painstaking care to devise practical arrangements for his interiors and to make the exteriors of his buildings reflect their interiors.

Wright also designed some of the furniture for his houses. In doing so, comfort, function, and integration with the total design were his chief criteria. Textures and colors in the environment were duplicated in the materials,

MASTERWORK

Wright—Kaufmann House

Frank Lloyd Wright is one of the greatest American artists in any medium. His primary message is the relationship of architecture to its setting, a lesson that some modern architects seem to have forgotten. Wright's buildings seem to grow out of, and never violate, their environment.

One of his most inventive designs is the Kaufmann House, Falling Water, at Bear Run, Pennsylvania (Fig. **17.25**). Cantilevered over a waterfall, its dramatic imagery is exciting. The inspiration for this house was probably the French Renaissance château of Chenonceaux, built on a bridge across the River Cher. However, "Falling Water" is no house built on a bridge. It seems to erupt out of its natural rock site, and its

beige concrete terraces blend harmoniously with the colors of the surrounding stone. Wright has successfully blended two seemingly dissimilar styles: the house is a part of its context, yet it has the rectilinear lines of the International Style, to which Wright was usually opposed. He has taken those spare, sterile boxes and made them harmonize with their natural surroundings.

Wright's great asset, and at the same time his greatest liability, was his myopic insistence on his own vision. He could work only with clients who would bend to his wishes. So, unlike many architects, whose designs are tempered by the vision of the client, what Wright built was Wright's, and Wright's only.

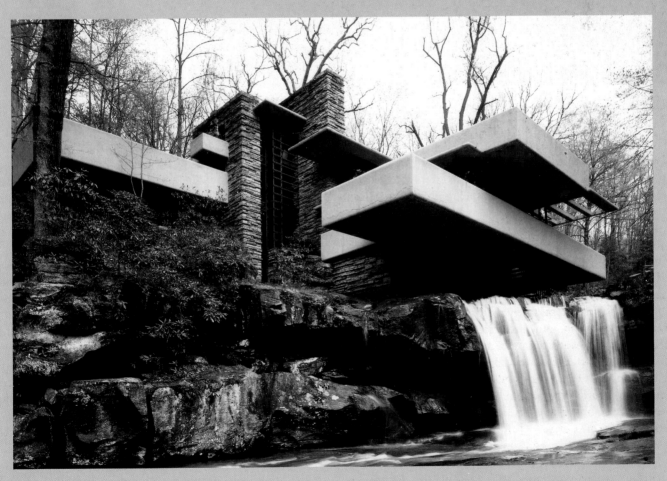

17.25 Frank Lloyd Wright, Kaufmann House, Falling Water, Bear Run, Pennsylvania, 1936–7.

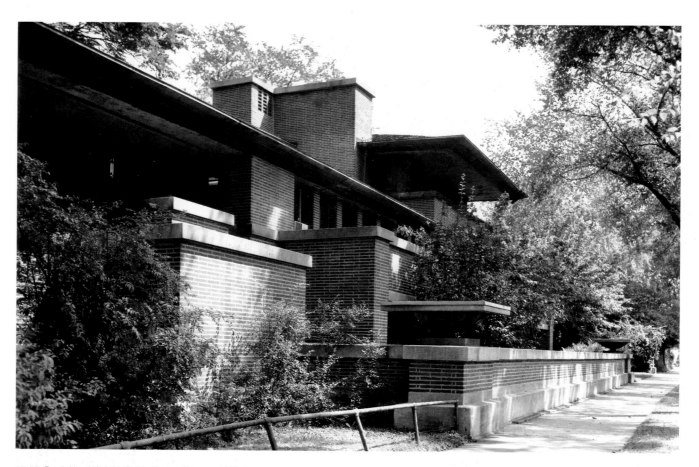

17.26 Frank Lloyd Wright, Robie House, Chicago, 1907–9.

including large expanses of wood, both in the house and for its furniture. He made a point of giving furniture several functions. Tables, for example, might also serve as cabinets. All spaces and objects were precisely designed to present a complete environment. Wright was convinced that houses profoundly influence the people who live in them, and he saw the architect as a "molder of humanity." Wright's works range from the simple to the complex, from the serene (Fig. **17.26**) to the dramatic (Fig. **17.25**), and from interpenetration to enclosure of space. He was always experimental, and his designs explore the various interrelationships between space and geometric design.

Wright's insistence on the integration of the context of the building and the creation of indoor space that was an extension of outdoor space led him to even more dramatic projects. The horizontality of the prairie style remains, but we see it in a completely different mode in the exciting Kaufmann House (Fig. **17.25**).

Other new concepts in design appeared in the works of Le Corbusier (luh kor-boo-ZYAY; 1887–1965) during the 1920s and 1930s. Le Corbusier was concerned with integrating structure and function, and he was especially interested in poured concrete. He demonstrated his belief that a

house was "a machine to be lived in" in several residences of that period. By "machine," Le Corbusier did not mean something depersonalized. Rather, he meant that a house should be efficiently constructed from standard, mass-produced parts, and logically designed for use, on the model of an efficient machine.

Le Corbusier had espoused a domino system of design for houses, using a series of slabs supported on slender columns. The resulting building was boxlike, with a flat roof, which could be used as a terrace. The Villa Savoye (Fig. **17.27**) combines these concepts in a building whose supporting structures free the interior from the necessity of weight-supporting walls. In many ways, the design of the Villa Savoye reveals a classical Greek inspiration, from its columns and human scale to its precisely articulated parts and coherent whole. The design is crisp and functional.

Many traditional approaches to architecture continued through the period. Cass Gilbert's Woolworth Building (Fig. **17.28**) is one such example. It has not only stimulated considerable discussion, including the appelation "Woolworth Gothic," but it has also inspired a wave of Gothic skyscrapers, including Howells and Hood's Tribune Tower in Chicago (1923–5).

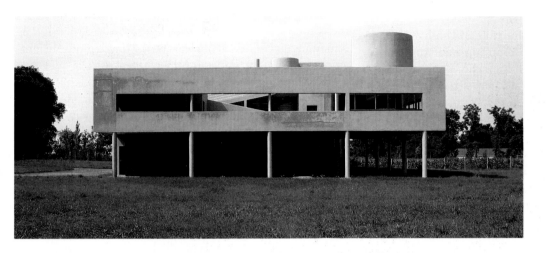

MUSIC

17.27 (*above*) Le Corbusier, Villa Savoye, Poissy, France, 1928–30.

Modern Traditionalism

Traditional tendencies continued through the 1930s and 1940s in various quarters, for example, in the music of the American William Schuman (1910–92). Schuman's symphonies have bright timbres and energetic rhythms, and focus on eighteenth- and nineteenth-century American folklore. The inspiration of the eighteenth-century American composer William Billings (1746–1800) figures prominently in Schuman's *William Billings Overture* (1943) and the *New England Triptych* (1956), which is based on three pieces by Billings. *American Festival Overture* (1939) is perhaps his most famous work. Traditional tonality also appears in the works of the Russian composer Sergei Prokofiev (sair-GAY prah-KOH-fyef; 1891–1953). With all its traditional tonality, however, Prokofiev's *Steel Step* reflected the encroachment of mechanization of the 1920s. The machine as a symbol for energy and motion found its way into music, and in *Steel Step* Prokofiev intentionally dehumanized the subject of his music in order to reflect contemporary life.

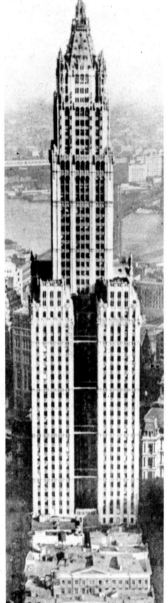

17.28 Cass Gilbert, The Woolworth Building, New York, 1913.

Departures

Hindemith

Paul Hindemith (HIN-duh-mith; 1895–1963) departed from traditional tonality in his compositions. He presented his systematized approach to problems of musical organization and their theoretical solutions in *The Craft of Musical Composition*. Hindemith's work was extremely chromatic and almost atonal. Although his system of tonality used centers, it did not include the concepts of major and minor keys. He hoped that his new system would become a universal music language, but it did not.

Hindemith was, however, extremely influential in twentieth-century composition, both as a composer and a teacher. His works are broad and varied, encompassing nearly every musical genre, including ten operas, art songs, cantatas, chamber music, requiems, and symphonies. *Kleine Kammermusik für fünf Bläser* is a delightful composition for five woodwinds in five contrasting movements. Its overall form is very clear, as are its themes. Its dissonant harmonies and untraditional tonalities typify Hindemith's works. Yet Hindemith criticized "esoteric isolationism in music," and he tried to write works that the general public could understand and that the amateur musician could play.

Bartók

The Hungarian composer Béla Bartók (BEL-luh BAHR-tohk; 1881–1945) took another nontraditional approach to tonality. He was interested in folk music, and a number of his compositions show those elements. Eastern European folk music does not use Western major/minor tonalities, and thus Bartók's interest in it and in nontraditional tonality in general went hand in hand. Bartók invented his own type of harmonic structure, which could accommodate folk melodies.

As nontraditional as some of Bartók's work is, however, he also employs traditional devices and forms. His style is precise and well structured, and he occasionally uses sonata form. He often develops his works from one or two very short motifs, and his larger works are unified by repeating thematic material. Bartók's textures are largely contrapuntal, with strong melodies but little conventional harmony, and dissonances occur frequently.

Bartók's employment of traditional devices was always bent to his own desires and nearly always lay outside the traditional tonal system. He contributed significantly to string quartet literature, and his six quartets each set out a particular problem which is then solved, using simple motifs combined with complex tonality. One characteristic of his melodic development was octave displacement, in which successive notes of a melody occur in different octaves. This device apparently came from the folk music in which he was so interested. When peasants found the notes of a melody too high or low, they simply jumped up or down an octave so as to sing them comfortably.

Rhythm also forms a notable feature of Bartók's music. His works tend to have significant rhythmic energy; he employs devices such as repeated chords and irregular meters to generate dynamic rhythms. He also uses polyrhythms, that is, various juxtaposed rhythms played at one time to create unique nonmelodic counterpoint.

Berg and Webern

Alban Berg (berkh; 1885–1935) was a close friend and disciple of Schoenberg, and his compositions are based on the serial technique. Berg's lyricism, however, despite their atonality, makes his works less disconnected than much serial music. Many of the characteristics of his work can be found in his *Lyric Suite* (1927), a string quartet in six movements, based on several different tone rows.

The opening movement of the *Lyric Suite* starts with a brief chordal introduction, followed by the first tone row (the main theme, played by the first violin). The second theme, derived from the tone row, is more peaceful. Both themes are then freely recapitulated, and the movement closes with a brief coda. The varied rhythm changes constantly between quadruple and duple meter. Much of the meaning of the piece depends on an accurate dynamic

rendering by each of the four string players; Berg indicates the volume and articulation he requires in great detail. The remaining five movements use contrasting tempos, heightening the dramatic impact of the whole work.

The story on which this piece is based, that is, its "program," alludes to an extramarital affair. This information, however, remained a secret for nearly fifty years. It was published for the first time only after the death of Berg's widow.

Anton Webern (VAY-burn; 1883–1945) was a friend of Berg's, and he did not live to see the significant influence of his relatively small output of music on composers throughout the world in the 1950s and '60s. His music is poetic, lyrical, and extremely original in its brevity, concentration, and quietude. His pieces typically last no more than two or three minutes. About half his compositions comprise choral works and songs; the rest was written for chamber orchestra or small chamber groups—for example, his Quartet for Clarinet, Tenor Saxophone, Violin, and Piano, Op. 22 (1930). He adopted his teacher Schoenberg's twelve-tone system and built upon it to achieve a "melody built of tone colors." Webern, in turn, became a point of departure for later composers who were fascinated by his use of texture, tone color, dynamics, and register as unifying elements.

Ives and Copland

The Americans Charles Ives and Aaron Copland both had experimental and highly personal styles.

Charles Ives (1874–1954) was so experimental that many of his compositions were considered unplayable, and did not receive public performances until after World War II. Content to remain anonymous and disinclined to formulate a "system," as Schoenberg did, Ives went unrecognized for many years. His melodies spring from folk and popular songs, hymns, and other, often familiar, material, which he treated in unfamiliar, complex ways. His rhythms are very irregular and are often written with only an occasional bar line to indicate an accent. His counterpoint is so dissonant that frequently it is impossible to distinguish one melodic line from another. Some of the tone clusters in his piano music are unplayable without using a block of wood to depress all the keys at once. Ives' experiments, such as *The Unanswered Question* (1908), employ ensembles placed in various locations to create stereophonic effects. Ives' work reflects his idea that all music relates to life's experiences and ideas, some of which are consonant and some dissonant.

Aaron Copland (1900–91) integrated American idioms—jazz, dissonance, Mexican folk songs, and Shaker hymns—into his compositions. The last of these figure prominently in Copland's most significant work, *Appalachian Spring* (1944). The theme and variations comprising the Shaker tune *Simple Gifts* (CD Track 21) reflect the Shaker text:

'Tis the gift to be simple, 'tis the gift to be free,
'Tis the gift to come down where we ought to be.

First written as a ballet, it was later reworked as a suite (set of movements) for symphony orchestra. Copland employed a variety of styles, some harmonically complex, some simple. He often used all the tones of the DIATONIC scale simultaneously, as he does in the opening chord of *Appalachian Spring*. His style is nonetheless traditionally tonal, and his unique use of rhythms and chords has been highly influential in twentieth-century American music.

THEATRE
Expressionism

In Chapter 16 we studied expressionism as a style in the visual arts. As seems always the case, visual art styles filter slowly into the theatre. The painters' expressionistic revolt against naturalism translated to the theatre most effectively in scenic design. For playwrights, expressionism proved merely an extension of realism or naturalism, but it allowed them to express their reactions to the universe more fully. August Strindberg (1849–1912), for example, turned inward to the subconscious in expressionistic plays such as the *Ghost Sonata*. In so doing, he created a "presentational" rather than "representational" style.

The plays of Ernst Toller (TAHW-luhr; 1893–1939) typify German expressionistic disillusionment after World War I. Toller's personal struggles, his communist idealism, and his opposition to violence are reflected in the heroine of *Man and the Masses* (1923). Sonia, a product of the upper class, leads a strike for peace. Her desire to avoid violence and bloodshed is opposed by the mob spirit (the "Nameless One"), who seeks just those results, and to destroy the peace the strike intends to achieve. For leading the disastrous strike, Sonia is imprisoned and sentenced to death.

Expressionism also found its way to America. Elmer Rice's *Adding Machine* (1923) introduces the viewer to Mr Zero, a cog in the great industrial machinery of twentieth-century life, who stumbles through a pointless existence. Finding himself replaced by an adding machine, he goes berserk, kills his employer, and is executed. Adrift later in the hereafter, he is too narrow-minded to understand the happiness offered to him there. He becomes an adding machine operator in heaven.

Epic Theatre

Theatre championing social action found a successful exponent in Bertolt Brecht (brehkht; 1898–1956) and his *epic theatre*. Although most of Brecht's plays were written before World War II, they were not produced until after it. With his Berliner Ensemble, Brecht brought his theories and productions to a wide audience. Drawing heavily on the expressionists, Brecht developed complex theories about theatre and its relationship to life, and he continued to mold and develop these theories until his death.

Brecht was in revolt against dramatic theatre. Essentially, he tried to move the audience out of the role of passive spectator and into a more dynamic relationship with the play. To this end, Brecht postulated three circumstances—*historification*, *alienation*, and *epic*.

Historification removed events from the lifelike present to the past in order to make the actions presented seem strange. According to Brecht, the playwright should make the audience feel that if they had lived under the conditions presented in the play, they would have taken some positive action. Understanding this, the audience should see that things have changed since then and thus they too can make changes in the present.

Brecht believed the audience should not confuse the theatre with reality. The audience should always watch the play critically as a comment on life. In order for the spectators to judge the action in the play and apply it to life outside, however, they must be separated—or *alienated*—from the play's events, even though they might be emotionally involved in them. Historification was one kind of alienation. Other devices could also be used to make things strange, such as calling attention to the make-believe nature of a production or inserting songs, film sequences, and so on. Brecht did not subscribe to the idea of a unified production. Rather, he saw each element as independent, and thus each was a device that could be employed to produce further alienation.

Finally, Brecht called his theatre "epic" because he believed that his plays resembled epic poems more than they did traditional drama. His plays present a story from the point of view of a storyteller, and they frequently involve narration and changes of time and place that might be accomplished with nothing more than an explanatory sentence.

Absurdism

Many artists of this period had lost faith in religion, science, and humanity itself. In their search for meaning, they found only chaos, complexity, grotesque laughter, and perhaps insanity. The plays of Luigi Pirandello (peer-an-

Martha Graham—*Appalachian Spring*

Social criticism as an artistic message came in with the Depression, and Martha Graham began to pursue topical themes. Her interest in the shaping of America led to her renowned dance piece *Appalachian Spring* (1944), set to the music of Aaron Copland (see the Music section of this chapter). *Appalachian Spring* deals, among other things, with the triumph of love and common sense over the fire and brimstone of American Puritanism. Martha Graham, herself, danced the principal role of The Bride, and the dancer/choreographer Merce Cunningham (see Chapter 18) danced the role of The Revivalist. Other roles in the dance include The Husbandman, The Pioneering Woman, and The Followers. Perhaps the best-known and best-loved of Graham's works, and the one with the finest score, *Appalachian Spring* takes as its pretext a wedding on the American frontier. The dance is like no actual ceremony or party, however. The movement not only expresses individual character and emotion, but it has a clarity, spaciousness, and definition that relate to the open frontier, which must be fenced and tamed.

Isamu Noguchi's (see p. 591) spare set (Fig. **17.29**) defines the stage: slim timbers that frame a house, a portion of wall, a bench, a platform with a rocker, a piece of fence, and a small, tilted disk. During the dance, the char-acters emerge to make solo statements; the action of the dance suspends while they reveal what is in their hearts. The Bride's two solos, for instance, suggest not only her joy but also her trepidation as she envisions her future. The four Followers rush about together with little steps and hops to provide a visual chorus of exclamations and "Amens." As Copland used American motifs in his score, so Graham drew subtly on steps from country dancing to express the frank vigor of these people.

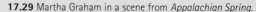
17.29 Martha Graham in a scene from *Appalachian Spring*.

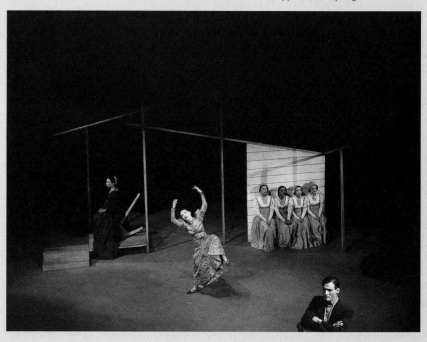

DEHL-lo; 1867–1936) obsessively ask the question "What is real?" with brilliant variations. *Right You Are If You Think You Are* (1917) presents a wife, living with her husband in a top-floor apartment, who is not permitted to see her mother. She converses with her daily, the mother in the street and the daughter at a garret window. Soon a neighbor demands an explanation from the husband. He answers, but so does the mother, who has an equally plausible but different answer. Finally, someone approaches the wife, who is the only one who can clear up the mystery. Her response, as the curtain falls, is loud laughter! Piran-dello's dismay at an incomprehensible world was expressed in mocking laughter directed at those who thought they knew the answers.

Pirandello's work was one factor in the emergence of a movement called "absurdism." A philosophy that posited the essential meaninglessness—or unknowable meaning—of existence, and thus questioned the meaning of any action, was also emerging. This philosophy, "existentialism," (see p. 549) also contributed to absurdist style, especially in the literary arts. From such antecedents came numerous dramas, the best-known of which were written by the French existentialist philosopher, writer, and playwright Jean-Paul Sartre (1905–80). Sartre held that there were no absolute or universal moral values and that humankind was part of a world without purpose. Therefore, men and women were responsible only to themselves. His plays attempted to draw logical conclusions from "a consistent atheism." Plays such as *No Exit* (1944) translate Sartre's existential views into dramatic form.

Albert Camus (kah-MOO; 1913–60) was the first writer to apply the term "absurd" to the human condition. This he took to be a state somewhere between humanity's aspirations and the meaninglessness of the universe which is the condition of life. Determining which way to take a chaotic universe is the theme of Camus's plays, such as *Cross-Purposes* (1944). Absurdism continued as a theatrical genre after World War II, and will be discussed further in the next chapter.

MODERN DANCE

Despite the notoriety of the young feminist Isadora Duncan, it was her contemporary Ruth St Denis and her husband, Ted Shawn, who laid more substantial cornerstones for modern dance in their Denishawn school. Much more serious than Duncan, Ruth St Denis numbered among her favorite books Kant's *Critique of Pure Reason* and Dumas's *Camille*. Her dancing began as a strange combination of exotic, oriental interpretations, and Delsartian poses. (Delsarte is a nineteenth-century system of gestures and postures that transmit feelings and ideas, originated by François Delsarte.) Ruth St Denis was a remarkable performer with a magnificently proportioned body. She manipulated it and various draperies and veils into presentations of line and form so gracefully that the fabric appeared to become an extension of the body.

The Denishawn school took a totally eclectic approach to dance. All traditions were included, from formal ballet to oriental and American Indian dances. The touring company presented wildly varied fare, from Hindu dances to the latest ballroom crazes. Branches of the school were formed throughout the United States, and the touring company occasionally appeared with the *Ziegfeld Follies*. By 1932, St Denis and Shawn had separated, and the Denishawn Company ceased to exist. Nevertheless, it left its mark on its pupils, if not always a positive one.

Among the first to leave Denishawn was Martha Graham (1893–1991), probably the most influential figure in modern dance. Although the term "modern dance" defies accurate definition, it remains the most appropriate label for the nonballetic tradition that Martha Graham came to symbolize. Graham found Denishawn unsatisfac-

tory as an artistic base. She did maintain the primacy of artistic individualism, however. As she said, "There are no general rules. Each work of art creates its own code."

Yet, principally because it tried so hard to be different from formal ballet, modern dance also developed its own conventions. Ballet movements were largely rounded and symmetrical. Therefore, modern dancers emphasized angularity and asymmetry. Ballet stressed leaps and based its line on toework, while modern dance hugged the floor and dancers went barefoot. As a result, the early works of Graham and others tended to be more fierce and earthy and less graceful. Beneath it all was the desire to express emotion. Martha Graham described her choreography as "a graph of the heart."

Graham's work progressed, through her own dancing and that of her company, as a reaction to specific artistic problems. Her early works were notorious for their jerks and tremblings, which Graham based on the natural act of breathing. She translated contractions and releases of inhaling and exhaling into a series of whiplash movements that expressly revealed energy and effort—unlike the ballet, where effort is concealed. Gradually, her style became more lyrical in line and movement, but passion was always its foundation.

Native American Dance

Most Native American dances are held for religious or ritualistic reasons. Medicine men dance to seek aid for the sick; hunters dance to attract game; and farming tribes dance to bring rain or to make the corn grow or ripen.

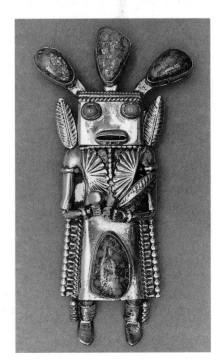

17.30 Navajo Kachina silver figure, representing a dancer, c. 1950. Private collection.

Some dances dramatize stories from the history or mythology of the tribe. Almost every occasion has an accompanying dance. Native Americans have separate dances for men and women as well as some in which men, women, and children take part. Dancers emphasize various movements of the feet and postures for the head (arms play a lesser role), and drums provide accompaniment. Each graceful movement reinforces the idea of oneness with the earth and natural environment.

The southwest provides two fairly common ceremonials: one, with a line of male dancers, each holding gourd rattles, and singing to their own accompaniment; a second, with dancers bedecked with colorful Kachina masks (Fig. **17.30**).

Usually the purpose of a Native American dance is serious, but often it becomes an occasion for fun and sociability, with clowns joining the dancers.

PHOTOGRAPHY

After World War I, as photography entered its second century, significant aesthetic changes occurred. Early explorations of photography as an art form tended to employ darkroom techniques, tricks, and manipulation that created works appearing staged and imitative of sentimental, moralistic paintings. The followers of such an aesthetic believed that for photography to be art, it must look like "art."

During the early years of the twentieth century, however, a new generation of photographers arose who determined to take photography away from the previous, pictorial style and its soft focus, and toward a more direct, un-manipulated, and sharply focused approach. Called "straight" photography, it expressed what its adherents believed was photography's unique vision. The principal American force behind the recognition of photography as a fine art was Alfred Stieglitz (STEEG-lits; 1864–1946). His own work gained recognition for his clarity of image and reality shots, especially of clouds and New York City architecture. In 1902, he formed the Photo-Secessionist group and opened a gallery referred to as 291 because of its address at 291 Fifth Avenue in New York City. In addition to showcasing photography, Stieglitz's efforts promoted many visual artists, including the woman who would become his wife, Georgia O'Keeffe (see page 556). He also promoted photography as a fine art in the pages of his illustrated quarterly, *Camera Work*.

Among the most famous of the adherents of straight photography was Ansel Adams (1902–84), who became a recognized leader of modern photography through his sharp, poetic landscape photographs of the American West (Fig. **17.31**). He was well known as a technical innovator and was a pioneer in the movement to preserve the wilderness. His work did much to elevate photography to the level of art. It emphasized sharp focus and subtle variety in light and texture, with rich detail and brilliant tonal differences. In 1941, he began making photomurals for the United States Department of the Interior, which forced him to master techniques for photographing the light and space of immense landscapes. He developed what he called the zone system, a means for predetermining the final tone of each part of the landscape.

17.31 Ansel Adams, *Mount Williamson in the Sierra Nevada*, 1945.

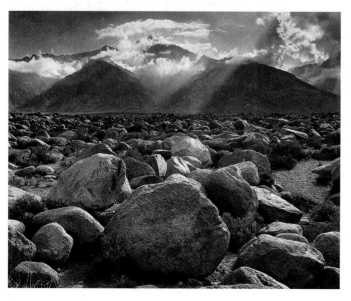

FILM

European Film

Film-making revived and spread rapidly throughout Europe after World War I. The German director Fritz Lang's futuristic *Metropolis* (1926) tells the story of life in the twenty-first century. Critics called the plot ludicrous, but marveled at the photographic effects. In France, film found its first real aesthetic theorist in Louis Delluc, and came to be regarded as a serious art form.

German expressionism made its mark in film as well as in the visual and other performing arts. In 1919, its most masterful example, Robert Wiene's (veen) *Cabinet of Dr Caligari* (Fig. **17.33**), astounded the film-going public. Macabre sets, surrealistic lighting effects, and distorted properties, all combined to portray a menacing postwar German world.

MASTERWORK

Dorothea Lange—*Migrant Mother*

Since the late nineteenth century, photographers had used photography to document social problems. During the Great Depression, a large-scale program in documentary photography began in the United States. Among the photographers using this approach, Dorothea Lange (1895–1965) helped develop an unsurpassed portrait of the nation. Noted for her ability to make strangers seem like familiar acquaintances, her work for the Farm Security Administration, including *Migrant Mother, Nipomo, California* (1936; Fig. **17.32**), graphically detailed the erosion of the land and the people of rural America during the Great Depression. Her work brought the plight of the poor to national attention. Her photographs of California's

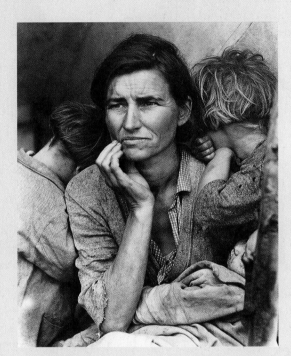

17.32 Dorothea Lange, *Migrant Mother, Nipomo, California*, 1936. Library of Congress, Washington D.C.

migrant workers, captioned with their own words, were so effective that the state established migrant worker camps to alleviate the suffering.

In this poignant photograph, Florence Thompson, a 32-year-old widow with ten children, looks past the viewer with a preoccupied, worried expression. With her furrowed brow and prematurely aged face, she captures the fears of an entire population of disenfranchised people. Two of her children lean on her for support, their faces buried disconsolately in their mother's shoulders. Lange consciously avoided including all of Thompson's children in the photograph because she did not wish to contribute to the widespread resentment of wealthier people in America about overpopulation among the poor.

In Russia Sergei Eisenstein (YZ-en-shtyn) wrote and directed the great film *Battleship Potemkin* (1925). This cruel story of the crew of the ship *Potemkin* contains one of the most legendary scenes in all cinema. A crowd of citizens is trapped on the great steps of Odessa between the Czar's troops and mounted Cossacks. The editing of the massacre scenes that follow is truly riveting. The sequence showing the carnage is a montage of short, vivid shots—a face, a flopping arm, a slipping body, a pair of broken eye glasses—deftly combined into a powerful whole.

The rise of Nazism in Germany had virtually eliminated the vigorous German film industry by the late thirties. Fritz Lang, however, had already produced his psychological thriller *M*, which employed subtle and deft manipulation of sound, including a Grieg *leitmotif*. Peter Lorre's performance as a child-murderer was significant.

The Rise of the Studio

The 1920s were the heyday of Hollywood. Its films were silent, but its extravagance, its star system, and its legions of starlets dazzled the world. It was the beginning of the big studio era—MGM, Paramount, Universal, Fox, and Warner Brothers all began. Fantastic movie houses that rivaled baroque palaces in their opulence were built all over the United States.

This was the era of Fairbanks and Pickford and an immigrant Italian tango dancer, whom the studio named Rudolph Valentino, who thrilled women in movies such as *The Sheik*. After Valentino's death, John Gilbert and his co-star (and, for a time, fiancée) Greta Garbo became matinee idols. On the lighter side were Harold Lloyd, Buster Keaton, and Laurel and Hardy.

Although the soundtrack had been invented many years earlier, and short talking films had been released, *The*

17.33 Robert Wiene, *The Cabinet of Dr Caligari*, 1919.

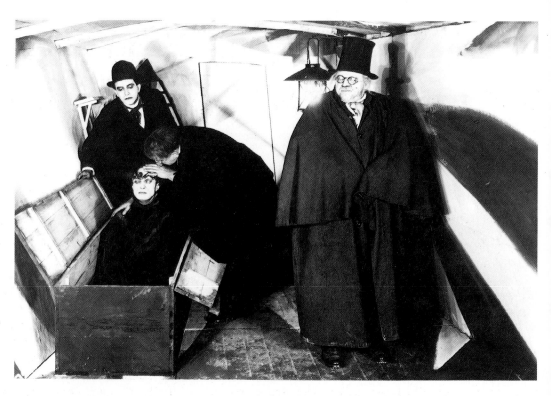

Jazz Singer in 1927 heralded the age of talkies with Al Jolson's famous line "You ain't heard nothin' yet!"

New Genres

The early thirties produced films about crime and violence. Films such as *Little Caesar* (1930), with Edward G. Robinson, kept Hollywood's coffers full during the Depression. But the gangster genre fell out of favor amid public cries that such glorified violence was harming American youth. The sexually explicit dialogue of Mae West added a titillating dimension to the cinema. But the Production Code—or censorship—was strengthened, and West was toned down.

The most popular star of the thirties, however, was created by Walt Disney. Mickey Mouse led a parade of animated characters in films. The Western continued, and in 1939, John Ford's classic, *Stagecoach*, made John Wayne the prototypical cowboy hero. This superbly edited film exemplified the technique of CUTTING WITHIN THE FRAME, which became a Ford trademark.

Chaplin continued to produce comedy into the thirties. *City Lights* (1931) was a silent relic in an age of sound, but its consummate artistry made it a classic. The story depicts Chaplin's love for a blind girl, who erroneously believes he is rich. He robs a bank and pays for an operation that restores her sight. He is apprehended and sent to prison. Years later she happens to cross a tramp being chased by a group of boys. Amused and yet saddened, she offers the tramp a coin and a flower. At the touch of his hand, she recognizes him, but she is stunned that her imagined rich and handsome lover is really nothing more than a comical tramp. The film ends with the knowledge that their relationship is doomed. Among the great comic sequences in this film is a scene in which Chaplin swallows a whistle at a society party, then, in a fit of hiccups, disrupts a musical performance and calls a pack of dogs and several taxicabs.

The epic of the decade was David O. Selznick's *Gone with the Wind*, a three-and-three-quarter-hour extravaganza with an improbable plot and stereotypical characters. The performances of Clark Gable, Vivien Leigh, Leslie Howard, and Olivia de Havilland, along with its magnificent cinematography, have made this film eternally popular.

Social Commentary

In the midst of World War II, film underwent radical change in form and content. In 1940, Darryl Zanuck produced and John Ford directed a film that stunned even Hollywood: John Steinbeck's *Grapes of Wrath*, an artistic visualization of Steinbeck's portrayal of the Depression. Here was social criticism with superb cinematography and compelling performances. Social commentary appeared again in 1941, with *How Green Was My Valley*, which dealt with exploited coal miners in Wales, and *Citizen Kane*, a grim view of wealth and power in the United States. This film, thought by some to be the best movie ever produced, blazed a new trail in its cinematic techniques. Orson Welles, its director and star, and Greg Toland, its cinematographer, brilliantly combined deep-focus photography, unique lighting effects, and rapid cutting.

Focal Point
The Bauhaus—Integration of the Arts

The Bauhaus (BOW-hows) is our Focal Point for this chapter because it represents a conscious attempt to integrate the arts into a unified statement. For the most part, the story of the Bauhaus and its goals will be told in the philosophy of its founder and primary visionary, Walter Gropius (VAHL-tur GROH-pee-us). Although it was secular in spirit, the Bauhaus represents a vision of artistic accomplishments, such as were seen in the great churches and palaces of the past—a true integration of vision wrapped in a common purpose. That vision may, in fact, be returning in the performance art of the last few years.

In Germany in the mid-1920s, and led by Walter Gropius and Adolph Meyer, the Bauhaus School of Art, Applied Arts, and Architecture approached aesthetics from the point of view of engineering. Experimentation and design were based on technological and economic factors rather than on formal considerations. The Bauhaus philosophy sought to establish links between the organic and technical worlds and thereby to reduce contrasts between the two. Spatial imagination, rather than building and construction, became the Bauhaus objective. The design principles of Gropius and Meyer produced building exteriors that were completely free of ornamentation. Several juxtaposed, functional materials form the external surface, underscoring the fact that exterior walls are no longer structural, merely a climate barrier. Bauhaus buildings evolved from a careful consideration of what people needed their buildings to do, while, at the same time, the architects were searching for dynamic balance and geometric purity (Fig. **17.34**).

In 1919 Walter Gropius (1883–1969) wrote what has been called the "Bauhaus Manifesto." The major thrust of his ideas was that "all the arts culminate in architecture." He was inspired by a vision of buildings as a new type of organic structure created by integrating all the arts and expressing the contemporary situation. What Gropius sought to do in his new vision was to bring back into the architectural environment the work of painters and sculptors—who, by the twentieth century, had been virtually excluded from the building crafts. Gropius wanted to create a new unity between art and technology, not by returning to the styles of the past, but, in fact, by abandoning contemporary artistic vocabulary—which he viewed as "sterile" and meaningless—and evolving a new architectonic outlook.

As he viewed the past, Gropius realized that ornamentation of buildings was considered the major function of the visual arts, and thus these arts had played a vital part in the creation of great architecture. However, in the twentieth century, visual art stood apart from architecture, as self-sufficient. Gropius believed that architects, painters, and sculptors needed to work together, exchanging ideas, to rediscover the many aspects of great building.

So, guided by this idea of a fundamental unity underlying all branches of design, Gropius founded the original Bauhaus during World War I. At the invitation of the grand duke of Sachsen-Weimar-Eisenach, Gropius took over the Weimar (VY-mahr) School of Arts and Crafts and the Weimar Academy of Fine Art. His primary plan was to shape instruction throughout the school so that students could be trained "to grasp life as a whole, a single cosmic entity," rather than to be trained in specialized classes. He tried to combine imaginative design and technical proficiency by producing a new type of artist–collaborator, who could be molded so as to achieve equal proficiency in design and technology. He made his students complete apprenticeships with the local building trades and insisted on manual instruction in order to provide the student with good all-round hand and eye training.

The Bauhaus workshops were laboratories for solving real problems. They sought to work out practical new designs for everyday goods and to improve models for mass production. All of this required a very special staff who had wide, general cultural backgrounds and skills in both practical application of design and in design theory. They needed to be able to build by hand and to translate designs into prototypes for mass production—two radically different skills. The Bauhaus philosophy maintained that the difference between industry and handicraft was due less to the nature of the tools involved than to the assignment of labor. That is, in handicraft, one person controls the entire process and product, while in industry the labor is subdivided among several individuals. For Gropius and the Bauhaus, these two approaches—handicraft and industry—were opposite poles that were gradually approaching each other. According to Bauhaus

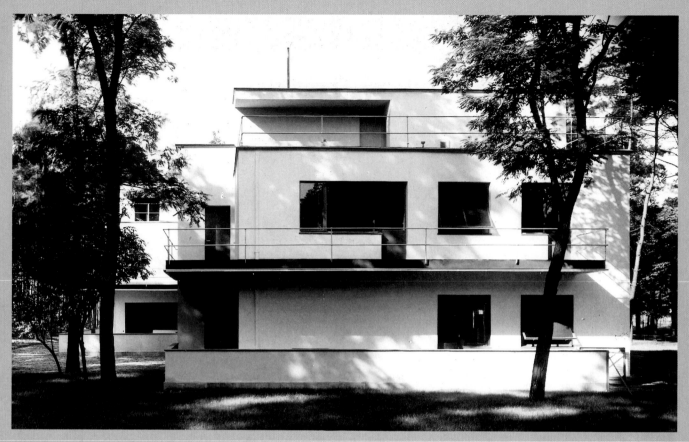

17.34 Walter Gropius, Professor Gropius's own house at Dessau, Germany, 1925.

thinking, in the future, handicraft would become chiefly preparation for evolving experimental new types and forms for mass production.

Gropius believed that talented craftspersons, who could turn out individual designs and market them, would always exist. However, the Bauhaus concentrated on a different direction, that would prevent human "enslavement by the machine by giving its products a content of reality and significance, and so saving the home from mechanistic anarchy." This also applied to architecture.[2]

During the years of its existence, the Bauhaus embraced a wide range of visual arts: architecture, planning, painting, sculpture, industrial design, and theatre stage design and technology. The Bauhaus sought a new and meaningful working relationship among all the processes of artistic creation, culminating in a new "cultural equilibrium," as Gropius described it, in the visual environment. Teachers and students worked together in a community effort, trying to become vital participants in the modern world. One of the fundamental precepts of the Bauhaus was that the teacher's own approach should never be imposed on the student. In fact, any attempt by the student to imitate the teacher was ruthlessly suppressed: stimulation from the teacher was solely to help students to find their bearings.

The Bauhaus was a synthesis of the arts, attempting the lofty goal of totally redesigning the visual environment by merging visual art and architecture. Although highly influential in its time, it soon became an isolated style of its own. Many famous artists participated in the Bauhaus School, but perhaps the intrinsic pluralism of the twentieth century and the constant striving for something "new" doomed the Bauhaus to a brief life. It was a synthesis— perhaps the only synthesis of its time—and a forerunner of the interdisciplinary art of the current age; however, the age itself made that synthesis impossible to sustain.

CHAPTER REVIEW

Critical Thought

What is the relationship between poverty and crime? In the Great Depression, when so many people had so little of material value, people could safely leave their doors unlocked. What is poverty? Is it lack of material things or a condition of the human spirit? Or is there some connnection?

Some of the disillusionment of the world from World War I through World War II, with its wars, dehumanization, and broken promises, can be seen in the art of the period. Certainly the anti-art art called dada brings home that idea. What we find, in addition, in the art of this time is something more personal and unreflective of the world around it: we find artists dabbling with the unconscious and subconscious mind. Some of the artists we have just studied do not care about our perceptions of the world we see around us, but care more about evocative images that stir something more primal in us.

When art gets so personal—or impersonal—it moves to a different plane from the one we might be used to, and that plane may or may not be a deeper one. Sometimes it offers nothing but self-centered drivel, sometimes it can be more profound than more "beautiful" or representational art, and sometimes it is difficult to know which is which because the language of images to which we are accustomed no longer applies.

Summary

After reading this chapter, you should be able to:

- Describe the condition of the world from 1914 to 1945, including specific references to economic factors, political situations, and military strategies.
- Explain the philosophies of pragmatism and existentialism and apply the latter to developments in literature and theatre.
- Discuss major writers of fiction and poetry.
- Characterize new styles in visual art and architecture arising during the period, including specific reference to individuals, styles, and works of art.
- Identify composers who pursued traditional and non-traditional pursuits in music by noting their approach to tonality, rhythm, and so on.
- Understand the characteristics of expressionism, absurdism, and epic theatre, including specific playwrights and productions.
- Discuss modern dance and film by noting specific movements, ideas, and practitioners.
- Apply the elements and principles of composition to analyze and compare individual works of art and architecture illustrated in the chapter.

CHAPTER EIGHTEEN

Postmodernism: The Pluralistic Age

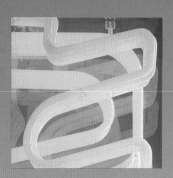

OUTLINE

A PLURALISTIC WORLD ORDER

THE VISUAL ARTS AND ARCHITECTURE
Abstract Expressionism
Pop Art
Op Art
Hard Edge
Photorealism and Conceptualism
Neo-Expressionism
Primary Structures
Abstraction
Found Sculpture and Junk Culture
Minimalism
Ephemeral and Environmental Art
  Installations
Light Art
Postmodernism
Neo-Abstraction
Video Art
"New" Realism
Architectural Modernism
Architectural Postmodernism

PLURALISM IN LITERATURE

MUSIC

THEATRE

FILM

DANCE

FOCAL POINT: AN OUTPOURING
OF ETHNICITY

VIEW

THE END OF HISTORY

In the physical world, things have changed drastically since the time of our Paleolithic ancestors, and the pace of change seems to be accelerating. In terms of the fundamentals of who we are as human beings, however, the changes seem almost superficial. The accumulation of material goods and the superficial gloss of technology may camouflage more important issues concerning what it means to be human and what it means to live a meaningful life. We can put a rover on Mars, but we cannot determine how to live in harmony with those around us.
We can clone a sheep, but we cannot eradicate ignorance.
At least one contemporary historian and scholar has suggested that we have come to the end of history. That challenging theory invites us to consider whether anything really "new" has happened to humanity at any time in history. The answers to questions about ourselves and our relationships to other people and an ultimate creator or force beyond us seem just as mysterious today as they were at the dawn of history.

Above Detail of Fig. **18.28**.

18.1 Louise Nevelson, *Black Wall*, 1959. Wood, 9 ft 4 ins × 7 ft 1¼ ins × 2 ft 1½ ins (264 × 217 × 65 cm). Tate Gallery, London. © ARS, New York and DACS, London 1999.

KEY TERMS

Some of the basic terms and concepts we will encounter in this chapter include the following:

Postmodernism, a broad description of cultural and artistic theory criticizing traditional culture, theory, and politics.

Abstract expressionism, an art style characterized by nontraditional brushwork and nonrepresentational subject matter.

Pop art, painting and sculpture employing subjects drawn from popular culture.

Op art plays on the possibilities offered by optics and perception.

Neo-expressionism, a visual art movement characterized by nightmarish and often repulsive images.

Hard edge—hard-edged abstraction—a painting style characterized by flat color areas with hard edges separating one color area from another.

Environmental art, art that attempts to create an inclusive experience for the viewer.

Aleatory, meaning chance or accidental. A term used for twentieth-century music in which the composer deliberately incorporates elements of chance.

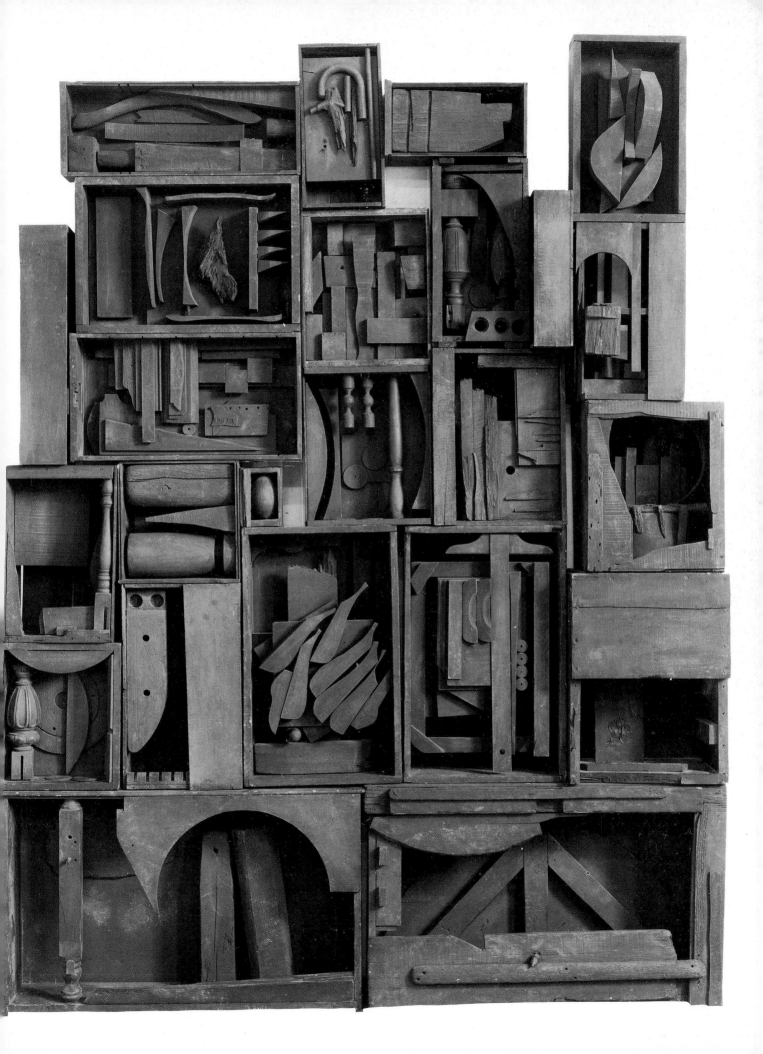

A PLURALISTIC WORLD ORDER

Our vision of ourselves and where we are going is probably as unclear to us as it was to our Paleolithic ancestors. As we are threatened with being drowned out by the clamor of our machines, overwhelmed by social problems, poisoned by our own waste, and swamped by the inane, we struggle to understand what it means to be human, turning to the arts of the past for inspiration, if not for answers. In the same spirit, we must also examine the art that is being created in our own time. As we strive to cope with our own finiteness from day to day, it is there that we may find the clues to who and what we are, and who we might become.

Increasingly, we recognize that even as our humanness unites us, there are manifold expressions of individuality in that togetherness. To paraphrase St Paul, the body that represents humanity is not all ears or eyes or feet. It takes diverse members, each with different purposes, to make a complete body. Thus, as the twentieth century closes and a new century begins, the evidence, indeed, the celebration, of pluralism—of difference—has become an important theme.

Decolonization

Before the end of World War II, a large portion of the globe, especially in what we call the Third World, existed under the colonial rule of outside nations. After World War II that order changed. During the late 1940s, decolonization was spurred by nationalist wars of independence, although the Dutch and the British, for example, had actually planned for the independence of their colonies in Egypt, India, and Malaysia. In the 1950s, as the Cold War

Map 18.1 The world economic situation in the early 1990s.

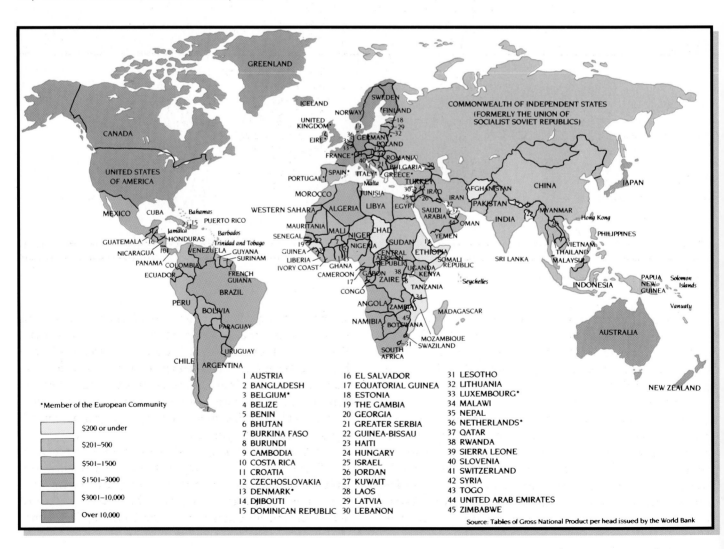

1 AUSTRIA	16 EL SALVADOR	31 LESOTHO
2 BANGLADESH	17 EQUATORIAL GUINEA	32 LITHUANIA
3 BELGIUM*	18 ESTONIA	33 LUXEMBOURG*
4 BELIZE	19 THE GAMBIA	34 MALAWI
5 BENIN	20 GEORGIA	35 NEPAL
6 BHUTAN	21 GREATER SERBIA	36 NETHERLANDS*
7 BURKINA FASO	22 GUINEA-BISSAU	37 QATAR
8 BURUNDI	23 HAITI	38 RWANDA
9 CAMBODIA	24 HUNGARY	39 SIERRA LEONE
10 COSTA RICA	25 ISRAEL	40 SLOVENIA
11 CROATIA	26 JORDAN	41 SWITZERLAND
12 CZECHOSLOVAKIA	27 KUWAIT	42 SYRIA
13 DENMARK*	28 LAOS	43 TOGO
14 DJIBOUTI	29 LATVIA	44 UNITED ARAB EMIRATES
15 DOMINICAN REPUBLIC	30 LEBANON	45 ZIMBABWE

*Member of the European Community

$200 or under
$201–500
$501–1500
$1501–3000
$3001–10,000
Over 10,000

Source: Tables of Gross National Product per head issued by the World Bank

	GENERAL EVENTS	LITERATURE & PHILOSOPHY	VISUAL ART & ARCHITECTURE	THEATRE & CINEMA	MUSIC & DANCE
1945					
	Hiroshima		Le Corbusier (**18.38**) Mies van der Rohe (**18.36**)	Beckett Miller Ionesco	Babbitt
	Korean War		Wright (**18.37**) Noguchi (**18.18**) Johnson (**18.36**) Pollock (**18.3**)	Williams Genet Rossellini	Parker Gillespie
	Start of Vietnam War		de Kooning (**18.4**) Rothko (**18.5**) Giacometti (**18.21**)	Hitchcock Fellini	Boulez Cage
	Cold War		Nervi (**18.39**) Fuller (**18.40**)	Kurosawa	Merce Cunningham Presley
1960					
	Decolonization	Wiesel Narayan	Hepworth (**18.19**) Nevelson (**18.1, 18.17**)	Bergman	Stockhausen
	Cuban missile crisis	Heller	Calder (**18.20**) Kosuth (**18.13**) Oldenburg (**18.8**)	Pinter	Foss
		Solzhenitsyn Yevtushenko	Segal (**18.10**) Warhol (**18.9**)		Berio Reich
	Arab nationalism	Momaday	Lichtenstein (**18.6**) Vasarély (**18.11**) Smithson (**18.25**) Nam June Paik (**18.31**)		Davis
1975					
		Abu-Khalid Khamis	Piano and Rogers (**18.43**) Shapiro (**18.29**) Bofill (**18.41**)	Spielberg	Penderecki Rorem
			Moore (**18.44**) Graves (**18.42**)	Churchill Wilson	
	Fall of Berlin Wall Demise of communism	Morrison Jones Pynchon	Frankenthaler (**18.7**) Clemente (**18.14**) Kiefer (**18.15**) Christo (**18.26**) Pfaff (**18.27**)		
	Gulf War		realism Pelli (**18.45**) Roberts (**18.34**)	Kushner Lee	Musique actuelle
2000					

Timeline 18.1 The late twentieth century.

polarized the entire world, violent popular revolutions challenged the remnants of colonialism in North Africa and southeast Asia. By the 1960s several African countries had undergone sweeping changes and had achieved independence with the more-or-less freely given consent of their previous overlords.

The effects of decolonization have been widespread and, to a large extent, problematical. Violent conflicts among tribal powers, oppressive military dictatorships, suppression of human rights, the use of unusually cruel weapons of war, and famine, for example, have replaced the injustices of colonial rule. Even today, with Eastern Europe having thrown off communism, the absence of any strong central authority has resulted in an explosion of ethnic violence that had lain dormant under the Soviets. Everywhere, those who have struggled for "freedom" have begun to learn that "independence" is not an automatic state of grace. Freedom has been confused with economic comfort, and when unrealistic expectations are not immediately fulfilled, disillusionment brings about more violent uprisings to no clear purpose.

In 1952, Alfred Sauvy, using an analogy referring to the Third Estate at the time of the French Revolution, called the emerging states that belonged to neither the Western nor the Eastern bloc, the "Third World." A Third World Movement emerged from the Bandung Conference of 1955, with the goal of bringing together subjugated peoples and dominated states in a common defense of their political interests and national security. Today the countries of the Third World do not constitute a unified bloc—the extreme diversity of their social formations, cultures, and histories make this impossible—but they have their own specific problems and strengths, and they represent pluralistic economic strategies and conditions that have yielded plural experiences and results.

The Cold War

After World War II, the United States and the Soviet Union dominated the world. The two former allies quickly grew apart as each sought to protect its sphere of influence from the other, and a period of tense conflict, sometimes called "peaceful coexistence," lasted for the next forty-five years.

The period of greatest conflict, the Cold War years of 1946–62, witnessed strain between the two great powers over the division of Germany, the Marshall Plan for the rebuilding of Europe, and the Berlin crisis, and the antagonism took an extended military form in Korea (1950–53). Toward the end of the 1950s, with the United States and the Soviet Union experiencing the beginnings of détente, the scene of international conflict shifted to Southeast Asia. The changing power relations between the USA, the USSR, and China destabilized the region after the French were thrown out of the area. The United States wanted to create in South Vietnam a military state like that in South Korea, which would be capable of resisting the communist insurgency. A strong anti-war movement in the United States and a strong offensive attack by the NLF (National Liberation Front), called the Tet Offensive, eventually spelled the end of American policy in South Vietnam.

After the late 1960s, another movement grew in importance, and that was the rise of Arab nationalism in the Middle East. Defeat in the 1967 Arab–Israeli war and the death of Egypt's President Nasser in 1970 left the door open for the return of religious leaders on the political scene. Fundamentalist protest grew strong on the disillusionment with progress and on the failure of various attempts at social and economic development, and, eventually, became a destabilizing factor.

A Unified Europe

As the Soviet Union under Mikhail Gorbachev (gahr-bah-chawf) and world communism in general disintegrated in the early 1990s, the large conflicts turned upon economics. The nations of Western Europe moved slowly but systematically toward an economically unified European community. In 1992 that movement was called into question by the European Community, because many of the partners disagreed about goals and operating details. Germany struggled to overcome the economic drag of its reunification. Providing aid to the former Soviet Union presented additional challenges for the European Community as well as for the individual states there.

Science and Liberty

As science and technology race on, questions of ethics and governmental control stubbornly resist clear solution. These vital concerns set the stage for military ventures, civil technology, and fundamental issues of individual liberty and social order. The development of nuclear weapons maintained by major and minor powers—of which Israel, Iran, Pakistan, India, and North Korea are only a few—rocket technology and "Star Wars" defenses, are threats to contemporary cultures that drain resources which might otherwise go to more civilized pursuits.

Who controls whom, how, and for what, remain critical issues as human knowledge and understanding of its applications expand. Who should control decisions about prolonging life through mechanical means? Who should control the dissemination of birth control devices and drugs such as the "abortion pill"? Is there a right to die and who has it? Is there a right to live, and who has that? These are a few of the difficult issues facing a pluralistic society with a rigid tradition of individual freedoms.

Another Millennium

The second half of the twentieth century is over. Societies exist in a global environment in which actions of even the smallest nation or single individual can have ramifications around the world that are often well beyond the importance of the original cause. The uncritical optimism spawned by the victory of democracy over totalitarianism in World War II has faded, to be replaced by a more realistic, if less positive, appreciation of social inequities within democracy itself. The inevitable conflict that arises when a state pursues individual liberties as well as social rights, and the question of where one ends and the other begins, are among the most vexing problems facing humankind. The questions of individual responsibility versus individual rights, and of accommodating minority differences while maintaining cultural integrity, plague every turn.

Multinational corporations function as supranational governments, and the creation of life in a test-tube is a scientific reality. Mechanization has assumed universal proportions, and computer-generated conclusions threaten

TECHNOLOGY: PUTTING DISCOVERY TO WORK

Robots

Robots—at least as an idea—occur in ancient mythology, and as long ago as 1738 a Parisian inventor made an artificial duck that quacked, ate grain, swam, and flapped its wings. The word Robot was coined in 1923 in Karel Čapek's (CHAH-pek) play *R.U.R.* (Rossum's Universal Robots), and it is the Czech word for worker. In the 1940s, Isaac Asimov, a science fiction writer, described the first benevolent robots, whose purpose was to serve humans.

The first actual robots derived from the work of Joseph Engelberger, a physicist devoted to Isaac Asimov, and the inventor George C. Devol. Engelberger had studied the development of digital controls, which had been used in World War II to aim and fire guns from ships, and which automatically adapted to changes in the position of the ship and the motion of the water. Devol had developed a Programmed Article Transfer device that Engelberger knew could become a robot. The two joined forces to create Unimates, robots that would replace humans in jobs that were tedious, limiting, and dangerous. After being turned down by everyone they approached, they eventually found a manufacturer willing to invest $25,000 in the experiment.

At first, the business was not successful, mainly because of the short-term view of economics taken by management (not the fear of losing jobs by labor). Today, Engelberger works to create and sell robots

designed for a service economy—for example, robots that can clean floors and toilets. One popular robot, called "Helpmate," is an all-purpose hospital aide that delivers meals, mail, and medicine, runs errands, gives directions, and speaks English (Fig. **18.2**). Engelberger's robots always conform to Asimov's three laws of robotics: (1) a robot must not harm a human being, nor through inaction allow one to come to harm; (2) a robot must always obey human beings, unless that is in conflict with the first law; (3) a robot must protect itself from harm, unless that is in conflict with the first or second laws.[1]

18.2 "Helpmate" robot being used to carry patients' meals at a hospital.

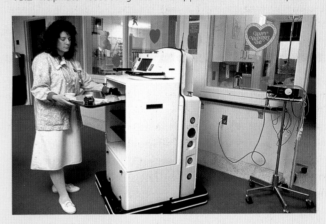

to replace human reason as the source of problem solving. Technocrats are poised to rule a world of individuals whose education, if any, has consisted solely of job training. Philosophy in many quarters is considered unproductive speculation, and usefulness alone has become the touchstone of value. In short, many of our contemporaries seem to have progressed to the point that they, in Oscar Wilde's cynical words, "know the price of everything and the value of nothing."

Postmodernism

At various points in this chapter, a term arises that, although we attempt to define it in specific terms relative to the art in question, needs attention before we examine the

sweep of the arts since World War II. That term is *postmodernism*. For more than twenty years, debates about postmodernism have dominated the cultural and intellectual scene in many fields. In aesthetic and cultural theory, arguments emerged over whether "modernism" in the arts was or was not dead and what sort of "postmodern" art was succeeding it. In philosophy, discussion centered upon whether or not the tradition of modern philosophy had ended and been replaced by a new "postmodern" philosophy associated with Nietzsche (see p. 503) and others. Eventually, the postmodern discussion produced new social and political theories, as well as theoretical attempts to define the multifaceted aspects of the postmodern phenomenon itself.

Basically, discourses about postmodernism raise issues that resist easy conclusions. Advocates of postmodernism

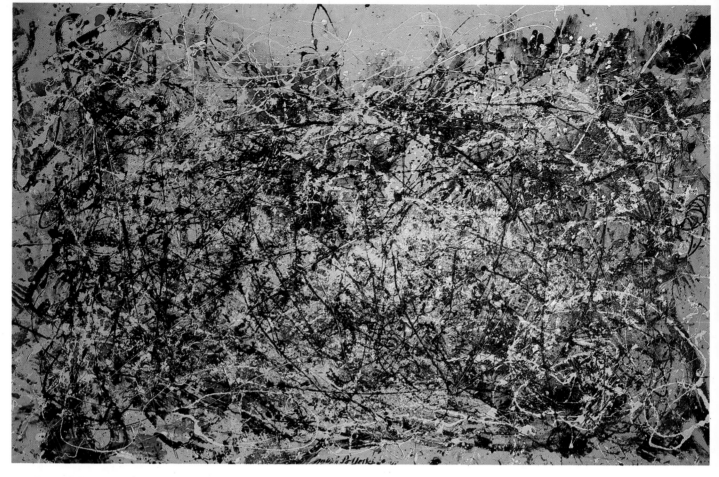

18.3 Jackson Pollock, *Number 1*, 1948. Oil and enamel on canvas, 5 ft 8 ins × 8 ft 8 ins (1.73 × 2.64 m). Museum of Modern Art, New York. Purchase. Photo: © 1998 Museum of Modern Art, New York. © ARS, New York and DACS, London 1999.

harshly criticize traditional culture, theory, and politics, and defenders of modernism respond either by ignoring the challenges, attacking postmodernism in return, or attempting to come to terms with new discourses and positions. Critics of postmodernism contend that it is a passing fad, a specious invention of self-seeking intellectuals, or an attempt to devalue the liberating theories and values of modernism.

In fact, there is no unified postmodern theory, or even a coherent set of positions. Rather, we find great diversity among theories often lumped together as "postmodern" and a great plurality—often contradictory—among postmodern positions. We certainly do not have the space to trace the issues in depth, but we must, at least, acknowledge them "up front," as it were.

The questions "What is modernism?" and "What is postmodernism?" are highly relevant to the twentieth century and its arts. "Modernity" is often conceptualized as the "modern age" and "postmodernity" as a term for describing the period that allegedly follows modernity. Modernity, as theorized by Marx and others, is a term for an historical period encompassing the epoch that follows the Middle Ages or feudalism. Modernism, then, might be defined as an attempt to overturn the feudal world and to produce a just and egalitarian social order that embodies

reason and social progress. Modernity enters everyday life through the dissemination of modern art, the products of consumer society, new technologies, and new modes of transportation and communication that have constituted the modern world. "Modernism" could be used to describe the art movements of the modern age (impressionism, art for art's sake, expressionism, surrealism, and other avant-garde movements).

Postmodern theorists, however, claim that in the contemporary high tech media society, emergent processes of change and transformation are producing a new, "postmodern," society that constitutes a novel state of history and a novel socio-cultural formation which requires new concepts and theories. "Postmodernism" would describe those diverse aesthetic forms and practices which come after and break with modernism. These forms include the architecture of Philip Johnson (see Fig. **18.36**), the musical experiments of John Cage (see p. 608), the art of Warhol (see Fig. **18.9**), the novels of Thomas Pynchon (see p. 607), and films such as *Blade Runner* or *Blue Velvet*. The debate centers on whether there is or is not a sharp conceptual distinction between modernism and postmodernism and the relative merits and limitations of these movements.

Therefore, postmodernism begins with a loss of faith in the dreams of modernism (the mindset that emerged during the Enlightenment, an optimistic faith in the idea that methodology of science could lead to meaningful understanding of people). Postmodernism, however, does not suggest anything to replace modernism. Rather, it invents a new and evolving language with words such as "metaphorical structuring," "deconstruction," and "metanarrative." As we work our way through this chapter, perhaps—just perhaps—this engaging and challenging dilemma will begin to coalesce for us in the art images we study.

THE VISUAL ARTS AND ARCHITECTURE

Abstract Expressionism

The first fifteen years following the end of World War II were dominated by a style called "abstract expressionism." The style originated in New York, and it spread rapidly throughout the world on the wings of modern mass communications. Two characteristics identify abstract expressionism. One is nontraditional brushwork, and the other is nonrepresentational subject matter. This complete freedom to reflect inner life led to the creation of works with high emotional intensity. Absolute individuality of expression and the freedom to be irrational underlie this style. This may have had some connection with the confidence inspired by postwar optimism and the triumph of individual freedom: as the implications of the nuclear age sank in, abstract expressionism all but ceased to exist.

The most acclaimed painter to create his own particular version of this style was Jackson Pollock (PAH-luhk; 1912–56). A rebellious spirit, Pollock came upon his characteristic approach to painting only ten years before his death. Although he insisted that he had absolute control, his compositions consist of what appear to be simple dripping and spilling of paint onto huge canvases, which he placed on the floor in order to work on them. His work (Fig. **18.3**), often called "action painting," conveys a sense of tremendous energy. The viewer seems to feel the painter's motions as he applied the paint.

Willem de Kooning (VIHL-uhm duh KOHN-ing; 1904–97) took a different approach to abstract expressionism. Sophisticated texture and heightened focal areas (Fig. **18.4**) emerged as de Kooning reworked, scraped off, repainted, and painted again. Yet this laborious work produced works that express spontaneity and free action.

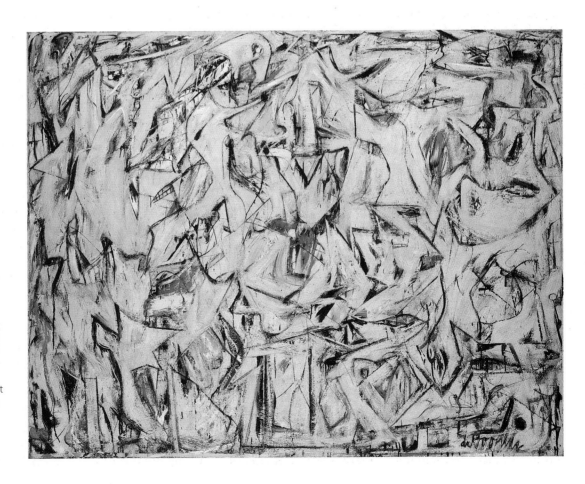

18.4 Willem de Kooning, *Excavation*, 1950. Oil on canvas, 6 ft 8¹/₈ ins × 8 ft 4¹/₈ ins (2.04 × 2.54 m). Courtesy the Art Institute of Chicago (Collection Mr and Mrs F.C. Logan Prize, Gift of Mr and Mrs Edgar Kaufmann Jr and Mr and Mrs Noah Goldowsky). © Willem de Kooning, ARS, New York, and DACS, London 1999.

The work has a ferocity and passion that tend to build in intensity as the eye moves from one focal area to the next.

Included among the work of the abstract expressionists is the *color-field* painting of Mark Rothko (1903–70), whose highly individualistic paintings follow a process of reduction and simplification (Fig. **18.5**). Rothko left all "memory, history, and geometry" out of his canvases. These, he said, were "obstacles between the painter and the idea." Rothko's careful juxtaposition of hues has a deep emotional impact on many viewers.

The abstract expressionist tradition continued in the work of Helen Frankenthaler (FRANK-en-thahl-ur; b. 1928), whose work we examine more closely in the Masterwork box associated with Figure **18.7**.

The emotionalism of abstract expressionism was followed by an explosion of styles: pop, op, hard edge, minimal, post-minimal, environmental, body, earth, video, kinetic, photorealist, and conceptual. We can describe only a few of these here.

Pop Art

Pop art, which evolved in the 1950s, concerned itself above all with representational images. The term "pop" was coined by the English critic Lawrence Alloway, and it simply meant that the subjects of these paintings are found in popular culture. The treatments of pop art also came from mass culture and commercial design. These sources provided pop artists with what they took to be the essential aspects of the visual environment that surrounded them. The pop artists themselves traced their heritage back to dada (see Chapter 17), although much of the heritage of the pop tradition continues to be debated.

18.5 Mark Rothko, *Number 10*, 1950. Oil on canvas, 7 ft 6³/₈ ins × 4 ft 9¹/₈ ins (2.3 × 1.45 m). Museum of Modern Art, New York (Gift of Philip Johnson). © Kate Rothko Prizel and Christopher Rothko/DACS 1999.
18.6 Roy Lichtenstein, *Whaam!*, 1963. Acrylic on canvas, 5 ft 8 ins × 13 ft 4 ins (1.73 x 4.06 m). Tate Gallery, London. © Estate of Roy Lichtenstein/DACS 1999.

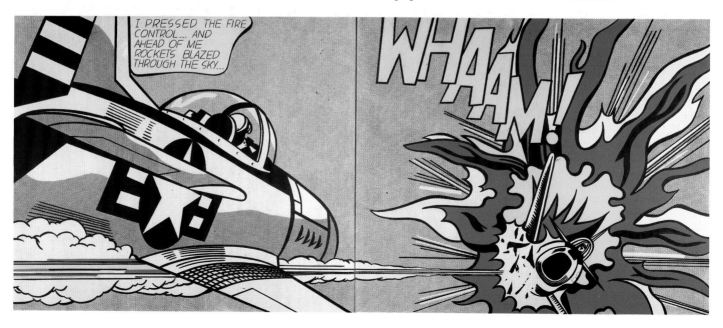

MASTERWORK

Helen Frankenthaler—*Buddha*

Helen Frankenthaler is probably the most recognized and celebrated of late twentieth-century women artists. A second-generation abstract expressionist, she began her painting career just as an earlier group of artists, including Jackson Pollock, Willem de Kooning, and Mark Rothko, were gaining widespread public attention.

Her innovative technique, seen in *Buddha* (Fig. **18.7**), involved pouring paint directly onto the unprimed surface of a canvas, allowing the color to soak into its support, rather than painting on top of an already sealed canvas, as was customary. This highly intuitive process, known as "stain painting," became the hallmark of her style and enabled her to create color-filled canvases filled with amorphous shapes that seemed to float on air. The image created thus has infinite potential meaning, apart from that suggested by whatever title Frankenthaler chooses, because the very freedom of the form means that viewers are free to choose their own associations. The viewer is, however, directed by the sensual quality of the work, whose fluidity and nonlinear use of color give it softness and grace. In her art, the process of pouring paint onto and over the canvas, allowing the flowing pigment to create its own shapes and edges, became a literal metaphor for experiences of nature. As a consequence, the works maintain powerful allusive qualities, even the impression of infinite space.

18.7 Helen Frankenthaler, *Buddha*, 1983. Acrylic on canvas, 6 ft 2 ins × 6 ft 9 ins (1.88 × 2.06 m) . Private collection. Courtesy Andre Emmerich Gallery, New York.

The compelling paintings of Roy Lichtenstein (LIK-ten-styn; 1923–97) are the most familiar examples of pop art (Fig. **18.6**). These magnified cartoon-strip paintings use the effect created by the dots of the screen that is used in color printing in comics. Using dot stencils about the size of a coin, Lichtenstein built his subjects, which are original, up into stark and dynamic, if sometimes violent, images.

Common, everyday objects serve as models for Claes Oldenburg (b. 1929). *Two Cheeseburgers, with Every-thing* (Fig. **18.8**) presents an enigma to the viewer. What are we to make of it? Is it a celebration of the mundane? Or is a serious comment on our age implicit in these objects? Certainly Oldenburg calls our attention to the qualities of design in ordinary objects by taking them out of their normal contexts and changing their scale.

The influence of the pop movement can also be seen in the plaster figures of George Segal (b. 1924). Working from plaster molds taken from living figures, Segal builds

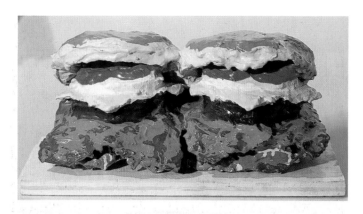

18.8 Claes Oldenberg, *Two Cheeseburgers, with Everything* (*Dual Hamburgers*), 1962. Burlap soaked in plaster, painted with enamel, 7 ins (17.8 cm) high. Museum of Modern Art, New York (Philip Johnson Fund). Photo: © 1998 Museum of Modern Art, New York.

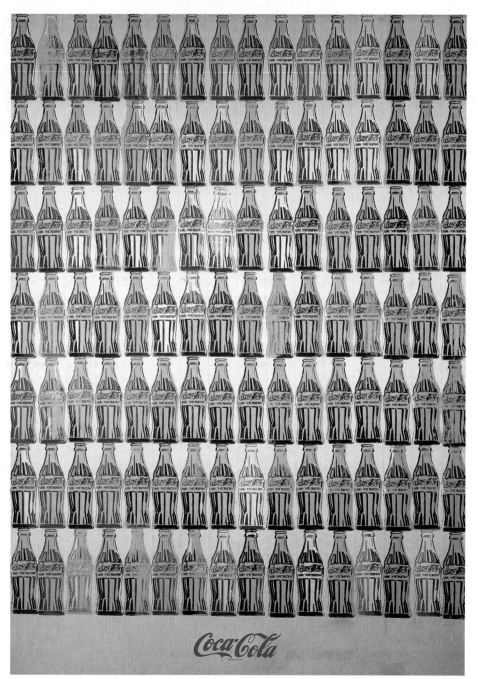

18.9 Andy Warhol, *Green Coca-Cola Bottles*, 1962. Oil on canvas, 6 ft 10 ins × 4 ft 9 ins (1.97 × 1.37 m). Whitney Museum of American Art, New York (purchase, with funds from the Friends of the Whitney Museum of American Art).
© The Andy Warhol Foundation for the Visual Arts, Inc./ARS, New York and DACS, London 1999.

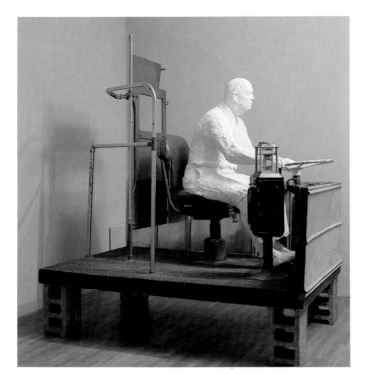

18.10 George Segal, *The Bus Driver*, 1962. Figure of plaster over cheesecloth; bus parts including coin box, steering wheel, driver's seat, railing, dashboard, etc. 6 ft 3 ins (1.91 m) high overall. Museum of Modern Art, New York (Philip Johnson Fund). © ADAGP, Paris and DACS, London 1999.

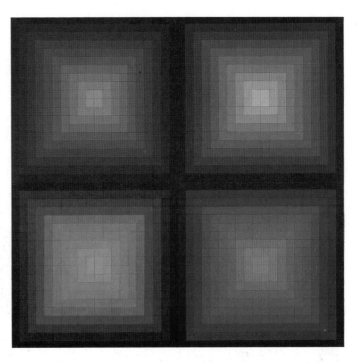

18.11 Victor Vasarély, *Arcturus II*, 1966. Oil on canvas, 5 ft 3 ins × 5 ft 3 ins (1.51 × 1.51 m). Hirshhorn Museum and Sculpture Garden, Smithsonian Institution, Washington, D.C. © ADAGP, Paris and DACS, London 1999.

scenes from everyday life with unpainted plaster images (Fig. **18.10**).

In the 1960s Andy Warhol (1928–87) focused on popular culture and contemporary consumerism in his ultra-representational art. The very graphic *Green Coca-Cola Bottles* (Fig. **18.9**) is a good example of his style. The starkness and repetitiousness of the composition are broken up by subtle variations. The apparently random breaks in color, line, and texture create moving focal areas, none of which is more important than another, yet each significant enough to keep the viewer's eye moving continuously through and around the painting. In these subtle variations, the artist takes an almost cubistlike approach to the manipulation of space and image.

Op Art

Op art plays on the possibilities offered by optics and perception. Emerging from work done in the 1950s, op art was an intellectually oriented and systematic style, very scientific in its applications. Based on perceptual tricks, the misleading images in these paintings capture our curiosity and pull us into a conscious exploration of what the optical illusion does and why it does it.

Victor Vasarély (vah-zah-ray-LEE; 1908–97) bends line and form to create a deceptive sense of three-dimensionality. Complex sets of stimuli proceed from horizontal, vertical, and diagonal arrangements. Using nothing but abstract form, Vasarély creates the illusion of real space.

The psychological effects of his images depend on extremely subtle repetition of shape and gradation of color. In *Arcturus II* (Fig. **18.11**), the symmetrical imagery seems to come into and out of focus because of the apparent brightness of the individual colors. Shape and color combine to create the optical experience, and what at first glance seems simple and straightforward, becomes complicated and deceptive. The more we look, the more we are convinced that we are "seeing things."

Hard Edge

Hard edge, or hard-edged abstraction, also came to its height during the 1950s and 1960s, in the work of Frank Stella (b. 1936), among others. Its flat color areas have hard edges which carefully separate one area from another. Essentially, hard edge is an exploration of design for its own sake. Stella often abandoned the rectangular format of most canvases in favor of irregular shapes in order to be

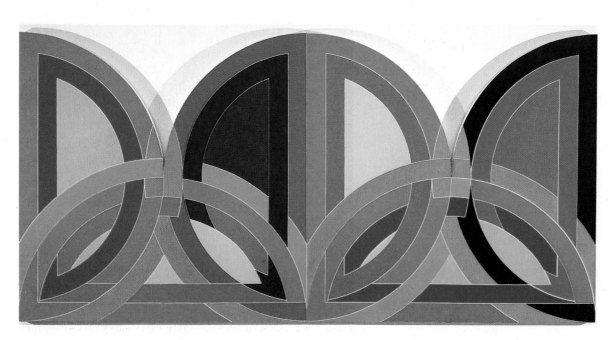

18.12 Frank Stella, *Tahkt-I-Sulayman I*, 1967. Polymer and fluorescent paint on canvas, 10 ft 1/4 in × 20 ft 2 1/4 ins (3.04 × 6.15 m). Pasadena Art Museum, California (Gift of Mr and Mrs Robert A. Rowan). © ARS, New York and DACS, London 1999.

sure that his paintings bore no resemblance to windows. The odd shape of the canvas thus became part of the design itself, as opposed to being a frame or a formal border within which the design was executed.

Some of Stella's paintings have iridescent metal powder mixed into the paint, and the metallic shine further enhances the precision of the composition. *Tahkt-I-Sulayman I* (Fig. **18.12**) stretches just over 20 feet (6 meters) across, with interspersed surging circles and half-circles of yellows, reds, and blues. The intensity of the surface, with its jarring fluorescence, counters the grace of its form, while the simplicity of the painted shapes is enriched by the variety of the repetitions.

Photorealism and Conceptualism

Photorealism is related to pop art in that it, too, relies on pre-existing images. As can be guessed from the name of the movement, it is a form of art that involves working directly from photographs, rather than from the original subjects. It came to the fore during the 1970s, in the work of people such as Richard Estes (b. 1932) and Chuck Close (b. 1940). Photorealism acknowledges the role that the camera plays in shaping our understanding of reality, and suggests obliquely that contemporary life is often centered more around manufactured than natural objects.

Conceptual art challenges the relationship between art and life in a different way, and, in fact, challenges the definition of art itself. Essentially anti-art, as was dada, conceptual art attempts to divorce the imagination from aesthetics. Ideas are more important than visual appearances. It insists that only the imagination and not the artwork is art. Therefore, artworks can be done away with. The creative process needs only to be documented by some incidental means—a verbal description, or a simple object such as a chair. But, of course, despite its claims, conceptual art depends on something physical to bridge the gap between the artist's imagination and the viewer's.

One and Three Chairs (Fig. **18.13**) by Joseph Kosuth (b. 1945) depicts three different realities. The first is that of the actual chair that sits between the photograph and the printed definition. The second reality is the lifesize photographic image of the same chair represented in the first reality. The third reality is the verbal description of the same chair. Using the third reality, we form in our mind an idea of the chair, and that might be termed a "conceptual reality." So the conceptual artwork, that is, the combination of actuality, photo image, and verbal description, presents a relationship "between an object and communicative methods of signifying that object."[2]

Neo-Expressionism

A recent controversial and momentarily successful movement has been called "neo-expressionism." One of its most notable adherents, the Italian Francesco Clemente (b. 1952), records images "that the rest of us repress." In *Untitled from White Shroud* (Fig. **18.14**), he forces the viewer to confront what may well be repulsive images. The painting has nightmarish qualities, and yet the fluid,

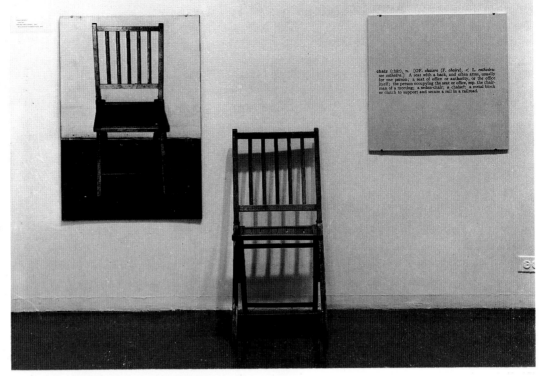

18.13 Joseph Kosuth, *One and Three Chairs*, 1965. Wooden folding chair, 32³/₈ ins (76.8 cm) high; photograph of chair, 36 × 24 ins (86.4 × 57.6 cm); photographic enlargement of dictionary definition of chair, 24 × 25 ins (57.6 × 60 cm). Collection, Museum of Modern Art, New York (Larry Aldrich Foundation Fund). Photo: © 1998 Museum of Modern Art, New York. © ARS, New York and DACS, London 1999.

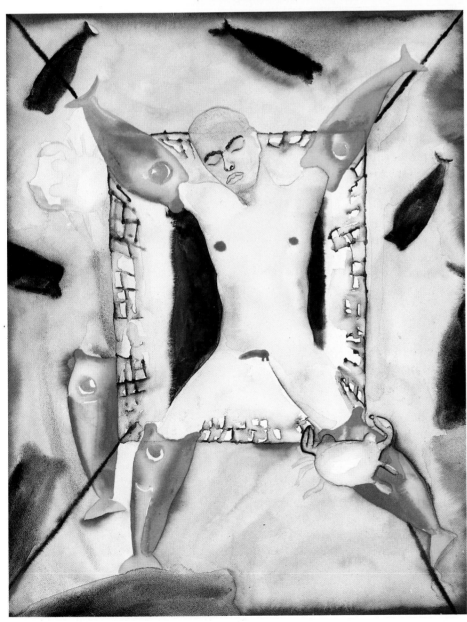

18.14 Francesco Clemente, *Untitled from White Shroud*, 1983. Watercolor. Kunsthalle, Basel, Switzerland.

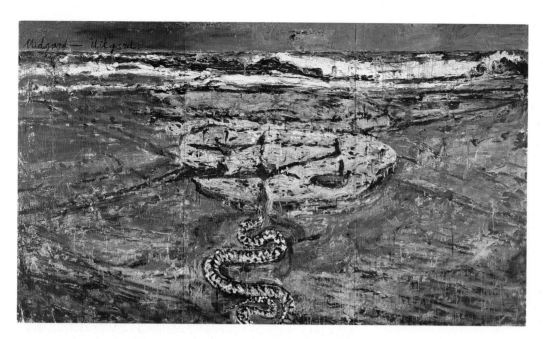

18.15 Anselm Kiefer, *Midgard*, 1980–5. Oil and emulsion on canvas, 11 ft 10 ins ×19 ft 9³/₄ ins (3.6 × 6.04 m). Carnegie Museum of Art, Pittsburgh.

18.16 David Smith, *Cubi XIX*, 1964. Stainless steel, 9 ft 5 ins (2.87 m) high. Tate Gallery, London. © Estate of David Smith/VAGA, New York/DACS, London 1999.

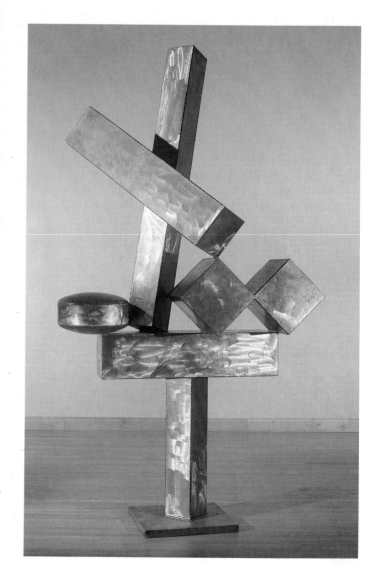

watercolor medium gives it a softened, translucent quality. The contrasts of the cool blues in the background and the bright red and yellow of the fishes capture our interest and successfully balance form and color.

Like the expressionists, neo-expressionists seek to evoke a particular emotional response in the viewer. German artist Anselm Kiefer (KEEF-urh; b. 1945) invests his work with strong emotive and empathetic content. In *Midgard* (Fig. **18.15**), he draws upon Nordic mythology to portray a desolate landscape of despair. "Midgard" means "middle garden," the term given by the Norse gods to the earth. In Nordic myth, the earth is destroyed by the Midgard serpent and other demons after three years of winter. Standing before this enormous painting, we find its scale and emotional power profoundly affecting. It takes up our whole field of vision and seems to surround us.

Primary Structures

The "primary structures" movement pursues two major goals: extreme simplicity of shapes and a kinship with architecture. A space–time relationship distinguishes primary structures from other sculpture. Viewers are invited to share an experience in three-dimensional space in which they can walk around and/or through the works. Form and content are reduced to their most "minimal" qualities.

Cubi XIX (Fig. **18.16**) by David Smith (1906–65) rises to nearly 10 feet (3 meters), and its seemingly precarious balance and its curious single cylinder convey a sense of urgency. Yet the work is in perfect balance. The texture of the luminescent stainless steel has a powerfully tactile

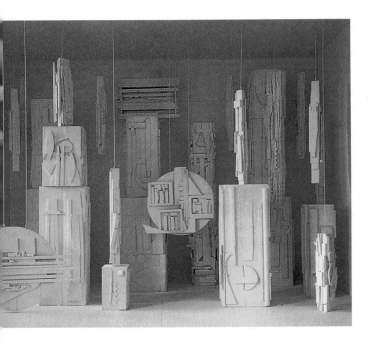

18.17 Louise Nevelson, *America—Dawn*, 1962. Painted wood, 18 × 14 × 10 ft (5.49 × 4.27 × 3.05 m). Art Institute of Chicago (Grant J. Pick Purchase Fund, 1967, 387). © ARS, New York and DACS, London 1999.

Abstraction

Less concerned with expressive content than other sculptors, Isamu Noguchi (ee-SAH-moo noh-GOO-chee; 1904–88) began experimenting with abstract sculptural design in the 1930s. His creations have gone beyond sculpture to provide highly dynamic and suggestive set designs for the choreography of Martha Graham (see p. 568), with whom he was associated for a number of years. Noguchi's *Kouros* figures (Fig. **18.18**) do seem to be abstractly related to archaic Greek sculpture, and they too exhibit exquisitely finished surfaces and masterly technique.

Another kind of abstraction of the human form

effect, yet it also creates a shimmering, almost impressionistic play of light. The forms are simple rectangles, squares, and a cylinder, and scale gives them a vital importance.

Louise Nevelson (1900–88) overcame the notion that sculpture was a man's profession because it involved heavy manual labor and became perhaps the first major woman sculptor of the twentieth century. In the 1950s, Nevelson began using found pieces of wood as her medium. At first miniature cityscapes, her work grew larger and larger. Painted a monochromatic flat black, *Black Wall* (see Fig. **18.1**) is a relief-like wall unit, whose pieces suggest the world of dreams. Their meaning remains a puzzle, although they make an intense appeal to the imagination.

Her *America—Dawn* (Fig. **18.17**) is similarly ambivalent. The decoration on her ivory-colored wooden blocks seems to have a primitive, mythic quality, but on the other hand we also sense the busy organization and sheer modernity of a circuit board or a complex machine. A Stonehenge or a city of skyscrapers?

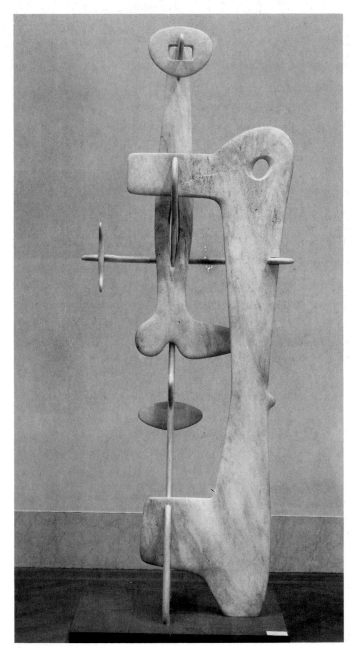

18.18 Isamu Noguchi, *Kouros* (in nine parts), 1944–5. Pink Georgia marble, slate base, about 9 ft 9 ins (2.97 m) high. Metropolitan Museum of Art, New York (Fletcher Fund, 1953).

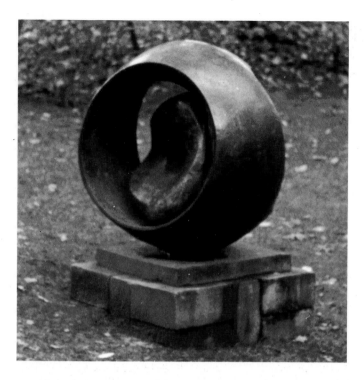

18.19 Dame Barbara Hepworth, *Sphere with Internal Form*, 1963. Bronze, 3 ft 4 ins (1.02 m) high. Collection, State Museum Kröller-Müller, Otterlo, The Netherlands.

appears in *Sphere with Internal Form* (Fig. **18.19**). Here Barbara Hepworth (1903–75) incorporates two sculptural devices—a small form resting inside a large, enclosing form, and the piercing of the form. Piercing gives the piece a sense of activity, as it admits light into the work and provides tonal contrasts.

The MOBILES of Alexander Calder (1898–1976; Fig. **18.20**) finally put abstract sculpture into motion. Decep-

18.20 Alexander Calder, *Spring Blossoms*, 1965. Painted metal and heavy wire, 4 ft 4 ins (1.32 m) high. Museum of Art, Pennsylvania State University. © ADAGP, Paris and DACS, London 1999.

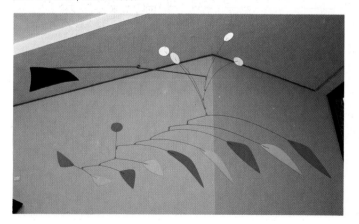

tively simple, these colorful shapes turn with the slightest air currents or by motors. Calder's pieces show us that sculpture can be created by the movement of forms in undefined space.

The figures of Alberto Giacometti (jah-koh-MET-tee; 1901–66) mark a return to objectivity. Giacometti was a surrealist sculptor in the 1930s, but he continued to explore the likeness of the human figure and the depiction of surface, as Figure **18.21** shows. Here form is reduced to its essence. The tortured fragmentation of the figure makes an emotional statement about what it feels like to be human in the contemporary world.

18.21 Alberto Giacometti, *Man Pointing*, 1947. Bronze, 6 ft 8½ ins (1.79 m) high. Museum of Modern Art, New York (Gift of Mrs John D. Rockefeller III). © ADAGP, Paris and DACS, London 1999.

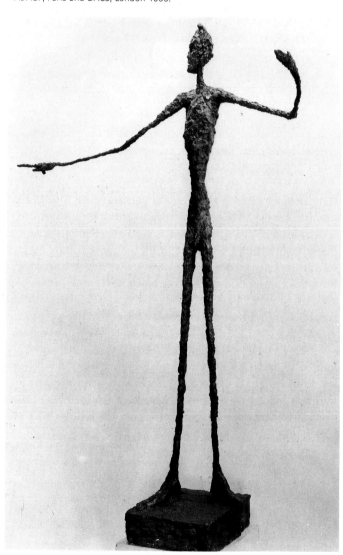

Pablo Picasso

Pablo Picasso (1881–1973) was born in Malaga, on the Mediterranean coast of Spain. He studied at the Academy of Fine Arts in Barcelona but had already mastered realistic technique, and had little use for school. At sixteen he had his own studio in Barcelona. In 1900 he first visited Paris, and in 1904 he settled there. His personal style began to form in the years from 1901 to 1904, a period often referred to as his blue period because of the pervasive blue tones he used in his paintings at that time. In 1905, as he became more successful, Picasso altered his palette, and the blue tones gave way to a terracotta color, a shade of deep pinkish red. At the same time his subject matter grew less melancholy and included dancers, acrobats, and harlequins. The paintings he did during the years between 1905 and 1907 are said to belong to his rose period (Fig. **16.25**).

Picasso played an important part in the sequence of different movements in the twentieth century. He said that to repeat oneself is to go against "the constant flight forward of the spirit." Primarily a painter, he also became a fine sculptor, engraver, and ceramist. In 1917 Picasso went to Rome to design costumes and scenery for Sergei Diaghilev's *Ballets russes* (see p. 531). This work stimulated another departure in Picasso's work, and he began to paint the works now referred to as belonging to his classic period, which lasted from about 1918 until 1925.

At the same time he was working on designs for the ballet, Picasso also continued to develop the cubist technique, making it less rigorous and austere. By the time he painted *Guernica*, his moving vision of the Spanish Civil War, the straight lines of early cubism had given way to curved forms. This huge painting (Fig. **18.23**), considered by many to be his masterpiece, was Picasso's response to the 1937 bombing by the Nationalist forces of the small Basque town of Guernica. He completed this emotional political statement in the same year. In it, as in many of his later pictures, distortions of form approach surrealism, but Picasso never called himself a surrealist. Picasso continued to work with incredible speed and versatility—as painter, ceramist, sculptor, designer, and graphic artist—into his nineties. The value of his estate was estimated at more than 500 million dollars when he died on 8 April 1973, in Mougins, France.

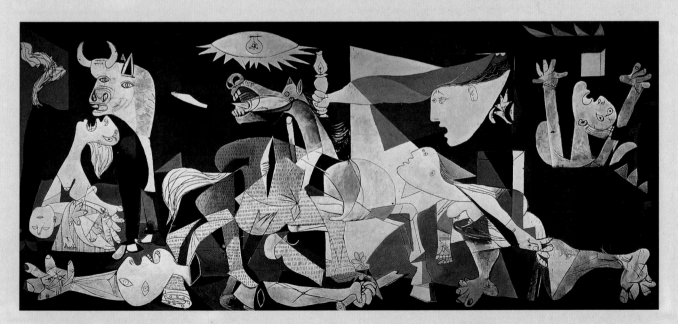

18.22 Pablo Picasso, *Guernica*, 1937. Oil on canvas, 11 ft 5¹/₂ ins × 25 ft 5³/₄ ins (3.5 × 7.8 m). Museo Nacional Centro de Arte Reina Sofia, Madrid.
© Succession Picasso?DACS 1999.

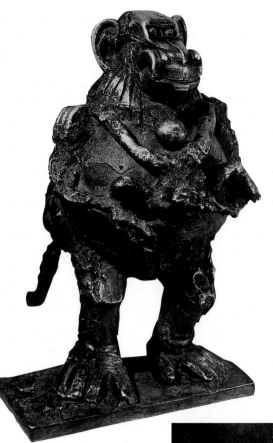

Found Sculpture and Junk Culture

Yet another approach to have emerged since World War II
is found sculpture—that is, objects taken from life and
presented as art for their inherent aesthetic value and
meaning. Perhaps developed out of cubist collages, the
movement called "junk culture" also took natural objects
and assembled them to create single artworks. Interpretations of this kind of assemblage art vary widely, but they
usually imply that the artist is making some value judgment on a culture to which built-in obsolescence and
throwaway materials are fundamental.

In Figure **18.23** we see a treatment of found objects by
Pablo Picasso. For *Baboon and Young*, he took a pair of
his son's toy cars and incorporated them into a humorous
parody.

Minimalism

In the late 1950s and 1960s, a style called "minimalism" in
painting and sculpture sought to reduce the complexity of

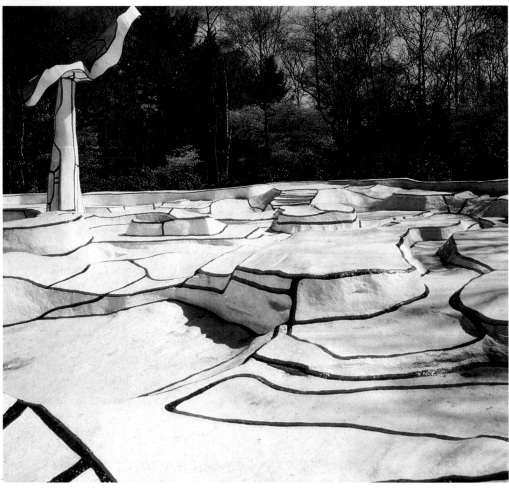

both design and content as far as possible. Instead, minimalist artists concentrated on nonsensual, impersonal, geometric shapes and forms. No communication was to pass between artist and respondent, no message was to be conveyed. Rather, the minimalists, such as Toby Smith, wanted to present neutral objects free of their own interpretations and leave response and "meaning" entirely up to the viewer.

Ephemeral and Environmental Art

Environmental art sets out to create an inclusive experience. In the *Jardin d'Émail* (zhahr-DAN day-MY; Fig. 18.24) by Jean Dubuffet (doo-boo-FAY; 1901–85), an area made of concrete is painted with white paint and black lines. Surrounded by high walls, the whole construction is capricious in form. Inside the sculptural environment we find a tree and two bushes of polyurethane. Here Dubuffet has tried to push the boundaries of art to their known limits, perhaps. He has consistently opted for chaos, for *art brut*—the art of children, psychotics, and amateurs. The *Jardin d'Émail* is one of several projects in which he has explored this chaotic, disorienting, and inexplicable three-dimensional form.

The dynamic and dramatic landscape of *Spiral Jetty* (Fig. 18.25) by Robert Smithson (1928–73), in the Great Salt Lake of Utah, is another example of environmental art. A number of concepts and ideas are represented here. The spiral shape represents the early Mormon belief that the Great Salt Lake was connected to the Pacific Ocean by an underground canal, which from time to time caused great whirlpools on the lake's surface. In addition, the jetty is intended to change the quality and color of the water around it, thereby creating a color-shift, as well as making a linear statement. Finally, the design is meant to be ephemeral as well as environmental. Smithson knew that eventually the forces of wind and water would transform, if not obliterate, the project. And, in fact, high water has submerged the jetty in recent years.

Designed to be transitory, *ephemeral* art makes its statement, then ceases to exist. Undoubtedly the largest works of sculpture ever designed were based on that concept. *The Umbrellas, Japan–USA, 1984–91* (Fig.

18.25 Robert Smithson, *Spiral Jetty*, 1969–70. Black rock, salt crystals, earth, and red water (algae), 160 ft (48.7 m) diameter; coil 1500 ft (457 m) long and 15 ft (4.6 m) wide. Great Salt Lake, Utah.

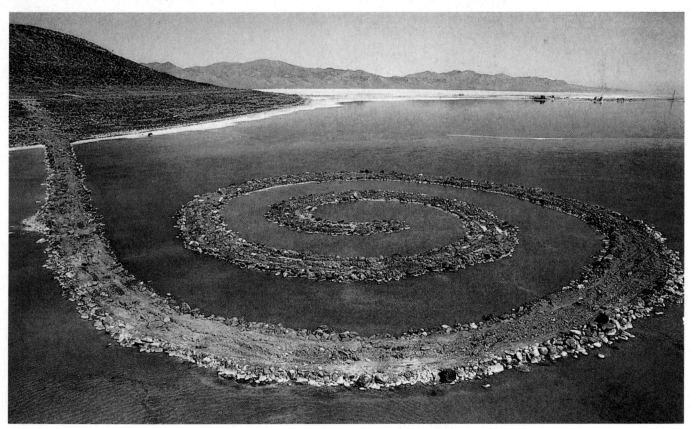

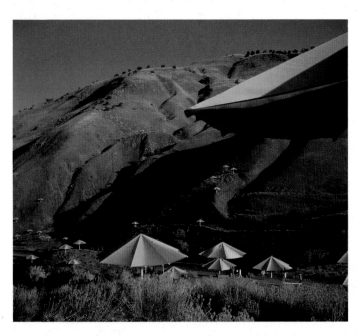

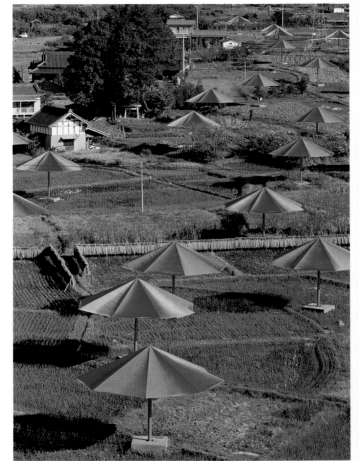

18.26 (*above* and *right*) Christo, *The Umbrellas, Japan–USA, 1984–91.*
Above: Valley north of Los Angeles, CA, 1,760 yellow umbrellas;   *Right:* Valley in prefecture of Ibaraki, Japan, 1,340 blue umbrellas. Combined length: 30 miles (48 km). © Christo 1991.

18.26) by Christo (Christo Jachareff, b. 1935) was an event and a process, as well as a sculptural work. In a sense, Christo's works are conceptual in that they call attention to the experience of art, rather than any actual permanent form. At the end of a short viewing period, *The Umbrellas* were removed and ceased to be.

Installations

"Environments" which have been expanded into room-size settings are now called "installations." The installations of Judy Pfaff (b. 1946) employ a variety of materials, including those of painting, in order to shape and charge architectural space. The art historian H.W. Janson likens her work to "exotic indoor landscapes," and finds her spontaneous energy similar to that of Jackson Pollock's action painting (see Fig. **18.3**). Nature seems to have inspired her installation *Dragons* (Fig. **18.27**). Swirling tendrils hang like brightly colored jungle foliage. Fiery reds predominate, although Pfaff uses the entire color spectrum. All this stands out against the white walls of the room. The sweeping diagonals seem carefully juxtaposed against linear verticals while, at the same time, a jumble of

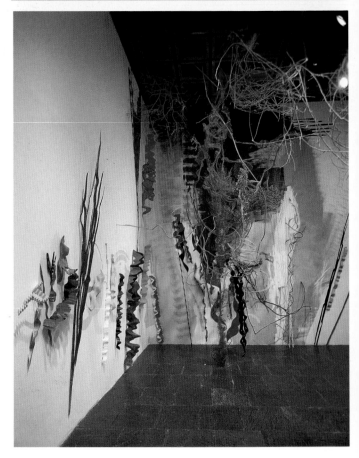

18.27 Judy Pfaff, *Dragons*, mixed media. Installation view at 1981 biennial, Whitney Museum of American Art, New York.

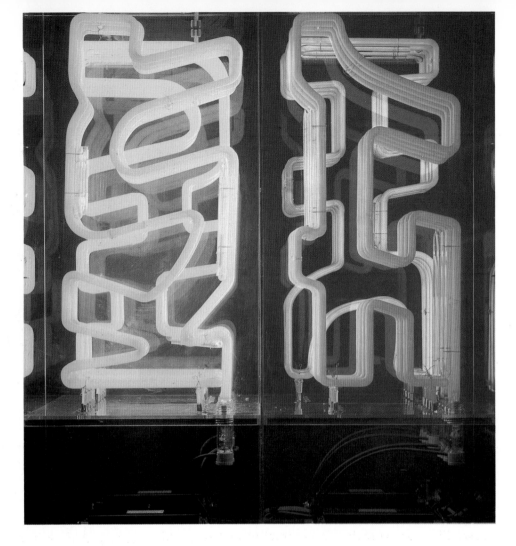

18.28 Chryssa, *Fragments for the Gates to Times Square*, 1966. Neon and plexiglas, 6 ft 9 ins × 2 ft 10½ ins × 2 ft 3½ ins (206 × 88 × 70 cm). Whitney Museum of American Art, New York (gift of Howard and Jean Lipman).

stringlike things in the far corner emanates confusion. The strong colors and proliferation of lines suggest that paint has been flung into space and, magically, suspended there.

Light Art

Since the 1960s, the use of light as an element in sculpture has gained in popularity. Its adherents see light as an independent aesthetic medium, and they use it in a variety of innovative ways.

Typical of artists working with light, (Varda) Chryssa (b. 1933) creates technically precise blinking neon sculptures using very simple shapes. Neon, so indicative of the commercialism and mechanization of modern life, serves as a symbolic comment on the modern era. Chryssa's (KRIS-uh) innovative constructions, such as *Fragments for the Gates to Times Square* (Fig. **18.28**), explore the experience of contemporary technology. Here stark color and linearity couple with intriguing depth in multiple rows of tubing and reflection from the plexiglas cases. His works also explore environmental space in a highly theatrical fashion, in this case surrounding the viewer with a garish ambience like that of Times Square or the Las Vegas Strip.

Postmodernism

The period from the late 1960s through the 1980s witnessed a variety of mostly individualistic reactions to the styles of the past—including the recent past of the twentieth century. Like the collective styles of the end of the nineteenth century, which were called post-impressionist, these "new" styles, which seem to have no common thread, have been lumped together as *postmodernist* styles. They are highly individualistic, although some artists prefer to return art to the anonymity of pre-Renaissance times. One recognizable aspect of the postmodernist styles appears to be a desire to return recognizable content or meaning to works of art, and the artists following these paths were reacting to what they felt was a clutter and lack of content in previous styles. To recount our earlier attribution from Ezra Pound, these artists sought to "make it new" and took great pains to be "different." The question of difference, however, became complicated by the fact that many, like the postmodernist architects, took great delight in eclectically borrowing from the past. They mixed old styles to create something "new." One common theme apparently shared by postmodernists is a basic concern for how art functions in society.

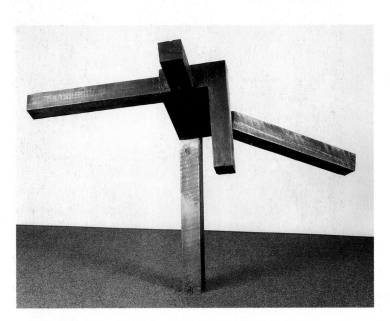

18.29 Joel Shapiro, *Untitled*, 1980–1. Bronze, 4 ft 4⁷/₈ ins × 5 ft 4 ins × 3 ft 9¹/₂ ins (1.34 × 1.62 × 1.15 m). Collection of the Whitney Museum of American Art, New York.

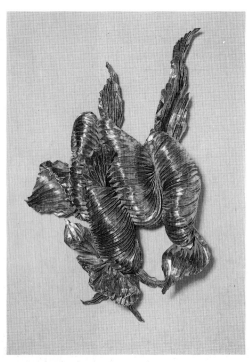

18.30 Lynda Benglis, *Passat*, 1990. Aluminum, 78 × 52 × 27 ins (198 × 132 × 68.5 cm). Paula Cooper Gallery, New York (photograph by Douglas Parker). © Lynda Benglis/DACS, London/VAGA, New York, 1999.

One artist who can represent this melange of styles is the sculptor Joel Shapiro. He was born, raised, and educated in New York, and his art gradually evolved into the production of miniature clay, glass, copper, and lead works shaped objectively. One particular aspect of his works illustrates the art of the 1980s—that is, the use of a variety of media and techniques, some of which are new and require new techniques. The mixture of media in previously untried ways provides new avenues of experimentation and mastery as well as providing works of art that have a different appearance from those of the past. Shapiro's works graduated from clusters of small geometric pieces—spread out on the floors of galleries in which the actual space in which they were assembled became an important element—to large-scale stick figures exhibiting precarious balance such as *Untitled* (Fig. **18.29**).[3] It is cast in metal but retains the texture and apparent construction methods of the wood from which it was originally constructed.

Neo-Abstraction

By the mid-1980s, other young artists sought to make their mark by reacting against the postmodernist trends. Their work returned to abstract and near-abstract works, including hard edge. These *neo-abstractionists*, like the postmod-

ernists, make up a loose confederation of mostly individualistic approaches. Like the postmodernists, the neo-abstractionists borrow freely from others by modifying or changing the scale, media, or color of older works to give them a new framework and, hence, new meaning. Occasionally, the new meanings include sarcasm and satire and often comment on the decadence of American society in the 1980s. An example is the work of Lynda Benglis, a painter who turned to sculpture. Her work also represents *process art*—that is, taking molten materials, letting them flow freely on the floor, and then adding color and/or shape to them. *Passat* (Fig. **18.30**) illustrates her recent work, in which she shapes knots, bows, and pleats into insectlike sculptures in shiny metal.

Video Art

Video Composition X by Nam June Paik (Payk; b. 1932) turned a large room into a garden of shrubbery, ferns, and small trees. As one looked up from the greenery, thirty television sets were all running the same program in unison. Bill Viola's *He Weeps for You* featured a drop of water forming at the end of a thin copper pipe and then falling on a drumhead. The image was blown up on a large television screen, and the sound of the falling drop was amplified into a thunderous boom. MIT's *Centerbeam* was a 220-foot

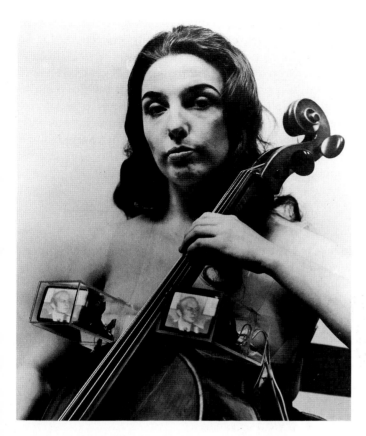

18.31 Nam June Paik, *TV Bra for Living Sculpture*, 1969. Performance by Charlotte Moorman with television sets and cello. Courtesy Holly Solomon Gallery, New York.

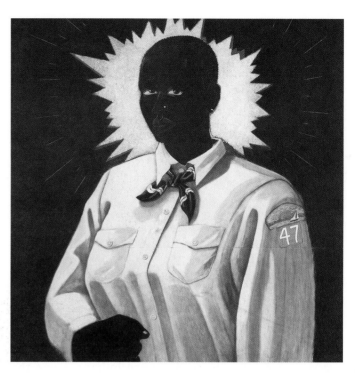

18.32 Kerry James Marshall, *Den Mother*, 1996. Acrylic on paper mounted on wood, 41 × 40 ins (104.1 × 101.6 cm). Collection of General Mills Corporation, Minneapolis, Minnesota. The Jack Shainman Gallery, New York.

(67-meter) long contraption using holograms, video, colored steam, and laser beams.

In fact, a wide-ranging genre of sculpture called "video art" emerged from the rebellions of the 1960s as a reaction against conventional broadcast television. Since then, inexpensive portable recording and playback video equipment has made it possible for this art form to flourish. Video art has moved from a nearly photojournalistic form to one in which outlandish experiments exploit new dimensions in hardware and imagery.

Nam June Paik is perhaps the most prominent of the video artists. His work pioneered the use of television imagery in performance and other multimedia art. It takes television well beyond its primary function of reproducing imagery. Indeed, Nam June Paik's video art creates its own imagery. In *TV Bra for Living Sculpture* (Fig. **18.31**), he creates interactive images of a performance of classical music and miniature televisions with their own images. The combined video and live situations function as a third, overriding experience. The effect is bizarre, startling, fascinating, and, unlike the moment captured in the illustration, constantly changing.

"New" Realism

The realistic style of the nineteenth century (see p. 504) returns from time to time, and in the late 1990s, we find its evidence in the work of a number of young and important painters. The first of these, Kerry James Marshall, employs conventional techniques and traditional approaches to figure depiction to illuminate personal and historical African American narratives. He looks into the particulars of African American daily living, from ordinary interpersonal exchanges to specifically political interaction. He tries to suggest that in his pictures there is something a little too right, too ordered. In *Den Mother* (Fig. **18.32**), such a sense of goodness pervades that we wonder if this could possibly be a portrait of a real individual, and in reality, Marshall has given us an archetype, an icon, *and* an oxymoron—an object more identifiable with white suburbs than black identity.

Mark Tansey (b. 1949) tries in his painting to find what he calls a new "technaphor"—that is, "a metaphorical technique for connecting subject matter and ideas." In *Soft Borders* (Fig. **18.33**), he takes four interrelated scenes, each seen from a different perspective, and brings them

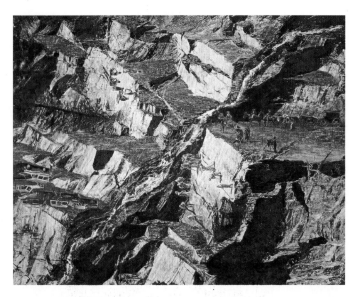

18.33 Mark Tansey, *Soft Borders*, 1997. Oil on canvas, 8 ft 8¹/₂ ins × 7 ft (2.65 × 2.13 m). Curt Marcus Gallery, New York.

together. A small tribe of American Indians shares the mountain with a band of surveyors, a tourist group, and a toxic waste removal crew. Tansey describes the scene as "a short history of the West from four different points of view."

Julie Roberts (b. 1963), a Welsh painter from London, takes a restrained approach to both realism and the drama

18.34 Julie Roberts, *Catholic/ Sacred and Profane Love*, 1996. Oil and acrylic on canvas, 5 ft × 5 ft (1.5 × 1.5 m). Sean Kelly Gallery, New York.

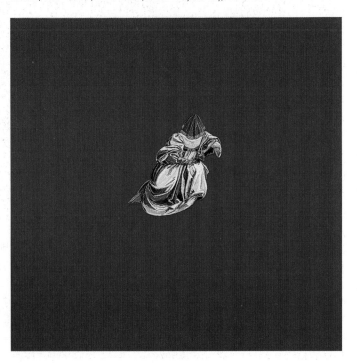

of human life. She leaves much to the viewer's imagination while creating an effective tension between the paint surface and the disturbing suggestions of the images. *Catholic/Sacred and Profane Love* (Fig. **18.34**) was inspired by a painting (of the same title) by Titian in the Borghese Gallery in Rome. Its references to sacrificial offerings, religious orthodoxy, and the papacy jar us with vibrant colors and dynamic diagonals. The covered visage of the figure mystifies as it causes us to contemplate its symbolism and relevance.

Architectural Modernism

In a sense, the task of evaluating contemporary architecture is the most difficult of all the arts. In our day, the human element in artistic creation has been blurred by the contributions of architectural firms rather than individual

18.35 Gordon Bunshaft (Skidmore, Owings, and Merrill), Lever House, New York, 1950–2.

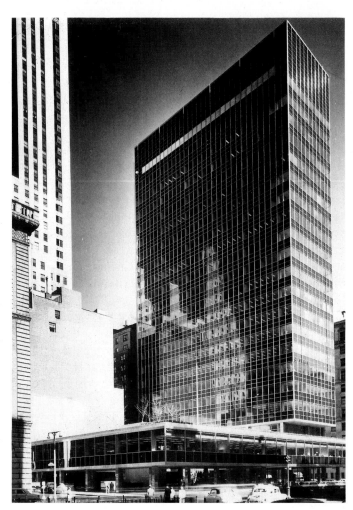

architects. In addition, the contemporary observer sees a sameness in the glass and steel boxes of the International Style that dominate our cities and easily misses some truly unique approach to design that is visible in some housing project in an obscure location.

The ten-year break in architectural construction during World War II separated what came after from what went before. The continuing careers of architects who had achieved significant accomplishments before the war soon bridged the gap, however. The focus of new building shifted from Europe to the United States, Japan, and even South America. The overall approach still remained modern, or international, in flavor.

A resurgence of skyscraper building occurred in the 1950s. Lever House (1951–2) in New York City (Fig. **18.35**) illustrates the glass-and-steel box approach that began then and continues today. A very important consideration in this design is the open space surrounding the tower. Created by setting the tower back from the perimeter of the site, the open space around the building creates its own envelope of environment, or its *context*. Reactions against, and alternatives to, the all-over glazing of the Lever Building have occurred throughout the last fifty years—aluminum surfaces pierced by small windows, for example. An intensification of the glazed exterior has also taken place, where metalized rather than normal glass forms the surface. Such an approach has been particularly popular in the Sun Belt, because metalized glass reflects the sun's rays and their heat. Whatever materials are used on the façade, however, the functional, plain rectangle of the International Style has continued as a standard architectural form.

The rectangle, which has so uniformly and in many cases thoughtlessly become the mark of contemporary architecture, leads us to the architect who, before World War II, was among its advocates. Ludwig Mies van der Rohe (LOOT-vik mees vahn dair ROH-e; 1886–1969) insisted that form should not be an end in itself but that the architect should discover and state the function of the building. Mies pursued those goals, taking mass-produced materials—bricks, glass, and manufactured metals—at their face value and expressing their shapes honestly. This was the basis for the rectangularization that is the common ground of twentieth-century architecture. His search for proportional perfection can be traced, perhaps, back to the German Pavilion of the Barcelona Exposition in 1929, and it was consummated in large-scale projects such as New York's Seagram Building (Fig. **18.36**).

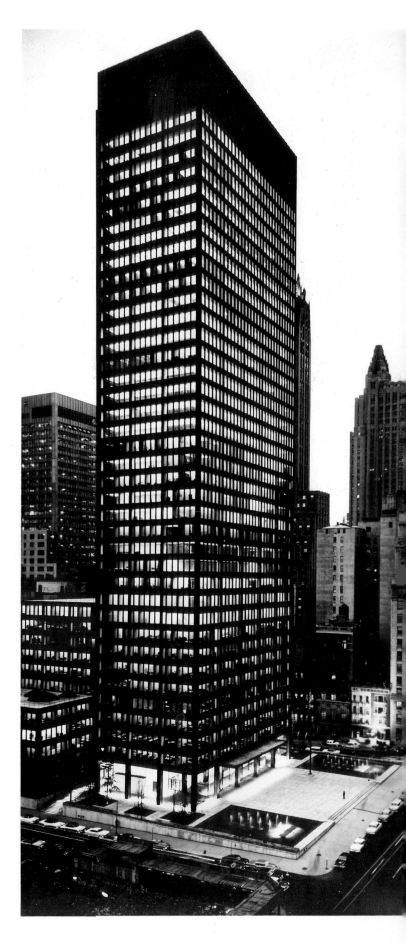

18.36 Mies van der Rohe and Philip Johnson, Seagram Building, New York, 1958.

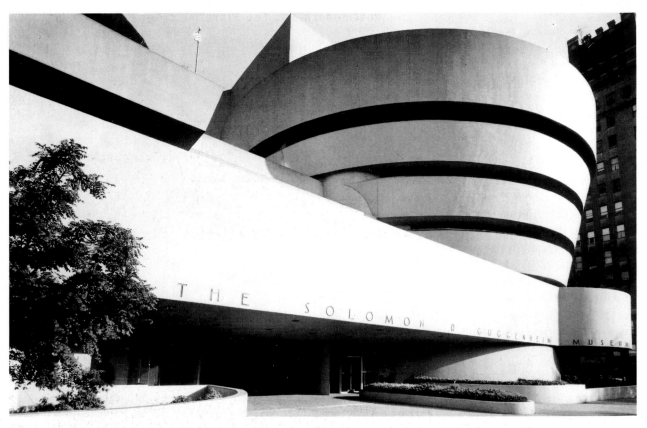

18.37 Frank Lloyd Wright, Solomon R. Guggenheim Museum, New York, 1942–59.

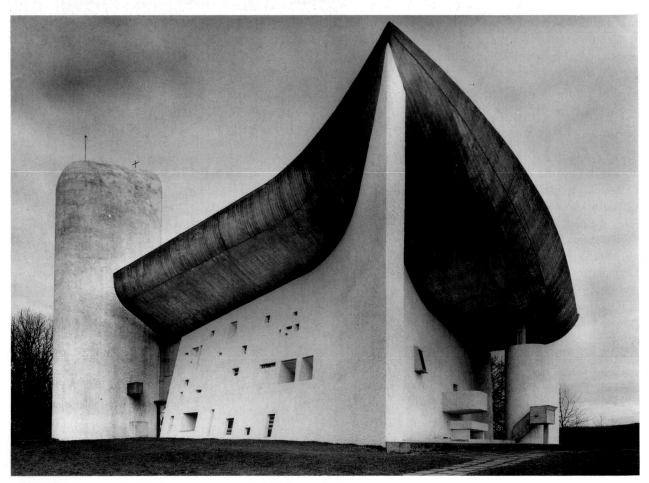

18.38 Le Corbusier, Notre Dame du Haut, Ronchamp, France, 1950–4, from the southeast.

18.39 Pier Luigi Nervi, Small Sports Palace, Rome, 1957.

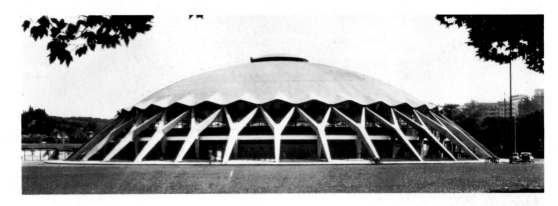

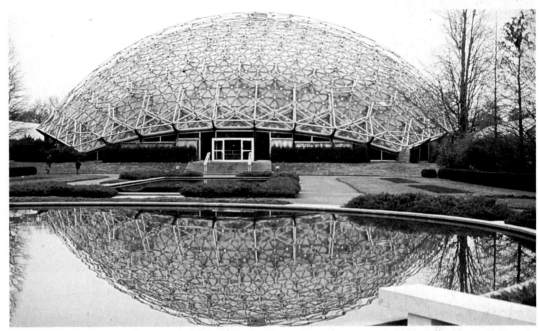

18.40 Richard Buckminster Fuller, Climatron, St Louis, 1959.

The simple straight line and functional structure that were basic to Mies' vision were easily imitated and readily reproduced. This multiplication of steel and glass boxes, however, has not overshadowed exploration of other forms. Contemporary design has ultimately answered in various ways the question put by Louis I. Kahn, "What form does the space want to become?"

In the case of Frank Lloyd Wright's Guggenheim Museum (Fig. **18.37**), space has become a relaxing spiral that reflects the leisurely progress one should make through an art museum. Eero Saarinen's (Ay-roh SAH-rin-en) Trans-World Airline Terminal emulates the shape of flight in its curved lines and spaces, carefully designed to accommodate large masses of people and channel them to and from waiting aircraft. (Shapes like this can be executed only using modern construction techniques and materials such as reinforced concrete.) Le Corbusier's dynamic church, Notre Dame du Haut (Fig. **18.38**), which is more like a piece of sculpture than a building, also suggests flight. The function of this pilgrimage church cannot easily be surmised from its form. Rather, the juxtaposed rectilinear windows and curvilinear walls and the overwhelming roof nestled lightly on thin pillars above the walls appear a "pure creation of the spirit."

Two other noteworthy architects have their own signatures, the arch of Pier Luigi Nervi (pee-AIR loo-EE-jee NAIR-vee; 1891–1979), and the dome of Richard Buckminster Fuller (1895–1983). The unencumbered free space of their work contrasts sharply with the self-contained boxes of the International Style. Nervi's Small Sports Palace (Fig. **18.39**) and Fuller's Climatron (Fig. **18.40**) illustrate the practical need for free space. They also illustrate the trend toward spansion architecture, which stretches engineering to the limits of its materials.

Architectural Postmodernism

Beyond these trends, contemporary architecture has been pluralistic. Postmodern, or "revisionist," architecture

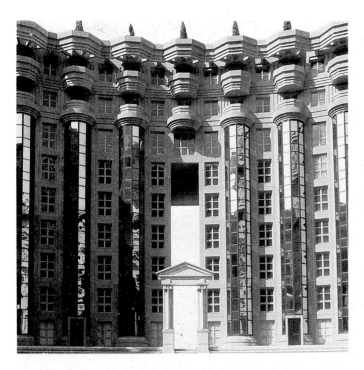

18.41 Ricardo Bofill, Palace of Abraxas, Marne-la-Vallée, near Paris, 1978–83.

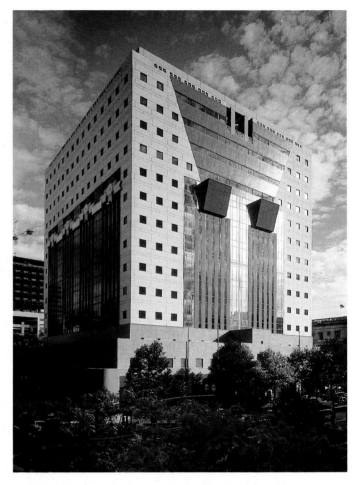

18.42 Michael Graves, Portland Public Office Building, Portland, Oregon, 1979–82.

takes past styles and does something new with them. The Spanish architect Ricardo Bofill (BOH-feel; b. 1939) and the Italian Aldo Rossi (b. 1931) both derive much of their architectural language from the past. As Bofill remarked, his architecture takes "without copying, different themes from the past, but in an eclectic manner, seizing certain moments in history and juxtaposing them, thereby prefiguring a new epoch." We see this eclectic juxtaposition in his public housing development called, with typical grandiosity, the Palace of Abraxas (Fig. **18.41**). Here columnar verticality is suggested by glass bays and by the cornice/capitals over them which give the appearance of a dynamic classicism. In Japan, postmodern architects such as Arata Isozaki (b. 1931) portray in their buildings the restrained elegance and style of traditional Japanese art. In the United States, Michael Graves (b. 1934) has reacted to the repetitive glass, concrete, and steel boxes of the International Style by creating a metaphorical allusion to the keystone of the Roman arch (Fig. **18.42**). The bright red pilasters suggest fluted columns, and fiberglass garlands recall both ART DECO and rococo.

Postmodern architecture focuses on meaning and symbolism, and it embraces the past. The postmodernist seeks to create buildings "in the fuller context of society and the environment." Function no longer dictates form, and ornamentation is acceptable. The goals of postmodern architecture are social identity, cultural continuity, and sense of place.

Another clear repudiation of the glass-and-steel box of the International Style and other popular forms in mainstream architecture can be seen in the design for the Pompidou (pohm-pee-DOO) Center in Paris (Fig. **18.43**). Here the building is turned inside out, with its network of ducts, pipes, and elevators color-coded and externalized, and its internal structure hidden. The interior spaces have no fixed walls, but temporary dividers can be arranged in any configuration that is wanted. The bright primary colors on the exterior combine with the serpentine, plexiglass-covered escalators to give a whimsical, lively appearance to a functional building. The Pompidou Center has become a tourist attraction rivaling the Eiffel Tower, and, while controversial, it has gained wide popular acceptance.

The highly colorful Piazza d'Italia (Fig. **18.44**), designed for the Italian-American community in New Orleans, comes alive at night with neon lighting that complements its columns, its temple front, and its fountain

18.43 Renzo Piano and Richard Rogers, Pompidou Center, Paris, 1971–8.

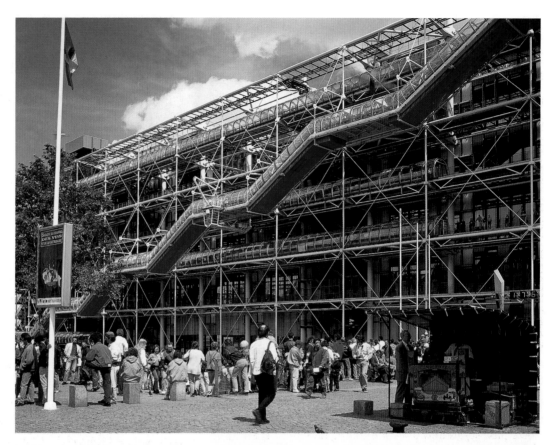

18.44 Charles Moore, Piazza d'Italia, New Orleans, 1978–9.

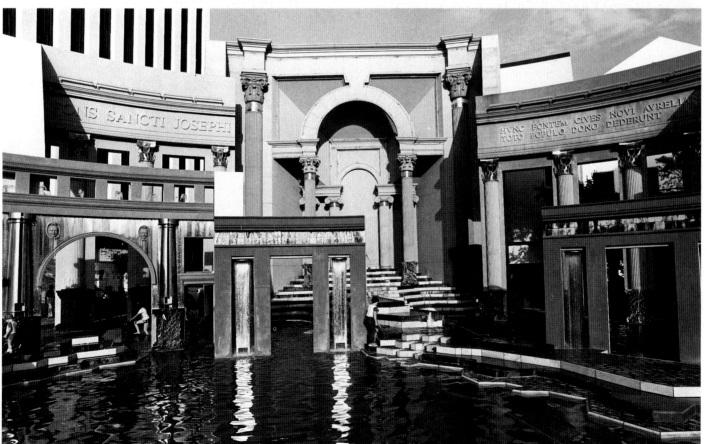

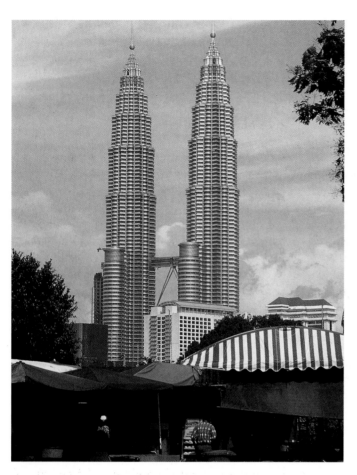

18.45 Cesar Pelli, Petronas Twin Towers, Kuala Lumpur City, 1997. Glass and steel, 1,483 ft (451.9 m) high.

that spills out onto a map of Italy. The architect, Charles Moore (b. 1925), was inspired by his conception of the "American dream," which he found embodied in Disneyland, and he applied that idea to this project.

The 88-story Petronas Twin Towers (Fig. **18.45**) were developed as an integral part of the Kuala Lumpur City Centre in Malaysia. Designed by Cesar Pelli and Associates, the twin towers symbolize strength and grace, using geometric principles typified in Islamic architecture. The 1,483-foot (451.9 m) Twin Towers are the world's tallest buildings. The two towers are linked by a 192-foot (58.4 m) double-decker skybridge at levels 41 and 42, 574 feet (175 m) above the street level. Apart from offices, the Twin Towers will also house among other things Petronas' science center, an art gallery, and an orchestra hall. The project is located at the former Selangor Turf Club, a 100-acre site in the heart of Kuala Lumpur's Golden Triangle. Some 50 acres of the site have been turned into tropical parkland, with the other 50 acres slotted for commercial development.

PLURALISM IN LITERATURE

In the field of literature, pluralism abounds. In fiction we find naturalism and realism, novels of manners, Southern fiction, Jewish fiction, black fiction, Western fiction, the beats, and metafiction. In poetry we find formalist/academic poets, black mountainists, San Francisco/beats, confessionalists, the New York poets, deep imagists, black poets and the independents. This wide-ranging nature of literature of the late twentieth century makes it impossible for us to do more than glance at a few luminaries. The age has been beset, at least briefly, by an approach to literary criticism called "deconstruction," which attempted to remove meaning from the work. Similarly, the literary theory of *intertextuality* asserts that a text has a quality of interdependence with all previous and future discourse—that is, every new literary text is an intersection of texts, has absorbed and transformed previous works, and will be, in turn, absorbed and transformed by future texts. *Poststructuralism,* based on deconstruction theories, centers on the idea that language is inherently unreliable and thus cannot possess absolute meaning in itself. Poststructuralists believe that all meaning resides in intertextuality. Nonetheless, amid the clamor of the times, we can find a cross-section of genres and styles, written by authors from every continent.

Following the horrors of World War II, various media have been used to try to document the inhumanity of Nazism, from documentary film and harrowing nonfiction to the short stories and novels of writers such as Elie Wiesel (b. 1928). Wiesel (vee-ZEHL) is a European Jew who survived incarceration in a concentration camp, and in his very moving autobiographical novel *Night* (1960) one gets a strong impression of the conflict between faith and human evil.

The American novelist Joseph Heller (b. 1923) also writes about the dreadful impact of modern warfare, but in a completely different style. Heller attacks it with black humor, satire, and a surrealistic streak that juxtaposes situations in bizarre ways. His most famous work is *Catch-22*, which pokes fun at bureaucracy as well as war.

India's foremost contemporary novelist, R.K. Narayan (b. 1906), writes in English for an international audience, and centers his fiction around middle-class life in southern India, painting a sympathetic but gently humorous portrait of social change, the struggle for identity, and the conflicts between generations.

Toni Morrison (b. 1931) is one of today's most celebrated authors. Her six major novels, *The Bluest Eye* (1969), *Sula* (1973), *Song of Solomon* (1977), *Tar Baby* (1981), *Beloved* (1987), and *Jazz* (1992) have received extensive national acclaim. She received the National Book

Critics Award in 1977 for *Song of Solomon* and the 1988 Pulitzer Prize for *Beloved*.

Morrison's novel *Jazz* is meant to follow *Beloved* as the second volume of a projected trilogy, although *Jazz* doesn't extend the story told in *Beloved* in a conventional way. The characters are new, and so is the location. Even the narrative approach is different. In terms of chronology, however, *Jazz* begins roughly where *Beloved* ended and continues the greater story Morrison wishes to tell of her people passing through their American experience, from the days of slavery in the 1800s to the present.

Full of tragedy and humor, *Jazz* continues many themes set out in *Beloved*: the individuals' struggle to establish and sustain a personal identity without abandoning their own history, and the clash between individual and community interests. Reading like a blues ballad from the age it suggests, *Jazz* is about a middle-aged couple—Joe Trace, waiter and door-to-door cosmetics salesman, and his wife, Violet, a home hairdresser—who migrate to Harlem from the rural South in the early 1900s and struggle with suffering and survival. The background portrays scenes of the brutal Virginia country life blacks endured as sharecroppers at the end of the nineteenth century. In contrast, Joe and Violet find the prospect of life in New York exciting, initially. Then reality sets in. Despite Joe's attachment to Violet, he falls in love with Dorcas, a teenager, and then kills her when she tries to leave him. No one wants to turn Joe in. At the funeral parlor, Violet attempts to slash Dorcas's face but is thrown out, running home and freeing her treasured birds. Later she establishes a relationship with Dorcas's mother.

Alexander I. Solzhenitsyn (sohl-zhuh-NEET-sin; b. 1918) is a Russian novelist and playwright. His fame gained impetus from his anti-Stalinist writings, particularly *One Day in the Life of Ivan Denisovich* (1962), and his other works, published in the United States, were not published in the Soviet Union under the communist regime. *August 1914*, in which he vociferously explores Russian participation in World War I, has tremendous sweep, power, and compassion. Solzhenitsyn was imprisoned after war service for an alleged slur on Stalin, and his subsequent work focused on the Soviet prison system, on which he writes with extremely human sensitivity and insight. He was expelled from the Soviet Writers' Union in 1969 because of his "radical" views. He defined these views in his undelivered acceptance speech for the 1970 Nobel Prize for literature: the indivisibility of truth and the "perception of world literature as the one great heart which beats for the concerns and misfortunes of our world."

Another Russian, the poet Yevgeny Alexandrovich Yevtushenko (yiv-tuh-SHENG-koh; b. 1933), became the spokesman for a younger generation of Russian poets, and his autobiographical work "Zima Junction" (1953) made him instantly famous and popular. He writes with a lyric tone of such quality that many of his poems have been set to music. His autobiography deals with the social and personal themes surrounding the important year 1953, when Stalin died, and he looks back on the past as it affects his present sensibilities on his return to his childhood home in Siberia (Zima). Yevtushenko's insights reveal a passionate love of his country and hopes for its future, his honesty, his sense of moral justice, and his refusal to be silenced by political dogma.

From the Middle East, the age of pluralism has produced women writers of great vision and courage. Fawziyya Abu-Khalid (b. 1955) came from a Westernized upper-middle-class family in Saudi Arabia. Her earliest poems, written when she was a young girl, were published in the local newspaper and were included in her first volume of poetry, published in Lebanon. Included in that volume was a poem with the provocative title "Until When Will They Go on Raping You on Your Wedding Night?" It was banned in Saudi Arabia.

One of the few popular poets to emerge from the United Arab Emirates is Zabyah Khamis (b. c. 1958). In 1987 she was arrested briefly by the security police, apparently because of several articles, including one on the status of women, and poems she had written that were critical of the UAE authorities. No charges were ever filed, but her arrest came amid a general clampdown of freedom of expression in several Gulf countries at the time. Among her recent collections are *Qasa'id Hubb* ("Love Odes"), which are written in traditional rhymes and meters.

Exemplary of postmodernism in literature is Thomas Pynchon (b. 1937), an American novelist and short story writer, who combines black humor and fantasy to portray human alienation in the chaos of modern society. His masterpiece, *Gravity's Rainbow* (1973), is based on the idea of conspiracy and filled with descriptions of paranoid fantasies, grotesque imagery, and esoteric mathematical language.

MUSIC

After World War II, music developed along several distinctly different lines, and the different schools became further polarized. Two general directions have been taken, one toward control and formality, and the other toward less control to the point of randomness and total improvisation. The serialism of Milton Babbitt (b. 1916) in America and Pierre Boulez (boo-LAY; b. 1925) in France are clear examples of a move toward tighter control and predetermination of events. The improvisational works of

Earle Brown (b. 1926) and the various approaches taken by John Cage (1912–92) exemplify a move away from composer control, leaving decisions to performers or to chance. At the same time, a number of composers have continued in more traditional styles, which stemmed from the musical principles of Hindemith, the neoclassicism of Stravinsky and Prokofiev, and the styles of Bartók and Copland.

Serialism

Postwar serialism reflects a desire to exert more control and to apply a predetermined hierarchy of values to all elements of a composition. Before the war, composers using the twelve-tone technique created a set, or row, of twelve pitches arranged in a specific order. Although the order could be manipulated in a number of ways, certain relationships between the pitches of the tone row were constant and provided the underlying structure and much of the flavor of this style. To some extent, structural decisions were made before the actual writing of the composition itself. The composer was then subject to fairly strict limitations on the selection of pitches as the work progressed, since all pitch order was pre-established.

Proponents of the technique argued that composers have always worked within limitations of some kind and that the discipline required to do so is an essential part of the creative problem-solving process. Opponents argued that writing music this way was more a mathematical manipulation that appealed to the intellect and less the function of a composer's ear.

Three Compositions for piano, by Milton Babbitt, written in 1947–8, is one of the earliest examples of serial technique applied to elements other than pitch. In this work, rhythm and dynamics are also predetermined by serial principles.

Aleatory Music

While some composers were developing techniques and even systems of highly controlled composition in the late 1940s, others went in the opposite direction. John Cage has been a major force in the application of ALEATORY, or chance, procedures to composition with works such as *Imaginary Landscape No. 4* for twelve radios and *The Music of Changes* (1951). Cage relied on the *I Ching*, or *Book of Changes*, for a random determination of many aspects of his works. (The *I Ching*, which dates from the earliest period of Chinese literature, contains a numerical series of combinations based on the throwing of yarrow sticks—not unlike the throwing of dice or coins.) The ultimate example of chance music is a piece that could be

considered nonmusical—Cage's *4' 33"* (1952)—in which the performer makes no sound whatever. The sounds of the hall, audience, traffic outside—that is, whatever occurs—forms the content of the composition.

Cage toured Europe in 1954 and 1958 and is thought to have influenced composers such as Boulez and Karlheinz Stockhausen to incorporate aspects of chance and indeterminacy into their music. Boulez's Third Piano Sonata and Stockhausen's *Klavierstück*, both dating from 1957, for example, give options to the performer concerning the overall form of the work or the order of specific musical fragments. But they are, for the most part, conventionally notated, and thus controlled.

Improvisation and *Musique Actuelle*

An open, improvisatory tradition was carried on by composers such as Lukas Foss, who wrote a suite for soprano and orchestra that includes jazz improvisation. He founded the Improvisation Chamber Ensemble, and a number of other improvisation groups sprang up in the United States during the 1960s. During this period, there was also intense exploration of new sound possibilities using both conventional and electronic instruments.

In the late 1990s, improvised music, viewed as the cutting edge of musical style, took the name *musique actuelle* (mue-ZEEK akt-yoo-EL). It freely draws on jazz and rock and exudes vibrancy, liveliness, and personal expression. Its literal translation means "current," and it represents a number of subfactions from various localities such as New York, San Francisco, Vancouver, Chicago, and Montreal. Illustrative of this approach is Gianni Gebbia (JAHN-ee GEHB-ee-ah) and his trio, whose music reflects one of the heroes of musique actuelle, Evan Parker. Gebbia's music integrates three strains, American jazz, free improvising, and traditional Sicilian music. Always in musique actuelle there seems to be a strain of humor—for instance, the vocalist in Gebbia's trio might alternate between phrases reminiscent of opera and phrases utilizing nasal whines and fearsome guttural groans in two simultaneous pitches.

Electronic Music

The development of the SYNTHESIZER and the establishment of the Columbia–Princeton Electronic Music Center provided an opportunity for composers such as Milton Babbitt to pursue the application and further development of primarily serial techniques. Many aleatory composers found electronic sound a congenial way to achieve their musical goals of indeterminacy, as John Cage did in *Imaginary Landscape No. 5*. Mainstream and jazz composers did not pay serious attention to the electronic medium until the 1960s, however.

Pluralism

In the 1960s and early 1970s, the "ultrarational" and "antirational" schools of music went to further extremes. The desire constantly to create something new also intensified, at times superseding most other considerations. Karlheinz Stockhausen (SHTOHK-how-zen; b. 1928), for example, became more interested in the total manipulation of sound and the acoustic space in which the performance was to take place. His work *Gruppen* (1957), for three orchestras, is an early example. As he became more and more interested in timbre modulation, his compositions—for example, *Microphonie I* (1964)—used more and more sound sources, both electronic and acoustic.

Elliott Carter (b. 1908) developed a highly organized approach toward rhythm often called "metric modulation," in which the mathematical principles of meter, standard rhythmic notation, and other elements are carried to complex ends. Carter's use of pitch is highly chromatic and exact, and his music requires virtuoso playing both from the individual and the ensemble.

Virtuoso playing produced an important composer–performer relationship in the 1960s, and many composers, such as Luciano Berio (BAIR-ee-oh; b. 1925), wrote specifically for individual performers, such as trombonist Stewart Dempster. In the same vein, percussionist Max Neuhaus (NEW-hows) was associated with Stockhausen, and pianist David Tudor with John Cage.

Experimentation with MICROTONES has been of interest to composers and music theorists throughout history, and many non-Western cultures employ them routinely. Microtones can be defined as intervals smaller than a half step. The usual Western system divides the octave into twelve equal half steps. But why might the octave not be divided into twenty-four, fifty-three, ninety-five, or any number of parts? The possibilities are limited only by our ability to hear such intervals and a performer's ability to produce them. Alois Haba experimented in the early part of the century with quarter tones (twenty-four per octave) and sixth tones (thirty-six per octave) and Charles Ives did much the same thing. A number of instruments were designed to produce microtones, and experimentation and composition have been carried out widely.

Composers also questioned the limitations of the traditional concert hall. Early work by Cage and others led to theatre pieces, multimedia or mixed media pieces, so-called danger music, biomusic, soundscapes, happenings, and total environments which might include stimulation of all the senses in some way. Thus the distinctions between the composer and the playwright, the film-maker, the visual artist, and so on, were often obscured.

Since the early 1960s, electronic instruments that can be used in live performance have had a powerful influence on music composition. Live performances were mixed with prerecorded tape in the 1950s, and by the 1960s, it became common to alter the sound of live performers by electronic means. Computer technology has been added to the composition and performance of music, and the options available through computer application are now virtually endless.

Theatre music, sometimes called "experimental music," may be relatively subtle, with performers playing or singing notated music and moving to various points on the stage, as in Berio's *Circles* (1960). Or it may be more extreme, as in the works of La Monte Young, where the performer is instructed to "draw a straight line and follow it," or to exchange places with the audience. In Nam June Paik's *Homage to John Cage*, the composer ran down into the audience, cut off Cage's tie, dumped liquid over his head, and ran out of the theatre. Later he phoned with the message that the composition had ended. Needless to say, such compositions contain a considerable degree of indeterminacy.

Some works were never intended to be performed, but only conceptualized, such as Nam June Paik's *Danger Music for Dick Higgins*, which instructs the performer to "creep into the vagina of a living whale" or Robert Moran's *Composition for Piano with Pianist*, which instructs the pianist to climb into the grand piano.

There was also a return to minimal materials. Stockhausen's *Stimmung* ("Tuning"), dating from 1968, has six vocalists singing only six notes. Minimal music can be defined as music which uses very little musical material, but often for an extended length of time. *One Sound* for string quartet by Harold Budd and the electronic piece *Come Out* (1966) by Steve Reich are clear examples. Reich's minimalism stressed the simple harmonic and highly repetitive melodic patterns of the music of India, Bali, and west Africa.

Many so-called "mainstream" composers continued writing throughout the 1960s and early 1970s. The source of much of this music is a combination of nineteenth-century Romantic tradition, the folk styles of Bartók and Copland, the harmonies of Hindemith, the tonal systems of Debussy and Ravel, and the neoclassicism of Prokofiev and Stravinsky. By this period, a noticeable element of controlled indeterminacy had crept into the music, however. The late 1960s and 1970s brought a greater acceptance of varying aesthetic viewpoints and musical styles as avant-garde techniques joined the mainstream.

One of America's leading composers through the end of the century, Ned Rorem (b. 1923) remained fairly traditional in style, focusing on his forte, the art song, a piece for voice based on a poetic text. He also has written five operas and many instrumental works. His works set to music poems ranging from international sources to the American poet Walt Whitman and many twentieth-century poets. Originally, his instrumental style was neoclassical, but in the 1960s he adopted serial techniques. His art songs remain traditional in style, striving for vocal lines that complement the text with clarity and directness, with picturesque accompaniments. As an example, his "The Shield of Achilles" begins with quick piano figures evoking the hammer blows in the making of the mythical shield. The figures return later to suggest execution posts being driven into the ground during World War II. At times the accompaniment ceases, leaving the voice alone to convey the mood of the text.

Freedom from melodic, rhythmic, and formal restraints appeared in jazz, and free jazz became the style of the 1960s. Saxophonist Ornette Coleman was one of its earliest proponents. Others, such as John Coltrane, developed a rhythmically and melodically free style based on more modal materials, while Cecil Taylor developed more chromatic music. In the mid to late sixties, Miles Davis arrived at a sophisticated blend of control and freedom in his *Bitches Brew* album of 1967. A number of musicians who originally worked with Miles Davis became leading artists in the 1970s, developing a style called "jazz-rock" or "fusion."

The Polish composer Krzysztof Penderecki (KRIS-tov pen-der-ET-skee; b. 1933) is widely known for instrumental and choral works, including a major composition, the *Requiem Mass* (1985). Most notably, Penderecki has experimented with techniques to produce new sounds from conventional stringed instruments.

His *Polymorphia* (1961) uses twenty-four violins, eight violas, eight cellos, and eight double basses. He has invented a whole new series of musical markings that are listed at the beginning of the score. In performance, his timings are measured by a stop watch and there is no clear meter. *Polymorphia* uses a free form, achieving its structure from textures, harmonies, and string techniques. The piece is dissonant and atonal.

It begins with a low, sustained chord. The mass of sound grows purposefully, with the entry of the upper strings, and then the middle register. Then comes a section of glissandos (slides), which can be played at any speed between two given pitches, or with what amounts to improvisation. A climax occurs, after which the sound tapers off. Then a number of pizzicato (plucked) effects are explored. Fingertips are used to tap the instruments, and the strings are hit with the palms of the hands, leading up

to a second climax. After another section, in which bowed, sustained, and sliding sounds are explored, a third climax is reached. After an almost total dearth of melody and defined pitch, the work ends with a somewhat surprising C major chord.

THEATRE

Realism

Realism flourished throughout the postwar era, most notably in the works of Tennessee Williams (1912–83) and Arthur Miller (b. 1915). Realism now included a great deal more than its nineteenth-century definition had allowed. It included more theatrical staging devices such as fragmented settings, and also many more nonrealistic literary and presentational techniques such as symbolism. As far as the theatre was concerned, stage realism and the realism of everyday life had parted company.

Tennessee Williams skillfully blended the qualities of realism with whatever scenic, structural, or symbolic devices were necessary to achieve the effects he wanted. His plays, such as *The Glass Menagerie* and *A Streetcar Named Desire*, deal sensitively with the psychological problems of common people. One of his great interests and strengths was character development, and this often carries his plays forward as he explores the tortured lives and the illusions of his larger-than-life characters.

Arthur Miller probed both the social and the psychological forces that destroy contemporary people in plays such as *Death of a Salesman*.

Absurdism

Following the work of Pirandello, Camus, and Sartre came a series of absurdists who differed quite radically from them. While early absurdists strove to bring order out of absurdity, the plays of Samuel Beckett, Eugène Ionesco, and Jean Genet all tend to point only to the absurdity of existence and to reflect the chaos in the universe. Their plays are chaotic and ambiguous, and their absurd and ambiguous nature makes direct analysis purely a matter of interpretation. *Waiting for Godot* (1958), the most popular work of Samuel Beckett (1906–89), has been interpreted in so many ways to suggest so many different meanings that it has become an eclectic experience in itself. Beckett, like minimalist sculptors, left it to the audience to draw whatever conclusions they wished about the work confronting them. The plays of Eugène Ionesco (U-ZHEN ee-oh-NES-koh; 1912–94) are even more baffling, using nonsense syllables and clichés for dialogue, endless and meaningless repetition, and plots that have no development. He called *The Bald Soprano* (1950) an "antiplay." The absurdist movement has influenced other playwrights and production approaches, from Harold Pinter to Edward Albee.

Performance Art and Postmodernism

Postmodern, as we have seen, implies a turn away from the qualities that characterized "modern" art. We may say the same about much contemporary theatrical production, and especially about a form of presentation called *performance art*. Performance art pushes the envelope of theatrical production in a variety of directions, some of which deny traditional concepts of theatrical production itself. It is a type of performance that combines elements from fields in the humanities and arts, from urban anthropology to folklore, and dance to feminism. Performance art pieces called "happenings" grew out of the pop art movement of the 1960s and were designed as critiques of consumer culture. European performance artists were influenced by the early twentieth-century movement of dada (see p. 553) and tended to be more political than their American counterparts. The central focus of many of the "happenings" was the idea that art and life should be connected (a central concept in postmodernism in general).

Because of its hybrid and diverse nature, there is no "typical" performance artist or work we can study as an illustration. We can, however, note three examples, which, if they do not typify, at least illumine this contemporary movement. The Hittite Empire, an all-male performance art group, performs *The Undersiege Stories*, which focuses on nonverbal communication and dance and includes confrontational scenarios. Performance artist Kathy Rose blends dance and film animation in unique ways. In a recent performance in New York, she creatively combined exotic dances with a wide variety of styles ranging from German expressionism to science fiction. The *New York Times* called her performance "visual astonishments." Playwright Rezo Abdoh's *Quotations from a Ruined City*, an intense and kinetic piece, features ten actors who act out outrage in fascinating, energetic fashion. The complicated, overlapping scenes, tableaux, and dances are punctuated by loud but unintelligible prerecorded voices. The piece combines elements depicting brutality, sadism, and sexuality. In the 1990s, performance art saw some difficult times because many people viewed it as rebellious and controversial for its own sake.

Caryl Churchill (b. 1938), a leading British postmodern playwright, addresses controversial issues of gender identity, economic justice, and political alienation in many of her plays. Churchill combines these critiques with dramatic inventions that challenge the boundaries of traditional theatre, critiquing the economic and social status quo and often reflecting her dissatisfaction with twentieth-century gender politics through thick layers of somewhat difficult language and innovative theatrical devices. In *Top Girls* (1982), for instance, Churchill depicts a dinner party hosted by a British woman in the early 1980s. This successful woman invites to the party five famous and courageous women, all of whom happen to be dead. The women share their stories, exploring age-old dichotomies between women's internal and external definitions of success and achievement. *Top Girls* was followed by *Fen* (1982), *Serious Money* (1987), *Mad Forest* (1990), and *The Striker* (1997).

Alternative Social Theatre

Among the avenues leading to theatre for and about particular social groups, we find *feminist, lesbian,* and *gay* theatre. *Feminist theatre* began as an alternative movement and proliferated during the 1970s. These activist women's productions tended to reflect radical techniques and agendas addressing women's subordinate position in the dominant culture. Their objective was political: to reform social and political systems and bring about women's equality. The feminist theatre began as a voice of radical feminism and its early manifestos. Its adherents sought a political restructuring of cultural power. New York's It's Alright to be a Woman Theatre, for example, changed the political movement's consciousness-raising format to performance and used the new public forum to help validate women's personal lives. Playwrights of the feminist theatre include Megan Terry and Roberta Sklar. At the Omaha Magic Theatre and the Women's Experimental Theatre (respectively), they brought to their productions many experimental innovations with theatrical form, including those of Bertolt Brecht (see p. 567). The visibility of women playwrights increased in the mainstream theatre of the 1980s and resulted in three Pulitzer Prizes during the decade: one each for Beth Henley (*Crimes of the Heart*, 1981), Marsha Norman (*Night Mother*, 1983), and Wendy Wasserstein (WAHS-er-steen) (*Heidi Chronicles*, 1989).

Lesbian Theatre refers to theatre for and by lesbians. Its presence dates essentially to 1968 and the alternative political theatre movement in Britain. One of the first important pieces of lesbian theatre came from the Gay Sweatshop, Britain's first gay theatre company. That play, *Any Woman Can* (1976), by Jill Posner, tells the story of "coming out." A separate women's company of the Gay Sweatshop produced its first piece, *Care and Control*, in

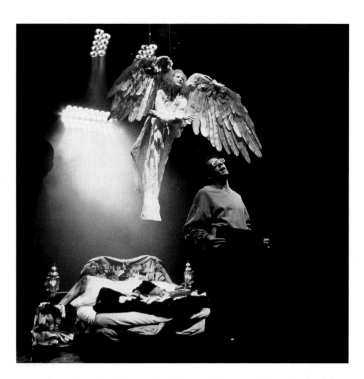

18.46 Scene from *Angels in America* ("Perestroika"), 1992. National Theatre, London, 1993.

1977. This play was developed by the company and scripted by Michelene Wandor. It was a documentary account of problems faced by lesbian mothers in custody cases. Lesbian theatre expanded during the 1970s and 1980s and tended to isolate itself in lesbian audiences in search of promoting a sense of community. Recent work by American performers Split Britches takes an aggressive attitude toward sexuality.

Gay Theatre is a term that describes theatre work by male homosexuals and usually refers to works from the 1960s onwards which feature overtly gay characters and situations and/or gay political protest. The liberalization of sexual attitudes in the period after World War II meant that sexuality could be explored as a central focus in drama. Actually, heterosexual playwrights such as Arthur Miller were among the first to include homosexual characters, although often from a negative perspective. Gay theatre's earliest works comprised low-budget productions in small theatres. One such theatre, Café Cino, in New York's Greenwich Village, produced the works of gay playwrights Doric Wilson and William Hoffman. Off-Broadway also accounted for Mart Crowley's *The Boys in the Band* (1968). The 1970s witnessed the founding of many gay theatre production companies throughout the United States and in Great Britain, and the number and strength of gay companies has grown with the growing gay community.

Much of the core of gay theatre has been socialist-political, but the AIDS epidemic has given it a new focus and objective: education. Among the latest to emerge as a figure in the gay theatre is Tony Kushner, whose huge, multidisciplinary epic of gay sex and politics, *Angels in America* (Fig. **18.46**), has been produced throughout the United States and Britain. The gay theatre occasionally reaches into mainstream, and plays such as *Torch Song Trilogy* and *La Cage au Folles* were hits on Broadway.

Angels in America is a two-part, seven-hour drama in which AIDS becomes a metaphor for the decay and salvation of America. The first part, "Millennium Approaches," ends with an angel crashing through a Manhattan ceiling to visit a man ravaged by AIDS. The second part, "Perestroika" (1993), resolves the drama of Part One in an uplifting and comic tone. Two AIDS-suffering but antithetical characters drive both plays. The first character is Prior Walter, a 31-year-old free spirit; the second character is Roy Cohn, a right-wing cynic. These two and others collide throughout, and the playwright, Kushner, eventually brings all his characters' conflicts to a peaceful resolution.

Kushner began writing *Angels* in 1987 as a comedy about the migrations of Jews, Mormons, and gays, but it quickly grew to epic proportions with the subtitle "A Gay Fantasia on American Themes." The play won the 1993 Pulitzer Prize for drama and several Tony awards. In 1994, Kushner completed *Slavs*, a lengthy one-act play dealing with themes related to the dissolution of the Soviet Empire.

FILM

International Film and the Demise of the Studio

As Italy recovered from World War II, a new concept in film set the stage for many years to come. In 1945, Roberto Rossellini's (rohs-sel-LEE-nee) *Rome, Open City* showed the misery of Rome during the German occupation. It was shot on the streets of Rome, using hidden cameras and mostly non-professional actors and actresses. Technically, the quality of the work was somewhat deficient, but its objective viewpoint and documentary style changed the course of cinema and inaugurated an important style called *neorealism*. The foreign film tradition remained dominated by this style into the 1960s, with works such as Fellini's (fel-LEE-nee) *La Strada* (1954) and *La Dolce Vita* (1960).

The stunning artistry of Japanese director Akiro Kurasawa's (kyoo-rah-SAH-wah) *Rashomon* (1951) and *Seven Samurai* (1954) penetrated the human condition. In 1986 he directed the spectacular film *Ran*, based on Shakespeare's *King Lear*. Heavy symbolism marked the films of Sweden's Ingmar Bergman. In works such as *The Seventh Seal* (1957), *Wild Strawberries* (1957), and *Virgin Spring* (1960), he delved into human character, suffering, and motivation. By the mid-1960s Bergman had assembled a team of actors who would appear in many of his subsequent films, among them Max von Sydow and Liv Ullmann. Autobiographical comments mark *Fanny and Alexander* (1983) and *After the Rehearsal* (1984). The same may be said about *The Best Intentions* (1992), about his parents' marriage, which Bergman wrote but did not direct.

International films and independent producers dominated from the 1960s on. Studios no longer undertook programs of film production, nor did they keep stables of contract players as they once did. Now each film was an independent project, whose artistic control was in the hands of the director. A new breed of film-maker came to prominence.

New Directors

More and more films are made for very specific and sophisticated audiences, and even movies made for commercial success have elements aimed at those in the know. Steven Spielberg's *Star Wars*, for example, consists of a carefully developed series of quotes from old movies and satires of them. Not recognizing these allusions does not hamper our enjoyment of the films, but knowing them certainly enhances the pleasure.

In the late 1990s, a new wave of film directors brought to the art flashy editing and sensibilities reflecting the changing tastes of audiences and a Hollywood scramble to find newer and more intense styles. Among the new wave are Bryan Singer (*The Usual Suspects*), Joel Schumacher (*Batman Forever*), Anthony Minghella (*The English Patient*), and others. Their styles have energy, directness, heightened intensity (fueled by MTV and Hong Kong action films), and a pursuit of the "language of the moment."

Among the many fine women film directors are Nancy Savoca and Beth B. Nancy Savoca is one of the most distinctive voices in American independent cinema, known for her thoughtful and often humorous examinations of women's lives. *Entertainment Weekly* (December 1997) called her film *True Love* one of the "50 Greatest Independent Films of All Time." Through such diverse media as film, video, sculpture and installation, Beth B has created a body of work that defies the very act of classification. B herself says, "People are comfortable when they can label and define you . . . but I don't want to be limited by boundaries."

DANCE
Modern

José Limón (lih-MOHN) and Martha Graham continued to influence dance well into the second half of the twentieth century. Limón's *Moor's Pavane* used Purcell's *Abdelazer* for its music. Based on Shakespeare's *Othello* and structured on the Elizabethan court dance, the *Pavane* is an unusual dramatic composition that sustains tension throughout the piece.

Martha Graham's troupe produced a radical and controversial choreographer who broke with many of the traditions of modern dance. Like John Cage, with whom he was closely associated, Merce Cunningham (b. 1919) incorporated chance, or aleatory, elements into his work. Cunningham uses the gestures of everyday activity as well as dance movements. He wants the audience to see dance in a new light, and, indeed, his choreography is radically different from anyone else's—elegant, cool, and severely abstract.

Works such as *Summerspace* and *Winterbranch* illustrate Cunningham's use of chance, or indeterminacy. To keep the dance fresh, he and his dancers rehearse different options and orders for sets. Then, sometimes by flipping a coin, he varies and intermixes parts in different orders from performance to performance. The same piece may appear totally different from one night to the next. Cunningham also uses stage space as an integral part of the performance and spreads the various focuses of a piece across various areas of the stage (unlike classical ballet, where the focus is isolated on center stage or downstage center alone). Thus Cunningham allows people in the audience to choose where to focus rather than choosing their focus for them. Finally, he allows each element of the performance to go its own way. The dancers rehearse without music and learn the count without any reference to it. The music, which can be anything, is added later, sometimes only when the curtain goes up. As a result, there is no beat-for-beat relationship that audiences have come to expect between music and footfalls in ballet and much modern dance.

Since 1954, another graduate of Martha Graham's troupe (and also of Merce Cunningham's) has provided another strong direction in modern dance. The work of Paul Taylor (b. 1930) has a vibrant, energetic, and abstract quality that often suggests primordial rites. Taylor, like Cunningham, uses strange combinations of music and movement in ebullient and unrestrained dances such as *Book of Beasts*. Unlike Cunningham, however, Taylor often uses traditional music, like that of Beethoven. The combination of esoteric musical forms with his wild, emotional movements creates confrontational works that viewers find challenging.

In this tradition of individual exploration and independence, there have been many accomplished dancer/choreographers, among them Alwin Nikolais (NI-koh-ly). His works—he designs the scenery, costumes, and lights and composes the music as well as the choreography—are mixed-media extravaganzas that celebrate the electronic age with spectacles compared by many to early court masques. Often the display is so dazzling that the audience loses the dancers in the lighting effects and scenic environment.

Another important figure is Alvin Ailey, a versatile dancer whose company is known for its unusual repertoire and energetic free movements. Twyla Tharp and Yvonne Ranier have both experimented with space and movement. James Waring has added Bach and 1920s pop songs to florid pantomimes and abstractions using Romantic point work.

Jazz Dance

With its roots in the black musical heritage, jazz dance nonetheless draws upon the broad experiments of modern dance. Its sources include "primitive" Africa and the urban ghetto. Its forms are not universally agreed upon, and, like modern dance, its directions are still in flux. Nevertheless, this form of dance has received significant attention throughout the United States (Fig. **18.47**). Choreographers such as Asadata Dafora Horton in the 1930s and Katherine Dunham and Pearl Primus in the 1940s were the pioneers of this form.

Ballet

It is virtually impossible even to name the many excellent contemporary ballet companies flourishing around the world. International tours of Europe's great companies, among them the Bolshoi, Great Britain's Royal Ballet, the Stuttgart, and the Royal Danish companies, make frequent trips to the United States, while American companies, notably the New York City Ballet, the American Ballet Theatre, and Dance Theatre of Harlem, are well received abroad. Crowds of American dance enthusiasts are found in the ballet houses of London, Moscow, Paris, and Vienna. In the United States and Canada, regional companies keep ballet traditions alive and fresh. Dance has become one of this country's most popular and growing art forms, with the availability of quality works growing each year.

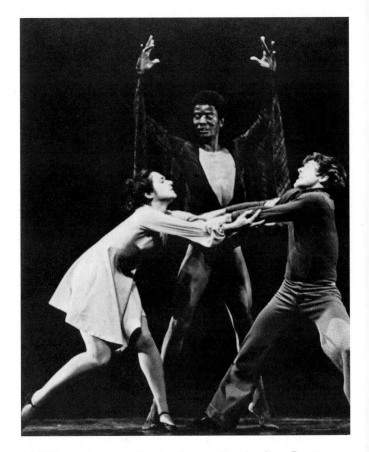

18.47 Choreographer: Jean Sabatine, *Nameless Hour*. Jazz Dance Theatre at Penn State. The Pennsylvania State University.

Postmodern

Rising in the 1960s, postmodern dance seeks the inter-relationships between art and life. The Judson Dance Theatre comprised an informal collective of experimentalists who rejected traditional choreography and technique in favor of open-ended scores and ordinary movement. There are no "typical" adherents, but one example surely is Deborah Hay (b. 1942), one of the style's pioneers. Hay defines dance broadly as "the place where I practice attention. . . . It's a kind of alertness in my body that I have at no other time. So dance for me is about playing awake."[4]

Most of Hay's work is playful, and "Voil," a forty-minute solo piece, requires the dancer to gallop and prance, engage in awkward gesticulations, and do storytelling, vocalizations (tongue clicks and gutteral rumblings), as well as other sorts of emotional outburst. The dance is "fierce, tentative, sorrowful, amazed, earnest, exasperated . . . [with] ugly faces and . . . silly kid's stuff."[5]

Focal Point
An Outpouring of Ethnicity

The title of this chapter is Postmodernism: The Pluralistic Age. We have already seen the wide diversity of artistic styles that the time since World War II produced: some of these stretch the traditional definitions and purposes of art almost to breaking point. However, pluralism in our society, as we are well aware, includes stretching the bounds of the way Americans think of their very society itself. Whatever importance the traditional Western canon of art and literature may have, ethnicity, positively or problematically, has taken on new emphasis. In some portions of the United States, traditional "minorities" are now the majority. Culture, of whatever tradition, is part of being, and it seems fitting that, in an age of pluralism, a focus on the arts of ethnic minorities should close our text.

Native American Poetry

Since World War II, Native Americans have struggled to avoid succumbing to a sense of despair about their culture's demise as it is assimilated into the general American "melting pot." Writers in particular have made the assault on such feelings a major focus of their works. In 1969, Scott Momaday's novel *House Made of Dawn* won a Pulitzer Prize and made a new generation of Native American writers aware of a powerful message: people caught between cultures can, despite a variety of problems, find ways to survive.

Paula Gunn Allen, a representative of many Native American writers, believes that Momaday's book created a new future for her: it "brought my land back to me." She believes that she and many Native Americans suffer from "land sickness"—that is, a deep sense of exile caused by the loss of their land and birthright. In the passages of *House Made of Dawn* she found that she shared a familiarity with the places Momaday described: "I knew every inch of what he was saying." It gave her the strength and inspiration—the will—to continue. In her poem "Recuerdo" she creates images of movement, loss, and of searching. She looks for a sense of "being securely planted."

Recuerdo
Paula Gunn Allen

I have climbed into silence trying for clear air
and seen the peaks rise above me like the gods.
That is where they live, the old people say.

I used to hear them speak when I was a child
and we went to the mountain on a picnic
or to get wood. Shivering in the cold air then
I listened and I heard.

Lately I write, trying to combine sound and memory;
searching for that significance once heard and nearly
    lost.
It was within the tall pines, speaking.
There was one voice under the wind—something in it
that brought me to terror and to tears. I wanted
to cling to my mother so she could comfort me,
explain the sound and my fear, but I simply sat,
frozen, trying to feel as warm as the campfire,
the family voices around me suggested I should.

Now I climb the mesas in my dreams.
The mountain gods are still, and still I seek.
I finger peyote buttons and count the stalks of
    sweetsage
given me by a friend—obsessed with a memory
that will not die.

I stir wild honey into my carefully prepared cedar tea
and wait for meaning to arise,
to greet and comfort me.

Maybe this time I will not away.
Maybe I will ask instead what that sounding means.
Maybe I will find that exact hollow
where terror and comfort meet.
Tomorrow I will go back and climb the endless
    mesas
of my home. I will seek thistles drying in the wind,
pocket bright bits of obsidian and fragments
old potters left behind.

Native American Ceramics and Painting

Pottery was the greatest of the prehistoric arts, and it continues today—even though it is now almost completely an aesthetic activity. Early pottery vessels, however, were designed for everyday use, and technique gave way to practical concerns—the time taken for exquisite finishing techniques was sacrificed in favor of getting the object into use. Today, clay bowls such as those made by Lucy Lewis reflect the time-honored traditions of southwest art, but they have risen in quality of finish and design to the status of

615

high art, and thus the culture has been sustained. Other artistic forms found among these peoples include silversmithing—the popular silver and turquoise jewelry is still made—and sand painting, which incorporates important religious meanings, so that many rituals cannot be performed without it.

In addition to the traditional materials of Native American art—that is, indigenous, easily accessible materials—contemporary Native American artists also work in the media of traditional artists—for example, watercolor. In Figure **18.48**, one of the foremost Navajo painters, Harrison Begay, documents typical Native American life, in this case, women picking corn. One aspect of Native American watercolor of the middle of the century that seems fairly typical is Begay's use of space—the painting stays on the surface plane and only the important subjects are depicted, with no background being shown. We are concerned only with the women and the corn, and no spatial environment is added. The subjects are rendered in two dimensions, and the only hint of space beyond the frontal plane—that is, three-dimensional space or perspective—is the diminutive size of the woman on the left. The horizon line, or viewer's eye level, is at the bottom of the painting.

Native American Music
Native American music continues to be an important aspect of cultural reality. For example, the music of the Inuit people has developed into a highly complex art form, exhibiting complex rhythms that use contrasting accents and meters. The tonal range of melodies tends to be limited, so that changes of pitch occupy only brief distances, thus creating a gentle, undulating quality. The style of Inuit music is often declamatory—that is, it is similar to the operatic technique of recitative in Western music.

Northwest coast Native American music has a number of unique qualities. The first of these is the concept of ownership of a song—that is, only the owner of a song can perform it. It is, however, possible to buy a song, to inherit it, or even to obtain it by murdering the owner, provided, of course, that the murderer could justify the claim. In addition, songs are owned by secret societies within the tribes. In musical terms, northwest Native American music requires part singing, and in a similar style to some African music, music of these tribes makes use of parallel harmonies and drone notes. The rhythms of this music tend toward strongly percussive and intricate patterns.

The songs of the southwest Native Americans, especially the Pueblos, reveal complex tonal arrangements. Songs are based on six- or seven-note scales and appear to keep within a rather low register—that is, the pitches stay among the low notes of the range. This is in contrast to the music of the Plains Indians, who tend to use high pitches

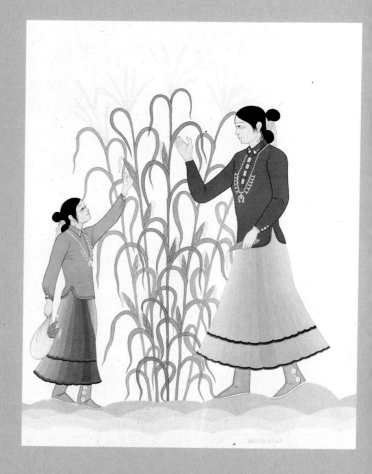

18.48 Harrison Begay, *Women Picking Corn*, mid-twentieth century. Watercolor, 15 × 11½ ins (38.1 × 29.2 cm). National Museum of the American Indian, Smithsonian Institution.

for their music. Nearly every social occasion, holy day, and ceremony has its own special music.

Native American Ritual/Theatre
The theatre of the Native American is rooted in communal celebrations and ancient rituals that reflect both religion and indigenous culture. The diversity of Native American tribal cultures has produced an equally diverse drama, which has at least two things in common: it is full of cosmic significance and it treats the "audience" as a participant rather than spectator. Among the varieties of Native American drama are one-person dramas of storytellers, improvisations of shamans, and the 100-hour-long celebrations of the Navajo chantways, which involve the entire community and comprise carefully designed costumes, words, gestures, movements, and songs. The potlatch drama of the coastal Northwest originally formed a mechanism for cementing the interrelationships of family and village by distribution of gifts by the wealthy.

African American Music—Jazz
Styles stemming from traditional jazz proliferated after

World War II, when there was a gradual move away from the big bands to smaller groups and a desire for much more improvisation within the context of the compositions. The term "be-bop" was coined as a result of the characteristic long-short triplet rhythm that ended many phrases, and the prime developers of this style were alto saxophonist Charlie "Bird" Parker (Fig. **18.49**) and trumpeter Dizzie Gillespie. The Cool Jazz style developed in the early 1950s with artists such as Miles Davis, and although the technical virtuosity of be-bop continued, a certain lyric quality, particularly in the slow ballads, was emphasized and, more importantly, the actual tone quality, particularly of the wind instruments, was a major distinction.

Were our space unlimited, we could look further into this African American form and include such gifted performers as Thelonius Monk, John Coltrane, and Cecil Taylor. John Coltrane, for example, whose personality and charisma were projected to black Americans in his albums *A Love Supreme*, *Ascension Meditations*, and those that followed, has had a tremendous influence on black society in the United States. These works acted as a spiritual reservoir for black people and have been hugely influential on jazz ever since.

African American Theatre

Mainstream

African American theatre began in the United States in 1821 in New York, where the African Theatre, founded by William Henry Brown, produced Shakespearean drama for both blacks and whites. Between then and the 1940s, a variety of experiences, both positive and negative, ranged from plays by black playwrights performed by black companies and plays by white playwrights for black casts to the demeaning tradition of the minstrel show. The 1940s witnessed progress in training and production by the American Negro Theatre at the Harlem Liberty Theatre. After World War II, the civil rights movement gave additional impetus to African American playwrights, productions, and actors, and out of this grew the Black Liberation Movement of the 1960s.

The realistic tradition in modern theatre gave rise to a number of African American playwrights. Garland Anderson wrote *Appearances*, the first black play to open on Broadway, in 1925. Other playwrights included Langston Hughes (see p. 551), Paul Green (1894–1981), and, most notably, Lorraine Hansberry (1930–65), whose masterful play *A Raisin in the Sun* dealt with crisis and redemption in the life of a black family on the south side of Chicago.

The Black Liberation Movement

The theatrical black liberation began in the 1960s, and continues to the present. One manifestation of the civil rights movement of the 1950s and 1960s was led by angry, militant blacks who espoused black consciousness. Many converted to the Black Muslim version of Islam, and many longed for a completely separate black nation. Radical groups talked about destroying Western society, and a number of African Americans turned toward Africa and sought a new identity in the Third World. In the 1980s, there was a change in self-description from "black" to "African American."

Many of these ideas were expressed in the dramatic works of playwrights such as LeRoi Jones, who became Imamu Ameer Baraka (b. 1934). His theatrical visions in *Dutchman* and *A Black Mass* dramatize the dangers of blacks allowing whites into their private lives and call for racial separation. Charles Gordonne's *No Place to Be Somebody* renews Baraka's cause, and espouses violence as

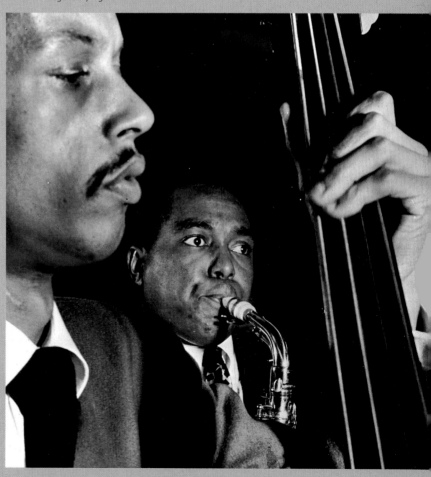

18.49 Saxophonist Charlie Parker in performance with Tommy Potter. Parker died prematurely in 1955, aged thirty-five, but by that time he was already a legendary figure.

legitimate action in the penetrating story of a fair-skinned black searching for his own racial identity.

Many new black theatre companies also emerged in the sixties. The Negro Ensemble Company, for example, founded by Douglas Turner Ward, is one enduring example. From that company came the moving production of *Home* (1979) by Samm-Art Williams (b. 1946).

[Home] traces the life of a Southern black, Cephus, from his farmboy youth, through escape to the big city, draft evasion and jail, joblessness and welfare, disease and despair, to his return to the honest labor and creative values on the farm. What makes *Home* more than a typical change-of-fortune melodrama are the poetic language and the conventions of its production format. Cephus is played by a single actor, but all the other roles—old, young, male, female, black, white—are played by two women who take on whatever role they wish by a simple costume addition. . . . Sometimes they are characters in Cephus's odyssey, other times they act as a chorus, helping the audience to collapse time and space and see the whole of Cephus's life from the larger viewpoint of American black history and culture. . . . The fact that the place itself never changes, though Cephus is constantly on the move, and the fact that the actors never change, though they play multitudes of different roles, suggest that "home" is right there all the time, ready to be grasped once the inner yearning is acknowledged, ready to be offered once others are willing to help, to extend themselves, to choose roles of grace instead of confrontation.[6]

The son of a white father and an African American mother, August Wilson (b. 1945) writes with an ear tuned to the rhythms and patterns of the blues and the speech of the black neighborhoods. Founder of the Playwrights Center in Minneapolis, his plays range from *Jitney* (1982) to a planned series of ten plays beginning with *Ma Rainey's Black Bottom* (1984). Wilson believes that the American black has the most dramatic story of all humankind to tell. His concern lies with the stripping away of important African traditions and religious rituals from blacks by whites. In plays such as *The Piano Lesson* (1987), he portrays the complexity of African American attitudes toward themselves and their past. The conflicts between black and white cultures and attitudes form the central core of Wilson's work and can be seen in plays such as *Fences*.

Fences treats the lives of black tenement-dwellers in Pittsburgh in the 1950s. Troy Maxson, a garbage collector, takes great pride in his ability to hold his family together and to take care of them. As the play opens, Troy discusses his challenge to the union concerning blacks' access to doing the same "easy" work as whites. He is frustrated and believes that he has been deprived of the opportunities to get what he deserves—and this becomes a central motif. He describes his wrestling match with death in 1941 when

he had pneumonia, and he also tells of his days in the Negro baseball leagues when he was not allowed to play in the majors—because of his race.

African American Writers

Earlier in the chapter, we met Toni Morrison, an African American novelist, poet, and short-story writer (see p. 606). Another contemporary African American writer is Gayl Jones (b. 1949), who grew up in the streets and segregated schools of Lexington, Kentucky. A graduate in English from Connecticut College and with two graduate degrees in writing from Brown University, she taught creative writing and African American literature at the University of Michigan from 1975 until 1983, when she left the United States. Her writings reflect black vernacular culture and treat the terror of constant sexual warfare, the obsessive extremes of sexuality and violence, and the joining of pleasure and pain. In her work, madness is not an ailment of an individual but of society. Her first novel, *Corregidora* (1975), tells the story of Ursa Corregidora, a descendant of the incest of the Portuguese slave owner of her maternal ancestors. Her husband's violence makes her incapable of having children, and she comes to the realization that "the ritual hatred for men found in the folklore of black women overlooks the perverse longing of all human beings for their own oppression."[7] Her second novel, *Eva's Man* (1976), was no less controversial. It tells the story of a horrendous sex crime committed by a woman who has been tormented by a lifetime of masculine sexual animosity. She recounts her story from a mental asylum and reveals the origins of her madness in everyday sexual violence.

African American Film-Makers

During the 1990s, independent films predominated, as we noted earlier in this chapter. Films by independent African American film-makers, with the exception of Spike Lee, have not shared the current explosion. Nonetheless, a good crop of contemporary African American artists has made their mark, and these artists show proficiency in several genres. *Jump the Gun* (1997), by English director Les Blair, tells the story of city dwellers in post-apartheid South Africa. *A Woman Like That*, directed by David E. Talbert, is a comedy about an ill-fated attempt to recover lost love. *Fakin' Da' Funk*, directed by Tim Chey, and also a feature film, explores the identity crisis of a Chinese-American adopted by a black family. *Soul Food* is George Tillman, Jr.'s story of a black family held together by a strong matriarch. Illustrative of documentaries directed by black artists is Keith O'Derek's *Straight from the Streets*, about West Coast rappers, with interviews with Ice T, Ice Cube, Cypress Hill, Snoop Doggy Dogg, and Dr Dre.

Hispanic Theatre

Theatre of the Spanish-speaking communities of America reflects and serves a diverse population. Among these, we will isolate three: *Chicano* theatre, *Nuyorican* theatre, and *Cuban-American* theatre. *Chicano theatre's* origins can be traced back to the arrival of the Spanish conquistadors of the sixteenth century. During the period of Spanish settlement and the centuries that followed, theatre played an important role in the culture. During the nineteenth century, both San Francisco and Los Angeles were major centers of Hispanic theatre. The advent of the railroad tied California, Texas, and Mexico City together to serve, through theatre, the culture and traditions of the local ethnic communities. Many traveling companies made regular tours to and from Mexico City. By the 1920s, flourishing Chicano theatres and productions explored the problems of adapting culturally and linguistically to a predominantly Anglo culture. Although Chicano theatre withered during the Great Depression and World War II, it rose during the civil rights struggles of the 1960s. In the summer of 1965, Luis Valdez joined Cesar Chavez to use improvisational theatre to underscore the plight of the migrant worker and give political impetus to the farm workers' strike in Delano, California. This led Valdez to form El Teatro Campesino (Farm Workers' Theatre).

Using Valdez as a model, a number of other Chicano theatre groups appeared during the 1960s and '70s, including Jorge Huerta's (WAR-tah) Teatro de la Esperanza ("Theatre of Hope"). A number of Hispanic playwrights have emerged as well, and these include women such as Estela Portillo Trambley, whose works include *Puente Negro*, *Autumn Gold*, and *Sor Juana*. Originally, Chicano theatre was written and performed in the linguistic tradition of the Chicano population. Lately, however, Chicano playwrights have turned more and more to English as their vehicle.

The curious label *Nuyorican theatre* applies to Puerto Rican culture in New York, which typically deals with bilingual and working-class situations. During the civil rights movements of the 1960s, young Puerto Rican writers and intellectuals began using the term as a means of affirming their own heritage as differing from Puerto Rico and the United States. This ethnic-consciousness produced a diversity of street theatre, prison productions, and small non-profit Hispanic theatres such as Teatro Repertorio Español and the Puerto Rican Traveling Theatre.

The term "Nuyorican" originally applied to the works of playwright–novelist Jaime Carrero in plays such as *Noo Jall* and *Pipo Subway No Sabe Reir*. Later Joseph Papp and a group of playwright–poets associated with the Nuyorican Poets' Cafe defined the term and developed it to exemplify the Nuyorican experience of workingclass Puerto Ricans in New York. Reaction against the term grew when themes of crime, drugs, abnormal sexuality, and generally aberrant behavior became associated with the movement.

Cuban-American theatre emerged as early as the nineteenth century in the Cuban-American communities of New York and Ybor City-Tampa, when groups of professional and amateur players such as that of Luis Baralt produced melodramas to raise money to support the war for Cuban independence from Spain. In the early twentieth century, a popular form called *obra buffa cubana*, or Cuban blackface, was produced by a number of Hispanic theatres and traveling companies. The strength of Cuban-American production led to the establishment in Tampa of the only Hispanic (Cuban) Federal Theatre Project during the 1930s. The Cuban Revolution of 1959, which brought Fidel Castro and communism to power in Cuba, resulted in large-scale theatrical activity in Cuban-American communities throughout the United States, but principally in Miami and New York. This activity was primarily political theatre of exile, and its adherents include José Cid Perez and José Sanchez Boudy. Their work focuses on opposition to Castro and a nostalgic longing for a world left behind. More recent Cuban-American playwrights, born in the United States, include Ivan Acosta and Dolores Prida. These playwrights are more likely to write in English as well as Spanish, and their themes include acculturation, bilingualism, culture conflict, and the generation gap between immigrants and their US-raised children.

Yiddish and Hebrew Theatre

Throughout the years, Yiddish- and Hebrew-language theatre companies and productions have ebbed and flowed in the Jewish community, particularly in New York. Currently these language-based productions are on the wane, but themes surrounding the Jewish experience continue to find their way into mainstream theatre. A good example is Joshua Sobol's play *Ghetto*, which explores (much like the movie *Schindler's List*) life in the Jewish ghetto of Vilna during the Holocaust of World War II. Basically a tragedy with music, *Ghetto* theatricalizes history to illustrate the indomitable Jewish cultural spirit.

Asian American Theatre

Ethnic Chinese theatres have existed in the United States since 1852, and Japanese theatres since the 1870s. In the 1960s, theatres dedicated to plays in English by Asian American playwrights began with the East-West Players in Los Angeles, the Asian American Theatre Workshop, and Yuriko Doi's Theatre of Yugen in San Francisco and in other theatres in Toronto and New York. Plays such as *M. Butterfly* (1988), in which Beijing Opera, an historic and highly conventionalized form, mixes with Puccini, have drawn some criticism from the Asian community for reinforcing stereotypes.

Critical Thought

Some of the fundamental issues we have just covered include differences among abstract, nonobjective, conceptual, ephemeral, and "chance" art. Each of these approaches places the artwork in a different position between the artist and the respondent. In abstract works visual effects are derived from objects in the "real world" but have been simplified or rearranged to satisfy the artists' purposes. The content in nonobjective art is wholly subjective or invented, and the ability to respond to the form within the art is an absolute must, whereas in conceptual art the idea behind the work is foremost and the product is somehow negligible. And so it goes. Compared to previous chapters, in which the entire chapter has explored a single style and encompassed one hundred or more years, we have just explored well over a dozen different styles in fewer than sixty years. In point of fact, in the last one hundred years, more art has been produced in the Western world than in all the previous millennia combined! Reviewing this material will take a bit of concentration and more than a little memory work, but these issues and outputs of the creative impulse comprise the "stuff" of the time in which we live. Perhaps in one hundred years much of what we offer for study in this chapter will have faded from the scene, relegated to insignificance; but it is too early for us to know and immaterial to try to judge the effects of time.

Summary

After reading this chapter, you should be able to:

- Discuss the conditions of world affairs from 1945 to the current year.
- Differentiate among all the visual art styles introduced in this chapter and identify major adherents and artworks, including ethnic considerations.
- Identify major writers and their works and styles.
- Characterize serialism, aleatory music, musique actuelle, electronic music, and other directions since World War II by noting specific composers and their works.
- Discuss late twentieth-century theatre genres, including alternative social theatre, performance art, and various ethnic theatre developments.
- Describe the major trends in film since World War II with specific references to international, new wave, and ethnic film-makers.
- Apply the elements and principles of composition to analyze and compare individual works of art and architecture illustrated in this chapter.

Glossary

a cappella. Choral music without instrumental accompaniment.

abacus. The uppermost member of the capital of an architectural column; the slab on which the architrave rests.

absolute music. Music that is free from any reference to nonmusical ideas, such as a text or program.

abstract, abstraction. Nonrepresentational; the essence of a thing rather than its actual appearance.

absurdism. A style dealing with life's apparent meaninglessness and the difficulty or impossibility of human communication.

academy. From the grove (the Academeia) where Plato taught; the term has come to mean the cultural and artistic establishment which exercises responsibility for teaching and the maintenance of standards.

accent. In music, a stress on a note. In the visual arts, any device used to highlight or draw attention to a particular area, such as an accent color. See also *focal point*.

action theatre. A contemporary phenomenon in which plays, happenings, and other types of performance are strongly committed to broad moral and social issues with the overt purpose of effecting a change for the better in society.

aerial perspective. The indication of distance in painting through use of light and color. Also called atmospheric perspective.

aesthetics. A branch of philosophy dealing with the nature of beauty and art and their relation to human experience.

affective. Relating to feelings or emotions, as opposed to facts. See *cognitive*.

aleatory. Chance or accidental. A term used for twentieth-century music in which the composer deliberately incorporates elements of chance.

allegory. Expression by means of symbols to make a more effective generalization or moral commentary about human experience than could be achieved by direct or literal means.

altarpiece. A painted or sculpted panel placed above or behind an altar to inspire religious devotion.

ambulatory. A covered passage for walking, found around the apse or choir of a church.

amphitheatre. A building, typically Roman, that is oval or circular in form and encloses a central performance area.

amphora. A two-handled vessel for storing provisions, with an opening large enough to admit a ladle, and usually fitted with a cover.

antiphonal. A responsive style of singing or playing, in which two groups alternate.

anthropomorphic. With human characteristics attributed to nonhuman beings, or things.

apse. A large niche or niche-like space projecting from and expanding the interior space of an architectural form such as a basilica.

arcade. A series of arches side by side.

arch. In architecture, a structural system in which space is spanned by a curved member supported by two legs.

archetype. An original model or type after which other similar things are patterned.

architrave. In post-and-lintel architecture, the lintel or lowest part of the entablature, resting directly on the capitals of the columns.

aria. An elaborate solo song found primarily in operas, oratorios, and cantatas.

Art Deco. An individual decorative art style that emerged between World War I and World War II. Its name was coined from the title of a Paris exhibit of 1925, the Exposition Internationale des Arts Décoratifs et Industriels Modernes. Art Deco style is characterized by slender forms, straight lines, and a sleekness expressive of modern technology.

art song. A solo musical composition for voice, usually with piano accompaniment.

articulation. The connection of the parts of an artwork. In music or speech, the production of distinct sounds.

artifact. An object produced or shaped by human workmanship.

Art Nouveau. A style of decoration and architecture first current in the 1890s, characterized by curvilinear floral forms.

atonality. The avoidance of tonal centers or keys in musical compositions.

atrium. An open courtyard within or related to a building.

avant-garde. A term used to designate innovators, the "advanced guard," whose experiments in art challenge established values.

balance. In composition, the equilibrium of opposing or interacting forces.

ballade. A verse form usually consisting of three stanzas of eight or ten lines each, with the same concluding line in each stanza, and a brief final stanza, ending with the same last line as that of the preceding stanzas. In musical composition, either a medieval French song, or a lyrical piano piece from the nineteenth century.

baroque. A seventeenth- and eighteenth-century style of art, architecture, and music that is highly ornamental.

barrel vault, tunnel vault. A series of arches placed back to back to enclose space.

basilica. In Roman times, a term referring to building function, usually a law court; later used by Christians to refer to church buildings and a specific form.

bel canto. An Italian baroque style of operatic singing characterized by rich tonal lyricism and brilliant display of vocal technique.

binary form. A musical form consisting of two sections.

biomorphic. Representing life forms as opposed to geometric forms.

bridge. A musical passage of subordinate importance played as a link between two principal themes.

buttress. A support, usually an exterior projection of masonry or wood, for a wall, arch, or vault.

cadence. In music, the specific harmonic arrangement that indicates the closing of a phrase.

canon. A body of principles, rules, standards or norms; a criterion for establishing measure, scale, and proportion. In music, a composition for two or more voices or instruments, where one enters after another in direct imitation of the first.

cantata. A type of composition developed in the baroque period, for chorus and/or solo voice(s) accompanied by an instrumental ensemble.

cantilever. Part of a beam or structure that projects beyond its support. A beam that is fixed at only one end.

capital. The transition between the top of a column and the lintel.

caryatid. A sculpted female figure standing in the place of a column.

catharsis. The cleansing or purification of the emotions through the experience of art, the result of which is spiritual release and renewal.

cella. The principal enclosed room of a temple; the entire body of a temple as opposed to its external parts.

chamber music. Vocal or instrumental music suitable for performance in small rooms.

chiaroscuro. Light and shade. In painting, the balance of light and shade across the whole picture. See also *modeling*. In theatre, the use of light to enhance plasticity of human and scenic form.

chorale. A Protestant hymn, for voices or organ.

chord. Three or more musical tones played at the same time.

choreography. The composition of a dance

work; the arrangement of patterns of movement in dance.

citadel. A fortress or a fortified place.

city-state. A sovereign state consisting of an independent city and its surrounding territory.

classical. Adhering to traditional standards. May refer to Greek and Roman art in which simplicity, clarity of structure, and appeal to the intellect are fundamental.

clerestory. A row of windows in the upper part of a wall.

cloister. A covered walk with an open colonnade on one side, running along the inside walls of buildings that face a quadrangle. A place devoted to religious seclusion.

coffer. A recessed panel in a ceiling.

cognitive. Facts and objectivity as opposed to emotions and subjectivity. See *affective*.

collage. An artwork constructed by pasting together various materials, such as newsprint, to create textures, or by combining two- and three-dimensional media.

colonnade. A row of columns usually spanned or connected by lintels.

colonnette. A small column-like vertical element or narrow, engaged column; colonnettes are usually attached to piers in buildings such as Gothic cathedrals. Colonnettes are decorative features.

color. In visual design, the hue or wavelength of light or pigment. In sound, the characteristic of an individual tone.

column. A cylindrical post or support which often has three distinct parts: base, shaft, and capital.

comedy. A theatre genre of complex qualities involving humor. Comedy may or may not involve laughter and may or may not end "happily"; compare *tragedy*.

commedia dell'arte. A type of comedy developed in Italy in the sixteenth century, characterized by improvisation from a plot outline and by the use of stock characters.

composition. The arrangement of line, form, mass, color, and so forth, in a work of art.

compression, compressive strength. In architecture, stress that results from two forces moving toward each other.

concerto. A composition for one or more solo instruments, accompanied by an orchestra, typically in three movements.

concerto grosso. A baroque composition for a small group of solo instruments and a small orchestra.

conjunct melody. In music, melody comprising neighboring notes in the scale. The opposite of *disjunct melody*.

consonance. The feeling of a comfortable relationship between elements of a composition. Consonance may be both physical and cultural in its ramifications. The opposite of *dissonance*.

continuo, basso continuo. In baroque music, a bass line played on a low melodic instrument, such as a cello, while a keyboard instrument

(or other chord-playing instrument) also plays the bass line and adds harmonies.

contrapposto, counterpoise. In sculpture, the arrangement of body parts so that the weight-bearing leg is apart from the free leg, thereby shifting the hip/shoulder axis.

Corinthian. A specific order of Greek architecture employing an elaborate leaf motif in the capital.

cornice. A crowning, projecting, architectural feature.

counterpoint. In music, two or more independent melodies played in opposition to each other at the same time.

crosscutting. In film, alternation between two independent actions that are related thematically or by plot to give the impression of simultaneous occurrence.

crossing. The area in a church where the transept crosses the nave.

cruciform. Arranged or shaped like a cross.

crypt. A vaulted chamber, wholly or partly underground, that usually contains a chapel. Found in a church under the choir.

cubism. A revolutionary art form from the early decades of the twentieth century involving the use of geometric shapes to represent objects and figures.

curvilinear. Formed or characterized by curved line.

cutting within the frame. Changing the viewpoint of the camera within a shot by moving from a long or medium shot to a close-up, without cutting the film.

Deism. A belief, based solely on reason, that God created the universe and, after setting it in motion, abandoned it, assuming no control over life or natural phenomena and giving no supernatural revelation.

dénouement. The section of a play's structure in which events are brought to a conclusion.

deposition. A painting or sculpture depicting the removal of the body of Christ from the cross.

design. A comprehensive scheme, plan or conception.

diatonic. Referring to the seven tones of a standard major or minor musical scale.

diptych. A painting on two hinged panels.

disjunct melody. In music, melody characterized by skips or jumps. The opposite of *conjunct melody*.

dissonance. The occurrence of inharmonious elements in music or the other arts. The opposite of *consonance*.

Doric. A Greek order of column having no base and only a simple slab as a capital.

dynamics. The various levels of loudness and softness of sounds.

echinus. In the Doric order, the round, cushion-like element between the top of the shaft and the abacus.

eclecticism. A combination of several differing styles in a single composition.

empirical. Based on experiments, observation, and practical experience, without regard to theory.

engaged column. A column, often decorative, which is part of and projects from a wall surface.

entablature. The upper portion of a classical architectural order above the column capital.

entasis. The slight convex curving on classical columns to correct the optical illusion of concavity which would result if the sides were left straight.

ephemeral. Transitory, not lasting.

epic. A long narrative poem in heightened style about the deeds and adventures of a hero.

étude. Literally, a study, a lesson. An instrumental composition, intended for the practice or display of some technique.

exposition. The introductory material or opening section of a play or a musical composition.

expressionism. A style of painting that seeks to express the artist's emotions rather than accurately represent line or form.

façade. The front of a building, or the sides, if they are emphasized architecturally.

fan vaulting. An intricate style of traceried vaulting, common in the late English Gothic style, in which ribs arch out like a fan from a single point such as a capital.

farce. A theatrical genre characterized by broad, slapstick humor and implausible plots.

fenestration. Windows or window-like openings in an architectural structure.

ferro-concrete. Concrete reinforced with rods or webs of steel.

fluting. Vertical ridges in a column.

flying buttress. A semi-detached buttress.

focal point, focal area. A major or minor area of visual attraction in pictures, sculpture, dance, plays, films, landscape design, or buildings.

foreground. The area of a picture, usually at the bottom, that appears to be closest to the viewer.

form. The shape, structure, configuration, or essence of something.

found object. An object taken from life that is presented as an artwork.

four-part harmony. A standard musical texture, where four tones fill out each chord.

framing tale. Overall unifying story within which one or more tales are related.

fresco. A method of painting in which pigment is mixed with wet plaster and applied as part of the wall surface.

frieze. The central portion of the entablature: any horizontal decorative or sculptural band.

fugue. Originated in the baroque period from a Latin word meaning "flight." A musical composition in a fixed form in which a theme is developed by counterpoint.

full-round. See *sculpture*.

genre. A category of artistic composition characterized by a particular style, form, or content.

geometric. Based on man-made patterns such as triangles, rectangles, circles, ellipses, and so on. The opposite of *biomorphic*.

Gesamtkunstwerk. A complete, totally

integrated artwork; associated with the music dramas of Richard Wagner in nineteenth-century Germany.

gesso. A mixture of plaster of Paris and glue, used as a base for low relief or as a surface for painting.

Greek cross. A cross in which all arms are the same length.

Gregorian chant. A medieval form of monophonic church music, also called plainchant or chant, sung unaccompanied, and named for Pope Gregory I.

groin vault. The ceiling formation created by the intersection of two tunnel or barrel vaults.

half cadence. A type of harmonic ending to a musical phrase which does not have a feeling of finality because it does not end on the home or tonic chord.

hamartia. The "tragic flaw" in the character of the protagonist of a classical tragedy.

harmony. The relationship of like elements such as musical notes, colors, and patterns of repetition. See *consonance* and *dissonance*.

Hellenistic. Relating to the time from the reign of Alexander the Great to the first century B.C.

heroic. Larger than lifesize.

hierarchy. Any system of persons or things that has higher and lower ranks.

hieratic. A style of depicting sacred persons or offices, particularly in Byzantine art.

hieroglyph, hieroglyphic. A picture or symbol of an object standing for a word, idea, or sound; developed by the ancient Egyptians into a system of writing.

homophony. A musical texture characterized by chordal texture supporting one melody. See *monophony* and *polyphony*.

horizon line. A real or implied line across the picture plane which, like the horizon in nature, tends to fix the viewer's vantage point.

hubris. Pride; typically the "tragic flaw" found in the protagonist of a classical tragedy. See *hamartia*.

hue. The spectrum notation of color; a specific, pure color with a measurable wavelength. There are primary hues, secondary hues, and tertiary hues.

humanism. A philosophy concerned with human beings, their achievements, and interests, as opposed to abstract beings and problems of theology; a cultural and intellectual movement occurring during the Renaissance focusing on humans and their capabilities.

humanitarianism. The ideas and philosophies associated with people who are concerned about human need and the alleviation of human suffering.

hymnody. The singing, composing, or study of hymns; the hymns of a particular period or church.

hypostyle. A building with a roof or ceiling supported by rows of columns, as in ancient Egyptian architecture.

icon. A Greek word meaning "image." Used to identify paintings which represent the image of a holy person.

iconography. The meanings of images and symbols.

idealization. The portrayal of an object or human body in its ideal form rather than as a true-to-life portrayal.

idée fixe. A recurring melodic motif representing a nonmusical idea; used by, among others, the composer Berlioz.

illumination. The practice of decorating the pages of books—especially medieval manuscripts—with colorful pictures or motifs.

improvisation. Music or other art produced on the spur of the moment, spontaneously.

intensity. The degree or purity of a hue. In music, theatre, and dance, that quality of dynamics denoting the amount of force used to create a sound or movement.

interval. The difference in pitch between two tones.

intrinsic. Belonging to a thing by its nature.

Ionic. A Greek order of column that has a scroll-like capital with a circular base.

jamb. The upright piece forming the side of a doorway or window frame.

key. A system of tones in music based on and named after a given tone—the tonic.

kouros. An archaic Greek statue of a standing, nude youth.

krater. A bowl for mixing wine and water, the usual Greek beverage.

kylix. A vase turned on a potter's wheel; used as a drinking cup.

lancet window. A tall, narrow window whose top forms a lancet or narrow arch shaped like a spear.

lantern. A relatively small structure on the top of a dome, roof, or tower, frequently open to admit light into the area beneath.

Latin cross. A cross in which the vertical arm is longer than the horizontal arm, through whose midpoint it passes.

leitmotif. A "leading motif" used in music to identify an individual, ideal, object, and so on; associated with Wagner.

lekythos. An oil flask with a long, narrow neck adapted for pouring oil slowly; used in funeral rites.

lied. German secular art song.

line. The basic building block of visual design; may be a thin mark, a color edge, or implied.

linear perspective. The creation of the illusion of distance in a two-dimensional artwork through the convention of line and foreshortening. That is, the illusion that parallel lines come together in the distance.

linear sculpture. See *sculpture*.

lintel. The horizontal member of a post-and-lintel structure in architecture, or a stone bridging an opening.

loggia. A gallery open on one or more sides, sometimes with arches or with columns.

lost-wax (cire-perdue). A method of casting sculpture in which the basic mold is created by using a wax model, which is then melted to leave the desired spaces in the mold.

low relief. See *sculpture*.

lyric. A category of poetry differentiated from dramatic or narrative. In music, the use of sensual sound patterns.

madrigal. An unaccompanied musical composition for two to five independent voices using a poetic text.

masonry. In architecture, stone or brickwork.

mass. Actual or implied physical bulk, weight, and density. Also, the most important rite of the Catholic liturgy, similar to the Protestant communion service.

medium (pl. media). The process employed by the artist. Also the binding agent used to hold pigments together.

melismatic. Music where a single syllable of text is sung on many notes.

melodrama. A theatrical genre characterized by stereotyped characters, implausible plots, and an emphasis on spectacle.

melody. In music, a succession of single tones; a tune.

metaphor. A figure of speech in which one object is used to represent another in order to imply characteristics.

microtone. A musical interval smaller than a half-step.

miniature. An artwork, usually a painting, done in very small scale.

mobile. A constructed structure whose components have been connected by joints to move by force of wind or motor.

mode. A particular form, style, or manner. In music, a scale; often used with reference to non-Western music.

modeling. The shaping of three-dimensional forms. Also the suggestion of three-dimensionality in two-dimensional forms.

modulation. The changing from one key to another in a musical composition.

monody. A style of musical composition in which one melodic line predominates; a poetic form expressing personal lament.

monolithic. Architecture or sculpture using a single large block of stone.

monophony. In music, a texture employing a single melody line without harmonic support.

montage. The process of making a single composition by combining parts of others. A rapid sequence of film shots bringing together associated ideas or images.

monotheism. The belief that there is only one God.

monumental. Works actually or appearing larger than lifesize.

mosaic. A decorative work for walls, vaults, floors, or ceilings, composed of pieces of colored material set in plaster or cement.

motet. A polyphonic musical composition based on a sacred text and usually sung without accompaniment.

motif, motive. In music, a short, recurrent melodic or rhythmic pattern. In the other arts, a recurrent element.

mural. A painting on a wall, usually large.

musique concrète. A twentieth-century musical approach in which conventional sounds are altered electronically and recorded on tape to produce new sounds.

narthex. A portico or lobby of an early Christian church, separated from the nave by a screen or railing.

naturalistic. Carefully imitating the appearance of nature.

nave. The great central space in a church, usually running from west to east, where the congregation sits.

negative space. Any opening in a work of sculpture.

neo-Attic. Literally, "new Greek." A reintroduction of the classical Greek and Hellenistic elements of architecture and visual art.

neoclassicism. Various artistic styles that borrow the devices or objectives of classical art.

niche. A recess in a wall in which sculpture can be displayed.

nimbus. The circle of radiant light around the head or figures of God, Christ, the Virgin Mary, and the saints.

nonobjective. Without reference to reality; may be differentiated from "abstract."

nonrepresentational. Without reference to reality; including abstract and nonobjective.

obelisk. A tall, tapering, four-sided stone shaft with a pyramidal top.

octave. In music, the distance between a specific pitch vibration and its double; for example, concert A equals 440 vibrations per second, the A one octave above that pitch equals 880, and the A one octave below equals 220.

oculus. A circular opening in the top of a dome.

oligarchy. Government by a small, select group.

opera. A lengthy work combining music and drama, fully staged with scenery and costumes.

opus. A single work of art.

oratorio. A large choral work for soloists, chorus, and orchestra, developed in the baroque period.

orchestra. A large instrumental musical ensemble; the first-floor seating area of a theatre; the circular playing area of the ancient Greek theatre.

organum. Singing together. Earliest form of polyphony in Western music, with the voices moving in parallel lines.

ornament. Anything used as a decoration or embellishment.

palette. In the visual arts, the composite use of color, including range and tonality.

palmette. A decoration taking the form or abstracting the form of a palm branch.

pantheon. A Greek word meaning all the gods.

pantomime. A genre of Roman drama in which an actor played various parts, without words, with a musical background.

pathos. The "suffering" aspect of drama usually associated with the evocation of pity.

pediment. The typically triangular roof piece characteristic of classical architecture.

pendentive. A triangular part of the vaulting which allows the stress of the round base of a dome to be transferred to a rectangular wall base.

performing arts. Music, theatre, and dance; in contrast to *visual arts*—painting and sculpture.

perspective. The representation of distance and three-dimensionality on a two-dimensional surface. See also *linear perspective* and *aerial perspective*.

picaresque. An artwork referring to the environment of rogues and adventurers.

piers. Upright architectural supports—usually rectangular.

pietà. A painting or sculpture of the dead Christ supported by Mary.

pigment. Any substance used as a coloring agent.

plainsong, plainchant. Medieval liturgical music sung without accompaniment and without strict meter.

plan. An architectural drawing that reveals in two dimensions the arrangement and distribution of interior spaces and walls, as well as door and window openings, of a building as seen from above.

plaque. A decorative or informative design placed on a wall.

plasticity. The capability of being molded or altered. In film, the capacity to be cut and shaped. In painting and theatre, the accentuation of dimensionality of form through chiaroscuro.

pointillism. A style of painting in which the paint is applied to the surface by dabbing the brush so as to create small dots of color.

polyphony. Literally, "many voiced." See *counterpoint.*

polyrhythm. The use of contrasting rhythms at the same time in music.

post-and-lintel. An architectural structure in which horizontal pieces (lintels) are held up by vertical columns (posts).

program music. Music that refers to nonmusical ideas through a descriptive title or text. The opposite of *absolute music.*

proportion. The relation, or ratio, of one part to another and of each part to the whole with regard to size, height, width, length, or depth.

proscenium. A Greek word meaning "before the skene." The plaster arch or "picture frame" stage of traditional theatres.

prototype. The model on which something is based.

psalmody. A collection of psalms.

putti. Nude male children—usually winged—especially shown in Renaissance and later art.

pylon. A gateway or a monumental structure flanking an entranceway.

quatrefoil. A carved ornament with four leaflets or lobes arranged around a common center.

rake. To place at an angle. A raked stage is one in which the floor slopes slightly upward from one point, usually downstage, to another, usually upstage.

realism. A style of painting, sculpture, and theatre based on the theory that the method of presentation should be true to life.

recitative. Sung monologue or dialogue, in opera, cantata, and oratorio.

reinforced concrete. See *ferro-concrete.*

relief. See *sculpture.*

repetition. How various elements are duplicated or alternated in a design.

representational. Art showing objects that are recognizable from real life.

requiem. A mass for the dead.

rhythm. The relationship, either of time or space, between recurring elements of a composition.

rib. A slender architectural support projecting from the surface in a vault system.

ribbed vault. A vault to which slender, projecting supports have been added. A structure in which arches are connected by diagonal as well as horizontal members. See *vault.*

rite. A customary form for conducting religious or other solemn ceremonies.

ritornello form. A baroque musical form in which a recurrent orchestral theme alternates with solo passages.

rondeau. A medieval French secular song based on a poetic form.

rondo form. A predominantly classical form of musical composition based around recurrence of the main theme, alternating with contrasting themes.

sarcophagus (plural **sarcophagi**). A stone coffin.

saturation. In color, the purity of a hue in terms of whiteness; the whiter the hue, the less saturated it is.

scale. In music, a graduated series of ascending or descending musical tones. In architecture, the mass of the building in relation to the human body.

schema. A summarized or diagrammatic representation.

sculpture. A three-dimensional art object. Among the types are 1. *cast*: created from molten material utilizing a mold. 2. *relief*: attached to a larger background. 3. *full-round*: freestanding. 4. *linear*: emphasizing linear items such as wire or tubing.

semidome. A roof covering a semicircular space; half a dome.

serial music. A twentieth-century musical style utilizing the tone row; can also employ serialization of rhythms, timbres, and dynamics.

sfumato. A smoky or hazy quality in a painting, with particular reference to Leonardo da Vinci's work.

shaft. The main trunk of a column.

shape. A two-dimensional area or plane with distinguishable boundaries.

silhouette. A form as defined by its outline.

skene. The stage building of the ancient Greek theatre.

skyphos. A two-handled ancient Greek drinking pot with an open top, tapering bowl, and flat, circular base.

sonata. Instrumental composition of the seventeenth through twentieth centuries, consisting of several movements.

statuary. Freestanding, three-dimensional sculpture.

still life. In the visual arts, an arrangement of inanimate objects used as a subject of a work of art.

strainer arch. An arch in an internal space that prevents the walls from being pushed inward.

stream of consciousness. A style of writing in which the author reveals character and event by expressing a continuous flow of a character's thoughts.

strophic form. Form of vocal music in which all stanzas of the text are sung to the same music.

stucco. A plaster or cement finish for interior and exterior walls.

style. The characteristics of a work of art that identify it with an artist, a group of artists, an era, or a nation.

stylized. A type of depiction in which verisimilitude has been altered for artistic effect.

stylobate. The foundation immediately below a row of columns.

suite. A grouping of musical movements, usually unrelated except by key.

symbol. A form, image, or subject standing for something else.

symmetry. The balancing of elements in design by placing physically equal objects on either side of a center line.

symphony. A lengthy orchestral composition, usually in four movements.

syncopation. In a musical composition, the displacement of accent from the normally accented beat to the offbeat.

synthesis. The combination of independent factors or entities into a compound that becomes a new, more complex whole.

synthesizer. An electronic instrument that produces and combines musical sounds.

temperament. In music, a system of tuning. Equal temperament—the division of the octave into twelve equal intervals—is the most common way of tuning keyboard instruments.

tempo. The rate of speed at which a musical composition is performed. In theatre, film, or dance, the rate of speed of the overall performance.

tensile strength. The ability of a material to resist bending and twisting.

text painting. See *word painting.*

theatricality. Exaggeration and artificiality; the opposite of *verisimilitude.*

theme. The subject of an artwork, whether melodic or philosophical.

timbre. The characteristic of a sound that results from the particular source of the sound. For example, the difference between the sound of a violin and the sound of the human voice, also called tone color.

toccata. A baroque keyboard composition intended to display technique.

tonality. In music, the specific key in which a composition is written. In the visual arts, the characteristics of value.

tondo. A circular painting.

tonic. In music, the root tone (*doh*) of a key.

tragedy. A serious drama or other literary work in which conflict between a protagonist and a superior force (often fate) concludes in disaster for the protagonist.

tragicomedy. A drama combining the qualities of tragedy and comedy.

transept. The crossing arm of a cruciform church, at right angles to the nave.

travertine. A creamy-colored type of calcium carbonate used as a facing in building construction.

triforium. The section of the nave wall above the arcade and below the clerestory windows.

triptych. An altarpiece or devotional picture composed of a central panel and two wings.

trompe l'oeil. "Trick of the eye" or "fool the eye." A two-dimensional artwork so executed as to make the viewer believe that three-dimensional subject matter is being perceived.

trope. A medieval dramatic elaboration of the Roman Catholic mass or other offices.

tunnel vault. See *barrel vault.*

twelve-tone technique. A twentieth-century atonal form of musical composition associated with Arnold Schoenberg.

tympanum. The space above the door beam and within the arch of a medieval doorway.

value, value scale. In the visual arts, the range of tonalities from white to black.

vanishing point. In linear perspective, the point on the horizon toward which parallel lines appear to converge and at which they seem to vanish.

variation. Repetition of a theme with small or large changes.

vault. An arched roof or ceiling usually made of stone, brick, or concrete.

verisimilitude. Lifelikeness or nearness to truth. The opposite of *theatricality.*

virtuoso. Referring to the display of impressive technique or skill by an artist or performer.

volute. A spiral architectural element found notably on Ionic and other capitals, but also used decoratively on building façades and interiors.

woodcut. A block of wood with an engraved design; a print made from such a piece of wood.

word painting. The use of language by a poet or playwright to suggest images and emotions; in music, the use of expressive melody to suggest a specific text.

Notes

See Further Reading for full bibliographical details of all cited works.

Chapter 3

1. Hofstadter and Kuhns, *Philosophies of Art and Beauty*, p. 4.
2. *Ibid.*
3. Fuller, *A History of Philosophy*, p. 172
4. Snell, *Discovery of the Mind: The Greek Origins of European Thought*, p. 247
5. *Ibid.*
6. Hamilton, trans. in *Three Greek Plays*
7. Hamilton, *op. cit.*
8. Arrowsmith, trans. in *The Complete Greek Tragedies*, vol. VI, New York: Random House, 1858

Chapter 4

1. From material provided by Alan Pizer
2. Fuller, *op. cit.*, p. 266
3. "Rings around the Pantheon," *Discover*, March, 1985, p. 12
4. Vergil, *The Aeneid*, trans. Theodore C. Williams, New York: Houghton Mifflin Co., 1938, p. 1
5. Andreae, *The Art of Rome*, p. 109

Chapter 5

1. McGiffert, *A History of Christian Thought*, p. 7
2. Fuller, *op. cit.*, p. 353
3. *Ibid.*
4. Hofstadter and Kuhns, *op. cit.*, p. 172

5. Barclay, *The Gospel of Luke*, pp. 15–16

Chapter 6

1. Garraty and Gay, *op. cit.*, p. 431
2. Roberts, *History of the World*, p. 321
3. Mango, *Byzantium*, p. 235
4. Nicoll, *The Development of Theatre*, p. 48

Chapter 8

1. Fuller, *op. cit.*, p. 377

Chapter 9

1. Transcribed by John Ockerbloom. A version from the MS in the British Museum edited by Grace Warrack, London: Methuen & Co. Ltd., 1901

Chapter 10

1. Hartt, *Italian Renaissance Art*, p. 187

Chapter 11

1. Hartt, *op. cit.*, p. 592
2. Campos (ed.), *Art Treasures of the Vatican*, p. 7

Chapter 13

1. Père Menestrier, in Vuillier, *A History of Dance*, New York: D. Appleton and Co., 1897, p. 90

Chapter 14

1. Helm, *Music at the Court of Frederick the Great*, p. 94

Chapter 15

1. Hofstadter and Kuhns, *op. cit.*, p. 381
2. Maas, *Victorian Painters*, p. 10

Chapter 16

1. Hamilton, *Nineteenth and Twentieth Century Art: Painting, Sculpture, Architecture*, p. 211

Chapter 17

1. Zitkala-Sa (Gertrude Bonnin), "The Soft-Hearted Sioux," (copyright 1989 The Arizona Board of Regents). Reprinted from *The Singing Spirit*, edited by Bernd C. Peyer, 1990
2. Gropius, *The New Architecture and the Bauhaus*, pp. 51–5

Chapter 18

1. Valerie-Anne Giscard d'Estaing and Mark Young (eds.), *Inventions and Discoveries 1993*, New York: Facts on File Inc., 1993, p. 220
2. Wilkins and Schultz, *Art Past Art Present*, p. 506
3. Otto G. Ocvirk *et al.*, *Art Fundamentals* (7th ed.), p. 309
4. *New York Times*, 30 May 1997
5. *Ibid.*
6. Kernodle and Pixley, *Invitation to the Theatre*, pp. 287–8
7. Arkin and Shollar (eds.), *Longman Anthology of World Literature by Women*, p. 1039

Further Reading

General

Bentley, Eric (ed.), *The Classic Theatre*, (4 vols), Garden City, NY: Doubleday Anchor Books, 1959

Braider, Christopher, *Refiguring the Real: Picture and Modernity in Word and Image: 1400–1700*, Princeton, NJ: Princeton University Press, 1993

Brockett, Oscar G., *History of the Theatre*, Boston: Allyn and Bacon, Inc., 1968

Chadwick, Whitney, *Women, Art, and Society*, New York: Norton, 1991

Clough, Shepard B. *et. al.*, *A History of the Western World*, Boston: D.C. Heath & Co., 1964

De la Crois, Horst, Tansey, Richard G., and Kirkpatric, Diane, *Gardner's Art Through the Ages* (9th ed.), San Diego, CA: Harcourt, 1991

Drinkwater, John, *The Outline of Literature*, London: Transatlantic Arts, 1967

Fuller, B.A.G., *A History of Philosophy*, New York: Henry Holt and Company, 1945

Garraty, John, and Gay, Peter, *A History of the World* (2 vols), New York: Harper & Row, 1972

Giscard d'Estaing, Valerie Anne, and Young, Mark (eds.), *Inventions and Discoveries 1993*, New York: Facts on File, Inc., 1993

Grout, Donald Jay, *A History of Western Music* (rev. ed.), New York: W.W. Norton & Co., Inc., 1979

Hartt, Frederick, *Art* (2 vols). Englewood Cliffs, NJ, and New York: Prentice Hall, Inc. and Harry N. Abrams, Inc., 1979

Hofstadter, Albert, and Kuhns, Richard, *Philosophies of Art and Beauty*, Chicago: University of Chicago Press, 1976

Honour, Hugh, and Fleming, John. *The Visual Arts: A History* (3rd ed.), Englewood Cliffs, NJ: Prentice Hall, Inc., 1992

Kamien, Roger, *Music: An Appreciation* (5th ed.), New York: McGraw-Hill, 1995

Kernodle, George and Portia, and Pixley, Edward, *Invitation to the Theatre* (3rd ed.), San Diego: Harcourt Brace Jovanovich, 1985

McNeill, William H., *The Shape of European History*, New York: Oxford University Press, 1974

Nicoll, Allardyce, *The Development of the Theatre* (5th ed.), London: Harrap & Co. Ltd, 1966

Ocvirk, Otto G., *et al.*, *Art Fundamentals* (7th ed.), Madison, WI: Brown & Benchmark, 1994

Pfeiffer, John E., *The Creative Explosion*, New York: Harper & Row, 1982

Roberts, J.M., *History of the World*, New York: Alfred A. Knopf, Inc, 1976

Sadie, Stanley (ed.), *The New Grove Dictionary of Music and Musicians*, Washington, D.C.; London: Macmillan, 1980

Sperry, Roger, *Science and Moral Priority: Merging Mind, Brain, and Human Values*, New York: Columbia University Press, 1983

Sporre, Dennis J., *The Art of Theatre*, Englewood Cliffs, NJ: Prentice Hall, 1993

Sporre, Dennis J., *Perceiving the Arts*, 5th ed. Englewood Cliffs, NJ: Prentice Hall, Inc., 1997

Vidal-Naquet, Pierre (ed.), *The Harper Atlas of World History*, New York: Harper & Row, 1986

Wilkins, David G., and Schultz, Bernard, *Art Past Art Present*, Englewood Cliffs, NJ, and New York: Prentice Hall Inc. and Harry N. Abrams, Inc., 1990

The Ancient World

Bataille, Georges, *Lascaux*, Switzerland: Skira, n.d.

Engel, Carl, *The Music of the Most Ancient Nations*, Freeport, NY: Books for Libraries Press, 1970

Frankfort, Henri, *Kingship and the Gods*, Chicago: University of Chicago Press, 1948

Graziosi, Paolo, *Palaeolithic Art*, New York: McGraw-Hill, 1960

Lange, Kurt, and Hirmer, Max, *Egypt*, London: Phaidon, 1968

Lloyd, Seton, *The Archaeology of Mesopotamia*, London: Thames & Hudson, 1978

Lommel, Andrea, *Prehistoric and Primitive Man*, New York: McGraw-Hill, 1966

Marshack, Alexander, *The Roots of Civilization*, New York: McGraw-Hill, 1972

Montet, Pierre, *Lives of the Pharaohs*, Cleveland: World Publishing Co., 1968

Moortgat, Anton, *The Art of Ancient Mesopotamia*, London: Phaidon, 1969

Murray, Margaret, *Egyptian Sculpture*, New York: Charles Scribner's Sons, 1930

Oppenheim, A. Leo, *Ancient Mesopotamia*, Chicago: University of Chicago Press, 1964

Powell, T.G.E., *Prehistoric Art*, New York: Frederick Praeger Publishers, 1966

Sachs, Curt, *The Rise of Music in the Ancient World*, New York: W.W. Norton & Co., 1943

Sandars, N.K., *Prehistoric Art in Europe*, Baltimore: Penguin Books, 1968

Smith, Hermann, *The World's Earliest Music*, London: W. Reeves, n.d.

Smith, W. Stevenson, *The Art and Architecture of Ancient Egypt*, Baltimore: Penguin Books, 1958

Archaic Greece and the Aegean

Beye, C.R., *Ancient Greek Literature and Society*, Ithaca: Cornell University Press, 1987

Boardman, J., *The Greeks Overseas*, Baltimore: Penguin, 1973

Boardman, J., Jasper, G., and Murray, O. (eds.), *The Oxford History of the Classical World*, Oxford: Oxford University Press, 1986

Finley, M.I., *Early Greece: The Bronze and Archaic Age*, New York: Norton, 1981

Graves, R., *The Greek Myths*, Garden City, NY: Doubleday, 1981

Groenewegen-Frankfort, H.A., and Ashmole, Bernard, *Art of the Ancient World*, Englewood Cliffs, NJ, and New York: Prentice Hall, Inc. and Harry N. Abrams, Inc., 1972

Janson, H.W., *A Basic History of Art* (4th ed.), Englewood Cliffs, NJ, and New York: Prentice Hall, Inc. and Harry N. Abrams, Inc., 1991

Snell, Bruno, *Discovery of the Mind: The Greek Origins of European Thought*, New York: Harper, 1960

Greek Classicism and Hellenism

Arnott, Peter D., *An Introduction to the Greek Theatre*, Bloomington, IN: Indiana University Press, 1963

Bieber, M., *The Sculpture of the Hellenistic Age*, New York: Columbia University Press, 1955

Boardman, J., *et al.*, *Greek Art and Architecture*, New York: Abrams, 1967

Burcket, W., *Ancient Mystery Cults*, Cambridge, MA: Harvard University Press, 1987

Grant, M., *From Alexander to Cleopatra: The Hellenistic World*, London: Weidenfeld & Nicolson, 1982

Hamilton, Edith, *Three Greek Plays*, New York: W.W. Norton & Co., Inc., 1965

Kjellberg, Ernst, and Saflund, Gosta, *Greek and Roman Art*, New York: Thomas Y. Crowell Co., 1968

Morford, M.P.O., and Lenardon, P.J., *Classical Mythology*, New York: Longman, 1977

Richter, Gisela, *Greek Art*, Greenwich, CT: Phaidon, 1960

Robertson, Martin, *A Shorter History of Greek Art*, Cambridge, UK: Cambridge University Press, 1981

The Roman Period

Andreae, Bernard, *The Art of Rome*, New York: Harry N. Abrams, Inc., 1977

Balsdon, J.P.V.D., *Rome: The Story of an Empire*, New York: McGraw Hill, 1970

Brendel, O.J., *Etruscan Art*, Baltimore: Penguin, 1978

Crawford, M., *The Roman Republic*, Cambridge, MA: Harvard University Press, 1982

Grant, M., *Roman Literature*, New York: Penguin, 1964

Henig, Martin (ed.), *A Handbook of Roman Art*, Ithaca, NY: Cornell University Press, 1983

Kjellberg, Ernst, and Saflund, Gosta, *Greek and Roman Art*, New York: Thomas Y. Crowell Co., 1968

Ward-Perkins, J.B., *Roman Imperial Architecture* (2nd ed.), New York: Penguin, 1981

Judaism and Early Christianity

Achtemeier, Paul (ed.), *Harper's Bible Dictionary*. San Francisco: Harper & Row, 1985

Anderson, Bernhard, *Understanding the Old Testament*, Englewood Cliffs, NJ: Prentice Hall, 1975

Andreae, Bernard, *The Art of Rome*, New York: Harry N. Abrams, Inc., 1977

Barclay, William, *The Gospel of Luke*, Philadelphia: Westminster Press, 1975

Bevan, G.M., *Early Christians of Rome*, London: Society for Promoting Christian Knowledge, 1927

Brown, P., *Augustine of Hippo*, London: Faber, 1967

Chadwick, H., *The Early Church*, New York: Penguin, 1967

Epstein, Isidore, *Judaism*, Middlesex, UK: Penguin Books, 1968

Frend, W.H.C., *The Rise of Christianity*, Philadelphia: Fortress Press, 1983

Henig, Martin (ed.), *A Handbook of Roman Art*, Ithaca, NY: Cornell University Press, 1983

Johnston, Leonard, *A History of Israel*, New York: Sheed & Ward, 1963

McGiffert, Arthur, *A History of Christian Thought*, New York: Charles Scribner's Sons, 1961

Milburn, Robert, *Early Christian Art and Architecture*, Berkeley: University of California Press, 1988

Wheeler, Robert Eric Mortimer, *Roman Art and Architecture*, New York: Frederick Praeger Publishers, 1964

Byzantium and the Rise of Islam

Armstrong, Karen, *Muhammad: A Western Attempt to Understand Islam*, San Francisco: HarperCollins, 1992

Bovini, G., *Ravenna Mosaics*, Greenwich, CT: New York Graphic Society Publishers, Ltd., 1956

Diehl, Charles, *Byzantium*, New Brunswick, NJ: Rutgers University Press, 1957

Dunlop, D.M., *Arab Civilization to A.D. 1500*, London: Longman, 1971

Esposito, John, *Islam: The Straight Path*, New York: Oxford University Press, 1991

Grabar, Andre, *The Art of the Byzantine Empire*, New York: Crown Publishers, Inc., 1966

MacDonald, William, *Early Christian and Byzantine Architecture*, New York: George Braziller, 1967

Mango, Cyril, *Byzantium*, New York: Charles Scribner's Sons, 1980

Rice, David Talbot, *The Art of Byzantium*, New York: Harry N. Abrams, Inc., n.d.

Sherrard, Philip, *Byzantium*, New York: Time Inc., 1966

Watt, W.M., *Muhammad: Statesman and Prophet*, New York: Oxford University Press, 1974

The Early Middle Ages

Beckwith, J., *Early Medieval Art*, New York: Praeger, 1973

Brondsted, Johannes, *The Vikings* (trans. Kalle Skov), New York: Penguin Books, 1960

Hoppin, Richard, *Medieval Music*, New York: W.W. Norton & Co., Inc., 1978

Jackson, W.T.H., *Medieval Literature: A History and a Guide*, New York: Collier Books, 1966

Knowles, David, *Christian Monasticism*, New York: McGraw-Hill, 1969

Rorig, F., *The Medieval Town* (trans. D.J.A. Matthew), Berkeley: University of California Press, 1969

Strayer, Joseph, and Munro, Dana, *The Middle Ages*, Pacific Palisades: Goodyear Publishing Co., 1970

Tierney, Brian, and Painter, Sidney, *Western Europe in the Middle Ages*, New York: Alfred A. Knopf, 1974

Zarnecki, George, *Art of the Medieval World*, Englewood Cliffs, NJ: Prentice Hall, Inc., 1975

The High Middle Ages

Barraclough, G., *The Medieval Papacy*, New York: Harcourt, Brace, & World, 1968

Bony, Jean, *French Gothic Architecture of the Twelfth and Thirteenth Centuries*, Berkeley: University of California Press, 1983

Bruzelius, Carline A., *The 13th-Century Church at St-Denis*, New Haven, CT: Yale University Press, 1985

Crosby, Sumner McKnight, *The Royal Abbey of Saint-Denis*, New Haven: Yale University Press, 1987

Daly, Lowrie, *The Medieval University: 1200-1400*, New York: Sheed & Ward, 1961

Esser, Kajetan, *Origins of the Franciscan Order* (trans. Aedan Daly and Irina Lynch), Chicago: Franciscan Herald Press, 1970

Hoppin, Richard, *Medieval Music*, New York: W.W. Norton & Co., Inc., 1978

Jackson, W.T.H., *Medieval Literature: A History and a Guide*, New York: Collier Books, 1966

Rorig, F., *The Medieval Town* (trans. D.J.A. Matthew), Berkeley: University of California Press, 1969

Singleton, Charles, *The Divine Comedy of Dante Alighieri* (6 vols), Princeton: Princeton University Press, 1972

Strayer, Joseph, and Munro, Dana, *The Middle Ages*, Pacific Palisades: Goodyear Publishing Co., 1970

Tierney, Brian, and Painter, Sidney, *Western Europe in the Middle Ages*, New York: Alfred A. Knopf, 1974

Zarnecki, George, *Art of the Medieval World*, Englewood Cliffs, NJ: Prentice Hall, Inc., 1975

The Late Middle Ages

Aston, M., *The Fifteenth Century: The Prospect of Europe*, New York: Harcourt, Brace, & World, 1968

Barraclough, G., *The Medieval Papacy*, New York: Harcourt, Brace, & World, 1968

Bishop, M., *Petrarch and His World*, Bloomington, Indiana University Press, 1963

Gottfried, Robert S., *The Black Death: Natural and Human Disaster in Medieval Europe*, New York: Free Press, 1983

Hofstatter, H.H., *Art of the Late Middle Ages* (trans. R.E. Wolf), New York: Abrams, 1968

Hoppin, Richard, *Medieval Music*, New York: W.W. Norton & Co., Inc., 1978

Hubert, J., Porcher, J., and Volbach, W.F., *The Carolingian Renaissance*, New York: George Braziller, 1970.

Jackson, W.T.H., *Medieval Literature: A History and a Guide*, New York: Collier Books, 1966

Janson, H.W., *A Basic History of Art* (4th ed.), Englewood Cliffs, NJ, and New York: Prentice Hall, Inc. and Harry N. Abrams, Inc., 1991

Kane, George, *Chaucer*, New York: Oxford University Press, 1984

Strayer, Joseph, and Munro, Dana, *The Middle Ages*, Pacific Palisades: Goodyear Publishing Co., 1970

Tierney, Brian, and Painter, Sidney, *Western Europe in the Middle Ages*, New York: Alfred A. Knopf, 1974

White, John, *Art and Architecture in Italy 1250–1400*, Baltimore: Pelican, 1966

Zarnecki, George, *Art of the Medieval World*, Englewood Cliffs, NJ: Prentice Hall, Inc., 1975

The Early Renaissance

Artz, Frederick, *From the Renaissance to Romanticism*, Chicago: University of Chicago Press, 1962

Brucker, Gene, *Renaissance Florence*, New York: Wiley, 1969

Burckhardt, Jakob, *The Civilization of the Renaissance in Italy*, New York: Harper Torchbooks, 1958

Cronin, Vincent, *The Florentine Renaissance*, New York: E.P. Dutton & Co., 1967

Fletcher, Jefferson, B., *Literature of the Italian Renaissance*, New York: The Macmillan Co., 1934

Gilbert, Creighton, *History of Renaissance Art Throughout Europe: Painting, Sculpture, Architecture*, New York: Harry N. Abrams, Inc., 1973

Hale, J.R., *Florence and the Medicis*, London: Thames & Hudson, 1977

Hartt, Frederick, *Italian Renaissance Art* (3rd ed.), Englewood Cliffs, NJ, and New York: Prentice Hall, Inc. and Harry N. Abrams, Inc., 1987

Keutner, Hubert, *Sculpture: Renaissance to Rococo*, Greenwich, CN: New York Graphic Society, 1969

King, Margaret, *Women of the Renaissance*, Chicago: University of Chicago Press, 1991

Kristeller, P.O., *Renaissance Thought: The Classic, Scholastic, and Humanist Strains*, New York: Harper Torchbooks, 1955

Staley, Edgcombe, *Famous Women of Florence*, London: Archibald Constable & Co., 1909

The High Renaissance and Mannerism

Artz, Frederick, *From the Renaissance to Romanticism*, Chicago: University of Chicago Press, 1962

Brown, Howard M., *Music in the Renaissance*, Englewood Cliffs, NJ: Prentice Hall, 1976

Campos, D. Redig de (ed.), *Art Treasures of the Vatican*, Englewood Cliffs, NJ: Prentice Hall, Inc., 1974

Cochrane, Eric, *The Late Italian Renaissance, 1525–1630*, New York: Harper Torchbooks, 1970

Fletcher, Jefferson, B., *Literature of the Italian Renaissance*, New York: The Macmillan Co., 1934

Gilbert, Creighton, *History of Renaissance Art Throughout Europe: Painting, Sculpture, Architecture*, New York: Harry N. Abrams, Inc., 1973

Hartt, Frederick, *Italian Renaissance Art* (3rd ed.), Englewood Cliffs, NJ, and New York: Prentice Hall, Inc. and Harry N. Abrams, Inc., 1987

Hay, Denys, and Law, John, *Italy in the Age of the Renaissance, 1380–1530*, London: Longman, 1989

Levey, Michael, *High Renaissance*, New York: Penguin, 1975

Oman, Sir Charles, *The Sixteenth Century*, Westport, CT: Greenwood Press, 1975

Plumb, J.H., *The Italian Renaissance*, New York: Harper Torchbooks, 1961

Stinger, Charles, *The Renaissance in Rome*, Bloomington: Indiana University Press, 1985

Renaissance and Reformation in Northern Europe

Artz, Frederick, *From the Renaissance to Romanticism*, Chicago: University of Chicago Press, 1962

Bainton, Roland, *Here I Stand: A Life of Martin Luther*, New York: New American Library, 1950

Brion, Marcel, *Dürer, His Life and Work*, New York: Tudor Publishing, 1960

Brown, Howard M., *Music in the Renaissance*, Englewood Cliffs, NJ: Prentice Hall, 1976

Fenlon, Iain (ed.), *The Renaissance*, Englewood Cliffs, NJ: Prentice Hall, 1989

Gilbert, Creighton, *History of Renaissance Art Throughout Europe: Painting, Sculpture, Architecture*, New York: Harry N. Abrams, Inc., 1973

Hall, A. Rupert, *The Revolution in Science 1500–1750*, London: Longman, 1983

Oman, Sir Charles, *The Sixteenth Century*, Westport, CT: Greenwood Press, 1975

Smart, Alastair, *The Renaissance and Mannerism in Northern Europe and Spain*, London: Harcourt, Brace Jovanovich, Inc., 1972

Snyder, J., *Northern Renaissance Art*, Englewood Cliffs, NJ: Prentice Hall, 1985

Spitz, Lewis (ed.), *The Protestant Reformation*, Englewood Cliffs, NJ: Prentice Hall, Inc., 1966

Thompson, S. Harrison, *Europe in Renaissance and Reformation*, New York: Harcourt, Brace & World, 1963

The Baroque Age

Bazin, Germain, *The Baroque*, Greenwich, CN: New York Graphic Society, 1968

Boyd, M., *Bach*, London: Dent, 1983

Braider, Christopher, *Refiguring the Real: Picture and Modernity in Word and Image: 1400–1700*, Princeton, NJ: Princeton University Press, 1993

Friedrich, C.J., *The Age of the Baroque: 1610–1660*, New York: Harper Torchbooks, 1961

Grimm, Harold, *The Reformation Era*, New York: Macmillan Co., 1954

Hall, A. Rupert, *The Revolution in Science 1500–1750*, London: Longman, 1983

Held, Julius, and Posner, D., *Seventeenth and Eighteenth Century Art*, New York: Harry N. Abrams, Inc., n.d.

Ogg, D., *Europe in the Seventeenth Century* (rev. ed.), New York: Collier Books, 1968

Van Der Kemp, Gerald, *Versailles*, New York: The Vendome Press, 1977

Willey, B., *The Seventeenth-century Background*, New York: Columbia University Press, 1967

Wolf, J.B., *Louis XIV*, New York: Norton, 1968

The Enlightenment

Conisbee, P., *Painting in Eighteenth-century France*, Ithaca, NY: Cornell University Press, 1981

Hampson, N., *A Cultural History of the Enlightenment*, New York: Pantheon, 1968

Held, Julius, and Posner, D., *Seventeenth and Eighteenth Century Art*, New York: Harry N. Abrams, Inc., n.d.

Helm, Ernest, *Music at the Court of Frederick the Great*, Norman, OK: University of Oklahoma Press, 1960

Hubatsch, Walther, *Frederick the Great of Prussia*, London: Thames & Hudson, 1975

Keutner, Hubert, *Sculpture: Renaissance to Rococo*, Greenwich, CN: New York Graphic Society, 1969

Pignatti, Terisio, *The Age of Rococo*, London: Paul Hamlyn, 1969

Schonberger, Arno, and Soehner, Halldor, *The Rococo Age*, New York: McGraw-Hill, 1960

Waterhouse, E., *Painting in Britain 1530–1790* (4th ed.), New York: Penguin, 1978

The Romantic Age

Booth, Michael, *Victorian Spectacular Theatre 1850–1910*, Boston: Routledge & Kegan Paul, 1981

Glasstone, Victor, *Victorian and Edwardian Theatres*, Cambridge, MA: Harvard University Press, 1975

Goethe, Johann Wolfgang von, *Faust: Part I* (trans. Philip Wayne), Baltimore: Penguin Books, 1962

Hamilton, George Heard, *Nineteenth and Twentieth Century Art: Painting, Sculpture, Architecture*, New York: Harry N. Abrams, Inc., 1970

Henderson, W.O., *The Industrialization of Europe, 1780–1914*, London: Thames & Hudson, 1969

Hewett, Bernard, *Theatre USA*, New York: McGraw-Hill Book Company, 1959

Hitchcock, Henry-Russell, *Architecture: Nineteenth and Twentieth Centuries*, Baltimore: Penguin, 1971

Katz, Bernard, *The Social Implications of Early Negro Music in the United States*, New York: Arno Press and The New York Times, 1969

Keck, George R., and Martin, Sherrill V., *Feel the Spirit*, New York: Greenwood Press, 1988

Krehbiel, Henry Edward, *Afro-American Folksongs*, New York: G. Schirmer, n.d. (c. 1914)

Maas, Jeremy, *Victorian Painters*, New York: G.P. Putnam's Sons, 1969

Muthesius, Stefan, *The High Victorian Movement in Architecture 1850–1870*, London: Routledge & Kegan Paul, 1972

Read, Benedict, *Victorian Sculpture*, New Haven: Yale University Press, 1982

Rowell, George, *The Victorian Theatre* (2nd ed.), Cambridge, UK: Cambridge University Press, 1978

The Beginnings of Modernism

Bohn, T.W., Stomgren, R.L., and Johnson, D.H., *Light and Shadows, A History of Motion Pictures* (2nd ed.), Sherman Oaks, CA: Alfred Publishing Co., 1978

Goldwater, R., *Symbolism*, New York: Harper & Row, 1979

Hamilton, George Heard, *Nineteenth and Twentieth Century Art: Painting, Sculpture, Architecture*, New York: Harry N. Abrams, Inc., 1970

Hayes, C.J.H., *A Generation of Materialism*, New York: Harper & Row, 1963

Henderson, W.O., *The Industrialization of Europe, 1780–1914*, London: Thames & Hudson, 1969

Hitchcock, Henry-Russell, *Architecture: Nineteenth and Twentieth Centuries*, Baltimore: Penguin, 1971

Leish, Kenneth W., *Cinema*, New York: Newsweek Books, 1974

Ostransky, Leroy, *Understanding Jazz*, Englewood Cliffs, NJ: Prentice Hall, Inc., 1977

Robinson, David, *The History of World Cinema*, New York: Stein & Day Publishers, 1973

Salzman, Eric, *Twentieth Century Music: An Introduction*, Englewood Cliffs, NJ: Prentice Hall, Inc., 1967

Tirro, Frank, *Jazz: A History*, New York: W.W. Norton & Co., Inc., 1977

Modernism

Arnason, H.H., *History of Modern Art*, Englewood Cliffs, NJ: Prentice Hall, Inc., 1977

Barrett, W., *Time of Need: Forms of Imagination in the Twentieth Century*, New York: Harper & Row, 1972

Golding, John, *Visions of the Modern*, Berkeley, CA: University of California Press, 1994

Griffiths, Paul, *A Concise History of Avant-Garde Music*, New York: Oxford University Press, 1978

Gropius, Walter (ed.), *The Theatre of the Bauhaus*, Middletown, CT: Wesleyan University Press, 1961

Gropius, Walter, *The New Architecture and the Bauhaus*, Cambridge, MA: M.I.T. Press, 1965

Hamilton, George Heard, *Nineteenth and Twentieth Century Art: Painting, Sculpture, Architecture*, New York: Harry N. Abrams, Inc., 1970

Hitchcock, Henry-Russell, *Architecture: Nineteenth and Twentieth Centuries*, Baltimore: Penguin, 1971

Knight, Arthur, *The Liveliest Art: A Panoramic History of the Movies* (rev. ed.), New York: Macmillan, Inc., 1978

Liddell Hart, B.H., *History of the Second World War*, New York: Putnam, 1971

Lippard, Lucy R., *Pop Art*, New York: Oxford University Press, 1966

Nyman, Michael, *Experimental Music: Cage and Beyond*, New York: Schirmer Books, 1974

Robinson, David, *The History of World Cinema*, New York: Stein & Day Publishers, 1973

Roters, Eberhard, *Painters of the Bauhaus*, New York: Frederick Praeger Publishers, 1965

Salzman, Eric, *Twentieth Century Music: An Introduction*, Englewood Cliffs, NJ: Prentice Hall, Inc., 1967

Shirer, William L., *The Rise and Fall of the Third Reich*, New York: Simon & Schuster, 1960

Postmodernism: The Pluralistic Age

Arkin, Marian, and Shollar, Barbara (eds.), *Longman Anthology of World Literature by Women*, New York: Longman, 1989

Arnason, H.H., *History of Modern Art*, Englewood Cliffs, NJ: Prentice Hall, Inc., 1977

Brindle, Reginald Smith, *The New Music: The Avant-Garde Since 1945*, London: Oxford University Press, 1975

Coryell, Julie, and Friedman, Laura, *Jazz-Rock Fusion*, New York: Delacorte Press, 1978

Dallmayr, Fred R., *Critical Encounters: Between Philosophy and Politics*, Notre Dame, IN: University of Notre Dame Press, 1987

Ernst, David, *The Evolution of Electronic Music*, New York: Schirmer Books, 1977

Golding, John, *Visions of the Modern*, Berkeley, CA: University of California Press, 1994

Griffiths, Paul, *A Concise History of Avant-Garde Music*, New York: Oxford University Press, 1978

Hitchcock, Henry-Russell, *Architecture: Nineteenth and Twentieth Centuries*, Baltimore: Penguin, 1971

Knight, Arthur, *The Liveliest Art: A Panoramic History of the Movies* (rev. ed.), New York: Macmillan, Inc., 1978

Nyman, Michael, *Experimental Music: Cage and Beyond*, New York: Schirmer Books, 1974

Robinson, David, *The History of World Cinema*, New York: Stein & Day Publishers, 1973

Salzman, Eric, *Twentieth Century Music: An Introduction*, Englewood Cliffs, NJ: Prentice Hall, Inc., 1967

Index

Aachen, Germany: Palatine Chapel 231–2, **7.28**, **7.29**
Aalto (Douglas) 558, **17.17**
Abdoh, Rezo: *Quotations from a Ruined City* 611
Abelard, Peter 241, 242–4
Abraham 142, 143
Abraham's Hospitality and the Sacrifice of Isaac (mosaic) 20 2, **6.29**
Absalom and Achitophel (Dryden) 409
absolutism 384, 392–5
abstract art/abstraction 538, 552–3, 598
abstract expressionism 576, 583–4
absurdism 538, 567–9, 610–11
Abu Bakr, Caliph 194
Abu–Khalid, Fawziyya 607
Achilles painter: lekythos 84, **3.5**
Acosta, Ivan 619
Acropolis, Athens 50, 56, 90, **3.15**; Parthenon 87, 89, 90, **3.1**, **3.9**, **3.10**, **3.16**, **3.17**; Propylaea 93, **3.20**; Theatre of Dionysus 99
"action painting" 583
Actium, battle of (31 B.C.) 120
Adams, Ansel 570; *Mount Williamson in the Sierra Nevada* **17.31**
Adding Machine (Rice) 567
Adler, Dankmar 517
Advancement of Learning (Bacon) 386
Aeneid (Vergil) 134–5, 137, 245
Aeschylus 95–6, 98, 99; *Agamemnon* 96; *Prometheus Bound* 107
Aesthetica (Baumgarten) 433, 440
aesthetics 74, 80, 433, 467–8
Africa: Benin sculptors 23; Igbo-Ukwu art 222, 560; Nok sculpture 94
African Americans: film-making 618–19; jazz 528, 617; literature 551, 552, 557–8, 618; painting 507; theatre 617–18
Agamemnon (Aeschylus) 96
Agra, India: Taj Mahal 404, **13.24**
Ahmad, Ustad: Taj Mahal 404, **13.24**
Aiken, Howard 547
Ailey, Alvin 614
Akhenaton (Amenhotep IV) 47, 48, **1.19**
Alaric 160, 177
Alba Madonna, The (Raphael) 334, **11.18**
Alberti, Leon Battista 296–7; Palazzo Rucellai 296, **10.6**
Alcuin of York 228
aleatory music 576, 608
Alexander the Great 81, 89, 100–1, 146, 147
Alexander VI, Pope 294, 323
Alexander Sarcophagus **3.27**
Alexandria 101, 102, 156, 180
alienation 567
allegory/allegories 234, 238, 255
alleluia 169
Allen, Paula Gunn 615
Alloway, Lawrence 584
Altar of Peace, Rome 137–8, **4.34**
Altar of Zeus, Pergamon 106, **3.33**
Altdorfer, Albrecht 369; *Battle of Alexander and Darius on the Issus* 369–70, **12.16**
alternative theatre 611–12
America-Dawn (Nevelson) 591, **18.17**
American Biograph 530
American Company 452

American Gothic (Wood) 557, **17.16**
Amiens Cathedral, France 248–9, **8.12**
amphitheatres, Roman 125–6
amphoras, Greek 60–1, 68, **2.1**, **2.8**, **2.9**, **2.21**
Anaximander 79
Andachtsbild 277
Angelico, Fra 305, 306; *Annunciation* 306, **10.20**
Angels in America (Kushner) 612, **18.46**
Anglicanism 375, 381
Ankara, Turkey: St Clement 192, **6.15**
Annunciation (Fra Angelico) 306, **10.20**
Annunciation, The (Pucelle) 281, **9.20**
Antecriste (play) 256
Anthemius of Tralles: Hagia Sophia 200, 202–3, 205, **6.30**, **6.33–6.36**
Antioch 156, 169, 180
Antiochus IV 146–7
Apollo Belvedere 320
Apollodorus of Damascus: Trajan's Column 125, **4.15**, **4.16**
Apoxyomenos (Lysippus) 92, **3.18**
Appalachian Spring (Copland) 566–7; dance piece (Graham) 568, **17.29**
Appert, Nicholas 464
Apuleius: *Golden Ass* 136
aqueducts, Roman 132, 133, **4.26**
Aquinas, St Thomas 181, 243, 244, 391
Ara Pacis (Altar of Peace), Rome 137–8, **4.34**
Arabian Nights, The 196–7
arcades 125, **4.18**
arches: Gothic 247; Norman 221; Roman 125; Roman triumphal 126, 132, 133, **4.27**; Romanesque 219
architecture 23–5; American 445, 515–17, 535–7, 562–4, 600–1, 603, 604; ancient Egyptian 43–4, 47–8; ancient Greek 67–8, 90, 92–3; Art Nouveau 517; Assyrian 41–2; Baroque 397–8, 400–1, 404–5, 418–19, 420; Bauhaus 573–4; British 219–21, 249–51, 376, 418–19, 420, 436, 476, 491–2; Byzantine 192, 200–3, 205; Carolingian 231–2; early Christian 166–7; French 221, 228, 231, 247–9, 258, 370–1, 400–1, 404–5, 436, 604; Georgian 436; German 273–4, 436, 457–8, 459–60, 473–4; Gothic 246–51, 258, 263, 273–7, **8.11**; Hellenistic 105–6; International Style 601, 603; Islamic 193, 197, 199; Italian 274–7, 295–9, 320, 338, 340, 342, 346–8, 370–1, 397–8; Japanese 604; Jewish 150–1; Mughal 404; neoclassical 442, 444–5; Norman 219–21; Palladian 338, 340; postmodern 603–4, 606; Renaissance 295–9, 338, 346–8, 370–1; revisionist 603–4; rococo 436; Roman 117, 125–6, 130–3, 139, 164–6; Romanesque 217–19; Romantic 476; Spanish 24, 517
Arcturus II (Vasarély) 587, **18.11**
arias 412
Ariosto, Ludovico 345; *Orlando Furioso* 345
Aristophanes 98, 99; *The Birds* 16;

Lysistrata 16, 98
Aristotle 81, 119, 133, 242, 244, 290, 386, **3.4**; *Poetics* 81–2, 96–7, 99
Armat, Thomas 529
Armory Show (New York, 1913) 556
Arneaux, J. A. 488
Arnolfini Marriage, The (van Eyck) 363, **12.8**
Arnolfo di Cambio 313
Arp, Jean 553
ars nova 264, 281–3
art: definitions 14–16; evaluations 17–18; functions 16–17; theories 80, 81–2, 123–4, 158, 433, 467–8
"art for art's sake", doctrine of 496, 511, 529
Art Nouveau 517
Art Workers' Guild 492
Arthur, King 244–5
Ascension of Muhammad, The 196, **6.22**
asceticism 211
Asheville, N. Carolina: Biltmore House (Hunt and Olmstead) 536–7, **16.41**
Ashton, Anthony 452
Ashurnasirpal II killing lions (relief) **1.6**
Asimov, Isaac 581
Aspects of Negro Life (Douglas) 558, **17.18**
Assommoir, L' (Zola) 523
Assumption of the Virgin (Titian) 335, **11.20**
Assyrians 41–2, 76, 146
Astor Place Company of Colored Tragedians 488
astronomy 294, 361–2, 386–7, 427
Atanasoff, John 547
Athens, Greece 56, 58, 59, 76, 77–9, 100, 103, 180; Dionysia 95; Lyceum 81; Temple of Olympian Zeus 105–6, **3.32**; *see also* Acropolis
atom, splitting the 548
atomic bombs 548
atomists 59
Attila the Hun 177
Auden, W. H. 552
Augustine, St 209, 210, 215
Augustine of Hippo, St 157–8, 226, 355, 391; *City of God* 157, 158
Augustus Caesar (Octavian) 119–21, 125, 134, 137–8, 142, **4.13**, **4.29–4.31**
Aurelius, Emperor Marcus 118, 121, 122–3; *Meditations* 122
Austen, Jane 479–80; *Pride and Prejudice* 480
Autun Cathedral, France 221, **7.18**
Auxerre, France: St-Germain 228, 231, **7.24**, **7.25**
axe, prehistoric 33, **1.2**
Aztecs 321–2

Babbitt, Milton 607; *Three Compositions* 608
Baboon and Young (Picasso) 594, **18.23**
Babylon/Babylonians 40, 58, 100, 146, 147
Babylonian Captivity (papacy) 271, 286
Bacchae, The (Euripides) 96
Bach, Carl Philipp Emanuel 448, 459
Bach, Johann Sebastian 374, 412, 413,

423, 448, 459; *Ein feste Burg ist unser Gott* 412, **13.31**; *Fugue in G minor* 411, **13.30**; *Well-Tempered Clavier* 410, 413
Bacon, Francis 386; *Advancement of Learning* 386
Bakst, Leon: costume designs 532, **16.38**
Balanchine, George 533
Baldacchino (Bernini) 397, **13.1**
ballad opera 452
ballades 255
ballate 283
ballet 28, 374, 414, 415–16, 454–6, 489–90, 527, 531–3, 614
Ballets russes 531–3, 593
balletts 382
balloon construction 25, **0.14**
Balzac, Honoré de: *Comédie Humaine* 481
Banjo Lesson, The (Tanner) 507, **16.10**
Baraka, Imamu Ameer 618
Baralt, Luis 619
Barber of Seville, The (Beaumarchais) 452, 453
Barber of Seville, The (Rossini) 486
Barberini Ivory 186, **6.11**
Barbizon School 504
Barcelona, Spain: Casa Batlló (Gaudí) 517, **16.24**
Baroque style 384, 433; architecture 397–8, 400–1, 404–5, 418–19, 420; dance 416; music 409–14, 419, 423; painting 393–5, 398–400, 405–8; sculpture 395–7, 400; theatre 419, 422
Barry, Sir Charles: Houses of Parliament, London 476, 491–2, **15.12**
Bartók, Béla 566, 608, 609
basilicas 140; Basilica of Constantine, Rome 165–6, **5.26**, **5.27**; early Christian 166–7, **5.28**, **5.29**; Paestum 68, **2.20**
baths, Roman 164–5, **5.25**
Battle of Alexander and Darius on the Issus (Altdorfer) 369–70, **12.16**
Battle of San Romano, The (Uccello) 308, **10.21**
Battleship Potemkin (Eisenstein) 571
Baudelaire, Charles: *Les Fleurs du Mal* 481
Bauhaus 552, 573–4
Baumgarten, Gottlieb: *Aesthetica* 433, 440
Beauchamps, Pierre 416
Beaumarchais, Pierre de: *The Barber of Seville* 452, 453; *The Marriage of Figaro* 452, 453
Beauvoir, Simone de 549
Beckett, Samuel 610; *Waiting for Godot* 610
Beckmann, Max: *Christ and the Woman Taken in Adultery* 521, **16.29**
Beethoven, Ludwig van 449, 451, 484; Piano Sonata in C minor 451, **14.30**; Symphony No. 5 451, **14.29**; Symphony No. 6 451, 483; Symphony No. 9 447, 449
Begay, Harrison: *Women Picking Corn* 616, **18.48**
Beggar's Opera (Gay) 452
Being and Nothingness (Sartre) 549

Benedict, St 210, 224
Benedictine order 210, 211, 225, 240
Benglis, Lynda 598; *Passat* 598, **18.30**
Benin sculptors 23
Beowulf 224
Bérain, Jean: *Dame en habit de ballet* 416, **13.34**
Berg, Alban 566; *Lyric Suite* 566
Bergman, Ingmar 613
Berio, Luciano 609; *Circles* 609
Berlin 459; Opera House 457–8
Berlioz, Hector: *Requiem* 484; *Symphonie Fantastique* 483, **15.17**; *The Trojans* 486
Bernard of Clairvaux, St 241
Bernini, Gian Lorenzo 395; *Baldacchino* 397, **13.1**; *David* 395–6, **13.9**; *The Ecstasy of St Theresa* 396–7, **13.10**; St Peter's Square statues 347, **11.38**
Bernward of Hildesheim, Bishop 218
Beth B 613
Bibiena family 414, **13.32**
Bible, the 147, 168, 355–6, 417
Billings, William 565
biography 27
Bird in Space (Brancusi) 559, **17.22**
Birds, The (Aristophanes) 16
Birth of a Nation, The (Griffith) 530–1, **16.36**
Birth of Venus, The (Botticelli) 310, **10.25**
Birth of the Virgin, The (Lorenzetti) 280, **9.19**
Bismarck, Otto von 501, 540
Bizet, Georges: *Carmen* 525–6, **16.33**
Black Death 266, 267, 269, 270, 284, 314
black-figure pottery, Greek 63, **2.10**
Black Liberation Movement (theatre) 617–18
Black Wall (Nevelson) 591, **18.1**
Blair, Les: *Jump the Gun* 618
Blasis, Carlo: *Code of Terpsichore* 489, **15.22**
Blissett, Francis **14.32**
Blue Nude (Matisse) 521–2, **16.30**
Blue Rider, The 522
blues 528
Boar Hunt (wall painting) 55, **2.3**
Boccaccio, Giovanni 271, 272; *Decameron* 272
Boccioni, Umberto: *Unique Forms of Continuity in Space* 520, **16.28**
Bofill, Ricardo 604; Palace of Abraxas 604, **18.41**
Bohr, Nils 502
Bologna, Italy 181; University 242
Bonheur, Rosa 475, 476; *Plowing in the Nivernais* 475, **15.9**
Bonnin, Gertrude 551; "The Soft-Hearted Sioux" 551–2
Book of the City of Ladies (Christine de Pisan) 272
Book of Hours of Jeanne d'Evreux (Pucelle) 281, **9.20**
Bordas, Caesar 179
Borghese, Pauline: *Pauline Borghese as Venus Victrix* (Canova) 442, **14.18**
Borodin, Mikhail: *In the Steppes of Central Asia* 484
Bosch, Hieronymus 364; *The Garden of Earthly Delights* 364–5, **12.10**
Boscoreale, Italy: villa bedroom 116, **4.4**
Botticelli, Sandro: *The Birth of Venus* 310, **10.25**; *La Primavera* (Spring) 309–10, **10.22**
Boucher, François 434; *Venus Consoling Love* 434–5, **14.6**
Boudy, José Sanchez 619
Boulez, Pierre 607, 608
Brahms, Johannes 485, **15.19**; *A German Requiem* 484–5; Symphony No. 3 484, **15.18**
Bramante, Donato: St Peter's 347,

11.40; Tempietto 338, **11.25**
Brancacci Chapel, S Maria del Carmine, Florence: Masaccio frescoes 303–5, **10.18**, **10.19**
Brancusi, Constantin 559; *Bird in Space* 559, **17.22**; *Mlle Pogany* 559–60, **17.21**
Braque, Georges 518, 519, 556
Brecht, Bertolt 567
Breughel *see* Bruegel
Brewton House, S. Carolina 445, **14.23**
Bridge, The 521, 522
Brighton, England: Royal Pavilion (Nash) 476, **15.11**
Britain 266, 267, 375–6, 427–8; architecture 219–21, 249–51, 376, 418–19, 420, 436, 476, 491–2; literature 224, 274, 376, 377–8, 386, 408–9, 445–7, 478–81, 550; music 381–2, 419; painting 376–7, 437, 439, 473–4, 492–4, 600; philosophy 388–90, 428, 468, 469, 549; science and technology 386, 387–8, 427–8, 465–6, 548; sculpture 562, 592; theatre 378–80, 419, 422, 452, 611
Broken Column, The (Kahlo) 556, **17.1**, **17.13**
Brontë, Charlotte: *Jane Eyre* 481
Brontë, Emily: *Wuthering Heights* 481
Bronzino (Agnolo di Cosimo di Mariano): *Portrait of a Young Man* 337, 371, **11.22**
Brown, Earle 608
Brown, Ford Madox: *Work* 499, **16.3**
Brown, William Henry 617
Brücke, Die ("The Bridge") 521
Bruegel, Pieter, the Elder 365; *Landscape with the Fall of Icarus* 365–6, **12.11**
Brunelleschi, Filippo 296; Florence Cathedral 274, 296–8, **10.7**, **10.8**; Foundling Hospital, Florence 298–9, **10.9**; Pazzi Chapel, S Croce, Florence 299, **10.10**; *Sacrifice of Isaac* 302, **10.14**
Bryennius, Nicephorus 180
Budd, Harold: *One Sound* 609
Buddha (Frankenthaler) 585, **8.6**
Buddhism 196; sculpture 255, **8.21**
Buffon, Georges 427
Bugiardini, Giuliano: *Michelangelo* **11.13**
Bunshaft, Gordon: Lever House, New York 601, **18.35**
Burckhardt, Jacob 290
Burghers of Calais, The (Rodin) 509, 511, **16.15**
Burnham, Daniel Hudson, and Root, John Wellborn: Monadnock Building, Chicago 515–16, **16.22**
Bus Driver, The (Segal) 585, 587, **18.10**
Buthyllus of Alexandria 136
Buxtehude, Dietrich 412
Byrd, William 382
Byron, Lord 478, 480; *Don Juan* 480
Byzantine Empire 176–80, 192–3, 194; architecture 192, 200–3, 205; dance 192; intellectualism 180–1; ivories 186, 188, **6.11–6.13**; literature 180, 186–7, 189–90; maps **6.1–6.3**; music 191–2; painting and mosaics 181–3, 185, 202; sculpture 186; theatre 190–1
Byzantium *see* Constantinople

Cabinet of Dr Caligari, The (Wiene) 570, **17.33**
Cabral, Pedro Alvares 321
Caesar, Julius 114, 119
Cage, John 582, 608, 609, 613; *4' 33"* 608; *Imaginary Landscape No. 4* 608; *Imaginary Landscape No. 5* 609
Calder, Alexander 592; *Spring Blossoms* **18.20**

calendars 270; Hellenic 57; Julian 114
Caligula, Emperor 121, 136
Callicrates *see* Ictinos
Calling of St Matthew, The (Caravaggio) 393–4, **13.6**
Callot, Jacques: etching **11.33**
Calvin, John/Calvinism 355, 359–60, 373, 381, 391–2, 430, **12.6**
Camargo, Marie Anne Cupis de 454
Camus, Albert 569
Canaan 142, 144
Candide (Voltaire) 430
Canova, Antonio 442; *Pauline Borghese as Venus Victrix* 442, **14.18**; *Perseus Holding the Head of Medusa* **0.1**
cantatas 410, 411–12
Canterbury Tales (Chaucer) 274
cantilever 24, **0.13**
cantus firmus 254–5
Čapek, Karel: *R.U.R.* 581
capitalism 288, 294
Caravaggio 393; *The Calling of St Matthew* 393–4, **13.6**; *The Death of the Virgin* 394, **13.7**
Carmen (Bizet) 525–6, **16.33**
Carolingian period 208, 211–12, 224, 227; architecture 231–2; manuscript illumination 228; map **6.3**; sculpture 231; wall painting 228, 231
Caroso, Fabrizio 374, **12.22**
Carrère and Hastings: Whitehall, Palm Beach 536, **16.40**
Carrero, Jaime 619
Carter, Elliott 609
Cartesianism 387, 390, 428
Carthage 113
Cassatt, Mary 509; *The Child's Bath* 509, **16.14**
Castiglione, Baldassare 344, **11.34**; *The Courtier* 344–5
Castle, The (Kafka) 550
Catch-22 (Heller) 606
Catherine of Siena, St 286, **9.23**; *The Dialogue* 286
Catholic/Sacred Profane and Love (Roberts) 600, **18.34**
Catullus 135–6
cave paintings 34, 35–6
cella 110, 117
cement, Roman 133
Centerbeam (MIT) 598–9
Cervantes, Miguel: *Don Quixote* 409
Cézanne, Paul 513, 519; *Mont Sainte-Victoire seen from Les Lauves* 513, **16.17**
Chabanon, Michel Paul de 448
Chadwick, Sir James 548
Chamberlain, Neville 546
Chambord, Château de 371, **12.17**
Chanson de Roland 224–6
Chaplin, Charlie 531; *City Lights* 572
Chardin, Jean-Baptiste Siméon 439–40; *Menu de Gras* 440, **14.15**
Charioteer (from Delphi) 85, **3.6**
Charlemagne 212, 227–8, 231; *Statuette of Charlemagne* 231, **7.4**
Charles I, King of England 392, 417–18, 419
Charles II, King of England 392, 409, 419, 422
Charles V, Holy Roman Emperor 323, 325, 340, 344, 358, 371
Charleston, S. Carolina: Miles Brewton House 445, **14.23**
Charlottesville, Virginia: Monticello (Jefferson) 445, **14.22**
Chartres Cathedral, France 258–9, 261, **8.24–8.30**
Chaucer, Geoffrey 274, **9.7**; *Canterbury Tales* 274
Chavez, Cesar 619
Chekhov, Anton 529
Chey, Tim: *Fakin' Da' Funk* 618–19
chiaroscuro 408

Chicago, Illinois: Carson, Pirie, and Scott Dept Store (Sullivan) 516–17, **16.23**; Monadnock Building (Burnham and Root) 515–16, **16.22**; Robie House (Wright) 564, **17.26**; Tribune Tower (Howells and Hood) 564
Chicano theatre 619
Child's Bath, The (Cassatt) 509, **16.14**
China 43, 321; Han tile 127, **4.14**; Ming nature 309, **10.23**; theatre 189, **6.14**
Chi-Rho monogram 160, 162, **5.18**
Chirico, Giorgio de 555; *The Nostalgia of the Infinite* 555, **17.12**
chivalry, medieval 234, 238–9
Chopin, Frédéric 482–3; Nocturne in E flat major 483, **15.16**
chorales 352, 373, 412
choreomania 284
Chrétien de Troyes 244
Christ *see* Jesus Christ
Christ and the Woman Taken in Adultery (Beckmann) 521, **16.29**
Christianity/Christian Church 152–6, 174; and architecture 166–7; and art 160, 162–4; and evolutionary theories 466; and Judaism 140, 173, 205; in Middle Ages 209–11, 239–41, 269, 270–1; and music 168–9, 191–2; in Roman Empire 118, 121, 123, 133, 142, 158–60; and theatre 190, 191, 226, 255–6; theology and philosophy 157–8, 242–4; *see also* papacy
Christine de Pisan 272–3
Christo (Christo Jachareff): *Running Fence* 15–16, **0.3**; *The Umbrellas, Japan-USA* 595–6, **18.26**
Chronicles... (Froissart) 272
Chroniques d'Angleterre (de Wavrin) 266, **9.2**
Chryssa 597; *Fragments for the Gates to Times Square* 597, **18.28**
Churchill, Caryl 611; *Top Girls* 611
Cicero 135
Cid, Le (Corneille) 415
Cimabue 279; *Enthroned Madonna with St Francis* **8.5**; *Madonna Enthroned* 279, **9.15**
cire-perdue see lost-wax casting
Cistercian order 241
cities, rise of 236
Citizen Kane (Welles) 572
City Lights (Chaplin) 572
City of God (Augustine) 157, 158
city-states, Italian 295
classicism 74, 433; in music 448–52
Clement VII, Pope 292, 344
Clemente, Francesco 588; *Untitled from White Shroud* 588, 590, **18.14**
Climatron, St Louis (Buckminster Fuller) 603, **18.40**
clocks 270, **9.5**
Clodion (Claude Michel) 435, 436; *Satyr and Bacchante* 436, **14.8**
Close, Chuck 588
Clouet, Jean: *Francis I* 371, **12.18**
Cluniac order 210–11, 241
Cluny Abbey, France 210–11, 219, 240, **7.14–7.17**
Cnidian Aphrodite (Praxiteles) 89, **3.13**
Coca-Cola 502
codices 215
Cold War 578–9, 580
Coleman, Ornette 610
Coleridge, Samuel Taylor 478–9; *Rime of the Ancient Mariner* 480
Cologne Cathedral: *Gero crucifix* 217, **7.10**
colonialism 320–1, 578–9; map **13.1**
color 22; color wheel 22, **0.6**; value scale 22, **0.7**
color-field painting 584
Colosseum, Rome 125–6, **4.20**, **4.21**
Coltrane, John 617

Columbus, Christopher 321, 325
Comédie Humaine (Balzac) 481
comedy: Greek 95, 97–8; Roman 117–18; *see also* farce
commedia dell'arte 318, 342–4
communication, art and 16, 18
Communist Manifesto, The (Marx and Engels) 465
Comnena, Anna 180
Comneni emperors 179, 189
Comnenus, Emperor Alexius 241
composition 20, 22
Composition (Miró) 20, **0.5**
Composition in White, Black, and Red (Mondrian) 553, **17.9**
computers 547
Comte, Auguste 469
conceptual art/conceptualism 588
concertos 25, 410
Confrérie de la Passion 311
Confucius 189
conquistadors 318
Constable, John 494
Constantine I, Emperor 122, 156, 159, 160, 176, 177, 208; head 160, **5.17**
Constantine V, Emperor 178, 179
Constantinople (Byzantium) 160, 174, 176–7, 179–80, 182–3, 205, 208, 241, 278, 291; University 179, 180, 181; *see* Istanbul
constructivists 552
contrapposto 85
Copernicus, Nicholas 386; *On the Revolutions of the Celestial Orbs* 361–2
Copland, Aaron 566, 608, 609; *Appalachian Spring* 566–7, 568
Corfu: Temple of Artemis 67, **2.18**
Corinthian order 74, 93, 105, **3.19**
Corneille, Pierre 414, 415; *Le Cid* 415
Corot, Jean-Baptiste-Camille 474, 528; *Volterra* 474, 476, **15.10**
corporations, multinational 580
Corregidora (G. Jones) 618
Cortés, Hernando 321–2, **11.2**
Cossutius 105
Counterfeiters, The (Gide) 550
Counter-Reformation 384, 390–1, 393
Couperin, François 447
Courbet, Gustave 504; *The Stone Breakers* 504, **16.6**
Courtier, The (Castiglione) 344–5
Cousin, Victor 496
Coysevox, Antoine 400; *The Great Condé* 400, **13.17**
Cranach, Lucas, the Elder: *Martin Luther* **12.3**
Cranach, Lucas, the Younger: *Martin Luther and the Wittenberg Reformers* **12.1**
Cranmer, Archbishop Thomas 281, 382
Crete: Minoan civilization 52–4
Crime and Punishment (Dostoyevski) 522–3
criticism, art 17–18
Cromwell, Oliver 360, 409, 414, 418, 419, 422
Crowley, Mart: *The Boys in the Band* 612
Crucifixion (Grünewald) 368–9, **12.15**
Crusades 179–80, 237, 241–2, 278, **8.3**; maps **8.2, 8.3**
Crystal Palace, London (Paxton) 476, **15.13**
Cuban-American theatre 619
Cubi XIX (D. Smith) 590–1, **18.16**
cubism 496, 517–19
cummings, e. e. 552
cuneiform writing 30, 38, **1.7**
Cunningham, Merce 613
Cuvilliès, Jean-François de: The Pagodenburg 436, **14.10**
Cynicism 102–3
Cyrus the Great 58, 146

Dada 519, 538, 553, 555
Dadd, Richard: *The Fair Feller's Master Stroke* 493–4, **15.25**
Dagulf Psalter 231, **7.26**
Dali, Salvador 555; *The Persistence of Memory* **17.11**
Damascus, Syria: Great Mosque 197, 199, **6.25, 6.26**
dance 28; ancient Greek 71, 99–100, 312; Baroque 416; Byzantine 192; folk 28, 531; Jewish 152; medieval 226, 284; modern 28, 531, 533, 569, 613–14; Native American 569–70; Roman 136; 16th-century 374; *see also* ballet
dance of death (*danse macabre*) 226, 270, 284
Dante Alighieri 245, 272, 291: *Divine Comedy* 245–6, **8.6**
Darius I, King of the Persians 58
Darius III, King of the Persians 100
Dark Abstraction (O'Keeffe) 556–7, **17.14**
Dark Ages 208
Darwin, Charles: *The Origin of Species* 466
Daughter of Pharaoh (ballet) 490
Daumier, Honoré: *The Third-Class Carriage* 507, **16.9**
David (Bernini) 395–6, **13.9**
David (Donatello) 301, **10.11**
David (Michelangelo) 23, 332, 333, **11.1, 11.16**
David, Jacques-Louis 440, 471; *The Death of Socrates* 440, **14.19**; *The Oath of the Horatii* 440, 443, **14.20**
David, King 146, 147, 151, 152; *King David and Four Dancers* (from St Gall) **10.26**
David Harping (from Oscott Psalter) 253–4, **8.20**
Davies, Arthur B. 556
Davis, Miles 617; *Bitches Brew* 610
Davis, Stuart 557; *Lucky Strike* **17.15**
De Architectura (Vitruvius) 116, 291, 342, 400
"Death, Be Not Proud" (Donne) 408–9
death masks, Roman 116
Death of Socrates, The (David) 440, **14.19**
Death of the Virgin, The (Caravaggio) 394, **13.7**
Debussy, Claude 524–5, 609; *Prélude à l'après-midi d'un faune* 525, 532, **16.32**
Decameron (Boccaccio) 272
de Chirico *see* Chirico, Giorgio de
decolonization 578–9
deduction 384, 387
Defense of Poesie, A (Sidney) 377
Defoe, Daniel: *Moll Flanders* 409; *Robinson Crusoe* 409
Déjeuner sur l'herbe (Manet) 504, 507, **16.8**
de Kooning *see* Kooning, Willem de
Delacroix, Eugène 474; *The 28th July: Liberty Leading the People* 474, **15.8**
Delian League 77–8
Deliverance of St Peter, The (Raphael) 334, 348, **11.19**
Delsarte, François 569
democracy 57, 78, 445; and law 110
Democritus 59
Demoiselles d'Avignon, Les (Picasso) 519, **16.26**
Dempster, Stewart 609
Den Mother (Marshall) 599, **18.32**
Denishawn school 569
Descent from the Cross, The (Rembrandt) 407, **13.26**
Descent from the Cross, The (Weyden) 363–4, 367, **12.9**
Deserted Village, The (Goldsmith) 446

despotism, enlightened 424, 457, 461
Dessau, Germany: Bauhaus 573–4, **17.34**
de Stijl 552
devil, the/devils 209, 256
Devol, George C. 581
Dewey, John 549
Diaghilev, Serge 527, 531, 533; Ballets russes 531–3, 593
Dialogue, The (St Catherine) 286
Diaspora, the 146
Diaz, Bartolomeu 294
Dickens, Charles 481; *Household Words* 493
Didelot, Charles 456
Diderot, Denis: *Encyclopedia* 429
Dido and Aeneas (Purcell) 419
Dignity and Impudence (Landseer) 493, **15.24**
Dijon, France: Chartreuse de Champol portal (Sluter) 277–8, **9.13**
Diocletian, Emperor 122, 156, 159–60; Baths 164–5, **5.25**
Diogenes 102
Diogenes of Babylon 119
Dionysus (from Parthenon) 87, 89, **3.10**
Dionysus, cult of 98, 99, 103, 116
Dipylon Vase 61, **2.9**
Discourse on Method (Descartes) 387
Discus Thrower (*Discobolus*) (Myron) 86, **3.8**
Disney, Walt 572
Divine Comedy (Dante) 245–6, **8.6**
divisionism 513
Doctor Faustus (Marlowe) 380
documentary films 27
Doges' Palace, Venice 276–7, **9.11**
dome construction 24, 130–1, 203, 296–9, **4.23, 6.31, 10.8**
Dome of the Rock, Jerusalem 197, **6.23, 6.24**
Domes Day (play) 256
Dominican order 244
Domitian, Emperor 126, 155
Don Juan (Byron) 480
Don Quixote (Cervantes) 409
Donatello 300–1; *David* 301, **10.11**; *Equestrian Monument to Gattamelata* 301, **10.12**; *Mary Magdalen* 315, **10.29**; *St George* 301, **10.13**
Donne, John 408; "Death, Be Not Proud" 408–9
Dorian mode 68
Doric order 67–8, 93, **2.19, 3.19**
Dormition of the Virgin (fresco) 182, **6.2**
Doryphorus (Polyclitus) 85, 87, 137, **3.7**
Dostoyevski, Feodor 522, 528, 549; *Crime and Punishment* 522–3
Douce Apocalypse 253, **8.19**
Douglas, Aaron 558; *Aalta* 558, **17.17**; *Aspects of Negro Life* 558, **17.18**
Dragons (Pfaff) 596–7, **18.27**
drama *see* theatre
Dryden, John 409; *Absalom and Achitophel* 409
Dual Hamburgers (Oldenburg) 585, **18.8**
Du Bois, W. E. B. 558
Dubuffet, Jean: *Jardin d'Émail* 595, **18.24**
Duccio 279; *Madonna Enthroned* 279–80, **9.16**
Duchamp, Marcel 519; *Nude Descending a Staircase, No. 2* 519, 555, 556, **16.27**
Dufay, Guillaume 372
Dumas, Alexandre 488
Duncan, Isadora 533, 569
Dunciad, The (Pope) 445
Dunham, Katherine 614
Dur Sharrukin (Khorsabad), Iraq: Sargon II's citadel 41–2, **1.10, 1.11**

Dura-Europos, Syria 149, **4.11, 5.4, 5.6**
Dürer, Albrecht 366–7; *Four Apostles* 368, **12.14**; *The Four Horsemen of the Apocalypse* 367–8, **12.13**; *Self-portrait* **12.12**
Durham Cathedral, England 221
Dutch painting 364–6, 405–8, 514–15, 552–3
Dvořák, Antonin: *The Noonday Witch* 484
Dying Gaul 103, **3.31**

Eakins, Thomas 507
Easton, William Edgar 488
economic systems 269–70, 431; capitalism 288, 294; *laissez-faire* 431–2, 465
Ecstasy of St Theresa, The (Bernini) 396–7, **13.10**
Edison, Thomas 529, 530
Egypt 42, 58, 100, 102, 103, 144, 224, 578, 580; architecture 47–8; map **1.3**; music 46; pyramids 30, 43–4, **1.13–1.15**; religion and mythology 42–3, 47, 103; sculpture 46, 48–9
Einstein, Albert 502, 518, 549
Eisenstein, Sergei: *Battleship Potemkin* 571
Eleanor of Aquitaine 238
electricity, harnessing of 464
electronic music 608–9
Elgard, Edward: *Falstaff* 484
"Elgin Marbles" 87
Eliot, T. S.: *The Waste Land* 552
Elizabeth I, Queen of England 375–6, 381–2, 392, 408
Elizabethan theatre 378–80
Embarkation for Cythera (Watteau) 434, **14.5**
Emerson, Ralph Waldo: *Representative Men* 362
Empedocles 59
empiricism 428
Encyclopedia (Diderot) 429
Enemy of the People, An (Ibsen) 16
Engelberger, Joseph 581
Engels, Friedrich 465
England *see* Britain
Enlightenment, the 424, 426, 429
Ennead (Plotinus) 123–4
Enslavement of the Indians (Rivera) 559, **17.19**
Enthroned Madonna with St Francis (Cimabue) **8.5**
environmental art 576, 595
ephemeral art 595–6
epic poetry 38, *see* Beowulf; Homer; Vergil
epic theatre 567
Epictetus 122–3
Epicureanism 102, 103, 122
Epicurus 103
Epidaurus, Greece: theatre 99, **3.24, 3.25**
Equestrian Monument to Gattamelata (Donatello) 301, **10.12**
Erasmus, Desiderius 355–7, 376, 391, **12.2**; *In Praise of Folly* 356
Erlking, The (Schubert) 482, **15.15**
Ernst, Max 553; *Woman, Old Man, and Flower* 553, 555, **17.10**
Essai sur l'architecture (Laugier) 444
Essay Concerning Human Understanding (Locke) 390
essays 27
Essays (Montaigne) 362
Estes, Richard 588
Etruscans 112; sculpture 112, **4.2**
Eucharides painter: amphora 68, **2.21**
Euclid 83
Euripides 95, 96, 99; *The Bacchae* 96; *Hecuba* 107–8
Eurydice (Peri) 414
Eva's Man (G. Jones) 618
Everyman (morality play) 283–4
evolutionary theories 466

Excavation (de Kooning) 583–4, **18.4**
existentialism 538, 549, 568–9
exploration 320–2
expressionism 496; in films 570; in painting 515, 521; in theatre 567
Eyck, Jan van 363; *The Arnolfini Marriage* 363, **12.8**
Every Man in his Humor (Jonson) 380

Faerie Queene, The (Spenser) 376, 378
Falconet, Étienne-Maurice 435; *Madame de Pompadour as the Venus of the Doves* 435–6, **14.7**
Falling Water (Kaufmann House), Bear Run, Pa (Wright) 563, 564, **17.25**
farce 288, 311–12
Faulkner, William 550–1
Faust: *Doctor Faustus* (Marlowe) 380; *Faust* (Goethe) 447
Fauvism 521–2
Fellini, Federico 612
feminist theatre 611
Fences (A. Wilson) 618
Ferdinand and Isabella 325
Fermi, Enrico 548, 549
Fernández de Navarrette, Juan: *St Peter and St Paul* **5.31**
Fertile Crescent 36
Feste Burg ist unser Gott, Ein (Bach) 412, **13.31**
feudalism 206, 212–13, 236, 237, 238, 240
Feuerbach, Ludwig: *The Essence of Christianity* 465
Fichte, Johann 467, 468
Ficino, Marsilio 291, 293, 310
fiction 27, *see* novels
Fielding, Henry 424, 446; *Joseph Andrews* 446; *Tom Jones* 446
films 27, 529–31, 570–2, 582, 612–13, 618–19
Finnegans Wake (Joyce) 550
Fiorilli, Tiberio 343
Flagler, Henry 535, 536
Flaubert, Gustave 481
Flemish art: music 372–3; painting 362–4; sculpture 277–8
Florence, Italy 245, 290, 292, 295, 313–17, **10.27**; Academy 291, 294, 310; Baptistery doors (*The Gates of Paradise*) 301–2, **10.16, 10.17**; Brancacci Chapel frescoes, S Maria del Carmine 303–5, **10.18, 10.19**; *Camerata* 413; Cathedral 274–5, 296–8, 313–14, **9.9, 10.7, 10.8**; Foundling Hospital 298–9, **10.9**; Palazzo Rucellai 296, **10.6**; Pazzi Chapel, S Croce 299, **10.10**; S Maria Novella (fresco) 304–5, **10.19**
Fokine, Mikhail 532
folk dance 28, 531
Fontainebleau, School of 371
Fontana, Domenico 347
Ford, John: *Grapes of Wrath* 572; *Stagecoach* 572
Foss, Lukas 608
found objects 553
found sculpture 595
Four Apostles (Dürer) 368, **12.14**
Four Horsemen of the Apocalypse, The (Dürer) 367–8, **12.13**
Fragments for the Gates to Times Square (Chryssa) 597, **18.28**
Fragonard, Jean-Honoré: *The Swing* 435, **14.1**
France 266–7, 325, 392, 393, 433, 469; architecture 221, 228, 231, 247–9, 258, 370–1, 400–1, 404–5, 436, 604; cave paintings 34, 35–6; dance 415–16, 454–6; literature 181, 224–6, 266, 272–3, 362, 429, 430, 481, 523–4, 549–50; music and opera 254–5, 283, 374, 447, 483–4, 486, 527, 532, 607, 608, 609; painting 252–3, 371, 398–400, 434–5, 439–40, 470–1, 472, 474–6,

504, 509–11, 513–14; *philosophes* 429; philosophy 468–9; sculpture 251, 258–9, 261, 400, 435–6, 509, 511; theatre 17–18, 311–12, 414–15, 452–3
Francesco di Giorgio: Palazzo Ducale, Urbino **10.4**
Francis of Assisi, St 243
Franciscan order 243
Franck, César 527
Frankenthaler, Helen 584, 585; *Buddha* 585, **8.6**
Franks 178, 212
Frederick I, King in Prussia 432
Frederick II ("the Great") 430, 433, 448, 457–60, **14.35**
Frederick II Hohenstaufen, Emperor 181
Frederick Barbarossa 181, 242
Frederick William, King of Prussia 432–3
French art *see* France
Freud, Sigmund 503, 504, 555, **16.5**; *The Interpretation of Dreams* 504
Friedrich, Caspar David: *The Wanderer above the Mists* **15.1**
Froissart, Jean: *Chronicles ...* 272
Frost, Robert 552
fugues 411; *Fugue in G minor* (Bach) 411, **13.30**
Fuller, Meta Vaux Warrick 558
Fuller, Richard Buckminster: Climatron 603, **18.40**
Futurism 519–20

Gainsborough, Thomas 439; *The Hon. Mrs Graham* 439, **14.13**; *The Market Cart* 439, **14.14**
Galileo Galilei 324, 386, 389
Garden of Earthly Delights, The (Bosch) 364–5, **12.10**
Gargas, France: engraved horse 34, **1.3**
Gaudí, Antoni 517; Casa Batlló, Barcelona 517, **16.24**
Gauguin, Paul 514; *La Orana Maria* 514, **16.19**
Gay, John: *Beggar's Opera* 452
Gay Sweatshop 611–12
gay theatre 612
Gebbia, Gianni 608
Gemma Augustea (cameo) **4.1**
Genet, Jean 610
genetics 503
Geneva, Switzerland 359, 360
genre painting 424, 439–40
Geometric vases 50, 60–1, **2.1**
Géricault, Théodore 471; *The Raft of the "Medusa"* 471, 472, **15.6**
German Requiem, A (Brahms) 484–5
Germany 325, 391, 392, 465, 500–1, 540–3, 544, 545–8, 549; architecture 273–4, 436, 457–8, 459–60, 573–4; expressionism 521, 570; film 570, 571; literature 224, 447, 482, 550; music and opera 373–4, 412, 413, 447–8, 481–2, 483–5, 487, 527–8; painting 366–70, 553; philosophy 428–9, 465, 466–8, 530, 549; sculpture 217; theatre 567
Gero crucifix 217, **7.10**
Gesamtkunstwerk 487, 488
Ghetto (Sobol) 619
Ghiberti, Lorenzo 302; *The Gates of Paradise* 302, **10.16, 10.17**; *Sacrifice of Isaac* 302, **10.15**
Ghirlandaio, Domenico 330
Giacometti, Alberto 592; *Man Pointing* 592, **18.17**
Gide, André: *The Counterfeiters* 550
Gilbert, Cass: Woolworth Building 564, **17.28**
Gilgamesh Epic 38
Gillespie, Dizzie 617
Giotto 278, 279, 280, 314; *The*

Lamentation 281, **9.18**; *Madonna Enthroned* 280, **9.17**
Giovanni da Bologna (Giambologna): *Mercury* 338, **11.24**
Girl Before a Mirror (Picasso) 22, **0.8**
Girl with a Red Hat, The (Vermeer) 408, **13.29**
Giselle (ballet) 490
Gislebertus: *Last Judgment* tympanum 221, **7.18**
Giza, Egypt: pyramid complex 44, **1.13–1.15**
Glackens, William 556
gladiators, Roman 118
Glorious Revolution 418
Godfrey, Thomas: *The Prince of Parthia* 452
"God's Wildering Daughter" (Sappho) 70
Goethe, Johann Wolfgang von 18, 424, 447, 496; "The Erlking" 482; *Faust* 447; *Die Leiden des jungen Werthers* 447, 469
Gogh, Vincent van 514–15; *Harvest at La Crau* 515, **16.20**; *The Starry Night* 20, 515, **16.21**
Gokstad ship 215, **7.7**
Golden Ass (Apuleius) 136
Golden Haggadah (miniature) **5.3**
Goldsmith, Oliver 446; *The Deserted Village* 446
Gone with the Wind (Selznick) 572
Good Shepherd, The (marble) 162–3, **5.21**
Gorbachev, Mikhail 580
Gordonne, Charles: *No Place to Be Somebody* 618
Gorgon Painter: Attic bowl 63, **2.10**
Gospel Books: Godescalc 228, **7.22**; St Médard of Soissons 228, **7.23**
Gospels 152–5, 191, 215–16; Synoptic 154
Gothic style 208, 234, 242; architecture 246–51, 258–9, 263, 273–7, **8.11**; painting 252–4; sculpture 251–2, 277–8; stained glass 246, 258, **8.26, 8.28**
Gounod, Charles 486
Goya, Francisco de 471; *The Third of May 1808* 471, 473, 559, **15.5**
Graham, Martha 569, 591, 613; *Appalachian Spring* 568, **17.29**
Grande Odalisque, La (Ingres) 471, **15.4**
Grapes of Wrath (Ford) 572
Graun, Karl Heinrich 457
Graves, Michael: Portland Public Office Building 604, **18.42**
Gravity's Rainbow (Pynchon) 607
Great Condé, The (Coysevox) 400, **13.17**
Great Depression 538, 545
Great Schism (1378) 271, 294
Great Train Robbery, The (Porter) 530
Great Wave off Kanazawa, The (Hokusai) 479, **15.14**
Greco, El (Domenikos Theotokopoulos) 394; *St Jerome* 394–5, **13.8**
Greece, ancient 50, 52, 54, 55–8; architecture 67–8, 90, 92–3, 99; city-states 56–7, 58, 77–8; dance 16, 71; drama and literature 16, 17, 69–71, 82–3, 95–9, 107–8; music 59, 68–9, 71, 84, 99; philosophies 59, 79–83; religion 58–9, 71, 79; sculpture 65–7, 85–9, 92, 100; theatre 16, 17, 71, 95–9, 107–8; vase painting 59–63, 68, 84; writing and language 57, 187; *see also* Athens; Hellenistic period
Green Coca-Cola Bottles (Warhol) 587, **18.9**
Gregorian chant 206, 223
Gregory I, Pope ("the Great") 206, 209, 210, 215, 223; *Book*

of Pastoral Care 209
Griffith, D. W.: *The Birth of a Nation* 530–1, **16.36**; *Intolerance* 531
Gringoire, Pierre: *Jeu du Prince des Sots* 311
Grogne, La (Grumbling) (Ruffe) **17.2**
Gropius, Walter 573–4; house, Dessau **17.34**
Grünewald, Matthias 368; *Crucifixion* (Isenheim Altarpiece) 368–9, **12.15**
Guernica (Picasso) 593, **18.22**
Guglielmo Ebreo 312
guilds 236, 269, 314
Gulliver's Travels (Swift) 445
Gutenberg, Johann 269

Haba, Alois 609
Hadrian, Emperor 121
Hagesandrus, Polydorus, and Athenodorus: *Laocoön and his Two Sons* 104–5, 320, **3.30**
Hagia Sophia, Istanbul 200, 202–3, 205, **6.30, 6.33–6.36**
Hajj 174, 193
Halicarnassus Mausoleum: frieze 89, **3.11**
Hall, Joseph 464
Hallenkirche 264, 274
Hals, Frans: *René Descartes* **13.2**
Hamlet (Shakespeare) 379
Hammurabi 40, 41; Code 40–1
Han dynasty painting 127
Hampton Court Palace, nr London 418–19, **13.35**
Handel, George Frederick 417, 419; *Messiah* 26, 419, **13.36**
Hannibal 113
Harbaville Triptych (ivory) 182, 188, **6.13**
hard edge painting 576, 587–8
Hardouin-Mansart, Jules: Versailles 401, **13.19, 13.20**
Harem Girl (Ingres) 471, **15.4**
Harlem Renaissance 557–8
Harlot's Progress, The (Hogarth) 437, **14.11**
Harvard Mark 1 calculator 547, **17.6**
Harvest at La Crau (van Gogh) 515, **16.20**
Hasmoneans 147
Hay, Deborah 614
Hayden, Palmer 558
Haydn, Franz Josef 448, 449; *Creation* 484; Symphony No. 3 449; Symphony No. 94 in G major 449–50, **14.24, 14.25**
He Weeps for You (Viola) 598
Hecuba (Euripides) 107–8
Hegel, Georg Wilhelm Friedrich 467–8, 549
Heidegger, Martin 549
Hellenes 57–8
Hellenistic period 74, 101, 146, 147; architecture 105–6; literature 102; philosophy and religion 102–3; sculpture 103–5; theatre(s) 102, 190
Heller, Joseph 606; *Catch-22* 606
hell/hellmouth, staging of 256–7
Hemingway, Ernest 551
Henley, Beth 611
Henri, Robert 556
Henry II, King of England 237, 242
Henry III, Emperor of Germany 241
Henry IV Receiving the Portrait of Maria de' Medici (Rubens) 398, **13.14**
Henry VII, King of England 267, 375
Henry VIII, King of England 354, 375, 376, 381, 382; *Henry VIII in Wedding Dress* (Holbein the Younger) 376, **12.24**
Hepworth, Barbara: *Sphere with Internal Form* 592, **18.19**
Heraclitus 79
Herbert, George 409; "Love Bade Me Welcome" 409

Herculaneum 124–5, 139, 433, 442, **4.12**
Hercules and Telephos (wall painting) 124, **4.10**
Herder, Johann Gottfried von 447
Hermes (marble) 116, **4.5**
Hermes and the Infant Dionysus (followers of Praxiteles) 89, **3.14**
Hero: steam turbine 102, **3.28**
Herod, King 142, 151
Herodotus: *History of the Persian Wars* 83
Hesiod 55, 69; *Theogony* 58, 71; *Works and Days* 69
hieratic style 174, 182
Hilary, bishop of Poitiers 169
Hildegard of Bingen 225
Hildesheim Cathedral, Germany: doors 218, **7.12**
Hilliard, Nicholas 377; *Youth Leaning Against a Tree with Roses* 377, **12.26**
Hindemith, Paul 565, 608, 609
Hippocrates 83
Hiroshige, Andō: *Maple Leaves at Mama...* 513, **16.18**
historification 567
History of the Persian Wars (Herodotus) 83
Hitchcock, Alfred 27; *North by Northwest* **0.16**
Hitler, Adolf 503, 544, 545–8
Hittite Empire 611
Hobbes, Thomas 388, 390; *Leviathan* 388–9
Hoffman, William 612
Hogarth, William 437; *The Harlot's Progress* 437, **14.11**; *The Rake's Progress* 437, **14.12**
Hokusai, Katsushika: *The Great Wave off Kanazawa* 479, **15.14**
Holbein, Hans, the Younger 376; *Erasmus of Rotterdam* **12.2**; *Henry VIII in Wedding Dress* 376, **12.24**; *Jane Seymour* 376–7, **12.25**
Hollywood 530, 571
Holy Trinity, The (Masaccio) 304–5, **10.19**
Home (Williams) 618
Homer: *Iliad* and *Odyssey* 54, 55, 58, 72–3
Hon. Mrs Graham, The (Gainsborough) 439, **14.13**
Horace 134, 135; *Odes* 135
Horatian Ode (Marvell) 409
horses/horse carts 236, **8.2**
Horton, Asadata Dafora 614
Houasse, René-Antoine: Salon d'Abondance ceiling, Versailles 404, **13.21**
Houdon, Jean-Antoine 440, 442; *Alexandre Brongniart* 440, **14.16**; *Louise Brongniart* 440, **14.17**; *Voltaire* 442, **14.4**
House Made of Dawn (Momaday) 615
Houses of Parliament, London (Barry and Pugin) 476, 491–2, **15.12**
Howells and Hood: Tribune Tower, Chicago 564
Hrosvitha 226, 290
Huber, Jean: *The Philosophes at Supper* 429, **14.3**
Huerta, Jorge 619
hues 22
Hughes, Langston 551, 557, **17.7**; "The Negro Speaks of Rivers" 551, 552; *Not Without Laughter* 551
Hugo, Victor 488
Huguenots 360, 391, 393
humanism/humanists 174, 181, 242, 264, 291, 293–4, 354–5
humanitarianism 437
humanities: definition 14
Hume, David 428
Hundred Years' War (1337–1453) 266

Hungary 322, 325; music 566
Huns 177
Hunt, Richard Morris: Biltmore House 536–7, **16.41**; The Breakers 536, **16.39**
Hunter, Richard 452
Huntsman, Benjamin 427–8
Huss, John 271, 354
hydraulos (water organ) 133, 168, **4.28**
Hyers, Anna and Emma 488
hymns 169, 191–2, 373

Ibsen, Henrik 528–9; *An Enemy of the People* 16
iconoclasm 179
Ictinos and Callicrates: Parthenon 90, **3.16**
idealism 107–8, 462, 466–8
idée fixe 483
idylls 102
Igbo-Ukwu: bronze roped pot 222, **7.20**; mask 560, **17.20**
Ignatius, St 156
Iliad (Homer) 54, 55, 58, 72–3
impressionism 496, 509–11; in music 524–5
improvisation (music) 608
Improvisation No. 30 (Kandinsky) 522, **16.31**
In the Dining Room (Morisot) 509, **16.12**
Ince, Thomas 531
individualism 234
induction 384, 386
Industrial Revolution 462, 464–5, 487
industrialization 269–70, 499
Ingres, Jean-Auguste-Dominique 470–1; *La Grande Odalisque* (*Harem Girl*) 471, **15.4**
Innocent X, Pope 393
"Innsbruck, I Must Leave Thee" (Isaac) 373
In Praise of Folly (Erasmus) 356
Inquisition, the 270, 386, 392
installations 596–7
International style: architecture 601, 603; sculpture (1400) 277
International Working Men's Association 499
Interpretation of Dreams (Freud) 504
Intolerance (Griffith) 531
inventions *see* science and technology
Ionesco, Eugène 610–11
Ionians 57, 58
Ionic order 74, 93, **3.19**
Isaac, Heinrich 373; "Innsbruck, I Must Leave Thee" 373–4
Isaiah, prophet 146, 148–9
Isaurian Emperors 178–9
Isenheim Altarpiece (Grünewald) 368–9, **12.15**
Islam/Islamic art 174, 193–4, 205; architecture 197, 199; literature 196–7; map **6.3**; manuscript illumination 196, **6.21, 6.22**; map **6.3**; mosaics 197, 199, **6.24, 6.25**
Isozaki, Arata 604
Israelites 142–4, 146, *see* Jews; Judaism
Istanbul, Turkey: Hagia Sophia, Istanbul 200, 202–3, 205, **6.30, 6.33–6.36**; Imperial Palace mosaic 183, **6.4**; Kariye Church **5.14**; St Mary Pammakaristos 192, **6.18**; St Theodosia 192, **6.16**; Theodosian obelisk 186, **6.10**
Italy: architecture 274–7, 295–9, 320, 338, 340, 342, 346–8, 370–1, 397–8; city-states 295; dance 312; literature 245–6, 271–2, 344–5; music and opera 283, 310, 320, 340–1, 486; painting 278–80, 303–6, 308–10, 326–30, 333, 334–8, 393–4; Papal States 294–5, 322–3; philosophy 291–4; sculpture 278, 300–2, 315, 320, 332, 333,

338, 347, 395–7, 520; theatre 567–8; *see also* Roman Republic and Empire; Rome
Ives, Charles 566, 609
ivories: Byzantine 186, 188, **6.11–6.13**; Carolingian 231, **7.26, 7.27**

James I, King of England, 417
James II, King of England 418
James, Henry 481
James, William 549
Janequin, Clément: chansons 374
Janson, H. W. 92, 596
Japan 321, 545, 548; architecture 604; films 612–13; Kabuki theatre 453, **14.31**; Noh drama 284, **9.22**; painting 479, 513, 515, **15.14**; sculpture 152, 255, **5.12, 8.21**
Jardin d'Émail (Dubuffet) 595, **18.24**
Jaspers, Karl 549
jazz 528, 608, 610, 617
Jazz (Morrison) 606, 607
jazz dance 614, **18.47**
Jazz Singer, The 572
Jefferson, Joseph **14.32**
Jefferson, Thomas 445; Monticello 445, **14.22**; Rotunda, University of Virginia **14.21**
Jemaa, head from 94, **3.22**
Jerome, St 224; *St Jerome* (El Greco) 394–5, **13.8**
Jerusalem 146, 156, 242; Dome of the Rock 197, **6.23, 6.24**; temples 146, 147, 150–1, **5.7–5.11**
Jesuits 321, 391, 398, 501
Jesus Christ 152–4, 205; as Pantocrator 153, **5.14**
Jewish Cemetery, The (van Ruisdael) 407–8, **13.28**
Jews 146–7, 155, 159, 270, 548, 606; art and architecture 149–52; music and dance 152; theatre 619; *see* Israelites; Judaism
Joan of Arc 266, 268, **9.3**
Johannsen, Wilhelm 503
John, St: Gospel 155
Johnson, Philip 582; Seagram Building, New York (with Mies van der Rohe) 601, **18.36**
Johnson, Dr Samuel 446
Johnson, William Henry 558
Jolson, Al 572
Jones, Gayl 618; *Corregidora* 618; *Eva's Man* 618
Jones, Inigo 422; stage design **13.40**
Jones, LeRoi 618
Jonson, Ben: *Every Man in his Humor* 380
Joplin, Scott 528
Joseph II, Emperor 431, 433
Joseph Andrews (Fielding) 446
Joshua 144, 148
Josquin des Prez 341, 372; *Ave Maria ... Virgo Serena* 372–3, **12.21**
Joyce, James: *Finnegans Wake* 550; *Ulysses* 550
Judah 146
Judaism 140, 147–9, 153, 173, 205
Judges 144
Judson Dance Theatre 614
Julian of Norwich 286; *Revelations of Divine Love* 286–7
Julius II, Pope 311, 323, 330, 338, 347; tomb 330
Justinian, Emperor 178, 190, 192, 200, 205; legal code 178, 181; *Emperor Justinian and his Court* (mosaic) 182, **6.3**
Juvenal 136

Kabuki theatre 453, **14.31**
Kachina masks 570, **17.30**
Kafka, Franz 549, 550
Kahlo, Frida 555; *The Broken Column* 556, **17.1, 17.13**
Kahn, Louis I. 603

Kandinsky, Vasily 522; *Improvisation No. 30* **16.31**
Kant, Immanuel 428–9, 466–7, 468, 496
Kaufmann House, Falling Water, Bear Run, Pa (Wright) 563, 564, **17.25**
Kayonaga, Torri: *Kabuki Scene* 453, **14.31**
Kean, Charles 488; *Richard II* **15.21**
Keats, John 478, 481
Kempe, Margery 285–6
Kepler, Johannes 294, 324, 386–7
Kerensky, Alexander 543
Khamis, Zabyah 607
Khorsabad, Iraq *see* Dur Sharrukin
Kiefer, Anselm 590; *Midgard* 590, **18.15**
Kierkegaard, Sören 549
Kirchner, Ernst Ludwig 521
knights, medieval 213, **7.5**
Knobelsdorff, Georg von: Sans Souci 459–60, **14.36–14.40**
Knossos, Crete: Palace of Minos 52, 53, **2.2**
Knox, John 360
Kokoschka, Oskar 522
Kollwitz, Käthe: *The Weaver's Cycle* 499, **16.2**
Kooning, Willem de 583; *Excavation* 583–4, **18.4**
korai 50, 66–7, **2.15, 2.16**
Koran, the 193, 194
Korean War 580
Kosuth, Joseph: *One and Three Chairs* 588, **18.13**
kouroi 50, 65–6, **2.13, 2.14**
Kouros (Noguchi) 591, **18.18**
Kresilas: *Pericles* **3.3**
Kritios Boy 67, 86, **2.17**
Kuala Lumpur City: Petronas Twin Towers (Pelli) 606, **18.45**
Kurasawa, Akiro 612–13
Kushner, Tony: *Angels in America* 612, **18.46**

Lady Playing the Cithara (wall painting) 115–16, **4.3**
La Flesche, Susette: "Nedawi" 523
Lamentation, The (Giotto) 281, **9.18**
Lance Bearer (Polyclitus) 85, 87, 137, **3.7**
Landini, Francesco 283
Landscape (Creswick) 494, **15.26**
Landscape with the Burial of Phocion (Poussin) 398–400, **13.15**
Landscape with the Fall of Icarus (Bruegel the Elder) 366, **12.11**
Landseer, Sir Edwin: *Dignity and Impudence* 493, **15.24**
Lang, Fritz: *M* 571; *Metropolis* 570
Lange, Dorothea 570; *Migrant Mother, Nipomo, California* 571, **17.32**
Laocoön and his Two Sons (Hagesandrus *et al.*) 104–5, 320, **3.30**
Lascaux caves, France: paintings 35–6, **1.1, 1.5**
Last Judgment tympanum (Gislebertus) 221, **7.18**
Last Supper, The (Leonardo) 327–8, **11.9**
Laue, Max von 502
Laugier, Abbé: *Essai sur l'architecture* 444
Laurana, Luciano: Palazzo Ducale, Urbino **10.4**
Lavoisier, Antoine 427
Lawrence, D. H. 550
Lawrence, T. E. 542
laws/legal codes: Byzantine 178, 179, 181; Greek 78; Hammurabi 40; Roman 118, 121, 122
Lawson, Ernest 556
Le Brun, Charles: Versailles 404, 405, **13.20**
Le Corbusier 564; Notre Dame du

Haut 603, **18.38**; Villa Savoye 564, **17.27**
legal codes *see* laws
Legalism 157
Legnani, Pierina 490
Leitmotifs 487, 526
lekythos (Achilles painter) 84, **3.5**
Lenin, V. I. 543, **17.3**
Leo I, Pope 156
Leo III, Emperor 178, 179
Leo III, Pope 212, 228
Leo IX, Pope 241
Leo X, Pope 323, 344, 358
Leo XIII, Pope 466
Leonardo da Vinci 294, 308, 320, 326, 329, 330, 371; *The Last Supper* 327–8, **11.9**; lathe 296, **10.5**; *The Madonna of the Rocks* 326–7, **11.7**; *Mona Lisa* 328, **11.11**; notebooks 324, **11.4**, **11.5**; *Virgin and Child with St Anne* 328–9, **11.10**; *Vitruvian Man* 291, **10.2**
Leoncavallo, Ruggiero: *I Pagliacci* 527
Leonin 254
Le Roy, Philibert: Versailles 400
lesbian theatre 611–12
Lescot, Pierre: Louvre wing 338, **11.26**
Leucippus 59
Le Vau, Louis: Versailles 400–1, 404–5, **13.18**, **13.19**
Leviathan (Hobbes) 388–9
Levites 149
Lewis, Lucy: ceramics 615–16
liberalism 389, 465
Liberty Leading the People (Delacroix) 474, **15.8**
Lichtenstein, Roy 585; *Whaam!* **18.6**
Lieder 352, 373–4, 481–2
light art 597
Ligugé monastery 211
Limón, José 613
Lincoln, Abraham 478
Lindisfarne Gospels 216, **7.8**
Linnaeus, Carolus 427
Lipchitz, Jacques 560; *Man with a Guitar* 560, **17.23**
Lippi, Fra Filippo 305
Liszt, Franz 482, 484, 485
literature 27; African American 551, 552, 557–8, 618; American 445, 523, 550–1, 552, 606, 607; Arabian 607; British 224, 274, 376, 377–80, 408–9, 445–7, 478–81, 550; Byzantine 180, 186–7, 189–90; existentialist 549; French 181, 224–6, 266, 272–3, 362, 429, 430, 481, 523–4, 549–50; German 224, 447, 550; Greek 69–71, 82–3; Hellenistic 102; Islamic 196–7; Italian 245–6, 271–2, 344–5; Jewish 606; medieval 224–6, 244–5; Native American 523, 551–2, 615; naturalist 523; pre-Romantic 424, 446–7; realist 522–3, 550; Renaissance 344–5; Roman 134–6, 137, 168; Romantic 478–9, 480–1; Russian 522–3, 529, 607; Spanish 409; Sumerian 38; symbolist 523–4
Livy 134, 135
Locke, Alain 558
Locke, John 389, 428, 430, 445; *An Essay Concerning Human Understanding* 390; *Treatises of Government* 389–90, 418
Lodi, Peace of (1454) 295
Lombard, Peter 244
London and environs 314, 381; Crystal Palace (Paxton) 476, **15.13**; Hampton Court Palace (Wren) 418–19, **13.35**; Houses of Parliament (Barry and Pugin) 476, 491–2, **15.12**; St Paul's Cathedral (Wren) 249, 408, 417, 418, 420, **13.37**–**13.39**; theatres 380, 452, 487, 488, **12.27**, **14.32**
Lorenzetti, Pietro 280; *The Birth of*

the Virgin 280, **9.19**
Lorsch Gospels 231, **7.27**
lost-wax (*cire perdue*) casting 23, 218, 222, **0.10**
Louis II, King of Bohemia 322
Louis IX, King of France 238, **8.3**; *Psalter of St Louis* 253, **8.18**
Louis XIV, King of France 392, 393, 400–1, 405, 414, 416, 430, 433
"Love Bade Me Welcome" (Herbert) 409
Loyola, St Ignatius 391
Lu Chi: *Winter* 309, **10.23**
Lucan 136
Lucky Strike (Davis) 557, **17.15**
Luke, St 216, 228, **5.13**, **7.22**; Gospel 152–3, 154, 155, 168
Luks, George 556
Lully, Jean-Baptiste: costume designs 416, **13.33**
Lumière brothers 529–30
Luther, Martin/Lutheranism 355, 357–8, 368, 373–4, 392, **12.1**, **12.3**, **12.4**; *Ein feste Burg ist unser Gott* 412
Luttrell Psalter **8.2**
Lyell, Sir Charles 465–6
lyric poetry 69, 70
Lyric Suite (Berg) 566
Lysippus 89; *Scraper* 92, **3.18**
Lysistrata (Aristophanes) 16, 98

M (Lang) 571
Maccabeus, Judas 147
Machaut, Guillaume de 283
Machiavelli, Niccolò 292, 314, 320, **10.3**; *The Mandrake* 311; *The Prince* 292
MacLise, Daniel: *The Marriage of Eva and Strongbow* 494, **15.27**
Maderno, Carlo: St Peter's, Rome 347–8, **11.42**
Madonna Enthroned (Cimabue) 279, **9.15**
Madonna Enthroned (Duccio) 279–80, **9.16**
Madonna Enthroned (Giotto) 280, **9.17**
Madonna of the Rocks, The (Leonardo) 326–7, **11.7**
Madonna with the Long Neck (Parmigianino) 337–8, **11.23**
Madrid, Spain: Zarzuela Race Track (Torroja) 24, **0.13**
madrigals 341, 413
Maeterlinck, Maurice 529
Magnus, Albertus 224
Makron: skyphos 63, **2.11**
Malevich, Kasimir 552–3; *Suprematist Composition: White on White* 553, **17.8**
Mallory, Thomas: *Le Morte d'Arthur* 244–5
Mlle Pogany (Brancusi) 559–60, **17.21**
Man and the Masses (Toller) 567
Man and Superman (Shaw) 529
Man Pointing (Giacometti) 592, **18.21**
Man with a Guitar (Lipchitz) 560, **17.23**
Mandragola (The Mandrake) (Machiavelli) 311
Manet, Edouard 504; *Déjeuner sur l'herbe* 504, 507, **16.8**
Manichaeism 157
Mann, Thomas: *The Magic Mountain* 550
mannerism 318; in architecture 338, 371; in music 341; in painting 336–8, 394; in sculpture 338
Mannheim orchestra 449
Manon Lescaut (Puccini) 527, **16.34**
mansion stages 256, **8.22**
Mantegna, Andrea 310; Camera degli Sposi **10.1**; *St James Led to Execution* 310, **10.24**
Mantua, Italy: Ducal Palace **10.1**

manuscript illumination: Byzantine 183, 185; Carolingian 228; Gothic 252–4; Islamic 196; medieval 213, 215–16, 281
Manutius, Aldus 356
Maple Leaves at Mama... (Hiroshige) 513, **16.18**
maps: Aegean **2.1**; ancient Egypt and Middle East **1.3**; ancient Greece **3.1**; Biblical lands **5.1**; Byzantine empire **6.1**–**6.3**; Carolingian empire **6.3**; colonial possessions (17th c.) **13.1**; Crusades **8.2**, **8.3**; early Christian world **5.3**; Europe **7.1**, **7.2**, **8.1**, **10.2**, **12.1**, **12.2**; Holy Roman Empire **11.1**; industrialized world (19th c.) **15.1**; Islam **6.3**; prehistoric sites **1.1**; Renaissance **10.1**, **10.2**; Roman Empire **4.2**, **4.3**, **5.5**; Roman Republic **4.1**; world economic situation (1990s) **18.1**; World War I **17.1**; World War II **17.2**, **17.3**
Marathon, battle of (490 B.C.) 76, 89, 93, 95
Maria Theresa, Archduchess 431, 433
Marie Antoinette 431, 433
Marius 114
Mark, St 228, **7.22**, **7.23**; Gospel 153, 154, 155; *St Mark Freeing a Christian Slave* (Tintoretto) 335–6, **11.21**
Mark Antony 120
Market Cart, The (Gainsborough) 439, **14.14**
Marlowe, Christopher 380; *Doctor Faustus* 380; *Tamburlaine the Great* 380
Marne-la-Vallée, France: Palace of Abraxas (Bofill) 604, **18.41**
Marriage of Eva and Strongbow, The (MacLise) 494, **15.27**
Marshall, Kerry James 599; *Den Mother* 599, **18.32**
Marsyas 84
Martel, Charles 194, 211
Martial 136
Martin, St 211
Martin, Jean-Baptiste: *Apollo* **14.33**
Marvell, Andrew 409; *Horatian Ode* 409
Marx, Karl/Marxism 462, 465, 581
Mary Magdalen (Donatello) 315, **10.29**
Mary *see* Virgin Mary
Masaccio (Tommaso di Giovanni) 303, 363; *The Holy Trinity* 304–5, **10.19**; *The Tribute Money* 303, 304–5, **10.18**
Mascagni, Pietro: *Cavalleria Rusticana* 527; *Il Piccolo Marat* 526
masks: African 560, **17.20**; Roman (death) 116
masques 419
Massine, Léonide 533
matches, invention of 169
materialism 59, 469
Mathematical Principles of Natural Philosophy (Newton) 387–8
mathematics and geometry 37, 59, 83
Matisse, Henri 521; *Blue Nude* 521–2, **16.30**
Matthew, St: Gospel 154, 155
Mazarin, Cardinal Jules 393, 416
measurement, standard 389, **13.4**
Mecca 193, 195; Kaaba 195
mechanism 519
Medici, Cosimo de' 291, 314, 315, **10.28**
Medici, Giovanni de' 314
Medici, Lorenzo de' 294, 295, 310, 316–17, 323, 330, **10.30**
Medici, Piero de' 315–16
Medici family 292
Meditations (Aurelius) 122
Mélies, Georges 530
melodrama 462, 488–9
Menander 102

Mendel, Gregor 466, 503
Mendelssohn, Felix 484; *Elijah* 484
Menu de Gras (Chardin) 440, **14.15**
Menzel, Adolf von: *Frederick's Flute Concert ...* **14.36**
Merbecke, John: *Booke of Common Praier* 381
Mercury (Giovanni da Bologna) 338, **11.24**
Mesopotamia 36–42, 52, 58; map **1.2**
Messiah (Handel) 26, 419, **13.36**
Metaphysical poets 408–9
Metropolis (Lang) 570
Mexico 321–2, 559
Meyer, Adolph 573
Meyerbeer, Giacomo 486
Michelangelo Buonarroti 15, 291, 320, 329, 330, **11.13**; *David* 23, 332, 333, **11.1**, **11.16**; *Pietà* 330, 333, **11.17**; St Peter's 347, **11.41**, **11.42**; Sistine Chapel frescoes 329, 330, 333, 348, **11.12**, **11.14**, **11.15**, **11.39**
microtones 609
Middle Ages 206, 208
Midgard (Kiefer) 590, **18.15**
Mies van der Rohe, Ludwig 601, 603; Seagram Building, New York (with Johnson) 601, **18.36**
Migrant Mother, Nipomo, California (Lange) 571, **17.32**
migration, European 498–9
Milan, Italy 295; Cathedral 275–6, **9.10**; S Maria delle Grazie (*Last Supper*) 327–8, **11.9**
Miller, Arthur 610, 612
Millet, Jean-François 504; *Woman Baking Bread* 504, **16.7**
milling machines 468, **15.2**
Milo of Crotona (Puget) 400, **13.16**
Milton, John 409; *Paradise Lost* 409
Minghella, Anthony 613
minimalism 594–5; in music 609
Minoan civilization 52–4
miracle plays 255, 256
Miró, Joan: *Composition 20*, **0.5**
Mirror of Simple Souls (Porète) 285
Mithra 124, **4.11**
Mithraism 124
mobiles 592
Modest Proposal, A (Swift) 445
Molière 415, 416; *Tartuffe* 17–18
Moll Flanders (Defoe) 409
Momaday, Scott: *House Made of Dawn* 615
Mona Lisa 328, **11.11**
monarchies, feudal 237–8
monasticism/monastic orders 206, 209–11, 240, 241
Mondrian, Piet 552, 553; *Composition in White, Black, and Red* 553, **17.9**
Monet, Claude 509; *On the Seine at Bennecourt* 509, **16.11**; *Rouen Cathedral, the Portal, Morning Sun, Harmony in Blue* **16.1**
Mongol rulers 196
Monk, Thelonius 617
Monophysitism 178
Mont Sainte-Victoire seen from Les Lauves (Cézanne) 513–14, **16.17**
Montaigne, Michel de 362; *Essays* 3623
Monteverdi, Claudio: *Orfeo* 414
Montezuma, Aztec ruler 321
Moore, Charles: Piazza d'Italia, New Orleans 604, 606, **18.44**
Moore, Henry 562; *Recumbent Figure* 562, **17.24**
morality plays 255, 283–4
Moran, Robert: *Composition for Piano with Pianist* 609
More, Sir Thomas 375, 376
Morisot, Berthe 509; *In the Dining Room* 509, **16.12**
Morley, Thomas 382; *Now is the Month of Maying* 382

Morris and Company 492
Morrison, Toni 606–7; *Jazz* 606, 607
Morte d'Arthur, Le (Mallory) 244–5
mosaics 174; Byzantine 182–3, 202, **6.1, 6.3–6.6, 6.29**; Islamic 197, 199, **6.24, 6.25**; Jewish **5.2**
Moses 142
mosques 193; Great Mosque, Damascus 197, 199, **6.25, 6.26**
motets 341
Moulin de la Galette, Le (Renoir) 510, **16.13**
Mount Williamson in the Sierra Nevada (Adams) 570, **17.31**
Mouton, Gabriel 389; table of measurement terminology **13.4**
movies *see* films
Mozart, Wolfgang Amadeus 423, 449, 450; Sonata No. 11 for piano 451, **14.28**; Symphony No. 40 in G minor 450–1, **14.26, 14.27**
Muhammad, Prophet 193–4, 196, 196
mummification 42
music and musical instruments 25–6; aleatory 576, 608; American 528, 566–7, 609, 610, 617; ancient Greek 59, 68–9, 71, 84, 99; ancient Egyptian 46, **1.17**; *ars nova* (14th c.) 281–3; atonal 524, 527–8; Austrian 449–51; Baroque 409–14, 419, 423; British 381–2, 419; Byzantine 191–2; classical 448–52; early Christian 168–9; electronic 608–9; French 254–5, 283, 374, 447, 483, 484, 524–5; German 373–4, 447–8, 449, 451, 483, 484–5, 565, 609; Gregorian chant 206, 223; Hungarian 566; impressionist 524–5; Jewish 152; Mannerist 341; medieval 223–4; Native American 616; Renaissance 320, 340–1, 372–3; Roman 133–4, 168, **4.3**; Romantic 481–7; Russian 484, 490, 524, 527, 565, 608; serialism 607, 608; Sumerian 38; 20th-century 565–7, 607–10; *see also* opera
musique actuelle 608
Muslims 241–2; in Spain 224, 242, 325; *see* Islam
Mussolini, Benito 546
Mycenae, Greece: Lion Gate 55, **2.4**
Mycenaean civilization 54–5
Myron 85; *Discus Thrower* 86, **3.8**
mystery cults 103, 116, 124
mystery plays 234, 255–6, 311, **8.23**
mysticism 241, 285–7

Nagasaki, Japan 321
Naples, Italy 295
Napoleon Bonaparte 442, 461, 469, 471, 473, **15.3**
Narayan, R. K. 606
Nash, John: Royal Pavilion, Brighton 476, **15.11**
nationalism 499, 500
Native Americans: ceramics 615–16; dance 569–70; literature 523, 551–2, 615; music 616; painting 616; ritual/theatre 616–17; sculpture 63
naturalism 496; in literature 523; in opera 525–7
Nausea (Sartre) 549
naval artillery 361, **12.7**
Nazianzus, Gregory: homilies 185, **6.7, 6.8**
Nazis 544, 545–8, 571, 606, **17.5**
Neanderthal people 36
Nefertiti 48, **1.20**
Negro Ensemble Company 618
"Negro Speaks of Rivers, The" (Hughes) 551, 552
neo-abstraction 598
neo-Attic sculpture 137–8
"neo-Byzantine" style 278–9

neoclassicism 384, 440; in architecture 442, 444–5; in painting 440, 442, 443; in sculpture 442
neo-expressionism 576, 588, 590
Neolithic period 32–3, 36
neo-Platonism 140, 157–8, 181, 291, 330
Nero, Emperor 121, 136
Nervi, Pier Luigi 603; Small Sports Palace, Rome 603, **18.39**
Netherlands, the 391; *see* Dutch painting
Neuhaus, Max 609
Nevelson, Louise 591; *America—Dawn* 591, **18.17**; *Black Wall* 591, **18.1**
New English Art Club 492
New Orleans 528; Piazza d'Italia (C. Moore) 604, 606, **18.44**
New York 583; Armory Show (1913) 556; Brooklyn Bridge 464; Central Park 537; Guggenheim Museum (Wright) 603, **18.37**; Lever House (Bunshaft) 601, **18.35**; Seagram Building (Mies van der Rohe and Johnson) 601, **18.36**; Trans-World Airline Terminal (Saarinen) 603; Woolworth Building (Gilbert) 564, **17.28**
Newcomen, Thomas 427
Newport, Rhode Island: The Breakers (Hunt) 536, **16.39**
Newton, Sir Isaac 387, 427, 430, **13.3**; *Mathematical Principles of Natural Philosophy* 387–8
Nibelungenlied 224
Nicholas V, Pope 294, 295, 347
Nicholas plays 256
Nietzsche, Friedrich 503, 581
Night (Wiesel) 606
Night Watch, The (Rembrandt) 304, 406, **13.27**
Nijinsky, Vaslav 532–3, **16.37**
Nike of Samothrace 103–4, **3.29**
Nikolais, Alwin 614
Nîmes, France: Pont du Gard 132, **4.26**
Nimrud 40
Nineveh 40
Nio (Unkei) 255, **8.21**
No Exit (Sartre) 569
Noguchi, Isamu 591; *Kouros* figures 591, **18.18**; set designs 568, 591, **17.29**
Noh drama, Japanese 284, **9.22**
Nok sculpture 94, **3.22**
nonrepresentational art 552–3, 538
Norman, Marsha 611
Norman architecture 219–21, **7.18**
North by Northwest (Hitchcock) 27, **0.16**
Nostalgia of the Infinite, The (de Chirico) 555, **17.12**
Not Without Laughter (Hughes) 551
Notre Dame, Paris 248–9, **8.9, 8.10**
novels 27, 409, 446–7, 479–80, 481, 522–3, 550–1, 606–7
Noverre, Jean-Georges 455–6
Now is the Month of Maying (Morley) 382
nuclear power 548–9, 580
Nude Descending a Staircase, No. 2 (Duchamp) 519, 555, 556, **16.27**
Number 1 (Pollock) 583, **18.3**
Number 10 (Rothko) 584, **18.5**
Nuremberg, Germany: Nazi rallies **17.5**; St Sebald 274, **9.8**
Nuyorican theatre 619

Oath of the Horatii, The (David) 440, 443, **14.20**
O'Derek, Keith: *Straight from the Streets* 619
Odes (Horace) 135
Odo of Metz: Palatine Chapel, Aachen 231–2, **7.28, 7.29**

Odyssey (Homer) 54, 55, 72–3
Oedipus the King (Sophocles) 96, 97
Offenbach, Jacques 486
oil painting 20, 362
O'Keeffe, Georgia 556, 558, 570; *Dark Abstraction* 556–7, **17.14**
Oldenburg, Claes 585; *Two Cheeseburgers, with Everything* 585, **18.8**
olive press 56, **2.5**
Olmec-style figurine 63, **2.12**
Olmstead, Frederick Law 537; Biltmore House 536–7, **16.41**
Olympic games 57–8
One and Three Chairs (Kosuth) 588, **18.13**
Onnes, Heike Kamerlingh 502
On the Fabric of the Human Body (Vesalius) 361
On the Gods (Protagoras) 79
On the Revolutions of the Celestial Orbs (Copernicus) 361–2
On the Seine at Bennecourt (Monet) 509, **16.11**
Op art 576, 587
opera 412–14, 486–7, 525–7
opéra comique 486, 526
Orana Maria, La (Gauguin) 514, **16.19**
Oration on the Dignity of Man (Pico della Mirandola) 293–4
Orbay, François d': Versailles 401
orchestras 449
orders, architectural: Corinthian 74, 93, 105, **3.19**; Doric 50, 67–8, 93, **2.19, 3.19**; Ionic 74, 93, **3.19**
Orfeo (Monteverdi) 414
organum 223
Orlando Furioso (Ariosto) 345
orthodoxy 174
Oscott Psalter 253–4, **8.20**
Ostrogoths 177
Ottoman Turks 291, 322, 325, 542
Ottonian period 208; manuscript illumination 216
Oxford University, England 242

Padua, Italy: Arena Chapel frescoes (Giotto) 281, **9.18**; *Equestrian Monument to Gattamelata* (Donatello) 301, **10.12**; University 361
Paestum, Italy: "Basilica" 68, **2.20**
pageant wagons 257
Pagodenburg, Schloss Nymphenburg (Cuvilliés) 436, **14.10**
Paik, Nam June 599; *Danger Music for Dick Higgins* 609; *Homage to John Cage* 609; *TV Bra for Living Sculpture* 599, **18.31**; *Video Composition X* 598
Paine, Thomas 445
painting: American 556–8, 585, 587–8; Baroque 393–5, 398–400, 405–8; British 376–7, 437, 439, 473–4, 492–4, 600; Byzantine 181–2, 192–3; Chinese 127, 309; dada 553, 555; Dutch 364–6, 405–8; early Christian 163; Flemish 362–4; French 252–3, 371, 398–400, 434–5, 439–40, 470–1, 472, 474–6, 504, 509–11, 513–14; German 366–70, 553; Greek (vases) 59–63, 68, 84; hard edge 587–8; impressionist 509, 510; Italian 278–80, 303–6, 308–10, 326–30, 333, 334–8, 393–4; Japanese 479, 513, 515; Jewish 149, 152; Mannerist 336–8, 394; Mughal 327; Native American 616; neoclassical 440, 442, 443; op art 587; pop art 584–5, 587; post-impressionist 511, 513–15; Pre-Raphaelite 493; realist 504, 507, 557, 599–600; Renaissance 326–9, 333, 334–6; rococo 433–5; Roman 114–16,

124–5; Romantic 470–6, 494; Russian 522; Spanish 20, 394–5, 471, 473, *see also* Picasso; surrealist 555; 20th-century 552–9, 583–90, 599–600; *see also* manuscript illumination
Paleolithic period 30, 34–6, **1.1, 1.5**
Palestrina, Giovanni Pierluigi da 340; *Pope Marcellus* Mass 340–1, **11.29**
Palladio, Andrea 338, 422, 445; Teatro Olimpico 342, **11.32**; Villa Rotonda 338, 340, **11.27**
Palm Beach, Florida: Whitehall (Carrère and Hastings) 536, **16.40**
Panini, Giovanni: *Interior of the Pantheon* **4.24**
Pantheon, Rome 24, 130–1, **4.22–4.24**
pantomime 136, 312, 343
papacy 156–7, 209, 241
Papal States 294–5, 322–3
paper 270
Papp, Joseph 619
Paradise Lost (Milton) 409
Parallel Lives (Plutarch) 135
Paris 251, 314, 374, 486; Louvre 338, **11.26**; Notre Dame 248–9, **8.9, 8.10**; Pompidou Center (Piano and Rogers) 604, **18.43**; Saint-Denis 247–8, 250, **8.7, 8.8, 8.15–8.17**; University 242, 244
Parker, Charlie "Bird" 617, **18.49**
Parma, Italy: Teatro Farnese 342
Parmigianino: *Madonna with the Long Neck* 337–8, **11.23**
Parthenon *see* Acropolis, Athens
Passat (Benglis) 598, **18.30**
Pasteur, Louis 503
pastoral poetry 102
Pathé, Charles 530
patronage 470, 492
Paul, St 140, 155, 168, 170, **5.31, 7.1**; letters 168, 170–2, 191
Paul III, Pope 330, 391
Pavlova, Anna 532
Pax Romana 110, 121–2, 159
Paxton, Sir Joseph: Crystal Palace, London 476, **15.13**
Pazzi Chapel, Santa Croce, Florence 299, **10.10**
Pelagius II, Pope 210
Pelli, Cesar: Petronas Twin Towers, Kuala Lumpur City 606, **18.45**
Peloponnesian War 78–9
Pemberton, Dr John S. 502, **16.4**
Penderecki, Krzysztof 610; *Polymorphia* 610
Perez, José Cid 619
performance art 611
Pergamon: Altar of Zeus 106, **3.33**
Peri, Jacopo: *Eurydice* 414
Pericles 78, 79, 90, **3.3**
Perotin 254–5
Persepolis 58, 100
Perseus Holding the Head of Medusa (Canova) **0.1**
Persians/Persian Wars 52, 58, 76, 83, 90, 93, 100, 124, 146, 194
Persistence of Memory, The (Dali) 555, **17.11**
perspective 288, 302, 342; aerial 281, 352, 362; linear 22, **0.9**
Peruzzi, Baldassare: stage design 342, **11.30**
Pesne, Antoine: *Frederick the Great...* **14.35**
Petchenegs 179
Peter, St 155, 156, **5.15, 5.31**
Petipa, Marius 490
Petrarch (Francesco Petrarca) 271–2, 291
"Petrine theory" 156
Petronius 136
Pfaff, Judy 596; *Dragons* 596–7, **18.27**
Pharisees 146
Phèdre (Racine) 415
Phidias 89; (?) *Riace Warrior* 89, **3.12**

Philip II, King of Macedonia 100
Philip II, King of Spain 325–6
Philip Augustus, King of France 237–8, 242
Philippi, battle of (42 B.C.) 119
Philistines 144, 146
philosophes 424, 429, **14.3**
philosophy/philosophers: ancient Greek 59, 79–83; British 388–90, 428, 468, 469, 549; Cartesianism 387, 390, 428; Christian 242–4; existentialism 549; French 468–9; German 428–9, 465, 466–8, 503, 549; Hellenistic 102–3; idealism 466–8; Italian 291–4; materialism 469; neo-Platonism 140, 157–8, 181, 291, 330; positivism 469; postmodern 581–2; pragmatism 549; Roman 118–19, 122–4
photography 570; social 571
Photorealism 588
Photo-Secessionists 570
Phrygian mode 68
physiocratic theory 431–2
Piano, Renzo (with Rogers): Pompidou Center, Paris 604, **18.43**
Piano Lesson, The (A. Wilson) 618
Picasso, Pablo 518–19, 533, 556, 593; *Baboon and Young* 594, **18.23**; *Les Demoiselles d'Avignon* 519, **16.26**; *Girl Before a Mirror* 22, **0.8**; *Guernica* 519, **18.22**; *Youth Riding* 519, **16.25**
Picnic, The (Manet) 504, 507, **16.8**
Pico della Mirandola, Giovanni: *Oration on the Dignity of Man* 293–4
Pierre Lunaire (Schoenberg) 528
Pietà 264; 14th-century 277, **9.12**
Pietà (Michelangelo) 330, 333, **11.17**
Pirandello, Luigi 567–8; *Right You Are If You Think You Are* 568
Piranesi, Giambattista: *Della Magnificenza ed Architettura dei Romani* 444; *S Paolo fuori le Mura* **5.29**
Pisa Cathedral, Italy: pulpits 278, **9.14**
Pisano, Giovanni: pulpits 278, **9.1**, **9.14**
Pisano, Nicola 278
Pistoia, Italy: Sant'Andrea (pulpit) **9.1**
Pius II, Pope 294, 295
Pius IX, Pope: *Syllabus of Errors* 466
plague *see* Black Death
plainchant/plainsong 206, 223
Planck, Max 502
Plato 80–1, 86; *Apology* 82–3; *The Republic* 80, 82, 99; *Symposium* 291; *see also* neo-Platonism
Plautus 117, 118
Plotinus 123, 157; *Ennead* 123–4
Plowing in the Nivernais (Bonheur) 476, **15.9**
Plutarch 135; *Parallel Lives* 135
Poe, Edgar Allan 478
Poetics (Aristotle) 81–2, 96–7, 99
pointillism 513
Poissy, France: Villa Savoye (Le Corbusier) 564, **17.27**
Poitiers, battle of (732) 194, 211
polis 50, 56–7
politics and religion 352
Pollock, Jackson 583; *Number 1* **18.3**
Polyclitus 85; *Lance Bearer* 85, 87, 137, **3.7**
Polyclitus the Younger: theatre at Epidaurus 99, **3.24**, **3.25**
Polymorphia (Penderecki) 610
Pompadour, Madame de 434; *Madame de Pompadour as the Venus of the Doves* (Falconet) 435–6, **14.7**
Pompeii 116, 124, 139, 433, 440, 442, **4.10**
Pompey 114
Pompidou Center, Paris (Piano and Rogers) 604, **18.43**

Pont du Gard, Nîmes 132, **4.26**
Pontormo, Jacopo: *Cosimo de' Medici* **10.28**
Pop art 576, 584–5, 587
Pope, Alexander 445
Pope Marcellus Mass 340–1, **11.29**
Porète, Marguerite: *Mirror of Simple Souls* 285
Porta, Giacomo della 338, 347, 397; *Il Gesù* 397–8, **13.11**, **13.12**
Porter, Edwin S. 530
Portland Public Office Building, Oregon (Graves) 604, **18.42**
Portrait of an Unknown Roman (marble) 116, **4.6**
Portrait of a Young Man (Bronzino) 337, 371, **11.22**
portraiture, Roman 116
positivism 469
Posner, Jill: *Any Woman Can* 611
post-and-lintel 24, 92, **4.27**
post-impressionism 496, 511, 513–15
postmodernism 576, 581–3; in dance 614; in sculpture 597–8
poststructuralism 606
Pound, Ezra 540; *The Cantos* 552
Poussin, Nicolas 398; *Landscape with the Burial of Phocion* 398–400, **13.15**
pragmatism 538, 549
Pratt, F. A. and Whitney, Amos: Lincoln Miller 469, **15.2**
Praxiteles 89; *Cnidian Aphrodite* 89, **3.13**; *Hermes and the Infant Dionysus* 89, **3.14**
precisionists 557
Prélude à l'après-midi d'un faune (Debussy) 525, 532–3, **16.32**
Prendergast, Maurice 556
Pre-Raphaelites 492, 493
pre-Romantic literature 424, 446–7
Prida, Dolores 619
Pride and Prejudice (Austen) 480
primary structures movement 590–1
Primavera, La (Botticelli) 309–10, **10.22**
Primus, Pearl 614
Prince, The (Machiavelli) 292
printing 269, 270, 294
Procopius of Caesarea 178, 187, 200, 205
Prodromic poems 189–90
program music 462, 483–4
Prokofiev, Sergei 565, 608, 609; *The Prodigal Son* 533; *Steel Step* 565
Prometheus Bound (Aeschylus) 107
Prophet, the *see* Muhammad, Prophet
Prophets, the 148–9
Propylea, Athens 93, **3.20**
Protagoras 79; *On the Gods* 79
Protestantism 391, 392, *see* Calvin; Luther; Reformation
Proust, Marcel 523–4; *Remembrance of Things Past* 524
psalters: Luttrell **8.2**; Oscott 253–4, **8.20**; St Louis 253, **8.18**
psychoanalysis 503, 504
Ptolemies 101, 102
Ptolemy I, ruler of Egypt 102, 103
Pu Qua workshop: *A Boy Selling Pipe Lighters and Matches* **5.30**
Puccini, Giacomo: *Manon Lescaut* 527, **16.34**; *Tosca* 527
Pucelle, Jean: *Book of Hours of Jeanne d'Evreux* 281, **9.20**
Puerto Rican theatre 619
Puget, Pierre: *Milo of Crotona* 400, **13.16**
Pugin, A. W. N.: Houses of Parliament, London 476, 491–2, **15.12**
Punic wars 113
Purcell, Henry 419; *Dido and Aeneas* 419
Pylades of Cilicia 136
Pynchon, Thomas 582, 607; *Gravity's Rainbow* 607

pyramids, Egyptian 30, 43–4, **1.13–1.15**
Pyrrho of Elis 103
Pythagoras 59, 99

quantum theory 502
Quo Vadis (film) 530
Quotations from a Ruined City (Abdoh) 611

Rabelais, François 290
Racine, Jean 414, 415; *Phèdre* 415
Radcliffe, Mrs 447
Raft of the "Medusa", The (Géricault) 471, 472, **15.6**
ragtime 528
Rahotep, Prince (painted limestone) 46, **1.16**
Rake's Progress, The (Hogarth) 437, **14.12**
Ranier, Yvonne 614
Rape of the Daughters of Leucippus (Rubens) 398, **13.13**
Rape of the Lock, The (Pope) 445
Raphael 334, 347; *The Alba Madonna* 334, **11.18**; *Castiglione* 344, **11.34**; *The Deliverance of St Peter* 334, 348, **11.19**; Loggia, Vatican 348, **11.43**
rationalism, systematic 384, 423
Ravel, Maurice 527, 609
Ravenna, Italy 181; S. Apollinare in Classe **5.1**; S Vitale 181, 182, 200–2, 203, **6.1**, **6.3**, **6.27–6.29**, **6.32**
realism 234, 496; in literature 522–3, 550; in painting 504, 507, 557, 599–600; in theatre 528–9, 610
rebus, fish (Christian) 162, **5.19**
Recumbent Figure (H. Moore) 562, **17.24**
red-figure pottery, Greek 63, **2.11**
Reformation, Protestant 325, 352, 354, 368
Reich, Steve: *Come Out* 609
relief sculpture 23
religion(s) 17, 50; ancient Egyptian 42–3, 47, 103; ancient Greek 58–9, 71, 79; Hellenistic 103; Islam 193–4; Mycenaean 54–5; Paleolithic 36; and politics 352; Roman 118, 124; 16th-century wars 391–2; Sumerian 38; *see* Christianity; Islam; Judaism
Rembrandt van Rijn 405, 407; *The Descent from the Cross* 407, **13.26**; *The Night Watch* 304, 406, **13.27**
Renaissance 288, 290, 318; architecture 295–9, 320, 338, 346–8, 370–1; dance 312; literature 344–5; music 310, 320, 340–1; painting 303–6, 308–10, 326–9, 333, 334–6; sculpture 300–2, 320, 332, 333; theatre 311–12, 341–4
Renoir, Pierre-Auguste 509, 510; *Le Moulin de la Galette* 510, **16.13**
Representation of Adam (mystery play) 256
Republic, The (Plato) 80, 82–3, 99
Restoration comedy 422
Revelation, book of 155, 168
Revelations of Divine Love (Julian of Norwich) 286–7
Rice, Elmer: *Adding Machine* 567
Richelieu, Cardinal 393, 415
Right You Are If You Think You Are (Pirandello) 568
Rigoletto (Verdi) 486, **15.20**
Rime of the Ancient Mariner (Coleridge) 480
Rimsky-Korsakov, Nikolai 524
Rite of Spring, The (Stravinsky) 527, 533
Rivera, Diego 555, 559; *Enslavement of the Indians* 559, **17.19**

Roberts, Julie 600; *Catholic/Sacred Profane and Love* 600, **18.34**
Robie House, Chicago (Wright) 564, **17.26**
Robinson Crusoe (Defoe) 409
robots 581, **18.2**
Rockefeller, John D. 535, 536
rococo style 424, 433; architecture 436; literature 445; painting 433–5; sculpture 435–6
Rodin, Auguste 509; *The Burghers of Calais* 509, 511, **16.15**
Rogers, Richard (with Piano): Pompidou Center, Paris 604, **18.43**
Roman Republic and Empire 112–14, 160; architecture 117, 125–6, 130–3, 139, 164–6; and Christianity 118, 121, 133, 158–60; dance 136; law 118, 121, 122; literature 134–6, 137, 168; maps **4.1–4.3**, **5.5**; music 133–4, 168, **4.3**; painting 114–16, 124–5; *Pax Romana* 110, 121–2, 159; philosophy 118–19, 122–4; religion 118, 124; sarcophagi 125, 164, **4.17**, **5.24**; sculpture 116, 125, 137–8, 160; theatre and blood sport 117–18, 121
Romance of Amir Hamza (Mughal manuscript) 327, **11.8**
romances, courtly 238, 244–5
Romanesque style 206, 208; architecture 217–19; sculpture 221, 223
Romanticism 431, 462, 467, 468, 469; in architecture 476; in dance 489–90; in literature 478–9, 480–1; in music 481–7; in painting 470–6, 494; in theatre 487–9
Rome 16, 110, 113–14, 121, 156, 160, 163–4, 176, 181, 320, 323, 325, 336, 340, 348, **4.9**; *Ara Pacis* (Altar of Peace) 137–8, **4.34**; Arch of Titus 126, 132, **4.25**; *Baldacchino*, St Peter's 397, **13.1**; Basilica of Constantine 165–6, **5.26**, **5.27**; Baths of Diocletian 164–5, **5.25**; catacomb paintings 163, **5.15**, **5.22**; Colosseum 125–6, 4.20, **4.21**; Forum of Augustus 137, **4.32**, **4.33**; Il Gesù 397–8, **13.11**, **13.12**; Old St Peter's Basilica 167, **5.28**; Pantheon 24, 130–1, **4.22–4.24**; S Paolo Fuori le Mura 167, **5.29**; St Peter's 338, 346, 347–8, **11.35–11.37**, **11.40–11.42**; Sistine Chapel 329, 330, 333, 348, **11.12**, **11.14**, **11.15**, **11.39**; Small Sports Palace (Nervi) 603, **18.39**; Tempietto, S Pietro in Montorio 338, **11.25**; Temple of Fortuna Virilis 117, **4.7**; Trajan's Column 125, **4.15**, **4.16**; Vatican 346–8
Romulus and Remus 112
Ronchamp, France: Notre Dame du Haut (Le Corbusier) 603, **18.38**
rondeaux 255
Röntgen, Wilhelm Conrad 502
Rorem, Ned 610
Rose, Kathy 611
Rosselli, Francesco: *View of Florence* **10.27**
Rossellini, Roberto: *Rome, Open City* 612
Rossi, Aldo 604
Rossini, Gioacchino 486; *The Barber of Seville* 486
Rothko, Mark 584; *Number 10* **18.5**
Rouault, Georges 522
Rouen Cathedral, the Portal, Morning Sun, Harmony in Blue (Monet) **16.1**
Rousseau, Jean-Jacques 424, 430, 431, 440, 446; *Social Contract* 431
Royal Academy, London 492
Rubens, Peter Paul 394, 398; *Henry IV Receiving the Portrait of Maria de' Medici* 398, **13.14**; *Rape of the Daughters of Leucippus* 398, **13.13**

Ruffe, L.: *La Grogne* (*Grumbling*) **17.2**
Ruisdael, Jacob van: *The Jewish Cemetery* 407–8, **13.28**
Running Fence (Christo) 15–16, **0.3**
Russia 542, 543, 580; film 571; literature 522–3, 529, 607; music 484, 490, 524, 527, 565, 608; painting 522

Saarinen, Eero: Trans-World Airline Terminal 603
Sabatine, Jean: *Nameless Hour* **18.47**
Sacrifice of Isaac (mosaic) 142, **5.2**
Sacrifice of Isaac (Brunelleschi) 302, **10.14**
Sacrifice of Isaac (Ghiberti) 302, **10.15**
Sadducees 146
St Alban's Cathedral, England 220–1, **7.18**
Saint-Denis, nr Paris 247–8, 250–1, **8.7, 8.8, 8.15–8.17**
St Denis, Ruth 569
St Gall, Switzerland: golden psalter **10.26**
St George (Donatello) 301, **10.13**
St Germain, Auxerre, France 228, 231, **7.24, 7.25**
St James Led to Execution (Mantegna) 310, **10.24**
St John of Patmos (from Douce Apocalypse) 253, **8.19**
St Mark's Cathedral, Venice 160, **5.16**
St Paul's Cathedral, London (Wren) 249, 408, 417, 418, 420, **13.37–13.39**
St Peter's, Rome 167, 338, 346, 347–8, **5.28, 11.35–11.37, 11.40–11.42**; *Baldacchino* 397, **13.1**
Saint-Saëns, Camille 527
St Sernin, Toulouse 217–19, **7.11, 7.13**
Saladin 242
Salamanca, Spain: University 242
Salamis, battle of (480 B.C.) 76
Salisbury Cathedral 249–51, 270, **8.1, 8.13, 8.14**
Sallé, Marie 454, **14.34**
Samochvalov, Alexandr: *Lenin Entering the Second All Russian Congress* **17.3**
Samuel, prophet 146, 148
Sans Souci Palace, Potsdam 457, 459–60, **14.36–14.40**
Sappho 69; "God's Wildering Daughter" 70
sarcophagi 110; early Christian 164, **5.24**; Roman 125, **4.17**
Sargon II, king of Assyria 41; citadel 41–2, **1.10, 1.11**
Sartre, Jean-Paul 549, 569; *L'Etre et le néant* 549; *La Nausée* 549; *No Exit* 569
Satie, Eric 533
Satyr and Bacchante (Clodion) 436, **14.8**
Saul, King 146, 152
Sauvy, Alfred 578
Savoca, Nancy 613; *True Love* 613
Savonarola, Girolamo 294
Scarlatti, Alessandro 412
Schelling, Friedrich 467, 468, 549
Schiller, Friedrich von 447
Schoenberg, Arnold 527–8; *Piano Suite*, Op. 25 528, **16.35**
Schopenhauer, Artur 468
Schubert, Franz 482, 484; *The Erlking* 482, **15.15**
Schumacher, Joel 613
Schuman, William 565
Schumann, Robert 485, 486
science and technology 83, 294, 360–2, 426, 427–8, 464, 465–6, 502–3, 580–1; cannons 361; clocks 102, 270; Coca-Cola 502; computers 547; crank-and-connecting rod system 296; domes 203; horse carts and harnesses 236; lathes 296;

lost-wax casting 23; matches 169; nuclear energy 548–9, 580; olive press 56; robots 581; screw threads 324; ships 215; steam engines/turbines 102, 427, 428, 464; tools 33; wheel 37
Scott, Sir Walter 480
Scraper (Lysippus) 92, **3.18**
Scribe, Eugène 486
sculpture 22–3; abstract 591–2; African 23, 94, 559–60; ancient Egyptian 46, 48–9; ancient Greek 65–7, 85–9, 92, 100; Baroque 395–7, 400; British 562, 592; Buddhist 255; Carolingian 231; early Christian 162–3; found 594; French 251, 258–9, 261, 400, 435–6, 509, 511; futurist 519–20; Etruscan 112; German 217; Gothic 251–2, 258–9, 261, 277–8; Hellenistic 103–4; impressionist 509, 511; Italian 278, 300–2, 315, 320, 332, 333, 338, 347, 395–7, 520; Japanese 152, 255 Mannerist 338; medieval 216–17; minimalist 594–5; Native American 63; neoclassical 442; prehistoric 34–5; primary structures 590–1; Renaissance 300–2, 320, 332, 333; rococo 435–6; Roman 116, 125, 137–8, 160; Romanesque 221, 223; Sumerian 39, 40; 20th-century 559–60, 562, 590–2, 594–5, 597–8
Sea Battle, The (Vroom) 326, **11.6**
Seasons, The (Vivaldi) 410
secularism 264, 266, 270
Segal, George: *The Bus Driver* 585, 587, **18.10**
Self-portrait (Dürer) **12.12**
Selznick, David O.: *Gone with the Wind* 572
Seneca 122
Sennet, Mack: comedies 531
serfs 213
serialism 607, 608
Serlio, Sebastiano 342, 376, 422; stage settings 342, **11.31**
Servetus, Michael 392
Seurat, Georges 513; *A Sunday Afternoon on the Island of La Grande Jatte* 513, **16.16**
Seymour, Jane: portrait (Holbein the Younger) 376–7, **12.25**
sfumato 318, 326
Shah Jahan 404
Shakespeare, William 378, 380, 487; *Hamlet* 379; *Richard II* **15.21**
Shang wine vessel 43, **1.12**
Shapiro, Joel 598; *Untitled* 598, **18.29**
Shaw, George Bernard 529; *Man and Superman* 529
Shawn, Ted 569
Shelley, Percy Bysshe 478, 480
Shepheardes Calendar, The (Spenser) 377
Shiites 193
Shinn, Everett 556
Shinto sculpture 152, **5.12**
Sidney, Sir Philip 377; *A Defense of Poesie* 377
Singer, Bryan 613
Sistine Chapel frescoes (Michelangelo) 329, 330, 333, 348, **11.12, 11.14, 11.15, 11.39**
Sixtus IV, Pope 294, 295, 316
skeleton frame structures 25, **0.14**
skepticism 102, 103
Sklar, Roberta 611
skyscrapers 515–17
Slave Ship, The (Turner) 473–4, **15.7**
Sloan, John 556
Sluter, Claus 277; Chartreuse de Champol portal 277–8, **9.13**
Smenkhkare and Meritaten (relief) 47, **1.18**

Smetana, Bedrich: *My Country* 484
Smith, Adam: *Wealth of Nations* 432
Smith, Bessie 528
Smith, David: *Cubi XIX* 590–1, **18.16**
Smith, Tony 595
Smithson, Robert: *Spiral Jetty* 595, **18.25**
Smythson, Robert: Wollaton Hall 376, **12.23**
Snell, Bruno: *Discovery of the Mind* 86
Sobol, Joshua: *Ghetto* 619
Social Contract (Rousseau) 431
socialism 499–500
Society of Jesus *see* Jesuits
Socrates 80, 82
Soft Borders (Tansey) 599–600, **18.33**
"Soft-Hearted Sioux, The" (Bonnin) 551–2
Solomon, King 146, 147, 150
Solon 78
Solzhenitsyn, Alexander 607
sonata form 448
sonatas 410, 448
"Song of Roland" 224–6
Sophocles 95, 96, 98, 99; *Oedipus the King* 96, 97
sophists 79, 82
Sopocani, Yugoslavia: church fresco 182, **6.2**
sotties 288, 311
Sound and the Fury, The (Faulkner) 550
Spain 325–6; architecture 24, 517; literature 409; Muslims (Moors) 224, 242, 325; painting 20, 394–5, 471, 473, *see also* Picasso
Spanish Armada 326, **11.6**
Sparta 56, 78–9
Spencer, Herbert 469
Spenser, Edmund 377–8; *The Faerie Queen* 376, 378; *The Shepheardes Calendar* 377
Sphere with Internal Form (Hepworth) 592, **18.19**
Spielberg, Steven: *Star Wars* 613
Spiral Jetty (Smithson) 595, **18.25**
Split Britches 612
Spring (Botticelli) 309–10, **10.22**
Spring Blossoms (Calder) 592, **18.20**
Spurgeon, Charles 558
stained-glass, Gothic 246, 258, **8.26, 8.28**
Star Wars (Spielberg) 613
Starry Night, The (van Gogh) 20, 515, **16.21**
steam engines 427, 428, 464
steam turbine, Hero's 102
steel 464
Steel Step (Prokofiev) 565
Stella, Frank 587–8; *Tahkt-I-Sulayman I* 588, **18.12**
Stibitz, George R. 547
Stieglitz, Alfred 558, 570
stigmata 234, 243
Stiris, Turkey: churches 192, **6.17**
Stockhausen, Karlheinz 608, 609; *Gruppen* 609; *Microphonie I* 609; *Stimmung* 609
stoicism 102, 103, 118–19, 122, 123, 136, 157
Stone Breakers, The (Courbet) 504, **16.6**
Stowe, Harriet Beecher: *Uncle Tom's Cabin* 488–9
Stradivari, Antonio 411
Strauss, Richard 482, 483; *Till Eulenspiegel* 483, 484
Stravinsky, Igor 524, 527, 608, 609; *Apollo* 533; *The Rite of Spring* 527, 533
stream of consciousness 550
Strindberg, August 567
Sturm und Drang movement 447
Suger, Abbot 241, 247, 250, 251
Suleiman I, Sultan ("the Magnificent") 322, **11.3**

Sulla 114
Sullivan, Louis 516–17, 562; Carson, Pirie, and Scott Dept Store, Chicago 517, **16.23**
Sumer/Sumerians 36, 37; art 37, 39, 40; literature 38; music 40; religion 38; writing 38
Sunday Afternoon on the Island of La Grande Jatte, A (Seurat) 513, **16.16**
Sunnites 193
Suprematist Composition: White on White (Malevich) 553, **17.8**
suprematists 552
surrealism 504, 538, 555
Susa 58
Sutton Hoo, England: ship burial 216, **7.9**
Swan Lake (ballet) 490
Swift, Jonathan 445; *Gulliver's Travels* 445; *A Modest Proposal* 445
Swing, The (Fragonard) 435, **14.1**
Sylphide, La (ballet) 489–90
symbolism: in literature 523–4, 529
symbols 16; early Christian 160, 162, **5.18, 5.19**
symmetry 22
symphonic poems 484
Symphonie Fantastique (Berlioz) 483, **15.17**
symphonies 25, 448–9, 450–1, 483, 484
synthesizers 608

tabula rasa 390
Tacitus 135
Taglioni, Filippo: *The Revolt in the Harem* 490
Taglioni, Marie 489–90, **15.23**
Tahkt-I-Sulayman I (Stella) 588, **18.12**
Taj Mahal, India 404, **13.24**
Talbert, David E.: *A Woman Like That* 618
Tallis, Thomas 382
Tamburlaine the Great (Marlowe) 380
Tanner, Henry O. 507; *The Banjo Lesson* 507, **16.10**
Tansey, Mark 599; *Soft Borders* 599–600, **18.33**
Tartuffe (Molière) 17–18
Taylor, Cecil 610, 617
Taylor, Paul 613
Tchaikovsky, Peter Ilyich 484, 490
technology *see* science and technology
Tell Asmar, Iraq: statues 39, 40, **1.8**
Tell el Amarna, Egypt 47–9
Tempietto (Bramante) 338, **11.25**
Ten Commandments 143, 144
Terence 117, 118, 226, 290
Terry, Megan 611
Tertullian 157
Tetrarchy, Diocletian's 159, 160, **5.16**
texture 23
Thales of Miletus 59, 79
Tharp, Twyla 614
theatre 26; absurdist 567–9, 610–11; alternative 611–12; American 452, 611, 612; ancient Greek 16, 71, 95–9, 107–8; Asian American 619; Baroque 419, 422; British 378–80, 419, 422, 452, 611; Chinese 189, **6.14**; Elizabethan 378–80; epic 567; expressionist 567; French 17–18, 414–15, 452–3; German 567; Hellenistic 102, 190; Hispanic 619; Italian 567–8; Japanese Kabuki 453; medieval 226, 234, 255–6, 283–4; Native American 616–17; realist 528–9, 610; Renaissance 311–12, 318, 341–4; Roman 16, 117–18, 121; Romantic 487–9; Yiddish and Hebrew 619
Themistocles 76
Theocritus 102
Theodora, Empress 178, 190, **6.1**
Theodoric, king of the Ostrogoths 177
Theodosius I 177; obelisk 186, **6.10**

Theogony (Hesiod) 58, 71
Theophanes Continuatus 187
Theophilus, Emperor 179
therapy, art as 17
Thespis 98
Third-Class Carriage, The (Daumier) 507, **16.9**
Third of May 1808 (Goya) 471, 473, 559, **15.5**
Third World, the 578–9
Thomas, Ambroise 486
Thomson, James: *The Seasons* 473
Thousand and One Nights, The 196–7
Thucydides 78, 83, 187
Till Eulenspiegel (Strauss) 483, 484
Tillman, George, Jr: *Soul Food* 619
Tintern Abbey (Wordsworth) 479
Tintoretto (Jacopo Robusti) 335; *St Mark Freeing a Christian Slave* 335–6, **11.21**
Titian (Tiziano Vecelli) 334–5; *Assumption of the Virgin* 335, **11.20**
Titus's Arch, Rome 126, 132, **4.25**
Toland, Greg 572
Toller, Ernst 567; *Man and the Masses* 567
Tom Jones (Fielding) 446
Top Girls (Churchill) 611
Torah, the 140, 147, 148
Torroja, Eduardo: Grandstand, Zarzuela Race Track 24, **0.13**
Toulouse, France: St Sernin 217–19, **7.11**, **7.13**
Toulouse-Lautrec, Henri de 519
Trajan, Emperor 121; Trajan's Column 125, **4.15**, **4.16**
Trambley, Estela Portillo 619
transubstantiation 352, 359, 360
Treatises of Government (Locke) 389–90, 418
Trent, Council of 391, 393
Trial, The (Kafka) 550
Tribute Money, The (Masaccio) 303, 304–5, **10.18**
Trinity, the 162, **5.20**
triremes, Greek 76, **3.2**
Trojans, The (Berlioz) 486
trompe l'oeil 110, 116
tropes 255, 256
troubadours 239
Tuby, Jean-Baptiste: Fountain of Apollo 405, **13.25**
Tudor, David 609
Tudors, the 267, 375–6
Turkey *see* Ankara; Constantinople; Istanbul; Ottoman Turks
Turner, Joseph Mallord William 473; *The Slave Ship* 473–4, **15.7**
Tutankhamun 48
TV Bra for Living Sculpture (Paik) 599, **18.31**
twelve-tone composition 527, 528
28th July: Liberty Leading the People (Delacroix) 474, **15.8**
Two Cheeseburgers, with Everything (Oldenburg) 585, **18.8**
tympana: Gothic 251, 261, **8.17**, **8.30**; Romanesque 221, 223, **7.18**, **7.19**
tyrants, Greek 57, 78

Uccello, Paolo 306, 308; *The Battle of San Romano* 308, **10.21**
Ulysses (Joyce) 550

Umbrellas, Japan-USA (Christo) 595–6, **18.26**
Uncle Tom's Cabin (Stowe) 488–9
Unique Forms of Continuity in Space (Boccioni) 520, **16.28**
United States 534–5, 542, 545, 547, 548, 580; architecture 445, 515–17, 535–7, 562–4, 600–1, 603, 604; films 571–2; literature 445, 523, 550–1, 606, 607; music 566–7, 609, 610; painting 556–8, 585, 587–8; theatre 452, 488; *see also* African Americans; Native Americans universities, medieval 242
Unkei: *Nio* 255, **8.21**
Ur, Iraq: he-goat 40, **1.9**
Urban II, Pope 241
Urbino, Italy 295, 344; Palazzo Ducale **10.4**
Uruk (Warka), Iraq 38
utilitarianism 496

Valdez, Luis 619
Valenciennes Mystery Play 256, **8.23**
Valentino, Rudolph 571
value (of color) 22, **0.7**
value judgments 17, 18
van der Zee, James 558
van Gogh, Vincent *see* Gogh, Vincent van
van Eyck, Jan *see* Eyck, Jan van
van Ruisdael, Jacob *see* Ruisdael, Jacob van
Vandals 160
Vanderbilt, Cornelius 535–6
Vanderbilt, George 536–7
Vasarély, Victor 587; *Arcturus II* 587, **18.11**
Vasco da Gama 294, 320–1
Vasco de Balboa 321
vase painting, Greek 59–63, 84
Vatican *see* Rome
vaults 24, **0.11**, **0.12**; groin 125; ribbed 221; tunnel 125, **4.19**
Venice, Italy 179, 180, 295, 356, 436; Doges' Palace 276–7, **9.11**; St Mark's Cathedral 160, **5.16**
Venus Consoling Love (Boucher) 434–5, **14.6**
Venus figures 30, 34–5, **1.4**
Verdi, Giuseppe 486; "*La donna è mobile*" 486, **15.20**
Vergil 134; *Aeneid* 134–5, 137, 245
verisimilitude 288, 300
verismo opera 526
Vermeer, Jan 408; *The Girl with a Red Hat* 408, **13.29**
Veron, Louis 486
Versailles, Palace of 400–1, 404–5, **13.18**–**13.23**; Fountain of Apollo 405, **13.25**
Versailles, Treaty of 543, 544, 546
Vesalius, Andreas 386; *On the Fabric of the Human Body* 361
Vézelay, France: Ste-Madeleine 221, 223, **7.19**
Vicenza, Italy: Teatro Olimpico (Palladio) 342, **11.32**; Villa Rotonda (Palladio) 338, 340, **11.27**
Victoria, Queen 491, 492

Victorians, the 491–4
Victory of Samothrace see Nike
video art 598–9
Video Composition X (Paik) 598
Vienna 431, 485
Vienna, Congress of 469
Vietnam War 580
Viking ships 215, **7.7**
Vindication of the Rights of Women, A (Wollstonecraft) 445
Viola, Bill: *He Weeps for You* 598
violins 410–11
Virgin and Child ivories 182,186, **6.12**
Virgin and Child with St Anne (Leonardo) 328–9, **11.10**
Virgin Mary cults 241, 256
Virgin of the Rocks, The (Leonardo) 326–7, **11.7**
Virginia, University of: Rotunda (Jefferson) 445, **14.21**
Visigoths 177
Vitascope, the 529
Vitruvian Man (Leonardo da Vinci) 291, **10.2**
Vitruvius: *De Architectura* 116, 291, 342, 400
Vitry, Philippe de 281
Vivaldi, Antonio 410; *The Seasons* 410
Voltaire 429, 430, 454, 457, 459, **14.4**; *Candide* 430
Volterra (Corot) 474, 476, **15.10**
Vroom, Hendrik Cornelisz: *The Sea Battle* 326, **11.6**

Wagner, Richard 482, 487, 527
Waiting for Godot (Beckett) 610
Wall Street Crash 545, **17.4**
Walpole, Horace 446–7
Walter, Johann 373
Wanderer above the Mists, The (Friedrich) **15.1**
Wandor, Michelene 612
Ward, Douglas Turner 618
Warhol, Andy 14, 582, 587; *Green Coca-Cola Bottles* 587, **18.9**
Waring, James 614
Wasserstein, Wendy 611
Waste Land, The (Eliot) 552
Watt, James 427; condensing chamber 427, 428, **14.2**
Watteau, Antoine 434; *Embarkation for Cythera* 434, **14.5**
Wavrin, Jean de: *Chroniques d'Angleterre* 266, **9.2**
Wealth of Nations (A. Smith) 432
Weaver, John 455
Weaver's Cycle, The (Kollwitz) 499, **16.2**
Webern, Anton 566
Welles, Orson: *Citizen Kane* 572
Well-Tempered Clavier (Bach) 410, 413
Weyden, Roger van der: *The Descent from the Cross* 363–4, 367, **12.9**
Whaam! (Lichtenstein) 585, **18.6**
wheel, invention of the 37
Whitman, Walt 478
Whitney, Eli 468
Wiene, Robert: *Cabinet of Dr Caligari* 570, **17.33**
Wiesel, Elie 606; *Night* 606
Willendorf, Woman from 34, **1.4**
William I, King ("the Conqueror") 237, 266

William I, Kaiser 500, 501
William II, Kaiser 501, 540, 541
William and Mary 418
William of Aquitaine 240
William of Champeaux 242
Williams, Samm-Art: *Home* 618
Williams, Tennessee 610
Williamsburg, Virginia: theatre 452
Wilson, August 618; *Fences* 618; *The Piano Lesson* 618
Wilson, Doric 612
Winckelmann, Johann 433, 440, 468
Winged Victory 103–4, **3.29**
Winter (Lu Chi) 309, **10.23**
Witt, Johannes 380
Wolgemut, Michael 367
Wollaton Hall, Nottingham, England 376, **12.23**
Wollstonecraft, Mary 445; *A Vindication of the Rights of Women* 445
Woman Baking Bread (Millet) 504, **16.7**
Woman, Old Man, and Flower (Ernst) 553, 555, **17.10**
women: mystics 285–7; status 40–1, 171–2, 213, 239
Wood, Grant 557; *American Gothic* 557, **17.16**
woodblock prints, Japanese 513, **14.31**, **16.18**
woodcuts (Dürer) 352, 367–8, **12.13**
Woolf, Virginia 550
Woolworth Building, New York (Gilbert) 564, **17.28**
Wordsworth, William 478–9; *Tintern Abbey* 479
Work (Brown) 499, **16.3**
Works and Days (Hesiod) 69
World War I 501, 538, 540, 541–3, 553
World War II 547–8
Wren, Sir Christopher 417, 418; Hampton Court Palace 418–19, **13.35**; St Paul's Cathedral 417, 418, 420, **13.37**–**13.39**
Wright, Frank Lloyd 517, 562, 564; Guggenheim Museum 603, **18.37**; Kaufmann House 563, 564, **17.25**; Robie House 564, **17.26**
writing: cuneiform 30, 38, **1.7**; Greek 57
Wycliffe, John 271

Xerxes I 58, 76

Yeats, William Butler 552
Yevtushenko, Yevgeny Alexandrovich: "Zima Junction" 607
Young, La Monte 609
Youth Leaning Against a Tree with Roses (Hilliard) 377, **12.26**
Youth Riding (Picasso) 519, **16.25**

Zanuck, Darryl 572
Zeno 103
"Zima Junction" (Yevtushenko) 607
Zola, Émile 470, 481, 523, 529; *L'Assommoir* 523
Zurich, Switzerland 358, 359
Zuse, Konrad 547
Zwingli, Ulrich 358–9, 373, **12.5**